PRESENT-VALUE INTEREST FACTORS FOR ONE DOLLAR, PVIF (continued)

Year	11%	12%	13%	14%	15%	16%	17%	18%	19%	20%
1	.901	.893	.885	.877	.870	.862	.855	.847	.840	.833
2	.812	.797	.783	.769	.756	.743	.731	.718	.706	.694
3	.731	.712	.693	.675	.658	.641	.624	.609	.593	.579
4	.659	.636	.613	.592	.572	.552	.534	.516	.499	.482
5	.593	.567	.543	.519	.497	.476	.456	.437	.419	.402
6	.535	.507	.480	.456	.432	.410	.390	.370	.352	.335
7	.482	.452	.425	.400	.376	.354	.333	.314	.296	.279
8	.434	.404	.376	.351	.327	.305	.285	.266	.249	.233
9	.391	.361	.333	.308	.284	.263	.243	.225	.209	.194
10	.352	.322	.295	.270	.247	.227	.208	.191	.176	.162
11	.317	.287	.261	.237	.215	.195	.178	.162	.148	.135
12	.286	.257	.231	.208	.187	.168	.152	.137	.124	.112
13	.258	.229	.204	.182	.163	.145	.130	.116	.104	.093
14	.232	.205	.181	.160	.141	.125	.111	.099	.088	.078
15	.209	.183	.160	.140	.123	.108	.095	.084	.074	.065
16	.188	.163	.141	.123	.107	.093	.081	.071	.062	.054
17	.170	.146	.125	.108	.093	.080	.069	.060	.052	.045
18	.153	.130	.111	.095	.081	.069	.059	.051	.044	.038
19	.138	.116	.098	.083	.070	.060	.051	.043	.037	.031
20	.124	.104	.087	.073	.061	.051	.043	.037	.031	.026
21	.112	.093	.077	.064	.053	.044	.037	.031	.026	.022
22	.101	.083	.068	.056	.046	.038	.032	.026	.022	.018
23	.091	.074	.060	.049	.040	.033	.027	.022	.018	.015
24	.082	.066	.053	.043	.035	.028	.023	.019	.015	.013
25	.074	.059	.047	.038	.030	.024	.020	.016	.013	.010
30	.044	.033	.026	.020	.015	.012	.009	.007	.005	.004
35	.026	.019	.014	.010	.008	.006	.004	.003	.002	.002
40	.015	.011	.008	.005	.004	.003	.002	.001	.001	.001
45	.009	.006	.004	.003	.002	.001	.001	.001	.000	.000
50	.005	.003	.002	.001	.001	.001	.000	.000	.000	.000

D1315232

PRINCIPLES OF MANAGERIAL FINANCE

Lawrence Kryzanowski
Concordia University

Devinder K. Gandhi
University of Calgary

Lawrence J. Gitman
Wright State University

HARPER & ROW, PUBLISHERS, New York
Cambridge, Philadelphia, San Francisco,
London, Mexico City, São Paulo, Sydney

1817

To Louise
—*Lawrence Kryzanowski*

To Nadia
—*Devinder K. Gandhi*

Sponsoring Editor: John Greenman
Project Editor: Nora Helfgott
Designer: T. R. Funderburk
Production Manager: Jeanie Berke
Compositor: Waldman Graphics Incorporated
Printer and Binder: Halliday Lithograph Corporation
Art Studio: Vantage Art, Inc.
Cover Design: Wanda Lubelska

Principles of Managerial Finance

Library of Congress Cataloging in Publication Data
Kryzanowski, Lawrence, 1946–
  Principles of managerial finance.

  Includes bibliographies and index.
  1. Business enterprises—Finance. 2. Corporations—
Finance. 3. Finance—Canada. I. Gandhi, Devinder K.
II. Gitman, Lawrence J. III. Title.
HG4026.K79   658.1'5   81-7162
ISBN 0-06-042348-X   AACR2

BRIEF CONTENTS

iii

DETAILED CONTENTS

Part Three: The Management of Working Capital   201

Chapter 7   AN OVERVIEW OF WORKING CAPITAL MANAGEMENT   205

x   Detailed Contents

Part Six: The Cost of Capital, Capital Structure, and Valuation   499

PREFACE

Although there are currently many basic finance texts written for Canadian students, we think there is still a need for a comprehensive text that is current in its coverage of the key concepts of financial management and that fully incorporates the essential characteristics of the Canadian environment into its presentations. Our book, the product of an equally shared venture, has been written to fill this need.

Content Features

Our coverage of the Canadian aspects of financial markets and institutions, taxation, working capital management, and short-term financings is one of the strengths of this text. This should be particularly evident after one has reviewed the chapters on the legal, operating, and tax environments (Chapter 2); sources of secured and unsecured short-term financing (Chapters 11 and 12); capital budgeting (Chapter 15); financial intermediaries and markets (Chapter 19); leasing (Chapter 20); and failure, rehabilitation, and liquidation (Chapter 26). For example, several illustrative examples included in the capital budgeting and leasing chapters incorporate tax shields based on *multiple-asset* capital cost allowance calculations. Although it would have been considerably easier and less time-consuming to present only single-asset capital cost allowance-based tax shield calculations, many of the unique features of the Canadian capital cost allowance system could not have been illustrated.

Principles of Managerial Finance was designed primarily for an introductory course at the undergraduate level. However, it may also be used effectively in a core MBA finance course and in executive development programs, especially if it is supplemented with cases and readings. Student feedback from classroom testing of the manuscript has confirmed the text's effectiveness for each of these purposes.

Other important features of the text are:

1 We have attempted to link discussions of various financial techniques and issues throughout the book to their theoretical foundations. We have done this by first developing theoretical concepts (especially those bearing on controversial topics such as the cost of capital, capital structure, and valuation), and then discussing the compromises and simplifications that practitioners must make to use those financial concepts in a practical setting. We have found in our own teaching that this approach both makes the study of finance interesting and enjoyable and prepares the student to effectively analyze case problems drawn from the real world. Since the text is addressed primarily to beginning students, we have relied minimally on mathematical constructs, preferring instead to challenge the student's intuition and power of logical thinking. For students who can handle mathematical rigor and are expecting to take advanced courses in finance, however, several explanatory mathematical footnotes and more challenging problems have been provided at appropriate places in the text.

2 We have emphasized the timely and emerging topics in financial management. For example, the text provides a comprehensive discussion of working capital management. Existing texts are concerned primarily with the longer-term aspects of financial management, and only secondarily with the day-to-day time-consuming aspects of a financial manager's job. In the present, prolonged period of tight money and high interest rates, the management of working capital has become critical to the survival of many businesses, both large and small. For this reason, *this text places equal emphasis on the management of a firm's short- and long-term assets and liabilities.*

Other contemporary developments, such as the importance of capital structure in a world of personal taxes (i.e., Miller's world), the significance of the Black-Scholes option pricing model for the valuation of contingent claims, and Roll's critical assessment of the capital asset pricing model, have also been discussed briefly.

3 Current financial management practices have been profoundly affected by inflationary conditions and changes in the international setting, and we have attempted to incorporate both elements into all chapters of the text. For example, a section in Chapter 15 illustrates the serious distortions that can result in the firm's capital investment decisions by its either ignoring or not properly accounting for inflation. Similarly, a section in Chapter 22 explores the sale of debt in international bond markets such as the Eurobond market.

4 We have also emphasized the realities of the Canadian marketplace; that is, the openness of the Canadian economy to external factors and the relatively small size of Canadian-based businesses. Thus, sections on the international and small business aspects of many topics are included in most chapters.

Pedagogical Features

ORGANIZATION

The entire book is structured around the balance sheet, viewed both horizontally and vertically, and the balance sheet is used repeatedly as a reference point. Each part of the text examines one or more portions of the firm's asset and/or liability structure, providing an explanation of corresponding aspects of the financial manager's function. Organizing the text in terms of balance sheet components provides a logical setting for exploring the key decision areas of financial management. It also permits incorporating several topics into those chapters to which they apply, rather than arbitrarily isolating them in separate chapters. Such topics include the effect of inflation, the implications for small businesses, and the international conduct of business. Emphasizing inflationary and international effects at many points helps to reflect the complex environment within which most practitioners operate, and it also ensures that students will be exposed to these often neglected subjects. As a self-test, ask yourself this question: When was the last time that I covered the chapters on small business finance and international finance in a basic introductory finance course?

The text contains 26 chapters organized into eight parts. Part One introduces the student to the world of finance. It discusses the fundamental valuation concepts and principles that provide a unifying link to the material covered in subsequent parts, and it reviews the legal, operating, and tax environments of business firms in Canada. Part Two is devoted to various aspects of financial planning and control. Part Three deals with the management of the firm's working capital. Part Four is concerned with short-term investing and financing decisions and with the major unsecured and secured sources of short-term financing available to Canadian business firms. Part Five deals with the management of fixed assets and capital budgeting. Part Six focuses on the cost of capital, capital structure, and valuation. Part Seven describes the Canadian financial system and markets as well as sources of long-term financing available to firms. Part Eight is devoted to the firm's external expansion (and, conversely, its possible failure) within the Canadian context.

Each part of the text is essentially a self-contained unit, which assures its users considerable flexibility. Various parts of the book may be taught in a sequence that best suits the particular instructor's preferences, course objectives, and time constraints. Optional sections in some chapters—clearly marked with bullets—cover topics that are relatively advanced and may be more difficult for students to understand. These sections have been included for well-prepared students planning to major in finance and may be omitted without loss of continuity in the basic coverage. Finally, the overall organization and the contents of the book make it suitable for either a one- or a two-term introductory course in finance.

EXAMPLES

Copious descriptive examples have been used throughout the book. They are sometimes presented as short cases based on contemporary difficulties or past experiences of Canadian businesses. Feedback from class testing of the manuscript showed that the content, number, placement, and method of presentation of the examples were all crucial to both the effective teaching and learning of the material.

QUESTIONS AND PROBLEMS

A comprehensive set of questions and problems at the ends of chapters will enable students to test their understanding of chapter content. The unusually large number of problems is designed to provide students with many self-testing opportunities and professors with a wide choice of problems for assignment. We believe that the use of good problems is one of the most pedagogically effective ways of clarifying financial concepts.

SELECTED SOURCES OF FINANCIAL INFORMATION

When working on research-oriented assignments, students need access to useful sources of information. Accordingly, as an aid to students, we have provided a list of auxiliary sources of financial and investment information on Canadian companies and industries in the appendix to Chapter 1.

Ancillary Materials

While writing each text chapter, the authors themselves prepared corresponding chapters in two supplementary manuals that accompany this text:

1 *Study Guide to accompany Principles of Managerial Finance.* This guide is designed to reinforce the text material. Each chapter of the guide contains a chapter summary, a chapter outline, a programmed self-test, and additional practice problems with detailed solutions.
2 *Instructor's Manual.* This manual provides answers to all end-of-chapter questions and problems in the text.

Acknowledgments

Numerous individuals have significantly contributed to the presentation of the material in this book. Only by receiving continual feedback from students, colleagues, and practitioners have we been able to create what we believe is a truly teachable Canadian textbook. If you or your students would like to write us about any matter pertaining to this text package, please do. We welcome constructive criticism and suggestions for the book's further improvement.

Harper & Row, Publishers, obtained the experienced advice of a large group of excellent reviewers. We appreciate their many suggestions and criticisms, which have had a strong influence on numerous aspects of this text. We are especially thankful to Larry Boyle, Concordia University; Andy Cann, Acadia University; Dennis Connelly, Saint Mary's University; L. T. Gallant, St. Francis Xavier University; James Hatch, University of Western Ontario; and To Minh Chau, Université du Québec à Montréal. In addition, the following practitioners have provided useful input: Donald Armitage, H. J. Cleland, Mario De Felice, Brian Neysmith, and Bill Speers.

We are also grateful to our colleagues for their encouragement, advice, and support throughout the preparation of the book. These include Lawrence Bessner, Larry Boyle, Bruce English, Jay Flynn, Yasar Geyikdgagi, George Lowenfeld, and Ken Riener of Concordia University; Philip Parr, Jack Schnabel, Edmund Sugars, and Bill Tilleman of the University of Calgary; and Suresh Srivastava. Professors Boyle and Sugars deserve special thanks for their patience in reading and commenting on most of the chapters.

We would also like to thank Marlene Lloyd and Debbie Gant, who did an excellent job of converting hundreds of pages of handwritten text into typed form. Nora Helfgott and the editorial staff of Harper & Row were most cooperative, and their contributions are sincerely appreciated. Devinder K. Gandhi would like to thank the Department of Finance, Faculty of Commerce, Concordia University, for providing him with the necessary stimulus for work conducted on this text during his stay at Concordia University.

Finally, our respective families have played most important roles in patiently providing the support and understanding needed during the writing of this book. To them we will be forever grateful.

LAWRENCE KRYZANOWSKI   DEVINDER K. GANDHI   LAWRENCE J. GITMAN

Part One

Introduction

BALANCE SHEET

Assets	Liabilities and Shareholders' Equity
Current Assets	Current Liabilities
Fixed Assets	Long-Term Debt
	Shareholders' Equity

This part of the text presents a general view of the finance function in the business firm. It also focuses on the legal organization of business entities and certain key concepts relating to the tax treatment of corporate and personal income. Part One contains two chapters. Chapter 1 provides a discussion of the scope, nature, and objective of the finance function within the business firm. It also presents a description of finance as a discipline and a brief overview of the contents and organization of the text. Chapter 2 discusses the legal and tax environments within which the firm operates. Specific attention is given to the corporate form of business organization. Together the two chapters in Part One should give the reader an understanding of the importance, the role, and the operating environment of the finance function in the business firm.

Chapter 1

THE SCOPE, NATURE, AND OBJECTIVE OF MANAGERIAL FINANCE

This chapter is intended to answer a number of important and basic questions—What is finance? What are the characteristics of finance as a discipline? What is the role and organizational structure of the finance function in a business firm? What are the functions and responsibilities of the financial manager? What is the primary objective of financial management? How can this objective be implemented? Such questions must be answered for a thorough understanding of the types of decisions made by financial managers and the decision-making processes and techniques used to make such decisions.

The chapter has four basic sections. The first section deals with finance as a discipline. It discusses what finance means and how finance is related to the fields of economics and accounting. The second section provides an overview of the finance function in order to answer two questions—What is the role and organizational structure of the finance function in a business firm? And what are the functions and responsibilities of the financial manager? The third section discusses the primary objective of financial management, including its measurement and implementation. The final section presents an overview of the text, the approach used to present the key concepts of financial management, and the rationale for that approach.

Finance As a Discipline

This section discusses what finance means, how finance has evolved as a discipline, and how finance is different from the closely related fields of economics and accounting.

5

WHAT IS FINANCE?

Finance is a body of principles, theories, and empirical findings dealing with the generation and allocation of scarce resources (primarily money) by various decision-making
units such as individuals, businesses, and governments. Finance deals with how these
parties allocate scarce resources through a market-pricing system that is based on the
valuation of risky assets (i.e., contingent claims). Thus, finance includes such topics as
personal finance, business or managerial finance, public finance, investment analysis
and management, capital market theory, financial institutions and markets, and international finance.

The basic financial problem faced by any decision-making unit, provided that it is
rational, is the same: Each decision maker must efficiently allocate (or use) its available
financial resources in order to maximize its well-being (or satisfaction) over its lifetime,
while simultaneously satisfying its budgetary constraint (i.e., total uses of funds must
equal total sources of funds). An individual's well-being is generally measured in terms
of the total satisfaction provided by a particular time sequence of consumption bundles
(i.e., the total consumption of all items such as food, clothing, and shelter).* Since an
individual's income for any particular period is likely to differ from his or her preferred
consumption for that period, an individual will invest any surplus (e.g., in cash, savings
accounts, bonds, common shares, or real estate) or fund any deficit (e.g., by selling
existing investments or obtaining a loan). In a certain world, such problems would be
neither difficult nor interesting to resolve; in an uncertain world, such problems are
both difficult and interesting to resolve. Thus, given an uncertain world, personal finance deals with how individuals should optimally divide their income between consumption and investment, how they should allocate surplus resources (i.e., funds not
needed for present consumption) to available investment opportunities, and how they
should fund deficits in order to provide for additional present consumption or investment.

Similarly, a rationally managed firm is faced with the basic financial problem of
efficiently allocating its available financial resources in order to maximize its well-being
over its lifetime, while simultaneously satisfying its budgetary constraint. As will be
discussed later in this chapter, a firm's well-being is generally measured in terms of the
wealth of its owners or shareholders. Like an individual, the firm's income (i.e., internally generated funds) for any particular time period is likely to differ from its planned
expenditures for that period. Thus, like an individual, the firm can invest any surplus
funds in cash or financial assets, or it can fund any shortfall by selling off its existing
assets or acquiring funds externally (i.e., by selling new shares or bonds, by leasing, or by
borrowing from the bank).†

The business firm is also different from the individual in at least three aspects. First,
the primary objective of the firm is the creation of wealth and not consumption per se.
Second, the firm can have an indefinite life. Finally, except for financial institutions, the
firm generally invests the greater proportion of its available funds in *real* assets (e.g.,
plant and equipment) rather than *financial* assets (e.g., shares and bonds).

---

*The specific measure used is the utility of total consumption.
†Unlike an individual, the firm also has the option of paying out any unneeded surplus funds to its
owners or shareholders in the form of dividends or share repurchases.

The existence of a well-developed financial system is important because it enables some individuals to use and control assets without owning them, and it enables other individuals to own assets without having to manage them. This facility for the separation of ownership and management reflects the fact that an individual's ability to succeed in business has no particular relationship with the same individual's ability to accumulate personal wealth. Thus, while an individual's ability to accumulate wealth depends on his or her initial endowment (e.g., inheritance) and rate of saving, an individual's ability to succeed in business depends upon other factors such as the willingness to bear and manage risk, promotional drive, and organizational and administrative expertise.

The study of financial institutions (such as the chartered banks) and the effect of governmental activities on the financial decisions of individuals and businesses is also an integral part of finance. Not only do governments and financial institutions have financial problems comparable to those of individuals and businesses, but they also enforce the laws and practices that govern the conduct of financial transactions. Thus a complete understanding of the constraints imposed by the Canadian legal and institutional setting is crucial to effective decision making by individuals and firms.

The primary concern of this text is managerial finance; that is, the financial management of profit-oriented businesses. However, since a firm's managers are agents of its existing shareholders and creditors, the managers will enhance their effectiveness if they fully understand the preferences, investment behaviour, and practices of individual and institutional investors and financial institutions.

EVOLUTION OF THE STUDY OF FINANCE

Prior to 1958, the finance literature was largely descriptive and legalistic. It concentrated mainly on the right-hand side of the balance sheet; that is, on raising funds, on business formations and combinations, and on the liquidation and rehabilitation of failing firms. The study of finance was profoundly affected in approximately 1958 with the publication of the seminal studies of Markowitz and of Tobin on the theory of portfolio selection, and of Modigliani and Miller on capital structure, cost of capital, and valuation.[1] Subsequently, the study of finance has become more analytical and quantitative, with particular emphasis being placed on decision making under uncertainty. The study of finance is continually evolving as the environment changes. For example, the advent of double-digit inflation in the late 1970s has resulted in the increased study of the impact of inflation on the financial operations of business firms.

FINANCE, ECONOMICS, AND ACCOUNTING

Finance is closely related to economics and accounting. Finance is essentially a branch of applied economics that has become highly specialized, decision-oriented, and technical. Finance also draws extensively on accounting concepts, practices, and numbers. In this section, we will briefly compare and contrast finance with economics and with accounting.

Finance and Economics The field of finance has adopted many of the basic assumptions, principles, and theoretical constructs initially developed by economics, and has applied them to explain the financial behaviour and decision-making practices of individuals and business firms. Thus, based on microeconomic theory, financial theories have been developed for efficiently managing a firm's assets and liabilities and for measuring the risk and value of a contingent claim (such as a common share).* Based on macroeconomic theory, partial equilibrium models have been developed to explain the pricing of risk and the movement of interest rates and foreign exchange rates.

One of the basic principles that has been adopted from economics and has been used extensively in finance is *marginal* (or incremental) *analysis;* that is, the principle that an investment (or action) should be undertaken only when its marginal benefits exceed its marginal costs. The importance of marginal analysis in making financial decisions will become apparent in the subsequent chapters of this text.

Finance and Accounting   In theory, accounting is primarily concerned with providing "accounting" information to facilitate the decision process utilized by rational managers in making asset and liability decisions and by rational investors in determining their consumption-investment plans. In practice, accounting, with the exception of managerial accounting, is primarily concerned with the recording, measuring, and reporting of financial transactions using generally accepted accounting principles (referred to as GAAP). The information generated by accounting may be historical (e.g., the balance sheet for the last fiscal year) or it may be predictive (e.g., the pro forma balance sheet for the end of the current fiscal year). The method of accounting commonly used to prepare financial statements is the *accrual* system, which is based on the premise that returns should be recognized at the point of sale and expenses as they are incurred. Revenues resulting from the sale of merchandise on credit, for which the actual cash payment has not yet been received, appear on the firm's financial statements as *accounts receivable,* a temporary asset. Expenses are treated in a similar fashion—that is, certain liabilities are established to represent goods or services that have been received but have not yet been paid for. These items are usually listed on the balance sheet as *accounts payable,* or *accruals.*

On the other hand, as noted earlier, finance is also concerned with rational decision making under uncertainty. Thus, finance is concerned with the use of information, provided predominantly by the accounting or management information system (M.I.S.), to make decisions so business firms and individuals can maximize their well-being. Thus, the accounting function can be viewed as a necessary input to the finance function. Of course, this does not mean that accountants never make decisions or that financial managers never gather data; rather, the primary emphasis of accounting and finance is on the functions indicated above.

Although accountants and financial managers essentially perform different tasks within a business firm, it is not unusual for a future financial manager to first enter the Canadian business community by accepting an accounting position with a firm. As the

---

Microeconomics (or price theory) deals with how economic units (i.e., individuals and businesses) make pricing and production decisions under differing behavioural assumptions and market structures. *Macroeconomics* deals with the measurement and prediction of the aggregate economic behaviour of such factors as production, consumption, savings, investment, and employment for a nation or group of nations.

accountant gains experience, he or she may become increasingly involved in providing advice on the various financial options being considered by the firm. Subsequently, the experienced accountant may desire to leave his or her advisory role in order to become a decision maker. Thus, he or she may take a position as a financial manager in the firm.

The Finance Function

Since most business decisions are measured in financial terms, it is not surprising that the financial manager plays a key role in the operation of the firm. Also, since there are financial considerations involved in nearly all business decisions, it is crucial that the nonfinancial decision maker has a basic understanding of finance and the finance function. Over the past ten or so years, the trend has been one in which more and more top executives are coming from the finance area.[2] In response to this trend most colleges and universities are experiencing increased enrollments in finance programs, both undergraduate and graduate. This trend clearly suggests that a strong understanding of financial management is a useful prerequisite for a successful business career. To gain the needed understanding of the finance function, we must look closely at its role within the firm and at the key characteristics and functions of the financial manager.

ORGANIZATION OF THE FINANCE FUNCTION

The size and importance of the finance function depends on a number of factors, such as the size of the business firm, the nature of the firm's business, the capabilities of the chief financial officer and his or her staff, and the capabilities of the firm's other officers, directors, and employees. In small firms, the finance function is generally performed by the president or the accounting department or both.* As a firm grows in size, the importance of the finance function typically results in the evolution of a separate finance department—an autonomous organizational unit linked directly to the company president through the *chief financial officer* (commonly called the vice-president of finance or the treasurer). Generally, two other financial officers report to the chief financial officer: the *treasurer*, who deals with the functions related to the *management of funds* (such as cash management, pension and trust management, forecasting financial needs, and maintaining relations with financial institutions and investors) and the *controller*, who deals with the functions related to the *management and control of assets* (such as profit analysis, planning and budgeting, cost and inventory control, accounting, and payroll).

Initially, the finance function may be concerned only with the credit function; that is, with evaluating, selecting, and following up on customers to whom credit is extended. As the organization grows, attention is given to the evaluation of the firm's financial position and working capital management. As the firm takes on a large scale of operations, the finance function expands to include decisions with respect to the acquisition

---

*Unfortunately, many small company presidents have limited competence in the finance function, as evidenced by the data on small business failures. Many of these individuals originally formed and promoted the business they presently manage to commercially exploit a new product idea or innovation (e.g., a snowmobile) or a marketable technical skill (e.g., personnel recruitment).

of fixed assets, obtaining funds to finance fixed assets, and the distribution of corporate earnings to owners.

GENERAL FUNCTIONS OF THE FINANCIAL MANAGER

The financial manager must be thoroughly familiar with financial theory and practice, and be knowledgeable about the closely related disciplines of accounting and economics. Since the business firm must operate in a competitive (and often internationally competitive) environment, knowledge of macroeconomics will provide the financial manager with insight into the monetary, fiscal, and economic stabilization policies of government, through which interest rates, exchange rates, regional incentives, tax policy, and general business conditions are established. More specifically, the financial manager should know the expected consequences of various levels of economic activity on his or her firm's profitability, liquidity, fund raising, and revenue-generating abilities.

The financial manager must actively participate in the ongoing development of the firm's internal management information system, so that its information output remains timely and useful for making financial decisions. The financial manager must be familiar with and must use external sources of information (see Appendix 1 at the end of this chapter for a brief summary of the external sources of financial information in a Canadian context). The financial manager must know the strengths and weaknesses of computers in processing and storing information. The financial manager must also have an increased knowledge of quantitative techniques, such as operations research and statistics, so that he or she can keep abreast of new theoretical and empirical developments published in the finance literature.

SPECIFIC FUNCTIONS OF THE FINANCIAL MANAGER

The financial manager has five specific functions. Each of these functions is discussed next.

Financial Analysis, Planning, and Control   This function is concerned with the transformation of financial data into a form that can be used to monitor the firm's financial position, to plan for future financing, to evaluate the need for increased productive capacity, and to determine what additional financing is required. Proper performance of this function is necessary if the financial manager is to carry out the other key functions of managing and controlling the firm's asset and financial structures.

Working Capital Management   This function is concerned with the day-to-day working capital (in particular, cash) requirements of the firm. It is an attempt to ensure that the firm has the necessary liquidity so that it can meet its obligations as they come due.

Managing the Firm's Asset Structure   The financial manager determines both the mix and the type of assets found on the firm's balance sheet. The *mix* refers to the number of dollars of current and fixed assets. Once the mix is determined, the financial manager must determine and attempt to maintain certain "optimal" levels of each *type* of current asset. He or she must also decide which are the best fixed assets to acquire and must know when existing fixed assets become obsolete and need to be replaced or modified.

Managing the Firm's Financial Structure   This function is concerned with the right-hand side of the firm's *balance sheet.* In performing this function, the financial manager must first determine the most appropriate mix of short-term and long-term financing, because this choice affects both the firm's profitability and overall liquidity. The financial manager must also determine which individual short-term or long-term sources, or financing combination, are best for the firm at a given point in time.

Distribution of Corporate Earnings to Owners   The financial manager must determine how much and in which way the firm should distribute its earnings to its owners or shareholders. More specifically, the financial manager must decide whether or not the firm should pay a cash dividend or repurchase shares, or whether or not it should declare a share dividend.

In terms of time spent, the financial manager generally devotes the most time to working capital management. His or her other time-consuming functions include advising on dividend policy, the administration of pensions, and public and investor relations.

Objectives of Financial Management

As discussed earlier in this chapter, the basic financial problem faced by a rationally managed firm is the efficient allocation of its available financial resources to maximize its well-being over its lifetime, while simultaneously satisfying its budgetary constraint. Unfortunately, when one attempts to enunciate the objectives of financial management in a more operational manner, the following basic questions arise: Whose well-being should be maximized? What effect, if any, does the social interest have on the objectives of financial management? Are the objectives of shareholders and management identical? How should this well-being be measured? How can the objectives of financial management be implemented?

WHOSE WELL-BEING?

The traditional economic and finance literature generally maintains that a business firm should be operated exclusively on behalf of its owners or shareholders. Since the owners or shareholders own the firm, it is argued that the firm should be managed so as to maximize the well-being of the firm's owners or shareholders. This traditional viewpoint is referred to as the *absolute parity of the owners' or shareholders' ownership interest in (or property right claim to) the firm.*

Validity of the Absolute Parity of the Owners' or Shareholders' Interest   It has been argued that the notion of the absolute parity of the owners' or shareholders' interest is not appropriate, because other parties (such as employees, creditors, government, and customers) also have some property right claims on the firm. This position has been aptly summarized by Donaldson as follows:

> The concept of *relative parity* may be employed by professional management in relating the conflicting interests of stockholders, employees, customers, the general public, government, and so on, to each other. Having abandoned the idea of absolute parity of the stockholder's interest, which existed only when management and ownership were one (and perhaps not even then), management continues to attach more weight to its responsibility to owners than to any other vested interest. This means, of course, that where a conflict of interest develops, management must determine how much of the stockholder's interest will be sacrificed in order to behave "more responsibly" toward other interests such as the labor union or the customer.[3]

While it is very difficult to determine whether or not this position is valid, it has been imposed on some firms. For example, in Germany there is legally imposed representation of unions on corporate boards (referred to as *co-determination*). Also, the financial troubles experienced by Chrysler Corporation in 1979 resulted in the appointment of the president of the United Auto Workers to Chrysler's board of directors.

Furthermore, it can be argued that the interests of these other parties can best be protected if they impose or negotiate contractual or legal constraints on the activities of a firm's management. This can be illustrated by the following example.

EXAMPLE   Big Lake Manufacturing Limited has two sources of capital in its capital structure—common equity and debt. The debt was issued five years ago at a time when Big Lake's future looked extremely promising. Big Lake is presently approaching bankruptcy, as can be seen from its current ratio (i.e., the ratio of current assets to current liabilities), which is now 0.4. An evaluation of Big Lake's financial condition indicates that its liquidation value would just fully satisfy the claims of its bondholders; that is, nothing would be left for its owners. Big Lake's management, which firmly belives in the absolute parity of its shareholders' interest, is aware of the firm's liquidation value and the consequences of bankruptcy. Thus, the firm's management is considering an investment in a very large and risky project, which has a very low probability of a very high payoff and a very high probability of being a total failure. Such an investment could only increase the well-being of the firm's shareholders. If it were unsuccessful, the firm's shareholders would not lose any more (because of limited liability) than they would now lose by the firm going into bankruptcy; and if it were successful, they would reap a large return. However, such an investment could only decrease the well-being of the firm's bondholders. If the project were unsuccessful, the bondholders would then lose all or a part of their claim on the firm; and if the project were successful, the bondholders would not gain since they do not share in the profits of the firm. Fortunately for the bondholders, their contractual agreement with the firm (referred to as a *trust indenture*) had a protective clause (referred to as a *restrictive covenant*) that stated that if the firm's current ratio dropped below 0.5, then all investment decisions had to be approved by the bondholders. Naturally, when Big Lake's management asked for such approval, the bondholders unanimously rejected the request.

Social Responsibility   The social responsibility argument is an alternate formulation of the argument that the absolute parity of the owners' or shareholders' interest is not appropriate. Proponents of this viewpoint argue that since business firms are partly responsible for the welfare of society, social considerations (such as minimizing pollution, maximizing worker safety, or saving energy) should also be an important company objective. Although this topic is probably more appropriately studied in a business policy course, it appears that the social interest is best protected if the government uses laws, regulations, and controls (and maybe even ownership) to protect the social interest, as has been the case in the railroad, airline, brokerage, cable television, broadcasting, and public utility industries. Thus, rationally managed firms can again concentrate solely on maximizing the well-being of their owners or shareholders, subject to the firm's budgetary constraint and any legally imposed constraints designed to protect the public interest.

The Effect of the Separation of Management from Ownership   Most of the traditional economic and financial literature accepts without question the hypothesis that business firms, even when ownership is diffused and separated from management, should be and are operated solely on behalf of their owners or shareholders. Others argue that there is obviously a separation between the *ownership* (*risk-bearing*) and *control* (*risk-taking*) functions of publicly traded firms.[4] Since the shareholders of these firms generally delegate the power to set corporate objectives and policies to management, there is no reason to believe that firm's management, which acts as an agent for the firm's owners or shareholders, will always act in the best interest of the firm's owners or shareholders. For example, a manager whose financial well-being depends upon his or her job performance and career mobility is likely to be more risk averse than an owner or shareholder who can hold a well-diversified portfolio of highly marketable securities.[5] In other words, the effect of the financial failure of the firm is generally more serious for its managers (especially those who have limited personal wealth) than for its owners or shareholders, especially if the latter hold well-diversified portfolios of securities.

In such *agency* relationships, the *principals* (i.e., the owners or shareholders) have a number of alternative courses of action for causing the *agent* (i.e., the firm's management) to act exclusively in the principal's interest.[6] These alternatives range from no action, to monitoring the activities of management (e.g., through the board of directors or speaking out at shareholders' meetings), to providing management compensation or incentive schemes (e.g., share options) that encourage managers to more closely align their interests with those of the firm's owners or shareholders.* However, it should be noted that even if the agent received all of his or her compensation in the form of shares of the firm, the agent would probably still not always act in the best interest of the firm's owners or shareholders. The agent would always receive part of his or her compensation in the form of nonsalary benefits, such as a secure pension plan, an endowed expense account, a large and lavish office, power, and a company-supplied automobile (or jet!).

When choosing between the alternatives, the owners or shareholders are faced with an economic decision in which the use of the marginal principle is appropriate. That is, the owners and shareholders should incur monitoring or compensation costs, or both, until their marginal cost is equal to their marginal benefit.

Like many relationships, the agency relationship between an existing management

---

*In the literature, this is referred to as the *incentive problem*.

team and a firm's shareholders is difficult to terminate. In practice, few outside take-overs or shareholder dissensions are even attempted since the promotional, legal, and other costs of such actions are often prohibitive. Furthermore, only a few of the attempted actions are successful. If the takeover is attempted through a large purchase of voting shares, much money is required; and if the takeover is attempted without a substantial purchase of voting shares, the dissenting group must individually contact and persuade a majority of the company's shareholders to vote at the annual meeting for the dissidents' proposed slate of directors. Unlike the existing management (and their board of directors), the dissidents are not entitled to use the firm's funds to defend their position by mailings and advertisements directed at shareholders.*

Although it is often difficult to ensure that a firm's management will always act exclusively in the best interest of its owners or shareholders, *the most appropriate objective of financial management is nonetheless the absolute parity of the owners' or shareholders' well-being.*

MEASURES OF WELL-BEING

There are two commonly proposed measures of the well-being of a profit-oriented firm's owners or shareholders: the firm's profits and the owners' or shareholders' wealth.[7] Each of these will now be discussed.

Maximization of Profits   The maximization of total profits has long been accepted in microeconomics as the best measure of the owners' or shareholders' well-being. For example, one of the basic assumptions of the model of perfect competition is that the goal of all firms is profit maximization and that no other goals are pursued.[8] Unfortunately, as will be shown in the following example, an objective of total profit maximization can in some cases decrease the owners' or shareholders' well-being.

EXAMPLE   Bellevue Coal Mining Limited has 100,000 common shares outstanding and had total profits of $200,000 for the past fiscal year. The firm invested proceeds from the sale of a 100,000 common share issue in projects yielding positive rates of return on equity. As a result of this new investment, Bellevue's total profits are expected to increase to $300,000 for the current fiscal year. Although Bellevue has increased its total profits by selling the additional common shares, are its shareholders "better off"?

An examination of the effect of the investment on Bellevue's earnings per share (eps) will show that its eps has been reduced from $2.00 per share (i.e., $200,000 ÷ 100,000 shares) to $1.50 per share (i.e., $300,000 ÷ 200,000 shares).† This would suggest that the original shareholders are, in fact, now "worse off"!

*If the dissident shareholders are successful in their takeover attempt, then, with the approval of shareholders, they can use company funds to reimburse themselves for the expenses incurred. For example, on July 14, 1980, the shareholders of Campbell Chibougamau Mines Ltd. approved (by a vote of 1.62 million to 168,911) to reimburse the dissident shareholder group for the following costs: $440,000 in printing and legal costs, and the interest on a $150,000 bank loan.
†In a later chapter, it will be shown that there will be a dilution in eps whenever the average return of the new investment projects is below the average return on the firm's existing projects.

This example illustrates that total profit maximization is an inappropriate measure of the owners' or shareholders' well-being because it can lead to situations where owners or shareholders are actually worse off. In a subsequent section, you will see that even if profits are more correctly interpreted as earnings per share, profit maximization is still an inappropriate measure of well-being.

Wealth Maximization   The maximization of wealth is generally accepted in finance as the best measure of the well-being of the owners or shareholders of a profit-oriented business.* The wealth of a firm's owners or shareholders should be defined as the discounted value of the after-tax cash flows paid out by the firm. In most instances, this is equivalent to the unadjusted total market value of a firm's common shares. However, for external transactions which involve a transfer of assets (e.g., cash dividends, share repurchases, and share rights) between the firm and its owners or shareholders, a firm's share value should be adjusted to reflect any cash or assets received or given up by the owners or shareholders as a result of the transaction. Summarizing, the maximization of a firm's share price is generally used in finance as the best operational measure of the well-being of the owners or shareholders of a profit-oriented firm.†

AN EVALUATION OF THE MEASURES OF WELL-BEING

In this section, we will show that wealth is the most appropriate measure of well-being; and therefore that the principle of maximizing the wealth of the firm's owners or shareholders is the most appropriate objective of financial management. Wealth maximization is the preferred approach for four basic reasons: it considers (1) the effect of future investment (i.e., profitable growth) opportunities, (2) timing of benefits, (3) risk, and (4) distribution of returns.

The Effect of Future Investment Opportunities   Profit maximization is essentially a short-run approach that does not consider the effect (i.e., present worth) of the future investment (i.e., profitable growth) opportunities of the firm. On the other hand, wealth maximization is essentially a long-run approach that does consider the effect of the future investment opportunities of the firm. In other words, the potential consequences of an ill-conceived short-run profit maximization strategy are likely to be reflected in the current share price, which will probably be lower than it would have been if the firm had pursued a longer-run strategy.‡

---

*This is based on Fisher's separation theorem, which can be paraphrased as follows: Given perfect and complete capital markets, production-investment decisions are governed solely by an objective market criterion (i.e., attained wealth), which is independent of individuals' time preference for consumption.
†In nonprofit-oriented organizations, the best measure is the maximization of the expected utility of the organization's contributors; in the public sector, it is the maximization of the expected utility of the decision makers' constituents.
‡This expectation is based upon the assumption that investors in the marketplace have perfect knowledge of the firm's short-run posture. This assumption, which underlies the basic theory of value, is discussed in greater detail in subsequent chapters.

EXAMPLE Four years ago, Harold Jenks purchased one common share of Alpha company and one common share of Beta Company, each at a price of $100. Both of the companies are in the same line of business. Although their profits have differed over the four-year period, each of the firms has paid an annual dividend of $1 per share. Alpha Company has earned an annual profit of $2 per share, while the Beta Company's annual profit has been $3 per share. The difference in earnings is attributed to the fact that Alpha Company has spent a great deal of money to develop an innovative new product, thereby lowering its profits. A share of Alpha Company is currently selling for $130, while a share of Beta Company sells for $110. This situation is not uncommon. The higher price of Alpha Company shares can be attributed to the expectation that the successful sale of the new product will provide increased future profits, which will more than compensate for the lower profits experienced during the development period. Harold's wealth in Alpha Company is greater than his wealth in Beta Company in spite of the fact that Beta Company's eps are larger.

This example should make it quite clear that the higher share price of Alpha Company has resulted from the fact that its short-term actions related to new-product development, although lowering short-run eps, is expected to result in higher future eps.

Timing of Benefits   The profit maximization approach generally fails to reflect differences in the timing (i.e., time value) of benefits, while wealth maximization considers such differences. Use of the profit maximization goal generally places a greater value on an investment that returns the highest total profits, while the wealth maximization approach explicitly considers the timing of benefits and their present value impact upon the firm's share price.[*] Thus, unless profit maximization is considered in terms of the present value of eps, wealth maximization recognizes the time preference of owners for the receipt of benefits sooner as opposed to later, while profit maximization does not.

EXAMPLE   The Wakaw Grain Company is attempting to choose between either of two machines. Both machines will provide benefits over a period of five years and are assumed to cost the same. The expected profits per share directly attributable to each of these machines are as follows:

Year	Machine A	Machine B
1	$ 0	$1.75
2	0	1.75
3	0	1.75
4	0	1.75
5	10.00	1.75
Total	$10.00	$8.75

[*]The basic constructs and techniques for valuing common shares are presented in subsequent chapters.

Although it appears, based solely upon the profit maximization objective, that machine A would be preferred, it is quite possible that once the differences in timing of benefits are considered, the impact of machine B on the owner's wealth would be greater than that of machine A. If we assume that the owners of the firm are required to earn 10 percent on their investments in the machines, certain financial analysis techniques will show that the impact of these investments on the share price would be a $3.21 per share increase with A and a $3.63 per share increase with B.* In other words, the use of the wealth maximization objective considers differences in the timing of benefits.

Risk   Profit maximization does not explicitly consider risk, while wealth maximization does give explicit consideration to differences in risk. A basic premise of financial management is that a trade-off exists between risk and return in that shareholders expect to receive higher returns from investments of higher risk, and vice versa.† Financial managers in attempting to maximize wealth must therefore consider the risk-return preferences of the firm's owners or shareholders.

EXAMPLE   Winnipeg Manufacturing Limited is considering expanding its production line into either of two new products, C or D. Product C is considered to be a relatively safe product to invest in, while product D is considered a highly risky fad item. After considering all costs, the two products are expected to provide the profits per share over their five-year lives as shown:

Year	Product C	Product D
1	$ 2.00	$ 2.20
2	2.00	2.20
3	2.00	2.20
4	2.00	2.20
5	2.00	2.20
Total	$10.00	$11.00

If we ignore any risk differences and use an earnings maximization approach, it would appear that product D is preferred. However, if one considers that product D is highly risky while product C represents a safe investment, the conclusion may not be so straightforward. The firm may only need to earn 10 percent on product C, while as compensation for the greater risk of product D it must earn 15 percent. Again by applying certain financial analysis techniques that reflect differences in timing of the earnings receipts, it is found that product C is likely to increase the share price by $7.58, while product D is likely to result in a $7.37 increase in share price. It should be clear that the wealth maximization approach reflects differences in the risks associated with the receipt of earnings.

*The financial analysis techniques alluded to here are fully developed in later chapters of the text. At this point, it is best merely to recognize that quantitative techniques for considering differences in timing are available.

†The trade-off between risk and return is discussed in a variety of chapters within this text. It is a concept that underlies nearly all aspects of financial theory.

In addition, profit maximization does not consider the risk of a firm's insolvency (i.e., the risk of not having the cash flows necessary to satisfy currently maturing obligations), while wealth maximization does give consideration to differences in insolvency risks.

EXAMPLE   James Thomas, who is the sole owner of a private frisbee business, sold his frisbees for $1.00 while incurring a production cost of $0.75.* He extended credit to his customers and required payment within 30 days of the date of sale. He based his level of production in each period on his estimates of the following period's sales. These estimates, which were quite accurate, indicated a steady increase in sales over the next three months. He paid all production costs during the period in which they were incurred. James was quite fortunate in that his customers always paid their accounts within the 30-day credit period. The following events occurred during the period January 1–April 1.

Jan. 1	Cash	$ 750
	Inventory (1,500 @ $0.75)	1,125
	Receivables	1,500

During January, he sold 2,000 frisbees and produced 2,500 more in order to have a 30-day supply as inventory. His profits were $500 ($0.25 · 2,000 units).

Feb. 1	Cash [$750 begin + $1,500 collected − (2,500 · $0.75) produced]	$ 375
	Inventory [(1,500 begin + 2,500 produced − 2,000 sold) · $0.75]	1,500
	Receivables (2,000 @ $1.00)	2,000

During February, sales increased to 2,500 units and production increased to 3,000 units. James's profits for the period were $625 ($0.25 · 2,500 units). His profits to date were $1,125.

Mar. 1	Cash [$375 begin + $2,000 collected − (3,000 · $0.75) produced]	$ 125
	Inventory [(2,000 begin + 3,000 produced − 2,500 sold) · $0.75]	1,875
	Receivables (2,500 @ $1.00)	2,500

During March, sales increased to 3,000 units and production to 3,500. This time, James's profits for the period were $750 ($0.25 · 3,000 units). His profits to date were $1,875.

Apr. 1	Cash [$125 begin + $2,500 collected − (3,500 · $0.75) produced]	$ 0
	Inventory [(2,500 begin + 3,500 produced − 3,000 sold) · $0.75]	2,250
	Receivables (3,000 @ $1.00)	3,000

On April 1, James was out of cash and was therefore unable to produce more frisbees, despite the profits he had recorded in all the preceding periods.

James's cash shortage resulted from the rapid growth in inventory and accounts receivable required to support his growing level of sales. He should have planned ahead to obtain financing, although he probably could have obtained the needed funds on short notice due to his proven profitability. Also, if the shares of James's business had been publicly traded, James would have realized from the drop in the market price of his firm's shares that profit maximization was not maximizing his wealth or the wealth of the firm's other shareholders.

*This example has been adapted from the article "How to Go Broke While Making a Profit," *Business Week*, April 28, 1956, pp. 46–54. In order to provide a clear understanding of the changes in cash, inventory, and accounts receivable, the computations of the account balances for each of the months precede the balance figures.

Distribution of Returns   Use of the profit maximization goal fails to consider that shareholders may wish to receive a portion of the firm's returns in the form of periodic dividend payments or share repurchases. In the absence of any preferences for dividends, and if all funds can be invested at a positive return, then the firm can only maximize profits from period to period by totally retaining all earnings. The wealth maximization strategy takes into consideration the possibility that many owners may place a value on the receipt of a *regular* dividend payment, and that investors may have a better use for funds than the firm.* For example, it may not be in the owners' best interest, if the firm increases its eps by retaining and reinvesting all its earnings in an 8-percent term deposit. This is the case if shareholders have the opportunity of reinvesting dividend payments at the same risk and a significantly higher return.

Thus, in the remainder of this text, it will be assumed that the *primary objective of financial management is to maximize the wealth of a firm's owners or shareholders, as measured by the market value of a firm's shares.*

IMPLEMENTATION

While maximizing the market price of a firm's shares is a theoretically sound objective, it can only be unambiguously implemented if the capital markets are efficient (i.e., securities are always correctly valued given the available information). Such markets exist when investors are rational and well informed, and make the same unbiased forecast of the future developments in the firm. *For firms trading in efficient markets, the financial decisions that maximize share price at any point in a firm's planning horizon will also maximize it at all other points of time. Thus, in efficient capital markets, it makes no difference if a firm's planning horizon differs from the planned investment horizon of its owners or shareholders.*

However, if capital markets are sometimes temporarily inefficient, as many practitioners believe, then an astute corporate management may be able to exploit such imperfections in order to increase the long-run wealth of its present owners or shareholders.† As will become evident in the remainder of this book, financial theory is based on the premise that capital markets are efficient, while many financial practices of practitioners are based on the belief that capital markets are sometimes temporarily inefficient.

An Overview of the Text

The text has eight basic parts, each of which is devoted to the explanation of some aspect of the financial manager's functions. The rationale for this overall organization is a

---

*One school of thought suggests that the payment of cash dividends has no effect on the value of a firm's shares; another suggests that cash dividend payments have an effect on the value of a firm's shares. A discussion of these positions is included in Chapter 24, which is concerned specifically with dividends and retained earnings.
†First, the reader should note that much of the empirical evidence does not support such a belief. And second, the reader should note that in such markets, management cannot maximize the wealth of all its present owners or shareholders unless all the owners or shareholders have an investment horizon identical to the firm's planning horizon.

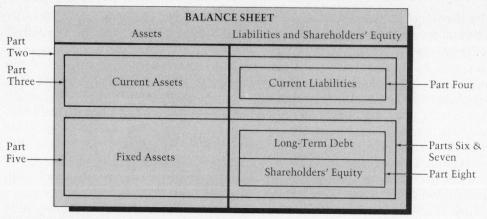

Figure 1.1   An overview of the major parts of the text.

simple balance-sheet approach, since the logical dissection and investigation of this statement provides the best structure for presenting the key principles of financial management. A brief description of the contents of Parts One through Eight is given next. These descriptions are summarized by Figure 1.1, which relates each part of the text to the firm's balance sheet.

PART ONE: INTRODUCTION

As indicated earlier, Part One sets the stage for a discussion of the key financial decision areas. This chapter has defined finance, has related finance to economics and accounting, has surveyed the finance function within the firm, and has determined the primary objective of financial management. Chapter 2 is devoted to a description of the legal organization of firms and a discussion of their operating and tax environments.

PART TWO: FINANCIAL ANALYSIS AND PLANNING

Part Two discusses the basic tools of financial analysis and planning. Special attention is given to the derivation, use, interpretation, and importance of such concepts as ratio analysis, leverage, sources and uses of funds, cash budgeting, and pro forma statements.

PART THREE: THE MANAGEMENT OF WORKING CAPITAL

Part Three is devoted to the management of the firm's current accounts, which is referred to as working capital management. The relationships between current assets and current liabilities are discussed, and certain strategies aimed at the efficient management of these items (e.g., accounts receivable) are highlighted.

PART FOUR: SOURCES OF SHORT-TERM FINANCING

Part Four discusses the key unsecured and secured sources of short-term financing available to the firm. The cost, the availability, and the pros and cons of these sources are discussed.

PART FIVE: FIXED-ASSET MANAGEMENT AND CAPITAL BUDGETING

Part Five is concerned with the management of fixed assets and capital budgeting. The mathematics of finance, capital budgeting fundamentals, capital budgeting techniques, and capital budgeting under risk are discussed in this part of the text. A knowledge of each of these areas is necessary for a thorough understanding of the management and selection of fixed-asset investments.

PART SIX: THE COST OF CAPITAL, CAPITAL STRUCTURE, AND VALUATION

Part Six is devoted to three important topics: the cost of capital, capital structure, and valuation. These topics are closely related and affect the long-term financing of the firm. The cost of capital is an important input to the capital budgeting process; capital structure and valuation both affect and are affected by the firm's cost of capital.

PART SEVEN: SOURCES OF LONG-TERM FINANCING

Part Seven describes the various financial intermediaries and markets as well as the sources of long-term financing available to firms. It discusses the cost, availability, inherent characteristics, and pros and cons of each of the following: leasing, long-term debt financing, preferred and common shares, convertible securities and warrants, and dividends and retained earnings.

PART EIGHT: EXPANSION AND FAILURE

Part Eight discusses two topics of interest to the financial manager, who must make decisions with respect to the firm's future: external expansion through acquisitions, amalgamations, and holding companies; and the alternatives available to the failed business firm.

Summary

This chapter has discussed the nature of finance as a discipline, the finance function and the role of the financial manager in the firm, and the objective of financial management, and has presented an organizational overview of the remainder of the text. Finance can be defined as a body of principles, theories, and empirical findings dealing with the generation and allocation of scarce resources (primarily money) by various decision-making units such as individuals, businesses, and governments. Finance deals with how these parties allocate scarce resources through a market-pricing system based on the valuation of risky assets (i.e., contingent claims). The basic financial problem faced by any decision-making unit is to efficiently allocate its available financial resources in order to maximize its well-being over its lifetime, while simultaneously satisfying its budgetary constraint. While an individual's well-being is generally measured in terms of the total satisfaction provided by a particular time sequence of consumption bundles, a firm's well-being is generally measured in terms of the wealth of its owners or shareholders.

Since most business decisions somehow must be measured in financial terms, the financial manager performs a highly important function within the firm. Of course, the degree of emphasis given to the finance function within a firm depends upon a number of factors such as the size of the firm, the value of the firm's business, the capabilities of the chief financial officer and his or her staff, and the capabilities of the firm's other officers, directors, and employees. In large firms, the finance function may be handled by a separate department; in small firms, it may be performed by the president, who is usually a jack-of-all-trades.

A financial manager must be thoroughly familiar with financial theory and practice and be knowledgeable about the closely related disciplines of accounting and finance. The accounting function can be viewed as a necessary input into the finance function. Thus, finance is concerned with the use of this accounting information, and other externally generated information, in order to make decisions so that business firms and individuals can maximize their well-being. An understanding of microeconomics is important because many of the financial theories that have been developed for efficiently managing a firm's assets and liabilities and measuring the risk and value of a contingent claim (e.g., a common share) are based on microeconomic theory. For example, marginal (or incremental) analysis is one of the basic principles that has been adopted from microeconomics and has been used extensively in finance. Macroeconomics provides the financial manager with an understanding of the effect of the monetary, fiscal, and economic stabilization policies carried out by government on his or her firm's profitability, liquidity, fund raising, and revenue-generating abilities. Some of the specific functions of the financial manager include financial analysis, planning and control, working capital management, managing the firm's asset structure, managing the firm's financial structure, and the distribution of corporate earnings to owners.

It is generally assumed that a business firm should be operated exclusively on behalf of its owners or shareholders. Some authors have argued that this notion of the absolute parity of the owners' or shareholders' interest is not appropriate, because other parties (such as employees, creditors, and government) also have some property right claim on the firm. It can be argued that the interests of these other parties are best protected if they impose or negotiate contractual or legal constraints on the activities of a firm's management. Since there is obviously a separation between the ownership (risk-bearing) and control (risk-taking) functions of publicly traded firms, a firm's management, who acts as an agent for the firm's owners or shareholders, may not always act in the interest of a firm's owners or shareholders (i.e., the principals). Thus, the owners or shareholders of a firm must monitor the activities of management and/or provide management compensation or incentive schemes that encourage the managers to more closely align their interests with those of the firm's owners or shareholders. Two commonly proposed measures of the well-being of a profit-oriented firm's owners or shareholders are the firm's profits and the owners' or shareholders' wealth. Even if profits are correctly interpreted as earnings per share (eps), wealth maximization is a preferred measure of well-being. It is a preferred measure because it considers the effect of future investment (i.e., profitable growth) opportunities, the timing of benefits, risk (including insolvency), and the distribution of returns. Thus, in this text, it is assumed that the primary objective of financial management is to maximize the wealth of a firm's owners or shareholders, as measured by the market value of the firm's shares.

This text is divided into eight major parts. Its organization parallels the organization of a firm's balance sheet. Part One provides an introduction that describes some of the key aspects (e.g., taxes) of the environment in which the financial manager operates. Part Two discusses the tools of financial analysis and planning. Part Three is concerned with the management of the firm's current assets and liabilities; this is referred to as working capital management. Part Four discusses the key unsecured and secured sources of short-term financing. Part Five is devoted to fixed-asset management and capital budgeting. Capital budgeting is concerned with the selection and justification of fixed-asset investments. Part Six discusses the cost of capital, capital structure, and valuation. These closely related topics are concerned with the makeup and cost implications of the firm's long-term financial structure. Part Seven is devoted primarily to the various types of long-term financing available to the firm. Part Eight discusses financial considerations related to business expansion and failure.

Questions

1.1 What is finance? What is the basic financial problem faced by any rational decision-making unit?

1.2 Describe the general relationship between finance and economics.

1.3 How does the financial manager depend on the accountant? How does the output of accounting act as an input for finance?

1.4 **a.** How does the finance function evolve within the business firm?
  b. Which two other financial officers report to the chief financial officer? What are their functions?

1.5 What are the five specific functions of the financial manager?

1.6 In financial management, whose well-being should be maximized? How can the interests of other parties best be protected?

1.7 It is sometimes argued that business firms are not operated exclusively on behalf of their owners or shareholders. Why?

1.8 What is an agency relationship? How can the principals cause the agent to act in their best interest?

1.9 What are the two commonly proposed measures of the well-being of a profit-oriented firm's owners or shareholders? Why is one of the measures a preferred measure of well-being?

1.10 Is it true that "if a firm is profitable, its survival is guaranteed"? Explain.

Notes

1. See Harry Markowitz, *Portfolio Selection* (New Haven, Conn.: Yale University Press, 1959); John Tobin, "Liquidity Preference as a Behavior Toward Risk," *The Review of Economic Studies* (February 1958), pp. 65–86; and Franco Modigliani and Merton H. Miller, "The Cost of Capital, Corporation Finance and the Theory of Investment," *American Economic Review* (June 1958), pp. 261–297.

2. Three relatively recent articles lend support to the belief that finance is currently the most common route to the top. See "The Controller: Inflation Gives Him More Clout with Management," *Business Week*, August 15, 1977, pp. 84–95; C. C. Burke, "A Group Profile of the Fortune 500 Chief Executives," *Fortune*, May 1976, pp. 172–177; and "Why the Financial Man Calls the Plays," *Business Week*, April 8, 1972, pp. 54–57.

3. Gordon Donaldson, "Financial Goals: Management vs. Stockholders," *Harvard Business Review* 41 (May–June 1963), p. 119. Reprinted by permission of the *Harvard Business Review*. Copyright © 1963 by the President and Fellows of Harvard College; all rights reserved.

4. For example, see R. Gordon, "Stockholdings of Officers and Directors in American Industrial Corporations," *Quarterly Journal of Economics* (August 1936), pp. 622–657; R. Gordon, "Ownership by Management and Control Groups in the Large Corporation," *Quarterly Journal of Economics* (May 1940), pp. 367–400; and J. Elliott, "Control, Size Growth, and Financial Performance in the Firm," *Journal of Financial and Quantitative Analysis* (January 1972), pp. 1309–1320.

5. This argument is supported by the psychologically based theories that corporate management are satisficers and not maximizers. See H. Simon, "Theories of Decision-Making in Economics and Behavioral Science," *American Economic Review* (June 1959), pp. 253–283.

6. Other examples of agency relationships include a trust deed trustee and the bondholders; a bankruptcy trustee and the bankrupt's creditors; and an underwriter and an issuing firm. The theory of agency is discussed in M. Jensen and W. Meckling, "Theory of the Firm: Managerial Behavior, Agency Costs and Ownership Structure," *Journal of Financial Economics* (October 1976), pp. 305–360.

7. Other measures have been proposed in the economics literature. For example, Baumol proposed sales revenue maximization as an alternative goal to profit maximization; and Marris proposed the maximization of the balanced rate of growth of the firm (i.e., the maximization of the rate of growth of demand for the products of the firm, and of the growth of its capital supply). See W. J. Baumol, *Business Behavior, Value and Growth* (New York: Harcourt Brace Jovanovich, 1967); and R. Marris, "A Model of the Managerial Enterprise," *Quarterly Journal of Economics* 77 (May 1963), pp. 185–209.

8. A. Koutsoyiannis, *Modern Microeconomics*, 2nd ed. (London: Macmillan Press, 1979). Also, see Roger LeRoy Miller, *Intermediate Microeconomics: Theory, Issues and Applications* (New York: McGraw-Hill, 1978), p. 160.

Suggested Readings

Anthony, Robert N., "The Trouble with Profit Maximization," *Harvard Business Review* 38 (November–December 1960), pp. 126–134.

Belkaoui, Ahmed, "The Impact of the Disclosure of the Environmental Effects of Organizational Behavior on the Market," *Financial Management* (Winter 1976), pp. 26–31.

Branch, Ben, "Corporate Objectives and Market Performance," *Financial Management* 2 (Summer 1973), pp. 24–29.

Brioschi, G., "How Olivetti's Treasury Department Functions," *Euromoney* (December 1974), pp. 53–55.

Burke, C. C., "A Group Profile of the Fortune 500 Chief Executives," *Fortune* (May 1976), pp. 172–177ff.

Caldwell, G. T. and J. R. Levesque, *The Chief Financial Officer and His Functions in Canadian Business* (Ottawa: The Conference Board in Canada, 1973).

"The Controller: Inflation Gives Him More Clout with Management," *Business Week* (August 15, 1977), pp. 84–95.

DeAlessi, Louis, "Private Property and Dispersion of Ownership in Large Corporations," *Journal of Finance* 28 (September 1973), pp. 839–851.

Dewing, Arthur S., *The Financial Policy of Corporations*, vol. 1, 5th ed. (New York: Ronald, 1953), chap. 1.

Donaldson, Gordon, "Financial Goals: Management vs. Stockholders," *Harvard Business Review* 41 (May–June 1963), pp. 116–129.

———, "Financial Management in an Affluent Society," *Financial Executive* 35 (April 1967), pp. 52–60.

Findlay, Chapman M. and G. A. Whitmore, "Beyond Shareholder Wealth Maximization," *Financial Management* 3 (Winter 1974), pp. 25–35.

Gerstner, Louis V. and Helen M. Anderson, "The Chief Financial Officer as Activist," *Harvard Business Review* 54 (September–October 1976), pp. 100–106.

Hill, Lawrence W., "The Growth of the Corporate Finance Function," *Financial Executive* 44 (July 1976), pp. 38–43.

Jensen, Michael C. and W. H. Meckling, "Theory of the Firm: Managerial Behavior, Agency Costs and Ownership Structure," *Journal of Financial Economics* (October 1976), pp. 305–360.

Lewellen, Wilbur G., "Management and Ownership in the Large Firm," *Journal of Finance* 24 (May 1969), pp. 299–322.

Mao, James C. T., "Survey of Capital Budgeting: Theory and Practice," *Journal of Finance* 25 (May 1970), pp. 349–360.

Masson, Robert Tempest, "Executive Motivations, Earnings, and Consequent Equity Performance," *Journal of Political Economy* 79 (November–December 1971), pp. 1278–1292.

Petty, William J. and Oswald D. Bowlin, "The Financial Manager and Quantitative Decision Models," *Financial Management* 5 (Winter 1976), pp. 32–41.

Pogue, Gerald A. and Kishore Lall, "Corporate Finance: An Overview," *Sloan Management Review* 15 (Spring 1974), pp. 19–38.

Solomon, Ezra, *The Theory of Financial Management* (New York: Columbia University Press, 1963), pp. 15–26.

Weston, J. Fred, "New Themes in Finance," *Journal of Finance* 24 (March 1974), pp. 237–243.

———, *The Scope and Methodology of Finance* (Englewood Cliffs, N.J.: Prentice-Hall, 1966).

"Why the Financial Man Calls the Plays," *Business Week* (April 8, 1972), pp. 54–57.

Selected Sources of Financial and Investment Information*

When gathering the data required in making a decision, the financial decision maker or analyst generally must consult a number of external sources of information. These sources are usually located in a company library, in a university or college library, or in a larger public library. A selection of the sources that provide information on Canadian companies, industries, and economic prospects are briefly discussed in this appendix.

Canadian-Based Financial and Investment Services

The Financial Post (FP) Corporation Card Service, Toronto, supplies information, such as the historical and current financial positions, on over 600 major investor-owned Canadian corporations. This consists of the basic (yellow) company cards (annual) and the current (white) information cards, which are issued as significant changes occur in the companies covered. Other information sources available from FP include: the *Dividend Service* (annual and monthly); the *Weekly Dividend Record and Investors' Diary*; the *Record of New Issues* (annual and updated); the *Record of Predecessor and Defunct Companies*; the *Record of Warrants and Convertible Securities* (annual and updated); the *Six Year Price Range* (annual); the *FP Investor's Handbook*; and the *FP Directory of Directors* (annual), which provides information on Canadian business executives and officers. In addition, the *FP Investment Data Bank* provides computerized financial and investment data in hard copy (i.e., in printed form) on approximately 275 major Canadian companies and 10 major Canadian industries.

The Canadian Business Service (CBS), Toronto, has since 1975 published the *Blue Book of CBS Stock Reports* (weekly), which provides a buy-hold-sell recommendation and a current record of

*We are grateful to Louise Carpentier, Government Publications Librarian, Concordia University, for preparing this appendix.

26

performance for the major Canadian corporations. CBS also provides the *Investment Reporter*, which contains information on the Canadian investment climate and on Canadian companies.

Dun & Bradstreet of Canada Ltd. (D&B), Toronto, publishes the *Canadian Book of Corporate Management* (annual), which deals with over 7,400 private and public companies; the *Key Business Ratios in Canada* (annual), which provides statistics on about 166 lines of business (e.g., retailing); the *Dun's Weekly Business Failures*; and the *Canadian Key Business Directory* (annual), which deals with about 10,000 businesses in Canada.

Bell and Howell (Canada) Ltd., has produced the *Canadian Financial Information Library (CAN–FIL)* on microfiche since 1970. It includes financial reports on over 2,500 listed and unlisted public companies, and financial reports of private companies.

Micromedia Limited, Toronto, has offered *The Insider* since 1980. This corporate information service is drawn from the corporate filings with the following regulatory bodies: The Ontario Securities Commission (OSC), the federal Department of Consumer and Corporate Affairs, and the U.S. Securities and Exchange Commission (SEC).

The *Blue Book of Canadian Business* (annual) has since 1976 provided surveys on about 2,700 Canadian companies and profiles of the leading Canadian companies.

R.R.S.P.-R.H.O.S.P.-R.R.I.F. Funds Performance Survey and Guaranteed Investments Annuities, Pirbeck Investment Measurement Ltd., provides ranking and performance evaluation of such funds.

American-Based Financial and Investment Services

Moody's Investors Service, New York, annually issues the following manuals: *Moody's Bank and Finance Manual, Moody's Industrial Manual, Moody's Municipal and Government (M&G) Manual, Moody's OTC Industrial Manual, Moody's Public Utility Manual*, and *Moody's Transportation Manual*. Canadian companies that are listed on U.S. stock exchanges are covered in these manuals. Companies included in a manual other than the *M&G Manual* are now indexed in *Moody's Complete Corporate Index*. Moody's also publishes *Moody's Bond Record, Moody's Dividend Record, Moody's Bond Survey*, and *Moody's Handbook of Common Stocks*.

Standard and Poor's (S&P) Corporation, New York, provides financial and investment information on Canadian corporations listed on American stock exchanges. Its publications include the *S&P Corporation Records* (6 volumes), which provide current information on individual corporations; the *S&P Register of Corporations, Directors and Executives* (annual), which supplies corporate data in the first of its three volumes; the *S&P Industry Surveys*, which in two volumes supplies data on various industries; the *S&P Analysts Handbook Composite Corporate Per Share Data by Industries*; and the *Standard NYSE Stock Reports*.

Value Line Investment Service surveys and reports on over 1100 companies. It also uses its own evaluation system to rank the companies according to their investment attractiveness.

Directories for Specific Businesses and Industries

The *Survey of Industrials, the Survey of Mines and Energy Resources*, and the *Financial Post 300* are prepared by the Financial Post. These alphabetical directories provide financial and corporate information on Canadian companies.

The *Canadian Mines Handbook* (annual) is an alphabetical directory of active and inactive Canadian mining companies. The *Canadian Mines Register of Dormant and Defunct Companies* and its *Supplements* (occasional) should be used in conjunction with the *Handbook*.

The *Sources of Funds Index* (bimonthly), published by SB Capital Corporation Ltd., is a register of fund sources for small and medium-sized Canadian businesses.

The *Franchise Annual* is a complete handbook and directory on Canadian (and American) franchisers. It also includes a "how to" section on franchising.

Who's Who in Canadian Finance supplies biographical information on financial managers and decision makers.

Indexes to Periodical Articles

The financial decision maker or analyst should minimize his or her search time by consulting the periodical indexes. The following periodical indexes are predominantly published monthly with an annual cumulation.

The *Canadian Business Periodicals Index* references articles on business, industry, and economics, which have been published in various Canadian periodicals. A corporate name index is provided in its second section.

The *Canadian Periodicals Index* references articles that have been published in a number of Canadian business journals.

Radar indexes about 130 Quebec periodicals; while *Periodex* indexes about 200 Canadian and foreign French-language periodicals.

The *F&S Index International* includes Canadian references (especially in its section 2 for countries). These include the *Financial Post, Globe and Mail Report on Business,* and the *Financial Times* (London).

The *Business Periodicals Index*, New York, references a number of Canadian business periodicals.

The *Public Affairs Information Service Bulletin*, New York, is a subject reference index on economic and social conditions. It indexes not only U.S., Canadian, and foreign periodicals but also books, government publications, agency reports, and pamphlets.

Indexes to Newspaper Articles

Since the latest financial and corporate information generally first appears in a newspaper, the financial decision maker or analyst should minimize his or her search time by consulting a newspaper index. Fortunately, the contents of a number of Canadian newspapers are readily accessible through the following published indexes.

The *Canadian News Index* (monthly), a continuation of the *Canadian Newspaper Index*, provides references to the contents of 30 major Canadian newspapers (and popular magazines) such as the *Halifax Chronicle-Herald*, the *Gazette* (Montreal), the *Toronto Star*, the *Globe and Mail*, the *Winnipeg Free Press*, the *Calgary Herald*, and the *Vancouver Sun*.

The *Canadian Business Periodicals Index* (discussed above) references the contents of the *Globe and Mail*, the *Financial Post*, and the *Financial Times of Canada*.

L'Index de l'actualité à travers la presse écrite indexes much of the contents of three French-language newspapers: *Le Devoir, Le Soleil,* and *La Presse.*

Federal Government Publications

The Canadian federal government publishes a wealth of statistical and financial information that is useful in corporate decision making.

Public and private companies. Generally, the federal government does not provide information on specific individual companies. Some notable exceptions are discussed next.

The *Financial Statement Fiche Service* is prepared by the Bureau of Corporate Affairs, Corporation Branch. It consists of a collection of microfiche of about 4,000 audited financial statements of companies filing with the bureau.

The Bureau of Corporate Affairs' *Bulletin—Canada Corporations* (monthly) provides a listing of the federal corporations that have filed financial statements, prospectuses, and take-over bids with the bureau.

The *Insolvency Bulletin* (monthly), issued by the Office of the Superintendent of Bankruptcy, contains useful information on bankruptcies in Canada.

The three-volume *Report of the Superintendent of Insurance for Canada* (annual) is published by Supply and Services Canada. It provides financial statements for federally regulated insurance companies.

Inter-Corporate Ownership, which is published occasionally by Statistics Canada, is an index of who owns or controls what in Canadian business.

In addition, firm-specific information is published by governmental Royal or special commissions and by governmental task forces. For example, the Royal Commission on Corporate Concentration prepared a series of *Studies—Background Reports* in 1976 (and subsequently) on such prominent corporations as Argus Corp. Ltd., Brascan Corp. Ltd., Domtar Ltd., Molson Companies Ltd., and Power Corporation of Canada Ltd.

Crown corporations. The Canadian federal government publishes financial information on its own crown corporations.

The *Annual Reports* of federal crown corporations (such as Petro-Canada) are usually published by Supply and Services Canada. Historical financial data for a particular crown corporation for a specific fiscal year is also found in Volume 3 (entitled "Financial Statements of Crown Corporations") of the *Public Accounts of Canada.* Pro forma financial data for a specific crown corporation for a specific fiscal year is available in the *Estimates* and the *Supplements,* published by the Treasury Board of Canada.

Aggregate economic and financial statistics. Aggregate data can be found in a number of Statistics Canada publications, which can be referenced from the *Statistics Canada Catalogues.* Such information can also be found in the monthly *Bank of Canada Review* and in the *Bank of Canada Weekly Financial Statistics.*

Provincial Government Publications

Each provincial government generally provides information on its own crown corporations and on insurance companies that are registered provincially. A useful tool to locate specific publications of the Canadian federal, provincial, and municipal governments is the *Microlog Index* (previously published as the *Profile Index,* the *Urban Canada Index,* and *Publicat*). In many libraries, titles that are listed in these indexes are available on microfiche and/or in hard copy.

Other Publications

Securities commission publications. The securities regulatory body (commonly called a securities commission) for each province generally publishes a weekly *Bulletin.* This publication contains information on the rulings of the body, on the regulatory actions taken by the body, on approved public issues of corporate securities, and on insider transactions.

Stock exchange publications. The Canadian stock exchanges generally publish a *Daily Record* (or *Bulletin*) or a monthly *Review* or both. These publications contain information on listings and delistings, on the regulatory actions taken by the exchange, and on share trading activity. It should be noted that the *Vancouver, Toronto,* and *Montreal Stock Exchange Reviews* are indexed in the *Canadian Business Periodicals Index* (discussed above).

Brokerage reports. Almost all of the Canadian brokerage houses prepare an analysis in report form on a specific company or industry for the use of their clients. For a listing of the brokerage firms (investment dealers) in a particular locale, refer to the yellow pages (in the telephone directory) of that locale. FP's *Investor Digest* publishes a weekly index of many of these reports.

On-Line Computerized Reference Services

A number of indexes to periodicals and newspaper articles are now stored on magnetic tape and are generally accessed by a librarian from a computer terminal. Although much of the information contained in these computer data bases is available from the hard-copy indexes discussed above, there are a number of advantages in performing a computerized as opposed to a manual reference search. These include: a reduced search time, a more complete search process, a more current index being searched, and a greater speed in obtaining the results of a search. The output of a search can also be obtained off-line in a hard-copy form. Some of the data bases containing financial and corporate references are the *Canadian Business Periodicals Index,* the *Canadian Newspaper Index,* the *F&S Indexes,* and the *Business Periodicals Index.*

Canadian-Based Computerized Financial and Investment Services

The *Financial Research Institute (FRI),* Montreal and Toronto, provides on-line access to current and comprehensive financial and investment information, such as daily trading statistics on the financial securities of corporations traded on the Montreal and Toronto Stock Exchanges. It also provides a number of computer packages to aid the financial and investment community in portfolio management, security analysis, detailed financial and corporate analysis, and economic analysis.

The *Financial Post Investment Databank* provides much of the FP hard-copy information discussed above on magnetic tape. It also provides the *Canadian Stock Market Tape* and the *Canadian Corporate Data Tape.*

CANSIM (Canadian Socioeconomic Information Management System) is a computerized data base that provides on-line access to Statistics Canada's socioeconomic data base. Both time series and cross-classified data series are available on this data base.

Other Guides to Sources of Information

The financial decision maker or analyst should also consult other guides to sources of Canadian financial and investment information. Two useful (and more comprehensive) guides are Barbara E. Brown (ed.), *Canadian Business and Economics: A Guide to Information/Sources d'information economiques et commerciales canadiennes* (Ottawa: Canadian Library Association, 1976); and Brian Land, *Sources of Information for Canadian Business* (Montreal: The Canadian Chamber of Commerce, 1978).

Chapter 2

THE LEGAL, OPERATING, AND TAX ENVIRONMENTS OF THE FIRM

To fully understand many financial decisions, a person must have a good understanding of the legal forms of business organization, their operating environments, the fund-raising implications, and the pros and cons of each. The basic assumption of this text is that the firm under study is a corporation; however, it is important to have a thorough understanding of the other forms of business organizations and their characteristics. Understanding the taxation procedure of noncorporate entities is also important. Since the primary emphasis in this book is on the corporate form of organization, it is important for the reader to understand both how corporate income is measured and how it is taxed. Such an understanding makes it easier to see why certain financial variables must be considered by the financial manager in making decisions about the asset or financial structure of the firm. A knowledge of income measurement and tax treatment is also of key importance in financial analysis and planning.

This chapter has four major sections. The first section describes the key aspects of the various forms of business organization, placing special emphasis on the corporation. The second section presents a brief discussion of the treatment of corporate income, covering the important topics of depreciation, capital cost allowance, interest, and dividends. The third section describes the main aspects of personal taxes. The final section discusses corporate taxes.

The Basic Forms of Business Organization

The three basic forms of business organization are the *sole proprietorship*, the *partnership*, and the *corporation*. Each of these forms will be evaluated individually. While the sole proprietorship is the most common form of business organization, the corporation is by far the most dominant form in terms of sales, earnings, and assets, especially in the industrial sector. For example, the 300 industrial companies ranked as the largest in terms of sales (or revenues) for 1978 by the *Financial Post* had sales of $145.8 billion, net income (before extraordinary items) of $7 billion, and assets of $171 billion.* On the other hand, Statistics Canada reported that all industrial organizations, excluding government enterprises, had sales of $191.3 billion, net income of $8.3 billion, and assets of $198 billion for 1978. Although these figures are not directly comparable, they do highlight the dominance of corporations—especially large corporations—in the Canadian economy.

SOLE PROPRIETORSHIPS

A *sole proprietorship* is a business that is owned by one person who operates it for his or her own profit. The typical sole proprietorship is a small firm, such as a neighbourhood grocery store, auto-repair shop, or shoe-repair business. Typically the proprietor, along with a few employees, operates the proprietorship. He or she normally raises all capital from personal resources or by borrowing. The majority of sole proprietorships are in the wholesale, retail, service, and construction industries.

Advantages of a Sole Proprietorship   The commonly cited advantages of a sole proprietorship, aside from being one's own boss, are as follows:

Ownership of All Profits   Many people do not like the idea of working for someone else and seeing their employer receive the profits from their efforts. The sole proprietorship allows the owner to receive the fruits of his or her efforts; however, he or she must also absorb the losses.

Low Organizational Costs   A sole proprietorship can be started without elaborate legal documents. At the most it need only obtain the necessary licences before it can begin to operate legally.

Tax Advantages   Typically the sole proprietor is not subject to any special types of taxes. The basic taxes he or she must pay are those on income, property, and payroll. The income of the sole proprietorship is taxed as personal income of the sole proprietor; in other words, the business is not viewed as being a separate entity. Certain carryback and carryforward rules for unused capital losses (to be discussed later in the chapter) are less restrictive in the case of sole proprietorships than for corporations. A recent amendment to the Income Tax Act allows salary paid to a spouse as a tax-deductible expense.

A Possible High Credit Standing   If the sole proprietor has any wealth, it is quite likely that the proprietorship will have a higher credit standing than a corporation of equal size, since the owner's wealth is not considered when a corporation's credit is analyzed.

*The *Financial Post*, "The 1979 ranking of Canada's 500 largest companies," June 16, 1979. The following two observations are also interesting. First, the first 200 companies on the list account for 94 percent of the 300's sales, 95 percent of the 300's net income, and 96 percent of the 300's assets. Second, of the 300 industrial companies, 101 are wholly owned by foreign parent companies, 54 are owned 50 percent or more by foreigners, and another 26 have lesser degrees of foreign ownership, but, in some cases, this is still sufficient to ensure effective control.

Other Advantages   Other advantages often cited for sole proprietorships are secrecy and ease of dissolution—secrecy because the owner is not required to disclose financial information publicly and ease of dissolution because a sole proprietorship can be dissolved simply by satisfying all the firm's financial obligations.

Disadvantages of a Sole Proprietorship   In many cases, the disadvantages may outweigh the advantages of this form of organization.

Unlimited Liability   The sole proprietor's total wealth, and not merely the amount he or she originally invested, can be used to satisfy creditors. Since the business is not independent of its proprietor, he or she may lose many personal assets in the process of satisfying the claims of creditors.

Limitations on Size   The financial fund-raising power of the sole proprietorship is limited to the amount one person can raise. Generally, this is not enough to permit larger-scale operations. The inability of the sole proprietor to raise needed capital often causes him or her to form a partnership or corporation.

Tax Disadvantages   Certain employee benefits, such as group insurance or medical coverage, can be claimed as tax deductible expenses by corporations but not by unincorporated businesses. Further, as will be shown later in this chapter, certain federal and provincial tax incentives for small Canadian businesses are offered only if such businesses are incorporated. It is also relatively more difficult for unincorporated businesses to defer income tax payments.

Other Disadvantages   A number of other disadvantages exist with a sole proprietorship. They are (1) difficulties in management resulting from the need to be a jack-of-all-trades; (2) a lack of opportunity for employees, since the usual long-run incentives for a good employee to stay with the firm cannot be provided; and (3) a lack of continuity when the proprietor dies.

PARTNERSHIPS

A partnership consists of two or more owners doing business together for a profit. Partnerships are typically larger than sole proprietorships but they are not generally large businesses. A partnership should be established with a formal agreement that covers (1) the name of the partnership; (2) the operational domain and business activities of the partnership; (3) the amount and timing of capital investments by each partner; (4) valuation, arbitration, and other procedures to be followed if a new partner is to be admitted to the partnership or an existing partner is to depart or to be expelled; (5) provisions for the payment of salaries and interest and for the distribution of profits and losses; (6) procedures to be followed if the partnership is to be dissolved; and (7) any restrictions on the outside private commercial activities of the partners. In the absence of a partnership agreement, the applicable legislation of the partnership's jurisdiction will dictate the terms of the partnership.

Thus, a formal partnership agreement is important, for if it is properly executed, it can aid in the resolution of many of the problems that may occur between partners.

General Partnerships   In a partnership, both profits and losses are shared according to a previous agreement. Therefore, a partnership is essentially an arrangement in which each partner can share the risk of loss in accordance with his or her risk preferences. A partnership in which the risk is shared symmetrically, in the sense that all the partners have unlimited liability, is called a *general partnership*. Thus, in a general partnership the personal assets of all the partners can be claimed when the firm defaults on its obligations. General partnerships are common among such professionals as lawyers, doctors, and accountants, since they have generally been precluded by legislation from incorporating. In essence, they have been denied the right to incorporate because of the desire of the provincial legislators not to limit the liability of each individual professional.

Limited Partnerships   This is a special type of partnership in which the liability of one or more, but *not* all, of the partners is limited to their original investment. That is, there must be at least one general partner whose liability is unlimited. The *limited partnership* is permitted in all provinces except Prince Edward Island and Nova Scotia. The limited partner is normally prohibited from being active in the management of the firm. Limited partnerships are often used in real estate development.* They are also being used more and more to fund the search for and development of oil and gas reserves. For example, the sale of *limited partnership units* in drilling funds was expected to raise $500 million in 1979.†

Advantages of a Partnership   The partnership is similar to the sole proprietorship with respect to taxes and organizational costs. A partner's income is taxed in the same manner as a sole proprietor's; and except for the possible legal cost of having a formal partnership agreement drawn up, the costs of organization are quite similar to those of the sole proprietorship. However, a partnership does have the following advantages over a sole proprietorship.

A Larger Amount of Capital   The financial resources of more than one individual normally provide higher amounts of capital than the sole proprietor can raise.

A Better Credit Standing   The credit standing of a partnership is higher than that of either a corporation or a sole proprietorship of similar size. This is because the personal assets of all the partners are available to satisfy the claims of creditors.

Other Advantages   A partnership is advantageous in the sense that more brainpower and management skills are available than in the sole proprietorship. Also, a partnership

---

*Since Canadian real estate investment trusts (REIT's) are unincorporated trusts, they have unit holders who do not have limited liability. To limit the unit holder's liability, all contracts with the REIT contain provisions that indemnify the unit holders from any losses beyond their initial investment.
†These investments are attractive to individual investors because of a 1976 federal budget tax amendment. Under the amendment, the ability to deduct petroleum exploration expenditures from income for tax purposes was extended to private investors. In addition, the applicable deduction was raised to a potential 100 percent of the funds raised, depending on the mix between exploration drilling expenses (100-percent deduction) and development expenses (30-percent deduction). As a result, more programs have provided the investor with an average first-year tax write-off of between 60 and 70 percent.

is more likely to retain good employees since it can give them the opportunity to become partners.

Disadvantages of a Partnership   Partnerships have a number of basic disadvantages which must be weighed against their advantages.

Unlimited Liability   Each of the general partners is liable for the partnership's debts. Partners are subject to *joint and several liability.* This means that if a partnership with three partners—A, B, C—fails, and net losses are greater than the liquidation value of the firm, and neither A nor B has any private resources other than their investment in the business, then the entire loss will fall on C if C has the assets to cover it. Partner C will, however, have a legal claim on A and B for the portion of their respective liabilities he or she has paid.

Limited Life   Technically, when a partner dies or withdraws, the partnership is dissolved. The articles of partnership should clearly provide the procedure to be followed if either of these events occurs.

Other Disadvantages   It is difficult for a partner to liquidate or transfer money invested in a partnership. The partnership, although it can grow to a larger size than a sole proprietorship, still has difficulty achieving large-scale operations.

   With regard to income taxes, similar rules apply to the partnership as to the proprietorship.

CORPORATIONS

A corporation is an entity created by law with separate and independent existence apart from its owners, who are referred to as shareholders. That is, a corporation is a "person" in that it can sue and be sued, make and be party to contracts, and acquire property in its own name. Although a large number of corporations are involved in wholesale and retail trade and in finance, insurance, and real estate, corporations in the manufacturing, utility, construction, transportation, mining, and oil refining businesses account for the largest portion of corporate business receipts and net profits.

   A corporation can be incorporated under federal or provincial law. In general, companies that intend to carry on business across Canada are incorporated federally; companies that intend to carry on business within a province are incorporated provincially. A provincially incorporated company may carry on business in provinces other than that of its incorporation if it registers as an extra-provincial company in each of the other provinces.

   A business incorporated in any province (except Alberta) or federally under the Canada Corporations Act must have either of the words "limited," "incorporated," or "corporation" appended to its title. For corporations registered in Alberta, only the word "limited" can be used.

   For Canadian tax purposes, corporations are divided into private and public corporations.* The distinction is spelled out in the Income Tax Act. In brief, a corporation is

---

*Corporations are also classified as being public or private, or alternatively as reporting or nonreporting for financial disclosure purposes.

defined as a public corporation if it has one or more classes of its shares listed on any of the prescribed Canadian stock exchanges. A resident corporation not meeting the above requirement and not controlled by one or more public corporations is deemed to be a private corporation.

Although the main concern of this book is with profit-oriented businesses, there are a number of "nonprofit" corporations in Canada that have been established to serve the broad public and private interest. For example, the Export Development Corporation is a federal crown corporation, which was set up to assist Canadian exporters; and the Ontario Development Corporation was established to assist businesses in central and southwestern Ontario.

Corporate Organization   The major parties in a corporation are the *common share-holders*, the *board of directors*, and the *officers*. Figure 2.1 depicts the relationship between these three groups. The common shareholders are the true owners of the firm. The board of directors is responsible for directing the affairs of the business. Final authority for the actions of the corporation is in the hands of the board of directors. The corporate officers are responsible for day-to-day operations. They are required to report periodically to the board of directors.

Shareholders   Since the common shareholders are the true owners of the firm, they vote periodically to select the board of directors and to make amendments to the corporate charter. The common shareholder has the following basic rights:

1 To receive dividends in proportion to his or her ownership
2 To hold or sell his or her share certificates*
3 To share in liquidation
4 To inspect the firm's books and records

In small corporations, it is quite likely that the board of directors consists of the shareholders, who also manage the business. In a large corporation with thousands of shareholders, the firm's executives do not usually own a large number of shares. Large numbers of shareholders result in separation of ownership and management. When there are large numbers of shareholders, management is more likely to consider the total operating environment of the firm and to attempt to maximize the owners' wealth by satisfying the needs of not only the owners but also employees, customers, suppliers, the general public, and the government.

Board of Directors   The individuals elected by the shareholders to manage the corporation on their behalf are referred to as *directors*. For federally incorporated corporations, a majority of the board members must be resident Canadians.† In order to ensure that the directors act in the best interests of the firm's shareholders, there are a number of duties that all directors must perform. These are given in both case law and in the Corporations Act of the relevant jurisdiction.

---

*Sometimes the right to purchase a pro rata portion of any new common share issue is also provided. However, in Canada this "preemptive" right is the exception rather than the rule.
†A resident Canadian is defined as either a Canadian citizen or a landed immigrant who has been a resident of Canada for more than six years.

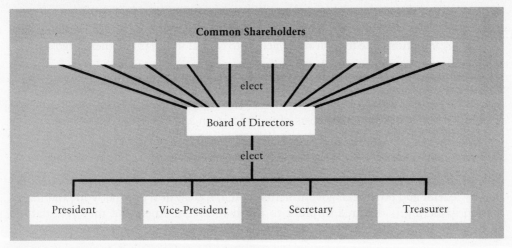

Figure 2.1   The general organization of a corporation.

Advantages of a Corporation   Since corporations dominate our economy, the corporate form of organization must have certain advantages over the sole proprietorship and the partnership. The principal advantages are listed below.

Limited Liability   The owners of a corporation have limited liability, which guarantees that they cannot lose more dollars than they have committed themselves to invest. In other words, a shareholder in a corporation bears risk that is limited to the loss of his or her investment. Thus, the corporation is similar to the partnership in one important respect: they are both mechanisms for sharing risk. However, the corporate form is unique in that it allows every owner (shareholder) to have the advantage of limited liability.*

Large Size   Since corporate shares can be made readily marketable and can be issued at low per-share prices, capital can be raised from many individuals through the sale of shares.

Transferability of Ownership   Corporate ownership is evidenced by share certificates, which can easily be transferred to new owners. Organized stock exchanges facilitate the sale or purchase of shares and the associated transfers of ownership.

Other Advantages   Corporations also have a few other advantages: (1) they have a long life, since a corporation is not dissolved by the death or withdrawal of shareholders; (2)

*This, however, may not be true in the case of small corporations operating in a risky environment. The owner-managers of such corporations, being typically small in number, may remain personally liable to creditors who, in order to reduce their risk, often demand personal guarantees in addition to the assets pledged by the corporation. Furthermore, shareholders of large corporations sometimes have to assume additional liability on a joint and several basis because of the requirements of customers, banks, financing institutions, or foreign governments. For example, the willingness to assume joint and several liability is often necessary to win a contract to deliver a large capital project, especially on a turn-key basis in a Middle East country.

professional managers can be hired to run the corporation, and if they do an unsatisfactory job they can be replaced; and (3) corporations can expand more easily than other types of organizations due to their ready access to capital markets and their large size.

Disadvantages of Corporations Corporations have certain disadvantages, particularly if they are public.

Organizational Expenses The costs of incorporation and the issuance of shares often prove to be a drawback to the corporate form of organization, especially for small businesses.

Government Regulation Since the corporation is a legal entity, it is subject to regulation by federal and provincial governments. Often, a great deal of paperwork and information gathering is required in order to fulfill the requirements of these regulatory agencies.

Other Disadvantages Other often-cited drawbacks of corporations are (1) a lack of personal interest in the firm by employees due to their often nonowner status, and (2) a lack of secrecy, since each shareholder must be provided with an annual report of the corporation's financial performance and financial position.

The Treatment of Corporate Income

As indicated in the introduction to this chapter, the emphasis in this text will be on the financial aspects of corporations. There are three basic reasons for this: (1) corporations, due to their generally large size, provide a workshop in which to examine the greatest number of financial concepts; (2) corporations are dominant in our capitalistic economy; and (3) business school graduates will most likely end up working in or with corporations. Since corporate performance is measured with respect to the net income shown on the firm's income statement, it is important to understand the basic concepts used in calculating that income. The key items to be examined are *depreciation, capital cost allowance, cash flows, interest,* and *dividends.*

DEPRECIATION AND CAPITAL COST ALLOWANCE

Corporations, as well as sole proprietorships and partnerships, are permitted to charge a portion of the cost of fixed assets to the annual revenues they generate. These costs show up as depreciation in the firm's accounting statements. The firm may report depreciation in any manner consistent with good business and accounting practice; but for tax purposes, the depreciation expense must be computed as capital cost allowance in accordance with the provisions set out in the Income Tax Act and the relevant regulations. Thus, capital cost allowance may bear no relationship with either the theoretically correct rate of depreciation or with the annual depreciation recorded in the firm's books. This is so because the objectives of our tax laws are not identical to those of financial reporting. For example, tax laws are often used to generate economic incentives for firms to invest in certain capital goods or regions of slow economic activity. This, of course, is not the objective of financial reporting.

Since the depreciation methods for reporting purposes can be found in most basic accounting texts, they will not be discussed here. The procedures for computing capital cost allowance (depreciation charges for tax purposes), however, will be discussed in a following section of this chapter.

Depreciation and Cash Flows   Chapter 1 noted that the financial manager is often more concerned with cash flows than with the net profits as reported on the income statement. To adjust the income statement to show cash flows from operations, all noncash charges must be added back. Noncash charges are expenses that are deducted on the income statement but do not involve an actual outlay of cash. Depreciation, amortization, and depletion allowances are examples of such charges.

The general rule for calculating cash flows from operations is

Cash flow from operations = net profits after taxes + noncash charges   (2.1)

Applying Equation 2.1 to the income statement for the ABC Company in Table 2.1 yields

Net profit after taxes	$12,000
Plus: Depreciation	5,000
Cash flow from operations	$17,000

However, this figure is only approximate, since not all sales are made for cash and not all expenses are paid when they are incurred.

Depreciation and other noncash charges shield the firm from taxes by lowering its taxable income. Many people do not accept depreciation as a source of funds; however, it is a source of funds in the sense that it is a "nonuse" of funds. Table 2.2 shows the income statement of the ABC Company Ltd. calculated on a cash basis in order to illustrate how depreciation shields income and acts as a nonuse of funds. Ignoring

Table 2.1   ABC Company Ltd. Income Statement

Sales		$100,000
Less: Return and allowances		5,000
Net sales		$ 95,000
Less: Cost of goods sold		45,000
Gross profit		$ 50,000
Less: Expenses		
General and administrative	$20,000	
Interest	5,000	
Depreciation	5,000	
Total		$ 30,000
Net profits before taxes		$ 20,000
Less: Federal taxes (40%)[a]		8,000
Net profit after taxes		$ 12,000

[a]Set at 40 percent for illustrative purposes only.

Table 2.2   ABC Company Ltd. Income Statement Calculated on a Cash Basis

Net sales		$95,000
Less: Cost of goods sold		45,000
Gross profit		$50,000
Less: Expenses		
General and administrative	$20,000	
Interest	5,000	
Depreciation	0	
Total		$25,000
Cash flow before taxes		$25,000
Less: Taxes[a]		8,000
Cash flow from operations		$17,000

[a]Taxes are based on the inclusion of depreciation, as in Table 2.1.

depreciation, except in determining the firm's tax liability, makes the resulting cash flow from operations equal to $17,000—the same figure we obtained earlier.*

The adjustment of the firm's net profits after taxes by adding back noncash charges such as depreciation will be used on numerous occasions in this text to determine cash flows.

Capital Cost Allowance   The portion of the cost of depreciable assets permitted as an annual tax-deductible expense is known as *capital cost allowance* (CCA).† Briefly, the deduction is calculated as follows: The firm's depreciable assets are classified into different classes or pools. Each class is treated separately for the purpose of CCA computations. Each class is assigned a fixed rate, which is called a *CCA rate*. Both the rates and the classification system are given in the Income Tax Regulations. In most cases,‡ the maximum amount of CCA permitted for a class is

---

*In other words, for the calculation of cash flow, depreciation expense is relevant only to the extent of determining the firm's tax liability. Since for tax purposes the depreciation expense is the capital cost allowance (CCA), the difference between the reported depreciation and the CCA-based depreciation is irrelevant for the calculation of cash flow.

†The Canadian Institute of Chartered Accountants (CICA) recommends that the difference between the tax charge based on the CCA deduction and the tax expense based on the depreciation expense for reporting purposes be shown on the income statement as *deferred taxes*. For an interesting study of the effect of the divergence between the tax depreciation and reported depreciation on the firm's cost of capital, see Eugene Brigham and James Pappas, *Liberalized Depreciation Practices and the Cost of Capital* (East Lansing, Mich.: MSU Public Utilities Studies, 1970). Briefly, their argument as to the effect on the cost of capital is as follows: Since the deductions claimed for tax purposes are usually greater than the reported depreciation charges in the early years of the asset's life, the tax expense on the income statement will exceed the taxes actually paid. In the later years, the situation may be reversed. Therefore, it is reasonable to consider the difference between the two amounts to be a deferment of taxes and not a true saving. Since the accumulated deferred tax is, in essence, an interest-free loan, it would affect the firm's cost of capital.

‡For certain classes of assets, CCA charges are computed on a straight-line basis. The annual straight-line CCA charge for an eligible asset is calculated by dividing the asset's capital cost by a prescribed

calculated by applying the prescribed CCA rate for the class to its year-end capital cost balance, which is referred to as *undepreciated capital cost* (UCC) balance.* The CCA claimed in the year is then deducted from the UCC balance at the end of the current taxation year in order to arrive at the UCC balance as of the beginning of the next taxation year. It is important to note that, unlike the accounting depreciation charge that is calculated for each asset, CCA is calculated for *the various classes of depreciable assets held by the firm*.† Examples of the calculation of the CCA are given next. In all of them, it is assumed that the firm's taxation year is identical to the calendar year.

No Purchase or Sale of Assets   In the following example, it will be assumed that no assets have been added to or sold from a particular asset class during the year for which the CCA is being calculated.

Example   Winnipeg Wires Ltd. began operations on January 1, 1973, by acquiring a building and certain wiring equipment for $190,000 and $10,000, respectively. Both assets are of Class 3, for which the prescribed CCA rate is 5 percent. No sale or further purchase of Class 3 assets was made up to 1975. The computations of the maximum CCA charges that the company was allowed to take under the Income Tax Act are shown in Table 2.3.

Table 2.3   CCA Charges for Winnipeg Wires Ltd.

Capital cost, 1973		$200,000
Less: CCA, 1973	(200,000 · .05) =	10,000
UCC, January 1, 1974		$190,000
Less: CCA, 1974	(190,000 · .05) =	9,500
UCC, January 1, 1975		$180,500
CCA, 1975	(180,500 · .05) =	9,025
UCC, January 1, 1976		$171,475

number of years that may or may not be equal to the asset's economic life. For example, for assets of Class 27 (air pollution control equipment), maximum CCA charges are permitted on a straight-line basis over two years—that is, at an annual rate of 50 percent.

*Capital cost is normally taken to be the original cost, except for assets acquired before 1949, for which it is the original cost less the straight-line depreciation accumulated up to 1948. The term capital cost for CCA purposes is discussed in the Department of Revenue's Interpretation Bulletin IT-174. It implies the full cost to the taxpayer of acquiring the asset, including legal, accounting, engineering, and other fees paid. If the payment is made in foreign currency, then the Canadian dollar equivalent of the amount paid will constitute the capital cost. Government grants are also normally credited to capital costs. Further, as per section 21 of the Income Tax Act, a taxpayer is allowed to add certain borrowing costs and interest paid to the cost of the asset, instead of claiming such items as a tax-deductible expense for the year. For a more detailed discussion, refer to Geoffrey M. Colley, *Tax Principles to Remember* (Toronto, CICA, 1978).

†However, this does not imply that once an asset has been included in its class, its capital cost becomes irrelevant in CCA calculations. How the cost of each individual asset enters into the CCA computations will be discussed later in this section of the chapter.

The CCA charge is always calculated on the year-end balance. In the present example, the UCC balance at the beginning of each year always equaled the year-end UCC balance because no new assets of the class were purchased; nor were any assets from the class sold during the years for which the CCA charges have been calculated. Notice that the UCC balance is declining and will continue to decline if no new assets of the class are added. For this reason, this method of calculating the CCA deduction is sometimes referred to as the *declining balance method*. Mathematical formulas for computing CCA charges and associated tax savings based on the declining balance method are developed in the Appendix to Chapter 15.

Purchase or Sale of Assets   If there is an addition of an asset to a class during a year, then the new asset's cost is added to the UCC balance as of the beginning of the year. If there is a sale of an asset from the class, the lower of the proceeds of the sale or the original cost of the asset is deducted from the presale UCC balance.* If at the end of the year the UCC balance for the asset class is positive and the class is continued (i.e., if not *all* the assets in the class have been disposed of), then no special tax treatment is called for. However, if this balance turns out to be negative, then its numerical value, referred to as *recaptured depreciation*, is deemed income for the year and is taxed at regular tax rates. In addition, the year-end UCC balance becomes zero.

Whether or not the proceeds of sale of an asset exceed the original cost of the asset is relevant in determining the amount that is to be recaptured. For example, suppose that the proceeds exceed the original cost. Then, in accordance with the prescribed rule, only a portion of the proceeds up to the original cost of the asset will be deducted from the presale UCC balance. The resulting balance, if negative, will constitute the amount of recaptured depreciation. The excess of the proceeds over the original cost will be considered a *capital gain* for tax purposes. On the other hand, if the negative UCC balance arises when the proceeds are less than the original cost, then there will be a recapture but no capital gain. The negative UCC balance, resulting from the sale of an asset(s), is considered to be an indication that the CCA deductions claimed in the past were in aggregate greater than the actual depreciation. The excess, therefore, is presumed to reflect overdepreciation and is brought back into the taxpayer's income as recaptured depreciation.

EXAMPLE   The Sindro Communications Ltd. acquired the following assets in 1974.

1 Building (Class 3, rate 5 percent), cost $395,000
2 Sound transmitter (Class 8, rate 20 percent), cost $62,000
3 Electrical generator (Class 8, rate 20 percent), cost $8,000

Class 3 and Class 8 each had a UCC balance of $5,000 before the three acquisitions were made. In September 1975, the company sold its sound transmitter for $10,000 and acquired a replace-

---

*For CCA purposes, proceeds are defined as the selling price minus any commissions, fees, or delivery costs incurred in connection with the sale of the asset.

ment, a Class 8 asset, for $18,000. In December 1976, the building, which was acquired in 1974, was sold for $400,000. It was replaced with a new Class 3 building, which cost $30,000. In the same month, the electrical generator acquired in 1974 was also disposed of for $4,400.

Using the procedure explained before, the maximum CCA charges allowed to the company as well as the related calculations of recaptured depreciation and capital gains are shown in Table 2.4.

Table 2.4   CCA Charges for the Sindro Communications Ltd.

	Class 3		Class 8
1974			
UCC, beginning of the year	$5,000		$5,000
Acquisitions	395,000		70,000
UCC, at year-end used for CCA charge	$400,000		$75,000
Less: CCA (400,000 · .05) =	20,000	(75,000 · .20) =	15,000
1975			
UCC, beginning of the year	$380,000		$60,000
Acquisitions	—		18,000
Assets sold:			
Less: Proceeds of sale or original cost	—		10,000
UCC, at year-end used for CCA charge	$380,000		$68,000
Less: CCA	19,000		13,600
1976			
UCC, beginning of the year	$361,000		$54,400
Acquisitions	30,000		—
Assets sold:			
Less: Proceeds of sale or original cost	395,000		4,400
Recapture	$4,000		—
Capital gains (400,000 − 395,000) =	5,000[a]		—
UCC, at year-end for calculating CCA charge	0		$50,000

[a]As will be explained later, only 50 percent of this amount (i.e., $2,500) will be added to income as a *taxable* capital gain.

The Class 3 building sold in 1976 generated proceeds of $400,000, which exceeded the original cost of the building by $5,000. This resulted in the $5,000 capital gain. Furthermore, the deduction of the proceeds up to the original cost ($395,000) from the presale Class 3 balance ($391,000) resulted in a negative UCC balance of $4,000 after the sale. Thus, the numerical value of this balance is shown as a recapture, and the Class 3 year-end UCC balance is reduced to zero.

If the building had been sold for less than its original cost, say for $392,000, then there would have been a recapture of $1,000 (i.e., $392,000 − $391,000), but no capital gain. It is also important to note that although the new Class 3 building was acquired in the last month of 1976, its capital cost was added to the preacquisition UCC balance as if the asset had been held by the firm for the entire year. Thus, when the prescribed CCA rate was applied to the year-end balance, the asset, in part, generated the maximum CCA allowed for the entire year. Unlike the pro rata deduction customary for depreciation calculations in the United States, a newly acquired asset's contribution to the annual CCA deduction is *not* a function of the number of months the asset was held during the year of interest. The CCA calculations for Class 8 were more straightforward, since there were no recaptures or capital gains. This is so because the UCC balance of the class remained positive throughout the period considered, and none of the assets sold generated proceeds in excess of their original costs.

Terminal Loss   Suppose that after the sale of an asset(s) from a class, there is no asset left in that class but there is still a positive year-end UCC balance for the class. In this case, the positive balance, referred to as the *terminal loss*, can be written off against income.* It should be emphasized that this provision operates only if the taxpayer owns no assets of the class at the end of the year.† The rationale for this provision is similar to that for recaptured depreciation. That is, the existence of a positive UCC balance, after all the assets have been disposed of, is considered to be an indication that the class was underdepreciated. Therefore, the terminal loss deduction is intended to enable the taxpayer to claim the amount of depreciation that should have been claimed but was not claimed in the past.

EXAMPLE   Suppose, in the previous example, that all the assets in Class 8, as of the end of 1976, were disposed of for $15,000 in 1977. Suppose also that no other Class 8 assets were acquired during 1977. Then the terminal loss deduction, available at the end of 1977, would be $35,000 ($50,000 − $15,000).‡

Accelerated Capital Cost Allowance   A firm's tax liability is affected significantly by the size of its capital cost allowance deductions. Consequently, in order to generate tax incentives for investment in certain types of machinery or products, the government has introduced several types of accelerated capital cost allowances. This has been done by allowing the CCA charges for certain classes to be computed on a straight-line basis over a prescribed number of years. For example, for Class 29, which includes certain manufacturing and processing machinery and equipment acquired after May 8, 1972, the CCA charges can be computed on a straight-line basis over two years.

---

*If the balance is negative, as explained earlier, it will be recaptured and treated as ordinary income.
†It is also important to note that the provision appears to imply that the deduction *must* be claimed in the year during which the terminal loss occurs, even if there is no income for the year against which to apply it. For details as to the interpretation of this provision, see Geoffrey M. Colley, *Tax Principles to Remember* (Toronto: CICA, 1978), pp. 17–18.
‡This calculation assumes that each asset's proceeds of disposal were less than its original cost so that no capital gains resulted from the disposal of assets from the class.

Capital Cost Allowance and Tax Planning   The distinction between the CCA charges and the depreciation expense calculated on the basis of customary depreciation methods becomes particularly significant in the matter of tax planning. Although the CCA rates are prescribed as maximum rates, the taxpayer is not required to claim the maximum allowance each year. Only a portion of the maximum, or no allowance at all, can be taken in any given taxation year. If the claim for any particular taxation year is less than the maximum, then the unabsorbed balance is allowed to be carried forward indefinitely to be claimed in future taxation years. The significance of this flexibility for planning tax payments can be shown by reviewing the following two examples.

EXAMPLE   Consider the situation of a firm that has incurred an operating loss and has therefore generated no tax liability for the year. In such a situation, the firm may find no tax advantage in claiming the maximum CCA allowed for the year.* Under the CCA system, the firm can defer its claim, in part or in whole, *indefinitely*.

EXAMPLE   Suppose that a firm expects a large tax liability arising from a recapture of a large negative year-end UCC balance for a particular class of its assets. If desired, this potential tax liability can be reduced by acquiring further assets of the class at any time during the year, up to the last day of the year. This is possible because under the CCA system, the year-end balance will be increased by the *full* cost of the assets purchased during the year as long as they were acquired before the end of the year.†

INTEREST AND DIVIDENDS

It is important to have a clear understanding of the difference in the treatment of interest and dividends. *Interest* is shown as an *expense* on the income statement and represents payments made by the firm to its creditors (lenders) for money borrowed. The repayment of a loan itself by a firm to a creditor does not represent interest and is not shown on the firm's income statement. The repayment must be from the firm's cash flows, but it does not affect the company's income since it merely represents the return of something that has been borrowed.

Dividends represent the distribution of earnings to the owners or shareholders of a corporation and are therefore not allowed as a tax-deductible expense to the firm. They must be paid from the firm's cash flows and are often deducted from the firm's net profits after taxes. Both interest and dividends are payments for funds, but interest is a payment for funds *temporarily* lent to the firm whereas dividends represent payment for *permanent* funds provided by the firm's owners. Moreover, dividend payments received by individuals must be claimed as personal income and are therefore subject to a

---

*Unless loss carryback and carryforward considerations dictate otherwise.
†There are, however, some exceptions; for example, if a building is acquired at a cost in excess of $50,000, a separate class or pool must be established.

Table 2.5   The Format of a General Income Statement

Sales
— Cost of goods sold
Gross profit
— Expenses other than interest
Operating profit or Earnings before interest and taxes (EBIT)
— Interest expense
Net profits before taxes or Earnings before taxes (EBT)
— Taxes
Net profits after taxes or Earnings after taxes (EAT)
— Preferred dividends
Earnings available for common shareholders (EAC)
—Common share dividends
To retained earnings

second tax in the form of a personal income tax. Dividends received by a corporation are to be included in the receiving corporation's income for tax purposes. However, if the dividends are received from a taxable Canadian corporation, then a receiving public corporation can determine its taxable income by deducting the amount of the dividend received from its net income before taxes.

A general income statement format is given in Table 2.5. This basic format will be used frequently throughout the text. One point to note is that before the common shareholders can receive dividends, the preferred shareholders' claims must be satisfied, since the preferred shareholders are given preference over the common shareholders in the distribution of dividends.

PERSONAL INCOME TAXES

The income of individuals is subject to taxation by both the federal and provincial governments. The province of Quebec levies a separate personal income tax. The procedures for determining taxes owed on personal income can be quite complicated and cannot be covered here.* Our discussion will be limited to the key aspects affecting corporate financial decisions. An understanding of these aspects should enable the reader to differentiate between the tax treatment given to individuals, which include sole proprietorships and partnerships, and that given to corporations.

COMPONENTS OF PERSONAL INCOME

The income of individuals is derived from several sources, such as salaries, dividends, interest, capital gains, and earnings from a sole proprietorship or partnership. After

---

*For various tax laws and their interpretations, applicable to both individuals and corporations, refer to the following major sources, available in most legislative and university libraries:

1 The Income Tax Act of Canada and the various provincial Income Tax Acts
2 The Income Tax Application Rules, 1971 (ITAR)
3 The Federal and Provincial Income Tax Regulations
4 Interpretation Bulletins, Information Circulars, and Advance Rulings issued by the Department of National Revenue and available to all taxpayers on request
5 Tax Review Board Decisions

certain prescribed computations, these forms of income are taxed at progressive rates; that is, higher levels of taxable income are taxed at higher rates. Since interest, dividends, and capital gains arise from ownership of capital assets, they require special attention in calculating net income (that is, income for tax purposes).* The entire amount of interest earned is to be included in the net income. Canadian dividends received are "grossed-up" before they are brought into income. The grossed-up amount equals 150 percent of the dividends received. The reasons for the gross-up will be explained in a subsequent section, which discusses the dividend tax credit.

CAPITAL GAINS AND LOSSES

A capital gain occurs when a capital asset is sold for more than its original cost.† The excess of the proceeds from sale over the original cost represents the amount of capital gain.

Many individuals are not affected by the legislation concerning capital gains or losses, since the types of property they own are not usually subjected to the capital gain provisions. This includes assets such as the individual's principal residence, and personal effects such as household goods and automobiles.‡ Examples of assets that are subject to capital gain taxation include shares, real estate, mortgages, and commodities.

For further guidance as to whether a gain arising from the sale or disposition of a property is to be considered a capital gain or ordinary income, refer to the sources given in the footnote on page 46. Essentially, a capital gain arises on the sale of a property that was held as an investment, rather than for the continued conduct of a business.

A capital loss§ results when a nondepreciable capital asset is sold for less than its original cost. For tax purposes, such losses are first netted against the capital gains realized in the year. If there is a net capital gain, then one-half of it is included as a *taxable capital gain* in the year's taxable income. In other words, in effect, capital gains are taxed at one-half the ordinary rate. ‖

If a net loss occurs, then one-half of the net loss up to a maximum of $2,000 can be deducted from other income of the year. The amount represented by one-half of the net loss is called the *allowable capital loss*. There is also a provision for carrying unused allowable capital losses back one year and forward to future years. This is how it works:

---

*The terms *net income* and *income for tax purposes* are used interchangeably in the tax literature. Briefly, net income is the taxpayer's income from all sources (computed in accordance with the tax laws) minus certain business expenses incurred in producing it.

†Prior to 1972, there was no tax on capital gains. For capital property purchased before 1972, there is a special rule provided for establishing the cost base against which to measure capital gains or losses. For details, see *Income Tax Application Rule 26 (3)*, the pamphlet "Capital Gains and Valuation Day," and "Valuation Day Prices of Publicly Traded Shares." Expenses incurred in making the sale are to be accounted for separately, and are not to be netted against the proceeds from the sale. See subsection 40(1) of the Income Tax Act for details. However, as noted earlier, Interpretation Bulletin IT-10SR explains that in calculating capital cost allowance, proceeds net of selling expenses are to be deducted from the presale UCC balance of the class from which the asset is sold.

‡For assistance, the reader is referred to Interpretation Bulletin IT-120R, "Principal Residence."

§Note that a loss arising from the sale of an entire class of depreciable assets is referred to as a *terminal loss*. This type of loss and its tax treatment was discussed earlier in the chapter.

‖ The effective tax rate on capital gain income is one-half the applicable marginal tax rate. The rate applies uniformly at every level of taxable income. However, this is not the case for dividends, as will be shown later in the discussion on the dividend tax credit.

First, the unused allowable capital loss of the current year is applied against the taxable capital gains (and up to $2,000 of other income) of the preceding year. If there is still an unabsorbed (unused) balance, it can be carried forward until it is claimed. This carry-forward is also restricted in that only up to $2,000 of the unabsorbed balance can be claimed against noncapital income of any particular future year. However, in the case of an individual, any allowable capital losses existing as of the date of the individual's death may be used against any other income.

DETERMINING TAXABLE INCOME

Taxable income can be determined by following essentially a three-step procedure. First, components of income from all sources are aggregated in the manner described above. This gives the total income accruing to the taxpayer.* Second, a variety of trade and business expenses can be deducted from the above total in order to determine net income. The essential criterion for expenses to be deductible is that they must have been incurred in producing the taxpayer's income. Finally, taxable income is arrived at by taking from net income a number of personal exemptions and deductions. We have already discussed an important deduction, which is the deduction of allowable capital losses carried over from previous years.† An offsetting deduction of particular interest is the interest, dividends, and capital gains deduction. In effect, this deduction entitles the taxpayer to an offsetting deduction, which is equal to the lesser of either $1,000 or the total amount of eligible interest income (from sources such as bank deposits, bonds, mortgages, and notes), eligible taxable dividends from taxable Canadian corporations, and taxable capital gains (before deducting allowable capital losses) on the disposition of Canadian securities.‡

PERSONAL INCOME TAX RATES

Taxable income constitutes the base upon which the federal personal income tax is levied. Because the income of individuals is taxed at progressive rates, the applicable tax

---

*It may be noted that not all the receipts accruing to the individual taxpayer are to be included in the total income figure. For example, the employer's contribution to the registered pension fund of an employee is not included. These contributions are brought back into the employee's income for tax purposes, when the pension benefits are later paid to him or her.

†There is also a deduction for noncapital (operating) losses incurred in the five years immediately preceding and in the year immediately following the current year. An interpretation of noncapital (operating) loss, as it applies to individual taxpayers, is provided in Interpretation Bulletin IT-232. Further, some of the exemptions and deductions are "indexed" in that they are increased in a prescribed relationship to the increases in the Consumer Price Index.

‡There are a number of provincial tax incentives designed to encourage taxpayer's to invest in resident Canadian business firms. For example, Ontario taxpayers investing in a corporation registered as a small business development corporation under the Ontario Small Business Development Corporations Act, 1979, are eligible for a 30-percent investment incentive grant from the province of Ontario. An example of such a company is Aurelian Small Business Developers Limited. The province of Quebec allows for a deduction of up to $15,000 in respect of an investment in a new share issue of a Quebec-based corporation.

Table 2.6 Federal and Quebec Personal Income Tax Rates for the 1978 Taxation Year

Federal rate	Quebec rate
6% on the first $761 of taxable income	13% on the first $577 of taxable income
$ 46 on $ 761 plus 16% on next $ 760	$ 75.01 on $ 577 plus 14% on the next $667
167 " 1,521 " 17% " " 1,521	168.39 " 1,244 " 15% " " " 771
426 " 3,042 " 18% " " 1,521	284.04 " 2,015 " 16% " " " 891
700 " 4,563 " 19% " " 3,042	426.60 " 2,906 " 17% " " " 1,030
1,278 " 7,605 " 21% " " 3,042	601.70 " 3,936 " 18% " " " 1,191
1,916 " 10,647 " 23% " " 3,042	816.08 " 5,127 " 19% " " " 1,377
2,616 " 13,698 " 25% " " 3,042	1,077.71 " 6,504 " 20% " " " 1,591
3,377 " 16,731 " 28% " " 4,563	1,395.91 " 8,095 " 21% " " " 1,840
4,654 " 21,294 " 32% " " 15,210	1,782.31 " 9,935 " 22% " " " 2,126
9,521 " 36,504 " 36% " " 22,815	2,250.03 " 12,061 " 23% " " " 2,458
17,735 " 59,319 " 39% " " 31,941	2,815.37 " 14,519 " 24% " " " 2,841
30,192 " 91,260 " 43% on remainder	3,497.21 " 17,360 " 25% " " " 3,284
	4,318.21 " 20,644 " 26% " " " 3,797
	5,305.43 " 24,441 " 27% " " " 4,388
	6,490.19 " 28,829 " 28% " " " 5,073
	7,910.63 " 33,902 " 29% " " " 5,864
	9,611.19 " 39,766 " 30% " " " 6,778
	11,644.59 " 46,544 " 31% " " " 7,836
	14,073.75 " 54,380 " 32% " " " 6,334
	16,100.63 " 60,714 " 33% " excess

SOURCE: Statistics Canada, *Principal Taxes in Canada*, 1978, CS 68-201E, pp. 14, 67.

rates given in Table 2.6 depend upon the taxpayer's level of taxable income.* Further, each province levies a tax on income earned in its jurisdiction, at a rate that it has stipulated. However, under certain fixed arrangements between the federal government and each of the provincial governments (except Quebec), the base (i.e., taxable income) for the provincial tax must be the same under the Provincial Income Tax Acts as it is under the Federal Act. Accordingly, except for Quebec, provincial taxes are calculated as a percentage of the basic federal income tax payable. For example, for 1978, Alberta had the lowest provincial tax rate, which was 38.5 percent of the federal income tax payable; and Newfoundland had the highest provincial tax rate, which was 57.5 percent of the federal income tax payable.

All the provinces except Quebec have their income taxes collected by the federal government. Since Quebec collects its own taxes, residents of Quebec must file two separate returns—one federal and one provincial. In order to reflect the fact that the federal government does not collect the taxes for Quebec, residents of Quebec are given a federal rebatement (reduction) of 16.5 percent on their federal tax calculation. In addition, the Quebec rules for computation of taxable income are quite similar to those

---

*A taxpayer's *average* tax rate is found by dividing the total taxes payable by his or her taxable income. A taxpayer's *marginal* tax rate is the rate of tax levied on an *additional* dollar of taxable income. Since the marginal tax rate is progressive, a taxpayer's average tax rate is always less than his or her marginal tax rate.

provided in the Federal Income Tax Act. The 1978 personal income tax rates for residents of Quebec are given in Table 2.6. The following example illustrates the calculation of federal personal tax.

EXAMPLE   Suppose Mr. Jean Chabot, a resident of New Brunswick, had a taxable income of $17,000 in 1978. From Table 2.6 we find that Mr. Chabot's federal tax payment in 1978 was equal to $3,377 on the first $16,731 of his taxable income plus 28 percent on each additional dollar of his taxable income above $16,731 (but below the upper limit of $21,294). Thus, Mr. Chabot's federal tax payment for the year 1978 was equal to $3,377 + .28 ($17,000 − $16,731) = $3,452.32.

DIVIDEND TAX CREDIT

Dividends received by individual shareholders from taxable Canadian corporations are subject to taxation.* This implies that the income of a corporation is taxed twice: once in the hands of the corporation and again in the hands of the shareholders, when and to the extent that such income is distributed in the form of dividends. The provision of the dividend tax credit—that is, a tax deduction permitted directly against federal tax otherwise payable—is intended to alleviate the effects of this double taxation.

The method prescribed for computing the amount of the tax credit is as follows: First, an amount called the "gross-up" is computed. It is equal to 50 percent of the dividends received. Then, the tax credit is calculated as 75 percent of the gross-up. The amount equal to 150 percent of the dividend received is referred to as the *grossed-up dividends* and is deemed to be investment income. Assuming that the $1,000 exemption for interest, dividends, and capital gains discussed earlier has already been utilized, the federal tax on the dividend income, before the tax credit is applied, equals the individual's marginal federal tax rate times the grossed-up amount. An illustration of the method of applying the tax credit is shown in Table 2.7. From the calculations shown, it is clear that the credit is designed to be of maximum benefit to individuals subject to relatively lower marginal tax rates, and that the impact of the tax credit declines sharply with increases in the taxpayer's marginal tax rate.

Notice that while the federal tax payable before the application of the tax credit increases from $900 to $2,700, the amount of the credit allowed remains constant at $1,125. This accounts for the reduced percentage of tax savings at higher marginal tax rates. Also, since the provincial income tax for each province (except Quebec) is calculated as a percentage of the federal income tax payable, the tax credit will reduce the provincial taxes as well.† Further, the effect of the credit will vary across provinces because of the differences in provincial income tax rates.

---

*The revision of the Income Tax Act in 1971 permitted certain surplus distributions as tax-free dividends. For further details, see section 83 of the Income Tax Act.

†No dividend tax credit is allowed under provincial income tax acts, except for Quebec. The dividend tax credit permitted under the Quebec act has been recently revised to parallel the federal dividend tax credit discussed here.

Table 2.7 Calculation and Application of the Dividend Tax Credit

	20%	30%	40%	60%[a]
Marginal federal tax rate	20%	30%	40%	60%[a]
Dividends received	$3,000	$3,000	$3,000	$3,000
Gross-up (50% dividends received)	1,500	1,500	1,500	1,500
Taxable amount (grossed-up dividends)	$4,500	$4,500	$4,500	$4,500
Federal tax before credit	900	1,350	1,800	2,700
Less: Dividend tax credit (75% of gross-up)	1,125	1,125	1,125	1,125
Federal tax payable	($225)[b]	$225	$675	$1,575
Effective federal tax rate	− 7.5%	7.5%	22.5%	52.5%
Percentage of federal tax savings	137.5%	75%	43.75%	12.5%

$$\left[\frac{\text{marginal federal tax rate—effective tax rate}}{\text{marginal federal tax rate}} \right]$$

[a]The 60 percent marginal federal tax rate is used here only for illustrative purposes. As indicated in Table 2.6, the highest marginal federal tax rate in 1978 was 43 percent.
[b]The negative $225 federal tax payable implies that the individual investor will receive a $225 tax credit against federal tax on his or her other income.

Corporate Taxes

In order to have a full understanding of corporate financial decisions, one must have a general understanding of the manner in which corporate income is taxed. There are two major sources of corporate income—ordinary business activities and property. Just as in the case of individuals, identification of the sources of income is important in determining a corporation's tax liability. A corporation can experience two types of tax losses, *operating losses* and *capital losses*,* which under certain limitations may be carried back and forward and applied against income in other years. The reader should not only understand these aspects of corporate taxes but should also have some familiarity with important tax incentives, such as the small business deduction and the investment tax credit. Finally, it should be noted that essentially the same basic procedure is used in determining taxable income of a corporation as was used for an individual. Aside from the rights of individuals to deductions such as personal exemptions and medical expenses, the difference exists mainly in the calculation of the taxable portions of certain components of income (which will be discussed next) and in the manner in which capital losses can be applied against income of other years.

CORPORATE TAXATION: SOURCES OF INCOME

For tax purposes, a corporation's income from ordinary business transactions is distinguished from income derived from its property. For example, it is only the first type of

---

*Strictly speaking, the losses resulting from the sale of *depreciable* capital assets are termed *terminal loss*. These losses can only be written off against income in the year in which they occur. The terminal loss deduction was discussed previously in the section dealing with capital cost allowance. The term *capital loss* refers to a loss from the sale of nondepreciable capital assets.

income, referred to as *active business income,* that qualifies for the small business deduction. By implication, income from royalties, dividends, interest, or similar sources is considered *passive,* unless the firm being considered is a money lending institution. As in the case of individuals, both interest and dividends received are to be included in net income. However, dividend income of corporations, unlike that of individuals, is not required to be grossed-up. Another principal source of corporate income is *net capital gains* defined in the preceding section. Again, like individuals, corporations are required to include only one-half of net capital gain in income. Finally, recaptured depreciation arising from the sale of depreciable capital assets is also included in income for tax purposes. This applies to both individuals and corporations.

PERMISSIBLE DEDUCTIONS

We have already considered four major deductions permitted against income—interest expense on debt issued,* CCA-based depreciation expense, the terminal loss deduction, and the deduction of dividends received from taxable Canadian corporations. Two other deductions of major significance are explained next. Note that a "deduction" is not the same as a "tax credit"; whereas a deduction is usually an expense deducted from income to reduce taxable income, a tax credit is a *direct* reduction against tax otherwise payable.

Operating (Noncapital) Losses   An operating loss occurs when a firm has negative before-tax profit. Taxpayers may carry such losses back one year and forward up to five years, to reduce taxable income.† As noted earlier, if these losses are not applied against current income, then they must first be applied against the earliest available income of a prior or subsequent year.

Capital Losses   The term *capital loss* and the calculation of the allowable capital loss were explained in the section dealing with personal taxation. Corporations, like individuals, can apply the allowable capital loss in the current year against the taxable capital gains in the previous year and in any subsequent year. However, unlike individuals, corporations cannot apply capital losses against noncapital income. In addition, if control of a corporation changes, capital losses cannot be carried forward against capital gains.

CORPORATE TAX RATES

The federal government and each province levies its own tax rate on income earned in the province.‡ However, federal and provincial taxable income in all provinces, except Quebec and Ontario, is determined under the federal Income Tax Act. Corporate tax, in

---

*Note that interest payments on income bonds are not tax deductible.

†Also note that since taxable income may include both the noncapital income and the taxable portion of income from capital gains, the above provision implies that the application of operating losses is not restricted to operating or noncapital income of the current or other years. For precise definition of the term "operating losses for tax purposes," see the Income Tax Act.

‡In addition, the four provinces of Quebec, Ontario, Manitoba, and British Columbia levy a tax on the paid-up capital of corporations operating within their boundaries. *Paid-up capital* is broadly defined to include share capital, surplus, long- and certain short-term debts, and reserves (other than those for depreciation, depletion, and doubtful debts).

Table 2.8 Provincial and Territorial Corporate Income Tax Rates for the 1978 Taxation Year

Province/territory	Provincial corporate tax rate (%)
Newfoundland	14, 12
Prince Edward Island	10
Nova Scotia	12
New Brunswick	12, 9
Quebec	12
Ontario	13, 10
Manitoba[a]	15, 11
Saskatchewan	14, 11
Alberta	11
British Columbia	15, 12
Northwest Territories	10

SOURCE: Statistics Canada, *Principal Taxes in Canada*, 1978, CS68-201E.
[a]Included in this tax rate is 1 percent to be used for municipal purposes.

either Quebec or Ontario, is computed under the tax statutes of those provinces. The provisions in the two statutes are very similar to those in the federal act. In addition, all provinces, except Quebec and Ontario and the Yukon territory, have their corporate taxes collected by the federal government.

The general federal tax rate for Canadian corporations is 46 percent. From this rate, a corporation deducts a uniform provincial tax rebatement of 10 percent. Thus, although the rebatement is the same for each of the provinces, the total (federal plus provincial) corporate tax rate varies from province to province, since the provincial rates vary.

The provincial and territorial income tax rates for the 1978 taxation year are given in Table 2.8. From the table, it is apparent that Prince Edward Island has the lowest provincial rate of 10 percent, and Manitoba and British Columbia have the highest provincial rate of 15 percent.*

Also, the provinces of Newfoundland, New Brunswick, Ontario, Manitoba, Saskatchewan, and British Columbia have dual rates of tax. In these provinces, the portion of income attributed to the province that qualifies for the small business deduction is subject to tax at the lower rate.

The differences in tax rates between provinces can influence corporate decisions. Two of these decisions are the location of a business and the setting of transfer prices for goods and services between geographically dispersed operating units of a company that conducts business intraprovincially.

TAX CREDITS

In practice, the effective tax rate for a corporation is lowered, since most corporations are eligible for one or more tax credits. Two of these credits, the investment tax credit and the small business deduction, will be discussed next.

*Thus, the effective total (federal plus provincial) corporate tax rate for 1978 varied from 46 to 51 percent.

INVESTMENT TAX CREDIT

The investment tax credit is allowed to both individuals and corporations for certain capital assets acquired between June 23, 1975, and June 30, 1980. It is applied on a regional basis. For most areas, it is calculated as 5 percent of the capital cost of the eligible assets. For certain designated regions in British Columbia, Saskatchewan, Manitoba, Ontario, and parts of Quebec, the rate is 7.5 percent. For the Gaspé region of Quebec and the Atlantic Provinces, the rate is as high as 10 percent.

Although the credit becomes available in the year in which the asset is acquired, the maximum amount of credit that can be claimed in a year is limited to the first $15,000 of federal tax otherwise payable, plus one-half of the federal tax in excess of $15,000. In other words, the maximum credit that can be claimed in a year is $15,000 + $\frac{1}{2}$ (federal tax otherwise payable − $15,000), which, simply stated, equals $\frac{1}{2}$ ($15,000 + federal tax otherwise payable). Any unused credit may be carried forward for up to five years and written off against federal taxes payable. Finally, it should be noted that, for capital cost allowance calculations, the capital cost of the applicable assets is reduced by the amount of the credit claimed.

The reduced capital cost implies that the maximum capital cost allowance charge, otherwise available, will also be reduced.* This will have the effect of increasing taxable income and therefore tax payable. Consequently, the benefit to the taxpayer from the credit will be partially offset due to reduced CCA charges.

EXAMPLE   Suppose a firm becomes eligible for an investment tax credit of $30,000 in 1979, and that its tax liability for the year before the credit is used is $36,000. Then the maximum amount of credit that can be claimed in 1979 is $\frac{1}{2}$($15,000 + $36,000) = $25,500. The unabsorbed balance of ($30,000 − $25,500) = $4,500 may be carried forward up to 1984 or until claimed, whichever occurs first.

SMALL BUSINESS DEDUCTION

The small business deduction is a federal tax credit available to relatively small Canadian-controlled private corporations. The tax rate for applicable income is calculated as follows: from the general federal tax rate of 46 percent, a small business deducts a federal small business deduction of 21 percent. Thus, the basic federal tax payable is reduced from 46 to 25 percent. From the basic reduced federal tax rate, the small business deducts the provincial tax abatement of 10 percent, and then adds the applicable provincial tax rate. However, since the provincial tax rates vary, the total (federal plus provincial) corporate tax rate for applicable small business income varies from province to province, as is illustrated in the following example. Note that although the small business deduction is referred to as a "deduction," it is actually equivalent to a direct tax reduction or tax credit against federal tax otherwise payable.

*As a general rule, such an adjustment is to be made for all depreciable assets purchased with any form of financial assistance received from a government, municipality, or other public authority.

EXAMPLE   Suppose that Newfoundland Hardware Ltd. and New Brunswick Hardware Ltd. operate solely in Newfoundland and New Brunswick, respectively. Also, suppose that during 1978, both firms only earned active income, all of which is taxable as small business income. What would be the total (federal plus provincial) corporate tax rates for the firms?

The solution to this example is summarized in Table 2.9. From the table, it is obvious that the differences in the tax rates are significant. In fact, Newfoundland Hardware Ltd. is being taxed at a rate which is approximately 12.5 percent $\{[(27 - 24)/24] \cdot 100\}$ higher than that for New Brunswick Hardware Ltd.

Table 2.9   Calculation of the Total Corporate Tax Rates for Newfoundland Hardware Ltd. and New Brunswick Hardware Ltd.

	Newfoundland Hardware Ltd.	New Brunswick Hardware Ltd.
General federal tax rate (%)	46	46
Less: Small business deduction (%)	21	21
Net federal tax rate (%)	25	25
Less: Provincial tax abatement (%)	10	10
Plus: Provincial tax rate (%)[a]	12	9
Total tax rate (%)	27	24

[a]These values are as given in Table 2.8.

Although the rules set out are rather involved, the amount of income eligible for the credit in any given taxation year is generally the lowest of the following:

(i) Active Canadian business income
(ii) $150,000 (called the *business limit*)
(iii) $750,000 *minus the cumulative deduction account balance* (CDA) *at the end of the immediately preceding year.*[*]

The rule provided for calculating the cumulative deduction account balance is also complex. Essentially what it involves is that beginning in 1972 the balance is to be increased by taxable active business income and decreased by four-thirds of taxable dividends paid out by the corporation. Simply stated, the rule implies that the reduced federal tax rate can be applied to a maximum of $150,000 of taxable active business income in a year; any amount in excess of $150,000 is to be taxed at the full corporate

[*]The simplified version of the rule described here does not cover all the possible situations. For example, if the eligible corporation's taxable income minus the sum of five-fourths of its foreign tax credit on investment income and twice its tax credit on foreign business income is less than each of three items listed above, then the base for the small business deduction will be this least amount. Also not covered is the situation where the corporation is associated with other Canadian-controlled corporations. The interested reader can refer to section 125 of the act for rules applicable in complex situations.

tax rate. Further, once the corporation has accumulated $750,000 of taxable active business income, referred to as the *total business limit*, the credit becomes unavailable.* The accumulated total may be reduced by paying taxable dividends. A simple example will illustrate the calculations involved.

EXAMPLE   Halifax Courier Ltd., a Canadian-controlled private corporation, began operations in 1979, and its taxable income for the year was $300,000. The forecasts of taxable income for the years 1980 through 1982 are $340,000, $150,000, and $280,000, respectively. All income earned by the corporation is active Canadian business income. The corporation plans to pay $27,000 in dividends in 1981. The calculation of the small business deductions available to the corporation are as in Table 2.10.

Table 2.10   Calculation of the Small Business Deduction

	1979	1980	1981	1982
Taxable active business income (i)	$300,000	$340,000	$150,000	$280,000
Taxable dividend payments	—	—	27,000	—
Business limit (ii)	150,000	150,000	150,000	150,000
Total business limit	750,000	750,000	750,000	750,000
Less: Cumulative deduction account balance	—	300,000	640,000	754,000[a]
Small business credit	31,500[b]	31,500[b]	23,100[c]	—

[a] Is equal to ($640,000 + $150,000) − $\frac{4}{3}$($27,000).
[b] Is equal to 21 percent of (ii), since (i) > (ii).
[c] Is equal to 21 percent of ($750,000 − $640,000) because $750,000 − $640,000 = $110,000 < (ii).

A particularly important point illustrated by this example is the restrictive nature of the rule for calculating the income eligible for the credit. For example, the company will not be able to claim any amount of the credit in 1982 since the CDA of $754,000 exceeds the total business limit of $750,000. However, if the dividend payment expected to be made in 1981 was increased to, say, $60,000, then $8,400 [[21{$750,000 − [$640,000 + $150,000 − $\frac{4}{3}$($60,000)]}]] would be available as a tax credit in 1982.

OTHER TAX CREDITS

A deduction on Canadian manufacturing and processing income is also available. By taking advantage of this deduction and the small business deduction, a small manufac-

*This limit is intended to restrict the availability of the credit to small Canadian corporations. The underlying assumption is that a reduced tax rate would provide a stimulus to small business development. This assumption, however, may not be valid in some situations. For example, it has been shown that reduced tax rates, under certain circumstances, may provide a disincentive to firms operating in risky environments. See D. K. Gandhi and Anthony Saunders, "Optimal Tax Structures and Risk Aversion," *International Review of Economics and Commerce* 26 (1979), pp. 286–291; E. D. Domar and R. A. Musgrave, "Proportional Income Taxation and Risk Taking," *Quarterly Journal of Economics* 58 (1944), pp. 388–422; and S. M. Ahsan, "Progression and Risk Taking," *Oxford Economic Papers* 26 (1974), pp. 318–328.

turing and processing Canadian-controlled corporation can reduce its federal tax rate to as low as 20 percent on the first $150,000 of its active business income.

TAX MATTERS PERTAINING TO EXPORT SALES

There is little in Canada's taxation policy that caters to export sales, since the Canadian tax system is based on a "closed economy" framework. Thus, unlike many of our competitors, Canadian tax law enactment and enforcement is based on domestic and not on global equity. As a result, Canada does not utilize indirect export tax incentives, such as the reduced taxation of export income* or the preferential taxation of off-shore income,† to stimulate export sales. The cumulative magnitude of the resultant benefits to non-Canadian exporters of their governmental incentives for export sales has been quantified by a Special Committee for U.S. Exports as in Table 2.11.

TAX PAYMENTS

Although the taxable income of a corporation and that of an owner of an unincorporated business is calculated by following substantially the same procedure, the timing of tax filings and payments may differ significantly.‡

The taxation year of individuals is the calendar year, but the individual tax returns must be filed by April 30 immediately following the taxation year. As noted earlier, the unincorporated business income is taxed as personal income of the individual owners. Thus, the desired fiscal period of the unincorporated business—the period over which the business income is computed—may not coincide with the legally prescribed taxation year of the individual owners.

Table 2.11 Effect of Certain Foreign Export Tax Practices

Country	Effect attributable to export tax incentives on a $10,000 export sale	
	Increase in after-tax profit	Possible export price reduction
Belgium	$300 (28.7%)	$330
Brazil	$200 (14.3%)	$223
France	$280 (28.0%)	$300
Ireland	$1,000 (100.0%)	$1,000
The Netherlands	$290 (27.9%)	$320
Spain	$65 (5.1%)	$90
U.S. (DISCs)	$240 (24.1%)	N.A.[a]

[a]Not available.

*For example, in Brazil and Ireland there are schemes ("tax holidays") to completely exempt the revenue from direct export sales from taxation.
†For example, France totally exempts foreign source income from taxable income. This encourages French companies to channel their exports through foreign-based sales offices or subsidiaries located in tax haven countries, so that profits can be subsequently repatriated in the form of tax-free dividends.
‡The timing of tax payments can significantly affect a firm's investment and short-term financing decisions. The former will be discussed in Chapter 16.

A corporation's fiscal period* is considered to be its taxation year. It need not coincide with the calendar year. For example, a corporation's fiscal period beginning on July 1, 1979, and ending on June 30, 1980, will be the corporation's 1980 taxation year. According to the act, a corporation must make monthly installment payments of taxes over a 14-month period, each installment being due on the last day of each month of the corporation's taxation year. The balance of tax, if any, is payable on the last day of the second month following the end of the taxation year. Late or insufficient installment payments and unpaid taxes bear interest.

Summary

This chapter has discussed taxes and the basic forms of business organization—the sole proprietorship, the partnership, and the corporation. Although sole proprietorships are the most common form of business organization, the corporation is the most dominant in terms of sales, earnings, and assets. Since the corporation is a legal entity, or person, its owners or shareholders have limited liability. They cannot lose more money than they have invested.

An understanding of a number of factors is important in measuring corporate income. Corporations, just as other forms of business, are permitted to allocate the historical cost of certain assets to offset future income. The most common of these noncash allocations are depreciation, amortization, and depletion allowances. Profits after taxes can be adjusted to show cash flows from operations by adding noncash charges (such as depreciation) to them.

The portion of the cost of depreciable assets permitted as an annual deduction for computing net income for tax purposes is called the *capital cost allowance*. While depreciation expense for reporting purposes may be calculated for each asset, capital cost allowance is calculated for the various *classes* of depreciable assets held by the firm. To encourage business to invest in certain types of machinery or products, the government allows several types of accelerated capital cost allowances. These allowances are determined by calculating the CCA charge for certain classes on a straight-line basis over a prescribed number of years.

Interest is a tax-deductible payment to lenders for money lent. It does not include return of the principal amount borrowed, which must be paid from the firm's after-tax cash flow. Dividends are payments made by the corporation to its owners or holders and they differ from interest in that they are not tax-deductible expenses for the firm. For corporations eligible for the small business deduction, dividend payments reduce the cumulative deduction account balance.

The income of individuals is derived from several sources, such as salaries, dividends, capital gains, and earnings from a sole proprietorship or a partnership. Income from the ownership of capital assets requires special attention in calculating net income for tax purposes. The entire amount of interest earned is to be included in net income. The

---

*The term *fiscal period* is defined in section 248 of the Income Tax Act. According to the section, a corporation is not allowed to choose a fiscal period of more than 53 weeks.

dividends are *grossed-up* before they are included in income. The grossed-up amount equals 150 percent of the dividends received.

When a capital asset is sold for more than its original cost, the difference between the proceeds from sale and the original cost is called a *capital gain*. A *capital loss* results when a nondepreciable asset, such as land or a financial asset, is sold for less than its original cost. For tax purposes, such losses are first netted against the capital gains realized in the year. Any "leftover" amount is called a *net capital gain*, and one-half of it is included in the year's taxable income as a *taxable gain*. In other words, in effect, capital gains are taxed at one-half the ordinary rate. If a net loss occurs, then one-half of the net loss, up to a maximum of $2,000, can be deducted from other income of the year. One-half of the net loss is called the *allowable capital loss*. Unused allowable capital loss of the current year is applied against the taxable capital gains and up to $2,000 of other income of the preceding year. If there is still an unabsorbed balance, it can be carried forward until claimed. However, only up to $2,000 of the unabsorbed balance can be claimed against noncapital income of any particular future year.

Taxable income of individuals and corporations can be determined by following essentially a three-step procedure. First, components of income from all sources are aggregated in the prescribed manner, in order to determine the taxpayer's total income. Second, a variety of trade and business expenses are deducted to determine net income. Finally, taxable income is arrived at by subtracting a number of exemptions and deductions from net income.

Taxable income is the base upon which the federal personal income tax is levied. Since the tax rate is progressive, the higher the taxable income, the higher the marginal rate of taxation. Each province levies a tax on taxable income earned in its jurisdiction at a rate that it has stipulated. However, except for Quebec, the base (i.e., taxable income) for the provincial tax must be the same as it is under the federal Income Tax Act. All the provinces, except Quebec, have their individual income taxes collected by the federal government, and Quebec and Ontario collect their own corporate taxes.

A tax credit (i.e., a tax deduction permitted directly against the taxes otherwise payable) available to individuals is the dividend tax credit. It is designed in such a way that it is of greater benefit to individuals in relatively lower income brackets.

There are two major sources of corporate income—ordinary business income and investment income that includes interest, dividends, and capital gains. Like individuals, corporations are required to include only one-half of their net capital gains in income. Major deductions from income to arrive at taxable income are interest expense, dividends from taxable Canadian corporations, capital cost allowance, and noncapital (operating) losses incurred in the five immediately preceding years and in the immediately following year.

The federal government and each province levies its own tax rate on income earned in each province. The general federal tax rate for Canadian corporations is 46 percent. From this rate, a corporation deducts a uniform provincial tax rebatement of 10 percent. Then the provincial tax rate is added, which is generally higher than 10 percent. Most corporations are eligible for the various tax credits, such as the investment tax credit and the small business deduction.

The taxation year of individuals is the calendar year. A corporation's fiscal period—

the period over which business income is computed—is considered to be its taxation year and it need not coincide with the calendar year. The act provides for monthly installment payments of taxes over a 14-month period, each installment being due on the last day of each month of the corporation's taxation year. The balance, if any, must be paid by the last day of the second month following the end of the taxation year.

Questions

2.1   What are the three basic forms of business organization? Which form of business organization is most common? Which form is dominant in terms of sales, earnings, and assets, especially in the industrial sector?

2.2   What different types of liability are related to the various forms of business organization? How do the terms *joint* and *several liability* relate to the business organization?

2.3   Explain the circumstances under which limited liability may, in effect, not provide a guarantee against creditor's claims to personal assets of corporate shareholders.

2.4   Why is a corporation often referred to as a legal entity? Who is responsible for chartering a corporation?

2.5   What are the owners of corporations called? Explain the basic rights of corporate owners. Explain the relationship between owners, directors, and officers of corporations.

2.6   In what respect does a corporation serve the same purpose as a partnership from the viewpoint of a risk-averse investor?

2.7   How do the various legal and organizational aspects of corporations facilitate their growth into large businesses?

2.8   In what sense does depreciation act as a cash inflow? How can a firm's after-tax profits be adjusted to show cash flow? What is the rationale for this adjustment?

2.9   Define *capital cost allowance*. What is the essential difference between capital cost allowance and depreciation charge for reporting purposes?

2.10 A firm sold two assets from the same CCA class, and then deducted the lesser of the following from the presale UCC balance of the class:
   a. Total proceeds of sale
   b. Original cost of the assets sold
   Did the firm apply the correct procedure for the calculation of the UCC balance after the sale? If not, explain with the help of a numerical example how the correct calculation would be made.

2.11 Explain whether or not a firm's cash flow from operations is affected by the difference between the depreciation reported on the income statement and the capital cost allowance claimed for tax purposes?

2.12 Can a firm pay both an ordinary tax and a capital gain tax on the sale of a depreciable asset at a price
   a. Greater than its original cost?
   b. Less than its original cost?
   Assume that other assets remain in the class after the sale.

2.13 What will be the tax advantages and disadvantages to the members of a partnership if their business is taxed as a corporation?

2.14 How are interest and dividends different? From what instruments do these types of payments arise? What are the tax implications (if any) of each of these types of payments?

2.15 Suppose you are a corporate shareholder with a very high marginal tax rate. Would you rather have the shares appreciate in value or receive the same dollar return in cash dividends? Explain your answer.

2.16 Briefly define
    a. Terminal loss
    b. Capital loss
    c. Tax credit

2.17 How do the average and marginal tax rates on an individual's taxable income differ? How are they calculated?

2.18 What are the differences between the standard straight-line method of tax depreciation and the same method for the CCA calculation for tax purposes for each of the following:
    a. A class, comprised of a single asset with a capital cost of $1,000, is to be depreciated over a two-year period.
    b. An asset of the same class is acquired toward the end of the first year.

Problems

Note: For all the following problems assume that the taxation years coincide with the calendar years.

2.1 The Lethbridge Electricals Ltd. acquired a piece of equipment on January 1, 19X1, for $100,000. The equipment, a Class 8 asset, is the only asset of its class on the company's books. The maximum CCA rate permitted for Class 8 is 20 percent on the declining balance. The company plans to acquire no further Class 8 assets in the future.
a. Calculate the maximum annual CCA deduction that the company can claim for the years 19X1 and 19X2.
b. Suppose the company sells the equipment at the beginning of 19X3. What will be the recaptured depreciation or capital gain or both arising from the sale in each of the following cases?

    (i) Proceeds of sale = $ 60,000
    (ii) Proceeds of sale = $ 70,000
    (iii) Proceeds of sale = $120,000

2.2 Mabou Movers Ltd. had the following UCC balances as of January 1, 1978.

Frame buildings (Class 6, CCA rate 10 percent)	$140,000
Automobiles and trucks (Class 10, CCA rate 30 percent)	$ 80,000

The company made no additions of depreciable assets in 1978, but in January 1979 certain automotive equipment, which was purchased for $8,000, was added to Class 10. On December 31, 1979, a frame building, which had been purchased in 1975 for $100,000, and a truck, which had cost $6,000 in 1974, were sold for $175,000, and $2,000, respectively. The company's practice is to claim the maximum permitted CCA charges each year. The company is subject to a corporate tax rate of 46 percent.

a. Prepare a schedule showing the calculations of CCA charges and the year-end UCC balances for each class for 1978 and 1979. Use the declining-balance method for calculating the CCA charges.

b. Compute the capital gains, if any, realized from the sale of assets in 1979. Also, calculate the increase in the firm's tax liability as a result of these capital gains.

c. Suppose on January 1, 1980, the company sells all its Class 6 and Class 10 assets for $40,000 and $38,000, respectively. What impact will the sale have on the firm's tax payable in 1980?

2.3   Clause and Kuzy Ltd. had the following UCC balances as of the beginning of 1978.

Building (Class 3, CCA rate 5 percent)	$700,000
Equipment and furniture (Class 8, CCA rate 20 percent)	$250,000

Early in 1978, the company purchased another Class 3 building and some additional Class 8 furniture for $50,000 and $20,000, respectively. In 1979, an electrical generator, a Class 8 asset, was acquired for $45,000. No depreciable assets were sold during 1978 and 1979. However, in 1980, the company plans to sell its older building for an estimated amount of $750,000 and to lease a new one. The original cost of the building was $750,000.

The company reported taxable income of $45,000 in 1978, after claiming the maximum CCA permitted in that year. In 1979, the company will show a loss of $27,000 for tax purposes if it claims the maximum CCA for the year. Since future business prospects appear to be excellent, a minimum net profit after taxes of $150,000 is expected in 1980. The company's executives are attempting to decide whether or not it would be advantageous for the firm to eliminate its 1979 loss by reducing its 1979 claim.

Assuming an overall corporate income tax rate of 46 percent in the years 1978 through 1980, what advice would you, as the company's tax consultant, offer to the firm's executives? Why?

2.4   The Soni Company Ltd. acquired manufacturing equipment in 1978 for $140,000. The equipment, a Class 8 asset, is to be used in the company's plant located in Charlettown, Prince Edward Island, and is eligible for the investment tax credit of 10 percent. Prior to 1978, the company did not own any Class 8 assets. The capital cost allowance rate applicable to the class is 20 percent on the declining balance. The company's federal tax payable for the year, before the application of the credit, was $17,000. Calculate the maximum possible tax savings that were available to the company for 1978 as a result of the application of the investment tax credit taken for the equipment purchased. Assume that the corporate income tax rate was 46 percent. Also, assume that the company claims the maximum CCA charges permitted each year.

2.5   Mr. Sanjay, the sole proprietor of a sporting goods store in downtown Calgary, earned a taxable income of $60,000 in 1978. The 1978 provincial income tax rate for Alberta was 38.5 percent of the federal income tax payable.

a. Compute the total federal and provincial income tax paid by Mr. Sanjay in 1978. Use Table 2.6 to determine the applicable personal marginal federal tax rate.

b. What would have been the total tax payable if Mr. Sanjay had incorporated his business in 1978? Assume that all of the $60,000 taxable income was eligible for the small business deduction.

2.6   The Lavigne Musical Company Ltd. began operations in 1980 and has projected the following income and operating (noncapital) losses for tax purposes for the years 1980 through 1986:

	Income	Operating loss
1980		$45,000
1981		$67,500
1982		$15,000
1983	$21,000	
1984		$ 6,000
1985	$60,000	
1986	$47,000	

Explain how the company will use its operating loss carryback and carryforward adjustments for the above years.

2.7   Red Deer Handicrafts Ltd., classified as a Canadian-controlled private corporation for tax purposes since 1977, reported 1978 taxable income of $200,000. The company buys handicrafts produced by local craftspeople in Alberta and has sale outlets in various parts of the province. Active Canadian business income earned by the company during its 1978 taxation year was $160,000. The cumulative deduction account of the company as of the end of 1977 was $215,000. What was the company's federal tax payable in 1978? Assume that the corporate income tax rate for the year was 46 percent and that the company was not eligible for any foreign tax credit.

2.8   Messrs. Gordon Roberts and Michael Dummer have received cash dividends of $6,000 each from a taxable Canadian corporation. Their dividend income will be subject to federal marginal income tax rates of 26 percent and 39 percent, respectively. Each individual will claim his $1,000 exemption on interest, dividends, and capital gains in calculating his taxes payable. Calculate and interpret the federal tax that will be paid by each individual on his dividend income.

Suggested Readings

Ahsan, S. M., "Progression and Risk Taking," *Oxford Economic Papers* 26 (1974), pp. 318–328.

Brigham, Eugene and James Pappas, *Liberalized Depreciation Practices and the Cost of Capital* (East Lansing, Mich.: MSU Public Utilities Studies, 1970).

Canadian Master Tax Guide (Toronto: CCH Canada Limited, 1979).

Domar, E. D. and R. A. Musgrave, "Proportional Income Taxation and Risk Taking," *Quarterly Journal of Economics* 58 (1944), pp. 338–422.

Gandhi, D. K. and A. Saunders, "Optimal Tax Structures and Risk Aversion," *International Review of Economics and Business* 26 (1979), pp. 286–291.

Geoffrey, M. Colley, *Tax Principles to Remember* (Toronto: CICA, 1978).

Maer, C. M., Jr., and R. A. Francis, "Whether to Incorporate," *Business Lawyer* 22 (April 1967), pp. 127–142.

Smith, Dan Troop, *Tax Factors in Business Decisions* (Englewood Cliffs, N.J.: Prentice-Hall, 1968).

Part Two

Financial Analysis and Planning

BALANCE SHEET	
Assets	Liabilities and Shareholders' Equity
Current Assets	Current Liabilities
Fixed Assets	Long-Term Debt
	Shareholders' Equity

This part of the text presents some of the basic tools of financial analysis and planning. Whereas the tools of financial analysis are devoted primarily to a historical evaluation of the firm, financial planning looks ahead to future operations. Both areas are quite important and, as indicated in Chapter 1, together comprise one of the functions of the financial manager. The four chapters in this part are devoted to the analysis of financial statements; operating, financial, and total leverage; sources and uses of funds and cash budgeting; and pro forma statements. Chapter 3 discusses the key ratios and techniques available for analyzing the firm's performance using data from its income statement and balance sheet. Chapter 4 presents the key concepts of breakeven analysis and defines and discusses operating, financial, and total leverage. Chapter 5 describes how and why sources and uses of funds statements and cash budgets are constructed. Chapter 6 describes both the shortcut and the more sophisticated approach for developing pro forma, or projected, financial statements. From this part the reader should gain an understanding of both the importance of financial analysis and planning and the techniques available to the financial manager for this purpose.

Chapter 3

THE ANALYSIS OF FINANCIAL STATEMENTS

The analysis of financial statements is typically devoted to the calculation of ratios in order to evaluate the past, current, and projected performance of the business firm. *Ratio analysis* is the most common form of financial analysis. It provides *relative* measures of the company's performance. A number of other techniques for measuring certain aspects of corporate performance are used, but the financial ratio is the one most commonly cited. The basic inputs to financial analysis are the firm's income statement and balance sheet for the period(s) to be examined.

This chapter has five major sections. The first section discusses the use of financial ratios, placing special emphasis on who uses financial ratios and how. The second section briefly describes the basic financial statements that are used to illustrate the calculation of key ratios. The third section describes how to calculate the various financial ratios and discusses their implications. The fourth section presents a discussion of the complete ratio analysis of the firm, which is used to illustrate the ratio computations in the third section of the chapter. The final section deals briefly with the impact of both inflation and a firm's non-Canadian operations on its financial statements and ratios.

The Use of Financial Ratios

Before we discuss the methods of calculating and interpreting financial ratios, it is important for the reader to have a basic understanding of the various parties interested in financial ratio analysis, the types of comparisons that are commonly made using financial ratios, and a few words of caution. The first part of this section briefly discusses the parties interested in ratio analysis of the firm and indicates their key areas of interest. The second section describes the two key types of ratio comparisons normally used. The third section offers a few words of caution related to the use of ratio analysis.

INTERESTED PARTIES

Ratio analysis of a firm's financial statements is of interest to a number of parties, especially *current and prospective shareholders, creditors,* and the firm's own *management*. The current and prospective shareholder is interested primarily in the firm's present and projected level of earnings. Although the shareholder's main concern is with profitability which affects share values, he or she also pays close attention to measures of liquidity and activity and leverage in order to determine the likelihood of the firm's continued existence and to evaluate the probability of receiving any distribution of the firm's earnings.

The firm's creditors are primarily interested in both the short-term liquidity of the firm and the ability of the firm to service its debts over the long run. Existing creditors want to assure themselves that the firm is liquid and that it will be able to make its interest and principal payments when due. Prospective creditors are concerned with determining whether the firm can support the additional debts that would result if they extended credit to the firm. A secondary interest of the present or prospective creditor is the firm's profitability; the creditor wants assurance that the firm is healthy and will continue to be successful.

The firm's management is concerned with all aspects of the firm's financial situation. Since it is aware of the types of things evaluated by owners and creditors, it attempts to operate in a manner that will result in ratios that will be considered favourable by both parties. If the firm is successful, its share price should remain at an acceptable level and its credit-worthiness should be unimpaired. In other words, the firm's ability to raise money through either the sale of shares or the issuance of debt (bonds) should be maintained at a reasonably high level. A collateral objective of the firm's management is to use ratios in order to monitor the firm's performance from period to period. Any unexpected changes are examined in order to isolate developing problems. Financial analysis provides the manager with the tools necessary to check continuously the pulse of the firm in order to implement corrective programs as soon as symptoms of future problems are found.

TYPES OF COMPARISONS

There are two basic ways in which financial ratios are used: (1) in a cross-sectional approach, and (2) in time-series analysis. The *cross-sectional approach* involves the comparison of different firms' financial ratios at the same point in time. The typical business firm is interested in how well it has performed in relation to its competitors. If the competitors are also corporations, then their financial statements should be available for analysis. Often the firm's performance will be compared to that of the industry leader. This comparison may allow the firm to uncover major operating differences, which, if changed, might increase the firm's efficiency. Another very popular type of cross-sectional comparison is a comparison of the firm's ratios to industry averages or standards. Major sources of data for industry averages are Dun & Bradstreet's Key Business Ratios, The Canadian Imperial Bank of Commerce, Financial Post Data Bank Services, trade associations, and various government agencies such as Statistics Canada. Table 3.1 provides a sample of key ratios across several industries in Canada.

Time-series analysis is done when the financial analyst measures a firm's performance over time. Comparison of the firm's current performance to past performance

Table 3.1   Selected Business Ratios for Selected Canadian Industries, 1978[a]

	Gross margin	Current ratio	Profit on sales	Collection period	Sales to inventory	Fixed assets to tangible net worth
	Percent	Times	Percent	Days	Times	Percent
All companies	30.9	1.13	5.33	58	5.9	92.6
Retail trade	27.0	1.42	3.60	15	6.8	53.1
Wholesale trade	19.1	1.29	1.97	44	6.2	37.7
Manufacturers	23.0	1.61	4.31	45	5.4	72.9
Construction	21.7	1.26	3.44	70	5.2	74.9
Service	—	1.01	4.5	56	—	129.4
Transport, storage, and utilities	—	1.02	5.4	56	—	265.4
Mining	41.0	1.48	12.07	48	7.2	57.1
Agriculture, forestry, and fishing	33.1	1.01	3.57	21	5.3	100.1

SOURCE: Dun & Bradstreet Canada Limited, 1978.

[a]These ratios are based on an analysis of a composite sample of audited financial statements published by the Business Finance Division of Statistics Canada. The statements were filed by corporations with the Department of National Revenue for income tax purposes for the taxation year 1974. These ratios are averages and include both profitable and unprofitable concerns.

utilizing ratio analysis allows the firm to determine whether it is progressing as planned. Developing trends can be seen by using multiyear comparisons; a knowledge of these trends should assist the firm in planning future operations. The theory behind time-series analysis is that the firm must be evaluated in relation to its past performance, any developing trends must be isolated, and appropriate action must be taken to direct the firm toward its immediate and long-term goals. Time-series analysis is often helpful in checking the reasonableness of a firm's projected financial statements. A comparison of current and past ratios to those resulting from an analysis of pro forma statements may reveal discrepancies or overoptimism in the pro forma statements.

WORDS OF CAUTION

Before we discuss specific ratios, four cautions are in order. First, a single ratio does not generally provide sufficient information to judge the overall performance of the firm; only when a group of ratios is used can reasonable judgments concerning the firm's overall financial condition be made.[1] If an analyst is not concerned with a firm's overall financial condition, but only with specific aspects of its financial position, then one or two ratios may be sufficient. Second, an analyst should be sure that the dates of the financial statements being compared are the same. If not, the effects of seasonality may cause erroneous conclusions and decisions. Third, it is best to use audited financial statements for performing ratio analysis; if the statements have not been audited there may be no reason to believe that the data contained in them presents an accurate reflection of the firm's true financial condition. Therefore the resulting ratios may be completely meaningless. Finally, it is important to recognize that interfirm comparisons of ratios are valid only when the ratios are constructed with comparable accounting information. Therefore, it is important to make sure that the data in the financial statements being compared have been developed in the same way.

Basic Financial Statements

The basic financial statements—the income statement and balance sheet—for the Phyllis Petroleum Company for the years 19X1 and 19X2 are presented in Tables 3.2 and 3.3. The statements will be used to demonstrate the calculation of the various financial ratios presented in the following sections. Data for the year 19X2 will be used for the calculation of most of the ratios.

These financial statements will be used throughout the remainder of this chapter to demonstrate the use of the ratios defined. In addition, we shall make two basic assumptions:

1 That 95 percent of the firm's sales is on credit and the remaining sales are made for cash.
2 That 80 percent of the cost of goods sold represents credit purchases while the remainder represent cash purchases.

These assumptions apply to the operations of the firm in both 19X1 and 19X2.

Table 3.2   Phyllis Petroleum Company Ltd. Income Statements

	For the year ending December 31	
	19X2	19X1
Sales	$3,073,538	$2,567,530
Less: Cost of goods sold	2,088,039	1,711,011
Gross profits	$985,499	$856,519
Less: Operating expenses		
Selling expense	$100,500	$108,089
General and administrative expenses	190,005	190,020
Lease expense	69,011	63,880
Depreciation and depletion charges	238,886	223,099
Total operating expense	$598,402	$585,088
Operating profits	$387,097	$271,431
Less: Interest expense	62,338	58,846
Net profits before taxes	$324,759	$212,585
Less: Taxes (rate = 29%)[a]	94,348	64,157
Net profits after taxes	$230,411	$148,428
Less: Preferred share dividends	10,000	10,000
Earnings available for common shareholders	$220,411	$138,428
Less: Common share dividends	98,195	97,598
To retained earnings	$122,216	$ 40,830

[a]The 29-percent tax rate for 19X2 results from the fact that the firm has certain special tax write-offs that do not show up directly on its income statement.

Table 3.3 Phyllis Petroleum Company Ltd. Balance Sheets

| | For the year ending December 31 | |
Assets	19X2	19X1
Current assets		
Cash	$ 362,970	$ 287,718
Marketable securities	68,162	50,764
Accounts receivable	502,695	383,854
Inventories	288,883	280,857
Total current assets	$1,222,710	$1,003,193
Property, plant, and equipment (at cost)[a]		
Land and buildings	$2,071,594	$1,902,962
Machinery and equipment	1,743,226	1,692,263
Furniture and fixtures	316,191	286,212
Vehicles	274,704	314,285
Other	98,352	96,183
Total fixed assets (at cost)	$4,504,067	$4,291,905
Less: Accumulated depreciation and depletion	2,172,008	2,056,249
Net property, plant, and equipment	$2,332,059	$2,235,656
Intangible assets	$ 42,004	$ 30,770
Total assets	$3,596,773	$3,269,619
Liabilities and shareholders' equity		
Current liabilities		
Accounts payable	$ 381,894	$ 270,159
Notes payable and current portion of long-term debt	79,378	58,992
Accruals	159,479	153,786
Total current liabilities	$ 620,751	$ 482,937
Long-term debts[b]	$1,022,437	$ 966,858
Total liabilities	$1,643,188	$1,449,795
Shareholders' equity		
Preferred shares—cumulative 5%, $100 par, 2,000 shares authorized and issued	$ 200,000	$ 200,000
Common shares—$2.50 par, 100,000 shares authorized, shares issued and outstanding in 19X2: 76,262; in 19X1: 76,244	190,655	190,610
Paid-in capital in excess of par on common shares	429,003	417,503
Retained earnings	1,133,927	1,011,711
Total shareholders' equity	$1,953,585	$1,819,824
Total liabilities and shareholders' equity	$3,596,773	$3,269,619

[a]In 19X2 the firm has a 6-year operating lease requiring annual beginning-of-year payments of $69,011. Four years of the lease have yet to run. In 19X1 the lease payment was $63,880; the upward adjustment in this payment in 19X2 is attributable to a number of improvements made to the leased property by the lessor at the company's request. Generally, a lease for a term of three or more years is considered a long-term lease.
[b]Annual principal repayments on a portion of the firm's total outstanding debt amount to $71,000.

Basic Financial Ratios

Financial ratios can be divided into three basic groups: liquidity and activity ratios, debt ratios, and profitability ratios. The first group of ratios relies most heavily on balance sheet data, the second group uses a mix of balance sheet and income statement data, while the third group relies primarily on income statement data. As a rule, the necessary inputs to a good financial analysis include, at minimum, the income statement and the balance sheet. The reader will find greatest emphasis placed on measures of liquidity and profitability, since these areas provide information most critical to the short-run operations of the business firm. If the firm cannot survive in the short run, one need not be concerned with the longer-term financial aspects of the firm. The debt ratios are useful only if one can assure one's self that the firm will successfully weather the short run. A creditor will not provide money if he or she does not feel the firm will be able to service the resulting debts.

MEASURES OF LIQUIDITY AND ACTIVITY

The *liquidity* of a business firm is measured by its ability to satisfy its short-term obligations *as they come due*. Liquidity refers to the firm's overall financing and reflects its ability to convert certain current assets and liabilities into cash.

Liquidity has two dimensions: the time required for conversion into cash and the probability of conversion into cash. The discussion of liquidity here will deal with both the overall liquidity of the firm and the liquidity (or activity) of specific current accounts.

Measures of the Overall Liquidity of the Firm   The three basic measures of a firm's overall liquidity are (1) net working capital, (2) the current ratio, and (3) the acid-test (quick) ratio.

Net Working Capital   The firm's net working capital is calculated by subtracting its current liabilities from its current assets. The net working capital for the Phyllis Petroleum Company in 19X2 was as follows:

$$\text{Net working capital} = \$1,222,710 - \$620,751 = \$601,959$$

This figure is not very useful for comparing the performance of different firms, but it is quite useful for internal control. Quite often the contract under which a long-term debt is incurred specifically states a minimum level of net working capital that must be maintained by the firm. This requirement is intended to force the firm to maintain sufficient operating liquidity and helps protect the creditor's loans. A time-series comparison of the firm's net working capital is often helpful in evaluating the firm's operations.

The Current Ratio   The current ratio is one of the most commonly cited financial ratios. It is expressed as follows:

$$\text{Current ratio} = \frac{\text{current assets}}{\text{current liabilities}}$$

The current ratio for the Phyllis Petroleum Company in 19X2 is

$$\frac{\$1,222,710}{\$620,751} = 1.97$$

A current ratio of 2.0 is generally considered to be acceptable, but the precise definition of an acceptable ratio is greatly dependent on the industry in which a firm operates. The acceptability of a current ratio is highly dependent on the predictability of the firm's cash flows. The more predictable the cash flows, the lower the current ratio required. For example, a current ratio of 1.0 would be considered acceptable for service industries and utilities, but it might be quite unacceptable for a manufacturing firm. The current ratio of 1.97 for the Phyllis Petroleum Company should be quite acceptable.

If the firm's current ratio is divided into 1.0, the resulting quotient subtracted from 1.0 and multiplied by 100 represents the percentage by which the firm's current assets can shrink without making it impossible for the firm to cover its current liabilities. For example, a current ratio of 2.0 means that the firm can still cover its current liabilities even if its current assets shrink by 50 percent.

The current ratio is much more useful for interfirm comparisons of liquidity than net working capital. For example, assume that there are two firms, A and B, with the following data:

Measure	Firm A	Firm B
Current assets	$100,000	$25,000
Current liabilities	80,000	10,000
Net working capital	20,000	15,000
Current ratio	1.25	2.5

On the basis of net working capital it appears that firm A is more liquid than firm B, even though current assets of firm B are 2.5 times its current liabilities while current assets of firm A are only 1.25 times its current liabilities. Therefore, in interfirm comparisons current ratios rather than levels of net working capital will reflect the relative liquidity positions of the firms more accurately.

A final point worthy of note is that whenever a firm's current ratio is 1.0, its net working capital is zero. If a firm has a current ratio of less than 1.0, it will have a negative net working capital. Net working capital is useful only in comparing the liquidity of the same firm over time and should not be used for comparing that of different firms; instead, the current ratio should be used.

The Acid-Test (Quick) Ratio   The acid-test ratio is similar to the current ratio except for the fact that it excludes inventory from the firm's current assets. The basic assumption of the acid-test ratio is that inventory is generally the least liquid current asset and should therefore be ignored. The acid-test ratio is calculated as follows:*

$$\text{Acid-test ratio} = \frac{\text{current assets} - \text{inventory}}{\text{current liabilities}}$$

*Sometimes the acid-test, or quick, ratio is defined as (cash + marketable securities + accounts receivable)/current liabilities. If a firm were to show items other than cash, marketable securities, accounts receivable, and inventory as current assets, its acid-test ratio might vary, depending on which method of calculation is used.

The acid-test ratio for the Phyllis Petroleum Company in 19X2 is

$$\frac{\$1,222,710 - \$288,883}{\$620,751} = \frac{\$933,827}{\$620,751} = 1.50$$

An acid-test ratio of 1.00 or greater is recommended. Again, what is considered an acceptable value depends highly on the industry in which the company operates. This ratio provides a better measure of overall liquidity than the current ratio only when a firm's inventory cannot easily be converted into cash.

Measures of the Liquidity, or Activity, of Specific Current Accounts[*]   Measuring the overall liquidity is generally not enough because the differences in the composition of a firm's current assets and current liabilities can significantly impact on the firm's "true" liquidity. For example, consider the following current portion of the balance sheets for firms X and Y.

Firm X

Cash	$ 0	Accts. pay.	$ 0	
Mktble. sec.	0	Notes pay.	10,000	
Accts. rec.	0	Accruals	0	
Inv.	20,000			
Total C.A.	$20,000	Total C.L.	$10,000	

Firm Y

Cash	$ 5,000	Accts. pay.	$ 5,000	
Mktble. sec.	5,000	Notes pay.	3,000	
Accts. rec.	5,000	Accruals	2,000	
Inv.	5,000			
Total C.A.	$20,000	Total C.L.	$10,000	

Although both firms appear to be equally liquid since their current ratios are both 2.00 (i.e., $20,000 ÷ $10,000), a closer look at the differences in the composition of current assets and liabilities suggests that firm Y is more liquid than firm X. This results for two reasons: (1) firm Y has generally more liquid assets in the form of cash and marketable securities than firm X, which has only a single and relatively illiquid asset in the form of inventory; and (2) firm Y's current liabilities are in general more flexible than the single current liability—notes payable—of firm X.

It is therefore important to look beyond measures of overall liquidity in order to assess the liquidity (or activity) of specific current accounts. A number of ratios are available for measuring the liquidity of the most important current accounts, which include inventory, accounts receivable, and accounts payable. The most common are discussed

[*]The term *activity* is often used to refer to the liquidity of specific accounts, or the quickness with which these accounts can be converted into cash. The terms *liquidity* and *activity* are used interchangeably to refer to the speed with which specific accounts turn over.

in the following pages. A basic simplifying assumption used in many of the calculations is that there are 360 days in the year and 30 days in each month.*

Inventory Turnover   The liquidity, or activity, of a firm's inventory is measured as follows:

$$\text{Inventory turnover} = \frac{\text{cost of goods sold}}{\text{average inventory}}$$

Applying this relationship to the Phyllis Petroleum Company for 19X2 yields

$$\text{Inventory turnover} = \frac{\$2,088,039}{\dfrac{\$288,883 + \$280,857}{2}} = \frac{\$2,088,039}{\$284,870} = 7.33$$

The resulting turnover is meaningful only when compared to that of other firms in the same industry or to the firm's past inventory turnover. A ballpark estimate cannot be given. An inventory turnover of 40.0 would not be unusual for a grocery store, whereas a common inventory turnover for an aircraft manufacturer would be 1.0. Differences in turnover rates result from the differing operating characteristics of various industries. Even within the same industry, interfirm comparisons of turnover rates will only be valid if the firms employ the same method of inventory valuation.

For example, other things being equal, the firm using LIFO for inventory valuation will likely have an inventory turnover ratio different from another firm using FIFO for inventory valuation. The most acceptable way to calculate average inventory is to use monthly figures. Often, however, the only data available is the year-end inventory figure.

Many people believe that the higher the firm's inventory turnover, the more efficiently it has managed its inventory. This is true up to a point beyond which a high inventory turnover may signal problems. For example, one way to increase inventory turnover is to carry very small inventories. However, such a strategy could result in a large number of stockouts (lost sales due to insufficient inventory), which could damage the firm's future sales. For each industry, there is a range of inventory turnover that may be considered good. Values below this range may signal illiquid or inactive inventories, while values above this range may indicate insufficient inventories and high stockouts.

The Average Age of Inventory   The average age of inventory represents how many days, on the average, an item remains in the firm's inventory. It is calculated as follows:

$$\text{Average age of inventory} = \frac{360}{\text{inventory turnover}}$$

The average age of inventory for the Phyllis Petroleum Company for 19X2 is

$$\frac{360}{7.33} = 49.11 \text{ days}$$

*Unless otherwise specified, a 360-day year consisting of twelve 30-day months is assumed throughout this text. This assumption allows some simplification of the calculations used to illustrate key principles.

The shorter the average age of the firm's inventory, the more liquid or active it may be considered. The average age of inventory can be thought of as the amount of time between the purchase of a raw material and the ultimate sale of the finished product. Viewed in this manner, it is useful for evaluating the purchasing, production, and inventory control functions of the firm.

The Accounts Receivable Turnover   The turnover of a firm's accounts receivable is a measure of their liquidity or activity. It is defined as follows:

$$\text{Accounts receivable turnover} = \frac{\text{annual credit sales}^*}{\text{average accounts receivable}}$$

In order to apply this ratio to the Phyllis Petroleum Company, the amount of credit sales must be determined. As indicated earlier, 95 percent of its sales are made on credit terms. Ninety-five percent of Phyllis's sales is $2,919,861.10 [.95($3,073,538)].

The accounts receivable turnover for the Phyllis Petroleum Company for 19X2 is

$$\frac{\$2,919,861.10}{\dfrac{\$502,695 + \$383,854}{2}} = \frac{\$2,919,861.10}{\$443,274.50} = 6.59$$

The higher the firm's accounts receivable turnover, the more favourable it is. A firm can increase its accounts receivable turnover by a very restrictive credit policy, but this strategy would not be recommended due to the lost sales that might result. The financial analyst should question especially high accounts receivable turnovers because they may signal poor credit policies.†

The Average Age of Accounts Receivable   The average age of accounts receivable, or *average collection period*, is a more meaningful figure to use in evaluating the firm's credit and collection policies than is the turnover of accounts receivable. It is defined as follows:

$$\text{Average collection period} = \frac{\text{average accounts receivable}}{\text{credit sales per day}}$$

The relationship between average collection period and accounts receivable is as follows:

$$\begin{aligned}
\text{Average collection period} &= \frac{\text{average accounts receivable}}{\dfrac{\text{annual credit sales}}{360}} \\[2ex]
&= 360 \cdot \frac{\text{average accounts receivable}}{\text{annual credit sales}} \\[2ex]
&= \frac{360}{\text{accounts receivable turnover}}
\end{aligned}$$

---

*Where information on credit sales is not available, total sales data may be an acceptable approximation.
†A discussion of the evaluation and establishment of credit policies is presented in Chapter 9, which is devoted solely to the management of accounts receivable.

The average collection period for the Phyllis Petroleum Company's accounts receivable for 19X2 is

$$\frac{360}{6.59} = 54.63 \text{ days}$$

The average collection period of accounts receivable is meaningful only in light of the firm's credit terms. If, for instance, the Phyllis Petroleum Company extends 30-day credit terms to its customers, an average collection period (age of accounts receivable) of 54.63 days would indicate a poorly managed credit or collection department, or both. If it extended 60-day credit terms, the 54.63 day average collection period would be quite acceptable.

The Accounts Payable Turnover   The turnover of accounts payable is similar to the turnover of accounts receivable. It measures the number of times accounts payable are converted into cash each year. It is defined as follows:

$$\text{Accounts payable turnover} = \frac{\text{annual credit purchases}}{\text{average accounts payable}}$$

Since annual credit purchases do not normally appear on balance sheets or income statements, they must be estimated by determining the percentage of the cost of goods sold that represents credit purchases. As indicated earlier, 80 percent of the Phyllis Petroleum Company's cost of goods sold represents credit purchases. This equals $1,670,431.20 [or .80($2,088,039)]. Using this figure, we can calculate the turnover of the company's accounts payable for 19X2.

$$\text{A/P turnover} = \frac{\$1,670,431.20}{\dfrac{\$381,894 + \$270,159}{2}} = \frac{\$1,670,431.20}{\$326,026.50} = 5.12$$

This figure is not quite as useful a measure as the average age of accounts payable.

The Average Age of Accounts Payable   The average age of accounts payable, or *average payment period*, is calculated as follows:

$$\text{Average age of A/P} = \frac{360}{\text{accounts payable turnover}^*}$$

The average age of accounts payable for the Phyllis Petroleum Company for 19X2 is

$$\frac{360}{5.12} = 70.31 \text{ days}$$

This figure is meaningful only in light of the average credit terms extended by the firm. If the Phyllis Petroleum Company's suppliers, on the average, have extended 30-day credit terms to the firm, an analyst might give it a low credit rating. However, if the firm has been generally extended 60-day credit terms, its credit would certainly be acceptable.

---

*At this point, the reader should recognize that the average age of accounts payable can be found by dividing 360 by the turnover. And, of course, given the average age, the turnover can be found by dividing it into 360.

Prospective lenders and suppliers of trade credit are especially interested in the average age of accounts payable, since it provides them with a feel for the bill-paying patterns of the firm.

Substituting the formula for the turnover of accounts payable into the denominator of the equation above gives us a one-step formula for determining the average age of accounts payable.

$$\text{Average age of A/P} = \frac{360 \cdot \text{average accounts payable}}{\text{annual credit purchases}}$$

Aging Accounts   *Aging* is a technique for evaluating the composition of *either* accounts receivable or accounts payable. It provides the analyst with information concerning the proportion of each type of account that has been outstanding for a period of time. By highlighting irregularities, it allows him or her to pinpoint the cause of collection or payment problems.

Aging requires that the firm's accounts receivable or payable be broken down into groups based on their point of origin; this breakdown is typically made on a month-by-month basis, going back three or four months.

EXAMPLE   Assume that a firm extends 30-day credit terms to its customers and on December 31 finds $200,000 of accounts receivable on its books. An evaluation of the $200,000 of accounts receivable results in the following breakdown:

			Days overdue			
Days	Current	0–30	31–60	61–90	Over 90	
Month	December	November	October	September	August	Total
Accounts receivable	$134,000	$16,000	$44,000	$4,000	$2,000	$200,000
Percentage of total	67	8	22	2	1	100

Since it is assumed that the firm gives its customers 30 days after the end of the month in which the sale is made to pay off their accounts, any December receivables still on the firm's books are considered current. November receivables are between zero and 30 days overdue, while October receivables are 31–60 days overdue, and so on.

The table shows that 67 percent of the firm's receivables are current, 8 percent are one month late, 22 percent are two months late, 2 percent are three months late, and 1 percent are more than three months late.* The only irregularity in these data is the high percentage of accounts receivable represented by October receivables. This indicates that some problem may have occurred in October, such as the hiring of a new credit manager or the acceptance of a new account that has made a large credit purchase it has not yet paid for. When accounts are aged and such a discrepancy is found, the analyst should determine its cause.

---

*The average age of the accounts receivable can be estimated by weighting the average age of each account by the percentage the account is of the total account, and then summing the weighted values. For example, the current (December) accounts would on average have an age of 15 days, the November

The benefit of aging lies in its ability to point up specific periods of apparent slowness in the collection or payment of accounts.

MEASURES OF DEBT

The debt position of the business firm indicates the amount of borrowed money that is being used in attempting to generate profits. Since the claims of the firm's creditors must be satisfied prior to the distribution of earnings to shareholders,* present and prospective shareholders pay close attention to both the degree of indebtedness and the ability to repay the debts the firm has incurred. Lenders are also concerned about the firm's degree of indebtedness and ability to service debts, since the more indebtedness present, the higher the probability that the firm will be unable to satisfy the claims of all its creditors. Management obviously must be concerned with indebtedness, since it recognizes the attention paid to it by these other parties and since it certainly does not wish to see the firm become insolvent.

Measures of the Degree of Indebtedness   The degree of indebtedness is typically measured using only balance sheet data. Three of the most commonly used measures of indebtedness are (1) the debt ratio, (2) the debt-equity ratio, and (3) the debt-to-total-capitalization ratio.

The Debt Ratio   This ratio measures the proportion of total assets provided by the firm's creditors and is calculated as follows:

$$\text{Debt ratio} = \frac{\text{total liabilities}}{\text{total assets}}$$

The debt ratio for the Phyllis Petroleum Company for 19X2 is

$$\frac{\$1,643,188}{\$3,596,773} = .457 = 45.7\%$$

This indicates that the company has financed 45.7 percent of its assets with debt. The higher this ratio is, the more financial leverage a firm has.† The following two ratios differ from the debt ratio in that they focus only on the firm's long-term debts.

---

accounts outstanding would have an average age of 45 days, and so on. Applying the given percentages, the average age is calculated

$$= .67(15 \text{ days}) + .08(45 \text{ days}) + .22(75 \text{ days}) + .02(105 \text{ days}) + .01(135 \text{ days})$$
$$= 10.05 + 3.60 + 16.50 + 2.10 + 1.35 = \underline{33.60} \text{ days}$$

This approximation can be applied in a similar fashion to an aging schedule of accounts payable.

*The law requires that creditors' claims be satisfied prior to those of the firm's owners. This only makes sense, since the creditor is providing a service (i.e., lending money) to the owners and is not required to bear the risks of ownership.

†*Financial leverage* refers to the degree to which a firm uses money requiring fixed payments to magnify the returns to the owners or to retain the firm's control in the hands of the existing owners. This topic is discussed at length in Chapters 4 and 18.

The Debt-Equity Ratio   This ratio indicates the relationship of the long-term funds provided by creditors to funds provided by the firm's owners.* It is commonly used to measure the degree of financial leverage of the firm. It is defined as follows:

$$\text{Debt-equity ratio} = \frac{\text{long-term debt}}{\text{shareholders' equity}}$$

The debt-equity ratio for the Phyllis Petroleum Company is

$$\frac{\$1,022,437}{\$1,953,585} = .523 = 52.3\%$$

This figure depends upon the type of business the firm is in. Firms with large amounts of fixed assets and stable cash flows, such as public utilities, typically have high debt-equity ratios; while other, less capital-intensive firms normally have lower debt-equity ratios. An industry average is a good figure against which to compare a firm's debt-equity ratio.

The Debt-to-Total-Capitalization Ratio   This ratio measures the percentage of the firm's *long-term* funds supplied by its creditors. The firm's long-term funds are referred to as its *total capitalization*. They include both long-term debt and the shareholders' equity. The ratio of debt to total capitalization is stated as follows:

$$\text{Debt-to-total-capitalization ratio} = \frac{\text{long-term debt}}{\text{total capitalization}}$$

The value of this ratio for the Phyllis Petroleum Company for 19X2 is

$$\frac{\$1,022,437}{\$1,022,437 + \$1,953,585} = \frac{\$1,022,437}{\$2,976,022} = .344 = 34.4\%$$

The ratio indicates that, of the firm's total long-term funds, 34.4 percent have been supplied by creditors.

Since there is great similarity between the debt-equity ratio and the ratio of debt to total capitalization, the analyst need use only one of these. In either case, the resulting value is meaningful only in light of the nature of the firm's operations and industry averages. The value of either of these ratios will be very different for a utility as compared to a grocery store, and care should be used in making comparisons.

Measures of the Ability to Service Debts   The ability to *service* debts refers to how readily a firm can meet the fixed contractual payments typically required on a scheduled basis over the life of a debt.† Debt results in obligations to meet scheduled fixed payments for interest and principal (or sinking-fund) payments.‡ Lease

---

*Sometimes the debt-to-equity ratio is calculated by using total debt in the numerator. Preferred shares may also be included under debt if the analysis is being made from the viewpoint of the common shareholders. This is so because preferred shares represent a senior claim from the standpoint of the common shareholders.

†The term *service* is used throughout this text to refer to the payment of interest and repayment of principal associated with a firm's debt obligations. When a firm services its debts, it pays, or fulfills, these obligations.

‡Information on sinking fund obligations may not be available to outside analysts.

payments as well as preferred dividend payments also represent scheduled payment obligations, which are quite similar to those required as part of many corporate debts. The firm's ability to meet certain fixed charges is measured using *coverage ratios.* Such ratios are of greatest interest to the firm's creditors, who are interested in its ability to service its existing debts or any additional proposed debts, or both. The lower the firm's coverage ratios, the more risky the firm is considered to be. "Riskiness" here refers to the firm's ability to meet its fixed obligations. If a firm is unable to meet these obligations, it will be in default and its creditors may seek immediate repayment. In most instances, this would force a firm into bankruptcy. The ability of coverage ratios to measure this type of risk makes their use quite common.* Of the three ratios discussed next, only the first two of these ratios devote attention solely to debt; the third ratio considers other fixed payment obligations in addition to debt service.

Times Interest Earned   This ratio is often called the firm's *total interest coverage ratio.* It measures the firm's ability to pay its contractual interest payments. The higher the value of this ratio, the better able the firm is to fulfill its interest obligations. Times interest earned is calculated as follows:

$$\text{Times interest earned} = \frac{\text{earnings before interest and taxes}}{\text{annual interest expense}}$$

Applying this ratio to the Phyllis Petroleum Company for 19X2 yields the following value:

$$\text{Times interest earned} = \frac{\$387,097}{\$62,338} = 6.21$$

The times interest earned for the Phyllis Petroleum Company is acceptable; as a rule, a value of at least 5.0 and preferably closer to 10.0 is suggested. If the firm's earnings before interest and taxes were to shrink by 84 percent $[(6.21 - 1.0) \div 6.21]$, the firm would still be able to pay the $62,338 in interest it owes. Thus it has a good margin of safety.

Total Debt Coverage   This ratio is similar to the interest coverage ratio, except that it measures not only the firm's ability to pay its interest charges but also its ability to repay the *principal* of loans or make scheduled *sinking-fund* payments. Often, as part of a bond or long-term loan agreement, a firm is required to make periodic payments of principal either to the lender or into a fund that is being accumulated so that the debt can be retired at maturity. The procedure for calculating the ratio is the same for either requirement. Since principal repayments are made on an after-tax basis, and interest is a pretax expenditure, the interest and principal payments must be measured on a common basis. It is easier to adjust principal payments to pretax equivalents in order to

---

*It is important to recognize that coverage ratios use data based upon the application of accrual concepts (discussed in Chapter 1) to measure what in a strict sense should be measured with cash flows. This occurs since debts are serviced using cash flows—not the accounting values shown on the firm's financial statements. But because it is difficult to determine cash flows available for debt service from the firm's financial statements, the calculation of coverage ratios as presented herein is quite common due to the ready availability of financial statement data.

calculate total debt coverage than to adjust both earnings before taxes and interest to after-tax equivalents. Table 3.4 presents a note on the calculation of the before-tax earnings necessary to achieve a stated amount of after-tax earnings. The table also illustrates the resulting relationship. The formula for the firm's total debt coverage is

$$\text{Total debt coverage} = \frac{\text{earnings before interest and taxes}}{\text{interest} + \text{principal payments} \left[1/(1-t)\right]}$$

where t = the corporate tax rate applicable to the firm's income.

Table 3.4   Calculating the Before-Tax Earnings Necessary to Achieve Given After-Tax Earnings

---

It is often necessary (especially when calculating coverage ratios) to determine the amount of before-tax earnings needed to achieve given after-tax earnings.

Let

EAT = the after-tax earnings desired
EBT = the before-tax earnings required in order to permit after-tax earnings to equal EAT
t = the tax rate on income

Looking at the bottom portion of the income statement, we have

Earnings before taxes	EBT
Less taxes	$-t \cdot$ EBT
Earnings after taxes	EAT

It can be seen above that

$$\text{EAT} = \text{EBT} - (t \cdot \text{EBT}) \tag{1}$$

Factoring EBT from Equation 1 yields

$$\text{EAT} = \text{EBT}(1 - t) \tag{2}$$

Solving for EBT yields

$$\text{EBT} = \frac{\text{EAT}}{1 - t} \tag{3}$$

Equation 3 gives the before-tax earnings necessary to have after-tax earnings of EAT dollars given a tax rate of t.

Example:

$$\text{Let EAT} = \$120$$
$$t = 25\%$$

How much must be earned before taxes to have after-tax earnings of $120?

Substituting the data into Equation 3, we get

$$\text{EBT} = \frac{\$120}{1 - .25} = \frac{\$120}{.75} = \$160$$

We can check our answer by the following simple calculation:
Check:	Earnings before taxes	$160
	Less: Taxes (25 percent)	40
	Earnings after taxes	$120

The term $1/(1 - t)$ is included in order to adjust the principal payment back to a pretax amount. If the Phyllis Petroleum Company is required to pay $71,000 annually into a sinking fund and the firm is in a 29-percent tax bracket, its total debt coverage ratio for 19X2 is

$$\frac{\$387,097}{\$62,338 + \$71,000[1/(1 - .29)]} = \frac{\$387,097}{\$62,338 + \$100,000} = \frac{\$387,097}{\$162,338} = 2.38$$

A total debt coverage ratio of 2.38 for the Phyllis Petroleum Company appears to be quite good.

It is important to recognize that this ratio, just like the interest coverage ratio, measures risk. The lower the ratio, the more risky the firm is from the lender's viewpoint. Although sinking-fund payments are not always made to the lender, they are usually a contractual requirement. This means that if a firm fails to make a sinking-fund payment it will be considered in default, just as it would be if it failed to repay the principal when it came due. A default normally permits the lender to call in his or her loan and often results in bankruptcy for the firm. This is why the ability of a firm to cover its interest and principal or sinking-fund payments is viewed as a measure of risk by prospective and existing creditors. An examination of the debt coverage ratio allows creditors to determine whether the firm is capable of handling any additional debts.

The Overall Coverage Ratio   The overall coverage ratio is quite similar to the total debt coverage ratio except that it includes any other fixed obligations, such as scheduled lease payments and preferred share dividends.* Since lease payments are tax-deductible expenditures they do not require any tax adjustment; the preferred share dividends, which must be paid from after-tax cash flows, must be adjusted for taxes. The formula for the overall coverage ratio is

Overall coverage ratio =

$$\frac{\text{earnings before lease payments, interest, and taxes}}{\text{interest + principal payments } [1/(1 - t)] + \text{lease payments} + \text{preferred dividends } [1/(1 - t)]}$$

Applying this formula to the Phyllis Petroleum Company data for 19X2 yields

Overall coverage ratio

$$= \frac{\$387,097 + \$69,011}{\$62,338 + \$71,000[1/(1 - .29)] + \$69,011 + \$10,000[1/(1 - .29)]}$$

$$= \frac{\$456,108}{\$245,434} = 1.86$$

The total coverage ratio is of interest not only to the firm's creditors but also to existing and prospective lessors, preferred shareholders, and common shareholders. It

*Although preferred share dividends, which are stated at the time of issue, can be "passed" (i.e., not paid) at the option of the firm's directors, it is generally believed that the payment of such dividends is necessary in order to impact favourably on the owners' wealth as reflected in the price of their shares. This text therefore treats the preferred dividend as if it were a contractual obligation not only to pay a fixed amount but also to make the payments as scheduled.

Table 3.5 Phyllis Petroleum Company Ltd. Percent Income Statements

		For the year ending December 31	
		19X2	19X1
	Sales	100.00%	100.00%
	Less: Cost of goods sold	67.94	66.64
(a)	Gross profit margin	32.06%	33.36%
	Less: Operating expenses		
	Selling expenses	3.27%	4.21%
	General and admin. expenses	6.18	7.40
	Lease expense	2.25	2.49
	Depreciation and depletion	7.77	8.69
	Total operating expense	19.47%	22.79%
(b)	Operating profit margin	12.59%	10.57%
	Less: Interest expense	2.02%	2.29%
	Net profits before taxes	10.57%	8.28%
	Less: Taxes	3.07%	2.50%
(c)	Net profit margin	7.50%	5.78%

measures the ability of the firm to cover all fixed financial charges. The higher it is, the safer are the interests of creditors, lessor(s), and preferred shareholders in the firm.

MEASURES OF PROFITABILITY

There are many measures of profitability. As a group, these measures allow the analyst to evaluate the firm's earnings with respect to a given level of sales, a certain level of assets, or the owners' investment. Attention is paid to the firm's profitability since in order to stay in existence it must be profitable. Creditors, owners, and, most important, management pay close attention to boosting the firm's profits due to the great importance placed on the earnings of the firm in the marketplace.

Percent Income Statements A common approach for evaluating profitability in relation to sales is the *percent income statement.** By expressing each item on the income statement as a percentage of sales, the relationship between sales and specific revenues and expenses can be evaluated. Percent income statements are especially useful in comparing a firm's performance for one year with that for another year. Percent income statements for 19X1 and 19X2 for the Phyllis Petroleum Company are presented in Table 3.5. An evaluation of these statements reveals that the firm's cost of goods sold increased from 66.64 percent of sales in 19X1 to 67.94 percent of sales in 19X2, resulting in a decrease in the gross profit margin from 33.36

*This statement is often referred to as a "common-size" statement. The same treatment is often applied to the firm's balance sheet to make it easier to evaluate changes in the asset or financial structure of the firm.

percent to 32.06 percent. However, thanks to a decrease in operating ex
22.79 percent in 19X1 to 19.47 percent in 19X2, the firm's net profit n
from 5.78 percent of sales in 19X1 to 7.50 percent in 19X2. The decrease in
in 19X1 more than compensated for the increase in the cost of goods so
crease in the firm's 19X2 interest expense (2.02 percent of sales as opposed
percent in 19X1) added to the increase in 19X2 profits.

Three commonly cited ratios of profitability can be read directly from the pe
income statement: (a) the gross profit margin, (b) the operating profit margin, and (c)
net profit margin.

The Gross Profit Margin   The gross profit margin indicates the percentage of each
sales dollar remaining after the firm has paid for its goods. The higher the gross
profit, the better, and the lower the relative cost of merchandise sold. The gross
profit margin is calculated as follows:

$$\text{Gross profit margin} = \frac{\text{sales} - \text{cost of goods sold}}{\text{sales}} = \frac{\text{gross profit}}{\text{sales}}$$

The value for Phyllis Petroleum Company's gross profit margin for 19X2 is

$$\frac{\$3,073,538 - \$2,088,039}{\$3,073,538} = \frac{\$985,499}{\$3,073,538} = 32.06\%$$

This value is shown on the percent income statement, Table 3.5.

The Operating Profit Margin   This ratio represents what are often called the *pure
profits* earned on each sales dollar by the firm. Operating profits are pure in the
sense that they ignore any financial or government charges (interest or taxes) and
measure only the profits earned by the firm on its operations. A high operating
profit margin is preferred.

The operating profit margin is calculated as follows:

$$\text{Operating profit margin} = \frac{\text{operating profit}}{\text{sales}}$$

The value for Phyllis Petroleum Company's operating profit margin for 19X2 is

$$\frac{\$387,097}{\$3,073,538} = 12.59\%$$

The Net Profit Margin   The net profit margin measures the percentage of each sales
dollar remaining after all expenses, including taxes, have been deducted. The higher
the firm's net profit margin, the better. The net profit margin is a quite commonly
cited measure of the corporation's success with respect to earnings on sales. "Good"
net profit margins differ considerably across industries. A net profit margin of 1
percent would not be unusual for a grocery store, while a net profit margin of 10
percent would be low for a jewelry store. The net profit margin is calculated as
follows:

$$\text{Net profit margin} = \frac{\text{net profits after taxes}}{\text{sales}}$$

The value of Phyllis Petroleum Company's net profit margin for 19X2 is

$$\frac{\$230,411}{\$3,073,538} = 7.50\%$$

The Total Asset Turnover   The total asset turnover indicates the efficiency with which the firm is able to use its assets to generate sales dollars. The higher a firm's total asset turnover is, the more efficiently its assets have been used. The total asset turnover is probably of greatest interest to the firm's management, since it indicates whether the firm's operations have been financially efficient. Other parties, such as creditors and prospective and existing owners, will also be interested in this measure. The firm's total asset turnover is calculated as follows:

$$\text{Total asset turnover} = \frac{\text{annual sales}}{\text{total assets}}$$

The value of the Phyllis Petroleum Company's total asset turnover for 19X2 is

$$\frac{\$3,073,538}{\$3,596,773} = 0.853$$

The Return on Investment (ROI) and the DuPont Formula   The return on investment, which is often called the firm's *return on total assets*, measures the overall effectiveness of management in generating profits with its available assets. The higher the firm's return on investment, the better. The return on investment is calculated as follows:

$$\text{Return on investment} = \frac{\text{net profits after taxes}}{\text{total assets}}$$

The value of the Phyllis Petroleum Company's return on investment for 19X2 is

$$\frac{\$230,411}{\$3,596,773} = 6.40\%$$

This value appears to be quite acceptable, but only when it is compared to industry averages can meaningful conclusions be drawn. The firm's return on investment can be calculated in an alternate fashion, utilizing the *DuPont formula*, which is written as follows:

$$\text{Return on investment} = \text{net profit margin} \cdot \text{total asset turnover}$$

The upper right-hand portion of Figure 3.1 presents a breakdown of this formula. Substituting the appropriate formulas into the equation and simplifying gives us the same values as those arrived at by the direct method:

$$\frac{\text{Net profits after taxes}}{\text{total assets}} = \frac{\text{net profits after taxes}}{\text{sales}} \cdot \frac{\text{sales}}{\text{total assets}}$$

If the values for the net profit margin and total asset turnover of the Phyllis Petroleum Company, calculated earlier, are substituted into the DuPont formula, the result is

$$6.40\% = 7.50\% \cdot 0.853$$

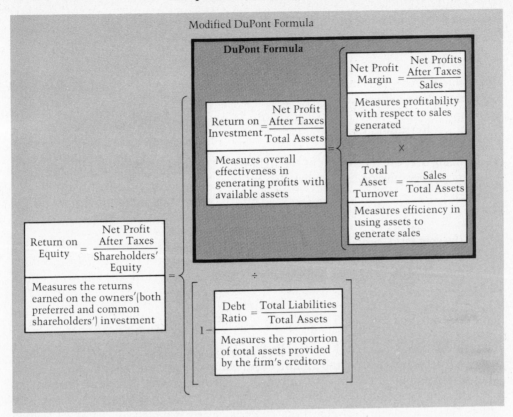

Figure 3.1   The DuPont and Modified DuPont formulas.

The DuPont formula allows the firm to break down its return on investment into a profit-on-sales component and an asset efficiency component. Typically, a firm with a low net profit margin has a high total asset turnover, which results in a reasonably good return on investment. Often, the opposite situation exists. The relationship between the two components of the DuPont formula will depend largely on the industry in which the firm operates.

Return on Equity (ROE) and the Modified DuPont Formula   The return on equity measures the return earned on the owners' (both preferred and common shareholders') investment.* Generally the higher this return, the better off are the owners. Return on equity is calculated as follows:

$$\text{Return on equity} = \frac{\text{net profits after taxes}}{\text{shareholders' equity}}$$

*This ratio includes preferred dividends in the earnings figures and preferred shares in the equity value, but because the amount of preferred share capital and its impact on a firm are generally quite small or nonexistent, this formula is a reasonably good approximation of the true owners', that is, the common shareholders', return.

The value of this ratio for the Phyllis Petroleum Company for 19X2 is

$$\frac{\$230,411}{\$1,953,585} = 11.79\%$$

This value, which seems to be quite good, could have been calculated using the *Modified DuPont formula*, which is

$$\text{Return on equity} = \frac{\text{net profit margin} \cdot \text{total asset turnover}}{(1 - \text{debt ratio})}$$

Recognizing that the numerator of the right-hand side of the equation is the return on investment, the equation can be rewritten as

$$\text{Return on equity} = \frac{\text{return on investment}}{(1 - \text{debt ratio})}$$

Use of the debt ratio (defined earlier as total liabilities/total assets) to convert the ROI to the ROE reflects the impact of leverage (i.e., use of debt) on the owners' return. Substituting the values for 19X2 into the Modified DuPont formula yields the following return on equity:

$$\frac{6.40\%}{(1 - .457)} = \frac{6.40\%}{.543} = 11.79\%$$

The value obtained using the Modified DuPont framework is the same as that calculated directly. The real strength of the Modified DuPont formulation is that it allows the firm to break its return on equity into a profit-on-sales component (net profit margin), an asset efficiency component (total asset turnover), and a use-of-leverage component (debt ratio). The relationship between these ratios is clearly depicted in Figure 3.1, which presents a breakdown of the Modified DuPont formula.

The Return on Common Shareholders' Equity   This ratio indicates the return earned on the *book value* of the common shareholders' equity (which includes retained earnings). The higher this ratio, the better the owners like it. It is calculated as follows:

Return on common shareholders' equity

$$= \frac{\text{net profits after taxes} - \text{preferred dividends}}{\text{shareholders' equity} - \text{preferred shareholders' equity}}$$

The value of this ratio for the Phyllis Petroleum Company for 19X2 is

$$\frac{\$230,411 - \$10,000}{\$1,953,585 - \$200,000} = \frac{\$220,411}{\$1,753,585} = 12.57\%$$

The numerator and denominator of this formula are often referred to as "earnings available for common shareholders" and "common shareholders' equity," respectively. Sometimes more meaningful results can be obtained by substituting the market value of the firm's equity into the denominator in order to calculate the yield, or return, on the current *market value* of the firm.

Earnings Per Share   The firm's earnings per share are generally of interest to the management and to current or prospective shareholders, since they are considered an important indicator of corporate success. High earnings per share are preferred. Earnings per share are calculated as follows:

$$\text{Earnings per share} = \frac{\text{earnings available for common shareholders}}{\text{number of common shares outstanding}}$$

The value of the Phyllis Petroleum Company's earnings per share for 19X2 is

$$\frac{\$220,411}{76,262} = \$2.89$$

This figure does not represent the amount of earnings actually distributed to shareholders. Also note that in some cases earnings per share may not be as simple to calculate as indicated by the preceding formula. The reader wishing to examine the complications that can arise should refer to the CICA (Canadian Institute of Chartered Accountants) Handbook, Section 3500.

Dividends Per Share*   This figure represents the amount of money distributed to each shareholder. It is calculated as follows:

$$\text{Dividends per share} = \frac{\text{dividends paid}}{\text{number of common shares outstanding}}$$

The dividends per share for 19X2 for the Phyllis Petroleum Company are

$$\frac{\$98,195}{76,262} = \$1.29$$

This figure indicates that owners of the company's 76,262 shares received dividends of $1.29 for each share owned. The many facets of dividends and dividend policy will be discussed fully in Chapter 24.

The Book Value Per Share   The book value per share indicates the minimum value of each share based on the assumption that all assets can be liquidated at least at their book value. Book value as used here represents the accounting value of the common shareholders' equity (i.e., the value shown on the firm's balance sheet). The book value per share can be thought of as the amount of money that would be received for each share owned if the firm's assets were sold at their book value and the proceeds remaining after all debts had been settled were distributed to the shareholders. The book value per share is calculated as follows:

$$\text{Book value per share} = \frac{\text{total common shareholders' equity}}{\text{number of common shares outstanding}}$$

---

*Dividends per share and the book value per share are not actually measures of profitability; rather, they measure values that reflect managerial action (in the case of dividends) and historical value (in the case of book value). They have been included here since they are often of interest to prospective and existing shareholders.

The book value per share for the Phyllis Petroleum Company for 19X2 is

$$\frac{\$1,953,585 - \$200,000}{76,262} = \frac{\$1,753,585}{76,262} = \$22.99$$

The reader should note that there is no "normal" relationship between market and book values per share. The reason for this is discussed in Chapter 18.

A Complete Ratio Analysis of Phyllis Petroleum Company

The 19X2 ratio values calculated in the preceding section of the chapter, and the ratio values calculated for 19X0 and 19X1 for the Phyllis Petroleum Company, along with the industry average ratios for 19X2, are summarized in Table 3.6. The table shows the formula used to calculate each of the ratios. Using these data, the three key aspects of Phyllis's performance—liquidity and activity, debt, and profitability—are discussed separately in the following paragraphs on both a time-series and cross-sectional basis.

LIQUIDITY AND ACTIVITY

The overall liquidity of the firm seems to exhibit a fairly stable trend and has been maintained at a level that is reasonably consistent with the industry average in 19X2. Phyllis's inventory management seems to have improved, performing at a level above the industry. The firm may be experiencing some problems with its accounts receivable. The average age of receivables seems to have crept up to a level above that of the industry; therefore, attention should be given to various aspects of the firm's credit management. The firm appears to be a bit slow in paying its bills. Although the trend seems to be towards improvement, Phyllis is paying nearly 14 days slower than the average firm in the industry. The payment procedures should be examined in order to make sure that the company's credit standing is not adversely affected. Overall, the firm's liquidity appears to be good, although some attention should be given to the management of accounts receivable and accounts payable.

DEBT

The firm's indebtedness seems to have increased over the 19X0–19X2 period and is currently at a level slightly above the industry average. Although this could be cause for alarm, a look at the coverage ratios seems to indicate that the firm's ability to meet debt service costs increased from 19X1 to 19X2 to a level that outperforms the industry. (Apparently in 19X1, the firm's increased indebtedness had caused a deterioration in its ability to adequately service its debts.) The same conclusion results from an analysis of Phyllis's overall coverage, which includes not only debt service but also lease payments and preferred share dividends. In summary, it appears that, although 19X1 was an off year, the firm's debt position—both in terms of degree of indebtedness and ability to service debts—is in good shape in 19X2.

Table 3.6 Summary of Phyllis Petroleum Company Ratios (19X0–19X2, including 19X2 industry averages)

Ratio	Formula	Year			19X2 industry average[a]
		19X0	19X1	19X2	
I. Liquidity and activity					
Overall firm liquidity					
Net working capital	current assets − current liabilities	$582,761	$520,256	$601,959	$426,900
Current ratio	$\dfrac{\text{current assets}}{\text{current liabilities}}$	2.04	2.08	1.97	2.05
Acid-test ratio	$\dfrac{\text{current assets − inventory}}{\text{current liabilities}}$	1.32	1.50	1.50	1.43
Liquidity, or activity, of specific accounts					
Inventory turnover	$\dfrac{\text{cost of goods sold}}{\text{average inventory}}$	5.10	6.00	7.33	6.50
Average age of inventory	$\dfrac{360}{\text{inventory turnover}}$	70.59 days	60.00 days	49.11 days	55.38 days
Accounts receivable turnover	$\dfrac{\text{annual credit sales}}{\text{average accounts receivable}}$	7.67	6.37	6.59	8.12
Average age of accounts receivable	$\dfrac{360}{\text{accounts receivable turnover}}$	46.94 days	56.51 days	54.63 days	44.33 days
Accounts payable turnover	$\dfrac{\text{annual credit purchases}}{\text{average accounts payable}}$	4.75	4.89	5.12	6.37
Average age of accounts payable	$\dfrac{360}{\text{accounts payable turnover}}$	75.79 days	73.62 days	70.31 days	56.51 days

93

Table 3.6 (*Continued*)

Ratio	Formula	Year			19X2 industry average[a]
		19X0	19X1	19X2	
II. Debt					
Degree of indebtedness					
Debt ratio	$\dfrac{\text{total liabilities}}{\text{total assets}}$	36.8%	44.3%	45.7%	40.0%
Debt-equity ratio	$\dfrac{\text{long-term debt}}{\text{shareholders' equity}}$	44.2%	53.1%	52.3%	50.0%
Debt-to-total capitalization	$\dfrac{\text{long-term debt}}{\text{total capitalization}}$	29.9%	34.7%	34.4%	33.3%
Ability to service debts					
Times interest earned	$\dfrac{\text{earnings before interest and taxes}}{\text{interest}}$	6.55	4.61	6.21	5.61
Total debt coverage	$\dfrac{\text{earnings before interest and taxes}}{\text{interest} + \text{principal}\,[1/(1-t)]}$	3.19	1.71	2.38	2.40
Overall coverage ratio	$\dfrac{\text{EBIT} + \text{lease payments}}{\text{int.} + \text{lease pay.} + [\text{prin.} + \text{pref. div}]\,[1/(1-t)]}$	2.65	1.42	1.86	1.54

III. Profitability

Gross profit margin	$\dfrac{\text{gross profit}}{\text{sales}}$	31.40%	33.36%	32.06%	30.00%
Operating profit margin	$\dfrac{\text{operating profit}}{\text{sales}}$	13.62%	10.57%	12.59%	10.00%
Net profit margin	$\dfrac{\text{net profit after taxes}}{\text{sales}}$	8.76%	5.78%	7.50%	6.40%
Total asset turnover	$\dfrac{\text{sales}}{\text{total assets}}$	.943	.785	.853	.754
Return on investment	$\dfrac{\text{net profit after taxes}}{\text{total assets}}$	8.26%	4.54%	6.40%	4.83%
Return on equity	$\dfrac{\text{net profit after taxes}}{\text{shareholders' equity}}$	13.07%	8.16%	11.79%	8.04%
Return on common shareholders' equity	$\dfrac{\text{earnings available for common}}{\text{common shareholders' equity}}$	12.88%	8.55%	12.57%	8.74%
Earnings per share	$\dfrac{\text{earnings available for common}}{\text{number of shares outstanding}}$	$3.26	$1.82	$2.89	$2.26
Dividends per share	$\dfrac{\text{total dividends paid}}{\text{number of shares outstanding}}$	$1.20	$1.28	$1.29	$1.50
Book value per share	$\dfrac{\text{book value of common}}{\text{number of shares outstanding}}$	$15.74	$21.25	$22.99	$18.75

aObtained from sources external to this chapter.

PROFITABILITY

Phyllis's profitability relative to sales in 19X2 was better than the average company in their industry, although it does not match its 19X0 performance. Although the gross profit margin in 19X1 and 19X2 was better than in 19X0, it appears that higher levels of operating and interest expenses in these latter years have caused the 19X2 net profit margin to fall below that of 19X0. Phyllis's 19X2 net profit margin is certainly quite favourable when viewed in light of the industry average. The firm's return on investment, return on equity, return on common share equity, and earnings per share seem to have behaved in a fashion similar to its net profit margin over the 19X0 to 19X2 period. The firm appears to have experienced either a sizable drop in sales between 19X0 and 19X1 or a rapid expansion in its assets during that period.

The total asset turnover points to a sizable decline in the efficiency of asset utilization between 19X0 and 19X1. Although in 19X2 this ratio rose to a level considerably above the industry average, it appears that the pre-19X1 level of efficiency has not yet been achieved. The owners' return as evidenced by the exceptionally high 19X2 levels of the return on equity and return on common share equity seem to suggest that the firm is performing quite well. The fact that earnings per share are not as far in excess of the industry average as these other measures of profitability suggests that during the 19X0–19X1 period the firm may have sold additional shares to finance the apparent expansion that took place during that period. The relatively stable level of dividends that are below the industry average suggests that the firm is growing: most growth firms pay out low percentages of dividends. The behaviour observed earlier in the 19X0–19X1 period suggests that, indeed, the firm does seem to reflect a growth posture. The firm's growing and high per-share book value also seems consistent with the firm's asset growth as well as its high level of retained earnings (i.e., low dividends relative to amount earned). In summary, it appears that the firm is growing and has recently gone through an expansion in assets, this expansion being financed through the use of debt as well as the sale of additional common shares. The 19X1–19X2 period seems to reflect a period of adjustment and recovery from the rapid growth in assets that occurred during the 19X0–19X1 period. The firm's sales, profits, and so forth seem to be growing with the increase in size of the operation. In short, the firm apparently is doing quite well in 19X2.

Other Issues

EFFECTS OF INFLATION

The preceding discussion implicitly assumed that the general level of prices remained stable over time. While this assumption has never been completely accurate, it has become increasingly unrealistic given the current high rates of general inflation. Consequently, conventional financial statements and ratios, unless appropriately adjusted for the effects of inflation, may not be acceptable as reliable indicators of a firm's performance during such periods.*

*Models for studying micro and macro financial behaviour assume that the data examined accurately reflects current competitive market prices. Hence, accounting statements that do not fulfill this as-

EXAMPLE The projected income statements of Crowchild Crafts Ltd. are given in Table 3.7. Furthermore, assume that:

1 The company began operations on January 1, 19X0, by acquiring (i) 12,000 units of inventory at $40 per unit; and (ii) a building for $250,000 with an estimated useful life of 25 years. Both for reporting and tax purposes, the building is to be depreciated on a straight-line basis.
2 The prices will remain stable during 19X0, and the firm will sell 6,000 units during the year at $60 per unit. The same number of units will be sold in 19X1, but general inflation during the year will cause an average increase of 20 percent in the selling price per unit; that is, the average selling price per unit will be $72 in 19X1.
3 The replacement cost of the inventory and building will also increase by 20 percent during 19X1 due to inflation.
4 The firm will use the FIFO (first-in, first-out) method of inventory valuation.
5 The selling and administrative expenses in 19X0 and 19X1 will be 5 percent of sales revenues in those years.
6 The effective income tax rate is 25 percent for 19X0 and 19X1.

Table 3.7 Crowchild Crafts Ltd. Projected Income Statements

	For the year ending	
	19X1	19X0
Sales	$432,000	$360,000
Less: Cost of goods sold	240,000	240,000
Gross profits	$192,000	$120,000
Less: Operating expenses		
Selling and administrative expenses (5% of sales)	$ 21,600	$ 18,000
Depreciation	10,000	10,000
Total operating expenses	$ 31,600	$ 28,000
Operating profits	$160,400	$ 92,000
Less: Taxes (25%)	40,100	23,000
Net income	$120,300	$ 69,000

The firm has projected an increase of $68,400 in operating profit for 19X1. However, this increase will result simply from inflated sales revenue in 19X1, and not from an increase in the physical volume of goods sold. Moreover, the operating profit projected for 19X1 is overstated in that it does not reflect the increased replacement costs of the firm's assets at the end of 19X1. For example, if the costs of goods sold and depreciation expenses were based on the replacement costs of inventory and building at the end of 19X1, Crowchild's operating profit in 19X1 would be reduced by $50,000 [i.e., .20 ($240,000 + $10,000)].

sumption cannot strictly meet the data needs of the financial analyst. Indeed such accounting data may result in misleading conclusions by the analyst. Unfortunately, complexities of inflation accounting are not easy to resolve, and the professional accounting bodies are still wrestling with the problem. Thus, the discussion presented here should be viewed merely as a very brief introduction to the nature of the various issues involved.

Several accounting approaches designed to minimize the preceding problem have been proposed.* One such approach requires all assets to be valued at replacement cost as soon as that is feasible. Accordingly, replacement costs are reflected in both the balance sheet and the income statement.† A second approach to account for the effects of inflation is the general price-level adjustment approach. Essentially, it requires that all financial statement items be adjusted for changes in the purchasing power of the dollar, by using a general price-level index.‡ All purchasing-power gains or losses are then shown on the income statement as monetary items.§ The price-level adjustment approach is appealing in that the adjusted statements will be expressed in dollars of the same (current) value. As such, the adjustments would enhance the comparability of accounting information over time. Furthermore, the approach requires no change in existing accounting principles. It merely calls for the adjustment of original cost data for general changes in the overall level of prices. In this sense, the approach is rooted in the historical cost basis. Major limitations of the approach arise from the use of an index of general price-level changes, because movements of prices of specific items will often differ from those of the index.

The foregoing discussion merely touches upon the problem of interpreting conventionally reported financial statements in an inflationary environment.‖ Essentially, the problem occurs because conventional financial statements are prepared by matching historical costs of assets—such as inventory, plant, and equipment—against current revenue.# There is a substantial body of literature that demonstrates that many firms, which had been reporting impressive growth in earnings over a long period of time, had in fact incurred losses when the effects of inflation were taken into account.

*A number of new proposals for dealing with this problem are currently being debated by the accounting profession. A discussion of these proposals is beyond the scope of this text. For a somewhat provocative discussion of the impact of inflation on financial operations and the need for modified procedures for preparing financial statements, refer to the various exposure drafts and discussion papers issued by professional bodies, such as the Canadian Institute of Chartered Accountants and the U.S. Financial Accounting Standards Board.

†Although the LIFO (last-in, first-out) method of inventory valuation is not strictly a replacement cost approach, the LIFO method results in a cost-of-goods-sold figure that is closer to replacement cost, and an income statement that is more representative of current values, in times of changing prices. However, closing inventory values may then be inaccurately based on out-of-date historical costs, since they may distort the asset values given on the balance sheet. If a replacement cost basis of inventory is used, then up-to-date information can be shown on both statements. It may also be noted that for tax purposes, the LIFO method of inventory valuation is presently not allowed in Canada.

‡Two well-known general price-level indices compiled by Statistics Canada are the Consumer Price Index and the Gross National Expenditure Implicit Price Index. It needs to be emphasized that the adjustments required under this approach are for changes in general increases in the level of prices. They are not for changes in the values of specific goods or services, due to fundamental changes in the demand and supply of those specific items.

§Monetary items are assets and liabilities that are contractually fixed or that are convertible into a fixed number of dollars regardless of changes in prices. These items include accounts and notes receivable as well as most forms of debt.

‖Some of the major Canadian companies providing inflation-adjusted financial statements include Bell Canada Ltd., Alcan Aluminum Ltd., Shell Canada Ltd., Imperial Oil Ltd., and John Labatt Ltd.

#Because of high rates of inflation since the late 1960s, the current replacement costs of fixed assets may far exceed the historical accounting costs. For example, it has been stated that the replacement costs of plant and equipment in the U.S. steel industry are about three times the historical cost. See *Business Week*, October 1, 1977, pp. 68–70.

EFFECTS OF NON-CANADIAN OPERATIONS

The preceding discussion implicitly assumed that a firm's operations were totally confined to Canada. For many Canadian firms, especially larger corporations, this assumption is unrealistic. These firms distribute consolidated financial statements that report on the financial position and income of the global operations of the firms.

Without appropriate adjustments, the ratios calculated from these consolidated financial statements may be unreliable indicators of the firms' performance. Specific areas that may require appropriate adjustments include the effect of different host-country reporting and tax regulations, and the effect of floating currency exchange rates.[2]

Summary

This chapter has presented a discussion of the importance, techniques, and interpretation of financial ratios. The use of financial ratios allows interested parties to make a relative evaluation of certain aspects of a firm's performance. Interested parties typically include prospective and existing shareholders and lenders as well as the firm's management. Owners and lenders are generally concerned only with certain aspects of the firm, whereas management must monitor many aspects of the firm in order to pinpoint any developing problems. Financial ratios are meaningful only when they are compared to other ratio values. Two types of comparison are common—cross-sectional and time-series. Cross-sectional comparisons involve comparing ratios calculated at a given point in time to similar ratios of another firm or an industry average. Values for industry averages are available from various sources. Cross-sectional comparisons allow the firm to determine how it is doing with respect to another closely related company or the industry as a whole. Time-series, or historical, comparisons merely involve comparing the firm's current performance to its performance at a different point in time to determine whether it is improving or deteriorating. Time-series comparisons are most useful for internal control purposes.

Certain cautions with respect to the use of ratios are in order. There is no absolutely correct value for any ratio. Each industry has certain characteristics that differentiate it from other industries. Even firms within a given industry may have different types of technology, scales of operations, or stages of distribution. The financial analyst should carefully analyze any differences between firms in attempting to determine which of a group of firms is the most financially sound. Often a company will develop its own ratios, tailored to its specific information requirements. The most important point to keep in mind is that ratios should be consistently applied to similar time periods in order to make the most accurate comparisons. The use of audited financial statements is strongly recommended, since unaudited statements do not offer any assurance of accuracy. Attention should also be given to any recognizable differences in accounting methods.

The most common ratios can be divided into three groups—measures of liquidity and activity, measures of debt, and measures of profitability. The overall liquidity or ability of the firm to pay its bills as they come due can be measured by its net working capital, its current ratio, or its acid-test ratio. The liquidity or activity of inventory can be measured by its turnover or average age, that of accounts receivable by the accounts receivable turnover or average age, and that of accounts payable by the accounts payable turnover or average age. Aging procedures can be applied to either accounts receivable or accounts payable to gain further insight into their liquidity. Debt ratios measure both the degree of indebtedness and the ability to service debts. The commonly used measures of indebtedness include the debt ratio, the debt-equity ratio, and the ratio of debt-to-total-capitalization. In general, the higher these ratios are, the more debt the firm has and the more financially risky it is. Measures of the ability to service debts and other contractual obligations such as interest, principal or sinking-fund payments, lease payments, and preferred dividends are provided by coverage ratios such as times interest earned, total debt coverage, and overall coverage. The higher these coverage ratios, the better able the firm is expected to be to meet its fixed-payment obligations.

A number of measures of profitability exist. Using a percent income statement, which shows all items as a percentage of sales, we can readily determine the firm's gross profit margin, operating profit margin, and net profit margin. Other measures of profitability include the total asset turnover, the return on investment, the return on equity, the return on common equity, and the earnings per share. The DuPont formula is useful in showing the relationship between a firm's net profit margin, its total asset turnover, and the return on investment. The Modified DuPont formula describes the interaction of leverage—the degree of indebtedness—on the return on investment in order to determine the return on equity. Dividends per share and the book value per share are sometimes calculated and considered important by the firm's shareholders.

In periods of general inflation, financial statements and ratios based on historical costs may lose much of their significance. A major problem is that in an inflationary environment, conventionally reported profits tend to be overstated as low historical costs of assets, such as inventory, plant, and equipment, are matched against sales revenue at current prices. Currently, several approaches are being considered by the accounting profession to account for the impact of inflation. One such approach requires all assets to be valued at their current replacement costs. Another approach is the general price-level adjustment approach. It requires that all financial statement items be adjusted to the purchasing power of the dollar prevailing at the time the statements are issued and that the purchasing power gain or loss on monetary items (assets and liabilities that are expected to be settled in specified amounts of cash regardless of changes in the purchasing power of the dollar) be reported on the income statement. As a result of such adjustments, financial statements are expressed in dollars of the same value. This, in turn, facilitates the comparison of financial statements over time.

Questions

3.1   How do the viewpoints held by a firm's current and prospective shareholders, creditors, and management with regard to financial ratio analyses of the firm differ? How can these viewpoints be related to the firm's fund-raising ability?

3.2   How can ratio analysis be used for cross-sectional and time-series comparisons? Which type of comparison would be most common for internal analysis? Why?

3.3   Why may analyses of a firm's ratios calculated at several points within the operating year lead to varying results? How might this problem be overcome?

3.4   Financial ratio analysis is often divided into three areas—measures of liquidity and activity, measures of debt, and measures of profitability. What is the purpose of these measures? Which is of greatest concern to prospective and existing creditors?

3.5   Is it true that a firm can always increase its current ratio by reducing its current liabilities with cash?

3.6   What is the best measure of the overall liquidity of a firm? (Discuss net working capital, the current ratio, and the acid-test ratio in your answer.)

3.7   What ratio can be used to measure the liquidity of a firm having very illiquid inventories and accounts receivable? How does it compare to the acid-test ratio?

3.8   Why does the use of averages in calculating various turnovers help to increase the accuracy of these measures? Can you relate the effect of averaging to the seasonal nature of many businesses?

3.9   What is the general relationship between (1) the turnover of inventory, accounts receivable, and accounts payable, and (2) the average ages of these items?

3.10   How can the average age of accounts receivable be used to evaluate the effectiveness of the firm's credit department? How can the average age of accounts payable be used for internal control purposes?

3.11   How does the process of aging either accounts receivable or accounts payable work? In what sense does aging accounts provide more information than calculating their average age?

3.12   What is the difference between the debt ratio, the debt-equity ratio, and the ratio of debt to total capitalization? Would lenders consider high values of these ratios more risky than low values? Why or why not?

3.13   What is the difference between times interest earned, total debt coverage, and the overall coverage ratio? How might the values of these measures and the various debt ratios be related?

3.14   How can one reconcile a firm having a high gross profit margin and a low net profit margin? To what must this situation be attributable?

3.15   What is the significance of the firm's return on investment (ROI)? Why is the ROI often considered a measure of both the firm's ability to generate profits through sales and the efficiency of its use of assets? Can this relationship be explained in light of the DuPont formula?

3.16   There are three areas of analysis or concern which are combined in the Modified DuPont formula. What are these concerns and how are they combined to explain the firm's return on equity (ROE)? Can this formula yield useful information through either cross-sectional or times-series analysis?

3.17   What is the difference between the return on common equity and earnings per share? How do each of these measures indicate the owner's returns from operations?

3.18   Explain briefly why reported profits tend to be overstated in an inflationary environment.

Problems

3.1   The Houston Corporation's total current assets, net working capital, and inventory for each of the past four years are as follows:

Ratio	19X0	19X1	19X2	19X3
Total current assets	16,950	21,900	22,500	27,000
Net working capital	7,950	9,300	9,900	9,600
Inventory	6,000	6,900	6,900	7,200

a. Calculate the firm's current and acid-test ratios for each year. Compare the resulting time series of each measure of liquidity (i.e., net working capital, the current ratio, and the acid-test ratio).

b. Comment on the firm's liquidity over the 19X0–19X3 period.

c. If you were told that the Houston Corporation's inventory turnover for each year in the 19X0–19X3 period and the industry averages were as follows, would this support or conflict with your evaluation in b? Why?

Inventory turnover	19X0	19X1	19X2	19X3
Houston Corporation	6.3	6.8	7.0	6.4
Industry average	10.6	11.2	10.8	11.0

3.2   The Davis Company Ltd. has sales of $4,000,000 and a gross profit margin of 40 percent. Its end-of-quarter inventories are as follows:

Quarter	Inventory
1	400,000
2	800,000
3	1,200,000
4	200,000

a. Calculate the firm's inventory turnover and the average age of inventory.

b. How would you evaluate the firm's liquidity, assuming it is in an industry with an average inventory turnover of 2.0?

3.3   An evaluation of the books of Gordon's Supply Company Ltd. shows the following end-of-year accounts receivable balance, which is believed to consist of amounts originating in the months indicated. The company had annual sales of $3,000,000 of which 80 percent are on a credit basis. The firm extends 30-day credit terms.

Month of origin	Amounts receivable
July	$ 3,875
August	2,000
September	34,025
October	15,100
November	52,000
December	193,000
Year-end accounts receivable	$300,000

a. Use the year-end total to evaluate the firm's collection system.

b. Age the accounts receivable in order to obtain additional information. What other observations can you make about the receivable collection policy?

c. If the firm's peak season is from July to December, how would this affect the validity of your preceding conclusion? Explain.

3.4 The Center City Bank is evaluating the Graham Corporation, which has requested a $4,000,000 loan in order to determine its leverage and the financial risk involved.

a. Based on the debt ratios for Graham, along with the industry averages and Graham's recent financial statements (presented in the following tables), evaluate and recommend appropriate action on the Graham request.

Income Statement
Graham Corporation
December 31, 19X1

Net sales		$30,000,000
Less: Cost of goods sold		21,000,000
Gross profits		$ 9,000,000
Less: Operating expenses		
Selling expense	$3,000,000	
Gen. and admin. expense	2,000,000	
Depreciation expense	1,000,000	
Total operating expense		6,000,000
Earnings before interest and taxes		$3,000,000
Less: Interest		1,000,000
Earnings before taxes		$2,000,000
Less: Taxes (.40)		800,000
Earnings after taxes		$1,200,000

Balance Sheet
Graham Corporation
December 31, 19X1

Assets	
Current assets	
Cash	$ 1,000,000
Marketable securities	3,000,000
Accounts receivable	12,000,000
Inventories	7,500,000
Total current assets	$23,500,000
Fixed assets	
Land and buildings	$11,000,000
Machinery and equipment	20,500,000
Furniture and fixtures	8,000,000
Total fixed assets	$39,500,000
Less: Accumulated depreciation	13,000,000
Net fixed assets	$26,500,000
Total assets	$50,000,000

Graham Corporation
Liabilities and Shareholder's Equity

Current liabilities	
Accrued liabilities	$ 500,000
Notes payable	8,000,000
Accounts payable	8,000,000
Total current liabilities	$16,500,000
Long-term debts[a]	$20,000,000
Shareholders' equity	
Preferred shares[b]	$ 2,500,000
Common shares	
(1 million shares at $5 par)	5,000,000
Paid-in capital in excess of par value	4,000,000
Retained earnings	2,000,000
Total shareholders' equity	$13,500,000
Total liabilities and shareholders' equity	$50,000,000

[a]Required annual principal payments are $800,000.
[b]25,000 shares of $4.00 cumulative outstanding.

Industry averages for 19X1

Debt ratio	0.51
Debt-equity ratio	1.07
Debt-to-total-capital ratio	0.46
Times interest earned	7.30
Total debt coverage	2.00
Overall coverage ratio	1.85

b. A percent income statement for the Graham Corporation's 19X0 operations is presented here. Develop and compare it to the 19X1 year-end percent income statement. Which areas require further analysis or investigation?

Percent Income Statement
Graham Corporation
December 31, 19X0

Net sales ($35,000,000)		100.0%
Less: Cost of goods sold		65.9%
Gross profits		34.1%
Less: Operating expenses		
Selling expense	12.7%	
Gen. and admin. expense	6.9%	
Depreciation	3.6%	
Total operating expense		23.2%
Earnings before interest and taxes		10.9%
Less: Interest		1.5%
Earnings before taxes		9.4%
Less: Taxes (40%)		3.8%
Earnings after taxes		5.6%

3.5 Use the following ratio information for Raimer Industries Ltd. and the industry averages for Raimer's lines of business to

a. Construct the modified DuPont model for both Raimer and the industry.
b. Evaluate Raimer (and the industry) over the three-year period.
c. For Raimer Industries, which areas require further analysis?

	Raimer		
Ratio	19X0	19X1	19X2
Debt ratio	.40	.43	.46
Net profit margin	.059	.058	.049
Total asset turnover	2.11	2.18	2.34

	Industry Averages		
Debt ratio	.40	.41	.39
Net profit margin	.054	.047	.041
Total asset turnover	2.05	2.13	2.15

3.6 Given the following financial statements, historical ratios, and industry averages, calculate the financial ratios of the Baker Company Ltd. for the most recent year, and its overall financial situation from both a time-series and a cross-sectional viewpoint. Evaluate the firm's liquidity, debt, and profitability by using the applicable ratios.

Income Statement
Baker Company Ltd.
December 31, 19X2

Net sales		
Cash		$ 300,000
Credit		9,700,000
Total		$10,000,000
Less: Cost of goods sold		7,500,000
Gross profit		$ 2,500,000
Less: Operating expenses		
Selling expense	$300,000	
General and admin.	700,000	
Depreciation	200,000	1,200,000
Operating profits		$ 1,300,000
Less: Interest expense		200,000
Profits before taxes		$ 1,100,000
Less: Taxes (40%)		440,000
Profits after taxes		$ 660,000
Less: Preferred share dividends		50,000
Earnings available for common		$ 610,000
Less: Common share dividends		200,000
To retained earnings		$ 410,000

Balance Sheet
Baker Company Ltd.
December 31, 19X2

Assets

Current assets		
Cash		$ 200,000
Marketable securities		50,000
Accounts receivable		800,000
Inventories		950,000
Total current assets		$ 2,000,000
Gross fixed assets	$12,000,000	
Less: Accumulated depreciation	3,000,000	
Net fixed assets		$ 9,000,000
Other assets		$ 1,000,000
Total assets		$12,000,000

Liabilities and shareholders' equity

Current liabilities		
Accrued liabilities		$ 100,000
Notes payable		200,000
Accounts payable[a]		900,000
Total current liabilities		$ 1,200,000
Long-term debts[b]		$ 3,000,000
Shareholders' equity		
Preferred shares[c]		$ 1,000,000
Common shares (40,000 shares at $75 par)		3,000,000
Paid-in capital in excess of par value		2,800,000
Retained earnings		1,000,000
Total shareholders' equity		$ 7,800,000
Total liabilities and shareholders' equity		$12,000,000

[a]Annual credit purchases of $6,200,000 were made.
[b]The annual principal payment on the long-term debt is $100,000.
[c]The firm has 25,000 shares of $2.00 preferred outstanding.

Historical Data
Baker Company Ltd.

| | Year | | Industry average |
Data	19X0	19X1	19X2
Current ratio	1.40	1.55	1.85
Net working capital	$760,000	$720,000	$1,600,000
Acid-test ratio	1.00	.92	1.05
Average age of accounts receivable	45.0 days	36.4 days	35.0 days
Inventory turnover	9.52	9.21	8.60
Average age of accounts payable	58.53 days	60.75 days	45.75 days
Debt ratio	0.20	0.20	0.30
Debt-equity ratio	0.25	0.27	0.39
Debt-to-total-capitalization ratio	0.22	0.22	0.27
Gross profit margin	0.30	0.27	0.25
Operating profit margin	0.12	0.12	0.10
Net profit margin	0.067	0.067	0.058
Total asset turnover	0.74	0.80	0.74
Return on investment	0.049	0.054	0.043
Return on common equity	0.078	0.085	0.084
Earnings per share	$8.65	$11.05	$7.45
Dividends per share	$2.60	$ 3.65	$2.46
Book value per share	$140	$150	$175
Times interest earned	8.2	7.3	8.0
Total debt coverage	4.8	4.5	4.5

Notes

1. Statistical testing of financial ratios has shown that certain ratios, as a group, can be used to predict failure and bankruptcy. See, for example, E. Altman, "Financial Ratios, Discriminant Analysis and the Prediction of Corporate Bankruptcy," *Journal of Finance* (September 1968), pp. 589–609. Statistical techniques have also been developed for the use of financial ratios in credit analysis. See, for example, J. Horrigan, "The Determination of Long-Term Credit Standing with Financial Ratios," *Empirical Research in Accounting: Selected Studies in Journal of Accounting Research* (1966), pp. 44–62. In Canada, there are two agencies that provide ratings of corporate bonds: The Canadian Bond Rating Service and Dominion Bond Rating Service.

2. A discussion of the treatment of these issues is beyond the scope of this text. The reader is referred to David K. Eiteman and Arthur I. Stonehill, *Multinational Business Finance*, 2nd ed. (Reading, Mass.: Addison-Wesley, 1979), chap. 15, for an excellent discussion of these issues.

Suggested Readings

Altman, Edward I., "Financial Ratios, Discriminant Analysis and the Prediction of Corporate Bankruptcy," *Journal of Finance* 23 (September 1968), pp. 589–609.

Beaver, William H., "Financial Ratios as Predictors of Failure," *Empirical Research in Accounting: Selected Studies in Journal of Accounting Research* (1966), pp. 71–111.

Benishay, Haskell, "Economic Information in Financial Ratio Analysis," *Accounting and Business Research* 2 (Spring 1971), pp. 174–179.

Carey, Kenneth J., "Persistence of Profitability," *Financial Management* 3 (Summer 1974), pp. 43–48.

Chang, Hui-Shyong and Cheng F. Lee, "Using Pooled Time-Series and Cross-Section Data to Test the Firm and Time Effects in Financial Analysis," *Journal of Financial and Quantitative Analysis* (September 1977), pp. 457–471.

Helfert, Erich A., *Techniques of Financial Analysis*, 4th ed. (Homewood, Ill.: Irwin, 1976), chap. 2.

Horrigan, James C., "A Short History of Financial Ratio Analysis," *Accounting Review* 43 (April 1968), pp. 284–294.

——, "The Determination of Long-Term Credit Standing with Financial Ratios," *Empirical Research in Accounting: Selected Studies in Journal of Accounting Research* (1966), pp. 44–62.

Jaedicke, Robert K. and Robert T. Sprouse, *Accounting Flows, Income, Funds and Cash* (Englewood Cliffs, N.J.: Prentice-Hall, 1965), chap. 7.

Lev, Baruch, *Financial Statement Analysis: A New Approach* (Englewood Cliffs, N.J.: Prentice-Hall, 1974), chaps. 2–5.

Meigs, Walter B., A. N. Mosich, Charles E. Johnson, and Thomas F. Keller, *Financial Accounting*, 3rd ed. (New York: McGraw-Hill, 1974), chap. 24.

Murray, Roger, "Lessons for Financial Analysis," *Journal of Finance* 26 (May 1971), pp. 327–332.

O'Conner, Melvin C., "On the Usefulness of Financial Ratios to Investors in Common Stock," *Accounting Review* 48 (April 1973), pp. 339–352.

Reiling, Henry B. and John C. Burton, "Financial Statements: Signposts As Well As Milestones," *Harvard Business Review* (November-December 1972), pp. 45–54.

Searby, Frederick W., "Return to Return on Investment," *Harvard Business Review* 53 (March-April 1975), pp. 113–119.

Seitz, Neil, *Financial Analysis: A Programmed Approach* (Reston, Va.: Reston Publishing Company, 1976).

Troy, Leo, *Almanac of Business and Industrial Financial Ratios* (Englewood Cliffs, N.J.: Prentice-Hall, 1979).

Viscione, Jerry A., *Financial Analysis: Principles and Procedures* (Boston: Houghton Mifflin, 1977).

Weston, J. Fred, "Financial Analysis: Planning and Control," *Financial Executive* 33 (July 1965), pp. 40–48.

Wright, Leonard T., *Financial Management: Analytical Techniques* (Columbus, Ohio: Grid, 1974), chap. 2.

Chapter 4

OPERATING, FINANCIAL, AND TOTAL LEVERAGE

The term *leverage* is quite commonly used to describe the firm's ability to use fixed-cost assets or funds to magnify the returns to its owners. Leverage occurs in varying degrees; the higher the degree of leverage, the higher the risk—but the higher the expected return as well. The term *risk* in this context refers to the degree of uncertainty associated with the firm's ability to cover its fixed-payment obligations. The level of leverage in the firm's structure greatly reflects the type of risk-return trade-off it makes. There are two types of leverage in most business firms—operating leverage and financial leverage. This chapter is devoted both to the discussion of each of these types of leverage and to their combination, which is referred to as *total leverage.*

The chapter has five basic sections. The first section briefly describes the income statement framework used to explain the concepts of operating, financial, and total leverage. The second section is devoted to the quite important topic of breakeven analysis. The third section develops the concept of operating leverage using a breakeven analysis framework. The fourth section discusses financial leverage in both algebraic and graphical contexts and introduces the concept of a financial plan. The final section of this chapter discusses total leverage, which reflects the combined impact of operating and financial leverage on the total risk of the firm.

An Income Statement Approach to Leverage

The two basic types of leverage can best be defined with reference to the firm's income statement. Table 4.1 presents a typical income statement format. The portion of the statement related to the firm's operating leverage and the portion related to its financial

Table 4.1   A General Income Statement Format

Operating leverage	Sales revenue
	Less: Cost of goods sold
	Gross profits
	Less: Operating expenses
	Earnings before interest and taxes (EBIT)
Financial leverage	Less: Interest
	Earnings before taxes (EBT)
	Less: Taxes
	Earnings after taxes (EAT)
	Less: Preferred share dividends
	Earnings available for common shareholders (EAC)

leverage are clearly labeled. *Operating leverage* is concerned with the relationship between the firm's sales revenue and its earnings before interest and taxes.* *Financial leverage* is concerned with the relationship between the firm's earnings before interest and taxes and the earnings available for common shareholders. Thus, the income statement reflects the combined effect of both types of leverage.

Breakeven Analysis

An understanding of the key aspects of breakeven analysis provides the framework from which the fundamental aspects of operating leverage can be described. *Breakeven analysis*, which is sometimes called *cost-volume-profit analysis*, is important to the firm since it allows the firm (1) to determine the level of operations it must maintain to cover all of its operating costs, and (2) to evaluate the profitability associated with various levels of sales. In order to understand fully breakeven analysis, it is necessary to analyze further the firm's operating costs. An examination of Table 4.1 reveals that in order to calculate the firm's earnings before interest and taxes, the firm's cost of goods sold and operating expenses must be subtracted from its sales revenue. The upper portion of the income statement can be recast as in Table 4.2.

Table 4.2   Operating Leverage and the Income Statement

Operating leverage	Sales revenue
	Less: Cost of goods sold
	Less: Operating expenses
	Earnings before interest and taxes (EBIT)

*The firm's earnings before interest and taxes are often referred to as the firm's *operating income*. Earnings before interest and taxes are used as the pivotal point in defining operating and financial leverage since they divide the firm's income statement into operating and financial portions.

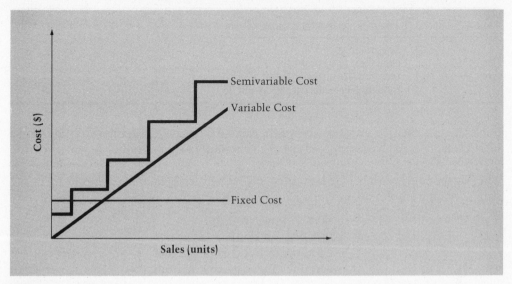

Figure 4.1 Types of costs.

TYPES OF COSTS

The firm's cost of goods sold and its operating expenses contain fixed- and variable-operating-cost components. In some cases, specific costs may have both fixed and variable elements. The resulting three types of costs are defined below. Figure 4.1 depicts each type graphically.

Fixed Costs The validity of categorizing certain costs as being fixed depends strictly on the time period under study. For example, in the short run, certain types of costs, such as depreciation, rent, and interest charges, can be regarded as being fixed periodic costs.

Variable Costs These costs vary directly with the firm's sales. Production and delivery costs are examples of variable costs.

Semivariable Costs Semivariable costs are partly fixed and partly variable.* One example of semivariable costs might be the sales staff's commissions. These commissions may be fixed over a certain range of volume and increase to higher levels for higher volumes.

DETERMINATION OF THE BREAKEVEN POINT

Using the classification scheme described above, the firm's cost of goods sold and its operating expenses can be grouped into fixed and variable costs.† The top portion of

---

*Semivariable costs are sometimes referred to as *semifixed costs*. Regardless of how these costs are labeled, they have the characteristics described here.
†Semivariable costs are ignored here and in the discussions that follow, since they can generally be broken down into fixed and variable components.

Table 4.3 Operating Leverage and Fixed and Variable Costs

Operating leverage	{	Sales revenue
		Less: Fixed operating costs
		Less: Variable operating costs
		Earnings before interest and taxes (EBIT)

Table 4.2 can then be recast as shown in Table 4.3. Using this framework, the firm's breakeven point can be determined either algebraically or graphically.

The Algebraic Approach   Utilizing the following variable names, the portion of the firm's income statement given in Table 4.3 can be represented as in Table 4.4:

$$X = \text{sales volume in units}$$
$$P = \text{sale price per unit}$$
$$F = \text{fixed operating cost per period}$$
$$V = \text{variable operating cost per unit}$$

Rewriting the algebraic calculations in Table 4.4 as a formula for earnings before interest and taxes yields Equation 4.1:

$$\text{EBIT} = P \cdot X - F - V \cdot X = P \cdot X - (F + V \cdot X) \tag{4.1}$$

Simplifying Equation 4.1 yields

$$\text{EBIT} = X(P - V) - F \tag{4.2}$$

The firm's *breakeven point* is defined as the level of unit sales at which all fixed and variable operating costs are covered; that is, the level at which EBIT equals zero.* Setting EBIT equal to zero and solving Equation 4.2 for the firm's breakeven sales volume, X_b, yields

$$X_b = \frac{F}{P - V} \tag{4.3}$$

This equation is used to find the firm's breakeven sales volume in units.

Table 4.4 Algebraic Terms in Breakeven Analysis

Item	Algebraic representation
Sales revenue	$P \cdot X$
Less: Fixed operating costs	$-F$
Less: Variable operating costs	$-V \cdot X$
Earnings before interest and taxes	EBIT

*The reader should recognize that the breakeven point defined in this chapter refers to the point at which *all operating costs are covered,* or where EBIT just equals zero. Quite often the breakeven point is calculated so that it represents the point where all operating and financial costs are covered. Our concern in this chapter is not with this overall breakeven point, although its calculation is quite similar.

EXAMPLE   Assume that a firm has fixed operating costs of $2,500, that the sale price per unit of its product is $10, and that its variable operating cost per unit is $5. Applying Equation 4.3 to these data yields

$$X_b = \frac{\$2,500}{\$10 - \$5} = \frac{\$2,500}{\$5} = 500 \text{ units}$$

At sales of 500 units or $5,000 (i.e., $10 · 500 units), the firm's EBIT should just equal zero.

In the preceding example, the firm will have positive EBIT for sales greater than 500 units and negative EBIT, or an operating loss, for sales less than 500 units.

The Graphical Approach   The firm's breakeven point can also be calculated graphically as in Figure 4.2 for the data in the preceding example. It has two base-line axes; one represents sales in units, and the other, sales in dollars. Breakeven charts can be presented using either of these axes, but the use of units is the simpler approach. A brief discussion of the calculation of the breakeven point in terms of dollars is presented in a subsequent part of this section.

In Figure 4.2, the firm's breakeven point is the point at which its total operating cost equals its sales revenue. Using the notation introduced earlier, we can define the equation for the total operating cost as follows:

$$\text{Total operating cost} = F + V \cdot X \qquad (4.4)$$

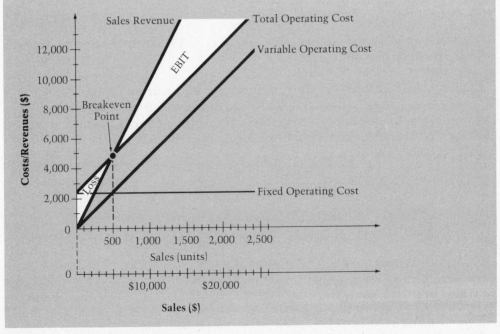

Figure 4.2   Graphical breakeven analysis.

Also depicted in Figure 4.2 are the firm's fixed and variable operating costs.

Figure 4.2 shows that a loss occurs when the firm's sales are less than 500 units ($5,000). For sales levels greater than the breakeven point, EBIT is greater than zero. The absolute amount of the loss increases as the level of sales decreases from the breakeven point; the absolute amount of EBIT increases as the level of sales increases beyond the breakeven point.

CHANGING COST RELATIONSHIPS AND THE BREAKEVEN POINT

A firm's breakeven point is sensitive to a number of variables, specifically, fixed operating costs, the sale price per unit, and the variable operating cost per unit. The effects of increases or decreases in each of these variables on the breakeven point are examined below.

Changes in Fixed Operating Costs   An increase in the firm's fixed operating costs will increase its breakeven point, and a decrease in its fixed operating costs will lower its breakeven point. For example, if we increased the fixed operating costs to $3,000, the breakeven point calculated using Equation 4.3 and the previous data would be

$$\frac{\$3,000}{\$10 - \$5} = 600 \text{ units}$$

If we decreased the fixed operating costs to $2,000, the breakeven point would be

$$\frac{\$2,000}{\$10 - \$5} = 400 \text{ units}$$

The effects of an *increase* in fixed operating costs to $3,000 on the firm's breakeven point are shown graphically in Figure 4.3.

Changes in the Sale Price Per Unit   An increase in the firm's unit sales price will lower the firm's breakeven volume, and a decrease in the firm's unit price will raise the firm's breakeven volume.* For example, if we increased the sales price to $12.50 per unit, the breakeven point calculated using Equation 4.3 and the previous data would become

$$\frac{\$2,500}{\$12.50 - \$5.00} = 333\tfrac{1}{3} \text{ units}$$

(The amount could be rounded to 333 units if fractional units cannot be sold.)

If we decreased the sales price to $7.50 per unit, the breakeven point would become

$$\frac{\$2,500}{\$7.50 - \$5.00} = 1,000 \text{ units}$$

*This discussion ignores the effects of changes in the unit sales price on the firm's sales volume; that is, it ignores the *price elasticity* of demand for the firm's products.

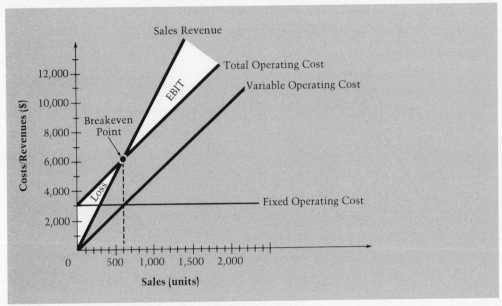

Figure 4.3 A breakeven graph for increased fixed operating costs.

The effects of an *increase* in the sales price to $12.50 per unit on the firm's breakeven point are shown graphically in Figure 4.4.

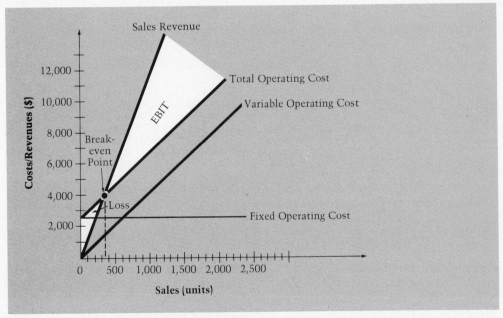

Figure 4.4 A breakeven graph for increased sale price.

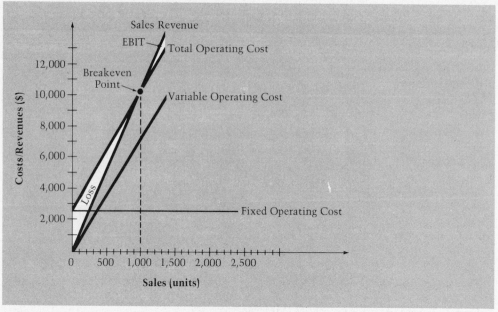

Figure 4.5   A breakeven graph for increased variable operating costs.

Changes in the Variable Operating Cost Per Unit   An increase in the firm's variable operating cost per unit will raise the firm's breakeven volume, while a decrease in the firm's variable operating cost per unit will lower the firm's breakeven point. For example, if we increased the variable operating cost to $7.50 per unit, the breakeven point calculated using Equation 4.3 and the previous data would become

$$\frac{\$2{,}500}{\$10.00 - \$7.50} = 1{,}000 \text{ units}$$

If we decreased variable operating cost to $2.50 per unit, the breakeven volume would become

$$\frac{\$2{,}500}{\$10.00 - \$2.50} = 333\tfrac{1}{3} \text{ units}$$

The effects of the *increase* in the variable operating cost per unit to $7.50 on the firm's breakeven point are illustrated graphically in Figure 4.5.

OTHER APPROACHES TO BREAKEVEN ANALYSIS

Although a wide variety of other approaches can be used to find the breakeven point, a brief discussion of alternative approaches is given next.

Breakeven in Dollars   When a firm has more than one product, each selling at a different price, it is useful to calculate the breakeven point in terms of dollars rather than in terms of units. Assuming that the firm's product mix remains relatively constant, the breakeven point can be calculated in terms of dollars by using a contribution margin approach. The *contribution margin* is defined as the portion of each sales dollar that remains after subtracting the variable costs incurred in generating that sales dollar. The following notation will be used in developing a formula for the dollar breakeven point:

S = total sales revenue in dollars
TV = total variable operating costs incurred to achieve S dollars of sales
F = total fixed operating costs incurred during the period in which S dollars of sales are achieved

In the case of a single-product firm, using the notation presented earlier, $S = P \cdot X$ and $TV = V \cdot X$.

The variable cost per dollar of sales can be represented as $TV \div S$. Since the unit sales price and variable cost per unit are assumed constant in the present discussion, the ratio $TV \div S$ remains constant at every level of sales. Subtracting the variable cost per dollar of sales, $TV \div S$, from one will yield the contribution margin, which reflects the per-dollar contribution toward meeting fixed operating costs and profits provided by each dollar of sales.

$$\text{Contribution margin} = 1 - \frac{TV}{S} \tag{4.5}$$

The EBIT at any particular level of dollar sales, D, can be found by multiplying the contribution margin by D, and subtracting the fixed costs, F. The similarity between Equation 4.6 and Equation 4.1 presented earlier

$$\text{EBIT} = D\left(1 - \frac{TV}{S}\right) - F \tag{4.6}$$

should be quite clear. To find the dollar breakeven point, D_b, we set EBIT equal to zero and solve Equation 4.6 for D to get*

$$D_b = \frac{F}{\left(1 - \dfrac{TV}{S}\right)} \tag{4.7}$$

*Note that in the case of a single product breakeven analysis, the dollar breakeven sales is simply P times unit breakeven sales. This can be seen by substituting $TV = VX$ and $S = PX$ in Equation 4.7 as follows:

$$D_b = \frac{F}{\left(1 - \dfrac{TV}{PX}\right)} = \frac{F}{\left(1 - \dfrac{VX}{PX}\right)} = P\left(\frac{F}{P - V}\right)$$

EXAMPLE Assume that during a period a firm has fixed operating costs of $100,000, total sales of $800,000, and total variable operating costs of $600,000. Applying Equation 4.7 to these data yields

$$D_b = \frac{\$100,000}{\left(1 - \dfrac{\$600,000}{\$800,000}\right)} = \frac{\$100,000}{.25} = \$400,000$$

Assuming the firm's product mix does not change at a $400,000 sales level, the firm will break even on its operation—its EBIT will just equal zero.

Cash Breakeven Analysis Because it is quite common for a firm's reported costs to result from the application of accrual concepts rather than a strict cash-flow approach, it is often useful to perform a cash breakeven analysis. This type of analysis recognizes that a firm's cash receipts and payments may not correspond with the recognition of income and expense. Although a variety of differences may result from the existence of accounts receivable and accounts payable, the key items requiring attention in the cash breakeven analysis are noncash charges such as depreciation. Any charges, such as these, that are included as part of the firm's fixed costs must be adjusted in preparing a cash breakeven analysis. The presence of such noncash charges as part of the firm's fixed costs tends to overstate the firm's breakeven point in terms of its ability to meet its cash obligations. Assuming that the firm has noncash charges, N, included in its fixed costs, Equation 4.3 can be rewritten for the cash breakeven point as follows:

$$\text{Cash breakeven point} = \frac{F - N}{P - V} \qquad (4.8)$$

EXAMPLE Assume that the firm presented in the example on page 113 had included in its fixed operating costs of $2,500, $1,500 of depreciation. Substituting this information along with the firm's $10 per unit sale price and $5 per unit variable operating cost into Equation 4.8 yields

$$\text{Cash breakeven point} = \frac{\$2,500 - \$1,500}{\$10 - \$5} = \frac{\$1,000}{\$5} = 200 \text{ units}$$

The firm's cash breakeven point of 200 units is considerably below the 500-unit breakeven point calculated earlier using accounting data. This difference can be seen graphically in Figure 4.6, in which point *A* represents the original breakeven point (500 units) and point *B* represents the cash breakeven point (200 units).

It is important to recognize that while the cash breakeven analysis provides a convenient mechanism for assessing the level of sales necessary to meet the firm's cash oper-

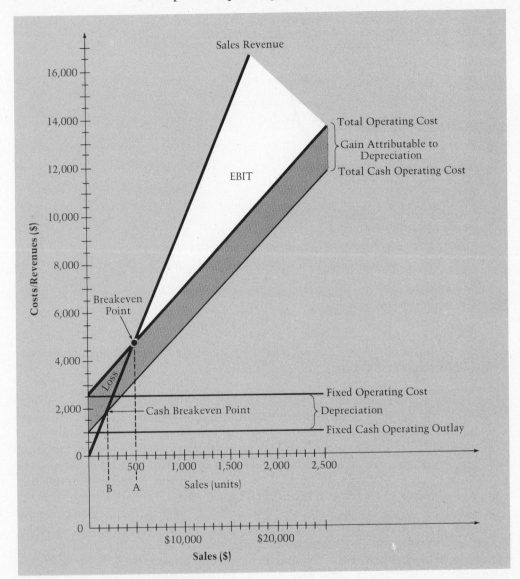

Figure 4.6   A cash breakeven analysis.

ating costs, it is not a substitute for detailed cash plans. Chapter 5 will provide a discussion of the more formal techniques available for analyzing and budgeting the firm's cash flows.

WEAKNESSES IN BREAKEVEN ANALYSIS

Although breakeven analysis is widely used by business firms, it has a number of inherent weaknesses. The major criticisms of this type of analysis stem from its as-

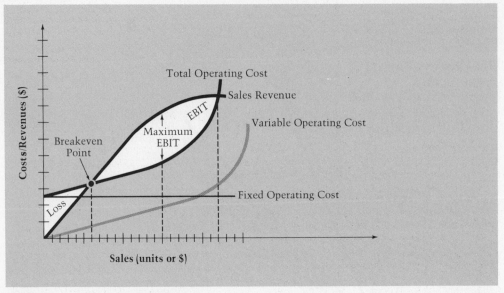

Figure 4.7 A nonlinear breakeven analysis.

sumption of linearity, its cost classifications, the difficulty of multi-product applications, and its short-term nature.

The Assumption of Linearity Generally, neither the firm's sale price per unit nor its variable cost per unit is independent of sales volume. In many cases, increases in sales beyond a certain point are achieved only by lowering the firm's price per unit. This results in a nonlinear concave-shaped, rather than a straight-line, total revenue function. In addition, the firm's variable operating cost per unit tends to increase as the firm approaches its capacity limit. This may result from a decrease in the efficiency of labour or an increase in overtime wages. Figure 4.7 shows a graphic breakeven analysis using nonlinear concave revenue and variable-operating-cost functions. It illustrates that when a firm has nonlinear sales revenue and variable-operating-cost functions, the maximum earnings before interest and taxes may occur at a level of sales below the obtainable maximum. An examination of the breakeven analysis with linear sales revenue and variable-operating-cost functions in Figures 4.2–4.6 indicates that as long as sales increase, profits will also increase; that is, in order to maximize EBIT, sales should be maximized. This relationship may not hold when one evaluates the situation using nonlinear revenue and cost functions. It should, however, be noted that since significant nonlinearities in the revenue and cost functions tend to occur only at the extreme levels, linear relationships may serve as acceptable approximations over the range of interest.

Cost Classifications A second weakness of breakeven analysis is the difficulty of classifying semivariable costs, which are fixed over certain ranges but vary between them. In some cases, it may not be possible to break these costs into fixed and variable components for breakeven analysis.

Multi-product Applications   A third weakness of breakeven analysis is the difficulty of applying it to multiple-product operations. If each product is analyzed separately, it may be difficult to divide the costs between products. Although the use of breakeven analysis using dollars instead of units partially overcomes this criticism, it does not allow the firm having a number of products to determine the level of sales required for each product in order to cover the related operating costs. More sophisticated multi-product breakeven models do exist, but will not be discussed here.

Short-Term Nature   A final weakness of breakeven analysis is its short-term nature. It is typically applied to one year's projected operations. If a firm makes a large outlay for advertising or research and development or incurs some other major expense whose benefits are not expected to be visible in the current period, these expenses will still add to the current period's total operating costs and raise the breakeven volume. Since the benefits of these outlays are not received in the current period, one may question their inclusion in the breakeven analysis for the current period.

Operating Leverage

Fixed operating costs, by definition, do not vary in the short run with variations in sales volume. Therefore, the effects of changes in sales volume on the firm's operating income (i.e., EBIT) are magnified due to the presence of fixed operating costs. The firm's operating leverage reflects the extent to which it utilizes fixed operating costs relative to variable costs in its cost structure. The income statement, when cast in the framework presented in Table 4.3, indicates the level of operating leverage present in the firm's cost structure.

OPERATING LEVERAGE ILLUSTRATED

Operating leverage can be illustrated conveniently using the data presented earlier (i.e., sale price, $P = \$10$ per unit; variable operating cost, $V = \$5$ per unit; fixed operating costs, $F = \$2,500$). Figure 4.8 presents the breakeven chart for these data, which was originally shown in Figure 4.2. It can be seen from the additional notations placed on the chart that as the firm's sales increase from 1,000 units to 1,500 units (X_1 to X_2), its EBIT increases from $2,500 to $5,000 (EBIT$_1$ to EBIT$_2$). In other words, a 50-percent increase in sales (i.e., 1,000 to 1,500 units) results in a 100-percent increase in EBIT ($2,500 to $5,000). Table 4.5 includes the data relating to Figure 4.8 as well as relevant data associated with a 500-unit sales level. Using the 1,000-unit sales level as a reference point, two cases can be illustrated.

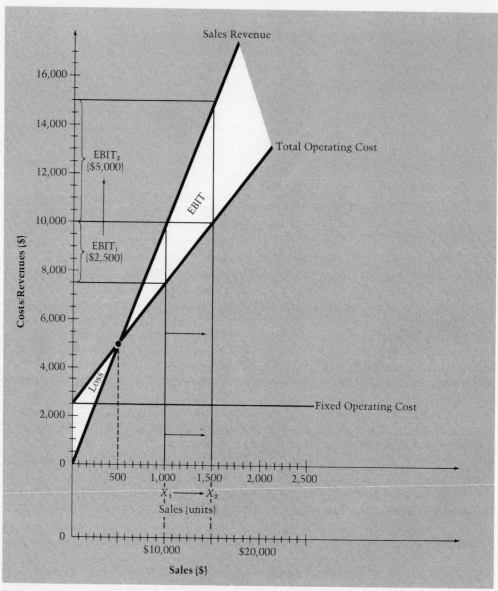

Figure 4.8   Breakeven analysis and operating leverage.

Table 4.5 EBIT for Various Sales Levels

	Case 2		Case 1
	−50%		+50%
Sales (in units)	500	1,000	1,500
Sales revenue[a]	$5,000	$10,000	$15,000
Less: Variable operating costs[b]	2,500	5,000	7,500
Less: Fixed operating costs	2,500	2,500	2,500
Earnings before interest and taxes (EBIT)	$ 0	$ 2,500	$ 5,000
	−100%		+100%

[a]Sales revenue = $10/unit · sales in units.
[b]Variable operating costs = $5/unit · sales in units.

CASE 1: A 50-percent *increase* in sales (from 1,000 to 1,500 units) results in a 100-percent *increase* in earnings before interest and taxes (from $2,500 to $5,000).

CASE 2: A 50-percent *decrease* in sales (from 1,000 to 500 units) results in a 100-percent *decrease* in earnings before interest and taxes (from $2,500 to 0).

These two cases illustrate the fact that operating leverage works in both directions. An increase in sales results in a greater than proportional increase in earnings before interest and taxes, while a decrease in sales results in a more than proportional decrease in earnings before interest and taxes.

MEASURING THE DEGREE OF OPERATING LEVERAGE (DOL)

The degree of operating leverage can be measured using the following equation:*

$$\text{DOL} = \frac{\text{percentage change in EBIT}}{\text{percentage change in sales}} \tag{4.9}$$

Whenever the percentage change in EBIT resulting from a given percentage change in sales is greater than the percentage change in sales, operating leverage exists. This means

*Since EBIT is close to zero near the breakeven level of sales, a small percentage change in the breakeven sales volume produces a relatively large percentage change in EBIT. The degree of operating leverage, therefore, is greatest near the breakeven point. In general, the closer the base sales level used is to the breakeven level of sales, the more operating leverage there is. A comparison of the operating-leverage ratio of two firms is valid only when the base level of sales used for each firm is the same.

that as long as DOL is greater than one, there is operating leverage. Applying Equation 4.9 to Case 1 and Case 2 yields the following results:*

$$\text{Case 1: } \frac{+100\%}{+50\%} = 2.0$$

$$\text{Case 2: } \frac{-100\%}{-50\%} = 2.0$$

For a given level of sales, the higher the value resulting from applying Equation 4.9, the greater the operating leverage.

A more direct formula for calculating the degree of operating leverage at a base unit-sales level X can be developed as follows:

$$\text{EBIT} = X(P - V) - F$$

If we denote the change in X by ΔX, then the change in EBIT is equal to $\Delta X (P - V)$, since F, P, and V do not change with changes in X. Therefore,

$$\text{DOL at base sales level } X = \frac{\text{percent change in EBIT}}{\text{percent change in } X}$$

$$= \frac{\dfrac{\Delta X (P - V)}{X (P - V) - F}}{\dfrac{\Delta X}{X}} \tag{4.10}$$

$$= \frac{X (P - V)}{X (P - V) - F}$$

Substituting $X = 1{,}000$, $P = \$10$, $V = \$5$, and $F = \$2{,}500$ into Equation 4.10 yields

$$\text{DOL at 1000 units} = \frac{1{,}000(\$10 - \$5)}{1{,}000(\$10 - \$5) - \$2{,}500} = \frac{\$5{,}000}{\$2{,}500} = 2.0$$

It should be clear that the use of Equation 4.10 provides a more direct method for calculating the degree of operating leverage than the approach illustrated using Table 4.5 and Equation 4.9.†

---

*Because the concept of leverage is *linear*, positive and negative changes of equal magnitude will always result in equal degrees of leverage when the same base sales level is used as a point of reference. This relationship holds for all types of leverage discussed in this chapter.

†When total dollar figures—instead of unit sales figures—are available, the following equation in which S = dollar level of base sales and TV = total variable operating costs in dollars can be used.

$$\text{DOL at base dollar sales } S = \frac{S - TV}{S - TV - F} \tag{a}$$

This formula is especially useful for finding the DOL for multi-product firms. It should be clear that since the case of a single product firm $S = P \cdot X$ and $TV = V \cdot X$, substitution of these values into Equation 4.10 would result in Equation (a).

Table 4.6 Operating Leverage and Increased Fixed Costs

	Case 2		Case 1
	−50%		+50%
Sales (in units)	500	1,000	1,500
Sales revenue[a]	$5,000	$10,000	$15,000
Less: Variable operating costs[b]	2,250	4,500	6,750
Less: Fixed operating costs	3,000	3,000	3,000
Earnings before interest and taxes (EBIT)	$ −250	$ 2,500	$ 5,250
	−110%		+110%

[a]Sales revenue was calculated as indicated in Table 4.5.
[b]Variable operating costs = $4.50/unit · sales in units.

FIXED COSTS AND OPERATING LEVERAGE

A change in the *relative* magnitude of fixed operating costs in the firm's cost structure can significantly affect the firm's operating leverage. For example, assume that the firm discussed in the preceding section is able to exchange a portion of its variable operating costs for fixed operating costs. This exchange results in the variable operating cost per unit being reduced from $5.00 to $4.50 while the fixed operating costs are increased to $3,000. Table 4.6 presents an analysis similar to that given in Table 4.5 using these new costs. Although the EBIT of $2,500 at the 1,000-unit sales level is the same as that before the shift in operating cost structure, it should be clear from Table 4.6 that by shifting to greater fixed costs (and lower variable costs) the firm has increased its leverage. The firm's DOL has increased from 2.0 to 2.2 as shown in the following equation:

$$\text{DOL at 1,000 units} = \frac{1,000(\$10 - \$4.50)}{1,000(\$10 - \$4.50) - \$3,000} = \frac{\$5,500}{\$2,500} = 2.2$$

Thus, it is clear that the higher the firm's fixed costs relative to its variable costs, the greater the degree of operating leverage.

Since leverage works both ways—it magnifies losses as well as gains—the shift in cost structure toward more fixed costs tends to increase the magnitude of potential losses. This increased risk is quite clear when one compares the breakeven points before and after the shift. Before the shift, the firm's breakeven point is found to be 500 units [i.e., $2,500 ÷ ($10 − $5)], while after the shift the breakeven point becomes 545 units [i.e., $3,000 ÷ ($10 − $4.50)]. The increased breakeven point reflects the fact that the firm must achieve a higher level of sales in order to meet the increased fixed operating costs.

OPERATING RISK

Operating risk is the risk of being unable to cover operating costs. We have seen that as a firm's fixed operating costs increase, the volume of sales necessary for it to cover all its operating costs increases. In other words, as a firm increases its fixed operating costs, the sales volume necessary to break even increases. Consequently, a firm may decide against heavy utilization of fixed assets in its production process because of the increased risk of not being able to achieve the higher breakeven sales volume associated with higher utilization of fixed assets.

On the other hand, in exchange for increasing levels of operating risk, the firm may achieve higher operating leverage. For example, a firm's automation of its production process increases its operating leverage in that it tends to lower its variable cost per unit by utilizing a higher level of fixed operating cost in its cost structure. As a result, the firm's EBIT increases at a faster rate with increases in sales volume.

In summary, an increase in operating leverage through increased fixed operating costs works both ways: It increases the firm's operating risk through a higher breakeven sales level and also magnifies the increase in the firm's operating return as sales increase. The choice of an appropriate leverage is, therefore, a critical management decision. A major factor in such a choice is the underlying variability in the firm's sales volume.

The greater the degree of a firm's operating leverage, the greater the impact of the firm's sales variability on its operating income (EBIT).* Consequently, firms with a high degree of sales variability are exposed to a high degree of operating risk. These firms avoid a high degree of operating leverage (and financial leverage, to be discussed below) to avoid increasing risk to unacceptable levels. On the other hand, firms with large and relatively stable sales, such as utilities and manufacturing firms with large domestic markets for their products, are likely to maintain high degrees of operating leverage. Unlike their American counterparts, Canadian manufacturing firms do not have a large domestic market. As a result, many Canadian companies that cannot expand their sales through exports tend to be relatively less capital intensive and therefore have relatively less operating leverage. Yet on the other hand, Canadian manufacturers with large export markets tend to be more closely matched with similar American firms in terms of capital intensiveness and operating leverage.

The risk-leverage relationship is also an important consideration for transnational corporations that have plants abroad. For example, the high political risk factors associated with a country in which a plant may be located may be mitigated through minimizing capital investment; that is, by following a labour intensive or lower fixed-to-variable-cost-ratio production strategy. Additionally, with such a strategy business risk is reduced through a lower breakeven point. The resulting lower operating leverage is, of course, the premium paid for offsetting the impact of political risk.

Financial Leverage

Financial leverage results from the presence of fixed *financial* charges in the firm's income stream.† These fixed charges do not vary with the firm's earnings before interest and taxes. An examination of the lower portion of Table 4.1 indicates that the two financial charges normally found on the firm's income statement are (1) interest on debt, and (2) preferred share dividends. Financial leverage is concerned with the effects of

---

*The variability of a firm's operating income is often referred to as the firm's *business* or *economic risk*.
†The term *trading on the equity* is often used interchangeably with *financial leverage*.

Table 4.7 The eps for Various EBIT Levels

	Case 2		Case 1
	−40%		+40%
EBIT	$6,000	$10,000	$14,000
Less: Interest (I)	2,000	2,000	2,000
Earnings before taxes (EBT)	$4,000	$ 8,000	$12,000
Less: Taxes (T) (40%)	1,600	3,200	4,800
Earnings after taxes (EAT)	$2,400	$ 4,800	$ 7,200
Less: Preferred share dividends (PD)	2,400	2,400	2,400
Earnings available for common (EAC)	$ 0	$ 2,400	$ 4,800

$$\text{Earnings per share (eps)} \quad \frac{\$0}{1,000} = \$0/\text{sh.} \quad \frac{\$2,400}{1,000} = \$2.40/\text{sh.} \quad \frac{\$4,800}{1,000} = \$4.80/\text{sh.}$$

−100%   +100%

changes in earnings before interest and taxes on the earnings available for the common shareholders. Throughout the following analysis, it is assumed that all preferred share dividends are paid. This assumption is required in order to measure the amount of money actually available to be distributed to common shareholders.*

Financial leverage is defined as the firm's ability to use fixed financial charges to magnify the effects of changes in earnings before interest and taxes on the firm's earnings per share (eps). Earnings per share are commonly considered instead of earnings available *for* common shareholders because eps measure the returns available to each shareholder; the calculation of earnings per share was discussed in Chapter 3. Taxes, as well as the financial costs of interest and preferred share dividends, are deducted from the firm's income stream. However, the taxes do not represent a fixed cost, since they change with changes in the level of earnings before taxes (EBT). Since taxes are a variable cost, they have no direct effect on the firm's financial leverage.

FINANCIAL LEVERAGE ILLUSTRATED

A firm expects earnings before interest and taxes of $10,000 in the current year. It has a $40,000 bond with a 5-percent coupon and an issue of 600 shares of $4.00 preferred outstanding; it also has 1,000 common shares outstanding. The annual interest on the bond issue is $2,000 (.05 · $40,000). The annual dividends on the preferred shares are $2,400 ($4.00/share · 600 shares). Table 4.7 presents the levels of earnings per share resulting from levels of earnings before interest and taxes of $6,000, $10,000, and $14,000 for a firm in the 40-percent tax bracket. Two situations are illustrated in the table.

---

*Preferred share dividends may be *passed* (unpaid) during a period, but only if no dividends are paid to the common shareholders. Preferred shares are generally such that unpaid dividends accrue and must be satisfied prior to any distribution of earnings to common shareholders. A more in-depth discussion of the characteristics of preferred shares is included in Chapter 22.

CASE 1:   A 40-percent *increase* in EBIT (from $10,000 to $14,000) results in a 100-percent *increase* in earnings per share (from $2.40 to $4.80).

CASE 2:   A 40-percent *decrease* in EBIT (from $10,000 to $6,000) results in a 100-percent *decrease* in earnings per share (from $2.40 to $0).

Table 4.7 indicates that financial leverage works in both directions and that financial leverage exists when a firm has fixed financial charges. The effect of financial leverage is such that an increase in the firm's EBIT results in a greater than proportional increase in the firm's earnings per share, while a decrease in the firm's EBIT results in a more than proportional decrease in the firm's eps. Note that in order to compare the degrees of financial leverage associated with different levels of fixed financial costs, the same base levels of EBIT must be used.

MEASURING THE DEGREE OF FINANCIAL LEVERAGE (DFL)

The degree of financial leverage can be measured in a fashion similar to that used to measure the degree of operating leverage. The following equation presents one approach for measuring DFL.

$$\text{DFL} = \frac{\text{percentage change in eps}}{\text{percentage change in EBIT}} \tag{4.11}$$

Whenever the percentage change in eps resulting from a given percentage change in EBIT is greater than the percentage change in EBIT, financial leverage exists. This means that whenever DFL is greater than 1, financial leverage exists. Applying Equation 4.11 to Case 1 and Case 2 yields

$$\text{Case 1: } \frac{+\ 100\%}{+\ 40\%} = 2.5$$

$$\text{Case 2: } \frac{-\ 100\%}{-\ 40\%} = 2.5$$

In both cases, the quotient is greater than 1 and financial leverage exists. The higher this quotient is, the greater the degree of financial leverage a firm has.

A more direct formula* for calculating the degree of financial leverage at a base level of EBIT is given by Equation 4.12.

$$\text{DFL for given EBIT} = \frac{\text{EBIT}}{\text{EBIT} - I - PD \cdot [1/(1 - t)]} \tag{4.12}$$

---

*The method for obtaining this formula is similar to that used in deriving the DOL formula given by Equation 4.10 from Equation 4.9.

Substituting EBIT = \$10,000, I = \$2,000, PD = \$2,400, and the tax rate (t = .40) into Equation 4.12 yields the following result:

$$\text{DFL at \$10,000 EBIT} = \frac{\$10,000}{\$10,000 - \$2,000 - \$2,400 \left[1/(1 - .40)\right]} = \frac{\$10,000}{\$4,000} = 2.5$$

Because financial leverage, like operating leverage, works in both directions, magnifying the effects of both increases and decreases in the firm's EBIT, higher levels of risk are again attached to higher degrees of leverage. High fixed financial costs thus increase the firm's financial leverage *and* its financial risk, and the financial manager must keep this in mind when making financing decisions.

A GRAPHICAL PRESENTATION OF A FINANCING PLAN

The term *financing plan* refers to the firm's mix of sources of long-term financing (e.g., long-term debt, preferred shares, and common shares). One such financing plan was used to illustrate financial leverage in Table 4.7. This financing plan can be illustrated graphically. Like other similar plans, it can be plotted as a straight line, since eps is a linear function of EBIT as follows:

$$\text{eps} = \frac{\text{EBIT} - I - T - PD}{n} \quad \text{where } n \text{ is the number of common shares outstanding}$$

$$= \frac{\text{EBIT} - I - t\,(\text{EBIT} - I) - PD}{n}$$

$$= \frac{(1 - t)\,\text{EBIT} - (1 - t)\,I - PD}{n}$$

Plotting two values of EBIT—\$10,000 and \$14,000—and their associated earnings per share of \$2.40 and \$4.80 gives us the line in Figure 4.9.

It is interesting to note that the line intersects the EBIT axis at \$6,000. This value of EBIT represents the level at which the firm's earnings per share are equal to zero. At levels of EBIT below \$6,000, the firm would have negative eps.[*] Mathematically, the intersection point with the EBIT axis can be found by letting

$$\text{eps} = \frac{(1 - t)\,\text{EBIT} - (1 - t)\,I - PD}{n} = 0$$

which gives

$$\text{EBIT} = I + \frac{PD}{1 - t}$$

at the intersection point. Substituting the appropriate values from Table 4.7, the point of intersection with the EBIT axis occurs at

$$\text{EBIT} = \$2,000 + \frac{\$2,400}{1 - .40} = \$6,000$$

[*]We have assumed for simplicity that the firm has no sinking-fund obligations on its outstanding debt. However, it should be noted that holding everything else constant, the sinking-fund payments will tend to shift the line to the left over time, since the interest to be paid will decline over time.

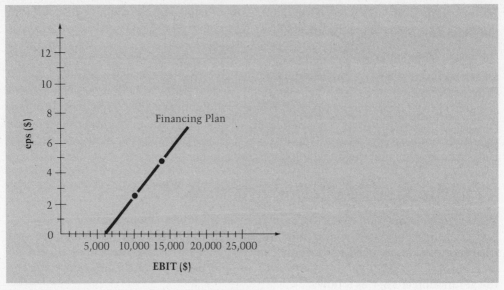

Figure 4.9   A graphical presentation of a financing plan.

A GRAPHICAL ILLUSTRATION OF DIFFERENT DEGREES OF FINANCIAL LEVERAGE: EBIT-eps ANALYSIS

The type of graphical presentation given in Figure 4.9 can be used to compare different levels of financial leverage under various financing plans. Suppose we want to compare the level of financial leverage under the financing plan in the preceding example with that of an alternate plan. The alternate plan involves $20,000 of 5-percent debt, 300 preferred shares with a per share dividend of $4.00, and 1,750 common shares. The two plans differ significantly with respect to their levels of fixed-cost components. With the alternate plan, the annual interest payment will be $1,000 (.05 · $20,000) and the annual preferred dividend payment will be $1,200 ($4/sh. · 300 sh.). In order to graph this plan, two sets of EBIT-eps coordinates are required. The eps associated with EBIT values of $10,000 and $14,000 are calculated as follows:

$$+ 40\%$$

EBIT	$10,000	$14,000
$-I$	1,000	1,000
EBT	$ 9,000	$13,000
$-T(40\%)$	3,600	5,200
EAT	$ 5,400	7,800
$-PD$	1,200	1,200
EAC	$ 4,200	$ 6,600

$$\text{eps} = \frac{\$4,200}{1,750} = \$2.40 \qquad \frac{\$6,600}{1,750} = \$3.77$$

$$+57\%$$

A 40-percent increase in the firm's EBIT will result in a 57-percent increase in eps. Applying Equation 4.12 to these values yields

$$\text{DFL at \$10,000 EBIT} = \frac{\$10,000}{\$10,000 - \$1,000 - \$1,200 \cdot [1/(1 - .40)]} = \frac{\$10,000}{\$7,000} = 1.4$$

The value of 1.4, when compared to the financial leverage value of 2.5 calculated earlier, indicates that the current plan has the lower degree of financial leverage. Each of these plans is graphed in Figure 4.10. The original plan, first graphed in Figure 4.9, is labeled plan A; the current plan is labeled plan B.

As Figure 4.10 illustrates, the slope of plan A is steeper than that of plan B. This indicates that eps under plan A, which has the higher DFL, are more sensitive to changes in EBIT than the eps under plan B. An important implication is that higher degrees of financial leverage are advantageous in terms of their impact on eps if EBIT rises and disadvantageous if it falls.

The point of intersection of each plan with the EBIT axis represents the amount of earnings before interest and taxes necessary for the firm to cover its fixed financial charges; that is, the point at which eps = 0. This point of intersection can be thought of as a *financial breakeven point*, since it represents the level of EBIT necessary for the firm to just cover its fixed financial charges. The breakeven EBIT for plan A is $6,000, and for plan B it is $3,000. In other words, earnings before interest and taxes of less than $6,000 with plan A or less than $3,000 with plan B will result in a loss, or negative eps.

The point labeled X in Figure 4.10 represents the point of intersection between plan A and plan B. It indicates that at a level of EBIT of $10,000, eps of $2.40 would result under either plan. At levels of EBIT below $10,000, plan B results in higher levels of eps; while at levels of EBIT above $10,000, plan A results in higher levels of eps. The usefulness of

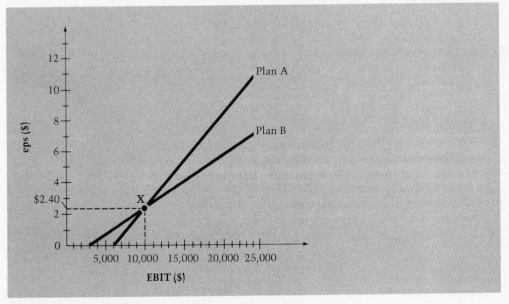

Figure 4.10 A graphical presentation of alternate financing plans.

this type of analysis is discussed in Chapter 18. It may, however, be noted here that eps is an important measure of the firm's performance and is closely watched by investors. The analysis of the effect of various financing plans on eps is, therefore, a useful approach. But the limitations of eps as a decision criterion in the selection of an optimal financing plan should not be overlooked. As we just observed, one plan may provide higher eps at one level of EBIT but less at another. Therefore, if EBIT is uncertain, eps as a decision criterion may not provide a clear-cut choice between various competing financing plans.

FINANCIAL RISK

Financial risk is the risk of being unable to cover financial costs. The discussion of financial leverage stressed the fact that as financial charges increase, the level of EBIT necessary to cover the firm's financial charges also increases. Increasing financial leverage results in increasing risk, since increased financial payments require the firm to maintain a higher level of EBIT in order to stay in business. If the firm cannot cover these financial payments, it can be forced out of business by creditors whose claims are unsettled.*

Financial leverage is often measured by a simple ratio such as the debt-equity ratio, times-interest earned, or the ratio of long-term debt plus preferred shares to total capitalization. Each of these ratios indicates the relationship between the funds on which fixed financial charges must be paid and the total funds invested in the firm.

Like operating leverage, financial leverage works in both directions. It increases the firm's risk since it places a greater burden on the firm in terms of fixed financial charges. On the other hand, it increases the expected return to owners at higher expected levels of EBIT. It is the responsibility of the financial manager to make decisions consistent with the maintenance of a desired degree of financial leverage.

Total Leverage: The Combined Effect

The combined effect of operating and financial leverage on the firm's risk can be assessed using a framework similar to that used to develop the concepts of operating and financial leverage. This combined effect, or *total leverage*, can be defined as the firm's ability to use fixed costs, both operating and financial, to magnify the effect of changes in sales on the firm's earnings per share. Total leverage therefore can be viewed as reflecting the total impact of the fixed costs on the firm's operating and financial structure. Operating leverage affects primarily the asset structure of the firm while financial leverage affects the relative proportions of various components in the firm's capital structure. From the standpoint of the income statement, operating leverage influences the risk-return trade-off present in the firm's operations, while financial leverage influences the risk-return trade-off present in the distribution of returns to various suppliers of long-term capital.

---

*Preferred shareholders do not have the power to force liquidation if their claims are unpaid. The problem with not paying preferred share dividends is that the common shareholders can receive no dividends.

Table 4.8   The Total Leverage Effect

	+ 50%	
Sales (in units)	20,000	30,000
Sales revenue[a]	$100,000	$150,000
Less: Variable operating costs[b]	40,000	60,000

$$DOL = \frac{60\%}{50\%} = 1.2$$

Less: Fixed operating costs	10,000	10,000
Earnings before interest and taxes (EBIT)	$ 50,000	$ 80,000

	+ 60%	
Less: Interest	20,000	20,000
Earnings before taxes	$30,000	$60,000
Less: Taxes (40%)	12,000	24,000

$$DFL = \frac{300\%}{60\%} = 5.0$$

Earnings after taxes	$18,000	$36,000
Less: Preferred share dividends	12,000	12,000
Earnings available for common	$ 6,000	$24,000
Earnings per share (eps)	$\frac{\$6,000}{5,000} = \$1.20/\text{sh.}$	$\frac{\$24,000}{5,000} = \$4.80/\text{sh.}$

	+ 300%	

[a]Sales revenue = $5/unit · sales in units.
[b]Variable operating costs = $2/unit · sales in units.

TOTAL LEVERAGE ILLUSTRATED

A firm expects sales of 20,000 units in the coming year and must meet the following: variable operating costs of $2.00 per unit, fixed operating costs of $10,000, interest of $20,000, and preferred share dividends of $12,000. The firm is in the 40-percent tax bracket and has 5,000 common shares outstanding. Table 4.8 presents the levels of earnings per share (eps) associated with the expected sales of 20,000 units and with sales of 30,000 units.

The table illustrates that as a result of a 50-percent increase in sales (20,000 to 30,000 units), the firm would experience a 300-percent increase in earnings per share ($1.20 to $4.80). Although not shown in the table, a 50-percent decrease in sales would, conversely, result in a 300-percent decrease in earnings per share. The linear nature of the leverage relationship accounts for the fact that sales changes of equal magnitude in opposite directions result in earnings per share changes of equal magnitude in the corresponding direction. At this point, it should be quite clear that whenever a firm has fixed costs—operating or financial—in its structure, the total leverage effect will exist.

MEASURING THE DEGREE OF TOTAL LEVERAGE (DTL)

The following equation presents one approach for measuring DTL.

$$DTL = \frac{\text{percentage change in eps}}{\text{percentage change in sales}} \tag{4.13}$$

Whenever the percentage change in eps resulting from a given percentage change in sales is greater than the percentage change in sales, DTL is greater than 1. The higher this quotient is, the greater the degree of total leverage a firm has.[*] Applying Equation 4.13 to the data in Table 4.8 yields

$$DTL = \frac{300\%}{50\%} = 6.0$$

A more direct formula for calculating the degree of total leverage at a given base level of sales, X, is given by Equation 4.14.

$$DTL \text{ at base sales } X = \frac{X(P - V)}{X(P - V) - F - I - PD \cdot [1/(1 - t)]} \tag{4.14}$$

Substituting $X = 20,000$, $P = \$5$, $V = \$2$, $F = \$10,000$, $I = \$20,000$, and $PD = \$10,000$, and the tax rate $(t = .40)$ into Equation 4.14 yields

DTL at 20,000 units

$$= \frac{20,000(\$5 - \$2)}{20,000(\$5 - \$2) - \$10,000 - \$20,000 - \$12,000 \cdot [1/(1 - .4)]}$$

$$= \frac{\$60,000}{\$10,000} = 6.0$$

Since total leverage, like operating and financial leverage, works in both directions, magnifying the effects of both increases and decreases in the firm's sales, higher levels of risk are attached to higher degrees of total leverage. High fixed costs thus increase the firm's total leverage *and* its total risk; the financial manager must keep this in mind when making both operating and financing decisions.

THE RELATIONSHIP BETWEEN OPERATING, FINANCIAL, AND TOTAL LEVERAGE

Though we shall not provide the proof here, it can be shown that the relationship between operating and financial leverage is a multiplicative rather than an additive one. The relationship between the degree of total leverage (DTL) and the degrees of operating (DOL) and financial (DFL) leverage is given by Equation 4.15.

$$DTL = DOL \cdot DFL \tag{4.15}$$

[*]This statement is true only when the base levels of sales used to calculate and compare such quotients are the same. In other words, the base level of sales must be held constant in order to compare the total leverage associated with different levels of fixed costs.

Substituting the values calculated for DOL and DFL, shown in the right-hand column of Table 4.8, into Equation 4.15 yields

$$DTL = 1.2 \cdot 5.0 = 6.0$$

The resulting degree of total leverage of 6.0 is the same value that was calculated directly in the previous section. Since there is a multiplier effect when the two forms of leverage are combined, a firm may maintain a high total leverage by combining high degrees of both operating and financial leverage, or the firm may moderate its total leverage position by balancing off high operating leverage against low financial leverage, or vice versa.

TOTAL RISK

In a relationship similar to operating leverage and operating risk and financial leverage and financial risk, total leverage reflects the total risk of the firm. The firm's *total risk* is therefore the risk associated with the ability to cover the firm's operating and financial costs. With increasing fixed operating and financial costs comes increasing risk since the firm will have to achieve a higher level of sales just to break even. On the other hand, the greater total leverage resulting from the increased fixed costs can provide higher levels of return than would otherwise be available.

Summary

Breakeven analysis is used to measure the level of sales necessary to cover a firm's total operating costs. The breakeven point can be measured in units or dollars of sales. It may be calculated algebraically or determined graphically. Below the breakeven point, the firm experiences a loss; above the breakeven point, the firm's earnings before interest and taxes are greater than zero. Breakeven points are sensitive to changes in fixed costs, variable costs, and the selling price of the firm's product. Increases in fixed operating costs, the variable cost per unit, and the sale price per unit increase the breakeven sales level and vice versa. Breakeven analysis can be performed on a cash basis by deducting any noncash expenses such as depreciation from the fixed costs and then determining the breakeven point. Breakeven analysis suffers from a number of weaknesses, chief among which are an assumption of linearity, the difficulty of classifying costs as required, the problems caused by multi-product situations, and its short-term nature.

Operating leverage is closely related to breakeven analysis. It is defined as the ability of the firm to use fixed operating costs to magnify the effects of changes in the firm's sales on its earnings before interest and taxes (EBIT). The higher the firm's fixed operating costs, the greater will be its operating leverage. The degree of operating leverage at a specified level of sales can be calculated in terms of unit or dollar sales volume. Since as the firm's fixed operating costs increase, the volume of sales necessary to cover these costs also increases, the firm's operating risk is directly related to its degree of operating leverage.

Financial leverage is defined as the ability of the firm to use fixed financial costs in order to magnify the effects of changes in earnings before interest and taxes (EBIT) on the firm's reported earnings per share (eps). The higher the firm's fixed financial costs—typically interest and preferred share dividends—the greater is its financial leverage. The degree of financial leverage at a given level of earnings before interest and taxes can be calculated in either of two ways. Financial leverage can be viewed graphically, and the level of earnings before interest and taxes necessary to cover all fixed financial charges can be considered a type of financial breakeven point. When various financing plans are graphed on a set of EBIT-eps axes, the differing levels of financial leverage are reflected in the slopes of the plans. The steeper the slope, the higher the financial leverage associated with a given financing plan. With increased fixed financial costs comes increased financial leverage. The risk associated with covering these financial charges is the firm's financial risk.

The total leverage of the firm is defined as the ability of the firm to use fixed costs—both operating and financial—to magnify the effects of changes in sales on earnings per share. Total leverage reflects the combined effect of operating and financial leverage on the firm. The degree of total leverage at a specified level of sales can be measured in either of two ways. It can also be found by multiplying the degree of operating leverage by the degree of financial leverage. The total risk of the firm, which is associated with its ability to cover fixed operating and financial costs, increases with increasing total leverage, and vice versa. The financial manager must consider the effect of operating and financial leverage on the total risk of the firm when making operating and financing decisions.

Questions

4.1   What is meant by the term *leverage*? With what type of risk is leverage generally associated?

4.2   What is the difference between operating and financial leverage as reflected in the firm's income statement?

4.3   What is the meaning of the firm's operating breakeven point? Does this breakeven point, as defined, consider financing costs? Does another breakeven concept account for coverage of all costs and, if so, how?

4.4   How can operating breakeven analysis be used to evaluate the feasibility of various types of operations and cost structures?

4.5   How do changes in the selling price of a product, the variable cost per unit, and fixed operating costs affect the firm's operating breakeven point?

4.6   One of the key weaknesses of breakeven analysis is the assumption of linear cost and revenue functions. Why may these functions actually be curvilinear? Can you graphically depict a curvilinear breakeven analysis?

4.7   How is operating leverage related to the firm's fixed and variable costs? Why are earnings before interest and taxes the pivotal variable in leverage analysis?

4.8   Why is increasing operating leverage also indicative of increasing risk? How does the ratio of the percentage change in EBIT to the percentage change in sales reflect this risk?

4.9   What is meant by financial leverage? What items on the firm's income statement affect the degree of financial leverage present in a given firm?

4.10   How can the ratio of the percentage change in earnings per share to the percentage change in EBIT be used to determine the degree of leverage present in a given firm?

4.11   How does a financial manager assess the firm's degree of financial leverage? Why is this measure important in evaluating various financing plans?

4.12   Why must the financial manager keep in mind the firm's degree of financial leverage when evaluating various financing plans?

4.13   What is the meaning of the firm's financial breakeven point? Is this affected by changes in operating costs?

4.14   What is the relationship between the slope of the graph of a financing plan, the financial breakeven point, and the financial leverage ratio? What do these measures reveal about the risk associated with a firm?

4.15   What is the relationship between operating leverage and operating risk? How is each of these related to the firm's breakeven point and risk-return trade-off?

4.16   What is the relationship between financial leverage and financial risk? How is each of these related to the firm's financial breakeven point and risk-return trade-off?

4.17   What is the relationship of total leverage to total risk? How is each of these related to the firm's total breakeven point and overall risk-return trade-off? How does one measure the degree of total leverage?

4.18   What is the general relationship between operating leverage, financial leverage, and the total leverage of the firm? Do both types of leverage complement each other? Why or why not?

Problems

4.1   The Alberta Press publishes the *Annual Alberta Almanac*. Last year, the book sold for $8.00 with variable cost per book of $6.00 and fixed costs of $40,000. How many books will they need to sell this year to achieve the breakeven point for their operating expenses given the following different circumstances?
a.   All figures remain the same as last year.
b.   Fixed costs increase to $44,000; all other figures remain the same as last year.
c.   The selling price increases to $8.50; all costs remain the same as last year.
d.   Variable cost per book increases to $6.50; all other figures remain the same.
e.   What conclusions about the operating breakeven point can be drawn from your answers?

4.2   Given the following price and cost data for each of the three firms R, S, and T, answer the questions below.

	R	S	T
Sale price per unit	$ 16	$ 14	$ 25
Variable operating cost per unit	$ 6	$ 9	$ 10
Fixed operating cost	$40,000	$20,000	$75,000

a.   What is the breakeven point in units for each firm?
b.   Compute the sales dollar breakeven level.
c.   Assuming $10,000 of each firm's fixed costs are depreciation, compute the cash breakeven point for each firm.
d.   How would you rank these firms in terms of their risk?

4.3   The Bush Company Ltd. sells its finished product for $9.00 per unit. Its fixed operating costs are $20,000 and the variable operating cost per unit is $5.00.

a. Calculate the firm's earnings before interest and taxes (EBIT) for sales of 10,000 units.
b. Calculate the firm's EBIT for sales of 8,000 and 12,000 units, respectively.
c. Calculate the percentage change in sales and associated percentage changes in EBIT for the shifts in sales indicated in **b**.

4.4 The Fiesta Paper Company Ltd. has fixed costs of $190,000, variable costs per unit of $8.00, and a selling price of $31.75 per unit.
a. Calculate the operating breakeven point in units and sales dollars.
b. Calculate the firm's EBIT at 9,000, 10,000, and 11,000 units, respectively.
c. Using 10,000 units as a base, what are the percentage changes in units sold and EBIT as sales move from the base to the other sales levels used in **b**?
d. Use the percentages computed in **c** to determine the degree of operating leverage (DOL).
e. Use the degree of operating leverage formula to determine the DOL at 10,000 units.

4.5 Wallace Wigits Ltd. has fixed operating costs of $60,000, variable operating costs of $5.75 per unit, and a selling price of $8.25 per unit.
a. Calculate the breakeven point in units.
b. Compute the degree of operating leverage (DOL) for the following unit sales levels: 25,000, 30,000, 40,000. Use the formula given in the chapter.
c. Graph the DOL figures you computed in **b** (on the y-axis) against sales levels (on the x-axis).
d. Compute the degree of operating leverage at 24,000 units; add this point to your graph.
e. What principle is illustrated by your graph and figures?

4.6 The Power Tool Corporation has $120,000 of 8-percent bonds outstanding, 1,500 preferred shares paying $5.00 dividends per share, and 4,000 common shares outstanding. Assuming the firm has a 40-percent tax rate, compute earnings per share (eps) for the following levels of EBIT:
a. $24,600
b. $30,600
c. $35,000

4.7 Canadian Barge has 400,000 common shares and $100,000 of bonds outstanding. The firm has a 40-percent tax rate.
a. Calculate the financial breakeven point if the interest rate on the bonds is 10 percent.
b. Calculate the financial breakeven point if the interest rate on the bonds is 8 percent.
c. Using **a** above, assume the firm has 1,000 outstanding preferred shares that pay a $6.00 dividend per share. What is the financial breakeven point?
d. Using **a** above, assume the firm has 1,000 preferred shares outstanding and the dividend is $5.40 per share. What is the financial breakeven point?

4.8 The Wonder Water Company Ltd. has EBIT of $45,000. Interest costs are $15,000 and the firm has 15,000 common shares outstanding. Assume a 40-percent tax rate.
a. Use the degree of financial leverage (DFL) formula to calculate the DFL for the firm.
b. Using a set of EBIT-eps axes, plot the Wonder Water financing plan.
c. Assuming the firm also has 1,000 preferred shares paying a $6.00 dividend per share, what is the DFL?
d. Plot the financing plan including the 1,000 preferred shares paying $6.00 per share dividend on the axes used in **b**.
e. Briefly discuss the graphs of the two financing plans.

4.9 Collins Electronics Ltd. is considering additional financing of $20,000. They currently have $100,000 of 6-percent bonds and 10,000 common shares outstanding. The firm can obtain the financing through a 6-percent bond issue or a sale of 1,000 common shares. If the firm expects EBIT to be $30,000 and has a 40-percent tax rate:

a. What would the degree of financial leverage (DFL) be under each financing plan?

b. Plot the two financing plans on a set of EBIT-eps axes.

c. At what level of EBIT does the bond plan become superior to the common share plan?

4.10 Johnson Manufacturing Ltd. produces small motors. Their fixed operating costs are $20,000, variable operating costs are $18 per unit, and the motors sell for $23 each. Johnson has $50,000 in 10-percent bonds and 20,000 common shares outstanding. The firm is in the 40-percent tax bracket.

a. What is Johnson's operating breakeven point in units?

b. What is Johnson's financial breakeven point?

c. What is Johnson's total breakeven point?

4.11 Rose Oil Cosmetics Ltd. produces skin-care products. It sells 400,000 bottles a year. Each bottle produced has a variable operating cost of $0.84, and sells for $1.00. Fixed operating costs are $28,000. The firm has current interest charges of $6,000 and preferred dividends of $2,000. The firm has a 40-percent tax rate.

a. Calculate operating (units), financial, and total breakeven points.

b. Use the degree of operating leverage (DOL) formula to calculate DOL.

c. Use the degree of financial leverage (DFL) formula to calculate DFL.

d. Use the degree of total leverage (DTL) formula to calculate DTL. Compare this to the product of DOL and DFL calculated in **b** and **c** above.

4.12 Firm A has a contribution margin of $0.30 per unit, has fixed costs of $6,000, and sells 100,000 units. Interest is $10,000 per year. Firm B has a contribution margin of $1.50 per unit, has fixed costs of $62,500, and sells 100,000 units. Interest is $17,500 per year. Assume both firms are in the 40-percent tax bracket.

a. Compute the degree of operating, financial, and total leverage for firm A.

b. Compute the degree of operating, financial, and total leverage for firm B.

c. Compare the relative risks of the two firms.

d. Discuss the principles of leverage illustrated in your answers.

Suggested Readings

Crowingshield, Gerald R. and George L. Battista, "Cost-Volume-Profit Analysis in Planning and Control," *N.A.A. Bulletin* 45 (July 1963), pp. 3–15.

Ghandi, J. K. S., "On the Measurement of Leverage," *Journal of Finance* 21 (December 1966), pp. 715–726.

Haslem, John A., "Leverage Effects on Corporate Earnings," *Arizona Review* 19 (March 1970), pp. 7–11.

Haugen, Robert A. and Dean W. Wichern, "The Intricate Relationship Between Financial Leverage and the Stability of Stock Prices," *Journal of Finance* 30 (December 1975), pp. 1283–1292.

Helfert, Erich A., *Techniques of Financial Analysis*, 4th ed. (Homewood, Ill.: Irwin, 1976), chap. 2.

Hugon, J. H., "Break-even Analysis in Three Dimensions," *Financial Executive* 33 (December 1965), pp. 22–26.

Jaedicke, R. K. and A. A. Robichek, "Cost-Volume-Profit Analysis Under Conditions of Uncertainty," *Accounting Review* 39 (October 1964), pp. 917–926.

Kelvie, W. E. and J. M. Sinclair, "New Technique for Break-even Charts," *Financial Executive* 36 (June 1968), pp. 31–43.

Krainer, Robert E., "Interest Rates, Leverage, and Investor Rationality," *Journal of Financial and Quantitative Analysis* 12 (March 1977), pp. 1–16.

Lev, Baruch, "On the Association Between Operating Leverage and Risk," *Journal of Financial and Quantitative Analysis* 9 (September 1974), pp. 627–642.

Percival, John R., "Operating Leverage and Risk," *Journal of Business Research* 2 (April 1974), pp. 223–227.

Pfahl, J. K., D. T. Crary, and R. H. Howard, "The Limits of Leverage," *Financial Executive* 38 (May 1970), pp. 48–56.

Raun, D. L., "The Limitations of Profit Graphs, Break-Even Analysis, and Budgets," *Accounting Review* 39 (October 1964), pp. 927–945.

Shalit, Sol S., "On the Mathematics of Financial Leverage," *Financial Management* 4 (Spring 1975), pp. 57–66.

Williams, George E., "The Other Side of Leverage," *Financial Executive* 39 (June 1971), pp. 46–48.

Chapter 5

SOURCES AND USES OF FUNDS AND CASH BUDGETING

It is often useful to develop certain financial statements as an aid in evaluating a firm's past or present performance. The source and use of funds statement (sometimes referred to as a *source and application of funds statement*) allows the financial manager to analyze the firm's historical sources and uses of funds. Occasionally, this statement is used for forecasting. Its major strength is its usefulness in evaluating the sources and uses of longer-term funds. A knowledge of the historical patterns of fund usage allows the financial manager to better plan his or her future intermediate and long-term funds requirements.

The *cash budget* is a forecasting tool that allows the financial manager to determine the short-term financial needs of the firm. It is often called a *cash forecast*, but the term "cash budget" will be used in this chapter. The cash budget is an important tool for evaluating the financial needs of seasonal businesses, since it is typically developed in a manner that permits the analysis of a firm's short-term financing needs on a month-by-month basis. Banks and other external lenders often require prospective borrowers of short-term funds to present a cash budget as part of their loan application. The cash budget is a key input to the firm's pro forma balance sheet and income statements, which are discussed in Chapter 6.

This chapter has two major sections. The first section is devoted to the development and interpretation of source and use of funds statements. Attention is given to the classification and adjustment of balance sheet changes in order to prepare both the source and use of cash and the source and use of net working capital statements. A discussion of the interpretation of these statements and the rationale for their preparation is also presented in the first section. The second section of the chapter discusses the importance, preparation, and interpretation of cash budgets. Emphasis is placed on the preparation of the sales forecast, which is the key input to the cash budget. A brief discussion of the incorporation of uncertainty into the cash budget is also included.

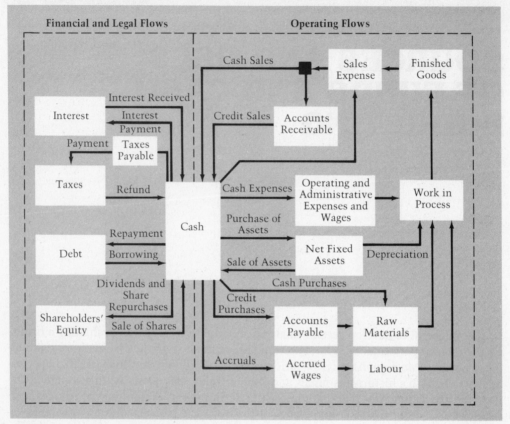

Figure 5.1 The flow of funds through the firm.

Source and Use of Funds Statements*

The term *funds* can be defined to mean either of two things—cash or net working capital. Both of these items are necessary for the firm to function effectively. The firm needs cash to pay bills. Net working capital is also necessary, especially in seasonal businesses, to provide a financial cushion for the payment of bills due in the near future. The use of net working capital in the development of the source and use of funds statement is based on the belief that noncash current assets, which by definition can be converted into cash in a short period of time, as well as cash, can be utilized to pay the firm's current liabilities. The source and use of cash statement provides much more detailed information than the source and use of net working capital statement.

Figure 5.1 is a diagram of the overall flow of cash through the business firm. It shows (1) operating flows, and (2) financial and legal flows. *Operating flows* relate to the firm's

*The Canadian Institute of Chartered Accountants (CICA) recommends that a firm should label this statement "Statement of Changes in Financial Position" in the annual report.

production cycle. Utilizing raw materials, labour, and depreciable assets, and incurring operating and administrative expenses such as salaries and rent, plus sales expenses, the firm produces and sells its finished goods. As Figure 5.1 shows, not all purchases are made for cash; rather, many are made on credit through the establishment of an account payable or accrual. Similarly, not all sales are made for cash; many are made on credit, producing accounts receivable.

The financial and legal flows depicted in Figure 5.1 include the payment and receipt of interest, the payment and refund of taxes, the incurrence or repayment of debt, the effect of distributions of earnings through the payment of dividends or share repurchases, and the cash inflow from the sale of shares. These flows differ from operating flows in that they are not directly related to the production and sale of the firm's products, but rather to the financing and tax payments of the firm. Although no division between operating flows and financial and legal flows will be made in the development of source and use of funds statements, the reader should recognize the difference between them. The breakdown of financial and operating flows in Figure 5.1 is consistent with the discussion of financial and operating leverage in Chapter 4.

CLASSIFYING SOURCES AND USES OF CASH

Sources of cash are items that increase a firm's cash, while *uses of cash* are items that decrease a firm's cash.

Sources   The basic sources of cash are

1 A decrease in an asset
2 An increase in a liability
3 Net profits after taxes
4 Depreciation and other noncash charges*
5 Sale of shares

A few points should be clarified with respect to these items.

Cash   The reader may wonder why a decrease in an asset, which would include a decrease in cash, is a source of cash. A decrease in the cash *balance* is a source of cash *flow* in the sense that if the firm's cash balance is decreased, the cash flow released must have gone toward some use of cash such as an increase in inventories or the repayment of debt.

Net Profits After Taxes and Noncash Charges   Chapter 2, Equation 2.1, and the discussion preceding it, explained why depreciation and other noncash charges must be con-

---

*In this section, depreciation (and the resulting cash flow) as reported in the financial statements of the annual report is used. However, it should be noted that there may be a difference between the depreciation expense reported in the annual report and the capital cost allowance used both in calculating the actual tax liability and in evaluating a capital expenditure proposal. For greater detail, refer to Chapter 2.

sidered cash inflows, or sources of funds.* Adding noncash charges back to the firm's net profits after taxes gives us the cash flows from operations as follows:

Cash flow from operations = net profits after taxes + noncash charges

In this chapter, net profits after taxes and noncash charges such as depreciation are treated as separate items in order to increase the informational content of the source and use of funds statement.

Uses   The most common uses of cash are

1 An increase in an asset
2 A decrease in a liability
3 A net loss
4 Payment of cash dividends
5 The repurchase or retirement of shares

A few points should be clarified with respect to these items.

Cash   Since all items in the source and use of cash statement attempt to measure changes in cash, it may be hard to understand that an increase in the asset cash can be a use of cash. An increase in the cash *balance* is a use of cash *flow* in the sense that if a firm's cash balance increases, this cash flow must come from some source of cash such as a decrease in inventories or an increase in a liability. For example, consider a firm that is confronted with two alternatives: (1) using cash to purchase inventory, or (2) putting the cash in its bank account. Both actions will consume cash, but the purchase of inventory will convert it into another type of asset, whereas the placement of cash in the firm's bank account will not. Both actions will increase the firm's assets and therefore must be considered uses of cash.

Net Losses   If a firm were to experience a net loss, this would result in a use of funds. It is possible for a firm to have a net loss but still have positive cash flows from operations if depreciation in the same period is greater than the net loss. This relationship is consistent with Equation 2.1.

ASSETS, LIABILITIES, AND SHAREHOLDERS' EQUITY

Except for cases described above, increases in assets are uses of funds and decreases in assets are sources of funds. It takes cash to increase assets, and cash is generated through the sale of a fixed asset or the collection of accounts receivable. Increases in liabilities are sources of funds and decreases in liabilities are uses of funds. An increase in a liability represents increased financing, which is expected to generate funds, while a decrease in a liability represents the repayment of a debt, which requires a cash outlay.

---

*Although depreciation will not, in effect, be a source of cash flows for those years in which a firm does not have sufficient sales revenues, it will enter into the cash-flow calculations. Depreciation will be charged against income even if it is only to increase the loss position, so that the firm can take advantage of the loss-carryforward/carryback provisions of the Income Tax Act (as discussed in Chapter 2).

One final preliminary point is that no direct shareholders' equity entries have been classified as sources or uses of funds; instead, entries for items that may affect the firm's shareholders' equity have appeared as net profits or losses after taxes, cash dividends, and the result of any sale or repurchase of shares. If the shareholders' equity entries were classified, they would be treated in the same fashion as are the liabilities. An increase in a shareholders' equity account would be treated as a source of funds, and a decrease in a shareholders' equity account would be treated as a use of funds. How shareholders' equity entries are treated on actual source and use of funds statements will be described later.

SPECIAL ADJUSTMENTS

A number of special adjustments are often required in making up a source and use of funds statement. Each of these adjustments stems from the nature of the financial statements used. The inputs required for preparing a source and use of funds statement are (1) an income statement for the most recent period, (2) a balance sheet for the most recent period, and (3) a balance sheet for the earlier period being used as a basis for comparisons. Adjustments can be expected relating to the following items.

Changes in Fixed Assets   Of all the firm's assets, *only* fixed assets require special attention. This is because there are two basic ways in which fixed assets may be shown on the balance sheet. The first way is more detailed and does not require any special attention. Assume that a firm has the following fixed-asset entries on its balance sheet and that depreciation of $500 is shown on the income statement for 19X1.

	19X0	19X1
Fixed assets	$9,500	$10,200
Less: Accumulated depreciation	4,200	4,700
Net fixed assets	$5,300	$ 5,500

In this case, the change in the firm's fixed assets is $700. This figure is easily obtained by taking the difference between the fixed assets for the current year (19X1) and those for the preceding year (19X0), ($10,200 − $9,500). The increase in fixed assets of $700 will appear as a use of funds on the firm's source and use statement. The difference between accumulated depreciation in 19X0 and 19X1 ($500) is equal to the depreciation expense on the firm's income statement.

A less detailed way of showing a firm's fixed assets on the balance sheet is to show only "net fixed assets." Assume that a firm has the net fixed assets indicated below and that $500 in depreciation was written off on its 19X1 income statement.

	19X0	19X1
Net fixed assets	$5,300	$5,500

To find the change (if any) in the firm's fixed assets when one is given this type of data, the following formula is used:

$$\Delta FA_t = NFA_t + Depr_t - NFA_{t-1} \tag{5.1}$$

where

ΔFA_t = the change in fixed assets in the current period t

NFA_t = the net fixed assets in the current period t

$Depr_t$ = the depreciation written off in the current period t

NFA_{t-1} = the net fixed assets in the preceding period $t - 1$

Applying Equation 5.1 to the data given above yields

$$\Delta FA_t = \$5,500 + \$500 - \$5,300 = \underline{\$700}$$

The result is the same as in the first case, but it has been obtained in an indirect fashion.

If the application of Equation 5.1 to the firm's financial statements results in a negative change in fixed assets, the amount of this decrease is entered as a source of funds in the source and use of funds statement. If a change of zero in the firm's fixed assets results, no fixed-asset entry is made on its source and use of funds statement.

Dividends   If the firm's cash dividend payments are shown on the income statement, they are readily available to be entered on the source and use of funds statement. However, in many instances, the last item shown on the firm's income statement is net profits after taxes. In this case the analyst should investigate further to determine whether any cash dividends were paid. Assume that a firm shows net profits after taxes of $5,000 for the current year (19X1) and that the shareholders' equity for the past year (19X0) and the current year (19X1) is as follows:

Shareholders' equity	19X0	19X1
Common shares	$40,000	$45,000
Retained earnings	30,000	33,000
Total	$70,000	$78,000

In this case, the firm's retained earnings have increased by $3,000 ($33,000 − $30,000), which accounts for only $3,000 of the $5,000 of net profits after taxes. The remaining $2,000 must therefore represent a dividend payment of $2,000. Equation 5.2 can be used to calculate the amount of cash dividends paid when they are not shown on the firm's income statement.

$$Cash\ div_t = NPAT_t - RE_t + RE_{t-1} \tag{5.2}$$

where

$Cash\ div_t$ = the cash dividend paid in period t

$NPAT_t$ = the net profits after taxes in period t

RE_t = the retained earnings at the end of period t

RE_{t-1} = the retained earnings at the end of period $t - 1$

Substituting the data above into Equation 5.2 yields

$$Cash \ div_t = \$5,000 - \$33,000 + \$30,000 = \underline{\underline{\$2,000}}$$

Shares   A firm may sell additional shares, repurchase outstanding shares, or retire existing shares. Preferred shares are most likely to be retired since they quite often have a call feature,* which gives the issuer the right to buy back shares in the future. In the case of both common and preferred shares, the amount purchased or sold can be determined by calculating the changes in the firm's shareholders' equity accounts, other than those in its retained earnings. An increase in shares is a source of funds, while a decrease is a use of funds. In the example in the preceding section, the firm's common shares increased from $40,000 in 19X0 to $45,000 in 19X1. This increase of $5,000 in common shares represents a sale of shares, which is shown as a source of funds on the firm's source and use of funds statement.

The following formula can be used to evaluate whether a sale or purchase of shares has occurred:

$$Shares_t = SE_t - SE_{t-1} - RE_t + RE_{t-1} \tag{5.3}$$

where

$Shares_t$ = the change (if any) in the value of the firm's shares outstanding

SE_t = the value of the firm's shareholders' equity in period t

SE_{t-1} = the value of the firm's shareholders' equity in period $t - 1$

RE_t and RE_{t-1} are defined as before

Applying Equation 5.3 to the previous figures yields

$$Shares_t = \$78,000 - \$70,000 - \$33,000 + \$30,000 = \underline{\underline{\$5,000}}$$

The $5,000 increase in shares will be shown as a source of funds of $5,000 on the source and use statement. If the firm were to repurchase or retire shares, a negative value would result that would be shown as a use of funds.

PRELIMINARIES TO THE PREPARATION OF A SOURCE AND USE STATEMENT

The simplified financial statements in Table 5.1 are used to illustrate the actual application of the adjustments discussed above to the preparation of source and use statements. The balance sheet is presented in a *stacked format,* with the assets followed by liabilities and the shareholders' equity, in order to simplify the development of the source and use of cash statement.

Classifying Sources and Uses   The suggested procedure for classifying items as sources or uses is illustrated below, using the XYZ Company as an example.

*An in-depth discussion of the various types of equity securities is provided in Chapter 22.

Table 5.1 Financial Statements for the XYZ Company

Balance Sheets

	Year ended	
	19X0	19X1
Assets		
Cash	$ 300	$ 400
Marketable securities	200	600
Accounts receivable	500	400
Inventory	800	500
Prepaid items	100	100
Total current assets	$1,900	$2,000
Net fixed assets	1,000	1,200
Total assets	$2,900	$3,200
Liabilities and shareholders' equity		
Accounts payable	$ 500	$ 600
Notes payable	700	400
Taxes payable	200	200
Accruals	0	400
Total current liabilities	$1,400	$1,600
Long-term debt	$ 400	$ 600
Preferred shares	$ 100	$ 100
Common shares	500	300
Retained earnings	500	600
Total shareholders' equity	$1,100	$1,000
Total liabilities and shareholders' equity	$2,900	$3,200

Income Statement

		19X1
Sales		$1,000
Less: Cost of goods sold		500
Gross profits		$ 500
Less: Expenses		
General and admin. expense	$100	
Depreciation	100	
Total		200
Profits before taxes		$ 300
Less: Taxes (40%)		120
Profits after taxes		$ 180

Table 5.2   A Classification of Asset and Liability (Balance Sheet)
Changes for the XYZ Company as Sources (S)
or Uses (U) of Funds

Item	Change ($)	Classification
Cash	+ 100	U
Marketable securities	+ 400	U
Accounts receivable	− 100	S
Inventory	− 300	S
Prepaid items	0	—
Net fixed assets	+ 200	—[a]
Accounts payable	+ 100	S
Notes payable	− 300	U
Taxes payable	0	—
Accruals	+ 400	S
Long-term debt	+ 200	S

[a]Not classified at this point in the analysis.

STEP 1:   Using the earliest time period as a base, calculate the balance sheet changes in all assets and liabilities.

STEP 2:   Using the classification scheme presented earlier, classify the changes in all asset and liability accounts, *except* net fixed assets, as either a source (S) or a use (U).

Table 5.2 presents the results of application of Steps 1 and 2 to the XYZ Company's balance sheet.

STEP 3:   Calculate the change in XYZ's fixed assets using Equation 5.1.

$$\text{Change in fixed assets} = \$1{,}200 + \$100 - \$1{,}000 = \underline{\$300}$$

Since the firm's fixed assets have increased, a use of funds of $300 results.

STEP 4:   Calculate the cash dividends paid, if they are not shown on the income statement, using Equation 5.2.

$$\text{Cash dividends} = \$180 - \$600 + \$500 = \underline{\$80}$$

The firm appears to have paid $80 in cash dividends in 19X1. This amount is entered as a use of funds on the source and use of funds statement.

STEP 5:   Calculate the change, if any, in the value of shares outstanding, using Equation 5.3.

$$\text{Change in the value of shares} = \$1{,}000 - \$1{,}100 - \$600 + \$500 = -\underline{\$200}$$

This decrease in the value of shares of $200 is shown as a use on the source and use statement. The change in the value of shares could have been calculated directly from the balance sheet, but the use of Equation 5.3 is suggested since shareholders' equity items are often grouped together on balance sheets.

Table 5.3 A Source and Use of Cash Statement for the XYZ Company

Sources		Uses	
Net profits after taxes	$ 180	Dividends	$ 80
Depreciation	100	Increase in fixed assets	300
Decrease in accounts receivable	100	Increase in cash	100
Decrease in inventory	300	Increase in marketable securities	400
Increase in accounts payable	100	Decrease in notes payable	300
Increase in accruals	400	Repurchase or retirement of shares	200
Increase in long-term debt	200		
Total sources	$1,380	Total uses	$1,380

PREPARING THE SOURCE AND USE OF CASH STATEMENT

The source and use of cash statement is prepared by listing all sources on the left and all uses on the right. The statement for the XYZ Company, based on the data developed in the preceding section, is presented in Table 5.3.

A number of points should be made about Table 5.3.

1 "Total sources" and "total uses" should be equal; if they are not, the analyst must have made an error.
2 Net profits after taxes are normally the first source listed and dividends are normally the first use. Ordering items on the source and use of cash statement this way makes it easy to calculate the change in the firm's retained earnings.
3 Depreciation and increases in fixed assets are shown second to make it easy to compare them. Placing depreciation just below net profits after taxes also makes the firm's cash flow from operations easily calculable.
4 The order of the remaining sources and uses of cash does not matter; the only requirement is that sources appear on the left side of the statement and uses on the right side.
5 The net change in the value of the firm's shareholders' equity can be calculated by adding any sales of shares or subtracting any repurchases or retirements of shares from the difference between the net profits after taxes and cash dividends. For the XYZ Company, the change in the value of shareholders' equity is −$100 ($180 − $80 − $200).

PREPARING THE SOURCE AND USE OF NET WORKING CAPITAL STATEMENT

The source and use of net working capital statement is quite similar to the source and use of cash statement, except that changes in current assets and current liabilities are not entered separately.* Instead, they are netted into a single entry—the change in net

---

*Some authors use the term *working capital* synonymously with what was defined in Chapter 3 as *net working capital.* This statement is therefore also commonly referred to as the source and use of working capital statement.

Table 5.4   The Change in Net Working Capital
for the XYZ Company

	19X0	19X1
Total current assets	$1,900	$2,000
Total current liabilities	1,400	1,600
Net working capital	$ 500	$ 400
Change in net working capital	−$100	

working capital. Many people prefer the source and use of net working capital statement to the source and use of cash statement because they believe the fluid nature of the firm's current accounts makes their individual inclusion pointless.

A decrease in net working capital is a source of funds, whereas an increase in working capital is a use of funds. From the balance sheet for the XYZ Company in Table 5.1, it can be seen that the firm's current assets, current liabilities, net working capital, and change in net working capital are as given in Table 5.4. The increase in current assets of $100, which was a use of funds, has been overpowered by the increase in current liabilities of $200, which was a source of funds. The net result of the $100 decrease in net working capital for the XYZ Company between 19X0 and 19X1 was a source of funds.

Table 5.5 presents a source and use of net working capital statement for the XYZ Company. The only noticeable difference between this statement in Table 5.5 and the source and use of cash statement in Table 5.3 is that the current asset and current liability entries have been replaced in Table 5.5 by a single entry—the change in net working capital. The balancing figures differ in the two types of source and use statements, but this does not have any significance for decision making.

The Source and Use Statements on a Percentage Basis

It is often useful to present the source and use statements on a percentage basis. Of course, before this can be done the statements must first be prepared in terms of dollars, as illustrated earlier. The presentation of source and use statements on a percentage

Table 5.5   A Source and Use of Net Working Capital Statement for the XYZ Company

Sources		Uses	
Net profits after taxes	$180	Dividends	$ 80
Depreciation	100	Increase in fixed assets	300
Decrease in net working capital	100	Repurchase or retirement of shares	200
Increase in long-term debt	200		
Total sources	$580	Total uses	$580

Table 5.6   A Percent Source and Use of Cash Statement for the XYZ Company

Sources		Uses	
Net profits after taxes	13.1%	Dividends	5.7%
Depreciation	7.2	Increase in fixed assets	21.8
Decrease in accounts receivable	7.2	Increase in cash	7.2
Decrease in inventory	21.8	Increase in marketable securities	29.0
Increase in accounts payable	7.2	Decrease in notes payable	21.8
Increase in accruals	29.0	Repurchase or retirement of shares	14.5
Increase in long-term debt	14.5		
Total sources	100.0%	Total uses	100.0%

basis should greatly simplify their interpretation, since such statements allow the analyst to get a feel for the relative contribution of each source and use to the firm's overall cash flow during the period covered by the statements. For example, Table 5.6 presents the source and use of cash statement in Table 5.3 on a percentage basis.

INTERPRETING SOURCE AND USE STATEMENTS

Source and use of cash and source and use of net working capital statements prepared either on a dollar or on a percentage basis allow the financial manager to analyze the firm's past funds flows. He or she will give special attention to the major sources and uses in order to determine whether any developments have occurred that are contrary to the firm's financial policies. Although specific causal relations between sources and uses cannot be determined from an analysis of these statements, they can point out certain types of inefficiencies. For example, large increases in inventories or accounts receivable may signal the existence of certain types of inventory or credit problems. Problems, or symptoms of developing problems, can be recognized and investigation into these problems initiated as a result of the analysis of source and use statements.

Analysis of the XYZ Company's source and use statements does not seem to indicate the existence of any problems. Both the sources and uses of funds seem to be distributed in a manner consistent with prudent financial management. Analysis of the source and use of cash statement seems to indicate great strength on the part of the firm. The majority of its funds have been generated by decreasing inventory and increasing accruals. Both these strategies are consistent with efficient financial management.* The major uses of funds have been an increase in fixed assets, an increase in marketable securities, and a decrease in notes payable. Each of these items reflects financial strength.

As indicated earlier, the financial manager may apply source and use analysis to projected financial statements in order to determine whether a proposed financing plan is feasible in the sense that the financing required to support the projected level of operations will be available.

---

*A thorough discussion of the management of working capital is presented in Chapters 7 through 10. After studying these chapters, the reader should be better able to interpret the source and use statements.

Cash Budgeting

The *cash budget*, or *cash forecast*, allows the firm to plan its short-term cash needs. Typically, attention is given both to planning for surplus cash and to planning for cash shortages. A firm expecting a cash surplus can plan short-term investments, whereas a firm expecting shortages in cash must arrange for needed short-term financing. Thus, the cash budget gives the financial manager a clear view of the timing of both the cash inflows and the cash outflows expected over a given period.

Typically, the cash budget is designed to cover a one-year period, although any time period is acceptable. The period covered is normally divided into intervals. The number and type of intervals depend greatly on the nature of the business. Firms with more seasonal and uncertain cash flows may use monthly intervals; firms with very stable patterns of cash flows may use either quarterly or annual intervals. If a cash budget is developed for a period greater than one year, less frequent time intervals may be warranted due to the difficulty and uncertainty of forecasting sales and associated cash items.

THE SALES FORECAST

The key input to any cash budget is the *sales forecast*. This is typically developed for the financial manager by the marketing department. Such forecasts can be based simply on mechanical and possibly subjective modifications of projections of historical patterns; or they can be based on detailed analysis of internal and external forecast data.*

After being assured of the "reasonableness" of the sales forecast, the financial manager estimates the monthly cash flows that will result from projected sales receipts and production- or inventory-related outlays. He or she also determines how much financing, if any, will be required to support the forecast level of production and sales, and whether and how it can best be obtained.

External Forecasts   An external forecast is based on the relationships that can be observed between the firm's sales and certain economic indicators such as the gross national product, new housing starts, and disposable personal income. Typically, forecasts containing these indicators from which the firm can estimate its future level of sales are readily available.

Internal Forecasts   Internally generated forecasts are based on a buildup of sales forecasts through the firm's sales channels. Typically, the salespersons in the field are asked to estimate the number of units of each type of product that they expect to sell in the coming year. These forecasts are collected by the district sales manager, who may adjust the figures using his or her own knowledge of specific markets or the salesperson's forecasting ability. Finally, adjustments may be made for additional internal factors such as production capabilities.

---

*A discussion of various mechanical forecasting techniques, such as regression, moving averages, and exponential smoothing, is not included in this text. The reader is referred to a basic statistics, econometrics, or management science text for a description of the technical side of forecasting. A few references on the subject have been included at the end of Chapter 6.

Table 5.7   The General Format of a Cash Budget

	Jan.	Feb.	...	Nov.	Dec.
Cash receipts					
Less: Cash disbursements	———	———	...	———	———
Net cash flow					
Add: Beginning cash			...		
Ending cash					
Less: Minimum cash balance	———	———	...	———	———
Required total financing			...		
Excess cash balance			...		

Firms generally use both external and internal forecast data in making up the final sales forecast. The internal forecast data provide insight into sales expectations, while the external forecast data provide a way of adjusting these expectations by taking into account general economic factors. The nature of a firm's products often affect the mix and types of forecasting methods it uses.

THE FORMAT OF THE CASH BUDGET

The general format of the cash budget is presented in Table 5.7. Each of its components will now be discussed individually.

Cash Receipts   Cash receipts include the total of all items from which cash inflows result in any given month. The most common components of cash receipts are cash sales, collections of credit sales, and other cash receipts.

EXAMPLE   The ABC Company is developing a cash budget for October, November, and December. Sales in August and September were $100,000 and $200,000, respectively. Sales of $400,000, $300,000, and $200,000 have been forecast for October, November, and December, respectively. Historically, 20 percent of the firm's sales have been for cash, 50 percent have generated accounts receivable collected after one month, and the remaining 30 percent have generated accounts receivable collected after two months. Bad-debt expenses have been negligible.* In December, the firm will receive a $30,000 dividend from shares in a subsidiary. The schedule of expected cash receipts for the company is given in Table 5.8. It contains the following items:

Forecast sales   This initial entry is *merely informational*. It has been provided as an aid in calculating other sales-related items.

Cash sales   The cash sales shown for each month represent 20 percent of the sales forecast for the month.

*Normally it would be expected that the collection percentages would total slightly less than 100 percent in order to reflect the fact that some of the accounts receivable would be uncollectible. In this example the sum of the collection percentages is 100 percent (i.e., 20% + 50% + 30%), which reflects the fact that all sales are assumed to be collected since bad debts are assumed to be negligible.

Table 5.8   A Schedule of Projected Cash Receipts for the ABC Company ($000 omitted)

	Aug.	Sept.	Oct.	Nov.	Dec.
Forecast sales	$100	$200	$400	$300	$200
Cash sales (.20)	$ 20	$ 40	$ 80	$ 60	$ 40
Collections:					
Lagged one month (.50)		50	100	200	150
Lagged two months (.30)			30	60	120
Other cash receipts					30
Total cash receipts			$210	$320	$340

Collection of credit sales   These entries represent the collection of accounts receivable resulting from sales in earlier months.*

Lagged one month   These figures represent sales made in the preceding month that generated accounts receivable collected in the current month. Since 50 percent of the current month's sales are collected one month later, the collections of accounts receivable with a one-month lag shown for September, October, November, and December represent 50 percent of the sales in August, September, October, and November, respectively.

Lagged two months   These figures represent sales made two months earlier that generated accounts receivable collected in the current month. Since 30 percent of sales are collected two months later, the collections with a two-month lag shown for October, November, and December represent 30 percent of the sales in August, September, and October, respectively.

Other cash receipts   These are cash receipts expected to result from sources other than sales. Items such as dividends received, interest received, proceeds from the sale of equipment, share and bond sale proceeds, and lease receipts may show up here. For the ABC Company, the only "other cash receipt" is the $30,000 dividend due in December.

Total cash receipts   This figure represents the total of all the cash receipt items listed for each month in the cash receipt schedule. In the case of the ABC Company, we are concerned only with October, November, and December; the total cash receipts for these months are shown in Table 5.8.

Cash Disbursements   Cash disbursements include all outlays of cash in the periods covered. The most common cash disbursements are

   Cash purchases
   Payments of accounts payable
   Payments of cash dividends
   Rent
   Wages and salaries
   Tax payments
   Capital additions
   Interest on debt
   Repayment of loans and sinking-fund payments
   Repurchases or retirements of shares

*Note that the experience of Canadian firms is that longer lead times are involved with the collection of foreign accounts receivable.

EXAMPLE   The ABC Company discussed in the preceding example has gathered the following data needed for the preparation of a cash disbursements schedule for the months of October, November, and December.

Purchases   The firm's purchases represent 70 percent of their sales; 10 percent of this amount is paid in cash, 70 percent is paid in the month immediately following the month of purchase, and the remaining 20 percent is paid two months following the month of purchase.*

Cash dividends   Cash dividends of $20,000 will be paid in October.

Rent   Rent of $5,000 will be paid each month.

Wages and salaries   The firm's wages and salaries can be calculated by adding 10 percent of its monthly sales to the $8,000 fixed-cost figure (i.e., the salary component).

Tax payments   Taxes of $25,000 must be paid in December.†

Capital additions   A new machine costing $130,000 will be purchased and paid for in November.

Interest payments   An interest payment of $10,000 is due in December.

Sinking-fund payments   A $20,000 sinking-fund payment is also due in December.

Repurchases or retirements of shares   No repurchase or retirement of shares is expected to occur during the October-December period.

The firm's cash disbursement schedule, based on the data above, is presented in Table 5.9. Some items in Table 5.9 are explained in greater detail in the following paragraphs.

Table 5.9   A Schedule of Projected Cash Disbursements for the ABC Company ($000 omitted)

	Aug.	Sept.	Oct.	Nov.	Dec.
Purchases (.70 · sales)	$70	$140	$280	$210	$140
Cash purchases (.10)	$ 7	$ 14	$ 28	$ 21	$ 14
Payments					
Lagged one month (.70)		49	98	196	147
Lagged two months (.20)			14	28	56
Cash dividends			20		
Rent expense			5	5	5
Wages and salaries			48	38	28
Tax payments					25
Capital additions				130	
Interest payments					10
Sinking-fund payments					20
Total cash disbursements			$213	$418	$305

*Unlike the collection percentages for sales, the total of the payment percentages should equal 100 percent since it is expected that the firm will pay off all of its accounts payable. In line with this expectation, the ABC Company's percentages total 100 percent (10% + 70% + 20%).

†To simplify the presentation, it has been assumed that the taxes are due only in December. As was discussed in Chapter 2, the most widely used option of paying corporate taxes is equal monthly installments of estimated annual taxes, where the monthly installments begin four months after the end of the firm's fiscal year.

Purchases   This entry is merely informational. The figures represent 70 percent of the fore-cast sales for each month. They have been included at the top of the exhibit to facilitate the calculation of the cash purchases and related payments.

Cash purchases   The cash purchases for each month represent 10 percent of the month's purchases.

Payments   These entries represent the payment of accounts payable resulting from purchases in earlier months.

Lagged one month   These figures represent purchases made in the preceding month that are paid for in the current month. Since 70 percent of the firm's purchases are paid for one month later, the payments lagged one month shown for September, October, November, and December represent 70 present of the August, September, October, and November purchases, respectively.

Lagged two months   These figures represent purchases made two months earlier that are paid for in the current month. Since 20 percent of the firm's purchases are paid for two months later, the payments lagged two months for October, November, and December represent 20 percent of the August, September, and October purchases, respectively.

Wages and salaries   These values were obtained by adding $8,000 to 10 percent of the *sales* in each month. The $8,000 represents the salary component; the rest represents wages.

The remaining items on the cash disbursements schedule are self-explanatory.

The Net Cash Flow, Ending Cash, Financing, and Excess Cash   A firm's *net cash flow* is found by subtracting the cash disbursements from cash receipts in each month. By adding beginning cash to the firm's net cash flow, the ending cash for each month can be found. Finally, subtracting the minimum cash balance from ending cash yields the required total financing or the excess cash.

INTERPRETING THE CASH BUDGET

The cash budget provides the firm with figures indicating the expected ending cash balance, which can be analyzed to determine whether a cash shortage or cash surplus is

EXAMPLE   Table 5.10 presents the ABC Company's cash budget, based on the cash receipt and cash disbursement data already developed for the firm. ABC's end-of-September cash balance was $50,000, and it wishes to maintain a minimum cash balance of $25,000.

In order for the ABC Company to maintain its required $25,000 ending cash balance, it will need to have borrowed $76,000 in November and $41,000 in December. In the month of October the firm will have an excess cash balance of $22,000, which can be placed in some interest earning form. The required total financing figures in the cash budget refer to "how much will have to be owed at the end of month"; they *do not* show the additional borrowing required during the month. In order to clarify the meaning of these financing figures, Table 5.11 presents a different approach to evaluating the firm's required financing.

Table 5.10 A Cash Budget for the ABC Company ($000 omitted)

	Oct.	Nov.	Dec.
Total cash receipts[a]	$210	$320	$340
Less: Total cash disbursements[b]	213	418	305
Net cash flow	$ (3)	$ (98)	$ 35
Add: Beginning cash	50	47	(51)
Ending cash	$ 47	$ (51)	$ (16)
Less: Minimum cash balance	25	25	25
Required total financing[c]	—	$ 76	$ 41
Excess cash balance[d]	$ 22	—	—

[a]From Table 5.8.
[b]From Table 5.9.
[c]Values are placed in this line when the "ending cash" is less than the "minimum cash balance" since in this instance financing is required.
[d]Values are placed in this line when the "ending cash" is greater than the "minimum cash balance" since in this instance an excess cash balance exists.

Table 5.11 Another View of the ABC Company's Financing Requirements ($000 omitted)

	Oct.	Nov.	Dec.
Net cash flow[a]	$ (3)	$(98)	$ 35
Add: Beginning cash	50	47	25
Less: Minimum cash balance	25	25	25
Less: Excess cash balance	22	0	0
Additional financing (repayment)	$ 0	$ 76	$(35)
Total financing	$ 0	$ 76	$ 41

[a]From Table 5.10.

expected to result in each of the months covered by the forecast. The ABC Company can expect a surplus of $22,000 in October, a deficit of $76,000 in November, and a deficit of $41,000 in December. Each of these figures is based on the internally imposed requirement of a $25,000 minimum cash balance.

The excess cash balance in October can be invested in marketable securities. The deficits in November and December will have to be financed by borrowing—typically, short-term borrowing. Since it may be necessary for the firm to borrow up to $76,000 for the three-month period evaluated, the financial manager should be sure that such financing will be available. The financial manager may request or arrange to borrow more than the maximum required financing indicated in the cash budget because of the uncertainty of the ending cash values, which are based on the sales forecast and other forecast values.

MEASURING THE UNCERTAINTY INHERENT IN THE CASH BUDGET

There are two ways of measuring the uncertainty inherent in the cash budget.* One way is by preparing several cash budgets—one based on a pessimistic forecast, one based on the most likely forecast, and a third based on an optimistic forecast. This type of sensitivity analysis approach allows the financial manager to get an idea of the "worst," "most likely," and "best" ending cash flows that can be expected. An evaluation of the ending cash flows of the pessimistic forecast will allow the financial manager to determine the amount of financing necessary to cover the most adverse situation. The use of three cash budgets, each based on different assumptions, should also give the financial manager a feel for the riskiness of alternatives so that he or she can make more intelligent short-term financial decisions.

A second and more sophisticated way of measuring the uncertainty inherent in the cash budget is by computer simulation. By simulating the occurrence of sales and other uncertain events, a probability distribution of the firm's ending cash flows for each month can be developed. The financial decision maker can then determine the amount of financing necessary to provide a desired degree of protection against a cash shortage.

CASH FLOW WITHIN THE MONTH

Since the cash flows presented in the cash budget have been shown only on a total monthly basis, the information it provides is not necessarily adequate for assuring

EXAMPLE   Table 5.12 presents the summary results of ABC Company's cash budget prepared for each month of concern for a pessimistic, most likely, and optimistic estimate of cash receipts and cash disbursements. The most likely estimate is based upon the expected outcomes presented earlier in Tables 5.8 through 5.11, while the pessimistic and optimistic outcomes are based upon the worst and best possible outcomes respectively. During the month of October, the ABC Company will need at a maximum $15,000 of financing while at best they will have $62,000 excess cash balance available for short-term investment. During November, their financing requirement will be between $0 and $185,000. They could experience an excess cash balance of $5,000 during November. The December projections reflect maximum borrowing of $190,000 with a possible excess cash balance of $107,000. By considering the extreme values reflected in the pessimistic and optimistic outcomes, the ABC Company should be better able to plan their cash requirements. For the three-month period, their peak borrowing requirement under the worst circumstances would be $190,000, which happens to be considerably greater than the most likely estimate for this period of $76,000.

---

*The term *uncertainty* is used here to refer to the variability of the outcomes that may actually occur. A thorough discussion of risk and uncertainty and the various techniques available for adjusting for them appears in Chapter 16. Although that chapter discusses uncertainty in light of capital budgeting, many of the techniques covered can easily be applied to cash budgeting.

Table 5.12 A Sensitivity Analysis of ABC Company's Cash Budget ($000 omitted)

	October			November			December		
	Pessi-mistic	Most likely	Opti-mistic	Pessi-mistic	Most likely	Opti-mistic	Pessi-mistic	Most likely	Opti-mistic
Total cash receipts	$ 160	$ 210	$ 285	$ 210	$ 320	$ 410	$ 275	$ 340	$ 422
Less: Total cash disbursements	200	213	248	380	418	467	280	305	320
Net cash flow	$ (40)	$ (3)	$ 37	$(170)	$ (98)	$ (57)	$ (5)	$ 35	$102
Add: Beginning cash	50	50	50	10	47	87	(160)	(51)	30
Ending cash	$ 10	$ 47	$ 87	$(160)	$ (51)	$ 30	$(165)	$ (16)	$ 132
Less: Minimum cash balance	25	25	25	25	25	25	25	25	25
Required total financing	$ 15	—	—	$ 185	$ 76	—	$ 190	$ 41	—
Excess cash balance	—	$ 22	$ 62	—	—	$ 5	—	—	$107

solvency. Often a firm will examine its pattern of daily cash receipts and cash disbursements in order to make sure that adequate cash is available for meeting bill payments as they come due. The following example illustrates the importance of monitoring daily cash flows in order to understand the importance of variations in net cash flows within a month.

EXAMPLE The ABC Company, presented in the preceding series of examples, found its actual pattern of cash receipts and cash disbursements during the month of October to be as shown in Table 5.13. It can be seen that, although the firm begins the month with $50,000 of cash and ends the month with $47,000 in cash, its cash balance is negative during the periods October 2 to October 11 and October 17 to October 22. It can be seen that the largest deficit of $72,000 occurs on October 4.

Based upon the cash budget presented in Table 5.10, it appears that the ABC Company will not require any financing during the month of October, since a $22,000 excess cash balance is expected. However, a look at the firm's daily cash flows during October makes it quite clear that additional financing will be required in order to make payments as they come due. The maximum financing required to meet daily cash-flow requirements during October is expected to be $72,000.

Table 5.13 Daily Cash Flows During October for the ABC Company
($000 omitted)

Date	Amount received	Amount disbursed	Cash balance[a]
1/10	Beginning balance		$50
2/10		$100	−50
4/10		22	−72
5/10	$65	15	−22
11/10	74		52
12/10	10	12	50
16/10		40	10
17/10	3	21	−8
22/10	35		27
26/10	20	1	46
29/10	3		49
31/10		2	47
Total	$210	$213	

[a]These figures represent ending cash balances without any financing.

The preceding example shows that while a firm's cash flows as reflected by the cash budget may be synchronized such that at month end receipts exceed disbursements, this still does not ensure that the firm can meet its daily cash requirements. Since a firm's cash flows are generally quite variable when viewed on a daily basis, effective cash planning often requires an analysis of daily cash flows. The greater the variability of the firm's cash flows from day to day, the greater the attention that must be paid to analyzing daily cash flows and preparing for daily cash-flow shortages.

Summary

This chapter has emphasized two financial statements that are quite helpful in analyzing the firm's past and future financial needs. The source and use of funds statement was discussed both on a cash and on a net working capital basis. In order to make these statements more easily interpreted, they can be prepared on a percentage basis, in which each source or use is stated as a percent of the total sources or uses. The importance of this statement lies in the ability it gives the financial manager to evaluate past or projected sources and uses of funds. Analysis of the types and magnitude of sources and uses of funds may uncover problems in some area of the firm's financing. The existence of high levels of accounts receivable and inventories or low levels of accounts payable that may not be consistent with the firm's overall objectives may be detected in such an analysis.

The cash budget, which is often called the cash forecast, is also discussed in this chapter. The value of developing a cash budget in order to forecast the firm's short-term financial needs is emphasized. The cash budget relies heavily on the sales forecast as an input. The ability to forecast cash flows and therefore financial needs is important to the business firm—especially the firm with a seasonal pattern of sales. Typically, the cash budget is prepared for a one-year period divided into monthly intervals. The less seasonal the business, the more infrequent the budget intervals required. The basic format of the cash budget is such that cash receipts and cash disbursements for each period can easily be netted against each other to get the net cash flow in each period. By adding beginning cash to the net cash flow, the ending cash can be estimated. After subtracting the minimum cash balance from the ending cash, the required total financing or excess cash balance can be determined. Any needed financing or surplus funds can therefore be planned for in light of this estimate.

Care is suggested in the preparation of the cash budget, since it is closely tied to forecast data. In order to measure the uncertainty inherent in the cash budget, the use of sensitivity analysis or computer simulation is suggested. One common sensitivity analysis approach involves preparing separate cash budgets based upon pessimistic, most likely, and optimistic estimates. It is important to recognize that the cash budget does not ensure that on a day-to-day basis the firm will be able to meet its cash requirements. Only by monitoring daily cash flows can this problem be effectively handled. The major difference between the cash budget and the source and use of funds statement is that the cash budget is a *short-term* financial *planning* tool, whereas the source and use of funds statement is typically a *historical* statement used for evaluating past funds flows to determine whether their pattern is consistent with the firm's long-term financial goals.

Questions

5.1   What are the key differences between the source and use of funds statement and the cash budget? How does this affect their use by the financial manager?

5.2   What is net working capital? What is the basic premise for using it in evaluating a firm's sources and uses of funds?

5.3   Sometimes the cash flows of a firm are divided into two groups—operating flows and financial and legal flows. What are the key differences between these flows? What are some examples of each type?

5.4   What is meant by "sources of cash"? What are the basic sources of cash for the typical firm?

5.5   Why are depreciation and noncash charges considered sources of cash to the firm?

5.6   What is meant by a "use of cash"? What are the basic uses of cash for the typical business firm?

5.7   Is it possible for a firm to have a net loss but still have positive cash flows from operations? Why or why not?

5.8   What are the three basic inputs for a source and use of funds statement?

5.9   How would the change in the firm's fixed assets be found in each of the following instances?

    a.   The firm's balance sheets are detailed and include data on its fixed assets, accumulated depreciation, and net fixed assets.

    b. The firm's balance sheets include only a net fixed-asset figure.

5.10 How might one determine whether a firm paid cash dividends in the current year when the cash dividend is not shown on the firm's income statement?

5.11 Given growth in sales due to inflation, what changes would you expect to find on a firm's balance sheet? How would such changes be reflected in a statement of sources and uses of funds?

5.12 What basic approach should be used in preparing a source and use of cash statement? What steps are required?

5.13 Why do people often argue that the source and use of net working capital statement is just as informative as the source and use of cash statement?

5.14 How is the source and use statement, presented on a percentage basis, prepared and used by the financial manager? Explain why the use of percentages might be especially helpful.

5.15 What is the purpose of the cash budget from the point of view of the financial manager?

5.16 The key input to the cash budget is a sales forecast. What is the difference between external and internal forecast data?

5.17 What general format is used for the cash budget?

5.18 How can the bottom lines of the cash budget be used to determine the firm's short-term borrowing and investment requirements?

5.19 Normally, uncertainty is present in the cash budget. What is the cause of this uncertainty?

5.20 How can sensitivity analysis and computer simulation aid the financial manager to reduce the uncertainty in the cash budget?

5.21 Even with a monthly cash budget, the firm may not be assured of solvency. What actions or analysis beyond preparation of the cash budget should the financial manager undertake to assure cash is available when needed?

Problems

5.1 Classify the following items as sources or uses of funds, or as neither.

Item	Change ($)	Item	Change ($)
Cash	+ 100	Accounts receivable	− 700
Accounts payable	− 1,000	Net profits	+ 600
Notes payable	+ 500	Depreciation	+ 100
Long-term debt	− 2,000	Repurchase of shares	+ 600
Inventory	+ 200	Cash dividends	+ 800
Fixed assets	+ 400	Sale of shares	+ 1,000

5.2 Using the following balance sheet data for Downing Cushion Company, indicate the change in fixed assets and classify this change as either a source or use of funds. Explain your answer.

a.

	19X0	19X1
Fixed assets	$60,000	$62,000
Less: Accumulated depreciation	− 18,000	− 23,000
Net fixed assets	$42,000	$39,000

b.

	19X0	19X1
Fixed assets	$50,000	$46,000
Less: Accumulated depreciation	− 18,000	− 23,000
Net fixed assets	$32,000	$23,000

5.3 Given the following balance sheet and income statement data for the Raney Russell Company:

a. Prepare and interpret a source and use of cash statement.
b. Prepare and interpret a source and use of net working capital statement.
c. Prepare and interpret a source and use of cash statement on a percentage basis.

Balance Sheet
Raney Russell Company
Years Ending December 31

Assets	19X0	19X1
Cash	$ 2,200	$ 2,800
Marketable securities	1,000	1,500
Inventory	3,600	3,900
Total current assets	$ 6,800	$ 8,200
Net plant and equipment	$15,000	$14,800
Total	$21,800	$23,000

Liabilities and shareholders' equity	19X0	19X1
Accounts payable	$ 1,500	$ 1,600
Notes payable—bank	2,500	3,000
Total current liabilities	$ 4,000	$ 4,600
Long-term debt	$ 5,000	$ 5,000
Common shares	$10,000	$10,000
Retained earnings	2,800	3,400
Total	$21,800	$23,000

Additional data	
Depreciation	$ 1,600
Earnings after taxes	$ 1,400

5.4 Use the following financial data for the Gold Equipment Company to

a. Prepare and interpret a source and use of cash statement.
b. Prepare and interpret a source and use of net working capital statement.
c. Prepare and interpret a source and use of cash statement on a percentage basis.

Balance Sheet
Gold Equipment Company
Years Ending December 31

Assets	19X0	19X1
Cash	$ 16,000	$ 15,000
Marketable securities	8,000	7,200
Accounts receivable	40,000	33,000
Inventory	50,000	82,000
Prepaid rent	2,200	1,100
Total current assets	$116,200	$138,300
Net plant and equipment	$285,000	$270,000
Total assets	$401,200	$408,300

Liabilities and shareholders' equity		
Accounts payable	$ 49,000	$ 57,000
Notes payable	16,000	13,000
Accruals	6,000	5,000
Total current liabilities	$ 71,000	$ 75,000
Long-term debt	$160,000	$150,000
Shareholders' equity	$170,200	$183,300
Total liabilities and equity	$401,200	$408,300

Income Statement
Gold Equipment Company
Year Ending December 31, 19X1

Sales		$600,000
Less: Cost of goods sold		460,000
Gross profit		$140,000
Less: Expenses		
General and administrative	$ 40,000	
Depreciation	30,000	
Total		70,000
Profits before taxes		$ 70,000
Less: Taxes		27,100
Profits after taxes		$ 42,900
Less: Cash dividends		20,000
To retained earnings		$ 22,900

5.5 A firm has actual sales of $65,000 in April and $60,000 in May. It expects sales of $70,000 in June and $100,000 in July and August, respectively. Assuming sales are the only source of cash inflows and half of these are for cash while the remainder are collected evenly over the following two months, what are the firm's expected cash receipts for July and August?

5.6   The Alberta Tire Company had sales of $50,000 in March and $60,000 in April. Forecast sales for May, June, and July are $70,000, $80,000, and $100,000, respectively. The firm has a cash balance of $5,000 on May 1. Given the following data prepare and interpret a cash budget for the months of May, June, and July.

(1) Twenty percent of the firm's sales are for cash, 60 percent are collected in the next month, the remaining 20 percent are collected in the second month following sale.
(2) The firm receives other income of $2,000 per month.
(3) The firm's actual or expected purchases are $50,000, $70,000, and $80,000 for the months of May through July, respectively.
(4) Rent is $3,000 per month.
(5) Wages and salaries are 10 percent of the previous month's sales.
(6) Cash dividends of $3,000 will be paid in June.
(7) Payment of principal and interest of $4,000 is due in June.
(8) A cash purchase of equipment costing $6,000 is scheduled in July.
(9) Taxes of $6,000 are due in June.

5.7   Archer Appliance Company's actual sales and purchases for September and October 19X0, along with its forecast sales and purchases for the period November 19X0 through April 19X1, are presented below.

Year	Month	Sales	Purchases
19X0	Sept.	$210,000	$120,000
19X0	Oct.	250,000	150,000
19X0	Nov.	170,000	140,000
19X0	Dec.	160,000	100,000
19X1	Jan.	140,000	80,000
19X1	Feb.	180,000	110,000
19X1	Mar.	200,000	100,000
19X1	Apr.	250,000	90,000

The firm makes 20 percent of all sales for cash and collects on 40 percent of its sales in each of the two months following the sale. Other cash inflows are expected to be $12,000 in September, February, and April, and $15,000 in January, February, and March. The firm pays cash for 10 percent of its purchases. It pays for 50 percent of its purchases in the following month and 40 percent of its purchases two months later.

Salaries and wages amount to 20 percent of the preceding month's sales. Rent of $20,000 per month must be paid. Interest payments of $10,000 are due in January and April. A principal payment of $30,000 is also due in April. The firm expects to pay cash dividends of $20,000 in January and April. Taxes of $80,000 are due in April. The firm also intends to make a capital outlay of $25,000 in December.

a. Assuming that the firm has a cash balance of $22,000 at the beginning of November, determine the end-of-month cash balances for each month from November through April.
b. Assuming that the firm wishes to maintain a $15,000 minimum cash balance, determine the monthly borrowing requirements or excess cash.
c. If the firm were requesting a line of credit in order to cover needed borrowing for the period of November to April, how large would this line have to be? Explain your answer.

•

5.8   Patterson's Parts Store expects to sell $100,000 in parts during each of the next three months. It is committed to accept monthly purchases of $60,000 during this time. Wages and salaries are $10,000 per month plus 5 percent of sales. Patterson's expects to make a tax payment of $20,000 in the next month, make a capital expenditure of $15,000 in the second month, and receive $8,000 of cash from the sale of an asset in the third month. All sales are for cash. Beginning cash balances are assumed to be zero.

a. Construct a cash budget for the next three months.

b. Patterson's only uncertainty is in the sales levels. If the most pessimistic sales figure is $80,000 per month and the most optimistic is $120,000 per month, what are the monthly minimum and maximum cash balances the firm can expect for each of the next three one-month periods?

c. Combine **a** and **b** into a sensitivity analysis for Patterson's Parts Store. Briefly discuss how these combined data allow the financial manager to plan for his financing needs.

Suggested Readings

Anthony, Ted F. and Hugh J. Watson, "Probabilistic Financial Planning," *Journal of Systems Management* 23 (September 1972), pp. 38–41.

Bogen, Jules I., Ed., *Financial Handbook*, 4th ed. (New York: Ronald, 1968), sect. 15.

Foulke, R. A., *Practical Financial Statement Analysis*, 6th ed. (New York: McGraw-Hill, 1968).

Gitman, Lawrence J. and Thomas M. Cook, "Cash Budgeting: A Simulation Approach," *Journal of the Midwest Finance Association* (1973), pp. 87–100.

Helfert, Erich A., *Techniques of Financial Analysis*, 4th ed. (Homewood, Ill.: Irwin, 1976), chaps. 1 and 5.

Jaedicke, Robert K. and Robert T. Sprouse, *Accounting Flows: Income, Funds, and Cash* (Englewood Cliffs, N.J.: Prentice-Hall, 1965), chaps. 5 and 6.

Lerner, Eugene M., "Simulating a Cash Budget," *California Management Review* 11 (Winter 1968), pp. 79–86.

Lynch, Richard M., *Accounting for Management: Planning and Control* (New York: McGraw-Hill, 1967), chap. 6.

Meigs, Walter B., A. N. Mosich, Charles E. Johnson, and Thomas F. Keller, *Financial Accounting*, 3rd ed. (New York: McGraw-Hill, 1974), chaps. 22 and 23.

Moore, Laurence J. and David F. Scott, "Simulation of Cash Budgets," *Journal of Systems Management* 24 (November 1973), pp. 28–33.

Packer, Stephen B., "Flow of Funds Analysis—Its Uses and Limitations," *Financial Analysts Journal* (July-August 1964), pp. 117–123.

Pan, Judy, Donald R. Nichols, and O. Maurice Joy, "Sales Forecasting Practice of Large U.S. Industrial Firms," *Financial Management* 6 (Fall 1977), pp. 72–77.

Pappas, James L. and George P. Huber, "Probabilistic Short-Term Financial Planning," *Financial Management* 2 (Autumn 1973), pp. 36–44.

Seitz, Neil, *Financial Analysis: A Programmed Approach* (Reston, Va.: Reston Publishing Co., 1976), chaps. 1 and 2.

Stone, Bernell K. and Robert A. Wood, "Daily Cash Forecasting: A Simple Method for Implementing the Distribution Approach," *Financial Management* 6 (Fall 1977), pp. 40–50.

Trumbull, Wendell P., "Developing the Funds Statement as the Third Major Financial Statement," *N.A.A. Bulletin* 45 (April 1963), pp. 21–31.

Viscione, Jerry A., *Financial Analysis: Principles and Procedures* (Boston: Houghton Mifflin, 1977), chaps. 2 and 3.

Welsch, Glenn A., Charles T. Zlatkovich, and John A. White, *Intermediate Accounting*, 4th ed. (Homewood, Ill.: Irwin, 1976), chap. 25.

Wright, Leonard T., *Financial Management: Analytical Techniques* (Columbus, Ohio: Grid, 1974), chaps. 3 and 4.

Chapter 6

PRO FORMA STATEMENTS

Pro forma statements are projected financial statements. Typically, such statements are financial forecasts for a firm's forthcoming fiscal year. The firm's pro forma income statement shows its expected revenues and costs for the coming year, while its pro forma balance sheet shows its expected financial position (i.e., its assets, liabilities, and shareholders' equity) at the end of the forecast period. Pro forma statements are not only useful in the internal financial planning process, but are also typically required by interested outside parties, such as current and prospective lenders, who want an estimate of the firm's financial position at the end of the coming period. A firm's actual performance can be evaluated with respect to these estimates in order to determine their accuracy and to make adjustments for any observed discrepancies. Pro forma statements differ from the cash budget in that they provide estimates not just of future cash requirements but of all assets, liabilities, equities, and income statement items.

This chapter has six major sections. The first section presents an overview of the entire budgeting process and relates the various budgeting inputs to pro forma statements. The second section is devoted to "simplified" approaches commonly used in the preparation of pro forma income statements and balance sheets. The third section describes the steps involved in preparing the additional data (budgets) that are used in the more "sophisticated" approach to the preparation of pro forma statements. In particular, the sales forecast, the production plan, the raw-material-usage plan, raw material purchases, direct labour requirements, factory overhead, operating expenses, the long-term financing plan, and the capital expenditure plan are developed in the third section. In the fourth and fifth sections, the pro forma income statement and the pro forma balance sheet, respectively, are developed using the sophisticated approach. The final section discusses the value of pro forma statements to small businesses.

Budgeting Inputs to Pro Forma Preparation

In order to prepare the firm's pro forma income statement and balance sheet correctly, certain preliminary budgets must be developed. This series of budgets begins with the firm's sales forecasts and ends with the cash budget. The total budgeting process, from the initial sales forecasts through the development of the pro forma income statement and balance sheet, is presented in a flow-chart format in Figure 6.1.

The key (and the most important input information) for the development of pro forma statements is the *sales forecast*. Although an accurate sales forecast is of the utmost importance, we shall assume in this chapter that a sales forecast has been made and is available for our use.*

Using the sales forecast as a basic input, a production plan is developed that takes into account the amount of "lead time" necessary to convert an item from a raw material into a finished good. The types and quantities of raw materials required during the forecast period can be estimated from the production plan. Based on these material usage estimates, a schedule of when and how much of each raw material to purchase can be developed. Also based on the production plan, estimates of the amount of direct labour required, in either man-hours or dollars, can be made. The firm's overhead outlays can also be estimated. Finally, the firm's operating expenses, specifically its sales and administrative expenses, can be estimated based on the level of operations necessary to support forecast sales.

Once this series of plans has been prepared, the firm's pro forma income statement can be developed. The firm's cash budget, based on monthly or quarterly breakdowns of cash receipts and disbursements, can also be created. With the pro forma income statement, the cash budget, the long-term financing plan, the capital expenditure plan, and the current period's balance sheet as basic inputs, the firm's pro forma balance sheet can be developed. The pro forma income statement is needed to find the projected change in retained earnings, depreciation, and taxes. Data on the firm's cash balance, notes payable, level of accounts receivable, and level of accounts payable can be obtained from the cash budget. The long-term financing plan provides information on changes in long-term debts and shareholders' equity attributed to the firm's financing decisions. The capital expenditure plan provides information regarding expected changes in the firm's fixed assets.

The preceding period's balance sheet is necessary in order to have initial values against which to measure changes in various balance sheet items, such as fixed assets, common shares, and retained earnings. The values for beginning cash, beginning accounts receivable, beginning inventory, and beginning debts are also derived from the most recent period's balance sheet. It is often quite helpful to compare the pro forma balance sheet to the current balance sheet to check the reasonableness of the forecast statement; a glaring discrepancy may exist that can be reconciled through further analysis.

---

*A discussion of various mechanical forecasting techniques, such as regression, moving averages, and exponential smoothing, is not included in this text. Refer to a basic statistics, econometrics, or management science text for a description of the technical side of forecasting. Some references on the subject have been included at the end of this chapter.

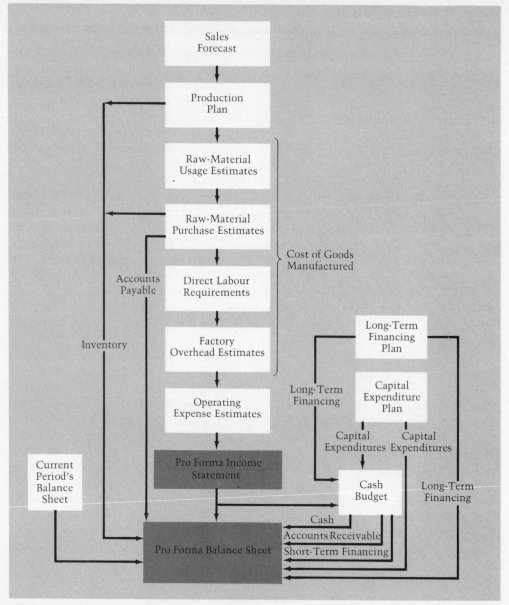

Figure 6.1 Budgeting inputs for pro forma statements.

A "Simplified" Approach to Pro Forma Preparation

Before treating a more "sophisticated" method for preparing pro forma statements, it is useful to discuss the commonly used and more naive methods for pro forma preparation. Since the procedures outlined by the flow chart in Figure 6.1 are quite tedious and time consuming, shortcut approaches often are used to get a feel for the firm's projected financial condition. Although the use of such simplified methods may not be as accurate as the longer approach, its appeal lies in its ease of application and its often surprising accuracy. Furthermore, this is often the only approach available to an outside analyst, such as a security analyst.

A variety of simplified approaches exist for preparing pro forma statements; the most popular are based upon the belief that the financial relationships reflected in the firm's historic financial statements will not change in the coming period. The most common of the shortcut pro forma preparation techniques is presented over the next few pages.

BACKGROUND INFORMATION

The inputs required for preparing pro forma statements using the simplified approach are recent financial statements and a sales forecast. A variety of assumptions must also be made when using this approach. Throughout this chapter we will examine DuBois Manufacturing Ltd., a company that manufactures and sells one basic product—widgets. DuBois has two basic models of widgets—model X and model Y. Although each model is produced by the same process, they require different amounts of raw material and labour. The products are produced from two raw materials—A and B.

Recent Financial Statements   The firm's income statement for the 19X0 operations is given in Table 6.1. It indicates that the firm paid $4,000 in cash dividends in the

---

Table 6.1   An Income Statement for DuBois Manufacturing Ltd.
for the Year Ended December 31, 19X0

Sales		
Model X (1,000 units at $20 each)	$20,000	
Model Y (3,000 units at $27 each)	81,000	
Total sales		$101,000
Less: Cost of goods sold		
Labour	$28,500	
Material A	8,000	
Material B	5,500	
Overhead	38,000	
Total cost of goods sold		80,000
Gross profits		$ 21,000
Less: Operating expense		10,000
Operating profits		$ 11,000
Less: Interest expense		1,000
Profits before taxes		$ 10,000
Less: Taxes (.20 · $10,000)		2,000
Profits after taxes		$ 8,000
Less: Common share dividends		4,000
To retained earnings		$ 4,000

Table 6.2   A Balance Sheet for DuBois Manufacturing Ltd. for the Year Ended December 31, 19X0

Assets		Liabilities and equities	
Cash	$ 6,000.00	Accounts payable	$12,000.00
Marketable Securities	4,016.40	Taxes payable	3,740.00
Accounts receivable	13,000.00	Other current liabilities	6,260.00
Inventory	15,983.60	Total current liabilities	$22,000.00
Total current assets	$39,000.00	Long-term debt	$15,000.00
Net fixed assets	51,000.00	Shareholders' equity	
		Common shares	$30,000.00
Total assets	$90,000.00	Retained earnings	$23,000.00
		Total liabilities and shareholders' equity	$90,000.00

most recent period of operation. The firm's balance sheet for the most recent period of operation, 19X0, is given in Table 6.2.

The Sales Forecast   The sales forecast for the coming year, 19X1, for the DuBois Company is given in Table 6.3. The unit sale prices given reflect an increase from $20 to $25 for model X and from $27 to $35 for model Y. These increases are required in order to cover the firm's anticipated increases in labour, overhead, and sales and administrative costs.

THE PRO FORMA INCOME STATEMENT

A simple way to develop a pro forma income statement is to use the percent-of-sale method. The first step in such a method is to identify those income statement items that can be expected to vary directly with sales. These include cost of goods sold and operating expenses. They do not include interest expense.*

Table 6.3   19X1 Sales Forecast for DuBois Manufacturing Ltd.

Unit sales	
Model X	1,500
Model Y	2,800
Dollar sales	
Model X ($25/unit)	$ 37,500
Model Y ($35/unit)	98,000
Total	$135,500

*Balance sheet items that can be expected to vary directly with sales include accounts receivable, inventory, fixed assets, accounts payable, and accruals. They do not include long-term liabilities (such as mortgages and bonds), common and preferred shares, and retained earnings. Although cash is generally treated as if it varies directly with sales, this is generally an inappropriate assumption for rapidly growing firms.

The second step is to forecast the income statement items that vary directly with sales, by utilizing the past relationship between each item and sales and the projected sales for the forthcoming period. The past relationships (percentages) used are generally the percentage of sales these items equaled in a previous year. For DuBois Manufacturing Ltd., these percentages are as follows:

$$\frac{19X0 \text{ cost of goods sold}}{19X0 \text{ sales}} = \frac{\$80,000}{\$101,000} = 79.2\%$$

$$\frac{19X0 \text{ operating expenses}}{19X0 \text{ sales}} = \frac{\$10,000}{\$101,000} = 9.9\%$$

First, it is necessary to assume that the firm will continue to pay $1,000 and $4,000 in interest and dividends, respectively, in 19X1. Then, applying the previous historic relationships (percentages) to DuBois's forecasted sales of $135,500 results in the pro forma income statement in Table 6.4.

Considering Types of Costs and Expenses It is important to recognize that the techniques used to prepare the pro forma income statement in Table 6.4 assume that all of the firm's costs are variable. The use of the historic (i.e., actual 19X0) ratios of cost of goods sold and operating expenses to sales assumes that for a given percent increase in future sales, the cost of goods sold and operating expenses will correspondingly increase so that the historic ratio of each of these items to sales is maintained. For example, as DuBois's sales increased by 34.2 percent (from $101,000 in 19X0 to $135,500 projected for 19X1), its cost of goods sold also increased by 34.2 percent (from $80,000 in 19X0 to $107,316 projected for 19X1). Because of this fixed percentage assumption, the firm's profits before interest and taxes also increased by 34.2 percent (from $11,000 in 19X0 to $13,769.50 projected for 19X1).

Table 6.4 A Pro Forma Income Statement, Using the Simplified Approach, for DuBois Manufacturing Ltd. for the Year Ended December 31, 19X1

Sales	$135,500.00
Less: Cost of goods sold (79.2%)	107,316.00
Gross profits	$ 28,184.00
Less: Operating expense (9.9%)	13,414.50
Operating profits	$ 14,769.50
Less: Interest expense	1,000.00
Profits before taxes	$ 13,769.50
Less: Taxes (.20 · $13,414.50)	2,753.90
Profits after taxes	$ 11,015.60
Less: Common share dividends	4,000.00
To retained earnings	$ 7,015.60

A broader implication of such an assumption is that a firm with no fixed costs can have no leverage. Thus, the greater the percentage of fixed costs in the firm's operating and financial structure, the larger the understatement of profits by using the simplified forecasting technique. A way to adjust for the presence of fixed costs, when using the simplified approach for pro forma income statement preparation, is to divide the firm's historic costs into fixed and variable components, and to utilize these resultant classifications in making the forecasts.

EXAMPLE   The ABC Company's past year and pro forma income statements, which are broken into fixed and variable cost components, are as follows:

ABC Company Income Statements

	Past year	Pro forma
Sales	$100,000	$120,000
Less: Cost of goods sold		
Fixed cost	20,000	20,000
Variable cost (.40 sales)	40,000	48,000
Gross profit	$ 40,000	$ 52,000
Less: Operating expense		
Fixed expense	5,000	5,000
Variable expense (.15 sales)	15,000	18,000
Operating profit (profit before interest and taxes)	$ 20,000	$ 29,000
Less: Interest (all fixed)	8,000	8,000
Profit before tax	$ 12,000	$ 21,000
Tax (.20 · profit before tax)	2,400	4,200
Profit after taxes	$ 9,600	$ 16,800

By breaking its costs and expenses into fixed and variable components, the ABC Company's pro forma income is expected to provide a more accurate projection. Had the firm treated all costs as variable, its pro forma profits before interest and taxes would equal 20 percent of sales, just as was the case in the last year ($20,000 profits before interest and taxes ÷ $100,000 sales). The profit before interest and taxes would therefore have been $24,000 (20% · $120,000 sales), instead of the $29,000 profit before interest and tax value found using the firm's fixed cost-variable cost breakdown.

The preceding example should make it clear that when using a simplified approach to pro forma income statement preparation, it is advisable to consider first the breakdown of costs and expenses into their fixed and variable components. Due to a lack of available data, the pro forma income statement prepared for DuBois Manufacturing Ltd. in Table 6.4 has to be based upon the unlikely assumption that all costs are variable. Therefore, its projected profits may be understated.

Table 6.5   A Pro Forma Balance Sheet, Expressed As a Percent of Sales, for DuBois Manufacturing Ltd. for the Year Ended December 31, 19X1

Assets		Liabilities and equities	
Cash	5.9	Accounts payable	11.9
Marketable securities	4.0	Taxes payable	3.7
Accounts receivable	12.9	Other current liabilities	6.2
Inventory	15.8	Long-term debt	—
Net fixed assets	50.5	Common shares	—
Total assets	89.1	Retained earnings	—
		Total liabilities and shareholders' equity	21.8

Assets as a percent of sales	89.1
Less: Spontaneous increase in liabilities	21.8
Percent of each additional dollar in sales that must be financed from nonspontaneous sources	67.3

THE PRO FORMA BALANCE SHEET

Two simplified approaches for developing the pro forma balance sheet are (1) using a percent-of-sales method, or (2) using judgmental estimates of the desired levels of certain balance sheet items. When either approach is employed, the levels of long-term liabilities and shareholders' equity are assumed to remain unchanged, and the firm's required financing is used as a balancing (plug) figure.*

PERCENT-OF-SALES FORECAST

The items that can be expected to vary directly with sales are tabulated as a percentage of sales in Table 6.5. For every $1.00 increase in sales, assets are expected to increase by $0.891, and spontaneous increases in current liabilities are expected to be $0.218. Thus, for each $1.00 increase in sales, DuBois Ltd. must obtain $0.673 (i.e., $0.891 − $0.218) of financing either from operations (retained earnings) or from external sources (issuance of debt or equity).

For DuBois Manufacturing Ltd., sales are expected to increase from $101,000 to $135,500, or by $34,500. Thus, DuBois Ltd. must obtain $23,218.50 ($34,500 · 67.3%) of additional financing to support the increased level of sales. From the pro forma income statement (Table 6.4), $7,015.60 will be from operations (retained earnings), *provided that there is no issuance of debt or equity by the firm during the period.* The remainder, $16,202.90, must be obtained by the issuance of debt or equity.†

*Note that these are contradictory assumptions. More specifically, if the firm's required financing for the period is greater than the retained earnings for the period, then the difference must be obtained by issuing either debt or equity.

†Note that the issuance of debt or equity will result in larger interest or dividend payments for the period. These in turn will lower the estimated retained earnings for the period, which increases the amount of the firm's required financing, and so on. Fortunately, this recursive relationship converges quickly.

To find the amount (if any) of external financing required when one is given this type of data, the following formula is used:

$$EFR_T = \frac{A_t}{S_t}(\Delta S_T) - \frac{L_t}{S_t}(\Delta S_T) - M_T S_T (1 - d_T) \qquad (6.1)$$

where

EFR_T = amount of external financing required for the forecast period T, where T is typically one year

A_t = value of the assets that increase spontaneously with sales on the latest balance sheet (for period t)

L_t = value of the liabilities that increase spontaneously with sales on the latest balance sheet (for period t)

S_t = sales on the latest income statement (for period t)

ΔS_T = forecasted change in sales for the forecast period T

M_T = forecasted after-tax profit margin for the forecast period T

S_T = forecasted total sales for the forecast period T

d_T = projected dividend payout percentage for the forecast period T

Substituting the data above into Equation 6.1 yields

$$EFR_T = (0.891)\,(\$34{,}500) - (0.218)\,(\$34{,}500) - (0.081)\,(\$135{,}500)\,(1 - 0.363)$$
$$\approx \$16{,}202.90$$

As expected, the result is the same as that calculated earlier.

The advantage of Formula 6.1 is that it can be easily used to measure the sensitivity of required external financing to alternate forecasts of sales, after-tax profit margins, or projected dividend payout percentages.

JUDGMENTAL FORECAST

In order to apply this approach, a number of judgmental estimates must be made:

1 A minimum cash balance of $6,000 is desired.
2 Accounts receivable will average three-fourths of a month's sales (i.e., an average age of accounts receivable of $30 \cdot .75 = 22.5$ days). Since DuBois's annual sales are projected to be $135,000, the accounts receivable should average $8,468.75 ($\frac{1}{16} \cdot$ $135,000) in any given month. (One-sixteenth represents three-fourths of a month expressed as a fraction of a year.)
3 The ending inventory should remain at a level of about $16,000, of which 25 percent (approximately $4,000) should be raw materials, while the remaining 75 percent (approximately $12,000) should consist of finished goods.
4 A frame building costing $20,000 will be purchased. The frame building will be the firm's only asset in Class 6, which has an applicable CCA of 10 percent. Thus, adding the $20,000 acquisition price of the frame building to the firm's current fixed assets of $51,000, and subtracting expected depreciation of $7,000 ($5,000 of depreciation for

all the classes of fixed assets currently held by the firm + $2,000 of depreciation to be taken on the new asset class, that is, the frame building) will yield net fixed assets of $64,000 at the end of the forecasted period.

5 Purchases are expected to represent approximately 20 percent of annual sales, which in this case would be approximately $27,000 (.20 · $135,500). The firm believes it can stretch the time it takes to pay its accounts payable to approximately 45 days. Thus, accounts payable should equal, on the average, one-eighth (i.e., 45 days ÷ 360 days) of the firm's purchases, or $3,375 ($\frac{1}{8}$ · $27,000).

6 Taxes payable are expected to equal the current year's tax liability, which is $2,753.90 on the pro forma income statement given in Table 6.4.

7 No change in other current liabilities is expected. They will remain at the level of the previous year, $6,260.

8 The firm's long-term debts and its common shares are expected to remain unchanged, at $15,000 and $30,000, respectively, since no issues, repurchases, or retirements of bonds or shares are planned.

9 Retained earnings will increase from the beginning level of $23,000 to $30,015.60. The increase of $7,015.60 represents the amount of retained earnings given in the pro forma income statement (Table 6.4).

A 19X1 pro forma balance sheet for DuBois Manufacturing Ltd., based on these estimates, is presented in Table 6.6.

Although the values shown in the pro forma balance sheets in Tables 6.5 and 6.6 provide a feel for the firm's financial position one year hence, more reliable estimates are expected to result from the application of the procedures reflected in the flow chart

Table 6.6 A Pro Forma Balance Sheet, Using the Simplified Approach for DuBois Manufacturing Ltd. for the Year Ended December 31, 19X1

Assets			Liabilities and equities	
Cash		$ 6,000.00	Accounts payable	$ 3,375.00
Marketable securities			Taxes payable	2,753.90
(unchanged)		4,016.40	Other current liabilities	6,260.00
Accounts receivable		8,468.75	Total current liabilities	$12,388.90
Inventories			Long-term debt	$15,000.00
Raw materials	$ 4,000.00		Shareholders' equity	
Finished goods	12,000.00		Common shares	$30,000.00
Total		16,000.00	Retained earnings	30,015.60
Total current assets		$34,485.15	Total liabilities and	
Net fixed assets		64,000.00	shareholders' equity	$87,404.50
Total assets		$98,485.15	Required external financing	
			(plug figure[a])	$11,080.65
			Total	$98,485.15

[a]The plug figure represents financing necessary to force the firm's balance sheet to balance. Due to the nature of the simplified approaches to preparing the pro forma balance sheet (especially for a growing firm), the balance sheet is not expected to balance without some type of adjustment.

given in Figure 6.1. While the simplified approaches are based on determining the effects desired, developing a balance sheet based on these effects, and balancing it with a plug figure, the longer and more sophisticated approach for pro forma preparation presented in a subsequent section of this chapter is based on determining the causes and then calculating the effects.

WEAKNESSES OF THE SIMPLIFIED APPROACHES

The basic weaknesses of the simplified approaches to pro forma statement preparation lie in (1) assuming that the firm's past financial condition is an accurate predictor of its future financial condition, and (2) assuming that the values of certain variables such as cash, inventory, and accounts receivable can be forced to take on certain "desired" values. These assumptions are quite questionable, especially for long-term forecasts, but due to the ease of the calculations involved, the use of simplified approaches similar to those illustrated is quite common.

NONMECHANICAL USE OF THE SIMPLIFIED APPROACH

In practice, the simplified approach to pro forma preparation should be applied, with appropriate adjustments being made for (1) the basic technology of the firm, (2) the logical validity of the relationship between sales and assets for the particular firm, and (3) the impact of expected changes in nonfirm (external) factors, such as the implementation of federal wage and price controls. For example, if a firm decides to enter into a product line that uses a different technology than the firm is presently using, then the historical relationships between assets and sales may not be relevant. Also, the possibility of a prolonged work stoppage by the firm's employees may invalidate the future usage of the past relationships between assets and sales.

The simplified approaches can also be supplemented by the use of more sophisticated statistical forecasting techniques, such as simple and multiple regression. However, as in all other applications of financial analysis, the *known* cost of using more refined techniques must be evaluated against the benefits of the *expected* increase in accuracy of using more sophisticated forecasting techniques.

The "Sophisticated" Approach to Pro Forma Preparation: Preliminary Budgets

In order to prepare pro forma statements using the longer, more sophisticated approach described by Figure 6.1, additional data—both historic and projected—are required. Using the background data along with the past financial statements and sales forecast presented earlier in Tables 6.1 through 6.3, DuBois Manufacturing Ltd. can prepare a variety of plans that act as inputs to the pro forma statements.

DEVELOPING BACKGROUND INFORMATION

As indicated in the preceding part of the chapter, Dubois Manufacturing Ltd. produces and sells two basic models of widgets—model X and model Y. Although each model is

Table 6.7 19X0 Labour and Material Costs/Unit for DuBois Manufacturing Ltd.

	Model	
	X	Y
Direct labour	$6.00	$7.50
Raw materials cost		
A	$2.00	$2.00
B	1.00	1.50
Raw-materials cost/unit	$3.00	$3.50

produced by the same process, they require different amounts of raw material and labour. As was shown in Table 6.1, DuBois's total 19X0 sales equaled $101,000.

Labour and Materials The labour and material requirements, along with the cost per unit, for each model are given in Table 6.7. As indicated in the table, each model of the product is made from two basic raw materials. Material A costs $2.00 per unit, and B costs $0.50 per unit. Direct labour costs $3.00 per hour. Using these values, Table 6.7 can be recast to show per unit labour and material requirements. This is done in Table 6.8.

Factory Overhead The firm's factory-overhead costs, which represent the outlays necessary to support production, totaled $38,000. These costs are itemized in Table 6.9. Factory overhead costs are normally applied to each product on the basis of the labour cost per unit, labour hours per unit, or floor space used. The DuBois Manufacturing Company allocated its factory overhead on the basis of direct labour costs. Table 6.10 presents a breakdown of the total overhead costs on a unit-cost basis, which will be used in the production planning phase of developing the firm's pro forma statements.

Table 6.8 19X0 Unit Labour and Material Requirements for DuBois Manufacturing Ltd.

	Model	
	X	Y
Direct labour (hours)	2.0	2.5
Raw materials (units)		
A	1.0	1.0
B	2.0	3.0

Note: All the unit figures were found by dividing the items in Table 6.7 by the cost per unit, which was $3.00 per labour hour, $2.00 per unit of raw material A, and $0.50 per unit of raw material B.

Table 6.9 A 19X0 Factory-Overhead Breakdown for DuBois Manufacturing Ltd.

Indirect labour	$ 6,000
Factory supplies	5,200
Heat, light, and power	2,000
Supervision	8,000
Maintenance	3,500
Engineering	5,500
Property and payroll taxes and insurance	2,800
Depreciation	5,000
Total factory overhead	$38,000

By adding the labour cost per unit and material cost per unit from Table 6.7 to the overhead allocation per unit from Table 6.10, the total cost per unit can be found. The total cost per unit for models X and Y is $16.98 and $21.00, respectively.

Operating Expenses The firm's operating expenses, which consist of sales and administrative expenses for the most recent year, are given in Table 6.11.

The Inventory Breakdown The inventory shown on the firm's 19X0 balance sheet (Table 6.2) consists only of raw materials and finished goods. No work-in-process inventory remains at the end of the year. Table 6.12 presents the firm's current inventory breakdown based on type of raw material and on model.

Table 6.10 A 19X0 Breakdown of Factory Overhead on the Basis of Direct Labour Costs for DuBois Manufacturing Ltd.

	Model	
Item	X	Y
(1) Direct labour cost/unit	$ 6.00	$ 7.50
(2) Number of units produced (sold)	1,000	3,000
(3) Total labour cost/model	$6,000	$22,500
(4) Total labour cost	$28,500	
(5) Percentage of total labour cost/model	21%	79%
(6) Overhead allocation	$7,980	$30,020
(7) Overhead allocation/unit	$ 7.98	$ 10.00

SOURCES: Item (1)—from Table 6.7.
       Item (2)—from Table 6.1.
       Item (3)—item (1) · item (2).
       Item (4)—sum of item (3) for models X and Y.
       Item (5)—item (3) for each model as a percentage of item (4).
       Item (6)—item (5) · total factory overhead ($38,000).
       Item (7)—item (6) ÷ item (2).

Table 6.11   19X0 Operating Expenses for DuBois Manufacturing Ltd.

Selling expense:		
Sales salaries	$3,000	
Freight out	800	
Advertising	1,200	
Total selling expense		$ 5,000
Administrative expense:		
Administrative salaries	$3,100	
Office supplies	700	
Telephone	300	
Professional fees	900	
Total administrative expense		5,000
Total 19X0 operating expenses		$10,000

DEVELOPING THE REQUIRED PLANS

The following sections are devoted to the development of the forecasts and plans required as inputs to the pro forma statements. (See Figure 6.1.)

The Production Plan   In order to estimate the required level of production for each model, the production plan for the year shown in Table 6.13 was drawn up. The firm's goal is to maintain in its finished goods inventory 8 percent of the expected sales for the coming year for each model. This would provide approximately one month's sales in inventory (since 8% · 12 months = .96 months). It can be seen from Table 6.13 that the firm will need to produce 1,300 model X's and 2,674 model Y's in order to fulfill the forecast sales demand while maintaining the desired level of finished goods in inventory.

Table 6.12   19X0 Inventory Breakdown for DuBois Manufacturing Ltd.

	Units	Dollars
Raw materials inventory		
Material A	600	$ 1,200.00
Material B	4,000	2,000.00
Total		$ 3,200.00
Finished goods inventory		
Model X	320	$ 5,433.60
Model Y	350	7,350.00
Total		$12,783.60
Total inventory		$15,983.60

Table 6.13   19X1 Production Plan by Model (in Units) for DuBois
Manufacturing Ltd.

	Model	
	X	Y
Desired ending inventory of finished goods	120	224
Add: Forecast sales	1,500	2,800
Total needs	1,620	3,024
Less: Beginning inventory of finished goods	320	350
Production required	1,300	2,674

Raw-Materials Usage   Using the production plan as an input, the firm's raw-materials requirements can be estimated. Multiplying the quantity of each raw material needed to produce a unit model (given in Table 6.8) by the number of units of each model required (given in Table 6.13) results in the total raw-materials requirements. The raw-materials requirements to the nearest unit can be calculated as follows:

$$\text{Material A} = 1(1,300) + 1(2,674)$$

$$= 3,974 \text{ units}$$

$$\text{Material B} = 2(1,300) + 3(2,674)$$

$$= 10,622 \text{ units}$$

The firm's management also wants an ending inventory of raw materials A and B of 500 and 3,000 units, respectively. The total purchases of each raw material can be estimated by simple addition, as in Table 6.14.

The required raw-materials purchases calculated in Table 6.14 can easily be converted into dollar figures by multiplying the unit requirements for raw materials A and B by

Table 6.14   19X1 Required Raw-Materials Purchases (in Units) for DuBois
Manufacturing Ltd.

	Raw material	
	A	B
Desired ending inventory of raw materials	500	3,000
Add: Required usage	3,974	10,622
Total requirement	4,474	13,622
Less: Beginning raw-materials inventory	600	4,000
Required raw-material purchases	3,874	9,622

the corresponding unit cost ($2.00 and $0.50, respectively).* Adding these costs together gives us the total annual raw-materials purchases in dollars.

$$\text{Purchase cost of material A} = \$2.00\,(3,874) \quad = \$\ 7,748.00$$
$$\text{Purchase cost of material B} = \ 0.50\,(9,622) \quad = \underline{\ \ \ 4,811.00}$$
$$\text{Total 19X0 raw-materials purchases} \quad = \underline{\$12,559.00}$$

Raw-Materials Purchases   An estimate of the firm's raw-materials purchase schedule, indicating when and how much of each raw material should be purchased, can be constructed. Since this company is in a relatively stable business, the raw-materials purchases are expected to occur in equal quarterly amounts. Thus, the total quarterly material purchase will be $(0.25)\ (\$7,748.00) + (0.25)\ (\$4,811.00) = \$3,139.75$.

Direct Labour   In Table 6.7 the direct labour cost per unit of each model, X and Y, was indicated to be $6.00 and $7.50 per unit, respectively, for 19X0. In 19X1 the direct labour rate will increase from $3.00 to $4.00. As a result, the per-unit direct labour costs for 19X1 for each model are as follows:

$$\text{Model X: } 2.0(\$4.00) = \$8.00/\text{unit}$$
$$\text{Model Y: } 2.5(\$4.00) = \$10.00/\text{unit}$$

Applying the per-unit labour costs to the production requirements in Table 6.13 results in the total labour costs associated with the production of each model. Table 6.13 indicated that 1,300 and 2,674 units of models X and Y, respectively, would have to be produced in the current period. Thus, the total direct labour costs for each model, along with the overall total annual direct labour cost, will be as follows:

$$\text{Model X: } \$8.00\ (1,300 \text{ units}) \quad = \$10,400$$
$$\text{Model Y: } \$10.00\ (2,674 \text{ units}) \quad = \underline{\ 26,740}$$
$$\text{Total annual direct labour cost} \quad = \underline{\$37,140}$$

As indicated in the preceding section, the firm produces its products at a constant rate throughout the year. One-fourth of the total annual direct labour cost is expected to be incurred each quarter. Dividing the total annual direct labour cost of $37,140, calculated above, by 4 yields quarterly direct labour costs of $9,285.

Factory Overhead   The firm's budgeted factory overhead for 19X1 is $50,000. This estimate was prepared by the firm's budgeting staff, with the aid of the firm's plant superintendent. The annual and quarterly totals for overhead are shown in Table 6.15.

---

*It has been assumed that the cost per unit of raw materials A and B will be the same in 19X1 as in 19X0.

Table 6.15   19X1 Budgeted Factory-Overhead Cost for DuBois Manufacturing Ltd.

Item	Annual	Quarterly
Indirect labour	$ 8,000	$ 2,000
Factory supplies	5,600	1,400
Heat, light, and power	3,200	800
Supervision	10,000	2,500
Maintenance	5,000	1,250
Engineering	7,200	1,800
Property and payroll taxes and insurance	4,000	1,000
Depreciation	7,000	1,750
Total factory overhead	$50,000	$12,500

A breakdown of these budgeted factory overhead costs on the basis of direct labour costs can be calculated for the projected level of sales. The technique used is similar to that used in Table 6.10. As Table 6.16 indicates, the overhead allocation per unit produced is $10.77 and $13.46 for models X and Y, respectively.

Operating Expenses   The firm has projected its total operating expenses in 19X1 to be $16,000 (see Table 6.17). Comparing the projected operating expenses with those of 19X0, given in Table 6.11, shows that the major factors contributing to the increased operating expenses are sales salaries and advertising expenses. The firm believes that by increasing these outlays it can meet the stiffened competition head-on, and thus maintain its market share for each of its models.

Table 6.16   19X1 Allocation of Budgeted Factory Overhead on the Basis of Direct Labour Costs for DuBois Manufacturing Ltd.

	Model	
Item	X	Y
(1) Total labour cost/model	$10,400	$26,740
(2) Total labour cost	$37,140	
(3) Percentage of total labour cost/model	28%	72%
(4) Overhead allocation	$14,000	$36,000
(5) Overhead allocation/unit	$ 10.77	$ 13.46

SOURCES: Item (1)—from section on direct labour.
       Item (2)—sum of item (1) for X and Y.
       Item (3)—item (1) for each model as a percentage of item (2).
       Item (4)—item (3) · budgeted factory overhead ($50,000).
       Item (5)—item (4) divided by the corresponding number of units of X and Y to be
          produced (1,300 and 2,674 units, respectively).

Table 6.17   19X1 Operating Expense Forecast for DuBois Manufacturing Ltd.

Selling expense:		
Sales salaries	$6,000	
Freight out	1,200	
Advertising	1,800	
Total selling expense		$ 9,000
Administrative expense:		
Administrative salaries	$4,000	
Office supplies	1,000	
Telephone	500	
Professional fees	1,500	
Total administrative expense		7,000
Total 19X1 operating expense forecast		$16,000

The Long-Term Financing Plan   The firm has not scheduled any changes in its long-term financing structure during 19X1. Any scheduled capital expenditures are expected to be paid for with funds generated internally from operations.

The Capital Expenditure Plan   The firm has scheduled one major capital expenditure, the purchase of a new frame building costing $20,000. As noted earlier, the new frame building will be the firm's only asset in Class 6, which has an applicable CCA of 10 percent. Thus, the depreciation charge for 19X1 will be $2,000. The frame building will be paid for in two equal installments—one in March and one in September.

The Pro Forma Income Statement

Using the preliminary budgets developed previously, DuBois's pro forma income statement can be developed. First, however, a number of preliminary calculations are necessary.

PRELIMINARY CALCULATIONS

Since the firm markets two models, each selling for a different price and requiring different cost inputs, both sales and the cost of goods sold require special attention. The cost of goods sold is especially important, since the cost per unit sold has increased from the 19X0 level. In our calculations, we shall assume that the firm has a FIFO inventory system; in other words, the oldest units are sold first.

Sales   The total sales revenue expected from the sale of models X and Y is $135,500 (see Table 6.3).

Table 6.18   The Unit Cost of Goods Manufactured in 19X1 for DuBois Manufacturing Ltd.

	Model	
	X	Y
Raw-materials cost/unit	$ 3.00	$ 3.50
Labour cost/unit	8.00	10.00
Overhead cost/unit	10.77	13.46
Total cost/unit	$21.77	$26.96

The Cost of Goods Sold   Since the per-unit cost of goods is expected to increase between 19X0 and 19X1, we must consider how much of the goods sold will be from the firm's inventory and how much will be manufactured during the period.

The Cost of Goods Sold from Inventory   Since the firm uses a FIFO (first-in, first-out) inventory system, the first 350 units of model X and first 350 units of model Y sold will cost $5,433.60 and $7,350.00, respectively. The total of these costs is $12,783.60. These figures can be obtained directly from Table 6.12.

The Cost of Goods Manufactured and Sold During the Period   By adding the material costs, the direct labour cost per unit, and the overhead cost per unit, the total cost per unit can be calculated. The total cost per unit for models X and Y is given in Table 6.18.

Table 6.13 indicated that 1,500 units of model X and 2,800 units of model Y will be sold during the current period. If 320 units of model X and 350 units of model Y come from the firm's beginning inventory, only 1,180 units (1,500 units − 320 units) and 2,450 units (2,800 units − 350 units) of models X and Y, respectively, will be produced and sold during the year. The cost of these units will be $25,688.60 (1,180 · $21.77) and $66,052.00 (2,540 · $26.96) for models X and Y, respectively. The total cost of producing and selling both models is $91,740.60.

The Cost of Goods Sold During the Period   The cost of goods sold during the period is the sum of the cost of goods sold from inventory ($12,783.60) and the cost of goods manufactured and sold during 19X1 ($91,740.60), which is $104,524.20.

THE STATEMENT

Since no change in DuBois's long-term capital structure is expected during 19X1, DuBois Manufacturing Ltd. will continue to pay $1,000 in interest* and $4,000 in dividends during 19X1.†

*This is based on the assumption that the firm will incur no additional debt during the period. As will be seen in a subsequent section of this chapter, this assumption is not valid, since the cash budget indicates that required financings (borrowings) of $15,228.85 and $5,433.10 are needed in the first and fourth quarters, respectively, of 19X1.

†The various types of dividend policies and their justification are thoroughly discussed in Chapter 24.

Table 6.19   A Pro Forma Income Statement for
DuBois Manufacturing Ltd. for the Year
Ended December 31, 19X1

Sales	$135,500.00
Less: Cost of goods sold	104,524.20
Gross profits	$ 30,975.80
Less: Operating expense	16,000.00
Operating profits	$ 14,975.80
Less: Interest expense	1,000.00
Profits before taxes	$ 13,975.80
Less: Taxes (.20 · $13,975.80)	2,795.16
Profits after taxes	$ 11,180.64
Less: Common share dividends	4,000.00
To retained earnings	$ 7,180.64

The pro forma income statement in Table 6.19 indicates that the company can expect its 19X1 profits after taxes to be $11,180.64. These profits seem to be quite good compared to the 19X0 profits of $8,000.00 indicated in Table 6.1. After paying $4,000.00 in cash dividends, the firm still has a sizable amount of funds to reinvest in the business. A meaningful analysis of the pro forma statement can be made by developing a percent income statement based on it and comparing it to the 19X0 percent income statement. Utilization of the ratios discussed in Chapter 3 may also provide additional information.

Comparing the Resulting Income Statement with the Simplified Approach   *If we assume that the $7,180.64 value for retained earnings calculated using the sophisticated forecasting approach is the correct one,* then the value for retained earnings, calculated by the simplified approach, has understated the actual value by $165.04 (i.e., $7,180.64 − $7,015.60), or 2.3 percent (i.e., $165.04 ÷ $7,180.64).* If the firm can tolerate this margin of error, the simplified approach may be useful; of course, use of the longer approach just illustrated is recommended. The basic advantage of the longer, sophisticated approach is that it considers changes in costs, prices, and expenses from one year to the next. The longer approach fits into the firm's overall budgeting and planning process, and key inputs to the firm's cash budget and pro forma balance sheet can be isolated in preparing the pro forma income statement.

The technique chosen by the firm for estimating the pro forma income statement is a function of the use of the statement, the stability of the firm's operations, and the expected level of economic activity. If the statement is to be used by a lender to evaluate the firm's loan application, greater accuracy is required than if the statement were merely being used for internal control purposes. A lender will want well-developed figures, and quite often it will examine the procedure used to prepare a statement. If the firm is in a very stable business and economic activity is expected to remain at current

---

*This result is consistent with the earlier discussion in which it was suggested that by using the percent-of-sales method to prepare pro forma income statements, the firm's profits would be understated when it had fixed costs. Since DuBois Manufacturing Ltd. does have fixed costs, this result is as expected.

levels, a projected income statement based on percentages developed from previous statements is quite likely to be acceptable. The higher the degree of volatility associated with a firm's operations, the greater the degree of care that should be taken in developing its pro forma income statement.

The Pro Forma Balance Sheet

At this point in the analysis, all the inputs for correctly developing the firm's pro forma balance sheet, except the firm's cash budget, are available. The cash budget is necessary since it presents the end-of-year cash and notes payable values. Also, in the process of developing the firm's cash budget, the ending accounts receivable and accounts payable can easily be calculated.

THE CASH BUDGET

A number of additional facts are required in order to calculate the firm's cash budget (Table 6.20).

1 The firm's projected sales (all on credit) are expected to be $27,500, $50,000, $35,000, and $23,000 in the first through the fourth quarters, respectively.
2 Seventy-five percent of the accounts receivable will be collected during the quarter of the sale; the remaining 25 percent will be collected during the following quarter. Bad debt expenses are therefore assumed to be negligible.
3 Sixty percent of the purchases of raw materials will be paid for in the current quarter; the remaining 40 percent will be paid for in the following quarter.
4 The payments for direct labour (wages), factory overhead (excluding depreciation), and operating expenses will be divided equally between the quarters.
5 The $1,000 interest payment will be made during December.
6 Taxes payable at the beginning of the year will be paid in equal quarterly installments of $935 ($3,740.00 ÷ 4).*
7 The firm wishes to maintain an ending cash balance of at least $6,000.

COMMENTS ON THE CASH BUDGET

Two pro forma balance sheet entries are readily available from the cash budget (Table 6.20)

1 Ending cash—the end-of-year cash balance, based on the various assumptions incorporated in the cash budget, is $6,000 (i.e., minimum cash balance of $6,000 plus excess cash balance of $0).
2 Notes payable—the end-of-year short-term borrowing (the fourth-quarter required total financing in the cash budget) is $5,433.10.

---

*The taxes-payable figure represents the end-of-19X0 taxes payable shown on the balance sheet in Table 6.2. It is assumed that these taxes of $3,740 are paid during the year 19X1, whereas the taxes incurred during 19X1 are paid in 19X2. Note that the assumption of equal quarterly installments is made only for illustrative purposes.

Table 6.20   The 19X1 Cash Budget for DuBois Manufacturing Ltd.

	1st Quarter	2nd Quarter	3rd Quarter	4th Quarter
Sales	$27,500.00	$50,000.00	$35,000.00	$23,000.00
Cash receipts				
75% for current sales	$20,625.00	$37,500.00	$26,250.00	$17,250.00
25% for previous quarter's sales	13,000.00[a]	6,875.00	12,500.00	8,750.00
Total receipts	$33,625.00	$44,375.00	$38,750.00	$26,000.00
Purchases	$ 3,139.75	$ 3,139.75	$ 3,139.75	$ 3,139.75
Cash disbursements				
60% for current purchases	$ 1,833.85	$ 1,883.85	$ 1,883.85	$ 1,883.85
40% for previous quarter's purchases	12,000.00[b]	1,255.90	1,255.90	1,255.90
Payroll—direct labour cost	9,285.00	9,285.00	9,285.00	9,285.00
Factory overhead (excluding depreciation)	10,750.00	10,750.00	10,750.00	10,750.00
Operating expense	4,000.00	4,000.00	4,000.00	4,000.00
Machine purchase	10,000.00	—	10,000.00	—
Interest payment	—	—	—	1,000.00
Cash dividend	—	—	—	4,000.00
Tax payment	935.00	935.00	935.00	935.00
Total disbursements	$48,853.85	$28,109.75	$38.109.75	$33,109.75
Net cash flow	($15,228.85)	$16,265.25	$ 640.25	($7,109.75)
Beginning cash	6,000.00	(9,228.85)	7,036.40	7,676.65
Ending cash	($9,228.85)	$ 7,036.40	$ 7,676.65	$ 566.90
Less: Minimum cash balance	6,000.00	6,000.00	6,000.00	6,000.00
Required total financing	$15,228.85	—	—	$ 5,433.10
Excess cash balance	—	$ 1,036.40	$ 1,676.65	—

[a]Beginning accounts receivable, from Table 6.2.
[b]Beginning accounts payable, from Table 6.2.

The end-of-period accounts receivable and accounts payable can easily be obtained from the preceding analysis.

Accounts Receivable   The end-of-period accounts receivable for the firm's pro forma balance sheet can be calculated by taking 25 percent of the fourth-quarter sales. This is consistent with the analysis used to develop receipts in the preceding section. Ending accounts receivable would therefore be 25 percent of $23,000, or $5,750.

Accounts Payable   The end-of-period accounts payable can be calculated in much the same way as the accounts receivable. Since 60 percent of the firm's purchases are paid for in the current quarter, and the remaining 40 percent are paid for in the following quarter, 40 percent of the fourth quarter's purchases will remain uncollected at the end of the fourth quarter. The fourth-quarter purchases were $3,139.75; 40 percent of this amount is $1,255.90. The ending accounts payable will therefore be $1,255.90.

Table 6.21 The Pro Forma Balance Sheet for DuBois Manufacturing Ltd. for the Year Ended December 31, 19X1

Assets			Liabilities and equities	
(1) Cash (Table 6.20)		$ 6,000.00	(6) Accounts payable	$1,255.90
(2) Marketable secur-			(7) Taxes payable	2,795.16
ities		4,016.40	(8) Notes payable	5,433.10
(3) Accounts			(9) Other current liabilities	6,260.00
receivable		5,750.00		
(4) Inventories			Total current	
(a) Raw materials	$2,500.00		liabilities	$15,744.16
(b) Finished goods	8,651.44		(10) Long-term debt	$15,000.00
			(11) Shareholders' equity	
Total		11,151.44	(a) Common shares	$30,000.00
Total current			(b) Retained earnings	$30,180.64
assets		$26,917.84	Total liabilities and	
(5) Net fixed assets		$64,000.00	shareholders' equity	$90,924.80[a]
Total assets		$90.917.84[a]		

[a]The total assets should equal the total liabilities and equities. That they do not is due to the rounding off of certain values in the analysis. However, the difference is insignificant; it is $6.96, which represents an error of less than .0077 percent.

THE STATEMENT

The pro forma balance sheet for DuBois Manufacturing Ltd. is presented in Table 6.21. The items in the statement were derived as follows:

1 Cash is obtained from the firm's cash budget (Table 6.20).
2 Marketable securities are assumed to have remained unchanged from the previous period's value, given in Table 6.2.
3 Accounts receivable are based on the cash budget (see the preceding section).
4 Inventories:
    a Raw materials—the value of the raw-materials inventory has been developed as follows:

Raw material	Ending inventory units	Cost/unit	Total
A	500	$2.00	$1,000
B	3,000	0.50	1,500
Total raw-materials inventory value			$2,500

    b Finished goods—the value of the finished-goods inventory has been found as follows:

Finished goods	Ending inventory units	Cost/unit	Total
X	120	$21.77	$2,612.40
Y	224	26.96	6,039.04
Total finished-goods inventory value			$8,651.44

5 Net fixed assets—this value has been calculated by adding the $20,000 outlay for a new frame building to the firm's beginning-of-period fixed assets of $51,000 (from Table 6.2), and then subtracting the current year's depreciation of $7,000 (from Table 6.15) from the total.

6 Accounts payable are based on the cash budget (see the preceding section of this chapter).

7 Taxes payable—this figure is the same as the firm's tax liability on the pro forma income statement (Table 6.19), $2,795.16.

8 Notes payable—this value is the same as the value for the fourth-quarter borrowing in the cash budget.*

9 Other current liabilities—this figure is the same as that given for the preceding year, since the firm's other current liabilities are expected to remain unchanged.

10 Long-term debt—this figure is the same as that given for the previous year, since no changes in this account are expected.

11 Shareholders' equity:

    a Common shares—this value is the same as that given for the previous year, since no changes in this account are expected.

    b Retained earnings—this value represents the $23,000.00 in retained earnings from the 19X0 balance sheet (Table 6.2) plus the projected increase in retained earnings of $7,180.64 from the 19X1 pro forma income statement (Table 6.19).

The pro forma balance sheet (Table 6.21) indicates that the firm's total assets are expected to increase by about $900 over the previous year's level of $90,000. The amount of change in the total assets is not nearly as important as the relationships between the items on the balance sheet. Ratio analysis of both the pro forma income statement and the balance sheet can be performed in order to evaluate the firm's expected liquidity or activity, debt position, and profitability. Source and use of funds statements can be developed using the pro forma balance sheet in order to determine whether the firm will obtain and use funds in a manner consistent with its overall financial policies.

COMPARING THE RESULTING BALANCE SHEET WITH THAT PRODUCED BY THE SIMPLIFIED APPROACH

Comparing the pro forma balance sheets prepared under each approach, significant differences in the balances shown for accounts receivable, inventories, accounts payable, and notes payable are seen to exist. Total assets in the sophisticated approach are $90,917.84, while in the simplified approach total assets are $98,485.15.

A decision maker should have a higher degree of confidence in the balance sheet developed using the sophisticated approach, since much more detail and fewer assumptions are required in the development of values. In sum, the basic difference between the two approaches is that the sophisticated approach requires determination of causes and calculation of effects; while the simplified approach determines the effects desired, develops a balance sheet based on these effects, and makes it balance using a plug figure. The approach used to prepare pro forma statements will depend upon the financial manager's need. For convenience, the simplified approach is recommended; while for accuracy, the sophisticated approach should be used.

*The notes payable figure in Table 6.21 is similar in purpose to that of the required external financing (plug) figure in Table 6.6.

COMPUTER-BASED FINANCIAL STATEMENT GENERATORS*

It is obvious from the preceding discussion that a large amount of "number crunching" must be performed to obtain complete and logically consistent pro forma financial statements. As a result, computer-based financial statement generators are one of the most widely used class of computer-based decision aids. Such generators range from simple computer programs performing simple accounting-type calculations to sophisticated models of the firm, which encompass special financing, depreciation, and tax subsystems to deal with the interdependent nature of these accounts.

With the aid of such computer-based models, pro forma statements can be derived for alternative sets of forecasts. Thus, by asking a variety of "what if" questions, management can evaluate the impact of different assumptions on the pro forma financial statements.

Even though these models can be very sophisticated, they must be used with care, since they have their shortcomings. Some of the practical shortcomings listed most often by users are inflexibility, excessive data-entry requirements, and understandability of directions for the use of the program. Two other shortcomings are first, the models may rely on relationships, which may not be valid for the forecast period, and second, the quality of the input data (and implicitly the program user). As is well known, no computer model will produce good output (forecasts) when given bad data (forecasts and assumptions) as input.

SMALL BUSINESSES

A pro forma balance sheet and income statement are two important documents that are used by credit officers in appraising the credit-worthiness of small businesses. In practice, the more supporting documents that the small business can supply, the more likely the credit officer is to find the application credit-worthy. For example, if possible, a small business should support its revenue projections by a competent market survey.

Summary

This chapter has illustrated procedures to be used in developing projected financial statements. Specific attention has been given to the pro forma income statement and pro forma balance sheet. The most critical input to these statements is a sales forecast. Based on this forecast, a production plan showing raw-material costs and usage, direct labour requirements, factory overhead, and operating expenses is developed. Using this plan, the firm's cost of goods sold can be calculated and a pro forma income statement developed. This statement provides the firm with a projected net income figure from which planned dividend payments can be deducted to obtain an estimate of retained earnings.

*For an interesting article on computer-based financial statement generators, the reader should refer to B. K. Stone, D. H. Downes, and R. P. Magee, "Computer-Assisted Financial Planning: The Planner-Model Interface," *Journal of Business Research* (September 1977), pp. 215–233.

The retained earnings figure from the pro forma income statement, the firm's most recent balance sheet, data on any planned long-term financing, planned capital expenditures, and the firm's cash budget can be used to prepare a pro forma balance sheet by using the more sophisticated and longer approach. The cash budget is a quite important input, since projections of the firm's ending cash, notes payable, accounts receivable, and accounts payable can easily be obtained from it.

Simplified approaches to developing pro forma income statements and balance sheets exist. A pro forma income statement can be developed using past percentage relationships between certain cost and expense items and the firm's sales, and then applying these percentages to the firm's forecast sales. Of course, the use of these historic percentages tends to suggest that all costs are variable—a situation that is unlikely to exist. A pro forma balance sheet can be estimated by determining the desired level of certain items and letting additional financing act as a balancing, or plug, figure.

The simplified approaches to pro forma preparation have appeal since they are more convenient, while the sophisticated approach to pro forma preparation should be superior in terms of accuracy. The basic difference between the two approaches can be summed up by saying that the sophisticated approach relies on the determination of causes in order to calculate effects; while the simplified approach is based on determining the effects desired, and then preparing pro forma statements consistent with them.

Pro forma statements are used for evaluating the firm's future performance. Not only are they useful for internal control, but lenders commonly use them in analyzing a firm before making a loan or deciding to extend a line of credit. Quite often ratio analysis is performed on pro forma statements in order to evaluate the firm's expected financial situation. Source and use of funds statements based on the pro forma statements are also often prepared.

Questions

6.1 What are pro forma financial statements?

6.2 What types of budgets are required in order to obtain the data necessary for the preparation of pro forma statements? What is the key input to this budgeting process?

6.3 Which of the pro forma statements must be developed first? Why? What necessary inputs to the pro forma statement preparation process are provided by the cash budget?

6.4 Why may the pro forma income statement prepared using the simplified method described in the chapter underestimate profits? How would this compare to the resulting statement using the sophisticated method?

6.5 What is the simplified approach to preparing a firm's pro forma balance sheet described in the chapter? What are the key assumptions necessary in using this approach?

6.6 What is the significance of the "plug figure" used in the preparation of a pro forma balance sheet using the simplified approach?

6.7 What is the essence of the percent-of-sales method of preparing pro forma balance sheets?

6.8 Why, in order to prepare pro forma statements, is it necessary to have both a unit and a dollar sales forecast by product?

6.9 What person or department of the firm is responsible for the development of each of the following items?
   a. The sales forecast
   b. The production plan
   c. The factory overhead budget
   d. Historical financial statements
   e. Pro forma statements

6.10 What items are generally included as part of the firm's manufacturing overhead cost?

6.11 On what basis is a firm's factory overhead cost commonly allocated to the various products produced? How do the three commonly used systems work?

6.12 What are the basic values required to determine the total cost per unit for each of a firm's products?

6.13 Why is it necessary to have a breakdown of the firm's inventory into raw materials (by type), work in process (by product), and finished goods (by product)?

6.14 What critical items used in the preparation of pro forma statements come from the firm's capital expenditure plan?

6.15 Why is the cost-of-goods-sold figure the most difficult item to calculate in preparing the pro forma income statement?

6.16 What reasons can be given to support the belief that the sophisticated approach to pro forma statement preparation considers both causes and effects, whereas the simplified approach is concerned only with effects?

6.17 How may the financial analyst wish to evaluate pro forma statements? What is his or her objective in evaluating these statements?

Problems

6.1 The O'Connor Corporation Ltd. wishes to apply the simplified method to prepare its financial plans. Using the following operating statements and the other information included,
   a. Prepare a pro forma income statement.
   b. Prepare a pro forma balance sheet.
   c. Analyze these statements and discuss the financing changes required.

Income Statement
O'Connor Corporation Ltd.
December 31, 19X0

Sales	$800,000
Less: Cost of goods sold	600,000
Gross profits	$200,000
Less: Operating expense	100,000
Profits before taxes	$100,000
Less: Taxes (40%)	40,000
Profits after taxes	$ 60,000
Less: Cash dividends	20,000
To retained earnings	$ 40,000

Balance Sheet
O'Connor Corporation Ltd.
December 31, 19X0

Assets		Liabilities and equities	
Cash	$ 32,000	Accounts payable	$100,000
Marketable securities	18,000	Taxes payable	20,000
Accounts receivable	150,000	Other current liabilities	5,000
Inventory	100,000	Total current liabilities	$125,000
Total current assets	$300,000	Long-term debt	$200,000
Net fixed assets	$350,000	Common shares	$150,000
Total assets	$650,000	Retained earnings	175,000
		Total liabilities and equity	$650,000

The following financial data are also available:

(1) The firm has estimated that its sales for 19X1 will be $900,000.
(2) The firm expects to pay $35,000 in cash dividends in 19X1.
(3) The firm wishes to maintain a minimum cash balance of $30,000.
(4) Accounts receivable represent approximately 18 percent of annual sales.
(5) The firm's ending inventory will change directly with changes in sales in 19X1.
(6) A new machine costing $42,000 will be purchased in 19X1. Total depreciation for 19X1 will be $17,000.
(7) Accounts payable will change directly in response to changes in sales in 19X1.
(8) Taxes payable will equal the tax liability on the pro forma income statement.
(9) Marketable securities, other current liabilities, long-term debt, and common shares will remain unchanged.

6.2   Tucker Tool has 19X0 sales of $10 million. It wishes to use the simplified method to analyze its expected performance and financing needs for the next year. Given the information below:

(1) The percent of sales for items which vary directly with sales are
    Cash 4%
    Receivables 12%
    Inventory 18%
    Net fixed assets 40%
    Accounts payable 14%
    Accruals 4%
    Net profit margin 3%
(2) No sale of common shares is expected.
(3) The dividend payout of 50 percent is expected to continue.
(4) Sales are expected to be $11 million in 19X1 and $12 million in 19X2.
(5) The December 31, 19X0, balance sheet follows:

Tucker Tool
Balance Sheet
December 31, 19X0
(in thousands)

Cash	$ 400	Accounts payable	$1,400
Marketable securities	200	Accruals	400
Accounts receivable	1,200	Other current liabilities	80
Inventory	1,800	Total current liabilities	$1,880
Total current assets	$3,600	Long-term debt	$2,000
Net fixed assets	$4,000	Common equity	$3,720
Total assets	$7,600	Total liabilities and equity	$7,600

a. Prepare a pro forma balance sheet dated December 31, 19X2.
b. Discuss the financing changes suggested by the statement prepared in a.

6.3 Use the following table to answer the following questions for a firm producing two products, P_1 and P_2, with two raw materials, RM_1 and RM_2.

	P_1	P_2	Total
Selling price per unit	$40.00	$28.00	
Number of units sold	5,000	8,000	
Sales revenue	$200,000	$224,000	$424,000
Direct labour cost per unit	$10.00	$6.00	
Material cost per unit RM_1	$7.00	$4.00	
RM_2	6.00	6.00	
Total	$13.00	$10.00	

Direct labour cost is $5.00 per hour, RM_1 costs $1.00 per-unit, RM_2 costs $0.50 per unit, factory overhead expense last year was $60,000.
a. What are the firm's historical per-unit labour and material requirements for each product?
b. Calculate the firm's overhead allocation per unit for each product. Round percentages and dollars to the nearest whole percentage and cent, respectively.
c. What is the total cost per unit for each product?

6.4 Use the following information for Morton Materials Ltd. for this problem, as well as Problems 6.5 and 6.6.
Morton Materials Ltd. produces two products, X and Y, with two raw materials, A and B, and direct labour. The production mix is listed below. The firm desires to hold 10 percent of annual sales as year-end finished goods inventory. The estimated overhead for the coming year is $70,000. The firm will maintain raw-material inventories of 3,000 and 6,000 units of A and B, respectively.

Inputs	Product X	Product Y
Raw material (units)		
A	3.0	1.0
B	4.0	6.5
Labour hours	2.0	1.5

Balance Sheet
Morton Materials Ltd.
(Last Year)

Assets		Liabilities and equities	
Cash	$ 20,000	Accounts payable	$ 15,000
Marketable securities	6,534	Taxes payable	8,828
Accounts receivable	25,000	Other current liabilities	18,000
Inventory	32,466	Total current liabilities	$ 41,828
Total current assets	$84,000	Long-term debt	$ 35,000
Net fixed assets	$116,000		
		Common shares	$ 80,000
Total assets	$200,000	Retained earnings	43,172
		Total liabilities and equity	$200,000

Income Statement
Morton Materials Ltd.
(Last Year)

Sales		
Product X	$128,000	
Product Y	200,000	
Total sales		$328,000
Less: Cost of goods sold		
Labour	$ 80,000	
Material A	48,000	
Material B	81,600	
Overhead	60,000	
Total cost of goods sold		269,600
Gross profits		$ 58,400
Less: Operating expense		16,000
Profits before taxes		$ 42,400
Less: Taxes		8,828
Profits after taxes		$ 33,572
Less: Cash dividends		13,000
To retained earnings		$ 20,572

Current Inventory Breakdown
Morton Materials Ltd.

Raw-materials inventory	Units	Dollars
Material A	2,000	$ 4,000
Material B	6,000	7,200
Total		$11,200
Finished-goods inventory		
Product X	350	$ 8,680
Product Y	620	12,586
Total		$21,266
Total inventory		$32,466

Sales Forecast (Coming Year)
Morton Materials Ltd.

Unit sales	
Product X	4,500
Product Y	9,000
Dollar sales	
Product X ($35)	$157,500
Product Y ($30)	270,000
Total	$427,500

a. Calculate the firm's production requirements for the coming year.
b. Calculate the firm's raw-material usage requirement for the next year, rounded to the nearest unit.
c. If direct labour costs are $3 per hour, and overhead estimates are $70,000, what is the expected cost per unit for the next period?

6.5 Using the information on Morton Materials Ltd. given in Problem 6.4, prepare a pro forma income statement for the firm assuming operating expenses will be $25,000, direct labour costs will be $4 per unit, cash dividends will be $15,000, the firm uses FIFO to value inventory, and the corporate tax rate is 40 percent. Assume the raw-material prices do not change.

6.6 Using the information on Morton Materials Ltd. given in Problems 6.4 and 6.5, prepare a pro forma balance sheet for the company for the coming year. Use the following information to prepare the balance sheet.

(1) The firm will purchase a new machine for $50,000.
(2) The firm desires to maintain a cash balance of $20,000.
(3) Accounts receivable should equal 5 percent of annual sales.
(4) Depreciation is expected to be $14,000, which is the same as the expected CCA for the year.
(5) Taxes payable will equal the coming year's tax liability as indicated on the pro forma income statement.
(6) Accounts payable should be approximately 5.5 percent of the annual cost of goods sold.
(7) Assume production and sales occur continuously over the year.

Suggested Readings

Ansoff, H. Igor, "Planning as a Practical Management Tool," *Financial Executive* 32 (June 1964), pp. 34–37.
Bogen, Jules I., Ed., *Financial Handbook*, 4th ed. (New York: Ronald, 1968), sect. 15.
Chambers, J. C., S. D. Mullick, and D. D. Smith, "How to Choose the Right Forecasting Technique," *Harvard Business Review* 49 (July-August 1971), pp. 45–74.
Chisholm, R. K. and G. R. Whitaker, Jr., *Forecasting Methods* (Homewood, Ill.: Irwin, 1971).
Gershefski, George W., "Building a Corporate Financial Model," *Harvard Business Review* (July-August, 1969), pp. 61–72.
Francis, Jack Clark and Dexter R. Rowell, "A Simultaneous Equation Model of the Firm for Financial Analysis and Planning," *Financial Management* 7 (Spring 1978), pp. 29–44.
Helfert, Erich A., *Techniques of Financial Analysis*, 4th ed. (Homewood, Ill.: Irwin, 1976), chap. 3.

Jaedicke, Robert K. and Robert T. Sprouse, *Accounting Flows: Income, Funds, and Cash* (Englewood Cliffs, N.J.: Prentice-Hall, 1965), chaps. 3 and 4.

Johnson, Timothy E. and Thomas G. Schmitt, "Effectiveness of Earnings Per Share Forecasts," *Financial Management* 3 (Summer 1974), pp. 64–72.

Lynch, Richard M., *Accounting for Management Planning and Control* (New York: McGraw-Hill, 1967), chap. 6.

Merville, Larry J. and Lee A. Tavis, "Long-Range Financial Planning," *Financial Management* 3 (Summer 1974), pp. 56–63.

Pappas, James L. and George P. Huber, "Probabilistic Short-Term Financial Planning," *Financial Management* 2 (Autumn 1973), pp. 36–44.

Parker, G. C. and E. L. Segura, "How to Get a Better Forecast," *Harvard Business Review* 49 (March-April 1971), pp. 99–109.

Preston, Gerald R., "Considerations in Long-Range Planning," *Financial Executive* (May 1968), pp. 44–49.

Ricketts, Donald E. and Michael J. Barrett, "Corporate Operating Income Forecasting Ability," *Financial Management* 2 (Summer 1973), pp. 53–62.

Schrieber, A., Ed., *Corporate Simulation Models* (Seattle: University of Washington, 1970).

Seitz, Neil, *Financial Analysis: A Programmed Approach* (Reston, Va.: Reston Publishing Co., 1976), chap. 2.

Stone, Bernell K., David H. Downes, and Robert P. Magee, "Computer-Assisted Financial Planning: The Planner-Model Interface," *Journal of Business Research* 5 (September 1977), pp. 215–233.

Viscione, Jerry A., *Financial Analysis: Principles and Procedures* (Boston: Houghton Mifflin Company, 1977), chap. 3.

Wagle, B., "The Use of Models for Environmental Forecasting and Corporate Planning," *Operational Research Quarterly* 22, No. 3., pp. 327–336.

Weston, J. Fred, "Forecasting Financial Requirements," *Accounting Review* 33 (July 1958), pp. 427–440.

Wright, Leonard T., *Financial Management: Analytical Techniques* (Columbus, Ohio: Grid, 1974), chap. 4.

Part Three

The Management of Working Capital

BALANCE SHEET	
Assets	Liabilities and Shareholders' Equity
Current Assets	**Current Liabilities**
Fixed Assets	Long-Term Debt
	Shareholders' Equity

This part of the text is devoted to working capital management. Working capital management is concerned with the management of the firm's current accounts, which include current assets and current liabilities. Efficiency in this area of financial management is necessary in order to assure the firm's long-term success and to achieve its overall goal; that is, the maximization of the owners' or shareholders' wealth. If the financial manager cannot manage the firm's working capital efficiently, these longer-run considerations become irrelevant. Short-term survival is a prerequisite to long-run success. Part Three consists of four chapters. Chapter 7 presents an overview of working capital management, in which some of the key considerations in working capital management are illustrated. Chapter 8 discusses the various aspects of cash and marketable securities management. Chapter 9 describes the key aspects of accounts receivable management, which include credit policies, credit terms, and collection policies. The final chapter in this part, Chapter 10, briefly discusses various inventory considerations and strategies for the financial manager.

Chapter 7

AN OVERVIEW OF WORKING CAPITAL MANAGEMENT

Working capital management is concerned with the management of the firm's current accounts, which include current assets and current liabilities. The management of working capital is one of the most important aspects of the firm's overall financial management. If the firm cannot maintain a satisfactory level of working capital, it is likely to become insolvent and may even be forced into bankruptcy. The firm's current assets should be large enough to cover its current liabilities in order to ensure a reasonable margin of safety.

The goal of working capital management is to manage each of the firm's current assets and current liabilities in such a way that an acceptable level of net working capital is maintained. The major current assets of concern in this text are cash, marketable securities, accounts receivable, and inventory. Each of these assets must be managed efficiently in order to maintain the firm's liquidity while not keeping too high a level of any one of them. The basic current liabilities of concern are accounts payable, notes payable, and accruals. Each of these short-term sources of financing must be cautiously managed to ensure that they are obtained and used in the best way possible. Individual current assets and current liabilities will not be discussed in this chapter; rather, attention will be given to the basic relationship between current assets and current liabilities. Subsequent chapters will devote attention to individual current assets and current liabilities.

This chapter is divided into four major sections. The first section presents an in-depth discussion of net working capital. Two alternate definitions of net working capital are discussed in light of the firm's financing. The second section develops, discusses, and illustrates the trade-off between profitability and risk associated with a firm's level of net working capital. Examples are used to illustrate the effects of changes in the level of current assets and current liabilities on the firm's profitability-risk configuration. The third section evaluates the effects of the firm's short-term–long-term financing mix on its net working capital and profitability-risk trade-off and discusses a number of financing mix strategies. The fourth section deals with working capital management in an international context.

Net Working Capital

The concept of net working capital was discussed in Chapter 3. The drawbacks of using net working capital to compare the liquidity of different firms were emphasized, giving special attention to the use of the current or acid-test ratio. The use of net working capital for evaluating the performance of the same firm over time is generally acceptable, as long as the firm's basic asset structure and business lines do not change drastically over the period.

THE COMMON DEFINITION

The most common definition of *net working capital* is the *difference between a firm's current assets and current liabilities.* As long as the firm's current assets exceed its current liabilities, it has net working capital. Most firms must operate with some amount of net working capital; how much depends largely on the industry. Firms with very predictable and stable cash flows, such as electric utilities, can operate with extremely low and even negative net working capital. Unfortunately, most firms cannot operate with negative levels of net working capital.

SOME AGGREGATE STATISTICS

Working capital statistics for selected Canadian industrial sectors are given in Table 7.1. From the table, it is evident that commitments by Canadian firms in current assets and current liabilities are a significant proportion of total assets, and of total liabilities and shareholders' equity, respectively.

   The significant differences between industrial sectors in both current asset and current liability composition, and in working capital positions, are also well illustrated in Table 7.1. For example, for industrial sectors with low levels of accounts receivable and inventories, such as utilities, current assets are 13.8 percent of total assets; while for those with high levels of accounts receivable and inventories, such as construction, current assets are 71.5 percent of total assets. Such differences reflect the nature of the two industrial sectors. Utilities require large long-term investments in the agents of production (such as plant and equipment); while construction firms require sizable short-term investments in work-in-progress and credit sales. Similarly, current liabilities account for 12.4 percent and 56.2 percent of total liabilities and shareholders' equity for the utilities and construction sectors, respectively, for the same year.

   The significance and rationale for the differences in the composition of both current assets and current liabilities between industrial sectors will be dealt with in subsequent chapters.

IMPLICATIONS OF THE WORKING CAPITAL CONCEPT

Underlying the use of net working capital (and other liquidity ratios) to measure a firm's liquidity is the belief that the greater the margin by which a firm's current assets cover

Table 7.1 Current Assets and Current Liabilities for Selected Canadian Industrial Sectors as a Percentage of Total Assets, and Total Liabilities and Shareholders' Equity, Respectively (based on 1976 figures)

				Industrial sector[a]				
Account	Total agriculture, forestry, & fishing (12,004)	Total mining (3,994)	Total manufacturing (29,233)	Total construction (37,061)	Total utilities (13,673)	Total wholesale trade (34,189)	Total retail trade (52,055)	All industries (325,218)[f]
Cash	3.7%	0.7%	1.1%	3.7%	0.8%	2.7%	4.1%	5.3%
Marketable securities[b]	3.8	4.2	3.8	5.0	3.7	3.2	2.7	7.5
Accounts receivable	5.2	6.5	15.5	27.1	5.1	25.9	11.1	8.9
Inventories	16.8	6.8	24.2	30.8	2.5	35.5	40.6	10.0
Other current assets[c]	3.9	5.5	6.2	4.9	1.7	6.8	5.4	16.1
Total current assets	33.4%	23.7%	50.8%	71.5%	13.8%	74.1%	63.9%	47.8%
Bank loans and other short-term loans[d]	16.5	3.5	8.9	26.2	2.9	19.9	16.0	29.6
Accounts payable	6.4	6.7	11.7	19.4	5.4	21.2	20.2	6.5
Taxes payable	1.1	1.5	1.5	1.7	0.2	1.3	1.4	0.7
Long-term debt due within one year	2.5	1.2	0.8	3.2	1.1	0.8	1.2	0.9
Other current liabilities[e]	4.9	3.1	7.9	5.7	2.8	12.2	6.4	3.9
Total current liabilities	31.4	16.0	30.8	56.2	12.4	55.4	45.2	41.6
Total liabilities	68.0%	49.1%	55.4%	76.1%	72.8%	69.4%	65.4%	73.7%

SOURCE: Statistics Canada, *Corporation Financial Statistics, 1976* (March 1979).
[a]The actual number of corporations in the corporate universe in Canada for each category is given in the parenthesis.
[b]Includes deposits and advances.
[c]Includes prepaid expenses, amounts due from affiliates, loans receivable, accrued trade receivables, receivables from employees, etc.
[d]Includes advances and prepayments.
[e]Includes taxes payable, valuation reserve, amounts due to affiliates, interest payable, foreign taxes payable, etc.
[f]The percentages in this column are highly affected by certain industrial sectors. For example, the "bank loans and other short-term loans" category is largely affected by the 49.5 percent value for the "total finance" industrial sector, which consisted of 85,753 corporations in 1976.

its short-term obligations (current liabilities) the better able it will be to pay its bills as they come due. This expectation is based on the belief that current assets are sources of *cash receipts*, while current liabilities are sources of *cash disbursements*. However, a problem arises because each current asset and current liability has a different degree of liquidity associated with it. Although the firm's current assets may not be converted into cash precisely when they are needed, the greater the amount of current assets present, the more likely it is that some current asset will be converted into cash in order to pay a debt that is due.

Since for nearly all firms cash inflows and cash outflows are not perfectly synchronized, some level of net working capital is necessary. The firm's cash outflows resulting from payment of current liabilities are relatively predictable. The firm generally learns when bills are due at the time that an obligation is incurred. For instance, when merchandise is purchased on credit, the credit terms extended to the firm require payment at a known point in time. The same predictability is associated with notes payable and accruals, which have stated payment dates. What is difficult to predict are the firm's cash inflows. Predicting when current assets other than cash and marketable securities will be converted into cash is quite difficult. The more predictable these cash inflows are, the less net working capital a firm requires. Firms with more uncertain cash inflows must maintain levels of current assets adequate to cover current liabilities (i.e., scheduled cash outflows).

EXAMPLE   For the GHI Company Ltd., which has the current position given in Table 7.2, the following situation may exist. All $600 of the firm's accounts payable, plus $200 of its notes payable and $100 in accruals, are due at the end of the current period. That this $900 in disbursements must be made is certain; how the firm will cover these disbursements is not certain. The firm can be sure that $700 will be available since it has $500 in cash and $200 in marketable securities, which can be easily converted into cash. The remaining $200 must come from the collection of an account receivable, or the sale of inventory for cash, or both.* The firm cannot be sure when either a cash sale or the collection of an account receivable will occur. Although customers who have purchased goods on credit are expected to pay for them by the date specified in the credit arrangement, quite often they will not pay until a later date. Thus the cash flows associated with the sale will not necessarily occur at the point in time they were expected.

Table 7.2   The Current Position of the GHI Company Ltd.

Current assets		Current liabilities	
Cash	$ 500	Accounts payable	$ 600
Marketable securities	200	Notes payable	800
Accounts receivable	800	Accruals	200
Inventory	1,200	Total	$1,600
Total	$2,700		

*A sale of inventory for credit would show up as a new account receivable, which could not be easily converted into cash. Only a *cash sale* will guarantee the firm that its bill-paying ability during the period of the sale has been enhanced.

Of course, some solution to this dilemma must exist. In order to have a higher probability of having sufficient cash to pay its bills, a firm should attempt to make sales, since in many cases sales will result in the immediate receipt of cash, and in other cases they will result in accounts receivable that will eventually be converted into cash. A level of inventory adequate to satisfy the probable demand for the firm's products should be maintained. As long as the firm is generating sales and collecting receivables as they come due, sufficient cash should be forthcoming to satisfy its cash payment obligations. The more accounts receivable and inventories there are on hand, the greater the probability that some of these items will be turned into cash.* As a rule, a certain level of net working capital is often recommended in order to ensure that a firm will be able to pay bills. The GHI Company has $1,100 of net working capital ($2,700 − $1,600), which will most likely be sufficient to cover all its bills. Its current ratio of 1.69 ($2,700 ÷ $1,600) should provide sufficient liquidity as long as its accounts receivable and inventories are relatively liquid.

AN ALTERNATE DEFINITION OF NET WORKING CAPITAL

An alternate definition of net working capital is *that portion of a firm's current assets financed with long-term funds.* This definition can best be illustrated by a special type of balance sheet, like that for the GHI Company presented in Figure 7.1. The vertical axis of the balance sheet is a dollar scale on which all the major items on the firm's balance sheet are indicated.

Figure 7.1 shows that the firm has current assets of $2,700, fixed assets of $4,300, and total assets of $7,000. It also shows that the firm has current liabilities of $1,600, long-

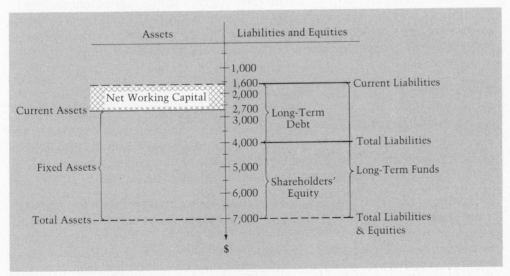

Figure 7.1   A special balance sheet for the GHI Company Ltd.

*It should be recognized that levels of accounts receivable or inventory can be too high, reflecting certain management inefficiencies. Acceptable levels for any firm can be calculated. The efficient management of accounts receivable and inventory is discussed in Chapters 9 and 10, respectively.

term debts of $2,400 ($4,000 − $1,600), and shareholders' equity of $3,000 ($7,000 − $4,000). Thus, the GHI Company's long-term funds equal $5,400. The portion of the firm's current assets that have been financed with long-term funds has been labeled "net working capital" in Figure 7.1. Since current liabilities represent the firm's sources of short-term funds, as long as current assets exceed current liabilities the amount of the excess must be financed with longer-term funds. The usefulness of this alternate definition will become more apparent in a later section of the chapter.

IMPORTANCE FOR SMALL BUSINESSES

Efficient working capital management is extremely important for small businesses, since they are often concentrated in retailing or the service industries, where large investments in fixed assets are not needed. Also, while a small business can minimize its fixed-asset investments by renting or leasing, it *cannot* avoid investments in current assets, such as cash, receivables, and inventories. In addition, a small business must necessarily rely heavily on short-term financings, because most small businesses have relative difficulty in accessing the long-term capital markets.

The Trade-Off Between Profitability and Risk*

A trade-off exists between a firm's profitability and risk. Profitability, in this context, is measured by profits after expenses; while risk is measured by the probability of a firm becoming *technically insolvent* (i.e., unable to pay bills as they come due). A firm's risk of becoming technically insolvent is most commonly measured using either the firm's level of net working capital or its current ratio. A firm's profits may be increased by (1) increasing its sales and (2) decreasing its costs, or both. Costs can be reduced by paying less for a good or a service, or by using existing resources more efficiently. Profits can also be increased by obtaining new resources and investing them profitably.

SOME BASIC ASSUMPTIONS

To illustrate the profitability-risk trade-off, a number of basic assumptions are made. The first concerns the nature of the firm being analyzed; the second concerns the nature of the relationship between a firm's net working capital position and the firm's risk of insolvency; the third concerns the differences in the earning power of assets; and the fourth concerns differences in the cost of various methods of financing.

The Nature of the Firm   For ease of exposition, we will refer primarily to manufacturing firms. However, this does not mean that the analysis only applies to manu-

---

*As was discussed in Chapter 1 (and to be discussed also in Chapter 18), the preferred conceptual approach for evaluating asset- and financing-mix decisions is to evaluate their effect on the *value of the firm, and not on the firm's profitability and risk.* The effect on the firm's market value provides an unambiguous measure of the owners' or shareholders' preference for various profitability-risk combinations. The profitability-risk trade-off approach, however, is generally used in practice because it is much easier to implement.

facturing firms. The same basic trade-off between profitability and risk also applies to other firms, such as retailing firms.

Relationship Between a Firm's Net Working Capital Position and Its Risk   In the following discussion, it is assumed that, if a firm's expected production, sales, factor prices, and selling prices are held constant, then *a firm's risk of insolvency will generally decrease as its net working capital increases.* In other words, if all other factors are held constant, the more net working capital, the more liquid the firm, and therefore the less likely it is to become technically insolvent. The relationship between liquidity, net working capital, and risk is such that if either net working capital or liquidity increases, the firm's risk will decrease, and vice versa.

The Earning Power of Assets   Although fixed assets represent the explicit (i.e., visible) earning assets of a firm, a firm's earnings are also generated by its current assets. Unfortunately, of the basic current assets, only marketable securities normally have a nonzero *explicit* return. The return from other current assets, such as cash, accounts receivable, and inventory, is *implicit;* that is, it is embodied in the stream of earnings generated by the firm's fixed assets. Thus, it is difficult to identify the specific contribution made by a (manufacturing) firm's current assets to the firm's earnings.

Nonetheless, a rational value-maximizing firm will strive to employ an "optimal" combination of current and fixed assets; that is, the particular combination at which the marginal risk-adjusted return on current assets equals that on fixed assets. Since current assets are generally considered to be less risky than fixed assets *for manufacturing firms,* it is assumed in the following discussion *that the firm expects to earn a higher return on fixed assets than on current assets.* Before proceeding, the reader should note that the expected return on fixed assets is higher than the expected return on current assets because it includes a premium to compensate for its greater risk.

The Nominal Cost of Financing   The firm can obtain its required financing from either current liabilities or long-term funds. Of the basic current liabilities, only notes payable normally have a stated cost, because notes payable represent the only negotiated form of borrowing. Accounts payable and accruals are cheaper nominal (i.e., explicit) sources of funds than notes payable, since they do not normally have any type of interest payment directly associated with them.

Historically, short-term funds have generally cost less than long-term funds. In the recent past, interest rates have been increasing and people have expected higher interest rates in the future.* Lenders with such expectations will typically provide short-term funds at rates below those charged for longer-term funds.† If interest rates are expected

---

*The relationship between the maturity of the debt and the interest rate on the debt is commonly referred to as "the term structure of interest rates."

†There have been periods when short-term interest rates have exceeded long-term rates, but these periods have been exceptions rather than the norm. The third quarter of 1973 through 1974, and the last quarter of 1979 and the first quarter of 1980, were periods during which the short-term rates were above long-term rates. This behaviour typically occurs during periods of "tight money" or economic recession. That is, it occurs generally during periods in which both long-term and short-term interest rates are relatively high.

to increase in the future, a lender will charge a high enough rate of interest on a longer-term loan to compensate for tying up a given amount of money for a long period, thus losing future opportunities to lend the same money at increased rates.

Therefore, whenever lenders believe that future interest rates will rise, short-term borrowing rates are less than long-term rates. When future rates are expected to decline from a currently high level, long-term rates are most often below short-term rates. Since increasing interest rates have prevailed in the most recent past, and since accounts payable and accruals are virtually interest-free, it is assumed below that *short-term funds are nominally cheaper than long-term funds* (i.e., the explicit cost of short-term funds is lower).

Financing Risks   Although short-term debt is generally cheaper than long-term debt, an additional risk is undertaken by a firm when it uses short-term debt. There are two underlying factors that account for this added risk. First, while long-term borrowings can be associated with relatively stable interest costs over time, short-term borrowings are generally associated with uncertain (fluctuating) interest costs over time. In fact, in periods of inflation with rising interest rates, the future short-term interest rates may exceed the present long-term rate for the entire life of the longer-lived instrument. In such situations, the effective (or real) cost of short-term funds would be greater than that for the long-term funds. Second, a firm that borrows heavily on a short-term basis may find itself unable to repay its debt as scheduled, or it may find that its financial position has deteriorated to the point where no lender will refinance its short-term loan. In such cases, the firm could be forced into bankruptcy.

Although this financial risk must also be considered in the trade-off decision between profitability and risk, we will not consider it in the rest of this chapter; that is, we shall *assume that the expected nominal cost of the firm's current liabilities is constant for the period under review.*

THE NATURE OF THE TRADE-OFF BETWEEN PROFITABILITY AND RISK

If a firm wants to increase its profitability, it must also increase its risk. If it wants to decrease risk, it must decrease profitability. The trade-off between these variables is such that regardless of how the firm increases its profitability through the manipulation of working capital, the consequence is a corresponding increase in risk as measured by the level of net working capital. The effects of changing current assets and changing current liabilities on the firm's profitability-risk trade-off will first be discussed separately.

Current Assets   The effects of the firm's level of current assets on its profitability-risk trade-off can be illustrated by using the ratio of the firm's current assets to its total assets.

Effects of an Increase in the Ratio   If all other factors are held constant, then as the ratio of current assets to total assets increases, both the profitability and risk of a firm decrease. A firm's profitability decreases because, as was discussed earlier, the expected return on the less risky current assets is lower than that on the more risky fixed assets. The risk of technical insolvency decreases because, assuming that the firm's current liabilities do not change, the increase in the firm's current assets will increase its net working capital.

Effects of a Decrease in the Ratio   The consequences of a decrease in the ratio of current to total assets are exactly the opposite of the results of an increase in the ratio.

EXAMPLE   The balance sheet for the GHI Company Ltd., which was presented in Figure 7.1, indicated the following levels of assets, liabilities, and equity:

Assets		Liabilities and equity	
Current assets	$2,700	Current liabilities	$1,600
Fixed assets	4,300	Long-term debts	2,400
		Equity	3,000
Total	$7,000	Total	$7,000

If the GHI Company earns approximately 2 percent on its current assets and 12 percent on its fixed assets, the current balance sheet configuration will allow it to earn approximately $570 [(2% · $2,700) + (12% · $4,300)] on its total assets. The firm's net working capital is currently $1,100 ($2,700 − $1,600). Its ratio of current assets to total assets is approximately .386 ($2,700 ÷ $7,000).

If the firm *decreases* this ratio by investing $300 more in fixed assets (and thus has $300 less in current assets), the new ratio of current to total assets is .343 ($2,400 ÷ $7,000). The firm's profits on its total assets will then be $600 [2% · ($2,400) + 12% ($4,600)]. Its net working capital will be $800 ($2,400 − $1,600).

As Table 7.3 indicates, as the firm's ratio of current to total assets decreases from .386 to .343, its profits on its total assets increase from $570 to $600. Its risk, measured by the amount of net working capital, increases, since its net working capital is reduced from $1,100 to $800. This supports our earlier conclusions concerning the profitability-risk trade-off as related to the firm's current assets.

Table 7.3   The Effects of a Change in GHI's Current Assets

Item	Initial value	Value after change
Ratio of current to total assets	.386	.343
Profits on total assets	$ 570	$ 600
Net working capital	$1,100	$ 800

Current Liabilities   The effects of changing the level of a firm's current liabilities on its profitability-risk trade-off can also be demonstrated using the ratio of the firm's current liabilities to its total assets.

Effects of an Increase in the Ratio   As the ratio of current liabilities to total assets increases, the firm's profitability increases. Profitability increases due to the decreased costs associated with using more lower-cost short-term financing and less higher-cost long-term financing. If current assets are assumed to remain unchanged, risk will increase due to the decrease in net working capital as current liabilities increase.

Effects of a Decrease in the Ratio   The consequences of a decrease in the ratio of current liabilities to total assets are exactly the opposite of the results of an increase in this ratio.

EXAMPLE   The balance sheet for the GHI Company Ltd. in the preceding section can also be used to show the effects of an *increase* in the firm's current liabilities. Initially the ratio of current liabilities to total assets is .229 ($1,600 ÷ $7,000). Assume that the firm's current liabilities cost approximately 3 percent to maintain, while the average cost of its long-term funds is 8 percent. Ignoring the changes made in the preceding example, the effect of shifting $300 from long-term funds into current liabilities will increase current liabilities to $1,900 ($1,600 + $300) and decrease long-term funds to $5,100 ($5,400 − $300). The new ratio of current liabilities to total assets will be .271 ($1,900 ÷ $7,000). The result of this change will be a decrease in *costs* from the current level of $480 [(3% · $1,600) + (8% · $5,400)] to $465 [(3% · $1,900) + (8% · $5,100)]. The firm's net working capital will decrease from the initial level of $1,100 to $800 ($2,700 − $1,900).

As Table 7.4 illustrates, as the firm's ratio of current liabilities to total assets increases from .229 to .271, the firm's profits increase by $15 (since its costs drop from $480 to $465). Meanwhile, the firm's risk increases, since its net working capital, or liquidity, decreases from $1,100 to $800.

Table 7.4   The Effects of a Change in GHI's Current Liabilities

Item	Initial value	Value after change
Ratio of current liabilities to total assets	.229	.271
Cost of financing[a]	$ 480	$ 465
Net working capital	$1,100	$ 800

[a]If sales are held constant, a decrease in any of the firm's costs will result in an equivalent increase in profitability.

Combined Effects   In the preceding two examples, the effects of a decrease in the ratio of current to total assets (Table 7.3) and the effects of an increase in the ratio of current liabilities to total assets (Table 7.4) were illustrated. Both changes, considered independently, were shown to increase the firm's profitability, while increasing its risk. Logically, then, the combined effect of these actions should be as is illustrated in Table 7.5.

As is given in Table 7.5, the combined effect of the two changes illustrated earlier is an increase in profits of $45 and a decrease in net working capital (liquidity) of $600 ($1,100 − $500). The trade-off here is obvious; the firm has increased its profitability by increasing its risk.

Table 7.5 The Combined Effects of Changes in GHI's Current Assets and Current Liabilities

Change	Change in profits	Change in net working capital
Decrease in ratio of current to total assets	+ $30	− $300
Increase in ratio of current liabilities to total assets	+ $15	− $300
Combined effect	+ $45	− $600

GHI's *initial net profit* of $90 can be viewed as being the difference between the initial profits on total assets and the initial cost of financing ($570 − $480). After the changes in current assets and current liabilities, the firm's profits on its total assets increase to $600, while the cost of financing decreases to $465. Its net profits therefore increase to $135 ($600 − $465).

Determining the Financing Mix

One of the most important decisions a financial manager makes is to determine how current liabilities will be used to finance current assets. One of the critical factors that must be kept in mind when making this decision is that only a limited amount of short-term financing (current liabilities) is available to any business firm. The amount of current liabilities available is limited by the dollar amount of purchases in the case of accounts payable, by the dollar amount of accrued liabilities in the case of accruals, and by the amount of seasonal borrowing considered acceptable by lenders in the case of notes payable. Lenders generally make short-term loans only to allow a firm to finance seasonal buildups of inventory or accounts receivable; *they generally do not lend short-term money for long-term uses.**

The firm's financing requirements can thus be broken into a permanent and a seasonal need. The permanent need, which consists of fixed assets plus the permanent portion of the firm's current assets, remains unchanged over the year; the seasonal need, which is attributable to the existence of certain temporary current assets, varies over the year. The relationship between current and fixed assets and permanent and seasonal funds requirements can be illustrated graphically with the aid of a simple example.

EXAMPLE The GHI Company's estimate of current, fixed, and total asset requirements on a monthly basis for the coming year are given in columns 1, 2, and 3 of Table 7.6. Columns 4 and 5 present a breakdown of the total requirement into its permanent and seasonal components. The permanent component (column 4) is the lowest level of total funds required during the period, while the seasonal portion is the difference between the total funds requirement (i.e., total assets) for each month and the permanent funds requirement.

*The rationale for, techniques of, and parties to short-term business loans are discussed in detail in Chapters 11 and 12. The primary sources of short-term loans to businesses, the chartered banks, make these loans for seasonal or self-liquidating purposes, such as temporary buildups of accounts receivable or inventory.

By comparing the firm's fixed assets found in column 2 to its permanent funds requirement given in column 4, it can be seen that the permanent funds requirement exceeds the firm's level of fixed assets. This result occurs because $800 of the firm's current assets are permanent, since they are apparently always being replaced. This value represents the maximum level of current assets that remains on the firm's books throughout the year. This value can also be found by subtracting the level of fixed assets from the permanent funds requirement ($13,800 − $13,000 = $800). The relationships presented in Table 7.6 are depicted graphically in Figure 7.2.

Table 7.6   Estimated Funds Requirements for the GHI Company Ltd.

Month	Current assets (1)	Fixed assets (2)	Total assets[a] (1) + (2) (3)	Permanent requirement (4)	Seasonal requirement (3) − (4) (5)
January	$4,000	$13,000	$17,000	$13,800	$3,200
February	3,000	13,000	16,000	13,800	2,200
March	2,000	13,000	15,000	13,800	1,200
April	1,000	13,000	14,000	13,800	200
May	800	13,000	13,800	13,800	0
June	1,500	13,000	14,500	13,800	700
July	3,000	13,000	16,000	13,800	2,200
August	3,700	13,000	16,700	13,800	2,900
September	4,000	13,000	17,000	13,800	3,200
October	5,000	13,000	18,000	13,800	4,200
November	3,000	13,000	16,000	13,800	2,200
December	2,000	13,000	15,000	13,800	1,200

[a]This represents the firm's total funds requirement.

There are three basic approaches to determining an appropriate financing mix—(1) the aggressive approach, (2) the conservative approach, and (3) a trade-off between the two.*

THE AGGRESSIVE APPROACH

The aggressive approach requires that the firm finance its short-term needs with short-term funds and long-term needs with long-term funds.† Seasonal variations in the firm's fund requirements are met from short-term sources of funds, while permanent financing needs are met from long-term sources of funds.

*It is important to recognize that the discussions that follow do not explicitly address the various types of financing used and currently found on the firm's books.
†The "aggressive" approach is used in this chapter to indicate a process of *matching* maturities of debt with the duration of each of the firm's financial needs.

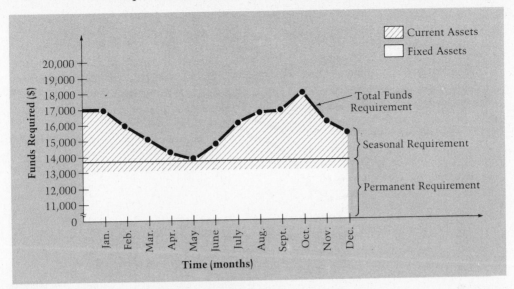

Figure 7.2   GHI Company's estimated funds requirements.

EXAMPLE   The GHI Company's estimate of its total funds requirements (i.e., total assets) on a monthly basis for the coming year has been given in Table 7.6, column 3. Columns 4 and 5 divide this total funds requirement into permanent and seasonal components.

The aggressive approach requires that the permanent portion of the firm's funds requirement be financed with long-term funds and the seasonal portion be financed with short-term funds, as is illustrated graphically in Figure 7.3.

Using the aggressive approach a firm's working capital would equal the portion of its current assets financed by long-term funds. Thus, the GHI Company's net working capital would amount to $800, which is the portion of its current assets financed using long-term funds (i.e., $13,800 permanent financing − $13,000 in fixed assets). This strategy would therefore be quite risky due to the low level of net working capital maintained.

Cost Considerations   If the cost of short-term funds needed by GHI in the example above is 3 percent and the cost of long-term funds is 8 percent, the cost of the financing plan can be estimated as follows:

The Cost of the Short-Term Funds   The cost of the short-term funds can be estimated by calculating the average annual short-term loan and multiplying this amount by the annual cost of short-term funds of 3 percent. The average annual short-term funds requirement can be estimated by dividing the sum of the monthly seasonal funds re-

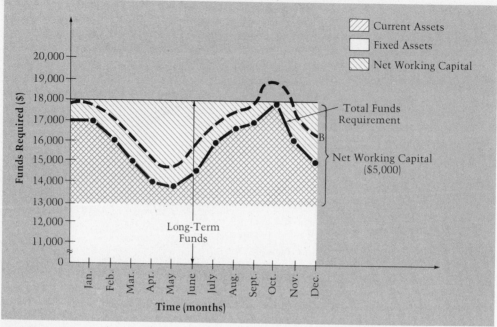

Figure 7.3 Applying the aggressive approach to the GHI Company's fund requirements.

quirements (column 5 in Table 7.6) by 12.* The sum of the seasonal funds requirements is $23,400, and the average short-term funds requirement is $1,950 ($23,400 ÷ 12). Thus the cost of short-term funds under this plan is $58.50 (3% · $1,950).

The Cost of the Long-Term Funds   The cost of the long-term funds can be calculated by multiplying the average annual permanent fund requirement of $13,800 (from column 4 in Table 7.6) by the annual cost of long-term funds of 8 percent. The resulting cost of long-term funds under the aggressive plan is $1,104 (8% · $13,800).

The Total Cost of the Aggressive Plan   The total cost of the aggressive plan ($1,162.50) can be found by adding the cost of the short-term funds ($58.50) and the cost of the long-term funds ($1,104). This figure will become more meaningful when compared to the cost of various other plans.

Risk Considerations   The aggressive plan operates with minimum net working capital since none of the firm's short-term seasonal needs are financed using long-term funds. For the GHI Company Ltd., the level of net working capital is therefore equal to $800, which is the amount of permanent current assets (i.e., $13,800 permanent requirement − $13,000 in fixed assets). The aggressive plan is risky not

---

*In calculating the average funds requirement, we have merely converted the monthly funds requirements into an equivalent balance for the entire year. In other words, instead of calculating the cost for each month and summing the monthly amounts, we have multiplied the average balance by the annual interest rate in order to find the annual interest cost.

only from the standpoint of low net working capital but also because the firm is drawing as heavily as possible on its short-term sources of funds to meet seasonal fluctuations in its funds requirements. If its total funds requirement actually turns out to be, say, the level indicated by the dashed line B in Figure 7.3, the firm may find it quite difficult to obtain a sufficient amount of short-term funds. Moreover, it may be impossible to obtain longer-term funds quickly enough to satisfy the firm's short-term needs.

THE CONSERVATIVE APPROACH

A very conservative approach would be to finance all the firm's projected funds requirements with long-term funds, and to use short-term funds in the event of an emergency or an unexpected outflow of funds. In practice, this approach could not be implemented, since some current liabilities (such as accounts payable and accruals) are virtually unavoidable. Furthermore, it would also be unwise for a firm to have no accounts payable and accruals, since these sources of funds are virtually costless.

In illustrating this approach, the distinction between payables and accruals will be ignored. For GHI a very conservative approach would involve meeting all the forecast funds requirements, even the entire $18,000 needed in October, with long-term funds; and reserving the use of short-term financing for contingencies.

EXAMPLE   Figure 7.4 shows graphically the application of the conservative approach to the estimated funds requirements for GHI given in Table 7.6. All the funds required over the one-year period, including the entire $18,000 forecast for October, are financed with long-term funds. The firm's net working capital, defined here as the portion of the firm's current assets financed by long-term funds, amounts to $5,000 ($18,000 − $13,000).* Any long-term financing in excess of the $13,000 in fixed-asset requirements provides net working capital.

Cost Considerations   The effects of this conservative approach on the firm's profitability can be measured by determining the cost of this financing plan. Since the average long-term financing balance with the conservative financing plan is $18,000, the total cost of this plan is $1,440 (8% · $18,000). Comparing this figure to the total cost of $1,162.50 using the aggressive approach indicates the more expensive nature of the conservative approach. The reason the conservative approach is so expensive can be seen by looking at Figure 7.4; the area above the total funds requirement line and below the long-term financing line (shown by diagonal lines going from left to right only) represents the level of funds not actually needed, but on which the firm is paying interest (i.e., the amount of excess funds available).†

---

*The level of net working capital is constant throughout the year since the firm has $5,000 in current assets that will be fully financed with long-term funds. Because the portion of the $5,000 in excess of the scheduled level of current assets is assumed to be held as cash, the firm's current asset balance will increase to this level.

†Note that it would be more realistic for the firm to "store" much of this excess liquidity in the form of marketable securities, which would lower the effective cost of this approach.

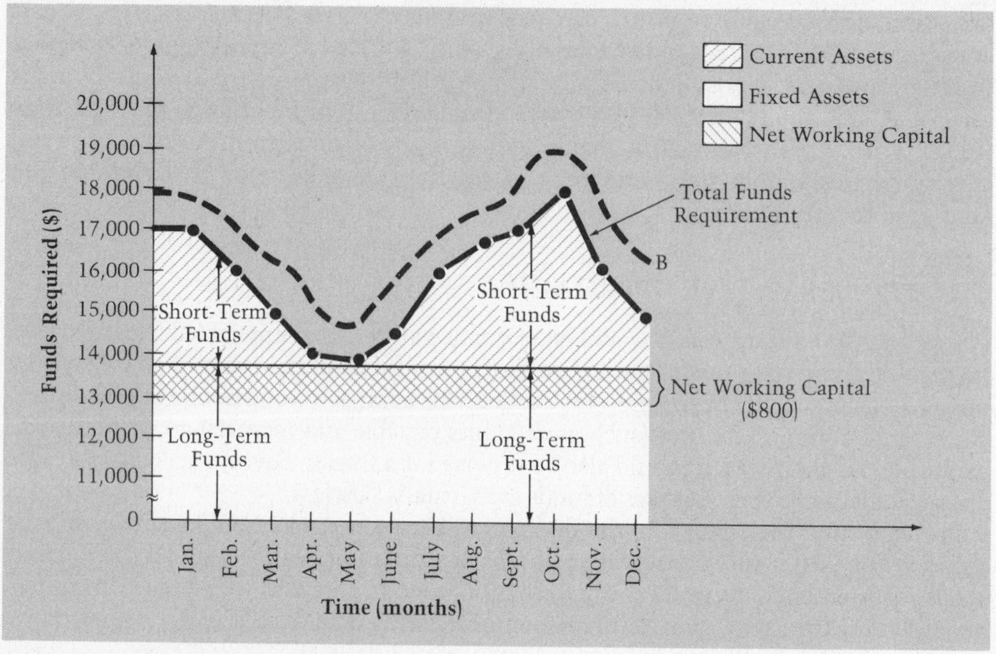

Figure 7.4   Applying the conservative approach to the GHI Company's fund requirements.

Risk Considerations   The $5,000 of net working capital (i.e., $18,000 long-term financing – $13,000 of fixed assets) associated with this plan should mean a very low level of risk for the firm. The firm's risk should also be lowered by the fact that the plan does not require the firm to use any of its limited short-term borrowing capacity. In other words, if the firm's total required financing actually turns out to be the level represented by the dashed line B in Figure 7.4, sufficient short-term borrowing capacity should be available to cover the unexpected financial needs and avoid technical insolvency.

Comparison with the Aggressive Approach   Unlike the aggressive approach, the conservative approach requires the firm to pay interest on unneeded funds, and is therefore less profitable than the aggressive approach. However, the aggressive approach is much more risky. The contrast between these two approaches should clearly indicate the trade-off that exists between profitability and risk. The aggressive approach provides high profits but also a high risk, while the conservative approach provides low profits and a low risk. A trade-off between these extremes should result in an acceptable financing strategy for most firms.

A TRADE-OFF BETWEEN THE TWO APPROACHES: THE INTERMEDIATE APPROACH

Most firms use a financing plan that lies somewhere between the high-profit–high-risk aggressive approach and the low-profit–low-risk conservative approach. The exact trade-off made between profitability and risk depends largely on the decision maker's attitude toward risk. One of many possible trade-offs in GHI Company's case is described below.

EXAMPLE After careful analysis, the GHI Company Ltd. has decided on a financing plan based on an amount of permanent financing equal to the midpoint of the minimum and maximum monthly funds requirement for the period. An examination of Table 7.6 reveals that the minimum monthly funds requirement is $13,800 (in May) and the maximum monthly funds requirement is $18,000 (in October). The midpoint between these two values is $15,900 [($13,800 + $18,000) ÷ 2]. Thus, the firm will use $15,900 in long-term funds each month and raise any additional funds required from short-term sources, as is given in Table 7.7.

Table 7.7 A Financing Plan Based on a Trade-off Between Profitability and Risk for the GHI Company Ltd.

Month	Total assets[a] (1)	Long-term funds (2)	Short-term funds[b] (3)
January	$17,000	$15,900	$1,100
February	16,000	15,900	100
March	15,000	15,900	0
April	14,000	15,900	0
May	13,800	15,900	0
June	14,500	15,900	0
July	16,000	15,900	100
August	16,700	15,900	800
September	17,000	15,900	1,100
October	18,000	15,900	2,100
November	16,000	15,900	100
December	15,000	15,900	0

[a]This represents the firm's total funds requirement from column 3 of Table 7.6.
[b]Whenever the level of total funds required is less than the level of long-term funds available, no short-term funds are needed.

Implementing this plan would result in net working capital as high as $2,900 ($15,900 long-term funds − $13,000 fixed assets). This level is between the high-risk level of the aggressive approach (which provides $800 of net working capital) and the low-risk position of the conservative approach (which provides $5,000 of net working capital).

Figure 7.5 graphically presents the trade-off described in Table 7.7, along with the plans based on the aggressive and the conservative approaches. The area (shown by diagonal lines going from left to right only) above the total funds requirement line and below the long-term financing line (line 3) represents the level of funds not actually needed but on which the firm is paying interest.

Cost Considerations The cost of the trade-off plan can be calculated as was explained before.

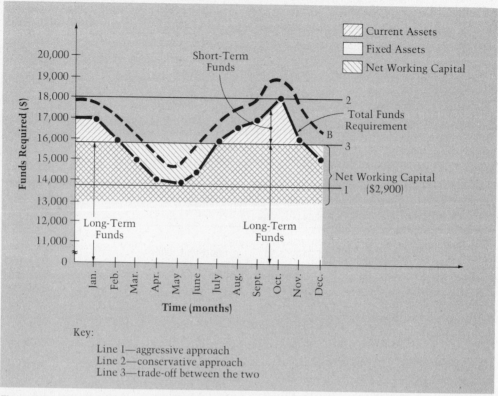

Figure 7.5 Three alternative financing plans for GHI Company Ltd.

The Cost of Short-Term Funds The sum of the seasonal funds requirements is $5,400. The average short-term funds requirement is thus $450 ($5,400 ÷ 12), and the cost of short-term funds with this plan is $13.50 (3% · $450).

The Cost of Long-Term Funds The cost of long-term funds of $1,272 is found by multiplying the average long-term fund requirement of $15,900 (from column 2 of Table 7.7) by the annual cost of long-term funds of 8 percent.

The Total Cost of the Trade-Off Plan The total cost of the trade-off plan is therefore $1,285.50 ($13.50 + $1,272.00).

Risk Considerations As Figure 7.5 shows, the trade-off plan is less risky than the aggressive approach but more risky than the conservative approach. With the trade-off plan, if the firm's total funds requirement is actually at the level given by line B in Figure 7.5, the likelihood that it will be able to obtain additional short-term financing is good, since a portion of its short-term financial requirements is actually being financed with long-term funds. With respect to cost, the trade-off plan falls between the aggressive approach, which has the lowest cost, and the conservative approach, which has the highest cost.

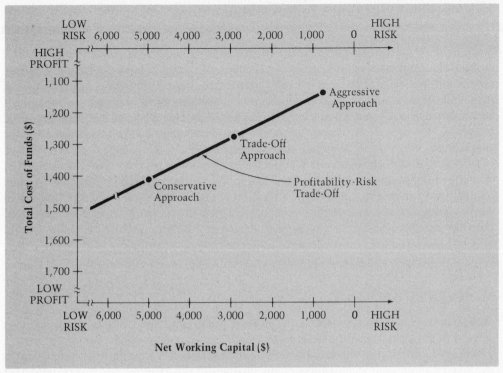

Figure 7.6   A graph of the profitability-risk trade-off for the GHI Company Ltd.

A SUMMARY COMPARISON OF APPROACHES

Table 7.8 and Figure 7.6 summarize the results of the analysis of each of the plans. Care should be used in analyzing Figure 7.6, since each of the axes measures two variables. As one moves to the left on the x-axis, risk decreases due to increasing net working capital. Unfortunately, profits also decrease, since one is also moving down the y-axis, and thus encountering increasing funds costs. The financial manager must choose the financing plan which suits his or her risk preferences.

Table 7.8   A Summary of the Results of the Three Financing Plans for the GHI Company Ltd.

Financing plan	Net working capital[a]	Degree of risk	Total cost of funds	Level of profits
Aggressive	$ 800.00	Highest	$1,162.50	Highest
Trade-off (intermediate)	$2,900.00	Intermediate	$1,285.50	Intermediate
Conservative	$5,000.00	Lowest	$1,440.00	Lowest

[a]These values represent the amount of net working capital provided by each financing plan as determined in the preceding examples.

International Working Capital Management

Financial executives of multinational firms must manage their working capital on a global basis. Such management involves the determination of both the level and monetary denomination of current assets and current liabilities. Thus, management of working capital on a global basis includes not only the problems and opportunities encountered on a domestic basis, but also the added problems caused by the fact that the monetary denomination of such accounts can be a major factor in minimizing the exposure to currency fluctuations and devaluation risks.

Working capital management practices designed to respond to the risks of foreign exchange fluctuations and devaluations can involve either specific contractual arrangements in the forward markets or the alteration of the composition and denomination of various current asset and liability accounts. Since the working capital management practices designed to reduce exposure to exchange loss are not cost-free, they should only be used up to the point where the efficiency or opportunity lost is not greater than the potential monetary loss of the exchange adjustment.

MONETARY BALANCE

Monetary assets are those assets, such as cash and accounts receivable, whose value is defined in terms of a fixed monetary unit (such as a Canadian dollar or a Japanese yen). *Monetary liabilities* are those obligations, such as accounts payable, which are payable in a fixed monetary unit, regardless of any changes in the value (or purchasing power) of that unit. Thus, a *monetary balance* is the difference between monetary assets and monetary liabilities for a specific monetary unit. A negative balance that occurs when monetary assets exceed monetary liabilities for a specific currency indicates that the firm is a net monetary creditor in that currency; a positive balance indicates that the firm is a net monetary debtor in that currency.*

To the extent that devaluation is associated with internal inflation, a multinational firm can maintain a net monetary debtor position to take advantage of an anticipated devaluation. If the devaluation occurs, the firm, being a net debtor in that currency, will gain.†

Insofar as is possible, a firm could obtain a net monetary debtor position by (1) the minimization of cash balances and other monetary assets in *"weak" ("soft") foreign currencies* by transferring these funds into *"strong" ("hard") currencies*; (2) the payment of outstanding hard currency debts on a first-priority basis; and (3) the incurrence of new liabilities denominated in weak currencies. For a multinational firm, much of this movement of funds can be accomplished largely by intracompany fund transfers. Unlike the payments between independent firms, the timing of intracompany payments between 100-percent owned subsidiaries of multinational firms can be accelerated or decelerated by management in order to benefit the overall organization.

---

*Currency and monetary unit are being used here interchangeably.
†If a specific currency is devalued, foreign debtors (borrowers) gain, while foreign creditors in that currency lose an equivalent amount.

Before protecting future revenues against foreign exchange risks, the multinational firm should match the time path of future receipts with that of future obligations denominated in the same currency. This should be done because only the balances, which result from the netting of various inflows and outflows of the same currency, need be protected from possible future adverse foreign exchange fluctuations.

Summary

This chapter has provided an in-depth look at the broad area of working capital management. Rather than looking at individual current assets and current liabilities, it has given specific attention to the relation between the two categories of accounts. The firm's net working capital, defined as the difference between its current assets and current liabilities, has been used as a focal point for analysis. The appropriate level of net working capital depends on the firm's cash-flow patterns. Firms maintain net working capital to provide a cushion between cash outflows and cash inflows. The significant differences between industrial sectors in working capital positions have been illustrated in this chapter by providing some working capital statistics for selected Canadian industrial sectors.

Net working capital is often used as a measure of the risk of technical insolvency by the firm. The more liquid a firm is, the less likely it will be unable to satisfy its current obligations as they come due. Since low levels of net working capital indicate a higher probability of insufficient liquidity, and vice versa, net working capital is a very useful measure of risk. Net working capital can also be defined as that portion of a firm's current assets financed with long-term funds.

In illustrating the profitability-risk trade-off related to the level of a firm's net working capital, we have made four basic assumptions: (1) that we are dealing with a manufacturing firm, (2) that a firm's risk of insolvency decreases as its net working capital increases, (3) that a firm expects to earn a higher return (before being risk-adjusted) on fixed assets than on current assets, and (4) that short-term funds are less expensive than long-term funds. The higher a firm's ratio of current-to-total assets, the less profitable the firm and the less risky. The converse is also true. The higher a firm's ratio of current liabilities to total assets, the more profitable and more risky the firm is. The converse of this statement is also true. These trade-offs between profitability and risk must be considered in evaluating a firm's net working capital position.

Since net working capital can be considered the portion of a firm's current assets financed by long-term funds, the mix between long-term and short-term financing is directly related to the profitability-risk trade-off and the firm's net working capital. By forecasting the firm's seasonal and permanent funds requirements, the financial manager can evaluate the consequences of various financing plans before deciding what portion of the company's current assets should be financed with long-term funds. The permanent need for funds is attributable to both fixed assets and the permanent portion of current assets, while the seasonal need is attributable to the existence of certain temporary current assets.

There are a number of approaches for determining an appropriate financing mix. The aggressive approach is a high-profit–high-risk financing plan, where seasonal needs are financed with short-term funds and permanent needs are financed with long-term funds. The conservative approach is a low-profit–low-risk financing plan, where all funds requirements are financed with long-term funds. Short-term funds are only used in emergencies. Most firms use a trade-off (or intermediate) approach whereby some of the firm's seasonal needs are financed with long-term funds.

International working capital management involves the determination of both the level and monetary denomination of current assets and current liabilities, in order to minimize the exposure of the firm to currency fluctuations and devaluation risks. For example, a multinational firm can maintain a net monetary debtor position, where current monetary liabilities exceed current monetary assets, in order to take advantage of an anticipated devaluation. Techniques for obtaining such a net monetary debtor position have been described in the chapter.

Questions

7.1 Why is working capital management considered so important by shareholders, creditors, and the firm's financial manager? What is the definition of net working capital?

7.2 What relationship would you expect to exist between the predictability of a firm's cash flows and its required level of net working capital?

7.3 Why are a firm's payments considered more predictable than its receipts?

7.4 Given that a firm's net working capital is sometimes defined as the portion of current assets financed with long-term funds, can you show diagrammatically why this definition is valid?

7.5 How are net working capital, liquidity, technical insolvency, and risk related?

7.6 Generally the cost of short-term borrowing is less than that of long-term borrowing. Why is it likely to be cheaper to incur current liabilities than to obtain long-term funds, even if the cost of short-term loans is greater than the cost of long-term funds?

7.7 Why is an increase in a firm's ratio of current to total assets expected to decrease both profits and risk as measured by net working capital?

7.8 How can changes in the ratio of a firm's current liabilities to total assets affect its profitability and risk?

7.9 How would you expect both an increase in a firm's ratio of current assets to total assets and a decrease in its ratio of current liabilities to total assets to affect its profits and risk? Why?

7.10 How can the differences between the returns on current and fixed assets and the cost of current liabilities and long-term funds be used to detemine how best to change a firm's net working capital?

7.11 What is the basic premise of the aggressive approach for meeting a firm's funds requirements? What are the effects of this approach on the firm's profitability and risk?

7.12 What is the conservative approach to financing a firm's funds requirements? What kind of profitability-risk trade-off is involved?

7.13 Why would a firm using the conservative approach be advised to finance no more than its projected peak financial need with long-term funds?

7.14 If a firm has a constant funds requirement throughout the year, which, if any, of the three financing plans is preferable? Why?

7.15 As the difference between the cost of short-term financing and long-term financing becomes smaller, which financing plan—aggressive or conservative—becomes more attractive? Would the aggressive or the conservative approach be preferable if the costs were equal? Why?

7.16 How would one apply the aggressive approach if one knew that only a certain amount of short-term financing, insufficient to cover the peak short-term need, would be available?

7.17 What are monetary assets and monetary liabilities? What is the significance of a negative monetary balance? How might a multinational firm take advantage of an anticipated devaluation in the monetary unit (currency) of one of its operations?

Problems

7.1 Last year, the NRC Corporation Ltd. had the following balance sheet:

Assets		Liabilities and equity	
Current assets	$ 6,000	Current liabilities	$ 2,000
Fixed assets	14,000	Long-term funds	18,000
Total	$20,000	Total	$20,000

The firm estimated that it earned 3 percent on current assets, current liabilities cost 6 percent, fixed assets earned 18 percent, and long-term funds cost 10 percent.

For the coming year, calculate the expected profits on total assets, financing costs, net profitability, current ratio, and ROI for each of the following circumstances:

a. There are no changes.

b. The firm shifts $1,000 from current assets to fixed assets, and $500 from long-term funds to current liabilities.

c. Discuss the changes in risk and return illustrated by **a** and **b** above.

7.2 The Badger Company Ltd. had the following balance sheet at the end of 19X0:

Assets		Liabilities and equity	
Current assets	$ 30,000	Current liabilities	$ 15,000
Fixed assets	90,000	Long-term funds	105,000
Total	$120,000	Total	$120,000

a. Calculate profits on total assets, financing costs, net profits, current ratio, and ROI for each of the following when the firm: (1) expects to earn 1 percent on current assets and 14 percent on fixed assets, and current liabilities cost 3 percent and long-term funds cost 10 percent; and (2) expects to earn 6 percent on current assets and 14 percent on fixed assets, and pay 6 percent on current liabilities and 9 percent on long-term funds.

b. The firm wishes to decrease net working capital by $10,000. This could be accomplished by decreasing current assets, increasing current liabilities, or a combination of the two. Under which circumstances—**a**(1) or **a**(2)—would you expect the greater reduction in current assets? Explain.

7.3 What is the average loan balance and the annual loan cost, given an annual interest rate on loans of 8 percent, for a firm with the total monthly borrowings given in the next table?

Month	Amount	Month	Amount
Jan.	$12,000	July	$6,000
Feb.	13,000	Aug.	5,000
Mar.	9,000	Sept.	6,000
Apr.	8,000	Oct.	5,000
May	9,000	Nov.	7,000
June	7,000	Dec.	9,000

7.4 International Tool Ltd. has forecast its total funds requirements for the coming year to be

Month	Amount	Month	Amount
Jan.	$2,000,000	July	$12,000,000
Feb.	2,000,000	Aug.	14,000,000
Mar.	2,000,000	Sept.	9,000,000
Apr.	4,000,000	Oct.	5,000,000
May	6,000,000	Nov.	4,000,000
June	9,000,000	Dec.	3,000,000

a. Calculate the financing costs for both the aggressive approach and the conservative approach for each of the following: (1) the cost of short-term funds is 5 percent, and the cost of long-term funds is 12 percent; and (2) the cost of short-term funds is 6 percent, and the cost of long-term funds is 8 percent.

b. Discuss the profitability-risk trade-offs associated with the aggressive plan and the conservative plan.

c. Which plan would more closely approximate your choice in a(1), and in a(2)? Why?

7.5 Petro-Gas Ltd. has forecast its seasonal financing needs for the next year as follows:

Month	Seasonal requirement	Month	Seasonal requirement
Jan.	$2,400,000	July	$ 800,000
Feb.	500,000	Aug.	400,000
Mar.	0	Sept.	0
Apr.	300,000	Oct.	300,000
May	1,200,000	Nov.	1,000,000
June	1,000,000	Dec.	1,800,000

Calculate the financing costs under the aggressive plan and the conservative plan and recommend one of the plans under the following conditions:

a. Short-term funds cost 4 percent, and long-term funds cost 12 percent.

b. Short-term funds cost 6 percent, and long-term funds cost 8 percent.

c. Both short-term and long-term funds cost 7 percent.

7.6 Mile High Enterprises Ltd. expects to need the following amounts of funds next year:

Month	Amount	Month	Amount
Jan.	$10,000	July	$10,000
Feb.	10,000	Aug.	9,000
Mar.	11,000	Sept.	8,000
Apr.	12,000	Oct.	8,000
May	13,000	Nov.	9,000
June	11,000	Dec.	9,000

a. What is the average amount of funding needed during the year?

b. If short-term financing costs 4 percent and long-term financing costs 10 percent, what will be the financing costs for the aggressive and conservative financing plans, respectively? *use trend analysis*

c. If the firm finances $10,000 with long-term financing, what will be the financing cost?

7.7 Snyder Supply has financing needs of $250,000 per month forecast for every month of the coming year. The cost of short-term financing is 6 percent, and the cost of long-term financing is 8 percent.

a. What are the costs of the aggressive and conservative financing plans?

b. Which plan is preferable and why?

Suggested Readings

Aigner, D. J. and C. M. Sprenkle, "On Optimal Financing of Cyclical Cash Needs," *Journal of Finance* 28 (December 1973), pp. 1249–1253.

Bean, Virginia L. and Reynolds Griffith, "Risk and Return in Working Capital Management," *Mississippi Valley Journal of Business and Economics* 1 (Fall 1966), pp. 28–48.

Beranek, William, *Working Capital Management* (Belmont, Calif.: Wadsworth, 1966).

Bierman, H., K. Chopra and J. Thomas, "Ruin Considerations: Optimal Working Capital and Capital Structure," *Journal of Financial and Quantitative Analysis* 10 (March 1975), pp. 119–128.

Bogen, Jules I., Ed., *Financial Handbook*, 4th ed. (New York: Ronald, 1968), sect. 16.

Cossaboom, Roger A., "Let's Reassess the Profitability-Liquidity Tradeoff," *Financial Executive* 39 (May 1971), pp. 46–51.

Glautier, M. W. E., "Towards a Reformulation of the Theory of Working Capital," *Journal of Business Finance* 3 (Spring 1971), pp. 37–42.

Jennings, Joseph A., "A Look at Corporate Liquidity," *Financial Executive* 39 (February 1971), pp. 26–32.

Knight, W. D., "Working Capital Management—Satisfying versus Optimization," *Financial Management* 1 (Spring 1972), pp. 33–40.

Mehta, Dileep R., *Working Capital Management* (Englewood Cliffs, N.J.: Prentice-Hall, 1974), chap. 1.

Merville, L. J. and L. A. Tavis, "Optimal Working Capital Policies: A Chance-Constrained Programming Approach," *Journal of Financial and Quantitative Analysis* 8 (January 1973), pp. 47–60.

Smith, Keith V., Ed., *Management of Working Capital: A Reader* (St. Paul. Minn.: West, 1974), readings 1, 30, and 34.

———, "State of the Art of Working Capital Management," *Financial Management* 2 (Autumn 1973), pp. 50–55.

Stancill, James McN., *The Management of Working Capital* (Scranton, Pa.: Intext, 1971), chaps. 1, 6, and 7.

Van Horne, James C., "A Risk-Return Analysis of a Firm's Working Capital Position," *Engineering Economist* 14 (Winter 1969), pp. 71–89.

Walker, Ernest W., "Towards a Theory of Working Capital," *Engineering Economist* 9 (January-February 1964), pp. 21–35.

Walter, James E., "Determination of Technical Solvency," *Journal of Business* 30 (January 1959), pp. 39–43.

Welter, Paul, "How to Calculate Savings Possible through Reduction of Working Capital," *Financial Executive* (October 1970), pp. 50–58.

Chapter 8

CASH AND MARKETABLE SECURITY MANAGEMENT

The management of cash and marketable securities is one of the key areas of working capital management. Since cash and marketable securities are the firm's most liquid assets, they provide the firm with the ability to pay bills as they come due. Collaterally, these liquid assets provide a pool of funds to cover unexpected outlays, thereby reducing the risk of a "liquidity crisis." Since the other major current assets (i.e., accounts receivable and inventory) will eventually be converted into cash through collections and sales, cash is the common denominator to which all liquid assets can be reduced.

Marketable securities represent short-term investments made by the firm to obtain a return on temporarily idle funds. When a firm recognizes that too large an amount of cash has been accumulated, it will often put a portion of the cash into an interest-earning instrument. Idle cash in the firm's checking account does not provide any interest income since chartered banks do not pay interest on demand deposits.* There are a number of highly liquid interest-earning instruments (referred to as marketable securities) that allow the firm to make a profit on its idle cash without sacrificing much of its liquidity.

This chapter has five sections. The first section is concerned with the firm's overall strategy with respect to the payment of accounts payable, the management of inventory, and the collection of accounts receivable. The second section provides a brief discussion of strategies for minimizing the firm's cash requirements. The third section discusses motives for holding marketable securities, aspects of marketability, and certain considerations with respect to the proportion of marketable securities held. The fourth section

---

*Business firms are being compensated for the "balances" they hold in chartered banks by receiving reduced activity fees or lower interest rates on loans or both. Thus, the explicit payment of interest on demand deposits would probably not significantly affect corporate banking relationships.

is devoted to a description of the characteristics, maturities, yields, and denominations of the most common marketable securities. The fifth section deals with some of the international aspects of cash and marketable security management.

The Efficient Management of Cash

The basic strategies that should be employed by the business firm in managing its cash are as follows:

1 Pay accounts payable as late as possible without damaging the firm's credit rating, but take advantage of any favourable cash discounts.*
2 Turn over inventory as quickly as possible, avoiding stockouts that might result in shutting down the production line or a loss of sales.
3 Collect accounts receivable as quickly as possible without losing future sales because of high-pressure collection techniques. Cash discounts, if they are economically justifiable, may be used to accomplish this objective.

The overall implications of these strategies for the firm can be demonstrated by looking at the cash turnover process.

CASH CYCLES AND CASH TURNOVERS

The *cash cycle* of a firm is defined as the amount of time that elapses from the point when the firm makes an outlay to purchase raw materials to the point when cash is collected from the sale of the finished good produced using those raw materials. The term *cash turnover* refers to the frequency of a firm's cash cycle during a year. The relationship between the cash cycle and cash turnover is similar to the relationship between the average age and turnover of inventory, accounts receivable, and accounts payable, discussed in Chapter 3. The concept of cash cycles and cash turnovers can be illustrated by a simple example.

EXAMPLE   The KLM Company Ltd. currently purchases all its raw materials on a credit basis and sells all its merchandise on credit.† The credit terms extended the firm currently require payment within 30 days of a purchase, while the firm currently requires its customers to pay within 60 days of a sale. The firm's calculations of the average age of its accounts payable and accounts receivable indicate that it is taking, on the average, 35 days to pay its accounts payable and 70 days to collect its accounts receivable. Further calculations reveal that, on the average, 85 days elapse between the point a raw material is purchased and the point the finished good is sold. In other words, the average age of the firm's inventory is 85 days.

*A discussion of the variables to consider in determining whether to take cash discounts appears in Chapter 11. A cash discount is often an enticement to pay accounts payable early in order to reduce the purchase price of goods.
†This assumption of all credit purchases and credit sales simplifies the cash management model. Although purchases and sales for cash could easily be incorporated into it, they have not been in order to convey the key cash management strategies with a minimum of algebraic complexity.

Cash cycle   The firm's cash cycle can be shown by a simple graph, as in Figure 8.1. There are 120 days between the cash outflow to pay the account payable (on day 35) and the cash inflow from the collection of the account receivable (on day 155). During this period, the firm's money is tied up.

At time zero the firm purchases raw materials, which are initially placed in the raw-materials inventory. Eventually the raw materials are used in the production process, becoming part of the work-in-process inventory. When the work in process is completed, the finished good is placed in the finished-goods inventory until it is sold. The total amount of time that elapses, on the average, between the purchase of raw materials and the ultimate sale of finished goods is the average age of inventory. In Figure 8.1, it is 85 days.

When the firm initially purchased the raw materials (on day 0), an account payable was established. It remained on the firm's books until it was paid, 35 days later. It was at this point that a *cash outflow* occurred. After the sale of the finished good (on day 85), the firm established an account receivable. This account receivable remained on its books until it was collected 70 days later. It was therefore 70 days after the item was sold, on day 155 (70 days beyond the 85th day, which was the day of sale) that a *cash inflow* occurred.

A firm's cash cycle is calculated by finding the average number of days that elapse between the cash outflows associated with paying accounts payable and the cash inflows associated with collecting accounts receivable. The cash cycle for the KLM Company is 120 days (155 days − 35 days).

Cash turnover   A firm's cash turnover can be calculated by dividing the cash cycle into 360, the assumed number of days in the year. The KLM Company's cash turnover is currently 3 (360 ÷ 120). The higher a firm's cash turnover is, the less cash the firm requires. The firm's cash turnover, like its inventory turnover, should be maximized. However, the firm does not want to run out of cash. The maintenance of a minimum amount of operating cash is discussed in the next two sections.

BANKING REQUIREMENTS FOR CASH BALANCES

Many firms must hold cash balances in order to satisfy their banking relationships. Since a bank provides many services to a firm, the bank must recoup the costs of the services that it provides to a firm. The bank can recoup its costs either by charging the firm with direct fees or by requiring the firm to hold maintenance balances. With the latter method, the bank must determine the average account balances necessary to provide sufficient income to compensate for the costs of the services rendered to their customers at no direct cost. (Naturally, the cost to the firm includes a profit loading for the bank.) These required balances are referred to as *maintenance balances.*

In addition, some bank loan agreements require compensating balances. For example, during "tight money" periods, banks have frequently insisted, as a condition for granting the loan, that borrowers maintain compensating balances equivalent to 10 percent of the loan amount. For the firm, the effective cost of the loan is increased whenever the compensating balance requirement results in the firm holding cash that it would not have held.

The present Bank Act stipulates that *compensating balances can not be used in a loan agreement unless the borrower has agreed to their use.* Generally, borrowers have

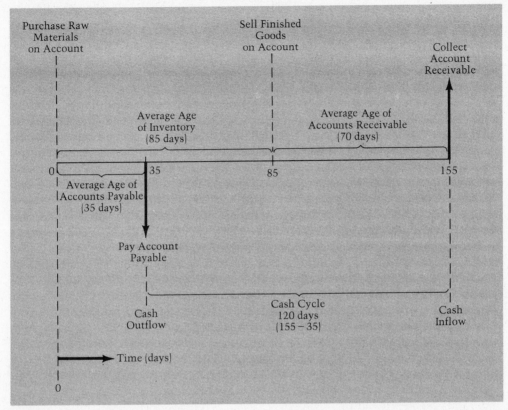

Figure 8.1 The KLM Company's cash cycle.

not objected to the inclusion of a compensating balance requirement in a loan agreement, since the borrowers know that compensating balances raise the effective rate of return to the lender.

Both maintenance and compensating balances can be determined as either (1) an absolute minimum level, above which the actual balance must always be; or (2) a minimum average balance for fixed periods, such as monthly periods. Fortunately for borrowers, the more stringent absolute minimum level requirement is seldom used in Canada.

DETERMINING A FIRM'S MINIMUM OPERATING CASH*

Because the firm must forego various opportunities to invest or repay debts in order to maintain a cash balance, the objective of the financial manager should be to operate in a

---

*The phrase "minimum operating cash" as used throughout this part of the chapter can more precisely be viewed as the "level of liquidity," which might be in the form of cash and marketable securities, needed to allow the firm to meet its payment obligations as they come due. Although the firm is expected to hold some part of its liquidity in marketable securities instead of cash, the phrase "minimum operating cash" is applicable, since to pay bills any liquidity warehoused in the form of a marketable security first will have to be converted into cash.

fashion that requires minimum cash. The amount of cash that will allow the firm to meet scheduled bill payments as they come due, and provide a margin of safety for making unscheduled payments or making scheduled payments when expected cash inflows are not available, must be planned for by the firm. This "cash," of course, can be held in the form of a demand deposit (i.e., checking account balance) or may be held in some type of interest-earning marketable security.

A variety of quantitative techniques, as well as rules of thumb, exist for the determination of the "optimum" cash balance.* The use of the cash budget, discussed in Chapter 5, presents a method for planning the firm's cash requirements; but it does not deal explicitly with the question of the appropriate cash balance level. The appropriate balance is the larger of (1) the cash required to meet both expected and unexpected cash requirements, or (2) the maintenance plus compensating balance requirements established by lenders.†

For the cases where the cash required to meet both expected and unexpected cash requirements is the larger, a common rule-of-thumb method for determining the firm's cash requirements is to set the minimum level of cash as a percentage of sales. For example, a firm wishing to maintain a cash balance equal to 8 percent of annual sales, which are expected to be $2,000,000, would maintain a balance of $160,000 (i.e., .08 · $2,000,000). More sophisticated approaches for determining necessary balances are based on the use of techniques such as calculus and statistics. For purposes of illustration, a simple yet appealing and practical technique is used to estimate the minimum liquidity level required. Using the framework already developed, the minimum level of operating cash needed by a firm can be estimated by dividing the firm's total annual outlays by its cash turnover rate.‡

EXAMPLE   If the KLM Company Ltd. (presented in the preceding example) spends approximately $12,000,000 annually on operating outlays, its minimum cash requirement is $4,000,000, ($12,000,000 ÷ 3). This means that if it begins the year with $4,000,000 in cash, it should have sufficient cash to pay bills as they come due. It should not have to borrow any additional funds in these circumstances. If the opportunity cost of holding cash is 5 percent, then the cost of maintaining a $4,000,000 cash balance will be $200,000 ($4,000,000 · .05) per year.

---

*It should be noted that the firm Johnson and Johnson has implemented an interesting technique, called the "treasury account," to minimize their idle cash balances.

†Although no empirical evidence is available on which is larger, experience suggests that the latter is generally the larger for manufacturing firms.

‡The logic of this calculation rests on the existence of the following equation for a firm's cash turnover:

$$\text{Cash turnover} = \frac{\text{total annual outlays}}{\text{average cash balance}}$$

Solving this equation for the average cash balance produces the following equation:

$$\text{Average cash balance} = \frac{\text{total annual outlays}}{\text{cash turnover}}$$

This model assumes that the *average* amount of cash required by the firm in order to operate is the same as the *minimum* amount.

Opportunity Cost Concept   The opportunity cost of 5 percent in the example above is based on the fact that the firm, if it were free to use the $4 million, could invest it in a riskless investment yielding a return of 5 percent per year or repay a debt costing 5 percent per year. Since there is a cost of maintaining idle cash balances, a firm should attempt to implement policies that will reduce the amount of operating cash it requires.

Analysis of the Cash Cycle Model   It is important to recognize that the discussion of cash cycles, cash turnover, and minimum operating cash is based on a number of limiting assumptions. One is that the technique explicitly ignores profit—the fact that inflows will actually exceed outflows. The model assumes that outflows equal inflows and therefore that no profit exists. Second, the model assumes that *all* outflows occur at the point at which the raw materials are paid for (i.e., payment of account payable). It should be clear that in actuality value will be added to the raw material at various stages throughout the production-sale process. This assumption tends to cause the actual cash requirement to be overestimated. Third, it is assumed that the firm's purchases, production, and sales occur at a constant rate throughout the year. In situations where this assumption is not valid, a firm's minimum cash balance can be estimated by using the cash turnover rate for the most cash-dependent period of operation. One should also recognize that the amount of uncertainty, or variability, in a firm's cash requirements will certainly affect the minimum level of operating cash maintained. Although for simplicity this uncertainty has been ignored here, the reader should be aware of the fact that the amount of cash held by a firm is a function of the uncertainty of its cash inflows and cash outflows. Although these limiting assumptions may subtract from the practical applicability of this technique, its use for illustrating the implementation of the recommended cash management strategies warrants its application in the following examples.

CASH MANAGEMENT STRATEGIES

The effects of implementing each of the strategies for efficient cash management mentioned earlier on the KLM Company Ltd. are described next.

Stretching Accounts Payable   KLM Company Ltd. can "stretch its accounts payable," by paying its bills as late as possible, without damaging its credit rating.

EXAMPLE   If KLM Company Ltd. can stretch the age of its accounts payable from the current average of 35 days to an average of 45 days, its cash cycle will be reduced to 110 days. Figure 8.2 illustrates this new cash cycle. By stretching its accounts payable 10 additional days, the firm increases its cash turnover rate from 3 to 3.27 (360 ÷ 110), and thus decreases its minimum operating cash requirement from $4,000,000 to approximately $3,670,000 ($12,000,000 ÷ 3.27). The reduction in required operating cash of approximately $330,000 ($4,000,000 − $3,670,000) represents an annual savings to the firm of $16,500 ($330,000 · .05), which is the opportunity cost of tying up that amount of funds.

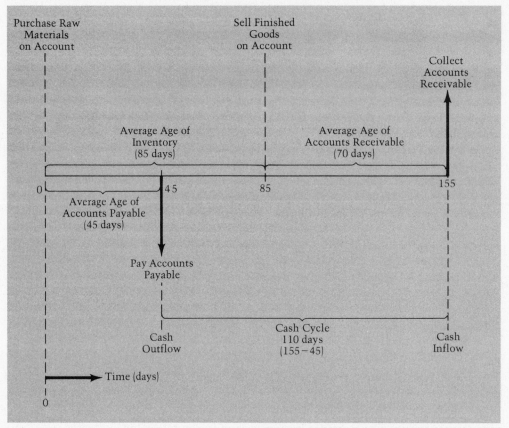

Figure 8.2 A cash cycle for the KLM Company Ltd. based on stretching the average age of accounts payable.

Although the payoff from stretching accounts payable for the KLM Company is clear, firms are quite often constrained as to the amount of stretching they can do. Only in instances where a firm's suppliers are highly dependent on the firm for a large portion of their business can a firm really capitalize on stretching accounts payable. Furthermore, had KLM's suppliers offered cash discounts for early payments, the firm might have found that the cheapest overall strategy would be to pay early and take the discount. Occasionally a supplier may let a young and growing customer stretch its accounts, based on the belief that helping the firm to grow will result in increased business in the future. (In periods of tight money such as 1974–1975, a firm's ability to stretch payables becomes limited, especially when the supplier can live without the customer's business.)

Efficient Inventory-Production Management Another way of minimizing required cash is to increase the inventory turnover rate by:

Increasing the Raw-Materials Turnover By using more efficient inventory control techniques, the firm may be able to increase its raw-materials turnover.

Decreasing the Production Cycle   By initiating better production planning, scheduling, and control techniques, the firm can reduce the length of the production cycle, and thus increase the firm's work-in-process inventory turnover.

Increasing the Finished-Goods Turnover   The firm can increase its finished-goods turnover by better forecasting of demand and by better planning of production to coincide with these forecasts.

EXAMPLE   If the KLM Company Ltd. manages to reduce the average age of its inventory from the current level of 85 days to 70 days—a reduction of 15 days—the effects on its minimum operating cash will be as follows. There will be a reduction of 15 days in the cash cycle, from 120 days to 105 days. (See Figure 8.3 for a graph of the new cash cycle.) The decreased average age of inventory will increase the annual cash turnover rate from the initial level of 3 to 3.43 (360 ÷ 105). The increased cash turnover rate results in a decrease in the firm's minimum operating cash requirement from $4,000,000 to approximately $3,500,000 ($12,000,000 ÷ 3.43). The reduction in required operating cash of approximately $500,000 ($4,000,000 − $3,500,000) represents an annual savings to the firm of $25,000 ($500,000 · .05).

Speeding the Collection of Accounts Receivable   Another way of reducing the firm's operating cash requirement is to speed up the collection of accounts receivable. Accounts receivable are a necessary cost to the firm, since the extension of credit to customers normally allows the firm to achieve higher levels of sales than it could by operating on a strictly cash basis. The actual *credit terms* extended by a firm are normally dictated by the industry in which it operates.* In industries where virtually undifferentiated products are sold, credit terms may be a critical factor in sales. Normally in these industries, all firms match the best credit terms given in order to maintain their competitive position. In industries where relatively differentiated types of products are sold, there may be a greater variance in credit terms between firms in the same industry.

   The firm's credit terms affect not only the pattern of collections but also credit policies and collection policies. *Credit policies* are the firm's criteria for determining to whom credit should be extended; *collection policies* determine the effort put forth by the firm to collect accounts receivable promptly. Changes in credit terms, credit policies, and collection policies can all be used to decrease the average collection period, while maintaining or increasing overall profits. Typically, the initiation of a cash discount for early payment, the use of more restrictive credit policies, or the initiation of more aggressive collection policies will decrease the average age of the firm's receivables. It is important that the firm consider the consequences of each or all of these actions on sales and profits beforehand. An example will help to clarify the effects of faster collections on the firm's minimum operating cash requirement.

*A discussion of various types of credit terms and their implications is presented in Chapter 9, which is devoted solely to the management of accounts receivable. Credit terms state when payment is due, and whether or not, and under what conditions, a cash discount is offered.

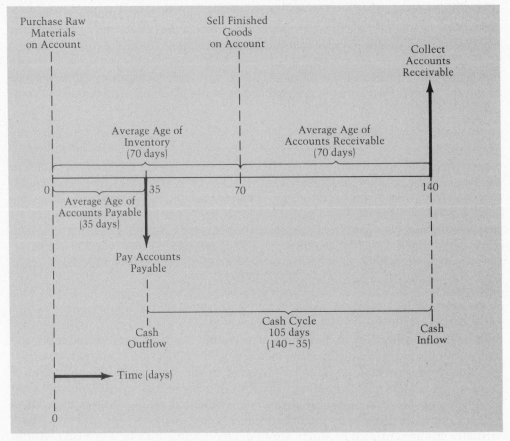

Figure 8.3   A cash cycle for the KLM Company Ltd. based on an increased inventory turnover.

EXAMPLE   If the KLM Company Ltd., by changing its credit terms, is able to reduce the average age of its accounts receivable from the current level of 70 days to 50 days, this will reduce its cash cycle by 20 days (70 days − 50 days). Figure 8.4 presents a graph of the new cash cycle. The decrease in the average age of accounts receivable raises the firm's annual cash turnover rate from the initial level of 3 to 3.60 (360 ÷ 100). The increased cash turnover results in a decrease in the firm's minimum operating cash requirement from $4,000,000 to approximately $3,333,000 ($12,000,000 ÷ 3.60). The reduction in required operating cash of approximately $667,000 ($4,000,000 − $3,333,000) represents an annual savings to the firm of approximately $33,350 ($667,000 · .05), if the released funds are invested at a rate of 5 percent.

COMBINING CASH MANAGEMENT STRATEGIES

The preceding discussions have illustrated the individual effects of implementing each of the suggested cash management strategies on the firm's overall operating cash requirement. In practice, firms would attempt to use all of these strategies to reduce

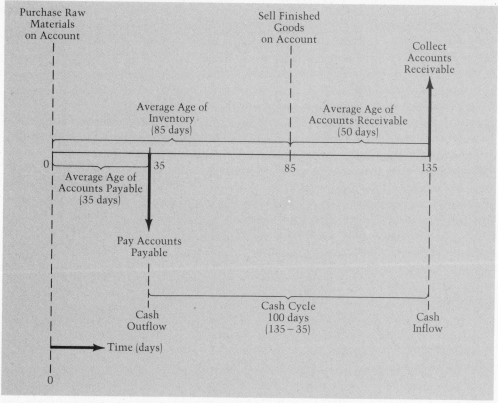

Figure 8.4   A cash cycle for the KLM Company Ltd. based on speeding up the collection of accounts receivable.

significantly their operating cash requirement. Using all of these strategies would have the following effects on the KLM Company.

EXAMPLE   If the KLM Company Ltd. simultaneously increased the average age of accounts payable by 10 days, decreased the average age of inventory by 15 days, and sped the collection of accounts receivable by 20 days, its cash cycle would be reduced to 75 days (120 days − 10 days − 15 days − 20 days). As Figure 8.5 illustrates, the firm's total cash cycle is shortened from 120 days to 75 days. Its annual cash turnover rate increases from 3 to 4.8 (360 ÷ 75). The increased cash turnover reduces the firm's minimum operating cash requirement from $4,000,000 to approximately $2,500,000 ($12,000,000 ÷ 4.8). The reduction in required operating cash of approximately $1,500,000 ($4,000,000 − $2,500,000) represents an annual savings to the firm of $75,000 ($1,500,000 · .05). This savings represents a sizable decrease in the firm's opportunity costs, from an initial level of $200,000 ($4,000,000 · .05) to $125,000 ($2,500,000 · .05).

The preceding examples have clearly shown the implications of each (and all) of the overall strategies for the efficient management of cash. However, when implementing these policies, care should be taken not to damage the firm's credit rating by overstretch-

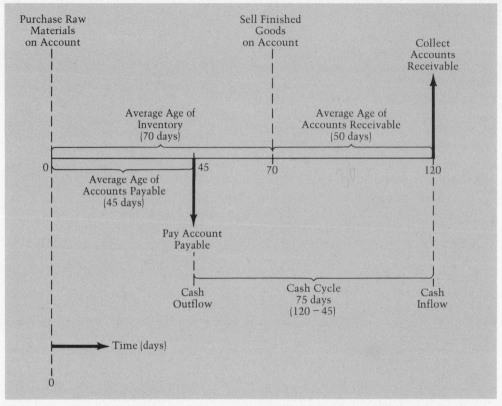

Figure 8.5   A cash cycle for the KLM Company Ltd. based on implementing all three cash management strategies simultaneously.

ing accounts payable, to avoid having a large number of stockouts or a production stoppage due to carrying too small an inventory, and to avoid losing sales due to overly restrictive credit terms, credit policies, or collection policies.

Refinements in the Cash Management Process

A number of additional and more specific techniques for the management of cash are also available.

COLLECTION PROCEDURES

The firm's objective with respect to accounts receivable should be not only to stimulate customers to pay as quickly as possible, but to convert customers' payments into a spendable form as quickly as possible. Two ways of reducing the amount of time that elapses between the customer's mailing of a payment and the point the funds become available to the firm for disbursement are discussed here.

Concentration Banking   Firms with regional sales outlets often designate certain of these offices as regional collection centers. Customers within these areas are required to remit their payments to these sales offices, which deposit these receipts in local banks. At certain times, or on a "when-needed basis," funds are transferred by wire from these bank branches to a *concentration*, or *disbursing, bank* from which bill payments are dispatched.*

Concentration banking is used to reduce the amount of time that elapses between the customer's mailing of a payment and a firm's receipt of the payment. Regionally dispersed collection centers should typically *reduce the mailing time*, since the collecting bank is on average closer to the point from which the check is sent.

In the United States, the banking system is quite fragmented, since the banking system ranges from statewide branch banking, as in California, to unit banking as in New York. Thus, in the United States, concentration banking should also reduce the time required for the customer's cheque to clear, since the customer's bank is likely to be in the same federal reserve district as the seller's bank.

On the other hand, the nationwide branch banking system in Canada facilitates the collection of cash from locations throughout Canada. Each nationwide Canadian bank has its own internal clearing system. Cheques are also cleared between banks in each of the major Canadian cities. In addition, the imprint of a standardized, machine-readable code on the cheques further facilitates cheque clearing in Canada. Thus, those firms dealing with nationwide banks have a maximum clearing delay of one to three days, even for locations as far apart as Nanaimo and Halifax.

The Lock-Box System   Another method of reducing the elapsed time between a customer payment and the actual receipt of the funds by the firm is the "lock-box system." In this system, the customer sends the payments to a post office box. The post office box is emptied by the firm's bank at least once or twice each business day. The bank opens the payment envelopes, deposits the cheques in the firm's account, and sends a deposit slip indicating the payments received, along with any enclosures, to the collecting firm. The lock boxes are normally geographically dispersed, and funds, when collected, are wired to the firm's disbursing bank.

The lock-box system is usually better than concentration banking, in that the time involved in the receipt and deposit of cheques by the firm may be greatly reduced, since the payments are received and deposited by the bank. The actual receipt of funds by the firm is recorded once the firm has received notification of the deposits from its lock-box bank.

Each lock-box bank charges the firm a fee or requires the firm to maintain a specified minimum deposit balance, or both. Thus, these costs must be evaluated with respect to the volume of cheques received and the amount of time saved to determine the economic feasibility of the lock-box system. Although lock-box systems are quite prevalent among larger retailers such as oil companies, which bill large numbers of customers throughout the country, lock-box systems are generally not economic for most companies.

---

*Most large firms disburse funds, or pay bills, only from certain banks. Normally, separate payroll and general expense accounts are maintained.

DISBURSEMENT PROCEDURES

The firm's objective with respect to accounts payable should be not only to pay slowly, but to slow down the availability of funds to suppliers and employees once the payment has been dispatched. The techniques used to slow down the withdrawal of funds from the firm's account generally are based upon *lengthening mail time* or *lengthening the clearing time* associated with the payment process, or both. In addition, accruals can be used by the firm to delay payments to certain of its suppliers of goods and services. Before proceeding to a discussion of these techniques, it should be noted that many business persons would consider one or more of the techniques as being *unethical.*

Lengthening Mail Delivery Time   When the date of postmark is considered the effective date of payment by a supplier, the firm may have an opportunity to lengthen mail delivery time. This can be done by placing payments in the mail at a location from which it is known that a great deal of time will likely elapse before the payment is received by the supplier. Typically, small towns that are not close to major highways and cities provide excellent opportunities to slow down mail delivery time. Another approach sometimes used is to mail payments to the suppliers' corporate headquarter's address rather than the post office box or collection center specified by the supplier.* If the firm can do this without violating the terms of sales specified by the supplier, the mail time may not directly be increased, but because most corporate headquarters cannot process receipts, the entire collection process for the supplier is slowed down, thereby slowing down the firm's payment.

Lengthening Clearing Time by Playing the Float   The term *float* refers to the amount of money tied up in cheques that have been written but have yet to be collected or paid on. Due to the presence of float in the banking system, many firms are able to "play the float," that is, to write cheques against money not currently in the firm's chequing account. Firms are able to play the float because they know that a delay will likely exist between the receipt and deposit of the cheque by their supplier and the actual withdrawal of funds from their chequing account. Playing the float is a method of consciously anticipating the resulting float associated with the payment process.

   Although playing the float is technically illegal, many firms use it to stretch their accounts payable.† Prosecution generally does not result, since the firm (or individual) either has the money in the account when the cheque clears or has arranged with its bank for overdraft privileges. By arranging for overdraft privileges, a firm can have cheques cleared even if the firm has insufficient funds in its account. In such cases, the

---

*A supplier's credit terms as well as any penalties associated with late payment are typically stated in the *invoice* that accompanies the shipment of merchandise. Of course, depending upon the supplier, the terms of the invoice may or may not be enforced. Knowledge of the strictness of enforcement of credit terms by suppliers is often useful for developing the firm's accounts payable strategies.

†Writing cheques against nonexistent funds is considered fraudulent, since it entails a misrepresentation of the amount of funds on deposit. If it can be proven that a firm or an individual has intentionally or with knowledge issued a cheque against a nonexistent balance, the firm or individual could be convicted of breaking the law.

bank automatically extends a loan to cover any deficit in the firm's account.* Three ways of playing the float are discussed next.

Paying from a Distant Bank   Some firms write their cheques for paying bills on a bank that is geographically removed from their supplier's bank in the hope that it will take longer for the cheque to clear. As noted above, this is not very effective in a Canadian context. Even if a firm does not pay bills from a distant bank, it may play the float for a few days, provided it protects itself by having an overdraft arrangement with its bank.

Use of Drafts   Another very effective, but seldom used, method to play the float is to use drafts. Unlike a cheque, which is payable upon demand, a draft can only be collected by the receiver after the draft has been received and approved by the issuer, and the issuer has deposited sufficient funds to cover the payment of the draft. In practice, both the receivers of the drafts and the banks themselves dislike drafts, because they find drafts to be an economically inefficient method of making payment.

Scientific Cheque-Cashing Analysis   Another way of playing the float, which may be used by more sophisticated firms, is to deposit a certain proportion of a payroll or payments in the firm's chequing account each day after the actual issuance of a group of payroll cheques. For example, if a firm can determine from historical data that only 25 percent of its payroll cheques are cashed on the day immediately following the issuance of the cheques, then only 25 percent of the value of the payroll needs to be in its chequing account one day later. The number of cheques cashed on each succeeding day can also be calculated, until the entire payroll is accounted for. Normally, in order to protect itself against any irregularities, a firm will place slightly more in its account than it needs to cover the expected cheque cashings.

Accruals   Another tool for stretching a firm's payments is accruals. *Accruals* are current liabilities that represent a service or good that has been received by the firm but not yet paid for. The most common accruals are wages, rent, and taxes. Just as a firm should stretch its accounts payable as much as possible without damaging its credit rating, so too it should attempt to arrange for the payment of wages, rent, taxes, and similar items as infrequently as possible.†

Since a firm cannot change the tax laws and most leases require frequent payments, payroll accruals provide the best opportunity for manipulation by the firm. Since firms do not pay employees in advance; the more infrequently a firm pays its employees, the better off it will be from the standpoint of cash flows. In actual fact, the employee can be thought of as extending credit to the firm and therefore temporarily financing a portion of the firm's assets. The firm should take advantage of opportunities to increase accruals to the extent that the constraints set by unions, the government, lessors, and others

*Both the maximum amount and the interest cost of overdraft loans must be agreed to by the bank and the firm beforehand. Furthermore, due to the absence of maintenance or compensating balances in the firm's account, the bank charges a higher rate of interest on overdraft loans.

†A further discussion of accruals, including a numerical example of the usefulness of accruals as a short-term source of financing, is included in Chapter 11.

allow such action; since the more of this type of credit the firm is extended, the less money it will need to operate.

Motives, Characteristics, and Proportion of Marketable Securities

Marketable securities are short-term money-market instruments that can easily be converted into cash.*

MOTIVES FOR HOLDING MARKETABLE SECURITIES

There are three basic motives for maintaining liquidity and therefore for holding marketable securities, which by definition represent a storehouse of liquidity. The type of marketable security a firm purchases will depend greatly on the motive for the purchase. The basic motives, which include the *transactions motive, safety motive,* and *speculative motive,* and the implications of each are as follows.

The Transactions Motive   Marketable securities that will be converted into cash to make some known future payment (such as income-tax payments) are said to be held for transactions purposes. Many firms that must make certain payments in the near future already have the cash with which to make these payments. In order to earn some return on these funds, they invest them in a marketable security with a maturity date that coincides with the required payment date.

The Safety (or Precautionary) Motive   Marketable securities held for safety are used to service the firm's cash account. These securities must be very liquid, since they are bought with funds that will be needed, though exactly when is unknown. They therefore protect the firm against the possibility of being unable to satisfy unexpected demands for cash.

The Speculative Motive   Marketable securities can be held for speculative reasons. Although such situations are not extremely common, some firms occasionally have excess cash (that is, cash not earmarked for any particular expenditures). Until the firm finds a suitable use for this money (say, investment in a new fixed asset, a dividend payment, or a repurchase of shares), it invests it in certain more speculative types of marketable securities. In many cases, these dollars are placed in long-term instruments, which do not fall within the category of marketable securities.

CHARACTERISTICS OF MARKETABLE SECURITIES

To be truly marketable a security must have two basic characteristics: (1) a ready market, and (2) no likelihood of a loss in value (safety of principal).

*The *money market* results from an intangible relationship between the demanders and suppliers of short-term funds, i.e., marketable securities. An in-depth description of the organization and operation of the money market is included in Chapter 19.

A Ready Market   The market for a security should have both breadth and depth in order to minimize the amount of time required to convert it into cash. Common definitions of marketable securities suggest that they are securities that can be converted into cash in a short period of time, typically a few days.

The Breadth of the Market   The *breadth* of a market is determined by the number of participants in it. A broad market is one that has many participants; a thin market is one that has few participants.

The Depth of the Market   The *depth* of a market is determined by its ability to absorb the purchase or sale of a large dollar amount of securities, within a relatively short period of time, with a minimum of price disruption. Although both characteristics are desirable, and generally exist together, it is much more important for a market to have depth than breadth in order for a security to be marketable.

No Likelihood of a Loss in Value (Safety of Principal)   The second key determinant of marketability is whether the market price received when liquidating a security deviates significantly from the amount invested. There should be little or no loss in the value of a marketable security over time. Consider a security recently purchased for $1,000. If it can be sold quickly for $500, does that make it marketable? No. According to the definition of marketability above, not only must the security be salable quickly, but it must be salable for close to the $1,000 initially invested. The risk associated with a loss in the value of the principal invested in a marketable security is probably the most important aspect of the marketable security selection process. Only those securities that can be easily converted into cash without experiencing any reduction in principal are candidates for short-term investment.

THE OPTIMUM PROPORTION OF MARKETABLE SECURITIES IN THE FIRM'S ASSET MIX

A major decision confronting the business firm is exactly what mix of cash and marketable securities should be maintained.* This decision is difficult to make because it involves a trade-off between the opportunity to earn interest on idle funds during the holding period and the cost of brokerage and management fees associated with the purchase and sale of marketable securities. For example, take the case of a firm paying $30 in brokerage and management fees to purchase and sell $5,000 worth of marketable securities yielding an annual return of 6 percent and held for one month. Since the securities are held for $\frac{1}{12}$ of a year, the firm earns interest of 0.5 percent ($\frac{1}{12} \cdot$ 6 percent), or $25 (.005 · $5,000). Since this is less than the $30 cost of the transaction, the firm should not have made the investment. This trade-off between interest returns and brokerage costs is a key factor in determining just what proportion of the firm's liquid assets should be held in the form of marketable securities.

---

*Numerous quantitative models for determining the optimum amounts of marketable securities to hold in certain circumstances have been developed. One of the most popular is based on the inventory theory underlying the EOQ model, which is described in Chapter 10. A discussion of these cash-marketable security models is beyond the scope of this text.

As the level of inflation has increased, the opportunity cost of holding idle cash balances has increased, since such balances have lost purchasing power at an increasing rate. Thus, during periods of high inflation, investments in marketable securities represent a defensive move to minimize the loss in the purchasing power of the funds held.

Small Businesses   As the above example illustrates, investment of small amounts of temporary surplus cash in marketable securities is generally not economic for small businesses, since the opportunity cost of the required management plus the actual transaction costs of buying and selling the marketable securities is generally larger than the expected returns on the funds invested. Nevertheless, the small business should realize some return, however modest, on idle cash balances by placing such idle funds in a savings or term-deposit account, or in federal treasury bills.*

The Basic Marketable Securities

This section presents a brief description of each of the most commonly held marketable securities. Yields on some selected "marketable" securities for August 2, 1979, are given in Table 8.1.

Table 8.1   Yields on Selected Securities for the Week Ending August 2, 1979

Security	Maturity period	Approximate yields August 2, 1979 %
Govt. of Canada Treasury bills	91 days	11.25 (average)
Govt. of Canada Treasury bills	182 days	11.28 (average)
Govt. of Canada bonds	short-term	10.25
Govt. of Canada bonds	medium-term	10.20
Govt. of Canada bonds	long-term	10.30
Certificates of deposit	1–3 months	11.45–11.55
Commercial paper	30–90 days	11.50–11.60
Banker's acceptances	30 days	11.50
Banker's acceptances	60 days	11.55
Bank term deposit accounts	30–59 days	10.50[a] & 11.50[b]
Bank term deposit accounts	60–89 days	10.75[a] & 11.55[b]
Bank swap deposits[c]	30–59 days	11.24
Bank swap deposits[c]	60–89 days	11.35

SOURCE: "Short Term Interest Rates," Head Office Investment Department, The Royal Bank of Canada; and the *Financial Post.*
[a]For deposits of $5,000 or more, and up to and including $100,000.
[b]For deposits greater than $100,000.
[c]For deposits of $100,000 or greater.

*Typically, amounts as small as $5,000 can be invested in term-deposit accounts for periods as short as 30 days.

GOVERNMENT ISSUES

The short-term obligations issued by the federal and provincial governments, which are available as marketable security investments, include treasury bills and bonds.

Treasury Bills   These are obligations of the federal (and sometimes the provincial) governments, and are issued weekly on an auction basis. The most common maturities are 91 and 182 days, although bills with one-year maturities are occasionally sold. Treasury bills are sold by competitive bidding, going to the highest bidder. Bids are tendered regularly by the Bank of Canada, the chartered banks, and the larger investment dealers. Because they are issued in bearer form, there is a strong secondary (resale) market for treasury bills. Furthermore, by arranging for a repurchase agreement with an investment dealer, a firm can sell its holding at a prespecified future date and price. Treasury bills are sold at a discount from their face value, the face value being received at maturity. Thus, the difference between the price at maturity and the purchase price provides the buyer of the treasury bill with a yield on his or her investment. The smallest denomination of federal treasury bills currently available is $1,000.* Since treasury bills are issues of a government, they are considered virtually riskless. For this reason, and because of the strong secondary market for them, treasury bills are probably the most popular marketable security. In addition, treasury bills constitute the central element in the Canadian money market, for the yield on other investments traded in this market are closely related to the yield on treasury bills.

Government of Canada Bonds   The government of Canada issues short-term bonds with maturities up to three years. A firm that purchases a government of Canada bond, which has less than one year left to maturity, is in the same position as if it had purchased a marketable security with an initial maturity of less than one year.

NONGOVERNMENT ISSUES

A number of additional marketable securities are issued by businesses and the financial institutions. These nongovernment issues typically have slightly higher yields than government issues, due to the slightly higher risks associated with them. The main nongovernment marketable securities are negotiable certificates of deposit, commercial paper, banker's acceptances, bank swapped deposits, and repurchase agreements.

Negotiable Certificates of Deposit (CD's)   The Canadian chartered banks offer their short-term obligations under a variety of names, such as certificates of deposit (CD's), term notes, and deposit receipts. The amounts, maturities, and means of interest payment are normally tailored to the initial investor's needs. The degree of liquidity varies from CD to CD. The yield on CD's is typically slightly above the yield offered on commercial paper of comparable maturity.

---

*Treasury bills are issued, according to need, by some of the provincial governments on an irregular basis. On August 31, 1979, the smallest denominations and rates for 91-day provincial treasury bills were Manitoba, $25,000, 11.49 percent; Newfoundland, $100,000, 11.57 percent; and Saskatchewan, $25,000, 11.49 percent. The corresponding federal treasury bill rate was 11.45 percent.

Commercial Paper   Commercial paper is a short-term, unsecured, interest-bearing promissory note issued by a corporation or finance company, which has a very high credit standing.* These instruments have maturities of anywhere from 24 hours to one year or longer. In addition, a firm can purchase commercial paper with a "put-option" feature; that is, the lender has the right to prepayment before maturity. The yield on high-grade commercial paper is usually somewhat above that offered on short-term government securities, of a comparable term to maturity.

Banker's Acceptances   A banker's acceptance is a commercial draft drawn on a chartered bank by a firm seeking funding for a specified export (or import) transaction. The firm's bank, by countersigning the draft, guarantees the payment of the draft, according to the terms and conditions stated on the acceptance. These instruments are usually sold at a discount to a money-market dealer. Since acceptances are generally virtually default-free and extremely liquid, the discount from face value is generally small.

Banker's acceptances are considered extremely liquid since money-market dealers, who both hold acceptances and need funds, can use acceptances as collateral for day loans from the chartered banks, or they can rediscount the acceptances at the Bank of Canada.

Although banker's acceptances are usually issued for periods that range from 30 to 90 days, they can have a maximum maturity of 180 days. Banker's acceptances, issued in multiples of $100,000, are considered as a part of a firm's line of credit. For providing the guarantee for the acceptance, the bank will charge the issuer of the acceptance a fee, referred to as a "stamping fee," that ranges between $\frac{1}{2}$ and 1 percent of the face value of the draft. The effective percent cost of acceptances to the issuer is the sum of the costs of the issue (i.e., the stamping fee plus the discount on the sale of the instrument to the money-market dealer) divided by the proceeds obtained by the issuer from the sale of the instrument to the money-market dealer.

A banker's acceptance is a very safe security, since as many as three parties may be liable for its payment at maturity. The yields on banker's acceptances are similar to those on CD's.

Bank Swapped Deposits   A bank swapped deposit is a short-term foreign currency (e.g., U.S.) deposit purchased with domestic (Canadian) dollars. The instrument is protected from exchange rate fluctuations through a swap, or hedge. The swap is accomplished by the simultaneous execution of two transactions: (1) the conversion of Canadian dollars into U.S. dollars to purchase the deposit; and (2) the forward sale of the U.S. dollar proceeds, at a specified exchange rate into Canadian dollars, to coincide with the maturity date of the deposit. An overall yield for swapped deposits is quoted by the chartered banks. The attractiveness of a swapped deposit depends upon the firm's (investor's) expectations for both international short-term interest rate differentials and forward exchange rate differentials.

---

*An in-depth discussion of commercial paper, from the point of view of the issuer, is deferred until Chapter 11, which is devoted to the various sources of unsecured short-term financing available to business.

Repurchase Agreements   A repurchase agreement is not a specific security; rather, it is an arrangement whereby a bank or security dealer sells specific marketable securities at a slight discount to a firm, and agrees to purchase the securities at a specified price at a specified future point in time. The investor is willing to accept the slightly lower rate of return, since the tailor-made maturity date assures the purchaser that he or she will have cash at a specified point in time. The actual securities involved may be any government or nongovernment issues. Repurchase agreements are ideal for marketable security investments made to satisfy the transaction motive.

International Cash and Marketable Securities Management

In international cash management, the number of opportunities include possible cash holdings in the domestic currencies of each of the countries in which a firm operates.[*] Although each division or subsidiary of the firm will generally hold its cash balances in the local currency, there are at least four reasons why this may not be in the overall corporate interest. First, due to existing or proposed foreign exchange restrictions, there may be undue delays in the conversion of local currency to make foreign payments. This, in turn, could result in the loss of trade discounts. Second, cash balances held in a "weak" local currency may be unduly exposed to a loss of value due to adverse foreign exchange movements. Third, as was noted in the previous chapter, certain economies of scale may be foregone if the management of cash holdings are not centralized. And finally, the opportunity cost of holding local cash balances may be high, either due to the unavailability of money-market instruments, or due to the lack of liquidity for the money-market instruments that are available.

Summary

Cash and marketable securities make up the firm's liquid assets. They give the firm the liquidity it needs to satisfy financial obligations as they come due. Cash is held in the form of currency and demand deposits at a chartered bank, both of which earn no interest. On the other hand, marketable securities provide a return.

The efficient management of cash is based on three basic strategies: (1) paying bills as late as possible without damaging the firm's credit rating, (2) managing the inventory-production cycle efficiently in order to maximize the inventory turnover rate, and (3) collecting accounts receivable quickly. Although certain constraints are placed on each of these strategies, maximizing the firm's cash turnover should increase the firm's profit by minimizing the level of operating cash (cash plus marketable securities) held by the firm.

Although the cash budget is useful for cash planning, decisions with respect to the

---

[*]Although a firm can hold cash balances in the currency of a country in which it has no economic dealings, this would probably be considered a speculative use of cash.

appropriate cash balance depend upon the magnitude of both expected and unexpected cash receipts and cash disbursements. The appropriate balance is the larger of (1) the cash required to meet both expected and unexpected cash requirements, or (2) the maintenance plus compensating balance requirements established by lenders. A variety of rules of thumb, as well as sophisticated quantitative models, exist for making such decisions. One practical approach is to relate the firm's cash turnover to the annual outlays.

Additional refinements in the cash management process (such as concentration banking, lock-box systems, lengthening mail time on payments, playing the float in the banking system, and managing accruals intelligently) can further increase the efficiency of cash management.

A firm holds marketable securities in order to earn interest on temporarily idle funds. Funds may be held in marketable securities (as well as cash) to satisfy a transactions motive, safety motive, or speculative motive. The transactions and safety motives are the most common. In order for a security to be considered marketable, it must have liquidity. In addition, the amount that can be realized by selling the security within a short period of time must be close to the amount invested initially. That is, the risks associated with the safety of principal must be quite low. The proportion of a firm's liquid assets made up of marketable securities depends on the trade-off between the interest earned during the holding period and the brokerage costs associated with purchasing and selling marketable securities. Thus, the investment of small amounts of temporary surplus cash in marketable securities is generally not economic for small businesses.

The most commonly held marketable securities are government issues such as treasury bills and bonds; and nongovernment issues such as negotiable certificates of deposit, commercial paper, banker's acceptances, bank swapped deposits, and repurchase agreements. Each of these has its own risk and yield characteristics. Government issues are the least risky, but have the lowest yield; nongovernment issues are more risky, but have higher yields.

Questions

8.1 What is the objective of the financial manager in cash management? What conditions must be satisfied in meeting this objective?

8.2 What role do marketable securities play in fulfilling the firm's overall objective of maximizing its owners' wealth? How does the presence of marketable securities in the firm's asset structure affect the risk associated with the firm?

8.3 What are the key strategies with respect to accounts payable, inventory, and accounts receivable for the firm that wants to manage its cash efficiently?

8.4 What is a firm's "cash cycle"? How are the cash cycle and cash turnover of a firm related? What should a firm's objectives with respect to its cash cycle and cash turnover be?

8.5 If a firm reduces the average age of its inventories, what effect might this action have on the cash cycle? on the firm's total sales? Is there a trade-off between average inventory and sales? Why?

8.6   "Stretching accounts payable" is often recommended in order to increase a firm's cash turnover. What does "stretching" imply? What two factors may limit the degree to which a firm can stretch its accounts payable?

8.7   How do a firm's credit terms, credit policies, and collection policies affect the minimum level of operating cash it requires?

8.8   What is concentration banking? How does it benefit a firm?

8.9   How does the lock-box system differ from concentration banking? What is the overall objective of both these arrangements?

8.10   How may a firm use "float" to reduce its cash requirements? What cautions are in order when taking advantage of float? Why?

8.11   What are the common types of accruals found on a firm's balance sheet? What is the general rationale for accruing certain items?

8.12   The three commonly cited motives for holding marketable securities are for the safety, transactions, and speculative motives. How do these motives differ?

8.13   What two characteristics are essential in a "marketable" security?

8.14   What are treasury bills? Why are they such attractive marketable securities? What maturities and denominations are common?

8.15   What is commercial paper? What kind of market is there for this security?

8.16   What are negotiable certificates of deposit and banker's acceptances? Is there any similarity between them?

8.17   What are bank swapped deposits? What accounts for their investment attractiveness?

8.18   Why might a repurchase agreement be attractive to a firm having a temporary excess of liquidity?

Problems

8.1   Western Supply Ltd. is concerned about managing cash in an efficient manner. On the average, accounts receivable are collected in 60 days, and inventories have an average age of 90 days. Accounts payable are paid approximately 30 days after they arise. The firm spends $30 million each year, at a constant rate. Assuming a 360-day year,
a.   Calculate the firm's cash cycle.
b.   Calculate the firm's cash turnover.
c.   Calculate the minimum cash balance the firm must maintain to meet its obligations.

8.2   The Denver Company Ltd. has an inventory turnover ratio of 12, accounts receivable turnover of 8, and an accounts payable turnover ratio of 9. The firm spends $1 million per year. Assuming a 360-day year,
a.   Calculate the firm's cash cycle.
b.   Calculate the firm's cash turnover.
c.   Calculate the minimum cash balance the firm must maintain to meet its obligations.

8.3   A firm collects accounts receivable, on the average, after 75 days. Inventory has an average age of 105 days and accounts payable are paid on an average of 60 days after they arise. What changes will occur in the cash cycle and cash turnover with each of the following different circumstances? Assume a 360-day year.
a.   The average age of accounts receivable changes to 60 days.
b.   The average age of inventory changes to 90 days.
c.   The average age of accounts payable changes to 105 days.
d.   All the circumstances above (**a** to **c**) occur simultaneously.

8.4 A firm is considering several plans that affect working capital accounts. Given the following five plans and their probable results, which one would you favour? Explain.

Plan	Change in average age of		
	Inventory	Accounts receivable	Accounts payable
A	+30 days	+20 days	+5 days Δ +45
B	+20 days	−10 days	+15 days Δ −5
C	−10 days	0 days	−5 days Δ −5
D	−15 days	+15 days	+10 days Δ +10
E	+5 days	−10 days	+15 days Δ −20

8.5 Watson Manufacturing Ltd. pays accounts payable on the tenth day after purchase. The average age of accounts receivable is 30 days and the average of inventory is 40 days. Annual cash outlays are approximately $18 million. The firm is considering a plan which would stretch its accounts payable by 20 days. If the firm can earn 7 percent on its investments, what annual savings can it realize by this plan. Assume no discount for early payment of trade credit and a 360-day year.

8.6 Consumer Products Corporation Ltd. sells to a national market and bills all credit customers from the Toronto office. Using a continuous billing system, the firm has collections of $1,200,000 per day. Under consideration is a concentration banking system that would require customers to mail payments to the nearest regional office.

Consumer Products estimates that the collection period for accounts will be shortened an average of 2.5 days under this system. The firm also estimates *annual* service charges and administrative costs of $125,000 will result from the proposed system. The firm can earn 9 percent on its investments.

a. How much cash will be made available for other uses if the firm accepts the proposed concentration banking system?

b. What savings will the firm realize on the 2.5-day reduction in the collection period?

c. Would you recommend the change? Explain your answer.

8.7 Manitoba Oil Ltd. feels a lock-box system can shorten its accounts receivable collection period by 3 days. Credit sales are $3,240,000 per year billed on a continuous basis. The firm has other investments with a return of 10 percent. The cost of the lock-box system is $9,000 per year.

a. What amount of cash will be made available for other uses under the lock-box system?

b. What net benefit (cost) will the firm receive if it adopts the lock-box system?

8.8 A large Quebec firm has annual cash disbursements of $360 million made continuously over the year. Although service and administrative costs would increase by $100,000, the firm is considering writing all disbursement cheques on a small bank situated on Vancouver Island. The firm estimates this will allow them an additional 1.5 days of cash usage. If the firm has a return on other investments of 8 percent, should they change to the distant bank? Why or why not?

8.9 Walter's Window has a weekly payroll of $250,000. The payroll cheques are issued on Friday afternoon each week. In examining the cheque cashing behaviour of its employees, it has found the following pattern:

Number of business days[a] since receipt of cheque	Percentage of cheques cleared
1	20
2	40
3	30
4	10

[a]Excludes Saturday and Sunday.

Given this information, what recommendation would you give the firm with respect to managing its payroll account? Explain.

8.10 A firm currently has a weekly payroll of $80,000. Thus, on the average, they have the use of $40,000 in accrued wages ($80,000 ÷ 2). If the firm changes to payment every two weeks, and can earn an annual rate of 12 percent on other investments, what savings, if any, could be obtained? Explain.

8.11 In order to purchase and sell $25,000 in marketable securities, a firm must pay $500. If the marketable securities have a yield of 9 percent annually, recommend purchasing or not if
a. The securities are held for one month.
b. The securities are held for three months.
c. The securities are held for six months.
d. The securities are held for one year.

8.12 Alice Piper is cash manager for Carousel Corporation Ltd. The cash budgets indicate excess cash of $20,000 will be available for the next 90 days. She is considering an investment of this sum in one of the instruments listed below. Calculate the expected rate of return for each and select the best investment. Explain your choice.
a. Common share costing $40 per share and paying a $2.00 annual dividend ($0.50 each quarter).
b. Preferred share that pays a $6.00 annual dividend ($1.50 each quarter), currently selling for $80 a share.
c. Municipal bonds issued by the city of Trois Rivieres, Quebec, maturing in 2005. These sell at par with an 8-percent annual coupon (2 percent per quarter).
d. Ninety-day commercial paper selling at 99 percent of face value (commercial paper sells at a discount).
e. A 90-day certificate of deposit paying 6-percent annual interest (1.5 percent per quarter).

Suggested Readings

Archer, Stephen H., "A Model for Determination of Firm Cash Balances," *Journal of Financial and Quantitative Analysis* 1 (March 1966), pp. 1–11.

Baumol, William J., "The Transactions Demand for Cash: An Inventory Theoretic Approach," *Quarterly Journal of Economics* 65 (November 1952), pp. 545–556.

Baxter, Nevins D., "Marketability, Default Risk, and Yields on Money-Market Instruments," *Journal of Financial and Quantitative Analysis* 3 (March 1968), pp. 75–85.

Calman, Robert F., *Linear Programming and Cash Management/CASH ALPHA* (Cambridge, Mass.: MIT Press, 1968).

Campbell, Tim and Leland Brendsel, "The Impact of Compensating Balance Requirements on the Cash Balances of Manufacturing Corporations: An Empirical Study," *Journal of Finance* 32 (March 1977), pp. 31–40.

DeSalvo, Alfred, "Cash Management Converts Dollars into Working Assets," *Harvard Business Review* (May-June 1972), pp. 92–100.

Gitman, Lawrence J., "Estimating Corporate Liquidity Requirements: A Simplified Approach," *The Financial Review* (1974), pp. 79–88.

——, D., Keith Forrester, and John R. Forrester, Jr., "Maximizing Cash Disbursement Float," *Financial Management* 5 (Summer 1976), pp. 15–24.

King, Alfred M., *Increasing the Productivity of Company Cash* (Englewood Cliffs, N.J.: Prentice-Hall, 1969), chaps. 4 and 5.

Kraus, A., C. Janssen and A. McAdams, "The Lock-Box Location Problem," *Journal of Bank Research* 1 (Autumn 1970), pp. 50–58.

Mehta, Dileep R., *Working Capital Management* (Englewood Cliffs, N.J.: Prentice-Hall, 1974), part 3.

Miller, Merton H. and Daniel Orr, "A Model of the Demand for Money by Firms," *Quarterly Journal of Economics* 80 (August 1966), pp. 413–435.

Orgler, Yair E., "An Unequal-Period Model for Cash-Management Decisions," *Management Science* 16 (October 1969), pp. 77–92.

——, *Cash Management* (Belmont: Wadsworth, 1970).

Pogue, Gerald A., Russell B. Faucett, and Ralph N. Bussard, "Cash Management: A Systems Approach," *Industrial Management Review* 2, No. 2 (1970), pp. 55–74.

Reed, Ward L., Jr., "Profits from Better Cash Management," *Financial Executive* 40 (May 1972), pp. 40–56.

Rutenberg, David P., "Maneuvering Liquid Assets in a Multinational Company: Formulation and Deterministic Solution Procedures," *Management Sciences* (June 1970), pp. B671–684.

Searby, Frederick W., "Use Your Hidden Cash Resource," *Harvard Business Review* 46 (March-April 1968), pp. 74–75.

Shanker, Roy J. and Andris A. Zoltners, "The Corporate Payment Problem," *Journal of Bank Research* 2 (March 1972), pp. 47–53.

Stancill, James McN., *The Management of Working Capital* (Scranton, Pa.: Intext, 1971), chaps. 2 and 3.

Stone, Bernell K., "The Use of Forecasts and Smoothing in Control-Limit Models for Cash Management," *Financial Management* 1 (Spring 1972), pp. 72–84.

Chapter 9

ACCOUNTS RECEIVABLE MANAGEMENT

Accounts receivable represent the extension of credit on an open account by the firm to its customers. In order to keep current customers and attract new ones, most manufacturing concerns find it necessary to offer credit. Credit terms may differ between industries, but firms within the same industry generally provide similar credit terms. Of course, exceptions do exist, since suppliers often provide more favourable credit terms to attract certain customers. Credit sales, which result in the establishment of accounts receivable, normally have associated credit terms requiring payment within a certain number of days. Although all accounts receivable are not collected within the credit period, most accounts receivable are converted into cash in considerably less than a year. Therefore, accounts receivable are considered to be part of the current assets of the firm.

Since most manufacturing firms find that accounts receivable represent a large portion of their current assets, a great deal of attention is normally given to the efficient management of these accounts. In the preceding chapter the benefits of efficient collection policies were illustrated with respect to the firm's cash requirements. It was shown that the more quickly a firm converted its accounts receivable into cash, the less operating cash it required. In this chapter, three aspects of accounts receivable management are evaluated in terms of their individual effects on the profitability and risk of a firm. These three aspects are credit policies, credit terms, and collection policies. The use of credit insurance for both domestic and export sales is also discussed. Lastly, the use of firm-specific and general credit cards are reviewed.

Credit Policies

A firm's credit policy provides the guidelines for determining whether to extend credit to a customer and how much credit to extend. The business firm must concern itself not only with the establishment of credit standards but with the correct use of these standards in making credit decisions. Appropriate sources of credit information and methods of credit analysis must be developed, as they are jointly important to the successful management of the firm's accounts receivable.

CREDIT STANDARDS

The firm's credit standards define the minimum criteria for the extension of credit to a customer. Such things as credit ratings, credit references, average payment periods, and certain financial ratios provide a numerical basis for establishing and enforcing credit standards for individual accounts. At this point in the chapter, however, our concern is not with the individual components of credit standards but with the relative restrictiveness of a firm's overall credit standards.

Key Variables   The major variables that should be considered in evaluating either the relaxation or tightening of credit standards are the changes in clerical expenses, the investment in receivables, the firm's bad debt expenses, and the volume of sales.

Clerical Expenses   If credit standards are relaxed, more credit will be extended and a larger credit department will be required to service the added accounts; if credit standards are tightened, less credit will be extended and a smaller credit department will be required to service accounts. In the analysis of the following sections, the relevant clerical costs are assumed to be included in the variable cost per unit.*

Investment in Receivables   There is a cost associated with carrying accounts receivable. Keeping the cost of funds constant, the higher the firm's average accounts receivable are, the more expensive they are to carry, and vice versa. Thus, a relaxation of credit standards can be expected to result in higher carrying costs, due to a higher average level of accounts receivable; and a tightening of credit standards can be expected to result in lower carrying costs. In addition, the cost associated with carrying accounts receivable will vary with the changes in the cost of funds over time.

The changes in the level of accounts receivable associated with changes in credit standards result from two factors—(1) changes in sales, and (2) changes in collections.† It is expected that as a firm relaxes its credit standards, sales will increase and thus there

---

*It is important to recognize that the clerical costs associated with changing credit standards are most likely *semivariable*. This is because the key ingredient of a credit department is *people*. As the department expands, certain points are reached at which new people must be employed, but between hirings the departmental cost remains fixed.

†Due to the forward-looking nature of accounts receivable analysis, certain items such as sales, collections, and bad debts resulting from changes in the management of accounts receivable must be estimated. The need to estimate these future values may introduce a great deal of uncertainty into the decision process. Thus, some sort of sensitivity analysis, as was discussed in Chapter 6, should be used to determine how sensitive the expected result is to possible error in the various forecasted values.

will be a high level of accounts receivable. When credit terms are relaxed, credit is extended to less credit-worthy customers, who will probably take longer to pay their bills. This, in turn, raises the average level of accounts receivable.*

In short, changes in sales and changes in collections work together to produce higher carrying costs for accounts receivable when credit standards are relaxed and reduced carrying costs for accounts receivable when credit standards are tightened. These basic reactions also occur when changes in credit terms or collection procedures are made. The effects of these other stimuli are discussed later in the chapter.

Bad Debt Expenses   Changes in credit standards should affect bad debt expenses. The probability (or risk) of acquiring a bad debt increases as credit standards are relaxed and decreases as credit standards become more restrictive. Bad debt losses are therefore expected to increase as credit standards are relaxed and to decrease as credit standards become more restrictive. The firm's required return on investments in accounts receivable is also expected to increase as the risk of bad debts increases.

Sales Volume   Changing credit standards can be expected to change the volume of sales. As credit standards are relaxed, sales are expected to increase; a tightening of credit standards is expected to reduce sales.

A firm's incremental costs, and thus profit margin, will also change as its rate of utilization of its capacity changes. Thus, the firm's credit policy will probably change with the firm's level of activity. When demand, and subsequently production, decreases, the firm will probably relax its credit standards and thus extend credit to less and less credit-worthy customers; when demand, and subsequently production, increases, the firm will probably tighten its credit standards and thus extend credit to more and more credit-worthy customers.

In summary, the basic changes and effects on profits expected to result from the *relaxation* of credit standards are tabulated as follows:

Item	Direction of change [increase (I) or decrease (D)]	Effect on profits [positive (+) or negative (−)]
Sales volume	I	+
Average collection period	I	−
Bad debt expense	I	−

If credit standards were tightened, the opposite effects would be expected.

Evaluating Alternative Credit Standards   The way in which credit standards are evaluated can be illustrated by a simple example.

---

*This relationship can also exist in the opposite direction. For example, changes in the level and cost of accounts receivable caused by the effects of inflation can result in a change in a firm's credit policies. More specifically, inflationary periods in Canada have generally been characterized by rapidly rising selling prices and costs, and by an effort by the federal government to combat inflation by the pursuit of a tight money policy. Thus, for the same unit volume of sales, firms have found that their dollar investment in accounts receivable has not only increased rapidly during an inflationary period but that it has also been more costly. As a result, some firms have tightened their credit (and collection) policies during inflationary times.

EXAMPLE   The XYZ Company Ltd. is currently selling a product for $10 per unit. Sales (all on credit) for the most recent year were 60,000 units. The variable cost per unit is $6, and the average cost per unit, given a sales volume of 60,000 units, is $8. The difference between the average cost per unit and the variable cost per unit of $2 represents the contribution of each of the 60,000 units toward the firm's fixed costs. Thus, the firm's total fixed costs must be $120,000.

The firm is currently contemplating a relaxation of credit standards that is expected to result in a 15-percent increase in unit sales, an increase in the average collection period from its current level of 30 days to 45 days, and no change in bad debt expenses.* The increase in clerical expenses is expected to be negligible. Since the firm has excess capacity, it can expand sales without incurring additional fixed costs. The firm's pretax required return on investments is 15 percent.

In order to determine whether the XYZ Company Ltd. should implement the proposed relaxation in credit standards, the effect on the firm's profit contribution from sales and the cost of the marginal investment in receivables must be calculated.

Additional profit contribution from sales   The firm's profit contribution from sales will increase by an amount equal to the product of the number of additional units sold and the profit contribution per unit. Since the first 60,000 units (i.e., the current level of sales) have absorbed all the firm's fixed costs, any additional units sold will cost only the variable cost per unit.† Sales are expected to increase by 15 percent, or 9,000 units. The profit contribution per unit will equal

Table 9.1   The Long Method of Calculating the Additional Profit Contribution from Sales for the XYZ Company Ltd.

Proposed plan	
Sales revenues	
69,000 units · $10	$690,000
Less: Costs	
Variable (69,000 units · $6)	414,000
Fixed (calculated earlier)	120,000
(1) Profits from sales	$156,000
Current plan	
Sales revenue	
60,000 units · $10	$600,000
Less: Costs	
Variable (60,000 units · $6)	360,000
Fixed (calculated earlier)	120,000
(2) Profits from sales	$120,000
Additional profit contribution with new plan [(1) − (2)]	$36,000

*Although the proposed relaxation in credit standards would likely increase the firm's bad debts, the effect is assumed negligible in this example. This assumption is made solely on the basis of computational convenience. Subsequent analyses will describe the appropriate treatment of bad debt expense changes in the accounts receivable decision process.

†It is being implicitly assumed that the firm is operating at a level of capacity at which it has constant variable costs and a constant inventory level over time.

the difference between the sale price per unit ($10) and the variable cost per unit ($6).* The total additional profit contribution from sales will be $36,000 (9,000 units · $4).

The approach used above is the quickest way to find the profit contribution from sales. There is also a longer approach, based on calculating the firm's costs and revenues at both the present and the proposed sales levels and finding the difference in profits at each level. This approach is presented in Table 9.1.

The cost of the marginal investment in accounts receivable   This cost can be calculated by finding the difference between the cost of carrying receivables before and after the introduction of the relaxed credit standards as follows:

Step 1: Calculate the average accounts receivable   Dividing the turnover of accounts receivable into the annual dollar credit sales gives us the average accounts receivable on the firm's books at any time during the year.† Currently the firm's accounts receivable turnover is 12 (360 ÷ 30), and it has credit sales of $600,000 ($10 per unit · 60,000 units). Under the proposed plan, the accounts receivable turnover would be 8 (360 ÷ 45) and the firm would have credit sales of $690,000 ($10 per unit · 69,000 units).

Average accounts receivable:

$$\text{Present plan}: \frac{\$600,000}{12} = \$50,000$$

$$\text{Proposed plan}: \frac{\$690,000}{8} = \$86,250$$

Step 2: Calculate the average investment in accounts receivable   The average figure for accounts receivable calculated above represents the average *book value* of receivables. Since accounts receivable reflect the *sales price* of goods, an adjustment must be made to determine how much the firm actually has invested in them (i.e., the firm's cost of accounts receivable).

If information is available on the sales price of goods, fixed costs, and variable costs, the average investment in accounts receivable is generally taken to be the variable cost associated with the level of accounts receivable.‡ This investment can be calculated by first determining what

*A discussion of the *profit contribution per unit* or *contribution margin* was presented as part of the discussion of breakeven analysis included in Chapter 4. It represents the amount of each sales dollar that is available for meeting fixed costs and profits. Since in the example the firm is assumed to be operating beyond its breakeven point, the amount by which the sale price per unit exceeds the variable cost per unit is viewed as contributing directly toward profits (or reducing losses).

†This calculation is based on transposing the expression for the turnover of accounts receivable presented in Chapter 3 as follows:

$$\text{Turnover of accounts receivable} = \frac{\text{annual credit sales}}{\text{average accounts receivable}}$$

$$\text{Average accounts receivable} = \frac{\text{annual credit sales}}{\text{turnover of accounts receivable}}$$

‡The average investment in accounts receivable can also be measured at the sales price of goods or services. This is a theoretically preferred measure for at least two reasons. First, when a firm evaluates a credit policy that shifts cash collections to credit collections (i.e., accounts receivable), the opportunity cost involved is the reduction in the firm's cash inflows (this reduction is equal to the sales price of the

Footnote continued on next page

percentage of the sales price represents the firm's marginal costs, and then multiplying the average receivables by this percentage. In order to calculate the percentage, the marginal cost per unit is divided by the selling price per unit. Thus, the percentage of marginal costs in each sales dollar is 60 percent [i.e., ($6/unit ÷ $10/unit) · 100%]. Multiplying the average accounts receivable calculated earlier by the corresponding marginal cost percentages for each plan results in the firm's average investment in accounts receivable as follows:

Average investment in accounts receivable:

Present plan: 60% · $50,000 = $30,000
Proposed plan: 60% · $86,250 = $51,750

Step 3: Calculate the relevant cost of the marginal investment in accounts receivable   The marginal investment in accounts receivable is the difference between the average investment in accounts receivable under the proposed plan and under the present plan. This is calculated as follows:

Marginal investment in accounts receivable:

Average investment with proposed plan:	$51,750
Average investment with present plan:	30,000
Marginal Investment:	$21,750

The marginal investment represents the amount of additional dollars the firm will have to tie up in accounts receivable if it relaxes its credit standards. The cost of investing an additional $21,750 in accounts receivable is found by multiplying this figure by 15 percent (i.e., the firm's required return on investment). Thus, the opportunity cost of the marginal investment in accounts receivable is $3,262.50 (i.e., $21,750 · 15%).

If information on the firm's fixed and variable costs, however, had not been available, then an approximate method of determining the average investment in accounts receivable is to divide the cost of sales by the turnover of accounts receivable for each plan as follows:

Average investment in accounts receivable:

$$\text{Present plan: } \frac{\$480,000}{12} = \$40,000$$

$$\text{Proposed plan: } \frac{\$534,000}{8} = \$66,750$$

---

goods or services). Thus, while the *explicit* cost of credit sales is less than the sales price, the *relevant* cost (i.e., the explicit plus implicit cost) must be equal to the cash collections (measured at the sales price) that were foregone by incurring the accounts receivable. Second, for a change in credit policy that results in cash collections instead of funds tied up in accounts receivable, the incremental increase in cash flows is equal to the actual cash sales receipts. For a more extensive discussion of these issues, see Joseph C. Atkins and Young H. Kim, "Comment and Correction: Opportunity Cost in the Evaluation of Investment in Accounts Receivable," *Financial Management* 6 (Winter 1977), pp. 71–74; Edward A. Dyl, "Another Look at the Investment in Accounts Receivable," *Financial Management* 6 (Winter 1977), pp. 67–70; and Tirlochan S. Walia, "Explicit and Implicit Cost of Changes in the Level of Accounts Receivable and the Credit Policy Decision of the Firm," *Financial Management* 6 (Winter 1977) pp. 75–78.

Using this approach, the marginal investment in accounts receivable is calculated as follows:
Marginal investment in accounts receivable:

Average investment with proposed plan:	$66,750
Average investment with present plan:	−40,000
Marginal investment	$26,750

The reader should note that this approach will overstate the relevant marginal investment in accounts receivable because it incorrectly includes a charge for fixed costs.

Making the Credit Standard Decision In order to decide whether the firm should relax its credit standards, the additional profit contribution from sales must be compared to the cost of the marginal investment in accounts receivable. If the additional profit contribution is greater than the marginal costs, the credit standards should be relaxed; otherwise, the current credit standards should remain unchanged. Since, for the XYZ Company, the additional profit contribution from the increased sales would be $36,000, which is considerably more than the cost of the marginal investment in accounts receivable of $3,262.50, the firm *should* relax its credit standards as proposed. The net addition to total profits resulting from such an action would be $32,737.50 (i.e., $36,000.00 − $3,262.50).

The technique described above for making a credit standard decision is quite commonly used for evaluating other types of changes in the management of accounts receivable as well. Other applications of this analytical technique are described later in the chapter. In the above example, it was assumed that the firm's bad debt expenses would be unaffected by the proposed change; in actuality these expenses would more likely change with changing credit standards. The inclusion of changes in bad debt expenses in accounts receivable analysis will also be dealt with later.

CREDIT ANALYSIS

Once the firm has established its credit standards, it must develop procedures for determining the credit-worthiness of a customer and for estimating the maximum amount of credit a customer is capable of supporting. Once this is done, the firm can establish a line of credit, stating the maximum amount the customer can owe the firm at any time. Lines of credit eliminate the necessity of checking a regular customer's credit each time a credit sale is made to that customer.

The depth of a firm's credit analysis to determine the credit-worthiness of each customer must be based on the costs and benefits of such an analysis. For example, while it would not be wise for a firm to spend $50 to investigate the credit-worthiness of a customer making a one-time $40 purchase, it may be wise to spend the $50 to investigate a customer expected to make credit purchases of $60,000 annually. The two basic steps in the credit investigation process are (1) obtaining credit information, and (2) analyzing the information in order to make the credit decision. Each step is discussed next.

Obtaining Credit Information The firm's credit department typically begins the credit evaluation process by requiring a credit applicant to provide certain financial and credit information and credit references. The firm then obtains additional credit information from other external sources. The major external sources of credit information are as follows:

Financial Statements Although no specific information with respect to past payment patterns is shown on a balance sheet or an income statement, insight into the firm's financial position may indicate the nature of its overall financial management. The willingness of the applicant firm to provide these statements may be indicative of its financial position. Audited financial statements are a must for the analysis of credit applicants desiring to make large credit purchases or to be extended lines of credit.

Dun & Bradstreet Dun & Bradstreet Canada Limited is the largest Canadian mercantile credit-reporting agency. It provides subscribers with a copy of a reference book containing credit ratings and keyed estimates of overall financial strength for approximately 4 million Canadian and U.S. firms. A sample reference book page, along with a key to the ratings, is given in Figure 9.1. For an additional charge, subscribers can obtain a Business Information Report on a specific company.* This report provides in-depth information on the firm's payments, finances, banking, history, and operations. When applicable, the Business Information Report also includes information on special events in the business, changes in the business, updates in the business's activities, and public filings such as suits, judgments, tax liens, and so forth. A sample report containing only the basic elements is presented in Figure 9.2.

Creditel of Canada Limited Creditel is the second largest Canadian mercantile credit-reporting agency. Since Creditel specializes in the mercantile paying habits of firms, it provides subscribers with specific information on the modes of payment and age of payables of prospective customers.

Direct Credit Information Purchases and Exchanges In addition to the previous sources, credit information is available from industry and trade associations, national credit associations, specialized credit bureaus, chambers of commerce, and better business bureaus. These organizations do not provide a national credit information service for all lines of business, since they are generally specialized by region, by industry, or by the size of the business firms on which they report.

By agreeing to provide credit information to a credit bureau on its present customers, a firm receives the right to make inquiries to the credit bureau concerning prospective customers. The reports obtained through these credit exchange relationships are factual rather than analytical. A fee is usually levied for each inquiry.

Another method of obtaining credit information, especially on payment patterns, is to solicit such information from other suppliers presently selling on credit to the applicant. Often the suppliers will respond affirmatively to such requests, if the firm agrees to reciprocate in the exchange of similar information.

---

*In 1979, the reference book contained listings on approximately 380,000 Canadian businesses. In addition, Business Information Reports were being maintained on approximately 425,000 Canadian businesses.

Bank Checking It may be possible for the firm's bank to obtain credit information from the applicant's bank. However, the type of information obtained is often vague, unless the applicant agrees to the release of such information. This is the case because the credit applicant's bank cannot disclose specific information such as account balances, loan balances, and so forth, without the consent of the applicant. Typically, an estimate of the firm's cash balance is provided. For instance, it may be found that a firm maintains a "high five-figure" balance.

Analysis of Credit Information A credit applicant's financial statements and accounts payable ledger can be used to calculate the firm's "average age of accounts payable." This figure can then be compared to the credit terms currently being extended to the firm. It may also be possible to age the applicant's accounts payable in order to obtain a better insight into its payment patterns. For customers requesting large amounts of credit or lines of credit, a thorough time-series ratio analysis of the firm's liquidity, debt, and profitability should be performed using the firm's financial statements, as was discussed in Chapter 3.

Dun & Bradstreet's reference book can be used for estimating the maximum line of credit to extend. Although Dun & Bradstreet provides *no* credit recommendations, it does suggest that 10 percent of a customer's "Estimated Financial Strength" (see Figure 9.1) be the maximum line of credit extended.* Additional data providing insight into the credit-worthiness of the customer can be obtained from the "Payments" section of the D & B Business Information Report (see upper portion of Figure 9.2).

The Credit Decision Ratios or other numerical credit evaluation schemes have been used by firms to judge a firm's credit-worthiness. In addition, statistical techniques, such as regression analysis and discriminant analysis, have also been used to judge credit-worthiness.† In practice, statistical methods have been a more useful decision aid for firms that have a large number of relatively small customers. Such firms include those engaged in retail sales, personal loans, and mortgage loans.

Although statistical credit evaluation schemes are gaining a wider acceptance, a key input to the final credit decision is still the financial analyst's *subjective judgment* of a firm's credit-worthiness. Experience provides a "feel" for the nonquantifiable aspects of the quality of a firm's operations. The analyst will add his or her knowledge of the character of the applicant's management, references from other suppliers, and the firm's historical payment patterns to any quantitative figures developed in order to determine its credit-worthiness. Generally, the final decision as to whether to extend credit to the applicant, and possibly what amount of credit to extend, is made by a credit review committee.

---

*However, Credit Clearing House, a division of Dun & Bradstreet, does provide credit recommendations to wholesalers on retail clothing and gift stores.

†Discriminant analysis is similar to regression analysis, except that it assumes that the observations under study originate from two or more universes (groupings). In discriminant analysis, a classification of the observations (e.g., loan applicants at a consumer loan company) into the groupings (e.g., credit-worthy and not credit-worthy) is based on a number of relevant factors (e.g., whether the applicant is self-employed, owns a home, etc.).

Explanation and Use of Listings

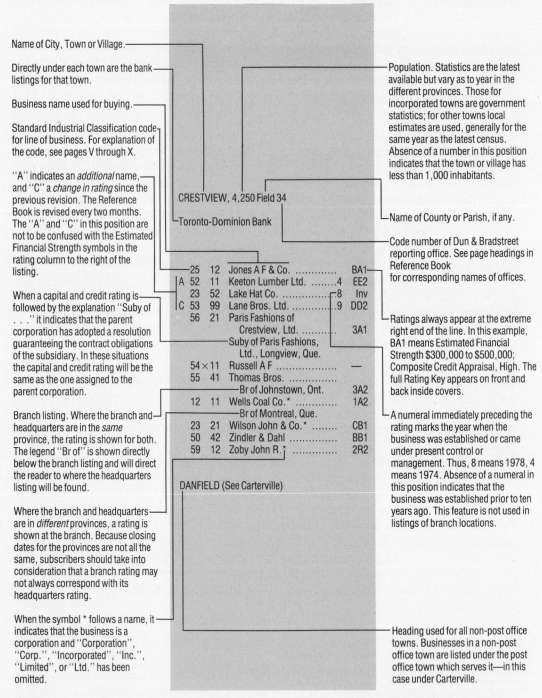

Name of City, Town or Village.

Directly under each town are the bank listings for that town.

Business name used for buying.

Standard Industrial Classification code for line of business. For explanation of the code, see pages V through X.

"A" indicates an *additional* name, and "C" a *change in rating* since the previous revision. The Reference Book is revised every two months. The "A" and "C" in this position are not to be confused with the Estimated Financial Strength symbols in the rating column to the right of the listing.

When a capital and credit rating is followed by the explanation "Suby of . . ." it indicates that the parent corporation has adopted a resolution guaranteeing the contract obligations of the subsidiary. In these situations the capital and credit rating will be the same as the one assigned to the parent corporation.

Branch listing. Where the branch and headquarters are in the *same* province, the rating is shown for both. The legend "Br of" is shown directly below the branch listing and will direct the reader to where the headquarters listing will be found.

Where the branch and headquarters are in *different* provinces, a rating is shown at the branch. Because closing dates for the provinces are not all the same, subscribers should take into consideration that a branch rating may not always correspond with its headquarters rating.

When the symbol * follows a name, it indicates that the business is a corporation and "Corporation", "Corp.", "Incorporated", "Inc.", "Limited", or "Ltd." has been omitted.

Population. Statistics are the latest available but vary as to year in the different provinces. Those for incorporated towns are government statistics; for other towns local estimates are used, generally for the same year as the latest census. Absence of a number in this position indicates that the town or village has less than 1,000 inhabitants.

Name of County or Parish, if any.

Code number of Dun & Bradstreet reporting office. See page headings in Reference Book for corresponding names of offices.

Ratings always appear at the extreme right end of the line. In this example, BA1 means Estimated Financial Strength $300,000 to $500,000; Composite Credit Appraisal, High. The full Rating Key appears on front and back inside covers.

A numeral immediately preceding the rating marks the year when the business was established or came under present control or management. Thus, 8 means 1978, 4 means 1974. Absence of a numeral in this position indicates that the business was established prior to ten years ago. This feature is not used in listings of branch locations.

Heading used for all non-post office towns. Businesses in a non-post office town are listed under the post office town which serves it—in this case under Carterville.

CRESTVIEW, 4,250 Field 34

Toronto-Dominion Bank

	25	12	Jones A F & Co.	BA1
A	52	11	Keeton Lumber Ltd. 4	EE2
	23	52	Lake Hat Co. 8	Inv
C	53	99	Lane Bros. Ltd. 9	DD2
	56	21	Paris Fashions of Crestview, Ltd.	3A1

Suby of Paris Fashions, Ltd., Longview, Que.

54 × 11	Russell A F	—
55	41	Thomas Bros.	

Br of Johnstown, Ont. — 3A2

12	11	Wells Coal Co.*	1A2

Br of Montreal, Que.

23	21	Wilson John & Co.*	CB1
50	42	Zindler & Dahl	BB1
59	12	Zoby John R.*	2R2

DANFIELD (See Carterville)

Figure 9.1 An excerpt from the Dun & Bradstreet Reference Book and Key to Ratings. (Source: Dun & Bradstreet, Inc. Reprinted by permission.)

Key to Ratings

	ESTIMATED FINANCIAL STRENGTH		COMPOSITE CREDIT APPRAISAL			
			HIGH	GOOD	FAIR	LIMITED
5A	$50,000,000	and over	1	2	3	4
4A	$10,000,000 to	49,999,999	1	2	3	4
3A	1,000,000 to	9,999,999	1	2	3	4
2A	750,000 to	999,999	1	2	3	4
1A	500,000 to	749,999	1	2	3	4
BA	300,000 to	499,999	1	2	3	4
BB	200,000 to	299,999	1	2	3	4
CB	125,000 to	199,999	1	2	3	4
CC	75,000 to	124,999	1	2	3	4
DC	50,000 to	74,999	1	2	3	4
DD	35,000 to	49,999	1	2	3	4
EE	20,000 to	34,999	1	2	3	4
FF	10,000 to	19,999	1	2	3	4
GG	5,000 to	9,999	1	2	3	4
HH	Up to	4,999	1	2	3	4

**CLASSIFICATION BASED ON BOTH
ESTIMATED FINANCIAL STRENGTH AND COMPOSITE CREDIT APPRAISAL**

FINANCIAL STRENGTH BRACKET

1   **$125,000 and over**
2   **20,000 to $124,999**

When only the numeral (1 or 2) appears, it is an indication that the estimated financial strength, while not definitely classified, is presumed to be within the range of the ($) figures in the corresponding bracket and while the composite credit appraisal cannot be judged precisely, it is believed to be "High" or "Good."

"INV," shown in place of a rating indicates that the report was under investigation at the time of going to press. It has no other significance.

ABSENCE OF RATING, expressed by two hypens (--), is not to be construed as unfavorable but signifies circumstances difficult to classify within condensed rating symbols. It suggests the advisability of obtaining a report for additional information.

**EMPLOYEE RANGE DESIGNATIONS IN REPORTS ON NAMES NOT LISTED
IN THE REFERENCE BOOK**

**KEY TO EMPLOYEE
RANGE DESIGNATIONS**

Certain businesses do not lend themselves to a Dun & Bradstreet rating and are not listed in the Reference Book. Information on these names, however, continues to be stored and updated in the D&B Business Information File. Reports are available on such businesses and instead of a rating they carry an Employee Range Designation (ER) which is indicative of size in terms of number of employees. No other significance should be attached.

ER 1	1000 or more	Employees
ER 2	500 - 999	Employees
ER 3	100 - 499	Employees
ER 4	50 - 99	Employees
ER 5	20 - 49	Employees
ER 6	10 - 19	Employees
ER 7	5 - 9	Employees
ER 8	1 - 4	Employees
ER N		Not Available

Dun & Bradstreet
84 Carlton Street, Toronto, Ont. M5B 1L6

Printed in Canada

08-2-5(7706)

Dun & Bradstreet

Please note whether name, business and street address correspond with your inquiry.

BUSINESS INFORMATION REPORT

BASE REPORT

SIC	D-U-N-S	©DUN & BRADSTREET	STARTED	RATING
59 43	20-155-5868	CD 34 JAN 28, 197–		
59 47	STANDARD SUPPLY	STATIONERY & GIFTS	1947	DDI
	CHARMAINE'S GIFTS			

165 CHINA ST.
OURTOWN ON
TEL 519 729-1141

CHARMAINE B. MALVIN   **PARTNERS**
LLOYD T. MALVIN JR

SUMMARY

PAYMENTS	DISC PPT
SALES	$119,519
WORTH	$40,096
EMPLOYS	3
RECORD	CLEAR
CONDITION	STRONG
TREND	UP

PAYMENTS

HC	OWE	P DUE TERMS	DEC 11 197–	SOLD
1100	300	2–10–30	Disc	Over 3 yrs
500	300	2–10–30	Disc Ppt	Over 3 yrs
300		30	Ppt	1 yr

FINANCE

On Jan 7 197– L.T. Malvin Jr., partner, submitted statement Dec 31

197–:

Cash	$ 8,524	Accts Pay	$ 702
Mdse	15,214		
Current	23,739	Current	702
Fixt & Equip	5,020		
R E	10,600	NET WORTH	40,096
Prepaid	1,439		
Total Assets	**$40,798**	**Total**	**$40,798**

REAL ESTATE	TITLE	VALUE	MTGE
Business property	Partners	$10,600	Clear

197– sales $119,519. Gross profit $55,238. Net profit $7,879. Fire insurance on merchandise and fixtures $20,000, on building $10,000.

Signed Jan 7 197– for STANDARD SUPPLY, by Lloyd T. Malvin Jr, partner.

-----0-----

During interview Malvin stated sales up 5% in 197–, and profit up by 2% during same year. These comments have been confirmed.

BANKING   Non-borrowing account. Balances average medium four figures. Relations satisfactory.

HISTORY   Style registered Jan 5 1950 by partners. Charmaine's Gifts is unregistered, used for advertising.
C.B. MALVIN, born 1903, married. 1938–1947 employed as bookkeeper-stenographer by Public Works Department. Purchased this business in 1947. Her husband, Lloyd Malvin, is employed by City Fire Department.
L.T. MALVIN JR, born 1927, married. Attended Speed Business College 1945–1946. Served Canadian Army 1946–1949. Employed by mother prior to 1950. Then became partner.

OPERATION   Retails stationery (60%), gifts, school supplies and greeting cards (40%). Terms 100% cash. Employs three, including the partners. LOCATION: Owns one-storey block building providing 6,200 square feet, in normal condition. Housekeeping good.
10-23 (14 66)

Figure 9.2   A Dun & Bradstreet Business Information Report. (Source: Dun & Bradstreet, Inc. Reprinted by permission.)

Performance Evaluation of the Credit Department   It is not easy to evaluate the performance of the credit department for control purposes. While the turnover of accounts receivable provides a measure of performance, it is probably too aggregated to provide effective control. A more refined but still indirect measure of collection experience is the aging of accounts receivable. With the aid of a computer, accounts receivable can be aged on a monthly basis.*

A more refined and direct measure is given by a tabulation of the distribution of collections by the age of the accounts at the time of their collection. Such a tabulation could contain the percentage of sales that were paid in less than 30 days, 30 to 60 days, and so on.

The above measures of accounts receivable management have a common problem. They attempt to measure the *net* efficiency of two aspects of accounts receivable management: the granting of credit and the collection of past due accounts. Thus, if a firm's credit standards and terms are lenient, its collection staff would probably be under great pressure to increase the collection of past due accounts.

Credit Terms

A firm's credit terms specify the repayment terms required of all credit customers.† Typically, a type of shorthand is used. For example, credit terms may be stated as 2/10 *net* 30, which means that the purchaser receives a 2-percent discount if the bill is paid within 10 days after the beginning of the credit period; if the customer does not take the cash discount, the full amount must be paid within 30 days after the beginning of the credit period. Credit terms cover three things: (1) the cash discount, if any (in this case 2 percent); (2) the cash discount period (in this case 10 days); and (3) the credit period (in this case 30 days). Changes in any aspect of the firm's credit terms may have an effect on its overall profitability. The positive and negative factors associated with such changes, and quantitative procedures for evaluating them, are presented in the following sections.

CASH DISCOUNTS

When a firm initiates or *increases* a cash discount, the following changes and effects on profits can be expected:

Item	Direction of change [increase (I) or decrease (D)]	Effect on profits [positive (+) or negative (−)]
Sales volume	I	+
Average collection period	D	+
Bad debt expense	D	+
Profit per unit	D	−

The sales volume should increase, since if a firm is willing to pay by day 10, the price per unit decreases. If demand is elastic, sales should increase as a result of this price decrease.

*A typical aging schedule for accounts receivable was given in Chapter 3.
†An in-depth discussion of credit terms as viewed by the recipient is presented in Chapter 11. The emphasis there is on the analysis of credit terms in order to evaluate trade credit as a source of financing. In this chapter, our concern is with credit terms from the point of view of the offerer.

The average collection period should decrease, thereby reducing the cost of carrying accounts receivable. The reduction in receivables results from the fact that some customers who did not previously take the cash discount will now take it. The bad debt expense should fall since, as people on the average pay earlier, the probability of a bad debt should decrease.* Both the decrease in the average collection period and the decrease in bad debt expense should result in increased profits. The negative aspect of an increased cash discount is a decreased profit margin per unit as more people take the discount and pay the reduced price. Decreasing or eliminating a cash discount would have opposite effects. The quantitative effects of changes in cash discounts can be evaluated by a method similar to that used to evaluate changes in credit terms.

EXAMPLE Assume that the XYZ Company Ltd., data on which were presented earlier, is contemplating initiating a cash discount of 2 percent for payment prior to day 10 after a purchase. The firm's current average collection period is 30 days, credit sales of 60,000 units are made, the variable cost per unit is $6, and the average cost per unit is currently $8. The firm expects that if the cash discount is initiated 60 percent of its sales will be on discount, and sales will increase by 15 percent to 69,000 units. The average collection period is expected to drop to 15 days. Bad debt expenses are assumed to be unaffected by the decision. The firm requires a 15 percent pretax return on investments.

The advantages of the cash discount plan for the firm are increased sales and a decreased average collection period. An additional 9,000 units will be sold, whose contribution to profits will be $36,000 (9,000 · $4). This is because the cost of these units is $6, while the sale price is $10. Using the previously discussed method of finding the average investment in accounts receivable under both the proposed cash discount plan and the present plan produces the following results:†

Average investment in accounts receivable:

$$\text{Present plan: } \frac{\$6 \ (60,000 \text{ units})}{12} = \$30,000$$

$$\text{Proposed plan: } \frac{\$6 \ (69,000 \text{ units})}{24} = \$17,250$$

With the cash discount, there is a reduction in the investment in accounts receivable of $12,750 (i.e., $30,000 − $17,250). The savings resulting from this reduction is $1,912.50 (i.e., 15% · $12,750). The total savings, or addition to profits, is therefore $37,912.50 (i.e., $36,000 + $1,912.50).

*This contention is based on the fact that the longer it takes a person to pay, the less likely it is that he or she will pay. The more time that elapses, the more opportunities there are for a customer to become technically insolvent or bankrupt. Therefore the probability of a bad debt is expected to increase directly with increases in the average collection period.
†The calculation of the investment in accounts receivable presented for both the present and proposed plan is not entirely correct. Technically, consideration should be explicitly given to the fact that the proposed action will change the payment pattern of existing customers, which means that not only will cost be recovered in a fashion different from before but the pattern of receipt of profit will also change. In other words, the old customers, who now pay earlier as a result of the firm offering the cash discount, cause the firm to receive not only its cost but also its profit sooner than would have occurred without such a credit term change. Technically, the analysis should be performed in a fashion that would value the firm's investment in receivables to existing customers that choose to take the cash discount at the *sales price* rather than at cost. Such an approach would more correctly measure the firm's cost or

The cost of the proposed cash discount is easily calculated by multiplying it by the dollar amount of sales on which it is taken. Since 60 percent of the sales are expected to be on the discount, the cost of the discount is as follows:

$$2\% \, (60\% \cdot \$690,000) = \$8,280$$

Comparing the savings of $37,912.50 to the $8,280 cost of the discount indicates that the firm will realize a net profit of $29,632.50 (i.e., $37,912.50 − $8,280). This type of analysis can also be applied to decisions concerning the reduction or elimination of cash discounts.

THE CASH DISCOUNT PERIOD

If the cash discount period were *increased,* the following changes could be expected:

Item	Direction of change [increase (I) or decrease (D)]	Effect on profits [positive (+) or negative (−)]
Sales volume	I	+
Average collection period due to nondiscount takers now paying earlier	D	+
Bad debt expense	D	+
Profit per unit	D	−
Average collection period due to discount takers still getting cash discount but paying later	I	−

benefits from implementation of a proposed credit term change. If we assume that 54 percent of the XYZ Company's existing customers will take the discount if offered, the *average investment in accounts receivable* would be calculated as follows in each case:

Present plan:
$$\frac{(.54)(\$10)(60,000 \text{ units}) + (1 - .54)(\$6)(60,000 \text{ units})}{12} = \frac{\$489,600}{12} = \$40,800$$

Proposed plan:
$$\frac{(.54)(\$10)(60,000 \text{ units}) + (1 - .54)(\$6)(60,000 \text{ units}) + (\$6)(9,000 \text{ units})}{24}$$
$$= \frac{\$543,600}{24} = \$22,650$$

The differences between these results and those found above are attributable to the fact that the change in the time-receipt pattern of profits from existing customers is reflected in this analysis while it was ignored above.

Anytime a change in credit terms, or some other aspects of accounts receivable management, is expected to change the payment pattern of existing customers, formal analysis should recognize that the firm's pattern of receipt of both cost *and* profit from these customers is being altered. Therefore, the investment in receivables for existing customers, whose payment patterns have been altered, should be measured at the sale price—not cost. For an excellent discussion of this point, the reader is referred to Edward A. Dyl, "Another Look at the Investment in Accounts Receivable," *Financial Management* 6, No. 4 (Winter 1977), pp. 67–70. In order to convey the key concepts throughout the remainder of this chapter without confusing the reader, the account receivable investment is calculated at cost regardless of whether or not the existing customers' payment pattern is altered by the given account receivable action.

The problem in determining the net effect of a change in the discount period are directly attributable to the two forces that affect the firm's average collection period. When the cash discount period is increased, there is a positive effect on profits because many people who did not take the cash discount in the past will now take it, thereby reducing the average collection period. However, there is also a negative effect on profits because people who already were taking the cash discount will be able to still take it and pay later, thus slowing down the average collection period. The net effect of these two forces on the average collection period is difficult to quantify.

If the firm were to shorten the cash discount period, the effects would be the opposite of those described above. Due to the many assumptions necessary to illustrate changes in the cash discount period analytically, no example of these effects is given.*

CREDIT PERIOD

Changes in the credit period also affect the firm's profitability. The following effects on profits can be expected from an increase in the credit period.

Item	Direction of change [increase (I) or decrease (D)]	Effect on profits [positive (+) or negative (−)]
Sales volume	I	+
Average collection period	I	−
Bad debt expense	I	−

Increasing the credit period should increase sales, the average collection period, and the bad debt expense. Thus, the effect on profits of the sales increase is positive, while the effect on profits of both the collection period and bad debt expense increases are negative. A decrease in the credit period is likely to have the opposite effects on profits.

EXAMPLE Assume that the XYZ Company Ltd. is considering increasing its credit period from 30 to 60 days. The average collection period, currently 45 days, is expected to increase to 75 days. Bad debt expenses, currently 1 percent of sales, are expected to increase to 3 percent. Sales (all on credit) are expected to increase by 15 percent to 69,000 units.† The selling price and variable cost per unit are $10 and $6, respectively. The firm's required return on investment is 15 percent.

*Since changes in the cash discount period may affect the payment pattern of existing customers, the refinement described in the footnote on pages 268–269 would also apply to the analysis of proposed cash discount period changes.
†Although all sales have been assumed to be made on credit throughout this chapter, the analytical techniques presented could easily be adapted to situations where only a portion of the firm's sales were made on credit. The simpler all-credit-sale assumption is used in order to avoid confusing the key issues by complicating the analytical procedure.

The key factor to be recognized when bad debt expenses are included in the analysis is that *the unit cost of a bad debt equals the sale price per unit.* The entire sale price is lost and must be deducted. This is due to the fact that the additional profit contribution from sales has been calculated on the assumption that the full sale price will be received.

A complete solution is given in Table 9.2. The analysis indicates that the additional profit contribution from sales of $36,000 covers the cost of the marginal investment in accounts receivable of $6,187.50,* and the marginal increase in the cost of bad debts of $14,700 by $15,112.50. This suggests that the change should be made. If the firm were contemplating a decrease in its credit period, the analysis would be similar to that presented in Table 9.2, but the negative and positive profit and cost values would be reversed.

Table 9.2   The Effects of an Increased Credit Period on the XYZ Company Ltd.

Additional profit contribution from sales (9,000 units) ($10.00 − $6.00)		$36,000.00
Cost of marginal investment in A/R[a]		
Investment with proposed credit period		
$\dfrac{(\$6.00)(69,000)}{4.8}$	$86,250	
Investment with present credit period		
$\dfrac{(\$6.00)(60,000)}{8.0}$	45,000	
Marginal investment in A/R	$41,250	
Cost of marginal investment in A/R		
(.15)($41,250)		($6,187.50)
Cost of marginal bad debts		
Bad debts with proposed credit period		
(.03)($690,000)	$20,700	
Bad debts with present credit period		
(.01)($600,000)	6,000	
Cost of marginal bad debts		($14,700.00)
Net profit from implementation of proposed plan		$15,112.50

[a]The denominators 4.8 and 8.0 in the calculation of the investment in accounts receivable for the proposed and present plans are the accounts receivable turnovers for each of these plans (360/75 = 4.8 and 360/45 = 8.0).

---

*Because changes in the credit period are likely to affect the payment pattern of existing customers, the refinement described in the footnote on pages 268–269 would apply to the analysis of proposed credit period changes.

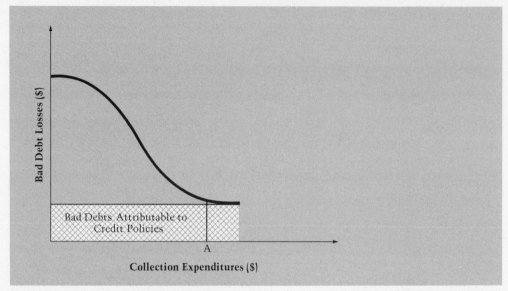

Figure 9.3   Collection expenditures and bad debt losses.

Collection Policies

The firm's collection policies are the procedures followed to collect accounts receivable when they are due. The effectiveness of the firm's collection policies can be partially evaluated by looking at the level of bad debt expenses. This level depends not only on the collection policies but on the credit policies on which the extension of credit is based. If one assumes that the level of bad debts attributable to the firm's credit policies is relatively constant, increasing collection expenditures can be expected to reduce the firm's bad debts, as is depicted in Figure 9.3. As the figure indicates, beyond point A additional collection expenditures will not reduce the firm's bad debt losses enough to justify the outlay of funds. The firm must determine the level of collection expenditures that is "optimal" from a cost-benefit viewpoint.

THE BASIC TRADE-OFFS

The basic trade-offs expected to result from a *tightening* of collection efforts are tabulated as follows:

Item	Direction of change [increase (I) or decrease (D)]	Effect on profits [positive (+) or negative (−)]
Bad debt expense	D	+
Average collection period	D	+
Sales volume	0 or D	0 or −
Collection expenditures	I	−

Increased collection expenditures should reduce the bad debt expense and the average collection period, thereby increasing profits. The costs of this strategy may include lost sales in addition to increased collection expenditures if the level of collection effort is too intense. In other words, if the firm pushes its customers too hard to pay their accounts, they may be angered and take their business elsewhere, thereby reducing the firm's sales.

The basic trade-offs described above can be evaluated numerically in a manner similar to that used to evaluate the trade-offs for credit standards and credit terms. By calculating the marginal cost of increased efforts and the decreased profit contribution from sales (if any) and comparing this to the savings from both reduced bad debt expenses and decreased investment in accounts receivable,* various strategies for increasing the level of collection effort can be assessed. An example of such an analysis is not included since the procedures are so similar to those illustrated earlier.

TYPES OF COLLECTION TECHNIQUES

As an account becomes more and more overdue, the collection techniques used become more personal and more strict. The basic collection techniques used are presented below in the order typically followed in the collection process.

Letters   After an account receivable becomes overdue a certain number of days, the firm normally sends a polite letter reminding the customer about his or her obligation. If the account is not paid within a certain period of time after the letter has been sent, a second, more demanding letter is sent. This letter may be followed by yet another letter, if necessary.

Telephone Calls   If letters prove unsuccessful, the company's credit manager may call the customer and personally request immediate payment. If the customer has a reasonable excuse, arrangements may be made to extend the payment period. A call from the company's attorney may be used if all else seems to fail.

Personal Visits   This technique is much more common at the consumer credit level, but it may be employed by industrial suppliers. Sending a local salesperson or a collection person to confront the customer can be a very effective collection procedure. Payment may be made on the spot.

Using Collection Agencies   A firm can turn uncollectible accounts over to a collection agency or an attorney for collection. The fees for this type of collection effort are typically quite high; the firm may receive less than fifty cents on the dollar for accounts collected in this way.

Legal Action   This is the most stringent step in the collection process. It is an alternative to the use of a collection agency. Not only is direct legal action expen-

---

*Because changes in collection effort are likely to impact on the payment patterns of existing customers, the refinement described in the footnote on pages 268–269 would also apply to the analysis of proposed collection effort changes.

sive, but it may force the debtor into bankruptcy, thereby reducing the possibility of future business from him without guaranteeing the ultimate receipt of the delinquent charges.

COST CONSIDERATIONS

Generally, the effort expended on collections depends upon the size of the account and the possibility of ultimate collection. A firm should usually not spend more on collection fees than the dollar value of the account to be collected. In fact, it may not even be worthwhile to spend more than the amount that the firm *expects* to collect.

Commercial entities, such as banks and sales finance companies, often are willing to spend more on their collection efforts than the actual sum to be collected. If these corporate entities were perceived by present customers as being willing to write off bad accounts, then some of their present customers might begin to withhold payments in the expectation of also being written off as a bad account.

COMPUTERIZATION OF ACCOUNTS RECEIVABLE MANAGEMENT

The use of computers to reduce the amount of manual effort involved in accounts receivable management is widespread. A computer can be programmed to monitor accounts receivable after a customer has been billed. If payment has not been received at certain predetermined points, collection letters are sent. After a prescribed number of these letters have been sent without any receipt of payment, a special notice will be generated, probably as part of a monthly report to the credit manager. At this point, the credit manager will use the above collection efforts to obtain payment.

Currently computers are being used not only to monitor accounts but also as an aid in the credit-decision process. Data on each customer's payment patterns are maintained and can be called for as needed to evaluate requests for renewed or additional credit by customers. A computer can also be used to monitor the effectiveness of the collection department by generating data on the status of outstanding accounts.

Credit Insurance

In addition to maintaining an efficient collection department, a firm can use credit insurance to ensure that it will be able to convert a major portion of its accounts receivable into cash. Credit insurance is designed to protect firms, such as manufacturers, from unusual (or extraordinary) credit losses. Such insurance may also be a prerequisite for a bank loan, which is secured by a lien on a firm's accounts receivable.

DOMESTIC SALES*

Since a firm's selling price should contain a markup, which is sufficient to cover normal credit losses, credit insurance is not designed to protect a firm against normal, or *pri-*

---

*Such insurance is obtainable from private-sector companies, such as the American Credit Indemnity Company.

mary, losses. A firm's primary loss is established by the credit insurance company, after a careful assessment of the bad debt loss experience of the firm and the industry in which the firm operates. For example, if the credit losses for firm A normally amount to one-half of 1 percent of sales for sales of $10 million, $50,000 ($10 million · 0.005) will be established by the credit insurance company as firm A's primary loss.

There are at least two important features that limit the amount of abnormal credit losses that a firm can transfer to the insurance company. First, the insurance company will require the firm to retain some percentage (typically 10 to 33 percent) of the net loss suffered, in order to prevent the firm from granting credit indiscriminately. The percentage retained by the firm is referred to as *coinsurance.* Second, the insurance company will limit its coverage on each individual account. Each limit will be based on the credit rating of the account (customer) at the time the goods purchased are shipped.

EXAMPLE   Based on a D & B rating of "BA" for B. C. Rod Ltd. at date of shipment, Canadian Credit Insurance Ltd. has set the credit coverage limit for sales to B. C. Rod at $10,000. If West Steel Ltd.'s policy has a 10 percent coinsurance clause, then what is the maximum amount that West Steel can lose on a $15,000 order placed by B. C. Rod?

The most that West Steel Ltd. can lose would be $6,000. This is its coinsurance loss of $1,000 (0.10 · $10,000) plus $5,000.

The cost of credit insurance has averaged about one-tenth of 1 percent of sales. The desirability of incurring this expense for a firm depends on (1) the relationship between the cost of the insurance and the expected cost of the covered losses, (2) management's level of risk aversion, and (3) the circumstances of the firm. For example, if a firm is not strong financially and can not self-insure, or if the firm is selling to a few large accounts, the firm may find credit insurance to be very attractive. On the other hand, if a firm is strong financially and its accounts are widely diversified, the firm may find credit insurance to be very unattractive. Also, if most of a firm's sales are to a small number of high credit-risks, credit insurance may be unavailable or prohibitive in cost.

EXPORT SALES

Selling in foreign markets has become more and more difficult due to increased foreign competition and exchange regulations. In order to remain competitive, Canadian exporters have consistently lessened their usage of irrevocable letters of credit. This, in turn, has exposed the Canadian exporting firm to additional commercial risks, and to political risks such as the possibility of war or revolution in the buyer's country.

In an effort to assist in minimizing the political and commercial risks associated with doing business internationally, specialized export credit institutions have developed in most countries. In Canada, this specialized institution is the Export Development Corporation, which was established under the Export Credit Insurance Act of 1944. EDC, as a federally owned crown corporation, provides export credit insurance for the risks which are not normally available from commercial (private) insurers, such as Marsh and

McLennan Ltd. and Reed Shaw Stenhouse Ltd.* Specific aspects of EDC's export credit insurance program are summarized in Table 9.3†

In 1978, EDC issued a record volume of $2.95 billion in export credit insurance on its own account. Furthermore, at the end of 1978, the corporation had more than 950 policies in effect for sales of goods and services to buyers in over 150 countries.‡

Table 9.3   Export Credit Insurance Program of the Export Development Corporation (EDC)

Principal risks covered:

(1) Commercial risks:
    (a) Insolvency of the buyer
    (b) Arbitrary nonacceptance by the buyer, not due to the fault of the seller
    (c) Protracted default
(2) Political risks:
    (a) Cancellation of an export licence, not due to the fault of the exporter
    (b) Cancellation of previously valid import authority or other restrictions by foreign government making imports impossible
    (c) Outbreak of war, hostilities, civil commotion, or other such occurrence, which prevents payment by the buyer

No separate political and commercial risk coverage is available.
No cost inflation (escalation) or foreign exchange fluctuation insurance is available.

Types of policies:

(1) Short-term (up to 180 days)
    For consumer goods and miscellaneous general commodities, two types of whole turnover insurance policies are:
    (a) Contract Policy (operating from date of order until date of payment)
    (b) Shipment Policy (operating from date of shipment until date of payment)
    For both types, credit limits are established for each foreign buyer and a total liability limit is established for the exporting corporation.
(2) Medium-term (up to 5 years)
    Specific contract policies are issued, covering individual contracts for the sale of capital goods and services.

Percentage of coverage:

Normally 85/15 coinsurance coverage on all export credit insurance policies.

Premium rates:

Vary by country, class of business, type of good, credit terms, exporter's previous loss experience, etc. For comprehensive policies is about $\frac{1}{2}$ to 1 percent.

Discretionary ceilings:

EDC provides exporters with a discretionary limit, below which orders by new customers need not be referred to EDC before being accepted for EDC insurance coverage.

---

*As a schedule D crown corporation, EDC can sue and be sued, and it can borrow funds on its own account.
†For a critical evaluation of EDC's export credit insurance program, see K. C. Dhawan and L. Kryzanowski, *Export Consortia: A Canadian Study* (Montreal: Dekemco Ltd., 1978).
‡Export Development Corporation, *1978 Annual Report.*

Use of Credit Cards

Both general and specific credit cards are used extensively in the retail field.

GENERAL CREDIT CARDS

General credit cards, such as Chargex (VISA) and Master Charge, are both sponsored and administered by the major Canadian financial institutions.* For the provision of a number of services, which are discussed below, the credit-card agency charges the retailer a percentage of his or her credit sales. Typically, the rates range between 2 and 5.5 percent, and are based on a matrix scale, which depends on monthly dollar sales volume of sales slips and average sales slip size. For large volume merchants, or those with unusually large ticket sizes, a "fixed" rate is most often negotiated.

If the only credit sales that a retailer honours are those on a general credit card, then the retailer can operate as if all his or her "credit" sales have been for cash. This results in the following four benefits for the retailer. First, the retailer will not have to finance accounts receivable, since he or she will receive cash immediately upon the deposit of the day's credit-card slips. Second, the retailer will generally not be exposed to losses from bad debts, since the risk of such losses will be shifted to the sponsoring financial institution(s). Third, the retailer will eliminate the costs associated with the credit investigation, credit approval, and collection aspects of credit sales. Fourth, the retailer can play the float on returned merchandise. If the retailer is slow in submitting refund slips, the retailer can use the receipts of a "prior but not cancelled sale" for a longer period of time.

A smaller retailer should honour a general credit card only if the cost savings resulting from the elimination of the credit granting function, plus the incremental benefit of the increased sales resulting from the acceptance of the card, are more than the costs associated with honouring the general credit card. These costs include not only the credit-card agency's fee, but also the costs associated with increased credit sales, resulting from previous cash customers now making purchases on the general credit card.

The acceptance of general credit cards also depends upon a retailer's particular circumstances. For example, a retailer who operates on a small margin in a price-competitive market may find the use of general credit cards unattractive; while a retailer who operates on a large markup may find the use of general credit cards attractive.

SPECIFIC CREDIT CARDS

Some of the large national department stores (such as Eatons and Simpsons) and gasoline retailers (such as Esso and Gulf) administer their own credit cards.† In general, these

---

*Master Charge is offered by the Bank of Montreal, Provincial Bank of Canada, Canada Trustco, and the members of the Canadian Cooperative Credit Society. Chargex is offered by the Royal Bank, Toronto Dominion Bank, Commerce Bank, National Bank, and the Bank of Nova Scotia. Whether the combined Provincial and National Banks will offer one or both cards is at present unresolved.

†Retailers such as the Bay honour general credit cards; others, such as Eatons, refuse to honour the general credit cards.

retailers have found that the term-financing of accounts receivable can be quite profitable, especially when carrying charges of 18–24 percent per annum are levied on overdue account balances.

Summary

This chapter has presented discussions and analyses of the important aspects of accounts receivable management. Since accounts receivable represent a sizable investment on the part of most firms, the efficient management of these accounts can provide considerable savings to the firm. The firm's overall objective with respect to the management of accounts receivable should not be merely to collect receivables quickly; attention should also be given to the benefit-cost trade-offs involved in the various areas of accounts receivable management. These areas are the determination of credit policies, credit terms, and collection policies.

Credit policies have two dimensions: credit standards and credit analysis. The basic trade-offs here are the cost of clerical efforts, the cost of investment in accounts receivable, the cost of bad debts, and the profit contribution from sales. Whenever credit standards are relaxed or tightened, these variables must be considered. Credit analysis, although not an exact science, is devoted to the collection and evaluation of credit information on credit applicants in order to determine whether they can meet the firm's credit standards. The subjective judgment of the credit manager is an important input to the credit decision. As noted in the chapter, it is difficult to evaluate the performance of the credit department for control purposes.

Credit terms have three components—the cash discount, the cash discount period, and the credit period. Changes in each of these variables affect the firm's sales, profits, average collection period, and bad debt expenses. The exact effects of a decision to change any of the three credit term components depend on the direction and degree of change. Analytical techniques for evaluating such decisions by assessing the benefit-cost trade-offs are available.

Collection policies determine the type and degree of effort exercised to collect overdue accounts. Decisions with respect to the level of collection effort depend upon the size of the account and the possibility of ultimate collection. A point exists beyond which additional collection expenditures do not provide an adequate return. Quantitative procedures for evaluating collection policies are available. The basic collection techniques include letters, telephone calls, personal visits, the use of collection agencies, and legal action. The actual methods used depend on the firm. With the widespread use of computers, a large portion of the accounts receivable management process has been automated, thereby eliminating much of the paperwork previously required.

A firm can use credit insurance to ensure that it will be able to convert a major portion of its accounts receivable into cash. Credit insurance is designed to protect a firm from unusual rather than primary losses. Thus, a firm will have to retain, or coinsure, some percentage of any losses suffered. For export credit sales, the Export Development Corporation (EDC) insures Canadian exporters against various commercial and political risks.

General credit cards, such as Chargex (VISA) and Master Charge are used extensively in the retail sector. Thus, for a fixed negotiated percentage of a retailer's credit sales, the credit agency will assume all aspects of credit sales by the retailer to his or her clients. Some large national retailers administer their own (specific) credit cards, since they have found that the term-financing of accounts receivable can be quite profitable.

Questions

9.1 What do the accounts receivable of a firm typically represent? How do credit terms relate to the firm's accounts receivable, and by what are they normally dictated?

9.2 What are a firm's credit standards? Why must a firm have credit standards, and on what basis are they normally established?

9.3 What key variables should be considered in evaluating possible changes in a firm's credit standards?

9.4 Why is a loosening of a firm's credit standards expected to
 a. Increase clerical expense?
 b. Increase the receivables investment?
 c. Increase bad debt expense?
 d. Increase sales?
 Would you expect the opposite events to occur as a result of tightening credit standards? Why?

9.5 What is meant by "the cost of the marginal investment in accounts receivable"? In what sense are accounts receivable viewed as an investment?

9.6 The payment habits of existing customers can affect the results of changes in credit terms and collection policies. Explain how changes in the payment habits of existing accounts can enter into the decision to change each of these.

9.7 How can the firm use the variable cost per unit, along with the corresponding average accounts receivable and sale price per unit, to determine its average investment in accounts receivable?

9.8 How does the firm's required return on investment enter into the evaluation of the effects of changes in credit policy on the firm's accounts receivable? What sort of comparison must be made?

9.9 Once a firm has established its credit standards, it must perform credit analysis of prospective customers for one or both of two possible reasons. What are these motives for credit analyses?

9.10 What are the basic sources of credit information for a business firm? Who is the key provider of mercantile credit information to business?

9.11 What is meant by a firm's credit terms? What do they determine?

9.12 What are the expected effects of a decrease in a firm's cash discount on the firm's sales volume, average collection period, bad debt expense, and per-unit profits?

9.13 What are the expected effects of an increase in the firm's cash discount period? Why may this decision prove quite difficult to quantify?

9.14 What are the expected effects of a decrease in a firm's credit period? What is likely to happen to its sales volume, average collection period, and bad debt expense?

9.15 When considering bad debts in the analysis of a possible change in a firm's credit policy or credit terms, how must the unit cost of a bad debt be viewed? Why?

9.16 How may a computer be used in both the management and collection of accounts receivable? Why is it difficult to use a computer to make credit decisions?

9.17 Why do firms use credit insurance? What credit losses are covered by credit insurance? What is meant by the term *coinsurance*?

9.18 What benefits are available to a retailer if he or she only accepts those credit sales that are on a general credit card?

Problems

9.1 A firm had sales of 30,000 units last year. Variable cost per unit was $23 and average cost per unit was $30. The firm expects to sell the product at $40 this year. Assume that the firm has excess capacity.
a. What are the firm's fixed costs?
b. If the firm expects sales to increase by 20 percent, what change in profits will result?
c. If the firm offers trade credit at the higher sales level, and all credit customers pay on the thirtieth day, what (average) level of accounts receivable will be shown on the firm's balance sheet? Assume a 360-day year.

9.2 Wilson Water Products currently has an average age of accounts receivable of 45 days and annual credit sales of $1 million. Assume a 360-day year and that the firm has excess capacity.
a. What is the firm's average accounts receivable balance?
b. If the variable cost of each product is 60 percent of sales, what is the average investment in receivables?
c. If the opportunity cost of the investment in accounts receivable is 12 percent, what is the total opportunity cost of the investment in accounts receivable.

9.3 Eastinghome Appliance currently has credit sales of $600 million per year and an average collection period of 60 days. Assume the price of Eastinghome's products is $100 per unit, variable costs are $55 per unit, and average costs are $85 per unit at the current level of sales. The firm is considering changing its credit policy. This will result in a 20-percent increase in sales and an equal 20-percent increase in the average collection period. The firm's opportunity cost on its investment in accounts receivable is 14 percent, and it has excess capacity.
a. What are the firm's fixed costs with and without the policy change?
b. Calculate the additional profits the firm will realize from new sales if it changes its credit policy.
c. What additional investment in accounts receivable will result?
d. Calculate the cost of the marginal investment in receivables.
e. Should the firm change its credit policy? What other information would be helpful in your analysis?

9.4 Nelson Menswear feels its credit costs are too high. By raising its credit standards, bad debts will fall from 5 percent of sales to 2 percent of sales. However, sales will fall from $100,000 to $90,000 per year. If the variable cost per unit is 50 percent of the sale price, fixed costs are $10,000, and the average investment in receivables does not change:
a. What will the reduction in profits be?
b. Should the firm raise its credit standards? Explain your answer.

9.5 Paul's Products currently makes all sales on credit and offers no cash discount. The firm is considering a 2-percent cash discount for payment within 15 days. The firm's current average collection period is 60 days, sales are 40,000 units, selling price is $45, variable cost per unit is $36, and average cost per unit is $40 (at the current sales volume). The firm expects the policy change to result in an increase in sales to 42,000 units (this 2,000 unit increase will be met from the firm's present excess capacity). After the change, 70 percent of the purchasers will take the discount, and the average collection period will be 30 days. If the firm's required rate of return on investments is 25 percent, should the proposed discount be offered?

9.6 Watson Scott is a financial manager of a large industrial products firm. The firm offers a 3-percent discount for payment within 10 days. The firm's average collection period is 28 days. It is Scott's contention that the discount should be dropped. Based on his estimates, the average collection period would only increase to 30 days, and the firm would save 3 percent on all accounts taking the discount. (Thirty percent of the firm's customers currently take the discount.) The marketing manager estimates that sales would drop from 21,000 to 20,000. The firm has a 20-percent required rate of return on investments. If the selling price is $22, average cost per unit is $20 (at the current sales volume), and variable cost is $17 per unit, should the firm discontinue the discount?

9.7 A firm is evaluating a credit policy change that would increase bad debts from 2 percent to 4 percent of sales. Sales are currently 50,000 units, the selling price is $20, variable cost per unit is $9, and average cost per unit is $11 (at the current level of sales). As a result of the change in accounts receivable policy, sales are forecast to increase to 60,000 units (the increase will be met from the firm's present excess capacity).
a. What are bad debts in dollars for the present and proposed plans?
b. Calculate the cost of the marginal bad debts to the firm.
c. Ignoring the profitability from increased sales, if the policy saves $3,500 and causes no change in the average investment in accounts receivable, would you recommend the policy change? Explain.
d. Considering *all* changes in costs and benefits, would you recommend this policy change? Explain.
e. Compare and discuss your answers in **c** and **d** above.

9.8 Armstrong Equipment Ltd. is considering an extension of its credit period from 30 to 60 days. All accounts pay on the net date. The firm currently bills $450,000 for sales, has $345,000 in variable costs, and has $45,000 in fixed costs. The change in the credit period is expected to increase sales to $510,000. Bad debt expense will increase from 1 percent to 1½ percent. The firm has a required rate of return on investments of 20 percent, and will meet its increased sales from present excess capacity.
a. What level of additional profitability on sales will be realized by the change?
b. What changes in bad debts and in the costs of financing in the investment in accounts receivable will the firm face?
c. Rework **a** and **b** above using the information given in footnote † on pages 268–269 of this chapter.
d. Why do the two techniques differ? Would you recommend this policy change based on either of these two methods of analysis?

9.9 The Rapp Rug Repair Company is attempting to evaluate whether the firm should ease collection efforts. The firm repairs 72,000 rugs per year at an average price of $32 each. Bad debt expenses are 1 percent and collection expenditures are $60,000. The average collection period is 40 days, the average cost per unit is $29 (at the current sales level), and the variable cost per unit is $28. By easing the collection efforts, Rapp expects to save $40,000 per year in collection expense. Bad debts will increase to 2 percent of sales, and the average collection period will increase to 58 days. Sales will increase by 1,000 repairs per year, and can be met from present excess capacity. If the firm has a required rate of return on its investments of 24 percent, what recommendation would you give the firm? Use your analysis to justify your answer.

Suggested Readings

Atkins, Joseph C. and Young H. Kim, "Comment and Correction: Opportunity Cost in the Evaluation of Investment in Accounts Receivable," *Financial Management* 6 (Winter 1977), pp. 71–74.

Block, Stanley B., "Accounts Receivable as an Investment," *Credit and Financial Management* 76 (May 1974), pp. 32–35, 40.

Dhawan, K. C. and Lawrence Kryzanowski, *Export Consortia: A Canadian Study* (Montreal: Dekemco Ltd., 1978).

Dyl, Edward A., "Another Look at the Investment in Accounts Receivable," *Financial Management* 6 (Winter 1977), pp. 67–70.

Greer, Carl C., "The Optimal Credit Acceptance Policy," *Journal of Financial and Quantitative Analysis* 2 (December 1967), pp. 399–415.

Herbst, Anthony F., "Some Empirical Evidence on the Determinants of Trade Credit at the Industry Level of Aggregation," *Journal of Financial and Quantitative Analysis* 9 (June 1974), pp. 377–394.

Kim, Young H. and Joseph C. Atkins, "Evaluating Investment in Accounts Receivable: A Wealth Maximizing Framework," *Journal of Finance* 33 (May 1978), pp. 403–412.

Lewellen, Wilbur G. and Robert O. Edmister, "A General Model for Accounts Receivable Control and Analysis," *Journal of Financial and Quantitative Analysis* 8 (March 1973), pp. 195–206.

Lewellen, Wilbur G. and Robert W. Johnson, "Better Way to Monitor Accounts Receivable," *Harvard Business Review* 50 (May-June 1972), pp. 101–109.

Long, Michael S., "Credit Screening System Selection," *Journal of Financial and Quantitative Analysis* 31 (June 1976), pp. 313–328.

Mao, James C. T. and C. Sarndal, "Controlling Risk in Accounts Receivable Management," *Journal of Business Finance and Accounting* 1 (Autumn 1974), pp. 395–403.

Mehta, Dileep R., "The Formulation of Credit Policy Models," *Management Science* 15 (October 1968), pp. 30–50.

———, *Working Capital Management* (Englewood Cliffs, N.J.: Prentice-Hall, 1974), part 1.

Oh, John S., "Opportunity Cost in the Evaluation of Investment in Accounts Receivable," *Financial Management* 5 (Summer 1976), pp. 32–36.

Poggess, William P., "Screen-Test Your Credit Risks," *Harvard Business Review* 45 (November-December 1967), pp. 113–122.

Schwartz, Robert A., "An Economic Model of Trade Credit," *Journal of Financial and Quantitative Analysis* 9 (September 1974), pp. 643–658.

Smith, D. W., "Efficient Credit Management with Time Sharing," *Financial Executive* 39 (March 1971), pp. 26–30.

Soldofsky, R. M., "A Model for Accounts Receivable Management," *Management Accounting* (January 1966), pp. 55–58.

Stone, Bernell K., "The Payments-Pattern Approach to the Forecasting and Control of Accounts Receivable," *Financial Management* 5 (Autumn 1976), pp. 65–82.

Walia, Tirlochan, S., "Explicit and Implicit Cost of Changes in the Level of Accounts Receivable and the Credit Policy Decision of the Firm," *Financial Management* 6 (Winter 1977), pp. 75–78.

Welshans, Merle T., "Using Credit for Profit Making," *Harvard Business Review* 45 (January-February 1967), pp. 141–156.

Wrightsman, Dwayne, "Optimal Credit Terms for Accounts Receivable," *Quarterly Review of Economics and Business* 9 (Summer 1969), pp. 59–66.

Chapter 10

INVENTORY MANAGEMENT

Inventories are necessary for a smooth functioning of the production-sale or purchase-sale process of the firm. A stock of both raw materials and work in process is required to ensure that required items are available when needed. Finished-goods inventories must be available to provide a buffer stock that will enable the firm to satisfy sales demands as they arise. In Chapter 8 it was indicated that, in order to minimize the firm's cash requirement, inventory should be turned over quickly, since the faster inventory is turned, the smaller the amount the firm must invest in inventory to satisfy a given demand for goods. This financial objective often conflicts with the firm's objective of carrying sufficient inventories to minimize stockouts and satisfy production demands. The firm must determine the "optimal" level of inventories that reconciles these conflicting objectives. The problem has been studied extensively and there exists a large body of specialized literature on the subject. Our goal in this chapter is to present some of the basic concepts and trade-offs involved in the firm's inventory decisions.

The chapter has three major sections. The first section is concerned with (1) the basic types of inventories held by firms, (2) conflicting objectives of various functional units within a firm with respect to control and management of inventory, (3) the concept of inventory as an investment, and (4) the relationship between inventory and accounts receivable. The second section discusses some of the basic concepts and techniques of inventory control. Although the techniques described in this section fall in the realm of production management, it is important for the financial manager to understand them because he or she is usually responsible for overall planning and budgeting of inventories. Finally, the third section demonstrates that the basic concepts of inventory control can be applied to the control and management of a firm's cash balances.

Characteristics of Inventory

A number of aspects of inventory require elaboration. One is the different types of inventory. Another is the different viewpoints of various organizational units of the firm concerning the appropriate levels of inventories. A third is the relationship between the level of inventory and the financial investment it involves. A fourth concerns the relationship between inventory and accounts receivable. Each of these four aspects of inventory will be evaluated in this section.

TYPES OF INVENTORY

The basic types of inventory held by manufacturing firms are raw-materials, work-in-process, and finished-goods inventories. The inventory of a wholesaler or retailer consists of only finished goods purchased from others. The discussion below is concerned primarily with the types of inventories held by manufacturing firms.

Raw Materials   Raw-materials inventory is necessary for the production of a manufacturer's final product. Stocks of raw materials allow manufacturers to benefit from the price advantages of bulk purchases and they facilitate production planning in times of uncertain supplies. The actual level of each raw material maintained depends on the lead time it takes to receive orders, the frequency of use, the dollar investment required, and the physical characteristics of the inventory itself. The lead time results from the lag between placement and receipt of items ordered. Therefore, the lead time is an important consideration in inventory decisions. The frequency with which an item is used in the production process must also be considered. The inventory of frequently used raw materials will generally be higher than the inventory of raw materials that are used relatively infrequently.

In the case of low-cost items such as nails, screws, and bolts, the lead time and frequency of use do not warrant a great deal of attention. Periodic orders of large lots of these items should simplify the inventory process. In the case of expensive raw materials, the lead time and frequency of use are much more important, since frugal management of these raw materials can significantly affect the firm's dollar investment in inventory.

Other factors affecting the level of raw materials are certain physical characteristics such as size or perishability. For example, an inexpensive item, which has a long lead time before orders are received and also has a short "shelf life," would not be ordered in large quantities.

Work in Process   The work-in-process inventory consists of all items currently being used in the production process. These are normally partially finished goods that are at some intermediate stage of production. Work-in-process inventory occurs because the production processes are not instantaneous. A direct relationship exists between the length of the firm's production process and its average level of work-in-process inventory: The longer the firm's production cycle, the higher the level of work-in-process inventory expected. A higher work-in-process inventory results in higher costs since the firm's money is tied up for a longer period of time. The total inventory cycle was defined in Chapter 8 as the amount of time that elapses from the initial purchase of a raw material to the ultimate sale of a finished good. The firm should try to minimize the length of this cycle while holding stockouts to a minimum. Efficient management of the production process should reduce the work-in-process inventory, which should speed the inventory turnover and reduce the firm's operating cash requirement.

The work-in-process inventory is the least liquid type of inventory. Generally, it is difficult to sell partially finished products. For this reason, the use of work-in-process inventories as collateral for loans is not common.* One other characteristic of work-in-process inventories is a buildup in value as an item is transformed from a raw material into a finished good through the production process. Raw materials are joined, labour is added, and overhead is allocated to the emerging finished product, causing the firm's dollar investment in the item to increase. A firm should move items through the work-in-process inventory quickly to quickly recover the outlays it has made for raw materials, labour, and overhead.

Finished Goods   The finished-goods inventory consists of items that have been produced but not yet sold. The level of finished goods is largely dictated by projected sales demands, the production process, and the investment made in finished goods. Firms typically maintain a *safety stock* of finished goods to allow for an unexpected increase in demand for a product or breakdowns in the production cycle. Scheduling production in a manner that provides sufficient finished goods to satisfy projected sales without creating excess inventories can minimize the firm's overall costs. Often the most efficient production quantities (those with the lowest production cost per unit) are larger than those needed to satisfy projected sales demands because of the high level of setup costs incurred in scheduling machines for smaller, and therefore, more frequent production runs.

Another important consideration with respect to the level of a finished-goods inventory is its degree of liquidity. Inventories of high-cost specialized finished goods that are expensive to warehouse should be scrutinized closely in order to keep inventory levels low. On the other hand, an inventory of standard low cost items that sell in a broad market can be safely carried at a relatively higher level.

FUNCTIONAL VIEWPOINTS REGARDING INVENTORY LEVELS

As indicated in Table 10.1, a major proportion of a firm's investment in current assets may be committed to inventories. Therefore, optimal management of inventories is an important concern of the financial manager. However, the financial manager's attempts to maintain optimality can be frustrated by subunits, such as marketing, production, and purchasing, which judge inventory management by their own objectives. The latter objectives are often different from those of the financial manager. As a result, suboptimal financial results and disagreements among the subunits, will occur if no effective countermeasures are taken. Before suggesting some appropriate countermeasures, a more detailed analysis of the cause of this conflict is necessary.

*This aspect of inventory management is discussed in Chapter 12.

Table 10.1   Inventories and Total Current Assets for a Sample of Major Canadian Corporations, As of December 31, 1978

Company	Inventory	Current Assets
Imperial Oil Ltd.	$618,000,000	$1,450,000,000
Hudson Bay Company Ltd.	$215,713,000	$ 501,919,000
Canadian General Electric Ltd.	$262,070,000	$ 532,129,000
Alcan Aluminum Ltd.	$984,550,000	$1,901,057,000

The financial manager's frame of reference is the welfare of the entire firm. Thus, he or she is interested in effectively managing all of the revenue and cost factors that affect cash flow and risk. In operating terms, the financial manager attempts to maximize the difference between the revenues and costs associated with inventory management, for a given level of risk.

On the other hand, the marketing manager is typically responsible for maximizing only gross revenues. Seldom does he or she have direct responsibility for the related costs associated with inventory management. Accordingly, the marketing manager may prefer large finished-goods inventories in order to minimize stockouts that result in lost sales, even though the added inventory costs of such a policy may exceed the added revenues generated by such a policy.

Similarly, the purchasing manager may prefer larger than optimal order sizes to obtain quantity discounts, to hedge against rising prices, or to ensure that no stockouts occur. Again, the added inventory costs of such a policy may exceed the benefits of such a policy.

Also, in order to achieve low production costs through larger production runs, the production manager may prefer to maintain finished-goods inventory at a high level. The resulting reduction in production costs may, however, be more than offset by increased inventory costs.

Thus, the financial manager must be concerned with preventing such financially suboptimal behaviour by individual functional areas. Preventative action may include budget controls, procedural guidelines, making functional managers responsible for all revenues and costs related to their function, changing jurisdictional boundaries, or changing managerial incentives. Furthermore, by making use of an on-line computer system, the financial manager may more easily monitor the quality of inventory decisions made by various subunits of the firm. Sophisticated automated inventory control systems are now available that not only coordinate many of the necessary functions related to the management and control of inventories but also determine the optimal order, or production quantities, in accordance with the overall investment criterion set by the firm.

A CLOSER VIEW OF INVENTORY AS AN INVESTMENT

On several occasions in the preceding discussions, references have been made to inventory as *an investment*. Inventory is an investment in the sense that it requires the firm to tie up its money. The analyses in Chapter 9 illustrated how the average investment in accounts receivable could be calculated using the turnover of accounts receivable and the cost of credit sales. The average investment in inventory can be calculated in a similar manner, as is shown in the following example.

EXAMPLE A firm is contemplating making larger production runs in order to reduce the high setup costs associated with production of its only product. The total *annual* reduction in setup costs that can be obtained has been estimated to be $15,000. Currently the firm's inventories turn over six times a year; with the proposed larger production runs, the inventory turnover rate is expected to drop to four. The larger production runs are not expected to have any effect on sales revenues. The cost of goods sold is expected to remain at the current level of $1,200,000. The firm has a required 20 percent return on investment. Should the firm implement the proposed system?

The first step in determining whether to increase the size of the production runs is to calculate the average investment in inventory under both the proposed and present system. The value of the firm's average inventory can be calculated, given the cost of goods sold and the inventory turnover, by the following formula:

$$\text{Average inventory} = \frac{\text{cost of goods sold}}{\text{inventory turnover}}$$

Since inventory is carried at cost on the firm's books, this formula can be used to calculate the average investment in inventory under both the proposed and the present system:*

Average investment in inventory:

$$\text{Proposed system: } \frac{\$1,200,000}{4} = \$300,000$$

$$\text{Present system: } \frac{\$1,200,000}{6} = \$200,000$$

The slower inventory turnover associated with the proposed system is due to the fact that, in the process of running larger lots, the firm must maintain higher average raw-materials, work-in-process, and finished-goods inventories. The result of this slower inventory turnover is a higher average investment in inventory than was previously required. It is the cost of the *incremental* investment† in higher average inventory that must be examined. This incremental investment is calculated by subtracting the present average investment ($200,000) from the average investment under the proposed system ($300,000). The marginal investment in inventory is therefore $100,000.

On this additional investment of $100,000 in inventory, the firm must earn 20 percent per year at a minimum, or $20,000. This can be viewed as the annual cost of carrying the higher inventories associated with the proposed system. Comparing the annual $20,000 cost of the system with the annual savings of $15,000 shows that the proposal should be *rejected*, since it results in a net annual loss of $5,000.

---

*Recall that in determining the firm's investment in accounts receivable it is necessary to take into account the fact that receivables are based on the sale price—not the cost—of the firm's products. Since inventory is carried on the firm's books at cost, no special adjustment is required to estimate the average investment in inventory.

†The term *cost* is used here to refer to the *opportunity cost* of the incremental investment required under the proposed system.

The procedure presented in this example should not be construed as a universal tool to be applied to all inventory decisions. It has been presented to illustrate a way of thinking, especially in the sense of recognizing the relationship between the level of inventory and the number of dollars invested in it. In general, the higher a firm's average inventories, the larger the dollar investment required, and vice versa. The similarity between the approach to evaluating accounts receivable investments and inventory investments should be recognized. The financial manager, in evaluating planned changes in inventory levels, should consider them from a cost-benefit standpoint.

THE RELATIONSHIP BETWEEN INVENTORY AND ACCOUNTS RECEIVABLE

The level and the management of inventory and accounts receivable are closely related. Generally in the case of manufacturing firms, when an item is sold, it moves from inventory to accounts receivable and ultimately to cash. Because of the close relationship between these current assets, the inventory management and accounts receivable management functions should not be viewed independently of each other. For example, the decision to extend credit to a customer can result in an increased level of sales, which can be supported only by higher levels of inventory and accounts receivable. The credit terms extended will also influence the investment in inventory and receivables, since longer credit terms may allow a firm to move items from inventory to accounts receivable. Generally there is an advantage to such a strategy, since the cost of carrying an item in inventory is greater than the cost of carrying an account receivable. This is true since the cost of carrying inventory includes, in addition to the required return on the invested funds, the costs of storing and insuring the physical inventory. This relationship can be shown using a simple example.

EXAMPLE   The Erker Company Ltd. estimates that the annual cost of carrying $1 of merchandise in inventory for a one-year period is $0.25, while the annual cost of carrying $1 of receivables is $0.15. The firm currently maintains average inventories of $300,000 and an average *investment* in accounts receivable of $200,000. The firm believes that by altering its credit terms, it can cause its customers to purchase in larger quantities on the average, thereby reducing its average

Table 10.2   Analysis of Inventory-Account Receivable Systems for the Erker Company Ltd.

		Present		Proposed	
	Cost/return	Ave.	Cost ($)	Ave.	Cost ($)
Item	(%) (1)	Bal. ($) (2)	(1)·(2) (3)	Bal. ($) (4)	(1)·(4) (5)
Average inventory cost	25	$300,000	$75,000	$150,000	$37,500
Average receivable investment	15	200,000	30,000	350,000	52,500
Total		$500,000	$105,000	$500,000	$90,000

inventories to $150,000 and increasing the average investment in accounts receivable to $350,000. The altered credit terms are not expected to generate new business, but will result only in a shift in the purchasing and payment patterns of existing customers. The costs of the present and proposed inventory-account receivable systems are calculated in Table 10.2.

This table shows that by shifting $150,000 of inventory cost to accounts receivable investment the Erker Company is able to lower the cost of carrying inventory and accounts receivable from $105,000 to $90,000—a $15,000 ($105,000 − $90,000) addition to profits. This profit is achieved without changing the level of average inventory and account receivable investment from its $500,000 total. Rather, the profit is attributed to a shift in the proportions of these current assets such that a larger portion of them is held in the form of accounts receivable, which is less costly than inventory to hold.

The preceding example should make it clear that inventory—especially finished goods—and accounts receivable are closely related. The financial manager should therefore consider the interactions between inventory and accounts receivable when developing strategies and making decisions related to the production-sales process. Although the balance of this chapter is concerned solely with inventory cost minimization decisions, the reader should recognize the potential suboptimality of such decisions from the viewpoint of overall working capital management.

Inventory Management and Control Techniques

This section presents a few production-oriented methods of inventory control. Although the concepts involved are not strictly financial, it is important that the financial manager understand them, since they have certain built-in financial costs. Three major areas of inventory control are discussed: (1) the type of control required, (2) the basic economic order quantity, and (3) the reorder point.

DETERMINING THE TYPE OF CONTROL REQUIRED: THE ABC SYSTEM

Most manufacturing firms find themselves confronted with virtually thousands of different inventory items. Many of these items are relatively inexpensive, while other items are quite expensive and account for a large portion of the firm's dollar investment. Some inventory items, although not especially expensive, turn over slowly and therefore require a high average dollar investment; other items, although they have a high unit cost, turn over rapidly enough to make the required investment relatively low.

A firm having a large number of items of inventory should in principle analyze each item in order to determine its approximate dollar investment in each. Research has indicated that for most manufacturing firms, the distribution of inventory items is similar to that shown in Figure 10.1. About 20 percent of the items in the inventory account for approximately 90 percent of the dollar investment in the inventory. The remaining 80 percent of the items account for only 10 percent. In response to this general

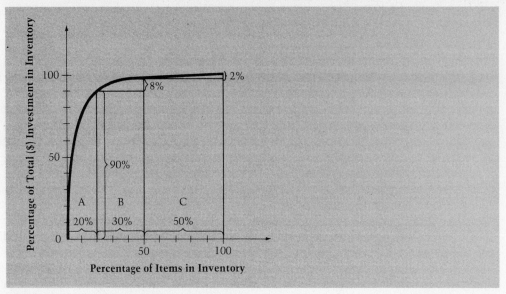

Figure 10.1 A sample distribution of inventory items.

characteristic of inventory of most manufacturing firms, the ABC approach to inventory control has been developed.

A firm using the ABC system of inventory control segregates its inventory into three groups, A, B, and C. The "A" items are the items in which it has the largest dollar investment. In Figure 10.1, this group consists of the 20 percent of the items of inventory that account for 90 percent of the firm's dollar investment. These are the most costly or slowest turning items of inventory. The "B" group consists of the items accounting for the next largest investment. In Figure 10.1, the "B" group consists of the 30 percent of the items accounting for about 8 percent of the firm's dollar investment. The "C" group typically consists of a large number of items accounting for a small dollar investment. In Figure 10.1, the "C" group consists of approximately 50 percent of all items of inventory but accounts for only about 2 percent of the firm's dollar investment in inventory. Such items as screws, nails, and washers would be in this group.

Dividing its inventory into A, B, and C category items allows the firm to determine the level and types of inventory control procedures needed. Control of "A" items of inventory should be most intensive due to the high dollar investments involved; they require the most sophisticated inventory control techniques. The "B" items can be controlled using relatively simpler techniques, and their inventory level can be reviewed less frequently than "A" items. The "C" items should receive a minimum of attention.

Finally, it should be recognized that the ABC system of inventory control cannot be universally applied. Certain items of inventory that are inexpensive but are critical to the production process and cannot be easily obtained may require special attention. These types of items must be treated as "A" items even though, using the broad framework described above, they would be "B" or "C" items. Although not perfect, the ABC system is an excellent method for determining the degree of inventory control effort to expend on each item of inventory.

THE BASIC ECONOMIC ORDER QUANTITY (EOQ) MODEL

A well-known model for determining the optimal order quantity for an item of inventory is the *economic order quantity* (EOQ) model. It takes into account various operating and financial costs and determines the order quantity that minimizes the firm's total inventory cost. The EOQ model is not only applicable to determining economic order quantities for inventory, but can also be used to determine the best production quantity. However, our concern here is to illustrate its use in inventory control.

The EOQ model presented here is based on the following major assumptions: (1) the inventory is ordered and delivered in equal lot sizes, (2) the usage or demand (in units) per period is known with certainty and is independent of the quantity ordered, (3) the purchase price per unit is independent of the quantity ordered,* (4) the rate at which inventory is used is steady over time, and (5) the orders placed to replenish inventory are received exactly when the inventory level reaches zero.

These highly *restrictive* assumptions are necessary in the most *simplified* version of the EOQ model. In the absence of the certain environment provided for by these assumptions, the firm may maintain a *safety stock* of inventory in excess of that necessary to meet expected usage in view of the expected lead time to receive an order.†

The discussion of the economic order quantity model here will cover (1) the basic costs included in the model, (2) a graphical approach, (3) a mathematical approach, and (4) the weaknesses of the model.

Basic Costs   Inventory costs‡ can be divided into two broad categories—order costs and carrying costs. Order costs include the fixed clerical costs of placing and receiving an order, and are normally stated as so many dollars per order.

Carrying costs are the variable costs of holding an item in inventory for a specified period of time. These costs are typically stated as so many dollars per unit per period. Carrying costs have a number of components such as storage costs, insurance costs, the cost of deterioration and obsolescence, and, most important, the opportunity cost of tying up funds in inventory. The *opportunity cost* is the *financial cost* component; it is the value of the returns that have been foregone in order to have the current investment in inventory. The total cost of inventory is defined as the sum of the order and carrying costs.

---

*An implication of this assumption is that quantity discounts which affect the purchase price per unit are not considered in the model as presented here.

†Models incorporating probability theory view annual usage, daily usage, and lead time as random variables. These models are quite complex mathematically, though they are built on the general EOQ framework discussed in this chapter. They can be used for determining the optimum order quantity, as well as the optimum level of safety stock. Unfortunately, most sophisticated models are difficult to implement because of their onerous data requirements. Therefore, reliance on the basic EOQ model presented here is quite common in developing practical inventory control systems.

‡Inventory purchase cost can be excluded from analysis because it is assumed to be independent of the order size.

EXAMPLE   An example may best illustrate the calculation of order costs, carrying costs, and the total cost for various order sizes. Assume that a firm has order costs of $50 per order and carrying costs of $1 per unit per year for an item. The annual order cost, carrying cost, and total cost if the firm uses 1,600 units of this item per year can easily be calculated. Table 10.3 presents the calculations for order quantities of 1,600, 800, 400, 200, and 100 units. A few points with respect to these calculations require clarification.

Table 10.3   Inventory Cost Calculations

Order quantity (units) (1)	Number of orders (2)	Cost/order (3)	Annual order cost (2) · (3) (4)	Average inventory (1) ÷ 2 (5)	Carrying cost/unit/yr. (6)	Annual carrying cost (5) · (6) (7)	Total cost (4) + (7) (8)
1,600	1	$50	$ 50	800	$1	$800	$850
800	2	$50	$100	400	$1	$400	$500
400	4	$50	$200	200	$1	$200	$400
200	8	$50	$400	100	$1	$100	$500
100	16	$50	$800	50	$1	$ 50	$850

1. The *number of orders* is obtained by dividing the order quantity into 1,600, the number of units of the item used annually.

2. The *average inventory* is calculated by dividing the order quantity by 2, since an amount of inventory equal to the order quantity once received is used at a constant rate until the inventory is depleted, at which point a new order is received. A graph of this pattern of inventory usage and replenishment is presented in Figure 10.2. The sawtooth pattern indicates the receipt of an order at each peak, while the negatively sloped lines represent the constantly diminishing inventory level. At t_1, t_2, and t_3 the inventory reaches zero; simultaneously, an order is received raising the inventory by an amount equal to the order quantity. The average inventory is equal to the order quantity divided by 2, since we have assumed that inventory is used at a constant rate.

A Graphical Approach   The objective of the EOQ approach is to find the order quantity that minimizes the firm's total inventory cost by balancing the order costs against carrying costs. The economic order quantity can be found graphically by plotting order quantities on the x-axis and carrying costs on the y-axis. Figure 10.3 shows the costs related to the example used in Table 10.3. The minimum total cost occurs at an order quantity of 400 units. Therefore, the economic order quantity is 400 units. The EOQ occurs at the point where the order cost line intersects the carrying cost line (i.e., at the point where the order cost equals the carrying cost). The total cost is minimized at the intersection point because the marginal value, or the slope of the order cost, equals the marginal carrying cost at the intersection point.*

---

*However, this is true only for the special case when the total ordering cost curve is a rectangular hyperbola and the total carrying cost is a straight line through the origin. Both of these conditions are met given the assumptions used in this chapter.

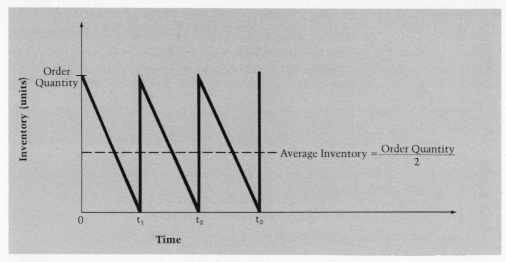

Figure 10.2   An inventory usage and replenishment cycle.

It is important to recognize the nature of the cost functions in Figure 10.3. The order cost function varies inversely with the order quantity. In other words, as the order quantity increases, the order cost for the period decreases, and vice versa. This can be explained by the fact that, since the usage for the period is fixed, if larger amounts are ordered, fewer orders and therefore lower order costs are incurred. Carrying costs are directly related to order quantities. The larger the order quantity, the larger the average inventory and therefore the higher the firm's carrying cost.

The total cost function exhibits a U shape, which means that a minimum value for the function exists. The total cost line represents the sum of the order costs and carrying costs for each quantity.

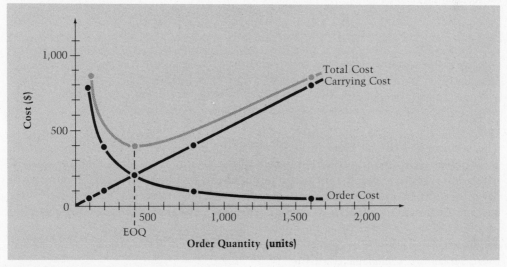

Figure 10.3   A graphical presentation of an EOQ.

A Mathematical Approach   For a mathematical derivation of the EOQ, let

$$S = \text{the usage in units per period}$$
$$O = \text{the order cost per order}$$
$$C = \text{the carrying cost per unit per period}$$
$$Q = \text{the order quantity}$$

The number of orders per period equals the usage during the period divided by the order quantity (i.e., S/Q); therefore,

$$\text{Order cost per period} = O \cdot S/Q \tag{10.1}$$

Since inventory is assumed to be used up at a constant rate, the average inventory level equals $Q/2$. This implies

$$\text{Carrying cost per period} = C \cdot Q/2 \tag{10.2}$$

The total inventory cost per period, T, is given by

$$T = O \cdot S/Q + C \cdot Q/2 \tag{10.3}$$

The optimal order quantity, Q^* (the EOQ), is the quantity that minimizes the total inventory cost, T. Therefore, Q^* can be found by setting the first derivative of the total cost function equal to zero,[*] which gives

$$Q^*(\text{EOQ}) = \sqrt{\frac{2SO}{C}} \tag{10.4}$$

As noted earlier, the EOQ occurs at the point where the order cost, SO/Q, equals the carrying cost, $CQ/2$. Therefore, Q^* can also be found by solving $SO/Q = C \cdot Q/2$ for Q. This also gives Equation 10.4.

EXAMPLE   Substituting the values for S, O, and C given in the earlier example (1,600, $50, and $1, respectively) into Equation 10.4 yields an EOQ of 400 units:

$$Q^* = \sqrt{\frac{2 \cdot 1,600 \cdot \$50}{\$1}} = \sqrt{160,000} = 400 \text{ units}$$

Comparing this result with the EOQ found graphically in Figure 10.3 indicates that both approaches result in the same value of 400 units. If the firm orders in quantities of 400 units, it will minimize its total inventory costs.

The Weaknesses of the EOQ Model   The EOQ model discussed here has certain weaknesses that are directly attributable to the assumptions on which it is based. The assumptions of a constant usage rate and the instantaneous replenishment of inventory stocks are quite suspect. Most firms maintain safety stocks as a buffer against an unusual increase in demand or slow deliveries, either of which could

[*]The first derivative, dT/dQ, is equal to $C/2 - SO/Q^2$. Also, since the second derivative, $d^2T/dQ^2 = 2SO/Q^3$, is positive, a minimum cost exists.

result in stockout costs. The assumption of a known annual demand for items is also questionable. Actually, a demand forecast is used to make the order quantity decision. Therefore, the EOQ formula is useful only when the demand can be forecast with a reasonable degree of accuracy.

THE REORDER POINT

Once the firm has calculated its economic order quantity, it must determine when to place an order. In the preceding EOQ model, it was assumed that orders are received instantaneously when the inventory level reaches zero. Actually, a reorder point is required that considers the lead time needed to place and receive orders. If the lead time is known with certainty, the reorder point can be determined as follows:

$$\text{Reorder point} = \text{lead time in days} \cdot \text{daily usage}$$

For example, if a firm knows that it requires 10 days to receive an order once the order is placed and it uses 5 units of inventory daily, the reorder point would be 50 units (i.e., 10 days · 5 units per day). As soon as the firm's inventory level reaches 50 units, an order will be placed for an amount equal to the economic order quantity. This order would be received exactly when the inventory level reaches zero. This reorder point formula is based on the assumptions of a fixed lead time and fixed daily usage. However, more sophisticated reorder point formulas, based on less restrictive assumptions are available.

●THE EOQ MODEL AND THE ECONOMIC CRITERION OF INVESTMENT*

The previous discussion of the EOQ model may lead the reader to believe that the model is purely an inventory cost minimization model. In this section, it will be shown that the model is consistent with the marginal cost/marginal revenue criterion for the evaluation of investment opportunities. To show this, the carrying cost per unit, C, must first be divided into its two components. The first component, iV, is equal to the opportunity cost of funds invested in inventory, i, times the purchase price (firm's investment) per unit of inventory, V. The second component, C', is all remaining carrying costs per unit, after the removal of i. It should be noted that if a firm finances investments in current assets with short-term funds (as was discussed in Chapter 7), then i may be operationally approximated by the interest cost of short-term borrowings.

The periodic *gross operating profit*, G, on investment in inventory is given by

$$G = PS - \left(VS + \frac{SO}{Q} + \frac{C'Q}{2} \right) \tag{10.5}$$

where the only new term, P, is the selling price per unit. The marginal increase in profit from a marginal increase in quantity is given by

$$\frac{dG}{dQ} = \frac{SO}{Q^2} - \frac{C'}{2} \tag{10.6}$$

●This section may be bypassed without loss of continuity.
*The discussion in this section has relied extensively on LeRoy D. Brooks, "Return on Investment As a Criterion for Inventory Models: Comment," *Decision Sciences* (October 1978), pp. 739–741.

Similarly, since the periodic average investment in inventory, I, is equal to $VQ/2$, the marginal increase in investment for a marginal increase in quantity is given by

$$\frac{dI}{dQ} = \frac{V}{2} \tag{10.7}$$

Therefore, the marginal return on the investment in inventory is given by dividing Equation 10.6 by Equation 10.7 to get

$$\frac{dG}{dI} = \frac{dG/dQ}{dI/dQ} = \frac{SO/Q^2 - C'/2}{V/2} \tag{10.8}$$

Since the optimal investment in inventory occurs when the marginal return on the investment in inventory is equal to its marginal (financing) cost,* then

$$\frac{SO/Q^2 - C'/2}{V/2} = i \tag{10.9}$$

Solving for Q^* in Equation 10.9 gives

$$Q^*(\text{EOQ}) = \sqrt{\frac{2SO}{C' + iV}} \tag{10.10}$$

This is identical to the solution obtained for the EOQ model in the previous section. That is, Equations 10.4 and 10.10 are identical, since $C = C' + iV$.

From Equation 10.10, it is apparent that there is an inverse relationship between the optimum order quantity and the opportunity cost of funds invested in inventory. That is, as the opportunity cost of funds increases, the optimum order quantity decreases. Thus, a firm with an EOQ-based inventory control system should hold less inventory as its cost of funds increases. This is consistent with observed business practice, for some firms do reduce their investment in inventory during periods of high interest rates.

APPLICATION OF THE EOQ CONCEPT TO CASH MANAGEMENT

If a firm has a forecast of its expected cash flows for a particular future period(s),† the firm can use the basic EOQ model structure discussed above to calculate the optimum average cash balance that it should maintain over the period. The firm can do this because a firm's cash balance is similar to an inventory of money, which is used by the firm to synchronize its cash inflows and outflows.

To illustrate, assume that (1) a firm's proceeds from its sales are all collected at the end of a specified period, (2) the firm invests the proceeds in short-term marketable securities, (3) the firm's cash transactions over the period occur continuously at a steady (even) rate over the period, and (4) the firm obtains C dollars of cash at the beginning of the period by selling marketable securities, in order to meet its projected volume of transactions payments, T, over the period. Thus, when the firm's cash balance reaches

---

*The marginal return, dG/dI, decreases with the level of investment, since $d/dI\,(dG/dI) = -8SO/Q^3V^2 < 0$. Therefore, the investment in additional units will be made until the marginal return equals i.
†Cash budgeting, which was discussed in Chapter 3, can be used to obtain such a forecast.

zero, it is replenished immediately by the cash proceeds, C, realized from the instantaneous sale of marketable securities.

In managing its cash balances, the firm incurs both ordering and carrying costs, as was the case in the EOQ model. For example, the fixed cost per order, b, involved in obtaining cash would be similar to the fixed order cost of the EOQ model. That is, there would be the fixed cost involved in selling marketable securities and there would be the variable cost involved in processing an order.[*] The cost of carrying cash, $iC/2$, would primarily be the opportunity cost resulting from the interest foregone, i, on the average cash balance, $C/2$, held over the period.[†]

In order to minimize the opportunity cost of holding cash, the firm would keep its average cash balance as low as possible by lowering its cash order size. But a lower cash order size would also imply a greater frequency of cash orders and therefore a higher total order cost, bT/C, per period.[‡] Therefore, the optimal cash order will be determined by balancing the ordering costs against the opportunity cost of holding cash. Accordingly, a mathematical calculation, similar to that used for the EOQ model, gives:

$$C^\star \text{ (optimal cash order)} = \sqrt{\frac{2bT}{i}} \qquad (10.11)$$

Although Equation 10.11 is derived from a set of rather restrictive assumptions, it does highlight the fact that the optimal average cash balance, $C^\star/2$, increases at a slower rate than the volume of cash transactions, T. For example, a doubling of the volume of transactions will only increase the optimal average cash balance to $\sqrt{2}$ or 1.4 times its former level. In other words, significant economies of scale are possible in the management of cash for transactions purposes. Similarly, the pooling of cash accounts, which were formerly held separately by the different units or divisions of a firm, can significantly reduce the average cash balance required by the firm for transaction purposes.[§] Although the administration of a centralized bank account may appear to be cumbersome and costly for decentralized firms, this may not be so in many cases. For example, the Canadian banking system is quite efficient in transferring funds between geographic areas.

---

[*]The broker's fee on the total value of security transactions, T, will not be affected by the cash order size C and can therefore be excluded from the analysis.

[†]If the other components of carrying cost are significant, they can also be incorporated into the analysis. Furthermore, the assumption that any reduction in the firm's cash holdings will be invested in short-term securities has been made merely for illustrative purposes. In practice, funds can sometimes be invested more profitably within the firm. Therefore, the opportunity cost per dollar of cash holdings may exceed the short-term interest rate. However, this will not alter the analysis in any fundamental way.

[‡]A lower cash balance may also result in costs of raising cash on short notice, or even technical insolvency on a very temporary basis. These costs are similar to the stockout costs. Inventory-type models of cash management, which incorporate comprehensive cost structures as well as probabilistic cash transactions, can be found in the references at the end of this chapter.

[§]Johnson and Johnson Ltd. and Northland Bank are two examples of Canadian companies that have utilized the concept of a centralized cash account. Johnson and Johnson refers to its centralized account as a "corporate treasury account." Northland Bank obtained its initial capitalization from Federated Cooperatives Ltd., which obtained the cash for making this equity investment by consolidating a number of accounts. These accounts had been formerly held separately by Federated's credit union members.

Summary

This chapter has discussed the basic concepts of inventory management. For many firms inventories represent a large fraction of total assets; therefore, considerable importance must be attached to efficient management of inventories.

The financial manager must consider the interrelationship that exists between inventory and accounts receivable when making production-sale decisions. Functional areas of the business firm tend to have conflicting objectives with respect to the appropriate inventory level. It is therefore important to design internal inventory control procedures that prevent financially suboptimal behaviour by individual functional areas.

Certain production-oriented techniques can be used to keep inventory levels and unit costs low with a minimum of stockouts. The ABC inventory control system is aimed at determining which inventories require the most attention. By dividing inventory into groups according to the dollar investment in various items, control techniques appropriate to each group can be applied.

One of the most common inventory control tools is the economic order quantity (EOQ) model. The economic order quantity is the order quantity that minimizes the firm's total inventory cost by balancing order cost against the operating and financial cost of carrying inventories. Once the optimal order quantity has been determined, the firm can set a reorder point, or the level of inventory at which an order will be placed. The EOQ concept can also be applied to specify the optimum average cash balance that the firm should maintain to meet its projected transaction payments over a specified period. This is possible because a firm's cash balance can be viewed as an inventory of money maintained to synchronize the firm's cash inflows and outflows over time.

Questions

10.1   What trade-off must the financial manager make with respect to the turnover of inventory, the inventory cost, and stockouts?

10.2   How is the level of finished-goods inventories dictated by the firm's production process? What kind of trade-off exists between the production cost per unit, the carrying cost of inventory, and the liquidity of inventory?

10.3   What is the financial manager's role with respect to the management of inventory? With what types of inventories is he or she primarily concerned?

10.4   What are the viewpoints of each of the following managers regarding the appropriate inventory levels?
   a.   Financial manager
   b.   Marketing manager
   c.   Production manager
   d.   Purchasing manager

10.5   In what sense can inventory be viewed as an investment? How might one calculate a firm's average investment in inventory?

10.6   Why is it important for the financial manager to understand production-oriented inventory control techniques? How does this fit into his or her overall goal of assuring efficient inventory management?

10.7   Explain the relationship between inventory and accounts receivable. What effects on inventory levels are likely to result from easing credit standards and lengthening credit terms? Distinguish between the immediate effects and longer-term effects.

10.8   What is meant by the ABC inventory control system? On what key premise is this system based? When is the system not recommended, and why?

10.9   In what instances may certain items of inventory have to be viewed as outside of the realm of the ABC system? What types of items would these be?

10.10   What is the EOQ model? What are its assumptions and objectives? To what group of inventory items is it most applicable? What costs does it consider? What financial cost is involved?

10.11   When can the average inventory be calculated by dividing the order quantity by two? Graph the depletion and replenishment of inventory and show the average level of inventory.

10.12   What is an EOQ? What are the basic weaknesses of the EOQ model described in the chapter?

10.13   What is the inventory reorder point? What key variables must be known in order to estimate the reorder point? How are these variables related?

10.14   What is the rationale for applying the EOQ concept to the management of a firm's transaction cash balance?

10.15   How would an increase in the general level of interest rates affect the inventory level of a firm?

10.16   a.   According to the EOQ cash order model discussed in this chapter, significant economies of scale are possible in the management of corporate transactions cash balances. Explain.

   b.   How will an increase in the general price level (inflation) affect the firm's transaction cash balance as determined by the EOQ cash order formula?

Problems

10.1   Ready Supply has 16 different items in its inventory. The average number of each of these items held, along with their unit costs, is listed below. The firm wishes to introduce an ABC inventory system. Suggest a breakdown of the items into classifications of A, B, and C. Justify your selection and point out items that could be considered borderline cases.

Item	Average number of units in inventory	Average cost per unit
1	1800	$ .54
2	1000	8.20
3	100	6.00
4	250	1.20
5	8	94.50
6	400	3.00
7	80	45.00
8	1600	1.45
9	600	.95
10	3000	.18
11	900	15.00
12	65	1.35
13	2200	4.75
14	1800	1.30
15	60	18.00
16	200	17.50

10.2   What is the firm's average investment in inventory in the following cases?

a.   The firm has sales of $25,000,000, a gross profit margin of 40 percent, and the average age of inventory is 45 days.

b.   The firm has an annual cost of goods sold of $200,000 and an inventory turnover ratio of 6.

c.   The firm's sales are $2 million, its gross profit margin is 20 percent, and its average age of inventory is 30 days.

10.3   Dayton Truck Parts has a net profit margin of 4 percent, a gross profit margin of 30 percent, and earnings after taxes of $20,000.

a.   What is its average investment in inventory if the average age of inventory is 45 days?

b.   What is its inventory turnover if the average investment in inventory is $80,000?

c.   What is its average age of inventory if the average investment in inventory is $56,000?

10.4   Nieman Brothers has sales of $200,000, a gross margin of 20 percent, and an average age of inventory of 45 days.

a.   What will be the change in the average investment in inventory if the firm's inventory turnover ratio changes to 7?

b.   If the firm's required rate of return on investments is 18 percent, what additional profits (or losses) result from the change in **a**?

10.5   International Pump is considering a production change that will reduce the average investment in inventory by $60,000. The changeover will cost $10,000 per year, and International's required rate of return on investment is 15 percent. Calculate the additional profits from this change and make a recommendation with respect to the proposed change.

10.6   Franklin Tire estimates the annual cost of carrying a dollar of inventory is $0.27, while the carrying cost of an equal investment in accounts receivable is $0.17. The firm's current balance sheet reflects its average inventory of $400,000 and average investment in accounts receivable of $100,000. If the firm can convince its customers to purchase in large quantities, the level of inventory can be reduced by $200,000, and the investment in receivables increased by the same amount. Assuming no change in annual sales, what addition to profits will be generated from this shift? Explain your answer.

10.7   Ottawa Textile uses 10,000 units of a raw material per year on a continuous basis. The firm estimates the cost of carrying one unit in inventory is $0.25 per year. Placing and processing an order for additional inventory costs $200 per order.

a.   What are annual ordering costs, carrying costs, and total costs of inventory if the firm orders in quantities of 1,000, 2,000, 3,000, 4,000, 5,000, 6,000, and 7,000 units, respectively?

b.   Graph ordering costs and carrying costs (y-axis) relative to quantity ordered (x-axis). Label the EOQ.

c.   Based on your graph, in what quantity would you order? Is this consistent with the EOQ equation? Explain why or why not.

10.8   Lyons Electronics purchases 100,000 units per month of one component. Monthly carrying costs of the item are 10 percent of the item's $2 cost. Fixed costs per order are $25.

a.   Determine the EOQ, average level of inventory, number of orders, and total cost of inventory under the following conditions: (1) no changes, (2) the carrying cost is zero, and (3) the ordering cost is zero.

b.   What do your answers illustrate about the EOQ model? Explain.

10.9   Columbus Gas and Electric (CG&E) is required to carry 20 days' average coal usage, which is 100 tons of coal. It takes 10 days between order and delivery. At which level of the remaining coal supply would CG&E reorder?

10.10   A firm uses 800 units of a product per year *on a continuous basis*. The product has carrying costs of $2 per unit and fixed costs of $50 per order. It takes 5 days to receive a shipment after an order is placed, and the firm wishes to hold in inventory 10 days' usage as a safety stock.
a. Calculate the EOQ.
b. Determine the average level of inventory.
c. Determine the reorder point.
d. Which of the following variables change in the event the firm does not hold the safety stock: (1) carrying costs, (2) ordering costs, (3) reorder point, (4) total inventory cost, (5) average level of inventory, (6) number of orders per year, or (7) economic order quantity? Explain.

10.11   Alberta Farm Supplies Ltd. has four divisions, each of which maintains its own separate transactions cash account. Transactions cash expenditures over the next month for each division are expected to be $40,000. An examination of the firm's records has revealed that the basic EOQ cash order model discussed in this chapter provides a reasonable description of the firm's transactions payment patterns. The firm has estimated that every dollar of cash held in the divisional transactions cash accounts will have an opportunity cost of $0.04 per month. The fixed cost per cash order for each division is estimated to be $50.

Management is contemplating the consolidation of the divisional cash accounts into a central account which will be accessible to each division for its transactions payments. Would you advise Alberta Farm Supplies to take this action? Explain.

Suggested Readings

Baumol, William J., "The Transactions Demand for Cash: An Inventory Theoretic Approach," *Quarterly Journal of Economics* 46 (November 1952), pp. 545–556.

Beranek, William, "Financial Implications of Lot-Size Inventory Models," *Harvard Business Review* 47 (January-February 1969), pp. 72–90.

———, *Working Capital Management* (Belmont, Calif.: Wadsworth, 1966).

Brooks, LeRoy D., "Return on Investment as a Criterion for Inventory Models: Comment," *Decision Sciences* 9 (October 1978), pp. 739–741.

Buffa, Elwood S., *Production-Inventory Systems: Planning and Control*, rev. ed. (Homewood, Ill.: Irwin, 1972).

Cook, Thomas M. and Robert A. Russell, *Introduction to Management Science* (Englewood Cliffs, N.J.: Prentice-Hall, Inc., 1977), chap. 11.

Hadley, G. and T. M. Whitin, *Analysis of Inventory Systems* (Englewood Cliffs, N.J.: Prentice-Hall, 1963).

Haley, Charles W. and Robert C. Higgins, "Inventory Control Theory and Trade Credit Financing," *Management Science* 20 (December 1973), pp. 464–471.

Hofer, C. F., "Analysis of Fixed Costs in Inventory," *Management Accounting* (September 1970), pp. 15–17.

Magee, John F., "Guides to Inventory Policy, I–III," *Harvard Business Review* 34 (January-February 1956), pp. 49–60; (March-April 1956), pp. 103–116; and (May-June 1956), pp. 57–70.

Mao, James C. T., *Quantitative Analysis of Financial Decisions* (New York: Macmillan, 1969), pp. 121–127.

Mehta, Dileep R., *Working Capital Management* (Englewood Cliffs, N.J.: Prentice-Hall, 1974), part 2.

Pinny, W. F., "Correcting a Misconception about EOQ," *Decision Sciences* 8 (October 1977), pp. 753–756.

Schiff, Michael, "Credit and Inventory Management—Separate or Together," *Financial Executive* 40 (November 1972), pp. 28–33.

Schiff, Michael and Z. Leiber, "A Model for the Integration of Credit and Inventory Management," *Journal of Finance* (March 1974), pp. 133–140.

Shapiro, Alan, "Optimal Inventory and Credit-Granting Strategies Under Inflation and Devaluation," *Journal of Financial and Quantitative Analysis* 7 (January 1973), pp. 37–46.

Snyder, Arthur, "Principles of Inventory Management," *Financial Executive* 32 (April 1964), pp. 16–19.

Stancill, James McN., *The Management of Working Capital* (Scranton, Pa.: Intext, 1971), chap. 5.

Starr, Martin K. and David W. Miler, *Inventory Control—Theory and Practice* (Englewood Cliffs, N.J.: Prentice-Hall, 1962).

Thurston, P. H., "Requirements Planning for Inventory Control," *Harvard Business Review* 50 (March-April 1972), pp. 67–71.

Vienott, Arthur F., Jr., "The Status of Mathematical Inventory Theory," *Management Science* 12 (July 1966), pp. 745–777.

Wagner, Harvey M., *Principles of Operations Research— with Applications for Managerial Decisions* (Englewood Cliffs, N.J.: Prentice-Hall, 1969), chaps. 9. and 19 and appendix 2.

Zink, Karl W., "How to Manage a System of Inventory Control," *Industrial Management* (May 1970), pp. 9–14.

Part Four

Sources of Short-Term Financing

BALANCE SHEET	
Assets	Liabilities and Shareholders' Equity
Current Assets	**Current Liabilities**
Fixed Assets	Long-Term Debt
	Shareholders' Equity

This part of the text is devoted solely to short-term financing or current liabilities. Most current liabilities result from the natural course of business; others are the result of negotiated short-term loans. Whereas spontaneous current liabilities are virtually unsecured, negotiated loans may be secured or unsecured, depending on the presence or absence of collateral backing. This section contains two chapters. Chapter 11 discusses the sources of unsecured short-term financing, which include spontaneous forms, such as accounts payable and accruals, and a negotiated form—the bank loan. Chapter 12 discusses the various types of secured short-term loans, such as bank loans. These are primarily loans secured by accounts receivable and inventory, although other forms of collateral are occasionally used. In both chapters, the emphasis is on the characteristics, cost, and availability of the various sources of short-term financing available to the business firm.

Chapter 11

SOURCES OF UNSECURED SHORT-TERM FINANCING

The availability of short-term financing to a business firm is of key importance to its continued existence. If the firm cannot sustain itself in the short run, the long run is of no consequence. Short-term financing, which consists of obligations that are expected to mature in one year or less, is required in order to support a large portion of a firm's current assets, such as cash, marketable securities, accounts receivable, and inventory. The discussion of cash budgeting and pro forma statements in Chapters 5 and 6, respectively, emphasized the importance of short-term financial planning. In Chapters 7 through 10 primary attention was given to the management of specific current assets, again emphasizing the importance of efficient financial management.

In this chapter, we shall discuss the characteristics of unsecured short-term financing. Unsecured short-term financing consists of funds raised by the firm without specifically pledging assets as collateral. These forms of financing show up on the firm's balance sheet as accounts payable, accruals, and notes payable. Accounts payable and accruals are spontaneous sources of short-term funds since they arise from the normal operations of the firm; notes payable, though sometimes unsecured, result from some type of negotiated borrowing by the firm's management.

This chapter has three basic sections. The first section discusses the spontaneous sources of short-term financing—accounts payable and accruals. Both of these can be manipulated to provide the firm with inexpensive financing. The second section is devoted to sources of unsecured short-term financing, which include bank financing, commercial and finance paper, customer advances, private loans, and nondomestic borrowings. A summary table, which presents the key facts related to each of the sources of unsecured short-term financing discussed in this chapter, is included as Table 11.4 at the end of the chapter.

Spontaneous Sources of Short-Term Financing

The two major spontaneous sources of short-term financing, accounts payable and accruals, result from normal business operations. As the firm's sales increase, accounts payable increase in response to the increased purchases required to produce at higher levels. Also in response to inceasing sales, the firm's accruals increase as wages and taxes rise as a result of greater labour requirements and the increased taxes on the increased earnings. There is normally no explicit cost attached to either of these current liabilities, although they do have certain implicit costs. The firm should take advantage of these often "interest-free" sources of short-term financing whenever possible.

ACCOUNTS PAYABLE

Accounts payable are generally created by the purchase of raw materials "on open account." Open-account purchases are the major source of unsecured short-term financing for business firms. They include all transactions in which merchandise is purchased but no formal note is signed evidencing the purchaser's liability to the seller. The purchaser by accepting shipped merchandise in effect agrees to pay the supplier the amount required by the supplier's terms of sale. The credit terms extended in such transactions are normally stated on the supplier's invoice, which often accompanies the goods shipped. These credit terms are of key importance to the purchaser and should be noted in planning all purchases.

Although the obligation of the purchaser to the supplier may not seem as legally binding as it would be if the supplier had required the purchaser to sign a note, there is no legal difference between the two arrangements. If a firm were to become bankrupt, a creditor who sold its goods on open account would have as strong a legal claim on the firm's assets as a creditor who held a note payable. The only advantage of using a note payable is that it gives the holder of the note stronger proof that merchandise had in fact been sold to the bankrupt firm. The use of notes for purchases of raw materials is quite rare; normally they are used only if a supplier has reason to believe that the character or credit-worthiness of a customer is questionable.

In this chapter, we shall deal solely with the use of accounts payable for purchasing raw materials. Among the most important aspects of accounts payable are the types of credit terms offered by suppliers, the costs that result from foregoing cash discounts, and the payoffs that may result from stretching accounts payable. The discussion of accounts payable here is presented from the viewpoint of the purchaser—not the supplier of trade credit.*

Credit Terms   The firm's credit terms state the credit period, the size of the cash discount, the cash discount period, and the date the credit period begins. Each of these aspects of a firm's credit terms is concisely stated in such expressions as "2/10 net 30 EOM." The terms contain all the key information concerning the length of the credit period (30 days), the cash discount (2 percent), the cash discount

---

*Chapter 9 presented an in-depth discussion of the various aspects of the firm's role as a supplier of credit. It highlighted the key strategies and considerations in extending credit to customers.

period (10 days), and the time the credit period begins (the end of the month). Although credit terms typically differ among industries, there are a number of commonly used terms, each of which is discussed separately below.

The Credit Period   The credit period is the number of days until payment in full is required. Credit periods usually range from zero to 120 days, although in certain instances longer credit periods are provided.*

No Credit Period   Often, suppliers do not extend credit to their customers, but instead require payment on delivery. The term COD, indicating "cash on delivery," is normally attached to these credit terms. Generally COD terms are extended only to customers believed to be questionable or unknown credit risks. In some instances, suppliers require payment before delivery. The term CBD, indicating "cash before delivery," is used to designate this type of arrangement. On contracted manufacturing jobs this type of arrangement is often referred to as "progress payments." For instance, if a firm contracts to have an addition built to its plant, it may agree to make payments at certain predetermined points prior to the completion of the entire project. COD and CBD terms *do not* actually represent extension of credit by the supplier to the customer and are *not* evidenced by an account payable on the purchaser's books.

The Net Period   Most credit terms include a net period that is typically referred to as "net 30 days," "net 60 days," and so on. The prefix *net* indicates that the face amount of the purchase must be paid within the number of days indicated from the beginning of the credit period. For example, the terms "net 30 days" indicate that the firm must make *full payment* within 30 days of the beginning of the credit period. (Once we have defined the beginning of the credit period, a more detailed example can be given.) A firm that stretches its accounts payable will pay beyond the stated credit period.

Seasonal Dating   Seasonal dating is a technique used by suppliers in seasonal businesses, such as clothing and sporting goods firms. It provides a considerably longer credit period than that normally extended, possibly as long as 180 days. The supplier ships finished goods to the purchaser in advance of the selling season, but does not require payment until shortly after the actual demand for the seasonal items is expected. Both parties to the transaction stand to gain from seasonal dating. The seller saves inventory carrying costs, since the seller often must manufacture the seasonal merchandise at a constant rate throughout the year. If sellers could not pass their inventory carrying costs on to their customers, they would have to absorb them.† The purchaser gains through assurances of having merchandise available for the peak season, but is not required to pay for it until the actual season arrives. As long as the purchaser has adequate inventory facilities, the use of seasonal dating works to the benefit of both parties concerned.

*The credit period is zero days when sales are made for cash.
†A commonly cited rule-of-thumb with respect to inventory carrying costs states that the cost of carrying an item in inventory for one year represents approximately 20 to 25—and even as much as 30—percent of the cost (or value) of the item. This suggests that very real savings may result for suppliers using seasonal dating.

Cash Discounts   If a cash discount is offered as part of the firm's credit terms, it is normally between 1 and 5 percent. It is actually a percentage deduction from the purchase price allowed the purchaser if payment is made within the cash discount period. A 2-percent cash discount indicates that the purchaser of $100 of merchandise need pay only $98 if it is paid within the discount period. Many purchasers will stretch their cash discounts by taking the discount even when paying after the cash discount period.

From the point of view of the supplier of credit, whose objective it is to collect the accounts receivable quickly, a cash discount provides an incentive for the purchaser to pay early. The reduction in proceeds due to the discount is compensated for by the speeding up of collections. The purchaser, whose objective is to stretch the accounts payable by paying as late as possible, must determine whether it is advantageous to take the cash discount and pay early. Techniques for analyzing the benefits of each alternative will be discussed in a later section.

The Cash Discount Period   The cash discount period specifies the maximum number of days after the beginning of the credit period that the cash discount can be taken. Typically, the cash discount period is between 5 and 20 days. In certain industries, more than one cash discount is offered. The discount period is shortest for the largest discount offered and longest for the smallest discount offered. Sometimes large customers of smaller firms use their position as key customers as a form of leverage, so that they can take cash discounts after the end of the cash discount period. Similarly, large firms sometimes allow certain customers to take cash discounts for payments beyond the end of the cash discount period. The first practice is ethically questionable and the second may be illegal, especially when it results in discriminatory pricing.

Since governmental buyers have tended to take cash discounts regardless of when payments were made, many suppliers have tended to eliminate cash discounts for governmental customers. Some suppliers have even attempted to decrease the average collection period for governmental accounts by charging interest on payments received beyond the net period.* Generally, this has not been successful, since the governmental purchasers either have refused to pay the interest penalty or have taken their business to more accommodating suppliers.

Generally in the insurance, professional services, and governmental sectors, no discount is offered. The standard credit terms are "net 30," with an interest penalty for payments made after 30 days.

During tight money periods, such as 1979–1980, many suppliers are approached by buyers to increase the cash discount for payments made within the cash discount period. On the other hand, other suppliers, such as the suppliers of heating oil, have begun offering a cash discount in order to deter firms from stretching their accounts payable.

---

*In general, private suppliers find that the average collection period for governmental accounts is much longer than private-sector accounts. For example, one Canadian firm reported that the average collection period for governmental accounts was almost two times that for its private-sector accounts.

The Beginning of the Credit Period   The beginning of the credit period is stated as part of the supplier's credit terms. It can be specified in various ways—as the date of the invoice, the end of the month, the middle of the month, or on receipt of the goods. The notation used is briefly described below.

The Date of the Invoice   This is one of the most common designations for the beginning of the credit period. Both the discount period and the net period are then measured with respect to the invoice date.

The End of the Month (EOM)   The notation EOM indicates that the credit period for all purchases made within a given month begins on the first of the month immediately following. These terms are quite common since they simplify record keeping on the part of the firm extending credit. The date of the invoice is recognized as the date of sale.*

The Middle of the Month (MOM)   The notation MOM indicates that the month is broken into two separate credit periods. The credit period for all sales made (i.e., invoices dated) between the first and fifteenth of the current month begins on the sixteenth of the month. The credit period for all sales made between the sixteenth and the thirtieth (or thirty-first) of the month begins on the first day of the month immediately following. These credit terms cause the firm's collections to be speeded up, since payments for purchases made prior to the fifteenth of the month are collected earlier than when EOM terms are offered. MOM terms are not commonly used. The following example may help clarify the difference between the various types of credit period beginnings.

EXAMPLE   The Grimes Company Ltd. made two purchases from a certain supplier offering credit terms of 2/10 net 30. One purchase was made on September 10 and the other on September 20. The payment dates for both purchases, based on credit periods that begin at various points, are given in Table 11.1. Both the payment dates if the firm takes the cash discount and the payment dates if it pays the net amount are shown.

Table 11.1   Payment Dates for the Grimes Company Given Various Assumptions

Beginning of credit period	September 10 purchase		September 20 purchase	
	Discount taken	Net amount paid	Discount taken	Net amount paid
Date of invoice	Sept. 20	Oct. 10	Sept. 30	Oct. 20
EOM	Oct. 10	Oct. 30	Oct. 10	Oct. 30
MOM	Sept. 25	Oct. 15	Oct. 10	Oct. 30

*Occasionally firms receive invoices prior to receiving the actual merchandise purchased. In these situations the beginning of the credit period is not tied to the invoice date, which could be 30 days prior to the receipt of goods.

Table 11.1 illustrates that, from the point of view of the recipient of trade credit, a credit period beginning at the end of the month is preferable in all cases. When the credit period begins on the date of the invoice, the credit recipient must pay earlier regardless of whether it takes the cash discount or pays the net amount. The difference between the MOM and EOM terms can be recognized by noting that, for the September 10 purchase, MOM terms require quicker payment than EOM terms. For the September 20 purchase, MOM and EOM terms result in the same payment dates.

Receipt of Goods (ROG)   Receipt of goods terms are commonly used when goods purchased may be received considerably later than the purchase date. This happens when merchandise is purchased from a geographically distant supplier and the shipping process takes a period of months. A large number of backorders, strikes, and other problems may also delay the receipt of goods. ROG terms indicate that the credit period does not begin until the purchaser has actually received the merchandise.

Credit terms are generally standardized within a given industry, since in order to maintain their competitive position, firms within an industry offer the same terms. In many cases the firms' stated credit terms are not the terms actually given to a customer; special arrangements or "deals" are made that provide certain customers with more favourable terms. This is often done in order to attract key accounts or to help a growing firm that is low on working capital. The prospective purchaser is wise to attempt to obtain credit term concessions from suppliers when making a purchase decision.

The Cost of Trade Credit   Although no explicit cost is levied on the recipient of trade credit, the firm extending the credit does incur a cost. Extending credit to customers requires the investment of money that could be used elsewhere, and this cost is indirectly passed on to the purchaser in the cost of the merchandise. In the same way that a supplier extends trade credit to a customer, so too the supplier's supplier generally extends trade credit, thereby helping the supplier to absorb a portion of the cost. A more in-depth discussion of trade credit from the point of the issuer (i.e., accounts receivable) was presented in Chapter 9.

Taking or Foregoing the Cash Discount   If a firm is extended credit terms that include a cash discount, it has two options. Its first option is to *take the cash discount*. Taking the cash discount will require the firm to pay earlier than it would have to if the discount were foregone. If a firm does intend to take a cash discount, it should pay on the last day of the cash discount period (as is assumed in subsequent analysis). There is no implicit cost associated with taking a cash discount.

EXAMPLE   The Russell Corporation purchased $1,000 worth of merchandise on February 27 from a supplier extending terms of 2/10 net 30 EOM. If the corporation takes the cash discount, it will have to pay $980 [$1,000 − .02($1,000)] on March 10. If it foregoes the discount, it will have to pay the full $1,000 on March 30. The factors involved in deciding whether or not the discount should be foregone are explained in the following section.

The second option open to the firm is to *forego the cash discount* and pay at the end of the credit period. Although there is no direct cost associated with foregoing a cash discount, there is an implicit cost because, in order to delay paying its bill for an additional number of days, the firm must forego an opportunity to pay less for the items it has purchased. If the cash discount is foregone, the firm should pay on the final day of the credit period (as is assumed in subsequent analysis). An overall strategy of paying as late as possible without damaging the firm's credit rating was discussed in Chapter 8. The cost of foregoing a cash discount can be illustrated by the following example.

EXAMPLE The Russell Corporation mentioned in the preceding example has been extended credit terms of 2/10 net 30 EOM. If it takes the cash discount on its February 27 purchase, payment will be required on March 10. If the cash discount is foregone, payment can be made on March 30. In order to keep its money (i.e., postpone payment) for an extra 20 days (from March 10 to March 30) the firm must forego an opportunity to pay $980 for its $1,000 purchase. In other words, it will cost the firm an extra $20 to delay payment for 20 days. Figure 11.1 shows the payment options open to the corporation.

In order to calculate the cost of foregoing the cash discount, the *true purchase price* must be viewed as the discounted cost of the merchandise, that is, $980. In order to avoid paying the $980 for an extra 20 days, the firm must pay $20 ($1,000 − $980). The annual percentage cost of foregoing the cash discount can be calculated using Equation 11.1.*

$$\text{Cost of foregoing cash discount} = \frac{CD}{1 - CD} \cdot \frac{360}{N} \qquad (11.1)$$

where

CD = the stated cash discount in percentage terms
N = the number of days payment can be delayed by foregoing the cash discount

Substituting the values for CD (.02) and N (20 days) into Equation 11.1 and solving results in a cost of foregoing the cash discount of 36.73 percent [(.02 ÷ .98) · (360 ÷ 20)]. A 360-day year is assumed.

A simple way to approximate the cost of a foregone discount is to use the stated cash discount percentage (2 percent for the Russell Corporation) in place of the first term of Equation 11.1. The smaller the cash discount, the closer the approximation is to the actual cost of foregoing the cash discount. Using this simplified approach, the cost of foregoing the cash discount for the Russell Corporation is found to be 36 percent [2% · (360 ÷ 20)].

Using the Cost of Foregoing a Cash Discount in Decision Making   There are a number of decisions with respect to cash discounts that may confront the financial manager. Each of these decisions can be illustrated by a simple example.

---

*Equation 11.1 as well as the related discussions are based upon the assumption that there is only one discount period. In the event that multiple discount periods are offered, calculation of the cost of foregoing the discount must be made for each payment alternative.

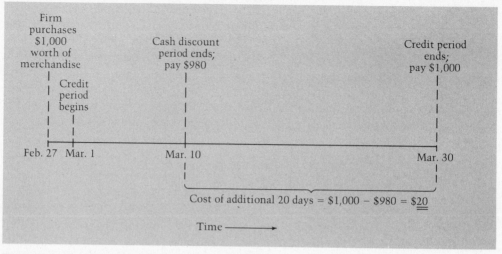

Figure 11.1   Payment options for the Russell Corporation.

EXAMPLE   The Gup Company Ltd. has four possible suppliers, each offering different credit terms. Except for the differences in credit terms, their products and services are undifferentiated. Table 11.2 presents the credit terms offered by each supplier (i.e., A, B, C, and D) and the cost of foregoing the cash discounts. The approximate method of calculating the cost of foregoing a cash discount has been used in order to simplify the analysis. Let us now see how the information in Table 11.2 might be used in three decision situations.*

Table 11.2   Cash Discounts and Associated Costs for the Gup Company

Supplier	Credit terms	Approximate cost of foregoing cash discount
A	2/10 net 30 EOM	36 %
B	1/10 net 55 EOM	8 %
C	3/20 net 70 EOM	21.6%
D	4/10 net 60 EOM	28.8%

CASE 1: A One-by-One Analysis   If the firm needs short-term funds, which are currently available from its chartered bank at 12 percent, and if each of the suppliers (A, B, C, and D) is viewed *separately*, which (if any) of the suppliers' cash discount will the firm forego? In order to answer

*The analysis of the various decisions implicitly assumes that the firm will continuously make purchases from the given supplier, since this permits the term of the loan provided to be aligned with the firm's actual financial need. In actuality, a 20-day loan obtained by foregoing a cash discount may not fulfill a firm's actual funds need.

this question, each supplier's terms must be evaluated as they would be if it were the firm's sole supplier. Thus, for supplier A, C, or D, the firm should take the cash discount, since in these three cases the cost of foregoing the discount is greater than the 12-percent cost of borrowing from the bank.

CASE 2: The Firm Must Forego a Discount   If the Gup Company knows that it must forego cash discounts, since it needs money and has no alternate sources of short-term financing, from which of its four alternative suppliers will the purchase be made? Since the cash discount must be foregone, all suppliers will be paid the full amount for their merchandise. Thus, the supplier that can be paid the latest is preferable. In this case, supplier C will be selected since it can be paid on day 70.

CASE 3: The Firm Must Take a Discount   If the Gup Company already has sufficient short-term financing, from which supplier should it make the purchase? In this situation, the chief consideration is *who can be paid the least the latest*. Table 11.3 presents the firm's options. The four alternatives can easily be reduced to two by comparing the terms of suppliers A, B, and D. Each of these suppliers requires payment on day 10, but supplier D is preferable since it requires payment of only 96 percent of the purchase price at that time. In other words, supplier D can be paid less than supplier A or supplier B at the same point in time.

Table 11.3   The Percentage of the Purchase Price Paid and Payment Dates When the Cash Discount Is Taken for the Gup Company

Supplier	Percentage of purchase price paid	Payment date
A	98	10
B	99	10
C	97	20
D	96	10

The comparison of suppliers C and D is not quite so straightforward. Supplier C can be paid 97 percent on day 20, and supplier D can be paid 96 percent on day 10. In order to delay payment 10 days, the firm must pay an additional 1 percent of the purchase price. In order to determine if supplier C is preferable to supplier D, the question of whether it is worth this much money (i.e., 1 percent) to delay payment 10 days must be answered. The cost of such an action is approximately 36 percent per annum [1% · (360 ÷ 10)]. Since the firm's cost of borrowing is 12 percent, it seems advisable for the firm to make its purchase from supplier D and avoid the 36 percent marginal borrowing cost.

The foregoing examples show that the cost of foregoing a cash discount is relevant only when evaluating a single supplier's credit terms in light of certain bank borrowing costs. In comparing various suppliers' credit terms, the cost of foregoing the cash discount is not the most important input to the decision process.

The Effects of Stretching Accounts Payable If a firm anticipates stretching accounts payable, the cost of foregoing a cash discount is reduced. Stretching accounts payable is sometimes suggested as a reasonable strategy for a firm as long as it does not materially damage its credit rating.

EXAMPLE The Russell Corporation, discussed earlier, was extended credit terms of 2/10 net 30 EOM. The cost of foregoing the cash discount, assuming payment on the last day of the credit period, was found to be approximately 36 percent [2% · (360 ÷ 20)]. If the firm were able to stretch its account payable to 70 days without damaging its credit rating, the cost of foregoing the cash discount would be only 12 percent [2% · (360 ÷ 60)]. Stretching accounts payable reduces the implicit cost of foregoing a cash discount. The firm might find that in view of its ability to stretch accounts payable, foregoing an otherwise attractive cash discount may be desirable.

ACCRUALS

The second spontaneous source of short-term financing for the business firm is accruals. Accruals are liabilities for services received for which payment has yet to be made. The most common items accrued by a firm are taxes and wages. The firm can manipulate both to some extent.*

Since accrued wages are virtually free sources of financing, a firm can save money by accruing as many dollars of wages as possible. Employees provide services for which they normally are not paid until a specified period of time—typically a week, two weeks, or a month—has elapsed. While the pay period for hourly employees is often governed by union regulations or provincial or federal law, the frequency of payment for other employees is at the discretion of the firm's management. The following example shows how wage accruals can be used to increase the firm's financing.

EXAMPLE The Smith Company currently pays its salaried employees every two weeks. The payroll for two weeks is normally about $3 million. If the firm's opportunity cost is 8 percent, how much would the firm save by changing the pay period from two weeks to one month? If the firm paid monthly, the payroll at the end of each month would be approximately $6 million. Currently the average amount accrued for the salaried payroll is $1.5 million ($3 million ÷ 2), since the accrued payroll is expected to increase at a constant rate until payment is actually made. For the first half of the payroll period, the accrued payroll will be below $1.5 million, and for the second half of the pay period it will be greater than $1.5 million.

Under the new plan, the average amount accrued would be $3 million ($6 million ÷ 2), using the same logic as above. Implementing the proposed plan would therefore increase the average amount of accruals by $1.5 million ($3 million − $1.5 million). This increase in average accrued salaries, in effect, increases the firm's free financing by $1.5 million. This amount of funds can now be used elsewhere at an opportunity cost of 8 percent. The annual savings from this change in the salary payment interval is $120,000 ($1,500,000 · .08).

---

*Since tax planning was discussed in Chapter 2, it will not be discussed further in this chapter.

In the case of accrued wages, the firm must be careful not to damage the morale of its employees by delaying the payment of wages for too long. Sometimes firms pay rent or lease expenses at the end of a lease period; if they do, these expenditures are accrued. The firm should use accruals as often as possible, keeping in mind any subjective costs associated with their use.

Sources of Unsecured Short-Term Funds

The five most common sources of negotiated short-term unsecured loans are unsecured bank loans, commercial and finance paper, customer advances, private loans, and non-domestic borrowings. All of these sources are not available to every business firm. The availability of these forms of financing depends largely on the nature, size, and operating environment of the firm.

UNSECURED SHORT-TERM BANK LOANS

Unlike the situation in the United States, most of the loans provided by the Canadian banking system are secured. There is little variation in the stated rates on unsecured bank loans, since risky firms do not obtain unsecured bank loans. In some instances, unsecured loans are available from foreign banks with offices in Canada. Thus, a detailed discussion of bank loans is left to the next chapter.

COMMERCIAL AND FINANCE PAPER

Commercial paper consists of short-term, unsecured promissory notes issued by firms having a high credit standing. Since generally only quite large firms of unquestionable financial soundness are able to issue commercial paper, there were about 200 corporations that were active in this market during 1978.* Most commercial paper has maturities ranging from 24 hours to 1 year or longer. Although there is no set denomination, most commercial paper is issued in multiples of $100,000 or more. It is interesting to note that although commercial paper is unsecured, the market expects the issuer of the paper to have available bank lines of credit to cover the dollar value of the paper outstanding. A large portion of the commercial paper is issued today by manufacturing firms.

Basically, *finance company paper* is quite similar to commercial paper. One difference is that finance paper is often secured by a pledge of receivables, which typically ranges from $112\frac{1}{2}$ to 125 percent of the value of the paper outstanding. Unsecured finance paper can generally only be issued if the paper's principal and interest is unconditionally guaranteed by the finance company's parent firm.

As was discussed in Chapter 8, business firms often purchase commercial and finance paper, which they hold as marketable securities to provide a reserve of liquidity. Chartered banks, individuals, insurance companies, pension funds, and other types of financial institutions also purchase commercial paper. In each case, the motive for purchasing

---

*Issuers of corporate paper include such companies as Bell Canada, Steinbergs, and MacMillan Bloedel.

the paper is the need to find an interest-earning medium in which to place temporarily idle funds.

Because most purchasers of commercial paper hold it to maturity, the secondary market for commercial paper is not well developed. In order to provide investors with the liquidity they desire, the issuing firm or selling dealer will agree to repurchase the paper at a discount price prior to maturity.

Commercial paper is generally considered a quite safe investment, since the issuers are considered to be very credit-worthy. However, issues of commercial paper have been known to go sour. For example, in August 1979, the Canadian Bond Rating Service Ltd. temporarily suspended its rating on the commercial paper of Chrysler Credit Canada Ltd., a subsidiary of Chrysler Canada. Interestingly, the suspension was primarily due to the publicity associated with the acute financial difficulties of the U.S. parent firm.

Interest on Commercial Paper   The interest paid by the issuer of commercial paper is determined by the size of the discount and the length of time to maturity. The calculation of the actual interest earned can be illustrated by a simple example.

EXAMPLE   The Howell Corporation has just issued $1 million worth of commercial paper that has a 90-day maturity and sells for $980,000. At the end of 90 days the purchaser of this paper will receive $1,000,000 for his or her $980,000 investment. The interest paid on the financing is therefore $20,000 on a principal of $980,000. This is equivalent to an annual interest rate for the Howell Corporation commercial paper of 8.16 percent [($20,000 ÷ $980,000) · (360 days ÷ 90 days)].

An interesting characteristic of commercial paper is that it *normally* has a yield below the prime bank lending rate. In other words, business firms are able to raise funds through the sale of commercial paper more cheaply than by borrowing from a bank. This is because many suppliers of short-term funds do not have the option of making low-risk business loans at the prime rate; they can invest only in marketable securities such as treasury bills and commercial paper. Since commercial paper is an extremely safe marketable security with a higher yield than treasury bills and most other marketable securities, it is a quite attractive investment to these investors.

Although the cost of borrowing through the sale of commercial paper is generally lower than the prime bank loan rate, one must keep in mind that interest on a bank loan is paid only on the outstanding balance. Since commercial paper, once issued, does not mature for a given period, the firm may pay interest on funds it does not actually need. A second point to recognize is that it is critical for a firm to maintain a good working relationship with its bank. Even if it is slightly more expensive to borrow from a bank, it may be advisable to do so in order to establish the necessary rapport with a banker. This strategy ensures that when money is tight funds can be obtained promptly through the firm's chartered bank.

The Sale of Commercial Paper   Commercial paper is sold either to or by investment dealers. For performing the marketing function, the dealer receives a commission of between one-eighth to one-fourth of 1 percent per annum of the face value of the paper placed with investors, such as other corporations, life insurance companies, or pension funds. If the dealer is not able to place the paper immediately, the dealer may purchase the paper for his or her own account with the expectation of reselling the paper later at a higher price.

Commercial Paper Substitutes   In February of 1978, the Bank of Montreal introduced a new plan to provide an alternative source of short-term funds for firms borrowing in the commercial paper market. The plan, designated the First Bank Acceptances with a Guaranteed Term Option, was designed for corporations that have been rated by the two Canadian rating services as either a No. 1 or No. 2 rating. Joseph Seagram & Sons Ltd., which carried the highest Dominion Rating of R1, was the first user of the plan.

CUSTOMER ADVANCES

A firm may be able to obtain short-term unsecured funds through customer advances. In other words, customers may pay for all or a portion of what they intend to purchase in advance of their receipt of the goods. In many situations where a large, expensive item is being custom manufactured, the customer may be more than willing to make an advance against the merchandise to finance a portion of its cost of production. In other instances, a customer may be highly dependent on a supplier for a key component and may therefore find it to his or her advantage to assure the supplier's success by providing financing in the form of an advance. In most instances, the supplier must request the advance from the customer.

PRIVATE LOANS

Short-term unsecured loans may also be obtained from shareholders of the firm. Wealthy shareholders in many smaller corporations may be quite willing to lend money to the firm to get it through a period of crisis. This type of arrangement makes sense from the viewpoint of the shareholder, who has a vested interest in the survival of the firm. Another form of private loan can be obtained by temporarily foregoing commissions for salespersons. Each of these types of loans involves the extension of unsecured credit to the firm by an interested or a concerned party.

NONDOMESTIC BORROWINGS

Larger corporations often borrow short-term in the international money markets, which are located in such major financial centers as New York, London, Zurich, and Frankfurt. A firm may access these markets for a number of reasons. For example, a firm may borrow in nondomestic markets in order to cover or hedge against the foreign exchange exposure encountered in managing its foreign accounts receivable. A firm may also borrow in a nondomestic market in order to take advantage of a lower interest rate. If a Canadian firm does not borrow in Canadian dollars, it should not ignore the fact that it is being exposed to exchange rate uncertainty, which could materially increase (or decrease) the real cost of a borrowing.

Table 11.4 Summary of Sources of Unsecured Short-Term Financing

Type of financing	Source	Cost/conditions	Characteristics
I. Spontaneous sources			
Accounts payable	Suppliers of materials	No explicit cost except when a cash discount is offered for early payment.	Credit extended on open account for 30–60 days. The largest source of short-term business financing.
Accruals	Employees and government	Free	Result from the fact that wages (employees) and taxes (government) are paid at discrete points in time after the service has been rendered. Hard to manipulate this source of financing.
II. Negotiated sources			
Bank loans	Chartered banks	Prime plus a small risk premium	Not common. Little variation in the stated rates, since unsecured loans are not available to risky firms.
Commercial paper	Investment dealers, other businesses, individuals, insurance companies, and other financial institutions.	Slightly below the prime rate of interest.	An unsecured short-term promissory note issued only by the most financially sound companies. It may be placed with or by investment dealers.
Customer advances	Customers having an interest in helping the firm survive.	Negotiable	Customers make advance payments on all or a portion of their planned purchases.
Private loans	Interested parties such as the firm's shareholders.	Negotiable	Extension of credit to the firm by an interested or concerned party.
Nondomestic borrowings	International money markets	Current rate in that market.	Exposes the borrower to exchange rate risks.

Summary

This chapter has described the more common sources of unsecured short-term financing for the business firm. Spontaneous sources of short-term unsecured financing result from the firm's normal business operations. Accounts payable, which are created by open-account purchases, are the primary source of short-term funds for the business firm. The terms of trade credit extended a firm may differ with respect to the credit period, cash discounts, cash discount period, and the beginning of the credit period. Each of these factors affects the firm's purchase decisions, although typically credit terms are standardized within a given industry.

Although there is no explicit cost associated with trade credit, there is an implied cost when a cash discount is offered. The cost of foregoing cash discounts affects the firm's decisions as to which suppliers to patronize as well as whether the discounts should be foregone. Policies with respect to cash discounts must be evaluated in light of the firm's ability to stretch accounts payable. Accruals, typically of wages or taxes, represent another spontaneous source of short-term funds. By accruing wages and taxes, the firm in essence delays payment for certain services. A firm should attempt to accrue as much as possible in light of certain behavioural and legal constraints.

Nonbank sources of unsecured short-term funds include the sale of commercial paper, customer advances, and private loans. Commercial paper can be issued only by large, financially strong firms. The other alternatives may be available to any firm regardless of its size. The cost of borrowing through the sale of commercial paper is generally lower than any alternate form of negotiated short-term unsecured borrowing.

Questions

11.1 What are the two key sources of spontaneous short-term financing for the business firm? Why are these sources considered spontaneous, and how are they related to the firm's sales? Do they normally have an explicit cost?

11.2 What are "credit terms"? How are credit periods, cash discounts, cash discount periods, and the beginning of a credit period defined?

11.3 What is a net period? What sort of payment is it concerned with?

11.4 What is meant by seasonal dating? Why is this sometimes considered advantageous to both the vendor and the purchaser of merchandise?

11.5 What are some of the labels used to designate the beginning of a credit period?

11.6 What costs are associated with the extension and use of trade credit? Who pays the cost of trade credit—the vendor or the purchaser? How?

11.7 Is there a cost associated with taking a cash discount? Is there any cost associated with foregoing a cash discount? Why or why not?

11.8 How is the decision whether to take a cash discount affected by the firm's opportunity cost of short-term funds?

11.9 What are accruals? What items are most commonly accrued by the firm? How attractive are accruals as a source of financing to the firm?

11.10 What factors must the firm consider in evaluating the use of accruals to obtain interest-free financing?

11.11   How is commercial paper used for raising short-term funds? Who can issue commercial paper? Who buys commercial paper? How is it sold?

11.12   Why is the cost of financing with commercial paper quite often less than the prime lending rate? Why don't firms raise all their short-term funds through the sale of commercial paper?

Problems

11.1   Determine when a firm must make payment for purchases made on the 25th day of November under each of the following credit terms.
a.   Net 30
b.   Net 30 EOM
c.   Net 45 MOM
d.   COD
e.   CBD

11.2   Determine the cost of foregoing discounts under each of the following terms of sale.
a.   2/10 net 30
b.   1/10 net 30
c.   2/10 net 45
d.   3/10 net 45
e.   1/10 net 60
f.   3/10 net 30
g.   4/10 net 180

11.3   Ann Daniels works in accounts payable for Penrod Industries. She has attempted to convince her boss to take advantage of the 3/10 net 45 discounts most suppliers offer, but her boss argues that the 3-percent discount is less costly than a short-term loan at 8 percent. Prove that either Ann or her boss is incorrect.

11.4   Upon accepting the position of chief executive officer and chairman of Canadian Cash Register, Robert Adamson changed the firm's weekly payday from Monday afternoon to the following Friday afternoon. The firm's weekly payroll was $10 million, and the cost of short-term funds was 9 percent. If the effect of this change was to delay cheque clearing by one week, what annual savings, if any, were realized here? Assume a 50-week year for computational purposes.

11.5   Stick Enterprises has obtained a 90-day bank loan at an annual interest rate of 12 percent. If the loan is for $10,000, how much interest (in dollars) will the firm pay?

11.6   Commercial paper is usually sold at a discount. Bell Ltd. has just sold an issue of 90-day commercial paper with a face value of $1,000,000. The firm has received $985,222.
a.   What effective *annual* rate will the firm pay for financing with commercial paper?
b.   If a brokerage fee of $9,612 has been charged by an investment dealer for selling the issue, what effective interest charge will the firm pay?

Suggested Readings

Baxter, Nevins D., *The Commercial Paper Market* (Princeton, N.J.: Princeton University Press, 1964).
Brosky, John J., *The Implicit Cost of Trade Credit and Theory of Optimal Terms of Sale* (New York: Credit Research Foundation, 1969).

Herbst, Anthony F., "A Factor Analysis Approach to Determining the Relative Endogeneity of Trade Credit," *Journal of Finance* 29 (September 1974), pp. 1087–1103.

Keehn, Richard H., "A Note on the Cost of Trade Credit and the Discriminatory Effects of Monetary Policy," *Journal of Finance* 29 (December 1974), pp. 1581–1582.

Laffer, Arthur B., "Trade Credit and the Money Market," *Journal of Political Economy* 78 (March-April 1970).

Little, J., *Euro-Dollars: The Money Market Gypsies* (New York: Harper & Row, 1975).

Robichek, Alexander A. and Stewart C. Myers, *Optimal Financing Decisions* (Englewood Cliffs, N.J.: Prentice-Hall, 1965), chap. 7.

———, Teichroew and J. M. Jones, "Optimal Short-Term Financing Decisions," *Management Science* 23 (September 1965), pp. 1–36.

Schwartz, Robert A., "An Economic Analysis of Trade Credit," *Journal of Financial and Quantitative Analysis* 9 (September 1974), pp. 643–658.

Stancill, James McN., *The Management of Working Capital* (Scranton, Pa.: Intext, 1971), chap. 6.

Chapter 12

SOURCES OF SECURED SHORT-TERM FINANCING

In Canada, most of the short-term credit needs of most Canadian businesses are provided by the chartered banks. Furthermore, it is customary for the Canadian chartered banks to require security for bank loans, unless the business borrower is in an extremely strong financial position. In general, the amount that a bank will lend to a firm depends on the amount of risk capital (equity) invested in that firm. A general heuristic rule used by the Canadian banking sector is to lend no more than one or two dollars for each dollar of risk capital (common equity) invested in the borrowing firm. The factoring and commercial financing firms supplement bank borrowings to Canadian businesses. They advance funds not only on the borrower's balance sheet ratios but also on the borrower's potential for profitable growth, the borrower's managerial capabilities, and the quality of the borrower's available security.

This chapter has six basic sections. The first section briefly discusses the nature and characteristics of secured short-term loans to business. The second and third sections deal with bank and nonbank sources of secured short-term funds, respectively. The fourth section discusses how accounts receivable may be used to obtain short-term funds. Both the use of accounts receivable as collateral for a short-term loan and the outright sale, or *factoring*, of accounts receivable are discussed in this section. The fifth section presents a discussion of the various methods of using inventories as collateral for short-term loans. The final section describes some other methods of securing short-term loans. A summary table depicting the key information on each of the sources of secured short-term financing is included as Table 12.3, at the end of the chapter.

Characteristics of Secured Short-Term Loans

A *secured loan* is a loan for which the lender requires *collateral*.* The collateral most commonly takes the form of a current asset, such as accounts receivable or inventory. The lender obtains a security interest in the collateral through the execution of a contract (security agreement) between it and the borrower. The security agreement indicates the collateral held against the loan.

The terms of the loan against which the security is held are attached to or are part of the security agreement. They specify the conditions required for the security interest to be removed, along with the interest rate on the loan, repayment dates, and other loan provisions. Although many people argue that holding collateral as security reduces the risk of the loan, lenders often do not view loans in this way. They recognize that by having an interest in collateral they can reduce losses in the instance the borrower defaults; however, as far as changing the probability that the borrower will default, the presence of collateral has little impact. Lenders require collateral because they want to be able to recover some portion of the loan proceeds in the event that default occurs. They do not want to have to administer and liquidate collateral; the lender would like to be repaid as scheduled. Also, a security requirement is not cost free. That is, the lender incurs the costs of inconvenience and administrative expense when he or she loans funds on a secured basis.

The remainder of this section presents a brief discussion of security registration requirements, the common types of security interests, and the nature of acceptable collateral for secured short-term loans.

SECURITY REGISTRATION REQUIREMENTS

The conditions under which credit is granted and the requirement for the registration of security requirements are under provincial jurisdiction. However, since federal legislation supersedes provincial legislation, federal requirements are applicable to those institutions under federal jurisdiction. Thus, all of the Canadian chartered banks operate under provisions, such as Section 88, of the Federal Bank Act.

While the taking of security has always been relatively easy and straightforward for the banking sector, it has not always been the case for the nonbanking sector. For example, in Ontario there were a number of statutes that required different and administratively cumbersome registration procedures for the taking of the various types of personal property as security.† With the recent passage of provincial legislation, based on the U.S. Uniform Commercial Code, there is now a standardized and simplified procedure for the general assignment (taking) of security for loans in Ontario. In all the other provinces, lenders continue to use their own general assignment agreements for

---

*The terms *security* and *collateral* are used interchangeably to refer to the items a borrower uses to back up a loan. Loan security or collateral may be any asset against which a lender, as a result of making a loan, has a legal claim that is exercisable if the borrower defaults on some provision of the loan. If the borrrower defaults, the lender can sell the security or collateral in order to satisfy his or her claim against the borrower. Some of the more technical aspects of loan defaults are presented in Chapter 26.
†Personal property includes such items as inventory, book debts (e.g., accounts receivable), marketable securities, equipment, and consumer goods.

the taking of loan security. However, in all provinces, if a general assignment agreement is to be legally effective, it must be registered with the appropriate registry office, and it must be publicly disclosed by being published in the financial press.

TYPES OF SECURITY INTERESTS

Three basic types of security interest are normally used in secured short-term loans to business borrowers. They are the floating lien, the trust receipt, and the warehouse receipt loan.

Floating Liens   A *floating lien* represents a general claim on a group of assets.* In the case of inventory, a floating lien provides the lender with collateral consisting of whatever items are in inventory at a given point in time. Specific items or accounts are not identified by serial number or debtor; rather, the lender has a claim on all items in the collateral grouping specified. Floating liens are useful when the collateral is constantly turning over and the dollar value of the average item of collateral is rather low. In this situation, the cost of specifically identifying and keeping track of each item of collateral would be prohibitive.

From the lender's standpoint, the floating lien is ideal for a firm that maintains, on the average, a fairly constant level of collateral. The collateral under the floating lien remains in the hands of the borrower, who also retains title to it. Since floating liens are so general, lenders typically will not lend heavily against them. Another reason for the small amount lent against this type of collateral is the expense and inconvenience associated with the liquidation of the collateral if the borrower defaults.

Trust Receipts   A *trust receipt loan* is a loan made against specific collateral that remains in the possession of the borrower. This type of arrangement can be made with respect to any asset, such as inventory or accounts receivable. A trust receipt loan backed by inventory is commonly referred to as *floor planning*. The lender, in this arrangement, takes a lien on the specific assets used as collateral. These assets are specifically identified in the security agreement either by serial numbers or by account names. The borrower normally retains title to or possession of the collateral.

The lender, in this arrangement, places *trust* in the borrower's integrity, and expects the borrower to provide notification immediately upon liquidation of any of the collateral. The borrower, upon the sale of collateral, must remit a certain amount of the proceeds to the lender or give additional collateral for the loan. If the borrower were to collect cash for the collateral and not remit funds to the lender, the lender would be holding *bogus collateral*.

In order to police trust receipt loans, the lender normally makes periodic checks on the borrower, taking an inventory of the collateral. If certain items of collateral cannot be found, the borrower is said to have broken the trust and can be considered in default of the loan.

---

*The term *lien* is a legal term meaning a claim on the property of another, such as a security interest against the payment of a legal debt. This is also commonly referred to as a *floating charge debenture*.

Trust receipt loans are typically made when a borrower has collateral that can be easily identified and each item has a reasonably large dollar value. This situation makes the trust receipt loan feasible; otherwise, a floating lien may have to be used. Since specific collateral can be more easily identified than a general claim (i.e., a floating lien), lenders are apt to lend a larger amount against a given amount of collateral under a trust receipt than under a floating lien arrangement. The most important consideration from the point of view of the lender is whether the borrower is trustworthy.

Warehouse Receipt Loans   The *warehouse receipt loan* is typically a loan secured with inventory. The borrower cannot sell any of the collateral without the lender's written permission. Typically, permission to sell an item held as collateral against this type of loan is granted only after the loan has been partially or fully repaid. The warehouse receipt loan provides the lender with the best position with respect to collateral—he or she has direct control over its disposition. This type of loan involves greater clerical costs than the floating lien; the increased cost is carried by the borrower. A lender is more likely to lend a larger amount against inventory under a warehouse receipt arrangement than under the other forms of security agreements mentioned earlier. Warehouse receipt loans will be discussed in more detail in the discussion of inventory as collateral.

WHAT CONSTITUTES ACCEPTABLE COLLATERAL?

A number of factors must be highlighted with respect to the characteristics desirable in collateral for secured short-term loans. These factors include the life of the collateral, the liquidity of the collateral, and the percentage advance.

The Life of the Collateral   Lenders of secured short-term funds prefer collateral that has a life closely related to the term of the loan. This requirement assures the lender that the security is sufficiently liquid to satisfy the loan in the event of a default. For short-term loans, the likely candidates as collateral are a firm's short-term or current assets, such as accounts receivable, inventories, and marketable securities. The use of fixed assets is better for long-term loans.

The strategy of securing short-term loans with current assets and long-term loans with fixed assets is similar to the aggressive strategy presented in Chapter 7, which suggested financing seasonal needs (primarily current assets) with short-term funds and financing permanent needs (primarily fixed assets) with long-term funds. By closely aligning the maturity (i.e., turnover) of the collateral with the loan maturity, the lender is assured of protection throughout the life of the loan and is somewhat assured that his or her funds can be readily recovered through liquidation of the collateral in the event that the borrower defaults on the loan.

The Liquidity of the Collateral   Another important consideration for the lender in evaluating possible collateral is its liquidity. Although current assets are the most common candidate as collateral for short-term loans, not all current assets are equally desirable. The desirability of various current assets is determined largely by the borrower's line of business. From our previous discussions of ratio analysis, we know that even within a given industry the liquidities of current assets often differ. Generally, the less acceptable collateral a firm has in the form of current assets, the less short-term money the firm is able to borrow on a secured basis.

Percentage Advances   Having determined the acceptable collateral of a given firm, the lender must determine what amount he or she is willing to lend against the value of this collateral, where typically this collateral value is taken to be the lower of historical cost or net realizable value. The desirable *percentage advance* is normally between 30 and 90 percent of the book value of collateral. It varies not only according to the type of collateral, but also according to the type of security interest being taken.

Percentage advances are low for floating liens and higher for trust receipt and warehouse receipt loans. They are low if the collateral is not very liquid and larger if the collateral is highly liquid. By accepting only a portion of the firm's current assets as collateral, the lender can isolate the faster-turning items, against which to make larger percentage advances. By selecting only acceptable assets and making loans equal to only certain percentages of the collateral's value, the lender adjusts the potential loss on the loan to an acceptable level. The lender can also set the interest rate at a level that provides adequate compensation for the probable risk attached to the loan.

Bank Sources of Secured Short-Term Funds

The Canadian chartered banks usually lend on a negotiated secured short-term basis to business firms.* To meet the competition from foreign banks operating in Canada, the chartered banks have been providing term loans (loans with maturities exceeding one year). The two major types of loans made by the chartered banks to business firms are the short-term self-liquidating working capital loan and the general working capital loan.

Self-liquidating working capital loans are intended merely to carry the firm through seasonal peaks in financing needs attributed primarily to buildups of inventory and accounts receivable. It is expected that as inventories and receivables are converted into cash, the funds needed to retire these loans will automatically be generated. In other words, the use to which the borrowed money is put provides the mechanism through which the loan is repaid. On the other hand, the *general working capital loan* is not self-liquidating, and therefore must be repaid from general profitability.

Banks lend short-term funds in three basic ways—(1) through notes, (2) through lines of credit, and (3) through revolving credit agreements. Each of these sources of funds is discussed below.

*No single firm (or industry) accounts for a significant share of the loans of the five major banks, because of their extremely large asset base. For example, the largest Canadian chartered bank, the Royal Bank of Canada, had assets that exceeded $50 billion in September 1979. Furthermore, the Royal Bank of Canada, the Canadian Imperial Bank of Commerce, the Bank of Montreal, the Bank of Nova Scotia, and the Toronto Dominion Bank are all ranked among the world's 50 largest banks.

NOTES

A *single-payment loan* can be obtained from a chartered bank by a credit-worthy business borrower. Typically, this type of loan is a "one-shot" deal made when a borrower needs additional funds for a short period but does not believe that this need will continue. The instrument resulting from this type of short-term loan is a *note*, which must be signed by the borrower. The note states the terms of the loan, which include the length of the loan (i.e., the maturity date) and the interest rate charged. This type of short-term note generally has a maturity of 30–90 days. The interest charged on the note is generally stated as a fixed percentage, tied in some fashion to the prime interest rate.

The *prime interest rate* is the lowest rate of interest charged on business loans by the Canadian chartered banks. The prime rate fluctuates with changing supply and demand relationships for short-term funds and is very dependent upon the rediscount rate set by the Bank of Canada.

Banks typically determine the rate charged on loans to various borrowers by adding some type of risk premium to the prime rate to adjust it for the borrower's "riskiness." This riskiness is a composite of the perceived business and financial riskiness of the borrower. The premium may be anything from 0 percent to 4 or more percent, although most secured short-term notes carry premiums of less than 2 percent.

LINES OF CREDIT

A *line of credit* is an agreement between a chartered bank and a business firm that states the amount of short-term borrowing the bank will make available to the borrower. A line of credit agreement is typically made for a period of one year and often places certain constraints on the borrower. A line of credit agreement is *not a guaranteed loan*, but indicates that if the bank has sufficient funds available it will allow the borrower to owe it up to a certain amount of money. The major attraction of a line of credit from the bank's point of view is that it eliminates the need to examine the credit-worthiness of a customer each time it borrows money.

The application to obtain a line of credit may require the borrower to submit such documents as its cash budget, its pro forma income statement, its pro forma balance sheet, and its recent financial statements. The bank will review these statements in order to determine if the firm needs the line of credit it is requesting and, if so, whether it will be able to repay the funds it seeks an option to borrow. If the bank finds the customer acceptable, the line of credit will be extended. A few characteristics of lines of credit require further explanation.

Interest Rates   The interest charge on a line of credit is normally stated as the *prime rate plus x percent*. A line-of-credit agreement is normally for a one-year period, and it is quite likely that the prime rate will change during this period. Thus, as the prime rate changes, the interest rate charged on new and old borrowing will automatically change.* The amount in excess of the prime interest rate a borrower is charged depends on its credit-worthiness.

---

*Since the banks not only adjust the interest rate charged on *new borrowing*, but they also adjust the rate charged against *outstanding loans* for changes in the prime rate, the borrower is not assured that the rate of interest at the time of borrowing will remain fixed over the maturity of the note. Thus, if the prime rate changes, so will the rate of interest charged over the remaining life of any loans outstanding.

EXAMPLE   The Raine Company is negotiating a line of credit with the Second Canadian Bank. After evaluating the Raine Company's financial statements, the bank sets an interest rate for the line of credit that is 2 percent more than the prime rate. The prime rate is currently $7\frac{1}{2}$ percent, so the Raine Company will have to pay $9\frac{1}{2}$ percent for current borrowing. If the prime rate drops to 7 percent in the future, the interest charge on Raine's borrowing will drop to 9 percent.

Interest Rate Computations   Once the rate of interest charged a given customer has been established, the method of computing interest should be determined. Interest can be paid when a loan matures or in advance. If interest is paid when a loan matures, the actual rate of interest paid (i.e., the *effective rate of interest*) is equal to the stated interest rate. When interest is paid in advance, it is deducted from the loan so that the borrower actually receives less money than it requested. Paying interest in advance therefore raises the effective interest rate above the stated rate.

EXAMPLE   Bressler Limited wants to borrow $10,000 at 8 percent for one year. If the interest on the loan is paid at maturity, the firm will pay $800 (.08 · $10,000) for the use of the $10,000 for the year. The effective rate of interest will therefore be

$$\frac{\$800}{\$10,000} = 8.00 \text{ percent}$$

If the money is borrowed at the same rate but interest is paid in advance, the firm will still pay $800 in interest, but it will receive only $9,200 ($10,000 − $800). The effective rate of interest in this case is

$$\frac{\$800}{\$9,200} = 8.70 \text{ percent}$$

Paying interest in advance thus makes the effective interest rate greater than the stated rate. Loans on which interest is paid in advance are often called *discount loans*. Most chartered bank loans to business require the interest payment at maturity.

The Amount of the Line   The amount of a line of credit is *the maximum amount the firm can owe the bank* at any point in time. Technically, it is possible for a firm to *borrow* more than the amount of its line of credit, but at no time can the *loan balance* exceed the line of credit.

EXAMPLE   The Holcomb Company has a line of credit of $1 million with its bank. The borrowing against this line of credit during the first six months of the year, along with cumulative borrowing, is given in Table 12.1. Although Holcomb's loan balance never exceeded its $1 million line of credit, it borrowed a total of $1.2 million during the six-month period.*

---

*If the average loan balance were to exceed the maximum line of credit, it would indicate that at some point during the period the firm borrowed more than the amount permitted by the line of credit. If the firm owed exactly the maximum amount allowed over the entire period, its average borrowing would equal that amount.

Table 12.1 The Holcomb Company's Borrowing Against Its Line of Credit

Month	Transaction Borrow	Repay	Loan balance
January	$ 200,000	0	$200,000
February	$ 600,000	0	$800,000
March	0	$ 200,000	$600,000
April	0	$ 100,000	$500,000
May	$ 400,000	0	$900,000
June	0	$ 900,000	0
Totals	$1,200,000	$1,200,000	

Restrictive Provisions   A bank normally includes certain restrictions as part of a line-of-credit agreement. The most common restrictions concern operating changes, compensating balances, and annual cleanups.

Operating Changes   In a line-of-credit agreement, a bank may retain the right to revoke the line if any major changes in the firm's operations occur. For example, the bank may reserve the right to approve any shifts in key managerial personnel or the nature of the firm's operations before they are initiated. It does this because changes in personnel or operations may affect the future success and debt servicing ability of the firm and could alter its status as an acceptable credit risk.

Compensating Balances   In order to ensure that the borrower will be a good customer, a short-term bank loan may require the borrower to maintain a compensating balance in a demand deposit account (i.e., a chequing account balance) equal to a certain percentage of the amount borrowed. Compensating balances of 10 percent are normally required. A compensating balance not only forces the borrower to be a good customer of the bank, but it *may* also raise the interest cost to the borrower, thereby increasing the bank's earnings.

EXAMPLE   A company has borrowed $1 million under a line-of-credit agreement. It must pay a stated interest charge of 8 percent and maintain a compensating balance of 20 percent of the funds borrowed, or $200,000, in its chequing account. Thus, it actually receives the use of only $800,000. In order to use the $800,000 for a year, the firm pays $80,000 (.08 · $1,000,000). The effective interest rate on the funds is therefore 10 percent ($80,000 ÷ $800,000), 2 percent more than the stated rate of 8 percent.

If the firm normally maintains a balance of $200,000 or more in its chequing account, then the effective interest cost will equal the stated interest rate of 8 percent. If the firm normally maintains a $100,000 balance in its chequing account, then only an additional $100,000 will have to be tied up, leaving it with $900,000 ($1,000,000 − $100,000) of usable funds. The effective interest cost in this case would be 8.89 percent ($80,000 ÷ $900,000). A compensating balance raises the cost of borrowing *only* if it is larger than the firm's normal cash balance.

Annual Cleanups   In order to ensure that money lent under a line of credit agreement is actually being used to finance seasonal needs, many banks require an annual cleanup. This means that the borrower must have a loan balance of zero for a certain number of days during the year. Sometimes more than one annual cleanup is required. Forcing the borrower to carry a zero loan balance for a certain period of time ensures that the short-term loans do not turn into long-term loans. A look back at Table 12.1 shows that the Holcomb Company cleaned up its loans during the month of June.

All the characteristics of a line-of-credit agreement are negotiable to some extent. A prospective borrower should attempt to negotiate a line of credit with the most favourable interest rate, for an optimal amount of funds, and with a minimum of restrictive provisions. The lender will attempt to get a good return with maximum safety.

REVOLVING CREDIT AGREEMENTS

A revolving credit agreement is nothing more than a *guaranteed line of credit*. It is guaranteed in the sense that the chartered bank making the arrangement guarantees the borrower that a specified amount of funds will be made available regardless of the tightness of money. It is not uncommon for a revolving credit agreement to be for a period greater than a year; two- or three-year agreements may be made.* The requirements for a revolving credit agreement are similar to those for a line of credit.

There are additional fees that may be levied by the bank on both revolving credit and line-of-credit arrangements. The first is referred to as a *commitment fee*. This fee is usually set at about $\frac{1}{2}$–$\frac{3}{4}$ percent (i.e., 0.005–0.0075) of the total line of the credit. Thus, it is independent of the amount of the credit actually used by the borrower. The second is referred to as a *standby fee*. This fee is calculated as a specified percentage of the unused portion of the credit. Thus, a firm may obtain a credit at prime, but the effective cost may be equal to prime plus 2 or 3 percent when all of the other fees are included.

SECURITY REQUIREMENTS

Many types of assets are acceptable as collateral to the Canadian chartered banks. In general, the forms of security accepted and the procedures followed by the chartered banks must conform to the provisions given in the Bank Act.

Section 88 of the Bank Act specifies that for manufacturing firms the chartered banks can lend on the security of both existing and future inventory. Under this section, a firm does not have to relinquish its control over the inventory it uses as security for the loan. Furthermore, the bank retains the same rights and priorities as if it had acquired a warehouse receipt or bill of lading.

Section 86 permits the chartered banks to accept warehouse receipts or bills of lading as security for a loan. These can cover any goods, wares, or merchandise, whether under

---

*Many authors classify the revolving credit agreement as a form of *intermediate-term financing*, where intermediate-term financing is defined as having a maturity of one to ten years. In this text, the intermediate-term financing classification is not used; only short-term and long-term classifications are made. Since many revolving credit agreements are often for more than one year, they can be classified as a form of long-term financing; however, they are discussed in this chapter due to their similarity to the line-of-credit agreement.

the control of a shipper or stored in an independent warehouse. Section 82 permits the chartered banks to accept hydrocarbons both in storage and in the ground as security for development loans to oil and natural gas producers.

Finally, the chartered banks can also accept pledged (or assigned) accounts receivable as security for bank loans. In fact, this is the most commonly used method of securing bank loans.

Bank loans are generally granted under Section 88 of the Bank Act as follows. First, a notice of intention to provide security under the section is registered with the provincial office of the Bank of Canada. This is necessary in order to establish that the bank has legal rights over the assets to be used as collateral. Second, the borrower must complete an application form. And finally, before the loan is officially approved, the borrower must sign a collateral security agreement and a loan agreement. In addition, subsequent to the granting of the loan, the bank may require the borrower to provide a statement of security. This statement reports on the status of the collateral at that point in time.

FLOATING CHARGE DEBENTURES

By using a floating charge debenture, a chartered bank obtains an exercisable claim on all the assets of the borrower. This includes all assets currently owned or those subsequently acquired by the borrower, which at the time the loan was approved had not already been pledged as security by the borrower to other lenders. Since under this arrangement direct control of the assets used as security remains with the borrower, a chartered bank must protect itself against a deterioration in the collateral value of these assets. The bank obtains such protection by including specific covenants, such as the requirement for quarterly financial reports, in the trust indenture. Thus, when a borrower defaults on the terms of the loan, the bank's floating charge becomes a fixed claim on all the remaining assets of the borrower.

Nonbank Sources of Secured Short-Term Funds

The primary sources of secured short-term nonbank funds for business are the factoring and commercial finance companies.

COMMERCIAL FINANCE COMPANIES

A *commercial finance company* is a financial institution without a bank charter that normally makes loans secured with accounts receivable, inventories, floating charge debentures on all assets, or chattel mortgages on fixed assets. Commercial finance companies also finance the installment purchase of commercial and industrial equipment by business firms. Commercial finance companies make secured loans both on a short- and long-term basis to businesses. The commercial finance companies include such firms as Canadian Financial Company, Laurentide Industrial Finance, and Traders Group Limited.

Borrowers in need of short-term financing usually rely on their chartered banks. In general, only when a firm's unsecured and secured short-term borrowing power from the chartered banks is exhausted will the firm approach a commercial finance company for additional secured borrowing. Because the commercial finance company typically ends up with higher-risk borrowers, its interest charges on secured short-term loans are generally higher than the charges levied by the chartered banks. Another reason for the slightly higher charges of commercial finance companies is the fact that a portion of their financing is often obtained through chartered bank borrowing at wholesale rates (approximately equal to prime, or prime plus one-quarter of one percent). Note that commercial finance companies are not permitted to hold demand deposits.

"SPLIT FINANCING"

When a firm needs more funds than its bank is willing to loan, a chartered bank and a commercial finance company may jointly provide the funds. This joint financing of a firm's short-term financing needs is referred to as *split financing*.

EXAMPLE Malbaie Artisan Ltd. needs to obtain a $300,000 operating line of credit. Suppose that the maximum credit line that Second Canadian Bank is willing to extend is $100,000. Also, suppose that Quebec Comfin Ltd. is only willing to provide the additional $200,000 for the credit line on a participation (split-financing) basis with the Second Canadian Bank. A typical split-financing arrangement would be organized as follows. Second Canadian Bank would provide $100,000 (one-third of the credit line) and Quebec Comfin Ltd. would provide the additional $200,000 (two-thirds of the credit line). Since Second Canadian Bank's loan would be guaranteed by Quebec Comfin, the bank would charge an interest rate of about 1 percent above prime. The bank would also be secured by a floating charge debenture on all of Malbaie Artisan's assets. Quebec Comfin would secure itself by taking an assignment of enough receivables, so that the total loan of $300,000 does not exceed 80–90 percent of the assigned receivables. Since the commercial finance company has a greater risk exposure than the bank, it would charge an interest rate of about $2\frac{1}{2}$ percent above prime.

The Use of Accounts Receivable As Collateral

Business firms commonly use two means of obtaining short-term financing with accounts receivable—pledging accounts receivable and factoring accounts receivable. Actually, only a pledge of accounts receivable creates a secured short-term loan; factoring really entails the "sale" of accounts receivable at a discount. Although factoring is not actually a form of secured short-term borrowing, it is discussed in this section since it involves the use of accounts receivable to obtain needed short-term funds.

PLEDGING (ASSIGNING) ACCOUNTS RECEIVABLE

A pledge or an assignment of accounts receivable is often used to secure a short-term loan. Because accounts receivable are normally quite liquid, they are an attractive form of short-term loan collateral for chartered banks, commercial finance companies, and factoring companies.

Types of Pledges   Accounts receivable are normally pledged on a *selective basis*. The prospective lender analyzes the past payment records of the firm's accounts to determine which accounts represent acceptable loan collateral. A lender will generally advance money only against those accounts determined to be acceptable credit risks. The lender can minimize his or her risk by being selective with respect to those accounts accepted as collateral. A lender is likely to advance as much as 90 percent (normally 80 percent) of the collateral's value against a pledge of selected accounts.

A second method of pledging accounts receivable is to take a lien on all the firm's accounts receivable. This type of *floating lien* arrangement is normally used when a firm has many accounts that, on the average, have only a small dollar value. In this case, the cost of evaluating each account separately in order to determine its acceptability would not be warranted. Instead, the lender places a lien on all the firm's accounts receivable. The lender in this situation keeps track of the total dollar amount of pledged accounts. Due to the difficulty of specifically identifying each item of collateral and therefore of policing this arrangement, the percentage advanced against a pledge of accounts receivable in general (a floating lien) is normally less than 50 percent of the book value of the accounts. This situation is more risky from the lender's viewpoint, since the borrower has opportunities to misrepresent accounts.

The Pledging Process   The process of pledging accounts receivable will be described with respect to pledging selected accounts, since this situation provides more scope for in-depth analysis. The four major steps in the pledging process are the selection of acceptable accounts, the adjustment of acceptable accounts, the determination of the advance, and the notification of and the collection of pledged accounts.

The Selection of Acceptable Accounts   The lender must first evaluate a firm's accounts receivable to determine their desirability as collateral. One consideration is whether the accounts are of sufficient size to warrant consideration as specific collateral. If the firm has many small accounts, the lender may extend only a floating lien.

Assuming that the firm has accounts of sufficient size to warrant consideration as specific collateral, the lender will investigate the firm's accounts receivable in order to determine which accounts are acceptable as collateral for a loan. The investigation will involve analyzing the past payment patterns of the various credit customers. The accounts receivable from those customers who appear to be good credit risks will be accepted as collateral. The lender may verify the existence and amount of the accounts by requiring a copy of the invoices. A list of the acceptable accounts, along with the billing dates and amounts, will be made by the lender. Typically a mark of some sort will be placed next to each pledged account in the borrowing firm's accounts receivable ledger.

If the borrowing firm requests a loan for only a fixed amount, the lender will need to select only enough accounts to secure the funds requested. Where the borrower desires the maximum loan available, the lender will evaluate all the accounts in order to determine the maximum amount of acceptable collateral.

EXAMPLE   The Second Canadian Bank is analyzing the Crowe Company's accounts receivable ledger in order to find acceptable collateral for a pledge of accounts receivable. Each of Crowe's accounts receivable, along with its age and its average payment period, is given in Table 12.2. Since Crowe extends credit terms of 2/10 net 30 EOM, the bank eliminates from further consideration all accounts that are currently overdue (i.e., whose age is greater than 30 days). This immediately eliminates the accounts of customers C, E, and I.

The second step in the bank's evaluation process is to analyze the historical payment patterns of the customers. After calculating the average payment period for each customer (given in the last column of Table 12.2), the Second Canadian Bank decides to eliminate customer B, whose account, although not currently overdue, normally requires 60 days to collect. Having eliminated the accounts of customers B, C, E, and I, the bank is left with $45,000 of acceptable accounts from customers A, D, F, G, and H (who owe $10,000, $4,000, $6,000, $14,000, and $11,000, respectively). The Crowe Company therefore has $45,000 of acceptable accounts receivable collateral. Each account used as collateral will be marked in the Crowe Company's ledger, and a list of the payment dates and amounts will be kept by the Second Canadian Bank.

Table 12.2   The Crowe Company's Accounts Receivable

Customer	Account receivable	Age[a]	Average payment period
A	$10,000	20 days	35 days
B	8,000	5 days	60 days
C	15,000	50 days	45 days
D	4,000	14 days	30 days
E	3,000	70 days	60 days
F	6,000	10 days	20 days
G	14,000	3 days	10 days
H	11,000	23 days	10 days
I	3,000	45 days	45 days

[a]Number of days since beginning of credit period.

The Adjustment of Acceptable Accounts   After selecting the acceptable accounts, the lender will normally adjust the dollar value of these accounts for expected returns or allowances. If a customer whose account has been pledged returns merchandise or receives some type of allowance, such as a cash discount for early payment, the amount of the collateral is automatically reduced. For protection from such occurrences, the lender will normally reduce the value of the acceptable collateral by a fixed percentage.

EXAMPLE   The $45,000 of acceptable accounts receivable selected by the Second Canadian Bank from the Crowe Company's books must be adjusted for returns and allowances. The bank decides, after evaluating the company's accounts, that a 5-percent adjustment is appropriate. After this adjustment, the Crowe Company has acceptable collateral of $42,750 [i.e., $45,000 · (1 − .05)].

The Determination of the Advance   Once the lender has determined the acceptable accounts and made adjustments for returns and allowances, the percentage to be advanced against the collateral must be determined based on the lender's overall evaluation of the quality of the acceptable receivables and the expected cost of their liquidation. For selected accounts receivable, this percentage will range between 50 and 90 percent, with banks near the lower end of the range and finance companies near the higher end. The more confident the lender is about the quality of the accounts, the larger the percentage advance that will normally be extended. However, since the lender in the event of default will have to absorb certain paperwork costs and the additional cost of liquidating the pledged accounts, he or she will rarely advance more than 90 percent of the value of accounts.

EXAMPLE   After a reexamination of the Crowe Company's acceptable accounts receivable *and* general operations, the Second Canadian Bank decides to advance 50 percent of the value of the adjusted acceptable collateral. This means that the bank will lend the company $21,375 (i.e., $42,750 · .50).

Notification and Collection   Pledges of accounts receivable are normally made on a *nonnotification* basis. This means that the customer whose account has been pledged is not notified of this action. Instead, the customer continues to remit payments to the firm. If a pledge of accounts receivable is made on a *notification* basis, the customer is notified to remit payments directly to the lender. Borrowers prefer nonnotification arrangements since their customers may construe the fact that their accounts have been pledged to mean that the firm is in financial difficulty. Although a notification arrangement is safer from the lender's viewpoint, the lender is normally willing to trust the borrower and lend on a nonnotification basis.

The nonnotification arrangement is a type of trust receipt loan, since the borrower collects and remits payments received on pledged accounts to the lender. In essence, the lender *trusts* that the borrower will remit payments on pledged accounts as they are received. If the borrower receives payment and does not remit it to the lender, the trust is broken and part of the collateral held by the lender becomes nonexistent. In order to police a trust arrangement, the lender will frequently check to see if the customers whose accounts have been pledged and are currently listed as uncollected have actually paid any of these accounts. A broken trust arrangement can seriously damage the borrower's future borrowing prospects. As the lender receives payments of accounts, the loan principal is reduced by the amount collected.

The Cost of Pledges of Accounts Receivable   The stated cost of a pledge of accounts receivable is normally 2–5 percent above the prime rate. In addition to the stated interest rate, a service charge of up to 3 percent may be levied. Although the interest payment is expected to compensate the lender for loaning the money, the service charge is needed to cover the administrative costs incurred by the lender. These administrative costs result from the need to inspect accounts, keep records of pledged accounts, make entries as collections of accounts are received, and generally police the lending arrangement.

Assignments As a Continuous Source of Financing   Quite often, a firm will use assigning accounts receivable, as a continuous source of financing. As accounts are collected, new accounts acceptable to the lender are substituted, allowing the firm to maintain a relatively constant loan balance with the lender. If the lender finds all the firm's accounts receivable acceptable and continuously takes them as collateral, he or she ends up financing all the firm's accounts receivable. The firm may find this arrangement quite beneficial from a cost standpoint.

Once the amount of acceptable accounts, the percentage advance (i.e., the loan principal), the interest cost, and other factors have been agreed upon, a note specifying the terms of the assignment is drawn up and signed by both parties. At the same time, a lien is filed on the pledged accounts. A statement of the lien is normally attached to the note. As remittances are received against assigned accounts, the lender records these receipts, thereby reducing both the amount of collateral and the amount of loan principal.

FACTORING ACCOUNTS RECEIVABLE

In the United States, factoring accounts receivable involves the outright sale of accounts receivable to a factor or other financial institution.* In Canada, factoring essentially involves the administration of the credit process by a factor or commercial finance company for a client firm. In addition, Canadian factoring may include credit payment guarantees by the factor of the approved accounts receivable generated by a client firm; and it may include a provision that allows the client firm to draw advances (borrow) against uncollected (and not due) accounts. Thus, while factoring accounts receivable does not actually represent a short-term loan, the latter form of Canadian factoring is quite similar to borrowing with accounts receivable as collateral. It should also be noted that factoring in Canada is similar to factoring in the United States only when it involves the credit payment guarantee and the client borrowing option.

The Factor   Factoring was introduced into Canada in the seventeenth century when the Hudson Bay Company provided guarantees to English merchants that they would be paid for goods shipped to North America. That is, the Hudson Bay Company acted as a factor when it paid the British merchants and subsequently collected from customers in North America. Later, because of the long credit period required by purchasers of apparel and textiles, factoring became well established in these industries in both Canada and the United States.† In 1949, the Canadian factoring industry consisted of one firm, which had an annual volume of approximately

---

*The use of bank credit cards such as Chargex (VISA) and Master Charge by retailers has some similarity to factoring, since the vendor accepting the card is reimbursed at a discount, on a nonrecourse basis, for purchases made using the card. In addition, in Canada the credit-granting decision is made by the bank card company and is often made by the factor. The major difference between factoring and bank cards is the timing of payments. While the vendor accepting the bank card is paid immediately on deposit of the day's credit sale slips, the firm factoring its accounts receivable is not paid until either its customers pay their accounts or the factor's guaranteed payment date elapses.

†Because of the seasonal nature of the sales of clothing and other textile items, textiles must be produced in large quantities well in advance of the selling season. Manufacturers use seasonal datings; they send

$25 million. In 1979, the nine member firms of the Factors and Commercial Financing Conference of Canada Inc. accounted for most of the factoring industry's estimated volume of $1.2 billion.*

Although the factor is the primary factoring institution, some commercial finance companies also factor accounts receivable. Since the present Bank Act does not allow the chartered banks to engage in factoring activities directly, many of the chartered banks have become involved in factoring by obtaining an equity interest in factoring companies.†

USERS OF FACTORING

In Canada, most factoring clients have annual sales volumes of $1–$5 million. Few clients have sales volumes that exceed $25 million. Most of these clients are either young, growth-oriented firms or older firms experiencing renewed growth that need more funds than the chartered banks are willing to provide.

The Factoring Agreement   A factoring agreement is normally drawn up stating the exact conditions, charges, and procedures for factoring. Typically, firms that factor accounts do so on a continuing basis. The factoring agreement covers nonrecourse, notification, selection procedures, assignment provisions, factor's reserves, payment dates, advances and surpluses, and factoring costs. The emphasis in the following sections will be on guaranteed-payment factoring.

Nonrecourse   Guaranteed-payment factoring is done on a *nonrecourse basis*. This means that the factor agrees to accept all credit risks; if the guaranteed accounts turn out to be uncollectible, the factor must absorb the loss. Only on rare occasions are factoring agreements made *with recourse.* Pledges of accounts receivable can be likened to a recourse arrangement since, if the borrower were to default and the lender liquidated the pledged accounts receivable for less than the loan principal, the lender would still have recourse to the borrower as a general creditor.

Notification   Guaranteed-payment factoring is normally done on a notification basis. Since the factor is guaranteeing the accounts, it seems only reasonable that payments be made directly to him or her. The customers whose accounts have been factored may not be directly advised that their accounts have been factored; they may simply be asked to make cheques payable to the factor or to send them to a

---

merchandise to purchasers as soon as it is produced to avoid inventory carrying costs, but they do not require payment until after the selling season begins. They therefore end up with very high levels of receivables, which they factor in order to get working capital for use in supporting the production and inventory outlays required to meet the next season's demand.

*Presently, factoring is common in the following industries: clothing, shoes, carpets, sporting goods, hi-fi equipment, furniture, lumber, plumbing supplies, and yard goods.

†The pending revisions to the Bank Act, if and when passed, will probably allow the chartered banks to enter the factoring industry directly through subsidiary firms.

new address. Regardless of how a factored account is camouflaged, the factor normally receives payment directly from the customer. The degree of secrecy regarding the arrangement depends largely on the firm's expectations with respect to how its customers may react to the fact that their accounts have been factored. The degree of secrecy required is incorporated in the factoring agreement.

Selection Procedures   A factor, like a lender against a pledge of accounts receivable, chooses accounts for guarantee, selecting only those accounts that appear to be acceptable credit risks. Where factoring is to be on a continuing basis, the factor will actually make the firm's credit decisions, since this will guarantee the acceptability of accounts. This situation is quite common, especially in the textile and clothing manufacturing industries.

Assignment Provisions   For guaranteed-payment factoring, the factor obtains a claim to the accounts being factored (personal property) by using an agreement referred to as a *general assignment*. As discussed earlier in this chapter, the factor ensures that the general assignment is legally effective by registering the assignment at the appropriate provincial registry office.

Factor's Reserves   After a factor selects the accounts to be included in a factoring agreement, a certain percentage of the total accounts are set aside to cover any returns or allowances or potential disputes against the merchandise sold. If a purchaser finds goods damaged or somehow not as specified, he or she may return the merchandise, thereby eliminating all or part of a factored account receivable. The factor normally holds a reserve of 10–20 percent of the amount factored as protection against these situations. The reserve is most important when a factor makes advances against accounts (which will be discussed in a following section).

Payment Dates   A factoring agreement specifies the payment dates for factored accounts. Unlike U.S. practice, maturity factoring is not common in Canada.* For guaranteed-payment factoring, the Canadian factor's obligation is to remit to the client as accounts are collected; or to remit to the client should the client's customers become financially insolvent; or to pay to the client at a predetermined date all accounts remaining uncollected—whichever of the three occurs first. This settlement date is set from 15 to 120 days (normally 90 to 120 days) after the due date of the client's invoices. A guaranteed-payment date of 120 days can be illustrated as follows. If a firm extends credit terms of "net 30," the last day of the firm's credit period will be 30 days after the date of the credit sale. The factor's guaranteed-payment date will thus be 120 days after the last day of the firm's credit period, or in other words, it will be 150 days after the date of the credit sale.

---

*Maturity factoring is equivalent to guaranteed-payment factoring when the guaranteed-payment dates are the end of the client's credit periods. Apparently, the guaranteed-payment date is set at a date after the end of the client's credit period, because Canadian customers have a history of poorer payment habits than U.S. customers.

EXAMPLE   Ross Ltd. has sold five accounts to a factor. All the accounts were due September 30. Each account, its amount, and its status on September 30 are given in the following table:

Account	Amount	Status
A	$10,000	Collected Sept. 20
B	4,000	Collected Sept. 28
C	50,000	Collected Sept. 29
D	8,000	Uncollected
E	12,000	Collected Sept. 20

As of September 30, the factor has received payment from suppliers A, B, C, and E. He or she therefore has already taken a fee, or discount, on each account and has remitted the balance to Ross Ltd. If Ross's credit terms to all accounts were "net 30 days," and the factor's guaranteed-payment date was 90 days, then the factor would not have to remit the $8,000 due on account D to Ross Ltd. on September 30. If account D continues to remain unpaid, the factor would not have to remit the $8,000 due on account D, less the factoring fee on this account, to Ross Ltd. until December 26.

Advances and Surpluses   A factor typically sets up an account similar to a bank deposit account for each customer. As the factor receives payment or as the guaranteed-payment dates arrive, he or she deposits money into the firm's account. The firm is free to withdraw this money as needed. If the firm leaves the money in the account, a *surplus* will exist on which the factor may pay interest. In other instances, the firm may need more cash than is available in its account. In order to provide the firm with immediate cash, the factoring agreement may specify that the client may borrow up to 90 percent of the value of approved invoices immediately upon shipment of the goods, or at any time thereafter. Interest, of course, is charged on any advances received from a factor. Since such advances are common, the factor normally holds a reserve of at least 10 percent against factored accounts.[*]

Factoring Costs   Factoring costs include factoring commissions, interest on advances, and interest on surpluses.

Factoring Commissions   Factoring commissions are payments to the factor for administrative costs of credit checking and collections, as well as for the risk assumed when guaranteeing accounts without recourse. Factoring commissions are typically stated as a $\frac{7}{8}$–$1\frac{1}{2}$ percent discount from the face value of factored accounts receivable. For accounts of wholesale jobbers, the typical range of commissions is $\frac{3}{4}$–1 percent of the face value of the accounts receivable factored. The particular rate charged depends on type of busi-

---

[*]If the factor makes an advance against factored accounts and some of the merchandise sold to one of the factored accounts is returned, he or she could be left with insufficient loan collaterial and in effect be extending a partially unsecured loan to the firm. Since this situation is not desirable, the factor maintains a reserve.

ness, number and average dollar value of customer invoices, the terms of sale, the degree of customer credit risk, and the nature of the client's industry.

Interest on Advances   The interest charge levied on advances is generally 2–2½ percent above the prime rate. It is levied on the actual amount advanced, only from the time the advance is taken until the prearranged due date for repayment of the advance.

Interest on Surpluses   Often a factor does not pay interest on surpluses or positive account balances in a factoring account. If interest is paid, it is generally about one-fourth of 1 percent above prime.

EXAMPLE   The Graber Company has recently factored a number of accounts. The factor holds 10-percent reserve, charges a 1-percent factoring commission, and charges 1 percent per month interest (i.e., 12 percent per year) on advances, payable at the end of each month. Graber wishes to obtain an advance on a factored account having a book value of $1,000 and due in 30 days. The proceeds to the company are calculated as follows:

Book value of account	$1,000
Less: Reserve (10% · $1,000)	100
Less: Factoring commission (1% · $1,000)	10
Funds available for advance	$ 910

The firm receives $910 now and expects to eventually receive the $80 reserve. In addition, Graber will have to pay $9.10 in interest at the end of each month for which the advance is outstanding.

Export Factoring   Most factors offer their factoring services to Canadian exporters. By being a member of Factors Chain International, the Canadian factor can arrange a factoring agreement for the factor's exporting client with a correspondent factor in the buying customer's country. Presently, most of the export factoring arranged by Canadian factors involves exports to the U.S. market.

Advantages and Disadvantages of Factoring   Factoring has certain advantages that make it quite attractive to many firms. One advantage is the ability it gives the firm to *turn accounts receivable immediately into cash* without having to worry about repayment. When a firm receives an advance, it does not have to make repayment. Once the factor collects the account or repayment obligation due, it merely retains the money. Another advantage of factoring is that it ensures a *known pattern of cash flows*. A firm that factors its accounts knows that it will definitely receive the cash flows from the accounts (less a factoring fee) by a certain date. This simplifies the firm's cash-flow planning.

If factoring is undertaken on a continuous basis, so that all accounts are sold to the factor, a couple of other advantages result. One is the elimination of the firm's credit department. The factor takes over the firm's credit analysis function when it determines which accounts are acceptable credit risks. Another advantage is the elimination of the firm's collection department. Since the factor normally accepts all credit risks, he or she must pay any collection costs and absorb any losses. The net result of continuous factoring is the elimination of the credit function and its related costs from the firm.

The disadvantages of factoring are considered to be its cost, the potential sacrifice of liquidity, and the associated implication of financial weakness. The stated costs of factoring are obviously higher than bank borrowing costs, but in light of the cost savings resulting from the elimination of many administrative and credit outlays, the net cost may not be high for the protection received. The sale of accounts receivable in order to obtain cash for meeting short-term obligations can result in a liquidity squeeze, since the sale might represent the sacrifice of the firm's long-run liquidity to satisfy its short-term obligations. Such an action could create a gap in the firm's anticipated cash flows since the current accounts receivable could be virtually eliminated from the books. This may not be a valid problem when the firm continuously factors all of its accounts receivable.

The validity of the belief that factoring accounts receivable is a sign of financial weakness that may damage future business if the firm's customers learn about it is quite difficult to assess. Each factoring agreement is unique, and the advantages and disadvantages of factoring for given firms can only be evaluated in light of the terms of the specific agreements drawn up. In general, small firms that cannot afford to carry professional credit and collection people on their payroll often find factoring quite feasible.

The Use of Inventory As Collateral

The chartered banks, when lending to manufacturing firms, can either lend under Section 88 or they can use inventory as security. Since Section 88 lending results in lower administrative costs, both parties in a loan transaction prefer a loan under Section 88.

For nonbank business loans or bank loans to nonmanufacturing firms, Section 88 lending is not applicable. Thus, in these instances short-term business loans are often made with inventory used as security. The desirability of using inventory as security for these loans results from the fact that the book value of inventory is used as the collateral value, and the book value is often less than the inventory's market value. (This discrepancy between book and market values is especially pronounced during periods of double-digit inflation!)

As will be discussed next, not all types of inventories are equally desirable as collateral.

CHARACTERISTICS OF INVENTORY

The desirability of inventory as collateral depends on its type, its physical properties, and its marketability.

Types of Inventory   Chapter 10 gave a description of three basic types of inventory—raw-materials, work-in-process, and finished-goods inventories. All types of inventories may be offered as collateral for a short-term loan, but typically only raw-materials or finished-goods inventories are considered acceptable (gold is an exception).

Physical Properties   Often inventory has certain physical properties that make it unacceptable as collateral. *Perishability* is one property that may cause inventory to be unacceptable collateral. If an inventory's value declines merely with the passage of time or if it requires special storage conditions, it may not be desirable as collateral. *Specialized* items may also be of questionable use as collateral if the market for them is small. Another property to be considered is the *physical size* of inventory. Very large items may not be desirable as collateral due to the expense associated with their transportation and storage.

Marketability   The most important characteristic of inventory that is being considered as loan collateral is marketability. If an inventory can easily be sold in the future at a price equal to at least current book value, then it is probably desirable as collateral. The marketability of inventory, of course, depends upon its physical properties. A warehouse of peaches may be quite marketable, but if the cost of storing and selling the peaches is high, they may not be desirable collateral.

The lender, in evaluating inventory as possible loan collateral, looks for items with very *stable market prices* that can be easily liquidated. Standardized or staple items of a durable nature are generally most desirable. These types of items have prices subject to small fluctuations; they have ready markets; and they have no undesirable physical characteristics.

FLOATING INVENTORY LIENS

The floating inventory lien is the most often used form of inventory security. A lender may be willing to secure a loan with inventory under a floating lien if the firm has a stable level of inventory that consists of a diversified group of merchandise, no single item of which has an excessively high dollar value. Since it is difficult for a lender to verify the presence of the inventory, he or she will generally advance less than 50 percent of the book value of the average inventory. Inventories of items such as auto tires, screws and bolts, and shoes are likely candidates for floating lien loans. The interest charge on a floating lien is about 4–6 percent above the prime rate.

TRUST RECEIPT INVENTORY LOANS

These loans against inventory are often made by manufacturers' financing subsidiaries to their customers.* *Floor planning* of automobile or equipment retailers is done under this arrangement. General Motors Acceptance Corporation of Canada Ltd. (GMAC), the financing subsidiary of General Motors of Canada Limited, grants these types of loans to its dealers. Under this type of loan arrangement the inventory, which normally consists of relatively expensive merchandise, remains in the hands of the borrowers.

---

*These manufacturers' subsidiaries are often referred to as *captive finance companies,* since they are wholly owned financing subsidiaries. Captive finance companies are especially popular in industries manufacturing consumer durable goods, since they provide the manufacturer with a useful sales tool as well as certain tax and borrowing advantages. For an interesting study on captive finance subsidiaries, see Gordon S. Roberts and Jerry A. Viscione, "Captive Finance Subsidiaries and the M-form Hypothesis," *The Bell Journal of Economics* 12 (Spring 1981), pp. 285–295.

In the case of a trust receipt loan, the borrower receives the merchandise and the lender advances anywhere from 80 percent to 100 percent of its cost. The lender files a lien on the items financed that contains a listing of each item along with its description and serial number. The borrower is free to sell the merchandise, but is required to remit the amount lent against each item along with accrued interest to the lender immediately after the sale is made; the lender then releases the lien on the item. The lender makes periodic checks of the borrower's inventory in order to make sure that all the required collateral is still in the hands of the borrower. The interest charge to the borrower is normally 2 percent or more above the prime rate.

WAREHOUSE RECEIPT LOANS

A *warehouse receipt loan* is an arrangement whereby the lender, which may be a chartered bank or a commercial finance company, receives control of the pledged collateral. Although this arrangement provides the lender with the ultimate degree of security, it is used infrequently.

Warehouse Receipt Lending Procedures   In the case of a warehouse receipt loan, the lender selects the inventory that is acceptable as collateral for the loan. Once the collateral has been selected, the lender hires a warehousing company to physically take possession of the inventory. Two types of warehousing arrangements are possible—terminal warehouses and field warehouses.

Terminal Warehouses   A *terminal warehouse* is one located in the geographical vicinity of the borrower. It is a central warehouse that is used to store the merchandise of various customers. A terminal warehouse is normally used by the lender when the inventory used as security is easily transported and can be delivered to the warehouse relatively inexpensively. When the goods arrive at the warehouse designated by the lender, the *warehouse official* checks the merchandise in, listing each item received on a *warehouse receipt*, noting the quantity, serial or lot numbers, and the estimated value. Once the warehouse official has checked in all the merchandise, he or she forwards the warehouse receipt to the lender, who advances a specified percentage of the collateral value to the borrower and files a lien on all the items listed on the receipt.

Field (Public) Warehouses   Under the *field warehouse* arrangement, the lender hires a field warehousing company to actually set up a warehouse on the borrower's premises or lease part of the borrower's warehouse. There are a number of companies that specialize in establishing field warehouses for a fee. The procedures followed by the field warehouse personnel are quite similar to those described above for terminal warehouses. The lender, on receipt of a warehouse receipt, advances a specified percentage of the collateral value to the borrower and files a lien on the pledged collateral. A field warehouse may take the form of a fence around a stock of raw materials located outdoors, it may consist of a roped-off section of the borrower's warehouse, or it may actually be a warehouse constructed by the warehousing company on the borrower's premises, a portion of which may have been leased by the warehousing company.

Table 12.3 Summary of Sources of Secured Short-Term Financing

Type of financing	Source	Cost/conditions	Characteristics
I. Bank sources			
Notes	Chartered banks	Prime plus 0–4% risk premium. Typical premium is less than 2%.	A single-payment note used to meet a funds shortage expected to last only a short period of time.
Lines of credit	Chartered banks	Prime plus 0–4% risk premium. Must clean up the line.	A prearranged borrowing limit under which funds, if available, will be lent to allow the borrower to meet seasonal needs.
Revolving credit agreements	Chartered banks	Prime plus 0–4% risk premium. Must pay commitment and standby fees.	A line-of-credit agreement under which the availability of funds is guaranteed. They are often two- or three-year agreements.
II. Accounts receivable collateral			
Pledging	Chartered banks and commercial finance companies	2–5% above prime, plus up to 3% in fees. Advance 50–90% of collateral value. Normally advance 80%.	Selected accounts receivable are used as collateral; the borrower is trusted to remit payments upon collection. Done on a nonnotification basis.
Factoring	Commercial finance companies and factors	$\frac{7}{8}$–1$\frac{1}{2}$% discount from face value of factored accounts. Interest on advances of 2–2$\frac{1}{2}$% above prime. Interest on surplus balances left with factor of 0%, or prime plus .25%.	Selected accounts are guaranteed—generally without recourse—by the factor. Factor will make advances against accounts sold but not yet scheduled for remittance to seller. Typically done on a notification basis.

Type of loan	Source	Cost	Description
III. Inventory collateral			
Floating liens	Chartered banks and commercial finance companies	4–6% above prime. Advance less than 50% of collateral value.	A loan against inventory in general for firms with stable inventory of a variety of inexpensive items.
Trust receipts	Manufacturer's captive financing subsidiaries, chartered banks, and commercial finance companies	2% or more above prime. Advance 80–100% of cost of collateral.	Loan against collateral that is relatively expensive and identifiable. Collateral remains in possession of borrower, who is trusted to remit proceeds to lender upon its sale. Often called *floor planning.*
Warehouse receipts	Chartered banks and commercial finance companies	4–6% above prime plus a 1–3% warehouse fee. Advance 75–90% of collateral value.	Inventory used as collateral is put in a terminal or field warehouse. A third party—a warehousing company—issues a warehouse receipt that is held by the lender. The warehousing company is an agent of the lender.
IV. Other collateral			
Shares and bonds	Chartered banks	1–5% above prime. Advance as much as 90% of market value of collateral.	Shares and bonds issued in bearer form and having a ready market with a stable market price are used as collateral. Lender takes possession and can liquidate the collateral in the event of default.
Comaker	Chartered banks	1–5% above prime.	The collateral is the borrowing power of a more financially sound firm or individual that cosigns the loan.

Field warehouses always have a guard stationed near the warehoused collateral. The guard or warehouse official is not permitted to release the collateral without written authorization from the lender.

The Loan Agreement   The actual lending agreement will specifically state the requirements for the release of inventory. As in the case of other secured loans, the lender accepts only collateral believed to be readily marketable and advances only a portion—generally 75 percent to 90 percent—of the collateral's value. The types of collateral normally found most acceptable for warehouse receipt loans are canned foods, lumber, coal, coke, refined products, and basic metal stocks. These products are acceptable because they are relatively nonperishable and are sold in well-developed and organized product markets. The loan agreement typically provides for the release of the lien on certain pledged items upon receipt of partial repayments of the loan. In general, warehouse receipts are not negotiable.

The Cost of Warehouse Receipt Loans   The specific costs of warehouse receipt loans are generally higher than those of any other secured lending arrangements due to the need to hire and pay a third party (the warehousing company) to guard and attend to the collateral. The basic interest charged on warehouse receipt loans generally ranges from 4 to 6 percent above the prime rate. In addition to the interest charge, the borrower must absorb the costs of warehousing by paying the warehouse fee, which is generally between 1 and 3 percent of the amount of the loan. These charges vary depending upon the size of the loan and other factors. The borrower is normally required to pay the insurance costs on warehoused merchandise.

Whenever warehouse receipt loans are arranged, it is important for the lender to select a reputable warehousing company. The warehousing company as the lender's agent is responsible for seeing that the collateral pledged is actually in the warehouse. There have been instances in the past when warehousing companies have fraudulently issued warehouse receipts against nonexistent collateral. If this happens, and the borrower defaults on the loan, the lender is in the same position as an unsecured creditor.

Other Types of Secured Loans

Other types of security for short-term loans include shares and bonds, comaker loans, chattel mortgages,* cash surrender values of life insurance, noncorporate assets, and government-guaranteed loans. The most common of these types of security are shares and bonds and comaker loans.

---

*A *chattel mortgage* is a lien on the personal or movable property of a borrower, such as equipment, machinery, and automobiles. Under this arrangement, the borrower retains control of the assets in security until there is a default on the terms of the loan. At that point, the lender assumes control of the assets being used as collateral for the chattel mortgage.

SHARE AND BOND COLLATERAL

Shares and certain types of bonds that are issued in bearer form can be assigned as collateral for a loan. *Bearer bonds* are bonds that can be transferred from one owner to another, instead of being issued only in the name of the initial owner like Canadian savings bonds. The lender, which is most commonly a chartered bank, of course is interested in accepting as collateral only those shares and bonds that have a ready market and a stable market price. Securities listed on the major exchanges are generally preferred. Lenders are likely to advance as much as 90 percent of the market value of the securities held as collateral. The lender takes possession of the collateral and receives the legal right to liquidate it if the borrower defaults on the terms of the loan agreement. The interest charges on loans secured with shares or bonds, or both, is normally between 1 and 5 percent above the prime rate.

COMAKER LOANS

Comaker loans arise when another party, who may have a vested interest in the firm's financial future, *cosigns* for the loan. Although no physical collateral is pledged against the loan, the borrowing power of a more financially sound party is used to back up the loan. If the borrower defaults, the comaker will be liable for the loan. A lender, which is typically a chartered bank, will make comaker loans only when certain of the financial soundness of the comaker. A comaker may be a wealthy shareholder, a supplier, a customer to whom the continued existence of the firm is important, or a friend of the firm. Interest rates charged on comaker loans are comparable to those charged on loans secured by shares and bonds.

Summary

This chapter has discussed the characteristics and basic types of secured short-term loans available to business. A lender can obtain a legal claim to certain collateral by filing a lien on the collateral, which can be removed only when the terms of the loan agreement have been met. A copy of the security agreement is made available to other lenders so that they will not attempt to secure a loan with collateral already being used as security. A lender can take a number of different types of security interests. A floating lien gives the lender a claim on general collateral. A trust receipt loan is made against specific collateral that remains under the control of the borrower. A warehouse receipt loan allows the lender to control the disposition of the loan collateral, which is typically inventory.

Short-term loan collateral is usually a current asset, such as accounts receivable, inventory, or shares and bonds whose maturity in effect liquidates the loan. Only a certain percentage of the collateral's value, determined by the lender's assessment of its liquidity and marketability, is advanced by the lender.

The major source of negotiated short-term secured loans to business is the chartered bank. A bank loan may take the form of a note, a line-of-credit, or a revolving credit agreement. Each of these arrangements has its own characteristics. The rate of interest charged under each of these arrangements is tied to the prime rate of interest; the premium above the prime rate is dependent upon the risk of the borrower as perceived by the bank. The line-of-credit and revolving credit agreements normally require compensating balances. The line of credit normally has an annual clean-up feature, while the revolving credit agreement requires that commitment and standby fees be paid. Each of these arrangements must be negotiated between the borrower and the bank.

Accounts receivable are the most common type of collateral for short-term secured loans. A pledge of accounts receivable is a type of trust arrangement whereby the lender advances a certain percentage of the book value of the accounts found to be acceptable. Accounts of average size are preferable. The borrower collects the pledged accounts and remits the payment to the lender, thereby reducing the loan balance on which interest is calculated. Accounts receivable can be factored to a factor or a commercial finance company. With guaranteed-payment factoring, the factor assumes the credit risks, and thus generally can collect nothing from the borrower if an account proves uncollectible. Customers whose accounts have been factored are generally notified to make payments directly to the factor; pledges of accounts receivable do not generally involve notification. The cost of factoring is greater than the cost of pledging accounts receivable since the factor takes the credit risks and performs certain administrative functions.

Inventory can be used as collateral under a floating lien, a trust receipt arrangement, or a warehouse receipt loan. In the case of a warehouse receipt loan, the collateral is placed in either a terminal or a field warehouse chosen by the lender and guarded on his or her behalf. The lender controls the collateral, which only he or she can release. The cost of warehouse receipt loans is high due to the fee that must be paid the warehousing company. This arrangement is quite safe for the lender.

Other types of collateral include shares and bonds, comaker loans, chattel mortgages, cash surrender values of life insurance, noncorporate assets, and government guarantees. Regardless of what method of security is used, the lender advances only a percentage of the book value of the collateral and levies interest and other charges as required. All terms and charges are explicitly stated in the loan agreement, which is a legal and binding contract. Liens filed against collateral become part of the loan agreement.

Questions

12.1   What are the key differences between unsecured and secured forms of short-term borrowing? In what circumstances do firms borrow short-term money on a secured basis?

12.2   What are the most common types of short-term loan collateral? How does a lender obtain a security interest in a firm's loan collateral?

12.3   Lenders evaluating the acceptability of short-term loan collateral are often concerned with its liquidity. How can a lender evaluate the liquidity of current assets?

12.4   On what basis is the "percentage advance" against acceptable collateral determined? Within what range is this percentage likely to fall?

12.5   What two key institutions provide secured short-term loans to business? Which institution charges the highest interest rates? Why?

12.6   What is the primary source of *negotiated* short-term loans to business? When are loans considered short-term self-liquidating loans?

12.7   What are the basic terms and characteristics of a note? How is the prime interest rate relevant to the cost of borrowing via notes?

12.8   What are line-of-credit agreements? How does a firm obtain a line of credit? What documents are useful to a banker evaluating an application for a line of credit?

12.9   What is the primary difference between the cost of interest paid at maturity and interest paid in advance?

12.10   What restrictive provisions are commonly included in a line-of-credit agreement? What are the basic motives for each of these restrictions? Is there any opportunity to negotiate these terms? Why or why not?

12.11   What is meant by a revolving credit agreement? How does this arrangement differ from the line-of-credit agreement? What type of fees are involved with a revolving credit agreement?

12.12   How does a lender determine which accounts receivable are acceptable as pledged collateral for a short-term loan?

12.13   What does the term *notification* refer to? Are pledges of accounts normally on a notification basis? How does the lender collect his money in a pledge (assignment) arrangement?

12.14   How is factoring different from a pledge of accounts receivable? What institutions provide factoring services to business?

12.15   What are the commonly cited advantages and disadvantages of factoring? What types of firms are most likely to find factoring a viable source of funds? Why?

12.16   The suitability of inventory as loan collateral generally depends on its type, its physical properties, and its marketability. How do each of these aspects of inventory affect its desirability as collateral?

12.17   What is a floating lien inventory loan? What sort of advances and costs are involved?

12.18   How does a typical trust receipt inventory loan arrangement work? Who makes these types of loans, and how are they policed?

12.19   How does a warehouse receipt lending arrangement work? What is the function of the warehouse personnel, and what types of warehouses are used?

12.20   What types of collateral, other than accounts receivable and inventory, are likely to be used to secure a short-term loan?

Problems

12.1   Bellevue Can Ltd. wishes to establish a prearranged borrowing agreement with its chartered bank. The bank's terms for a line of credit are 3 percent over the prime rate, and the borrowing must be reduced to zero for a 30-day period. For an equivalent revolving credit account, the rate is 2.80 percent over prime with fees of .5 percent on the average unused balance. With both loans, the compensating balance is 20 percent. The prime rate is currently 8 percent.

a.   What is the effective interest cost of the line of credit?

b.   What is the effective cost of the revolving credit account if, on the average, the amount of borrowing is one-half the guaranteed amount?

c.   Under what conditions does the revolving credit account have a lower/higher effective interest rate than the line of credit?

d.   If the firm does expect to borrow an average of half the prearranged funds, which arrangement would you recommend for the borrower? Explain why.

12.2 A financial institution lends a firm $10,000 for one year at 10 percent on a discounted basis and requires compensating balances of 20 percent of the face value of the loan. Determine the effective annual interest rate associated with this loan.

12.3 Moose Jaw Castings (MJC) is attempting to obtain the maximum loan possible using its accounts receivable as collateral. The firm extends net 30-day credit. The amounts owed MJC by its 12 credit customers, the average age of each account, and the customers' average payment periods are as follows:

Customer	Account receivable	Average age of account	Average payment period of customer
A	$37,000	40 days	30 days
B	42,000	25 days	50 days
C	15,000	40 days	60 days
D	8,000	30 days	35 days
E	50,000	31 days	40 days
F	12,000	28 days	30 days
G	24,000	30 days	70 days
H	46,000	29 days	40 days
I	3,000	30 days	65 days
J	22,000	25 days	35 days
K	62,000	35 days	40 days
L	80,000	60 days	70 days

a. If the bank will accept all accounts that can be collected in 45 days or less as long as the customer has a history of paying within 45 days, which accounts will be acceptable? What is the total dollar amount of accounts receivable collateral? (Accounts receivable that have an average age greater than the customer's average payment period are also excluded.)

b. In addition to the conditions in **a**, the bank recognizes that 5 percent of credit sales will be lost to returns and allowances. Also, the bank will only lend 80 percent of the acceptable collateral (after adjusting for returns and allowances). What level of funds would be made available through this lending source?

12.4 Windsor Plate and Glass Ltd. wishes to borrow $80,000 from the Second Canadian Bank, using its accounts receivable to secure the loan. The bank's policy is to accept as collateral any accounts that are normally paid within 30 days of the end of the credit period so long as the average age of the account is not greater than the customer's average payment period. Windsor Plate's accounts receivable, their average ages, and the average payment period for each customer are given below. The company extends terms of net 30 days.

Customer	Account receivable	Average age of account	Average payment period of customer
A	$20,000	10 days	40 days
B	6,000	40 days	35 days
C	22,000	62 days	50 days
D	11,000	68 days	65 days
E	2,000	14 days	30 days
F	12,000	38 days	50 days
G	27,000	55 days	60 days
H	19,000	20 days	35 days

a. Calculate the dollar amount of acceptable accounts receivable collateral held by Windsor Plate and Glass.

b. The bank adjusts collateral by 10 percent for returns and allowances; what is the level of acceptable collateral under this condition?

c. The bank will advance 75 percent against the firm's acceptable collateral (after adjusting for returns and allowances). What amount can Windsor Plate and Glass borrow against these accounts?

12.5 Dynamic Finance factors the accounts of the Russell Allen Company. All eight factored accounts are listed below with the amount factored, the due date, the guaranteed-payment date, and the status as of May 30. Indicate the amounts that Dynamic should have remitted to Russell Allen as of May 30, as well as the dates of those remittances. Assume the factor's commission is 2 percent.

Account	Amount	Date due	Guaranteed-payment date	Status on May 30
A	$200,000	May 30	June 14	Collected, May 15
B	90,000	May 30	June 14	Uncollected
C	110,000	May 30	June 14	Uncollected
D	85,000	June 15	June 30	Collected, May 30
E	120,000	May 30	June 14	Collected, May 27
F	180,000	June 15	June 30	Collected, May 30
G	90,000	May 15	May 30	Uncollected
H	30,000	June 30	July 15	Collected, May 30

12.6 Duff Duds wishes to receive an *advance* from its factor on an account of $100,000 due in 30 days. The factor holds a 10-percent factor's reserve, charges a 2-percent factoring commission, and charges 16-percent annual interest on advances.

a. Calculate the maximum dollar amount of interest to be paid.

b. What amount of funds will the firm actually receive?

12.7 The Sable Oil Company Ltd. factors all of its accounts. The factor charges a 1-percent factoring commission, holds a 15-percent reserve, and charges 10-percent interest on advances. Sable wishes to receive an advance against the following accounts as of September 1:

Account	Amount	Date due
A	$ 60,000	September 30
B	100,00	September 30
C	120,000	September 30
D	75,000	September 30
E	40,000	September 30

a. Calculate the actual amount the firm can borrow.

b. Calculate the maximum dollar amount of interest that must be paid.

c. Why might the actual interest cost be less than the amount calculated in **b**?

12.8 New Brunswick Manufacturing Ltd. is considering obtaining funding through advances against receivables. Total credit sales are $12 million, terms are net 30 days, and payment is made on the average in 30 days. Eastern Bank will advance funds under a pledging arrangement for 15-percent annual interest. On the average, 80 percent of credit sales will be accepted as collateral. Friendly Finance offers factoring on a nonrecourse basis for a 2.5-percent factoring commission, charging 1 percent per month on advances, and requiring a

20-percent factor's reserve. Under this plan, the firm would factor all accounts and close its credit and collections department, saving $300,000 per year.

a. What is the effective interest rate and the average amount of funds made available under pledging and under factoring?

b. What other effects must be considered in choosing either of these plans?

c. Which plan do you recommend and why?

12.9 Prescott Turbine Company faces a liquidity crisis—they need a loan of $100,000 for 30 days. Having no source of unsecured borrowing, the firm must find a secured short-term lender. The firm's accounts receivable are quite low, but its inventory is considered liquid and reasonably good collateral. The book value of the inventory is $300,000.

1. Intercity Bank will make a trust receipt loan against the $120,000 finished-goods inventory. This loan costs 6 percent plus a ¼-percent administration fee. The average amount owed over the month is expected to be $75,000.

2. Second Canadian Bank is willing to lend against a blanket lien on a maximum of one-half of the book value of inventory for the 30-day period at an annual interest rate of 8 percent.

3. North Mall Commercial Finance Limited will lend an amount equal to 85 percent of the finished-goods balance and charge 9-percent interest on the outstanding loan balance. A ½ percent warehousing fee will be levied against the amount borrowed. The average loan balance is expected to be $60,000.

a. Assuming $100,000 is borrowed in each case, calculate the cost of each of the proposed plans.

b. Which plan do you recommend? Why?

c. If the firm had made a purchase of $100,000 for which it had been given terms of 1/10 net 40, would it increase the firm's profitability to forego the discount and not borrow as recommended in **b**? Why or why not?

Suggested Readings

Abraham, Alfred B., "Factoring—The New Frontier for Commercial Banks," *The Journal of Commercial Bank Lending* 53 (April 1971), pp. 32–43.

Addison, Edward, "Factoring: A Case History," *Financial Executive* (November 1963), pp. 32–33.

Adler, M., "Administration of Inventory Loans Under the Uniform Commercial Code," *The Journal of Commercial Bank Lending* 52 (April 1970), pp. 55–60.

Andrews, Victor L., "Captive Finance Companies," *Harvard Business Review* 42 (July-August 1964), pp. 80–92.

Berger, Paul D. and William K. Harper, "Determination of an Optimal Revolving Credit Agreement," *Journal of Financial and Quantitative Analysis* 8 (June 1973), pp. 491–498.

Bogen, Jules I., Ed., *Financial Handbook*, 4th ed. (New York: Ronald, 1968), sect. 16.

Campbell, Tim S., "A Model of the Market for Lines of Credit," *Journal of Finance* 33 (March 1978), pp. 231–244.

Crane, Dwight B. and William L. White, "Who Benefits from a Floating Prime Rate?" *Harvard Business Review* 50 (January-February 1972), pp. 121–129.

D'Agostino, R. S., "Accounts Receivable Loans—Worthless Collateral?" *The Journal of Commercial Bank Lending* (March 1970), pp. 34–42.

Daniels, Frank, Sidney Legg, and E. C. Yueille, "Accounts Receivable and Related Inventory Financing," *Journal of Commercial Bank Lending* 53 (July 1970), pp. 38–53.

Dennon, Lester E., "The Security Agreement," *Journal of Commercial Bank Lending* 50 (February 1968), pp. 32–40.

Edwards, R. E., "Finance Companies and Their Creditors," *Journal of Commercial Bank Lending* 54 (October 1971), pp. 2–10.

Fisher, D. J., "Factoring—An Industry on the Move," *The Conference Board Record* 9 (April 1972), pp. 42–45.

Gordon, R. L., "Talking Business with a Banker," *Financial Executive* 35 (February 1967).

Griffin, Norris S., "Factoring Meets Canadian Banks' Short-term Needs," *American Banker* (July 25, 1979).

Grover, Warren and Donald Ross, *Materials on Corporation Finance* (Toronto: Richard De Boo Limited, 1979).

Harris, Duane G., "Some Evidence on Differential Lending Practices at Commercial Banks," *Journal of Finance* 28 (December 1973), pp. 1303–1311.

Hayes, Douglas A., *Bank Lending Policies: Domestic and International* (Ann Arbor, Mich.: University of Michigan, 1971).

Holmes, W., "Market Values of Inventories—Perils and Pitfalls," *Journal of Commercial Bank Lending* 55 (April 1974), pp. 30–36.

Naitove, Irwin, *Modern Factoring* (New York: American Management Association, 1969).

Peters, D. "Competition and Canada's Banking Structure," *The Banker* (October 1971), p. 23.

Quarles, J. Carson, "The Floating Lien," *Journal of Commercial Bank Lending* 53 (November 1970), pp. 51–58.

Rogers, Robert W., "Warehouse Receipts and Their Use in Financing," *Bulletin of the Robert Morris Associates* 46 (April 1964), pp. 317–327.

Stancill, James McN., *The Management of Working Capital* (Scranton, Pa.: Intext, 1971), chap. 6.

Stone, Bernell K., "Allocating Credit Lines, Planned Borrowing, and Tangible Services Over a Company's Banking System," *Financial Management* 4 (Summer 1975), pp. 65–78.

———, "The Cost of Bank Loans," *Journal of Financial and Quantitative Analysis* 7 (December 1972), pp. 2077–2086.

Wellman, M. T., "Field Warehousing—Protective Measures," *Robert Morris Associates Bulletin* 47 (March 1965), pp. 302–312.

Wishner, Maynard, "Coming Significantly Larger Rates for Secured Corporate Financing," *Financial Executive* 45 (May 1977), pp. 18–23.

Part Five

Fixed-Asset Management and Capital Budgeting

BALANCE SHEET

Assets	Liabilities and Shareholders' Equity
Current Assets	Current Liabilities
Fixed Assets	Long-Term Debt
	Shareholders' Equity

This part of the text is devoted to one of the key areas of financial management—fixed-asset management and capital budgeting. The concepts and techniques underlying this topic are often viewed as the backbone of contemporary financial management. Chapter 13 is devoted to the key mathematical concepts of finance. An understanding of many of these concepts is necessary in order to grasp the various capital budgeting techniques; others are used in later parts of the text. Chapter 14 describes certain fixed-asset management strategies and presents the terminology and fundamentals of capital budgeting. Special emphasis is placed upon determination of relevant cash-flow streams. Chapter 15 describes and discusses the key techniques of capital budgeting. Chapter 16 discusses capital budgeting under risk. It covers techniques for evaluating capital budgeting projects under risk and includes a discussion of risk and return which places emphasis on the Capital Asset Pricing Model (CAPM).

Chapter 13

THE MATHEMATICS
OF FINANCE

In order to understand the various techniques of capital budgeting and other interest-related financial concepts, one needs an understanding of certain algebraic relationships associated with interest calculations. The key calculations are the determination of compound interest and the present value of future cash flows. Compound interest calculations are needed to evaluate future sums resulting from an investment in an interest-earning medium. Compound interest techniques are also quite useful in evaluating interest and growth rates of money streams.

Discounting, or the calculation of present values, is inversely related to compounding. It is of key importance in the evaluation of future income streams associated with capital budgeting projects. An understanding of both compound interest and present value is needed to calculate the payments required to accumulate a predetermined future sum or for amortizing loans or calculating loan payment schedules. A thorough knowledge of discounting and present values is also helpful in understanding the techniques for finding internal rates of return and yields to maturity, both of which are discussed in subsequent chapters.

This chapter explains the terminology, concepts, calculations, and tables used in finding compound interest and present values. The reader should not fear these topics, for they are conceptually and algebraically quite simple. An understanding of the concepts presented in this chapter will provide the key to understanding the capital budgeting techniques presented in Chapters 14 through 16 as well as the discussions of the cost of capital, capital structure, valuation, leasing, bond refunding, valuing convertible securities, business combinations, and business rehabilitation included in later parts of the text.

This chapter has three basic sections. The first section discusses compound interest, the second is devoted to present-value calculations, and the final section presents some important applications of compound interest and present-value techniques.

Compound Interest

Compound interest is most commonly thought of in reference to various savings institutions. These institutions quite often advertise the fact that they pay "compound interest at a rate of x percent" or "x-percent interest compounded semiannually, quarterly, weekly, or daily." In this section, we shall discuss three types of compounding: annual compounding, intrayear compounding, and finding the compound value of a stream of equal payments known as an annuity.

ANNUAL COMPOUNDING

The most common type of compounding is *annual compounding*. Interest is *compounded* when the amount earned on an initial deposit (the *initial principal*) becomes *part* of the principal at the end of the first compounding period. The term *principal* refers to the amount of money on which *interest* is paid.

The Calculation of Compound Interest   The actual method by which interest is compounded annually can be illustrated by a simple example.

EXAMPLE   If Steve Saver places $100 in a savings account paying 8-percent interest compounded annually, at the end of one year he will have $108 in the account. This $108 represents the initial principal of $100 plus 8 percent ($8) in interest. The amount of money in the account at the end of the first year is calculated using Equation 13.1.

$$\text{Amount of money at end of year 1} = \$100(1 + .08) \qquad (13.1)$$
$$= \$108$$

If Steve were to leave this money in the account for another year, he would be paid interest at the rate of 8 percent on the new principal of $108. At the end of this second year, there would be $116.64 in the account. This $116.64 would represent the principal at the beginning of year 2 ($108) plus 8 percent of the $108 (i.e., $8.64) in interest. The amount of money in the account at the end of the second year is calculated using Equation 13.2.

$$\text{Amount of money at end of year 2} = \$108(1 + .08) \qquad (13.2)$$
$$= \$116.64$$

Substituting the right side of Equation 13.1 for the $108 figure in Equation 13.2 gives us Equation 13.3.

$$\text{Amount of money at end of year 2} = \$100(1 + .08)(1 + .08)$$
$$= \$100(1.08)^2 \qquad (13.3)$$
$$= \$116.64$$

The basic relationship in Equation 13.3 can be generalized to find the amount of money after any number of years. Let

F_n = the amount of money at the end of year n
P = the initial principal
i = the annual rate of interest paid on the account
n = the number of years the money is left in the account

Using this notation, a general equation for the amount of money at the end of year n can be formulated.

$$F_n = P(1 + i)^n \qquad (13.4)$$

The usefulness of Equation 13.4 for finding the amount of money, F_n, in an account paying i-percent interest compounded annually for n years if P dollars were deposited initially can be illustrated by a simple example.

EXAMPLE   James Frugal has placed $800 in a savings account paying 6-percent interest compounded annually. He wishes to determine how much money will be in the account at the end of five years if he withdraws neither the principal nor interest during the five-year period. Substituting $P = \$800$, $i = .06$, and $n = 5$ into Equation 13.4 gives him the amount at the end of year 5.

$$F_5 = \$800(1 + .06)^5 = \$800(1.338) = \$1,070.40 \qquad (13.5)$$

James will have $1,070.40 in the account at the end of year 5.

COMPOUND INTEREST TABLES

In order to simplify compound interest calculations, compound interest tables have been compiled. A table of the amount generated by the payment of compound interest on an initial principal of $1 is given as Appendix Table A-1. This table, labeled "The compound-value interest factors for one dollar," provides a value for $(1 + i)^n$ in Equation 13.4 for various values of i and n.* This portion of Equation 13.4 is called the *compound-value interest factor*, or $CVIF_{i,n}$.

$$\text{Compound-value interest factor} = CVIF_{i,n} = (1 + i)^n \qquad (13.6)$$

By accessing the table with respect to the annual interest rate, i, and the appropriate number of years, n, the factor relevant to a particular problem can be found. A sample portion of Table A-1 is given in Table 13.1. An example will illustrate the use of this table.

*This table is commonly referred to as a "compound interest table" or a "table of the future value of $1." As long as the reader understands the source of the table values, the various names attached to it should not create confusion since one can always make a trial calculation of a value for one factor as a check.

Table 13.1   The Compound-Value Interest Factors for One Dollar, $CVIF_{i,n}$

Year	5.00 percent	6.00 percent	7.00 percent	8.00 percent	9.00 percent	10.00 percent
1	1.050	1.060	1.070	1.080	1.090	1.100
2	1.102	1.124	1.145	1.166	1.188	1.210
3	1.158	1.191	1.225	1.260	1.295	1.331
4	1.216	1.262	1.311	1.360	1.412	1.464
5	1.276	1.338	1.403	1.469	1.539	1.611
6	1.340	1.419	1.501	1.587	1.677	1.772
7	1.407	1.504	1.606	1.714	1.828	1.949
8	1.477	1.594	1.718	1.851	1.993	2.144
9	1.551	1.689	1.838	1.999	2.172	2.358
10	1.629	1.791	1.967	2.159	2.367	2.594

Note: All table values have been rounded to the nearest one-thousandth; thus, calculated values may differ slightly from the table values.

EXAMPLE   James Frugal, whom we discussed in the preceding example, has placed $800 in his savings account at 6-percent interest compounded annually. He wishes to find out how much would be in the account at the end of five years and does so by the cumbersome process of raising $(1 + .06)$ to the fifth power. Using the table for the compound value of $1 (Table 13.1 or Table A-1), he could find the compound-value interest factor for an initial principal of $1 on deposit for five years at 6-percent interest compounded annually without performing any calculations. The appropriate factor, $CVIF_{6\%,5 \text{ yrs.}}$, for 6 percent and five years is 1.338. Multiplying this factor, 1.338, by his actual initial principal of $800 would then give him the amount in the account at the end of year 5, $1,070.40. The usefulness of the table should be clear from this example.

Three important observations should be made about the table for the compound value of one dollar. The first is that the factors in the table represent factors for determining the compound value of one dollar *at the end of the given year.* Second, *as the interest rate increases for any given year, the compound-value interest factor also increases.* Thus, the higher the interest rate, the greater the future sum. The third point is that *for a given interest rate the compound value of a dollar increases with the passage of time.* The relationships between various interest rates, the number of years interest is earned, and compound-value interest factors are illustrated in Figure 13.1. Note that for an interest rate of 0 percent, the compound-value interest factor always equals 1. In this event, the compound-value always equals the initial principal.

INTRAYEAR COMPOUNDING

The preceding section was devoted solely to the annual compounding of interest. Quite commonly, interest is compounded more often. This behaviour is particularly noticeable in the advertising of savings institutions, which compound interest semiannually, quarterly, monthly, daily, or even continuously. This section first discusses semiannual

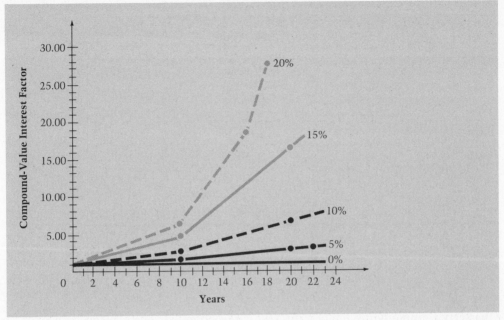

Figure 13.1   Interest rates, time, and compound-value interest factors used to find the compound value of one dollar.

and quarterly compounding and then presents a general equation for intrayear compounding. It also explains how to use compound-value interest tables in these situations.

Semiannual Compounding   When interest is compounded semiannually, there are two compounding periods within the year. Instead of being paid the stated interest rate once a year, one is paid one-half of the stated interest rate twice a year.

EXAMPLE   Steve Saver, who was discussed in an earlier example, has decided to place his $100 in a savings account paying 8-percent interest compounded semiannually. If he leaves his money in the account for two years, he will be paid 4-percent interest compounded over four periods— each six months long. Table 13.2 presents the calculations required to determine the amount Steve will have at the end of two years.

As the table shows, at the end of one year, when the 8-percent interest is compounded semiannually, Steve will have $108.16. At the end of two years, he will have $116.99. Note that the semiannual compounding at an annual interest rate of 8 percent results in the same value of $108.16 at the end of the first year as annual compounding at an annual interest rate of 8.16 percent. In other words, because of semiannual compounding the *effective* annual interest rate (8.16 percent) is higher than the *nominal* or stated annual interest rate (8 percent). In general, the greater the number of times per year interest is compounded, the larger the difference between the effective annual interest rate and the nominal annual interest rate. The reader should also

Table 13.2   The Results of Investing $100 at 8-Percent Interest Compounded Semiannually over Two Years

Period	Beginning principal (1)	Compound-value interest factor (2)	Amount at end of period (1) · (2) (3)
6 months	$100.00	1.04	$104.00
1 year	104.00	1.04	108.16
18 months	108.16	1.04	112.49
2 years	112.49	1.04	116.99

recall from Chapter 11 that the effective rate of interest is higher than the stipulated rate of interest on discount loans (that is, loans on which interest is paid in advance).

Quarterly Compounding   When interest is compounded quarterly, one is paid one-fourth of the stated interest rate four times a year.

EXAMPLE   Steve Saver, after further investigation of his savings opportunities, has found an institution that will pay him 8 percent compounded quarterly. If he leaves his money in this account for two years, he will be paid 2-percent interest compounded over eight periods—each of which consists of one-fourth of a year. Table 13.3 presents the calculations required to determine

Table 13.3   The Results of Investing $100 at 8-Percent Interest Compounded Quarterly over Two Years

Period	Beginning principal (1)	Compound-value interest factor (2)	Amount at end of period (1) · (2) (3)
3 months	$100.00	1.02	$102.00
6 months	102.00	1.02	104.04
9 months	104.04	1.02	106.12
1 year	106.12	1.02	108.24
15 months	108.24	1.02	110.40
18 months	110.40	1.02	112.61
21 months	112.61	1.02	114.86
2 years	114.86	1.02	117.16

the amount Steve will have at the end of two years. As the table shows, at the end of one year, when the 8-percent interest is compounded quarterly, Steve will have $108.24. This implies that even though the nominal annual rate of interest is 8 percent, the effective annual rate of interest, due to quarterly interest compounding, will be equal to 8.24 percent. At the end of two years Steve will have $117.16.

Table 13.4 presents comparative values for Steve Saver's $100 at the end of years 1 and 2 given annual, semiannual, and quarterly compounding at the 8-percent rate. As the table shows, the *more frequently interest is compounded, the greater the amount of money accumulated*. In other words, the greater the frequency of compounding, the higher the effective annual interest rate relative to the nominal annual interest rate.

Table 13.4   The Results of Investing $100 at 8 Percent for One and Two Years Given Various Compounding Periods

End of year	Compounding period		
	Annual	Semiannual	Quarterly
1	$108.00	$108.16	$108.24
2	116.64	116.99	117.16

A General Equation for Intrayear Compounding   It should be clear from the preceding examples of semiannual and quarterly compounding that, if m equals the number of times per year interest is compounded, Equation 13.4 (our formula for annual compounding) can be rewritten as

$$F_n = P \left(1 + \frac{i}{m} \right)^{m \cdot n} \tag{13.7}$$

If $m = 1$, Equation 13.7 reduces to Equation 13.4. Thus, if interest is compounded annually (i.e., once a year), Equation 13.7 will provide the same results as Equation 13.4. The general applicability of Equation 13.7 can be illustrated with a simple example.

EXAMPLE   In the preceding examples, the amount that Steve Saver would have at the end of two years if he deposited $100 at 8-percent interest compounded semiannually and quarterly was discussed. For semiannual compounding, m would equal 2 in Equation 13.7, while for quarterly compounding m would equal 4. Substituting the appropriate values for semiannual and quarterly compounding into Equation 13.7 would yield

1. *For semiannual compounding*

$$F_2 = \$100 \left(1 + \frac{.08}{2} \right)^{2 \cdot 2} = \$100(1 + .04)^4$$
$$= \$116.99$$

2. For quarterly compounding

$$F_2 = \$100 \left(1 + \frac{.08}{4}\right)^{4 \cdot 2} = \$100(1 + .02)^8$$
$$= \$117.16$$

As one would expect, the results in this example are the same as those given earlier in Tables 13.2 and 13.3.

If the interest were compounded monthly, weekly, or daily, m would equal 12, 52, or 365, respectively. In all these cases of multiple intrayear compounding, the effective annual interest rate i', given the nominal or stated annual interest rate i, can be derived from Equation 13.7,* as follows: Let $P = \$1$, $n = 1$ year. Then F_1 from Equation 13.7 becomes equal to $\$1 (1 + i/m)^m$. Since F_1 represents an amount equal to \$1 plus accumulated interest at the end of 1 year, when the interest is compounded m times a year, the implied effective interest rate, i', is given by Equation 13.8.

$$i' = \left(1 + \frac{i}{m}\right)^m - 1 \tag{13.8}$$

---

*Equation 13.7 can also be modified to develop the formula for *continuous compounding* (i.e., compounding every microsecond) and the formula for the associated effective annual rate of interest. These formulas are very useful for theoretical work in finance. Also, since many Canadian banks and credit unions are now using daily compounding, the formula for the calculation of the effective annual interest rate under continuous compounding can be used to approximate the effective annual interest rate under daily compounding. In the literature of finance, which employs continuous compounding, the number of years is represented by t (time). Substituting t for n in Equation 13.7, the compound value F_t is given by

$$F_t = P\left(1 + \frac{i}{m}\right)^{m \cdot t}$$
$$= P\left[\left(1 + \frac{i}{m}\right)^{m/i}\right]^{i \cdot t}$$

If we replace m/i by k, then we can rewrite the above equation as

$$F_t = P\left[\left(1 + \frac{1}{k}\right)^{k}\right]^{i \cdot t}$$

Because compounding is continuous, m tends to infinity $(m \to \infty)$, and given interest i, $k \to \infty$. Therefore, for the case of continuous compounding the above equation, in the language of calculus, can be restated as

$$F_t = P\left[\lim_{k \to \infty}\left(1 + \frac{1}{k}\right)^{k}\right]^{i \cdot t}$$

It is well known that the bracketed term approaches e, where e is equal to 2.718. . . . Therefore, the compound value, F_t, when the interest is compounded continuously, is given by

$$F_t = Pe^{it} \tag{1}$$

For some types of financial problems (e.g., the Gordon valuation model discussed in Chapter 17), the symbol g (growth rate) is used instead of the interest rate i.

Letting $P = \$1$ and $t = 1$ year in Equation 1 above, $F_1 = e^i$. Therefore, the effective annual rate of interest i' under continuous compounding is given by

$$i' = e^i - 1 \tag{2}$$

EXAMPLE Using the data in the preceding example, the effective annual interest rate, i', earned by Steve Saver on his deposit at 8 percent, compounded semiannually can be calculated by substituting the nominal interest rate $i = .08$ and $m = 2$ in Equation 13.8. Thus, the effective annual interest rate i' is given by

$$i' = \left(1 + \frac{.08}{2}\right)^2 - 1$$
$$= (1 + .04)^2 - 1$$
$$= 1.0816 - 1$$
$$= .0816 \text{ or } 8.16 \text{ percent}$$

which is the same as the effective annual interest rate calculated earlier without using Equation 13.8.

If the interest rate had been compounded daily, then the effective annual interest rate, i', would be equal to $(1 + .08/365)^{365} - 1$. This calculation can be made with the aid of a computer. An approximation of the effective annual interest rate under *daily* compounding can be obtained by using the formula for the calculation of the effective annual interest rate under *continuous compounding*, which is given by Equation 2 in the footnote on page 368 (i.e., $i' = e^i - 1$). Substituting $i = .08$ in the equation $i' = e^i - 1$, we find that the effective annual interest rate, i', under continuous compounding equals $e^{.08} - 1$. Using a financial calculator, $e^{.08} = 1.0833$ (approximately). Therefore, i' under continuous compounding equals $1.0833 - 1 = .0833$ or 8.33 percent. Thus, the effective annual rate of interest under *daily* compounding is approximately equal to 8.33 percent. It should be noted that the 8.33 percent effective annual interest rate under continuous compounding compares closely with the 8.16 percent and 8.24 percent effective annual interest rates under semiannual and quarterly compounding, respectively.

Using a Table for Intrayear Compounding The table of the compound value of one dollar, Table A-1, can be used to simplify the calculations required by Equation 13.7. Instead of indexing the table for i percent and n years, as we do when interest is compounded annually, we index it for $(i \div m)$ percent and $(m \cdot n)$ years. In this way, we deal with the number of compounding periods and the rate appropriate to each period. The usefulness of the table is usually somewhat limited, since only selected rates for a limited number of years can be found. The table can commonly be used to calculate the results of semiannual and quarterly compounding (i.e., when $m = 2, 4$), but when more frequent compounding is done, the aid of a computer may be necessary to solve Equation 13.7. The following example will clarify the use of the compound interest table for intrayear compounding.

EXAMPLE In the earlier examples, Steve Saver wished to find the compound value of $100 invested at 8 percent compounded both semiannually and quarterly for two years. The number of compounding periods, m, was 2 and 4 in each of these cases, respectively. The values by which the table for the compound value of $1 is accessed, along with the compound-value interest factor in each case, are as follows:

Compounding period	m	Percentage $(i \div m)$	Years $(m \cdot n)$	Compound-value interest factor from Table A-1
Semiannual	2	.08 ÷ 2 = .04	2 · 2 = 4	1.170
Quarterly	4	.08 ÷ 4 = .02	4 · 2 = 8	1.172

Multiplying each of the factors by the initial $100 deposit results in a value of $117.00 (i.e., 1.170 · $100) for semiannual compounding and value of $117.20 (i.e., 1.172 · $100) for quarterly compounding. The corresponding values found by the long method are $116.99 and $117.16, respectively. The discrepancy can be attributed to the rounding of values in the table.

THE COMPOUND VALUE OF AN ANNUITY

An *annuity* is a stream of equal cash flows. These cash flows can be either received or deposited by an individual in some interest-earning form. The calculations required to find the compound value of an annuity on which interest is paid at a specified rate compounded annually can be illustrated by a simple example.

EXAMPLE   Mary Jones wishes to determine how much money she will have at the end of 5 years if she deposits $1,000 annually, at the end of each year, in a savings account paying 7-percent interest. As Table 13.5 shows, at the end of year 5, Mary will have $5,751 in her account. Column 2 of the table indicates that, since the deposits are made at the end of the year, the first deposit will earn interest for four years, the second for three years, and so on. The compound value interest factors in column 3 correspond with these interest-earning periods and the 7-percent rate of interest.

Table 13.5   The Value of a $1,000 Five-Year Annuity Compounded at 7 Percent

End of year	Amount deposited (1)	Number of years compounded (2)	Compound-value interest factor from Table A-1 (3)	Future sum (1) · (3) (4)
1	$1,000	4	1.311	$1,311
2	1,000	3	1.225	1,225
3	1,000	2	1.145	1,145
4	1,000	1	1.070	1,070
5	1,000	0	1.000	1,000
Amount at end of year 5				$5,751

Simplifying the Calculations   The calculations required in the preceding example can be simplified somewhat since each of the factors is actually multiplied by the same dollar amount. The actual calculations required in the preceding table can be expressed as follows:

$$
\begin{aligned}
\text{Amount at end of year 5} &= \$1,000(1.311) + \$1,000(1.225) \\
&\quad + \$1,000(1.145) + \$1,000(1.070) \\
&\quad + \$1,000(1.000) \\
&= \$5,751 \\
&= \text{sum of the compound values of} \\
&\quad \text{each of the payments}
\end{aligned}
\tag{13.9}
$$

Factoring out the $1,000, Equation 13.9 can be rewritten as

$$
\begin{aligned}
\text{Amount at end of year 5} &= \$1,000(1.311 + 1.225 + 1.145 + 1.070 \\
&\quad + 1.000) \\
&= \$1,000\,(5.751) \\
&= \$5,751
\end{aligned}
\tag{13.10}
$$

Equation 13.10 indicates that in order to find the compound value of the annuity, the annual amount must be multiplied by the sum of the appropriate compound-value interest factors.

Using a Compound Value of an Annuity Table Appendix Table A-2 simplifies even further the calculations required to find the compound value of an annuity. A portion of Table A-2 is given in Table 13.6. The factors in this table are derived by summing the terms in parentheses in equations like Equation 13.10. In the case of Equation 13.10, this results in Equation 13.11.

$$
\text{Amount at end of year 5} = \$1,000(5.751) = \$5,751 \tag{13.11}
$$

The values in the table are based on the assumption that deposits are made at the end of the year. If S_n equals the compound value of an n-year annuity, A equals the amount to be deposited annually at the end of each year, and $CVIFA_{i,n}$ represents the appropriate *compound-value interest factor for an n-year annuity compounded at i percent*, the relationship between these variables can be expressed as follows:

$$
S_n = A \cdot (CVIFA_{i,n}) \tag{13.12}
$$

Table 13.6 The Compound-Value Interest Factors for a One-Dollar Annuity, $CVIFA_{i,n}$

Year	5.00 percent	6.00 percent	7.00 percent	8.00 percent	9.00 percent	10.00 percent
1	1.000	1.000	1.000	1.000	1.000	1.000
2	2.050	2.060	2.070	2.080	2.090	2.100
3	3.152	3.184	3.215	3.246	3.278	3.310
4	4.310	4.375	4.440	4.506	4.573	4.641
5	5.526	5.637	5.751	5.867	5.985	6.105
6	6.802	6.975	7.153	7.336	7.523	7.716
7	8.142	8.394	8.654	8.923	9.200	9.487
8	9.549	9.897	10.260	10.637	11.028	11.436
9	11.027	11.491	11.978	12.488	13.021	13.579
10	12.578	13.181	13.816	14.487	15.193	15.937

In Mary Jones' case, the interest factor for the compound value of a $1 annuity with a five-year life at 7 percent can be obtained from Table A-2 and multiplied by the $1,000 deposit. Multiplying the table value of 5.751 by $1,000 results in a compound value for the annuity of $5,751. The following example further illustrates the usefulness of Table A-2.

EXAMPLE   Randa Middleton wishes to determine the sum of money she will have in her savings account, which pays 6-percent annual interest, at the end of 10 years if she deposits $600 at the end of each year for the next 10 years. The appropriate interest factor $CVIFA_{6\%, 10 \text{ yrs.}}$ for the compound value of a 10-year annuity at 6 percent is given in Table A-2 as 13.181. Multiplying this factor by the $600 deposit results in a future sum of $7,908.60. The simple calculations required to find the compound value of an annuity using Table A-2 should be clear from this example.

Present Value

It is often useful to determine the "present value" of a future sum of money. This type of calculation is most important in the capital budgeting decision process, which is discussed in Chapters 14 through 16. The concept of present value, like the concept of compound interest, is based on the belief that the value of money is affected by when it is received. The axiom underlying this belief is that a dollar today is worth more than a dollar that will be received at some future date. In other words, the present value of a dollar that will be received in the future is less than the value of a dollar in hand today. The actual present value of a dollar depends largely on the earning opportunities of the recipient and the point in time the money is to be received. This section explores the present value of single amounts, mixed streams of cash flows, and annuities.

THE PRESENT VALUE OF A SINGLE AMOUNT

The process of finding present values, or *discounting cash flows*, is actually the inverse of compounding. It is concerned with answering the question "If I can earn i percent on my money, what is the most I would be willing to pay for an opportunity to receive F_n dollars n years from today?" Instead of finding the future amount (i.e., compound value) of present dollars invested at a given rate, discounting determines the present value of a future amount, assuming that the decision maker has an opportunity to earn a certain return, i, on his or her money. This return is often referred to as the *discount rate, the cost of capital*, or *an opportunity cost.** These terms will be used interchangeably in this text. The discounting process can be illustrated by a simple example.

---

*The theoretical underpinning of this "cost of capital," as it relates to the business firm's evaluation of capital budgeting proposals, is discussed in depth in Chapter 17.

EXAMPLE Mr. Jones has been given an opportunity to receive $300 one year from now. If he can earn 6 percent on his investments in the normal course of events, what is the most he should pay for this opportunity? To answer this question, we must determine how many dollars must be invested at 6 percent today to have $300 one year from now. Letting P equal this unknown amount, and using the same notation as in the compounding discussion, the situation can be expressed as follows:

$$P(1 + .06) = \$300 \tag{13.13}$$

Solving Equation 13.13 for P gives us Equation 13.14,

$$P = \frac{\$300}{1.06} \tag{13.14}$$

$$= \$283.02$$

In other words, the "present value" of $300 received one year from today, given an opportunity cost of 6 percent, is $283.02. Mr. Jones should be indifferent to whether he receives $283.02 today or $300.00 one year from now. If he can receive $300 one year hence, by paying less than $283.02 today, he should, of course, do so.

A Mathematical Expression for Present Value The present value of a future sum can be found mathematically by solving Equation 13.4 for P. In other words, one merely wants to obtain the present value, P, of some future amount, F_n, to be received n years from now, assuming an opportunity rate of i. Solving Equation 13.4 for P gives us Equation 13.15.

$$P = \frac{F_n}{(1 + i)^n} = F_n \left[\frac{1}{(1 + i)^n} \right] \tag{13.15}$$

The similarity between this general equation for present value* and the equation in the preceding example (Equation 13.14) should be clear. The use of Equation 13.15 can be illustrated by a simple example.

*The present value for the case when the interest is compounded m number of times per year can also be obtained by solving Equation 13.7 for P, which gives:

$$P = F_n \left[\frac{1}{\left(1 + \dfrac{i}{m}\right)^{m \cdot n}} \right]$$

From Equation 13.8 for the calculation of the effective annual interest rate i', $(1 + i/m)^m = (1 + i')$. Therefore, $P = F_n/(1 + i')^n = F_n/(1 + \text{the effective annual interest rate})^n$. When interest is compounded continuously, the present value P will equal $F_t/e^{it} = F_t e^{-it}$. This follows from Equation 1 of the footnote on page 368. Also, from Equation 2 of that footnote, $e^i = 1 + \text{the effective annual interest rate } i'$ under continuous compounding. Therefore, $P = F_t/e^{it} = F_t/(1 + i')^t$.

EXAMPLE   Jim McCarthy wishes to find the present value of $1,700 that will be received eight years from now. Jim's opportunity cost is 8 percent. Substituting $F_8 = \$1,700$, $n = 8$, and $i = .08$ into Equation 13.15 yields Equation 13.16:

$$P = \frac{\$1,700}{(1 + .08)^8} \tag{13.16}$$

In order to solve Equation 13.16, the term $(1 + .08)$ must be raised to the eighth power. The value resulting from this time-consuming calculation is 1.851. Dividing this value into $1,700 yields a present value for the $1,700 of $918.42.

Present-Value Tables   In order to simplify the present-value calculation, tables of present-value interest factors can be used. The table for the *present-value interest factor for one dollar*, $PVIF_{i,n}$, gives values for the expression $1/(1 + i)^n$ where i is the discount rate and n is the number of years involved. Table A-3 in the appendix presents present-value interest factors for various discount rates and years. A portion of Table A-3 is presented in Table 13.7. We can, by letting $PVIF_{i,n}$ represent the appropriate factor from Table A-3, rewrite Equation 13.15 as follows:

$$P = F_n \cdot (PVIF_{i,n}) \tag{13.17}$$

This expression indicates that in order to find the present value, P, of an amount to be received in a future year, n, we have merely to multiply the future amount, F_n, by the appropriate present-value factor from Table A-3. An example should help clarify the use of Equation 13.17.

EXAMPLE   Jim McCarthy, whom we met in the preceding example, wishes to find the present value of $1,700 to be received eight years from now, assuming an 8-percent opportunity cost. Table A-3 gives us a present-value interest factor for 8 percent and eight years, $PVIF_{8\%, 8 \text{ yrs.}}$, of .540. Multiplying this factor by the $1,700 yields a present value of $918. This value is $0.42 less than the value obtained using the long method. This difference is attributable to the fact that the table values have been rounded off to the nearest one-thousandth.

A few other points with respect to present-value tables are also important. First, *the present-value interest factor for a single sum is always less than one;* only if the opportunity cost was zero would this factor equal one. Second, Table A-3 shows that *the higher the opportunity cost for a given year, the smaller the present-value interest factor* is. In other words, the greater an individual's opportunity cost, the less an amount to be received in a certain future year is worth today. Finally, observation of the table values for a given discount rate indicates that *the farther in the future a sum is to be received, the less it is worth presently.* The relationships between various discount rates, discount periods, and present-value interest factors are illustrated in Figure 13.2. The reader should note that given a discount rate of 0 percent the present-value interest factor always equals one, and therefore the future value of the funds equals their present value.

Table 13.7   The Present-Value Interest Factors for One Dollar, $PVIF_{i,n}$

Year	5.00 percent	6.00 percent	7.00 percent	8.00 percent	9.00 percent	10.00 percent
1	.952	.943	.935	.926	.917	.909
2	.907	.890	.873	.857	.842	.826
3	.864	.840	.816	.794	.772	.751
4	.823	.792	.763	.735	.708	.683
5	.784	.747	.713	.681	.650	.621
6	.746	.705	.666	.630	.596	.564
7	.711	.665	.623	.583	.547	.513
8	.677	.627	.582	.540	.502	.467
9	.645	.592	.544	.500	.460	.424
10	.614	.558	.508	.463	.422	.386

Comparing Present Value and Compound Interest   A few important observations must be made with respect to present values. One is that the expression for the present-value interest factor for i percent and n years, $1/(1 + i)^n$, is the inverse of the compound-value interest factor for i percent and n years, $(1 + i)^n$. This observation can be confirmed by dividing a present-value interest factor for i percent and n years,

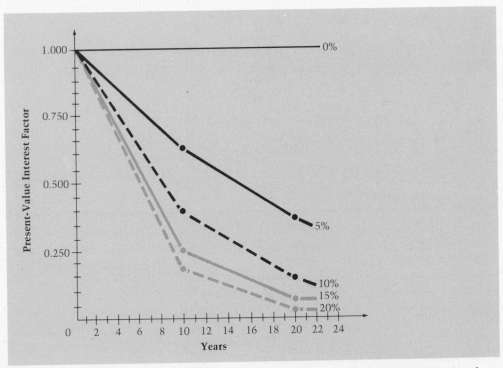

Figure 13.2   Discount rates, time, and present-value interest factors used to find the present value of one dollar.

$PVIF_{i,n}$ into 1 and comparing the resulting value to the compound-value interest factor given in Table A-1 for i percent and n years, $CVIF_{i,n}$. The two values should be equivalent. Because of the relationship between present-value interest and compound-value interest factors, we can find the present-value interest factors given a table of compound-value interest factors and vice versa. The compound-value interest factor from Table A-1 for five years and 10 percent is 1.611. Dividing this value into 1 yields .621, which is the present-value interest factor given in Table A-3 for five years and 10 percent.

UNEVEN STREAMS OF CASH FLOWS

Quite often, especially in capital budgeting problems, there is a need to find the present value of a stream of cash flows to be received in various future years. Two basic types of cash-flow streams are possible—the uneven stream and the annuity. An *uneven stream* of cash flows reflects no particular pattern, while an *annuity* is a pattern of equal annual cash flows (i.e., the cash flows are the same each year). Since certain shortcuts are possible in finding the present value of an annuity, uneven streams and annuities will be discussed separately.

In order to find the present value of an uneven stream of cash flows, all that is required is to determine the present value of each future amount in the manner described in the preceding section and then sum all the individual present values to find the present values of the stream of cash flows. A simple example should clarify this process.

EXAMPLE   The CAM Company has been offered an opportunity to receive the following stream of uneven cash flows over the next five years:

Year	Cash flow
1	$400
2	800
3	500
4	400
5	300

If the firm must earn 9 percent, at minimum, on its investments, what is the most it should pay for this opportunity?

In order to solve this problem, the present value of each individual cash flow discounted at 9 percent for the appropriate number of years is determined. The sum of all these individual values is then calculated to get the present value of the total stream. Table 13.8 presents the calculations required to find the present value of the cash-flow stream, which turns out to be $1,904.60. CAM should not pay more than $1,904.60 for the opportunity to receive these cash flows, since paying $1,904.60 would provide exactly a 9-percent return.

Table 13.8   The Present Value of a Stream of Uneven Cash Flows

Year	Cash flow (1)	P.V. interest factor[a] (2)	Present value (1) · (2) (3)
1	$400	.917	$ 366.80
2	800	.842	673.60
3	500	.772	386.00
4	400	.708	283.20
5	300	.650	195.00
Present value of stream			$1,904.60

[a]Present-value interest factors at 9 percent are from Table A-3.

EXAMPLE   The Delco Company is attempting to determine the most it should pay to purchase a particular annuity. The firm requires a minimum return of 8 percent on all investments; the annuity consists of cash inflows of $700 per year for five years. Table 13.9 shows the long way of finding the present value of the annuity. This procedure yields a present value of $2,795.10, which can be interpreted in the same manner as for the uneven cash-flow stream in the preceding example.

Table 13.9   The Long Method for Finding the Present Value of an Annuity

Year	Cash flow (1)	P.V. interest factor[a] (2)	Present value (1) · (2) (3)
1	$700	.926	$ 648.20
2	700	.857	599.90
3	700	.794	555.80
4	700	.735	514.50
5	700	.681	476.70
Present value of annuity			$2,795.10

[a]Present-value interest factors at 8 percent are from Table A-3.

ANNUITIES

The present value of an annuity can be found in a manner similar to that used on an uneven stream. However, due to the nature of an annuity, a shortcut is possible and is demonstrated next.

Simplifying the Calculations   The calculations used in the preceding example can be simplified by recognizing that each of the five multiplications made to get the individual present values involved multiplying the annual amount ($700) by the appropriate present-value interest factor, as follows:

$$
\begin{aligned}
\text{P.V. of annuity} &= \$700(.926) + \$700(.857) + \$700(.794) \\
&\quad + \$700(.735) + \$700(.681) \\
&= \$2,795.10 \\
&= \text{the sum of the present values} \\
&\quad \text{of each of the payments}
\end{aligned}
\tag{13.18}
$$

Simplifying Equation 13.18 by factoring out the $700 yields Equation 13.19.

$$
\begin{aligned}
\text{P.V. of annuity} &= \$700(.926 + .857 + .794 + .735 + .681) \\
&= \$2,795.10
\end{aligned}
\tag{13.19}
$$

Thus, the present value of an annuity can be found by multiplying the annual amount received by the sum of the present-value interest factors for each year of the annuity's life.

A Table of Present Values for an Annuity   Appendix Table A-4 is a table of *present-value interest factors for a one-dollar annuity* for specified rates and years. A portion of this table is presented in Table 13.10. The interest factors in the table are derived by summing the terms in the parentheses in equations like Equation 13.19. In the case of Equation 13.19, this results in Equation 13.20.

$$
\text{P.V. of annuity} = \$700(3.993) = \$2,795.10
\tag{13.20}
$$

The interest factors in Table A-4 actually represent the sum of the first n present-value interest factors in Table A-3 for a given discount rate. If P_n equals the present value of an n-year annuity, A equals the amount to be received annually at the end of each year, and

Table 13.10   The Present-Value Interest Factors for a One-Dollar Annuity, $PVIFA_{i,n}$

Year	5.00 percent	6.00 percent	7.00 percent	8.00 percent	9.00 percent	10.00 percent
1	.952	.943	.935	.926	.917	.909
2	1.859	1.833	1.808	1.783	1.759	1.736
3	2.723	2.673	2.624	2.577	2.531	2.487
4	3.546	3.465	3.387	3.312	3.240	3.170
5	4.329	4.212	4.100	3.993	3.890	3.791
6	5.076	4.917	4.767	4.623	4.486	4.355
7	5.786	5.582	5.389	5.206	5.033	4.868
8	6.463	6.210	5.971	5.747	5.535	5.335
9	7.108	6.802	6.515	6.247	5.995	5.759
10	7.722	7.360	7.024	6.710	6.418	6.145

$PVIFA_{i,n}$ represents the appropriate value for the *present-value interest factor for a one-dollar annuity discounted at i percent for n years*, the present value of the annuity can be found by the following equation:

$$P_n = A \cdot (PVIFA_{i,n})$$ (13.21)

The problem presented earlier involving the calculation of the present value of a five-year annuity of $700 assuming an 8-percent opportunity cost can be easily worked out with the aid of Table A-4 and Equation 13.21. The present-value interest factor for a $1 annuity in Table A-4 for 8-percent and five years, $PVIFA_{8\%,5yrs.}$ is 3.993. Multiplying this factor by the $700 annuity provides a present value for the annuity of $2,795.10. A simple example may help clarify the usefulness of Table A-4 in finding the present value of an annuity.

EXAMPLE   The Saskatchewan Mining Company Ltd. expects to receive $160,000 per year at the end of each of the next 20 years from a new mine. If the firm's opportunity cost of funds is 10 percent, what is the present value of this annuity? The appropriate interest factor for the present value at 10 percent for a 20-year annuity, $PVIFA_{10\%,20\ yrs.}$, is found in Table A-4 to be 8.514. Multiplying this factor by the $160,000 cash flow results in a present value of $1,362,240.

Applying Compound Interest and Present-Value Techniques

Compound interest and present-value techniques have a number of important applications in addition to those we have discussed. Five of these applications will be presented in this section. They are (1) the calculation of the deposit needed to accumulate a future sum, (2) the calculation of amortization on loans, (3) the determination of interest and growth rates, (4) the determination of bond values, and (5) the calculation of the present value of perpetuities.

DEPOSITS TO ACCUMULATE A FUTURE SUM

Often an individual may wish to determine the annual deposit necessary to accumulate a certain amount of money at a particular future point in time. Suppose a person wishes to purchase a house five years from now and recognizes that an initial down payment of $4,000 will be required at that time. He or she wishes to make equal annual end-of-year deposits in an account paying annual interest of 6 percent, so the amount of an equal annual deposit (annuity) that will result in a sum equal to $4,000 at the end of year 5 must be determined. The solution to this problem is closely related to the process of finding the compound value of an annuity. The compound value of an n-year annuity, S_n, was found earlier by multiplying the annual deposit, A, by the appropriate interest factor from Table A-2, $CVIFA_{i,n}$. The relationship between the three variables was given by Equation 13.12, which is rewritten below as Equation 13.22.

$$S_n = A \cdot (CVIFA_{i,n})$$ (13.22)

We can find the annual deposit required to accumulate S_n dollars, given a specified interest rate, i, and a certain number of years, n, by solving Equation 13.22 for A. Isolating A on the left side of the equation gives us

$$A = \frac{S_n}{CVIFA_{i,n}}$$ (13.23)

EXAMPLE   In the problem stated earlier in this section, an individual wished to determine the equal annual end-of-year deposits required to accumulate $4,000 at the end of five years given an interest rate of 6 percent. Table A-2 indicates that the compound-value interest factor for an annuity at 6 percent for five years, $CVIFA_{6\%,5\ yrs.}$, is 5.637. Substituting $S_5 = \$4,000$ and $CVIFA_{6\%,5\ yrs.} = 5.637$ into Equation 13.23 yields an annual required deposit, A, of $709.60 (i.e., $4,000 ÷ 5.637). If $709.60 is deposited at the end of each year for five years at 6 percent, then there will be $4,000 in the account at the end of the five years.

LOAN AMORTIZATION

The phrase *loan amortization* refers to the determination of the equal annual loan payments necessary to provide a lender with a specified interest return, and repay the loan principal, over a specified term. The loan amortization process involves finding the future payments (over the term of the loan) whose present value at the loan interest rate just equals the amount of initial principal borrowed. Lenders use loan amortization tables to find these payment amounts. In the case of home mortgages, these tables are used to find the equal monthly payments necessary to amortize or pay off the loan at a specified interest rate over a 20- to 35-year period.

The discussion here will deal only with the amortization of loans on which annual end-of-year payments are made. Amortizing a loan actually involves creating an annuity out of a present sum. For example, an individual may borrow $6,000 at 10 percent and agree to make equal annual payments over seven years. In order to determine the size of the payments, the seven-year annuity discounted at 10 percent that has a present value of $6,000 must be determined. This process is actually the inverse of finding the present value of an annuity.

Earlier in this chapter the present value, P_n, of an n-year annuity of A dollars was found by multiplying the annual amount, A, by the present-value interest factor for an annuity from Table A-4, $PVIFA_{i,n}$. This relationship, which was originally expressed as Equation 13.21, is rewritten as Equation 13.24 as follows:

$$P_n = A \cdot (PVIFA_{i,n})$$ (13.24)

To find the equal annual payment, A, required to pay off or amortize the loan, P_n, over a certain number of years at a specified interest rate, we need to solve Equation 13.24 for A. Isolating A on the left side of the equation gives us

$$A = \frac{P_n}{PVIFA_{i,n}}$$ (13.25)

EXAMPLE In the problem stated at the start of this section, an individual wished to determine the equal annual end-of-year loan payments necessary to fully amortize a $6,000, 10-percent loan over seven years. Table A-4 indicates that the present-value interest factor for an annuity corresponding to 10 percent and seven years, $PVIFA_{10\%,7 \text{ yrs.}}$, is 4.868. Substituting $P_7 = \$6,000$ and $PVIFA_{10\%,7 \text{ yrs.}} = 4.868$ in Equation 13.25 and solving for A yields an annual loan payment of $1,232.54 (i.e., $6,000 ÷ 4.868). In order to repay the principal and interest on a $6,000, 10-percent, seven-year loan, equal annual end-of-year payments of $1,232.54 are necessary.

DETERMINING INTEREST AND GROWTH RATES

It is often necessary to calculate the compound annual interest or growth rate associated with a stream of cash flows. In doing this, either compound interest or present-value tables can be used. The preferred approach, using compound interest tables, is described in this section. The simplest situation is where one wishes to find the rate of interest or growth in a cash-flow stream. This case can be illustrated by a simple example.

EXAMPLE Tom Richards wishes to find the rate of interest or growth of the following stream of cash flows*

Year	Amount	
19X4	$1,520	4
19X3	$1,440	3
19X2	$1,370	2
19X1	$1,300	1
19X0	$1,250	

Interest has been earned (or growth experienced) for four years. In order to find the rate at which this has occurred, the amount received in the latest year (19X4) is divided by the amount received in the earliest year (19X0). This gives us the compound-value interest factor for four years, $CVIF_{i,4 \text{ yrs.}}$, which is 1.216 ($1,520 ÷ $1,250). The interest rate in Table A-1 associated with the factor closest to 1.216 for four years is the rate of interest or growth rate associated with the cash flows. Looking across year 4 of Table A-1 shows that the factor for 5 percent is exactly 1.216; therefore, the rate of interest or growth rate associated with the cash flows given is 5 percent.†

Sometimes one wishes to determine the interest rate associated with an equal-payment loan. For instance, if a person were to borrow $2,000, which was to be repaid in

---

*Since the calculations required for finding interest rates and growth rates, given certain cash flow or principal flow streams, are the same, this section refers to the calculations as those required to find interest *or* growth rates.

†If the $CVIF_{i,4 \text{ yrs.}}$ had been 1.200 instead of 1.216, then the value of i would have to be obtained by interpolation. Interpolating, one would obtain

$$\begin{bmatrix} 5\% & 1.216 \\ i\% & 1.200 \\ 4\% & 1.170 \end{bmatrix} \quad \text{or} \quad \frac{i - .04}{.05 - .04} = \frac{1.200 - 1.170}{1.216 - 1.170}, \text{ which gives } i = .0465 \text{ or } 4.65\%.$$

equal annual end-of-year amounts of $514.14 for the next five years, he or she might wish to determine the rate of interest being paid on the loan. Referring back to Equation 13.24 shows that $P_5 = \$2,000$ and $A = \$514.14$. Rearranging the equation and substituting these values results in a present-value interest factor for a 5-year annuity, $PVIFA_{i,5\ yrs.}$ of 3.890:

$$PVIFA_{i,5\ yrs.} = \frac{P_5}{A} = \frac{\$2,000}{\$514.14} = 3.890 \tag{13.26}$$

The interest rate for five years associated with a factor of 3.890 in Table A-4 is 9 percent; therefore, the interest rate on the loan is 9 percent.

DETERMINING BOND VALUES

Corporate bonds, which are discussed in greater detail in Chapter 21, typically pay interest semiannually. Often it is necessary to determine the value, or current worth, of a bond. The cash flows from a bond consist not only of the interest inflows every six months, but also of the cash flow resulting from payment of the face value at maturity. Since the interest payments on a bond occur periodically throughout its life, it is easiest to calculate the present value of this annuity-type cash flow separately from the present value of the principal payment at maturity. Since interest is paid semiannually, the factors involved in the calculation of the present value of the semiannual interest annuity, are one-half the annual discount rate and twice the number of years.

EXAMPLE   In order to find the value of a 20-year bond with a 10-percent coupon, paying interest semiannually and having a face value of $1,000, we must first find the present value of the 40 semiannual interest payments. Since the bond pays $100 (i.e., 10 percent of $1,000) in interest per year, the semiannual payments are $50 each (i.e., $\frac{1}{2}$ of $100). In order to find the present value of the 40 semiannual $50 payments, the *market discount rate*, which reflects the return currently available on bonds of similar risk and maturity, must be used. In this case we will assume that the market discount rate equals 10 percent, which happens to be equal to the bond's coupon rate. Since the interest is compounded semiannually over the 20 years, the present-value interest factor for an annuity for 5 percent and 40 years, $PVIFA_{5\%,40\ yrs.}$, from Table A-4 is used. This present-value interest factor is 17.159, which when multiplied by $50 gives us a present value for the interest cash flows of $857.95. This value results from viewing the interest payments as a 40-year annuity discounted at 5 percent.

The present value of the $1,000 maturity value is found by multiplying the $1,000 by the present-value interest factor for $1 to be received 40 years from now at 5-percent. The use of 40 years and 5 percent is consistent with the 5-percent *semiannual* interest compounding over a 20-year period with the stated or nominal interest rate (i.e., coupon rate) of 10 percent described above. The factor in Table A-3 for 5 percent and 40 years, $PVIF_{5\%,40\ yrs.}$, is .142. Multiplied by the $1,000 maturity value, it gives us a present value for that sum of $142. Adding the present value of the interest ($857.95) to the present value of the maturity value of the bond ($142) gives us a value for the bond of $999.95. Since the market discount rate is assumed to be 10 percent, which equals the coupon rate on the bond, the bond's value of $999.95 is equal (except for a slight rounding error) to its face value of $1,000. Should the market discount rate be higher than 10 percent, the bond value would be less than its $1,000 face value, and vice versa. Note that the effective annual interest rate on the bond equals $(1 + .10/2)^2 - 1 = (1 + .05)^2 - 1 = 1.1025 - 1 = .1025$ or 10.25%. The effective rate is greater than the coupon rate of 10 percent due to semiannual compounding.

PERPETUITIES

A *perpetuity* is an annuity with an infinite life, or in other words, an annuity that never stops providing its holder with "*x* dollars" at the end of each year. It is often necessary to find the present value of a perpetuity. The present-value interest factor for a perpetuity discounted at the rate *i* is defined by Equation 13.27.

$$\text{Present-value interest factor for a perpetuity at } i\% = \frac{1}{i} \qquad (13.27)$$

In other words, the appropriate factor is found merely by dividing the discount rate (stated as a decimal) into 1. The validity of this method can be seen by looking at the factors in Table A-4 for 8 percent, 10 percent, and 20 percent. As the number of years approaches 50, the value of these factors approaches 12.500, 10.000, and 5.000, respectively. Substituting .08, .10, and .20 (for *i*) into Equation 13.27 gives us factors for finding the present value of perpetuities at these rates of 12.500, 10.000, and 5.000. An example may help clarify the application of Equation 13.27.

EXAMPLE   An individual wishes to determine the present value of a $1,000 perpetuity discounted at 10 percent. The appropriate present-value interest factor can be found by dividing 1 by .10, as prescribed by Equation 13.27. The resulting factor, 10, is then multiplied by the annual cash inflow of $1,000 to get the present value of the perpetuity, $10,000. In other words, the receipt of $1,000 every year for an indefinite period is worth only $10,000 today if a person can earn 10 percent on investments. This is because, if the person had $10,000 and earned 10 percent interest on it each year, $1,000 a year could be withdrawn indefinitely without affecting the initial $10,000, which would never be drawn down.

Summary

This chapter has discussed the key mathematical concepts of finance. Specific attention has been given to compound interest, present value, and certain applications of the techniques for calculating compound interest and present value. Compound interest is an important concept in measuring the value of future sums. When interest is compounded, the initial principal or deposit in one period along with the interest earned on it becomes the beginning principal of the following period, and so on. Interest can be compounded annually, semiannually, quarterly, monthly, weekly, daily, or even continuously. The more frequently interest is compounded, the larger the future sum that will be accumulated. If F_n equals the future sum at the end of year n, P equals the initial principal, m equals the number of times per year interest is compounded, i equals the stated annual rate of interest, and n equals the number of years over which the money earns a return, then

$$F_n = P \left(1 + \frac{i}{m} \right)^{m \cdot n}$$

and the effective annual interest rate i', given the nominal annual interest rate i, equals $(1 + i/m)^m - 1$. Whenever interest is compounded annually, m equals 1. The effective annual interest rate i' in the case of continuous compounding equals $e^i - 1$.

Table A-1 in the Appendix presents the compound-value interest factors used in the annual compounding of interest at various rates for periods from 1 to 50 years. This table can also be used to evaluate the benefits of compounding interest more frequently than annually. Table A-2 in the Appendix provides an easier method for finding the compound value of an annuity by multiplying the amount of the annuity by the appropriate factor.

Present value represents the inverse of compounding. When a person finds the present value of a future amount, he or she determines what amount of money today would be equivalent to the given future amount, considering the fact that he or she can earn a certain return on the invested money. As long as a person can earn a return at a rate greater than 0 percent, the present value of a future cash flow is less than its future value. If P equals the present value of a future amount, F_n, to be received n years from now and interest can be earned at i percent per year, the formula for present value is

$$P = \frac{F_n}{(1 + i)^n} = F_n \left[\frac{1}{(1 + i)^n} \right]$$

The present-value interest factor is represented by the term in brackets. Table A-3 in the Appendix presents these factors for various discount rates, i, and years, n. Occasionally it is necessary to find the present value of a stream of cash flows. Uneven streams consist of any cash-flow pattern other than an annuity, which is a pattern of equal annual cash flows (i.e., the cash flows are the same each year). For uneven streams, the individual present values must be found and summed. In the case of an annuity, the present value can be found using the present-value interest factor for an annuity from Table A-4 in the Appendix. Multiplying the appropriate interest factor from Table A-4 by the annual cash flow gives us the present value of the annuity.

By manipulating the equations for the compound value and present value of single amounts and annuities in certain ways, the deposits needed to accumulate a future sum, loan amortization payments, interest and growth rates, and bond values can be calculated. Although differing calculations are required in each case, the basic approach is derived from the concepts of compound interest and present value. The present value of a perpetuity, which is an annuity with an infinite life, can be calculated by multiplying the annual cash flow by (1 divided by the appropriate discount rate).

Techniques for calculating compound values and present values are most important in the financial decision-making process. These techniques are of critical importance in the capital budgeting decision process and in analyses of the cost of capital, capital structure, valuation, leasing, bond refunding, valuing convertible securities, business combinations, and business rehabilitation. Subsequent parts of this text will draw on compound-interest and present-value concepts in analyzing decisions in these areas.

Questions

13.1 How is the compounding process related to the payment of interest on savings? What is the general equation for the future amount, F_n, in year n if P dollars are deposited in an account paying i-percent annual interest?

13.2 How are compound-value interest tables arranged? How may they be used to calculate the future amount generated by a current deposit? At what point in time in each period have the values shown in the compound-value tables been calculated?

13.3 What effect would a decrease in the interest rate or an increase in the holding period of a deposit have on the future amount available? Why?

13.4 What effect does compounding interest more frequently than once a year have on the future amount generated by a current sum? Why?

13.5 If interest is compounded m times a year at a stated rate i over n years, what is the expression for the future amount, F_n? Can you explain this equation?

13.6 How may the table for the compound-value interest factor for one dollar be used for calculating the future amount of a present sum when interest is compounded more often than annually?

13.7 What is meant by the term "compound value of an annuity"? How are the factors in the table for the compound value of an annuity developed, and how may the table be used to find the compound value of an annuity?

13.8 What is meant by the phrase "the present value of a future sum"? How are present-value and compound interest calculations related?

13.9 What is the equation for the present value of a future amount, F_n, to be received in year n assuming that the firm's cost of capital is i? How is this equation different from the equation for the compound value of one dollar?

13.10 How may the table of interest factors for the present value of one dollar be used for calculating present values? How could present values be calculated using the table for the compound value of one dollar?

13.11 What effect do increasing (1) costs of capital and (2) increasing time periods have on the present value of a future sum? Why?

13.12 How can the present-value tables be used to find the present value of an uneven stream of cash flows? Why can the present value of an annuity be found by summing the individual present-value interest factors and mutiplying the sum by the annual amount received?

13.13 How is the table of interest factors for the present value of an annuity used? How could this table be developed from the table of interest factors for the present value of one dollar?

13.14 How can the size of the equal annual end-of-year deposits necessary to accumulate a certain future amount in a specified future year be determined? How might one of the financial tables discussed in this chapter aid in this calculation?

13.15 How can a loan requiring equal annual end-of-year payments be amortized over its stated life at a given rate? How might one of the financial tables in this chapter be used to simplify this calculation?

13.16 Which financial tables would be used to find (1) the growth rate associated with a stream of cash flows and (2) the interest rate associated with an equal-payment loan? How would each of these be calculated?

13.17 If bond interest is paid semiannually, how can one determine a bond value? Which table(s) are required to calculate this?

13.18 What is a perpetuity? How might the factor for the present value of such a stream of cash flows be determined?

Problems

13.1 For each of the following cases, calculate the amount of money that will be available at the end of the deposit period if the interest rate is compounded annually for the given period of years.

Case	Amount	Interest rate	Period (years)
A	$ 200	5%	20
B	$ 4,500	8%	7
C	$10,000	9%	10
D	$25,000	10%	12
E	$37,000	11%	5
F	$40,000	12%	9

13.2 An individual borrows $200 to be repaid in 8 years with 14-percent annually compounded interest. The loan may be repaid at the end of any earlier year with no prepayment penalty.
a. What amount would be due if the loan is repaid at the end of year 1?
b. What is the repayment at the end of year 4?
c. What amount is due at the end of the eighth year?

13.3 Using annual, semiannual, and quarterly compounding periods, calculate the future sum and the effective annual interest rate if $5,000 is deposited
a. At 8 percent for 5 years.
b. At 12 percent for 5 years.
c. At 8 percent for 10 years.
d. Calculate the effective annual interest rate for each of the above parts, assuming *daily* interest compounding. Use the continuous compounding approximation discussed in the chapter.

13.4 Nancy Jackson has $10,000 that she can deposit in any of three savings accounts for a three-year period. Bank A pays interest on an annual basis; Bank B pays interest twice each year; and Bank C pays interest each quarter. If all banks have a stated annual interest rate of 8 percent, but follow the different interest payment practices above, what sum would Ms. Jackson have at the end of the third year leaving all interest paid on deposit in
a. Bank A
b. Bank B
c. Bank C

13.5   Jay Martin has been offered a future payment of $500 three years from today. If his opportunity cost is 7 percent compounded annually, what value would he place on this opportunity?

13.6   A hypothetical Quebec savings bond can be converted at $25 at maturity six years from purchase. If the Quebec bonds are to be competitive with Canada Savings Bonds paying 6 percent annual interest (compounded annually), at what price will the province sell its bonds? Assume no cash payments on savings bonds prior to redemption.

13.7   Julio Lopez has $1,500 to invest. His investment counselor suggests an investment that pays no explicit interest, but will return $2,000 at the end of three years.
a.   What annual rate of return will Mr. Lopez earn with this investment?
b.   Mr. Lopez is considering another investment of equal risk, which earns a return of 8 percent. Which investment should he take, and why?

13.8   If one deposits $75 in his or her credit union at the end of each quarter for the next 10 years, and the credit union pays 8-percent interest on the balance on deposit at the end of each year, determine the sum the individual will have if no interest is withdrawn, and:
a.   The credit union pays interest annually.
b.   The credit union pays interest semiannually.
c.   The credit union pays interest quarterly.

13.9   What initial sum would one need to deposit at 10-percent annual interest in order to pay out $85 at the end of each of the next six years, at which time the account would have a zero balance?

13.10   What amount should an individual pay for a bond with a $1,000 face value, maturing in six years, paying a coupon yield of 2 percent each six months (4-percent annual interest paid semiannually) if the market rate of interest on equally risky bonds is 10-percent (annual) paid semiannually?

13.11   Calculate the present value of a $500-face-value bond paying quarterly interest at an annual rate of 10 percent and having a 10-year maturity if the market rate of interest is 12 percent (annual) paid quarterly.

13.12   Calculate the value of each of the following bonds, all of which pay interest semiannually.

Bond	Face value	Coupon rate	Maturity	Market rate
A	$ 100	12%	10 years	8%
B	$ 500	10%	15 years	10%
C	$1000	8%	20 years	12%

13.13   Jerry Carney has an opportunity to purchase any of the following cash flows at the prices given. What recommendation would you make, assuming that Mr. Carney can earn 10 percent on his investments?

Project	Price	Cash flow	Year of receipt
A	$18,000	$30,000	5
B	$ 600	$ 3,000	20
C	$ 3,500	$10,000	10
D	$ 1,000	$15,000	40

13.14 You are given the following series of cash flows:

	Cash flows		
Year	A	B	C
1	$500	$1,500	$2,500
2	560	1,550	2,600
3	640	1,610	2,650
4	720	1,680	2,650
5	800	1,760	2,800
6		1,850	2,850
7		1,950	2,900
8		2,060	
9		2,170	
10		2,280	

a. Calculate the compound growth rate associated with each cash-flow stream.
b. If year 1 values represent initial deposits in a savings account paying annual interest, what is the rate of interest on each account?
c. Compare and discuss the growth rates and interest rates found in **a** and **b**, respectively.

13.15 A retirement home at Marineworld Estates now costs $35,000. Inflation is expected to cause this price to increase at 6 percent per year over the 20 years before J. R. Rogers retires. How much will he need to save each year at an annual rate of 10 percent to have the cash to purchase his home upon retirement?

13.16 Young Daniel Markham will be attending the University of Calgary in 19 years. Total university expenses will be $10,000 per year, payable at the beginning of each of the four years he will attend university. How much will his parents need to save in each of the next 19 years, at 6-percent annual interest, to pay for Daniel's education? Assume a 6-percent annual interest rate throughout and no contribution from the parents after year 19.

13.17 Given the following data, determine for each of the following perpetuities:
a. The appropriate present-value interest factor.
b. The present value.

Perpetuity	Annual amount	Discount rate
A	$ 20,000	8%
B	$100,000	10%
C	$ 3,000	6%
D	$ 60,000	5%

13.18 Bob Sherill has been shopping for a loan to finance the purchase of his new car. He has found three possibilities that seem attractive and wishes to select the one having the lowest interest rate. The information available with respect to each of the three $5,000 loans follows.

Loan	Principal	Annual payment	Life (years)
A	$5,000	$1,352.81	5
B	$5,000	$1,543.21	4
C	$5,000	$2,010.45	3

a. Determine the interest rate that would be associated with each of the loans.
b. Which loan should Mr. Sherill take?

Suggested Readings

Bierman, Harold, Jr., Charles P. Bonini, and Warren H. Hausman, *Quantitative Analysis for Business Decisions*, 5th ed. (Homewood, Ill.: Irwin, 1977), chap. 21.

Bierman, Harold, Jr., and Seymour Smidt, *The Capital Budgeting Decision*, 4th ed. (New York: Macmillan, 1975), chaps. 1 and 4.

Boness, A. James, *Capital Budgeting* (New York: Praeger, 1972).

Cissell, Robert, Helen Cissell, and David C. Flaspohler, *Mathematics of Finance*, 5th ed. (Boston: Houghton Mifflin, 1978).

Clayton, Gary E. and Christopher B. Spivey, *The Time Value of Money* (Philadelphia: Saunders, 1978).

Draper, Jean E. and Jane S. Klingman, *Mathematical Analysis* (New York: Harper & Row, 1967).

Grant, Eugene L. and W. Grant Iverson, *Principles of Engineering Economy*, 6th ed. (New York: Ronald, 1976), pp. 25–61.

Hart, William L., *Mathematics of Investment*, 5th ed. (Lexington, Mass.: Heath, 1975).

Jean, William H., *Capital Budgeting: The Economic Evaluation of Investment Projects* (Scranton, Pa.: Intext, 1969).

Johnson, R. W., *Capital Budgeting* (Dubuque, Iowa: Kendall/Hunt, 1977).

Levy, Haim and Marshall Sarnat, *Capital Investment and Financial Decisions* (Englewood Cliffs, N.J.: Prentice-Hall, 1978), chap. 2.

Mao, James C. T., *Quantitative Analysis for Financial Decisions* (New York: Macmillan, 1969).

Merrett, A. J. and Allen Sykes, *Capital Budgeting and Company Finance* (London: Longmans, 1966).

Osteryoung, Jerome, *Capital Budgeting: Long-Term Asset Selection*, 2nd ed. (Columbus, Ohio: Grid, 1979), chap. 3.

Peterson, David E., A *Quantitative Framework for Financial Management* (Homewood, Ill.: Irwin, 1969).

Quirin, G. David, *The Capital Expenditure Decision* (Homewood, Ill.: Irwin, 1967).

Solomon, Ezra, "The Arithmetic of Capital-Budgeting Decisions," *Journal of Business* 29 (April 1956), pp. 124–129.

Wright, M. G., *Discounted Cash Flow*, 2nd ed. (London: McGraw-Hill, 1973).

Chapter 14

FIXED-ASSET MANAGEMENT AND CAPITAL BUDGETING FUNDAMENTALS

Typically, the largest dollar investment maintained by a manufacturing firm is in fixed assets. Some fixed assets are a necessity for the manufacturing firm, since without them, production would be a virtual impossibility. There are two major classes of fixed assets—plant and equipment. It is possible for a manufacturing firm to operate without any fixed assets on its balance sheet by leasing plant or equipment, or both. However, the emphasis in this chapter will be on owned fixed assets. A discussion of leased fixed assets is presented in Chapter 20.

The level of fixed assets maintained by a manufacturing concern is somewhat dependent on the nature of the firm's production processes. Aside from raw materials, the major inputs to the production process are overhead and labour. The majority of the firm's overhead cost is attributable to its plant and equipment. Some firms, such as electric utilities, require high levels of fixed assets and relatively low labour inputs to produce their finished product. This type of firm is often referred to as *capital intensive*.

Other firms require high labour inputs and fewer fixed assets in order to produce a finished good. Manufacturers of electrical equipment that requires a great deal of hand assembly and soldering are examples of labour *intensive* firms.

Fixed assets are quite often referred to as *earning assets*, since they generally provide the basis for the firm's earning power. Without plant and equipment, the manufacturing firm could not produce a product. Current assets such as cash, accounts receivable, and inventory do not directly give the manufacturing firm earning power; only in the case of a merchandising concern could these assets be considered the firm's earning base.

This chapter discusses the key concepts involved in the management of the firm's fixed assets. The first section is devoted to the financial considerations involved in the acquisition, maintenance, and replacement of fixed assets. The second section of the chapter is devoted to basic capital budgeting concepts and terminology. The final section discusses procedures for developing the data needed to evaluate capital expenditure alternatives. The main objective in this chapter is to develop the groundwork for Chapter 15, which will present the basic techniques used to select capital expenditure projects.

Managing Fixed Assets

Since fixed-asset investments represent sizable outlays to manufacturing firms, a great deal of attention must be given to decisions involving not only the initial outlay for purchasing a given asset, but also subsequent outlays associated with the asset. Fixed assets by definition have lives longer than a year and therefore represent a long-term financial commitment by the firm. As time passes, they may require an overhaul or replacement. This section of the chapter is concerned with the nature of capital expenditure decisions, the authorization of capital expenditures, and the origin and path of capital expenditure proposals.

CAPITAL EXPENDITURES

A *capital expenditure* is an outlay made by the firm that is expected to produce *benefits over a period of time greater than one year*. While fixed-asset outlays are capital expenditures, not all capital expenditures result in receipts of fixed assets. A $60,000 outlay for a new machine, with a usable life of 15 years, is a capital expenditure; so is an outlay for advertising that produces benefits over a long period. However, outlays for advertising are not normally capitalized as a fixed asset on the firm's balance sheet.* In this chapter we shall be concerned primarily with capital expenditures for fixed assets. Although the motives for making capital expenditures may differ, the techniques for evaluating them remain the same. The basic motives for capital expenditures are to acquire, replace, or modernize fixed assets; or to obtain other less-tangible long-term benefits. Each of these motives is described below.

Expenditures to Acquire Assets   Probably the most common motive for a capital expenditure is the acquisition of fixed assets. A growing firm often finds it necessary to acquire new fixed assets rapidly. As the firm's growth slows and it reaches maturity, most of its capital expenditures will be for the replacement of obsolete or worn-out assets.

The classic example of a capital expenditure decision involves a firm that is operating at full capacity and is unable to fulfill the demand for its products. It must evaluate alternative capital expenditure proposals in order to determine how best to increase its productive capacity. The proposals include the acquisition of an existing facility, an addition to the firm's current facility, or construction of a totally new facility. Techniques for making such a decision are presented in Chapter 15.

*Some firms do, in effect, capitalize advertising outlays if there is reason to believe the benefit of the outlay will be received at some future date. The capitalized advertising may appear as a deferred charge such as "deferred advertising expense," which is then amortized over the future. Expenses of this type are often deferred for reporting purposes in order to increase reported earnings, while for tax purposes, the entire amount may be expensed to reduce the firm's tax liability.

Expenditures to Replace Assets   The replacement decision is quite common in more mature firms. This type of capital expenditure does not always result from the outright failure of a piece of equipment or the inability of an existing plant to function efficiently. The need to replace existing assets must be examined periodically by the firm's financial manager. For example, each time a machine requires a major repair, the outlay and benefits for the repair must be evaluated against the outlay and benefits from replacing the machine.

It should not take a breakdown to stir the financial manager to consider the replacement of fixed assets. As a machine becomes unable to meet required performance standards, or becomes inefficient compared to new-generation machines, the benefits, of replacement should be evaluated. Due to electronic advances, numerically and computer-controlled machines have made many existing machines obsolete. New materials also contribute to the obsolescence of machinery. If replacing an existing machine with a new machine would permit the firm to produce the same product at a lower cost, the firm should analyze the costs and benefits of this change.

Expenditures for Modernization   The modernization of fixed assets is often an alternative to their replacement. Firms needing additional productive capacity may find that both replacing and modernizing existing machinery are suitable solutions to the capacity problem. Modernization may involve rebuilding, overhauling, or adding to an existing machine or facility.

Modernization decisions must be viewed in light of the relevant costs and benefits. Although the cost of modernizing a machine or physical facility may well be justified by the benefits, the financial manager must be certain that other alternatives have been considered. In some cases, the cost of modernizing assets may exceed the cost of replacing them. In other cases, although the cost of modernization may be less than the cost of replacement, replacement may be preferable since it results in the receipt of benefits over a longer period of time.

Expenditures for Other Purposes   Some capital expenditures do not result in the acquisition or transformation of tangible fixed assets; rather, they may involve a long-term commitment of funds by the firm in expectation of a future return. These types of capital expenditures include outlays for advertising, research and development, management consulting, and new product development. Advertising outlays are expected to provide benefits in the form of increased future sales. Research and development outlays are expected to provide future benefits in the form of new product ideas. Management consulting outlays are expected to provide returns in the form of increased profits from increased operating efficiency. New product development is expected to contribute to a product mix that will maximize the firm's overall returns.

AUTHORIZING CAPITAL EXPENDITURES

The amount of proposed capital expenditures can differ significantly. Some, such as the purchase of a hammer, do not require large outlays. The purchase of a hammer that will provide benefits for three years is by definition a capital expenditure, even if it costs only

Table 14.1 A Scheme for Delegating Capital Expenditure Decision Authority

Size of expenditure	Decision-making authority
Over $100,000	Board of directors or specified top management committee
$50,000–$100,000	President and/or chairperson of board of directors
$20,000–$50,000	Vice president in charge of division
$5,000–$20,000	Plant manager
Under $5,000	Persons chosen by plant manager

$8.* The purchase of a new machine costing $20,000 is also a capital expenditure, since the machine is also expected to provide long-run returns. The actual dollar outlay and the importance of a capital item determine the organizational level at which the capital expenditure decision is made.

Dollar Outlay Firms typically delegate capital expenditure authority on the basis of certain dollar limits. Typically, the board of directors reserves the right to make final decisions on capital expenditures requiring outlays beyond a certain dollar limit, while the authority for making smaller expenditures is delegated to other organizational levels. An example of such a scheme is presented in Table 14.1. The table illustrates that as the dollar value of outlays decreases, the decision-making authority moves to lower levels within the organization. The actual breakdown of decision-making authority differs from one organization to the next and depends directly on the size of the organization. Generally, there is less delegation of decision-making authority in smaller organizations than in larger ones.

The top management committee mentioned in Table 14.1 generally consists of high-level officers and members of the board of directors. This special committee, which is sometimes called an executive committee, an advisory committee, an operations committee, or a planning committee, often has the final authority for approving proposals concerning plant expansion, subsidiary acquisitions, and any other actions that would require a major financial commitment by the firm.

Critical Expenditures Firms operating under critical time constraints in production or under costly restart procedures often find it necessary to provide for exceptions to a dollar outlay scheme for making capital expenditure decisions. In such firms, the plant manager is often given the power to make capital expenditure decisions necessary to keep the production line moving even though they entail larger

---

*Even though purchases of items such as hammers are known to provide benefits over a period greater than a year, they are treated as expenditures in the year of purchase. There is a certain dollar limit beyond which outlays are capitalized and depreciated rather than expensed. This dollar limit depends largely on what Revenue Canada will permit. In accounting, the issue of whether to expense or capitalize an outlay is resolved using the *principle of materiality*, which suggests that any outlays that are deemed material (i.e., large) relative to the firm's scale of operations should be capitalized; others should be expensed in the current period. Of course, the firm, by expensing instead of capitalizing outlays, avoids the clerical work required to set up and maintain a capital cost allowance schedule for the item, while at the same time receiving the maximum tax relief in the year in which the outlay is made.

outlays than he or she would normally be allowed to authorize. Large critical expenditures must be evaluated from a cost-benefit or marginal-cost–marginal-revenue standpoint. For example, if a critical machine breaks and the cost of its repair is high, it is advisable for the decision maker to evaluate the possibility of replacing the machine. These types of decisions must be made in light of losses that would result from a shutdown, the cost of repairs versus the cost of replacement, and the duration and dollar amount of the benefits that would result from replacement.

THE ORIGIN AND PATH OF CAPITAL EXPENDITURE PROPOSALS

Proposals for capital expenditures are made by people at all levels within a business organization. Many firms require the originator of a capital expenditure proposal to fill out certain forms indicating the estimated costs and benefits. The actual path the proposal follows as it travels from the originator to the ultimate decision maker(s) differs from one organization to another. Two patterns are quite common.

Minor Expenditures   Proposals for minor expenditures typically go from the originator to a reviewer at some higher level in the firm. The reviewer's function is to check the accuracy and utility of the proposal, making sure that the information it contains is correct. If the reviewer is satisfied with the accuracy of the proposal, he or she passes it on to a decision maker, who may be a department head or plant manager. The decision maker then determines whether the proposed expenditure should be made. In the case of outlays critical to the continuation of production, the proposal-review process may be bypassed.

Major Expenditures   Proposals for major expenditures go from the originator to a reviewer at a top management level. These proposals generally originate at the top management level and are reviewed by a high-level committee to check that the proposal being considered meets the minimum standards of the firm, that estimates of cost and benefits are reasonable and conclusive, and that the calculations are accurate. The decision whether a proposal should be implemented is made on the basis of the data submitted, minimum acceptance standards of the firm, relevant subjective factors, and any financial constraints present.

Capital Budgeting Fundamentals

Capital budgeting refers to the total process of generating, evaluating, selecting, and following up on capital expenditure proposals. While the preceding section of this chapter described the generation and flow of proposals, this section is devoted to the basic concepts and terminology used in the capital budgeting decision environment. Attention is given to the interdependencies between projects, the availability of funds, and the types of investment decisions made.

PROJECT INTERDEPENDENCE

The firm may be confronted with a number of different types of decision-making situations, depending on the relationships between the projects it is considering. Thus, projects can be economically independent, economically dependent, mutually exclusive, or statistically dependent.

Economically Independent Projects   An investment project is *economically independent* of another project if its *operating* cash flows and the likelihood of its acceptance are not affected by the acceptance or nonacceptance of the other project, and vice versa. The economic independence of projects is important for capital budgeting decision making because, in principle, only those projects that are economically independent of the firm's existing or prospective investments can be evaluated independently.

Economically Dependent Projects   An investment project is *economically dependent* on another project if its operating cash flows or the likelihood of its acceptance are affected by the acceptance or nonacceptance of the other project.

Economic dependencies generally exist among projects that share common facilities, such as land, factory, or transactions cash, or common input or output markets. For example, two identical apartment houses built for old-age pensioners would probably be economically dependent on each other because they are *competitive* projects. Thus, either one or the other or both might experience lower cash flows than would be the case if they were built to rent to different markets. On the other hand, two projects, such as an apartment house and an adjacent parking facility, could generate increased cash flows even if they were constructed to serve the same clientele. These latter projects are *complementary* projects. Economic dependencies also occur when the output of one project is input to another project. For example, oil companies, by integrating their oil production and refining facilities, can often ensure that there is a more stable supply of crude oil to their refineries. This, in turn, generally results in greater economies of utilization and therefore a lower cost of production for each barrel of refined oil.

From the above discussion, it should be clear that an investment that is economically dependent on another investment cannot be evaluated in isolation from the other. Therefore, in theory, a firm should evaluate all the possible combinations (portfolios) of currently or potentially available interdependent projects to determine its optimal portfolio of capital projects. Since absolute economic independence occurs very rarely and most firms usually have to consider many investment proposals, such portfolio evaluations can be enormously difficult and costly.* Therefore, in practice, financial managers generally consider only the most important dependencies.

---

*For example, a firm with just 10 interdependent investment proposals would have to evaluate as many as 1,024 (2^{10}) combinations in order to identify the single best combination. The number of combinations to be evaluated will be more than 3 billion with just 30 proposals to consider! Since it is not uncommon for a firm to be faced with 30 or more interdependent proposals, the practical difficulties and cost of applying the portfolio approach should be obvious.

EXAMPLE   Edmonton Tool Ltd. is considering the development of a new machine that would be partially competitive with the firm's existing machines. In order to recognize the economic dependencies between the new machine and the firm's existing machines, the firm's financial vice-president, Mrs. Nimmi Kanwal, should theoretically consider all the possible combinations of the new machine with the firm's existing machines. However, in practice, Mrs. Kanwal evaluates the investment in the new machine by itself, after she has adjusted the new machine's cash flows for its effect on the future cash flows of the firm's existing machines. Since the acceptance of the new machine will result in a reduction in sales (and thus cash revenues) for the firm's existing machines, the estimated amount of these lost revenues should be subtracted from the new machine's expected cash inflows.

Mutually Exclusive Projects   An extreme case of economic dependence arises when the projects being considered are *mutually exclusive.* A group of projects are mutually exclusive when the acceptance of one of the projects in the group eliminates all the other projects in the group from further consideration. For example, if an oil company has three alternative pumps available for pumping oil from a specific reservoir, then the investments in the three pumps would be mutually exclusive. If each of these alternatives satisfies the company's minimum acceptance criteria, then some technique will have to be used to determine which of the three pumps is the "best" investment. The development and illustration of such techniques will be presented in Chapter 15.

Statistical Dependence Between Project Cash Flows   It is important to recognize that economic dependence refers to the interdependencies between the operating costs and revenues of projects, and *not* to the *statistical dependence* of the cash flows of projects in an environment of uncertainty. Under uncertainty, two or more investments can be both economically independent and statistically dependent. As will be shown in Chapter 16, statistical dependence generally occurs between investment projects when the projects' cash flows are similarly affected by common external factors, such as the business cycles in the economy.

It is important to recognize that interdependencies between the financing costs of investments are not included in the definition of the term "economic dependence." Thus, if the cost of financing the firm's existing investments increases because of the acceptance of another investment and vice versa, but the operating cash flows are not affected, then the investments are not economically dependent. Generally, this type of interdependence between projects is reflected in the discount rate at which projects are discounted.

Types of Investment Decisions

Investment decisions can be categorized into two groups: *accept–reject decisions* and *ranking decisions.* As discussed before, the only decision that usually must be made for an economically independent project is whether or not to accept the project. However, in some situations it is also necessary to evaluate whether or not a project is more desirable than alternative projects. The situations under which the ranking of proposed projects becomes necessary are (1) when the projects are mutually exclusive, and (2) when the firm is operating in an environment of capital rationing.

When the firm has numerous projects under consideration, the total funds required for all acceptable projects may exceed the amount of funds available. In such a situation, it becomes necessary to rank the acceptable projects on the basis of some predetermined criterion. These criteria are discussed in Chapter 15.

When the firm is considering a number of projects, some of which are mutually exclusive and some of which are independent, the proper approach is to reduce the mixed group of projects to a group of independent projects by determining the "best" of each group of mutually exclusive projects. Thus, all acceptable remaining independent projects can be selected if the firm has unlimited funds. If capital must be rationed, then the group of acceptable projects that maximizes the firm's overall rate of return should be accepted. The decision-making techniques that can be used in these situations are presented in Chapter 15.

EXAMPLE   A firm with no constraint on its current investment budget must evaluate eight projects—A through H. Projects A, B, and C are mutually exclusive; projects G and H are also mutually exclusive; and the remaining projects—D, E, and F—are economically independent of each other and the other projects. The projects, along with their rates of return, are listed.

Project	Status	Rate of return
A }		16%
B }	Mutually exclusive	19%
C }		11%
D	Independent	15%
E	Independent	13%
F	Independent	21%
G }	Mutually exclusive	20%
H }		17%

In order to evaluate these projects, the best of the mutually exclusive groups must first be determined. On the basis of the given rate of return figures, project B would be selected from mutually exclusive projects A, B, and C, since it has the highest return of this group; and project G would be preferred to project H since it has the higher return. After the selection of the best of the two groups of mutually exclusive projects, the five (three projects—A, C, and H—will have been eliminated) remaining independent projects can be ranked on the basis of their rates of return as follows:

Rank	Project	Rate of return
1	F	21%
2	G	20%
3	B	19%
4	D	15%
5	E	13%

Since there is no ceiling on the firm's investment budget, all acceptable projects would be undertaken. However, if there is a budget constraint, then some of the acceptable projects may not be undertaken. Under capital rationing, the above ranking will be useful in choosing a combination of projects that will provide maximum returns. In principle, a firm should accept all projects that satisfy its investment criteria. There are, however, situations in which a firm may choose to limit its investment budget and hence not undertake all acceptable projects. For example, a firm may have numerous acceptable investments but may decide not to increase its capital budget through outside financing—borrowing or sale of new shares—in order to avoid incremental financial risk or the dilution of voting control. The need to ration capital may also result from practical problems, such as time lags involved in raising new capital.*

Developing the Relevant Data

The most important step in the evaluation of an investment project is the estimation of the project's cash flows. However, it should be noted that the benefits and costs from some projects are not easily quantifiable in dollar terms. For example, a massive advertising program or a donation to a symphony orchestra may be undertaken to maintain a firm's image and reputation in the marketplace. Measuring the benefits of such investments in dollar terms can be an exceedingly difficult, if not an impossible, task. Our concern here is with the evaluation of those projects for which the benefits and costs can be quantified in dollar terms.

RATIONALE FOR USING CASH FLOWS

Cash flows, rather than "accounting profits," are used because they directly affect the firm's ability to pay bills or purchase assets. Accounting profits and cash flows are not identical, because of the presence of certain noncash charges such as depreciation on the firm's income statement. Therefore, income can change without any corresponding change in cash flow. For example, many firms with growing investments in plant and equipment experience shortages of cash, although their accounting profits are growing rapidly. Therefore, an investment evaluation procedure should be based on the evaluation of cash flows and not accounting profits.

Another major reason for the use of cash flows is that the receipt of cash is a clearly defined and measurable occurrence, whereas the measurement of corporate income presents numerous unresolved allocational and measurement problems. Thus, the use of the cash-flow approach allows us to minimize these measurement problems.[1]

*It should be recognized that though our concern here is with financial constraints, organizational problems of obtaining and training additional personnel may also limit a firm's ability to undertake all acceptable projects. However, in many small firms, especially young firms with low current cash inflows and limited access to regular capital markets, the need to ration capital arises mainly from nonavailability of funds.

USE OF INCREMENTAL CASH FLOWS

In evaluating a proposed project, we are concerned with the additional or *incremental* cash flows that will be generated by undertaking the project. In other words, the cash flows that would occur regardless of whether the project is accepted or rejected should not be included in the analysis.

EXAMPLE Suppose that a proposed project would use some excess space in a building presently owned by a firm. Whether or not the proposed project should be charged for the use of the excess space depends upon whether or not the firm has an alternative use for the excess space during the life of the project. If no alternative use exists, then all costs attributable to the excess space should be treated as *sunk costs* and should not be charged to the project. If an alternative use exists (or may exist), then the use of the excess space for the proposed project may have an opportunity cost. The opportunity cost would be the additional expenditure that the firm may have to incur in acquiring space for the alternative use. In this case, the opportunity cost of the space should be included as part of the proposed project's cash outflow at the time the expenditure will be made.

The remainder of this chapter is devoted to the development of procedures for measuring the relevant cash flows associated with proposed capital expenditures. Cash-flow patterns are discussed, the concept of "initial investment" is examined, and a technique for determining the incremental, after-tax cash flows associated with a capital expenditure project is illustrated.

TYPES OF CASH-FLOW PATTERNS

Cash-flow patterns associated with capital investment projects can be classified as simple or nonsimple. Another classification is as an annuity or an uneven stream.

Simple Cash Flows The simple cash-flow pattern consists of an initial cash outflow followed by a series of cash inflows. This pattern is associated with many types of capital expenditures. For example, a firm may spend $1,000 today and as a result expect to receive cash inflows of $200 at the end of each year for the next eight years. This simple cash-flow pattern is diagrammed in Figure 14.1. All simple cash-flow patterns can be diagrammed in this way.

Nonsimple Cash Flows A nonsimple cash-flow pattern is any cash-flow pattern in which an inital outlay is not followed by a series of inflows. Alternating inflows and outflows and an inflow followed by outflows are examples of nonsimple cash-flow patterns. A common type of nonsimple cash-flow pattern results from the purchase of an asset that generates cash inflows for a period of years, is overhauled, and again generates a stream of cash inflows for a number of years. For example, the purchase of a machine may require an initial cash outflow of $2,000 and generate cash inflows of $500 each year for four years. In the fifth year after the purchase, an outlay of

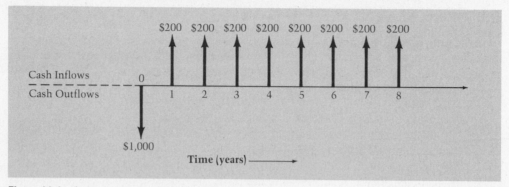

Figure 14.1   A simple cash-flow pattern.

$800 may be required in order to overhaul the machine, after which it generates inflows of $500 each year for five years. This nonsimple pattern of cash flows is illustrated in Figure 14.2.

Difficulties may arise in evaluating projects involving a nonsimple pattern of cash flows. The discussions in the remainder of this chapter and in the following chapters will be limited to the evaluation of simple cash-flow patterns.

Annuity and Uneven Stream   The term *annuity* is commonly used to describe a pattern of cash inflows that are the same every year. In other words, an annuity is a series of *equal annual* cash inflows. A stream of cash inflows that is not an annuity is referred to as an uneven stream of cash inflows. As pointed out in Chapter 13, the techniques required to evaluate cash inflows are much simpler to use when the pattern of inflows is an annuity.

INITIAL INVESTMENT

The term *initial investment* refers to the net cash outlay used in evaluating a prospective capital expenditure. It is calculated by netting out all outflows and inflows occurring at

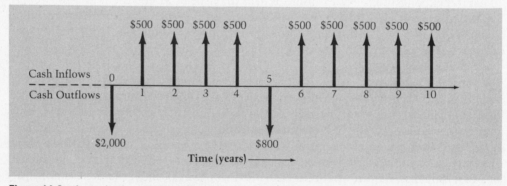

Figure 14.2   A nonsimple cash-flow pattern.

Table 14.2   The Basic Format for Determining the
                 Initial Investment

Acquisition cost of the new asset
− Proceeds from the sale of the replaced asset(s)
± Taxes associated with the proposed project

= Initial investment

the time the project is initiated. It should, however, be noted that there is no strict definition for the term "initial investment." In practice, the cash flows that occur close to the outset of a project, and are nonrecurring in nature, are generally classified as part of the initial investment.

Typically, a capital project involves the acquisition of a fixed asset for the expansion of the firm's productive capacity or for the replacement of the firm's old assets. Therefore, the basic components to be considered in determining the initial investment in a capital project are (1) the cost of acquiring the new asset,* (2) the proceeds (if any) from the sale of the replaced asset(s), and (3) the taxes (if any) resulting from the acquisition and/or sale of asset(s). The basic format for determining initial investment is given in Table 14.2. The initial investment generally does not require a tax adjustment. A situation in which a tax adjustment is necessary is illustrated in the following example.

EXAMPLE   The Topan Company Ltd. plans to replace one of its old machines just before the end of its current taxation year.† The new machine will cost $15,000 and will increase the company's maximum permissible capital cost allowance (CCA) deduction for the current taxation year by $500. The company plans to take the maximum CCA allowed.‡ The old machine is expected to be sold for $1,000 immediately after the acquisition of the new machine. The corporate tax rate is at 40 percent.

We note that even though the new machine will be acquired just before the end of the firm's current taxation year, under the capital cost allowance system, the company will be able to claim the full amount of the incremental CCA deduction of $500 at the end of the year.§ The tax savings resulting from this incremental CCA deduction will amount to $200 (i.e., 40 percent of $500).

---

*The Income Tax Act permits the inclusion of installation costs in the asset's cost for capital cost allowance (CCA) purposes. The cost permitted for CCA deductions is referred to as the *capital cost.*
†As noted in Chapter 2, a corporation's taxation year need not coincide with the calendar year. However, for the sake of simplicity, throughout this text they are assumed to be identical.
‡Recall that under the CCA system, the CCA rates are presented as maximum rates but the firm can defer its CCA claim in any given year, in part or in whole indefinitely. The situations in which a firm may find it advantageous to do so are illustrated in Chapter 2. For expository convenience, throughout the remainder of this and the following chapters, we assume that the maximum permitted CCA is taken.
§The timing of the initial investment can be an important consideration in making actual investment decisions. For example, individual investors often make their investments in MURBs (multiple urban residential building units) as close as possible to the end of their taxation year.

Therefore, the initial cash outlay for the new machine will be calculated as follows:

Acquisition cost of the new machine	$15,000
Less: Proceeds from the sale of the old machine	1,000
Less: Tax saving (assuming that the proceeds from this saving are received by the firm immediately)	200
Total	$13,800

We have considered the tax effect of the incremental CCA deduction on the initial investment only. The tax effects of the incremental CCA deductions in subsequent years will be reflected in the future cash flows associated with the project.

If *net* working capital had increased with the adoption of the project, then this increase would have been included in the initial investment. Furthermore, if any incremental *net* working capital is expected to be recovered at the end of the life of the project, then it should be considered as part of the project's cash inflow at that time.

CALCULATION OF CASH FLOWS

For an economic evaluation of an investment project, the benefits and *operating* costs associated with the project are measured on a period-to-period, incremental, after-tax cash-flow basis. Each period's benefits and operating costs over the estimated life of the project are netted to obtain the project's *after-tax net cash flows.*[*] Since in this chapter and the following chapters we are dealing only with simple projects, all the after-tax net cash flows from operations after the initial period will be positive. Thus, they will frequently be referred to as *cash inflows.*[†]

As noted previously, cash inflows represent dollars that can be spent and are therefore quite different from after-tax profits, which, as explained in Chapter 1, are not necessarily available for paying the firm's bills. A general rule for converting the firm's after-tax profits into cash flows was illustrated in Chapter 2. It was shown that the annual cash flow was calculated by adding noncash charges, such as depreciation, to the annual profits after taxes. It was also noted that the depreciation charges reported by a firm may differ from the CCA deductions made for tax purposes, but the difference does *not* affect the firm's annual cash flows. Therefore, in the calculation of cash inflows, we use CCA, since it affects the firm's tax payments and hence cash flows.

As a result, the *incremental after-tax net operating cash flow* (referred to as cash inflow) resulting from an investment project for any given year can be calculated as

---

[*]Sometimes it is possible to structure the analysis of an investment in terms of before-tax cash flows and arrive at the same results as would be obtained from an analysis based on after-tax cash flows. See, for example, W. Beranek, "The Cost of Capital, Capital Budgeting and the Maximization of Shareholders Wealth," *Journal of Financial and Quantitative Analysis* (March 1975), pp. 1–21.

[†]Although for analytical convenience cash inflows are often calculated on an annual basis, they may, and indeed usually do, occur on a continuous basis. Fortunately, the use of annual cash inflows will generally provide fairly accurate results.

$$\text{cash inflow} = \text{incremental after-tax operating income}$$
$$+ \text{incremental CCA}$$
$$= (1 - t)(\Delta R - \Delta C - \Delta CCA) + \Delta CCA \qquad (14.1)$$

or

$$\text{cash inflow} = (1 - t)(\Delta R - \Delta C) + (t \cdot \Delta CCA) \qquad (14.2)$$

where

$$t = \text{corporate tax rate}$$
$$\Delta R = \text{incremental revenue}$$
$$\Delta C = \text{incremental operating costs, other than incremental CCA}^\star$$
$$\Delta CCA = \text{incremental CCA}$$

Equations 14.1 and 14.2 give identical results. However, analytically Equation 14.2 is particularly useful because it represents the cash inflow as the sum of two separate components. The first component, $(1 - t)(\Delta R - \Delta C)$, represents the after-tax increase in cash operating income from the project. The second component represents the tax-saving effect of the ΔCCA deduction. The tax-saving effect of the ΔCCA deduction is often referred to as the *tax-shield* effect of undertaking a capital investment. As shown in Equation 14.2, the tax shield can be calculated independently.

The following example illustrates the use of Equation 14.2 for the calculation of cash inflows from a capital project.

EXAMPLE   The Hatch Company Ltd. is considering a proposal for the acquisition of a new fixed asset at a cost of $250,000. The economic life of the proposed asset is estimated to be five years, with an expected salvage value of zero at the end of that time.† If acquired, the proposed asset will be the only asset of its class on the company's books and the CCA deductions for the asset will be taken on a straight-line basis over its useful life.‡ The company's projections of revenues and cash operating costs (excluding CCA) for each of the five years, with and without the asset, are given in Table 14.3. Calculations of the annual cash flows that would be generated by the asset are summarized in Table 14.5. The asset will generate an incremental CCA deduction (ΔCCA) of $50,000 (i.e., $250,000/5) for each of its five years of useful life. ΔR (incremental revenue) and ΔC (incremental operating costs, excluding CCA) resulting from the acquisition of the asset for each of the five years are shown in Table 14.4. Table 14.5 shows the calculations of annual cash inflows based on Equation 14.2.

---

*Some operating costs (expenses) for which cash outlays are made may not be tax-deductible. However, to keep the present discussion simple, we have assumed that all operating costs are tax-deductible.
†Note that the actual salvage value at the end of the asset's life may turn out to be different from the salvage value expected *at the time the investment decision is made.* This difference will affect the firm's CCA-based tax savings. However, at the time of the decision, the actual salvage value is seldom known with certainty. Accordingly, the evaluation of the project will be based on the expected and not the actual salvage value.
‡For certain classes such as 27, 29, and 34, CCA can be claimed on a straight-line basis over *two* years. The assumption of straight-line CCA deductions over the asset's *five-year life* in the present example is being made to simplify the analysis. Examples dealing with more than one asset in a class and the calculation of the CCA deductions on the declining balance basis using special formulas are given in Chapter 15.

Table 14.3   The Hatch Company Ltd.'s Revenues and Cash Operating Costs (Excluding CCA) With and Without the Proposed Asset

Year	Projected revenue	Projected operating cost (excl. CCA)
With proposed asset:		
1	$2,520,000	$2,300,000
2	2,520,000	2,300,000
3	2,520,000	2,300,000
4	2,520,000	2,300,000
5	2,520,000	2,300,000
Without proposed asset:		
1	2,200,000	1,990,000
2	2,300,000	2,110,000
3	2,400,000	2,230,000
4	2,400,000	2,250,000
5	2,250,000	2,120,000

Table 14.4   Calculations of Incremental Revenues and Incremental Operating Costs (Excluding CCA)

Year	ΔR	ΔC (excl. ΔCCA)
1	$320,000[a]	$310,000[b]
2	220,000	190,000
3	120,000	70,000
4	120,000	50,000
5	270,000	180,000

[a]ΔR for year 1: $320,000 = $2,520,000 − $2,200,000; ΔR for each of the years 2 through 5 is calculated in the same way.
[b]ΔC for year 1: $310,000 = $2,300,000 − $1,990,000; ΔC for each of the years 2 through 5 is calculated in the same way.

Table 14.5   Calculations of Cash Inflows

Year	$(1-t)(\Delta R - \Delta C)$ (incremental after-tax cash operating income) (1)	ΔCCA (2)	$t \cdot CCA$ (tax saving) (3) = 40% of (2)	Cash inflow (incremental after-tax net operating cash flow) (4) = (1) + (3)
1	$ 6,000[a]	$50,000	$20,000	$26,000
2	18,000	50,000	20,000	38,000
3	30,000	50,000	20,000	50,000
4	42,000	50,000	20,000	62,000
5	54,000	50,000	20,000	74,000

[a]$(1-t)(\Delta R - \Delta C)$ for year 1: $6,000 = (1 − .40) [$320,000 − $310,000]; $(1-t)[\Delta R - \Delta C]$ for each of the years 2 through 5 is calculated in the same way.

The foregoing example illustrates the calculation of cash inflows when the incremental CCA deductions resulting from the acquisition of an asset are determined on a straight-line basis. For most classes of depreciable assets, however, capital cost allowances are taken on the basis of the declining balance method discussed in Chapter 2. Calculations of cash inflows in the latter case tend to be somewhat more complicated and will be illustrated in Chapter 15.

Finally, the incremental cash-flow approach illustrated here permits the calculation of cash flows from an investment in a more direct fashion than the more detailed approach using an income statement format. This incremental approach has the virtue of better focussing one's attention on the fact that it is the *difference* in the firm's cash flows, rather than the absolute cash flows resulting from an investment, that determine the economic worth of the investment to the firm.

Summary

This chapter has been devoted to certain key concepts regarding the management and analysis of fixed assets. Various motives were discussed for capital expenditures, which are outlays that generate benefits over a period greater than a year. Some capital expenditures are made in order to acquire new assets for expansion; others result from the need to replace or modernize existing facilities. Another group of capital expenditures, the results of which do not necessarily show up as fixed assets on the firm's balance sheet, are those made for advertising compaigns, research and development projects, and the like. Regardless of the motive for making a capital expenditure, the basic format for analyzing capital expenditure proposals remains the same.

The authority to make capital expenditures is typically delegated on the basis of the dollar outlays involved. Generally there is a maximum dollar amount a given manager can expend. Procedures for the review of all capital expenditures are a normal part of the capital expenditure process. Often capital expenditure decisions involving large dollar outlays are made by a committee of top executives. Proposals for capital expenditures must be closely scrutinized because of the long-term commitments they entail.

An investment project may be either economically dependent or independent. A project is economically dependent on another project if its operating cash flows or the likelihood of its acceptance are affected by the acceptance or nonacceptance of the other project. A project is economically independent if its operating cash flows or the likelihood of its acceptance is not affected by the acceptance or nonacceptance of the other project, and vice versa. Only those projects that are economically independent of the firm's existing or prospective investments can be evaluated independently. An extreme form of economic dependence arises when the projects being evaluated are mutually exclusive; that is, when the acceptance of one project eliminates the other projects from consideration. Sometimes firms have only limited funds for capital investments and must ration them between carefully selected projects. In order to make investment decisions when capital must be rationed or proposals are mutually exclusive, projects must be ranked. Independent project decisions can be made using an accept–reject criterion when funds are unlimited.

The relevant data necessary for making capital budgeting decisions are the initial investment and the incremental after-tax cash inflows associated with a given proposal.

The initial investment is the initial outlay required, taking into account all installation costs, liquidation values, and taxes. Incremental after-tax cash inflows are the additional cash flows received as a result of implementing a proposal. Cash flows are used instead of after-tax profits since cash, not paper profits, pays the bills and permits additional investments. Two basic approaches exist for determining the relevant cash inflows. One approach uses the income statement format to estimate the relevant cash inflows; the other is a shortcut approach that directly adjusts changes in revenues, cash operating costs (i.e., excluding CCA), and taxes in order to determine the relevant cash inflows. Only simple cash flows, which consist of an initial outlay followed by cash inflows, are dealt with in this text. Annuities, which provide simple patterns of equal annual cash inflows, simplify the analysis of capital expenditures.

Questions

14.1 What does the fact that a firm is described as "capital intensive" reveal about its production process and level of fixed assets? Why?

14.2 What is a capital expenditure? How does the definition of a capital expenditure suggest that all fixed-asset outlays are capital expenditures?

14.3 What are the key motives for capital expenditures? Which motive is most commonly cited?

14.4 What sort of expenditure might be referred to as a "critical capital expenditure"? Why might the decision authority with respect to these outlays bypass the traditional decision channels?

14.5 How does the term *capital budgeting* relate to capital expenditures? What are key aspects of this process?

14.6 What two situations with respect to the availability of funds may be faced by the firm attempting to make capital budgeting decisions? Which of these situations is most common? Why?

14.7 What are the two basic categories of investment decisions? Under what conditions is it necessary to rank investment opportunities?

14.8 Why must an investment project be evaluated on the basis of *incremental after-tax cash flows* expected from the project? Why not use accounting profits instead of cash flows?

14.9 How should changes in working capital resulting from an investment project be treated in evaluating the project?

14.10 A firm is considering an investment project that would use one of the firm's existing facilities. Should the firm consider the costs associated with this existing facility in the analysis of the project?

14.11 What is the difference between simple and nonsimple cash-flow patterns? Can you diagram a simple and a nonsimple pattern of cash flows? Which of these patterns is easiest to work with?

14.12 What is meant by the term *initial investment* in the context of the capital budgeting decision? With simple cash-flow patterns, when does the initial investment occur?

14.13 What is the difference between annuities and uneven streams of cash flows? Why is it important to recognize the existence of an annuity?

14.14 When is a project considered to be economically dependent on another project? Why is it important to examine whether a proposed project is economically dependent on or independent of other projects?

14.15 How should overhead expenses that will be allocated to a prospective project for accounting purposes be treated in evaluating the project?

Problems

14.1 For each of the following projects, determine the after-tax net cash flow for each year.

a. A project that will generate annual after-tax cash benefits and costs of $25,000 and $5,000, respectively, for the next 18 years.

b. A project that will yield annual cash benefits of $300,000 for each of the next 10 years. Operating cash outlays will be $20,000 for each year except year 6, when an overhaul requiring an additional cash outlay of $100,000 will be required.

14.2 The Potters Publishing Company Ltd. is considering replacement of its old printing machine at the beginning of the next year. The market value of the old machine at the beginning of the next year is expected to be $12,000. The new machine will cost the company $52,000. The company's maximum permissible CCA deduction for the next year will be increased by $10,000 as a result of the replacement. The corporate tax rate is at 40 percent.

a. Determine the initial investment in the new machine.

b. What will be the effect on the initial cash outlay if the old machine is replaced just before the *end* of the next year. Assume that the company will claim the maximum CCA allowed for the next year and the market value of the old machine and the cost of its replacement will not change.

14.3 A firm is evaluating the acquisition of an asset costing $64,000, having $8,000 in installation costs, and having no salvage value at the end of its six-year life. If acquired, it will be the only asset of its CCA class held by the company and the CCA deductions for it will be taken on a straight-line basis.

a. Determine the incremental CCA deductions resulting from the acquisition of the proposed asset.

b. If the firm has a 40 percent tax rate, what effect do the incremental CCA deductions have on the firm's cash inflow? Explain your answer.

c. Assuming that the asset will increase the firm's revenues from $70,000 to $90,000 and reduce the firm's operating costs (excluding CCA) from $10,000 to $9,000 for each year of its six-year life, calculate the cash inflows that should be used in evaluating the acquisition of the asset.

14.4 The Oshawa Castings Company Ltd. is considering a proposal for the replacement of its old equipment. The old equipment was purchased 4 years ago at a cost of $10,000. It is included in a single asset class and the CCA deductions for it are being taken on a straight-line basis with no salvage value at the end of its estimated useful life of 10 years. Currently, the asset can be sold for $2,000. The new equipment will cost the company $8,000. It is expected to last six years with no salvage value at the end of that time. It is of the same asset class as the old equipment. As such, the CCA deductions for it can also be taken on a straight-line basis over its useful life. It is estimated that for each year of its useful life it will increase the company's revenues by $45,000 and reduce its labour, material, and other direct costs by $5,000. The corporate tax rate is at 40 percent.

a. Calculate the initial investment in the new machine.
b. Calculate the incremental CCA deductions and the resulting annual tax savings that would be generated from the replacement of the old machine.
c. Calculate the annual cash flows that the company should use in evaluating the replacement proposal.

14.5 Boyle Company Ltd. is considering a proposal for the acquisition of new manufacturing equipment at the beginning of 19X1. The equipment will cost $12,000 (including installation cost) and is expected to last five years with no salvage value at the end of that time. The equipment, classified as a Class 27 asset, qualifies for accelerated CCA deductions on a straight-line basis at a rate of up to 50 percent per year. The equipment will have no effect on the company's revenues but will decrease its labour costs from $100,000 to $80,000 for each of the five years of its life. Assuming that the company claims the maximum CCA allowed for any given year, calculate
a. The initial investment required for the equipment.
b. The incremental CCA deductions and the associated tax savings that would be generated if the equipment is purchased.
c. The cash inflows attributable to the equipment.

Notes

1. For a provocative discussion of this issue, see Willis R. Greer, Jr., and Michael F. O'Neill, "The Impact of Accounting Income Streams on Investment Project Value," *The Engineering Economist* 22 (Winter 1977), pp. 119–130.

Suggested Readings

Abdelsamad, Maustafa, *A Guide to Capital Expenditure Analysis* (New York: American Management Association, 1973).

Aplin, Richard D. and George L. Casler, *Capital Investment Analysis* (Columbus, Ohio: Grid, 1973), chap. 5.

Beranek, William, "The Cost of Capital, Capital Budgeting and the Maximization of Shareholders Wealth," *Journal of Financial and Quantitative Analysis* (March 1975), pp. 1–20.

Bierman, Harold, Jr. and Seymour Smidt, *The Capital Budgeting Decision*, 4th ed. (New York: Macmillan, 1975), chaps. 1, 5, 6, and 7.

Boersema, J. M., *Capital Budgeting Practice Including the Impact of Inflation* (Toronto: CICA, 1978).

Bogen, Jules I., Ed., *Financial Handbook*, 4th ed. (New York: Ronald, 1968), sect. 17.

Cooley, Phillip L., Rodney L. Roenfeldt, and It-Keong Chew, "Capital Budgeting Procedures Under Inflation," *Financial Management* 4 (Winter 1975), pp. 18–27.

Greer, Jr., R. Willis, and Michael F. O'Neill, "The Impact of Accounting Income Streams on Investment Project Value," *The Engineering Economist* 22 (Winter 1977), pp. 119–130.

Hastie, K. Larry, "One Businessman's View of Capital Budgeting," *Financial Management* 3 (Winter 1974), pp. 36–44.

Horngren, Charles T., *Accounting for Management Control: An Introduction*, 4th ed. (Englewood Cliffs, N.J.: Prentice-Hall, 1978), chaps. 12 and 13.

Hunt, Pearson, *Financial Analysis in Capital Budgeting* (Boston: Harvard University Graduate School of Business Administration, 1964).

Johnson, Robert W., *Capital Budgeting* (Dubuque, Iowa: Kendall/Hunt, 1977).

Mayer, Raymond R., *Capital Expenditure Analysis for Managers and Engineers* (Prospect Heights, Ill.: Waveland, 1978).

Meyers, Stephen L., "Avoiding Depreciation Influences on Investment Decisions," *Financial Management* 1 (Winter 1972), pp. 17–24.

Murdick, Robert G. and Donald D. Deming, *The Management of Corporate Expenditures* (New York: McGraw-Hill, 1968).

Oakford, Robert V., *Capital Budgeting* (New York: Ronald, 1970).

Osteryoung, Jerome S., *Capital Budgeting: Long-Term Asset Selection*, 2nd ed. (Columbus, Ohio: Grid, 1979), chaps. 1 and 2.

Petty, J. William, David F. Scott, Jr., and Monroe M. Bird, "The Capital Expenditure Decision-Making Process of Large Corporations," *Engineering Economist* 20 (Spring 1975), pp. 159–172.

Porterfield, James T. S., *Investment Decisions and Capital Costs* (Englewood Cliffs, N.J.: Prentice-Hall, 1965), chap. 2.

Schnell, James S. and Roy S. Nicolosi, "Capital Expenditure Feedback: Project Reappraisal," *Engineering Economist* 19 (Summer 1974), pp. 253–261.

Spies, Richard R., "The Dynamics of Corporate Capital Budgeting," *Journal of Finance* 29 (June 1974), pp. 829–845.

Weaver, James B., "Organizing and Maintaining a Capital Expenditure Program," *Engineering Economist* 20 (Fall 1974), pp. 1–36.

Westfall, Othel D., "Evaluation of the Equipment Replacement Alternative," *Financial Executive* (August 1963), pp. 29–32.

Chapter 15

CAPITAL BUDGETING CONCEPTS AND TECHNIQUES

The two preceding chapters, Chapters 13 and 14, have provided the necessary background for a discussion of capital budgeting concepts and techniques. Chapter 13 presented the key mathematical concepts used in various interest-related aspects of finance, and discussed the meaning and methods of calculating future and present values. Chapter 14 presented a general approach to finding the relevant cash flows associated with a given project so that capital budgeting decision criteria can be applied. Emphasis was placed on simple cash-flow patterns, which consist of an initial outlay (cash outflow) followed by a series of net cash inflows. The initial investment in a capital project was defined as the net cash outlay required at the time of initiating the project. The relevant cash inflows were defined as the incremental after-tax net operating cash inflows (i.e., the combined incremental after-tax cash operating incomes and the tax savings for each period) and the salvage value expected to result from the investment.

As in Chapter 14, our examples will be based on the assumption that all investment projects have simple net cash-flow patterns (i.e., an initial cash outlay followed by a series of net cash inflows), but we will use the more general term "net cash flows" instead of "net cash inflows" when referring to the future cash flows associated with an investment project. The term "net cash flows" allows for the real-life possibility that when all the various cash inflows and outflows are netted (summed up) for a particular time period, the resulting value (net cash flow) can either be positive (i.e., an inflow) or negative (i.e., as outflow). However, since we are only dealing with simple investments, all the future net cash flows associated with a project will be positive, and thus the two terms may be used interchangeably.

The emphasis in this chapter will be on the presentation and illustration of the use of the present-value techniques to evaluate the relevant net cash flows expected to be generated from various capital expenditure proposals.

The chapter is divided into four sections. The first section presents the capital budgeting evaluation criteria that are commonly used today. The second section discusses project selection under conditions of capital rationing. The third section is concerned with the evaluation of capital projects involving tax shields based on the declining balance method for calculating capital cost allowances. The chapter concludes with a brief discussion of capital budgeting in an inflationary environment.

Methods for Evaluating Capital Expenditure Proposals

A number of methods are used for ranking as well as for determining the acceptability or nonacceptability of capital expenditure proposals. We shall discuss only four of the most commonly used methods, known as the *payback period,* the *net present value,* the *internal rate of return,* and the *benefit–cost ratio* (also referred to as the *profitability index*). The last three are often referred to as *discounted cash-flow (DCF) methods.**

We shall use the same basic problem to illustrate the application of all the methods discussed in this chapter. The problem concerns the Bosco Company Ltd., which is currently contemplating two mutually exclusive projects, A and B, each project requiring an initial investment of $60,000. The net cash flows expected from each of these projects for each year of their six-year lives are presented in Table 15.1.

The analysis of these alternatives on the following pages is approached with a view to both making an "accept–reject" decision and "ranking" the alternatives. The analysis of project A is simpler than that of project B, since the net cash flows for project A are an "annuity" while those for project B are an "uneven stream." No capital rationing is assumed.

Table 15.1   Capital Expenditure Data for the Bosco Company Ltd.

Initial investment year	Project A $60,000 net cash flows	Project B $60,000 net cash flows
1	$20,000	$50,000
2	20,000	22,000
3	20,000	11,325
4	20,000	2,000
5	20,000	180
6	20,000	20

*A number of "accounting rate of return" or "average rate of return" methods with several variations have also been discussed in the literature and are used in practice. However, these accounting-based methods are generally considered deficient compared with the DCF methods discussed here. For a relatively recent survey of the various capital project evaluation methods used in practice, see Lawrence J. Gitman and John R. Forrester, Jr., "A Survey of Capital Budgeting Techniques Used by Major U.S. Firms," *Financial Management* 6, No. 3 (Spring 1977), pp. 66–71.

PAYBACK PERIOD

Payback periods are commonly used to evaluate proposed investments. The payback period is the number of years required to recover the initial investment. It is calculated by figuring how long it takes to recover the initial investment. For instance, in the case of project A, $60,000 must be recovered. After one year, $20,000 will be recovered; after two years, a total of $40,000 will be recovered. At the end of the third year, exactly $60,000 will be recovered (i.e., $40,000 total from years 1 and 2 plus the $20,000 recovered in year 3). The payback period for project A is therefore exactly 3 years. In the case of any annuity, such as project A, the payback period can be found by merely dividing the initial investment by the annual net cash flow (i.e., $60,000 ÷ $20,000).

Calculation of the payback for project B proceeds as follows. In year 1, the firm will recover $50,000 of its $60,000 initial investment. At the end of year 2, $72,000 will be recovered. Since the amount received by the end of year 2 is more than the initial investment of $60,000, the payback period is somewhere between one and two years. Only $10,000 (i.e., $60,000 − $50,000) need be recovered during the second year. Actually, $22,000 is recovered. Thus, only about 45.5 percent of the net cash flow (i.e., $10,000 ÷ $22,000) is needed to complete the payback of the initial $60,000 investment.* The payback period for project B is therefore about 1.45 years (i.e., 1 year + about 45.5 percent of year 2). Project B would be preferred to project A since the former has a shorter payback period (i.e., 1.45 years versus 3 years). In general, shorter payback periods are preferred. Often companies use a maximum payback period as an initial screening device. Projects with longer payback periods are rejected; the remaining projects are evaluated using some more sophisticated capital budgeting techniques.

The Pros and Cons of Using Payback Periods   First, the payback period ignores the time value of money, which implies that under the payback method the financing costs of investments are ignored. A second weakness of this approach is its failure to recognize cash flows that occur after the payback period. This weakness can be illustrated using the two investment opportunities given in Table 15.2.

Table 15.2   Calculation of the Payback Period for Two Alternative Investment Projects

	Project X	Project Y
Initial investment	$10,000	$10,000
Year	Net cash flow	
1	$5,000	$3,000
2	5,000	4,000
3	1,000	3,000
4	100	4,000
5	100	3,000
Payback period	2 yrs.	3 yrs.

*This method of finding fractional payback periods implicitly assumes that the net cash flows from the project are received continuously at a constant rate instead of discretely throughout the year. Although this may not be the case, this method is believed to provide an acceptable estimate of payback periods.

The payback period for project X is two years; for project Y, it is three years. Strict adherence to the payback approach suggests that project X is preferable to project Y. However, if we look beyond the payback period, we see that project X returns only an additional $1,200 ($1,000 in year 3, $100 in year 4, and $100 in year 5), while project Y returns an additional $7,000 ($4,000 in year 4 and $3,000 in year 5). Based on this information it appears that project Y is preferable to X. The payback approach ignores the net cash flows in years 3–5 for project X and years 4–5 for project Y.

A reason many firms use the payback period as a decision criterion, or as a supplement to sophisticated decision criteria, is that it is a rough measure of risk. The payback period reflects the liquidity of a project and thereby the risk of recovering the initial investment.* The more liquid an investment is, the less risky it is assumed to be, and vice versa. Companies making international investments in countries having high inflation rates, unstable governments, or other problems use the payback period as a primary decision criterion because of their inability to forecast or measure such risks.[1]

DISCOUNTED CASH-FLOW (DCF) METHODS

Discounted cash-flow methods give explicit consideration to the concept of the *time value of money* discussed in Chapter 13. The time value principle is incorporated by discounting future net cash flows at an appropriate (percentage) discount rate. The discount rate used in the DCF analysis of a project is the current *after-tax* cost of funds required to finance the project. This rate is referred to as the project's cost of capital and represents the minimum rate of return on the project that will leave the firm's existing market value unchanged. In the following chapter, it will be shown that a project's cost of capital depends on the degree of risk inherent in its cash flows.† In this chapter, we shall assume that any new investment will have the same business risk (i.e., operating cash-flow risk) as the firm's existing mix of investments and that it will not significantly affect the firm's financial risk. Under these assumptions the cost of capital applicable to the firm viewed as a portfolio of investments is also applicable to new investments. Therefore, the discount rate used will be the firm's overall cost of capital, which will simply be referred to in this chapter as the firm's "cost of capital."‡

---

*The liquidity of a capital project is determined by the speed with which the firm recovers the initial investment. The reader may recall the discussion in Chapter 7, which indicated that liquidity and risk are somewhat related. The more liquid a project (i.e., the quicker the payback) the less the risk, and vice versa. The longer one must wait to recover an investment, the higher the possibility of a calamity, and vice versa.

†The discussion of risk and uncertainty and specifically the use of certainty equivalents and risk-adjusted discount rates in Chapter 16 will explain how projects involving different degrees of risk must be evaluated (i.e., how the net cash flows should be adjusted or discounted, or both). In this chapter, net cash-flow estimates represent the *expected* future net cash flows.

‡As will be explained in Chapter 17, the term *firm's overall cost of capital* refers to the *after-tax* weighted-average cost of capital. It is calculated as a weighted average of the *current* after-tax *marginal* costs of the types of capital required to finance an investment having the same business risk as the firm's existing portfolio of investments. Since the current *marginal* costs and not the historical costs of the required funds are used in the weighted-average calculation, the overall cost of capital is sometimes referred to as the *marginal* weighted-average cost of capital or simply marginal cost of capital (MCC). In this chapter, for the sake of simplicity, we are assuming that the firm's MCC will remain constant with each incremental dollar of capital expenditure, thus permitting us to use a constant cost of capital for *all* investments to be considered.

A second important point is that since financing costs (adjusted for corporate income taxes) are reflected in the discount rate, cash flows used in the DCF analysis are the after-tax net *operating* cash flows generated by the investment.* Consequently, interest on debt and the tax savings resulting from the tax-deductibility of interest are not included in the net cash flows as defined above. In other words, the tax component of a project's cash flow stream is calculated as though the project were financed entirely with equity funds.

NET PRESENT VALUE (NPV)

The net present value of a project is given by

$$\begin{aligned}NPV &= \text{present value of future net cash flows} \\ &\quad - \text{ initial investment} \\ &= PV - I \\ &= \frac{C_1}{(1 + k)} + \frac{C_2}{(1 + k)^2} + \cdots \frac{C_n}{(1 + k)^n} - I\end{aligned}$$

where

$C_1 = $ net cash flow in period 1
$C_2 = $ net cash flow in period 2 (and so forth)
$I = $ the initial investment†
$k = $ the cost of capital, expressed as a percentage rate

The NPV of a project represents the economic worth of the project in terms of today's dollars. The comparison of the relative worth of projects having different patterns of multiperiod cash flows becomes possible because the NPV method yields a single dollar figure for each project.

The Decision Criterion   The decision-making criterion when the net present-value approach is used to make "accept–reject" decisions is as follows: *If NPV ≥ 0, accept the project; otherwise, reject the project.* If NPV equals zero, the project is just earning the cost of capital and can therefore be viewed as marginally "acceptable."

---

*See Chapter 14 for a discussion of the specification of cash flows in investment analysis. Note that the net cash flows used in the payback period evaluations are also the after-tax net operating cash flows. It should also be pointed out that, although it is possible to structure a DCF analysis of a project on a before-tax basis and arrive at the same results as would be obtained from an after-tax analysis, the calculations involved tend to be relatively complex. See, for example, W. Beranek, "The Cost of Capital, Capital Budgeting and Maximization of Shareholder Wealth," *Journal of Financial and Quantitative Analysis* (March 1975), pp. 1–21. Also, for a relatively recent and somewhat controversial viewpoint on the specification of cash flows and discount rates in the DCF analysis, see Fred D. Arditti and Haim Levy, "The Weighted Average Cost of Capital As a Cutoff Rate: A Critical Analysis of the Classical Textbook Weighted Average," *Financial Management* 6, No.1 (Spring 1977), pp. 24–34.

†Since in this chapter we are considering only simple investments (defined in Chapter 14), the initial investment is automatically stated in terms of today's dollars. If the capital expenditures for a project are spread over time, then the initial investment term I can be replaced by the present value of the capital expenditures, or future capital expenditures can be reflected in the future net cash flows.

If NPV is greater than zero, the firm will earn a return greater than its cost of capital. Therefore, acceptance of a project with positive NPV will increase the market value of the firm and thus the wealth of the firm's shareholders, which is the objective of the financial manager. The increase in the firm's value will equal the amount of the NPV. In the case of mutually exclusive projects, the project with the highest NPV, if it is positive, should be accepted.

EXAMPLE   The net present-value approach can be illustrated using the Bosco Company Ltd. cash-flow data presented in Table 15.1. If the firm has a 10-percent cost of capital, the net present values for projects A and B can be calculated as in Table 15.3. These calculations are based on the application of the techniques presented in Chapter 13. The results show that the net present values of projects A and B are, respectively, $27,100 and $13,616. Both projects, if independent, are acceptable, since their net present values are greater than zero. If the projects were being ranked, project A would be considered superior to B, since it has a higher net present value (i.e., $27,100 vs. $13,616).

Table 15.3   The Calculation of NPV's for the Bosco Company's Capital Expenditure Alternatives

Project A		Project B			
		Year	Net cash flows (1)	P.V. interest factor, PVIF[b] (2)	Present value (1) · (2) (3)
Annual net cash flows	$20,000	1	$50,000	.909	$45,450
PV annuity interest		2	22,000	.826	18,172
factor (PVIFA)[a]	4.355	3	11,325	.751	8,505
PV	87,100	4	2,000	.683	1,366
− I	60,000	5	180	.621	112
NPV	$27,100	6	20	.564	11
		P.V.			$73,616
		− I			60,000
		NPV			$13,616

[a]From Table A-4, for 6 years and 10 percent.
[b]From Table A-3, for given year and 10 percent.

INTERNAL RATE OF RETURN (IRR)

The internal rate of return (sometimes referred to as simply the "rate of return") criterion is defined as *the rate of discount that equates the present value of the future net cash flows from the project to the initial investment associated with the project*. The IRR, in other words, is the discount rate that equates the NPV of an investment opportunity with zero. Mathematically, letting r signify the IRR, the project's IRR is the rate r that satisfies the following equation:

$$\frac{C_1}{(1 + r)} + \frac{C_2}{(1 + r)^2} + \cdots \frac{C_n}{(1 + r)^n} - I = 0$$

The Decision Criterion   The decision criterion when the IRR is used in making "accept–reject" decisions is as follows: *If* IRR $\geq$ *cost of capital, accept the project; otherwise, reject the project.* In order for a project to increase the firm's value, the IRR must exceed the firm's cost of capital.* When IRR equals the cost of capital, the project can be viewed as marginally acceptable. In accepting such a project, the firm is seeking expansion with no incremental impact on the wealth of its share-holders. In the case of mutually exclusive projects, the project with the highest IRR, if it is greater than the firm's cost of capital, should be accepted.

Calculating the IRR   The IRR must be calculated using a trial-and-error technique. Calculating the IRR for an annuity is considerably easier than calculating the IRR for an uneven stream of cash flows. The steps involved in calculating the IRR in each case are described below. The Bosco Company Ltd. cash-flow data are used in the examples. Most large firms have computer programs which calculate the IRR by using iterative convergent computational techniques.

For Annuities   Finding the IRR for an annuity involves the following steps:

STEP 1: Calculate the Payback Period for the Project.   This payback period can be interpreted as the present-value factor for a one-dollar annuity over the project's life (i.e., PVIFA).†

---

*For this reason, the firm's cost of capital is sometimes referred to as the "cutoff" or "hurdle rate" for projects having the same risk as the firm's existing portfolio of investment projects. It should also be noted that since the cash flows used in the IRR calculation are on an after-tax basis, the calculated IRR will be tax-adjusted. Furthermore, from the cash inflow Equation 14.2 developed in Chapter 14, it should be clear that in general the tax-adjusted IRR will not equal $(1 -$ tax rate$)$ times the before-tax IRR (i.e., IRR determined on the basis of before-tax cash flows).

†To illustrate, suppose a project with an initial investment of I dollars generates a net (positive) cash flow of C dollars per year for n years. Then, by definition, the internal rate of return, r, is given by

$$I = \frac{C}{(1 + r)} + \frac{C}{(1 + r)^2} + \cdots \frac{C}{(1 + r)^n}$$

which gives

$$\frac{I}{C} \text{ (i.e., the payback period)} = \frac{1}{(1 + r)} + \frac{1}{(1 + r)^2} + \cdots \frac{1}{(1 + r)^n}$$

$$= PVIFA \text{ of an } n\text{-year annuity discounted at rate } r.$$

For $n = \infty$ (i.e., for level perpetual annual net cash flows C), the payback period, $I/C = 1/r$. It is interesting to note that the previous result allows us to use the DCF criteria of NPV and IRR to establish the maximum acceptable payback period for a project with level perpetual annual net cash flows. To illustrate, let k be the appropriate discount rate (i.e., cost of capital). For a project to be acceptable on the basis of the IRR criterion, r must exceed k. That is, $1/r < 1/k$. Since, for a project with level perpetual annual net cash flow C and initial investment I, $1/r = I/C$ (i.e., the payback period), $1/r < 1/k$ implies that the maximum acceptable payback period for the project equals $1/k$.

STEP 2: Use the PVIFA Table A-4 and Find, for the Life of the Project, the Factor Closest to the Payback Period Determined in Step 1.   This is the IRR to the nearest 1 percent.

EXAMPLE   Steps 1 and 2 can be illustrated by applying them to the cash-flow data for project A of the Bosco Company Ltd. given in Table 15.1. The payback (or present-value annuity factor, PVIFA) for the Bosco Company is 3.000 years (i.e., \$60,000 ÷ \$20,000). According to Table A-4, the factors closest to 3.000 for 6 years are 3.020 (for 24 percent) and 2.951 (for 25 percent). The value closest to 3.000 is 3.020; therefore, the IRR for project A, to the nearest 1 percent, is 24 percent. The actual value, which is between 24 and 25 percent, could be found by interpolation;* it is 24.29 percent. For our purposes, however, values rounded to the nearest 1 percent are acceptable.

Since the Bosco Company has a cost of capital of 10 percent, project A, with an IRR of approximately 24 percent, is acceptable (i.e., 24 percent IRR > 10 percent cost of capital).

For an Uneven Stream of Net Cash Flows   The IRR for an uneven stream of net cash flows is considerably more difficult to calculate manually. One way to simplify the process is to use the following series of steps, which involves the use of a "fake annuity" as a starting point.

STEP 1:   Calculate the average annual net cash flow and interpret it as the annual net cash flow of a "fake annuity."

STEP 2:   Divide the average annual net cash flow into the initial outlay in order to get a "fake payback period."

STEP 3:   Use Table A-4 and the fake payback period in the same manner as described in Step 2 for the preceding annuity calculation to find the IRR of the fake annuity. The result will be a *very rough* first approximation of the true IRR of the project with the uneven stream of net cash flows.

STEP 4:   Using the IRR from Step 3 as the discount rate, calculate the net present value of the uneven-stream project.

STEP 5:   If the resulting NPV is greater than zero, subjectively raise the discount rate; if the resulting NPV is less than zero, subjectively lower the discount rate. Continue this process until you have found two discount rates that cause the NPV to be positive and negative, respectively, and are within one percentage point of each other. Whichever of these two rates causes the NPV to be closest to zero will provide the IRR to the nearest 1 percent. A more exact IRR can be found by interpolation. However, given that the cash-flow estimates are usually quite uncertain, an IRR that is accurate to within about $\frac{1}{2}$ percent will be sufficient for most project evaluations in practice. A subjective feel for the amount of adjustment needed in the last step cannot be taught, but as one works through a number of these uneven-stream problems, one tends to develop such a feel.

*As discussed in Chapter 13, *interpolation* is a mathematical technique used to find intermediate or fractional values when only integer data are provided. Since interest factors only for whole percentages are included in the financial tables in Appendix A of this text, interpolation is required to calculate more precisely the internal rate of return.

EXAMPLE   The application of the previous five-step procedure, which essentially is a trial-and-error process for finding the internal rate of return of an uneven stream of cash flows, can be illustrated using the Bosco Company's project B cash-flow data presented in Table 15.1.

STEP 1   Summing the net cash flows for years 1 through 6 results in total net cash flows of $85,525, which, when divided by the number of years in the project's life (i.e., 6), results in an average annual net cash flow or "fake annuity" of approximately $14,254.

STEP 2   Dividing the initial outlay of $60,000 by the average annual net cash flow of $14,254 (calculated above) results in a "fake" payback period (or present value of an annuity factor, PVIFA) of 4.21 years.

STEP 3   In Table A-4, the PVIFA factor closest to 4.21 for six years is 4.231, which corresponds to the factor for a discount rate of 11 percent. The starting estimate of the IRR is therefore 11 percent.

STEP 4   Using 11 percent as the discount rate, the NPV of the project will be found as follows:

Year	Net cash flow (1)	P.V. interest factor (PVIF) @ 11% (2)	Present value (1) · (2) (3)
1	$50,000	.901	$45,050
2	22,000	.812	17,864
3	11,325	.731	8,279
4	2,000	.659	1,318
5	180	.593	107
6	20	.535	11
		PV	72,629
		− I	60,000
		NPV	$12,629

STEP 5   Since the net present value of $12,629 calculated in Step 4 is rather high, the discount rate should be increased substantially. After a few trials, the reader will find that the project's NPV at a discount rate of 26 percent will equal approximately $79, as follows:

Year	Net cash flow (1)	P.V. interest factor (PVIF) @ 26% (2)	Present value (1) · (2) (3)
1	$50,000	.794	$39,700
2	22,000	.630	13,860
3	11,325	.500	5,663
4	2,000	.397	794
5	180	.315	57
6	20	.250	05
		PV	$60,079
		− I	60,000
		NPV	$ 79

The previous calculations indicate that the NPV of $79 for an IRR of 26 percent is reasonably close to, but still greater than, zero. Thus, a slightly higher discount rate should be tried. Since we are so close, let's try 27 percent. As the following calculations show, the net present value from an IRR of 27 percent is — $655.

Year	Net cash flows (1)	P.V. interest factor (PVIF) @ 27% (2)	Present value (1) · (2) (3)
1	$50,000	.787	$39,350
2	22,000	.620	13,640
3	11,325	.488	5,527
4	2,000	.384	768
5	180	.303	55
6	20	.238	05
		PV	$59,345
		− I	60,000
		NPV	− $ 655

Since 26 and 27 percent are the discount rates that are within one percentage point of each other and give positive and negative net present values, the trial-and-error process can be terminated. The IRR we are seeking is the discount rate for which the NPV is closest to zero. For this project, 26 percent causes the NPV to be closer to zero than 27 percent, so 26 percent is the IRR we shall use. If interpolation were used, a more precise figure for the IRR would be 26.08 percent.

Project B is acceptable since its IRR of approximately 26 percent is greater than the Bosco Company's 10-percent cost of capital. This is the same conclusion as was reached using the NPV as the criterion. It is interesting to note that the IRR criterion suggests that project B is preferable to A, which, as shown earlier, has an IRR of approximately 24 percent. This conflicts with the rankings of the projects obtained earlier using the NPV criterion. Such conflicts are not unusual; there is no guarantee that the NPV and the IRR criteria will rank projects in the same order. Also, note that both the projects have IRR's greater than the firm's cost of capital. Therefore, both of them will be acceptable if they were independent. *As a general rule, the NPV and the IRR criteria (as well as the benefit–cost ratio or profitability index criterion, to be discussed shortly) yield identical accept–reject decisions in the case of economically independent projects.* *

*It is simple to demonstrate this result mathematically. Consider a project with the initial investment I, cost of capital k, and expected future net cash flows C_i $(i = 1, 2, \ldots n)$. The project's IRR by definition is given by

$$\text{NPV} = 0 = \frac{C_1}{(1 + \text{IRR})} + \frac{C_2}{(1 + \text{IRR})^2} + \cdots \frac{C_n}{(1 + \text{IRR})^n} - I$$

It is clear from the above equation that

IRR $> k$ implies NPV > 0 and vice versa; and
IRR $\leq k$ implies NPV ≤ 0 and vice versa.

The first relationship means that if a project is acceptable on the basis of the IRR criterion, then it is also acceptable on the basis of the NPV criterion, and vice versa. The second relationship shows that the converse of the above statement is also true.

• CONFLICTS BETWEEN NPV AND IRR RANKINGS

The foregoing example shows that the NPV and IRR can give contradictory project rankings. There are basically two situations in which the conflicts can occur: (1) when the initial outlay or cost of one project differs from that of the other; and (2) when the time patterns of future cash flows from the two projects differ. Two situations in which the cash-flow time patterns can differ are when the expected lives of the projects differ or when the cash flows of one project increase over time while those of the other decrease. We will illustrate the conflict in the first situation by using a rather extreme example.

EXAMPLE   Project M requires an initial outlay of $100 and returns $180 one year later; while project N requires an initial outlay of $10,000 and returns $12,000 one year later. Assume that the cost of capital is 15 percent. Which project would you rather have?

Project M has an IRR of 80 percent (given by x in the equation $100 = \$180/(1 + x)$), whereas project N has an IRR of only 20 percent (given by y in the equation $\$10,000 = \$12,000/(1 + y)$). Therefore, project M is more desirable than project N on the basis of the IRR criterion. On the other hand, project M's NPV equals only $56.6 (i.e., $180 · PVIF$_{.15,1\ yr.}$ of .87 − $100) as against project N's NPV of $440 (i.e., $12,000 · PVIF$_{.15,1\ yr.}$ of .87 − $10,000). Since N ranks higher than M on the basis of the NPV criterion, this contradicts the projects' IRR ranking obtained earlier. Although this is an unrealistic example, it does illustrate rather dramatically that when projects differ in scale, contradictory NPV and IRR rankings *may* occur.*

The basic cause of the conflict is the fact that the use of the NPV and IRR criteria require different assumptions about the rate of return at which future cash inflows from projects can be reinvested. Under the NPV rule, the discount rate (i.e., the cost of capital) is by definition the rate at which a firm can reinvest funds profitably. The IRR rule, on the other hand, *implicitly* assumes that the reinvestment rate equals the IRR itself, since the net cash flows are discounted at the IRR.†

• This section may be bypassed without loss of continuity, as may end-of-chapter problems preceded by bullets.

*There are techniques we can use to make identical project choices from conflicting NPV and IRR rankings of mutually exclusive projects. One commonly used technique in such a situation is to use the following two steps:

(1) Arrange projects in ascending order of their sizes (i.e., initial outlays) and calculate the *incremental* initial outlays and *incremental* future net cash flows that would be generated if the smaller project were rejected.

(2) Find the NPV or the IRR implied by the incremental initial outlay and the incremental net cash flows. If this NPV is positive (i.e., if the IRR exceeds the cost of capital), then the larger project should be selected; if not, then the smaller project is more desirable.

A detailed discussion of the incremental analysis of such project evaluations is beyond the scope of this text. An illustrative example is provided in the following section. Also, some simple problems are provided at the end of the chapter to challenge the ambitious student. An excellent treatment of the incremental approaches to investment decisions can be found in Charles W. Haley and Lawrence D. Schall, *The Theory of Financial Decisions* (New York: McGraw-Hill, 1980), chap. 3, pp. 43–72.

†To see this analytically, consider the general IRR equation.

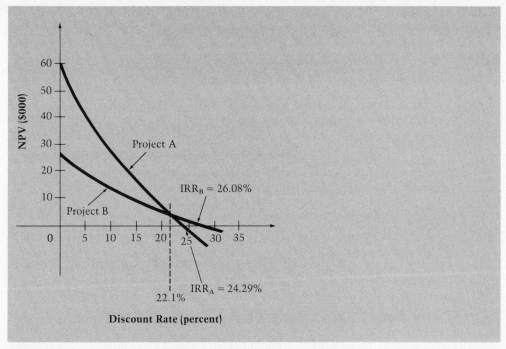

Figure 15.1   Net present-value profiles for projects A and B.

To understand how the difference in the reinvestment rate assumptions implied in the two rules can cause conflicting rankings, let us compare Bosco Company's projects A and B (described in Table 15.1) at varying discount rates. A graph depicting a project's NPV for various discount rates is called its *net present-value profile.* The NPV profiles of projects A and B are presented in Figure 15.1. The IRR is, by definition, the discount rate at which the NPV equals zero. Therefore, the IRR's of projects A and B are given by the intersections of their NPV profiles with the horizontal axis at 24.29 percent and 26.08 percent, respectively. Thus, as noted earlier, project B is superior to project A on the basis of their IRR's, and the two projects' implied reinvestment rates are their IRR's

$$I = \frac{C_1}{(1 + \text{IRR})} + \frac{C_2}{(1 + \text{IRR})^2} + \cdots \frac{C_n}{(1 + \text{IRR})^n}$$

This equation can equivalently be written as:

$$I(1 + \text{IRR})^n = C_1(1 + \text{IRR})^{n-1} + C_2(1 + \text{IRR})^{n-2} + \cdots C_n$$

or

$$I(1 + \text{IRR})^{n+x} = C_1(1 + \text{IRR})^{n+x-1} + C_2(1 + \text{IRR})^{n+x-2} + \cdots C_n(1 + \text{IRR})^x$$

for any arbitrarily chosen number $x \geq 0$. In other words, the above equation states that the initial investment I will earn a rate of return equal to the IRR *if and only if* each net cash flow can be reinvested until an arbitrarily specified period at a rate equal to the IRR. It is in this precise sense that we can state that the use of the IRR rule *implicitly* assumes the reinvestment of net cash flows at the IRR itself.

of 26.08 percent and 24.29 percent, respectively. *The cost of capital does not affect this ranking because the IRR's are determined independently of the cost of capital.* ∗

On the other hand, in the NPV evaluation of a project, the cost of capital is specified explicitly *in advance* of the evaluation and represents the discount rate or the reinvestment rate for future cash flows generated by the project. Therefore, the NPV rankings can change with a change in the cost of capital (the discount rate). For example, as indicated in Figure 15.1, at a discount rate greater than approximately 22.1 percent (the point where the NPV profiles cross over each other),† project B will have a greater NPV than project A and therefore will be rated as being more desirable than project A. Also, this NPV ranking of the two projects will be consistent with their IRR ranking. For any discount rate less than the cross-over point rate of 22.1 percent, project A will rank higher than project B because of its higher NPV. Such a ranking would conflict with the IRR ranking.

To understand why the above conflict occurs, let us examine the NPV profiles of the projects more closely. Project B's NPV profile starts out at a lower NPV than project A's. However, since project B's larger net cash flows occur earlier than those for project A, project B's NPV falls *less* rapidly with an increase in the discount rate than A's NPV. Thus, at relatively high discount rates (i.e., the discount rates to the right of the cross-over rate of 22.1 percent), the NPV of project B becomes greater than that of A, resulting in an NPV ranking consistent with the IRR ranking. But, at relatively low discount rates, the discounting effect of time is not severe enough to offset A's relative advantage of higher initial NPV. Thus, A's NPV remains higher than B's until the cross-over point, which contradicts the IRR ranking.

Since a change in the discount rate is also an equivalent change in the reinvestment rate assumed in the NPV evaluations, the above result can be interpreted as follows: At any reinvestment rate to the right of the cross-over rate the NPV and IRR rankings will be identical.‡ However, when the reinvestment rate is relatively low and is below the cross-over rate, the rankings become contradictory. This permits us to generalize that *the NPV and IRR rankings of any two projects will be in conflict if the NPV profiles of the projects cross over at some rate higher than the cost of capital (i.e., higher than the reinvestment rate implied in the NPV evaluations of the projects).*§

∗It is only when we judge the acceptability or nonacceptability of a project that we need an explicit specification of the cost of capital. Some authors regard this as an advantage of the IRR method over the NPV method, since in situations where the cost of capital cannot be specified accurately enough for project *selection*, one can at least rank the projects using the IRR rule as a ranking criterion.

†The discount rate associated with the cross-over point in the NPV profiles is referred to as the "Fisher's rate of return." It serves as a reference point for determining when a change in the discount rate or cost of capital will give the same or conflicting NPV and IRR rankings.

‡We do not have to consider discount rates greater than 24.29 percent for comparing the NPV and IRR rankings. This is so because at discount rates greater than 24.29 percent, project A has negative NPV's and therefore becomes ineligible as a candidate for ranking.

§This is true only if the expected reinvestment rate can appropriately be regarded as being equal to the cost of capital used in the NPV evaluations of the projects to be ranked. See, for example, Richard L. Myer, "A Note on Capital Budgeting Techniques and the Reinvestment Rate," *Journal of Finance* 34 (December 1979), pp. 1251–1254. Furthermore, in some situations more than one cross-over point may occur. Here, for illustrative purposes, we have dealt with a relatively simple situation. For a classical discussion of the problem see J. Hirshleifer, "On the Theory of Optimal Investment Decisions," *Journal*

● THE REINVESTMENT RATE ASSUMPTION
AND THE RELIABILITY OF NPV AND IRR RANKINGS

In the preceding discussion we saw that although the NPV and IRR rules will give the same signals for accept–reject decisions, this may not be the case for ranking decisions. Therefore, the question that we now must answer is: Which of the two rules should we rely on for making ranking decisions? Let us answer this question in the context of the following simplified example that involves the use of the terminal value concept discussed in Chapter 13.*

EXAMPLE   A firm wishes to select between two mutually exclusive projects, A and B, each requiring an initial outlay of $2,000. The net cash flows expected from these projects are as follows:

| Year | Net cash flows | |
	Project A	Project B
1	0	$2,400
2	0	0
3	$2,970	0

A simple calculation will show that project B has a higher IRR than project A (20 percent versus 14 percent). Therefore, the firm would select project B on the basis of the IRR rule. This decision would indeed be correct if project B's net cash flow of $2,400 at the end of the first year can be reinvested at the project's IRR of 20 percent.† But if, at the end of the first year, the reinvestment rate for the cash inflow of $2,400 turns out to be less than 20 percent, then the selection of project B *may*, in retrospect, prove to be incorrect.

To illustrate, suppose the firm, at the end of the first year, finds that the $2,400 net cash flow can only be invested to yield 11 percent after taxes. Then the terminal value of this net cash flow at the end of the third year would amount to only $2,956.80 (i.e., $2,400 · $CVIF_{.11,2 \text{ yrs.}}$ of 1.232).

---

of Political Economy 66 (August 1958), pp. 95–103. Also note that projects A and B in the above illustration had equal lives and involved the same initial outlay. As such, the difference in the timing of their future net cash flows created the situation for the conflict in their NPV and IRR rankings. We leave it as an exercise for the reader to verify that in the earlier example of project M and N requiring different initial outlays, the projects' NPV and IRR rankings were different because their NPV profiles crossed over at a rate of approximately 19.4 percent, which is higher than the cost of capital of 15 percent that was used in the NPV evaluation of the projects.

• This section may be bypassed without loss of continuity.

*Recall from Chapter 13 that the present value and the terminal value are equivalent concepts for evaluating investment proposals. We have chosen to use the terminal value concept here because it is particularly convenient for what we desire to illustrate in this section of the chapter.

†This can be seen from the fact that both projects require the same initial outlay, but project B's cash flow of $2,400, reinvested at 20 percent will, at the end of the third year, yield a terminal value of $3,456.00 (i.e., $2,400 · $CVIF_{.20,2 \text{ yrs.}}$ of 1.44), which exceeds project A's terminal cash flow of $2,970 at the end of the third year.

This is less than the $2,970 terminal value of the net cash flow of project A. Since both projects require the same initial outlay, it is clear that project B should have been ranked as being inferior to project A.*

Thus, we find that if the reinvestment rate differs from the IRR, the IRR can give a misleading assessment of one project relative to another. Ranking errors can also occur with the NPV rule if the actual reinvestment rate is different from the assumed reinvestment rate (i.e., the discount rate). To illustrate, suppose that the firm has estimated that it will be able to reinvest the net cash flows from either project at 12 percent. Then, using this rate as the discount rate in the NPV calculations, project B will again be rated as superior to project A because its NPV of $143.20 (i.e., $2,400 \cdot PVIF_{12,1\ yr.}$ of .893 − $2,000) will exceed project A's NPV of $114.64 (i.e., $2,970 \cdot PVIF_{12,3\ yrs.}$ of .712 − $2,000). But as we saw earlier, this ranking will prove to be incorrect if the best available opportunity to invest project B's net cash flow of $2,400 at the end of the first year was at a yield of 11 percent after taxes.†

Based on this example, we find that the reliability of both the NPV and IRR rankings depends critically on the reliability of their reinvestment rate assumptions. The issue, in essence, is which of the two rules as a ranking criterion makes a more acceptable reinvestment rate assumption? A widely accepted view to date has been that the assumption of reinvestment at the cost of capital is theoretically a better assumption than that implied in the IRR rule. It is therefore generally recommended that the NPV rule should be preferred.‡ Arguments in support of this recommendation include:

1 With the IRR, the *implied* reinvestment rate varies with each project's calculated IRR. This implicit assumption that funds released from one project will be reinvested at one rate and those from another at a different rate is logically unsound. With the NPV rule, on the other hand, the implied reinvestment rate (i.e., the cost of capital) remains the same for each project.§ Thus, the NPV rule compares projects on a consistent basis.

*Indeed, it is possible to show that project B would prove to be superior to project A only if its net cash flow of $2,400 at the end of the first year could be reinvested at a rate greater than a certain minimum rate (i.e., Fisher's rate of return). Because of the highly simplified situation being discussed here, it is possible to determine this minimum rate algebraically by observing that this rate is simply the reinvestment rate x at which the terminal value of $2,400 at the end of the third year just equals project A's terminal cash flow of $2,970. That is, it is found by solving for x in the equation $2,400 \left(1 + x\right)^2 = $2,970, which readily gives $x = 11.3$ percent (approximately). The reader can easily verify that this minimum rate of 11.3 percent represents the cross-over rate for the NPV profiles of the projects under consideration.

†For this reason some authors advocate the use of modified definitions of NPV and IRR using terminal values of intermediate cash flows with *varying* reinvestment rates over time. While this approach is theoretically appealing, it is difficult to implement because it requires estimation of multiple reinvestment rates. A discussion of the approach is beyond the scope of this text. For an excellent theoretical exposition of the approach, see William H. Jean, "Terminal Value or Present Value in Capital Budgeting Programs," *Journal of Financial and Quantitative Analysis* 6 (January 1971), pp. 649–652.

‡For an illustrative example that shows that under certain conditions the use of the IRR rule is more appropriate for selecting among mutually exclusive investments, see the article by Myer cited earlier in the footnote on page 422.

§This is true only if the investments to be evaluated have similar operating cash-flow risk (business risk) and similar financing. As indicated earlier in this chapter, we are assuming that the firm's new investments will not affect its financial risk and will have the same business risk as the firm's current investments. Under these conditions the firm's cost of capital will be applicable to all new investments.

2 The IRR of an investment is calculated without an *explicit* consideration of reinvestment opportunities available in the market. Yet the use of the IRR rule requires us to *implicitly* assume that the opportunities will exist to reinvest the net cash flows from *any* project at that project's IRR! For projects with very high or very low IRR's, this implicit reinvestment assumption may be unrealistic. In contrast, the NPV rule assumes that the actual reinvestment for any project will take place at the market determined *opportunity* cost of capital. This assumption is theoretically more appealing and in general more realistic.

3 It is not unusual for a project with mixed patterns of cash flows to have more than one IRR. When this occurs difficult problems of interpretation result. Furthermore, some projects may have cash-flow patterns for which mathematically the IRR's do not even exist. This technical problem causes theoretical difficulties that do not occur when one uses the NPV rule.

It should, however, be pointed out that, despite the theoretical problems associated with the IRR rule, evidence suggests* that financial managers (of large corporations) commonly use IRR over NPV. Finally, since a variety of methods and techniques have been developed to avoid the theoretical pitfalls of the IRR, its widespread use should not be viewed as reflecting a lack of sophistication on part of financial decision makers.

PROFITABILITY INDEX OR BENEFIT–COST RATIO

The benefit–cost ratio (B/C ratio), or the profitability index (PI) as it is sometimes called, is defined as

$$\text{B/C ratio} = \frac{\text{present value of net cash flows } (PV)}{\text{initial investment } (I)}$$

Since NPV $= PV - I$ implies that $PV = I + NPV$,

$$\text{B/C ratio} = \frac{I + NPV}{I}$$

This ratio measures the present value of benefits per dollar of investment.†

The Decision Criterion   The decision criterion when the B/C ratio is used to make "accept–reject" decisions is as follows: *If B/C ratio $\geq$ 1, accept the project;* other-

---

Since a firm's new investments, in general, can be expected to be of the same risk class as the firm's current investments, the statement made here is generally valid. Furthermore, even if the cost of capital in the NPV evaluations varies because of differences in projects' risks, the NPV comparisons are consistent insofar as the risk adjustments of the cost of capital occur in the market on a consistent basis.

*For example, see the article cited in the footnote on page 411 for a discussion of the survey evidence with respect to the capital budgeting decision-making practices used by major U.S. firms. For a Canadian survey, see C. G. Hoskins and M. J. Dunn, "The Economic Evaluation of Capital Expenditure Proposals Under Uncertainty: The Practice of Large Corporations in Canada," *Journal of Business Administration* (Fall 1974), pp. 44–45.

†If the capital expenditures are expected to be spread over time, then *I* can be taken to be the present value of those expenditures. It also should be noted that the B/C ratio or the profitability index is sometimes defined as *NPV/I*. The two definitions are, however, equivalent with respect to both accept–reject and ranking decisions. In the *NPV/I* ratio definition, a project is accepted if its *NPV/I* ratio is positive; whereas in the *PV/I* ratio definition, it is accepted if its *PV/I* exceeds 1.

wise, reject the project. When the B/C ratio for a project equals 1, the project can be viewed as marginally acceptable. It should be apparent from the definition of the B/C ratio that when the B/C ratio is greater than 1, the NPV is greater than zero; and when the B/C ratio is less than 1, the NPV is less than zero. Therefore, the NPV and B/C ratios give the same "accept–reject" decisions. In a fashion similar to that described for NPV, the acceptance of projects having B/C ratios greater than 1 will enhance the value of the firm.

EXAMPLE   Benefit–cost ratios for the Bosco Company Ltd. can be easily determined using the present values calculated in Table 15.3. The B/C ratios for projects A and B, respectively, are 1.45 (i.e., $87,100 ÷ $60,000) and 1.23 (i.e., $73,616 ÷ $60,000). Since both these ratios are greater than 1, both projects are acceptable. Ranking the projects on the basis of their B/C ratios indicates that on a *relative basis* project A is preferable to project B, since A returns $1.45 present value for each dollar invested. This ranking is the same as that obtained using NPV's. However, *the condition of conflicting rankings by these two techniques is not unusual*, especially when the initial investments differ.

Conflicting Rankings with the NPV and PI Criteria   The following example illustrates the possibility of conflicting rankings using net present values and benefit–cost ratios as ranking criteria.

EXAMPLE   The Digby Company Ltd., in the process of evaluating two mutually exclusive projects, X and Y, developed the information given in the following table:

	Project X	Project Y
(1) Present value of net cash flows	$30,000	$60,000
(2) Initial outlay	20,000	45,000
(3) Net present value [(1) − (2)]	$10,000	$15,000[a]
(4) Benefit–cost ratio [(1) ÷ (2)]	1.50[a]	1.33

[a]Preferred project using respective technique shown.

The results of the analysis indicate that both the projects are acceptable, since their NPV's are greater than zero and their B/C ratios are greater than 1. If the projects were ranked on the basis of NPV's, project Y would be preferable; but if the projects were ranked on the basis of B/C ratios, project X would be preferable. Which investment should be preferred? In other words, should the firm use the NPV approach on an *absolute* basis and adopt project Y, or on a *relative* basis and adopt X? To answer this question, let us consider the two projects on an incremental basis as follows:

Project	Initial outlay	NPV
Y	$45,000	$15,000
X	20,000	10,000
Incremental flows (Y − X)	$25,000	$ 5,000

From this calculation, it is clear that by choosing X over Y on the basis of the B/C ratio, the firm would be passing up the opportunity of making an *incremental* investment of $25,000 that would generate a *positive* NPV of $5,000. Therefore, the choice of X would be inconsistent with shareholders' wealth maximization. As such, the NPV-based selection of project Y is superior.

Capital Rationing

In Chapter 14, we observed that the need to ration capital may arise whenever there is a budget ceiling on the amount of funds available for investment during a given period of time. A limit on the size of the capital expenditure budget may arise from the nonavailability of additional funds from external sources (referred to as *hard capital rationing*). It may also be imposed by the top management of the firm in order to achieve certain policy objectives, such as the preservation of corporate control and/or the achievement of orderly growth (referred to as *soft capital rationing*).*

A capital constraint implies that some proposals that might have otherwise been acceptable are either forgone or postponed. Under capital rationing the objective is to select the subset of available projects that provides the greatest profitability and uses up the available capital. Thus, for the present value approach, the objective is to maximize the net present value subject to the constraint that the available capital budget is not exceeded.† Essentially, this approach requires the enumeration of all the subsets of acceptable projects that meet the budget constraint and then the selection of the subset with the largest total NPV. If the number of available projects is large, then the above procedure can be carried out by using certain programming techniques described briefly in the following section. Programming techniques can be applied regardless of whether or not the projects are economically independent of one another.‡ However, if the projects are economically independent, then the subset of the projects with the highest total NPV under the budget constraint can be selected by the following simple procedure: *Rank all the available projects in descending order of their profitability indices*

---

*It is important to determine whether or not a given situation calls for capital rationing. For example, if a firm is in a situation where it is not able to raise funds at an acceptable cost because its investment opportunities are perceived to be unattractive in terms of their risk-return trade-offs, then the situation is not that of capital rationing. Rather, in such a situation the firm should use its current high cost of capital to evaluate its current investment opportunities. It should also be pointed out that large firms with profitable investment opportunities rarely, if ever, encounter hard capital rationing in the real world. If hard capital rationing exists, it is more likely to be encountered by small firms. In fact, it is often alleged that the small firm typically has limited access to external funds and usually faces an inflexible market-determined capital constraint.

†A single-period (i.e., current period) capital constraint is being assumed in the above discussion. Advanced methods to handle multiperiod capital constraints are available but are not discussed in this text. For an excellent discussion of the multiperiod capital constraint problem, the reader is referred to the references listed at the end of this chapter.

‡The concepts of economic independence and dependence of projects were explained in Chapter 14. In general, absolute economic independence of projects is a rare occurrence. It is largely a matter of management's judgment whether or not the dependencies in a given situation are significant enough to be included in the analysis. Thus, we are assuming that the projects are approximately economically independent in the above discussion.

(PI's) and then select acceptable projects (those with profitability indices greater than 1) until the available capital budget is exhausted.

It should be recognized that often the projects selected on the basis of the above procedure will not entirely exhaust the available investment budget. In such a case, it is necessary to examine projects close to the budget limit (i.e., the marginal projects) in order to ensure that the selected projects do indeed maximize the total NPV. The following example illustrates the procedure.

EXAMPLE   The Maritimes division of the Canada Manufacturing Corporation has been allocated $500,000 for capital investments during the current year. The divisional management has identified six investment opportunities, all of which are economically independent of one another. The data for these investments are as shown in Table 15.4.

Table 15.4   Profitability Index Procedure for Capital Rationing

Project	Initial outlay (I)	NPV	PV = I + NPV	PV/I
A	$200,000	$160,000	$360,000	1.80
B	150,000	75,000	225,000	1.50
C	100,000	40,000	140,000	1.40
D	20,000	7,000	27,000	1.35
E	150,000	30,000	180,000	1.20
F	16,000	−4,000	12,000	.75

First, notice that project F has a negative NPV and thus a *PV/I* ratio of less than 1. Therefore, it would be rejected at the very outset of the selection process. Using the profitability index project selection method, the Maritime division would start its selection by choosing the project with the largest profitability index. It would then select projects of successively lower profitability indices until project D. At that point, the funds available for investment would be reduced to $30,000 [i.e., the budget limit of $500,000 − ($200,000 + $150,000 + $100,000 + $20,000)]. Since this remaining amount of $30,000 is less than the initial outlay of $150,000 required for project E, project E cannot be undertaken even though it has a positive NPV.* It can also be readily verified that the combination of projects A through D would indeed yield the largest total NPV of $282,000 (i.e., $160,000 + $75,000 + $40,000 + $7,000), given the budget constraint of $500,000. For example, if projects A, B, and E are undertaken, the budgeted funds of $500,000 (i.e., $200,000 + $150,000 + $150,000) would be fully utilized. However, these projects would provide an NPV of only $265,000 (i.e., $160,000 + $75,000 + $30,000), which is $17,000 less than the total NPV of $282,000 expected from projects A, B, C, and D.

However, suppose that project E's NPV were $50,000 instead of $30,000 shown in Table 15.4. In this case, project E would have a PI of approximately 1.33 [i.e., ($150,000 + $50,000)/ $150,000], which is still less than project D's PI of 1.35. Again, using the profitability index

---

*Any funds left over in the capital budget after the selection of the most profitable group of projects (with maximum total NPV) can be viewed as being invested in a project that earns a rate of return equal to the firm's opportunity cost of capital (i.e., in a project with NPV = 0).

method, A through D would be selected and E would be rejected. However, it would now be more profitable to select E and to reject C and D, since the combined NPV of $282,000 of A, B, C, and D would now be less than the combined NPV of $285,000 (i.e., $160,000 + $75,000 + $50,000) of A, B, and E. In this case, the profitability index method is not appropriate for selecting from among the *marginal investments* C, D, and E. Thus, when this approach is used, the NPV contribution of alternate combinations of marginal investments (i.e., the investments close to the budget ceiling) should be evaluated.

The current example shows that when the total required investment in positive NPV projects exceeds some capital constraint, acceptability of projects is governed by the constraint and not by the cost of capital used in the NPV calculations. To illustrate, suppose that the firm in our example had a capital constraint of $620,000 instead of $500,000. This additional $120,000, together with the $30,000 remaining after acceptance of project D, would have permitted acceptance of E. Thus, the $500,000 capital constraint resulted in the rejection of E, which in turn forced the firm to forego the $30,000 increase in net present value associated with the acceptance of E. In other words, the rejection of E implies that the budget constraint had the effect of raising the cutoff (hurdle) rate above the cost of capital.

• CAPITAL RATIONING AND MATHEMATICAL PROGRAMMING

Mathematical programming techniques are used for optimizing some objective subject to certain constraints. Capital rationing problems, as we saw above, represent situations of constrained maximization, since the objective is to select the group of projects with the maximum net present value subject to a capital budget constraint. Generally, integer programming is used instead of linear programming so that the results will all be in terms of whole projects.*

If it is possible to undertake fractions of projects through participation in joint ventures, consortia, or syndicates, then the capital rationing problem may be formulated using linear programming. Programming approaches to capital budgeting under multiperiod capital and noncapital constraints are often used in the oil industry for scheduling of refinery operations. These approaches have great versatility but they can be difficult to implement because firms often have inadequate knowledge of future investment opportunities and capital constraints. Assuming a single-period budget constraint, the basic integer programming problem can be stated as follows:†

$$\text{Maximize } b_1 X_1 + b_2 X_2 + \cdots + b_n X_n$$

• This section may be bypassed without loss of continuity.

*The integer programming algorithm described here is a form of zero-one integer programming, which permits the decision variable to take values of only 0 or 1. Since at most we want to accept a project only once, this integer programming algorithm is used to solve capital rationing problems. For a detailed discussion of programming solutions to capital budgeting problems, see the references listed at the end of this chapter.

†Because the full amount of the capital budget, C, is assumed to represent the initial investment, by maximizing the present value of net cash flows resulting from projects the firm is providing for maximum net present value.

when

$$c_1X_1 + c_2X_2 + \cdots + c_nX_n \le C \qquad X_i = 0, 1 \text{ (for all } i = 1, n)$$

where

b_i (for $i = 1, n$) = the present value of the net cash flows from project i

X_i (for $i = 1, n$) = a decision variable which can have a value of either 0 or 1 depending on whether the project is accepted ($X_i = 1$) or rejected ($X_i = 0$)

c_i (for $i = 1, n$) = the initial investment required for project i

C = the amount of budget available for investment during the current period

n = the number of projects considered

Using certain integer programming algorithms, the acceptable projects (those for which $X_i = 1$) can be determined. Computer programs are available to solve these algorithms. The following example shows how the basic single-period integer programming problem is set up.

EXAMPLE   The Antigonish International Ltd. has five projects competing for the firm's fixed-capital budget of $250,000. The initial outlay and the present value of the future net cash flows associated with each of these projects is as follows:

Project	Initial outlay	PV of net cash flows
A	$ 80,000	$100,000
B	70,000	112,000
C	100,000	145,000
D	60,000	79,000
E	110,000	126,500

The integer programming formulation of the problem is designed to select the group of projects with the maximum NPV subject to the current capital budget constraint of $250,000. It can be formulated as follows:

$$\text{Maximize } 100,000X_A + 112,000X_B + 145,000X_C + 79,000X_D + 126,500X_E$$

when

$$80,000X_A + 70,000X_B + 100,000X_C + 60,000X_D + 110,000X_E \le 250,000$$

$$X_i = 0, 1 \text{ (for } i = A,E)$$

The solution to this problem is $X_A = 1$, $X_B = 1$, $X_C = 1$, $X_D = 0$, and $X_E = 0$. Thus projects A, B, and C should be accepted and projects D and E should be rejected.

Capital Budgeting Under the Declining Balance Method of CCA Calculations

For most classes of depreciable assets, capital cost allowances are calculated by using the declining balance method that was illustrated in Chapter 2. Since under the declining balance method, the CCA-based tax savings can occur in perpetuity, the cash-flow analysis of a capital project can become rather cumbersome. The following two examples illustrate many of the complications involved. These examples draw heavily on the CCA calculation procedures discussed in Chapter 2; the reader may therefore wish to review those procedures before going through these examples.

THE PURCHASE OF A NEW ASSET

The example discussed next deals with the capital budgeting evaluation of the purchase of a new asset.

EXAMPLE   The Debbie Designers Ltd. is considering the purchase of a new piece of equipment at the beginning of 19X1 at a cost of $100,000. The economic life of the equipment is expected to be four years with an estimated salvage value of $20,000 at the end of that time. It is estimated that the equipment will increase cash revenues by $60,000 and labour costs by $20,000 during each year of its four-year life. The equipment will be included in the firm's Class 8 pool for which the maximum CCA rate of 20 percent is allowed on the declining balance. The company intends to take the maximum CCA allowed. It is expected that subsequent to the disposal of the equipment at its salvage value, the undepreciated capital cost (UCC) balance for Class 8 will remain positive and that there will still be some assets left in the class. The corporate tax rate is 40 percent and the firm's cost of capital is 10 percent. The firm expects no change in its working capital as a result of the purchase.

Should the company purchase the new equipment? The analysis required for this decision involves the following steps:

STEP 1: Initial investment   Since the equipment will not be replacing any of the firm's existing assets, no proceeds from the sale of existing assets need be considered in calculating the initial investment in the new equipment. Furthermore, since the tax effects of the incremental CCA deductions (ΔCCA's) resulting from the equipment will occur in the future (beginning from the year-end 19X1), the initial investment will require no tax adjustment. Consequently, the initial investment in the proposed equipment will simply equal its acquisition cost of $100,000.

STEP 2: Net cash flows*   The calculations of the net cash flows resulting from the purchase of the proposed equipment are summarized in Table 15.7. The tax savings components of the net cash flows are calculated in Tables 15.5 and 15.6. The acquisition cost of the equipment ($100,000) will be added to the existing Class 8 UCC balance (i.e., the UCC balance prior to the

---

*Since we are dealing with simple cash-flow patterns (i.e., investments for which all future net cash flows are either zero or positive), we could refer to the net cash flows as being net cash inflows.

Table 15.5 ΔCCA Deductions and Associated Tax Savings for Years 19X1–19X4

Year	ΔUCC (1)	ΔCCA (to be claimed at year-end) (2) = 20% of (1)	$t \cdot \Delta CCA$ (tax savings) (3) = 40% of (2)	ΔUCC remaining after deduction of ΔCCA (4) = (1) − (2)
19X1	$100,000	$20,000	$8,000	$80,000
19X2	80,000	16,000	6,400	64,000
19X3	64,000	12,800	5,120	51,200
19X4	51,200	10,240	4,096	40,960

acquisition of the equipment). The resulting increase in the UCC balance (ΔUCC_o) will generate incremental CCA deductions (ΔCCA's), and therefore tax savings beginning at the end of 19X1. The ΔCCA deductions and the associated tax savings for the years 19X1 through 19X4 are shown in Table 15.5. As indicated in this table, the ΔUCC balance left at the end of 19X4 will be $40,960. This balance after the sale of the equipment at the beginning of 19X5 will be reduced to $20,960 (i.e., $40,960 − $20,000).* The firm will be able to claim ΔCCA deductions in future years on this remaining balance even if the equipment will no longer be part of the firm's Class 8 pool. Since this residual ΔUCC balance will never be fully expensed under the declining balance method, it will generate ΔCCA deductions and therefore tax savings in perpetuity (beginning from the end of 19X5).† These perpetual ΔCCA deductions and tax savings are shown in Table 15.6.

Table 15.6 ΔCCA Deductions and Associated Tax Savings *After* the Sale of the Equipment

Year	ΔUCC (1)	ΔCCA (to be claimed at year-end) (2) = 20% of (1)	$t \cdot \Delta CCA$ (tax savings) (3) = 40% of (2)	ΔUCC remaining after deduction of ΔCCA at year-end (4) = (1) − (2)
19X5	$20,960	$4,192.00	$1,676.80	$16,768.00
19X6	16,768	3,353.60	1,341.44	13,414.40
Limiting values	↓ ∞	↓ 0	↓ 0	↓ 0

*In Chapter 2, we noted that if there is a sale of an asset from a class, the lower of the proceeds of sale or the original cost of the asset sold, is deducted from the presale UCC balance of the class. In the present example, the original cost of the machine ($100,000) exceeds the proceeds of the sale ($20,000). Therefore, the presale ΔUCC balance is reduced by $20,000. This reduction will reduce the ΔCCA-based tax shields in future years.

†This is true only if subsequent to the sale of the equipment, the UCC balance of Class 8 of which the equipment was a part *remains positive and the class continues* (i.e., other assets remain in the class after the sale of the machine). This is the case in our example. To illustrate this point, suppose that the Class 8 UCC balance after the sale was positive but that there was *no* asset left in the class. In that case, the UCC balance will be treated as a terminal loss, and will be used to reduce the firm's taxable income in 19X5. Therefore, the entire tax savings from the ΔUCC balance of $20,960 (included in the aggregate Class 8 UCC balance) will occur in 19X5 and not in future years. If the UCC balance after the sale was negative, then regardless of whether or not there are assets left in the class it would be recaptured and taxed as ordinary income in 19X5. The amount to be recaptured in 19X5 will be reduced

Finally, the annual net cash flows (excluding the cash flow from the sale of the equipment at its salvage value) expected to result from the equipment are summarized in Table 15.7. Using Equation 14.2 developed in Chapter 14, the net cash flow for each year from 19X1 through 19X4 is stated as the sum of incremental after-tax cash operating income, $(1 - t)(\Delta R - \Delta C)$, and the tax saving, $t \cdot \Delta CCA$, for the year. For each of the four years, $(1 - t)(\Delta R - \Delta C)$, equals $24,000 [i.e., $(1 - .40)(\$60,000 - \$20,000)$].

Table 15.7   Annual Net Cash Flows (Excluding Salvage Value)

Year	Incremental after-tax cash operating income $(1 - t)(\Delta R - \Delta C)$ (1)	Tax savings $t \cdot \Delta CCA$ (2)	Net cash flow (excluding salvage value) (3) = (1) + (2)
19X1	$24,000	$8,000	$24,000 + $8,000
19X2	24,000	6,400	24,000 + 6,400
19X3	24,000	5,120	24,000 + 5,120
19X4	24,000	4,096	24,000 + 4,096
19X5	—	1,676.8	1,676.8
19X6	—	1,341.44	1,341.44
	↓	↓	↓
Limiting value:	∞	0	0

The tax savings shown in Table 15.7 for the years 19X1 through 19X4 are taken from column 3 of Table 15.5. Note that Table 15.7 also includes the tax savings for the years 19X5 and onwards, as given in Table 15.6. Since these tax savings are part of the net cash-flow stream resulting from the equipment, they must not be ignored in the analysis.

STEP 3: Salvage value   The sale of the equipment at its salvage value at the beginning of 19X5 will generate a cash inflow of $20,000. Since this is an incremental flow, it must be included in the analysis.

STEP 4: Calculation of NPV

NPV = present value of net cash flows − initial investment

= present value of incremental after-tax cash operating income

    + present value of tax savings + present value of salvage value

    − initial investment

$$= \frac{\$24,000}{(1 + .10)} + \frac{\$24,000}{(1 + .10)^2} + \frac{\$24,000}{(1 + .10)^3} + \frac{\$24,000}{(1 + .10)^4}$$

$$+ \text{present value of tax savings} + \frac{\$20,000}{(1 + .10)^4} - \$100,000$$

---

by the residual balance of $20,960. Therefore, in this case also, the tax savings (resulting from the reduction in the recapture) on the $20,960 will be realized in 19X5 and not in subsequent years. Note that a negative UCC balance at the beginning of 19X5 *could* occur if, for example, Class 8 were a single-asset class and the asset was sold for more than its book value (UCC) at the time of sale.

$$= \$24,000 \cdot PVIFA_{.10,4 \text{ yrs.}} + \text{present value of tax savings}$$

$$+ \$20,000 \cdot PVIF_{.10,4 \text{ yrs.}} - \$100,000$$

$$= \$24,000 \cdot 3.17 + \text{present value of tax savings} + \$20,000 \cdot .683 - \$100,000$$

$$= \$76,080 + \text{present value of tax savings} + \$13,660 - \$100,000$$

Fortunately, the calculation of the present value of the infinite series of tax savings can be simplified by using the following formula (derived in the appendix to this chapter):

$$\text{Present value of tax savings} = \frac{\Delta UCC_o \cdot d \cdot t}{k + d} - \frac{S \cdot d \cdot t}{k + d} \cdot \frac{1}{(1 + k)^n}$$

where ΔUCC_o is the incremental UCC balance resulting from the acquisition of the asset, and

d = CCA rate
k = cost of capital
S = salvage value
n = number of years after which the asset is sold

The salvage value appears in this formula because it affects the tax savings *after* the asset is disposed of.

In this example, $\Delta UCC_o = \$100,000$, $t = .40$, $n = 4$, $d = .20$, $k = .10$, and $S = \$20,000$. Therefore, the present value of the tax savings

$$= \frac{\$100,000 \cdot .20 \cdot .40}{.10 + .20} - \frac{\$20,000 \cdot .20 \cdot .40}{.10 + .20} \cdot \frac{1}{(1.10)^4}$$

$$= \$26,666.7 - \$5,333.3 \cdot .683$$

$$= \$23,024.1$$

Substituting this value into the expression for NPV and summing gives: NPV = \$12,764.10. Since the NPV is positive, the proposed equipment should be purchased. Also note that since the example involves an accept–reject type of decision, the NPV and the IRR criteria should give the same decision. To illustrate, let us calculate the IRR on the investment in the proposed equipment. By definition, the IRR is the discount rate at which NPV = 0. Therefore, it is obtained by solving for IRR in the following equation:

$$NPV = 0 = \left[\frac{\$24,000}{(1 + IRR)} + \frac{\$24,000}{(1 + IRR)^2} + \frac{\$24,000}{(1 + IRR)^3} + \frac{\$24,000}{(1 + IRR)^4} \right]$$

$$+ \left[\frac{\$100,000 \cdot .20 \cdot .40}{IRR + .20} - \frac{\$20,000 \cdot .20 \cdot .40}{IRR + .20} \cdot \frac{1}{(1 + IRR)^4} \right]$$

$$+ \left[\frac{\$20,000}{(1 + IRR)^4} \right] - \$100,000$$

By trial and error, the IRR would be found to be approximately equal to 15 percent. Since the IRR exceeds the firm's cost of capital, the proposed equipment should be purchased. This is the same decision as was arrived at by using the NPV criterion.

THE REPLACEMENT OF AN EXISTING ASSET

The example discussed next deals with the capital budgeting evaluation of the purchase of a new asset to replace an existing asset.

EXAMPLE   The president of Cann Printers Ltd. is considering a proposal for the replacement of one of the company's old printing machines at the beginning of 19X1. The old machine was originally purchased at a cost of $60,000 and it is expected to last until the end of 19X4. Its salvage value at the beginning of 19X5 is expected to be $5,000. Its market value at the beginning of 19X1 is expected to be $10,000. The new machine will cost the company $210,000 (including installation costs) and it is expected to last for four years (i.e., until the end of 19X4). It is estimated that the new machine will increase the company's cash revenues from $120,000 to $130,000 and reduce its labour and other cash costs from $80,000 to $60,000 for each of the four years of its useful life. Furthermore, the president believes that the *new* machine could be sold at its estimated salvage value of $20,000 at the beginning of 19X5. Both the new and the old machines are Class 5 assets. The prescribed maximum CCA rate for Class 5 is 10 percent on the declining balance. The Class 5 UCC balance at the beginning of 19X1, without the new machine, is expected to be $80,000. The replacement of the old machine will not affect the company's working capital requirements. The corporate tax rate is at 40 percent and Cann's cost of capital is 10 percent.

Should Cann Printers Ltd. replace the old machine? The analysis required for the replacement decision faced by the president of Cann Printers Ltd. can be made by calculating the NPV of the incremental net cash flows that would be generated if the old machine is replaced. This can be calculated by following the same four-step procedure as was used in the preceding example. It is assumed that the company claims the maximum CCA permitted in any given year; that after the disposal of the new machine at the beginning of 19X5, the Class 5 UCC balance will remain positive; and that there will still be some assets left in the class for all future time periods.

STEP 1: Initial investment   The initial investment is calculated as follows:

Acquisition cost of the new machine (including installation cost)	$210,000
Less: Proceeds from the sale of the old machine	10,000
Total	$200,000

STEP 2: Net cash flows   The calculation of the future net cash flows associated with the replacement decision are summarized in Tables 15.8–15.11. Table 15.8 shows that the replacement of the old machine will generate an incremental UCC balance (ΔUCC_o) of $200,000 as of the beginning of 19X1. Based on this ΔUCC_o balance, the ΔCCA deductions and the tax savings resulting from these deductions for the years 19X1–19X4 are shown in Table 15.9. As indicated in this table, the ΔUCC balance left at the end of 19X4 will be $131,220. The sale of the new machine at the beginning of 19X5 will generate *incremental* proceeds of sale of $15,000 (i.e., $20,000 − $5,000).

Therefore, the ΔUCC balance of $131,220 left at the end of 19X4 is reduced by the incremental proceeds of sale to obtain a ΔUCC balance of $116,220 (i.e., $131,220 − $15,000) at the beginning of 19X5. Because of the declining balance method, this residual ΔUCC balance will generate ΔCCA deductions and therefore tax savings in perpetuity (beginning at the end of 19X5). These perpetual ΔCCA deductions and tax savings are shown in Table 15.10.

Table 15.8   Incremental UCC Balance (ΔUCC_o) Resulting from the Replacement of the Old Machine

UCC before replacement (i.e., at the beginning of 19X1)	$ 80,000
Acquisition cost of the new machine	210,000
Less: Proceeds of sale or original cost of the old machine	10,000
UCC after replacement	$280,000

Therefore, ΔUCC_o = UCC after replacement $-$ UCC before replacement[a]
= $280,000 $-$ $80,000
= $200,000

[a]It should be noted that the ΔUCC_o balance equals the difference between the acquisition cost of the new machine and the proceeds of the sale of the old machine (i.e., $210,000 $-$ $10,000). This will always be the case (regardless of the UCC balance before replacement), whenever the proceeds of the sale of the replaced asset are less than its original cost as in the present example.

Table 15.9 ΔCCA Deductions and Associated Tax Savings for the Years 19X1–19X4

Year	ΔUCC (1)	ΔCCA (to be claimed at year-end) (2) = 10% of (1)	$t \cdot \Delta CCA$ (tax savings) (3) = 40% of (2)	ΔUCC remaining after deduction of ΔCCA at year-end (4) = (1) − (2)
19X1	$200,000	$20,000	$8,000	$180,000
19X2	180,000	18,000	7,200	162,000
19X3	162,000	16,200	6,480	145,800
19X4	145,800	14,580	5,832	131,220

Table 15.10 ΔCCA Deductions and Associated Tax Savings *After* the Sale of the New Machine

Year	ΔUCC (1)	ΔCCA (to be claimed at year-end) (2) = 10% of (1)	$t \cdot \Delta CCA$ (tax savings) (3) = 40% of (2)	ΔUCC remaining after deduction of ΔCCA at year-end (4) = (1) − (2)
19X5	$116,220	$11,622	$4,649	$104,598
19X6	104,598	10,459.8	4,184	94,138.2
↓	↓	↓	↓	↓
Limiting value: ∞	0	0	0	0

[a]The values are approximate due to rounding errors.

Finally, the annual net cash flows (excluding the cash flow from the incremental salvage value) that will be generated if the old machine were replaced are summarized in Table 15.11. Based on Equation 14.2 developed in Chapter 14, the net cash flow (excluding salvage value) for each year from 19X1 through 19X4 is stated as the sum of the incremental after-tax cash operating income, $(1 - t)(\Delta R - \Delta C)$, and the tax saving, $t \cdot \Delta CCA$, for the year. Since for each year from 19X1 through 19X4, $\Delta R = \$10,000$ (i.e., $\$130,000 - \$120,000$) and $\Delta C = \$-20,000$ (i.e., $\$60,000 - \$80,000$), $(1 - t)(\Delta R - \Delta C) = \$18,000$ [i.e., $(1 - .40)(\$10,000 - (-\$20,000))$] for each of these years. Note that ΔC is negative because replacement of the old machine will *reduce* the cash operating costs of the firm.

Table 15.11 Annual Net Cash Flows (Excluding Salvage Value)

Year	Incremental after-tax cash operating income $(1 - t)(\Delta R - \Delta C)$ (1)	Tax savings $t \cdot \Delta CCA$ (2)	Net cash flow (excluding salvage value) (3) = (1) + (2)
19X1	$18,000	$8,000	$18,000 + $8,000
19X2	18,000	7,200	18,000 + 7,200
19X3	18,000	6,480	18,000 + 6,480
19X4	18,000	5,832	18,000 + 5,832
19X5	—	4,649	$4,649
19X6	—	4,184	4,184
$\downarrow$	—	$\downarrow$	$\downarrow$
Limiting value: ∞	—	0	0

STEP 3: Incremental salvage value (ΔS) If the old machine is not replaced, then its sale at its salvage value at the beginning of 19X5 will generate a cash inflow of $5,000. If it is replaced, then the sale of the new machine at its salvage value will generate a cash inflow of $20,000 at the beginning of 19X5. Thus, the replacement decision will result in an incremental disposal cash inflow of $15,000 (i.e., $20,000 − $5,000) at the beginning of 19X5 (i.e., four years after the replacement of the old machine).

STEP 4: Calculation of NPV

NPV = present value of net cash flows − initial investment

$\quad$ = $18,000 \cdot PVIFA_{.10,4 \text{ yrs.}}$ + present value of tax savings

$\quad\quad$ + [incremental salvage value (ΔS) of $15,000 \cdot PVIF_{.10,4 \text{ yrs.}}$] − $200,000

$\quad$ = $18,000 (3.17) + present value of tax savings + $15,000 (.683) − $200,000

The present value of the tax savings can be calculated by using the formula used in the preceding example, except that in the present example we must substitute ΔS (the incremental salvage value) for S in the formula.

In the present example, $t = .40$, $n = 4$, $d = .10$, $k = .10$, $\Delta S = \$15,000$, and $\Delta UCC_o = \$200,000$. Therefore, substituting these values into the formula we obtain:

$$\text{Present value of tax savings} = \frac{\Delta UCC_o \cdot d \cdot t}{k + d} - \frac{\Delta S \cdot d \cdot t}{k + d} \cdot \frac{1}{(1 + k)^n}$$

$$= \frac{.40 \cdot \$200,000 \cdot .10}{.10 + .10} - \frac{.40 \cdot \$15,000 \cdot .10}{.10 + .10} \cdot \frac{1}{(1.10)^4}$$

$$= \$37,951$$

Substituting this value into the expression for NPV we obtain NPV = $57,060 + $37,951 + $10,245 − $200,000 = −$94,744. Since the NPV is negative, the old machine should not be replaced.* We leave it as an exercise for the reader to verify that the IRR of the project is less than 10 percent (the cost of capital).

● Inflation and Capital Budgeting

Not so long ago, inflation was not an issue in investment analysis. Most firms simply ignored the effects of inflation on their investment decisions because inflation rates were low. This may have been a reasonable approach in the past, but at current high rates of inflation in Canada and in most other countries there may be significant distortions in capital investment decisions if the expected inflationary trend is either ignored or is not properly accounted for in the investment evaluation process. Let us illustrate this point with the help of a simplified example.

EXAMPLE   A firm is considering the acquisition of a piece of equipment at a cost of $50,000. The equipment is expected to last five years with no salvage value at the end of that time. If acquired, it will constitute a single-asset class on the company's books and the CCA deduction on it will be taken on a straight-line basis over its five-year life. The data developed for the evaluation of the contemplated investment are as follows:

1 Without the adjustment for the effects of the current inflationary trend in the economy, the equipment, for each year of its life, is expected to increase annual cash revenues and cash operating costs by $120,000 and $100,000, respectively.
2 Based on the forecasts of the inflationary trend available from government and private sources, the annual rate of general inflation is expected to be 10 percent during the equipment's life of five years. However, management feels that the general inflationary trend will affect the above

---

*The reader will recognize that the replacement decision is really a ranking decision (old versus new asset). Thus, in evaluating the replacement decision in the above example on the basis of the new machine's *incremental* cash flows, we have used the incremental analysis method outlined in the footnote on page 420.

● This section may be bypassed without loss of continuity.

two elements of the equipment's cash-flow stream to different degrees: The incremental annual cash revenue (ΔR) is expected to grow at an annual rate of 6 percent and the incremental cash operating costs (ΔC) at 8 percent.

3 The firm estimates that the *current* cost of capital required to finance the equipment will equal 15 percent and the corporate tax rate is 40 percent.

Suppose the company uses cash-flow data that has *not* been adjusted for the effects of anticipated inflation. Then the incremental after-tax net operating cash flows expected from the project will be as shown in Table 15.12. The NPV of the project, using the expected cost of capital of 15 percent as the discount rate, equals $3,632 [i.e., $16,000 $\cdot$ $PVIFA_{.15,5yrs.}$ − $50,000].

Table 15.12   Cash Flows *Without* Adjustment for Expected Inflationary Trend[a]

	Year 1	Year 2	Year 3	Year 4	Year 5
Increase in cash revenue (ΔR)	$120,000	$120,000	$120,000	$120,000	120,000
Less: Increase in cash operating costs (ΔC)	100,000	100,000	100,000	100,000	100,000
Increase in cash operating income ($\Delta R - \Delta C$)	20,000	20,000	20,000	20,000	20,000
Increase in after-tax cash operating income $(1 - t)(\Delta R - \Delta C)$	12,000[b]	12,000	12,000	12,000	12,000
Plus: Tax savings from incremental CCA deductions ($t \cdot \Delta CCA$)	4,000[c]	4,000	4,000	4,000	4,000
Net cash flows (i.e., incremental after-tax net operating cash flows)	$ 16,000	$ 16,000	$ 16,000	$ 16,000	$ 16,000

[a]The figures in this table have been rounded off to the nearest dollar.
[b]$(1 - t)(\Delta R - \Delta C) = (1 - .40) \cdot \$20,000 = \$12,000$.
[c]$t \cdot \Delta CCA = .40 \cdot$ annual straight-line CCA deduction $= .40 \cdot \$50,000/5 = \$4,000$.

Since the NPV is expected to be positive, the project will be accepted. However, notice that while the cash-flow data used in the NPV calculation does *not* include an adjustment for the effects of expected general inflation, *the estimated current cost of capital used as the discount rate will reflect the market's inflationary expectations.* * The cost of capital will reflect the market's expectations of inflation, because inflation erodes the purchasing power of the investors' investment.

---

*This relationship is known as the *Fisher effect.* In the present context this relationship implies that the current cost of capital to the firm will exceed the expected rate of inflation in the economy. Also, note that although we have incorporated only the *expected* rate of inflation in the analysis, the uncertainty of the future rate of inflation will also be reflected in the cost of new capital. For more details, see Thomas E. Copeland and J. Fred Weston, *Financial Theory and Corporate Finance* (Don Mills, Ontario: Addison-Wesley 1979), chap. 3, pp. 57–59.

Thus, in order to protect themselves from the reduction in the purchasing power of their investment, a firm's capital suppliers will seek compensation for this reduction by requiring higher rates
of returns on their investments in the firm's securities than would be the case in the absence of
general inflation.*

Now suppose that the company evaluates the project using the cash-flow data that includes the
adjustment for the effects of anticipated inflation. The calculations required for the adjustment are
summarized in Table 15.13. The *actual* (i.e., nominal) incremental cash revenue for year n, due to
the inflation-induced growth rate of 6 percent, will equal the unadjusted incremental cash revenue
for the year n multiplied by $(1 + .06)^n$. For example, the actual incremental cash revenue for year
3 in Table 15.13 is \$142,920 [i.e., \$120,000 $\cdot$ $(1 + .06)^3$ or \$120,000 $\cdot$ $CVIF_{.06.3 \text{ yrs.}}$]. The
adjustment of the given unadjusted incremental cash costs, using the applicable inflationary
growth rate of 8 percent, is made in a similar manner.

Table 15.13   Inflation-Adjusted Cash-Flow Data[a]

	Year 1	Year 2	Year 3	Year 4	Year 5
Increase in cash revenue (ΔR)(inflationary growth at 6%)	\$127,200	\$134,880	\$142,920	\$151,440	\$160,560
Less: Increase in cash operating expenses (ΔC)(inflationary growth rate at 8%)	108,000	116,600	126,000	136,000	146,900
Increase in cash operating income ($\Delta R - \Delta C$)	19,200	18,280	16,920	15,440	13,660
Increase in after-tax cash operating income $(1 - t)(\Delta R - \Delta C)$	11,520[b]	10,968	10,152	9,264	8,196
Plus: Tax savings from incremental CCA deductions $(t \cdot \Delta CCA)$[b]	4,000[c]	4,000	4,000	4,000	4,000
Net cash flows (i.e., incremental after-tax net operating cash flows)	\$ 15,520	\$ 14,968	\$ 14,152	\$ 13,264	\$ 12,196

[a]The figures in this table have been rounded off to the nearest dollar.
[b]$(1 - t)(\Delta R - \Delta C) = (1 - .40)(\$19,200) = \$11,520$ calculated in a similar manner for years 2–5.
[c]Capital cost allowances are permitted on the basis of the historical costs of the assets involved. Therefore, the tax saving
element of the cash-flow stream is not adjusted for the expected general inflation.

The NPV of the project based on the inflation-adjusted cash flows (shown in the last row of
Table 15.13) is now given by

---

*To illustrate this point, suppose an investment will return \$100 this year and \$100 next year. If the
general price level rises 10 percent between now and next year, the inflow of \$100 next year will have
a purchasing power in terms of today's dollar of only about \$90.90 (i.e., \$100/\$110). Such losses of
purchasing power induce investors to demand higher returns on their investments.

$$\text{NPV (inflation-adjusted)} = \$15,520 \cdot PVIF_{.15,1 \text{ yr.}} \text{ of } .87 + \$14,968 \cdot PVIF_{.15,2 \text{ yrs.}} \text{ of } .756$$

$$+ \$14,152 \cdot PVIF_{.15,3 \text{ yrs.}} \text{ of } .658 + \$13,264 \cdot PVIF_{.15,4 \text{ yrs.}} \text{ of } .572$$

$$+ \$12,196 \cdot PVIF_{.15,5 \text{ yrs.}} \text{ of } .497 - \$50,000$$

$$= -\$2,222 \text{ (approximately)}$$

Since this NPV, which represents the net benefit to the firm's shareholders in terms of current dollars, is negative, the project should be rejected. This is a reversal of the earlier decision that was based on the unadjusted cash-flow data. It shows that if the firm were to ignore the expected inflationary effects on the project's incremental cash-flow stream, it would make an erroneous project evaluation. In this regard, note that the unadjusted cash-flow data was revised upward using a higher inflation-induced growth rate for the incremental cash expenses than for the incremental cash revenues (8 percent vs. 6 percent).* As a consequence, the expected NPV of the project became negative ($-\$2,222$). *Thus, a project that is considered acceptable in a noninflationary environment may not be acceptable when inflationary effects on the various components of the project's cash flows are taken into account.*

The CCA-based tax savings in Table 15.12 were not adjusted for the anticipated inflation, because the tax laws do not permit upward revision of capital costs (and, therefore, of capital-cost allowances) to allow for increases in the replacement values of existing assets caused by inflation.[2] It should be obvious from Table 15.12 that the upward adjustment of *all* the unadjusted components of the project's expected cash-flow stream (ΔR , ΔC , and $t \cdot \Delta CCA$) at the *same* expected rate of inflation will yield a positive NPV instead of the negative NPV obtained by using the approximately adjusted cash-flow data in Table 15.13. This example illustrates *that simple adjustments of the after-tax net cash flows at an estimated rate of general inflation can lead to misleading investment decisions.*

---

*It has often been argued that firms "mark up" increases in costs and then pass the resultant amount along to their customers in the form of higher prices. Thus, if mark-up pricing is used by a firm and costs increase due to inflation, then revenues (i.e., cash inflows) should increase at a faster rate than costs (i.e., cash outflows). Therefore, a project's net cash flow (i.e., the difference between its cash inflows and outflows), and thus its IRR, should increase with an increase in inflation. [If the inflation is fully anticipated, it is not clear whether the firm is better off, because the cost of capital (discount rate), k, is also an increasing function of anticipated inflation!]

While investment decision making is *ex ante*, and thus uses expected values, a post audit is *ex post* and thus uses realized or actual values. Thus, inflation, which was unanticipated *ex ante*, will cause an investment project's realized return to exceed its expected return (i.e., increase its actual IRR over its expected IRR). In other words, inflation, which was unanticipated *ex ante*, should favourably affect the *ex post* performance of an investment project (i.e., increase its actual IRR over its expected IRR). This could complicate a post audit of an investment project, because an investment decision that *ex ante* had an IRR $< k$ but was nonetheless undertaken erroneously could have an acceptable *ex post* performance (IRR $> k$) because actual inflation exceeded anticipated inflation. For a discussion of the sensitivity of a firm's net operating income to inflation, see R. A. Kessel and A. A. Alchian, "The Meaning and Validity of the Inflation-Induced Lag of Wages Behind Prices," *American Economic Review* (March 1960); and Moon K. Kim, "Inflationary Effects in the Capital Investment Process: An Empirical Examination," *The Journal of Finance* 34, No. 4 (September 1979), pp. 941–950.

The analysis in the preceding example shows that if a firm expects continuing general inflation, the firm should evaluate its investment opportunities on the basis of the following general principles:

1 It should use the actual or *nominal* dollar cash flows (i.e., cash flows that reflect the anticipated effects of inflation).
2 The nominal dollar cash flows should generally not be obtained by simply adjusting after-tax net operating cash flows by using an average or expected *general* rate of inflation (as measured, for example, by the consumer price index).*
3 Each component of the cash-flow stream should be estimated separately using that component's particular inflation-induced growth rate because inflation will generally influence each component differently.
4 As in the case of no inflation, the appropriate discount rate to employ is the firm's *current* cost of capital because this rate will reflect the market's inflationary expectations.

Summary

This chapter has been devoted to a description of the basic capital budgeting concepts and techniques. A widely used investment evaluation criterion that does not rely on discounted cash-flow (DCF) concepts is the payback period. Under the payback criterion, a project is accepted if it returns the project's initial cash outlay within a specified period of time. This method ignores the time value of money and the cash flows beyond the payback period. It is, however, useful as an initial screening device for investments. Firms with serious liquidity problems or firms engaged in international investments subject to considerable political and other risks may find payback a useful criterion.

Discounted cash-flow (DCF) techniques for capital budgeting consider the time factor in the value of money, and their use is consistent with the objective of maximizing shareholders' wealth. The net present-value (NPV) approach measures the difference between the present values of inflows and the initial outlay (or present value of the outlays if they are spread over time) in order to determine the desirability of a project. If the net present value of a project is greater than or equal to zero, it is considered acceptable; if the net present value is less than zero, the project must be rejected. The benefit–cost ratio or profitability index is defined as the ratio of the present value of future net cash flows to the initial investment. It therefore shows the *relative* profitability of a project or the present value of benefits per dollar invested in the project. Projects are acceptable if their benefit–cost ratios are greater than or equal to one; otherwise they should be rejected. The internal rate of return (IRR), the discount rate that equates the net present value of a project with zero, is also used as a basis for capital budgeting decision making. If this rate is greater than or equal to the firm's cost of capital, a project is acceptable; otherwise it must be rejected.

*This is particularly important because prices of many important goods and services purchased by business firms are not included in the price indices (such as the consumer price index), which are commonly employed to measure the *average* rate of inflation in the entire economy.

Each of the DCF capital budgeting techniques somehow uses the cost of capital in its decision criterion. In the case of the net present-value and benefit–cost ratio approaches, the cost of capital is used to discount the cash flows in order to calculate these measures. In the case of the internal rate-of-return method, the cost of capital is compared to the project's internal rate of return in order to determine its acceptability. Each of these capital-budgeting techniques provides the same accept–reject decision for a given project, but there can be conflicts between the rankings of projects using these various techniques. The basic conflict in ranking between net present value and internal rate of return results from the internal rate of return's implicit assumption that future cash flows from an investment can be reinvested at the internal rate of return. Although the net present-value technique is often considered to be more theoretically acceptable than the internal rate of return, the internal rate of return is commonly used by major firms.

Capital rationing occurs when there are insufficient funds available to finance all acceptable projects. A limit on the size of the capital expenditure budget may arise from the nonavailability of funds from external sources or may be imposed by the top management of the firm in order to preserve corporate control or to achieve orderly growth, or both. When faced with capital rationing, the firm should adopt that subset of investments within its capital constraint that has the highest total NPV. If the projects to be considered are economically independent, then the firm can make such a selection by ranking the projects in descending order of their profitability indices and then selecting the acceptable projects until the capital budget is exhausted. If the projects selected on the basis of the above procedure do not exhaust the entire investment budget, then the projects close to the budget limit (i.e., the marginal projects) must be examined to ensure that the selected projects do indeed maximize the total NPV subject to the budget constraint. If the total NPV is not the maximum possible, then different groups of projects, including marginal projects, should be tested to find the group that provides the maximum total NPV under the budget constraint.

Finally, under conditions of expected general inflation, a firm should evaluate its investment opportunities on the basis of the following general principles. It should use the actual dollar cash flows (i.e., the cash flows that reflect the anticipated effects of general inflation). These cash flows should generally not be estimated by simply adjusting the after-tax net operating cash flows by using an average or expected general rate of inflation. Instead, each component of the cash-flow stream should be adjusted by its own inflation-induced growth rate, because inflation generally influences each component differently. As in the case of no inflation, the appropriate discount rate to employ is the firm's *current* cost of capital, because this rate reflects the market's inflationary expectations.

Questions

15.1 What is the payback period? Is it calculated using after-tax profits or cash flows? What are the pros and cons of using the payback period to measure an investment's attractiveness?

15.2 In what situations is the payback method useful?

15.3   How does the passage of time affect the value of money? How are compound interest and discounting related?

15.4   What is meant by the phrase "the present value of $X to be received n years from now"? How is the present value of a future sum related to compounding?

15.5   How can the present value of an uneven stream of cash flows be calculated?

15.6   What is the essential difference between the DCF capital-budgeting techniques and the non-DCF techniques such as the payback period?

15.7   What is meant by the phrase "net present value"? How may it be used in making accept–reject decisions? How is NPV calculated?

15.8   How is the benefit–cost ratio or profitability index computed? What is the criterion for judging the acceptability of investments when using B/C ratios? What do B/C ratios signify? What is an investment's B/C ratio when its net present value equals zero?

15.9   Do the benefit–cost ratio and the net present-value approaches to capital budgeting always agree with respect to both the acceptability and ranking of investments? Why or why not?

15.10   What is the internal rate of return of an investment? How is it used to determine the acceptability of a project?

15.11   In attempting to find the internal rate of return for a project, what must one do if the present value of future net cash flows discounted at a given rate is greater than the initial investment? Why?

15.12   Do the NPV and IRR approaches to capital budgeting always agree with respect to the acceptability and ranking of projects? Can you explain your answer graphically?

15.13   There is disagreement with respect to the theoretical and practical superiority of the NPV and IRR methods of evaluating capital expenditures. Briefly discuss the arguments favouring each of these techniques.

15.14   When mutually exclusive projects have different rankings using NPV and IRR, which project would be preferred? Explain your answer. In which situation do conflicting project rankings arise?

15.15   What is meant by "capital rationing"? In which situations does it occur? What does it imply with respect to project selection?

15.16   Is capital rationing consistent with the criterion of shareholders' wealth maximization?

15.17   Comment briefly on the integer and linear programming approaches to capital rationing. What are the major practical difficulties in applying programming approaches to capital budgeting problems under capital rationing?

15.18   What general principles should a firm follow in evaluating an investment opportunity under conditions of continuing general inflation?

Problems

15.1   The Lee Corporation Ltd. is considering a capital expenditure that requires an initial investment of $42,000 and generates net cash flows of $7,000 per year for 10 years. The company has established a maximum payback standard of 8 years.
a.   Determine the payback period for this project.
b.   Should the company accept the project? Why or why not?

15.2   Prince George Company Ltd. uses a 5-year maximum payback standard. The firm is considering the purchase of a new machine and must choose between the two. The first machine requires an initial investment of $14,000 and generates annual net cash flows of $3,000 for each of the next 7 years. The second machine requires an initial investment of $21,000 and provides an annual net cash flow of $4,000 for 20 years.

a. Determine the payback period for each machine.

b. Comment on the acceptability of the machines assuming they are independent projects.

c. Which machine should the firm accept on the basis of the payback period criterion and why?

d. Do the machines in this problem illustrate any of the criticisms of using payback?

15.3 Bonnie's Beauty Aids is evaluating a new fragrance mixing machine. The asset requires an initial investment of $24,000 and will generate net cash flows of $5,000 per year for eight years. For each of the following cost of capital rates, (1) calculate the net present value, (2) indicate whether to accept or reject the machine, and (3) explain your decision.

a. 12 percent

b. 10 percent

c. 14 percent

15.4 A firm can purchase a fixed asset for a $13,000 initial investment. If the project yields an annual net cash flow of $4,000 for four years,

a. Determine the maximum cost of capital the firm can have and still accept the project (closest whole percentage rate).

b. Determine the net present value of the project assuming the firm has a 10-percent cost of capital.

c. Determine the benefit–cost ratio assuming the firm has a 10-percent cost of capital.

15.5 Calculate the net present value and benefit–cost ratio for the following 20-year projects. Assume that the firm's cost of capital is 14 percent.

a. Initial investment is $10,000; net cash flows are $2,000 per year.

b. Initial investment is $25,000; net cash flows are $3,000 per year.

c. Initial investment is $30,000; net cash flows are $5,000 per year.

15.6 Prince Albert Manufacturing Enterprises Ltd. has been given the following figures for a long-term project it is considering. The initial investment will be $18,250 and the project is expected to yield net cash flows of $4,000 per year for seven years. The firm has a 10-percent cost of capital.

a. Determine the net present value of the project.

b. Determine the benefit–cost ratio for the project.

c. Determine the internal rate of return for the project.

d. Would you recommend that Prince Albert accept or reject the project? Explain your answer.

15.7 Moncton Machine Tool Ltd. accepts projects earning more than the firm's 15-percent cost of capital. It is currently considering a 10-year project that provides annual net cash flows of $10,000 and requires an initial investment of $61,450.

a. Determine the IRR of this project.

b. How many years of net cash flows would it take to make this project just acceptable (i.e., have an IRR of 15 percent)?

c. With the given life, initial investment, and cost of capital, what is the minimum annual net cash flow the project must generate in order to be acceptable?

15.8   Compare the PI (profitability index) and NPV rankings of the following two projects. Which project would you prefer? Why?

	Initial investment	NPV
Project X	$40,000	$8,000
Project Y	10,000	5,000

15.9   A project requires an initial investment of $5,000 and is expected to generate net cash flows of $2,000, $2,500, and $1,500 over its three-year life. The project's IRR equals approximately 10 percent. Show that the IRR is equivalent to the rate of return on the *unrecovered* portion of the initial investment for the beginning of each year of the project's life.

15.10   Consider the project in Problem 15.9 again. Assume that its net cash flows are known with certainty. Suppose you are able to take a bank loan at a cost of 8 percent in order to finance this project. Show that by undertaking this project you will realize a gain (in present value terms) equal to the project's NPV, after you have repaid the principal and the interest charges on the loan from the project's net cash flows.

15.11   You are given the following information for two mutually exclusive projects, A and B.

Cash flows

Year	Project A	Project B
19X0	− $16,500 (initial investment)	− $32,500 (initial investment)
19X1	4,500	7,500
19X2	4,500	7,500
19X3	19,500	37,500

a. If the firm's cost of capital is 15 percent, rank the projects on the basis of their NPV's and their IRR's.
b. Do the rankings differ? If they do, which project would you choose?
c. Draw the NPV profiles of the two projects.
d. If a choice was based on the IRR ranking of the project, what criticisms would you propose?
e. What general conclusion do you draw from your answer to part **b**?
f. Would you accept both the projects if they were economically independent?

15.12   Rebecca Company Ltd. is considering two mutually exclusive projects, A and B, based on the following information.

Cash flows

Year	Project A	Project B
19X0	− $4,000 (initial investment)	− $4,000 (initial investment)
19X1	800	800
19X2	800	4,800
19X3	4,800	0

a. If Rebecca's cost of capital is 15 percent, rank the projects on the basis of the NPV and IRR criteria.

b. Why should Rebecca not choose between the projects on the basis of the IRR ranking determined in **a**?

c. What general conclusion can be drawn from your explanation in part **b**?

•**15.13**   The Sonya Company Ltd. plans to replace one of its old machines *just before the end of its current taxation year.* The new machine will cost the company $100,000. The old machine was originally purchased at a cost of $120,000 and is expected to be sold for $80,000 immediately after the acquisition of the new machine. Both the new and the old machines belong to an asset class for which the maximum capital cost allowance (CCA) can be taken at an annual rate of 20 percent on the declining balance. The company plans to claim the maximum CCA allowed. The year-end undepreciated capital cost balance (UCC), if the old machine is not replaced, is expected to be $40,000. The company expects no change in its working capital as a result of the replacement decision. The tax rate for the company is 40 percent. Calculate the initial cash outlay required for the new machine.

•**15.14**   The High River Machine Tools Company Ltd. is reviewing a proposal for the replacement of one of its old machines at the beginning of 19X1. The old machine was originally acquired six years ago at a cost of $10,000. It is expected to last until the end of 19X4, when its salvage value will be $500. If replaced, its market value at the time of its replacement is expected to be $2,000. The new machine will cost the company $18,000. Its useful life is expected to be four years, with a salvage value of $15,000 at the end of that time. Both the existing machine and the proposed replacement are Class 9 assets. The maximum CCA rate applicable to Class 9 is 25 percent on the declining balance. The company plans to claim the maximum CCA allowed in any given year. It is expected that the Class 9 UCC balance at the beginning of 19X1, without the new machine, will be $20,000. The corporate tax rate is at 40 percent. Assume that after the disposal of the new machine at its salvage value, the Class 9 UCC balance will always remain positive, and that the company will always have some assets in Class 9.

a. Calculate the initial investment required for the new machine.

b. Calculate the incremental UCC (ΔUCC_o) that will be generated if the old machine is replaced.

c. Calculate the incremental CCA deductions ($\Delta CCA's$) and the associated tax savings based on the calculation of ΔUCC_o in part **b**.

d. The company has estimated that the new machine will result in an increase in cash revenues of $4,000 and an increase in cash operating costs of $800 for each of the four years of its useful life. Calculate the annual net cash flows that the company should use in evaluating the replacement proposal.

e. Calculate the NPV of the replacement project assuming the firm's cost of capital is 10 percent.

f. What would the NPV of the project be if the old as well as the new machine had salvage values of zero at the end of 19X4?

g. What would the NPV of the project be if each machine were eligible for CCA deductions on a straight-line basis and had a salvage value of zero at the end of its useful life? What conclusion would you draw from a comparison of the NPV calculated in this part with the NPV calculated in part **f**?

•**15.15**   The management of New Brunswick Lumber Company Ltd. is considering automation of its production and scheduling operations at the beginning of 19X1. It is estimated that the development of the automation program will require a before-tax outlay of $100,000. Under the existing tax laws, this outlay will be considered a capital cost and will be added to the firm's Class 10 UCC balance for CCA purposes. The prescribed maximum CCA rate for Class 10 is 30 percent on the declining balance. The development of the automation program will also require the use of the firm's computer, which is currently not being utilized at its full capacity. Except for its use in the development of the automation program, the firm envisages no alternative way of using its excess computing facilities in the foreseeable future. It is also not possible to rent out the excess capacity. The company has estimated that the implementation of the automation program will reduce its before-tax production costs by $20,000 per year for 10 years (i.e., for years 19X1–19Y0). The corporate tax rate is 40 percent and the company's cost of capital is 10 percent.

Should the company develop the automation program? Assume that the Class 10 UCC balance will always remain positive, that there will always be some assets left in the class, and that the company will claim the maximum CCA permitted in any given year.

•15.16   Due to certain policy considerations, Kapahi Retailers Inc. is currently operating under a self-imposed capital expenditure limit of $1 million. It has identified five potential sites to locate new retail outlets in the Atlantic Provinces. These sites are so far apart from each other that there would be essentially no market overlaps between the outlets being considered. Furthermore, management feels that no operating economies are likely to result from integrating any two or more of the contemplated outlets.

The initial outlays and the net present values associated with the outlets under consideration are as follows:

Investment	Initial outlay	NPV
Outlet 1	$150,000	$112,500
Outlet 2	360,000	3 252,000
Outlet 3	480,000	288,000
Outlet 4	330,000	1 429,000
Outlet 5	270,000	2 297,000

Which outlets should Kapahi select?

• 15.17   As the financial analyst for Apex Tooling Ltd., you are to evaluate whether or not Apex should acquire a new piece of equipment for its machining division. The capital cost of the equipment is $100,000 and it is expected to have a five-year life. At the end of the five years, the equipment will have no resale value. The equipment will be recorded as a single-asset CCA class and CCA deductions for it will be taken on a straight-line basis over the equipment's five-year life.

The equipment is expected to increase cash revenues by $45,000 each year. The inflation-induced growth rate for cash revenues is expected to be 8 percent per year. If the equipment is acquired, Apex will have to hire a new employee to operate it. The new employee will be paid $15,000 per year. Recent wage settlements indicate that this salary will be subject to a 10 percent inflation rate. Apex's current cost of capital is 12 percent and the corporate tax rate is 40 percent. Determine the NPV of the project.

Notes

1. The payback method can also be considered as a "rough" measure of the rate at which uncertainty of cash flows from a risky project is resolved. For an excellent discussion of this point see H. Martin Weingartner, "Some New Views on the Payback Period and Capital Budgeting Decisions," *Management Science* 15 (August 1969), pp. 376–386; and Harold Bierman, Jr., and Warren H. Hauseman, "The Resolution of Investment Uncertainty Through Time," *Management Science* 18 (August 1972), pp. 654–662.

2. For a discussion of the implications of this restrictive tax provision in the context of capital budgeting decisions in public utilities see Milford Tysseland and Devinder K. Gandhi, "Depreciation, Inflation and Capital Formation in Public Utilities: One Possible Approach Toward Solution," *The Quarterly Review of Economics and Business* 19 (Spring 1979), pp. 99–113. For a general discussion of the inflationary effects of depreciation on investments, see J. Van Horne, "A Note on Biases in Capital Budgeting Induced by Inflation," *Journal of Financial and Quantitative Analysis* (January 1971), pp. 653–658.

Suggested Readings

Arditti, D. Fred and Haim Levy, "The Weighted Average Cost of Capital As a Cutoff Rate: A Critical Analysis of the Classical Textbook Weighted Average," *Financial Management* 6, No. 1 (Spring 1977), pp. 24–34.

Bacon, Peter W., "The Evaluation of Mutually Exclusive Investments," *Financial Management* 6 (Summer 1977), pp. 55–58.

Beranek, W., "The Cost of Capital, Capital Budgeting and Maximization of Shareholders' Wealth," *Journal of Financial and Quantitative Analysis* (March 1975), pp. 1–21.

Bernhard, Richard H., "Mathematical Programming Models for Capital Budgeting—A Survey, Generalization and Critique," *Journal of Financial and Quantitative Analysis* 4 (June 1969), pp. 111–158.

Bernardo, John S. and Howard P. Lanser, "A Capital Budgeting Decision Model with Subjective Criteria," *Journal of Financial and Quantitative Analysis* 12 (June 1977), pp. 261–275.

Bierman, Harold, Jr., and Warren H. Hauseman, "The Resolution of Investment Uncertainty Through Time," *Management Science* 18 (August 1972), pp. 654–662.

Bierman, Harold, Jr., "A Reconciliation of Present Value Capital Budgeting," *Financial Management* 6 (Summer 1977), pp. 52–54.

Bierman, Harold, Jr., and Seymour Smidt, *The Capital Budgeting Decision*, 4th ed. (New York: Macmillan 1975), chaps. 2, 3, and 8.

Brigham, Eugene F., "Hurdle Rates for Screening Capital Expenditure Proposals," *Financial Management* 4 (Autumn 1975), pp. 17–26.

Copeland, E. Thomas and Fred J. Weston, *Financial Theory and Corporate Finance* (Don Mills, Ontario: Addison-Wesley 1979), chap. 3, pp. 57–59.

Doenges, R. Conrad, "The Reinvestment Problem in Practical Perspective," *Financial Management* 1 (Spring 1972), pp. 85–91.

Donaldson, Gordon, "Strategic Hurdle Rates for Capital Investment," *Harvard Business Review* 50 (March-April 1972), pp. 50–58.

Elton, Edwin, "Capital Rationing and External Discount Rates," *Journal of Finance* (June 1970).

Fogler, H. Russell, "Overkill in Capital Budgeting Techniques?" *Financial Management* 1 (Spring 1972), pp. 92–96.

———, "Ranking Techniques and Capital Rationing," *Accounting Review* 47 (January 1972), pp. 134–143.

Fremgen, James M., "Capital Budgeting Practices: A Survey," *Management Accounting* (May 1973), pp. 19–25.

Gitman, Lawrence J. and John R. Forrester, Jr., "A Survey of Capital Budgeting Techniques Used by Major U.S. Firms," *Financial Management* 6 (Fall 1977), pp. 66–71.

Hoskins, C. G. and M. J. Dunn, "The Economic Evaluation of Capital Expenditures Proposals Under Uncertainty: Practice of Large Corporations in Canada," *Journal of Business Administration* (Fall 1974), pp. 44–55.

Jean, William H., "On Multiple Rates of Return," *Journal of Finance* 23 (March 1968), pp. 187–192.

———, "Terminal Value or Present Value in Capital Budgeting Problems," *Journal of Financial and Quantitative Analysis* 6 (January 1971), pp. 649–652.

Kessel, R. A. and A. A. Alchian. "The Meaning and Validity of the Inflation-Induced Lag of Wages Behind Prices," *American Economic Review* (March 1960).

Klammer, Thomas, "Empirical Evidence of the Adoption of Sophisticated Capital Budgeting Techniques," *Journal of Business* 45 (July 1972), pp. 387–397.

Levy, Haim and Marshall Sarnat, *Investment and Financial Decisions* (Englewood Cliffs, N.J.: Prentice-Hall, 1978).

Lewellen, Wilbur G., H. P. Lanser, and J. J. McConnell, "Payback Substitutes for Discounted Cash Flow," *Financial Management* 2 (Summer 1973), pp. 17–25.

Mao, James C. T., "The Internal Rate of Return as a Ranking Criterion," *Engineering Economist* 11 (Winter 1966), pp. 1–13.

Merville, L. J. and L. A. Tavis, "A Generalized Model for Capital Investment," *Journal of Finance* 28 (March 1973), pp. 109–118.

Myer, L. Richard, "A Note on Capital Budgeting Techniques and the Reinvestment Rate," *Journal of Finance* 34 (December 1979), pp. 1251–1254.

Nelson, Charles R., "Inflation and Capital Budgeting," *Journal of Finance* 31 (June 1976), pp. 923–931.

Osteryoung, Jerome, *Capital Budgeting: Long-Term Asset Selection,* 2nd ed. (Columbus, Ohio: Grid, 1979).

Robichek, Alexander A., Donald G. Ogilivie, and John D. C. Roach, "Capital Budgeting: A Pragmatic Approach," *Financial Executive* 37 (April 1969), pp. 26–38.

Rychel, Dwight F., "Capital Budgeting with Mixed Integer Linear Programming: An Application," *Financial Management* 6 (Winter 1977), pp. 11–17.

Sarnat, M. and H. Levy, "The Relationship of Rules of Thumb to the Internal Rate of Return: A Restatement and Generalization," *Journal of Finance* 24 (June 1969), pp. 479–489.

Schwab, Bernhard and Peter Lusztig, "A Comparative Analysis of the Net Present Value and the Benefit-Cost Ratios as a Measure of the Economic Desirability of Investments," *Journal of Finance* 24 (June 1969), pp. 507–516.

Tysseland, Milford and Devinder K. Gandhi, "Depreciation, Inflation and Capital Formation in Public Utilities: One Possible Approach Toward Solution," *The Quarterly Review of Economics and Business* 19 (Spring 1979), pp. 99–113.

Van Horne, James C., "A Note on Biases in Capital Budgeting Introduced by Inflation," *Journal of Financial and Quantitative Analysis* 6 (January 1971), pp. 654–658.

Weingartner, H. Martin, *Mathematical Programming and the Analysis of Capital Budgeting Problems,* (Englewood Cliffs, N.J.: Prentice-Hall, 1963).

———, "Some New Views on the Payback Period and Capital Budgeting Decisions," *Management Science* 15 (August 1969), pp. 594–607.

Present Value of Tax Savings Under the Declining Balance Method of CCA Calculations

In the preceding chapter, it was shown that under the declining balance method the incremental CCA deductions (ΔCCA's) from a capital project can occur in perpetuity. We shall now develop a formula that simplifies the calculation of the present value of tax savings derived from the perpetual ΔCCA deductions. As a first step, let us consider the case of a project that involves the acquisition of a depreciable asset that will never be sold.

$$\text{Let } \Delta UCC_o = \text{the incremental undepreciated capital cost balance}$$
$$\text{resulting from the acquisition of the asset at time o}^*$$

$d =$ the maximum CCA rate applicable to the class to which the asset belongs (it is assumed that the firm will take the maximum CCA permitted in any given year)

$t =$ the applicable tax rate

$k =$ the firm's after-tax cost of capital

Table A15.1 shows the calculation of ΔCCA's and the associated tax savings, $t \cdot \Delta CCA$'s, that will be generated from the acquisition of the asset.

Generalizing from the calculations in Table A15.1:

$$\Delta CCA \text{ at the end of year } n = \Delta UCC_o \cdot (1 - d)^{n-1} \cdot d \text{ (from Column 2)}$$

$$\text{Tax saving at the end of year } n = \Delta UCC_o \cdot (1 - d)^{n-1} \cdot d \cdot t \text{ (from Column 3)}$$

Thus, the present value of tax savings

$$= \frac{\Delta UCC_o \cdot d \cdot t}{(1 + k)} + \frac{\Delta UCC_o \cdot (1 - d) \cdot d \cdot t}{(1 + k)^2} + \cdots \frac{\Delta UCC_o \cdot (1 - d)^{n-1} \cdot d \cdot t}{(1 + k)^n} + \cdots$$

$$= \frac{\Delta UCC_o \cdot d \cdot t}{(1 + k)} \left[1 + \frac{1 - d}{1 + k} + \cdots \left(\frac{1 - d}{1 + k} \right)^{n-1} + \cdots \right]$$

---

*This will equal the original capital cost of the asset except when the investment tax credit is claimed for the asset. In this case, the amount of the credit taken must be subtracted from the original capital cost for capital cost allowance purposes. See Chapter 2 for a detailed discussion of this point.

Table A15.1

Year	Incremental UCC: base for calculations of ΔCCA (1)	ΔCCA (to be claimed at year-end) (2)	$t \cdot \Delta CCA$ (tax savings) (3)	Incremental ΔUCC remaining after deduction of ΔCCA at year-end (4) = (1) − (2)
1	ΔUCC_o	$\Delta UCC_o \cdot d$	$\Delta UCC_o \cdot d \cdot t$	$\Delta UCC_o - \Delta UCC_o \cdot d = \Delta UCC_o \cdot (1 - d)$
2	$\Delta UCC_o \cdot (1 - d)$	$\Delta UCC_o \cdot (1 - d) \cdot d$	$\Delta UCC_o \cdot (1 - d) \cdot d \cdot t$	$\Delta UCC_o \cdot (1 - d) - \Delta UCC_o \cdot (1 - d) \cdot d = \Delta UCC_o \cdot (1 - d)^2$
3	$\Delta UCC_o \cdot (1 - d)^2$	$\Delta UCC_o \cdot (1 - d)^2 \cdot d$	$\Delta UCC_o \cdot (1 - d)^2 \cdot d \cdot t$	$\Delta UCC_o \cdot (1 - d)^2 - \Delta UCC_o \cdot (1 - d)^2 \cdot d = \Delta UCC_o \cdot (1 - d)^3$
● ● ● ● ● ● ●	● ● ● ● ●	● ● ● ● ●	● ● ● ● ●	● ● ● ● ●
$n \rightarrow$	$\Delta UCC_o \cdot (1 - d)^{n-1}$	$\Delta UCC_o \cdot (1 - d)^{n-1} \cdot d$	$\Delta UCC_o \cdot (1 - d)^{n-1} \cdot d \cdot t$	$= \Delta UCC_o \cdot (1 - d)^n$
Limiting values ∞	$\rightarrow 0$	$\rightarrow 0$	$\rightarrow 0$	$\rightarrow 0$

The expression in the large brackets is the sum of an infinite but convergent geometric series with a common ratio of $(1 - d)/(1 + k) < 1$. Using the well-known formula for the summation of such a series, the sum of the terms in the large brackets will be found to be equal to

$$\left\{\frac{1}{1 - \dfrac{1 - d}{1 + k}}\right\} \quad \text{or} \quad \frac{1 + k}{k + d}$$

Therefore, the present value of tax savings

$$= \frac{\Delta UCC_o \cdot d \cdot t}{1 + k} \cdot \frac{1 + k}{k + d}$$

$$= \frac{\Delta UCC_o \cdot d \cdot t}{k + d} \tag{A15.1}$$

The above formula can be modified to deal with the case when the asset is expected to be sold for a salvage value of S dollars after n years and the CCA class from which the asset is being sold includes more than one asset. In such a case, the proceeds of sale (salvage value) will reduce the ΔUCC balance of the class *as of the beginning of year $n + 1$.* In that case, this will have the effect of reducing the ΔCCA deductions and the resulting tax savings for year $n + 1$ and thereafter. If the ΔUCC balance after the sale remains positive and there are still some assets left in the class after the sale,* then the discounted value of the reduction in tax savings, as of the beginning of year $n + 1$ (or the end of year n), will equal $(S \cdot d \cdot t)/(k + d)$. (This follows immediately by applying the logic of the formula given by Equation A15.1.) Converting $(S \cdot d \cdot t)/(k + d)$ to its present value, $[(S \cdot d \cdot t)/(k + d)] \cdot [1/(1 + k)^n]$ (i.e., the value at the time when the asset is to be acquired) and subtracting it from the right-hand side of Equation A15.1, we find that the present value of tax savings derived from ΔCCA's resulting from an asset that is expected to be sold for a salvage value of S dollars after n years equals

$$\frac{\Delta UCC_o \cdot d \cdot t}{k + d} - \frac{S \cdot d \cdot t}{k + d} \cdot \frac{1}{(1 + k)^n} \tag{A15.2}$$

In the case of a project involving the replacement of an old asset, the formula given by Equation A15.2 above will have to be modified to

$$\text{Present value of tax savings} = \frac{\Delta UCC_o \cdot d \cdot t}{k + d} - \frac{\Delta S \cdot d \cdot t}{k + d} \cdot \frac{1}{(1 + k)^n} \tag{A15.3}$$

where

$\Delta UCC_o =$ the incremental UCC balance resulting from the replacement of the old asset at time o

$\Delta S =$ the incremental salvage value at the end of n years (i.e., the salvage value of the new asset after n years if the old asset is replaced minus the salvage value of the old asset after n years if it is not replaced)

---

*If the UCC balance becomes negative after the sale, or if there are no assets left in the class after the sale, then the computation of the present value of the tax shield will become more cumbersome. As explained in Chapter 2, the recapture of CCA, capital gains and capital losses, may have to be recognized in such situations.

Chapter 16

CAPITAL BUDGETING UNDER RISK

In Chapter 15, the key concepts and techniques of capital budgeting were discussed. Although the "risk" associated with a project's cash flows was not dealt with explicitly in Chapter 15, it was implicitly assumed that each evaluated project was of average risk; that is, each project was such that its acceptance did not change the risk characteristics of the firm. Stated differently, since the projects evaluated in Chapter 15 were implicitly assumed to be of the same business (i.e., systematic) risk as the firm's existing assets, they were all evaluated using the firm's overall cost of capital.

In practice, few projects evaluated by a firm are of average risk. Thus, it is important to have a basic understanding of the key considerations in and techniques for explicitly incorporating risk into the analysis of the firm's capital budgeting projects. In this chapter, attention is focused on the basic concepts, the measurement of a project's risk, the risk-time relationship, the risk-return relationship, the capital asset pricing model (CAPM), and the project-by-project approaches to risk adjustment.

These topics are presented in five separate sections. The first section discusses the basic concepts of risk and uncertainty, sensitivity analysis of risk, and the use of probabilities. The second section discusses the risk measurement process from both visual and statistical viewpoints. The third section discusses the risk-time relationship, the risk-time function, and the nature of portfolio risk. The fourth and possibly most important section briefly describes the market-determined relationship between risk and return, or the capital asset pricing model (CAPM). From the CAPM, the determination of the security (or asset) market line is discussed. The last section presents a number of project-by-project risk adjustment techniques, including the subjective approach, certainty equivalents, risk-adjusted discount rates, and the capital asset pricing model. Decision trees and Monte Carlo simulation, which are two analytical techniques for generating the information required to make risk adjustments, are also discussed in this

section of the chapter.

Basic Risk Concepts

In order to have some appreciation of the basic problems associated with project risk, it is useful to understand the basic risk-related concepts and to understand why differences in project risk must be considered in capital budgeting. In this section, the terms risk and uncertainty are discussed, and two techniques—sensitivity analysis and the use of probabilities—are presented.

RISK AND UNCERTAINTY

Throughout this text the terms *risk* and *uncertainty* are used interchangeably to refer to the variability of returns (or cash flows) associated with a given project. For instance, a capital budgeting project in which the government contractually guarantees the firm $1000 per year for 10 years has no risk, since there is no variability associated with the cash flows. On the other hand, a capital budgeting project that may generate cash inflows of anywhere from $0 to $2,000 per year is very risky due to the high variability of the cash inflows.

The difference between risk and uncertainty as defined by the statistician is related to the decision maker's knowledge of the probabilities, or chances, of certain outcomes or cash flows occurring. *Risk* exists when the decision maker is able to estimate the probabilities associated with various outcomes (i.e., an objective probability distribution), normally from historical data. For instance, if a person wishes to determine the probabilities associated with various occupancy rates in an apartment complex, he or she can develop a distribution of probabilities based on historical data gathered on similar projects. *Uncertainty* exists when the decision maker has no historical data from which to develop a probability distribution and must make educated guesses in order to develop a *subjective probability distribution*. For example, if the proposed project is completely new to the firm, the decision maker, through research and consultation with others, may be able to assign probabilities subjectively to various outcomes.*

SENSITIVITY ANALYSIS OF RISK

One of the simplest ways of considering the risk (or uncertainty) of a project is to use sensitivity analysis. *Sensitivity analysis* involves using a number of possible outcomes in evaluating a project. The basic procedure is to evaluate a project using a number of possible cash inflow estimates to get a "feel" for the variability of the associated outcomes. One of the most common sensitivity approaches is to estimate the worst (i.e., most pessimistic), the most likely, and the best (i.e., most optimistic) outcomes associated with a project. In this case the risk of a project is reflected by the *range*, found by subtracting the pessimistic outcome from the optimistic outcome. The larger the range for the given project, the more variability or risk it is said to have.

---

*Since most decision makers believe that it is valid to use subjective probability distributions, the methodology of financial decision making is drawn essentially from statistical decision theory.

EXAMPLE   Goodwear Tire Ltd. is attempting to evaluate two mutually exclusive projects, A and B, each requiring an initial investment of $10,000 and both having *most likely* annual cash inflows of $2,000 per year for the next 15 years. The firm's cost of capital is 10 percent. In order to obtain some insight into the riskiness of these projects, management has also made pessimistic and optimistic estimates of the annual cash inflows associated with each project. The three cash inflow values for each project along with their ranges are given in Table 16.1. Comparing the ranges of project cash inflows, it can be seen that project A appears to be less risky than project B, since its range of $1,000 is less than the range of $4,000 for project B.

Table 16.1   Goodwear Tire's Projects A and B

	Project A	Project B
Initial investment	$10,000	$10,000
Cash inflow estimates		
Pessimistic	$ 1,500	$ 0
Most likely	$ 2,000	$ 2,000
Optimistic	$ 2,500	$ 4,000
Range	$ 1,000	$ 4,000

Using the techniques presented in Chapter 15 for evaluating average-risk investments, the net present value of each project at the 10-percent cost of capital can be calculated for each of the possible cash inflows. The results are presented in Table 16.2, which is a *payoff matrix* indicating, for each possible outcome (or *state of nature*), the associated payoff.

Table 16.2 illustrates that sensitivity analysis can produce some useful information about projects that appear equally desirable on the basis of the most likely estimates of their cash inflows. Comparing the range of net present value for project A ($7,606) with that of project B ($30,424), it should be clear that project A is less risky (i.e., has a smaller range) than project B. The actual choice will depend upon the decision maker's attitude toward risk. A decision maker who is averse to risk of loss will take project A. On the other hand, a more risk-taking decision maker may take project B in order to have the possibility of receiving a return with a high net present value. The same type of sensitivity analysis could have, of course, been applied more directly to the cash inflows themselves, as was illustrated in Table 16.1

Table 16.2   A Payoff Matrix of NPV's for Projects A and B

Outcomes (states of nature)	Net present value	
	Project A	Project B
Possible cash inflows (outcomes)		
Pessimistic	$1,409	− $10,000
Most likely	$5,212	$ 5,212
Optimistic	$9,015	$20,424
Range	$7,606	$30,424

ASSIGNING PROBABILITIES TO OUTCOMES

Probabilities are used to assess more accurately the risk involved in a project. The *probability* of an event occurring may be thought of as the *percentage chance* of a given outcome. In other words, if it has been determined that an outcome has an 80-percent probability of occurrence, it is expected that the given outcome will occur eight out of ten times. If an outcome has a probability of 100 percent, it is certain to occur; outcomes having a probability of zero will never occur. By assigning probabilities to a project's outcomes, the *expected value* of the outcomes can be calculated. *

The expected value of a project is a weighted average outcome, in which the weights used are the probabilities of the various outcomes. Although the expected value may never be realized, it gives the average outcome from repeating a project a large number of times or from undertaking a large number of similar projects. The most difficult aspect of determining expected values is the estimation of the probabilities associated with the various outcomes. Regardless of whether these probabilities are estimated *objectively* or *subjectively,* the expected value is calculated in the same manner. The expected value calculation can be illustrated using the cash inflows† for projects A and B, which were presented in Table 16.1.

EXAMPLE   An evaluation of past pessimistic, most likely, and optimistic estimates of the state of the economy by Goodwear Tire Ltd. indicates that 25 percent of the time the pessimistic outcome occurred; 50 percent of the time the most likely outcome occurred; and 25 percent of the time the optimistic outcome occurred. Thus, the probabilities of the pessimistic, most likely, and optimistic outcomes occurring this time are 25 percent, 50 percent, and 25 percent, respectively. The sum of these probabilities must equal 100 percent; that is, they must be based upon all the alternatives considered. Table 16.3 presents the calculations required to find the expected values of the cash inflows and NPV's for projects A and B.

A number of important points should be recognized in Table 16.3. First, the probabilities for all of the possible outcomes of each project sum to 1. Second, since the states of nature labeled "possible outcomes" are the same for projects A and B, the associated probabilites are the same for each project. Third, the expected cash inflow values are equivalent to the most likely estimate

---

*Decisions based on choosing the highest expected value are appropriate in a few business situations. For example, it is appropriate in insurance decision making when the following three conditions are satisfied: (1) the situation is replicable and repetitive in nature; (2) successive realizations are independent of preceding realizations; and (3) the difference between any two possible outcomes is not large. †Much of this chapter will be devoted to risk as reflected in a project's cash inflows rather than its associated net present value. This approach is often preferred since the risk of most projects is introduced through their cash inflows rather than through their initial investments, which are often known with certainty. The only difference between using cash inflows rather than net present value is that the initial investment has not been subtracted from the present value of the cash inflows in order to determine the net present value. Since the projects used throughout the next few pages require the same initial investment of $10,000 and are discounted at the same rate (10 percent), conclusions relating to project risk can be drawn more directly using the cash inflow data. Had the probabilities been attached to the NPV's from Table 16.2, the same answers for expected NPV as those found using cash inflows in Table 16.3 would have resulted.

Table 16.3   Expected Values of Cash Inflows and NPV'S for Projects A and B

Possible outcomes	Probability (1)	Cash inflows (2)	Weighted value (1) · (2) (3)
Project A			
Pessimistic	0.25	$1,500	$ 375
Most likely	0.50	2,000	1,000
Optimistic	0.25	2,500	625
	1.00	Expected cash inflows	$2,000

Expected NPV = 7.606[a] ($2,000) − $10,000 = $5,212

Project B			
Pessimistic	0.25	$ 0	$ 0
Most likely	0.50	2,000	1,000
Optimistic	0.25	4,000	1,000
	1.00	Expected cash inflows	$2,000

Expected NPV = 7.606[a] ($2,000) − $10,000 = $5,212

[a]The present-value interest factor for an annuity (PVIFA) with a 15-year life discounted at 10 percent is 7.606.

for each project because each project has a symmetrical distribution of outcomes. Finally, the most likely estimates for each project are equivalent. *

Measuring Project Risk

By measuring the risk of capital budgeting projects, one will be better able to differentiate between those projects with identical expected returns. One's ability to compare projects with different returns is also greatly enhanced, since one can get some feel for the type of risk-return trade-offs offered by the projects. In order to measure project risk, a decision maker must be able to differentiate between the variability of project returns. In this section, two related methods of measuring project risk are discussed. The first method is a visual one that requires the development of probability distributions. The second method uses statistical measures to get a more concrete index of project variability, or risk.

PROBABILITY DISTRIBUTIONS

Comparing the probability distributions associated with different projects allows the decision maker to get some "feel" for any differences in the risk of the projects. A

*Since this example has been designed to highlight certain aspects of risk, the expected and the most likely cash inflow values for the two projects have been made equal. The reader should note that this is generally not the case when two projects are being compared.

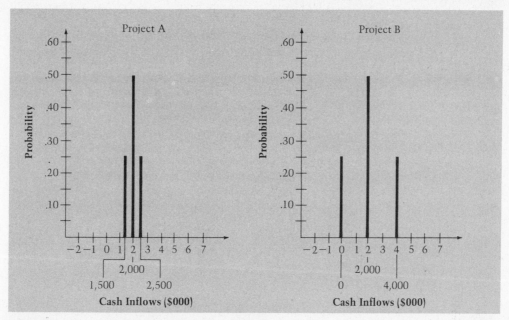

Figure 16.1   Bar charts for project A and B's cash inflows.

probability distribution can be graphed by plotting possible outcomes and associated probabilities on a set of outcome-probability axes.

The simplest type of probability distribution is the *bar chart,* or *discrete probability distribution,* which shows only a limited number of outcome-probability coordinates. The bar charts for projects A and B are shown in Figure 16.1. A comparison of the two charts shows that although both projects have the same expected value of cash inflows, the range of cash inflows is much more dispersed for project B than for project A—$4,000 versus $1,000.

A more descriptive probability distribution for a project can be developed by obtaining the probabilities associated with every possible outcome. By obtaining all of the possible cash inflow outcomes and their associated probabilities, a *continuous probability distribution* can be developed. This type of distribution can be thought of as a bar chart for a very large number of outcomes.* Figure 16.2 presents the continuous probability distributions for projects A and B.

In the bar charts in Figure 16.1, projects A and B had the same probability (i.e., 50 percent) of cash inflows of $2,000. In the continuous distribution, these probabilities change due to the large number of additional outcomes considered. The area under each of the curves up to and including a certain value is equal to the cumulative probability of achieving at least that value. Thus, the total area under each of the curves sum to 1, which means that 100 percent of the outcomes, or all the possible outcomes, have been

*In order to develop a continuous objective probability distribution, one must have data on a large number of historical occurrences of the event. Then, by developing a frequency distribution indicating how many times each outcome has occurred over the given time horizon, one can convert this data into a probability distribution.

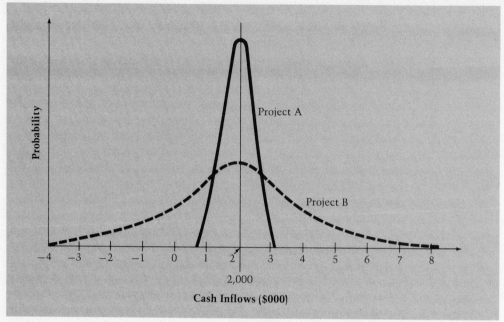

Figure 16.2 Continuous probability distributions for project A and B's cash inflows.

considered. Often probability distributions such as those in Figure 16.2 are converted into *cumulative probability distributions,* which allow the decision maker to determine easily the probability of obtaining at least some value.* It is important to note in Figure 16.2 that, although projects A and B have the same expected cash inflow value ($2,000), the distribution of cash inflows for project A is much tighter, or closer to the expected value, than that for project B. The distribution of cash inflows for project A has less *dispersion* than the distribution of cash inflows for project B.

USING STATISTICS FOR MEASURING RISK

Instead of visually observing the variability of project returns, we can use certain statistical (i.e., summary) measures of risk.† The most common statistical measure of project

---

*A probability distribution can be converted into a cumulative probability distribution by determining the probability associated with obtaining at least each given value and plotting the cumulative probability of all occurrences less than or equal to the given value against the associated outcome.
†Risk is typically viewed as the variability, or dispersion, of values around an expected value. This is consistent with the definition of risk up to the Middle Ages, which was "chance" or "luck" (both good and bad). Since many authors now define risk as the chance of "hazard" or "ruin" or "danger of loss," they believe that risk is only present when outcomes are below a target (e.g., the expected) value, since only outcomes below the target value are deemed to be undesirable. Accordingly, these authors suggest that a risk measure such as semivariance should be used. See, for example, James C. T. Mao and John F. Brewster, "An $E-S_h$ Model of Capital Budgeting," *Engineering Economist* 15 (January-February 1970), pp. 103–121. Although this latter approach may result in a better measure of risk, the common approach is to view risk as determined by the variability on either side of the expected value, since the greater this variability, the less confident one can be of the outcomes associated with a project.

risk is the *standard deviation* from the mean or expected value of the distribution of returns.

The Standard Deviation   The standard deviation of a distribution of project returns represents the square root of the average squared deviations of the individual observations from the expected value. The first step in calculating the standard deviation of a distribution is to find the expected value, $\overline{E}$, which is given by

$$\overline{E} = \sum_{i=1}^{n} E_i \cdot P_i \tag{16.1}$$

where

E_i = the outcome for the ith case

P_i = the probability of occurrence of ith outcome

n = the number of outcomes considered

The calculation of the expected value of cash inflows, $\overline{E}$, for projects A and B were presented in Table 16.3. The expected value for each project's cash inflows was found to be $2,000.

The expression for the standard deviation* of the probability distribution, σ, is given by

$$\sigma = \sqrt{\sum_{i=1}^{n} (E_i - \overline{E})^2 \cdot P_i} \tag{16.2}$$

The standard deviation represents the square root of the sum of the squared product of each deviation from the expected value, $\overline{E}$, multiplied by the associated probability of occurrence. Table 16.4 presents the calculation of the standard deviations for the cash inflows for projects A and B, based on the data presented earlier. Statistically, if the probability distribution is *normal*, 68 percent of the outcomes will lie between ± 1 standard deviation from the expected value, 95 percent of all observations will lie between ± 2 standard deviations from the expected value, and 99 percent of all observations will lie between ± 3 standard deviations from the expected value.†

Our primary concern with standard deviations or variances lies in their use as indexes to measure the risks of various projects. In fact, a very popular decision criterion has

---

*The formula commonly used to find the standard deviation, σ, in a situation where all of the outcomes are known, but their related probabilities have not been determined, is

$$\sigma = \sqrt{\sum_{i=1}^{n} \frac{(E_i - \overline{E})^2}{n}}$$

where n is the number of observations. Since outcomes and related probabilities are often available when analyzing capital budgeting proposals, the formula given in Equation 16.2 is emphasized in this chapter.

†A probability distribution that is *normal* is symmetrical around the expected value. This type of distribution is best viewed graphically, in which case it resembles a bell-shaped curve. Tables of values indicating the probabilities associated with various deviations from the expected value of a normal distribution can be found in any basic statistics text.

Table 16.4   The Calculation of the Standard Deviation of the Cash Inflows for Projects A and B

Project A

i	E_i	$\overline{E}$	$E_i - \overline{E}$	$(E_i - \overline{E})^2$	P_i	$(E_i - \overline{E})^2 \cdot P_i$
1	$1,500	$2,000	−$500	$250,000	.25	$62,500
2	2,000	2,000	0	0	.50	0
3	2,500	2,000	500	250,000	.25	62,500

$$\sum_{i=1}^{3} (E_i - \overline{E})^2 \cdot P_i = \$125,000$$

$$\sigma_A = \sqrt{\sum_{i=1}^{3} (E_i - \overline{E})^2 \cdot P_i} = \sqrt{\$125,000} = \underline{\$353.55}$$

Project B

i	E_i	$\overline{E}$	$E_i - \overline{E}$	$(E_i - \overline{E})^2$	P_i	$(E_i - \overline{E})^2 \cdot P_i$
1	$ 0	$2,000	−$2,000	$4,000,000	.25	$1,000,000
2	2,000	2,000	0	0	.50	0
3	4,000	2,000	2,000	4,000,000	.25	1,000,000

$$\sum_{i=1}^{3} (E_i - \overline{E})^2 \cdot P_i = \$2,000,000$$

$$\sigma_B = \sqrt{\sum_{i=1}^{3} (E_i - \overline{E})^2 \cdot P_i} = \sqrt{\$2,000,000} = \underline{\$1,414.21}$$

been developed by Markowitz for comparing investment alternatives based on their expected returns and variances (or standard deviations) of return. Markowitz's *expected return-variance* (also referred to as the *mean-variance* or *E–V*) *rule* is to choose project A over project B if (1) the expected return of A is at least equal to that of B, when the variance of A is less than the variance of B; or (2) the expected return of A exceeds that of B when the variance of A is not greater than that of B.* Thus, by using Markowitz's expected return-variance criterion, we can confirm that project A is preferred to project B. Both have the same expected values (i.e., $2,000), while project A is less risky than project B. Project A has a smaller standard deviation (i.e., $353.55 vs. $1,414.21), and hence variance, than project B.

If projects A and B had been such that project A had both a smaller expected value and variance than project B, or vice versa, then the *E–V* criterion could not be used directly to choose between the two projects. In that case, one could use either *mathematical programming techniques* (which are briefly discussed later in this chapter) or in some cases the *coefficient of variation* to choose between the two projects.†

---

*The *E–V* criterion derives its validity from the fact that in many cases it can be used in place of the theoretically preferred, but nonoperational, expected utility criterion. For further details on the utility foundation of the *E–V* criterion, the reader should refer to Harry Markowitz, *Portfolio Selection* (New York: Wiley, 1959).

†It should be noted that the coefficient of variation is a theoretically correct measure of risk only if the distribution of returns is lognormal and investors are risk-averse. See Haim Levy, "Stochastic Dominance Among Log Normal Prospects," *International Economic Review* (October 1973).

The Coefficient of Variation The coefficient of variation, V, is calculated simply by dividing the standard deviation, σ, for a project by the expected value, $\overline{E}$, for the project as follows:

$$V = \frac{\sigma}{\overline{E}} \tag{16.3}$$

The coefficients of variation for projects A and B are 0.177 ($353.55 ÷ $2,000) and 0.707 ($1,414.21 ÷ $2,000.00). The higher the coefficient of variation, the more risky the project. Project B is therefore more risky than project A. Since both these projects have the same expected value, the coefficient of variation has not provided any more information than was provided by the standard deviation.

The coefficient of variation is often useful in comparing projects having different expected values, because it provides a relative and not an absolute measure of risk. A simple example will illustrate this point.

EXAMPLE A firm is attempting to select the least risky of two mutually exclusive projects—X and Y. The expected value, standard deviation, and coefficient of variation for each of these project's cash inflows are as follows:

Statistics with respect to cash inflows	Project X	Project Y
(1) Expected value	$12,000	$20,000
(2) Standard deviation	$ 9,000[a]	$10,000
(3) Coefficient of variation (2) ÷ (1)	0.75	0.50[a]

[a]Preferred project using the given risk measure.

If the firm were to compare the projects solely on the basis of their standard deviations, it would prefer project X to project Y, since project X has a lower standared deviation than Y ($9,000 vs. $10,000). Comparing the coefficients of variation of the projects shows that management may be making an error in accepting project X in preference to project Y, since the relative dispersion or risk of the projects as reflected in the coefficient of variation is lower for project Y than for project X (0.50 vs. 0.75). This example should make it clear that the coefficient of variation provides a relative measure of risk, while the standard deviation provides an absolute measure of risk.*

Risk and Time

Time is an important consideration in evaluating the risk in a capital budgeting project. When capital budgeting projects were originally discussed in Chapter 14, the key factor that differentiated capital expenditures from operating expenditures was the amount of time over which the benefits from the expenditure were expected to be received. Capital expenditures have benefits received over a period greater than one year; operating ex-

---

*Note that when the risks of two projects having the same expected value are being compared, the risk rankings based on the standard deviation and coefficient of variation will agree.

penditures have benefits received over a period of up to one year. In order to evaluate these capital expenditures, consideration must be given to the fact that future industry and economic factors may greatly affect the project outcomes. In this section, the time-related aspects of risk will be discussed. The first part will discuss the general risk-time relationship; the second part will discuss portfolio risk, which is indirectly tied to the time-related risk associated with projects.

RISK AS A FUNCTION OF TIME

Risk must be viewed not only with respect to the current time period, but *as a function of time.* Although the cash inflows associated with a given project may be expected to resemble an annuity, and therefore to have similar expected values, it is not unusual to find that they have differing degrees of risk over time. Even in the cases where the expected values are not believed to be equal in each year, the probability distributions of cash inflows will probably become more dispersed with the passage of time due to the difficulty of accurately forecasting future outcomes.* Generally, the *farther into the future one forecasts cash flows, the more variable* and therefore the more risky one considers the forecasted values to be.

Figure 16.3 depicts increasing dispersion in returns with the passage of time, assuming that the expected value of each year's cash inflows are equal. A band representing ± 1 standard deviation, σ, from the expected value, $\overline{E}$, is indicated in the figure.

PORTFOLIO RISK

Thus far attention has been devoted only to the evaluation of the time-related risk for a single project. However, since the firm has a *portfolio* of projects (i.e., assets), it may not be appropriate to view the risk of a proposed project as being independent of that of existing projects, especially if the firm's goal is to maximize its owners' or shareholders' wealth.

There are two opposing viewpoints on whether portfolio risk effects should be considered when evaluating a capital expenditure. The *risk-interdependence* viewpoint maintains that portfolio risk effects should be considered; while the *risk-independence* viewpoint maintains that portfolio risk effects can be ignored. Each of these viewpoints will be discussed below.

Corporate Portfolio Effects Are Important   According to this viewpoint, new capital budgeting proposals must be considered in light of both existing projects and other proposed projects, and the projects selected must be those that best *diversify,* or reduce, the firm's risk (i.e., standard deviation) for a given level of expected return. Thus, *efficient diversification will make the risk of a group, or portfolio, of projects less than the sum of the risk of the individual projects.*

In order to diversify risk in order to create an *efficient portfolio*—one that allows the firm to achieve the maximum expected return for a given level of risk or to minimize

---

*Forecast errors are only normal since, in most situations, there are many uncontrollable factors such as labour strikes, inflation, and wars that are difficult if not impossible to predict but that can have a very real effect on the firm's future cash inflows.

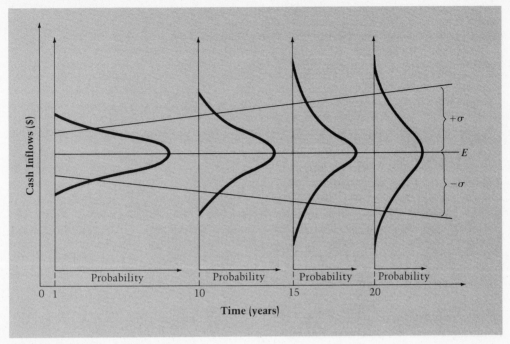

Figure 16.3 Risk as a function of time.

risk for a given level of expected return—the concept of correlation must be understood. *Correlation* is a statistical measure that indicates the relationship between series of numbers (such as the cash inflows or returns of various projects).

If two series move together, they are *positively correlated;* if the series are counter-cyclical, or move in opposite directions, they are *negatively correlated.* The statistical measure of correlation, the *correlation coefficient* or *rho* (i.e., ρ), has a range of $+1$ for perfectly positively correlated series and -1 for perfectly negatively correlated series. These two extremes are depicted for series M and N in Figure 16.4. The perfectly positively correlated series move exactly together, while the perfectly negatively correlated series move in exactly opposite directions. The existence of perfectly negatively correlated projects is, however, quite rare.

To diversify project risk and thereby reduce the firm's overall risk, the best projects to combine or add to the existing portfolio of projects are those that have a negative (or low-positive) correlation with existing projects. By combining negatively correlated projects, the overall variability of returns or risk, σ, can be reduced. The result of diversifying to reduce risk (i.e., the standard deviation of returns) by combining two negatively correlated projects, F and G, which both have the same expected return, $\overline{E}$, is illustrated in Figure 16.5. This figure shows that a portfolio containing projects F and G will have the same expected return, $\overline{E}$, but a lower standard deviation of return, σ, than either of the two projects taken separately.

The reader should recognize that even if projects are not negatively correlated, diversification occurs as long as the projects combined are *not* perfectly correlated. Thus, holding the amount invested in each project in the portfolio constant, the lower the

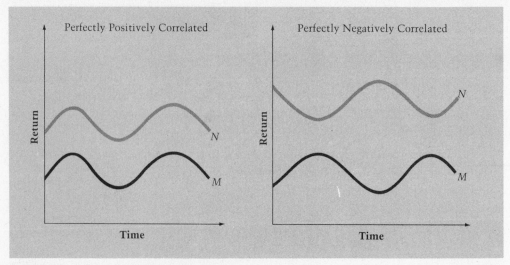

Figure 16.4 The correlation between series M and N.

positive correlation between the projects to be combined into a portfolio, the lower the resulting combined standard deviation.*

As shown in Figure 16.6, the creation of a portfolio by combining two perfectly positively correlated projects can not reduce the portfolio's overall risk below the risk of the least risky project. On the other hand, the creation of a portfolio by combining two

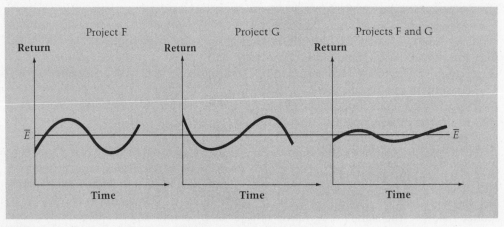

Figure 16.5 Combining negatively correlated projects to diversify risk.

*Some projects are uncorrelated; that is, they are completely unrelated in the sense that there is no statistical relationship between their returns. Combining uncorrelated projects can reduce risk—not as effectively as combining negatively correlated projects, but more effectively than combining positively correlated projects. Since the correlation coefficient for uncorrelated projects is zero, it is the midpoint between perfect positive and perfect negative correlation.

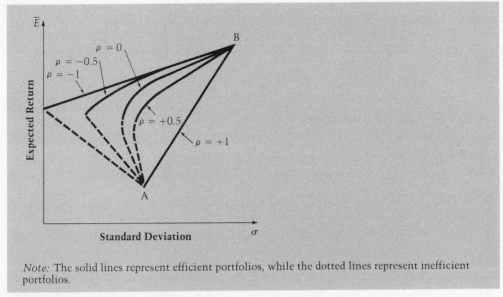

Figure 16.6   Relationship between the expected return and risk of a portfolio.

projects that are perfectly negatively correlated can reduce the portfolio's total risk to a level below that of either of the component projects. Combining projects with correlations less than perfect positive correlation (i.e., a ρ of $+1$) can therefore reduce the overall risk of a portfolio.* Examples of perfect positive and negative correlation might be a meat packer acquiring another meat packer and a meat packer acquiring a vegetarian chain of restaurants, respectively.

Thus, according to the risk-interdependence viewpoint, the value of a capital budgeting project depends on the covariances of its return with the returns of other projects that have been or may be undertaken by the firm. The procedure for implementing this approach is no different than that required when creating a portfolio of securities. Its basic features are illustrated in the following example.

---

*Mathematically, the mean-variance effects of diversification can be derived as follows. First, assume that a firm will form a portfolio of two completely divisible projects, A and B, where x_A is the proportion of the firm's wealth invested in project A and $(1 - x_A)$ is the proportion of the firm's wealth invested in project B. Also assume that the expected returns and standard deviations of return for projects A and B are ($\overline{E}_A$ and σ_A) and ($\overline{E}_B$ and σ_B), respectively. Then the expected return on the firm's portfolio of projects, $\overline{E}$, is given by

$$\overline{E} = x_A\overline{E}_A + (1 - x_A)\,\overline{E}_B$$

and the portfolio's variance of return, σ^2, is given by

$$\sigma^2 = x_A^2\sigma_A^2 + (1 - x_A)^2\sigma_B^2 + 2x_A(1 - x_A)\,\rho_{AB}\,\sigma_A\,\sigma_B$$

It should also be noted that $\rho_{AB}\,\sigma_A\,\sigma_B$ is equal to the covariance between E_A and E_B [as denoted by Cov $(E_A,\,E_B)$] since ρ_{AB} is by definition equal to Cov $(E_A,\,E_B)/\sigma_A\,\sigma_B$.

EXAMPLE   Table 16.5 presents the expected cash inflows from three different projects—X, Y, and Z—over the next five years along with their expected values and standard deviations. It can be seen that each of the projects has an expected value of 30 and a standard deviation of 14.14. The projects therefore have equal risk and equal return although their cash-inflow patterns are not necessarily identical. A comparison of the cash-inflows patterns of projects X and Y should disclose that they are perfectly negatively correlated since they move in exactly opposite directions over time. Comparing projects X and Z, it should be clear that they are perfectly positively correlated since they move in precisely the same direction (note that in this example the cash inflows for X and Z are identical).*

Table 16.5   Cash Inflows, Expected Values, and Standard Deviations for Projects X, Y, and Z and Portfolios XY and XZ

| | Projects | | | Portfolios | |
| | | | | XY[a] (50%X plus 50%Y) | XZ[b] (50%X plus 50%Z) |
Year	X	Y	Z		
19X1	10	50	10	30	10
19X2	20	40	20	30	20
19X3	30	30	30	30	30
19X4	40	20	40	30	40
19X5	50	10	50	30	50
Statistics:					
Expected value	30	30	30	30	30
Standard deviation[c]	14.14	14.14	14.14	0	14.14

[a]Portfolio XY, which consists of 50 percent of project X and 50 percent of project Y, illustrates *perfect negative correlation*, since these two cash-inflow streams behave in completely opposite fashions over the five-year period.
[b]Portfolio XZ, which consists of 50 percent of project X and 50 percent of project Z, illustrates *perfect positive correlation*, since these two cash-inflow streams behave identically over the five-year period.
[c]Since the probabilities associated with the returns are not given, the formula given earlier in Equation 16.2 could not be used to calculate the standard deviations, σ. Instead the more general formula,

$$\sigma = \sqrt{\frac{\sum_{i=1}^{n} (E_i - \overline{E})^2}{n}}$$

where E_i = return i, $\overline{E}$ = expected value of the returns, and n = the number of observations, was used.

Portfolio XY   By combining equal portions of projects X and Y—the perfectly negatively correlated projects—portfolio XY (shown in Table 16.5) is created.† The risk in the portfolio

*It is *not* necessary for cash-inflow streams to be identical in order for them to be perfectly positively correlated. Identical cash-inflow streams are used in this example in order to permit the concepts to be illustrated in the simplest, most straightforward fashion available. Any cash-inflow streams that move (i.e., vary) exactly together—regardless of the relative magnitude of the cash inflows—are perfectly positively correlated.
†The projects may not in actuality be divisible. However, for illustrative purposes, it has been assumed that each of the projects—X, Y, and Z—are divisible and can be combined with other projects to create portfolios. This assumption is made only to permit the concepts, again, to be illustrated in the simplest, most straightforward fashion.

created by this combination (as reflected in the standard deviation) is reduced to zero, while the expected cash inflow remains at 30. Since both of the projects had the same expected cash-inflow values, are combined in equal parts, and are perfectly negatively correlated, the combination results in the complete elimination of risk. Whenever projects are perfectly negatively correlated, an optimum combination (similar to the 50–50 mix in the case of projects X and Y) exists for which the resulting standard deviation will equal zero.

Portfolio XZ   By combining equal portions of projects X and Z—the perfectly positively corre- lated projects—portfolio XZ (shown in Table 16.5) is created. The standard deviation, or risk, of this portfolio, which remains at 14.14, is unaffected by the combination. Also, the expected cash inflow remains at 30. Whenever perfectly positively correlated projects such as X and Z are combined, the standard deviation of the resulting portfolio cannot be reduced below that of the least risky project. In fact, the maximum portfolio standard deviation will be that of the more risky project, and the minimum portfolio standard deviation will be that of the less risky project.

The portfolio approach to capital budgeting is implemented by using *mathematical programming techniques* (such as quadratic programming). Although an in-depth dis- cussion of the actual mechanics of the technique is beyond the scope of this text, it is important to note that the procedure is extremely difficult to operationalize. Some of the difficulties encountered include (1) the nondivisibility of capital budgeting projects; (2) difficulties in collecting necessary data (i.e., the expected returns, variances, and covariances for *all* existing and proposed projects); and (3) the computational difficulties in solving realistic problems.

Corporate Portfolio Effects Are Unimportant   According to this viewpoint, diver- sification per se is not an appropriate corporate objective for firms that attempt to maximize the wealth of their owners or shareholders. This applies to diversification benefits whether they are achieved by internal expansion (i.e., capital expenditures) or by external expansion (i.e., business combinations).

This *risk-independence* or *value-additivity principle* can be explained as follows. Suppose a firm is evaluating project B; that V_B is project B's market value when it is traded separately in the capital market; that the firm's market value without project B is V_A; and that the firm's market value after the adoption of project B is V_{A+B}. Then the risk-independence or value-additivity principle states that: $V_{A+B} = V_A + V_B$. That is, the market value of the firm with the project is no more (or no less) than the market value of the firm without the project plus the market value of the project traded sepa- rately in the capital market.

As shown analytically by Myers, risk-independence is a general property of capital market equilibrium under uncertainty, when capital markets are both perfect and com- plete.[1] That is, since investors can create their own diversification at the same cost as the firm, they will not pay a premium for corporate diversification.*

---

*Risk independence is consistent with the notion that the market value of a project depends upon the covariance of its returns with the returns of other projects. However, in equilibrium, market prices will be determined by the investment opportunities that are available to investors, and not by those available to firms.

For firms that attempt to maximize the market price of their shares, risk-independence implies that the risk characteristics of each capital budgeting project can be evaluated independently of the other projects that have been or may be undertaken by the firm. Thus, if the principle holds and there are no physical interdependencies among projects (i.e., the evaluated projects are not "competitive" or "complementary" projects), then the firm's capital budgeting procedure can be greatly simplified. In other words, the firm can evaluate projects on a project-by-project basis, instead of calculating the firm's market value for every possible combination of projects it can hold. Note that this is a very important result, because *the NPV rule is valid under uncertainty only if the risk-independence or value-additivity principle holds.* Thus, the validity of the procedures used to adjust for project risk on a project-by-project basis, which are discussed in a later section of this chapter, depend upon the validity of the risk-independence principle.*

Practice[2]   The risk-independence principle may be violated in a number of practical situations. First, it may be violated when the value of the project being evaluated is large in comparison to the value of the firm's existing assets. Second, it may be violated when the scale and/or risk characteristics of the project's incremental cash flows are unanticipated by the market. And finally, it may be violated if the firm's shareholders do not hold diversified portfolios and/or the shareholders cannot dispose of their share holdings. Since the satisfaction of these conditions is more likely for proprietorships or small, closely held corporations than for large, widely held public corporations, corporate portfolio effects are probably important for proprietorships and small, closely held corporations and are probably unimportant for widely held public corporations.

Risk and Return: Capital Asset Pricing Model (CAPM)

Over the past 15 or so years,[3] a great deal of theory has been developed with respect to risk-return trade-offs. In Chapter 7, this type of trade-off was discussed as it related to the management of the firm's working capital. It was shown that a firm's profitability would be expected to increase as the firm decreased its liquidity, which would increase the risk of technical insolvency, and vice versa. The broader and more important aspect of risk is the overall pricing of a firm's risk by investors in the marketplace. An understanding of this risk is important since it significantly impacts on the firm's investment and financing policies. A basic theory with respect to risk and return is commonly referred to as the *capital asset pricing model (CAPM)*. It was developed primarily to explain the behaviour of financial asset prices (primarily securities) under conditions of equilibrium in capital markets. It was also used to provide a mechanism whereby investors could readily assess the impact of a proposed security investment on their overall portfolio risk and return. Although the theory cannot be easily applied to the internal capital budgeting project-selection process, it does provide useful insights into the na-

---

*This is not always the case for the IRR rule, even under certainty.

ture of the risk-return trade-offs that must be considered as part of the capital budgeting process. This section of the chapter describes the basic CAPM in order to provide an intuitive understanding of the risk-return trade-offs involved, not only in capital budgeting decisions, but also in all types of financial decisions. The use of the CAPM in capital budgeting will be discussed in a later section of this chapter.

ASSUMPTIONS OF THE MODEL

The basic capital asset pricing model not only assumes that the market is perfect, but it also makes several assumptions about the way investors behave. Although these assumptions appear to be unrealistic, empirical studies have tended to support the reasonableness of the relationships described by CAPM.[4] The basic assumptions are discussed next.

Perfect Markets   The marketplace in which investors make transactions in securities (or assets) is assumed to be perfect and thus efficient. This means that at any point in time all investors have the same costless information regarding securities and that this information is accurate. There are no restrictions on investment, no taxes, and no transactions cost. None of the investors are assumed to be large enough to have a significant impact on the prevailing market prices of assets. The supply of assets is fixed, and all assets are assumed to be perfectly divisible and to have complete liquidity. Furthermore, it is generally assumed that all investors can borrow or lend an unlimited amount of funds at the risk-free rate of interest, R_F.

Investor Characteristics and Preferences   Investors are all assumed to view securities in light of a common ownership (or holding) period that is typically one year. Investors are assumed to choose among alternative portfolios of assets solely on the basis of expected return and risk of return of those portfolios.

Investors are also assumed to prefer to earn higher (vs. lower) returns, while, at the same time, they are averse to risk, preferring lower (vs. higher) risk. In general, they will prefer to invest in securities offering the highest return for a given level of risk or the lowest risk for a given level of return. They are assumed to measure return using the expected value and measure risk using the standard deviation. At any point in time, all investors are assumed to have the same (homogeneous) expectations about the future returns and risks of all assets.

THE CAPITAL MARKET LINE (CML)

It is important to understand the market-determined relationship between return and risk. Since every investor is assumed to have the same expectations and to be able to borrow or lend at the same rate of interest, every investor must face the same investment situation. Thus, all investors will agree on what constitutes the optimal or best combination of risky assets. Since all outstanding assets must be held by investors, and all investors agree on the *same* best portfolio of risky assets, then in equilibrium the optimal combination of risky securities must include all outstanding assets. That is, the optimal combination of risky assets must be the market portfolio.

Without the previous assumptions, the market may not necessarily be efficient and the equilibrium model derived in the next section may not necessarily be valid. Thus, as noted by Roll,[5] the efficiency of the market portfolio and the capital asset pricing model are inseparable, joint hypotheses. One cannot test one hypothesis without testing the other hypothesis.

The Equation   Since the risk-free asset and the market portfolio are not correlated, the capital market line (CML) must be a linear combination of the risk-free asset and the market portfolio of risky assets. The equation of the CML is given by

$$\overline{K}_p = R_F + \left[\frac{\overline{K}_m - R_F}{\sigma_m} \right] \sigma_p \tag{16.4}$$

where

$\overline{K}_p$ = the investors' required (or expected) return on efficient portfolio p, where p is a portfolio on the capital market line

R_F = the rate of return on a risk-free security, which is usually assumed to be the expected return on a government of Canada treasury bill

$\overline{K}_m$ = the expected rate of return on the market portfolio

σ_m = the standard deviation of return for the market portfolio

σ_p = the standard deviation of return for efficient portfolio p.

The term in brackets in Equation 16.4 is the slope of the CML, and can be taken as a measure of the market price (reward) for bearing one unit of risk. Thus, Equation 16.4 can be stated in words as follows: The expected return on an efficient portfolio of assets is equal to the risk-free rate plus the product of the market reward (or premium) for bearing a unit of risk multiplied by the amount of risk undertaken.

The Graph: The Capital Market Line (CML)   The CML can be depicted as in Figure 16.7. It reflects for each level of risk the required (expected) return in the marketplace. In the graph, risk as measured by the standard deviations of return, σ_p, is plotted on the x-axis and the required returns, $\overline{K}_p$, are plotted on the y-axis. Note that since the CML represents the highest expected rate of return for each level of risk, *all portfolios of assets must lie either on or below the line.*

THE SECURITY MARKET LINE (SML)

In equilibrium, *the above simple relationship* between expected return and risk *only holds for efficient portfolios*; that is, portfolios that are perfectly diversified. Thus, the relationship does not hold for inefficient portfolios nor does it hold for individual assets. Therefore, it is necessary, if one wants to evaluate capital projects, to examine the market-pricing relationship for both inefficient portfolios and individual assets.

This relationship will be discussed in the following four sections. The first section

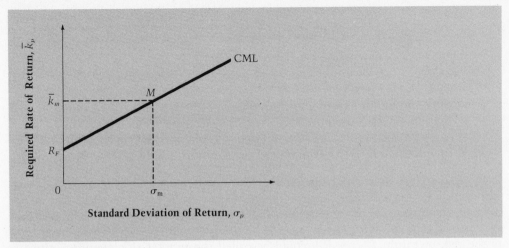

Figure 16.7   The capital market line (CML).

will discuss the types of risks involved with individual assets. The second section presents an equation for the security market line, and the third section defines and describes the beta coefficient, which is an index of nondiversifiable risk. The final section graphically depicts the security market line.

Types of Risk   A security's (or asset's) risk is said to consist of two components—diversifiable and nondiversifiable risk. *Diversifiable risk*, sometimes referred to as *unsystematic risk*, represents the portion of an asset's risk that can be eliminated through diversification. It results from the occurrence of uncontrollable or random events such as labour strikes, lawsuits, regulatory actions, loss of a key account, and so forth. The events that cause firms to have diversifiable risk vary from firm to firm; they are therefore unique to the given firm. *Nondiversifiable risk*, also called *systematic risk*, is attributed to forces that affect all firms and are therefore not unique to the given firm. Factors such as war, inflation, international incidents, and political events account for an asset's nondiversifiable risk. This risk can be assessed relative to the risk of one of the most diversified portfolios of securities, shown in the previous section to be the *market portfolio.*

Because any investor can create a portfolio of assets that will diversify away all diversifiable risk, the market does not provide a risk premium for any nondiversifiable risk that an investor assumes. Thus, the only *relevant* risk for an investor or firm is nondiversifiable risk.[6] Any investor (or firm) therefore must be concerned solely with the nondiversifiable risk, which reflects the contribution of an asset to the risk of the portfolio. This risk is not the same for each asset, but rather different assets will affect the portfolio differently.

Because nondiversifiable risk differs from asset to asset, its measurement is important in order to allow investors to select assets offering the desired risk-return characteristics to be included in their portfolios. The security market line provides a mechanism for relating risk and return for individual securities (assets).

The Equation   The security market line, which gives the risk-return pricing relationship for asset j, is given in Equation 16.5.

$$\overline{k}_j = R_F + b_j \cdot (\overline{k}_m - R_F) \qquad (16.5)$$

where

$\overline{k}_j$ = the required (or expected) return on asset j
R_F = the rate of return required on a risk-free security
b_j = the beta coefficient or index of nondiversifiable (relevant) risk for asset j
$\overline{k}_m$ = the required rate of return on the market portfolio of assets

It should be clear from the equation that the required return on an asset, $\overline{k}_j$, is an increasing function of beta, b_j, which reflects the relevant risk. In other words, the higher the risk, the higher the required return, and vice versa. The model can be broken into two parts: (1) the risk-free rate, R_F; and (2) the *risk premium*, $b_j \cdot (\overline{k}_m - R_F)$. The portion of the risk premium, $(\overline{k}_m - R_F)$, could be called the *market risk premium*, since it represents the premium that the investor must receive if he or she held a portfolio of assets that had a nondiversifiable risk level equal to the market (that is, b_j equal to 1). It should also be noted that Equation 16.5 is often referred to as the *Sharpe formulation of the capital asset pricing model*.

Beta Coefficient   In order to assess an asset's nondiversifiable risk, its *beta coefficient*, b, must be determined. The beta coefficient for an asset can be found by regressing an asset's historic returns with the returns for the market portfolio.* The market returns typically are measured by the average return on all (or a large sample of) assets. The Toronto Stock Exchange's 300 Stock Composite Index, or some other

---

*The empirical measurement of beta is approached using regression analysis in order to estimate the regression coefficients, a_j and b_j, in an asset's *characteristic line*, which is given by

$$k_j = a_j + b_j k_m + e_j$$

where

k_j = the return on security j
a_j = the intercept, which includes but does not necessarily equal the risk-free rate, R_F
b_j = the beta coefficient, which equals $\dfrac{Cov(k_j, k_m)}{\sigma_m^2}$

where

$Cov(k_j, k_m)$ = covariance of the return on security j, that is k_j and the market portfolio, k_m
σ_m^2 = variance of the market portfolio
k_m = the rate of return on the market portfolio of securities, which is usually measured by using the TSE index
e_j = random-error term, which reflects the diversifiable or unsystematic risk of security j

Note that the previous equation is often referred to as the *single-factor market model*. Because of the somewhat rigorous calculations involved in finding betas, the interested reader is referred to an advanced managerial finance or investments text for a more detailed discussion of this topic. Published security betas can be found in a variety of sources such as *Value Line*, as well as from one of the corporate clients of the Montreal-based Financial Research Institute.

market index, is commonly used to measure the market return. The beta coefficient can be viewed as an index of the degree of responsiveness or volatility of an asset's return with the market return. The beta for the market is equal to 1; all other betas are viewed relative to this value. Asset betas may take on values that are either positive or negative; positive betas are much more common than negative betas. The majority of betas fall between .2 and 2.0. Table 16.6 gives some selected beta values and their associated interpretations.

EXAMPLE   Alter Corporation Ltd. wishes to determine the required return on an average-risk asset that has a beta of 1.5. The risk-free rate of interest is found to be 7 percent, while the return on the market portfolio of assets is 11 percent. Substituting $b_{AC} = 1.5$, $R_F = 7$ percent, and $\bar{k}_m = 11$ percent into Equation 16.5 yields a required return,

$$\bar{k}_{AC} = 7\% + 1.5 \cdot (11\% - 7\%) = 7\% + 6\% = \underline{\underline{13\%}}$$

The market risk premium of 4 percent (i.e., $11\% - 7\%$), when adjusted for the asset's index of risk (beta) of 1.5, results in a risk premium of 6 percent (i.e., $4\% \cdot 1.5$) which, when added to the 7-percent rate of return expected on a risk-free security, results in a 13-percent required return. It should be clear that, other things being equal, the higher the beta, the greater the required return, and vice versa. Also note that the firm's overall cost of capital is equal to 13 percent, since the firm's beta must also be equal to 1.5.

The Graph: The Security Market Line (SML)   The security market line (SML) can be depicted graphically as a straight line, as in Figure 16.8. It reflects for each level of nondiversifiable risk (i.e., beta) the required return in the marketplace. In the graph, risk as measured by beta, b, is plotted on the x-axis and required returns, $\bar{k}$, are plotted on the y-axis.

Table 16.6   Selected Betas and Their Associated Interpretations

Beta	Comment	Interpretation[a]
2.0		Twice as responsive, or risky, as the market. An aggressive asset.
1.0	Move in same direction as market (cyclical)	Same response or risk as the market.
.5		Only half as responsive as the market. A conservative asset.
0		Unaffected by market movement.
−.5		Only half as responsive as the market.
−1.0	Move in opposite direction to market (counter cyclical)	Same response or risk as the market.
−2.0		Twice as responsive as the market. A defensive asset.

[a]A share that is twice as responsive as the market will experience a 2-percent change in its return for each 1-percent change in the return of the market portfolio; while the return of a share that is half as responsive as the market will change by $\frac{1}{2}$ percent for each 1 percent change in the return of the market portfolio.

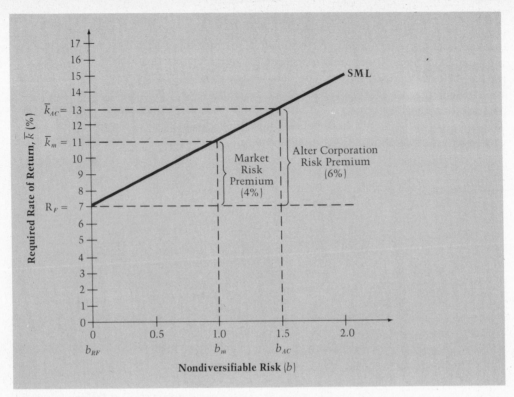

Figure 16.8 The security market line (SML) with Alter Corporation (AC) data shown.

EXAMPLE In the preceding example for the Alter Corporation, the risk-free rate, R_F, was 7 percent and the required return on the market portfolio, $\overline{k}_m$, was 11 percent. *Since the betas associated with R_F and $\overline{k}_m$, b_F and b_m, are by definition zero and one, respectively, the SML can be plotted using these two sets of coordinates.* Figure 16.8 presents the security market line (SML) resulting from plotting the coordinates given. As traditionally shown, the security market line in Figure 16.8 presents the required or expected returns associated with all positive betas. The market risk premium of 4 percent (i.e., $\overline{k}_m$ of 11 percent minus R_F of 7 percent) has been highlighted. Using the beta for the Alter Corporation, b_{AC}, of 1.5, its corresponding required return, $\overline{k}_{AC}$, has also been noted as 13 percent. Also shown in the figure is the Alter Corporation's risk premium of 6 percent ($\overline{k}_{AC}$ of 13 percent minus R_F of 7 percent). It should be clear from this figure that for assets with betas greater than one, the risk premium is greater than that for the market risk; while for assets with betas less than one, the risk premium is less than that for the market risk.

SOME COMMENTS ON CAPM

Although the capital asset pricing model (CAPM) was developed primarily for use in creating efficient portfolios of securities, it can be and has been adapted to making capital budgeting and other types of internal financial decisions, such as determining a firm's cost of capital or evaluating a firm's performance.* The use of the model's basic constructs in capital budgeting is discussed in a following section. The key concept that should result from the preceding discussion is that a risk-return trade-off, which sometimes may be difficult to quantify, exists. When making financial decisions, an awareness of this risk-return trade-off, and an attempt to somehow capture and consider the risk involved, should provide for better financial decisions.

Adjusting for Project Risk on a Project-by-Project Basis ⟵NO THIS

The discussion thus far has been devoted primarily to the problems of measuring risk and evaluating certain risk-related considerations. In this section, some techniques that are used in practice to adjust for project risk in capital budgeting on a project-by-project basis are presented. The key techniques discussed are the subjective approach, certainty equivalents, risk-adjusted discount rates, and the CAPM. In addition, two analytical techniques—decision trees and Monte Carlo simulation—that can be used to generate the information required to make risk adjustments are also discussed. Before proceeding to the discussion of these techniques, the importance of adequately and realistically adjusting for risk is shown in the following example.

EXAMPLE[7]   In 1979, the Port Cartier mill of International Telephone and Telegraph Corporation's Canadian subsidiary, Rayonier Quebec Inc., became IT&T's Edsel. With the closing of the mill, which was on a site 850 kilometres northeast of Montreal, the New York-based IT&T lost an estimated $600 million before taxes and $475 million after taxes. This loss was essentially the result of not adequately accounting for the risks of the project in the capital expenditure decision and of a poor implementation of the investment project. More specifically, an obsession with the opportunity to obtain a huge stand of timber caused IT&T's decision makers to downplay the following risks: (1) the mill was to be the largest mill the firm had ever built; (2) the mill was to incorporate unproven technology; (3) the mill was to be built in an unfamiliar and hostile climate (this results in the growth of many unusable trees that make logging operations difficult and costly); and (4) the future market for the mill's product, chemical cellulose, was very uncertain. Also, the project's estimated *expected* cost was $120 million (the *actual* cost was $250 million). (Thus, for the project to have been accepted, the firm's *required risk-adjusted rate of return* for this project must have been *less* than 10–13 percent!) Furthermore, the engineering of the plant was below average, and the mill was plagued by ongoing labour problems. At least some of these labour problems were caused by the fact that the management of Rayonier lacked the "cultural sensitivities" necessary for working with the French-speaking workers of the region. Note that this example also shows the nature of the investment risks encountered in making investment decisions in other countries, that is, internationally.

---

*The *ex post* form of the SML is often used as a benchmark for the evaluation of an asset's performance. However, as noted by Roll: (1) if performance is measured as a departure from the SML for an index that is *ex post* efficient, then no asset will exhibit an abnormal performance due to the mathematics of the efficient set; (2) if performance is measured relative to indexes that are *ex post* inefficient, then conflicting and incorrect rankings of portfolio performance are possible; and (3) although the only legitimate test of the CAPM is whether or not the market portfolio is mean-variance efficient, such a test cannot be unambiguous because the market portfolio can not be measured. See Richard Roll, "A Critique of the Asset Pricing Theory's Tests," *Journal of Financial Economics*, (March 1977), pp. 129–176; and "Ambiguity when Performance Is Measured by the Securities Market Line," *The Journal of Finance* 33, No. 4 (September 1978), pp. 1051–1069.

THE SUBJECTIVE APPROACH

The subjective approach to risk adjustment involves calculating the net present value of a project and then making the capital budgeting decision on the basis of the calculated NPV and the decision maker's subjective evaluation of the project's risk. Projects having similar net present values when discounted at the same rate, but believed to have differing degrees of risk, can easily be selected using this approach; whereas projects having differing net present values when discounted at the same rate, and believed to have differing degrees of risk, are much more difficult to select. Two of the major deficiencies of this approach are as follows. First, since no formal procedure is used to measure risk, it is unlikely that projects of the same risk will be consistently considered as being equivalent using the subjective approach. Second, since the actual decision made is based on the decision maker's return-risk trade-off, and not the market-determined trade-off, such decision making will generally not lead to the maximization of the wealth of the firm's shareholders or owners.

The first deficiency can be rectified somewhat by using sensitivity analysis (such as pessimistic, most likely, and optimistic estimates of a project's outcomes) to generate the information required to calculate a formal measure of project risk (such as the variance or the coefficient of variation). It can also be rectified somewhat by using decision trees or Monte Carlo simulation in order to generate the information required in order to calculate a formal measure of project risk.

Decision Trees   Some capital budgeting opportunities involve a sequence of decisions over time. The decision tree is an analytical technique for making sequential decisions among alternatives in an objective and consistent manner. Decision trees are diagrams that permit the various decision alternatives and payoffs, as well as their probabilities of occurrence, to be mapped out in a clear and easy-to-analyze fashion. They get their name from their resemblance to trees with a number of branches. (See Figure 16.9 for the decision tree for a simple accept-reject decision at the outset of a project.)*

Generally in a decision tree analysis, the payoffs associated with each course of action are weighted by the associated probability; the weighted payoffs for each course of action are summed; and the expected value of each course of action is then determined. If risk is to be ignored, then the alternative providing the highest expected value is selected; if risk is to be considered, then it must be explicitly measured. Common project-specific measures of risk, when using a decision tree analysis, are the variance and the coefficient of variation of NPV.

EXAMPLE   Elroy's Ltd. wishes to choose between two projects, I and J. To make this decision, Elroy's management has gathered the necessary data, which are depicted in the decision tree given in Figure 16.9. Project I requires an initial investment of $120,000. The calculation in column 4, based on the present values of cash inflow in column 3 and associated probabilities in column 2, gives an expected present value of cash inflows of $130,000. Project I's expected net

---

*In the case of sequential decisions, conditional probabilities must be determined, and in general the analysis is much more sophisticated than that described herein.

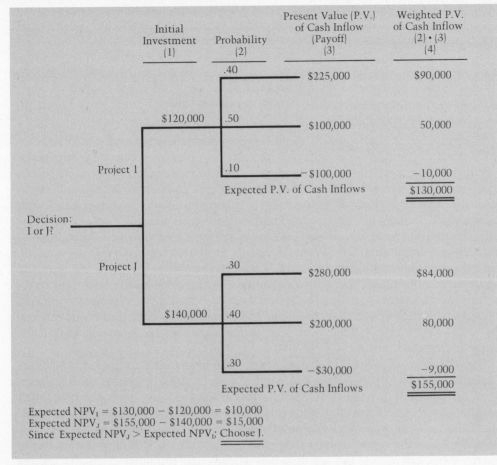

	Initial Investment (1)	Probability (2)	Present Value (P.V.) of Cash Inflow (Payoff) (3)	Weighted P.V. of Cash Inflow (2) • (3) (4)
		.40	$225,000	$90,000
	$120,000	.50	$100,000	50,000
Project I		.10	–$100,000	–10,000
			Expected P.V. of Cash Inflows	$130,000

Decision: I or J?

	Initial Investment (1)	Probability (2)	Present Value (P.V.) of Cash Inflow (Payoff) (3)	Weighted P.V. of Cash Inflow (2) • (3) (4)
Project J		.30	$280,000	$84,000
	$140,000	.40	$200,000	80,000
		.30	–$30,000	–9,000
			Expected P.V. of Cash Inflows	$155,000

Expected NPV$_I$ = $130,000 – $120,000 = $10,000
Expected NPV$_J$ = $155,000 – $140,000 = $15,000
Since Expected NPV$_J$ > Expected NPV$_I$; Choose J.

Figure 16.9   Decision tree for Elroy's choice between projects I and J.

present value, which is calculated below the decision tree, is therefore $10,000. If Elroy's management ignores risk, it would prefer project J because its expected net present value of $15,000 is greater than the expected net present value of project I of $10,000. If Elroy's management considers risk, it would have to explicitly measure the risk of each project. The expected value, standard deviation, and coefficient of variation for each of these projects' NPV's is given in the following table:

Statistics with respect to NPV	Project I	Project J
(1) Expected value	$10,000	$ 15,000[a]
(2) Standard deviation	$92,033[a]	$100,921
(3) Coefficient of variation (2) ÷ (1)	9.20	6.73[a]

[a]Preferred project solely using this measure.

A major problem often encountered when using decision trees is that the number of branches becomes unmanageable when the technique is used to analyze realistic capital budgeting problems.

Monte Carlo Simulation   Monte Carlo simulation is a statistically based approach for generating a probability distribution of project outcomes (such as net cash flow) or measures of profitability (such as NPV). While sensitivity analysis is more appropriate when evaluating the effect of the variation in a specific variable on a project's profitability, Monte Carlo simulation is more appropriate when evaluating the combined effect of simultaneous variations in many variables on a project's profitability.

Before actually performing a Monte Carlo simulation for a specific project, certain tasks must be performed. First, each of the variables that is expected to significantly affect the net cash flow of the project must be identified. These include such factors as market share, selling price per unit, and maintenance costs. Second, a subjective probability distribution must be gathered for each of the identified variables. For example, a market share distribution would generally be obtained from the marketing department; and a maintenance cost distribution would generally be obtained from the maintenance department. And finally, the mathematical relationship used to combine the various cash-flow components to obtain the project's net cash flow must be programmed. Any interdependencies between variables both within and across time periods, or between the values of the same variable over time, should be incorporated into the formulated mathematical relationship.

After the above tasks have been completed, the Monte Carlo simulation can be run. Generally, 200–300 iterations are run. During each of these iterations, the computer, based on randomly generated numbers, draws a specific value from the probability distribution of each of the identified variables for each year of the project's estimated life. Then, in accordance with the programmed mathematical relationship, the computer combines the various values in order to generate the net cash-flow stream for the project. After calculating the net cash-flow stream, the computer calculates the net present value or the internal rate of return of the stream. Thus, for each and every iteration, one specific NPV (or IRR) value is calculated. After the desired number of iterations have been completed, a probability distribution of NPV or IRR values is outputed. A simplified flowchart of the steps involved in simulating the distribution of NPV's for a project are presented in Figure 16.10. Note that although only netted cash inflows and outflows are shown in Figure 16.10, most computer-based simulations utilize a number of cash-inflow and cash-outflow variables.*

From the distribution of output values, regardless of how they are measured, the decision maker can determine not only their expected value but also the probability of

---

*The cash-inflow components are such things as the number of units sold, the sale price per unit, and collection patterns of receivables. The cash-outflow components include such items as maintenance costs, payments for raw materials, and wages. Sophisticated simulation models for capital budgeting consider the probability distribution of these and other cash flow components. For an algorithm and implementation evaluation of the technique for an actual proposed plant expansion by a major Canadian natural resource firm, see Lawrence Kryzanowski, Peter Lusztig, and Bernhard Schwab, "Monte Carlo Simulation and Capital Expenditure Decisions—A Case Study," *Engineering Economist* 18 (Fall 1972), pp. 31–48.

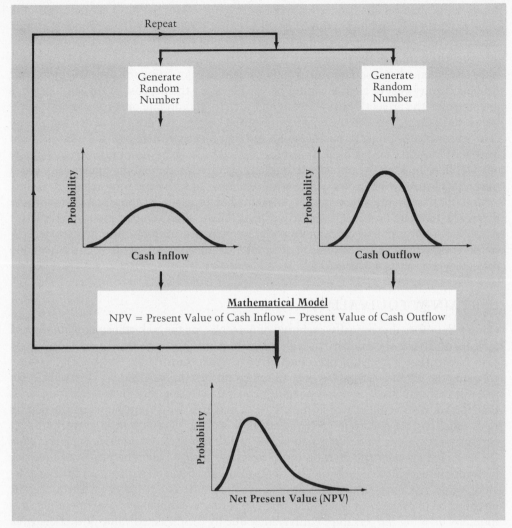

Figure 16.10   A simplified flowchart of a net present-value Monte Carlo simulation.

achieving, exceeding, or not achieving a given value. The output of a Monte Carlo simulation is a useful decision aid for at least three reasons. First, the output can aid a financial manager in assessing the accuracy with which future cash flows can be forecasted. Second, the output can be used in *risk positioning*; that is, in classifying projects as being of high, low, or average risk. And finally, the output, if properly summarized, can aid a financial manager in making capital expenditure decisions.

Monte Carlo simulation has a number of possible deficiencies. First, while the technique generates the data required to calculate a project's total risk, it does not generate the data required to calculate a project's business (i.e., nondiversifiable) risk. Thus, if the technique is to be used, the user must assume that the observed variability of project outcomes is a reasonably accurate proxy for the project's "true" business risk.* Second, since practitioners find it difficult to use the output generated by the technique, simple summary measures must accompany the technique's output. Third, it is difficult to interpret the output of the technique. For example, if a distribution of net present values is desired, then what discount rate should be used in calculating the net present values? An opportunity cost of capital cannot be used because the purpose of the simulation is to determine the project's business risk and thus its appropriate opportunity cost; similarly a risk-adjusted discount rate cannot be used because the purpose of the simulation is to determine the project's business risk and thus its appropriate risk-adjusted discount rate; and a risk-free rate of interest cannot be used because by discounting at such a rate one would be making the unrealistic implicit assumption that all the uncertainty about the project's future cash flows will be resolved between today and tomorrow.[8]

Nonetheless, the most appropriate discount rate to use in a Monte Carlo simulation is the risk-free rate of interest, since it adjusts for the time value of money and not for risk. And finally, unless abandonment is programmed into a simulation model, extremely unfavourable outcomes are generally not meaningful, because firms abandon projects when the "going gets tough."

CERTAINTY EQUIVALENTS

One of the most theoretically preferred approaches for the risk-adjusted evaluation of projects is the use of certainty equivalents. A *certainty equivalent* is that single certain cash payoff that a decision maker requires to make him or her indifferent between choosing the certain cash payoff and an uncertain cash payoff; that is, a distribution of possible cash payoffs. The name *certainty equivalent* is appropriate because it provides that certain cash value at which the decision maker is indifferent between the certain cash value and an uncertain cash value. For a specific distribution of cash flows, the certainty-equivalent value for a risk-averse decision maker would always be less than the expected value of the distribution of the cash flows. Thus, the positive difference between the expected value of the distribution and the decision maker's certainty-equivalent value gives a measure of how risk-averse the decision maker is. For a specific distribution of cash flows, a decision maker's certainty-equivalent adjustment factor is found by dividing the certainty-equivalent value by the expected value of that distribution. For a risk-averse decision maker, the certainty-equivalent adjustment factor will be less than one.

In evaluating projects using this approach, the decision maker first adjusts for risk by converting the expected cash flows to their corresponding certainty equivalents. This is generally done by multiplying each expected cash flow by the decision maker's corresponding certainty-equivalent factor. Then, the certainty-equivalent cash-flow values are discounted at the risk-free rate to get their net present values.† The risk-free rate, R_F,

---

*Since empirical studies have found a reliable level of association between systematic risk and various measures of earnings volatility, this assumption is somewhat reasonable. See Stewart C. Myers, "The Relationship Between Real and Market Measures of Risk and Return," in I. Friend and J. Bicksler, Eds., *Studies in Risk and Return* (Cambridge, Mass.: Ballinger, 1976).

†Alternatively, the internal rate of return could be calculated for the certainty-equivalent cash flows and then compared to the risk-free rate in order to make the accept-reject decision.

is used to discount the cash-flow certainty equivalents, since these values are the result of adjusting for the risks contained in the unadjusted cash flow stream.

The certainty-equivalent approach has a number of possible deficiencies. First, the certainty-equivalent factors used must be those used by the market in converting risky sums into their certainty equivalents. Second, it is difficult to obtain market-determined certainty-equivalent factors, even if the CAPM is used (as discussed below).

EXAMPLE   Spalding Sporting Goods is attempting to choose the best of two possible advertising campaigns—S and T. Both campaigns require initial investments of $200,000; Campaign S is quite conservative while campaign T is rather innovative and bold. The theory underlying campaign T is such that either people will be offended and not purchase the product, or they will be pleased and purchase the product. Each campaign is expected to provide equal annual benefits over a five-year period. Campaign S has expected benefits of $75,000 per year, while campaign T has expected benefits of $80,000 per year. Table 16.7 presents the expected cash inflows, the certainty-equivalent adjustment factors the firm believes applicable to each of them, and the resulting certainty-equivalent cash inflows, which are found by multiplying the cash inflow for each of the five years by the associated certainty-equivalent adjustment factors. The certainty-equivalent cash inflows for campaigns S and T are given in columns 3 and 6, respectively, of the table.

Table 16.7   Expected Cash Inflows, Certainty-Equivalent Adjustment Factors, and Certainty-Equivalent Cash Inflows for Campaigns S and T for Spalding Sporting Goods

	Campaign S			Campaign T		
Year	Expected cash inflows (1)	Certainty-equivalent adjustment factors[a] (2)	Certainty-equivalent cash inflows (1) · (2) (3)	Expected cash inflows (4)	Certainty-equivalent adjustment factors[a] (5)	Certainty-equivalent cash inflows (4) · (5) (6)
1	$75,000	1.00	$75,000	$80,000	.90	$72,000
2	75,000	1.00	75,000	80,000	.80	64,000
3	75,000	.90	67,500	80,000	.70	56,000
4	75,000	.90	67,500	80,000	.60	48,000
5	75,000	.80	60,000	80,000	.50	40,000
		NPV @ 6% = $92,455			NPV @ 6% = $39,792	

[a]These values were market-determined.

Upon investigation, Spalding's management estimated the prevailing risk-free rate of return, R_F, to be 6 percent. Using the 6-percent risk-free rate to discount the certainty-equivalent cash inflows for each of the campaigns (S and T) results in the net present values of $92,455 for campaign S and $39,792 for campaign T. Therefore, campaign S is preferred to campaign T. It is interesting to note that had the cash inflows not been adjusted for risk, campaign T would have been preferred to campaign S because of its higher annual expected inflows for the same initial investment. The usefulness of the certainty-equivalent approach for risk adjustment should be quite clear; the only difficulty lies in the need to estimate the certainty-equivalent adjustment factors.

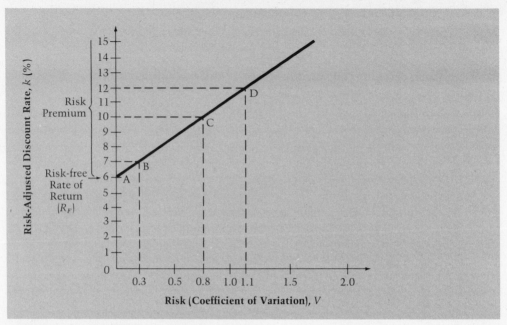

Figure 16.11 A hypothetical market indifference curve.

RISK-ADJUSTED DISCOUNT RATES

Another approach for risk adjustment involves the use of risk-adjusted discount rates. Instead of adjusting the cash inflows for risk as was done using the certainty-equivalent approach, the risk-adjusted discount rate approach adjusts the discount rate.* To adjust the discount rate, it is necessary to develop the function (or relationship) that gives the minimum return required by the market for each level of project business risk; that is, the minimum required return-risk function that leaves the market value of a firm unchanged.

Since risk independence is being assumed, there are two commonly proposed methods of calculating the required return-risk function for capital budgeting projects (i.e., real assets)—the capital asset pricing model (CAPM) and the market indifference curve approach.† The CAPM is further discussed in the next section of the chapter.

A *market indifference curve* can be developed by using the variance or coefficient of variation as a measure of project risk. As depicted in Figure 16.11, a market indifference curve provides the relationship between the risk-adjusted discount rate, k, and project

---

*The risk-adjusted discount rate approach can be applied when using the internal rate of return as well as net present value. If the IRR is used, the risk-adjusted discount rate becomes the cutoff rate that must be equaled or exceeded by the IRR for the project to be accepted. When using net present value, the projected cash inflows are merely discounted at the risk-adjusted discount rate.

†If risk interdependence is assumed, then a proposed project's marginal contribution to the overall risk of the firm's existing portfolio of assets must be considered. For example, Quirin proposes that one should analyze a project's impact on the present coefficient of variation of the firm. See G. David Quirin, *The Capital Expenditure Decision* (Homewood, Ill.: Irwin, 1967).

risk as measured by the coefficient of variation, V. Unlike the SML, which has theoretical underpinnings, the market indifference curve is assumed to begin at the risk-free rate of return, R_F (point A in the figure) and to increase linearly as project risk increases. Given the hypothetical market indifference curve, a riskless project (i.e., $V = 0$) should be discounted at the riskless rate (6 percent); while projects such as B, C, and D, which have a greater level of risk (i.e., $V > 0$), should be discounted at higher risk-adjusted rates. More specifically, the risky projects B, C, and D, which have coefficients of variation of 0.3, 0.8, and 1.1, must offer minimum risk-adjusted rates of return of 7, 10, and 12 percent, respectively, if their acceptance is to leave the firm's market value unchanged. In other words, the risk-adjusted rates of return, k, represent the firm's minimum cutoff rates for projects of various levels of risk.

If we assume that the firm's present portfolio of assets is represented by point C, then the firm's overall cost of capital is 10 percent. Thus, the reader should again note that the overall cost of capital for the firm (i.e., the cost of capital that reflects the overall or average business risk of the firm's existing assets) cannot be used as the appropriate discount rate for evaluating nonaverage-risk capital budgeting projects. In addition, it should be noted that the firm's overall cost of capital will change over time since the new projects accepted by the firm are likely to change the firm's business risk. A simple example should help to clarify how the risk-adjusted rate of return, k, can be used to evaluate capital budgeting projects.

EXAMPLE Spalding Sporting Goods (presented in the preceding example) wishes to use the risk-adjusted discount rate approach to determine whether to increase its sales by accepting either of two advertising campaigns—S and T. In addition to the data presented earlier, Spalding's management has estimated that the standard deviation of campaign S's benefits is $22,500, while the standard deviation of benefits for campaign T is $64,000. Figure 16.11 represents the current market indifference curve.

The first step in evaluating the campaigns is to calculate their coefficients of variation. The coefficient of variation for campaign S is 0.30 (i.e., $22,500 ÷ $75,000); while the coefficient of variation for campaign T is 0.80 (i.e., $64,000 ÷ $80,000). According to Figure 16.11, the risk-adjusted discount rate for campaign S is 7 percent; for campaign T, it is 10 percent. Due to the more certain nature of campaign S, its risk premium is only 1 percent (i.e., 7% − 6%); for campaign T the risk premium is 4 percent (i.e., 10% − 6%). The net present value of each campaign, using its risk-adjusted discount rate, is calculated as follows:

Campaign S

$$\text{NPV} = \$75,000 \text{ (P.V. of an annuity, 5 years at 7\%)} - \$200,000$$
$$= \$75,000 \,(4.100) - \$200,000$$
$$= \$107,500$$

Campaign T

$$\text{NPV} = \$80,000 \text{ (P.V. of an annuity, 5 years @ 10\%)} - \$200,000$$
$$= \$80,000 \,(3.791) - \$200,000$$
$$= \$103,280$$

Apparently, campaign S is preferable to campaign T since it has a higher risk-adjusted net present value. This is the same result obtained earlier using the certainty-equivalent approach. Had the discount rates not been adjusted for risk, campaign T would have been preferred to campaign S because of its higher annual expected inflows for the same initial investment. The usefulness of risk-adjusted discount rates should now be clear; the real difficulty with this approach lies in estimating the market indifference curve.

Using the risk-adjusted discount rate approach has a number of possible deficiencies. First, in order to use a project's coefficient of variation or standard deviation as the appropriate measure of a project's risk, the user of this approach must assume that the project's standard deviation is a reasonably accurate proxy for the project's "true" business risk. Second, when the firm is choosing among alternative investment opportunities, whose acceptance will materially change the average-risk level of the firm, then it may be more appropriate to simultaneously determine both the appropriate discount rate and the optimal mix of investments. Third, using a fixed risk-adjusted discount rate to evaluate a multiperiod cash-flow stream may not be appropriate, because it makes an implicit assumption that the risk of the project's cash flows are increasing at a constant rate over time.

THE CAPITAL ASSET PRICING MODEL (CAPM)

The basic concepts of the capital asset pricing model were discussed earlier in the chapter. In this section, we will discuss the use of the CAPM in evaluating capital budgeting projects (i.e., real assets). Since in a perfect capital market individual and corporate risk diversification are perfect substitutes, a proposed capital budgeting project can be evaluated as if it is risk-independent. Thus, in such a world, risky assets should be evaluated solely in terms of their own expected return and their own nondiversifiable (i.e., systematic) risk as measured by beta. In other words, the appropriate discount or cutoff rate for evaluating risky capital budgeting projects is equal to the risk-free rate plus a risk premium that depends solely on the project's beta.[*]

When using the CAPM to evaluate capital budgeting projects, it is necessary to derive the security market line for real assets; that is, the return-risk pricing relationship for projects in terms of the market portfolio, m. Thus, the minimum required return for project j is given by:

$$\overline{k}_j = R_F + \hat{b}_j \cdot (\overline{k}_m - R_F) \tag{16.6}$$

where $\hat{b}_j$ is the estimated slope of the characteristic line between the returns from project j and those from the market portfolio.

It is interesting to note that $\overline{k}_j$ does not depend upon the firm undertaking the invest-

[*]Since a portfolio beta is a linearly weighted combination of the betas of the assets in the portfolio, only the betas of the individual assets are needed to measure the systematic risk of a portfolio. In other words, it is not necessary for the firm to solve a quadratic programming problem in order to find its efficient portfolio of assets.

ment; that is, given the project's systematic risk, *the market-determined required rate of return on the project is the same for all firms that are considering an investment in the project.* On the other hand, the expected IRR or NPV of the project is likely to differ between firms, because different firms will derive different incremental cash flows from the adoption of the project. These differences will occur because the incremental cash flow derived by a specific firm from the adoption of the project will depend upon such factors as the specific firm's management, efficiency, expertise, and tax status.

Application   The minimum required return for project j (i.e., $\bar{k}_j$) can either be used as the risk-adjusted discount rate or as the required cutoff rate when evaluating project j. Thus, project j would be accepted if either its expected IRR exceeds its minimum required return, $\bar{k}_j$; or its risk-adjusted NPV is positive.

The difficulty encountered in applying this approach lies in the estimation of a project's beta. Since a project's stream of annual returns over its lifetime is needed to estimate its beta, it is necessary to estimate the annual changes in the project's market value over its lifetime. Alternatively, it may be possible to obtain some proxy measure of a project's systematic risk by identifying publicly traded assets with similar risk characteristics. Thus, if one can identify one or more publicly held companies with similar systematic-risk characteristics as the evaluated project, then obtaining an appropriate proxy measure of the project's systematic risk is reasonably straightforward. This is illustrated in the following example.

EXAMPLE   Tasty Ale Ltd. is considering the formation of an oil and gas subsidiary. As there are a number of oil and gas companies with publicly traded shares and similar risk characteristics as the proposed subsidiary, the financial manager of Tasty Ale has simply determined the average beta for those companies which most closely resemble the expected systematic-risk characteristics of Tasty Ale's new venture. He then calculated the required rate of return for the oil and gas venture using Equation 16.6. That is, given a calculated average beta of 1.4, an expected market return of 20 percent, and a risk-free rate of 10 percent, the financial manager found that the minimum required rate of return for the new venture would be

$$\bar{k} = 0.10 + (0.20 - 0.10) \cdot 1.4 = 24 \text{ percent}$$

The financial manager would accept the oil and gas venture if its expected IRR exceeds $\bar{k}$; or if its NPV is positive when it is calculated using $\bar{k}$ as the appropriate risk-adjusted discount rate. It is important to note that $\bar{k}$ would not be the appropriate discount rate for all of the projects involved in Tasty Ale's new oil and gas subsidiary. It would only be the appropriate rate for those projects that have the same business risk as the subsidiary; that is, it would only be appropriate for the firm's "average-risk" oil and gas projects.

If one cannot identify a publicly traded company with similar systematic-risk characteristics as the evaluated project, then obtaining an appropriate proxy measure of the project's systematic risk is not feasible. In that case, one must attempt to estimate beta directly. This will be nearly impossible to do, unless there is a well-developed product market for the real asset being evaluated. Generally, such markets exist only for those assets that are leased (see Chapter 20 for greater details). Therefore, when evaluating the desirability of assets such as office space or computer hardware, the financial manager can obtain the resale values of "used" assets of various ages from a fairly well-developed (but not necessarily efficient) secondary market. After collecting these resale values, the financial manager must first estimate the annual holding period returns for the evaluated asset over its lifetime, and then use this information in Equation 16.6 to estimate the project's beta.

Critique   The CAPM approach to the evaluation of risky capital budgeting projects is subject to a number of possible deficiencies.[9] First, it is generally difficult to identify one or more publicly traded companies that have systematic risk characteristics similar to the project being evaluated. Furthermore, while an estimate of the project's level of systematic risk is generally needed to identify the similar-risk publicly traded companies, the purpose of identifying similar systematic-risk companies is to determine the project's level of systematic risk. Second, because the (product) market for real assets is not generally efficient, the resale values of such assets is probably a "poor" measure of their "true" value. Product markets are generally inefficient because not all participants have the same and/or accurate information about such assets; such information is costly; the assets are often relatively large, indivisible, and illiquid; transaction costs are significant; often one or more firms are large enough to have a significant impact on the prevailing market prices of real assets; and firms active in these markets generally have different expectations about the future returns and risks of such assets.*

Summary

This chapter has presented a discussion of capital budgeting under risk. Because the cash inflows associated with capital budgeting projects are future cash inflows, an understanding of risk is most important to making good capital budgeting decisions. The terms *risk* and *uncertainty* are often used interchangeably to refer to the variability of project outcomes. Statistically, risk is present when the probability distribution of outcomes is known, while uncertainty is present when the probability distribution is unknown. The terms are used interchangeably in this text. Two approaches often used to get a "feel" for project risk are sensitivity analysis and the use of probabilities. Sensitivity analysis involves evaluating various estimates of project outcomes such as the most pessimistic, most likely, and most optimistic. The range is often used to quantify risk by measuring the dispersion of these potential outcomes. A more sophisticated approach would be to assign probabilities to the various outcomes either objectively or subjectively to determine the expected value, the standard deviation, and the coefficient of variation of the project outcomes.

Risk can be assessed visually by drawing either a bar graph or the entire probability distribution (if sufficient data are available) associated with a project's outcomes. To obtain a more concrete measure of project risk, statistical measures of variability can be

---

*Product markets must be inefficient; otherwise assets traded in such markets would not systematically promise positive risk-adjusted net present values.

used. Two statistics that provide a measure of project risk are the standard deviation and the coefficient of variation. The coefficient of variation, which is the standard deviation of the project outcomes divided by the expected value of the project outcomes, provides a relative measure of project risk.

The timing of returns also affects project risk. In general, the farther into the future cash inflows are to be received, the greater the variability of these cash inflows. Another time-related consideration is portfolio risk, which is concerned with the time-related relationship between project cash inflows. The correlation between projects in a portfolio, which is the degree to which their returns vary together, greatly affects the overall risk of the portfolio. Capital budgeting projects whose returns are negatively correlated provide the best combination for minimizing overall risk. There are two opposing viewpoints on whether portfolio risk effects should be considered when evaluating a capital expenditure. The risk-interdependence viewpoint maintains that portfolio risk effects should be considered; while the risk-independence viewpoint maintains that portfolio risk effects can be ignored.

One of the key considerations in financial decision making involves the trade-off between risk and return. In a world of perfect capital markets, the only relevant risk is the nondiversifiable risk, which is attributable to changes in some common underlying factor such as the economy. The diversifiable risk, which is attributed to the firm itself and results from the occurrence of uncontrollable or random firm-related events, can be eliminated through diversification. The nondiversifiable risk can be measured by beta, which is an index that relates the responsiveness or comovement of an asset's return to that of the market. Betas may be positive or negative; most are positive and less than 2.0. The security market line gives the risk-return relationship for individual assets. Letting $\overline{k}_j$ = the required (or expected) return on an asset j, R_F = the risk-free rate of return, b_j = the index of nondiversifiable risk (or beta) for asset j, and $\overline{k}_m$ = the required return on the market portfolio, the security market line is given by the following equation:

$$\overline{k}_j = R_F + b_j \cdot (\overline{k}_m - R_F)$$

The required return on asset j, $\overline{k}_j$ can be viewed as the sum of the return on a risk-free asset, R_F, plus a risk premium, $b_j \cdot (\overline{k}_m - R_F)$, which reflects the asset's (relevant) risk relative to the market. Graphically, the security market line (SML) depicts, for each level of nondiversifiable risk (i.e., beta), the associated required return. Although the CAPM is difficult to apply to real assets, the type of risk-return relationship depicted by the capital asset pricing model must be considered when making capital budgeting decisions in order to provide for the wealth maximization of owners.

A number of techniques to adjust for project risk in capital budgeting on a project-by-project basis exist. The subjective approach involves calculating the net present value of a project and then making the capital budgeting decision on the basis of the calculated NPV and the decision maker's subjective evaluation of the project's risk. Techniques such as sensitivity analysis, decision trees, or Monte Carlo simulation can be used to generate the information required by the decision maker in order to more formally measure a project's risk. The certainty-equivalent approach provides a mechanism whereby risky cash flows can be adjusted to their certainty-equivalent amounts, and then discounted at a risk-free rate to evaluate a project. Risk-adjusted discount rates, which are the discount rates required in the marketplace in order to compensate for project risk, can also be used. The two commonly proposed methods of calculating the required return-risk function for capital budgeting projects are the market indifference curve approach and the capital asset pricing model (CAPM) approach.

Questions

16.1   Why is it important for a decision maker to have some feel for the risk or uncertainty associated with capital budgeting projects? What kind of capital budgeting project would have certain nominal returns?

16.2   What is the difference between the terms *risk* and *uncertainty* as defined by a statistician? What kind of probability distributions are associated with each of these states?

16.3   What is the sensitivity analysis approach for dealing with project risk? What is one of the most common methods used to evaluate projects using sensitivity analysis. Define and describe the role of the *range* as an aid in sensitivity analysis.

16.4   What is a payoff matrix? What are the two dimensions of this matrix? How can a payoff matrix be used to evaluate risk?

16.5   What is meant by "the probability of an event occurring"? What do probabilities of zero and one indicate about outcomes? Why?

16.6   How does a plot of the probability distribution of outcomes allow the decision maker to get a "feel" for project risk? What is the difference between a bar chart and a continuous probability distribution?

16.7   What does the standard deviation of a distribution of project outcomes indicate? What relationship exists between the size of the standard deviation and the degree of project risk?

16.8   What is the coefficient of variation? How is it calculated? Why may the coefficient of variation be a better basis for comparing the risk associated with different projects than the standard deviation?

16.9   What general relationship is expected to exist between project risk and time? To what factor(s) is this behaviour attributable? Why?

16.10   Should the firm be viewed as having a portfolio of projects when it is evaluating capital budgeting projects?

16.11   What are correlation coefficients? When do perfect positive and perfect negative correlations exist? Which is more desirable for effective diversification? Why?

16.12   How does diversification of risk in the project selection process allow the firm to combine two risky projects in such a fashion that the risk of the portfolio is less than the risk of each of the individual projects in it? What is an efficient portfolio?

16.13   What is a basic theory with respect to risk and return? Upon what assumptions is this theory based?

16.14   Explain the difference between nondiversifiable and diversifiable risk. Why would one argue that nondiversifiable risk is the only *relevant* risk?

16.15   What is a *beta coefficient*? How can a beta coefficient be measured or estimated?

16.16   Using the beta coefficient as the measure of nondiversifiable risk, what is the equation for the security market line (SML)? Explain the meaning of each variable.

16.17   What graphical representation is used to depict the risk-return trade-off given by the CAPM for inefficient portfolios? Define the axes and construct a graph for a risk-free rate of 5 percent and a market rate of return of 10 percent.

16.18   How may decision trees be used in considering project risk? Do they provide for the measurement of risk? Explain.

16.19   What is the basic Monte Carlo simulation approach for generating a distribution of project outcomes or measures of profitability? How does Monte Carlo simulation provide the decision maker with useful decision-making inputs?

16.20   Explain the concept of certainty equivalents.

16.21   Using the NPV framework, what changes are necessary to utilize the certainty-equivalent approach to evaluate risky capital expenditures?

16.22   What is a market indifference curve? What is plotted on each axis?

16.23   How can a risk-return function be used to determine the risk-adjusted discount rate used in evaluating a project? What must be known in order to determine the risk-adjusted discount rate? Why?

16.24   What relationship must be derived when using the CAPM to evaluate capital budgeting projects? How is this relationship used in evaluating capital budgeting projects? What is a major difficulty encountered in applying this approach to the evaluation of capital budgeting projects?

Problems

16.1   Klauer Pharmaceutical Ltd. is in the process of evaluating two mutually exclusive additions to their processing capacity. The firm's financial analysts have developed pessimistic, most likely, and optimistic estimates of the annual cash inflows associated with each project. These estimates are as follows:

	Project A	Project B
Initial investment	$8,000	$8,000
Cash inflow estimates		
Pessimistic	$ 200	$ 900
Most likely	1,000	1,000
Optimistic	1,800	1,100

a.   Determine the range of annual cash inflows for each of the two projects.

b.   Assume the cost of capital for the firm is 10 percent, and the projects should have 20-year lives. Construct a sensitivity table for the *net present values* of the estimates. Include the range of NPV's for each project.

c.   Do **a** and **b** give consistent views of the risk of the two projects? Explain.

d.   Which project would you recommend and why?

16.2   Micro-Pub Ltd. is considering the purchase of one of two new microfilm cameras—R or S. Both should provide benefits over a 10-year period, and each has a required investment of $3,000. Management has constructed the following table of estimates of probabilities and cash inflows for pessimistic, most likely, and optimistic results:

	Camera R		Camera S	
	Amount	Probability	Amount	Probability
Initial investment	$3,000	1.00	$3,000	1.00
Cash Inflow				
Pessimistic	$ 500	.25	$ 400	.20
Most likely	750	.50	750	.55
Optimistic	1,000	.25	1,200	.25

a. Determine the range of cash inflows for each camera.
b. Determine the expected cash inflow for each camera.
c. Which camera do you consider the more risky? Discuss the nature of the risk-return trade-off associated with these cameras.

16.3   Whitney's Western-Wear, a clothing manufacturer, is considering a new line of female headwear. The following table summarizes the cash inflows and probabilities for the two lines under consideration:

| Market acceptance | Probability | Cash inflow | |
		Line A	Line B
Very poor	.05	$ 100	$ 75
Poor	.15	250	125
Average	.60	800	850
Good	.15	1,350	1,475
Excellent	.05	1,500	1,625

Use the table to
a. Construct a bar chart for each line's cash inflows.
b. Calculate the expected value of each line's cash inflows.
c. Evaluate the relative riskiness of each clothing line's cash inflows using the bar charts.

16.4   Using the net present values (NPV) and associated probabilities for two projects—X and Y—summarized in the following table,
a. Prepare bar charts for the two projects' net present values.
b. Calculate and compare the expected net present values of the projects.
c. Compare the riskiness of the two projects. (Use the range to measure riskiness.)

| Project X | | Project Y | |
NPV ($)	Probability	NPV ($)	Probability
−15,000	.01	−20,000	.00
0	.03	−10,000	.02
15,000	.03	0	.04
25,000	.05	10,000	.06
30,000	.15	20,000	.08
35,000	.50	30,000	.15
40,000	.15	40,000	.35
45,000	.05	50,000	.20
55,000	.03	60,000	.05
70,000	.00	70,000	.03
		80,000	.01
		90,000	.01
		100,000	.00

16.5   A firm is considering two projects; their cash inflow probability distributions are summarized:

Project A		Project B	
Cash inflow	Probability	Cash inflow	Probability
$100	.10	$100	.10
200	.20	300	.80
300	.40	500	.10
400	.20		
500	.10		

a. Determine the range for each distribution of project cash inflows.
b. Determine the expected cash inflow from each project.
c. Determine the standard deviation of each project's probability distribution of cash inflow.
d. Discuss the information the financial manager gains from each of the measures calculated previously.

16.6 Robin Parker must decide which of two projects is best for her firm. By using probability estimates, she has determined the following information:

Statistic	Project A	Project B
Expected NPV	$24,000	$18,000
Standard deviation	$36,000	$32,000

a. Complete the table by computing the coefficient of variation for each project.
b. Explain to Ms. Parker why the standard deviation and coefficient of variation give different rankings of risk.

16.7 Weber Tool Ltd. must choose between two asset purchases. The cash-inflow data and related probabilities given below summarize the firm's analysis.

Project 473		Project 297	
Cash inflow ($)	Probability	Cash inflow ($)	Probability
100	.05	−100	.01
150	.10	100	.04
200	.10	200	.05
250	.15	300	.10
300	.20	400	.15
350	.15	450	.30
400	.10	500	.15
450	.10	600	.10
500	.05	700	.05
		800	.04
		1,000	.01

a. For each project, compute
   (1) The range of cash inflow.
   (2) The expected value of cash inflow.
   (3) The standard deviation of cash inflow.
   (4) The coefficient of variation of cash inflow.
b. Construct a bar chart of each distribution of cash inflow.
c. Which project would you consider to have the lower relative risk and why?

16.8 The project cash inflows for four projects—A through D—forecast for the period 19X1–19X8 are given in the following table:

Year	A	B	C	D
19X1	$2,000	$ 7,000	$15,000	$18,000
19X2	3,000	8,000	15,000	17,000
19X3	4,000	9,000	15,000	16,000
19X4	5,000	6,000	15,000	15,000
19X5	4,000	5,000	15,000	17,000
19X6	3,000	7,000	15,000	18,000
19X7	2,000	9,000	15,000	19,000
19X8	5,000	10,000	15,000	20,000

a. Indicate for each of the project combinations (AB, AC, AD, BC, BD, and CD) whether the returns are positively correlated, negatively correlated, or not correlated.
b. Calculate the average cash inflows and standard deviation of cash inflows for each project. Hint: to calculate the standard deviation, σ, with these data, employ the formula found in the footnote on page 461, which uses the same notation that was used in Equation 16.2 of the chapter:

$$\sigma = \sqrt{\frac{\sum_{i=1}^{n} (E_i - \overline{E})^2}{n}}$$

c. Calculate the average cash inflows and standard deviation of cash inflows for project combinations AB and AD. (See hint in b).
d. What conclusions about the portfolio effects of combinations of projects can be drawn from your preceding work? Explain.

16.9 The Jenkins Box Ltd. must consider several investment projects using the capital asset pricing model (CAPM). Using the following table and the security market line (SML),
a. Calculate the expected rate of return and risk premium each project must produce given its level of nondiversifiable risk.
b. Graph the security market line (required rate of return relative to nondiversifiable risk) for all projects listed in the table.
c. Discuss the relative nondiversifiable risk of projects A through E.

Project	Expected rate of return	b value
Risk-free asset	5%	0
Market portfolio	12%	1.00
Asset A	—	1.50
Asset B	—	.75
Asset C	—	2.00
Asset D	—	0
Asset E	—	− .50

16.10 The Emory Board-Games Ltd. can bring out one of two new games this season. The *Signs Away* game has a higher initial cost but also has a higher expected return. *Monopolistic Competition*, the alternative, has a slightly lower intitial cost but also has a lower expected return. The probabilities and present values associated with each game are listed in the following table.

Game	Initial investment	PV of cash inflows	Probabilities
Signs Away	$140,000		1.00
		$320,000	.30
		220,000	.50
		− 80,000	.20
Monopolistic Competition	$120,000		1.00
		$260,000	.20
		200,000	.45
		− 50,000	.35

a. Construct a decision tree to analyze the two games.
b. Which game would you recommend (following a decision-tree analysis)?
c. Has your analysis captured the differences in project risk? Explain.

16.11 Creighton Castings Ltd. has compiled the following information on a capital expenditure proposal:

(1) The projected cash inflows are normally distributed with a mean of $36,000 and a standard deviation of $9,000.
(2) The projected cash inflows are normally distributed with a mean of $30,000 and a standard deviation of $6,000.
(3) The firm has an 11-percent cost of capital.
(4) The probability distributions of cash inflows and cash outflows are not expected to change over the project's 10-year life.

Describe how the preceding data could be used to develop a Monte Carlo simulation model for finding the net present value of the project.

16.12 Westchester Ball Valve Ltd. has constructed the table given below that gives expected cash inflows and certainty-equivalent adjustment factors for these cash inflows. These values are for a new machine that is expected to last five years and requires an initial investment of $100,000. The firm has a 10-percent cost of capital and the risk-free rate is 7 percent.
a. What is the unadjusted net present value?
b. What is the certainty-equivalent net present value?
c. Should the firm accept the project? Explain.

Year	Expected cash inflow	Certainty-equivalent adjustment factors
1	$35,000	1.0
2	35,000	.8
3	35,000	.6
4	35,000	.6
5	35,000	.2

16.13 A firm is considering a risky project that requires an initial investment of $1,000,000 and will have expected after-tax cash inflows of $200,000 per year for the next 10 years. The firm uses a 10-percent cost of capital for projects of average risk, but feels this project requires an additional premium of 4 percent.
a. Should the firm accept the project? Why or why not?
b. At what risk premium (above the 10-percent rate) would the project be acceptable?

5 ?.

16.14 Preston Tire Ltd. has recently investigated market risk-return trade-offs and has assembled the following data:

Coefficient of variation	Market discount rate
0.0	6%
0.2	7%
0.4	8%
0.6	9%
0.8	10%
1.0	11%
1.2	12%
1.4	13%
1.8	15%
2.2	17%

a. Construct a graph of the market indifference curve. Be sure to clearly label the axes and indicate the area of risk premiums.

b. The firm is evaluating the following two projects. Both have four-year lives and require initial investments of $4,000.

Project A		Project B	
Annual cash inflow ($)	Probability	Annual cash inflow ($)	Probability
−2,000	.25	− 100	.20
2,000	.50	1,600	.50
6,000	.25	3,000	.30

(1) Determine the expected value, standard deviation, and coefficient of variation for each of the two projects' cash inflows.

(2) Use the market indifference curve to determine the appropriate risk-adjusted discount rate for each project. (Adjust to the nearest $\frac{1}{2}$ percent.)

(3) Which project do you recommend and why?

Notes

1. See Stewart C. Myers, "Procedures for Capital Budgeting Under Uncertainty," *Industrial Management Review* 9 (Spring 1968), pp. 1–15. Also, see Lawrence D. Schall, "Asset Valuation, Firm Investment, and Firm Diversification," *Journal of Business* 45 (January 1972), pp. 11–28. An arbitrage-type argument, similar to that used in Chapter 18, will ensure that this result will occur.

2. This section is based on Stewart C. Myers, "Procedures for Capital Budgeting Under Uncertainty," *Industrial Management Review* 9 (Spring 1968), pp. 1–15.

3. The key development of this theory is generally attributed to William F. Sharpe, "Capital Asset Prices: A Theory of Market Equilibrium Under Conditions of Risk," *Journal of Finance* 19 (September 1964), pp. 425–442; and John Lintner, "The Valuation of Risk Assets and the Selection of Risky Investments in Stock Portfolios and Capital Budgets," *The Review of Economics and Statistics* (February 1965), pp. 13–37. A variety of authors have significantly advanced, refined, and tested this theory.

4. In general, the empirical support is much stronger for U.S. than Canadian security markets. The U.S. evidence includes Marshall E. Blume and Irwin Friend, "A New Look at the Capital Asset Pricing Model," *Journal of Finance* 28 (March 1973), pp. 19–33; Eugene F. Fama and J. D. MacBeth, "Risk, Return and Equilibrium: Some Empirical Tests," *Journal of Political Economy* (1973), pp. 607–636; and Fischer Black, Michael C. Jensen, and Myron Scholes, "The Capital Asset Pricing

Model: Some Empirical Tests," in Michael C. Jensen (ed.), *Studies in the Theory of Capital Markets* (New York: Praeger, 1972), pp. 79–124. The Canadian evidence includes R. A. Morin, "Capital Asset Pricing Theory: The Canadian Experience" (Unpublished Ph.D. dissertation, University of Pennsylvania, 1976); and L. Kryzanowski, "Misinformation and Regulatory Actions in the Canadian Capital Markets: Some Empirical Evidence," *The Bell Journal of Economics* 9, No. 2 (Autumn 1978), pp. 355–368.

5. Richard Roll, "A Critique of the Asset Pricing Theory's Tests," *Journal of Financial Economics* 4 (March 1977), pp. 129–176.

6. Empirical studies have found that portfolios of 15–20 randomly selected securities will on average diversify away approximately 90 percent of the diversifiable risk. Two interesting studies are those of W. H. Wagner and S. C. Lau, "The Effect of Diversification on Risk," *Financial Analysts Journal* 26 (November-December 1971), pp. 48–53; and John Evans and Stephen H. Archer, "Diversification and the Reduction of Dispersion: An Empirical Analysis," *Journal of Finance* 23 (December 1968), pp. 761–767.

7. This example is based on various sources. For example, see Carol J. Loomis, "How I.T.T. Got Lost in a Big Bad Forest," *Fortune*, December 17, 1979, pp. 42–47, 50, 52, 54.

8. For greater details, see Robert H. Keeley and Randolph Westerfield, "A Problem in Probability Distribution Techniques for Capital Budgeting," *Journal of Finance* 27 (June 1972), pp. 703–709. Also, see Harold Bierman, Jr., and Warren H. Hausman, "The Resolution of Investment Uncertainty Through Time," *Management Science* 18 (August 1972), pp. 654–662.

9. For a discussion of a number of other difficulties, see Stewart C. Myers and Stuart M. Turnbull, "Capital Budgeting and the Capital Asset Pricing Model: Good News and Bad News," *Journal of Finance* 32 (May 1977), pp. 321–333.

Suggested Readings

Bierman, Harold, Jr., and Jerome E. Hass, "Capital Budgeting Under Uncertainty: A Reformulation," *Journal of Finance* 28 (March 1973), pp. 119–130.

Biger, Nahum, "The Assessment of Inflation and Portfolio Selection," *Journal of Finance* 30 (May 1975), pp. 451–468.

Blume, Marshall, E., "On the Assessment of Risk," *Journal of Finance* 26 (March 1971), pp. 95–117.

Boersema, J. M., *Capital Budgeting Practice Including the Impact of Inflation* (Toronto: CICA, 1978).

Carter, E. Eugene, *Portfolio Aspects of Corporate Capital Budgeting* (Lexington, Mass.: Heath, 1974).

Evans, John and Stephen H. Archer, "Diversification and the Reduction of Dispersion: An Empirical Analysis," *Journal of Finance* 23 (December 1968), pp. 761–767.

Findlay, M. Chapman III, Arthur E. Gooding, and Wallace Q. Weaver, Jr., "On the Relevant Risk for Determining Capital Expenditure Hurdle Rates," *Financial Management* 5 (Winter 1976), pp. 9–16.

Gitman, Lawrence J., "Capturing Risk Exposure in the Evaluation of Capital Budgeting Projects," *Engineering Economist* 22 (Summer 1977), pp. 261–276.

Grayson, C. Jackson, "The Use of Statistical Techniques in Capital Budgeting," in Alexander A. Robichek, Ed., *Financial Research and Management Decisions* (New York: Wiley, 1967), pp. 90–132.

Greer, Willis R., "Theory versus Practice in Risk Analysis: An Empirical Study," *Accounting Review* 49 (July 1974), pp. 496–505.

Harvey, R. K. and A. V. Cabot, "A Decision Theory Approach to Capital Budgeting Under Risk," *Engineering Economist* 20 (Fall 1977), pp. 37–49.

Hertz, David B., "Investment Policies That Pay Off," *Harvard Business Review* 46 (January-February 1968), pp. 96–108.

———, "Risk Analysis in Capital Investment," *Harvard Business Review* 42 (January-February 1964), pp. 95–106.

Hillier, Frederick S., "A Basic Model for Capital Budgeting of Risky Interrelated Projects," *Engineering Economist* 17 (Fall 1971), pp. 1–30.

Jensen, M. C., Ed., *Studies in the Theory of Capital Markets* (New York: Praeger, 1972).

Keeley, Robert H. and Randoph Westerfield, "A Problem in Probability Distribution Techniques for Capital Budgeting," *Journal of Finance* 27 (June 1972), pp. 703–709.

Kryzanowski, Lawrence, "Misinformation and Regulatory Actions in the Canadian Capital Markets: Some Empirical Evidence," *The Bell Journal of Economics* 9 (Autumn 1978), pp. 355–368.

———, Peter Lusztig, and Bernhard Schwab, "Monte Carlo Simulation and Capital Expenditure Decisions—A Case Study," *Engineering Economist* 18 (Fall 1972), pp. 31–48.

Lessard, Donald R. and Richard S. Bower, "Risk-Screening in Capital Budgeting," *Journal of Finance* 28 (May 1973), pp. 321–338.

Lewellen, Wilbur G. and Michael E. Long, "Simulation versus Single-Value Estimates in Capital Expenditure Analysis," *Decision Sciences* 3 (1972), pp. 19–33.

Magee, John F., "Decision Trees for Decision-Making," *Harvard Business Review* (July-August 1964), pp. 126–136.

———, "How to Use Decision Trees in Capital Investment," *Harvard Business Review* (September-October 1964), pp. 79–96.

Mao, James C. T. and John F. Brewster, "An E-S_h Model of Capital Budgeting," *Engineering Economist* 15 (January-February 1970), pp. 103–121.

Markowitz, H., *Portfolio Selection* (New York: Wiley, 1959).

Miller, Robert B. and Dean W. Wichern, *Intermediate Business Statistics: Analysis of Variance, Regression and Time Series* (New York: Holt, Rinehart, and Winston, 1977).

Modigliani, Franco and Gerald A. Pogue, "An Introduction to Risk and Return," *Financial Analysts Journal* (March-April 1974), pp. 68–80 and (May-June 1974), pp. 69–86.

Morin, Roger A., "Capital Asset Pricing Theory: The Canadian Experience" (Unpublished Ph.D. dissertation, University of Pennsylvania, 1976).

Myers, Stewart C., "Procedures for Capital Budgeting Under Uncertainty," *Industrial Management Review* 9 (Spring 1968), pp. 1–15.

——— and Stuart M. Turnbull, "Capital Budgeting and Capital Asset Pricing Model: Good News and Bad News," *Journal of Finance* 32 (May 1977), pp. 321–333.

Osteryoung, Jerome S., Elton Scott, and Gordon S. Roberts, "Selecting Capital Projects with the Coefficient of Variation," *Financial Management* 6 (Summer 1977), pp. 65–70.

Porter, R. Burr, Roger P. Bey, and David C. Lewis, "The Development of a Mean-Semi-Variance Approach to Capital Budgeting," *Journal of Financial and Quantitative Analysis* 10 (November 1975), pp. 639–650.

Robichek, Alexander A. and Stewart C. Myers, "Conceptual Problems in the Use of Risk-Adjusted Discount Rates," *Journal of Finance* (December 1966), pp. 727–730.

Roll, Richard, "A Critique of the Asset Pricing Theory's Tests," *Journal of Financial Economics* 4 (March 1977), pp. 129–176.

———, "Ambiguity When Performance Is Measured by the Securities Market Line," *Journal of Finance* 33 (September 1978), pp. 1051–1069.

Sharpe, William F., "Capital Asset Prices: A Theory of Market Equilibrium Under Conditions of Risk," *Journal of Finance* 19 (September 1964), pp. 425–442.

———, *Portfolio Theory and Capital Markets* (New York: McGraw-Hill, 1970).

Stapleton, R. C., "Portfolio Analysis, Stock Valuation and Capital Budgeting Decision Rules for Risky Projects," *Journal of Finance* 26 (March 1971), pp. 95–117.

Van Horne, James C., "Capital Budgeting Decisions Using Combinations of Risky Investments," *Management Science* 13 (October 1966), pp. 84–92.

Wagner, Wayne H. and Sheila Lau, "The Effect of Diversification on Risk," *Financial Analysts Journal* 26 (November-December 1971), pp. 48–53.

Weston, J. Fred, "Investment Decisions Using the Capital Asset Pricing Model," *Financial Management* 2 (Spring 1973), pp. 25–33.

The Cost of Capital, Capital Structure, and Valuation

The Cost
of Capital,
Capital Structure,
and Valuation

BALANCE SHEET	
Assets	Liabilities and Shareholders' Equity
Current Assets	**Current Liabilities**
Fixed Assets	**Long-Term Debt**
	Shareholders' Equity

This part of the text covers three important and closely related topics—the cost of capital, capital structure, and valuation. The cost of capital, which represents the firm's average cost of money, is an important input to the capital budgeting process; the firm's capital structure and valuation affect, and are affected by, its cost of capital. The first chapter in this part, Chapter 17, is devoted to the cost of capital. It presents an in-depth discussion of the underlying theory, methods of calculation, and application of the cost of capital for a hypothetical firm. Chapter 18 discusses both capital structure and valuation. It describes the basic theories and some of the mathematical techniques for evaluating the mix of long-term debt and equity financing of a firm.

Chapter 17

THE COST OF CAPITAL

In the preceding chapters, we developed various techniques and concepts for evaluating investment alternatives. In the discussion of discounted cash-flow (DCF) techniques of capital budgeting, it was assumed that the appropriate cost of capital used as the discount or cutoff rate for evaluating capital expenditure proposals was known. In this chapter, we tackle the difficult task of first defining the term *cost of capital*, and then explaining how to calculate a specific measure of the firm's cost of capital, known as the firm's *overall* or *weighted average cost of capital*.

An estimate of the firm's cost of capital is of critical importance to the financial manager, not only for evaluating the firm's investment projects but also for other important financial decisions such as those related to lease financing, bond refunding, capital structure mix, acquisitions, and amalgamations. These topics will be discussed in following chapters.

This chapter is divided into four major sections. The first section explains the assumptions under which a firm's cost of capital can be measured as a weighted average of the costs of its individual or specific sources of capital, such as debt, preferred shares, common equity, and depreciation. The second section discusses the methods for estimating the explicit opportunity or marginal cost to the firm of each of the above four specific sources of capital. This section also briefly discusses how the financial manager can check the accuracy of his or her estimate of the firm's cost of equity capital. The third section illustrates how the individual costs of the firm's specific sources of capital can be combined to obtain the firm's overall or weighted average cost of capital for evaluating new investments. The final section briefly discusses the choice and timing of corporate financings.

The reader should note at the outset that there are still a number of unresolved analytical problems associated with the specification and measurement of the cost of capital. Thus, the following discussion will be more valuable to financial managers in terms of its insights and qualitative guidance than for its use in providing exact quantitative answers to specific questions.

Definition and Basic Assumptions

DEFINITION

A firm's cost of capital is the rate of return the firm must earn on its existing investment in order for its market value (and hence the market value of the shareholders' equity) to remain unchanged. It can also be viewed as the *minimum rate of return that the firm must earn on new investment in order to satisfy all of the firm's suppliers of capital.* Acceptance of a project with an expected (risk-adjusted) rate of return that is lower than the cost of capital will lower the market value of the firm, and vice versa.

OVERALL OR WEIGHTED AVERAGE COST OF CAPITAL

Under the two basic assumptions discussed next, a firm's cost of capital is equal to the weighted average of the specific costs of the various types of capital used to finance the firm's total investment. The weights used in the weighted average cost of capital calculation are given by the proportion of each type of capital in the firm's long-run target capital structure that reflects the firm's long-run financing policy.

ASSUMPTIONS

The first basic assumption is that the business or operating risk of the firm's new investments is the same as the business risk of the firm's existing mix of investments; that is, that the firm does not alter its business risk by undertaking new investments.* *Thus, the measure of the cost of capital developed in this chapter is valid only for evaluating those projects that do not significantly change the firm's business risk.*† If a firm accepts a relatively large project that has considerably more business risk than the firm's existing mix of investments, then the suppliers of funds to the firm will likely raise the cost of their funds. This is so because the probability of the suppliers of funds receiving the expected returns on their money is decreased. A creditor will charge higher interest on loans if the probability of receiving periodic interest payments and the principal from the borrowing firm is decreased. Common shareholders will require the

---

*The term *business risk* is sometimes also referred to as *economic risk*. For a detailed discussion of the concept of business risk and its determinants, see Chapter 4. As discussed in that chapter, a firm's business risk is associated with the variability of the firm's EBIT (earnings before interest and taxes) stream, because EBIT does not in general depend upon how the firm is financed (except in the case of financial institutions).

†In the terminology of the capital asset pricing model developed in Chapter 16, the overall or weighted average cost of capital can be used to evaluate only those projects that do not affect the firm's *systematic* or *nondiversifiable* risk. An investment (such as a diversification project) that is expected to carry the firm into a new risk class should be evaluated against the cost of capital characteristic of firms in that new risk class.

firm to offer higher returns as compensation for increases in the uncertainty of receiving dividend payments or any appreciation in the market value of their shares. In other words, an increase in the firm's business risk will increase the specific marginal costs of each of the firm's sources of financing, and vice versa. A firm's use of its weighted average cost of capital for evaluating its new investments is based on a simplifying assumption that its current business risk will remain essentially unaltered by the new investments.

The second basic assumption is that the new investments do not affect the financing policies of the firm. More specifically, it is assumed that the firm seeks to maintain a *long-run target capital structure* (or financing mix) which it believes to be optimal in the long run, and that all new investment projects are financed so as to maintain this target capital structure.

The firm's financing mix or capital structure affects its financial risk. Firms with high levels of long-term debt relative to equity are considered to be riskier than firms with lower ratios of long-term debt to equity. It is the contractual fixed-payment obligations associated with debt financing that make a firm financially risky. The greater the amount of interest and principal (or sinking-fund) payments a firm must make in a given period, the higher the operating profits required to cover these charges. If a firm fails to generate sufficient revenues to cover financial charges, it may be forced into bankruptcy. As we indicated in the discussion of financial leverage in Chapter 4, the higher the firm's financial leverage, the greater the firm's financial risk.

As a firm's capital structure shifts toward a more highly levered position, the increased financial risk associated with the firm is recognized by suppliers of funds. They compensate for this increased risk by charging higher rates of interest or requiring greater returns. In short, they react in much the same way as they would to increasing operating risk. Thus, the assumption of maintaining a constant target capital structure over some long-run planning horizon is necessary to isolate the specific costs of the various forms of financing (i.e., the costs of long-term debt, the costs of common equity, etc.).

UNDERLYING RATIONALE OF THE WEIGHTED AVERAGE COST OF CAPITAL

Suppose that the above two assumptions are satisfied. Then the rationale underlying the use of the weighted average cost of capital as a measure of the minimum acceptable rate of return on the firm's new investments can be illustrated by the following simplified example.

EXAMPLE The Sigmund Company Ltd. is considering an investment requiring an initial cash outlay of $600,000. The investment has the same business risk as the typical investment undertaken by the firm in the past. Currently, the firm's capital structure is comprised of $24,000,000 of debt with a current cost of 10 percent, and $36,000,000 of common equity with a required rate of return or cost of equity of 15 percent. After analyzing its business and a number of other factors,* the firm has determined that this capital structure is the firm's long-term optimal target

*A detailed discussion of the major determinants of a firm's capital structure is presented in Chapter 18.

capital structure. Accordingly, the firm plans to raise 40 percent of the required initial outlay for the investment by issuing 10-percent bonds and the remaining 60 percent by issuing new common shares for which the required rate of return is 15 percent.* The firm's annual cash flow from operations, *before* making the investment, is expected to be $7,800,000 in perpetuity.

For simplicity assume that the project will generate constant annual operating cash flows over an infinite horizon and that no earnings are retained. Also, assume that there are no corporate taxes and no flotation costs associated with the new bond issue. Based on these assumptions, Table 17.1 summarizes the analysis required to determine the minimum rate of return on the proposed investment that will leave the value of the firm's existing equity unchanged.

Table 17.1   The Sigmund Company's Operating Cash Flows

	Before the proposed investment (1)	Proposed investment (2)	*After* the proposed investment (3) = (1) + (2)
Capital structure:			
Debt (10%)	$24,000,000	$240,000[a]	$24,240,000
Equity	$36,000,000	$360,000[a]	$36,360,000
	$60,000,000	$600,000	$60,600,000
Cash flows:			
Operating cash flow	$ 7,800,000	$ 78,000	$ 7,878,000
Interest	2,400,000	24,000	2,424,000
Dividends	5,400,000	54,000	5,454,000

[a]$360,000 (new common share equity) = 60% of $600,000 (total cash outlay required for the new investment). Similarly, $240,000 = 40% of $600,000.

From the calculations shown in the table, we find that *without* the proposed investment, the firm's existing shareholders will receive their required annual rate of return of 15 percent (i.e., $5,400,000/$36,000,000),† after annual interest payments of $2,400,000 (i.e., 10% of $24,000,000) have been made to the firm's existing bondholders. The minimum cash returns from the new investment must just cover the interest cost on new bonds and the required 15-percent return on new equity, without affecting the amount of dividends being paid to the old shareholders. Therefore, the minimum acceptable annual cash flow from the proposed investment equals $78,000 [i.e., ($240,000 · 10%) + ($360,000 · 15%)].

If the annual cash return expected to be generated by the new investment is less than $78,000, the investment should be rejected, and vice versa. For example, suppose the expected annual

---

*The rate of return investors require on a security is sometimes referred to as the *market capitalization rate*, because this is the rate at which investors discount (i.e., capitalize) future cash flows from the security when establishing its market value.

†As explained in Chapter 13, the rate of return, r, on an investment, I, with perpetual level annual cash flows, C, is given by $r = C/I$.

cash returns from the investment were $48,000; then the firm's total annual cash flow after the investment would equal $7,848,000. This means that after the firm has made the annual interest payment of $2,424,000 (column 3) to its existing and new bondholders, the earnings available for dividends will be reduced to $5,424,000 (i.e., $7,800,000 + $48,000 − $2,424,000). In this case, the common shareholders' rate of return after the investment has been made will decline from 15 percent to approximately 14.92 percent (i.e., $5,424,000/$36,360,000). On the other hand, if the investment's annual cash returns were expected to be, say, $120,000 (i.e., greater than the minimum acceptable cash returns of $78,000), then the existing shareholders would be better off. In this case, after paying $2,424,000 as annual interest, the total annual cash flow available for payment to the common shareholders, after the investment has been made, will rise to approximately 15.12 percent (i.e., $5,496,000/$36,360,000).

From the preceding calculations, it is clear that in order for the value of the existing equity to remain unchanged, the proposed investment must provide an annual cash return of $78,000; that is, a rate of return of $78,000/$600,000 = .13 or 13 percent. By definition, this percentage return is equal to the firm's cost of capital, which can be expressed as

$$\frac{\$240,000}{\$600,000} \cdot 10\% + \frac{\$360,000}{\$600,000} \cdot 15\% = .40 \cdot 10\% + .60 \cdot 15\%$$
$$= .13$$

Thus, the cost of capital of 13 percent represents a weighted average of the specific costs of the individual sources of financing the project, where each individual financing source is weighted by its proportion in the firm's long-run target capital structure (i.e., 40 percent long-term debt and 60 percent common equity). Moreover, the firm's *preinvestment* overall or weighted average cost of capital based on the *current marginal* costs of debt and equity capital, and their proportions in the firm's existing capital structure (which, by assumption, is the firm's long-run target capital structure), must also equal 13 percent (i.e., {[$24,000,000/($24,000,000 + $36,000,000)] · 10%} + {[$36,000,000/($24,000,000 + $36,000,000)] · 15%}).

*Thus, if the two basic assumptions discussed above are satisfied, then the minimum acceptable rate of return on the firm's new investment is equal to the current average cost of financing the firm's existing investment.**

Finally, it should be noted that it is the *current marginal costs* rather than the historical or average costs of the firm's various sources of financing that are relevant for the calculation of the overall or weighted average cost of capital for evaluating new investments. It is for this reason that the firm's weighted average cost of capital is sometimes referred to as the *marginal weighted average cost of capital*. It provides the appropriate measure of the marginal cost of capital (the cutoff or discount rate) for evaluating the firm's new *average-risk* investments.†

---

*For simplicity we have ignored the consideration of flotation costs and corporate tax effects (such as the interest-tax shield) in the above analysis. This, however, does not affect the basic concepts illustrated in the example. The impact of corporate income tax and flotation costs on a firm's weighted average cost of capital will be considered in the following section of the chapter.

†An "average-risk project" is defined as the project having the same business risk as the typical or average investments undertaken by the firm historically.

THE POOL-OF-FUNDS APPROACH
TO THE DETERMINATION OF THE OVERALL COST
OF CAPITAL

In the preceding section it was assumed that the firm finances all its new investments according to its target proportions of debt and equity. Unfortunately, in practice, firms do not generally raise capital in predetermined proportions of debt and equity to finance each new project. Actual raising of long-term funds is generally "lumpy"; that is, in the short-run, firms generally finance a specific project with a specific source of financing. In some cases, the financing arrangements are an integral part of the investment opportunity itself. For example, in a real estate investment a mortgage loan on the assets generally provides a major part of the required funds. Thus, even though a firm may have specified a target capital structure, it will, in the short-run, tend to deviate from this long-run goal because of certain practical considerations. Therefore, it has sometimes been argued that the explicit marginal cost of the specific source of financing used for a specific project should be used as the cutoff or discount rate for evaluating the project, and that the firm's overall cost of capital should not be used. As illustrated in the following example, a major criticism of this argument is that it fails to consider the long-run implications of the firm's current financing and leads to an arbitrary measure of the cutoff rate for evaluating new investments.

EXAMPLE   Suppose that the Sigmund Company from the preceding example plans to finance the proposed investment *exclusively* with the 10-percent $600,000-bond issue, and that the rate of return on the investment is expected to be 12 percent. If the investment's 12-percent rate of return is compared with the 10-percent cost of debt financing, then the project would be acceptable. However, if it is compared with the firm's overall cost of capital of 13 percent, the project would be rejected. In essence, the issue is which is the appropriate cost of funds for evaluating the project? Should the project be judged against the explicit marginal 10-percent cost of its specific source of financing or against the firm's overall or marginal weighted average cost of 13 percent that reflects the firm's long-run financing policy (as represented by its target capital structure)? Let us investigate this critical question in some detail.

By financing the project with the bond issue, the firm will be increasing the proportion of debt in its capital structure and, hence, its financial risk. The resulting increase in its financial risk will, in turn, increase the cost of the firm's future debt and/or equity financing. Clearly, such *incremental* future effects will not be accounted for if the firm measures the project only against the directly observable or *explicit* 10-percent cost of the bond issue. To put it another way, by increasing the proportion of debt this year, the firm will be using up some of its potential for obtaining relatively low-cost debt in future years. Therefore, at some point in time in the future, the firm will find it prudent to raise relatively expensive equity capital to prevent the debt ratio from becoming too large relative to its business or operating risk. Clearly then, the explicit 10-percent cost of the bond issue does not represent the "true" marginal cost of financing the project.* Rather, the true

---

*Because of the tax deductibility of the interest cost of debt, the effective marginal cost of the bond issue will be lower than the 10-percent interest rate on the bond. This fact, however, does not affect the main thrust of the discussion in the example.

marginal cost of the bond issue is its explicit 10-percent interest cost plus its *implicit* cost due to its potential incremental impact on the firm's future financing costs. Similarly, if the project is financed exclusively with a new common share issue, the explicit cost of the issue will overstate the true marginal cost of financing the project, since the issue will provide a foundation for future issues of relatively less expensive debt.

Moreover, if the firm follows the policy of evaluating a project against the explicit marginal cost of the specific source of financing the project, then its cost of capital (i.e., the explicit marginal cost of the specific source of financing used) will fluctuate sharply as it finances one project with the sale of bonds, the next with common equity, the third with preferred shares, and so on. Such a randomly fluctuating "cost of capital" will lead to inconsistent decision making. For example, in some time periods, a relatively low-return project may be accepted while a relatively high-return project may be rejected, simply because a different source of funds was arbitrarily chosen to finance each project. Thus, the project in our example will be accepted if its rate of return of 12 percent is compared with the 10-percent cost of the bond issue. However, if the firm had arbitrarily decided to finance this particular project with new common equity at a cost of 15 percent, the project would be rejected even if it promised a return of, say, 14 percent.

Abuses possible under the policy of appraising investments by assigning specific sources of capital to specific investments should now be self-evident. A decision maker could arbitrarily accept a particular project by arbitrarily comparing that project's expected return with the specific source of funds having the lowest explicit marginal cost; and he or she could arbitrarily reject a particular project by arbitrarily comparing that project's expected return with the specific source of funds having the highest explicit marginal cost. In a decentralized decision-making organizational structure with many decision makers, the abuses would be compounded.

Thus, it is generally recommended that the firm should evaluate its average-risk investment projects against an overall weighted average cost of funds that reflects its long-run target financing policy; and that the firm, as an ongoing concern, should ignore minor deviations over time from its long-run target financing policy; that is, it should calculate its cost of capital *as if* all its investments are financed out of a common pool of funds with constant proportions for each source of funds.*

The cost of capital measured as a weighted average cost of capital under the pool-of-funds approach will reflect the unobservable (and therefore difficult to measure) implicit costs of financing because in order to maintain a stable capital structure, the firm must continuously supplement relatively cheaper debt financing with equity financing, and vice versa. In other words, a firm's (marginal) weighted average cost of capital, under the

---

*The firm should, however, reassess its long-term financing policy from time to time due to anticipated changes in factors such as government policies, tax legislation, and general capital market conditions. The changes in these factors will generally affect the relative costs (and therefore the overall or weighted average cost) of the firm's various sources of financing. The adjective *long-term* in the above discussion refers to some specified and distant decision horizon of the firm. Thus, the firm's target capital structure should not be viewed as being static over time but as a step function that evolves over an infinite horizon. For an excellent development of this point, see Haim Levy and Marshall Sarnat, *Capital Investment and Financial Decisions* (Englewood Cliffs, N.J.: Prentice-Hall, 1978), pp. 251–254.

pool-of-funds approach, will closely approximate the true marginal cost of financing the firm's new average-risk investments.

The Cost of Specific Sources of Capital

In order to estimate the firm's overall cost of capital, we need to estimate the explicit marginal or opportunity cost of each individual type of financing source used by the firm. Our concern is only with the long-term sources of funds available to a business firm, because it is generally safe to assume that these sources supply the permanent financing of the firm.* Long-term financing supports the firm's fixed-asset investments, which, so it is assumed, have been selected using appropriate capital budgeting techniques.

The three major external sources of long-term funds for a corporation are long-term debt, preferred shares, and common shares. The two major internal sources are new equity obtained from retained earnings and the funds generated by depreciation charges.† Techniques for determining the specific after-tax marginal costs of each of these sources of financing are presented on the following pages. Although these techniques develop precisely calculated values of specific as well as weighted average costs, it is important to recognize that the resulting values are at best *rough approximations* due to the numerous assumptions and forecasts that underlie them.

THE COST OF LONG-TERM DEBT (BONDS)

The cost of long-term debt has two basic components.‡ One is the annual interest; the other arises from the amortization of discounts or premiums paid or received when the debt is initially issued. In order to simplify the calculations in this section, *annual* fixed interest payments on noncallable debt issues, with no sinking-fund requirements, are assumed.§ Also, for ease of exposition, corporate tax effects on the cost of debt will initially be ignored.

---

*Current liabilities, which are not costless in an opportunity-cost sense, can be ignored in the overall cost of capital calculation if the firm uses the capital budgeting approach that nets the working capital required for a project against that project's initial investment when evaluating the project. This generally accepted approach was the one used in discussing the evaluation of capital projects in Chapter 14.

†Other sources of long-term funds include deferred taxes, government grants, and financial leases.

‡Note that a firm may employ different forms of debt with varying maturities and terms. For example, a firm can issue different types of bonds, such as ordinary bonds, income bonds, mortgage bonds, retractable bonds, and extendable bonds to accommodate the varying preferences of long-term lenders. In addition, the interest payment on each type of debt can be fixed or variable. For simplicity, we shall refer to a single cost of debt in the discussion to follow, but a firm's cost of debt will generally be a weighted average of the individual costs of the various types of debt included in the firm's capital structure. An alternative to calculating the average cost of debt is to view each type of debt as a separate source of financing and to include it as a part of the weighted average cost of capital calculation. A detailed discussion of the various types of long-term debt and their costs is presented in Chapter 21. In Chapter 20, it is explained that financial leases can also be viewed as a form of long-term debt financing.

§Interest on bonds is typically paid *semiannually*. The assumption of annual payments is made in order to simplify the required calculations, while still conveying the key concepts. A discussion of how to treat bonds paying semiannual interest was included in Chapter 13.

Net Proceeds   Most corporate long-term debt is incurred through the sale of bonds. The net proceeds from the sale of a bond are the funds received from the sale after all underwriting and brokerage fees have been paid. Sometimes the net proceeds from the sale of a bond are greater than the bond's *face, or maturity, value.* This is generally true when the stated interest on the bond (the *coupon rate*) is greater than interest associated with other, similar-risk and term debt instruments. The bond is sold for a *premium* (more than its face value) in order to align the actual interest yield with the yields prevailing in the market. Bonds sold for less than their face value, or at a *discount,* have stated interest rates (coupon rates) below the prevailing rates for similar-risk and term debt instruments. Selling bonds at a discount puts the effective yield to the purchaser on a par with yields of similar-risk and term debt instruments. Underwriting and brokerage costs reduce the net proceeds from the sale of a bond at a premium, at a discount, or at its par (i.e., face) value.

EXAMPLE   The Jerry Company Ltd. is contemplating selling $10,000,000 worth of 20-year, 9-percent bonds, each with a face value of $1,000. Since similar-risk and term debt instruments are yielding more than 9 percent, the firm must sell the bonds for $980 (i.e., at a discount of 2 percent of the par value) to compensate for the low coupon rate. The investment dealer underwriting the bond issue receives a fee of 1 percent of the face value of the bond (i.e., 1% · $1,000, or $10).* Additional issue expenses per bond are $10. The net proceeds to the firm from the sale of each bond are therefore $960 (i.e., $980 − $10 − $10).

Calculating the Cost of Debt   The before-tax cost of debt can be found by determining the internal rate of return on the bond cash flows. From the issuer's point of view this value can be referred to as the before-tax *cost-to-maturity.*† The before-tax cost-to-maturity is calculated using the internal rate-of-return techniques presented in Chapter 15. It represents the annual before-tax percentage cost of the debt to the firm.

EXAMPLE   In the preceding example the net proceeds of a $1,000, 9-percent, 20-year bond were found to be $960. Although the cash flows from the bond issue do not appear to have a simple cash-flow pattern, the calculation of the annual cost is quite simple. Actually, the cash-flow pattern is exactly the opposite of a simple pattern associated with investment projects, since it consists of an initial inflow (the net proceeds) followed by a series of annual outlays (the interest

---

*An investment dealer *underwrites* a bond issue when he or she buys it at a discount from the issuer and sells it on behalf of the issuer. The discount compensates the underwriter for acting as a middleman. An in-depth discussion of the underwriting function is included in Chapter 19.

†The internal rate of return on a bond investment when viewed by a purchaser—not issuer—is referred to as *yield-to-maturity (YTM),* since it presents the investor's return from purchasing the bond at a given price and holding it until maturity. It is computed from the market value of the bond and *promised* payments (i.e., payments of interest and principal). The YTM of a bond purchased at its par value equals the coupon rate associated with the bond.

payments) plus the repayment of the principal at the end of the bond's 20-year term. The cash flows associated with the Jerry Company's bond issue are as follows:

End of year(s)	Cash flow
0	$ 960
1–20	−$ 90
20	−$1,000

The initial $960 inflow is followed by annual interest outflows of $90 (i.e., 9% of $1,000) over the 20-year life of the bond. In year 20 an outflow of $1,000, representing the repayment of the principal, occurs. The before-tax cost of the debt can be determined by finding the discount rate that equates the present value of the outflows with the initial inflow. Applying the trial-and-error-techniques of Chapter 15 for finding the internal rate of return results in an approximate before-tax cost-to-maturity of 9.47 percent.

As discussed in Chapter 2, interest payments on debt are permitted as a tax-deductible expense. As such, the before-tax cost of debt must be adjusted downwards to reflect the fact that it is a tax-deductible expense. The before-tax debt cost, k_b, can be converted to an after-tax debt cost, k_i, by the following equation:*

$$k_i = k_b(1 - t) \tag{17.1}$$

The t represents the corporate tax rate.

EXAMPLE   The before-tax debt cost for the Jerry Company, which is subject to a 40-percent corporate tax rate, is 9.47 percent. Applying Equation 17.1 results in an after-tax debt cost of 5.68 percent [i.e., 9.47% (1 − .40)]. Typically, the cost of debt is considerably less than the cost of any of the alternate forms of long-term financing. This is because the interest expense is tax deductible.†

---

*This equation is exact only when the net proceeds from a bond issue equal the bond's par value; that is, when k_b is equal to the coupon rate on the bond. Thus, when a bond is sold to the public at a price different from its par value and/or underwriting and issue expenses associated with the bond are significant, the after-tax cost given by the equation should be regarded as a *first approximation*. However, for maturities of over 10 years, the equation will generally provide a good approximation. This is so because the impact (in percentage terms) of flotation costs on the specific cost of a bond issue diminishes sharply with the increase in the number of years to maturity of the bond. Also, note that issue expenses and bond discounts paid to the public can, under certain conditions, be treated as a tax-deductible expense. For simplicity, we have ignored these tax shields in the illustrative calculation of the after-tax cost of debt in this chapter. A detailed discussion of the tax aspects of issue expenses, underwriting costs, and discounts is presented in the bond refunding section of Chapter 21. Finally, Equation 17.1 assumes that the firm will be able to benefit fully from the interest tax shield.

†For a somewhat controversial viewpoint that questions the generally accepted procedure of using the after-tax cost of debt (to reflect the interest tax-shield effect) in calculating a firm's after-tax weighted average cost of capital, see Fred D. Arditti, "The Weighted Average Cost of Capital: Some Questions on Its Definition, Interpretation and Use," *Journal of Finance* 28 (September 1973), pp. 1001–1007; and

A Shortcut for Approximating the Cost of Debt   The cost of long-term debt can also be approximated using a shortcut approach that bypasses the need to find the internal rate of return of the cash flows associated with borrowing. This approach involves determining the average annual outflow, which consists of taking the annual interest plus the amortization of any premium or discount, and dividing this outflow by the average amount borrowed. If

$$I = \text{the annual interest payment in dollars}$$
$$N_b = \text{the net proceeds from the sale of a bond}$$
$$n = \text{the term of the bond in years}$$

then the approximate *before-tax* debt cost for a bond with a $1,000 face value can be found by the following equation:

$$\text{Approximate before-tax debt cost} = \frac{I + \dfrac{\$1,000 - N_b}{n}}{\dfrac{N_b + \$1,000}{2}}$$

The first term in the numerator of the previous equation represents the annual interest, the second term in the numerator represents the annual amortization of any premium or discount, and the denominator represents the average amount borrowed.

EXAMPLE   Substituting the appropriate values from the Jerry Company example into the approximation formula results in an approximate *before-tax* debt cost of 9.39 percent. Converting this value to an after-tax basis using Equation 17.1 results in an approximate after-tax debt cost of 5.63 percent. The accuracy of this approximation can be seen by comparing the approximate value of 5.63 percent to the after-tax debt cost of 5.68 percent calculated earlier. The reader may want to use this approximation in making rough calculations of the after-tax cost of debt.

THE COST OF PREFERRED SHARES*

Preferred shares represent a special type of ownership interest in the firm. Preferred shareholders must receive their *stated* dividends prior to the distribution of any earnings

---

Fred D. Arditti and Haim Levy, "The Weighted Average Cost of Capital as a Cutoff Rate: A Critical Analysis of the Classical Textbook Weighted Average," *Financial Management* 6, No. 1 (Spring 1977), pp. 24–34. Rebuttals to these two articles, however, have demonstrated that there is no real contradiction between the "new" procedure suggested in the two articles and the generally accepted textbook procedure for calculating an after-tax weighted average cost of capital. See, for example, the comments by M. Chapman Findlay III, R. Richardson Pettit, and several others in the *Journal of Finance* 30 (June 1975), pp. 881–889. In addition, for an excellent discussion of the various specifications of a project's cash flows and the cutoff or discount rate that lead to the same accept-reject decision, see Timothy J. Nantell and C. Robert Carlson, "The Cost of Capital as a Weighted Average," *Journal of Finance* 30 (December 1975), pp. 1343–1355; and William Beranek, "The Cost of Capital, Capital Budgeting and Maximization of Shareholder Wealth," *Journal of Financial and Quantitative Analysis* 10 (March 1975), pp. 1–21. Also see problem 14 at the end of this chapter.

*As discussed in Chapter 22, preferred shares are more properly referred to as preference shares.

to common shareholders. Since preferred shares represent a form of ownership, and a business firm is viewed as a "going concern," the proceeds from the sale of preferred shares are expected to be held for an infinite period of time. A complete discussion of the various characteristics of preferred shares will be presented in Chapter 22. However, one aspect of preferred shares that requires clarification at this point is preferred share dividends.

Preferred Share Dividends   The amount of preferred share dividends that must be paid each year before earnings can be distributed to common shareholders may be stated either in dollars or as a percentage of each share's *par*, or *face, value*.

Dollar Amounts   Most preferred dividends are stated as "*x* dollars per year." When dividends are stated this way, the share is often referred to as "*x*-dollar preferred shares." A $4 preferred share is expected to pay preferred shareholders $4 in dividends each year on each preferred share owned.

Percentage Amounts   Sometimes preferred share dividends are stated as an annual percentage rate. This rate represents the percentage of the share's par, or face, value that equals the annual dividend. For instance, a 4-percent preferred share with a $100 par value would be expected to pay an annual dividend of $4 a share. Before calculating the cost of preferred shares, any dividends stated as percentages should be converted into annual dollar dividends.

Calculating the Cost of Preferred Shares   The cost of preferred shares is calculated on the basis of the following considerations: (1) since preferred shares generally have no maturity date,* the stream of expected preferred dividend payments can be viewed as a perpetuity for most classes of preferred shares issued by the firm; (2) preferred dividends can be treated as fixed costs to the firm, since firms ordinarily are not expected to issue preferred shares without intending to pay regular dividends; and (3) since preferred dividend payments are not allowed as a tax-deductible expense to the issuer, they require no tax adjustment.

Given the above considerations, the cost of *new* preferred shares to the firm is given by the discount rate (k_p) that equates the present value of the perpetual and level per-share dividend payment (D_p) with the net proceeds per share (N_p) received by the firm. Thus, using the present value formula for a perpetuity developed in Chapter 13, the (marginal) cost of new preferred shares to the firm can be determined by solving the following equation:

$$N_p = \frac{D_p}{k_p}$$

which gives

$$k_p = \frac{D_p}{N_p} \qquad (17.2)$$

---

*As will be discussed in Chapter 22, firms sometimes issue a class of preferred shares known as *term preferred shares*. These shares either have a *fixed* maturity date or have a number of provisions designed to alter the maturity date or the stated fixed dividend rate. In the present discussion, we are considering only those preferred shares which have no maturity date and have a stated fixed dividend rate.

In accordance with the principles discussed earlier in the chapter, the cost of the firm's *outstanding* preferred shares should be estimated by dividing the per-share dollar dividend by the *current* market price per share. If a firm has more than one class of preferred shares outstanding, then the cost of the preferred shares can be estimated as the weighted average of the current costs of each class of preferred shares.

EXAMPLE   The Eric Company Ltd. intends to sell a $4 preferred share at $100 per share, and expects to incur underwriting and issuing expenses of $3 per share. The net proceeds per share from the sale will equal $97.* If the preferred issue will be a perpetuity, the cost of the preferred issue to the firm, calculated using Equation 17.2, will be equal to 4.12 percent (i.e., $4 ÷ $97).

EXAMPLE   The Jerry Company Ltd. is contemplating issuance of 9-percent preferred shares that are expected to sell for $85.00 per share. The cost of issuing and marketing the shares is expected to be $3.00 per share. The firm would like to determine the cost of the preferred share issue. The first step in finding this cost is to calculate the dollar amount of preferred share dividends, since the dividend is stated as a percentage of the share's $85.00 face value. The annual dollar dividend is $7.65 (i.e., 9% of $85.00). The net proceeds from the proposed sale of shares can be found by subtracting the underwriting costs from the sale price. This gives us a value of $82.00 per share. Substituting the annual dividend, D_p, of $7.65 and the net proceeds, N_p, of $82.00 into Equation 17.2 gives us the cost of preferred shares, which is 9.33 percent (i.e., $7.65 ÷ $82.00). Comparing the Jerry Company's 9.33-percent cost of preferred shares (which is already on an *after-tax* basis, since preferred dividends are not a tax-deductible expense) to its 5.68-percent *after-tax* cost of debt calculated earlier shows that the preferred shares are more expensive. This is generally the case since the interest cost of debt is tax-deductible.†

THE COST OF COMMON EQUITY CAPITAL

The cost of a firm's common equity capital is defined as the minimum rate of return currently required by the firm's common shareholders on their investment, given the firm's current business and financial risks. The cost of common equity is much more difficult to measure than the cost of debt or the cost of preferred shares. Unlike these fixed-income securities, a firm's common shares do not promise a fixed stream of cash

---

*For the sake of simplicity, this calculation ignores the tax shields, if any, associated with the issuing and underwriting expenses on the new preferred issue. The calculations can be easily extended to include such tax effects as may be applicable under the existing tax laws.

†Although investors experience greater risks with preferred shares than with bonds of the same firm, a firm's before-tax cost of preferred shares is now generally lower than that of bonds. This is due to the fact that while interest is taxed at the investor's marginal tax rate, preferred dividends are tax free for intercorporate dividend payments, and the dividend tax credit makes the effective tax rate on dividends very low for investors in the low-marginal tax brackets. However, the firm's after-tax cost of preferred shares is still significantly higher than that of long-term debt. This is due to the fact that interest on long-term debt is tax-deductible, while preferred dividends must be paid from earnings after tax. (See Chapter 2 for a detailed discussion of the dividend tax credit provision under the Canadian Income Tax Act.)

payments. Therefore, the rate of return investors expect on a firm's common shares (and correspondingly, the cost of equity capital to the firm) is entirely dependent on the shareholder's *expectations* as to future performance and risk of the firm.* Since expectations are not directly observable and change over time, the cost of equity capital is a particularly difficult rate to measure. Although several approaches to estimate the cost of equity capital have been suggested, only two of them will be discussed here. The first uses the well-known share price valuation model known as the Gordon valuation model. The second uses the security market line equation discussed in Chapter 16.† As will be shown, both the approaches provide only approximate estimates of the cost of equity, since both approaches make a number of simplifying assumptions and both require that a number of very difficult forecasts be made.

The Gordon Valuation Model and the Cost of Equity Capital   The Gordon share-price valuation model is based on the premise that the value of a share to investors is the present value of *all* future dividends *expected* to be paid by the issuing firm to the holder of the share.‡ Thus, for an ongoing firm,

$$P_0 = \frac{D_1}{(1 + k_e)^1} + \frac{D_2}{(1 + k_e)^2} + \cdots \frac{D_n}{(1 + k_e)^n} + \frac{D_{n+1}}{(1 + k_e)^{n+1}} + \cdots \frac{D_\infty}{(1 + k_e)^\infty} \quad (17.3)$$

where

$$P_0 = \text{the current price (or market value) of a common share}$$
$$D_t(t = 1,\infty) = \text{the per-share dividend expected at the end of year } t \text{ §}$$
$$k_e = \text{the cost of common equity capital (i.e., the shareholders'}$$
$$\text{required rate of return or the rate at which investors discount}$$
$$\text{the expected future per-share dividends to calculate } P_0)$$

Relationship with the "Dividend-Plus-Future-Price" Approach   Valuation Equation 17.3 is consistent with the "dividend-plus-future-price" approach to valuation of common shares. This can be seen by rewriting the equation as follows:

$$P_0 = \frac{D_1}{(1 + k_e)^1} + \frac{D_2}{(1 + k_e)^2} \cdots + \frac{D_n}{(1 + k_e)^n}$$
$$+ \frac{D_{n+1}}{(1 + k_e)^{n+1}} + \frac{D_{n+2}}{(1 + k_e)^{n+2}} + \cdots \frac{D_\infty}{(1 + k_e)^\infty}$$

*The terms *expected rate of return* and the *required rate of return* on common equity capital are often used interchangeably. However, note that these two rates are equal only under conditions of market equilibrium. It is also important to note that the expected rate of return to common shareholders is not an accounting-type cost to the firm. Rather, it is an *opportunity cost* to common shareholders in the sense that they could sell their shares and earn their required rate of return by reinvesting the proceeds from the sale in another common share investment of the same risk class as the present investment.
†Other approaches include the "synthetic approach" (Vickers, Lerner, and Carleton), contingent-claims (option) pricing approach (Black and Scholes), and arbitrage-pricing model (Ross).
‡Not all earnings are paid out as dividends, but it is expected that those earnings that are retained and reinvested will boost future dividends. At infinity a *liquidating*, or final, dividend is expected, which actually represents the distribution of the firm's assets. Since the firm is viewed as a going concern with an infinite life, the liquidating dividend does not have to be specified.
§For the market *as a whole*, $D_t(t = 1,\infty)$ represents the dividends per share expected by the *marginal* (i.e., price-determining) investor.

$$= \frac{D_1}{(1 + k_e)^1} + \frac{D_2}{(1 + k_e)^2} \cdots + \frac{D_n}{(1 + k_e)^n}$$

$$+ \frac{1}{(1 + k_e)^n} \left[\frac{D_{n+1}}{(1 + k_e)^1} + \frac{D_{n+2}}{(1 + k_e)^2} + \cdots \frac{D_\infty}{(1 + k_e)^\infty} \right] \tag{17.4}$$

The bracketed term on the right-hand side of Equation 17.4 represents the discounted value (as of the end of *any* given year n) of the expected per-share dividends from year $n + 1$ and onwards. Therefore, this discounted value represents the expected price per share, P_n, at the end of year n (or alternatively, at the beginning of year $n + 1$), given today's (i.e., time 0) per-share dividend expectations of investors. Thus, Equation 17.4 can be simplified to get:

$$P_0 = \left[\frac{D_1}{(1 + k_e)^1} + \frac{D_2}{(1 + k_e)^2} + \cdots \frac{D_n}{(1 + k_e)^n} \right] + \frac{P_n}{(1 + k_e)^n} \tag{17.5}$$

In words, Equation 17.5 shows that the value of a share to an investor, who expects to sell the share at the end of year n, equals the present value of the expected dividends during the holding period of n years plus the present value of the expected market price of the share at the end of the holding period. Thus, investors' expectations of capital gain or loss (depending on the sign of $P_n - P_0$) are based on their current expectations of future dividends and are *implicitly* embodied in valuation Equation 17.3 and, therefore, in Equation 17.5.

Simplified Form of the Gordon Valuation Model Valuation Equation 17.3 can be solved for k_e, the cost of equity capital, given P_0 (which is easily determined because it is observable) and a forecast of the perpetual dividend stream $D_t(t = 1, \infty)$.* However, in practice, it is extremely difficult to forecast the future dividend stream expected by investors.† If future dividend payments per share are currently expected to grow (or decline) on average at a *constant* compound annual rate g over the firm's life (assumed to be indefinite), then Equation 17.3 can be simplified[1]

if $k_e > g$,

to

$$P_0 = \frac{D_1}{k_e - g} \tag{17.6}$$

Rearranging terms, and solving for k_e, gives

$$k_e = \frac{D_1}{P_0} + g \tag{17.7}$$

---

*Since dividend payments are not allowed as a tax-deductible expense to the firm, they are a cash outflow *after* the payment of corporate income tax. Accordingly, k_e unlike the interest cost of debt, needs no explicit tax adjustment when used in the weighted average cost of capital calculations. Furthermore, k_e will also be risk-adjusted, since investors' uncertainty and therefore risk perception as to future dividends (and price P_n at the end of any year n) is reflected in P_0.

†A firm's dividend payments are discretionary payments (determined by the firm's board of directors). This fact adds to the difficulty of forecasting $D_t(t = 1, \infty)$.

Equation 17.7 can be stated in words as follows: The cost of *existing* equity capital to the firm is equal to the expected *dividend yield* for the current year (i.e., D_1/P_0), plus the expected constant perpetual dividend growth (or decline) rate g. Of course, Equation 17.7 will provide a realistic estimate of k_e only if the expectations of investors are such that the per-share dividends, on average, are expected to grow (or decline) perpetually at a constant rate. For example, such an assumption is reasonable if a firm had a consistent per-share dividend growth rate in the past, and there are reasons to believe that the trend will continue indefinitely into the future.* Also, it is important to note that g, and therefore k_e, will reflect investors' current expectations of future inflationary increases in the firm's sales revenues and operating costs.†

EXAMPLE The Jerry Company Ltd. wishes to estimate its cost of common share equity capital, k_e. The prevailing market price, P_0, of its common shares is $50 per share. The firm expects to pay a dividend per share, D_1, of $1.50 at the end of 19X8. The dividends paid on the outstanding common shares over the past six years are given below. It is expected that this past pattern of dividend payments will continue indefinitely into the future.

Year	Dividend per share
19X7	$1.37
19X6	1.25
19X5	1.13
19X4	1.03
19X3	0.95
19X2	0.85

Although six dividend payments are shown, they represent only five years of growth. The average growth rate, g, of the per-share dividends over the five-year period (from 19X2 to 19X7) is given by $.85 (1 + g)^5 = 1.37, which gives $(1 + g)^5$ or *CVIF* = 1.61 (i.e., $1.37/$0.85). Looking across Table A-1 (given at the end of the text) for the compound-value interest factor, *CVIF*, for five years, the factor closest to 1.61 occurs at 10 percent. Therefore, the average historical annual growth rate g over the past five years equals 10 percent,‡ which is expected to

---

*Conceptually, the constant growth rate assumption is reasonable when a firm raises no new external capital and retains a constant proportion b of its annual earnings for reinvestment at an average rate of return r. Under these circumstances Equation 17.7 becomes

$$k_e = \frac{(1 - b)E_0}{P_0} + br$$

where E_0 is the current earnings per share and br is the perpetual long-run average growth rate g in per-share dividends (and earnings, since b is assumed to be constant). This result, developed by Gordon, is sometimes used to estimate g for firms with historically stable b and r. However, note that a necessary condition for the validity of this equation is that $br < k_e$. This, in turn, implies that for $0 < b < 1$ (i.e., for any positive retention rate b, which is less than 100 percent), r can be less than or equal to k_e, or greater than k_e, but it cannot be $\geq k_e/b$.

†Recall the discussion in the section on capital budgeting under inflation in Chapter 15 where we pointed out that the discount rate (the cost of capital) needs no explicit adjustment for anticipated inflation since market rates take into account inflationary expectations.

‡Techniques for finding growth rates using CVIF Table A-1 were discussed in Chapter 13.

continue for the foreseeable future. Substituting $D_1 = \$1.50$, $P_0 = \$50$, and $g = .10$ into Equation 17.7 results in the cost of Jerry Company's *existing* equity capital as calculated in the following equation:

$$k_e = \frac{\$1.50}{\$50} + .10$$

$$= .03 + .10 = 13 \text{ percent}$$

Model Application: Nondividend-Paying Growth Companies   The expected dividend growth factor, g, in Equation 17.7 is also the expected share-price growth rate or *capital gains rate*.* This can be illustrated by the following example.

EXAMPLE   Assume that the Jerry Company Ltd., which was discussed in the preceding example, actually pays D_1, the expected \$1.50 dividend per share at the end of 19X8. Then the *currently expected* market price P_1, at the end of 19X8 (i.e., after the payment of D_1), can be calculated by using the share-price valuation Equation 17.6 (i.e., the Gordon valuation model). Substituting $k_e = .13$ (which was calculated in the preceding example), D_2 (i.e., the currently expected per-share dividend at the end of 19X9) $= \$1.50 (1 + .10) = \$1.65$, and $g = .10$ into Equation 17.6 gives $P_1 = \$55$ (i.e., \$1.65/.13 $-$ .10). Thus, given investors' present (i.e., end of 19X7) expectation of g, the share price is expected to grow from now to the end of 19X8 by 10 percent (i.e., (\$55 $-$ \$50)/\$50). This *presently* expected 10-percent rate of price appreciation represents the presently expected capital gains rate. It is equal to the expected 10-percent per share dividend growth rate. This result will hold for any holding period horizon of n years.[2] The calculations involved in the example can be diagrammed as follows:

year-end 19X7	year-end 19X8	year-end 19X9
↑ _current year_ ↑	↑	↑
$P_0 = \$50 \longrightarrow$	$D_1 = \$1.50 \longrightarrow$	$D_2 = \$1.50 (1 + .10)$
$k_e = \dfrac{\$1.50}{\$50} + .10$	Expected $P_1 = \dfrac{\$1.65}{.13 - .10}$	$= \$1.65$
$= .03 + .10 = .13$	$= \$55$	

Note that P_1 is the expected market price based on investors' *present* expectations of the perpetually growing per-share dividend stream $D_2, D_3, \ldots D_{n-1}, D_n, \ldots$. The share price at the end of 19X8 will equal the currently expected price $P_1 = \$55$ only if there is no change in the expectation regarding $D_2, D_3, \ldots$ from now till the end of 19X8.

The preceding example shows that Equation 17.7 can also be written as

$$k_e = \frac{D_1}{P_0} + \text{expected capital gains (or loss) rate} \qquad (17.8)$$

---

*As indicated earlier, this is implicit in Equation 17.5, which was derived from general share-price valuation Equation 17.3.

Equation 17.8 can be used to provide an explanation of why shares of corporations that pay no dividends command positive market prices. This occurs because the shareholders of corporations that presently pay no dividends expect to earn their required rate of return primarily through capital gains; that is, they expect the reinvestment of earnings by the nondividend-paying firm to increase future dividends and thereby increase the terminal value of their shares.

Although Equation 17.7 (when stated in the equivalent form 17.8) provides a plausible explanation of why shares of a nondividend-paying corporation command a positive market value, it cannot easily be applied to estimate k_e of such a corporation. In order to apply Equation 17.7 to such companies, the analyst faces an extremely difficult task of estimating the timing and amounts of ultimate dividend payments. In fact, this dividend may be a liquidating dividend at some future distant date when either the assets of the firm are liquidated, or the firm as a going concern is sold in the market place.

One approximate way to deal with this estimation problem is to estimate the historical growth rate in the market price per share of the nondividend-paying firm* and use this rate as a proxy for the rate of return investors expect to receive from the growth in the market price of their shares. Since the presently nondividend-paying firm's expected future per-share dividend payments are reflected in its expected share-price growth rate, the historical growth rate in the market price per share of the company can be used as an approximation of its cost of equity capital.† Such a procedure, however, should not be applied to companies that clearly cannot be expected to sustain their past high growth rate indefinitely into the future.

EXAMPLE   The Phyllis Informatics Inc., a firm engaged in the fast-growing mini-computer business, has historically reinvested all of its earnings and has paid no dividends to its shareholders. Since the company's opportunities for profitable reinvestment of its earnings are expected to continue unchanged for the foreseeable future, investors do not expect the company to pay dividends for a long period of time in the future. The market price per share of the company's common shares over the past five years has appreciated at an average annual compound rate of 15 percent. Based on such factors as the general projection of sales and profit margins in the mini-computer business,‡ investors expect the historical 15-percent average growth rate in the price of the company's shares to continue into the distant future. Since the company is not expected to pay dividends for the foreseeable future, the 15-percent share-price growth rate can be used as an approximation of the shareholder's expected rate of return. This value is equal to the company's cost of equity capital.

*Such estimates, for example, are often made by institutional investors and pension fund portfolio managers seeking growth stock portfolios.
†Alternatively, under certain circumstances, the past trend in *earnings* per share may be satisfactorily used to predict the expected future growth rate in dividends. For example, young firms generally finance their initial growth predominantly through the retention of earnings. Therefore, future dividend expectations of investors in these firms are typically based on the past trend in the earnings of these firms rather than on the past trend in their dividend payments.
‡Such projections are commonly used by professional security analysts for developing forecasts of earnings and dividend growth rates of major companies.

Model Application: Companies with Varying Growth Rates   The constant perpetual growth assumption of the Gordon valuation model may be roughly accurate for some companies, particularly those with a low to moderate current growth rate. However, for others, future business prospects may be such that the extrapolation of their past rate of growth into the future would be clearly inappropriate. For these companies, the general valuation Equation 17.3 must be modified in order to estimate k_e. This is illustrated in the following example.

EXAMPLE   Talwar International Inc. is currently trading at $100 per share. The company has just paid a dividend, D_0, of $5 per share. The company's future per-share dividend payments are expected to grow at a rate of 10 percent for the next five years and afterwards at a rate of 6 percent in perpetuity. Under these circumstances, Talwar's cost of equity capital can be obtained by solving the following equation for k_e:*

$$\$100 = \frac{\$5(1 + .10)}{(1 + k_e)} + \frac{\$5(1 + .10)^2}{(1 + k_e)^2} + \frac{\$5(1 + .10)^3}{(1 + k_e)^3}$$

$$+ \frac{\$5(1 + .10)^4}{(1 + k_e)^4} + \frac{\$5(1 + .10)^5}{(1 + k_e)^5}$$

$$+ \left[\frac{\$5(1 + .10)^5 (1 + .06)^1}{(1 + k_e)^6} + \frac{\$5(1 + .10)^5 (1 + .06)^2}{(1 + k_e)^7} \right.$$

$$\left. + \cdots \frac{\$5(1 + .10)^5 (1 + .06)^\infty}{(1 + k_e)^\infty} \right]$$

Complicated equations such as the above can easily be programmed and should be solved by the financial manager on a computer terminal.

Model Application: Mature Companies   If investors expect per-share dividends to be a constant amount D dollars per year in the future (i.e., if expected $g = 0$), the Equation 17.7 simply reduces to

$$k_e = \frac{D}{P_0} \tag{17.9}$$

A firm's annual per-share dividend payments will remain constant in the future only if two conditions are met. First, the firm's future annual earnings (i.e., after the deductions of interest, depreciation, and taxes) must remain at their current level E_0. Second, the firm must pay out *all* of its earnings in dividends. Thus, the cost of equity capital to

*The last term in the equation, $[\$5(1 + .10)^5 (1 + .06)^\infty]/(1 + k_e)^\infty$, will approach zero only if the expected 6-percent dividend growth rate beyond the fifth year is less than k_e. If this condition is satisfied, then the right-hand side of the equation will be an infinite convergent geometric series, and the equation will yield a meaningful solution because the sum of the bracketed expression with an infinite series of terms will converge to $[\$5(1 + .10)^5 (1 + .06)]/[(1 + k_e)^5 (k_e - .06)]$.

a nongrowth firm, expected to pay a constant annual dividend per share in the future, can be estimated by its current earnings-to-price ratio, E_0/P_0.*

Model Application: Declining Companies   As is shown in the following example, Equation 17.7 can be used to estimate k_e for companies that have a perpetual constant rate of decline of dividends per share.

EXAMPLE   Horse and Buggy Manufacturing Inc. wishes to determine the cost of its existing common share equity capital, k_e. The prevailing market price of its common shares is $6.50 per share. Investors expect the firm to pay a dividend per share, D_1, of $1.50 at the end of the current year. The dividends paid on the outstanding common shares over the past six years have decreased at an average annual rate of 10 percent and are expected to continue to decline at this rate in the future. Substituting $D_1 = \$1.50$, $P_0 = \$6.50$, and $g = -.10$ into Equation 17.7 results in the cost of common equity, calculated as follows:

$$k_e = \frac{\$1.50}{\$6.50} + (-.10)$$

$$= .23 - .10$$

$$= .13$$

Although the 13-percent cost of the Horse and Buggy's existing common share equity capital is the same as that of the Jerry Company (calculated in an earlier example), we find that there is a major difference in the makeup of that return for the common share investors in the two companies. For example, Horse and Buggy's common shareholders that have a one-year holding period horizon expect their return to consist of a 23-percent dividend yield and a 10-percent capital *loss*;[3] while in the case of the Jerry Company, investors with an identical one-year horizon expect their return to consist of a 3-percent dividend yield and a 10-percent capital *gain*. It is not uncommon for a declining firm (e.g., a firm mining a single depletable ore body) to pay a relatively large annual dividend yield to its investors.†

The above result for the Horse and Buggy Company can be obtained as follows. Horse and Buggy's shareholders currently expect the price per share at the end of their one-year holding period to be equal to:

$$P_1 = \frac{D_2}{k_e - g} = \frac{D_1(1 + g)}{k_e - g} = \frac{\$1.50(1 - .10)}{.13 - (-.10)} = \frac{\$1.35}{.23} = \$5.87$$

This gives a currently expected *capital loss* rate of ($6.50 − $5.87)/$6.50, which equals 10 percent (except for a minor rounding off error). Thus, the one-year holding period expected return

---

*This also applies to a firm that, instead of paying out all of its earnings in dividends, reinvests a proportion of the earnings in investments with $NPV = 0$; that is, reinvests its retained earnings at a rate of return just equal to its cost of capital.

†For example, the indicated dividend yield for Pine Point Mines Ltd., as reported in the *Financial Post* on July 5, 1980, was 20.9 percent (i.e., an indicated dollar dividend of $7.00 divided by the week's closing share price of $33½). For the year ended December 31, 1979, Pine Point Mines, a company mining a single ore body in the Northwest Territories, had earnings of $9.52 per share. Similarly, the indicated dividend yields for Gibraltar Mines and Vestgron Mines were 17.6 and 22.5 percent, respectively.

equals the expected dividend yield of 23 percent for the current year *minus* the expected capital loss rate of 10 percent on a share investment over the year. The calculations in the example can be diagrammed as follows:

year-end 0   year-end 1   year-end 2

$k_e = \dfrac{D_1}{P_0} + g$ ⟶ $D_1 = \$1.50$ ⟶ $D_2 = \$1.50(1 - .10)$

current year (holding period)

$= \dfrac{\$1.50}{\$6.50} + (-.10)$ $P_1 = \dfrac{\$1.35}{.13 - (-.10)}$ $= \$1.35$

$= .23 - .10 = .13$ $= \$5.87$ (approx.)

Using the CAPM to Measure the Cost of Common Equity Capital   Another approach for measuring k_e, the cost of a firm's existing common equity capital, involves the use of the capital asset pricing model, CAPM, which was described in Chapter 16. Using the security market line equation developed in Chapter 16, we can depict the relationship between the shareholders' required rate of return (which represents the firm's cost of existing common equity capital k_e) and the firm's nondiversifiable risk, as reflected by its index of nondiversifiable or systematic risk, by the following equation.*

$$k_e = R_F + [E(k_m) - R_F] \cdot b \qquad (17.10)$$

where

$R_F =$ The required rate of return on a risk-free
security, which is commonly measured by the yield on a
short-term Canadian government security such as
a treasury bill.

$E(k_m) =$ The expected rate of return on the market portfolio
of assets that can be measured as the average rate
of return on a well-diversified portfolio.
The Toronto Stock Exchange's 300 Stock Composite Index
(TSE-300) is commonly used to measure $E(k_m)$.

$b =$ The nondiversifiable or systematic risk or beta
of the firm's common shares.

From the discussion of CAPM in Chapter 16, it should follow that a firm's beta measures the firm's nondiversifiable risk in terms of the covariance of the return on the firm's common shares with the return on the market portfolio. It should also be noted that the CAPM approach can also be used to estimate the specific costs of preferred

---

*For a more complete development and discussion of CAPM, refer back to the discussion of risk and return in Chapter 16. Comparison of Equation 17.10 and Equation 16.5 will show a few minor differences in notation. These were made merely to simplify the current discussion of the cost of capital; they do not alter the model in any way.

shares and debt. However, most of the practical applications of the CAPM have involved only common shares. Several large U.S. institutional investors are reportedly using beta values in their investment portfolio decisions.[4]

EXAMPLE   The Jerry Company, which calculated its cost of common equity capital, k_e, using the Gordon model in a preceding example, also wishes to calculate this cost using the capital asset pricing model, CAPM. From information provided the firm by its investment advisors along with the firm's own analyses, it is found that the risk-free rate, R_F, equals 7.00 percent; the firm's beta, b, equals 1.50; and the average rate of return on the TSE–300, as an approximation of $E(k_m)$, equals 11.00 percent. Substituting these values into the CAPM (i.e., Equation 17.10), they have estimated the cost of common equity capital, k_e, as follows:

$$k_e = 7.00\% + 1.50(11.00\% - 7.00\%) = 7.00\% + 6.00\% = 13.00\%$$

The 13.00-percent cost of common equity capital represents the required return of investors on the Jerry Company common shares. This required return, which is the same as that found using the Gordon model in a preceding example,* represents the return that must be earned by investors in order to adequately compensate them for the nondiversifiable or relevant risk of the firm. The 13.00-percent cost of common equity capital can be viewed as consisting of a 7.00-percent risk-free rate plus a 6.00-percent risk premium, which reflects the fact that the Jerry Company's common share investors' return is 1.50 times more volatile than that on the market portfolio.

The Cost of New Issues of Common Shares   Since our purpose in finding the firm's overall cost of capital is to determine the after-tax cost of *new* funds required for financing projects, attention must be given to the cost of *new* issues of common shares. Two methods for finding the current cost of existing common shares were described in the preceding parts of this section. Assuming that new funds are raised over time in the same proportions as those given by the firm's target capital structure, the only additional data required for finding the cost of new common share issues are the underwriting and selling costs associated with them. It is quite likely that, in order to sell a new common share issue, the sale price will have to be below the current market price (i.e., *underpriced*), thereby causing the per-share net proceeds from the sale of shares to be less than the current market price, P_o. Another factor that may reduce these proceeds is an underwriting fee paid for marketing the new issue.†

The cost of new issues of common shares can easily be calculated by introducing the percentage reduction in the current market price attributable to *flotation costs* (i.e.,

---

*The agreement between the cost of common equity capital, k_e, of 13.00 percent calculated using CAPM and the 13.00-percent cost found earlier using the Gordon model has been intentionally so arranged in order to avoid any problems that may arise from differing values. In actual situations, the cost of common equity capital, calculated using these alternate approaches, will not necessarily agree due to certain underlying differences in the models.

†These aspects are discussed in greater detail in Chapter 19.

underpricing costs and underwriting fees after the appropriate tax adjustments have been made)* into the Gordon model equation for determining the cost of existing common shares k_e. If we let f represent the after-tax *percentage* reduction in the current market price expected as a result of underpricing and underwriting charges on a new common share issue, the cost of the new issue, k_c, can be expressed as follows:

$$k_c = \frac{D_1}{(1 - f)P_0} + g \qquad (17.11)$$

The cost of new equity issues will be greater than the cost of existing equity as long as f in Equation 17.11 is greater than zero.† Also note that $(1 - f)P_0$ represents the (after-tax) *net proceeds* from the sale of a new issue of common shares. It is sometimes more convenient to substitute the dollar amount of net proceeds into the denominator rather than calculate the flotation percentage, f.

EXAMPLE   In the example using the Gordon model, an expected dividend, D_1, of $1.50, a current market price, P_0, of $50.00, and an expected growth rate of dividends, g, of 10.00 percent, were used to calculate the Jerry Company's cost of existing common share equity capital, k_e, which was found to be 13.00 percent. In order to determine its cost of a new common share issue, k_c, the Jerry Company with the aid of its advisors have estimated that on average new shares can be sold for $49.00. The $1.00 per-share (i.e., $50.00 per-share market price–$49.00 per-share average sale price) underpricing is necessary due to the competitive nature of the market for securities. A second cost associated with a new issue is an after-tax underwriting fee of $0.75 per share. The total after-tax flotation costs per share are therefore expected to be $1.75 (i.e., $1.00 per-share underpricing plus $0.75 per-share after-tax underwriting costs).

Expressing the dollar flotation cost of $1.75 per share as a percentage of the current market price of $50.00 per share results in a flotation percentage, f, of 3.50 percent (i.e., $1.75 per share ÷ $50.00 per share). Substituting f = 3.50 percent, D_1 = $1.50, P_0 = $50.00, and g =

*Under certain conditions, underwriting and issue expenses on new common share issues may be permitted as a tax-deductible expense to the firm. To simplify the exposition here and to concentrate on the development of a basic framework for analysis, we are assuming that all the appropriate tax adjustments of the underwriting and issue costs have been made. A detailed discussion of the tax treatment of underwriting and issue costs on new issues of securities is presented in Chapters 19 and 21.

†Underwriting and issue costs increase the marginal costs of a firm's specific sources of capital and therefore increase the firm's overall cost of capital used as a discount rate for evaluating the firm's new average-risk investments. However, since the underwriting and issue costs do *not* affect the timing, magnitude, or riskiness of a project's future operating cash flows, the appropriate discount rate, which, in principle, must be commensurate with the riskiness of the project's cash flows, should also be independent of the underwriting and issue costs. Accordingly, the generally accepted procedure of adjusting the component marginal costs of funds (and therefore adjusting the overall cost of funds as a discount rate) becomes somewhat questionable. For a rigorous development of this point and its implications for DCF evaluations of investment projects, see John R. Ezzel and R. Burr Porter, "Flotation Costs and the Weighted Average Cost of Capital," *Journal of Financial and Quantitative Analysis* (September 1976), pp. 403–413.

10.00 percent into Equation 17.11 results in a cost of new common shares, k_c, shown as follows:

$$k_c = \frac{\$1.50}{(1 - .0350) \cdot (\$50.00)} + .10 = \frac{\$1.50}{\$48.25} + .10 = .031 + .10$$

$$= .1310$$

$$= 13.10\% \text{ (approximately)}$$

Since the common share dividends are paid from after-tax cash flows, no further tax adjustment is required.

The Cost of Retained Earnings   Firms frequently finance a large proportion of their long-term capital investments internally out of retained earnings.* Since earnings not retained for reinvestment would be paid out in dividends to common shareholders, the use of retained earnings by a firm is equivalent to the use of additional equity capital obtained from the firm's existing common shareholders. A firm's cost of retained earnings must, therefore, be viewed in terms of the rate of return the firm's shareholders currently require on the firm's common equity. In other words, the use of retained earnings by a firm involves an *opportunity cost* to its shareholders in that they could have received the earnings as dividends and purchased additional shares in this or other firms of comparable risk to earn their expected or required rate of return. Thus, conceptually, the cost of retained earnings, k_r, to a firm can be defined as the rate of return, k_e, that shareholders' currently require on the firm's common equity. That is,

$$k_r = k_e \tag{17.12}$$

Note that k_e equals the cost of the firm's existing common equity capital. It is not necessary to adjust the cost of retained earnings for underwriting and issue costs. By obtaining new equity capital from retained earnings, the firm bypasses these costs.

EXAMPLE   The cost of the Jerry Company's existing common share equity capital, k_e, was calculated to be 13.00 percent in an earlier example. Based on Equation 17.12, the Jerry Company's (opportunity) cost of retained earnings, k_r, also equals 13.00 percent. Thus, the Jerry Company's cost of retained earnings is lower than the cost of a new common share issue that was calculated earlier to be equal to 13.10 percent. The reason is the absence of flotation costs in financing projects with retained earnings.

Moreover, the actual cost of retained earnings (in an opportunity cost sense) will tend to be less than the shareholders' required rate of return, k_e. The reason is that if a shareholder is paid

---

Retained earnings refer to the part of the firm's *current* earnings that are plowed back into the business for reinvestment, and not to the balance sheet retained earnings account that represents the total of all earnings retained by the firm up to the present point in time.

dividends, he or she generally would have to first pay taxes on the dividends* and then pay brokerage fees in order to reinvest the *after-tax* dividend income to earn his or her required rate of return, k_e. To illustrate these considerations, let us assume that a firm is contemplating distribution of its current year's earnings in dividends; that all of its shareholders pay the same effective marginal tax rate, t (i.e., the marginal tax rate net of the dividend tax credit) on their dividend receipts; and that all of the firm's shareholders will incur an average per-dollar brokerage cost, b, in reinvesting their after-tax dividend income. Given these assumptions, each shareholder will be able to reinvest only a fraction, $[(1 - t)(1 - b)(\$1)]$, of each dollar paid in dividends by the firm. This implies that if the firm were to retain its current year's earnings, it would need to earn a rate of return of only $(1 - t)(1 - b)k_e$ on the retained earnings in order to leave its shareholders as well off as they would be if the earnings were paid out and reinvested by the shareholders themselves to earn their required rate of return, k_e, on investments of similar risk as the firm. In other words, the firm's internal opportunity cost, k_{re}, of retaining its current earnings will be given by

$$k_{re} = k_e(1 - t)(1 - b) \tag{17.13}$$

The value of k_{re} is less than the value of k_e whenever t and/or b are greater than zero.

EXAMPLE   If the effective marginal tax rate on the dividend income of shareholders in the Jerry Company is 20 percent and the average brokerage fees are 3 percent, then the cost of retained earnings for the company can be found by substituting the appropriate values into Equation 17.13 as follows:

$$k_{re} = (.1300)(1 - .20)(1 - .03) = (.1300)(.80)(.97) = .1009 = 10.09\%$$

The resulting cost of retained earnings of 10.09 percent is greater than the 9.33-percent cost of preferred shares, but less than the 13.10-percent cost of new common share equity calculated earlier. This type of cost relationship generally prevails.

The previous equation provides a useful insight. It shows that retained earnings may provide a cheaper source of financing than floating a new common share issue. However, the simplifying assumptions made in developing the equation should not be overlooked. First, the analysis ignores the possibility that reinvestment of earnings may increase the market value of the firm's shares (barring changes in the general level of share prices), and therefore that the shareholders might have to pay capital gains taxes if they were to

---

*As noted in Chapter 2, dividends received by individual shareholders from taxable Canadian corporations are subject to taxation. However, due to the provision of the dividend tax credit, which is available to all individual investors, the *effective* marginal tax rate (i.e., the marginal tax rate net of the dividend tax credit) on the dividend income becomes progressively lower with decreasing marginal tax rates and is reduced to zero for individuals in very low income tax brackets. On the other hand, the effective marginal tax rate on the dividend income of individuals in very high income tax brackets may nearly equal the applicable marginal tax rate.

sell their shares.[5] Second, it was assumed that each of the firm's shareholders will be subject to the same effective marginal tax rate on his or her dividend income. While this assumption may be an acceptable approximation for closely held firms, it is not likely to be the case for firms with widely dispersed shareholdings—that is, in a situation where the common shareholders of a firm face widely varying effective tax rates on their dividend incomes. In these circumstances Equation 17.13 can only be used to obtain a rough estimate of a firm's k_{re} by using, for example, an estimate of the effective tax rate of the firm's "typical" shareholder or the average effective tax rate of the firm's controlling shareholders. Alternatively, due to the difficulty of estimating the average tax rate of shareholders and estimating the percentage brokerage cost, practitioners often use Equation 17.12 (i.e., $k_r = k_e$), recognizing that it will provide an overly conservative estimate of the opportunity cost of retained earnings. Similarly, in subsequent sections of this chapter, a firm's cost of retained earnings will be estimated using Equation 17.12, which gives $k_r = k_e$.

Checking the Accuracy of the Cost of Equity Capital Estimates As noted before, the cost of equity capital can never be determined precisely, because factors such as the expected growth rate of dividends are unobservable and must be forecasted. Thus, a financial manager will want to "check" the accuracy of his or her estimates. For users of the Gordon valuation model, two methods of making such a check are (1) an investor-opinion survey, and (2) the use of the security market line, which was discussed in the previous section.

Obviously, the first method is the most direct means of determining the rate of return investors require on an investment in the common equity of the firm.[6] Two disadvantages of investor-opinion surveys are (1) cost, and (2) the fact that the results are strictly a measure of investors' expectations on the date of the survey.* If the firm's business risk and/or financial risk changes subsequent to the date of the survey, the usefulness of the survey findings are lessened. Thus, this technique may be most useful for mature, stable firms such as public utilities.

THE COST OF DEPRECIATION

For many firms, particularly capital-intensive firms such as public utilities, depreciation charges are a significant source of funds for financing new investments. Although such funds, unlike the firm's other sources of capital, do not appear on the liability side of the balance sheet, they should not be regarded as costless to the firm for the following reason: Depreciation represents a gradual recovery of the capital that was invested in the past. The original investment was financed out of the firm's common pool of funds, which by assumption is maintained at the constant long-run target proportions of each source of capital used by the firm. Thus, the use of depreciation-generated funds involves a cost to the firm equal to the firm's overall or weighted average cost of capital.

*A firm could minimize the cost of conducting such a survey if the firm restricted its survey to present owners or shareholders and the survey questionnaire was mailed as part of the mailing of the annual report to the firm's owners or shareholders.

Alternatively, if the firm has no profitable investments on the horizon, it can distribute its depreciation-generated funds in such a way that it keeps its capital structure (and therefore its financial risk) unchanged.* In so doing, the firm's remaining capital would still have a percentage cost equal to its weighted average cost of capital. Moreover, the firm's future financing charges would be reduced by an amount equal to the weighted average cost of capital multiplied by the amount of the depreciation-generated funds distributed. In this sense, the use of depreciation-generated funds for reinvestment can be viewed as involving a percentage opportunity cost to the firm which is equal to its weighted average cost of capital.

Interestingly, the preceding discussion suggests that the inclusion of depreciation as a specific source of capital will have no effect on the calculation of the firm's weighted average cost of capital based on the firm's nondepreciation sources of capital. For this reason, depreciation as a source of capital is ignored in calculating the firm's overall cost of capital.

EXAMPLE   Suppose a firm's current capital structure (excluding depreciation as a source of capital) consists of $2 million of debt with a current cost of 10 percent and $3 million of common equity with a current cost of 15 percent. Also assume that these proportions of debt and equity are close to the firm's long-run optimal target proportions. Then the firm's weighted average cost of capital excluding consideration of depreciation will equal 13 percent {i.e., [($2 million/$5 million) · .10] + [($3 million/$5 million) · .15] }. Now suppose that the firm's accumulated depreciation currently equals $1 million. If this amount is included as an additional source of capital with an (opportunity) cost of 13 percent, then the firm's weighted average cost of capital will be calculated as

$$\frac{\$2 \text{ million}}{\$6 \text{ million}} \cdot .10 + \frac{\$3 \text{ million}}{\$6 \text{ million}} \cdot .15 + \frac{\$1 \text{ million}}{\$6 \text{ million}} \cdot .13$$

$$= \frac{.10}{3} + \frac{.15}{2} + \frac{.13}{6}$$

$$= .13$$

which equals the 13-percent weighted average cost of capital calculated without using depreciation as a source of funds.†

*Distribution of depreciation-generated funds in this manner implies that the firm would be decreasing its scale without altering its financial risk.
†Note that although, for illustrative purposes, we have used specific figures in the example, the result is a general one because any average value (the weighted average cost of capital in the present case) remains unaltered when subjected to a marginal increase (or decrease) equal to the average value. Also note that since the use of depreciation-generated funds, like financing through retained earnings, enables the firm to avoid the various underwriting and issuing costs associated with the issuance of new securities, the cost of depreciation-generated funds to the firm equals the weighted average cost of the firm's *existing* capital sources.

Calculating the Weights or Proportions

After the explicit marginal opportunity costs of specific sources of capital have been estimated, the proportions or weights to be used in calculating the firm's overall or weighted average cost of existing or new capital must be calculated. As pointed out earlier, the proportions used should be consistent with the firm's long-run financing policy (i.e., with the firm's long-run target capital structure), even though in the short run the firm may deviate temporarily from its target proportions because of certain practical considerations. How to calculate the firm's long-run target proportions is an important and somewhat controversial problem. One way to address the problem is to assume that the firm's existing historical target structure is close to its long-run target capital structure and then to use the proportions embodied in the existing capital structure. However, implementing this approach results in still another problem: Should the existing proportions be measured in terms of their book values using the firm's balance sheet or should they be measured in terms of their current market values? Resolving this problem will be the subject of the remainder of this section.

BOOK VALUE WEIGHTS

The use of book value weights assumes that the firm's new financing will be directed toward maintaining over time the same proportions of each source of capital as the firm currently has on its balance sheet. Book value weights are commonly used to estimate the weighted average cost of the firm's existing capital, particularly by external analysts who generally have to rely on public financial information. For example, regulatory commissions in establishing a fair rate of return for the regulated firm, often approximate the firm's weighted average cost of capital by using the firm's published financial statements. The calculations involved in estimating a firm's book value weighted average cost of capital for evaluating new investments are illustrated in the following example.

EXAMPLE   Earlier in the chapter the costs of the Jerry Company's various sources of financing were calculated to be as follows:

After-tax cost of debt, $k_i = 5.68$ percent

Cost of preferred shares, $k_p = 9.33$ percent

Cost of new common shares, $k_c = 13.10$ percent

Cost of retained earnings, $k_r = 13.0$ percent*

First, notice that since we are interested in the calculation of the Jerry Company's weighted average cost of capital for evaluating *new* investments, in keeping with the principle of using the marginal costs discussed earlier, the relevant cost of equity capital to use in the weighted average cost of capital calculation will be the relatively higher 13.10-percent marginal cost of the new

*As indicated earlier at the end of the discussion of cost of retained earnings, 13 percent is a conservative estimate of the cost of retained earnings to the firm under discussion.

common shares rather than the 13.0-percent (opportunity) cost of equity capital drawn from retained earnings.* The book values of the Jerry Company's capital sources and their weights are shown in Table 17.2. Using these book value weights and the marginal costs of the company's debt, preferred share and new common shares given above, the weighted average cost of capital for evaluating the company's new average-risk investments will be calculated as .30 · .0568 + .20 .0933 + .50 · .1310 = .1012 or 10.12 percent. The book values in column 1 of Table 17.2 are taken from the Jerry Company's balance sheet (not shown here). In view of the 10.12-percent cost of capital, the firm should accept all average-risk projects with an expected internal rate of return greater than 10.12 percent or, alternatively, all average-risk projects whose net present value at the discount rate of 10.12 percent is positive.

Table 17.2 Book Value Weights of the Jerry Company's Capital Sources

Source of capital	Book value (1)	Weight (percentage of total book value of capital) (2)
Long-term debt	$15,000,000	.30
Preferred shares	10,000,000	.20
Equity: 800,000 shares at $25 each	25,000,000	.50
Retained earnings $5,000,000		

MARKET VALUE WEIGHTS

Although book value weights are often used in practice, their use can be questioned on theoretical grounds. A major criticism is that as historical figures they reflect sunk costs and are therefore irrelevant for current financial decisions. On the other hand, the current market values of a firm's capital sources reflect the rates of return investors *currently* require on the firm's securities, given the firm's present business and financial risks. Thus, a weighted average cost, computed using market value proportions and current market rates (after they have been adjusted for relevant tax effects), provides a conceptually appealing and the best current estimate of the appropriate measure of the firm's cost of capital. Such a measure recognizes the fact that the return relevant to the firm's owners and creditors is the return on the market values and not on the book values of the firm's outstanding securities. Therefore, when the book values of a firm's existing capital components differ significantly from the market values, the use of book value weights will seriously misstate the firm's "true" cost of capital. The following example illustrates this point.

*Obviously, if a firm plans to issue no new common shares and the equity portion of its new financings is expected to be drawn entirely from its retained earnings, then the cost of retained earnings, k_r, will be the appropriate measure of the firm's cost of equity capital to be included in calculating its new average-risk investments.

EXAMPLE   Using the Jerry Company data presented earlier, along with the market values of the firm's sources of capital, gives us the firm's weighted average cost of capital (developed in Table 17.3) for evaluating the firm's new investments.

The firm's common shares, reflecting the firm's growth potential perceived by investors, are currently trading at $50 per share. The firm's debt capital, however, has a market value practically equal to its book value because its initial yield-to-maturity equals the current yield-to-maturity on comparable debt instruments.* Notice that the market value of the firm's equity capital in Table 17.3 is shown only as the market value of the firm's common shares rather than as common shares plus retained earnings as in Table 17.2. This is done because retained earnings are already reflected in the market value of the firm's common shares.† The weighted average cost of capital of 10.71 percent computed with the market value weights is greater than the 10.12-percent weighted average cost of capital calculated using book value weights. This usually is the case whenever the market value of a firm's equity capital exceeds its book value (as in the present example). This is so because generally the relatively more expensive equity capital receives a greater weight in the market value weighted average cost of capital calculation. If the book value weighted average cost of capital were used, some projects would be accepted that would be unacceptable based on the market value approach. For example, an average-risk project with a 10.50-percent internal rate of return would be accepted using the book value weighted average cost of capital of 10.12 percent, while the same project would be rejected using the market value weighted average cost of capital of 10.71 percent.

Table 17.3   Calculation of the Weighted Average Cost of Capital for the Jerry Company Ltd. Using Market Value Weights

Source of capital	Market value (1)	Percentage of total market value of capital (2)	Cost (3)	Weighted cost (2) · (3) (4)
Long-term debt	$15,000,000	21.4%	5.68%	1.216%
Preferred shares	15,000,000	21.4	9.33	2.000
Equity: 800,000 common shares at $50 each	40,000,000	57.2	13.10	7.490
	$70,000,000	100.0%		10.710% (approximately)
Weighted average cost of capital is 10.71%.				

Although conceptually appealing, market value weights are difficult to implement. The difficulty lies in the fact that market values, particularly those of common shares, are subject to continuous wide fluctuations. In turn, these fluctuations cause significant

---

*The market value of untraded securities (privately placed debt, for example) can be approximated by using current market prices of traded securities of comparable risk and, in the case of bonds, a comparable term-to-maturity.

†From the discussion of the cost of a firm's retained earnings presented earlier in the chapter, it should be clear that the market takes into account the firm's retained earnings when placing a value on the firm's common shares.

variations in the market value weighted average cost of capital over time. It is, therefore, necessary to average or *normalize* market values in order to obtain a stable and operationally useful weighted average cost of capital. On the other hand, book value weights are relatively more stable over time and thus are easier to compute than the market value weights.

● MARKET VALUE WEIGHTS: A CONCLUDING COMMENT

Though market value weights are more appropriate for the calculation of a weighted average cost of capital, the issue continues to be controversial. The controversy essentially revolves around the unsettling question of whether or not investors measure financial risk in terms of book value proportions of debt-to-equity instead of the theoretically correct market value proportions. The relevance of this question can be illustrated by a simple example.

EXAMPLE   Suppose the Jerry Company in the preceding example raises an additional $10 million to finance a new investment in market value proportions (given in Table 17.3) of new long-term debt, preferred shares, and common shares. Then book value weights of the firm's capital sources *after* the new financing program will become 28.57-percent debt, 20.30-percent preferred shares, 42.90-percent common shares, and 8.30-percent retained earnings.* It is clear from these new weights that the new financing has shifted the firm's book value capital structure toward a lower proportion of debt (28.57 percent versus 30.00 percent shown in Table 17.2). With continued new financing according to the market value weights, the book value mix of the capital structure will converge to the market value mix (Table 17.3).

If investors judge the firm's financial risk in terms of its market value proportions of debt-to-equity, then the use of the market value weighted average cost of capital clearly seems to be appropriate. However, if the financial risk is measured primarily in terms of book value proportions of debt-to-equity, then the reduced book debt-to-equity ratio (caused by the new investment being financed with a market value debt-to-equity proportion which is lower than the existing balance sheet debt-to-equity proportion) will lower the perceived financial risk of the firm. This, in turn, may lower the component *marginal* costs and therefore the overall cost of capital to the firm.

•This section may be bypassed without loss of continuity.

*These weights (after the new financing) are calculated as follows:

$$\text{Book value weight of debt} = \frac{\$15,000,000 \text{ (from Table 17.2)} + 21.4\% \text{ of } \$10,000,000}{\$50,000,000 + \$10,000,000}$$

$$= .2857$$

$$\text{Book value weight of preferred shares} = \frac{\$10,000,000 + 21.4\% \text{ of } \$10,000,000}{\$50,000,000 + \$10,000,000} = .2030$$

$$\text{Book value weight of common shares} = \frac{\$20,000,000 + 57.2\% \text{ of } \$10,000,000}{\$50,000,000 + \$10,000,000} = .4290$$

$$\text{Book value weight of retained earnings} = \frac{\$5,000,000}{\$50,000,000 + \$10,000,000} = .0830$$

Consequently, the market value weighted average cost of capital, which must be calculated *before* an additional financing occurs, may not reflect the appropriate cost of capital to the firm for evaluating the new project. Thus, if new investments are financed with market value proportions that are different from the existing book value proportions, and if investors judge the firm's financial risk on the basis of its book value proportions, then the new investment will alter the risk characteristics of the firm from the viewpoint of investors. Consequently, the market value weighted average cost of capital cannot (strictly speaking) be applied to evaluate new investments, because, as discussed earlier, it provides a valid cutoff or discount rate for only those average-risk investments that do *not* affect the firm's existing business or financial risk.

Interestingly, an analogous argument can be made in the case where book value weights are used by a firm and investors judge the firm's financial risk primarily on the basis of the market value proportions of debt-to-equity in the firm's capital structure.

The Choice and Timing of Corporate Financings

In theory, since capital markets are assumed to be efficient (i.e., securities are always correctly valued given the available information), the firm should always attempt to remain at (or close to) its long-run target capital structure. If the firm must, in the short run, deviate from this long-run goal because of certain practical considerations that were discussed earlier, the firm should not expect to be any better (or worse) off by choosing one particular financing alternative over another at any particular point in time, or by advancing or delaying the implementation of a particular financing alternative to take advantage of more "favourable" market conditions.*

Although the empirical evidence suggests that capital markets are reasonably efficient, it is obvious that in practice financing decisions are influenced by the belief of practitioners that capital markets are sometimes temporarily inefficient. In other words, at any particular point in time, corporate managers believe that one (or more) financing source is incorrectly priced by the market; and thus, that they can minimize their cost of capital by choosing or avoiding particular types of financing alternatives, and/or by advancing or delaying particular types of financings in order to correspond to more "favourable" capital market conditions.† There are many examples of such corporate decision-making behaviour. Five of these examples are (1) corporate management may issue debt rather than equity, and thus overrepresent debt in the capital structure, because they perceive the firm's equity as being undervalued; (2) corporate management may issue equity during "hot" new issue markets because they perceive the price of equity as being reasonably priced (if not overpriced!); (3) corporate management may

---

*The former issue is also discussed in the section entitled "Rationale for Various Classes of Securities" in Chapter 22. In addition, the reader should note that if the firm intends to increase its business risk in the future by investing in more risky projects, and thus to move to a different optimal target capital structure, it can effect a transfer of wealth from the new bondholders to its shareholders by issuing new debt and concealing the fact that it intends to increase its business risk. See S. C. Myers, "Determinants of Corporate Borrowing," *Journal of Financial Economics* (November 1977), pp. 147–176.

†Note that the disclosure laws, which are discussed in Chapter 19, attempt to ensure that such decisions are not made on the basis of material nonpublic information.

repurchase their firm's outstanding common shares because they believe that such shares are being underpriced in the market; (4) corporate management may issue convertible debentures as a form of delayed equity financing because they perceive the firm's equity as being temporarily undervalued; and (5) corporate management may acquire other firms because they perceive the acquisition of such firms in a "depressed" financial market as being a superior investment opportunity to purchasing similar assets in the market for real assets (e.g., plant and equipment).

The decision-making problem implicit in the previous discussion has been aptly summarized as follows:

> Given a firm's asset base and/or growth in assets and the manager's beliefs about
> market conditions, is there an optimal way in which to vary the mix and
> characteristics of the liabilities used to finance the firm?[7]

Unfortunately, the financial literature provides little guidance for such decision making, since it has focused primarily on the historical costs of the various sources of financing, the factors that affect the various sources of financing, and the forecasting of the future cost of each source of financing.[8]

A similar issue, which may affect the choice and timing of corporate financings, is whether or not the marginal cost for each dollar of a specific source of new financing, raised in a relatively *short* time period, is constant (i.e., horizontal) or increasing (i.e., upward sloping), assuming that the firm raises the funds in such a manner as to maintain its existing target capital structure. Generally, finance theory assumes that capital markets are perfect and therefore that the marginal cost schedule for any specific source of new financing is horizontal; while practitioners believe, or act as if they believe, that the schedule is upward sloping (i.e., that the marginal cost of each additional dollar raised increases as the size of the issue increases).* Thus, as depicted in Figure 17.1,

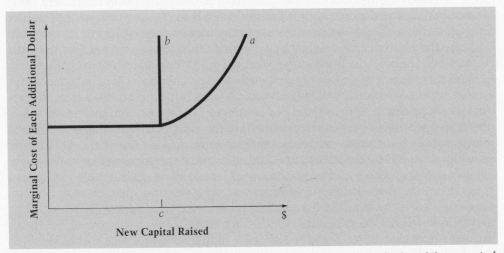

Figure 17.1   Relationship between the marginal cost of a specific source of new funds and the amount of new funds raised.

---

*As discussed in Chapter 19, many government programs and agencies (such as the Federal Business Development Bank) are often predicated on the belief that this is especially true for small businesses.

curve *a* represents the case where the marginal cost schedule increases gradually with the amount of funds raised; and curve *b* represents the case of "hard" capital rationing (i.e., beyond point *c*, the cost of raising an additional dollar is prohibitive). Since financing and investment decisions can no longer be separated when the marginal cost schedule is upward sloping, and thus must be solved simultaneously, we will not pursue the topic further in this text.[9]

Summary

This chapter has presented the basic concept of a firm's cost of capital as the minimum rate of return that the firm must earn on new investment from the viewpoint of its capital suppliers. A firm's cost of capital, as a cutoff or discount rate for evaluating the firm's new investments, can be measured as a weighted average of the current marginal or opportunity costs of the firm's individual sources of capital. The two basic assumptions underlying this measure of the cost of capital are (1) the business or operating risk of the firm's new investments is the same as the business risk of the firm's existing mix of investments, and (2) the new investments are financed in the firm's long-run target capital structure proportions (i.e., weights).

Although firms actually raise capital in "lumps" (i.e., by a specific source of financing), the firm should not evaluate a specific project against the marginal cost of the specific source of funds used to finance it. Instead, as an ongoing concern, the firm should view all its investments as being financed out of a common pool of funds with constant (target) proportions of each source of capital.

The three key external sources of long-term funds to a corporation are long-term debt, preferred shares, and common shares. The explicit marginal cost of each of these sources can be derived as the discount rate (internal rate of return) that equates the present value of the expected after-tax cash outflows with the funds received by the firm (i.e., the net proceeds to the firm after adjustments have been made for the underwriting and issue costs and the associated tax-shields, if any). Using this approach, the after-tax marginal cost of a bond issue to the firm can be estimated as $[(1 - \text{corporate tax rate}) \cdot k_b]$, where k_b represents the before-tax cost of the bond issue. The marginal cost of preferred shares equals the annual per-share preferred dividend divided by the net proceeds from the sale of a share. The cost of equity capital can be derived from the Gordon share-price valuation model, which is based on the premise that the value of a share to investors is the present value of all future dividends expected to be paid on the share. This model embodies the notion of expected capital gain or loss from the sale of a share at the end of any given holding period. If a firm's annual per-share dividend is, on average, expected to grow (or decline) perpetually at a constant rate, then the firm's cost of equity capital equals the sum of the expected dividend yield plus the expected annual growth rate. The cost of a new common share issue to the firm is higher than the cost of the firm's existing equity capital because of the presence of flotation costs. The cost of preferred shares, as well as the cost of common equity capital, need no explicit tax adjustment, since dividends are paid out of the firm's after-tax cash flows.

Another method of estimating the cost of common equity capital is based on the security market line equation (SML) developed in Chapter 16. According to this equation, the cost of equity equals the risk-free rate plus a risk premium commensurate with the systematic or nondiversifiable risk of the firm's common shares.

The two major internal sources of financing to a firm are retained earnings and depreciation. These two sources of funds are assigned specific costs because a firm's use of these funds involves an opportunity cost to the firm's shareholders. The opportunity cost, k_r, of retained earnings is defined as the rate of return shareholders currently require on the firm's existing common equity capital. This definition provides a conservative estimate of k_r because it ignores the brokerage costs associated with the reinvestment of cash dividends by shareholders as well as shareholders' personal tax considerations. The opportunity cost of depreciation-generated funds equals the weighted average cost of the firm's existing capital. As such, the cost of depreciation can be ignored when computing the firm's weighted average cost of capital.

A firm's weighted average cost of capital can be computed by using either book value or market value weights. The use of market value weights is theoretically correct because the market values of a firm's capital sources reflect the rates of return investors currently require on the firm's securities. The book values, as historical figures, reflect sunk costs and are therefore irrelevant for the firm's current financial decision making.

Although financial theory assumes that capital markets are efficient (i.e., that the prices of securities instantaneously and fully reflect all available relevant information), financial managers often time their financings based on the belief that capital markets are sometimes temporarily inefficient. The timing of a firm's financings may also be influenced by the belief that, in the short run, the marginal cost schedule of any specific source of financing is upward sloping. Financial theory, however, assumes that a firm can raise an unlimited amount of any type of new capital at the same marginal cost during all time periods (i.e., the capital markets are perfect).

Questions

17.1 How is the cost of capital used in the capital budgeting process? Specifically, how is it connected with the net present-value, benefit-cost ratio, and internal rate-of-return techniques for determining a project's acceptability?

17.2 What is meant by the cost of capital for a firm? What effect will accepting projects earning less than the cost of capital have on the firm's value?

17.3 Why, in using the cost of capital for evaluating investment alternatives, was it assumed that the acceptance of proposed projects would not affect the business risk of the firm?

17.4 What is financial risk? Why is it necessary to assume that the firm's financial structure remains unchanged when evaluating the firm's cost of capital? Why is this assumption awkward?

17.5 "In accordance with the marginal principle, an investment proposal should be accepted if its rate of return is expected to be greater than the marginal cost of funds required to finance the investment. Thus, if a project is to be financed with a new bond issue, it should be accepted if its rate of return is expected to be greater than the after-tax interest cost of the bond issue." Do you agree with this statement?

Explain your answer, assuming that the project will not affect the firm's current business risk and that the bond will be sold at its par value.

17.6 Under what conditions would one expect all the firms in the same industry to have approximately the same cost of capital?

17.7 A firm maintains stable market value proportions of its various capital sources. Would you expect the firm's weighted average cost of capital to remain stable over time? Explain.

17.8 Suppose a firm has two types of outstanding bond issues B_1 and B_2. How will you calculate the average cost to the firm of these two bond issues?

17.9 What is meant by the net proceeds from the sale of a bond? In what circumstances is a bond expected to sell at a discount or premium?

17.10 "The major challenge in measuring the cost of capital is estimating the cost of common equity capital." Why?

17.11 How would one calculate the cost of preferred shares? Why do we concern ourselves with the net proceeds from the sale of the new shares instead of the total value at which the shares were sold?

17.12 Why does the cost of common equity capital to the firm require no tax adjustment, whereas the cost of debt does? Is it necessary to adjust the cost of preferred equity for taxes?

17.13 What is meant by *underwriting* and *underpricing* costs? How does the cost of each affect the firm's cost of equity capital? How is the firm's cost of equity adjusted for these two factors?

17.14 What major assumptions underly the Gordon model for the cost of common equity, k_e?

17.15 "The cost of common equity capital as derived from the Gordon dividend valuation model is risk-adjusted." Why is this so?

17.16 "The cost of equity capital as derived from the Gordon dividend valuation model needs no explicit tax adjustment when included in the firm's weighted average cost of capital calculation." Why?

17.17 How would you explain the fact that the common shares of companies that pay no dividends have positive market values? How would you estimate the cost of equity capital for a nondividend paying firm? Explain.

17.18 As of January 1, 1980, the indicated dividend yield for the Labrador Mining Company Ltd. was 25 percent. Does this *necessarily* mean that the cost of common equity for the company is as high as or above 25 percent? Explain your answer using Equation 17.8, which was derived in the chapter.

17.19 Explain the rationale for assigning a specific cost to retained earnings as a source of capital.

17.20 What is the rationale for assigning a specific cost to depreciation as a source of capital to the firm? What is the specific cost of depreciation-generated funds?

17.21 Why is the use of market value weights considered to be a conceptually preferred approach? What is the major practical difficulty in using market value weights?

17.22 How would you explain the fact that financial managers time their financings (i.e., delay or advance financing issues)?

Problems

17.1 For each of the following $1,000 bonds, assuming annual interest payment and a 40-percent tax rate, calculate the *after-tax* cost to maturity using

a. The standard approach and
b. The approximate method discussed in the chapter.
c. Compare the costs calculated for each bond in **a** and **b**.

Bond	Life	After-tax underwriting fee	Discount (−) or premium (+)	Coupon rate
A	20 years	$25	$ − 20	8%
B	16 years	$40	$ + 10	10%
C	15 years	$30	$ − 15	7%
D	25 years	$15	par	6%
E	22 years	$20	$ − 60	5%

17.2   The Swift Current Company Ltd. has just issued preferred shares. They have an 8-percent annual dividend and a $100.00 par value, and were sold at $97.50 per share.
a. Calculate the after-tax cost of the preferred shares.
b. If the firm had sold the preferred shares with a 6-percent annual dividend per share and had netted (after taxes) $90 per share, then what would their after-tax cost have been?

17.3   Determine the after-tax cost of preferred shares for each of the following cases.

Preferred shares	Par value	After-tax underwriting costs	Annual dividend per share
A	$100	$5.00	7%
B	$ 80	$3.50	8%
C	$ 75	$4.00	$5.00
D	$ 60	5%	$3.00
E	$ 40	$2.50	9%

17.4   Chasham Musicals Ltd. wishes to measure the cost of a new common share issue. The firm's common shares are currently selling for $57.50 per share. Investors expect the firm to pay a $2.00 dividend per share (i.e., D_1) at the end of the current year. The dividends per share for the past five years are as follows, and this past trend in dividends is expected to continue for the foreseeable future.

Year	Dividend per share
19X8	$1.96
19X7	$1.88
19X6	$1.82
19X5	$1.76
19X4	$1.73

After adjustment for after-tax issue costs per share, the firm expects to net $52.00 per share on a new common share issue.
a. Determine the expected growth in dividends per share based on its historical growth rate.
b. Determine the percentage market price the firm actually receives.
c. Determine the cost of the new common share issue.
d. Determine the cost of retained earnings to the firm (ignore investors' brokerage costs and personal taxes).

17.5   The Nadia Crafts Corporation is a relatively young company that has financed its past growth predominantly through retention of its earnings. To date, it has paid no dividends to its shareholders. Investors expect the company's opportunities for profitable reinvestment of its earnings (i.e., after the deduction of interest, depreciation and taxes) to remain unchanged for a long period into the future. Therefore, investors expect the company to pay either no dividend or a negligible one in the future. The history of the company's earnings and market price per share is as follows:

Year	Price per share	Earnings per share
19X9	$61.10	$6.10
19X8	$53.00	$5.32
19X7	$46.30	$4.70
19X6	$40.30	$4.06
19X5	$35.50	$3.58
19X4	$30.00	$3.10
19X3	$26.40	$2.68
19X2	$23.10	$2.32
19X1	$20.00	$2.00

What is the company's estimated cost of equity capital?

17.6   For the following firms, calculate the cost of retained earnings (ignoring investors' brokerage costs and personal taxes) and the cost of new common share equity. Use the Gordon model.

Firm	Current market price per share	Expected dividend growth rate	Projected dividend per share next year	After-tax cost of underwriting per share	Underpricing per share
A	$100	8%	$2.25	$1.00	$2.00
B	$ 40	4%	$1.00	$1.50	$ .50
C	$ 85	6%	$2.00	$2.00	$1.00
D	$ 38	2%	$2.10	$1.70	$1.30

17.7   The Yellowknife Development Corporation's common shares are currently selling for $100 per share. The corporation has just paid a dividend, D_0, of $4 per share. Based on the forecasts of the inflationary trend in the economy, the annual general inflation rate is anticipated to be at least 10 percent for many years to come. Given these inflationary expectations in the market, management feels that it is reasonable to assume that investors expect a long-run average annual growth rate of about 12 percent in the company's future per-share dividend payments.
a.   What is Yellowknife's estimate of its existing equity capital?
b.   Suppose, as part of the financing plan for a new average-risk project, Yellowknife issues 50,000 common shares at their prevailing par value of $100 per share. Also suppose that after-tax underpricing and underwriting costs amount to $200,000. What is the cost of the new common share issue to Yellowknife?
c.   What is the appropriate cost of equity capital to use in calculating Yellowknife's overall or weighted average cost of capital for evaluating the project? If the firm maintains a long-run target capital structure, should the firm evaluate the project against its (marginal) cost of equity capital calculated in part **b**? Explain.

d. Suppose the contemplated project were financed partly from the current year's retained earnings and partly from the new common-share issue, what is the relevant cost of equity capital to use in calculating the appropriate discount rate for evaluating the project? Discuss briefly.

e. Suppose the equity portion of Yellowknife's current and new project financings is expected to come entirely out of its current and future years' retained earnings. In that case what is the appropriate cost of equity capital to use in calculating the firm's weighted average cost of capital for evaluating the contemplated project? Explain your answer briefly.

17.8 The Fort Murry Realty Ltd. is presently trading at $66 per share. Given the current business and financial risk characteristics of the company and the current capital market conditions, investors require a 15-percent rate of return on the company's common shares. The company has just paid a dividend, D_0, of $3 per share.

a. Determine the long-run average annual growth rate in dividend per share that is currently (at time 0) being expected by the company's common shareholders.

b. Suppose, due to a sudden downturn in the real estate sector of the economy, investors now (at time 0) expect the future per-share dividend payments of the company to decline at an average annual rate of 6 percent but, in view of their alternative investment opportunities, they still require a 15-percent rate of return on the company's common shares. How will this change in investors' expectations affect the market price of the company's common shares?

17.9 Alpha and Beta Corporations are currently trading at $50 and $25 per share, respectively. The dividend per share paid by the Alpha Corporation over the last several years has increased at an average annual rate of 10 percent; whereas that paid by the Beta Corporation has decreased at that rate. This past trend in the per-share dividend payments of both the corporations is expected to continue indefinitely into the future. The dividend payment of the Alpha Corporation at the end of the current year is expected to be $2 per share; whereas that of the Beta Corporation is expected to be $6 per share.

a. Compare the specific costs of equity capital for the two corporations.

b. What is the essential difference in the makeup of the expected rate of return on the common shares of the two corporations? For illustrative convenience, assume that the current common-share investors in the two corporations will sell their shares at the end of a one-year holding period.

17.10 The index of nondiversifiable risk (i.e., beta) for Blairmore Pop Works (BPW) Ltd. equals 1.5. Assume that the firm's optimal target capital structure is 100 percent equity financing. If the risk-free rate of return is 10 percent, and the currently expected rate of return on the market (as measured by the Toronto Stock Exchange's 300 Stock Composite Index) is 18 percent, then using the CAPM

a. Calculate the cost of common equity capital.

b. What market risk premium is included in the firm's cost of common equity capital?

c. Should an average-risk project that promises a rate of return of 23 percent be accepted or rejected? Explain.

d. Should *all* projects with expected rates of return that are less than the firm's cost of capital (calculated in part **a**) be rejected? Why or why not?

e. Calculate the appropriate cost of capital for evaluating a new investment project that has a greater systematic risk than the average systematic risk of the firm's existing assets. Assume that the appropriate beta for the new investment is 2.0.

17.11   Trois Rivières Company Ltd. has on its books the following amounts and specific after-tax current costs for each type of capital:

Type of capital	Book value	Specific cost
Long-term debt	$100,000	4.25% (after tax)
Preferred equity	50,000	5.85%
Common equity	650,000	9.75%

Calculate the firm's book value weighted average cost of capital.

17.12   The Cool Airconditioning Company Ltd. has compiled the following information:

Type of capital	Book value	Market value	Specific cost
Long-term debt	$4,000,000	$3,840,000	4.50% (after tax)
Preferred shares	40,000	60,000	8.25%
Common share equity	1,060,000	3,000,000	12.50%
	$5,100,000	$6,900,000	

a.   Calculate the weighted average cost of capital using book value weights.
b.   Calculate the weighted average cost of capital using market value weights.
c.   Compare the answers obtained in **a** and **b**. Explain the differences.

17.13   The Alberta Heritage Company Ltd. wishes to estimate the appropriate discount rate for evaluating one of its new resource development projects that requires an initial outlay of $20 million. The project's operating cash-flow risk (i.e., business risk) is expected to be approximately the same as the company's current operating risk (i.e., business risk). The company's existing capital structure, measured in market value proportions, is comprised of 40-percent long-term debt, 10-percent preferred shares, and 50-percent common equity capital. Management believes this financing mix to be the optimal one for the company and wishes to maintain it in the future.

The company plans to finance the project through its current year's retained earnings and new capital raised in the capital market. Considering the company's current operating and financial risk and the current conditions in the capital markets, Mr. Phillip Laugheed, the company's financial vice-president, has developed the following estimates:

(1)   The company could sell 10-year $1,000-face-value bonds, having a 10-percent annual coupon, for $980 less an underwriting fee of 3-percent of the face value of the bonds. These estimates reflect all the necessary tax shields with respect to the bond discount and underwriting fee.

(2)   The company could issue 10-percent preferred shares at $100 per share with an after-tax issue cost of $1 per share.

(3)   Common shares could be sold to the public at $50 per share with after-tax issue costs of 4 percent. Investors expect the $2 dividend that has just been paid (i.e., D_0) to grow at an average annual rate of 11 percent. (This growth rate is just above the currently anticipated future general rate of inflation of 10 percent.)

The company is subject to a 40-percent corporate tax rate.

a.   Compute the specific cost of each source of financing being considered by the company. (Use the approximate method discussed in the chapter for calculating the specific cost of debt.)

b.   Compute the discount rate that the company should use to evaluate the contemplated project.

   c. Should the company accept the project, assuming it would increase the company's after-tax net operating cash flow by $2 million per year in perpetuity?

   d. What will the increase or decrease in the market value of the company's common equity capital be if the project is accepted? Will the acceptance of the project be consistent with the firm's objective of maximizing shareholders' wealth?

   e. Suppose the firm had $20 million of depreciation charges this year and the firm had considered these charges *explicitly* as a specific source of capital for financing the project. What effect, if any, would this have had on the discount rate calculated in part **b**?

•17.14 Mr. Don Quixote, as a sole proprietor of Wuthering Heights Resorts, owns a non-depreciable ocean-front property purchased several years ago for $50,000. Currently, the property can be sold for $1 million. However, Mr. Quixote, a man of unerring business instinct, has resisted the temptation of selling the property. Instead, he is contemplating the development of the property into a sailing- and surfing-oriented recreation spot. The development, which will be called "The Impossible Dream Enclave," will require an initial outlay of $4 million. Based on his forecast of the project's expected cash flows, a major Canadian bank is willing to lend Mr. Quixote the $4 million at an annual fixed interest rate of 10 percent. Considering his alternative investment opportunities, Mr. Quixote requires a minimum before-tax return of 20 percent on his investment in the project.

   a. What will the dollar value of Mr. Quixote's investment in the project be?

   b. Assume that the project is expected to generate level operating cash flows in perpetuity. What is the *minimum* annual *before-tax* operating cash flow that the project must generate in order for Mr. Quixote to earn a 20-percent *before-tax* return on his investment in the project?

   c. Calculate and interpret the *minimum acceptable* before-tax rate of return on the project.

   d. Assume that Mr. Quixote's marginal tax rate is 20 percent and that he would be able to fully deduct the interest on the $4 million debt for tax purposes. Calculate and interpret the minimum acceptable *tax-adjusted* rate of return on the project.

   e. It is generally recommended in the capital budgeting literature that in the discounted cash-flow evaluation of a project, only the *operating* cash flows of the project should be discounted, and that the *financing* flows and the associated tax effects (such as the interest tax shield) should be reflected in the discount rate. Suppose Mr. Quixote does not follow this general recommendation and specifies his project's cash flows as: The project's after-tax operating cash flows *plus* the interest tax shield on the $4 million debt.[10] Then, what discount rate should Mr. Quixote use to evaluate his project in order to obtain the same NPV for the project as he would if he were to use the generally recommended procedure? What general conclusion would you draw with respect to the DCF method of evaluating capital investments from your calculations?

Notes

1. For the interested reader, the calculations necessary to derive Equation 17.6 from Equation 17.3 follow.

Let D_0 = the per-share dividend payment made *just before the start of the current period 1.*

Then,

$$D_1 = D_0(1+g), D_2 = D_1(1+g), \text{ which equals } D_0(1+g)^2$$

similarly

$$D_3 = D_0(1+g)^3, \ldots D_n = D_0(1+g)^n, \ldots$$

•This problem is rather complex and should therefore be attempted only after one has thoroughly grasped the concept of the cost of capital.

Thus, Equation 17.3 can be written as:

$$P_0 = \frac{D_0(1+g)^1}{(1+k_e)^1} + \frac{D_0(1+g)^2}{(1+k_e)^2} + \cdots \frac{D_0(1+g)^\infty}{(1+k_e)^\infty}$$

(1)

$$= \frac{D_0(1+g)}{(1+k_e)}\left[1 + \left(\frac{1+g}{1+k_e}\right) + \left(\frac{1+g}{1+k_e}\right)^2 + \cdots \left(\frac{1+g}{1+k_e}\right)^\infty\right]$$

The bracketed expression on the right-hand side of this equation is an infinite geometric series with the common factor $(1+g)/(1+k_e)$. If we assume that $g<k_e$, then $(1+g)/(1+k_e)<1$ and the series becomes convergent. Using the well-known formula for the sum of an infinite convergent geometric series, the bracketed expression sums to

$$\frac{1}{1 - \left(\dfrac{1+g}{1+k_e}\right)} = \frac{1+k_e}{k_e-g}$$

Using this result, Equation 1 can be written as

$$P_0 = \frac{D_0(1+g)}{(1+k_e)} \cdot \frac{(1+k_e)}{(k_e-g)}$$

$$= \frac{D_0(1+g)}{(k_e-g)}$$

$$= \frac{D_1}{k_e-g}$$

If $g=k_e$, then the formula will yield an infinitely large value for P_0; and if $g>k_e$ and $D_1>0$, then $P_0=-\infty$. Both of these results have no realistic economic interpretation. Thus, the assumption that $g<k_e$ is a necessary condition for a meaningful application of this formula. Finally, from Equation 1 in this note it is clear that since the term $[(1 + g)/(1 + k_e)]^n$ declines sharply with increasing n, the impact of an underestimation or overestimation of g (provided the estimated value is less than k_e) on P_0 diminishes sharply with the distance in the future. Hence, the usefulness of the formula as an approximation of P_0 (and therefore of k_e in the derived Equation 17.7). Also note that for $g<0$ (i.e., expected rate of *decrease* in annual per-share dividends), the necessary condition $g<k_e$ is automatically satisfied.

2. To illustrate this analytically, note that the expected share price growth rate (i.e., the expected capital gains rate) during *any* given year n equals:

$$\frac{P_n - P_{n-1}}{P_{n-1}} = \frac{P_n}{P_{n-1}} - 1$$

$$= \frac{D_0(1+g)^{n+1}}{D_0(1+g)^n} - 1$$

$$= (1+g) - 1$$

$$= g$$

Also note that the *dividend yield* for any year n, given *current* investors' expectations of g, equals

$$\frac{D_0(1+g)^n}{P_{n-1}} = \frac{D_0(1+g)^n}{P_0(1+g)^{n-1}} = \frac{D_0(1+g)}{P_0} = \frac{D_1}{P_0}$$

Thus, even though in Equation 17.7 we need to substitute only the current year's expected dividend yield, which is easily calculated because P_0 is observable, it should be remembered that in terms of *current* investors' expectations, the expected dividend yield for any year n equals the expected dividend yield for the current year, D_1/P_0.

3. Note that even though the per-share dividend payment of the Horse and Buggy Company is *currently* expected to decline at an annual rate of 10 percent, the dividend *yield* (D_n/P_{n-1}) for any year n is

currently expected to remain constant over the future years. This occurs because, as was shown by Equation 17.8, *both* the dividend per share and price per share are expected to decline at the same rate of 10 percent. To illustrate, $D_n = D_0(1 - .10)^n = D_1(1 - .10)^{n-1} = \$1.50(1 - .10)^{n-1}$; and $P_{n-1} = P_0(1 - .10)^{n-1}$. Therefore, given investors' expectations as of today, the dividend yield for *any* year *n*, equals

$$\frac{D_n}{P_{n-1}} = \frac{\$1.50(1 - .10)^{n-1}}{P_0(1 - .10)^{n-1}} = \frac{\$1.50}{P_0} = \frac{\$1.50}{\$6.50} = .23$$

and the expected rate of return for year *n* on a common share of the company equals .23 − .10 = .13. Similar calculations apply to the expected rate of return on the common shares of the Jerry Company. Thus, the one-year holding period horizon assumption in the example was made only for illustrative convenience.

4. For a discussion of an application of the CAPM to the rate of return determinations for public utilities, see Howard E. Thompson, "On the Use of Beta in Regulatory Proceedings: An Empirical Examination," *The Bell Journal of Economics* (Spring 1978), pp. 239–248. Also, see Robert Litzenberger, Krishna Ramaswamy, and Howard Sosin, "On the CAPM Approach to the Estimation of a Public Utility's Cost of Equity Capital," *The Journal of Finance* 35 (May 1980), pp. 369–383. For an application of the CAPM to the financial planning model of a large firm, see B. E. Davis, G. J. Caccappolo, and M. A. Chaudry, "An Econometric Planning Model for American Telephone and Telegraph Company," *The Bell Journal of Economics and Management Science* (Spring 1973), pp. 29–56.

5. For an analysis of the impact of differential capital gains and dividend income taxation on the firm's cost of capital, see Myron J. Gordon and L. T. Gould, "The Cost of Equity Capital with Personal Income Taxes and Flotation Costs," *Journal of Finance*, (September 1978), pp. 1201–1212; and M. J. Gordon and L. T. Gould, "The Cost of Capital: A Reconsideration," *Journal of Finance* (June 1978), pp. 849–862.

6. For an interesting Canadian application, see John T. Bart, "The Nature of the Conflict Between Transactors' Expectations of Capital Gain," *Journal of Finance* 33 (September 1978), pp. 1095–1107. Also, see Harold Bierman, Jr., and Clayton P. Alderfer, "Estimating the Cost of Capital, A Different Approach," *Decision Sciences* 1 (January-April 1970), pp. 40–53.

7. Jerome Baesel and Dwight Grant, "Timing Policy for Corporate Capital Structure," *Proceedings* ASAC Conference (Montreal 1980), p. 1.

8. Exceptions include the paper referred to in note 7; and John D. Cragg and Nevins D. Baxter, "The Issuing of Corporate Securities," *Journal of Political Economy* 78 (November-December 1970), pp. 1310–1324.

9. For an excellent discussion of this topic see Stewart C. Myers, "Interactions of Corporate Financing and Investment Decisions—Implications for Capital Budgeting," *Journal of Finance* 29 (March 1974), pp. 1–23.

10. This method of specifying a project's cash flows for corporate investments is, for example, recommended in D. Arditti and Haim Levy, "The Weighted Average Cost of Capital as a Cut-off Rate: A Critical Analysis of the Classical Textbook Weighted Average," *Financial Management* 6, No. 1 (Spring 1977), pp. 24–34.

Suggested Readings

Ang, James S., "Weighted Average versus True Cost of Capital," *Financial Management* 2 (Autumn 1973), pp. 56–60.

Arditti, Fred D., "Risk and the Required Return on Equity," *Journal of Finance* 22 (March 1967), pp. 19–36.

———, "The Weighted Average Cost of Capital: Some Questions on Its Definition, Interpretation and Use," *Journal of Finance* 28 (September 1973), pp. 1001–1008.

Arditti, Fred D. and Haim Levy, "The Weighted Average Cost of Capital As a Cutoff Rate: A Critical Analysis of the Classical Textbook Weighted Average," *Financial Management* 6 (Fall 1977), pp. 24–34.

Arditti, Fred D. and Milford S. Tysseland, "Three Ways to Present the Marginal Cost of Capital," *Financial Management* 2 (Summer 1973), pp. 63–67.

Bart, John T., "The Nature of the Conflict Between Transactors' Expectations of Capital Gain," *Journal of Finance* 33 (September 1978), pp. 1095–1107.

Baesel, Jerome and Dwight Grant, "Timing Policy for Corporate Capital Structure," Proceedings ASAC Conference, Montreal, 1980.

Beranek, William, "The Cost of Capital, Capital Budgeting, and the Maximization of Shareholder Wealth," *Journal of Financial and Quantitative Analysis* 10 (March 1975), pp. 1–21.

———, "The Weighted Average Cost of Capital and Shareholder Wealth Maximization," *Journal of Financial and Quantitative Analysis* 12 (March 1977), pp. 17–32.

Bierman, Harold J. and Clayton P. Alderfer, "Estimating the Cost of Capital: A Different Approach," *Decision Sciences* 1 (January-April 1970), pp. 40–53.

Brennan, Michael J., "A New Look at the Weighted Average Cost of Capital," *Journal of Business Finance* 5, No. 1 (1973), pp. 24–30.

Brigham, Eugene F. and Myron J. Gordon, "Leverage, Dividend Policy, and the Cost of Capital," *Journal of Finance* 23 (March 1968), pp. 85–103.

Brigham, Eugene F., Myron J. Gordon, and Keith V. Smith, "The Cost of Capital and the Small Firm," *Engineering Economist* 13 (Fall 1967), pp. 1–26.

Cragg, John D. and Nevins D. Baxter, "The Issuing of Corporate Securities," *Journal of Political Economy* 78 (November-December 1970), pp. 1310–1324.

Davis E. B., G. J. Caccappolo, and M. A. Chaudry, "An Econometric Planning Model for American Telephone and Telegraph Company," *Bell Journal of Economics and Management Science* (Spring 1973), pp. 29–56.

Elton, Edwin J. and Martin J. Gruber, "The Cost of Retained Earnings—Implications of Share Repurchase," *Industrial Management Review* 9 (Spring 1968), pp. 87–104.

Ezzell, John R. and R. Burr Porter, "Flotation Costs and the Weighted Average Cost of Capital," *Journal of Financial and Quantitative Analysis* 11 (September 1976), pp. 403–414.

Findlay III, Chapman M., "The Weighted Average Cost of Capital," *Journal of Finance* 30 (June 1975), pp. 879–880.

Gordon, Myron J., *The Investment, Financing and Valuation of the Corporation* (Homewood, Ill.: Irwin, 1962).

———, "The Cost of Capital: A Reconsideration," *Journal of Finance* (June 1978), pp. 849–862.

Gordon, Myron J. and L. T. Gould, "The Cost of Equity Capital with Personal Income Taxes and Flotation Costs," *Journal of Finance* (September 1978), pp. 1201–1212.

———, and Paul J. Halpern, "Cost of Capital for a Division of a Firm," *Journal of Finance* 29 (September 1974), pp. 1153–1163.

Grinyer, John R., "The Cost of Equity, the C.A.P.M. and Management Objectives Under Uncertainty," *Journal of Business Finance and Accounting* 3 (Winter 1976), pp. 101–121.

Haley, Charles W., "Taxes, the Cost of Capital, and the Firm's Investment Decisions," *Journal of Finance* 20 (September 1971), pp. 901–917.

Henderson, Glenn V., "Shareholder Taxation and the Required Rate of Return on Internally Generated Funds," *Financial Management* 5 (Summer 1976), pp. 25–31.

Keane, Simon M., "Some Aspects of the Cost of Debt," *Accounting and Business Research* (Autumn 1975), pp. 298–304.

Lawrenz, David W., "The Effects of Corporate Taxation on the Cost of Equity Capital," *Financial Management* 5 (Spring 1976), pp. 53–57.

Levy, Haim and Marshall Sarnat, *Capital Investment and Financial Decisions* (Englewood Cliffs, N.J.: Prentice-Hall, 1978), pp. 251–254.

Lewellen, Wilbur G., *The Cost of Capital* (Dubuque, Iowa: Kendall/Hunt, 1976).

———, "A Conceptual Reappraisal of Cost of Capital," *Financial Management* 3 (Winter 1974), pp. 63–70.

Lintner, John, "The Cost of Capital and Optimal Financing of Corporate Growth," *Journal of Finance* 18 (May 1963), pp. 292–310.

Litzenberger, Robert, Krishna Ramaswamy, and Howard Sosin, "On the CAPM Approach to the Estimation of a Public Utility's Cost of Equity Capital," *Journal of Finance* 35 (May 1980), pp. 369–383.

Melnyk, Z. Lew, "Cost of Capital As a Function of Financial Leverage," *Decision Sciences* (July-October 1970), pp. 327–356.

Modigliani, Franco and Merton Miller, "The Cost of Capital, Corporation Finance and the Theory of Investment," *American Economic Review* 48 (June 1958), pp. 261–296.

Myers, Stewart C., "Determinants of Corporate Borrowing," *Journal of Financial Economics* (November 1977), pp. 147–176.

———, "Interactions of Corporate Financing and Investment Decisions—Implications for Capital Budgeting," *Journal of Finance* 29 (March 1974), pp. 1–23.

Nantell, Timothy J. and C. Robert Carlson, "The Cost of Capital As a Weighted Average," *Journal of Finance* 30 (December 1975), pp. 1343–1355.

Petry, Glenn H., "Empirical Evidence on Cost of Capital Weights," *Financial Management* 4 (Winter 1975), pp. 58–65.

Pettit, Richardson R., "The Weighted Average Cost of Capital: Some Questions on Its Definition, Interpretation and Use: Comment," *Journal of Finance* 30 (June 1975), pp. 881–882.

Porterfield, James T. S., *Investment Decisions and Capital Costs* (Englewood Cliffs, N.J.: Prentice-Hall, 1965).

Reilly, Raymond R. and William E. Wecker, "On the Weighted Average Cost of Capital," *Journal of Financial and Quantitative Analysis* 8 (January 1973), pp. 123–126.

Robichek, Alexander A. and Stewart C. Myers, *Optimal Financing Decisions* (Englewood Cliffs, N.J.: Prentice-Hall, 1965).

Solomon, Ezra, "Measuring a Company's Cost of Capital," *Journal of Business* 28 (October 1955), pp. 240–252.

Taggart, Robert A., Jr., "Capital Budgeting and the Financing Decision: An Exposition," *Financial Management* 32 (Summer 1977), pp. 59–64.

Thompson, Howard E., "On the Use of Beta in Regulatory Proceedings: An Empirical Examination," *Bell Journal of Economics* (Spring 1978), pp. 239–248.

Vickers, Douglas, "The Cost of Capital and the Structure of the Firm," *Journal of Finance* 25 (March 1970), pp. 35–46.

Chapter 18

CAPITAL STRUCTURE AND VALUATION

Capital structure, valuation, and the cost of capital are all closely interrelated topics. In the preceding chapter, the cost of capital was calculated based on the assumptions that the firm would effectively remain at its long-run optimal capital structure and that it would not change its business risk over time. In turn, these assumptions imply that in the long run the firm will raise additional capital in the same proportions of debt and equity as presently exists in its optimal (i.e., target) capital structure. Valuation was also referred to in the preceding chapter in the discussion of the cost of specific sources of capital, such as common equity capital.

In this chapter, the basic concepts and theories of capital structure, and the relationship between a firm's capital structure, value, and cost of capital are discussed. The important issues of whether or not an "optimal" capital structure exists will also be critically examined by examining the effect of alternate capital structures on the total value of the firm. Since the capital structure decision essentially involves a consideration of how much debt (and other fixed-income securities) a firm should use, the capital structure decision is often referred to in the financial literature as the "debt-capacity" decision. Practical application of techniques for valuing a firm will be discussed in greater detail in Chapter 25, which deals with acquisitions, amalgamations, and holding companies.

This chapter is divided into five basic sections. The first section deals with some of the key concepts encountered in making capital structure decisions, and argues that the wealth of the firm's owners or shareholders is the preferred measure of the impact of alternative capital structures. The second and third sections are devoted to the presentation of the traditional, and the Modigliani and Miller (MM) views, respectively, of the impact of alternative capital structures on a firm's value and cost of capital. The fourth section critically reviews a number of possible explanations for observed capital structures. The final section deals with the implications of the capital structure theories for practice, as well as with the techniques and guidelines used by practitioners in making capital structure decisions.

The Nature of the Capital Structure Decision

This section of the chapter deals with some of the basic concepts involved in the capital structure decision. More specifically, it discusses capital structure components, the factors that influence the capital structure decision, and the two commonly proposed methods of measuring the impact of alternative capital structures.

CAPITAL STRUCTURE COMPONENTS

In the preceding chapter, *capital structure* was defined as the permanent (i.e., long-term) financing of the firm; that is, the financing of the firm from various specific sources other than current liabilities.* The costs of specific sources of funds—such as debt, preferred equity, and common equity—were calculated in the preceding chapter. The right-hand side of the following simplified balance sheet indicates the basic breakdown of the firm's capital structure into its various components.

Balance sheet

Assets	Current liabilities Long-term debt	}	Debt capital	}	Capital
	Shareholders' equity Preferred shares Common shares Retained earnings	}	Equity capital		

Debt Capital *Debt capital* includes any type of long-term funds borrowed at a specified fixed or variable rate for a fixed or variable (but generally finite) term. The debt can be secured or unsecured, senior or subordinated, and it can be raised through various means such as the sale of bonds or through a negotiated long-term loan. Larger firms generally have more than one type of debt outstanding. In the preceding chapter, the explicit after-tax cost of debt capital was found to be considerably less than the cost of any other specific source of long-term financing. The "cheapness" of debt capital is attributable to the fact that as creditors, holders of such debt generally have the least risk of any long-term contributors of capital. Debt

---

*Current liabilities, which are not costless in an opportunity-cost sense, can be ignored in both the capital structure decision and the cost of capital calculation, if the firm uses the capital budgeting approach that nets the working capital of a specific project against the project's initial investment when evaluating that project. Alternatively, such funds could be included in both the capital structure decision and the cost of capital calculation, if the firm uses the capital budgeting approach that does *not* net the working capital requirements of a specific project against the project's initial investment when evaluating that project. Although the two approaches should result in similar decisions, the discussion in this chapter follows the first approach—it ignores current liabilities when evaluating alternate capital structures.

holders have the highest priority of claim against any earnings or assets available for payment; they have the strongest contractual claim against the firm for such payments; and their return (i.e., interest payments) are tax-deductible expenses to the firm. The characteristics of the various types of long-term debt instruments are discussed in greater detail in Chapter 21.

Equity Capital   *Equity capital* consists of the long-term funds provided by the firm's owners or shareholders. Unlike borrowed funds that must be repaid at a specified date, equity capital is expected to remain in the firm for an indefinite period of time. All equity capital takes a secondary (i.e., subordinated) position to debt capital with respect to the distribution of operating income and the liquidation of assets in the event of bankruptcy. This generally makes the returns on equity capital more uncertain than the returns on debt capital, and thus this higher risk must be compensated for with higher expected returns.

The three basic sources of equity capital to the firm are preferred shares, common shares, and retained earnings. Most corporate financial managers do not consider preferred shares as being equity; they consider preferred shares as being a substitute for debt. From the common shareholders' viewpoint, preferred shares carry a senior claim on both the receipt of income (i.e., cash dividends) and the distribution of assets. As discussed in Chapter 17, the marginal cost of each of these sources of equity capital to a firm differs. New issues of common equity are generally the most expensive, followed by retained earnings, and then preferred shares. A detailed discussion of the characteristics of the various types of equity is presented in Chapters 22 through 24.

FACTORS THAT INFLUENCE THE CAPITAL STRUCTURE DECISION

Due to its apparent "cheapness," debt capital appears to be an extremely attractive source of funds. In fact, it appears that the overall cost of funds to the firm would decrease, and thus the expected return to equity holders would increase, with an increasing use of debt. Therefore, it would seem logical to use as much debt as possible; that is, 100 percent debt financing.

However, additional debt would also increase the uncertainty of returns to equity holders. Since equity holders expect a higher return to accompany an increased risk, the objective of the capital structure decision must be to obtain the optimal trade-off between expected return and risk. Thus, the relevant measures of return and risk—and the consequences of ignoring risk—are discussed next.

Return Stream   The characteristics of the stream of returns generated by the assets of an ongoing firm are important considerations in making the capital structure decision. The generally accepted measure of the stream of returns generated by a firm's assets is the firm's stream of pretax operating income (i.e., earnings before interest and taxes, or EBIT). This measure is appropriate because it does not mix financing effects and their associated tax effects with investment effects. In other words, EBIT represents the stream of returns generated by the firm's assets before the deduction of either interest or taxes. Since interest payments depend upon the manner by which projects have been financed, and thus on management's attitude towards the firm's target capital structure, any return measure that is net of interest payments depends on the firm's capital structure. Similarly, since taxes paid by a firm depend on factors, such as the tax environment and the tax shield from interest expense, any return measure that is net of taxes will also depend on the firm's capital structure.

Risk   The risks of both the stream of returns generated by the assets of an ongoing firm and by the way the firm is financed are important considerations in making the capital structure decision. Both of these risks will be discussed next—the former is called business risk, the latter is called financial risk.

Business Risk   *Business risk*, or what is commonly referred to as *economic* or *operating risk*, is measured by the variability of a firm's EBIT. This type of risk was examined in Chapter 4, where it was defined in terms of the probability distribution of EBIT (i.e., $\tilde{X}$) generated by the firm's assets.* The business risk of a firm is the result of many factors— some unique to the firm, some common to all the firms in the same industry, and some dependent on the general state of the economy. Some of the important factors include fluctuation in demand; variability in the selling prices of a firm's goods or services; changes in the costs of inputs (e.g., rapidly rising oil prices); the ability to adjust prices for changes in costs (especially inflation); the level of operating leverage; the rate of technological innovation (or conversely, technological obsolescence); the level of competition; the state of labour relations; and international exposure. As a result, business risk varies not only from industry to industry, but also among the firms in a given industry. Although investment decisions significantly impact upon the firm's business risk, firms cannot totally control their business risk. Thus, the business risk of a firm will change somewhat over time, even if the firm maintains its assets unchanged. Business risk is practically independent of the firm's financing decisions; that is, variations in EBIT are generally independent of the firm's financial leverage.†

Financial Risk   Financial risk and financial leverage were discussed in detail in Chapter 4. *Financial risk* is generally defined as the additional variability introduced into the stream of per-share earnings by the use of financial leverage. *Financial leverage* is generally defined as the use of financing sources, which have a contractually fixed cost that must be paid according to a fixed schedule, in order to magnify the effects of changes in the firm's EBIT on the firm's earnings per share (eps). Financial risk is determined by the relationship between the firm's debt and equity capital, since the only "fixed" financial charge the firm must pay is interest on debt. As the amount of debt increases, so do the

---

*The " ~ " indicates that X is a random variable.

†At extremely high levels of debt-to-equity and poor economic conditions, a firm's capital structure may affect its EBIT stream. More specifically, firms that are having difficulty servicing a large debt load may face a real threat of bankruptcy, and thus may forego profitable investment opportunities. In addition, the firm's EBIT stream may be affected because such firms may have difficulty obtaining trade credit; may be unable to attract or retain competent employees without paying premium salaries; and may be overly anxious to meet the excessive contract demands of their unionized employees in order to avoid a work stoppage.

fixed payments required, and so does financial risk. The effect of financial leverage on the variability of a firm's eps distribution, and thus on its financial risk, is illustrated in the following example. Note that the example would not have been changed materially if preferred shares had been used instead of debt, provided that it was assumed that management considered it necessary to make the preferred dividend payments.

EXAMPLE   Radium Hot Water Ltd. has two alternative financing plans to raise $100,000 to finance a new health spa. Plan 1 consists of the issue of 4,000 common shares at $25 per share; and plan 2 consists of the issue of 2,000 common shares at $25 per share and $50,000 of bonds at a 6-percent interest rate. The impacts of these proposed financing plans on the firm's eps, for various possible levels of EBIT, are given in Tables 18.1a and 18.1b. Since the financing and investment decisions are independent, the probability distribution of EBIT is unaffected by the choice of the financing alternative.

Table 18.1a   The Impact of Financing Plan 1 on the eps of Radium Hot Water Ltd. for Various Levels of EBIT

Probability of EBIT, $P(X)$	0.05	0.20	0.50	0.20	0.05
EBIT, X	$2,000	$5,000	$10,000	$15,000	$18,000
Tax @ 40%	800	2,000	4,000	6,000	7,200
Earnings available for common, EAC	$1,200	$3,000	$6,000	$9,000	$10,800
Shares outstanding, N	4,000	4,000	4,000	4,000	4,000
eps	$0.30	$0.75	$1.50	$2.25	$2.70

Table 18.1b   The Impact of Financing Plan 2 on the eps of Radium Hot Water Ltd. for Various Levels of EBIT

Probability of EBIT, $P(X)$	0.05	0.20	0.50	0.20	0.05
EBIT, X	$2,000	$5,000	$10,000	$15,000	$18,000
− Interest, I	3,000	3,000	3,000	3,000	3,000
EBT	$(1,000)	$2,000	$7,000	$12,000	$15,000
− Taxes @ 40%	(400)[a]	800	2,800	4,800	6,000
EAC	$(600)	$1,200	$4,200	$7,200	$9,000
Shares outstanding, N	2,000	2,000	2,000	2,000	2,000
eps	$(0.30)	$0.60	$2.10	$3.60	$4.50

[a]The availability of a tax credit in full is assumed.

The calculation of the means, variances, and coefficients of variation of the probability distributions of eps for plans 1 and 2 are presented in Table 18.2. Although variance is generally used to measure variability, the coefficient of variation is the more appropriate measure in this example, because it allows us to compare the relative variability of the two eps distributions, given that they have different means (i.e., different expected values). While the coefficient of variation of EBIT measures business risk, the coefficient of variation of eps measures the total risk borne by the shareholders. As is evident from Table 18.2, the total risk of plan 1—the coefficient of variation of eps of 0.41—is identical to its business risk—the coefficient of variation of EBIT of 0.41. Since plan 2 contains debt financing and thus financial risk, the total risk of plan 2—the coefficient of variation of eps of 0.58—is greater than its business risk—the coefficient of variation of EBIT of 0.41. Thus, whenever debt (or preferred shares) is used to finance a project, the total risk borne by the common shareholders becomes greater than the business risk. This additional risk is referred to as *financial risk*.

Table 18.2 The Impact of Financing Plans 1 and 2 on the eps of Radium Hot Water Ltd. for the Expected Level of EBIT

	Plan 1	Plan 2
Expected EBIT, $\overline{X}$	$10,000.00	$10,000.00
Standard deviation of EBIT, σ_x	$ 4,049.69	$ 4,049.69
Coefficient of variation of EBIT, $\sigma_x / \overline{X}$	0.41	0.41
Expected eps, eps	$1.50	$2.10
Variance of eps, V_{eps}	$0.37	$1.48
Standard deviation of eps, σ_{eps}	$0.61	$1.22
Coefficient of variation of eps, $\sigma_{eps} / \overline{eps}$	0.41	0.58

The above example illustrates that both the expected eps and the variability of eps increase with an increase in financial leverage (i.e., with an increase in the proportion of debt-to-equity financing), provided that the investment decision is economically justified and does not depend upon the financing decision.* That is, *for a given probability distribution of EBIT, the resulting expected value and variability (risk) of eps is increased by financial leverage.*

MEASUREMENT OF THE IMPACT OF ALTERNATIVE CAPITAL STRUCTURES

Basically, the choice of a particular capital structure or new financing alternative involves choosing that capital structure or financing alternative that will maximize the well-being of a firm's owners or shareholders. As discussed in detail in Chapter 1, there are two commonly proposed measures of the well-being of a profit-oriented firm's owners or shareholders: the firm's eps and the owners' or shareholders' wealth. Each of these will now be discussed.

Impact on the Firm's eps   This accounting-based measure for evaluating the effect of alternative capital structures or new financing proposals was discussed in Chapter 4, where it was referred to as an EBIT-eps analysis. When using this approach, the financial manager first estimates a single value for EBIT, and then calculates the

*The evaluation of investment decisions (i.e., capital budgeting projects) was discussed in Chapters 14, 15, and 16.

eps for each level of financial leverage or for each financing proposal. The financial manager then selects the level of financial leverage that maximizes eps. As discussed in Chapter 1, eps maximization is not an appropriate measure of well-being because it does not consider such factors as risk. This is best illustrated by the following example.

EXAMPLE   The eps distribution for each financing plan for Radium Hot Water Ltd. was determined in the preceding example. It is also graphically depicted in Figure 18.1.

Susie Wong is the financial vice-president of the firm. As shown in Figure 18.2, if Susie assumes an optimistic EBIT value of more than $6,000, then the firm's eps will be maximized by adopting plan 2. In this case, the EBIT-eps analysis is biased toward the financing option with the greatest financial leverage (i.e., plan 2). If Susie assumes a pessimistic EBIT value of less than $6,000, then the firm's eps will be maximized by adopting plan 1. In this case, the EBIT-eps analysis is biased toward the financing option with the least financial leverage (i.e., plan 1). If Susie assumes a EBIT value of $6,000, then both of the financing plans will yield the same eps. (Note that the calculation of this indifference point was discussed in Chapter 4. Basically, it involves solving for the level of EBIT at which the eps values of both financing plans are equal.)

A decision based on the expected EBIT of $10,000 would lead to the acceptance of financing plan 2—the financing plan with debt. However, this could be inappropriate because if the actual EBIT was $2,000, then the firm might not be able to pay its interest commitment. This, in turn, could lead to financial distress. Therefore, the evaluation of alternative financing plans by measuring their impact on a firm's eps is not appropriate, since this measure does *not* adequately handle financial risk (including the increased risk of insolvency).*

Impact on the Wealth of a Firm's Owners or Shareholders   In the preceding section, it was demonstrated that for any given level of business risk (i.e., for any given distribution of EBIT), the higher the proportion of debt in a firm's capital structure, the larger the mean, the variance, and the coefficient of variation of earnings per share. This finding, along with the assumption that investors are in general risk averse, leads to the conclusion that, if other things are held constant, the required rate of return on equity capital will increase as the proportion of debt used by a firm increases. In other words, as the proportion of debt in the capital structure increases, the cost of equity capital will increase.

While the marginal return of an additional dollar of debt financing is directly observable, it is obvious that the *effective* marginal cost of the additional dollar of debt financing is not directly observable, since this cost is equal to or greater than the *explicit* or *direct* marginal cost of debt, k_i, which was calculated in Chapter 17. More specifically, debt financing generally has an *implicit* or *indirect* cost equal to the risk premium the

---

*One of the shortcomings of using accounting flows (i.e., EBIT) instead of cash flows (i.e., operating cash flows) is that the inclusion of debt in a firm's capital structure may lead to liquidity problems that are not revealed by an analysis of accounting flows. For example, a firm may have a liquidity problem if its operating cash flow is insufficient to cover interest charges as well as sinking-fund requirements. This aspect is considered in greater detail in a later section of the chapter.

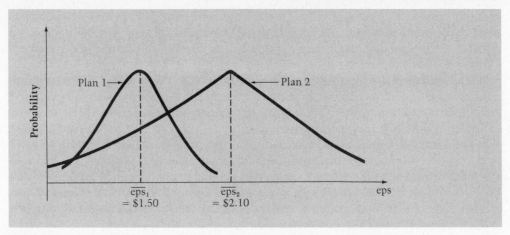

Figure 18.1   The impact of the financing plans on the eps of Radium Hot Water Ltd.

firm's owners or shareholders require for bearing the financial risk caused by employing debt in the firm's capital structure.

Based on the discussion of the objective of financial management in Chapter 1, the *net impact of alternative capital structures or financing plans is best measured by its effect on* the wealth of the firm's owners or shareholders, as measured by *the total market value of a firm's common shares*. Unlike eps, the market value incorporates

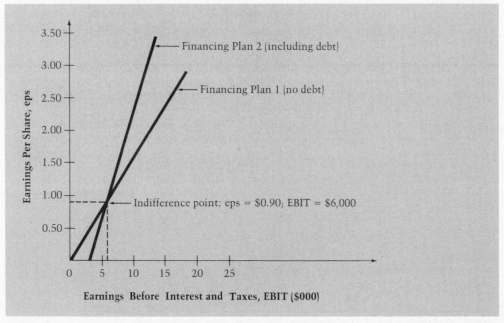

Figure 18.2   Indifference analysis of the impact of the two financing plans on the eps of Radium Hot Water Ltd. for various levels of EBIT.

both the expected return and financial risk consequences of alternative capital structures or financing plans. Thus, if all other factors are held constant, the optimal capital structure is the one that maximizes share values (or alternatively, minimizes the firm's overall weighted average cost of capital).

The existence of an "optimal" capital structure, which would lead to a maximum market value and a minimum cost of capital, has been the subject of extensive debate. As in many other controversial issues (e.g., dividend policy) in finance, there are basically two opposing points of view. At one extreme, there is the traditional viewpoint that maintains that there is an optimal capital structure, because the implicit cost of debt *does not* (for moderate amounts of debt) *offset* the advantage of using low explicit-cost debt financing; at the other extreme, there is the "uncorrected" Modigliani-Miller (MM) viewpoint that maintains that there is no optimal capital structure because the implicit cost of debt is such that it *always exactly offsets* the advantage of using low explicit-cost debt financing.

A discussion of the two opposing viewpoints is the subject matter of the next two major sections of this chapter. In order to provide some insight into what is meant by an "optimal capital structure," we shall begin by examining the assumptions and cost functions that are part of the traditional theory of capital structure.

Capital Structure and Valuation: The Traditional Viewpoint

Although the traditional viewpoint is more judgmental than analytical, it does seem to conform to the observed capital structure makeups of most business firms, as is given in Table 18.3. In other words, this position does seem to correspond with the observation

Table 18.3   Debt-to-Common-Equity Ratios for Selected Canadian Industries

Line of business	Debt-to-equity ratio based on	
	Book values	Market values
Communications and media	0.19	0.09
Consumer products	0.37	0.43
Industrial products	0.50	0.50
Management companies	0.95	1.44
Merchandising	0.83	0.70
Metals and minerals	0.53	0.44
Oil and gas	0.35	0.25
Paper and forest products	0.66	0.77
Pipelines	1.60	1.31
Real estate and construction	0.08	0.10
Transportation	0.95	1.50
Utilities	1.36	1.48

SOURCE: Compiled from data given in *Performance Summaries, Major Canadian Industries* (McLeod Young Weir Ltd., 1977). Based on data for 1976.

that firms in different lines of business employ different proportions of debt and equity. Thus, as expected, regulated industries such as the utilities and pipelines, which have very stable and predictable sale revenue and EBIT patterns (i.e., low business risk), have the highest leverage ratios. Industries such as oil and gas, communications and the media, and real estate and construction, which have very volatile sale revenue and EBIT patterns (i.e., high business risk), have the lowest leverage ratios.*

ASSUMPTIONS

The basic traditional approach to capital structure is based on the following simplifying assumptions.

Financing Through Debt and Equity   The traditional approach assumes that only two sources of financing are available to the firm—debt and equity. This assumption simplifies graphical representation of the analysis since only two dimensions are required. Also, to simplify the discussion, we will assume that the *debt* is *perpetual* and that it carries a *fixed-coupon rate.*

No-Growth Firm   The assumption of no-growth ensures that the firm's investment strategy can be taken as being given, and thus the analysis can concentrate exclusively on the effects of alternative capital structures.

A 100-Percent Dividend Payout   The firm is assumed to pay out *all* earnings in the form of cash dividends. This assumption is consistent with the no-growth firm assumption.

No Income or Capital Gains Taxes   This assumption simplifies the analysis, but does not detract from the general relationships. The introduction of corporate taxes results in an interest tax shield from debt financing and a CCA tax shield from CCA deductions.

Fixed Distribution of Earnings Before Interest and Taxes (EBIT) over Time   The distribution of EBIT is assumed to be the same for all future time periods, so that the expected value and variance (i.e., business risk) of EBIT are constant over time. This assumption is appropriate for a no-growth firm, and it allows us to isolate the effects of financial risk (i.e., financial leverage). If either expected EBIT or the variance of EBIT were allowed to vary, then a different "optimum" capital structure would exist for each different distribution of EBIT.

Changes in Financial Leverage   It is assumed that the firm decreases its financial leverage by selling shares and using the proceeds to retire bonds, or increases its financial leverage by issuing bonds and using the proceeds to retire shares. It is also assumed that these changes are costless—that there are no issue or transaction costs

---

*It should be noted that because of the nature of the industry, large amounts of short-term debt are used in the real estate and construction industry.

in issuing or retiring bonds or shares. Keeping the total amount of capital constant makes it easier to isolate the effects of a changing capital structure "mix" on the firm's value.

Although many of these assumptions are unrealistic, many of them can be relaxed without materially changing the implications of the basic traditional approach to capital structure.* On the other hand, these assumptions are extremely useful in formulating a simple model that is able to convey a basic understanding of capital structure theory.

COST FUNCTIONS NEEDED TO FIND THE VALUE OF THE FIRM

The value of the firm is determined by adding the market value of the firm's debt to the market value of its equity. Once the firm's market value has been determined, its overall cost of capital, or overall *capitalization rate*, can be found. The calculation of each of these items is described below, using a simple example.

The Cost of Debt Function According to the basic traditional approach, the explicit cost of debt, k_i, remains constant with moderate usage of financial leverage. At some point, lenders will begin to perceive the firm as having become financially more risky, and thus the cost of debt function will become upward sloping. This cost of debt function is presented graphically in Figure 18.3. Leverage is measured on the x-axis (the horizontal axis) by the ratio of the market value of debt, B, to the market value of equity, S.

The market value of the firm's debt is calculated by capitalizing (i.e., discounting) the constant annual dollar interest payments made to debt holders, which are expected to be constant over an infinite time horizon, at the firm's cost of debt.† As discussed in Chapter 13, an *infinite* stream of constant annual dollar interest payments can be capitalized at a given rate by dividing the annual interest payments by the capitalization rate, k_i (in this case, the cost of debt).‡

The Cost of Equity Function According to the basic traditional approach, the general relationship between the cost of equity, k_e, and leverage is presented in Figure 18.3. The cost of equity increases with increasing leverage, but much more rapidly than the cost of debt. The increase in the cost of equity occurs because market participants recognize that the cash dividends expected to be paid by a firm must be discounted at a higher rate as leverage increases in order to compensate for the higher degree of financial risk associated with their investment.

As discussed in Chapter 17, the market value of the firm's equity is calculated by capitalizing (i.e., discounting) the cash dividends expected to be paid to the firm's equity

---

*The effect of relaxing some of these assumptions will be examined in a later section of this chapter.
†The term *capitalize* is commonly used to refer to the process of converting a future stream of cash flows into its present value. This is done merely by discounting the cash flows at the appropriate cost of capital, or *capitalization rate*. The capitalization rate is largely a function of how the market views the risk of the firm. It is the same as the required return and risk-adjusted discount rate discussed in Chapter 16.
‡As was discussed in Chapter 13, this is merely the procedure for finding the present value of a *perpetuity* (i.e., an annuity with an infinite life).

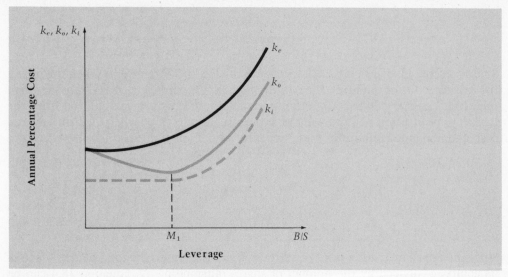

Figure 18.3   The traditional position on the cost of debt, the cost of equity, and the overall cost of capital functions.

holders at the firm's cost of equity. These cash dividends are expected to be constant over an infinite time horizon. As discussed in Chapter 13, an *infinite* stream of equal cash dividends can be capitalized at a given rate by dividing the annual cash dividends by the capitalization rate, k_e (in this case, the cost of equity).

The Overall Cost of Capital Function   The overall cost of capital, or overall capitalization rate, k_o, is found by first determining the total market value of the firm, V, and then using V and $\overline{X}$ (i.e., the firm's expected EBIT) to determine at what rate the expected EBIT must have been capitalized in order for the firm's market value to equal V (i.e., $B + S$). Thus,

$$k_o = \frac{\overline{X}}{V} \tag{18.1}$$

Figure 18.3 shows the function for the firm's overall (or weighted average) cost of capital.* It also shows the firm's cost of debt and cost of equity functions. The point labeled "M_1" represents the "optimal" leverage for the firm, since it is at this point that the firm's overall capitalization rate, k_o, reaches a minimum, and the market value of the firm reaches a maximum.† This can be shown by rearranging Equation 18.1 as

---

*The overall and weighted average cost of capital are one and the same. The term *overall cost of capital* is used here since it is used in the theoretical literature.

†This implies that a value-maximizing firm should strive to attain and remain at its optimal capital structure, since this structure will minimize the firm's overall cost of capital. Thus, once the firm has reached its optimal capital structure, it should subsequently finance all its investments out of its common pool of funds so as to maintain its optimal capital structure proportions of debt and equity. However, as was discussed in Chapter 17, the optimal capital structure is in practice only a target value, because at any moment in time the firm will deviate somewhat from its optimal capital structure due to practical considerations.

follows:

$$V = \frac{\overline{X}}{k_o} \qquad (18.2)$$

Since expected EBIT (i.e., $\overline{X}$) is held constant, the lower the value of k_o, then the higher the market value of the firm. *The optimal capital structure is therefore that at which the overall cost of capital, k_o, is minimized.* Like the market value of the firm, the market price of a firm's equity will also be at a maximum value when the firm's overall cost of capital is at a minimum value, and vice versa. Equation 18.2 can be rewritten as:

$$V = S + B = \frac{\overline{X}}{k_o} \qquad (18.3)$$

or

$$S = \frac{\overline{X}}{k_o} - B \qquad (18.4)$$

Since the per-share market price of a firm's equity is equal to the total market value of its equity, S, divided by the number of shares outstanding, N, Equation 18.4 can be rewritten as

$$P = \frac{S}{N} = \frac{1}{N}\left(\frac{\overline{X}}{k_o} - B\right) \qquad (18.5)$$

Thus, for a *fixed* value of $\overline{X}$, Equation 18.5 states that the market price per share is at a maximum value when the overall cost of capital is at a minimum value, and vice versa.

Thus, it is important to emphasize that *the three objectives of maximizing the market value of a firm, maximizing the per-share market price of a firm's equity, and minimizing a firm's overall cost of capital are all equivalent and interchangeable objectives.* An example may help to clarify the traditional approach.

EXAMPLE   Windsor Silver Plating Ltd. currently has earnings before interest and taxes (i.e., EBIT) of $16,000. Since Windsor Silver Plating expects not to grow, its level of EBIT is expected to remain at its current level over the firm's infinite life. The firm currently has $50,000 of outstanding debt which carries an 8-percent coupon rate. For the firm's current capital structure, the cost of debt, k_i, is 8 percent and the cost of equity, k_e, is 12 percent. The current market value of the firm, V, can be found as follows:

$$
\begin{aligned}
\text{EBIT} &= & \$16,000 \\
-I &= (\$50,000 \cdot .08) = & 4,000 \\
\hline
\text{EAC} = D &= & \$12,000 \\
S &= \frac{\$12,000}{.12} = & \$100,000 \\[2mm]
B &= \frac{\$4,000}{.08} = & 50,000 \\
\hline
V = S + B &= & \$150,000
\end{aligned}
$$

Substituting the current market value of the firm (i.e., $150,000) into Equation 18.1, gives the overall cost of capital of 10.67 percent (i.e., $16,000 ÷ $150,000). The debt-equity ratio (B/S) in this case equals 0.50 (i.e., $50,000 ÷ $100,000).

The firm is considering increasing its financial leverage by issuing an additional $20,000 of debt and using the proceeds to retire that amount of equity. If it does sell this additional debt, the firm will have debt on the books at a value of $70,000. The firm's cost of debt, k_i, will rise to 9 percent due to the increased financial risk of the new debt-to-equity structure. (Figure 18.3 presented the general relationship between the cost of debt and leverage.) The cost of equity, k_e, will increase to 14 percent, as a result of the increased financial leverage. (Figure 18.3 presented the general relationship between the cost of equity and leverage.) Because of the change in its capital structure, the market value of Windsor Silver Plate will change as follows:

$$
\begin{array}{lll}
\text{EBIT} = & & \$16,000.00 \\
-I = & & \underline{\$\ 5,800.00^*} \\
\hline
\text{EAC} = D = & & \$10,200.00 \\
& S = \dfrac{\$10,200}{.14} = & \$72,857.14 \\
& & \\
& B = \dfrac{\$5,800}{.09} = & \$64,444.44 \\
& & \\
V = & S + B = & \underline{\underline{\$137,301.58}}
\end{array}
$$

The overall capitalization rate will rise to 11.65 percent (i.e., $16,000.00 ÷ $137,301.58), and the debt-equity ratio will rise to 0.88 (i.e., $64,444.44 ÷ $72,857.14).

Although the optimal capital structure for the firm in the previous example was not found, it is obvious that the optimal debt-equity ratio must be less than 0.88. At that ratio, the market value of the firm is $137,301.58; while at a debt-equity ratio of 0.50, it is $150,000.00.† However, the nature of the traditional relationship between the cost of debt, k_i, the cost of equity, k_e, and the resulting overall cost of capital, k_o, should now be clear. Referring to Figure 18.3 may help relate this example to traditional capital structure theory. This section should also have given one an appreciation of the relationship between the firm's cost of capital and the owners' or shareholders' total wealth. The lower the firm's overall, or weighted average, cost of capital, the higher is the total wealth (as measured by the market) of the firm's owners or shareholders in the firm. Or in other words, given a fixed capital budget and fixed investment opportunities, the less the firm's money costs, the greater the total NPV will be from investing that capital budget.

---

*Total annual interest payment = (0.8) ($50,000) + (0.9) ($20,000).

†One way to find the optimal capital structure would be to find, through trial and error, the debt-equity ratios on either side of a given debt-equity ratio that result in lower valuations than the middle ratio. The optimum debt-equity ratio would be somewhere between the two outside ratios. More sophisticated mathematical or graphical techniques could also be used to estimate the optimal capital structure.

ALTERNATIVE FORMULATIONS OF THE TRADITIONAL VIEWPOINT

A number of alternative formulations of the traditional model have been proposed. One such alternative formulation is represented graphically in Figure 18.4(a). In this formulation, it is argued that the cost of equity function does not rise until some critical value of the debt-equity ratio is reached. That is, prior to this critical point, the increased financial risk of additional debt is either not perceived or is considered to be insignificant by equity investors. Thus, up to point "M_2," the implicit cost of debt does not adversely affect the market price of equity. Thus, the firm's optimal capital structure (i.e., M_2) for this formulation has a greater B/S ratio than that for the previous formulation (i.e., $M_2 > M_1$).

According to still another formulation of the traditional approach, the overall cost of capital, k_o, is saucer-shaped, as is shown in Figure 18.4(b). Hence, there is a range of optimal capital structures within which financial leverage has no effect on the value of the firm.

• Capital Structure and Valuation: The Modigliani and Miller (MM) Viewpoint

In 1958, Modigliani and Miller (MM) published their seminal paper on the cost of capital, corporate valuation, and capital structure. As indicated in Chapter 1, the paper profoundly affected the study of corporation finance. In fact, it has probably been the single most important contribution to the theory of corporation finance in the last 25 years.

ASSUMPTIONS

The MM approach to capital structure is based on the following simplifying assumptions.

Financing Through Debt and Equity   The MM approach assumes that only two sources of financing are available to the firm—*risk-free* debt and (risky) equity. It is also assumed that the debt is *perpetual* and that it carries a *fixed-coupon rate.*

No-Growth Firms   The assumption of no-growth means that each firm will have no new *net* investment (i.e., each firm will just maintain the economic value or earning power of its existing assets). As a result, each firm will pay out 100 percent of its cash earnings in the form of *cash* dividends, and the EBIT and cash dividend streams of all firms will be perpetuities.

No Income or Capital Gains Taxes   It is assumed that there are no taxes on the income or capital gains of individuals or corporations.

•This section may be bypassed during the first reading of the chapter.

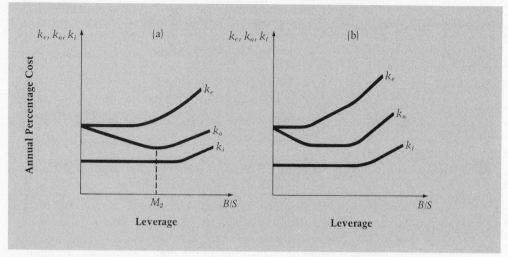

Figure 18.4   Alternative traditional positions on the overall cost of capital function.

Fixed Distribution of Earnings Before Interest and Taxes (EBIT) over Time   The distribution of a firm's EBIT is assumed to be the same for all future time periods. Thus, the expected value and variance (i.e., business risk) of EBIT are constant over time.

Firms Can Be Classified into Homogeneous Risk Classes   MM assumed that firms could be classified, according to their business risk, into homogeneous risk classes. By this, MM meant that the expected EBIT of firms in the same risk class are perfectly correlated and therefore differ by, at most, a "scale factor."*

No Bankruptcy Costs   It is assumed that bankruptcy is costless.

Perfect Capital Markets   The assumptions and implications of perfect capital markets are discussed in Chapters 16 and 19. These assumptions can be briefly summarized as follows: (1) transactions are *frictionless* (i.e., there are no transaction costs in issuing, retiring, or trading the firm's financial claims)†; (2) all existing and prospective investors have complete, identical (i.e., *homogeneous*), and costless information about the EBIT distributions of all firms; (3) all assets are perfectly divisible and marketable; (4) all market participants (i.e., investors and firms) can borrow or lend an unlimited amount of funds at the risk-free rate of interest; (5) all market participants are rational wealth maximizers; and (6) no market participant is large enough to have any impact on market prices.

---

*As discussed earlier in the chapter, two distributions that differ by a scale factor will have the same coefficient of variation.
†Although the existence of transaction costs could impede the arbitrage process, the effects of arbitrage could be achieved simply by investors biasing the investment of new funds to undervalued firms.

Although many of these assumptions are unrealistic, it will be shown in a later section that relaxing them does not really change the major conclusions reached by MM.

COST OF CAPITAL FUNCTIONS

Based on the above assumptions, MM derived the overall cost of capital function and the cost of equity capital function. Before proceeding to a discussion of each of these functions, it should be noted that MM's cost of debt capital function, k_i, is horizontal because it is assumed to be equal to the risk-free rate of interest.

The Overall Cost of Capital Function   The overall cost of capital function is given by MM's first (i.e., irrelevance) proposition, which can be worded as follows:

> The market value of any given firm is independent of its capital structure and is given by capitalizing its expected return (i.e., its expected EBIT) at the rate, k_o, appropriate to its risk class. That is, the overall cost of capital, k_o, to any firm is completely independent of its capital structure and is equal to the capitalization rate of a pure equity stream of its risk class.

Before presenting the "arbitrage" proof of this proposition, we will present a graphical representation of a firm's cost of capital functions and will discuss the implications of this proposition.

Graphical Representation of the Cost of Capital Functions   The cost of capital functions, according to MM, can be graphically represented as in Figure 18.5. This shows that, since the explicit cost of debt function, k_i, is constant, the overall cost of capital function, k_o, can be constant only if the cost of equity function, k_e, is a linearly increasing function of financial leverage. In fact, as will be shown later in

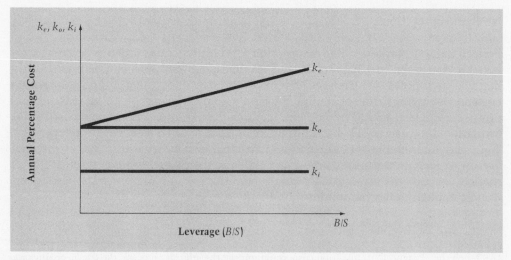

Figure 18.5   The MM position on the cost of debt, the cost of equity, and the overall cost of capital functions.

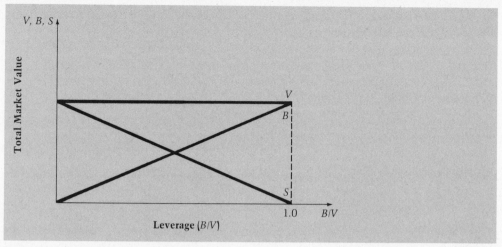

Figure 18.6   The MM position on the market value of the firm, the market value of its debt, and the market value of its equity.

the chapter, the slope of the cost of equity function must be such that the overall cost of capital, k_o, remains constant.

The market value functions, according to the MM position, can be graphically represented as in Figure 18.6. In the figure, it is shown that, since the market value of debt increases with increasing leverage, the total value of the firm can be constant only if the value of the firm's equity is a linearly decreasing function of the firm's financial leverage.

Implications of MM's First Proposition   According to MM's first proposition, the market value of any firm is given by

$$V = \frac{\overline{X}}{k_o} \qquad (18.6)$$

where V is the market value of the firm (i.e., the sum of the market value of a firm's debt, B, and the market value of a firm's equity, S)[*]; $\overline{X}$ is the firm's expected EBIT; and k_o is the firm's overall cost of capital (i.e., overall capitalization rate given its business risk). Equation 18.6 can be rewritten as

$$k_o = \frac{\overline{X}}{V} \qquad (18.7)$$

Since $\overline{X}$ is assumed to be constant, Equations 18.6 and 18.7 imply that the market value of the firm, V, is at a maximum value when the firm's overall cost of capital, k_o, is at a minimum value, and vice versa.

For a leveraged firm, the firm's $\overline{X}$ will be divided in its entirety between the firm's debt holders and equity holders. In other words, a portion of $\overline{X}$ equal to $k_i B$ will be paid to the firm's debt holders in the form of cash interest payments; and the remainder of $\overline{X}$ (i.e.,

---

[*]Given MM's assumptions, the market and book values of a firm's debt will be the same.

$\overline{X} - k_iB)$, will be paid to the firm's equity holders in the form of cash dividends. Thus, Equation 18.7 can be rewritten as:

$$k_o = \frac{\overline{X} - k_iB}{V} + \frac{k_iB}{V}$$

or

$$k_o = \left(\frac{\overline{X} - k_iB}{S}\right)\left(\frac{S}{V}\right) + k_i\frac{B}{V} \tag{18.8}$$

However, since the cost of equity, k_e, is equal to $(\overline{X} - k_iB)/S$, then Equation 18.8 can be rewritten as:

$$k_o = k_e\frac{S}{V} + k_i\frac{B}{V} \tag{18.9}$$

This shows that the *overall cost of capital and the weighted average cost of capital are identical.*

Thus, in order to show that an optimal capital structure exists for a given $\tilde{X}$, it is necessary to show that a particular capital structure will result in a higher market value for the firm (or a higher per-share market price or a lower cost of capital) than that for all other possible capital structures.

"Arbitrage" Proof of Proposition 1*   The rationale behind proposition 1 is simply that, in an efficient capital market, the market value of a whole should not be dependent upon how the whole is divided. Conceptually, such a statement can be proven in the following three steps: (1) make the statement of the proposition explicit; (2) determine if a market equilibrium is consistent with the violation of the proposition; and (3) determine the effects of violations of the proposition's underlying assumptions. The underlying logic of this procedure and the arbitrage logic is best illustrated by first using an example that does not deal with a capital structure decision.

EXAMPLE   Nick Donnello is a Montreal street vendor of hot dogs (often referred to as "steamies"). Nick believes that the market for hot dogs satisfies all of the MM assumptions; and in particular, transactions (i.e., combining the individual components of a hot dog into the whole hot dog, or the reverse process) are assumed to be costless. Furthermore, Nick can either buy a whole hot dog or he can buy the only two components of a hot dog (i.e., the bun and the frankfurter) separately. For the hot dog market, the proposition can be made explicit as follows:

---

*Arbitrage means simultaneously buying and selling the same good, or its perfect substitute, for a profit. The importance of the arbitrage argument in analytically solving many of the problems of finance cannot be overemphasized. In Chapter 1 it was stated that finance deals with how various parties allocate scarce resources through a market-pricing system based on the valuation of risky assets. The existence of no profitable arbitrage opportunities is essential to the equilibrium of such market-pricing systems and the efficient valuation of risky assets. For example, an arbitrage-type argument was fundamental in the derivation of the Black-Scholes option pricing model, which is discussed in Chapter 22, and in the derivation of the Ross arbitrage pricing model.

Proposition: price (whole hot dog) = price (bun) + price (frankfurter)

Thus, the market-pricing relationship implies that if the price of a bun is $0.40 and the price of a frankfurter is $0.60, then the price of the whole hot dog, on average, should be $1.00. Implicit in this statement is that if, for any reason, the pricing relationship is violated (i.e., the market is in *disequilibrium*), then market forces will tend to bring prices back into line (i.e., into *equilibrium*).

What happens if the proposition is violated? There are two possibilities: either Nick can buy a whole hot dog for more than the sum of the cost of a bun and a frankfurter, or he can buy a whole hot dog for less than the sum of the cost of a bun and a frankfurter. In either case, Nick will have an incentive to engage in arbitrage transactions.

If the first case exists (i.e., a whole hot dog costs $1.10, while a bun costs $0.40 and a frankfurter costs $0.60), then Nick would have a profitable "arbitrage" opportunity. That is, he could buy a bun and a frankfurter for a combined cost of $1.00 and then sell the whole hot dog for marginally less than $1.10. Such arbitrage activities by Nick (and all the other rational street vendors) would drive the price of a whole hot dog to its equilibrium price of $1.00.

If the second case exists (i.e., a whole hot dog costs $0.90, while a bun costs $0.40 and a frankfurter costs $0.60), then Nick would have a profitable "arbitrage" opportunity. That is, he could buy a whole hot dog for a cost of $0.90 cents and then sell their two components (i.e., the bun and the frankfurter) for a combined price of $1.00. Again, such arbitrage activities by Nick (and all the other rational street vendors) would drive the market price of a whole hot dog to its equilibrium price of $1.00. Thus, only when the proposition is *not* violated, is there *no* incentive for Nick and other market participants to make arbitrage transactions.

Of course, in practice, Nick may find that "small" deviations from the proposition (i.e., market equilibrium) do not lead to profitable arbitrage opportunities. For example, there may be institutional restrictions against vendors combining buns and frankfurters into whole hot dogs or dividing whole hot dogs into buns and frankfurters. There also may be significant implicit costs, risks, or transaction costs associated with making arbitrage transactions that may impede such transactions from driving prices into equilibrium.

In a similar manner, the firm's capital structure decision is whether or not the total value of the firm (as measured by the capitalized value of its expected EBIT) is dependent upon the sum of the value of the cash payments the firm makes to its bondholders (as measured by the capitalized value of the firm's total cash interest payment) and the value of cash dividend payments the firm makes to its shareholders (as measured by the capitalized value of the firm's total cash dividend payment). Thus, MM's proposition 1 states that the market value of the firm (i.e., the total market value of the firm's real assets) is independent of how the returns generated by the firm's assets are shared among holders of debt and holders of equity. This is best illustrated by the following example.

EXAMPLE Ottawa Info Ltd. (firm A) and Hull Info Ltd. (firm B) are identical in all respects, except for their financial structures. Ottawa Info is unleveraged and has 1,000 common shares outstanding at a 20-percent cost of equity. Hull Info is leveraged. The firm has $40,000 of risk-free debt outstanding at a 12-percent coupon rate and 600 common shares outstanding. The expected earnings before interest and taxes (i.e., $\overline{EBIT}$) for each firm is $20,000. Further, suppose that all of MM's assumptions hold, and that perfect capital markets for trading both debt and equity claims exist.

The MM proposition 1 implies that

$$V_A = V_B = S_B + B_B$$

or

$100,000$ (i.e., $20,000 \div 0.20$) $= 60,000$ (i.e., $100,000 - 40,000$) $+ 40,000$

What happens if this proposition is violated? There are two possible types of violations: (1) the value of the unleveraged firm can be less than the value of the leveraged firm (i.e., $V_A < V_B$); or (2) the value of the unleveraged firm can be greater than the value of the leveraged firm (i.e., $V_A > V_B$).

Type 1 violation   Suppose that the market values of firms A and B are such that $V_A < S_B + B_B$ or $100,000 < 66,000 + 40,000$. Then the calculation of the cost of equity and the overall capitalization rate for both of the firms is given in Table 18.4.

Suppose that Jane Smith owns 10 percent of the equity (i.e., 60 shares) of firm B. She could sell her 10-percent equity interest in firm B for $6,600 (i.e., 60 shares · $110 per share). She could then buy 10 percent of the equity (i.e., 100 shares) of firm A for $10,000 (i.e., 100 shares · $100 per share) by investing $6,000 of her own money and borrowing $4,000 at 12 percent on her own account (referred to as *home-made leverage*).* By these "arbitrage" transactions, Jane

Table 18.4   Calculation of the Cost of Equity and the Overall Capitalization Rate for Firms A and B, when $V_A < V_B$

	Firm A (*unleveraged*)	Firm B (*leveraged*)
Total value of the firm, V	$100,000	$106,000
Value of debt, B	0	40,000
Value of equity, S	$100,000	$ 66,000
No. of shares outstanding, N	1,000	600
Market price per share, P	$ 100	$ 110
Expected EBIT, $\overline{X}$	$ 20,000	$ 20,000
– Interest, I	0	$ 4,800
Expected cash payment to equity holders, $\overline{D}$	$ 20,000	$ 15,200
Cost of equity, $k_e = \overline{D}/S$[a]	20.0%	23.0%
Overall capitalization rate, $k_o = \overline{X}/V$	20.0%	18.9%

[a]Note that this is consistent with the method used to calculate the marginal cost of equity in Chapter 17. More specifically, this is equivalent to the Gordon dividend valuation model, when markets are frictionless and the firm has a zero expected growth rate. Note also that $\overline{D} = \overline{EAC}$, since the firm is assumed to follow a 100-percent dividend payout policy.

*For example, Jane could buy the shares using margin (which is discussed in Chapter 19) or she could "borrow" by selling bonds from her portfolio. Also, the arbitrage activities can be conducted by financial intermediaries instead of individuals.

Table 18.5   Calculation of Jane Smith's Total Investment and Expected Dollar Return Before and After the "Arbitrage" Transactions

	Pre-transactions	Post-transactions
Market value of personal equity holding	$6,600	$10,000
— Personal loan	0	4,000
Personal investment	$6,600	$ 6,000
Prepersonal financing expected dollar returns	$1,520[a]	$ 2,000[b]
— Interest payment on personal loan	0	480[c]
Expected dollar return	$1,520	$ 1,520

[a]10% · $15,200.
[b]10% · $20,000.
[c]12% · $4,000.

would *reduce her total investment* by $600 (i.e., $6,600 − $6,000) *without changing either her expected return* of $1,520 [i.e., (10% · $15,200) = (10% · $20,000) − (12% · $4,000)] or the variance of return of her investment portfolio.* The calculation of the expected return before and after her transactions is summarized in Table 18.5.

In addition, the financial risk borne either directly or indirectly by Jane Smith has not changed. Before the transactions, Jane owned a portion of firm B's assets that were subject to a debt claim of $4,000 for every $10,600 invested. After the transactions, Jane owns a portion of firm A's assets, which are by assumption equivalent to firm B's assets, which are encumbered by $4,000 of personal debt for every $10,000 invested in firm A (the remaining $600 is also available for investment in firm A). The only difference between the two positions is that in the latter situation the debt is borne by Jane on her personal account, while in the former situation it is borne by firm B acting as Jane's agent.†

Thus, investors in firm B, like Jane Smith, will have an incentive to sell their equity in firm B and to invest in the equity of firm A. Thus, the market price of firm B's equity will fall relative to the market price of firm A's equity until the firms have an identical market value (i.e., $V_B = V_A$).

Type 2 violation   Suppose that the market values of firms A and B are such that $V_A > S_B + B_B$; or $100,000 > $54,000 + $40,000. Then the calculation of the cost of equity and the overall capitalization rate for both firms is given in Table 18.6.

Suppose that Bill Smith, who is more risk averse than his wife, owns 10 percent of the equity (i.e., 100 shares) of firm A. He could sell his 10-percent equity interest in firm A for $10,000 (i.e., 100 shares · $100 per share). He could then buy 10 percent of the equity (i.e., 60 shares) of firm B for $5,400 (i.e., 60 shares · $90 per share) and 10 percent of the debt of firm B for $4,000 (i.e., 10% · $40,000). By these "arbitrage" transactions, Bill would *reduce his total investment* by

---

*According to MM, this cost minimization proof of their proposition 1 is more general than (and thus preferable to) their original proof. See Franco Modigliani and Merton H. Miller, "Reply to Heins and Sprenkle," *American Economic Review* 59 (September 1969).

†Note that this assumes that *home-made leverage* and *corporate leverage* are *perfect substitutes*. It is equivalent to assuming that capital markets are perfect.

Table 18.6   Calculation of the Cost of Equity and the Overall Capitalization Rate for Firms A and B, when $V_A > V_B$

	Firm A (unleveraged)	Firm B (leveraged)
Total value of the firm, V	$100,000	$94,000
Value of debt, B	0	40,000
Value of equity, S	$100,000	$54,000
No. of shares outstanding, N	1,000	600
Market price per share, P	$ 100	$ 90
Expected EBIT, $\overline{X}$	$ 20,000	$20,000
− Interest, I	$ 0	$ 4,800
Expected cash payment to equity holders, $\overline{D}$	$ 20,000	$15,200
Cost of equity, $k_e = \overline{D}/S$	20.0%	28.1%
Overall capitalization rate, $k_o = \overline{X}/V$	20.0%	21.3%

$600 (i.e., $10,000 − $9,400) *without changing either his expected dollar return* of $2,000 [i.e., (10% · $20,000) = (10% · $15,200) + (10% · $4,800)] or the *variance of return* on his investment.

In addition, the financial risk borne either directly or indirectly by Bill Smith has not changed materially. Before the transactions, Bill owned a portion of firm A's assets that were subject to no debt claim. After the transactions, Bill owned a portion of firm B's assets that were subject to a debt claim of $4,000 for every $5,400 of equity. However, since Bill owned $5,400 of firm B's equity and $4,000 of firm B's debt, Bill neutralized the financial risk he had to bear (i.e., his offsetting personal holding "undid" the corporate leverage).

Thus, investors in firm A, like Bill Smith, will have an incentive to sell their equity in firm A and to invest in the equity of firm B. Thus, the market price of firm A's equity will fall relative to the market price of firm B's equity until the firms have identical market values (i.e., $V_A = V_B$).

The previous example shows that, given MM's assumptions, the exploitation of arbitrage opportunities will ensure that proposition 1 holds. Thus, there will be no optimal capital structure for a firm, because the total market value of a firm (and thus its overall cost of capital) will not depend upon the firm's capital structure.

The Cost of Equity Function   The cost of equity function is given by MM's second proposition, which can be worded as follows:

> The cost of equity capital, k_e, is equal to the appropriate capitalization rate, k_o, for a pure equity stream in the risk class, plus a premium related to financial risk equal to the debt-to-equity ratio times the spread between k_o and the cost of debt k_i.

Equation 18.9 was given earlier as

$$k_o = k_e (S/V) + k_i (B/V) \tag{18.9}$$

Solving for k_e, and using the fact that $V = B + S$, we get

$$k_e \left(\frac{S}{V}\right)\left(\frac{V}{S}\right) = k_o \left(\frac{B + S}{S}\right) - k_i \left(\frac{B}{V}\right)\left(\frac{V}{S}\right)$$

$$k_e = k_o \left(\frac{B}{S}\right) + k_o - k_i \left(\frac{B}{S}\right) \qquad (18.10)$$

$$= k_o + (k_o - k_i)\frac{B}{S}$$

Thus, proposition 2 states that the firm's cost of equity capital increases *linearly* with an increase in its use of debt (as measured by its debt-to-equity ratio), and that the premium investors require for bearing the *implicit* cost of the added debt is given by $(k_o - k_i)\,B/S$.

This result was implicitly shown in the preceding example. In that example, it was shown that as financial leverage increases, both the expected rate of return and variance of return on equity increase. Furthermore, since MM's proposition 1 states that shareholders neither gain nor lose as a result of increased financial leverage, the incremental risk (i.e., the implicit cost of added debt as measured by the increase in the cost of equity) and the incremental return (i.e., the benefits of adding low explicit-cost debt) must exactly offset each other. Thus, the overall cost of capital must remain constant.

The Relationship Between a Firm's Investment and Financing Decisions   If the firm's overall cost of capital is independent of the firm's capital structure, then MM have shown that a firm's investment decisions will be unrelated (i.e., independent) of its financing decisions. More specifically, in their proposition 3, MM state that

> The cutoff point for investment by the firm, of a given risk class, will in all cases be k_o and will be completely unaffected by the type of security used to finance the investment.

The implications of this proposition are illustrated in the following two examples.

EXAMPLE   Sigmund Publishing Ltd. is a pure equity-financed firm. The firm's overall cost of capital, k_o, is 12 percent, and its future expected EBIT is $240,000.00. In order to finance an average-risk investment opportunity (i.e., an investment having the same business risk as the firm), which requires an initial cash outlay of $100,000.00 and promises a 10-percent return, the firm would borrow funds at a cost of 8 percent. Suppose that the financial vice-president of Sigmund considers the investment and its financing to be related and thus measures the investment against the explicit cost of its specific source(s) of financing. Under such circumstances, the investment opportunity would be found acceptable, since its expected return of 10 percent is greater than its explicit financing cost of 8 percent. However, the calculations, which are summarized in Table 18.7, show that the per-share market price of the firm's equity decreased from $5.00 to $4.96 when the proposed project was accepted. In essence, the market has lowered the firm's per-share market price because the firm has accepted a project that promises a rate of return less than the firm's overall cost of capital.

Table 18.7   Effect of the Acceptance of the New Average-Risk Investment on the Per-Share Market Price of Sigmund Publishing Ltd.

	Pre-acceptance	Post-acceptance
Expected EBIT from existing assets	$240,000	$240,000
+ Expected EBIT from new average-risk investment	0	10,000
Total expected EBIT	$240,000	$250,000
Overall cost of capital, k_o	0.12	0.12
Total market value of the firm, V	$2,000,000	$2,083,333.33
− Market value of debt, B	0	100,000.00
Market value of equity, S	$2,000,000	$1,983,333.33
Expected earnings per share, $\overline{eps}$	$0.60	$0.605
Number of shares outstanding, N	400,000	400,000
Per-share market price of equity, P	$5.00	$4.96

EXAMPLE   Michele Library Services Ltd., which is in the same business risk class as Sigmund Publishing Ltd., has a capital structure consisting of 50 percent debt and 50 percent common equity (200,000 common shares outstanding). The firm's expected EBIT, cost of debt, and the overall cost of capital are the same as that given in the preceding example. The firm has an average-risk investment opportunity that requires an initial outlay of $100,000.00 and promises a return of 13 percent. Equation 18.10 can be used to determine the firm's current cost of equity, k_e, as follows:

$$k_e = k_o + (k_o - k_i)\ B/S$$
$$= .12 + (.12 - .08) \cdot 1$$
$$= .16$$

Table 18.8   Effect of the Acceptance of the New Average-Risk Investment on the Per-Share Market Price of Michele Library Services Ltd.

	Pre-acceptance	Post-acceptance
Expected EBIT from existing assets	$240,000	$240,000
+ Expected EBIT from new average-risk investment	0	13,000
Total expected EBIT	$240,000	$253,000
Overall cost of capital, k_o	0.12	0.12
Total market value of the firm, V	$2,000,000	$2,108,333.33
− Market value of debt, B	1,000,000	1,000,000.00
Market value of equity, S	$1,000,000	$1,108,333.33
Expected earnings per share, $\overline{eps}$	$0.80	0.79
Number of shares outstanding, N	200,000	220,000
Per-share market price of equity, P	$5.00	$5.04

The firm will finance the new average-risk investment by selling 20,000 shares at their current market price of $5.00. Suppose that the financial vice-president of the firm considers the investment and its financing to be related and thus measures the investment against the explicit cost of its specific source(s) of financing. Under such circumstances, the investment opportunity would not be found to be acceptable since its expected return of 13 percent is less than the equity financing cost of 16 percent. However, the calculations, which are summarized in Table 18.8, show that the per-share market price of the firm's equity would have increased from $5.00 to $5.04 if the proposed project had been accepted. In essence, the market would have increased the firm's per-share price, because the firm would have accepted a project which promised a rate of return that was greater than the firm's overall cost of capital. Thus, the dilution in the firm's eps would have been more than offset (as determined by the market) by the decrease in the firm's financial leverage.

Note from the previous example that although the firm's overall cost of capital is independent of its capital structure, it is not independent of its business risk. Thus, *the firm's overall cost of capital, given the firm's present business risk class, is only appropriate for evaluating the firm's average-risk investment opportunities* (i.e., those investment opportunities that have the same business risk as the firm). For the firm's investment opportunities that are not of the same business risk as the firm, the firm must use one of the risk-adjustment techniques discussed in Chapter 16.

• Possible Explanations for Observed Capital Structures

As discussed in the immediately preceding section of this chapter, MM's irrelevance proposition (i.e., the market value of a firm is independent of its capital structure) can be logically proven by using an "arbitrage" argument. In an earlier section of the chapter, the observed capital structures of a number of Canadian industries were presented. If capital structure is irrelevant, as MM propose, then how can the prevailing capital structures of Canadian firms be explained?

In this section of the chapter, a number of potential explanations for observed capital structures are reviewed. Since the existence of risky debt, or the market imperfections that arise from risky debt, are most often used to explain observed capital structures, the discussion will begin with the effect, if any, of risky debt on MM's irrelevance proposition.

THE EXISTENCE OF RISKY DEBT

One of the frequently criticized assumptions of the MM approach is the assumption that corporate debt is risk free (i.e., default free). If corporate debt is risky, it has been argued that current debt holders can incur a risk that the firm may transfer wealth from debt holders to equity holders through financial rearrangements. Of course, in a perfect

•This section may be bypassed during the first reading of the chapter.

capital market, debt holders will be fairly compensated for incurring this additional risk and thus MM's irrelevance proposition will not be invalidated.

In an imperfect but efficient capital market, it has been shown that MM's irrelevance proposition is not invalidated if there are perfectly enforceable "me-first" rules.[1] A *me-first rule* is a contractual arrangement or agreement that gives the firm's claimants (e.g., bondholders) veto power over any change in the investment and/or financing policy of the firm whenever such a change adversely affects the market value of the claimants' claim on the firm's cash flows and/or assets. An example of such a me-first rule was the restrictive covenant in the trust indenture of the Big Lake Manufacturing Ltd. example presented in Chapter 1.

If the firm issues risky debt without a me-first rule, it has also been shown that MM's irrelevance proposition is not invalidated if investors have the ability to create *"home-made limited liability."*[2] That is, if investors and firms have "equal" access to capital markets, a firm's financial actions cannot affect the portfolio opportunities available to investors, because investors can either do or undo the effects of such actions on their personal accounts.*

CORPORATE TAXES, BANKRUPTCY COSTS, AND OPTIMAL CAPITAL STRUCTURES

One of the common textbook explanations of observed capital structures (and for resolving the traditional and MM viewpoints) is that corporate debt policy requires an optimal trade-off between the present value of tax savings due to the tax deductibility of interest payments and the present value of potential bankruptcy costs. Each of these factors will now be discussed.

Corporate Taxes and Optimal Capital Structures   In a world with no taxes, the choice of capital structure was shown by MM to be irrelevant, since a firm's value and overall cost of capital remain constant, regardless of the degree of financial leverage employed by the firm. In a world with corporate taxes, MM show that a firm's market value and overall cost of capital become linearly dependent on its capital structure.† In this section, the relationship between the market value of a firm and its degree of financial leverage will be derived for a world with corporate taxes.

Market Value of an Unleveraged Firm   Based on Equation 18.6, the market value of an unleveraged firm, in a world of corporate taxes, is given by

$$V_u = \frac{\overline{X}(1 - T_c)}{k_o^u} = \frac{\overline{X}^T}{k_o^u} \tag{18.11}$$

---

*The underlying logic of this argument is similar to that of the home-made leverage argument discussed earlier in the chapter. An investor could create home-made limited liability by setting up an incorporated holding or investment company.

†It should be emphasized that MM regard the tax deductibility of interest as the only advantage of debt financing; whereas the proponents of the traditional approach regard debt financing as being advantageous even in a world of no taxes. See Franco Modigliani and Merton H. Miller, "Corporation Income Taxes and the Cost of Capital: A Correction," *American Economic Review* 53 (June 1963), pp. 433–443.

where V_u is the market value of the unleveraged firm; $\overline{X}$ is the firm's expected earnings before interest and taxes (i.e., EBIT); $\overline{X}^T$ is the firm's expected earnings before interest, but after taxes (i.e., EBIAT); k_o^u is the average cost of capital to an unleveraged firm; and T_c is the corporate tax rate.

Present Value of the Interest Tax Savings   Since corporate interest payments are deductible from expected EBIT (which is assumed to be constant), increases in a firm's financial leverage will reduce a corporation's tax payment, and thus will increase the *aggregate* amount a firm can pay out to its debt holders and equity holders. Stated differently, due to the tax savings of interest payments, the expected EBIAT of a leveraged firm is given by

$$\overline{X}^T = \overline{X}(1 - T_c) + T_c k_i B \qquad (18.12)$$

Thus, the overall value of the firm and the per-share market price of its equity should also increase as a firm's financial leverage increases. In fact, the market value of a leveraged firm will increase by the present value of the perpetual stream of tax savings due to the tax deductibility of interest payments (i.e., by $T_c k_i B / k_i = T_c B$). The value-adding impact of these tax savings is illustrated by the following example.

EXAMPLE   Hillcrest Mining Ltd. is a profitable company that has issued $10,000,000 of perpetual debt at an interest rate of 12 percent. The firm's corporate income tax rate is 40 percent. Thus, Hillcrest Mining's annual tax saving due to deducting the annual interest payment of $1,200,000 (i.e., 12% · $10,000,000) from taxable income is $480,000 (i.e., 0.40 · $1,200,000). Since the risk characteristics of the interest tax savings are essentially the same as those of the interest payments on the firm's debt, the present value of the $480,000 perpetuity is found by discounting that stream at 12 percent. Thus, the present value of the perpetual annual tax savings of $480,000 is $4,000,000 (i.e., $480,000 ÷ 0.12).

Market Value of a Leveraged Firm   The expected annual earnings before interest, but after taxes (i.e., expected EBIAT) available for distribution to a firm's debt and equity holders, in a world of corporate taxes, thus consists of a risky amount, $\overline{X}(1 - T_c)$, and a constant amount, $T_c k_i B$. Since the risky portion of a leveraged firm's EBIAT is identical to the EBIAT of an unleveraged firm (with the same business risk), they both must have the same risk (i.e. variance). Therefore, the appropriate capitalization rate for the risky portion of a leveraged firm's EBIAT is k_o^u; and, as discussed above, the appropriate capitalization rate for the constant portion is k_i. Hence, the market value of a leveraged firm, in a world with corporate taxes, is given by

$$V_L = \frac{\overline{X}(1 - T_c)}{k_o^u} + \frac{k_i T_c B}{k_i} = V_u + T_c B \qquad (18.13)$$

Thus, the value of a leveraged firm is equal to the value of an identical unleveraged firm having the same business risk plus the present value of the interest tax savings on the firm's debt. As shown in Figure 18.7, an important consequence of considering

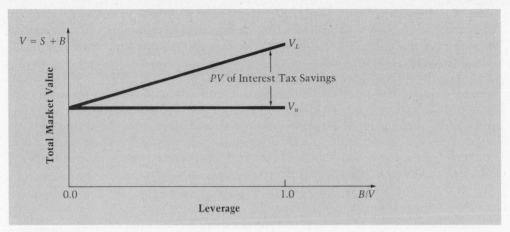

Figure 18.7   The MM position on the market value of the firm in a world with corporate taxes.

corporate taxes is that the value of the firm increases linearly with financial leverage. Thus, the "optimal" capital structure for *all* firms is 100-percent debt financing (i.e., a ratio of B/V of 1.0)!*

Although the implication of the above is that all firms should be 100-percent debt financed, few, if any, firms follow such a policy. This may be explained by the importance of another factor, such as the cost of financial failure (i.e., technical insolvency or bankruptcy).

Bankruptcy Costs and Optimal Capital Structures   MM assumed that financial failure is costless, and thus that its occurrence does not affect the amount available to pay out to debt holders and equity holders.† If financial failure reduces the aggregate amount available to be paid out to bond and equity holders, then the market value of the firm will be reduced. The magnitude of this reduction will be equal to the present value of the expected costs of financial failure.

The costs of financial failure include (1) the administrative and legal costs of commercial arrangements or liquidations, (2) the difference between the market value of the firm as a going concern and its realized value in liquidation, (3) the costs of suboptimal investment decisions made in an attempt to forestall bankruptcy,‡[3] and (4) the loss of tax credits in bankruptcy.[4] Unfortunately, it is not known whether or not expected bankruptcy costs are large enough to be economically significant because there are no reliable empirical estimates of the magnitude of total bankruptcy costs.§ In fact, Miller

---

*Similarly, it can be shown that the weighted average cost of capital decreases linearly with increases in financial leverage and that it reaches its minimum at 100-percent debt financing.
†Financial failure is discussed in greater detail in Chapter 26.
‡Jensen and Meckling note that when risky debt is outstanding, there is an incentive for shareholders to expropriate debt holders' wealth by making investment decisions that will increase the default risk of existing debt.
§A "rough" estimate of the cost of bankruptcy is given by the cost of avoiding such costs; that is, the cost of insuring the firm's earnings against bankruptcy outcomes. The net present value of the insurance premium and the benefits obtained would measure the cost of bankruptcy. However, this insurance premium cost would have to be adjusted for any administrative costs built into the premium.

argues that bankruptcy costs should be economically insignificant because it is in the best economic self-interest of all of the firm's claimants to reduce them.[5]

The Trade-Off If the MM logic is accepted, and corporate taxes and the costs of bankruptcy are introduced into the analysis, then a decision maker is faced with the trade-off shown in Figure 18.8. The maximum value of the firm is reached when the marginal principle is satisfied; that is, when the marginal increase in the present value of the interest tax savings equals the marginal increase in the present value of possible future costs of bankruptcy.

To many academics and practitioners, the implications of Figure 18.8 are so logically appealing that they can accept them without question. Thus, some of these individuals conclude that once the existence of corporate taxes and bankruptcy costs is accepted the MM and traditional positions can be reconciled. However, in the absence of conclusive empirical evidence,[6] are there any other critical assumptions of the MM approach that are violated in practice?

PERSONAL INCOME TAXES

Miller argues that the above discussion has omitted an important market imperfection; that is, the existence of personal taxes.[7] He assumes that personal income from equity is not taxed and that the personal tax rate on debt is progressive and extends on either side of the corporate rate. Based on these assumptions, Miller demonstrates that the differential tax treatment between personal incomes from equity and debt offsets the favourable tax treatment of corporate interest payments. Thus, when both personal and corporate taxes are allowed within a general equilibrium model, the tax incentive for

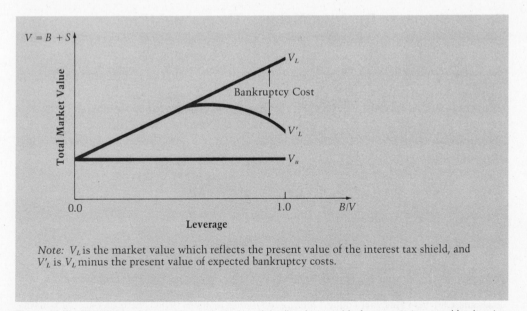

Note: V_L is the market value which reflects the present value of the interest tax shield, and V'_L is V_L minus the present value of expected bankruptcy costs.

Figure 18.8   The MM position on the market value of the firm in a world of corporate taxes and bankruptcy costs.

corporate leverage is nonexistent for any particular firm.* However, Miller notes that an optimal debt-equity ratio for the corporate sector as a whole will exist. Summarizing Miller's findings, *the value of any firm is independent of the specific capital structure that it happens to adopt; and it is not obvious what causes individual firms to issue risky debt when there is no tax advantage at the individual firm level.*

MANAGERIAL INCENTIVES

Recently, some authors have incorporated managerial self-interest within the theory of capital structure. They have advanced two explanations as to why firms issue risky debt when there is no tax advantage associated with debt. The first explanation deals with *owner-manager firms,* in which the owner-managers are both irreplaceable and not concerned about the well-being of suppliers of *outside* capital, especially after the needed outside capital has been raised.[8] According to this explanation, owner-managers will expropriate the wealth of suppliers of outside capital whenever they can by drawing down excessive nonpecuniary benefits, or by making investments that increase the risk, but not the expected return, of outside suppliers of capital.

The second explanation focuses on the existence of *asymmetric* (i.e., unequal) information between insiders and outsiders.[9] In this explanation, the insiders (i.e., managers and entrepreneurs) possess inside information about the firm's business risk and profitability, which they convey to outsiders (i.e., suppliers of outside capital) by *financial signalling.* Thus, a relatively high degree of financial risk signals that the firm has a relatively low degree of business risk, and vice versa. Thus, in order to ensure that such signals are valid, outsiders (i.e., principals) must monitor the activities of their managers (i.e., the agents), as was discussed in Chapter 1.

Capital Structure Decision Making: Theory and Practice

In the preceding sections of the chapter, the two opposing theories on the effect of alternative capital structures on a firm's market value, cost of capital, and choice of financing instruments were presented and were critically reviewed. However, the *practical* implications of these theoretical findings for corporate financial decision making were not discussed explicitly. In this section of the chapter, we will therefore discuss the implications of these theoretical findings to practice, and the techniques and guidelines used by practitioners in making capital structure and financing decisions.

ANALYSIS OF THE EFFECT ON A FIRM'S eps

Many practitioners continue to evaluate the effect of alternative capital structures (or financing packages) by using an EBIT-eps analysis. As was demonstrated earlier in the

---

*Litzenberger and Van Horne, by assuming that both interest and dividends are taxed at the personal rate, and that capital gains are not taxed, conclude that *there is a net tax advantage* associated with debt financing. See R. H. Litzenberger and J. C. Van Horne, "Elimination of Double Taxation of Dividends and Corporate Financial Policy," *Journal of Finance* 33 (June 1978). The reader should note that the Canadian taxation environment appears to more closely resemble Miller's world. Refer to Chapter 2 for an extensive discussion on personal and corporate taxation.

chapter, this technique is biased toward debt capital, especially when the decision maker assumes that business conditions will be normal, interest rates will not be excessive, and only corporate taxes are relevant. It was also demonstrated earlier in the chapter that this technique is generally not consistent with the objective of financial management (i.e., the maximization of the wealth of the firm's owners or shareholders) because it does not consider risk. Thus, in the capital structure irrelevance worlds of MM and of Miller, the particular choice of capital structure (or financing package), which maximizes the firm's eps for a given EBIT, will be irrelevant for maximizing the firm's value. In the traditional or MM (with corporate taxes and bankruptcy cost) world, the particular choice of capital structure (or financing package) that maximizes the firm's eps will probably not maximize its market value.

Although an analysis of the effect of alternative capital structures (or financing plans) on the firm's *value* is *strongly recommended*, practitioners will probably continue to make such decisions by using an EBIT-eps analysis. Thus, we recommend that an EBIT-eps analysis only be used in conjunction with a cash-flow analysis, so that the trade-off between profitability and the risk of capital inadequacy can be made explicit.

ANALYSIS OF THE EFFECT ON A FIRM'S NET CASH FLOW

Many financial managers (especially with larger firms) supplement an EBIT-eps analysis with some type of cash-flow analysis. A cash-flow analysis is essential to determine a firm's ability to meet *fixed* contractual obligations, such as interest and sinking-fund payments, in order to determine if a firm can avoid financial insolvency under adverse business conditions.

A financial manager can evaluate a firm's ability to meet *fixed* contractual obligations either by using certain rules of thumb or by using a formal cash-flow analysis. For example, Donaldson identified two rules of thumb that guide financial managers in controlling the risk of insolvency.[10] The first rule limits the principal amount of long-term debt to a fixed percentage of the combined value of debt and equity; while the second rule indirectly regulates the amount of debt by specifying an upward limit on the "fixed-charge coverage" ratios.

A formal cash-flow analysis helps in assessing the extent to which a financing plan influences the firm's risk of insolvency. Although it may appear that an emphasis on cash-flow considerations is inconsistent with the objective of maximizing the wealth of a firm's owners or shareholders, this is not totally so. Insofar as insolvency inflicts a cost on a firm's owners or shareholders, it is in the best interest of the firm's owners or shareholders that some attention be given to minimizing the net present value of expected bankruptcy costs. Thus, firms with very volatile EBIT streams are generally willing to pay a fee to ensure the availability of a reserve of unused short-term borrowing power (e.g., a confirmed line of credit).

ANALYSIS OF THE EFFECT ON THE FIRM'S MARKET VALUE

As was shown throughout this chapter, the effect of alternative capital structures *should* be assessed by their impact on a firm's market *value*. In this section, we will discuss the practical implications of the theoretical findings for corporate financial decision making under two possible worlds—a world with corporate taxes and bankruptcy costs, and a Miller world with corporate taxes, bankruptcy costs, and personal taxes.

World with Corporate Taxes and Bankruptcy Costs   As was shown earlier, if the MM logic, corporate taxes, and the cost of bankruptcy are assumed to adequately reflect reality, then the maximum value of the firm is reached when the marginal increase in the present value of the interest tax savings equals the marginal increase in the present value of the expected costs of bankruptcy. Thus, in such a world, all tax-paying risky firms will have an optimal capital structure that includes some debt capital. Such firms should review their optimal capital structure whenever they change their risk of bankruptcy (e.g., by an increase in business risk), or whenever there is a change in the rate of corporate taxation or in the manner in which interest payments can be deducted from corporate income.

Furthermore, in such a world, firms can attempt to be "near" their optimal capital structure by adhering to the following two rules of thumb: (1) Borrow the maximum available at the prime (interest) rate, and (2) borrow the maximum consistent with an "A" rating.[11] Both of these rules are an attempt to locate the point at which the cost of capital functions (i.e., the k_i and k_e functions) begin to rise rapidly.

*Small Corporations**   Since small corporations are taxed at a lower effective rate than large corporations, the market value-adding impact due to the tax savings of interest payments will be much less for small corporations than for large corporations. In addition, it would be expected that the relative magnitude of bankruptcy costs would be higher for small as compared to large corporations. Thus, one would expect that the optimal proportion of debt-to-equity for small corporations, holding business risk constant, would be much lower than for large corporations.†

Firms in Tax Havens‡   Since firms in tax havens are *not* subject to corporate taxation, they should have *no* incentive to issue corporate debt on their own account. However, if such firms are subsidiaries of multinational parent companies that are subject to corporate taxation, then one would expect that financial arrangements would be made between the parent and subsidiary so that the potential interest tax shield is not lost.

World with Corporate Taxes, Bankruptcy Costs, and Personal Taxes (i.e., Miller's World)   As was discussed earlier, in a world with corporate taxes, bankruptcy costs, and personal taxes, Miller has demonstrated that the value of a firm is independent of the specific capital structure that it happens to adopt. In other words, investors are "indifferent" with regard to the capital structure adopted by a firm.

---

*The following discussion may also apply to sole proprietorships and partnerships. Since for unincorporated businesses interest payments are deductible on personal account, the following discussion will apply whenever the owner's marginal tax rate is less than the corporate tax rate for incorporated businesses. For greater details on the small business tax deduction refer to Chapter 2.

†Small firms, subject to extreme business risks, might even have a "negative" leverage ratio. That is, they might raise more equity than is required for normal expenditures so that they can hold a risk-free asset.

‡As discussed in Chapter 20, the shifting of potential interest tax savings from the user of the asset to the lessor is one of the possible reasons for lease financing.

However, given the separation of management and ownership, this does not mean that a firm's management will be indifferent to the various alternative capital structures that the firm could adopt. Thus, management can choose the "optimal" capital structure that maximizes its welfare *without* adversely affecting the welfare of its owners or shareholders. If the compensation of one firm's management depends upon accounting-based measures, such as profits, then we would expect that management to be biased toward a high debt-to-equity ratio; while if the compensation of another firm's management depends upon the stability of eps, then we would expect that management to be biased toward a low debt-to-equity ratio.

CHOICE, MATURITY, AND TIMING DECISIONS

As we stressed in the previous chapter, since capital markets are assumed to be efficient, the financial manager should not be concerned with maturity, choice, and/or timing decisions. More specifically, the financial manager should not expect his or her firm to be any better or worse off by choosing one particular financing alternative over another at any particular point in time; or by choosing one particular maturity over another at any particular point in time; or by advancing or delaying the implementation of a particular financing alternative to take advantage of more "favourable" market conditions. While it is obvious that in practice financing and capital structure decisions are influenced by the belief of practitioners that capital markets are sometimes temporarily inefficient, the financial literature provides little rigorously derived guidance for such decision making.

Summary

In this chapter, we have discussed the basic concepts and theories of capital structure and the relationship between a firm's capital structure, value, and cost of capital. The important issue of whether or not an "optimal" capital structure exists was critically examined by determining the effect of alternative capital structures on the total value of the firm. A firm's capital structure is determined by the mix of long-term funds it maintains. The basic sources of long-term funds are long-term debt, preferred equity, common equity, and retained earnings. The simplest way to analyze capital structure effects is to assume that the firm has a simple capital structure consisting of only debt and equity capital.

The objective of the capital structure decision is to obtain the optimal trade-off between expected return and risk. The generally accepted measure of the stream of returns is the firm's earnings before interest and taxes (i.e., EBIT). The relevant risks are business risk (i.e., the risk inherent in the stream of EBIT) and financial risk (i.e., the risk generated by the way the firm is financed). For a given business risk, it was shown that an increase in financial leverage will increase both the expected value and risk of earnings per share (eps). Since eps maximization does not consider risk (i.e., the implicit or indirect cost of debt financing), this measure is not appropriate for evaluating the desirability of alternative capital structures or new financing proposals. Thus, the desirability of alternative capital structures or financing plans is best measured by examining their effects on the wealth of the firm's owners or shareholders, as measured by the total market value of a firm's common shares.

The controversy over the existence of an optimal capital structure for firms is as yet unresolved in the literature of finance. The traditional approach to capital structure is based on a number of simplifying assumptions, and maintains that the optimal capital structure for a firm is that for which the firm's overall cost of capital is minimized. Both the cost of debt and the cost of equity are increasing functions of leverage. The cost of debt, under the traditional approach, however, only increases after a certain debt-to-equity ratio has been exceeded.

Although the Modigliani and Miller (MM) approach to capital structure is also based on a number of simplifying assumptions, MM argue that in the no-corporate-tax world, the market value of the firm is independent of its capital structure, and that a firm's value is found by capitalizing the firm's expected EBIT at the overall cost of capital that is appropriate given the firm's business risk class. This capitalization rate is the one that is appropriate to an all equity-financed firm of the same risk class. MM use an "arbitrage" argument to prove their result. If capital structure is irrelevant, it was shown that the three objectives of maximizing the market value of a firm, maximizing the per-share market price of a firm's equity, and minimizing a firm's overall cost of capital are all equivalent and interchangeable objectives. It was also shown that a firm's cutoff rate for evaluating investments is its overall cost of capital, and that the appropriate rate for evaluating a specific project is completely unaffected by the specific mix of financing the firm uses to finance that specific project.

Although capital structure is irrelevant in a MM nontax world, there must be an explanation for the observed capital structures of Canadian firms. Potential explanations for observed capital structures are the existence of risky debt or the market imperfections that arise from risky debt. If MM's logic is accepted, and the existence of corporate taxes and the costs of bankruptcy are also accepted, then an optimal capital structure will exist for tax-paying risky firms. This optimum will occur at the point where the marginal increase in the present value of the interest tax savings equals the marginal increase in the present value of the expected costs of bankruptcy. However, if as Miller argues, personal taxes are also assumed to exist, then it can be shown that once again the value of a firm is independent of the specific capital structure that it happens to adopt. Managerial self-interest can also be used to explain the observed capital structures of firms.

Although an analysis of the effect of alternative capital structures (or financing plans) on the firm's value is strongly recommended, practitioners will probably continue to use an EBIT-eps analysis. Such an analysis should be done only in conjunction with a cash-flow analysis, so that the trade-off between profitability and the risk of capital inadequacy can be made explicit.

Questions

18.1   What is financial leverage? How is it related to the firm's debt and equity capital? Why is it difficult to estimate the firm's financial leverage accurately using a debt-capital/equity-capital breakdown?

18.2   What are the advantages and disadvantages of using financial leverage?

18.3   Explain what is meant by "business risk" and "financial risk." Does a grocery store or a women's clothing store have greater business risk?

18.4   Which is more likely to have a higher degree of financial leverage: a bakery or a cosmetic store?

18.5   Discuss the major limitation of using an EBIT-eps analysis to evaluate alternate capital structures. What approach overcomes this limitation?

18.6   It is observed that firms in different industries use a different proportion of debt in their capital structures. Explain.

18.7   How is the total value of the firm determined? If this value is known, along with the firm's EBIT, how can the firm's overall capitalization rate be calculated? What is the significance of the overall capitalization rate?

18.8   Although a greater proportion of debt reduces the overall cost of capital in a world with corporate taxes, firms refrain from using a high proportion (e.g., 100 percent) of debt. Why?

18.9   Explain the term *home-made leverage*. Is home-made leverage a perfect substitute for corporate leverage?

18.10 What is the optimal capital structure in a world with no bankruptcy costs and no corporate or personal taxes? What is the optimal capital structure in a world with significant bankruptcy costs and no corporate or personal taxes? How would you graph the relationship between a firm's value and its debt-to-value ratio in each of these worlds?

18.11 "In the traditional theory of capital structure, a firm's investment and financing decisons are inseparable." Discuss the implications of this statement for the cutoff or discount rate used by a firm to evaluate its average-risk investments.

18.12 What theoretical arguments would you advance in support of the view that a firm's investment decisions should be considered to be independent of its financing decisions? Briefly explain your answer.

18.13 "MM's capital structure irrelevance proposition rests on a critical assumption that an investor's personal leverage (i.e., home-made leverage) is a perfect substitute for corporate leverage." To what extent, in your view, does this assumption approximate reality? Briefly discuss the implications of your answer.

18.14 Assume that we are in MM's world of no corporate or personal taxes and no bankruptcy costs. In such a world, MM have shown that the market value of any given firm is independent of its capital structure and is given by capitalizing its expected return (i.e., EBIT) at the rate, k_o, appropriate to its risk class. Can this overall cost of capital (i.e., k_o) be used, without being adjusted, to evaluate *all* of the firm's proposed investment projects? What happens to each of the following if the firm accepts a large, higher than average risk investment project:

a.   Business risk
b.   The overall cost of capital

Problems

18.1   Parkland Dancing Studio Ltd. is evaluating each of the following three financing plans:

Plan 1—issue 10,000 common shares at $10 per share

Plan 2—issue 5,000 common shares at $10 per share and $50,000 of debt at a 6-percent interest rate

Plan 3—issue 3,000 common shares at $10 per share and $70,000 of debt at a 6-percent interest rate

The firm's expected EBIT is $20,000. Assuming that markets are perfect (i.e., no issue costs or taxes), calculate the eps for each of the three financing plans.

18.2   Assume that the Parkland Dancing Studio Ltd. is taxed at a 40-percent rate, and all other factors remain unchanged:
a. Recalculate the eps for each of the three financing plans given in Problem 18.1.
b. Does the introduction of corporate income taxes change the eps ranking of the three financing plans?

18.3   Parkland Dancing Studio Ltd. intends to replace the 6-percent debt in financing plans 1 and 2 (given above in Problem 18.1) with 6-percent preferred shares.
a. Calculate the eps for each of the financing plans if there are no corporate income taxes.
b. Calculate the eps for each of the financing plans if corporate income is taxed at a 40 percent rate.
c. Does the use of preferred shares in place of debt change the eps ranking of the three plans when there are *no* corporate income taxes?
d. Does the use of preferred shares in place of debt change the eps ranking of the three plans when there are corporate income taxes?

18.4   Majestic Boot Manufacturing Ltd. is evaluating each of the following financing plans to raise $200,000:

> Plan 1—issue 10,000 common shares at $20 per share
> Plan 2—issue 5,000 common shares at $20 per share, and $100,000 of debt at an 8-percent interest rate

The firm's income tax rate is 40 percent, and its distribution of EBIT is given as follows:

Probability	EBIT
0.05	$ 5,000
0.20	10,000
0.50	20,000
0.20	30,000
0.05	35,000

a. Show that the variability of eps is increased by the use of financial leverage.
b. Based on the expected value of EBIT, which plan would result in the highest eps?
c. Suppose that the actual EBIT for the current period turns out to be $5,000, and that the firm must meet all financing charges from the EBIT generated during the current period. Will Majestic be affected adversely if it adopts plan 1 now? If it adopts plan 2 now?

18.5   The earnings before interest and taxes (EBIT), interest (I), equity capitalization rate (k_e), and overall cost of capital (k_o) are tabulated below for firms A through E. Assume that taxes are zero and that the traditional approach to capital structure is valid.

Firm	EBIT	I	k_e	k_o
A	$ 110,000	$11,000	6.7%	6.0%
B	$ 880,000	$10,000	8.2%	7.2%
C	$ 230,000	$20,000	7.4%	6.6%
D	$1,200,000	$33,000	10.2%	8.5%
E	$ 660,000	$40,000	9.8%	7.0%

a. Determine the market value of each firm's common shares.
b. Determine the total market value of each firm.
c. Determine the market value of each firm's bonds.

18.6 Collins Equipment Ltd. has an expected EBIT of $96,000. The firm has $360,000 of outstanding 7-percent bonds. The firm's equity capitalization rate is 10 percent. Use the traditional approach to answer the following. (Note: ignore taxes and assume that the market value of debt is $360,000.)

a. What is the current value of the firm?
b. Calculate the firm's overall or weighted average cost of capital, k_o.
c. Determine the firm's market debt-equity ratio.
d. The firm is considering an increase in its financial leverage. The plan is to sell $120,000 in bonds and retire an equal amount of shares. The increase in leverage will increase the cost of debt to 8 percent and the cost of equity to 12 percent. Should the firm adopt this plan? Explain your answer. Assume that the interest rate on the presently outstanding debt is variable; that is, that the interest rate on the presently outstanding bonds will be increased to 8 percent.

18.7 Red River Cup Ltd. has earnings before interest and taxes of $700,000. The firm currently has outstanding debt of $4,200,000 at a cost of 6 percent. Its cost of equity is estimated to be 11 percent. Use the traditional approach to answer the following. (Note: Ignore taxes and assume that the interest rate on comparable debt currently yields 6 percent.)

a. What is the current value of the firm?
b. Calculate the firm's overall or weighted average cost of capital.
c. Determine the firm's market debt-equity ratio.
d. If the firm reduces its leverage by selling $1,000,000 in equity and retiring an equal amount of debt, the cost of debt will not change, but the cost of equity is expected to fall to 9.5 percent. Would you recommend the reduction in leverage? Why or why not?

18.8 St. John's Sea Capers Ltd., which has earnings before interest and taxes, EBIT, of $80,000, is attempting to evaluate a number of possible capital structures. Although the firm recognizes that it cannot determine its optimal capital structure, there are five possible capital structures it wishes to consider. These capital structures, along with their associated debt and equity capital costs, are given below. (Note: ignore taxes.)

Capital structure	Debt in capital structure	Cost of debt	Cost of equity
A	$100,000	5%	8.00%
B	$200,000	5%	8.25%
C	$300,000	6%	8.50%
D	$400,000	7%	9.00%
E	$500,000	9%	10.50%

a. Calculate the firm's value for each of the capital structures.
b. Calculate the debt-equity ratio and overall capitalization rate for each structure.
c. Tabulate the results of **a** and **b**.
d. Using this data, graph the firm's debt, equity, and overall cost functions.
e. Which capital structure would you recommend? Why?

•18.9   Fargo Package Delivery Ltd. requires $50,000 to start up operations in Southern Ontario. Fargo's earnings before interest and taxes from the Southern Ontario operation are expected to be $80,000. The required initial investment can be raised by any one of the following five alternatives:

(1) The issue of $50,000 of common shares
(2) The issue of $40,000 of common shares and $10,000 of 8-percent debt
(3) The issue of $30,000 of common shares and $20,000 of 8-percent debt
(4) The issue of $20,000 of common shares and $30,000 of 8-percent debt
(5) The issue of $50,000 of 8-percent debt

The overall cost of capital for a firm in the same business risk class as Fargo is 10 percent. Assume that Fargo is not subject to corporate income taxes and that the MM approach to capital structure is valid.
a. Calculate the market value of Fargo's equity for each of the five alternative financing plans.
b. Calculate Fargo's cost of equity for each of the five alternative financing plans.

•18.10   Assume that the corporate tax rate for Fargo Package Delivery Ltd. is 40 percent, and that all other information remains unchanged from question 18.9. If the cost of equity for an unleveraged firm in the same business risk class as Fargo is 12 percent, then calculate
a. The market value of the firm for each of the five alternative financing plans.
b. The cost of equity capital for each of the five alternative financing plans.
c. The overall cost of capital for each of the five alternative financing plans.

•18.11   Firms U and L are identical in all respects, except for their capital structures. Firm U is unleveraged, whereas firm L has $200,000 of debt outstanding at a 7.5-percent interest rate. The expected EBIT for both firms is $50,000, and both firms pay out 100 percent of their earnings available for common shareholders. Firm U's overall cost of capital is 12.5 percent. Firms U and L have 20,000 and 10,000 shares outstanding, respectively. Suppose that you have a portfolio consisting fo 1,000 shares of firm L, and that there are no corporate or personal income taxes.
a. If the market prices of U's and L's common shares are $20 and $21, respectively, how can you reduce your invested funds without altering either the expected return or risk of your investment?
b. If the total transaction costs of such a series of arbitrage transactions were $1,200, would arbitrage still be profitable?

•18.12   Halifax Metal Works Ltd. has 50-percent debt and 50-percent equity in its capital structure. The firm's cost of debt is 8 percent, and its expected EBIT is $50,000. The overall cost of capital for an all-equity firm in the same business risk class is 12.5 percent. The firm has an average-risk investment opportunity that requires an initial outlay of $10,000 and promises a 10-percent return. The firm could finance the new average-risk investment by either (1) borrowing $10,000 at 8 percent or (2) issuing $10,000 of new common equity at the current market price per share. The firm currently has 50,000 common shares outstanding, and it pays no corporate income taxes.

•Problems 18.9–18.12 may be bypassed.

a. Should the firm accept the new average-risk investment opportunity?
b. If the answer to **a** is yes, how should the average-risk investment opportunity be financed?
c. Does this mean that all projects that promise a 10-percent return will be found acceptable/unacceptable by the firm?

Notes

1. Eugene F. Fama and Merton H. Miller, *The Theory of Finance* (New York: Holt, Rinehart and Winston, 1972).
2. Andrew H. Chen and E. Han Kim, "Theories of Corporate Debt Policy: A Synthesis," *The Journal of Finance* 34 (May 1979), pp. 371–384.
3. See Michael C. Jensen and W. H. Meckling, "Theory of the Firm: Managerial Behavior, Agency Costs and Ownership Structure," *Journal of Financial Economics* (October 1976), pp. 305–360.
4. For an analysis of the loss of tax credits in bankruptcy on firm valuation, see M. J. Brennan and E. S. Schwartz, "Corporate Income Taxes, Valuation and the Problem of Optimal Capital Structure," *Journal of Business* (January 1978).
5. M. H. Miller, "Debt and Taxes," *Journal of Finance* (May 1977), pp. 261–275.
6. The empirical literature on this question is very inconclusive. See Franco Modigliani and Merton H. Miller, "Some Estimates of the Cost of Capital to the Electric Utility Industry, 1954–57," *American Economic Review* 56 (June 1966), pp. 333–391; J. Fred Weston, "A Test of Cost of Capital Propositions," *Southern Economic Journal* 30 (October 1963), pp. 105–112.
7. See Merton H. Miller, "Debt and Taxes," *Journal of Finance* (May 1977), pp. 261–275.
8. See Michael C. Jensen and W. H. Meckling, "Theory of the Firm: Managerial Behavior, Agency Costs and Ownership Structure," *Journal of Financial Economics* (October 1976), pp. 305–360.
9. S. A. Ross, "The Determination of Financial Structure: The Incentive Signalling Approach," *Bell Journal of Economics* (Spring 1977).
10. Gordon Donaldson, *Corporate Debt Policy* (Boston: Harvard University Graduate School of Business Administration, 1961).
11. These rules of thumb are taken from Gordon Donaldson, *Corporate Debt Policy* (Boston: Harvard University Graduate School of Business Administration, 1961), pp. 97–100.

Suggested Readings

Barges, Alexander, *The Effect of Capital Structure on the Cost of Capital* (Englewood Cliffs, N.J.: Prentice-Hall, 1963).

Baron, D. P., "Default Risk, Homemade Leverage, and the Modigliani-Miller Theorem," *American Economic Review* (March 1974).

Baxter, Nevin D., "Leverage, Risk of Ruin and the Cost of Capital," *Journal of Finance* (September 1967), pp. 395–403.

Brennan, Michael J. and Eduardo S. Schwartz, "Corporate Income Taxes, Valuation and the Problem of Optimal Capital Structure," *Journal of Business* (January 1978).

Chen, Andrew H., "Recent Developments in the Cost of Debt Capital," *Journal of Finance* (June 1978).

———, and E. Han Kim, "Theories of Corporate Debt Policy: A Synthesis," *Journal of Finance* 34 (May 1979), pp. 371–384.

Donaldson, Gordon, *Corporate Debt Capacity* (Boston: Harvard University Graduate School of Business Administration, 1961).

———, "New Framework for Corporate Debt Policy," *Harvard Business Review* (March-April 1962). Reprinted in the *Harvard Business Review* (September-October 1978), pp. 149–164.

DeAngelo, Harry and Ronald W. Masulis, "Leverage and Dividend Irrelevancy Under Corporate and Personal Taxation," *Journal of Finance* 35 (May 1980), pp. 453–464.

Fama, Eugene F., "The Effect of a Firm's Investment and Financing Decisions on the Welfare of Its Securityholders," *American Economic Review* (June 1978).

———, and Merton H. Miller, *The Theory of Finance* (New York: Holt, Rinehart and Winston, 1972).

Gordon, Myron J., *The Investment, Financing and Valuation of the Corporation* (Homewood, Ill.: Irwin, 1962).

Hamada, R. S., "Portfolio Analysis, Market Equilibrium and Corporation Finance," *Journal of Finance* (March 1969).

Haugen, Robert A. and Dean W. Wichern, "The Intricate Relationship Between Financial Leverage and the Stability of Stock Prices," *Journal of Finance* 30 (December 1975), pp. 1283–1292.

Jensen, Michael C. and William H. Meckling, "Theory of the Firm: Managerial Behavior, Agency Costs and Ownership Structure," *Journal of Financial Economics* (October 1976), pp. 305–360.

Kim, E. Han, "A Mean-Variance Theory of Optimal Capital Structure and Corporate Debt Capacity," *Journal of Finance* (March 1978), pp. 45–64.

———, Wilbur G. Lewellen and John J. McConnell, "Financial Leverage Clienteles: Theory and Evidence," *Journal of Financial Economics* 7 (March 1979).

Kraus, Allan and Robert Litzenberger, "A State-Preference Model of Optimal Financial Leverage," *Journal of Finance* (September 1973), pp. 911–922.

Leland, H. E. and D. H. Pyle, "Informational Asymmetries, Financial Structure, and Financial Intermediation," *Journal of Finance* (May 1977).

Litzenberger, Robert H. and James C. Van Horne, "Elimination of the Double Taxation of Dividends and Corporate Financial Policy," *Journal of Finance* 33 (June 1978).

Masulis, Ronald, "Effects of Capital Structure Change on Security Prices" (Ph.D. Dissertation, The University of Chicago, 1977).

Miller, Merton H., "Debt and Taxes," *Journal of Finance* (May 1977), pp. 261–275.

Modigliani, Franco F. and Merton H. Miller, "The Cost of Capital, Corporation Finance, and the Theory of Investment," *American Economic Review* 48 (June 1958), pp. 261–297.

———, "Corporation Income Taxes and the Cost of Capital: A Correction," *American Economic Review* 53 (June 1963), pp. 433–443.

Myers, Stewart C., "Determinants of Corporate Borrowing," *Journal of Financial Economics* (November 1977), pp. 147–176.

Patterson, Cleveland S., "An Empirical Investigation of the Determinants of Corporate Capital Structure Decisions" (Unpublished Ph.D. Dissertation, McGill University, 1980).

Ross, Stephen A., "The Determination of Financial Structure: The Incentive Signalling Approach," *Bell Journal of Economics* (Spring 1977).

Scott, J. H., "A Theory of Optimal Capital Structure," *Bell Journal of Economics* (Spring 1976), pp. 33–54.

Solomon, Ezra, *The Theory of Financial Management* (New York: Columbia University Press, 1963).

Stiglitz, J. E., "On the Irrelevance of Corporate Financial Policy," *American Economic Review* (December 1974), pp. 851–866.

Taggart, Robert A., Jr., "A Model of Corporate Financing Decisions," *Journal of Finance* 32 (December 1977), pp. 1467–1484.

Warner, James B., "Bankruptcy Costs: Some Evidence," *Journal of Finance* (May 1977), pp. 337–347.

———, "Bankruptcy, Absolute Priority, and the Pricing of Risky Debt Claims," *Journal of Financial Economics* (May 1977), pp. 239–276.

Weston, J. Fred, "A Test of Cost of Capital Propositions," *Southern Economic Journal* 30 (October 1963), pp. 105–112.

Part Seven

Sources of Long-Term Financing

BALANCE SHEET

Assets	Liabilities and Shareholders' Equity
Current Assets	Current Liabilities
Fixed Assets	**Long-Term Debt**
	Shareholders' Equity

This part of the text discusses the various types of long-term financing available to the business firm. These include leasing, debt, preferred and common shares, convertible securities and warrants, and dividends and retained earnings. There are six chapters. Chapter 19 describes the types and functions of financial intermediaries and the markets for short- and long-term financing. It sets the stage for the following five chapters by its description of the market for long-term funds. Chapter 20 describes leasing as a form of long-term financing. Chapter 21 discusses long-term debt financing, including long-term loans and the sale of bonds. Chapter 22 discusses the key aspects of preferred and common shares. Chapter 23 describes the nature and uses of convertible securities and warrants that are often used to enhance the firm's ability to obtain long-term funds. Finally, Chapter 24 discusses dividends and retained earnings, two closely related factors in financing decisions. The key emphasis in this part of the text is on the various forms of long-term financing as viewed by the corporate fund raiser.

Chapter 19

FINANCIAL INTERMEDIARIES AND MARKETS

A corporation does not operate in a financial vacuum; on the contrary, it operates in close contact with the various financial intermediaries and markets. This close relationship to the various financial media allows the firm to obtain needed financing and also to invest idle funds in various financial instruments. Large corporations find it necessary to frequent the financial marketplace, while small corporations may visit these markets relatively infrequently. Regardless of the size of the firm, the various financial media act as clearing mechanisms, matching the suppliers and demanders of funds and giving a structure to the fund-raising and investing process.

The emergence of strong financial intermediaries and markets is greatly responsible for the existence of large-scale business firms. Without some mechanism through which idle funds could be attracted by firms needing funds for investment in current and fixed assets, companies such as Moore Corporation Ltd. and the Molson Companies Ltd. would have been unable to reach their current size. Not only do these financial media make funds available, but they also allocate funds through the pricing mechanism. In general, firms that have greater uncertainty of their future prospects must compensate suppliers of funds by providing higher returns, and vice versa.

In this chapter, we shall discuss the key aspects of both financial intermediaries and financial markets. A broad understanding of the nature and role of these financial media will give the reader a better understanding of the firm's financing decisions. The chapter has five basic sections. The first section discusses the broad framework of financial intermediaries and markets and their role in our economy. The second section is devoted solely to a discussion of the money market. The third section presents a brief discussion of the key aspects of capital markets. The fourth section presents a discussion of the function and importance of the investment dealer as an underwriter in capital markets. Finally, the last section briefly discusses the role of investor relations in the operations of Canadian companies.

Financial Intermediaries and Markets: An Overview

There are three external ways by which available funds can be transmitted to firms requiring funds. One way is through a *financial intermediary*, which is an institution that accumulates and then distributes savings to those needing funds. Another way is through financial markets—organized forums where the suppliers and demanders of funds can make transactions. A third way in which funds can be transferred from a saver to an investor is through a direct (or private) placement arrangement. Due to the unstructured nature of direct placements, we shall focus primarily on financial intermediaries and financial markets in this section of the chapter. However, the direct placement of funds is not unusual—especially in the case of debt instruments and preferred shares for larger companies; and debt, preferred, and common shares for smaller companies.

FINANCIAL INTERMEDIARIES

Financial intermediaries, or *financial institutions*, channel the savings of various parties into loans or investments.* The process by which savings are accumulated by financial institutions and then lent or invested is generally referred to as *intermediation*.† Many financial institutions directly or indirectly pay savers interest on deposited funds; others provide services for which they charge depositors. (For example, the chartered banks levy service charges on chequing accounts, thereby indirectly charging depositors in these accounts.) Some financial intermediaries accept savings and lend this money to their customers; others accept savings and then invest the funds in earning assets such as real estate or shares and bonds; and still others both lend and invest money. In most instances, a financial intermediary must operate within certain legal constraints on the type of loans or investments, or both, that can be made. A brief discussion of the key participants in financial transactions and the key institutions acting as intermediaries follows.

Key Participants in Financial Transactions   The key suppliers and demanders of funds are individuals, businesses, and governments. The role of each of these in financial transactions is discussed separately next.

Individuals   The savings of individual household units placed in certain financial institutions provide these institutions with a large portion of the funds they lend or invest. Individual savings may be kept in a chequing or a savings account in a chartered bank, or in savings accounts in a caisses populaire or credit union. They may be used to

---

*When a financial institution receives deposits or borrows money, it can either lend the money out directly or invest it in other types of earning assets such as real estate or shares and bonds. Some institutions primarily make loans, while others primarily invest their money. In this chapter the terms "loans" and "investments" are used interchangeably to mean the placement of funds in some type of earning financial instrument.

†During inflationary periods, the process of *disintermediation* may take place. This occurs when depositors withdraw their funds from financial institutions in order to invest them in higher-yielding marketable securities.

purchase life insurance, contributed to pension funds, or used to make other types of deposits. Individuals not only act as suppliers of funds to intermediaries, but they also obtain funds in the form of consumer, business, and mortgage loans from various intermediaries. Individuals may borrow money from chartered banks, caisses populaires, credit unions, life insurance companies, and other institutions. In summary, individuals can be viewed as both suppliers of funds to, and demanders of funds from, financial intermediaries. The important point to recognize is that individuals as a group are *net suppliers*. They save more money than they borrow, thereby providing funds for use by others.

Businesses   Business firms also place some of their funds with financial intermediaries, primarily in chequing accounts with various chartered banks. Firms, like individuals, also obtain funds from various financial institutions. They obtain funds primarily from chartered banks, commercial finance companies, life insurance companies, and trusteed pension funds. They borrow more money than they save.

Governments   The government of Canada maintains cash balances with the Bank of Canada, the chartered banks, and banks in a few foreign countries. However, most of the federal government's daily cash receipts and disbursements are transacted through its account with the Bank of Canada. The federal government does not borrow funds directly from financial institutions, but does obtain needed financing through the financial markets. Provincial and local governments behave similarly by maintaining bank deposits and raising needed financing in the financial markets. When one considers the savings and borrowings of various levels of government in the financial marketplace, governments, like business firms, are typically *net demanders* of money. They borrow because they spend more than they generate in taxation.

Key Private Sector Financial Intermediaries   Financial intermediaries can be divided into two groupings—private sector financial intermediaries and public sector financial intermediaries. The private sector financial intermediaries include the chartered banks, the Quebec savings banks, caisses populaires and credit unions, finance companies, trust companies, life insurance companies, investment companies, pension funds, and venture capital companies. These intermediaries are discussed below.

Chartered Banks   The *chartered bank* is an important financial intermediary. It accepts both demand (chequing) and time (savings) deposits, which it then loans out directly to borrowers or through the financial markets. As was discussed in Chapters 11 and 12, the traditional type of loan made by a chartered bank is the short-term secured business loan. However, with the ongoing removal of the provisions in the Bank Act that restrict the bank's ability to be active in long-term borrowings, and with the rapid growth in the asset size of the Canadian banks, the chartered banks have been placing more emphasis on term loans. A chartered bank will often syndicate a large term loan by forming a financing group made up of a number of banks and other financial institutions, each providing a certain percentage of the total loan. Term loans are generally syndicated in order to spread, or diversify, the risks of a large loan.

The advantages of chartered bank term loans include the establishment of a working relationship with a banker, advice and counsel from experts in business loans, a source of credit information on customers, and the establishment of a possible source of information on business combinations. Their disadvantages include the need to divulge confidential information and the general control given the lender by the provisions of the loan agreement. Many of these advantages and disadvantages are present in term loans from other financial institutions as well.

The chartered banks also provide mortgage loans to individuals and have become the largest single source of personal loans. Thus, the chartered banks are an important financial intermediary, especially in accumulating funds from individuals and lending them to business.

The Quebec Savings Banks   The only remaining Quebec savings bank, the Montreal City and District Savings Bank, was originally incorporated in the pre-Confederation period as a mutual savings bank. Although the bank presently has a federal charter, it is governed by the Quebec Savings Bank Act. Its most important source of funds is deposits and its most important uses of funds are mortgage loans and government securities.*

Caisses Populaires and Credit Unions   *Caisses populaires* and *credit unions* are provincially chartered savings and credit cooperatives that deal primarily with the transfer of funds between members.† Historically, the first caisses populaires closely followed the concept of the European savings banks, which were oriented toward inducing the virtues of thrift and mutuality; while the first credit unions closely followed the concept of the European people's banks, which were oriented toward cooperation, self-help, and the democratic structure of management.

Membership in a caisse populaire or credit union is generally based on some common bond, such as working for the same employer, attending the same church, or being part of the same parish. In general, these organizations accept members' savings deposits and then lend the majority of their funds to other members, who typically use the money to purchase durable goods, homes, or home improvements. Historically, the caisses populaires have concentrated their member loans in the form of residential first mortgages. Since the caisses populaires have considered it a moral obligation to assist with the financing of local institutions, they have also placed a sizable proportion of their assets in the bonds issued by municipalities and school boards.

On the other hand, the credit unions have engaged primarily in consumer loans and residential first mortgages. The credit unions do, however, make some business loans on terms comparable to those offered by banks, since the credit unions have similar risk and liquidity constraints as those encountered by the chartered banks, due to their similar method of financing. Most of these business loans are for small locally oriented firms and cooperative enterprises.

---

*With the pending revisions to the Quebec Savings Bank Act, the bank will be able to finance small business, to offer commercial loans, to raise the maximum amount of personal loans, to finance itself on the bond market, and to extend its field of banking activities to non-Quebec locations.
†At the end of 1978, the Federation de Quebec des Caisses Populaires Desjardins, with assets of $8.8 billion and 1,250 affiliated caisses, had approximately 36.7 percent of the total assets of the Canadian credit union and caisse populaire movement.

Finance Companies   There are two main types of finance companies—consumer loan companies and commercial finance companies. The former generally only make secured cash loans to consumers who cannot obtain credit elsewhere. Many of these consumer loan companies are subsidiaries or affiliates of commercial finance companies. Commercial finance companies provide financing of most durable goods, such as automobiles; wholesale financing, such as the financing of inventory of automobiles; commercial financing, such as the financing of accounts receivable and inventory; factoring of accounts receivable; and the financing of equipment purchases by manufacturing firms.*

On term loans from a finance company, the borrower is generally required to make a specified down payment followed by equal installment payments over the life of the loan. Title to the equipment may or may not initially pass to the borrower. The interest-plus-service-charge cost of term loans from finance companies is generally higher than the cost of long-term loans from other sources.

Trust Companies   *Trust companies* are financial intermediaries that provide a variety of executor, administrative, and trustee services. They are the only entity permitted to act in a *fiduciary capacity*; that is, to hold assets in trust. The funds administered by trust companies can be put into one of three groups—estates, trusts, and agency funds; guaranteed funds; and company funds. In addition, trust companies are becoming more active in other financial fields. For example, most trust companies accept both chequable and nonchequable demand accounts, term deposits, and guaranteed investment certificates. Trust companies invest primarily in conventional residential mortgage loans and the bonds of provincial and municipal governments. Only a small proportion of their funds are invested in corporate shares.

Life Insurance Companies   Life insurance companies provide two basic services—protection, by spreading risks over time and across individuals and organizations, and a means for accumulating savings. Since annual cash inflows (premiums) seldom equal cash outflows for all types of insurance policies, life insurance companies must invest any current positive net cash flows in order to accumulate funds to cover future cash outflows (claims). Furthermore, life insurance companies must invest the premiums received from endowment life insurance policies and annuity contracts in such a manner that they can cover their contractual obligations to provide the policy or contract holder with the fixed payment(s) which he or she was promised.†

When channelling such funds to seekers of funds in the capital markets, life insurance companies must abide by the statutory regulations set out by both federal and provincial authorities, since they are both registered with the federal government and licensed by the provincial government. In general, life insurance companies have preferred to con-

---

*The manufacturer or seller of equipment may finance long-term installment sales to business firms directly. The characteristics of manufacturers' loans to customers are similar to those of loans made by commercial finance companies. Some manufacturers have their own commercial financing subsidiaries.
†While life insurance protects the beneficiaries of the insured against the financial difficulties from the insured dying too early, an annuity contract protects the annuitant against the financial difficulties caused by living longer than expected. It should also be noted that income-averaging annuities can sometimes be used to alter, and even reduce, the stream of tax payments over the life of the annuity.

centrate most of their investment in mortgage loans and long-term government and corporate bonds.

Life insurance firms, such as Prudential Insurance Company, also make term loans, with maturities of 10–15 years. The basic covenants and terms of insurance company loans are the same as for bank loans. Sometimes, when the amount to be borrowed is large, a syndicate of insurance companies and banks will jointly make the loan; the insurance companies will provide the longer maturities and the banks the shorter maturities. The major advantages of insurance company loans over bank loans are the longer terms available from insurance companies and the fact that insurance company loans are generally fixed-rate loans while the chartered bank loans are generally variable-rate loans. The basic disadvantage of insurance company loans is that the rate of interest charged is in many cases slightly higher than that charged on chartered bank loans.

Investment Companies   There are two basic types of investment companies—investment trusts or closed-end funds, and mutual or open-end funds. Both of these types of investment companies are financial intermediaries who sell their own securities to investors and use the proceeds to acquire other financial claims. Unlike most of the other financial intermediaries, the claims they sell (ordinary shares) are almost identical to the major assets (equity) they hold. Closed-end investment companies will be discussed next, while open-end investment companies will be discussed in a subsequent section of this chapter.

Three rather typical and well-known closed-end investment companies are Argus Corporation, Roy Nat Ltd., and the Canada Development Corporation. *Roy Nat Ltd.* was founded in 1962 to provide term debt financing, equity financing, and equity leasing to small and medium-sized Canadian businesses. Its shareholders include the Royal Bank of Canada, Banque Canadienne Nationale, Montreal Trust, General Trust of Canada, and Canada Trust. Roy Nat provides funds for expenditures on plant and equipment, working capital, refinancing, and the acquisition of other companies. These funds are provided through the provision of secured term loans and the purchase of mortgage bonds, debentures, income bonds, convertible securities, and common shares. The size of Roy Nat's term financings generally range from $25,000 to $5,000,000; while the size of its common share or convertible positions have generally been around $150,000, and have not exceeded $400,000. Roy Nat will invest in any stage subsequent to the prototype (or model) stage of a firm's growth. Roy Nat provides lease financing through a wholly owned subsidiary, Roy Nat Leasing Ltd.

The *Canada Development Corporation (CDC)* was incorporated by the federal government in 1971.* Although the federal government continues to be the major shareholder of CDC shares, the *CDC Act* does specify that the government's equity position may ultimately be reduced to the point where 90 percent of the voting shares are held by Canadian citizens and residents. While CDC is profit oriented, its primary orientation is to take equity positions in firms that are undertaking large development projects with long lead times, especially in sectors such as high technology, natural resources, and transportation. A secondary orientation is to invest in situations that will lead to a more substantial Canadian-controlled presence in international markets. CDC has also not

---

*CDC was *not* incorporated as a Crown corporation.

only invested in these selected sectors directly (for example, its equity investment in Texas Gulf) but also provided significant amounts of venture capital indirectly to business ventures through its equity interests in three closely held venture capital firms.*

Pension Funds   *Pension funds* are set up so that employees of various institutions can receive income after retirement. There are numerous types of pension plan arrangements. Quite often employers contribute to a pension fund, matching in some way the contributions of their employees; occasionally employer contributions are based on a profit-sharing arrangement. In essence, pension funds represent an accumulation of savings that will be disbursed in future years. Pension fund dollars are loaned or invested in numerous areas. Some of the money is transferred directly to various borrowers, but the majority of it is lent or invested via the financial markets. Private pension funds invest a small portion of their funds in term loans to large business. These loans are generally mortgage loans to large firms. The terms and costs of pension fund loans to business firms are similar to those of life insurance company loans.

Venture Capital Companies   A *venture capitalist* is any individual or institution that provides "high-risk" debt or equity capital, which is unavailable from traditional sources, for the growth (or seed funding) of small businesses at any stage before they go public. There are approximately 60–70 active venture capital firms in Canada. The portfolios of these venture capitalists are predominantly comprised of equity investments. Other types of financial assets held include convertible debentures and debentures with warrants. Since most firms that approach a venture capitalist have a limited performance record, most venture capitalists consider an assessment of the management of the firm seeking funds to be the most crucial variable in deciding whether or not funds should be advanced.[1]

Others   The financial intermediaries described above are the key financial institutions in the Canadian economy. Other important financial intermediaries include the provincial treasury branches (e.g., in Alberta and Ontario), mortgage loan companies, general (property and casualty) insurance companies, and charitable and endowment funds.

It is not surprising that the above private sector intermediaries have found it easier, and often more efficient, to deal predominantly with the domestic financing needs of the larger public firms. As a result, Canadian exporters of all sizes, and Canadian small and medium-sized businesses for domestic operations, have encountered difficulties in obtaining long-term financings on reasonable terms and conditions from Canadian intermediaries. This, in turn, has resulted in the introduction of a number of governmental assistance programs, some of which are discussed next.

Key Public Sector Financial Intermediaries[2]   The key public sector financial intermediaries include the Canada and Quebec Pension Plans, the federally guaranteed loan plans, the Federal Business Development Bank, the Export Development Corporation, Regional Development Programs, and various provincial development corporations.[3]

*In 1977, these three companies—Venturetek International Ltd., Innocan Investments Ltd., and Ventures West Capital Ltd.—had combined total assets of approximately $100 million.

Canada and Quebec Pension Plans   The two universal pension plans in Canada are the *Canada Pension Plan* and the *Quebec Pension Plan,* to which most of us belong. While the proceeds of the Canada Pension Plan are invested almost exclusively in nonnegotiable, nontransferable, and nonassignable debt securities issued by the provinces or the Crown corporations, such is not the case for the proceeds of the Quebec Pension Plan. The majority of the latter's funds are invested by the Quebec Deposit and Investment Fund (QDIF) in securities which are publicly offered and have market-determined yields, such as private sector equities. Thus, the QDIF manages the single largest institutional portfolio of Canadian equities in Canada.

Federally Guaranteed Loan Plans   Through various pieces of legislation, the federal government has extended loan guarantees to householders, small businesses, fishermen, and students. Under most of these plans, no government funds are involved; the federal government merely guarantees to reimburse the lender for all loan defaults up to an annual maximum.

The *Small Business Loans Act* is especially of interest to us. Under the provisions of the Act, all chartered banks and other approved lenders (such as credit unions, caisses populaires, Alberta treasury branches, and trust companies) are authorized to make government-guaranteed loans to small businesses. These loans can be for the purchase or modernization of equipment or premises, or for the purchase of land, but cannot be for the refinancing of existing debts or working capital requirements. Loans of up to $75,000 may be made to small business enterprises engaged in manufacturing, wholesale or retail trade, service businesses, construction, transportation, or communications, whose gross revenues during the fiscal year of application did not exceed $1,500,000. Generally, these loans cannot be more than 80–90 percent of the cost of the project to be financed and must be repaid within 10 years. The rate of interest on these loans is fixed at prime plus 1 percent. In 1978–1979, the government guaranteed $200,000,000 in small business loans under the Act.

The Federal Business Development Bank   The next public sector financial intermediary, *The Federal Business Development Bank* (FBDB), is a Schedule-D Crown corporation, which reports to Parliament through the Federal Minister of Industry, Trade, and Commerce. FBDB was established to assist in the creation and growth of small business enterprises across Canada by providing them with financial and management services.*
It was also originally formed to provide term loans to Canadian manufacturing firms, since the Bank Act at that point in time prohibited the chartered banks from engaging in term lending to business.

FBDB provides such services to almost every type of new or existing Canadian business, which cannot obtain other sources of financing on reasonable terms and conditions. Based on the particular needs of the business, FBDB will provide loans, loan guarantees, equity financing, or any combination of these forms of financing. When loans are involved, FBDB usually takes a first charge on fixed assets as security and charges an interest rate of prime plus 1 percent. When equity is involved, FBDB will

---

*In addition to its financial services, FBDB provides management services to small businesses. These include CASE (Counseling Assistance for Small Enterprises), management training, and information services.

normally take a minority interest and is willing to have its equity repurchased later on mutually agreeable terms. The majority of FBDB's customers obtain funds to acquire buildings, equipment, or land; other customers obtain funds for increasing working capital, establishing new businesses, financing change of ownership, or repaying term obligations.

Although FBDB's junior capital commitments have grown to $19.8 million in 1979, they still only represent 1.1 percent of the net value of FBDB's loan and investment portfolio. Much of this has been undertaken by FBDB in the form of "equity-sweeteners" and ancillary clauses in FBDB's traditional loan contracts. The fact that junior capital commitments do not represent a larger proportion of FBDB's loan and investment portfolio may not be due to excessive risk aversion on the part of FBDB's management, but it may merely reflect the typical unwillingness of small businessmen to sell equity to "outsiders."

The Export Development Corporation   The *Export Development Corporation (EDC)*, and its credit insurance programs, were discussed in Chapter 9. Here we will briefly discuss EDC's role as a provider of export financing.

EDC does not provide short-term export finance; nor does it *officially* offer financing for medium-term credits. In order to facilitate the medium-term financing needs of Canadian exporters, EDC officially only provides unconditional guarantees to financial institutions for the risks incurred in financing either the Canadian-based seller or the non-Canadian buyer. The absence of short-term export financing is especially difficult on small Canadian exporters. More specifically, these small firms find it difficult to negotiate a sufficiently generous discounting or credit facility with the chartered banks, particularly as it relates to short-term (up to 180-day) export paper.

EDC provides long-term loans to foreign borrowers by separate loan agreements and confirmed lines of credit. Specific aspects of EDC's long-term export finance program are summarized in Table 19.1. In 1978, EDC incurred an additional $1.1 billion in export loans and guarantees.

Regional Development Programs   The *Federal Department of Regional Economic Expansion (DREE)* provides incentives for the establishment, modernization, or expansion of manufacturing and certain other facilities through the *Regional Development Incentives Act (RDIA)*. These incentives are provided to increase or maintain employment in specific regions of Canada which, because of slower rates of growth, high levels of unemployment, low income, and low labour participation rates, have been *designated* as areas that need special economic measures to encourage industrial development.

A firm engaged in manufacturing or processing may qualify for direct grants, loan guarantees, or repayable incentives under the program.* For a particular project, the incentives obtained by a firm will depend upon the geographical location, size, and nature of the project, and upon whether or not the project involves new facilities or the expansion of existing facilities. Thus, the ceiling on incentives for new plants or new plant expansion is 25 percent of approved capital cost plus $5,000 per direct job created; while the ceiling on incentives for plant modernization or volume expansion is 20

---

*Certain service industries may qualify for loan guarantees on new facilities.

Table 19.1 Export Development Corporation: Long-Term Export Finance Program

Credit granting agency	Export Development Corporation (EDC). There is also a voluntary EDC—chartered banks protocol agreement, known as Participatory Export Financing Arrangement (PEFA).
Purpose of credit	(1) For long-term credit, export of capital goods and related engineering services (not feasibility studies) with a Canadian-content (labour and material) which is normally not less than 80 percent of the portion financed by EDC.
	(2) For medium-term credit, EDC provides unconditional guarantees to financial institutions for risks incurred by them in financing either the Canadian-based supplier or the foreign buyer. These guarantees may be issued on insured or insurable exports of capital goods or services. Guarantees may also be provided to banks for specific goods or services. Guarantees may also be provided to banks for specific loans to cover the material and labour costs in the manufacture of capital goods insurable as medium-term exports.
Length of credit/recipient	Long-term credit (over 5 years). Buyer credit only (however, the funds can be disbursed directly to the Canadian exporter or supplier).
Percentage financed	Down payment (normally 15 percent) is required.
Required security	A guarantee from a guarantor or guarantors acceptable to EDC.
Credit instrument	Not known.
Interest charge/other costs	Approximate range of charges is as follows:
	(1) EDC: Interest rate: between 9 percent and 10 percent p.a. fixed (for Cdn. dollar loans). Stand by fee: 1/2 percent p.a. on undisbursed amounts. Administrative fee: 1/5 percent p.a. Guarantee fee: 3/4 percent p.a.
	(2) Bank Participants: Interest rate: market rate for borrower (for Canadian dollar loans, on a Canadian floating prime-plus basis). Commitment fee: 1/2 percent p.a. on undisbursed amounts. Management fee: 3/4 percent p.a. on outstanding amounts.

SOURCE: K.C. Dhawan and L. Kryzanowski, *Export Consortia: A Canadian Study* (Montreal: Dekemco Ltd., 1978), p. 136.

percent of the approved capital cost of the project. In 1978, DREE distributed $77 million in grants and contributions.

Provincial Development Corporations   In 1973, the British Columbia government established the B.C. Development Corporation. Subsequently, all the provinces established similar public agencies to provide financing, incentive grants, and other services to qualified businesses wishing to locate new or expand existing manufacturing plants within their province. The rationale for establishing these agencies is to stimulate and spread the benefits of industrial development across a province, especially to regions with low economic growth. Generally, these provincial agencies attempt to provide financial support when it is not available from other sources on reasonable terms and conditions. A notable exception was the Manitoba Development Corporation, which publicly maintained that it was *not* a lender of the last resort.

The provincial development corporations include the Newfoundland and Labrador Development Corporation, the Industrial Enterprises Incorporated of Prince Edward

Island, the Nova Scotia Development Board (NSRDB), Industrial Estates Limited of Nova Scotia, Department of Commerce and Development and Provincial Holdings Ltd. of New Brunswick, the Quebec Development Corporation (QIDC), the Ontario Development Corporation (ODC), Northern Ontario Development Corporation (NODC), Eastern Ontario Development Corporation (EODC), the Manitoba Development Corporation (MDC), the Saskatchewan Economic Development Corporation (SEDCO), the Alberta Opportunity Company,[4] and the British Columbia Development Corporation (BCDC). Specific details of these programs will not be discussed here.[5] For such details, one is referred to the particular provincial agency of interest.

FINANCIAL MARKETS

Financial markets permit the demanders and suppliers of short-term and long-term loans and investments to transact business directly. Whereas the loans and investments of financial intermediaries are made without the direct knowledge of the fund suppliers (i.e., savers), suppliers in the financial marketplace know exactly where their funds are being lent or invested. The two key financial markets are the *money market* and the *capital market*. Transactions in short-term debt instruments or marketable securities take place in the money market. Long-term securities (shares and bonds) are traded in the capital market.

THE RELATIONSHIP BETWEEN FINANCIAL INTERMEDIARIES AND FINANCIAL MARKETS

It is quite common to find financial intermediaries actively participating in both the money market and the capital market, as both suppliers and demanders of funds. Figure 19.1 depicts the general flow of funds through and between financial intermediaries and financial markets. From the figure, it is obvious that the operational efficiency of the financial intermediaries that participate in the financial markets is important in the functioning of the financial markets. Thus, *operational efficiency* measures the relative cost incurred by a financial intermediary in providing intermediation services between the suppliers and demanders of funds in financial markets.

The individuals, businesses, and governments that supply and demand funds may be domestic or foreign. In some instances there may be legal constraints on the operations of certain institutions in the financial marketplace. Because of the key importance of the money and capital markets to the business firm, the next two sections of this chapter will be devoted solely to these topics.

The Money Market

The money market is a market for the suppliers and demanders of financial instruments with maturities of less than three years. Trading is not housed in some central location, although the majority of money market transactions culminate in the major financial centers, such as Toronto, Montreal, Vancouver, and Calgary. Most money market transactions are made in marketable securities.

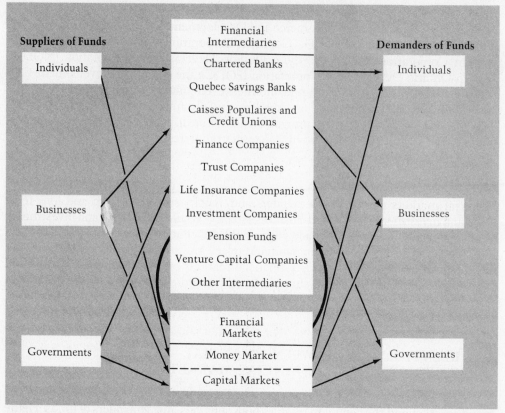

Figure 19.1 Financial intermediaries and markets.

THE OPERATION OF THE MONEY MARKET

Since the money market is not centrally located, suppliers and demanders of short-term funds are typically matched through the facilities of the major authorized dealers, who are in constant telephone contact with each other.* Thus, a firm wishing to purchase a certain marketable security may telephone its brokerage firm or dealer, which will then attempt to buy the securities by contacting a dealer known to "make a market" or deal in the security.† Regardless of whether a business or government is issuing a money market instrument (demanding short-term funds) or purchasing a money market instrument (supplying short-term funds), one party must go directly to another party or use a middleman such as a money market dealer or brokerage firm to make the transaction.

---

*These authorized dealers enjoy a special arrangement with the Bank of Canada. That is, when it is necessary, the Bank of Canada as a lender of last resort will supply these dealers with temporary credit.
†Although the terms *broker* and *dealer* are often used interchangeably, they are different. Since a broker acts as an agent for his or her client, the broker buys or sells securities for the client's account. The dealer purchases the securities from the seller and then attempts to resell them to a buyer. Thus, while a broker does not take title to the securities and is remunerated by commissions, the dealer takes title to the securities and is remunerated by the spread between the buying (bid) price and the selling (ask) price.

The key to successful transactions in the money market is knowing which dealer is willing to buy or sell a given instrument at a certain time. Firms that make frequent transactions in the money market become aware of the dealers in the market, while firms that make less frequent transactions generally have to pay a broker to facilitate a transaction. The *secondary or resale market* for marketable securities is no different from the *primary or initial issue market* with respect to the basic transactions made.

MONEY MARKET INSTRUMENTS

The key money market instruments were briefly described in Chapter 8. It is important to have a general understanding of the key characteristics of these instruments. One characteristic common to all of them is their liquidity. The yields on these securities reflect directly the "tightness" or "looseness" of money, as determined by the forces of supply and demand and by the Bank of Canada. Differences in yield between various instruments result from the different degrees of "risk" associated with the issuers.

The Capital Markets

Capital markets are created by a number of institutions and arrangements that allow the suppliers and demanders of *long-term funds* to make transactions. Included among these transactions are transactions in the debt and equity issues of businesses and the debt issues of local, provincial, and federal governments. Capital markets are of key importance to the long-run growth and prosperity of business and government organizations, since they provide the funds needed to acquire fixed assets and implement programs aimed at ensuring the organizations' continued existence. The backbone of the capital markets is the various security exchanges that provide a marketplace for debt and equity transactions.

Capital markets aid those segments of the economy that need capital to acquire plant and equipment to obtain funds from the numerous savers in the economy. Just as financial intermediaries collect savings from numerous parties and lend them to acceptable borrowers, so too do the capital markets permit the conversion of savings into investment. They permit individuals, businesses, governments, and financial institutions to channel their savings into long-term loans or purchases of equity in businesses, government, and financial institutions.

The key factor differentiating money and capital markets is that the capital markets provide long-term funds for the firm, while the money market provides short-term financing.

THE FUNCTIONS OF SECURITY MARKETS

The securities markets that make up the capital markets actually perform a number of important functions, such as allocating scarce capital, creating a continuous market, determining and publicizing security prices, and aiding in new financing.

Allocating Scarce Capital   A key function of the securities markets is to help in allocating scarce funds to the best uses and users. That is, by disclosing the price behaviour of various securities and requiring the disclosure of certain corporate financial data, they allow prospective and existing investors to assess risk-return trade-offs and to move their funds into the most promising investments. An allocationally efficient market is one that allocates funds to the most productive use and users. Thus, *allocational efficiency* measures the ability of a market to maintain equivalent rates of return (or financing costs) on investments of equal risk.

Creating a Continuous Market   A securities market helps in the creation of a continuous market for securities at a price that is not very different from the securities *correct equilibrium (intrinsic) price.* The continuity of security markets provides securities with the liquidity necessary to attract investors' funds. A continuous market also reduces the volatility of security prices, further enhancing their liquidity.

Determining and Publicizing Security Prices   Security markets both determine and publicize security prices. The price of an individual security is determined by what is bought and sold, or the demand of and supply for the security. A capital market brings together buyers and sellers from all geographic areas while still affording them some anonymity. This helps to ensure a price that reflects the true or intrinsic value of the security. Changing evaluations of a firm, of course, cause changes in the supply of and demand for its securities and ultimately result in a new price for the securities. Since the prices and other relevant information on securities are readily available to interested parties, investors can use this public information to make better purchase and sale decisions. When the security prices on a market always "fully reflect" all available public information, that market is *informationally efficient.*

Aiding in New Financing   Security markets also provide firms with a method of obtaining new financing. Since the markets are continuous, thereby ensuring investor liquidity, new capital can be raised through new security issues. Of course, not all firms have access to those markets in order to raise new capital, but the presence of securities markets does give certain firms direct access to the savings of individuals, other firms, and financial institutions in order to finance new capital expenditures. Without these markets, new capital could be obtained only through direct negotiations with holders of large amounts of money. This obviously would be quite tedious and operationally inefficient.

SECURITIES REGULATION

An understanding of securities regulation is necessary for a financial officer for the following reasons. First, securities laws and regulations have a substantial effect on the ease, costs, and terms of public financings. Second, securities laws and regulations affect the type and costs of the financial disclosures which a firm must make. Third, the protection perceived by investors from securities regulations may influence the willingness of investors, especially small investors, to purchase and hold securities. And finally, the securities laws and regulations give the personal liabilities that corporate officers and directors may face if they violate corporation disclosure and insider trading provisions.

Most of the securities legislation in Canada is incorporated in the Securities and Companies Acts of each province. This results from the fact that, unlike the United States, Canadian securities regulation is under provincial jurisdiction. The two exceptions are the sections in the Federal Criminal Code, which deal with securities in the areas of fraud and fraudulent disclosure, and the Dominion Companies Act, which regulates federally incorporated companies.

Each of the 10 provincial securities acts is administered by a provincial securities commission or similar body.* Each securities commission is also responsible for the general supervision of any stock exchange situated within its province. Thus, the Ontario Securities Commission (OSC) is responsible for the Toronto Stock Exchange (TSE). Although each commission operates independently, the burden of *clearing* (getting approval of) prospectuses in more than one Canadian province has been reduced, since most provincial commissions abide by the uniform National Securities Policy.†

The two basic aims of security regulation are to improve the economic performance (efficiency) of securities markets and to maintain equitable (fair) treatment among all market participants. Historically, regulators have attempted to achieve these two basic aims through two regulatory approaches—full, continuing, and timely disclosure requirements, and control of conduct regulations.

Full Disclosure   Full disclosure is intended to prevent financial manipulation in the marketplace and to provide investors with enough information to enable them to arrive at their own rational decisions. For new issues, Canadian securities commissions generally do not judge the merits or the quality of the issue but only ensure that all purchasers of the new issue are sufficiently informed to make a reasoned investment decision. Consistent with this philosophy, most securities acts have a withdrawal provision. For example, under the Ontario Securities Act, a purchaser has 90 days within which he or she can nullify a new issue purchase, if there were material errors or omissions in the prospectus.

However, for very risky issues, such as penny mining and oil issues, the commissions have sometimes insisted that full disclosure was not sufficient. In such cases, they have either refused to approve a new issue or have caused an issuer to improve the terms of an offer before the issuer's prospectus was accepted. When such a behaviour was based on administrative convenience—that is, the minimization of public criticism—there was probably an underallocation of funds to such ventures.

Continuing Disclosure   To ensure that secondary markets are informationally efficient, most provincial securities acts have general disclosure requirements for public companies. These include regular reporting of insider trading, mandatory filing of annual and quarterly financial statements, mandatory solicitation of proxies,

---

*In the United States, securities regulation is administered by a federal agency, the Securities and Exchange Commission (SEC).

†This includes the provinces of British Columbia, Alberta, Saskatchewan, Manitoba, Ontario, Quebec, New Brunswick, and Prince Edward Island.

and the mandatory provision of information circulars to shareholders prior to the annual meeting.

Timely Disclosure   Timely disclosure is concerned with the public announcement of new material information, such as a proposed takeover or amalgamation bid. It is designed to ensure that information regarding a firm is not withheld from the public at the same time that persons who have such information are profiteering by buying from or selling to an unknowing public.

For this reason, most of the Canadian exchanges and securities commissions maintain a timely disclosure policy. Most of these policies contain a release mechanism by which companies that experience a material change or event can withhold public disclosure of the information if the officers of the company feel that disclosure would be injurious to the company. However, if share price movements suggest that insiders are trading based on that information, or that the information has already been leaked to the market, then the officers of the company must immediately disclose that information.

Control of Conduct Regulations   These regulations deal with the type of behaviour considered to be acceptable for new and existing participants in the securities markets. The regulations deal with items such as the suitability of those wishing to enter the brokerage industry, the conduct of those already in the brokerage industry, the structure of commission rates, and the protection of investors by ensuring the maintenance of a sound financial position by those financial intermediaries providing services in the securities industry.

Regulatory Enforcement of Provisions   A corporate or individual violation of the provisions of a securities act or other securities regulations may result in a regulatory action. The primary regulatory actions used are moral suasion, interruption of the trading privileges of specific individuals or brokerage firms, interruption of *all* trading for a security, and fines levied against individuals or brokerage houses.*

CHARACTERISTICS OF SECURITY MARKETS

Security markets are the key institutions making up the capital markets. Many people refer to these markets as "stock markets"; however, this phrase is somewhat misleading since *shares*, bonds, and options may be traded on these markets. There are two key types of security markets—organized exchanges and the over-the-counter markets.

Organized Security Exchanges   *Organized security exchanges* are centrally located organizations on whose premises securities are traded. The key Canadian exchange is the Toronto Stock Exchange (TSE), which accounted for approximately 81 percent

---

*For unlisted shares, an interruption of all trading in a security is referred to as a *cease trading order*. For listed shares, trading interruptions can be further classified as delayed openings, trading delays, trading halts, trading suspensions, and delistings. For an empirical test of the effectiveness of trading suspensions in Canadian markets, see Lawrence Kryzanowski, "The Efficacy of Trading Suspensions: A Regulatory Action Designed to Prevent the Exploitation of Monopoly Information," *The Journal of Finance* 34, No. 5 (December 1979), pp. 1187–1200.

of the total value of shares traded on the Canadian exchanges in 1979. The TSE has its own building, membership, disclosure, and trading rules. Other active Canadian exchanges include the Montreal Stock Exchange (MSE), the Vancouver Stock Exchange (VSE), the Alberta Stock Exchange (ASE), and the Winnipeg Stock Exchange.* With the possible exception of the MSE, these exchanges deal primarily in the trading of securities with local or regional appeal. Since most of the exchanges are modeled after the Toronto Stock Exchange, a brief discussion of the TSE's membership and policies with regard to listing securities, trading activity, and reporting market activity is in order.

Membership   Membership in the Toronto Stock Exchange is expensive. In order to become a member, an individual or firm must own a seat on the exchange. The word "seat" is used only figuratively, since members trade securities standing up. A total of 126 "seats" make up the "ownership" of the TSE. The record high price of $140,000 for a seat on the TSE was paid in 1959. Recently, seats have sold in the $20,000–$30,000 range. Most seats are owned by brokerage firms, and many brokerage firms own more than one seat. Each firm designates one of its officers as a "member seatholder." For every seat it owns, a firm can have up to 5 attorneys or traders on the floor of the exchange. No firm can own more than 4 active seats (i.e., the right to more than 20 traders). However, in the corporate decision making of the exchange, any particular firm has a vote for each seat owned up to a maximum of three seats. Membership on the other stock exchanges is obtained in a similar manner, but the cost of a seat is generally less and the other requirements are often not as strict.

Listing Policies   To become listed on an organized stock exchange, a public company must file an application for listing. Many firms are *interlisted*; that is, listed and actively traded on more than one exchange.† The Toronto Stock Exchange has the most stringent listing requirements. In 1979, over 800 listed companies accounting for over 1,200 issues were traded on the TSE. Due to the different business activities of companies listed on the TSE, specific minimum listing requirements apply to each of three company categories—industrials or general; mines; and oil and gas. In order to be eligible for listing on the TSE, an industrial company must satisfy the following four requirements: First, the company must have at least 200,000 shares in the hands of the public (i.e., held by noninsiders), and there must not be fewer than 300 public holders of at least one board lot. Second, the market value of publicly held issued shares must be at least $1,000,000. Third, the company must have earned at least $200,000 before taxes in the immediately preceding year, and must have earned an average of at least $200,000 before income taxes over the immediately preceding three years. Fourth, the company must have net

---

*In 1979, the total value and volume of shares traded on the four major Canadian exchanges were TSE, $18.73 billion and 1.39 billion shares; MSE, $2.67 billion and 180 million shares; VSE, $1.48 billion and 920 million shares; and ASE, $240 million and 90 million shares. The MSE has a greater total dollar value but a smaller volume of traded shares than the VSE, because a much higher proportion of senior (i.e., higher-priced) securities are listed and traded on the MSE. The largest North American exchanges are the New York Stock Exchange (NYSE) and the American Stock Exchange (AMEX), both of which are headquartered in New York City.

†For interlisted shares, the market price on the various markets at any point in time is nearly the same because of arbitrage. The reader should refer to Chapter 18 for a discussion of arbitrage.

tangible assets of $1,000,000 and sufficient working capital to carry on its business. In addition, the company must be willing to pay a listing fee. If listed firms do not continue to meet certain requirements, they may be *delisted* from the exchange. The listing requirements of the other exchanges are in general more lenient than those of the TSE.

Whether or not a firm gains financially by having its shares listed is unknown. Generally, financial officers of the larger firms believe that the financial advantages of listing exceed the financial disadvantages. The alleged advantages include free advertising and publicity; and cheaper cost of funds due to enhanced prestige and reputation, increased share liquidity, and a greater market following. The major disadvantages of listing are the initial listing fee, the annual listing fees paid to the exchange, and the costs of producing the information required to maintain the listing.

Trading Activity   Trading is carried out on the floor of the exchange. Around the perimeter of the floor are telephones and telegraphs, used primarily to transmit buy and sell orders from brokers' offices to the exchange floor and back again once an order has been executed. All trades are made on the floor of the exchange by the designated representatives of the occupants of seats. Only these people can make transactions on the floor. Trades are made primarily in *board lots* and not in *odd lots* (lots of less than a board lot).* Certain specialists known as *odd-lot brokers* make odd-lot transactions. The general procedure for placing and executing an order can be described by a simple example.

EXAMPLE   Sally Jones, who has an account with Wood Gundy Ltd. in Montreal, wishes to purchase 200 shares of Northern Telecom Ltd. at the prevailing market price. Sally calls her account executive,† Abe Cohen of Wood Gundy, and places her order. Abe immediately has the order transmitted to the Toronto headquarters of Wood Gundy, which immediately forwards the order to the Wood Gundy clerk on the floor of the exchange. The clerk dispatches the order to one of the firm's representatives, who goes to the appropriate trading post, executes the order at the best possible price, and returns to the clerk, who then transmits the execution price and confirmation of the transaction back to the brokerage office. Abe is then given the relevant information and passes it along to Sally. Abe then has certain paperwork to do.

Only a matter of minutes may be required for an order, once placed, to be executed, thanks to sophisticated telecommunication devices. A sale of securities would have been handled in a similar manner.

All transactions on the floor of the exchange are made through an auction process, without the aid of a specialist. The goal is to fill all *buy orders* at the lowest price and to fill all sell orders at the highest price, thereby giving both purchasers and sellers the best possible deal. The actual auction process is quite complicated. New security issues and

---

*A board lot is generally as follows: 1,000 shares for securities selling under $0.10; 500 shares for securities selling at $0.10 or above, but under $1.00; 100 shares for securities selling at $1.00 or above, but under $100.00; and 10 shares for securities selling at $100.00 or above.

†The title "account executive" is often used to refer to an individual who traditionally has been called a "stockbroker." The account executive title is believed to add respectability to the position and change the image of the stockbroker from that of a salesperson to that of a personal financial manager who provides diversified financial services to his or her clients.

1979 High	Low	Stock	Div	Days High	Low	Close	Ch'ge	Vol
22$\frac{7}{8}$	12$\frac{1}{8}$	Noranda	1.00	22\frac{1}{8}$	21$\frac{7}{8}$	22	+ $\frac{1}{8}$	32095
68	35	Norbaska		44	42	44	+ 1	2000
34	16$\frac{1}{2}$	Norcen	.80	32\frac{3}{8}$	32$\frac{1}{4}$	32$\frac{1}{2}$		14712
59$\frac{1}{2}$	44	Norcn 288	2.88	$58	57	57	− $\frac{1}{2}$	2150
24	6	Norlex		24	22	23	+ 2	47000
10$\frac{1}{2}$	6	Normick P	.60	7\frac{1}{2}$	7$\frac{1}{4}$	7$\frac{1}{2}$	+ $\frac{1}{4}$	400
22$\frac{5}{8}$	8$\frac{1}{2}$	NC Oils		$21	21	21		2500
95	43$\frac{1}{2}$	N Canada		95	90	95	+ 5	10500
54$\frac{1}{2}$	36	Nor Tel	1.00	$52	52	52	− $\frac{1}{4}$	150
10$\frac{5}{8}$	6	Northgat		10\frac{5}{8}$	9$\frac{3}{4}$	10$\frac{5}{8}$	+ 1$\frac{1}{8}$	21866
355	15	Northid		124	112	115	+ 5	528000
65	30	N Beauc		45	45	45	+ 6$\frac{1}{2}$	500
14$\frac{5}{8}$	8	NS Savngs	.40	$8	8	8	− $\frac{3}{8}$	850
46$\frac{1}{2}$	20$\frac{3}{4}$	Nowsco W	.36	$46	45$\frac{3}{4}$	46		700
17	6$\frac{1}{4}$	Nu-Wst A	.30	14\frac{3}{8}$	14$\frac{1}{4}$	14$\frac{3}{8}$	− $\frac{1}{8}$	2700
70	16$\frac{1}{2}$	Nufort Res		70	69	70	+ 1	25166
48$\frac{1}{4}$	26	Numac	.20	45\frac{1}{2}$	44$\frac{1}{2}$	45$\frac{1}{2}$	+ 1$\frac{1}{2}$	8720
36	17	OPI A	p .15	$36	36	36		150
17$\frac{1}{4}$	450	Oakwood P		14\frac{3}{4}$	14$\frac{3}{8}$	14$\frac{5}{8}$	+ $\frac{3}{8}$	2700
305	137	Obrien		237	225	233	+11	27040
33$\frac{1}{2}$	13$\frac{5}{8}$	Ocelot A		27\frac{3}{4}$	27$\frac{5}{8}$	27$\frac{5}{8}$	− $\frac{3}{8}$	250
33	13$\frac{5}{8}$	Ocelot B		27\frac{7}{8}$	27$\frac{1}{2}$	27$\frac{3}{4}$	− $\frac{1}{4}$	5700
400	104	Onaping		400	340	400	+55	24850
9$\frac{3}{4}$	7	Oshawa A	.42	8\frac{3}{4}$	8$\frac{1}{8}$	8$\frac{5}{8}$	+ $\frac{1}{2}$	3040

Figure 19.2   Toronto Stock Exchange stock price quotations. SOURCE: "Report on Business," *The Globe and Mail*, December 28, 1979.

large block trades of listed firms are generally handled in a special way, so that the market can absorb the shares without putting undue pressure on the share's price.[6]

Reporting Market Activity   Information regarding the trading of listed securities on organized exchanges is reported in various financial and nonfinancial media. Most big city newspapers report the daily activity on major exchanges, although the key source of share price information on listed securities is the *Globe and Mail's* "Report on Business."[*] Figure 19.2 presents an example of some TSE listings from the *Globe and Mail*. Reporting these data daily enhances investor confidence in the continuity of the security markets.

To see exactly what share price information is reported, suppose we take a closer look at the data on Northern Telecom Ltd. (Nor Tel) shares outlined in Figure 19.2. The first two columns, labeled "High" and "Low," contain the highest and lowest price at which the shares traded during the current year. (Unless a $ sign is present, the price is in cents.) The figure immediately following the company's abbreviated name is the cash dividend expected to be paid in 1979, $1.00. The next entries are the "High," "Low," and "Close," which contain the highest, lowest, and last (closing) price, respectively, at which the shares traded on December 27. The prices of shares trading at $5.00 or over per share are quoted and traded in eighths of a dollar.[†] The next column gives the net change between the current day's closing price and the closing price on the preceding day. Northern Telecom Ltd. closed at 52, down $\frac{1}{4}$ on December 27, 1979, which means that it must have closed at 52 $\frac{1}{4}$ (i.e., $\frac{1}{4}$ point higher) on December 24 (the preceding trading day). The

*There is a one-day lag in reporting. This means that the December 27, 1979, transactions are reported in the December 28, 1979, issue of the *Globe and Mail*. Also, the weekly *Financial Post* publishes a weekly stock market report for all Canadian Stock Exchanges.

†Although the smallest divisor of security prices for trades at $5 per share or above is one-eighth, the fractions are rounded off whenever possible. In other words, two-eighths, four-eighths, and six-eighths are expressed as one-fourth, one-half, and three-fourths, respectively.

final column gives the daily volume; 150 shares of Northern Telecom Ltd. were traded on December 27, 1979. Not all price quotations are as easy to read as is the case for Northern Telecom, since quite often various symbols and numbers may be found in the listing between the name and dividend columns. The specific definition of these symbols is given in the legend that accompanies the stock market listing. For example, the small "p," associated with OPI A, indicates that $0.15 in dividends has been paid to date in the latest 12-month period.

The Over-the-Counter Exchange The over-the-counter exchange is not a specific institution; rather, it is a way of trading securities other than on an organized security exchange.* The over-the-counter exchange (OTC) is the result of an intangible relationship among the purchasers and the sellers of securities. Active traders in this market are linked by a telecommunications network. The prices at which securities are traded over the counter are determined by both competitive bids and negotiation. The actual process depends on the general activity of a security. A numerical majority of shares are traded over the counter, as are all government and corporate bonds. Bonds are traded over the counter because most bond trades involve the exchange of large blocks between institutional investors.

The *bid* and *ask* prices quoted on the OTC market represent, respectively, the highest price offered to purchase a given security and the lowest price at which it is offered for sale. Some traders, known as *broker-dealers, make* markets in certain OTC securities by offering to buy or sell them at stated prices. Thus, in order to trade OTC securities, purchasers and sellers must find each other through brokers, or through known market makers in the securities. The financial press obtains daily high and low prices and volumes for unlisted mines and industrials from the Investment Dealers Association of Canada (IDA).

OPTION MARKET

An options market is a market where investors can buy or sell contracts that give the holder the right to purchase or sell the common shares of certain Canadian listed shares during a specified period of time. An option is merely a contract between two investors that gives its owner the right to *buy* (a *call option*) or *sell* (a *put option*) the common shares of a particular company before the expiry date of the option at the option's exercise (striking) price. The *striking* price, as given in the option contract, is the price at which the owner of the option can buy or sell a common share. The two Canadian option markets were established in September 1975 on the Montreal Stock Exchange and in March 1976 on the Toronto Stock Exchange. Subsequently, the TSE and MSE jointly established the Trans-Canada Option Inc. to guarantee execution of option contracts, and to provide for the clearance of option contracts. In 1979, 1.4 million option contracts, worth $577.8 million, were transacted by these two Canadian option markets.

---

*Two additional types of markets—the third market and the fourth market—have developed in the United States. The *third market* involves the trading of listed shares by institutional investors on the over-the-counter market. The *fourth market* involves the direct trading of shares between institutional investors, without the use of a financial intermediary or financial market.

Option trading is best illustrated by an example, which for ease of exposition assumes that an option is exercisable for one common share of a firm.

EXAMPLE   On December 27, 1979, one common share of the Bank of Montreal closed at $24\frac{7}{8}$. On the same day, a call option to purchase one common share of the Bank of Montreal by February 1980 sold at $0.60; and a put option to sell one common share of the Bank of Montreal by February 1980 sold at $0.90. Thus, if the call option was purchased at $0.60, the price of a Bank of Montreal share would have to rise from its price of $24⅞ to above $25½ ($24.88 + 0.60) before the call option purchaser would make a before-commission profit. Similarly, if the put option was purchased at $0.90, the price of a Bank of Montreal share would have to drop below $23⅜ ($24.88 − 0.90) before the put option purchaser would make a before-commission profit.

SPECIAL SHARE TRANSACTIONS

Two special types of stock market transactions often made by a common share investor are *margin purchases* and *short selling.** These transactions are aimed at stimulating market activity and adding additional continuity to the securities markets.

Margin Purchases   The appropriate regulatory agency (e.g., an exchange) sets *margin requirements* that specify how much of the dollar price of a security purchase the purchaser must have, and how much he or she is permitted to borrow. Although the agency could depress or stimulate activity in the securities markets by raising or lowering margin requirements, this is seldom done.

Margin purchases must be approved by a broker. The brokerage firm then lends the purchaser the needed funds and retains the securities purchased as collateral. Some brokerage firms have "in-house" margin requirements that are more restrictive than required by regulation. Present margin requirements are 50 percent for common shares and 10 percent for corporate bonds. Margin purchasers, of course, must pay interest at a specified rate on the amount they borrow.

EXAMPLE   Sue Saskatoon wishes to purchase on margin 200 shares of Northern Telecom at $52 per share. If the margin requirement is 50 percent, Sue will have to pay 50 percent of the total purchase price of $10,400 ($52/share · 200 shares), or $5,200. The remaining $5,200 of the purchase price will be lent to Sue by her brokerage firm. Sue will, of course, have to pay interest to her broker on the $5,200 she borrows, along with the appropriate brokerage fee.

Short Selling   Most people, when they think of security transactions, think of "buying low and selling high." These types of *long* transactions are most common;

---

*There are numerous other types of orders and trades that can be made on the security exchanges. For information on them, refer to an elementary investments text. A few of these texts are referenced at the end of this chapter.

but there are some individuals who engage in *short selling*, which can be thought of as "selling high and buying low." Long transactions are made in anticipation of price increases, whereas *short transactions are made in anticipation of price decreases*. When an individual sells a security short, his or her broker borrows the security from someone else and then sells it on the short seller's behalf. These borrowed shares must be replaced by the short seller in the future. If the short seller can repurchase the shares at a lower price in the future and then return them to their owner, his or her profit will be the difference between the proceeds of the initial sale and the repurchase price. If the short seller ends up repurchasing the shares at a higher price than he or she sold them for, the short seller sustains a loss. There are numerous rules and regulations that govern short sales.

EXAMPLE   Stan Saskatoon wishes to sell short 100 shares of Northern Telecom at $52.25 per share. His broker borrows the shares and sells them, receiving proceeds of $5,225.00 ($52.25/share · 100 shares). If the price of the shares drops, as Stan expects it to, and he repurchases the shares at $39.00 per share, Stan will make a profit, since the cost of replacing the shares, $3,900.00 ($39.00/share · 100 shares) is less than his initial proceeds of $5,225.00. Stan's profit will be $1,325.00 ($5,225.00 − $3,900.00). If the share price rises above $52.25 per share and Stan repurchases it at, say, $56.00 per share, he will sustain a loss of $375.00 [($56.00/share · 100 shares) − ($52.25/share · 100 shares)]. When Stan, or any person, sells short, he is betting on a price decline; if wrong, the short seller will suffer a loss. Stan, of course, will have to pay brokerage fees on his short sale transaction.

MUTUAL FUNDS

A mutual fund is a common form of an open-end investment company.* The attractiveness of mutual funds lies in their ability to provide the small investor with the benefits of diversification, professional portfolio management, and skilled timing of purchases and sales. By purchasing a broad group of securities, the mutual fund attempts to maximize the return for a given level of risk. An individual owning one share in a mutual fund would probably be unable to obtain so diversified an investment in any other way, since it would require a large amount of money for him or her to assemble a portfolio similar to that of the mutual fund. Thus, a mutual fund allows the investor to buy a small portion of a diversified portfolio of securities for a modest outlay.

Distribution of Securities

Although firms could issue securities and sell them directly to investors, most firms utilize the services of a financial intermediary to distribute securities. Since firms usually do not have a well-organized selling organization and are not experts in the pricing

---

*A *mutual fund* sells its shares to the public and redeems these shares at a value representing their claim on the firm's total portfolio. Mutual funds are attractive in that they are open-ended. New shares can be sold as they are demanded by investors, so that the size of the fund increases or decreases with demand.

and marketing of securities, most firms find that it is more operationally efficient to use an underwriter to price and market security issues.

In the United States, the investment banker is responsible for underwriting and distributing securities. The name "investment banker" is somewhat misleading, since an investment banker is neither an investor nor a banker, since he or she neither makes long-term investments nor guards the savings of others. Instead, acting as a middleman between the issuer and seller of new security issues, the investment banker purchases securities from corporations and governments and markets them to the public. The First Boston Corporation and Merrill Lynch, Pierce, Fenner and Smith are two large American investment banking firms that are active in distributing Canadian securities in the U.S. capital markets.

In Canada, the *investment dealer* is generally responsible for providing the services provided by the American investment banker. Similarly, like many of the American investment banking firms such as Merrill Lynch, Canadian investment dealers also provide brokerage services and research to both individuals and institutional investors. Wood Gundy Ltd. and McLeod Young Weir International Ltd. are two of the largest Canadian investment dealers active in underwriting and distributing securities.

Before proceeding further, it should be noted that although the distribution of securities is generally handled by an investment dealer, other parties can underwrite and distribute securities. For example, the directors and officers of small firms sometimes underwrite and distribute their firm's securities to the public. In this chapter, we shall assume that the underwriter is an investment dealer, and thus we will use the two terms interchangeably.

THE FUNCTIONS OF THE INVESTMENT DEALER

The functions of an investment dealer include underwriting security issues, advising clients, and bearing risk.

Underwriting   When an investment dealer agrees to underwrite a security issue, he or she guarantees the issuer that the issuer will receive at least a specified minimum amount of proceeds from the issue. The dealer expects to make a profit by buying the securities at a lower price than he or she plans to sell them for. However, the dealer bears the risk of a downward price movement, or not being able to sell all or part of the issue, during the period from the time of purchase to the time of sale of the issue.

EXAMPLE   The First Big Corporation has agreed to underwrite a new $50 million common share issue for the Taxaco Oil Company. It has agreed to purchase the shares for $48 million. Since First Big must pay Taxaco $48 million for the shares, it must attempt to sell the shares for net proceeds of at least $48 million. Actually, it will attempt to sell the shares for at least $50 million, thereby obtaining a $2 million commission. If it is unable to raise $50 million, the investment dealer will lose its $2 million commission and possibly part of the $48 million spent for the shares initially. In some cases, a security issue can be sold in a few days; in other, less fortunate situations, months are required to negotiate a sale. The investment dealer therefore bears the risk of unfavourable price changes before the issue is sold as well as the risk of being unable to sell part or all of the issue.

Many security issues are not underwritten; rather, they are *privately placed* or sold on a *best efforts* basis. These functions may also be handled by an investment dealer.

Private Placement   Private placement occurs when an investment dealer arranges for the direct purchase of a new security issue by an individual, several individuals, an institution, or a group of institutions. The investment dealer is then paid a commission for acting as a middleman in the transaction.

Best Efforts   In the case of some public offerings, the investment dealer may not actually underwrite the issue; rather, the dealer may use his or her resources to sell the securities on a *best efforts* basis. In this case, the dealer does not take on the risk associated with underwriting and his or her compensation is based on the number of securities sold.

Advising   The investment dealer performs an advisory function by analyzing the firm's financial needs and recommending appropriate means of financing. Since an investment dealer has a feel for the pulse of the securities markets, he or she can provide useful advice on new issues, acquisitions, amalgamations, and refinancing decisions.

Risk Bearing   As indicated in the discussion of the underwriting function, the investment dealer accepts the risk of price changes and a market collapse between the time of purchase and the time of sale of securities. There is always the possibility that he or she will be "stuck" with a large amount of the securities. In some instances, he or she may be able to sell the securities only at a price lower than the initial purchase price.

THE ORGANIZATION OF AN UNDERWRITTEN SECURITY DISTRIBUTION

The investment dealer's functions of underwriting security issues, advising clients, and bearing risks come into play as a result of a logical sequence of events. The process begins with selecting an investment dealer; proceeds through conferring with the issuer, preparing the preliminary prospectus, forming the banking and selling groups, registering the prospectus, signing the underwriting agreement, and distributing the issue; and ends with the stabilizing of the market price during and subsequent to the distribution period. The sequence and approximate timing of these activities is depicted in Figure 19.3. Each of these activities is described below.

Selecting an Investment Dealer   A firm needing additional capital market financing initiates the fund-raising process by selecting a *lead* or *principal* investment dealer to advise, underwrite, and therefore bear the risk of the new issue. The investment dealer is generally chosen by the issuing firm, but may be selected through *competitive bidding*. In the case of competitive bidding, the investment dealer(s) with the highest bid obtains the right to underwrite the issue. When the issuer chooses the investment dealer, the security issue is called a *negotiated offering*. In

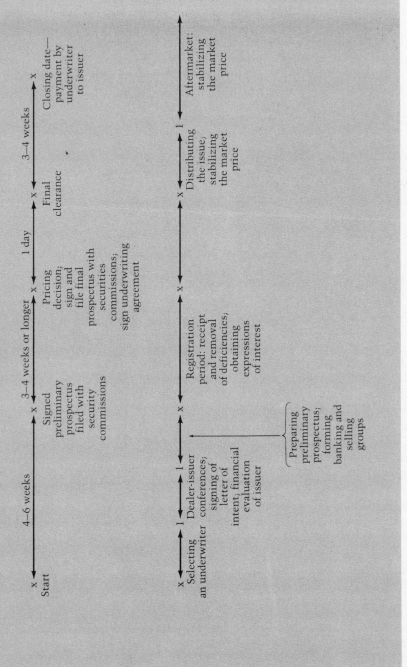

Figure 19.3 Sequence and approximate timing of the activities involved in the primary distribution of securities.

Canada, issuing firms generally choose a dealer with whom they have an established underwriting relationship.

Conferring With the Issuer   Once selected, the *lead* investment dealer(s), the officers of the issuing firm, and their legal counsel hold a number of meetings to determine how much capital should be raised, and in what form this capital should be raised. During this period of time, a *letter of intent** is signed, and the investment dealer analyzes the issuer's financial position and proposed disposition of the funds to be raised to ensure that the firm is financially sound and that the proposed expenditures are justifiable. After the board of directors of the issuing firm agrees to a proposed method of financing, the preparation of the preliminary prospectus begins.

Preparing the Preliminary Prospectus   A number of meetings are then held to prepare the preliminary prospectus. The preliminary prospectus contains the audited financial statements of the issuing firm and full, true, and plain disclosure of all other material facts relating to the proposed offering of securities. Items dealing with the issue, which at this point of time are not included in the prospectus draft, include the price and size of the issue and the underwriter's commission.

Forming the Banking Group   While preparing the preliminary prospectus, the lead investment dealer(s) will invite other interested investment dealers to join the *banking group* or *underwriting syndicate*. Members of the banking group accept some of the underwriting risk of the issue, since they agree to purchase a specific proportion of the issue from the underwriting group. It should be noted that the banking group is not fixed until the signing of the banking-group arrangement. This is done on the day of final clearance of the prospectus.

In Canada, the banking group is likely to be assembled based on past relationships between the principal underwriter and other investment dealers.† Thus, once a particular underwriter and banking group have handled an issue of a particular issuer, each group member expects to have an identical percentage participation in the future issues of the same issuer.

A specified percentage of each member's participation is withheld by the principal underwriter for sale to the 100-plus financial institutions on the so-called *exempt list*. This is done to avoid unnecessary duplication of selling effort and possible price cutting by members of the banking group when dealing with large potential purchasers of the issue. Generally, the specified percentage withheld for sale to the exempt list is highest for bonds (about 50 percent) and lowest for common equity.

Forming the Selling Group   For larger issues, the lead underwriter may also form a selling group to assist with the sale of the issue. Selling group members, unlike the members of the banking group, act as brokers for the issue. That is, they assume

---

*This letter broadly describes the terms and size of the proposed new issue and is a conditional offer by the dealer to purchase the issue.
†The names of the members of the banking group are listed in the prospectus. To highlight the prestige attached with being the principal underwriter(s), the only name(s) on the cover of the propectus is often that of the principal underwriter(s).

no risk and are paid a certain amount (commission) for each security sold.* Thus, a series of dealer prices emerge as the marketing organization for the issue becomes more elaborate. This is illustrated in the following example.

EXAMPLE   As the principal underwriter for a bond issue for Taxaco Oil Company, First Big Corporation purchased each $100.00 of face value of bonds at $97.00. These bonds were resold at $97.75 and $98.50 to the banking and selling group members, respectively. Casual dealers purchased the bonds for resale from First Big at $99.25. Members of the exempt list and the public purchased the bonds at the retail price of $100.00.

Registering the Prospectus   When the preliminary prospectus has been signed by all parties, it is filed with the securities commissions in all the provinces in which the underwriter intends to sell the issue. Subsequently, the commissions' staffs analyze the preliminary prospectus to determine if there are any factual omissions or misrepresentations in the filed prospectus. After reviewing the preliminary prospectus for three to four weeks or longer, each commission may file a *list of deficiencies* or may request additional information from the issuing firm or underwriter.

After receiving the letter of deficiencies, the underwriter attempts to rectify the deficiencies. The underwriter does this through meetings with the issuer and the security commissions' staff. Once all the commissions indicate that all deficiencies have been satisfied, the preparation of the final prospectus is initiated.

An important aspect of the issue that must be resolved at this point is the price of the issue. Thus, the principal underwriter and the issuing firm meet after the close of the financial markets to agree upon the price of the issue. For a primary issue of common shares for a company with outstanding shares that are already publicly traded, the issue price is based on the day's closing price. For a primary issue of common shares for a company with no publicly traded shares, the issue price is based on the valuation principles given in Chapter 17. For new issues of bonds, the issue price is based on the closing market yields for similar debt instruments. Naturally, in all of these pricing decisions, there is a conflict of interest between the underwriter and the issuer; that is, the underwriter attempts to negotiate a low issue price, while the issuer attempts to negotiate a high issue price. During the next day, the final prospectus is signed by all parties and is filed with the various provincial securities commissions.

During the registration period, the underwriters and the other members of the banking and selling groups cannot sell the issue. However, they can measure the likely saleability of the issue by obtaining *expressions of interest* from potential buyers of the issue, including the institutions on the exempt list. The interest expressed by institutions on the exempt list is referred to as the *institutional book*.

Signing of the Underwriting Agreement   The issuer and the underwriter also sign the underwriting agreement on the day the final prospectus is filed. This agreement

---

*The selling group is usually compensated in the same fashion as the underwriter. In other words, the selling group buys the securities at a discount from the sale price and profits from the *spread* between the price at which it purchases and the price at which it sells the security. However, since the selling group assumes no risk, it operates on a smaller discount than the underwriter or banking group.

specifies the terms and conditions under which the underwriter will purchase the issue from the issuing firm. The *closing date,* or the date on which the underwriter must purchase the issue, is specified in the underwriting agreement. Generally, the closing date is from three to four weeks after the final clearance of the prospectus by all securities commissions.

Most underwriting agreements also have *opting (market) out clauses,* which give the underwriter the option to terminate the underwriting without paying a penalty to the issuer. Generally, an underwriter can opt out of an underwriting if (1) there is a regulatory action (as discussed earlier) that restricts the trading or distribution of the issue; (2) there is a change, before the fourth day after final clearance of the prospectus, that seriously affects or may affect the financial markets or the firm; and (3) there is a material change during the distribution period that causes the final approved prospectus to become incorrect or misleading.

Distribution of the Issue   Generally, within one or two days after the filing of the final prospectus, all the applicable securities commissions will have given final clearance to the final prospectus. *Approval of a prospectus by one or more security commissions does not mean that the security is a good investment; it only indicates that the facts presented in the prospectus accurately reflect the firm's true position.*

After obtaining final clearance, the banking and selling groups and casual dealers can begin to legally sell the issue. If the issue is sold out, it is considered *oversubscribed;* if all the shares are not sold immediately, it is said to be *undersubscribed.*

Stabilizing the Market Price During Distribution   Once an issue has been offered for sale, the banking group may stabilize the market price of the issue so that the entire issue can be sold at the initial offering price. By placing orders to buy the security, the underwriting group can maintain the demand for the issue and therefore keep the market price at the desired level.* Also, in order to stabilize the price in the *after-market* (that is, the period after the distribution is completed), the banking group may *oversell the issue* (that is, sell more securities than were available for sale). Stabilizing the market price during the distribution period is in the best interests of both the issuer and the banking group, since it reduces the group's risk, thereby lowering the issuance cost charged the issuer.

Stabilizing the Market Price in the After-Market   Once the distribution of an issue has been completed, the banking group may continue to stabilize the price of the issue to ensure an orderly and continuous after-market. Stabilizing the price during the after-market often consists of the banking group buying shares to cover the *short position* of the group, which was *caused by initially overselling* the issue.

THE COST OF UNDERWRITING SERVICES

The investment dealer is compensated by purchasing the security issue at a discount from the proposed sale price. The discount on an individual per-bond or per-share basis

---

*These activities, sometimes referred to as *price-pegging,* are legal under the Canadian criminal code.

is referred to as the *spread.* The size of the spread depends on the cost of investigations, printing, registration, the discount to the banking group, and the discount given to the selling group. The cost of an issue is a function of two basic components—administrative cost and underwriting cost. Generally, the larger the issue, the lower the overall cost in percentage terms. It is also generally true that the overall flotation cost for common shares is highest, with preferred shares and bonds following in that order. The overall flotation cost ranges from as little as 1 percent of the total proceeds on a large bond issue to as much as 20 percent or more of the proceeds on a small common share issue. The size of an issue affects the cost in that large issues have a lower percentage cost due to economies of scale. The type of security issued affects the cost because it affects the ease with which large blocks can be placed with one purchaser. These differences are shown in Table 19.2.[7] The firm contemplating a security issue must therefore weigh the cost of public sale against the cost and feasibility of private placement, which is briefly described in the next section.

PRIVATE PLACEMENT

The *private* or *direct placement* of a security issue with the purchaser can sometimes be negotiated by a business firm. Often, however, the advice of an investment dealer is required to price the issue correctly. In such cases, the dealer will receive a commission, which depending on the size of the issue and the services to be provided, will range between $\frac{1}{4}$ and $1\frac{1}{2}$ percent.

A private placement usually reduces issuance and administrative costs. For example, the filing of a private placement memorandum with the securities commissions is a much less demanding reporting requirement than filing a prospectus for a public offering. It also may provide both the issuer and the buyer with a great deal of flexibility. For example, the borrower may arrange to draw funds at more convenient future points in time; while the buyer of the issue may be able to obtain better security or more protective covenants than would be obtained in a public offering.

There are two potential disadvantages with private placements. First, the issuing company bears the underwriting risk. Any investment dealers who are involved generally only act as agents. Second, the required returns or yields on private placements are

Table 19.2 Canadian Underwriters' Compensation

Size of issue	Type of issue	Percentage compensation[a]		
		Average	Medium	Range
Under $3 million	debt	4.62	4.90	1.00–10.00
	preferred shares	6.05	4.77	3.50–11.00
	common equity	8.43	9.09	2.00–14.00
Over $3 million	debt	2.82	2.85	0.50–5.00
	preferred shares	4.75	4.00	3.50–6.50
	common equity	6.98	6.38	5.00–10.00

[a]Compensation calculated by taking average gross underwriter discount as a percentage of net proceeds.
SOURCE: *I.D.A. Brief to the Porter Commission*, Volume II, June 1962, p. E-14.

generally a little higher than those on comparable public issues. This is due to a lack of marketability for private placements.

Private placement of common shares is sometimes made through share options or purchase plans. *Share options* are generally extended to management and permit it to purchase a certain number of shares of their firm at a specified price over a stated period of time. These options are intended to stimulate managerial actions that increase the long-run success of the firm. *Share purchase plans* are a fringe benefit occasionally offered to a firm's employees. They allow the employees to purchase the firm's shares at a discount or on a matching basis with the firm absorbing part of the cost. Both of these plans provide equity capital and at the same time increase employee motivation and interest in the company.

Investor Relations[8]

Many Canadian public companies have personnel assigned to investor relations. Often these individuals are either a part of or report directly to senior management. *Investor relations* involves the dissemination of firm-related information (such as the award of a large contract) and nonfirm-related information (such as the corporation's viewpoint on the value of new pollution control regulations) to past, present, and future suppliers of corporate capital in order to perpetuate or encourage their financial involvement in the firm.* The objectives of investor relations are to minimize a firm's cost of capital by maximizing the firm's exposure and credibility in the marketplace, and to influence shareholders to act as an external pressure group on their legislators when governmental legislation is against the corporate interest. For example, MacMillan Bloedel Ltd. sponsored a series of mini-documentary commercials that directly emphasized how the firm was reducing waste and preserving forest resources and that indirectly implied that the government should be careful in its regulation of the forestry industry.

The growing importance of investor relations is depicted by the growth of the U.S.-based National Investor Relations Institute (NIRI). From a little over 10 corporate members in 1969, it has grown to over 900 in 1979. Furthermore, most of the corporate executives who are responsible for investor relations for the Fortune 500 firms are members of the NIRI.

Summary

This chapter has presented a discussion of the institutions and markets that allow the funds of savers to be channeled into the hands of those who need funds for investment purposes. The forums in which this activity takes place are the financial intermediaries and markets. Financial intermediaries or institutions channel the savings of various individuals, businesses, and governments into the hands of demanders of these funds.

---

*It should be noted that all firm-related disclosures must conform to provincial security regulations. Generally, these regulations prohibit firms or their employees, who are not registered with the appropriate securities commissions, from any act, solicitation, advertisement, or negotiation that would further trading in their own securities.

The key private sector financial intermediaries include the chartered banks, caisses populaires and credit unions, finance companies, trust companies, life insurance companies, investment companies, pension funds, and venture capital companies. The key public sector financial intermediaries and programs include the Canada and Quebec Pension Plans, the federally guaranteed loan plans, the Federal Business Development Bank, the Export Development Corporation, Regional Development program, and various provincial development corporations. The private sector intermediaries either lend out their funds directly to individuals, businesses, and governments or channel them to these same parties via loans and investments made in the capital markets. These intermediaries sometimes go into the capital markets to raise money to supplement the funds obtained directly from savers.

There are two components of the financial market. The short-term market is known as the money market. It is created by the intangible relationship between suppliers and demanders of short-term funds (maturities less than three years). The key instruments of the money market include all the so-called marketable securities, such as treasury bills, negotiable certificates of deposit, commercial paper, banker's acceptances, and repurchase agreements. Participants in the money market include individuals, businesses, government, and financial institutions.

The capital market is the market where long-term debt and equity capital is raised. This market is of key importance to new capital formation in our economy. It is made up of both the organized security exchanges and the over-the-counter exchange. These exchanges allocate scarce capital, create a continuous market, determine and publicize security prices, and aid firms in obtaining new financing. There are a number of organized Canadian exchanges, the largest of which is the Toronto Stock Exchange. Each of these exchanges allows only members to make transactions in listed securities, which are securities that have met some predefined standards. The results of trading activity in securities listed on the major exchanges are reported daily in financial news media such as *The Globe and Mail Report on Business.* The over-the-counter exchange is not a specific institution, but there is a telecommunications network between active participants in this market. Markets also exist where investors can buy or sell options. Securities can be traded in the capital markets not only by normal purchase and sale transactions but by margin purchases and short selling. These are only two of the special types of stock market transactions that can be made. Mutual funds enable individuals to purchase ownership in a portfolio of securities.

Investment dealers make it easier for firms to raise long-term debt and equity funds in the capital markets. The investment dealer underwrites or sells total issues of securities, receiving compensation in the form of a spread between the price at which he or she purchases and sells a security issue. Occasionally the investment dealer does not accept all the risk of an issue, instead being paid a commission for privately placing an issue or selling whatever is possible. Investment dealers also provide advice to the issuer of new securities. Generally the principal investment dealer chosen by a firm will share the risk of a large issue by forming a banking group, which consists of other investment dealers. Before a new issue can be sold, all applicable provincial security commissions must give final clearance to the issue, since securities regulation is under provincial jurisdiction in Canada. The investment dealer aids in pricing an issue and usually forms a selling group to market the issue. The cost of underwriting services is a function of the size of the issue and the type of security being sold. The investment dealer's knowledge of the market is quite important to the issuer. An alternative to the use of an investment dealer is the direct or private placement of a security issue in the hands of a single or small group of purchasers. Even in the case of a direct placement, though, an investment dealer is often used in an advisory capacity. Most Canadian public companies have senior personnel assigned to investor relations.

Questions

19.1 What are financial intermediaries and financial markets? What is the fund-raising alternative to these media?

19.2 Who are the key participants in the financial intermediation process? Indicate which are net savers and which are net borrowers.

19.3 How do caisses populaires and credit unions operate?

19.4 What role do life insurance companies and pension funds play in lending and investing funds? Are these institutions important sources of funds to business?

19.5 What relationship exists between financial intermediaries and financial markets? Why does it exist?

19.6 What is the money market? Where is it housed? How does it differ from the capital markets?

19.7 What are the capital markets? What role do securities exchanges play in this market? How is membership on these exchanges obtained, and how do they operate?

19.8 How does the over-the-counter market operate? How does it differ from the organized security exchanges? How is it linked? What are *bid* and *ask* prices?

19.9 What are margin purchases and short sale transactions? Who controls margin requirements? When is an individual likely to make a short sale?

19.10 What is an *option*? What is the difference between a *call* and a *put* option? What is meant by the *striking price*?

19.11 What is a mutual fund? Why are they attractive to investors?

19.12 What is an investment dealer, and what are his or her functions as an underwriter?

19.13 What events occur between the time an issuer decides to raise capital and the ultimate sale of the securities by the investment dealer?

19.14 What happens during the prospectus registration period?

19.15 How does an investment dealer attempt to stabilize the market price of a new issue? Are there any legal requirements regarding this activity?

19.16 How is an investment dealer compensated for his or her underwriting-related services? How are underwriting costs affected by the size and type of an issue?

19.17 Explain the *private placement* of a security issue. What securities typically would be considered for private placement? Under what conditions would the firm decide on using private placement rather than a firm underwriting?

19.18 What is *operational efficiency*? What is *allocational efficiency*? What is *informational efficiency*?

Problems

19.1 Given the following quotations for Harlequin Enterprises Ltd. (ticker symbol 'HQE') and Skyline Hotels Ltd. (ticker symbol 'SKY'), from the Thursday, January 10, *The Globe and Mail*, answer questions **a** through **g** for HQE and SKY, respectively.

| $21\frac{3}{4}$ | $13\frac{7}{8}$ | Harlequin | .56 | $20\frac{1}{2}$ $20\frac{1}{4}$ | $20\frac{3}{8}$ | $-\frac{1}{8}$ | 13130 |
| 430 | 245 | Skyline H | | 290 285 | 285 | -5 | 900 |

a. On what day did the trading activity occur?
b. What are the highest and lowest prices at which the shares sold on the day quoted?
c. What was the last or closing price at which each share was traded on the day quoted?
d. How large a dividend is expected for each share in the current year?
e. What are the highest and lowest prices at which each share has traded in the current year?
f. How many shares of each firm were traded on the day quoted?
g. How much, if any, of a change in the price took place between the day quoted and the preceding trading day?

19.2   For each of the following cases, indicate how much money Paula Lipski would have to put up in order to make the given transaction, if the stated margin requirements were applicable.

Case	Number of shares	Price per share($)	Margin requirement
A	100	$23\frac{1}{4}$	55%
B	80	$41\frac{1}{2}$	40%
C	900	94	60%
D	100	$22\frac{1}{8}$	35%
E	250	$14\frac{7}{8}$	65%
F	400	62	20%

19.3   Wayne Marcotti is considering purchasing shares on margin. He has the following information. Use it to answer the next questions.

Security	Number of shares	Price per share ($)	Margin requirement	Interest on margin	Holding period of shares
A	100	25	20%	10%	3 months
B	50	$28\frac{1}{2}$	40%	9%	6 months
C	200	$37\frac{1}{4}$	60%	12%	1 month
D	450	$16\frac{7}{8}$	55%	8%	4 months

a. How much money will he have to put up in each case?
b. For each case, what amount of interest would he owe if he sells at the end of the given holding period?

19.4   Winston Ross, on February 2, 19X0, purchased 400 shares of CBA at $23\frac{1}{2}$ and 300 shares of DZC at $44\frac{7}{8}$. The margin requirement at the time was 40 percent and the interest rate on margin purchases was 9 percent.
a. If Winston used the maximum amount of margin available, how much of his own money would he need for the purchase?
b. If he sold the shares on June 2, 19X0, how much interest would he pay on his margin account?
c. If the total brokerage fees for the purchase and sale were $62.50, and he sold CBA for $23 and DZC for $49\frac{3}{8}$, considering all costs, how much did Winston net from his original purchases?
d. What was his rate of return on his *invested capital?*

e. What would his net return have been if he had not bought on margin?
f. What would his return on *invested capital* have been if he had *not* bought on margin?

19.5   Consider each of the following cases:

	Case			
	A	B	C	D
Number of shares purchased	300	150	150	80
Price per share ($)	31	$62\frac{1}{2}$	$62\frac{1}{2}$	254
Brokerage fees (total)	$60	$100	$100	$90
Margin requirement	65%	55%	55%	45%
Margin interest rate	9%	8%	8%	9%
Holding period	6 months	9 months	9 months	12 months
Sale price per share ($)	$37\frac{1}{4}$	55	70	302

a. Calculate the amount of money the purchaser must put up in each case assuming he or she uses the full amount of margin available.
b. Calculate the margin interest charged for the specified holding period.
c. Calculate the net profit (i.e., the proceeds after brokerage and margin costs) in each case.
d. Determine the return on *invested capital* earned by the purchaser in each case.
e. Calculate the net profit in each case assuming margin is *not* used.
f. Determine the return on *invested capital* assuming margin was *not* used.
g. What conclusions can you draw with respect to the risk-return trade-off provided by the use of margin? Explain this in light of cases B and C.

19.6   Chung Li is considering the purchase of the common shares of Mountain Pass Food Processing Ltd. She has $8,000 to invest and the shares are currently selling at $50 per share.
a. How many shares can she purchase if the margin requirement is
(1) 100 percent?
(2) 50 percent?
(3) 10 percent?
b. From **a**, what conclusions with respect to the effects of changes in the margin requirements on the ability to purchase securities can be drawn?

19.7   For each of the following cases indicate
a. The short profit or loss made (prior to brokerage fees).
b. The net profit after all costs.

Case	Number of shares	Price ($) at which shares sold short	Price ($) at which shares repurchased	Broker's commission
A	100	50	55	$ 25
B	700	80	70	$280
C	300	$23\frac{7}{8}$	$32\frac{1}{4}$	$120
D	1000	$32\frac{1}{2}$	$32\frac{1}{4}$	$180

19.8   Ray Glaser, who is a real gambler, cannot decide whether to take a long or a short position in a given security. The shares are currently selling for $48 per share.
a. How much would Ray lose or gain if he bought 200 shares and later sold them for $54 per share?

b. How much would he have lost or gained had he taken a short position if the shares were repurchased at $54 per share?

c. Answer **a** and **b**, assuming that the shares were sold or repurchased at $38 per share.

d. If Mr. Glaser does some research into future share price movements, what market expectation will cause him to take a long position and what expectation will justify selling short? Explain. Is there an implicit assumption here, dealing with the relationship between the share and the market?

19.9   Given the following securities and expected prices now and six months from now, indicate whether you would take a long or short position in each firm, and how much per share would be earned in each case if the expected prices matched the actual prices.

Firm	Current price per share ($)	Expected price per share ($) 6 months from now
A	44	50
B	37	$32\frac{1}{2}$
C	$14\frac{1}{4}$	$18\frac{1}{2}$
D	$19\frac{1}{8}$	22
E	47	47

19.10   The Gray Company is interested in selling common shares in order to raise capital for plant expansion. The firm has consulted the First Maritime Company, a large underwriting firm, which believes the shares can be sold for $80 per share. The underwriter, on investigation, has found that its administrative costs will be 2 percent of the sale price and its selling costs will be $1\frac{1}{2}$ percent of the sale price. If the underwriter requires a profit of 1 percent of the sale price, how much will the *spread* have to be in *dollars* in order to cover the underwriter's costs and profit?

19.11   The Philip-Marrow Company Ltd. wishes to raise $100 million to be used in the acquisition of Unsoda Soft Drinks. The company has estimated that the $100 million should provide an amount sufficient to make the acquisition after paying the underwriter. The underwriter, Morris Lunch & Co., believes it can sell the 100,000 bonds at their $1,000 face value. The underwriter estimates that its administrative costs will be $3.5 million. It also must sell the bonds at a $\frac{3}{4}$ of 1 percent discount from their face value to members of the selling group. (No banking group will be formed.) Morris Lunch's gross underwriting spread will thus be the sum of the estimated administrative costs, the selling group discount, and a further 1 percent underwriting cost charge based on the bonds' face value.

a. Calculate the per-bond gross underwriting spread.

b. How much will Philip-Marrow Company Ltd. net from the issue (given the spread in **a**)?

c. How much will the selling group receive? How much will the underwriter receive?

d. Describe the nature of the underwriter's risk assuming that this is *not* a private placement or best efforts offering.

Notes

1. Lawrence Kryzanowski and Roger Giraldeau, "Venture Capital Management: A Survey of Attitudes Towards Selection Criteria," *American Journal of Small Business* 2 (July 1977), pp. 29–37. For a comprehensive review of Canadian sources of venture capital, see Peter McQuillan and Howard Taylor, *Sources of Venture Capital in Canada* (Ottawa: Department of Industry, Trade and Commerce, 1977).

2. An extremely useful source of information on governmental assistance to business is *ABC: Assistance to Business in Canada* (Ottawa: Board of Economic Ministers, 1979). Also, since governmental assistance programs are continually being dropped, added, and modified, the *reader should refer to the official text of each program for current information on each of the programs.*

3. Two other programs of interest are the Enterprise Development Program (EDP) and the Program for Export Market Development (PEMD). EDP is an extensive program of assistance to small and medium-sized Canadian businesses. It is designed to assist firms undertaking highly risky innovative, adjustment, restructuring, or modernization projects that are expected to generate high rates of return. PEMD encourages Canadian suppliers of goods and services to enter new export markets, or to undertake additional development activities in existing export markets. Under the PEMD program, the government makes financial contributions to Canadian exporters when it deems that there is a proven need to share the risk of developing or monitoring overseas markets (sections B, C, and D of the program), bidding on capital projects of unusual size or complexity (section A), unusual international competition (all sections), or to operate an export consortium to obtain sales opportunities abroad (section E).

4. The $5-billion-plus Alberta Heritage Trust Fund entered the corporate lending field in 1979. Loans of $1 million or more at commercial interest rates were made available only to firms doing or planning to do business in Alberta. The fund was also considering the provision of venture capital funding to smaller businesses.

5. For example, the QIDC provides assistance to qualified Quebec manufacturers and processors by means of low-interest term loans, loan guarantees, forgiveable loans, construction and leasing of plants, leasebacks, direct equity investment, and export assistance.

6. Close found little adverse price effects associated with large block secondary issues and trades, which qualified for a volume discount, on the TSE and MSE. See Nicholas Close, "Price Reaction to Large Transactions in the Canadian Equity Markets," *Financial Analysts Journal* (November-December 1975), pp. 50–57. On the other hand, some institutions have found that the ability of Canadian exchanges to handle large block trades is sometimes quite limited. In such cases, member brokers have had to divide blocks into smaller lots so that they could be transacted on two or more exchanges.

7. Shaw, in a study of underwriting costs for the period 1966–1968, found a linear relationship between underwriting costs and issue size. This absence of scale economies was quite surprising. See David Shaw, "The Cost of Going Public in Canada," *Financial Executive* (July 1969), pp. 20–28. The reader should note that, given the date of these studies, the costs cited are probably no longer representative of the actual costs.

8. Based on Lawrence Kryzanowski and Patricia E. Moran, "The Role of Investor Relations in the Operations of Canadian Public Companies," *Cost and Management* (July-August 1979), pp. 11–15.

Suggested Readings

Amling, Frederick, *Investments: An Introduction to Analysis and Management*, 4th ed. (Englewood Cliffs, N.J.: Prentice-Hall 1978).

Close, Nicholas, "Price Reaction to Large Transactions in the Canadian Equity Markets," *Financial Analysts Journal* (November-December 1975), pp. 50–57.

Curley, Anthony J. and Robert M. Bear, *Investment Analysis and Management* (New York: Harper & Row, 1979).

D'Ambrosio, Charles A., *Principles of Modern Investments* (Chicago, Ill.: Science Research Associates, 1976).

Dyl, E. and M. Joehnk, "Competitive versus Negotiated Underwriting of Public Utility Debt," *The Bell Journal of Economics* (Autumn 1976), pp. 680–689.

Ederington, Louis H., "Negotiated versus Competitive Underwriting of Corporate Bonds," *Journal of Finance* 31 (March 1976), pp. 17–28.

Francis, Jack Clark, *Investments: Analysis and Management*, 2nd ed. (New York: McGraw-Hill, 1976).

Government of Canada, *1964 Report of the Royal Commission on Banking and Finance* (Ottawa: Queen's Printer, 1964).

———, *ABC: Assistance to Business in Canada* (Ottawa: Board of Economic Ministers, 1979).

Hamilton, James L., "Marketplace Organization and Marketability: NASDQ, the Stock Exchange, and the National Market System," *Journal of Finance* 33 (May 1978), pp. 487–503.

Hayes, Samuel III, "Investment Banking Power Structure in Flux," *Harvard Business Review* (March-April 1971), pp. 136–152.

Jacobs, Donald P., Loring C. Farwell, and Edwin H. Neave, *Financial Institutions*, 5th ed. (Homewood, Ill.: Irwin, 1972).

Johnson, Keith B., T. Gregory Morton, and M. Chapman Findlay III, "An Empirical Analysis of the Flotation Cost of Corporate Securities, 1971–1972," *Journal of Finance* 30 (June 1975), pp. 1129–1133.

Kryzanowski, Lawrence, "The Efficacy of Trading Suspensions: A Regulatory Action Designed to Prevent the Exploitation of Monopoly Information," *The Journal of Finance* 34 (December 1979), pp. 1187–1200.

Logue, Dennis E. and John R. Lindvall, "The Behavior of Investment Bankers: An Econometric Investigation," *Journal of Finance* 29 (March 1974), pp. 203–215.

McQuillan, Peter, *Going Public in Canada* (Toronto: The Canadian Institute of Chartered Accountants, 1971).

—— and Howard Taylor, *Sources of Venture Capital in Canada* (Ottawa: Department of Industry, Trade and Commerce, 1977).

Neufeld, E., *The Financial System of Canada* (Toronto: Macmillan, 1972).

Peters, R., *Economics of the Canadian Corporate Bond Market* (Montreal: McGill–Queen's University Press, 1971).

Shapiro, Eli and Charles R. Wolf, *The Role of Private Placements in Corporate Finance* (Boston: Division of Research, Graduate School of Business Administration, Harvard University, 1972).

Sharpe, William F., *Investments* (Englewood Cliffs, N.J.: Prentice-Hall, 1978).

Shaw, David, "The Cost of Going Public in Canada," *Financial Executive* (July 1969), pp. 20–28.

——, "The Performance of Primary Common Stock Offerings: A Canadian Comparison," *Journal of Finance* (December 1971), pp. 1101–1113.

Stevenson, Richard A. and Edward H. Jennings, *Fundamentals of Investments* (St. Paul, Minn.: West, 1976).

Stoll, Hans R. and Anthony J. Curley, "Small Business and the New Issues Market for Equities," *Journal of Financial and Quantitative Analysis* 5 (September 1970), pp. 309–322.

Tinic, Seha M. and Richard R. West, "Marketability of Common Stocks in Canada and the U.S.A.: A Comparison of Agent versus Dealer Dominated Markets," *The Journal of Finance* 29 (June 1974), pp. 729–746.

——, *Investing in Securities: An Efficient Markets Approach* (Reading, Mass.: Addison-Wesley, 1979).

Van Horne, James C., *The Function and Analysis of Capital Market Rates* (Englewood Cliffs, N.J.: Prentice-Hall, 1970).

Chapter 20

LEASING

Leasing involves obtaining the use of specific fixed assets, such as land and equipment, without actually receiving title to them. The *lessee* (user) receives the services of the assets *leased* by the *lessor*, who owns the assets. In exchange for the use of the assets, the lessee makes a series of fixed periodic payments to the lessor. The lease payment is treated as a tax-deductible expenditure by the lessee; lease receipts are treated as revenues by the lessor.

The popularity of leasing has increased over the past 20 years. Many firms offering a wide variety of deals have become lessors. Leasing of assets is now quite common in fields such as computers, real estate, transportation, manufacturing equipment, and equipment for oil fields and mining operations.

The use of leasing as a source of financing can best be understood by comparing the lease to the purchase of a specific asset. If a firm wishes to obtain the service of a specific asset, it has, in general, two basic alternatives: to purchase the asset or to lease it. Sometimes leasing may be the only alternative. To mention a few cases, leased land is the only land available in Canada's national parks. Oil rights in Alberta must be leased from the government (except in the almost nonexistent case where title to the land antedates the present law on mineral and oil rights). Certain dock facilities for ocean freighters can only be acquired through leasing.

Leasing is discussed in this section of the text because it has many of the characteristics of long-term financing. The chapter is divided into four basic sections. The first section describes some of the important characteristics of leases such as the types of leases and lease arrangements, the legal requirements of leases, and the lease contract. Because the types of assets leased and the lease arrangements vary widely, the discussion in this section is of a general nature. The second section examines the use of leasing as a source of financing and discusses the costs and capital structure implications of leasing. The third section presents a framework for analyzing the lease-purchase decision. The chapter concludes with a critical appraisal of certain advantages and disadvantages commonly associated with the use of leasing as a source of financing.

Characteristics of Leases

Leasing arrangements can take a number of different forms. This section discusses both the most common types of leases and various leasing arrangements. The common provisions of a lease, such as maintenance clauses, are discussed here. Also described in this section are the legal requirements of leases and the general provisions of the lease contract.

BASIC TYPES OF LEASES

There are two basic types of lease arrangements, namely, *operating leases* and *financial leases*. Financial leases are often called *capital leases.* An operating lease is generally a short-term contractual arrangement. The primary difference between operating and financial leases is that a financial lease is a relatively long-term arrangement that cannot be canceled at the option of the lessee; whereas an operating lease can generally be canceled by giving proper notice to the lessor.

Operating Leases   An operating lease is normally a contractual arrangement whereby the lessee agrees to make periodic payments to the lessor over the lease period. The lease period is generally less than the estimated future life of the asset at the time of leasing. Such leases are generally *cancelable* at the option of the lessee. A firm will, therefore, tend to acquire assets under operating leases if its operations are subject to rapid changes or if the assets involved are subject to a relatively high rate of technological obsolescence. Under the terms of an operating lease, the lessee-firm can generally shift the entire risk of possible technological obsolescence associated with the leased asset to the lessor.

Computer systems are prime examples of assets whose relative efficiency is expected to diminish with new technological developments; the operating lease is therefore a commonly used leasing arrangement for computers. Other types of assets involved in operating leases include heavy specialized equipment, copying machines, automobiles, and cash registers. Since the operating lease is normally for a period less than the asset's usable life, the total payments made by the lessee under this type of lease are generally *less* than the initial cost of the leased asset to the lessor. The lessor expects to recover the asset's cost through repeated renewals of the original lease or through subsequent leasing arrangements with other user firms and the residual value of the asset. In some instances, the lease contract may give the lessee an option to purchase the leased asset at the end of the lease period at a price specified in the contract.

Financial (or Capital) Lease   A financial (or capital) lease is a *longer-term* lease than an operating lease. Financial leases are *noncancelable* unless the lessor and the lessee agree to the cancellation. Thus, under a financial lease, even if the lessee at some point in time during the term of the lease does not require the service of the leased asset, it will be contractually obliged to make payments over the entire life of the lease contract. Financial leases are commonly used for leasing land, buildings, and large pieces of fixed equipment.

The noncancelable feature of the financial lease makes it quite similar to certain types of long-term debt.* The lease payments, like payments of interest and principal, constitute a fixed obligation of the lessee; and just as in a debt contract, a default on the lease payments can result in insolvency and bankruptcy court action. Furthermore, like debt interest payments, fixed contractual charges under a lease contract provide financial leverage and affect the firm's financial risk.

Another distinguishing characteristic of the financial lease is that the lease period is generally closely aligned with the productive life of the asset. Therefore, if the salvage value of the asset is expected to be negligible, then the lessee, over the lease period, must make a series of lease payments—the sum of which is greater than the lessor's investment in the asset to allow the lessor to earn his or her required rate of return on investment.† In the remainder of this chapter, our focus will be on financial leases, since this type of lease results in an inescapable financial commitment on the part of the lessee firm. Because of the binding nature of financial leases, a firm must be very careful in making financial lease commitments. Some financial leases give the lessee an option to renew the lease at reduced lease payments or to purchase the leased asset at the expiration of the original lease at a specified price.

Leveraged Lease A relatively recent form of lease, known as a *leveraged lease*, involves three participants: (1) the lessor, (2) the lessee, and (3) the lender or lenders. This arrangement serves as a source of financing of assets requiring relatively large capital outlays and arises as follows. The firm requiring the use of a fixed asset negotiates the price and other relevant terms with a manufacturer. It then arranges for a lessor who buys the asset from the manufacturer and simultaneously executes an agreement to lease the asset from the lessor. A portion of the purchase price of the asset, say 20 percent, is provided by the lessor (referred to as the *investor*). The remaining 80 percent is provided by a lender, usually a financial institution. The loan is generally secured by a mortgage on the asset and the assignment of the lease payments. In addition, sometimes the loan is also guaranteed by the lessee.

Since, in the previous type of arrangement, the lessor's investment in the asset is levered by borrowing, the lease is referred to as a *leveraged lease.* In return for his or her investment, the lessor (owner) receives periodic lease payments, the tax benefits of incremental capital cost allowance deductions resulting from the asset,‡ and the invest-

---

*Some authors classify financial leases as *intermediate-term financing,* where the intermediate term is assumed to represent a period of 1–10 years. In this text the intermediate-term classification is not used; rather, any debt having a maturity of greater than 1 year is classified as *long term.*

†Leasing companies often finance assets to be leased with term loans (discussed in Chapter 21) from financial institutions by using lease contracts as security. Due to the current uncertainty as to future rates of inflation and interest rates, many term loans from Canadian financial institutions provide for variable interest rates aligned to fluctuations in the prime rate. As a result, the lease contract may also provide for variable lease payments related to movements in the general level of interest rates.

‡There exist situations in which the full purchase price of the asset may not be permitted as the capital cost for capital cost allowance deductions. For example, a ruling by the Department of National Revenue stipulates that the lessor, to claim the capital cost allowances on the full cost of the asset, must ultimately be liable for the funds provided by the lender or lenders.

ment tax credit (if any) associated with the asset, and makes payment on debt (interest and principal). From the lessee's viewpoint, a leveraged lease requires the same analysis as a financial lease. The lessee's essential obligation is to make periodic lease payments to the lessor over the lease term in return for the right to use the asset over that period.[1]

THE ACQUISITION OF LEASED ASSETS

Two primary techniques for obtaining assets to be leased are used by lessors. In essence, the method of acquiring assets depends largely on the desires of the prospective lessee. The two most common techniques are direct leases and sale-leaseback arrangements.

Direct Leases A direct lease results when a firm leases an asset it did not previously own. The lessor may be the actual manufacturer of the asset, or it may be a leasing firm or subsidiary that acquires the assets from the manufacturer and then leases them to the lessee. A lessee will normally specify the manufacturer, model number, and other relevant characteristics of the asset it wishes to lease.

Sale and Leaseback A sale and leaseback arrangement results when a firm sells an asset it currently owns to another party who agrees to lease the asset back to the firm immediately after the sale. The asset is usually sold at approximately its market value. The buyer-lessor secures the title to the asset and thereby a claim on the incremental CCA deductions resulting from the asset as well as the asset's residual value at the end of the lease period. The type of arrangement is quite common in real estate leasing. For example, hotels are often sold and leased back by hotel management companies. A sale and leaseback arrangement is normally initiated by a firm that needs funds for operations. By selling an existing asset to a lessor and then leasing it back the lessee receives cash for the asset immediately, while at the same time becoming obligated to make fixed periodic payments for the services of the leased asset. The sale-leaseback of an existing old asset provides the firm with a mechanism whereby the firm's liquidity can be increased.

The periodic lease payments charged the lessee will be set by the lessor at a level that allows the lessor to recover his or her investment in the leased asset and obtain his or her required rate of return on the dollars invested. Note that a sale and leaseback arrangement is similar to a financial lease, except that in the case of a financial lease the leased equipment is generally new and the lessor buys it from a manufacturer or distributor rather than from the user firm.

MAINTENANCE PROVISIONS

A lease agreement normally specifies whether the lessee is responsible for maintenance of the leased assets. *Operating leases* normally include maintenance clauses requiring the lessor to maintain and service the leased assets. For this reason, operating leases are sometimes referred to as *service leases*.

Maintenance normally includes not only repairs, but also insurance and tax payments on leased assets. The lessor, of course, will include in the lease payment sufficient compensation for the expected maintenance costs of the leased assets. Since operating leases are relatively short-term agreements, the lessor is generally able to accurately estimate the maintenance outlays expected for the duration of the lease.

Financial leases almost always require the lessee to pay maintenance costs. In other words, the lease payment under a financial lease is generally a payment for the use of the asset only. Since the term of a financial lease is normally closely aligned with the expected life of the leased asset (except in the case of land), the lessee's position is quite similar to that of an owner; therefore, the responsibility and cost of maintaining the asset is placed in his or her hands. Since a financial lease is a long-term agreement, it would be quite difficult, if not impossible, for the lessor to estimate maintenance costs for the asset's life so that they could be fairly reflected in the lease payment. The costs of maintenance are therefore borne by the lessee.

Any of the above types of leases can be written as either a net or a gross lease. A *net lease* is a lease under which the property taxes, maintenance, and insurance expenses on the leased asset are borne by the lessee. Under a *gross lease*, these expenses are borne by the lessor. However, since the lease contract is a negotiable contract, a lease may be arranged so that some of the expenses—say maintenance costs—are to be borne by the lessee; while the lessor bears the remaining expenses, such as the property taxes and insurance. Financial leases are normally written as net leases.

RENEWABILITY

Generally the lessee is given the option to renew a lease at its expiration. Renewal options are especially common in operating leases, since they have shorter lives relative to the useful lives of the assets leased. Lease payments are normally lower after the renewal of the lease than during the initial lease period.

TYPES OF LESSORS

The lessor can be one of a number of parties. In operating lease arrangements, the lessor is likely to be the manufacturer of the leased item. Generally manufacturers such as IBM and Telex have their own leasing divisions, which are responsible for negotiating leases for their products. Independent leasing companies also exist and engage in financing a wide variety of equipment. Using the lease contract as security, they often borrow funds from pension funds, banks, insurance companies, and other financial institutions. Since a leasing company engaged in general leasing can spread its financial risk over several firms in a variety of industries, it may be able to offer a financial institution better credit-worthiness than the lessee firm. Lease financing is also available through certain provincial corporations and agencies as an incentive provision; for example, the Ontario Development Corporation assists businesses seeking to locate or expand in certain slow-growth areas of Ontario by identifying and acquiring general purpose buildings and then leasing them back to the businesses. There are also specialized leasing companies such as Roy Marine Leasing Ltd., which engage in leasing only particular types of equipment. The leasing industry also includes partnerships of individuals in high tax brackets seeking CCA-based tax advantages as lessors. Financial leases are often offered by large financial institutions, such as life insurance companies, which are especially active in real estate leasing. In Canada, under the current Bank Act, chartered banks cannot directly be involved in leasing services. However, they are involved indirectly through partial ownership of leasing companies. For example, the Canada Dominion Leasing Corporation is partly owned by the Bank of Montreal. Under the pending revision of the Bank Act, the chartered banks will be permitted to participate directly in the leasing business.

LEGAL REQUIREMENTS OF LEASES

In order to prevent the buyer and seller of an asset from using a leasing arrangement as a disguise for what is actually an installment loan or installment sales contract (that is, the case where the user of the asset becomes the legal owner of the asset on full payment of any financing provided by the seller), the Department of National Revenue requires that certain conditions must be met for a particular contract to be defined as a legitimate lease contract. The essential requirement is that the lease payments do not include an amount that implies that the lessee is, in effect, purchasing an ownership interest in the underlying asset through payment on an installment basis. The department's concern stems from the fact that the full lease payment is tax-deductible, whereas in the case of an installment loan only the interest component of the payment is tax-deductible. As such, to obtain high current tax deductions, a firm could arrange for a "lease" requiring high initial lease payments over the lease period with an option to purchase the asset for a nominal amount at the end of the lease period. The following example will illustrate this point.

EXAMPLE   Saskatchewan Potash Ltd. has arranged for a 10-year lease on a piece of equipment costing $100,000. The terms of the lease call for lease payments of $20,000 per year for the first 6 years and $2,000 per year for the remaining 4 years. The lease also provides for an option by which Saskatchewan Potash can purchase the leased equipment for $100 at the end of the 10-year lease period. Such an arrangement for tax purposes would most likely be deemed by the Department of National Revenue as an installment sales contract for the equipment, not as a genuine lease. The lease contract would probably be considered a lease by the tax authorities only if Saskatchewan Potash could establish that the equipment's value declined more or less commensurately with the decline in the lease payments for the last 4 years of the lease period. Thus, a lease providing for a purchase option to the lessee is considered a legitimate lease only if the lease payments realistically represent rental value, and the option price reflects a reasonable estimate of the market value of the leased asset at the end of the lease period. The Department of National Revenue has issued guidelines in the form of Interpretation Bulletin IT-233 on how to determine whether or not a contract represents a genuine lease agreement. If a lease is not considered a true lease by the tax authorities, the lessee is required to allocate each payment to a principal and an interest portion for tax purposes.

THE LEASE CONTRACT

The key items in the lease contract normally include the term of the lease, provisions for its cancellation, lease payment amounts and dates, renewal features, purchase clauses, maintenance and associated cost provisions, and other provisions specified in the lease negotiation process. As we indicated in the preceding discussion, many provisions are optional. A lease can be cancelable or noncancelable, but if cancellation is permitted the penalties must be clearly specified. The lease may be renewable. If it is, the renewal procedures and costs should be specified. The lease agreement may provide for the purchase of the leased assets either during the contract period or at the termination of the lease. The costs and conditions of the purchase must be clearly specified. In the case of operating leases, it is likely that maintenance costs, taxes, and insurance will be paid by the lessor. In the case of a financial lease these costs will generally be borne by the lessee. The bearer of these costs must be specified in the lease agreement.

The consequences of missing a payment or violating any other lease provision must also be clearly stated in the lease contract. The consequences of violation of the agreement by the lessor must also be specified in this contract. Sometimes the lease contract contains a protective provision requiring the lessee to provide lease insurance to the lessor through a company specializing in insuring that the lease payments will be made. In the case of default on the part of the lessee, the insurer pays off the lessor. Once the lease contract has been drawn up and agreed to by the lessor and the lessee, the notarized signatures of these parties binds them to the terms of the contract.

Leasing As a Source of Financing

Leasing is considered a source of financing provided by the lessor to the lessee. The lessee receives the service of a certain fixed asset for a specified period of time, while in exchange for the use of this asset the lessee becomes committed to a fixed periodic payment. It is the fixed financial obligation of the lessee to the lessor that forces us to consider a lease—specifically a financial lease—as a form of financing. The only other way the lessee could obtain the services of the given asset would be to purchase it outright, and the outright purchase of the asset would require financing. Again, fixed—most likely periodic—payments would be required. The lessee might have sufficient funds to purchase the asset outright without borrowing, but the funds used would not be "free" since there is an opportunity cost associated with the use of cash. It is the fixed payment obligation for a set period that forces us to view the financial lease as a source of long-term financing. Although at this point the rationale for leasing may seem no different than that for borrowing when a cash purchase cannot be made, certain other considerations with respect to the lease-purchase decision do exist.

The two major topics discussed in this section are the cost of leasing and the accounting treatment of leases. An understanding of these topics should help to clarify some of the subjective considerations in the leasing decision.

LEASE COSTS

To discuss the lease cost as viewed by the lessee, lease payments, their timing, and their tax implications must be considered. Each of these items is briefly discussed below.

Tax Considerations   Lease payments are fully deductible as an expense for federal income tax purposes. However, any particular lease payment is deductible only in *the period in which the service for which the payment is made is received.* Furthermore, if the lease provides an option to the lessee firm to purchase the leased asset at the end of the lease period and the option is exercised, then the firm at that point in time becomes entitled to the tax shield from the incremental CCA deductions from the asset. The exercise price of the option becomes the capital cost for the calculation of the incremental CCA deductions.

The lease payment received by the lessor must be treated as part of the lessor's taxable income. But, being the legal owner of the leased asset, the lessor is entitled to the tax shield resulting from the incremental CCA deductions generated by the asset. In addition, the lessor, as an owner of the asset, also receives the benefit of any investment tax credit for which the asset may be eligible.*

It should, however, be noted that effective May 25, 1976, the federal government has introduced certain "loss limitation rules"† that limit the capital cost allowances for leased equipment to the lessor's "net rental income."‡ Net rental income is broadly defined as income from all *leased* assets minus overhead expenses and interest charges on debt incurred by the lessor in financing the leased assets.

Clearly, the above restriction diminishes the profitability of leasing for many lessors because it prohibits the use of incremental capital cost allowances on leased equipment against income that cannot directly be attributed to their leasing business. In other words, the lessor cannot shelter from taxes income from sources other than his or her leasing business. In certain situations, the restriction makes leasing a less attractive source of financing for the lessee. Consider, for instance, a situation in which a firm requires the use of an asset but it anticipates future profit levels that will not allow it to fully utilize the incremental capital cost allowances associated with the ownership of the asset. In such a situation, it may be relatively advantageous for the firm to enter into a lease arrangement with a lessor, who can realize the full tax benefits provided by the incremental capital cost allowances resulting from the asset and is also willing to pass back part of the benefits to the firm through a reduction in lease payments.§ However, if the capital cost allowance restriction discussed above applied to the asset, then the lessor may not be able to take full advantage of the tax shelter associated with the capital cost allowances from the asset. As a consequence, the lessor would demand relatively higher lease payments than it would if the asset were free from the restriction. In other words, the capital cost allowance limitation provides a disincentive to the user-firm to enter into a leasing arrangement for the assets. Thus, by introducing the capital cost allowance restriction, the government may have caused leasing of certain assets to be less competitive than the alternative of borrowing to purchase those assets. The existing

---

*The rules set out in the Income Tax Act for claiming the investment tax credit were discussed in Chapter 2.

†These rules are set out in the Income Tax Regulations 1100(15) to 1100(20) and closely parallel the rules for rental real estate. Leasing property is broadly defined in Regulation 1100(17).

‡More precisely, the leased equipment is segregated and included in a separate CCA class and the maximum CCA for the equipment equals the lesser of "net rental income" or incremental CCA calculated by applying the maximum CCA rate permitted for the entire class.

§A firm not subject to taxation, such as a crown corporation, or a firm unable to use its investment tax credit, may negotiate similar leasing arrangements with lessors who can benefit from the tax credits and/or the tax shields provided by the capital cost allowances on the assets required by the lessee-firm.

tax legislation also discourages leasing from nonresident lessors, because of the 25-percent Canadian withholding tax on lease payments to nonresidents.

Advance Payments   A lessor normally requires the first lease payment at the start of the lease period. In general, each payment is required in advance. For example, in the case of yearly payments, the lessee will be required to make the lease payment for any particular year at the beginning of that year, although the services of the leased asset for that year will not yet have been received. In evaluating lease-purchase decisions, it is important to clearly specify when lease payments are to be made. However, the tax laws permit the deduction of a lease payment only in the period in which the lease benefits have been received and not when the lease payments have been made. Thus, making a lease payment in advance may cause the actual tax benefits of the lease payment to lag behind the actual cash outlay. In actual practice, however, the effect of these lags on the lease evaluation process may not be very significant because of monthly corporate tax payments.

EXAMPLE   The Northland Suppliers Ltd. has recently entered into a leasing agreement with the St. John's Leasing Company Ltd. The agreement requires Northland to make annual beginning-of-year payments of $39,535.88 for the next 12 years. In exchange, Northland will receive the use of a 20,000-square-foot warehouse. Northland is subject to a 40-percent tax rate. The payment pattern required, the tax benefits and the cash outflows for Northland over the life of the lease are given in Table 20.1. The lag in the tax benefits resulting from the advance payment can be seen in the table.[2]

Table 20.1   Lease-Related Cash Flows for the Northland Suppliers Ltd.

End of year(s)	Lease payment (1)	Tax benefit[a] (2)	After-tax cash outflow (1) − (2) (3)
0	$39,535.88	$ 0	$39,535.88
1-11	39,535.88	15,814.35	23,721.53
12		15,814.35	(15,814.35)

[a]40% tax rate.

Lease Payment Calculations   Lease payments must be set at a level that will allow the lessor to recover the full cost of the asset plus an adequate return over the term of the lease. The calculation of the required lease payments is based on the present-value concepts developed in Chapter 13. The example given next illustrates the necessary calculations for a simplified situation.

EXAMPLE Dorval Corporation Ltd. has decided to lease a piece of equipment costing $274,300.00 under a 12-year noncancelable lease from Cornwal Leasing Company Ltd. The equipment is expected to have no residual value at the end of the lease period. Cornwal requires lease payments that would fully amortize the equipment's cost over the lease period and would yield a 12-percent return over that period. As is customary, each lease payment is required in advance.

Before calculating the annual lease payment, it is important to note that since a lease payment for any given year is made at the start of that year, the 12 payments will consist of an initial (beginning of year 1 or time 0) payment followed by 11 end-of-year payments. The beginning of any year is considered to be equivalent to the end of the immediately preceding year. Equation 20.1 equates the equipment's cost of $274,300.00 with the present value of the annual lease payments, x, discounted at the required return of 12 percent:

$$\$274,300 = 1.00x + 5.938x \tag{20.1}$$

Since present-value tables are based on year-end cash flows, the present-value factor for the end of the year 0 (the beginning of year 1) payment is 1.000. The remaining 11 payments can be viewed as an 11-year annuity, since they are made at the end of years 1 through 11. The present-value interest factor for an annuity, PVIFA, with an 11-year life discounted at 12 percent is 5.938 (the coefficient of the second term on the right side of Equation 20.1). Solving Equation 20.1 for x, we find that the annual lease payment, x, equals $39,535.88.

It is important to note that the annual payment calculated in the above example actually represents the *after-tax cash inflow* that the lessor must receive annually in order to earn a 12-percent return on his or her initial investment of $274,300 in the equipment to be leased. In a competitive leasing market, the lessor would tend to lower the annual lease payment in order to adjust for the tax benefits of incremental CCA deductions and any investment tax credit associated with the asset. To simplify the analysis, we have assumed that the lessor does not adjust the required lease payments for these tax benefits.

ACCOUNTING TREATMENT OF LEASES

Since lease payments are allowed as a tax-deductible expense, they appear on the lessee-firm's income statement.* Therefore, by referring to a firm's income statement, one can determine if an asset is being leased by a firm. However, if the leased assets or the liabilities under the lease contracts are not disclosed on a firm's balance sheet, then the full impact of the firm's outstanding leases on its financial condition may be unclear. This point can be illustrated through an example.

*In the case of operating leases the Canadian Institute of Chartered Accountants (CICA) requires future minimum lease payments (i.e., lease payments exclusive of insurance, maintenance charges, and any provincial sales taxes) to be disclosed in the notes to the financial statements of lessees both in total and for each of the five succeeding years. Leases with initial terms of less than one year need not be disclosed.

EXAMPLE   The Sherbrooke Company Ltd. has decided to replace one of its old machines at the beginning of 19X1. The new machine will cost the company $100,000 and will increase its capital cost allowance deduction for the year 19X1 by $10,000. Its useful life is expected to be 10 years with no salvage value at the end of that time. The firm is considering whether to acquire the new machine under a 10-year financial lease requiring annual beginning-of-year payments of $15,000, or to borrow-purchase the machine with $100,000 of 9-percent bonds. Table 20.2 presents the firm's 19X1 income statement and balance sheet as they would appear under the two financing options. It is assumed that the firm will not record the lease, if it is undertaken, as an asset or a liability on its balance sheet.*

Table 20.2   Financial Statements for the Sherbrooke Company Ltd. (19X1)

Income statement	With borrowing-to-purchase	With leasing[a]
Sales	$500,000	$500,000
Less: Cost of goods sold	300,000	300,000
Gross profits	$200,000	$200,000
Less: Selling, general, and administrative expenses	80,000	80,000
Less: Depreciation expense (CCA)	50,000	40,000
Lease expense	0	15,000
Interest expense	25,000	16,000
Profits before taxes	$ 45,000	$ 49,000
Less: Taxes (.40)	18,000	19,600
Profits after taxes	$ 27,000	$ 29,400
Balance sheet		
Current assets	$ 60,000	$ 60,000
Fixed assets (net)	340,000	240,000
Total assets	$400,000	$300,000
Current liabilities	$ 30,000	$ 30,000
Long-term debt	220,000	120,000
Total liabilities	$250,000	$150,000
Shareholders' equity	150,000	150,000
Total liabilities and shareholders' equity	$400,000	$300,000

[a]The firm has a 10-year lease on machinery requiring beginning-of-year payments of $15,000 for the next 10 years. The lease is noncancelable.

---

*To isolate the purely financing effects of the two options, it is assumed that the replacement of the old machine under either of the financing alternatives will not affect the firm's revenues, cost of goods sold, and selling, general, and administrative expenses. It is also assumed that the firm uses the same method for calculating its tax depreciation (CCA) and the depreciation expense for reporting purposes.

Table 20.3 presents a number of financial ratios calculated from the data in Table 20.2. As indicated in this table, the firm's debt-equity ratio would be lower under the leasing alternative than under the borrowing-to-purchase alternative. Therefore, the firm would appear to have relatively lower financial risk and therefore greater borrowing capacity under the leasing alternative.* This measure of financial risk is misleading because the contemplated financial lease would create a long-term contractual obligation similar to that created under the borrowing-to-purchase alternative. The difference in the two debt-equity ratios occurs simply because the equivalent-debt liability that would be created under the leasing alternative is not recorded on the firm's balance sheet as a loan or a debt security of the firm.

Table 20.3   A Comparison of Borrowing and Leasing Alternatives for the Sherbrooke Company Ltd. Using Ratio Analysis

Ratio	With borrowing-to-purchase	With leasing
Debt-equity	1.47	0.80
Total asset turnover	1.25	1.67
Average rate of return on investment	6.75%	9.80%
Rate of return on shareholders' equity	18.0%	19.6%

Table 20.3 also shows that under the leasing alternative the firm's asset turnover ratio, the return on shareholders' equity, and the average rate of return on assets are all relatively higher. Therefore, under the leasing alternative, the firm would appear to be more efficient in its use of assets and would also seem to have greater earning power. However, all of these differences are artificial, since they all result from the same omission—that is, they all result from the fact that the capitalized value of the leasing obligation was not reported on the firm's balance sheet.

Because of this problem, the Canadian Institute of Chartered Accountants (CICA) requires that *a lease that transfers substantially all of the benefits and risks of ownership related to the leased property from the lessor to the lessee should be accounted for as a capital lease by the lessee and that the lessee should account for a capital lease as an asset and an obligation.*† To implement this recommendation, the gross amount of assets under capital leases and related amortization should be shown on the asset side of

*It is easily verified that the firm's coverage ratio (i.e., times interest earned) would also be relatively higher under the leasing alternative. This again suggests that leasing rather than borrowing-to-purchase would have less of an effect in reducing the firm's ability to incur additional debt. However, the fixed charges over the lease period are as much a contractual obligation as the payment of interest and principal under the borrowing-to-purchase alternative. For this reason, we suggested in Chapter 3 that in case of a firm holding leased assets, the overall coverage ratio, which includes lease payments as well as other fixed charges, more realistically depicts a firm's ability to meet its fixed-charge or contractual obligations than the times-interest coverage ratio.

†A lease where the benefits and risk of ownership related to the leased property are substantially retained by the lessor is to be accounted for as an operating lease by the lessee. For a detailed list and illustration of the CICA requirements regarding accounting for lease transactions and the various disclosure requirements with respect to capital and operating leases, see Alan D. Stickler and Dunlop J. Bruce, *Financial Statement Presentation Requirements and Practices in Canada* (Butterworths, 1979).

the balance sheet. The present value of *minimum* future lease payments (i.e., lease payments exclusive of insurance, maintenance charges, and any provincial sales taxes), discounted at an appropriate discount rate, should be shown on the liability side of the balance sheet.* Disclosure of a capital lease directly on the balance sheet in the above manner is referred to as *lease capitalization*. Such a disclosure will enable the firm's suppliers of funds to more easily assess the firm's true financial condition. Lease capitalization is illustrated in the following example.

EXAMPLE   The lease of the Sherbrooke Company Ltd., which was described in the preceding example, can be capitalized merely by determining the present value of the future lease payments (assuming that they represent the minimum lease payments as defined above). However, the rate at which the payments should be discounted is still a somewhat controversial issue.† If the company were to use its incremental borrowing rate of 9 percent as the discount rate, the present value (i.e., the capitalized value) of the lease would be approximately $104,925 [i.e., $15,000 + $15,000 · $PVIFA_{.09, 9 \text{ yrs.}}$ or $15,000 + $15,000 · 5.995]. If the capitalized value of the lease is added to both the firm's assets and its long-term liabilities, the ratios calculated for both the borrowing and leasing alternatives will be approximately equal. This will provide a more accurate reflection of the firm's true financial position.

Lease Versus Purchase Decision

The lease versus purchase decision can be illustrated by considering the following situation. A firm, on the basis of capital budgeting procedures, has decided to acquire an asset. Having made this decision using the techniques discussed in Chapters 14 and 15, the firm is now considering how to *finance* the acquisition of the asset. If a financial lease is one possible method of financing, then the choice between leasing and alternative methods of financing the asset should depend upon a comparison of the net costs of each possible financing alternative. Since, as discussed earlier, a lease commitment is not only very similar to debt but is also generally regarded as such by the firm's suppliers of funds, the most reasonable approach would be to compare the leasing alternative with the alternative of owning the asset by purchasing it with borrowed funds.‡ The form of financing that most closely approximates lease financing is the term loan (a type of loan that is negotiated directly between borrower and lender and has a maturity of more than

*The CICA has also recommended that any portion of lease obligations payable within one year out of current funds should be included in current liabilities.

†The majority view seems to be that the discount rate for lease capitalization should be closely related to the cost of financing associated with the outright purchase alternative. The CICA has established certain guidelines with respect to the appropriate rate for capitalizing leases. Briefly, the appropriate discount rate is considered to be the lower of the lessee's incremental borrowing rate or the interest rate implicit in the lease. The interested reader is referred to the CICA Handbook, 3065.03(m), (p), and 3065.16 for these guidelines.

‡The reader will recall that the financial lease is noncancelable over the term of the lease. For a comparison of a cancelable lease and a purchase option, see David O. Jenkins, ''Purchase or Cancelable Lease,'' *Financial Executive* 38 (April 1970), pp. 26–31.

one year).* For this reason, a financial lease is typically evaluated against a term loan to be repaid over a period of time equal to the life of the lease. Since these alternatives involve payments over time, they can be compared on the basis of their net costs defined as the present values of their net after-tax costs or cash outflows. Thus, the alternative with the lower present value of net after-tax cash outflows will be financially more attractive to the user of the asset.

There is still considerable disagreement among financial theorists on which discount rate should be used in computing the present values under two alternatives.[3] The discount rates recommended in the literature range from the after-tax cost of debt to the firm's overall or weighted average cost of capital. Most analysts, however, recommend that when leasing is viewed purely as a financing decision, the firm's *after-tax* interest rate on borrowed funds is the rate to use in discounting the *after-tax* cash flows of both alternatives. Arguments used to support this discount rate include:

1 Most cash flows under either alternative are contractually predetermined and therefore relatively certain.† Thus, they should be discounted at a relatively low rate in keeping with the principle that the discount rate should reflect the degree of risk inherent in the cash flows involved.‡

2 The tax savings components of the cash flows of either alternative also involve a low degree of uncertainty, because the probability that a well-managed firm will fail to benefit from the available tax shields is minimal. The firm will be able to take full advantage of the tax shields of the two alternatives as long as it has sufficient taxable income. But even if it fails to earn sufficient taxable income in any particular year, the tax loss carryforward–carryback provisions, as well as the provisions for indefinite deferal of CCA claims (discussed in Chapter 2), provide a reasonable degree of assurance that the tax-deductible items will not be lost although the timing of their applications might change slightly. Furthermore, if we assume that the probability of failing to fully exploit tax shields approximately equals the probability of the firm's bankruptcy, the firm's after-tax cost of borrowed funds should be the appropriate discount rate for calculating the present value of the tax savings under either alternative.

RESIDUAL VALUE

When a firm chooses to lease rather than to own an asset, the firm foregoes the benefit of whatever *residual value* the asset might have at the end of the lease period. Thus, the expectation of a high residual value will increase the desirability of owning relative to leasing. Consequently, when an asset is expected to have some residual value at the end

---

*Because the lessor retains title to the asset, an even closer approximation would be a collateralized term loan. A detailed discussion of the various types of term loans is presented in the next chapter.

†This, however, is not the case, when due to uncertainty as to future rates of inflation and interest rates, the lease contract or the term loan provide for variable payments aligned to movements in the general level of interest rates. The residual value estimate of the asset at the time of the lease-purchase decision also tends to be relatively uncertain. The matter of the appropriate discount rate for residual value cash flows is discussed later in this section.

‡This same principle was used in Chapter 16, when we discussed the evaluation of capital projects involving risky cash flows.

of the lease period, an estimate of the residual value should be treated as cash inflow under the purchase alternative. However, as we saw in Chapter 15, the proceeds from an asset's residual value reduce CCA-based tax savings expected from the asset. Therefore, such losses in tax savings should also be considered in the cash-flow analysis of the purchase alternative.*

Finally, the cash flow expected from the residual value is likely to be the least predictable element of the cash-flow stream under the purchase alternative. Therefore, this cash flow should be discounted at a rate higher than the after-tax cost of debt to adjust for its relatively higher risk. A relatively simple approach to account for the risk associated with this cash flow is to estimate the *minimum* value that can reasonably be expected and then to discount this value at the after-tax cost of debt.[4]

Table 20.4 summarizes the cash flows attributable to the leasing and the borrowing-to-purchase alternatives. The method for comparing these alternatives on the basis of the present values of their after-tax cash outflows is illustrated in the examples following the table. The analysis to be presented is from the viewpoint of the lessee-user.

Table 20.4 Cash Flows Attributable to Leasing and Borrowing-to-Purchase Alternatives from the Viewpoint of the Lessee-User

Leasing	Borrowing-to-purchase
Outflows Lease payments. Any after-tax maintenance expenses on the asset paid by the lessee. Purchase price of the asset at the end of the basic lease period, if the lease provides the purchase option to the lessee and the option is exercised.	*Outflows* Loan amortization payments. After-tax maintenance expenses on the asset.
Inflows Tax shields resulting from the deductibility of lease payments. CCA-based tax savings if the option to purchase the asset exists and is exercised by the lessee. The option price will constitute the capital cost for purposes of CCA deductions and the associated tax savings.	*Inflows* Tax shields from the interest components of the loan amortization payments. Investment tax credit, if any, taken in accordance with the procedure discussed in Chapter 2. Residual value of the asset at the end of the lease period. Tax savings from the incremental CCA deductions resulting from the asset. These savings must be adjusted for the tax effect of the proceeds from the residual value. Furthermore, as indicated in Chapter 2, where an investment tax credit is taken, the capital cost of the asset must be reduced by the amount of the tax credit for purposes of calculating CCA deductions.

*A simple formula for the calculation of the present value of the declining balance CCA-based tax savings, adjusted for the tax effect of the residual value, was developed in the Appendix to Chapter 15.

EXAMPLE The Athabasca Company Ltd. has decided to acquire a piece of equipment costing $24,000. Discussions with various manufacturers of the equipment and leasing companies have shown that the equipment can be either leased or purchased for cash. The purchase alternative would be financed by a 15-percent, five-year loan requiring equal end-of-year installment payments. The leasing alternative would require the firm to sign a five-year noncancelable lease requiring annual lease payments to be made in advance. The lease would not provide Athabasca with an option to purchase the equipment at the end of the lease period. The lease payments would be set at a level that would amortize the cost of the equipment over the lease period and would provide the lessor with a 14-percent return on that amount. All maintenance, insurance, and other such costs would be borne by Athabasca. If purchased, the equipment will be recorded as a single asset capital cost allowance class and the CCA deductions on it will be taken on a straight-line basis over its useful life of five years. The equipment does not qualify for the investment tax credit and its residual value at the end of five years is expected to be zero. The firm's tax rate is at 40 percent. Should the firm lease or borrow-to-purchase the equipment? The answer to this question requires the following analysis:

After-tax cash outflows: leasing The after-tax cash outflows associated with leasing are relatively easy to calculate. If the periods in which lease payments are made are aligned with the periods in which the resulting tax benefits occur, the after-tax cash outflows for each period of the lease's life can be found simply by determining the difference between the lease payment and the tax savings in each period. The required calculations can be carried out in the following two steps.

STEP 1: Finding the annual lease payment Substitution of the appropriate values for this problem into Equation 20.1 results in:

$$\$24,000 = 1.000x + 2.914x$$

The coefficient 2.914 represents the present-value interest factor for an annuity, PVIFA, from Table A-4 for four years discounted at 14 percent. Simplifying the equation and solving for x yields an annual lease payment of approximately $6,132.*

STEP 2: Finding the cash outflows Table 20.5 presents the after-tax cash outflows associated with each of the five years of the lease agreement. Column 3 of the table presents the relevant cash outflows associated with the lease. The cash inflow of $2,453 shown for year 5 is due to the fact that no actual lease payment is made at the end of year 5 and the tax savings from the *beginning* of the year 5 lease payment are realized at the end of that year.

After-tax cash outflows: borrowing-to-purchase The calculation of the after-tax cash outflows under the borrowing-to-purchase alternative can be carried out in the following three steps.

STEP 1: Calculating the interest payments Since only the interest expense portion of the loan payments is allowed as a tax-deductible expense, it is necessary to split each loan payment into its interest and principal components. The required calculations are presented in Table 20.6.

---

*As noted earlier, the value referred to here as the lease payment may not represent the lessor's actual cash-inflow requirement. This is so because, for the sake of simplicity, we are assuming that the lessor is not passing along any of the tax benefits of ownership of the machine to the lessee through a reduction in the required lease payments.

Table 20.5 After-Tax Outflows Associated with Leasing Alternative

Year ended	Lease payment (1)	Tax savings from lease payment[a] (2)	After-tax cash outflow (1) − (2) (3)
0	$6,132	$ 0	$6,132
1	6,132	2,453	3,679
2	6,132	2,453	3,679
3	6,132	2,453	3,679
4	6,132	2,453	3,679
5	0	2,453	(2,453)

[a]Tax savings are calculated by multiplying the tax rate (.40) by the lease expense deductible in the year indicated.

The annual loan payment can be calculated as follows.*

$$\$24,000 = \text{annual payment} \cdot PVIFA_{.15,5 \text{ yrs.}}$$
$$= \text{annual payment} \cdot 3.352$$

which gives

$$\text{annual payment} = \frac{\$24,000}{3.352}$$
$$= \$7,160 \text{ (approximately)}$$

Table 20.6 Determining Interest and Principal Components of Loan Payments

Year	Loan payment (1)	Beginning-of-year principal (2)	Payments Interest .15 · (2) (3)	Payments Principal (1) − (3) (4)	End-of-year principal (2) − (4) (5)
1	$7,160	$24,000	3,600	3,560	20,440
2	7,160	20,440	3,066	4,094	16,346
3	7,160	16,346	2,452	4,708	11,638
4	7,160	11,638	1,746	5,414	6,224
5	7,160	6,224	934	6,226	—[a]

[a]The values in this table have been rounded to the nearest dollar, which results in a slight difference ($2) between the beginning-of-year-5 principal (in column 2) and the principal payment (in column 4).

*For a discussion of various loan amortization techniques, refer back to Chapter 13.

Table 20.7 After-Tax Cash Outflows Associated with Borrowing-to-Purchase Alternative

Year	Loan payment (1)	ΔCCA (2)	Interest (3)[a]	Total deductions (2) + (3) (4)	Tax shield .40 · (4) (5)	After-tax cash outflow (1) − (5) (6)
1	$7,160	$4,800	$3,600	$8,400	$3,360	$3,800
2	7,160	4,800	3,066	7,866	3,146	4,014
3	7,160	4,800	2,452	7,252	2,901	4,259
4	7,160	4,800	1,746	6,546	2,618	4,542
5	7,160	4,800	934	5,734	2,294	4,866

[a]From Table 20.6, column 3.

STEP 2: Calculating the incremental CCA deductions resulting from the equipment Since the equipment is not eligible for the investment tax credit, the incremental CCA deductions (ΔCCA's) from the equipment will simply equal $4,800 per year (i.e., $24,000/5). These deductions are shown in column 2 of Table 20.7.

STEP 3: Calculating the after-tax cash outflows Table 20.7 presents the calculation of the after-tax cash outflows of the borrowing-to-purchase alternative. Column 5 of the table shows the annual tax savings that will result from the tax deductibility of the interest payments and the ΔCCA deductions calculated, respectively, in Steps 1 and 2 above. Column 6 of the table shows the annual after-tax cash flows obtained by subtracting the tax savings from the annual loan payments of $7,160.

Comparing the leasing and borrowing-to-purchase alternatives As indicated earlier, the choice between the leasing and borrowing-to-purchase alternatives requires a comparison of their net costs defined as the present values of their after-tax cash outflows. The present values of both the alternatives using the after-tax interest cost of 9 percent [i.e., (1 − .40)15%] are shown in Table 20.8. As shown in this table, the net cost of leasing is lower than the net cost of the borrowing-to-purchase alternative (i.e., $16,455 vs. $16,528).* Therefore, the firm should lease instead of borrowing to purchase the equipment.

A few points should be clarified with respect to the calculation of the net cost of the borrowing-to-purchase alternative:

1 The net cost of this alternative can be thought of as the present value (PV) of *after-tax* loan repayments (i.e., loan repayments net of interest cost tax shields) minus the PV of the tax savings from the incremental CCA deductions. Since the after-tax loan repayments imply an

---

*In comparing the two alternatives, we have not considered the expected maintenance, insurance, and other such expenses on the equipment. The reason for ignoring these expenses in the analysis is that these expenses will be borne by Athabasca under either alternative. However, if these expenses were expected to be different under the two alternatives, then the expected difference and the associated tax effects would have to be considered in the analysis. For the sake of simplicity, it was assumed that no differences existed.

Table 20.8   Present Values of the After-Tax Cash Outflows Associated with Leasing and Borrowing-to-Purchase Alternatives

	Leasing			Borrowing		
Year	After-tax cash outflows[a] (1)	Present-value factors[b] (2)	Present-value of after-tax outflows (1) · (2) (3)	After-tax cash outflows[c] (4)	Present value factors (5)	Present value of after-tax outflows (4) · (5) (6)
0	$6,132	1.000	$6,132	$ 0	1.000	$ 0
1	3,679	.917	3,374	3,800	.917	3,485
2	3,679	.842	3,098	4,014	.842	3,376
3	3,679	.772	2,840	4,259	.772	3,288
4	3,679	.708	2,605	4,542	.708	3,216
5	(2,453)	.650	(1,594)	4,866	.650	3,163
		Total	$16,455		Total	$16,528

[a]From column 3, Table 20.5.
[b]From Table A-3, PVIF, for 9 percent and the corresponding year.
[c]From column 6, Table 20.7.

after-tax interest rate of 9 percent, their PV obtained by using the *same* rate of 9 percent as the discount rate will equal the original amount of the loan, that is, $24,000. This is illustrated by the calculations shown in Table 20.9 (the minor difference is due to the rounding off of the computations in the table).

Table 20.9[a]   After-Tax Cash Outflows Excluding Tax Savings from Incremental CCA Deductions

Year	Loan payment[b] (1)	Interest[c] (2)	Tax shield (3) = .40 · (2)	After-tax cash outflow (4) = (1) − (3)	Present value factor at 9 percent (5)	Present value of after-tax cash outflows (6) = (4) · (5)
1	$7,160	$3,600	$1,440	$5,720	.917	$5,245
2	7,160	3,066	1,226	5,934	.842	4,996
3	7,160	2,452	981	6,179	.772	4,770
4	7,160	1,746	698	6,462	.708	4,575
5	7,160	934	374	6,786	.650	4,411
					Total	$23,997

[a]The values in this table have been rounded off to the nearest dollar.
[b]From Table 20.6, column 1.
[c]From Table 20.6, column 3.

As a result, the calculation of the net cost of the borrowing-to-purchase alternative simply reduces to

Amount of the loan − PV of the CCA-based tax savings

or

$$\$24{,}000 - \$7{,}469 \ (\text{i.e.}, \ .40 \cdot \$4{,}800 \cdot PVIFA_{.09,5 \text{ yrs.}}).$$

This equals $16,531. Except for the minor difference of $3 due to rounding errors, this is the same value that was obtained earlier in Table 20.8.

2 In this example, a specific loan repayment schedule requiring equal annual payments is assumed. However, if the discount rate used in the analysis is the same after-tax interest cost of 9 percent, the particular repayment schedule chosen will not affect the PV of the loan payments. To illustrate, suppose the loan repayment schedule was specified as interest payments of $3,600 (i.e., 15% of $24,000) per year for five years and the repayment of the principal in a lump sum at the end of the fifth year. With this repayment schedule, the after-tax annual interest payments will equal $2,160 [i.e., $(1 - .40) \cdot \$3{,}600$], and the PV of the entire after-tax loan repayment stream will equal

$$\$2{,}160 \cdot PVIFA_{.09,5 \text{ yrs.}} + \$24{,}000 \cdot PVIF_{.09,5 \text{ yrs.}}$$

i.e.,

$$\$2{,}160 \cdot 3.89 + \$24{,}000 \cdot .650$$

i.e.,

$$\$8{,}402 + 15{,}600$$

i.e.,

$$\$24{,}002$$

which, except for the minor difference of $2 due to the rounding off of computations, equals the PV or the original amount of the loan.

From the above, it is apparent that the method of loan repayment will not affect the PV of the after-tax cash outflows or the net cost of the borrowing-to-purchase alternative.

●CCA-BASED TAX SHIELDS IN MORE REALISTIC LEASE VERSUS BORROWING-TO-PURCHASE EVALUATIONS

In order to simplify the calculations, the CCA-based tax shield component of the cash flows of the purchase alternative in the preceding example was calculated by assuming that the equipment was expected to have no residual value at the end of its useful life and that CCA deductions on it were to be taken on a straight-line basis. It was also assumed that the equipment did not qualify for any investment tax credit. The following example illustrates the calculation of the CCA-based tax shield in a more realistic setting.

•This section may be bypassed without loss of continuity.

EXAMPLE The Athabasca Company Ltd., discussed in the preceding example, finds that its situation has been modified as follows. First, the equipment to be acquired will be included in the company's Class 8 asset pool for which CCA deductions will be claimed at the prescribed maximum rate of 20 percent on the declining balance. Second, the residual value of the equipment at the end of its useful life of five years (i.e., at the beginning of the sixth year) is estimated to be $1,880. The company feels that this residual-value estimate is fairly certain, and that it will be appropriate to discount the cash inflow from the residual value and the associated tax outflows at the after-tax interest rate on the loan required to purchase the equipment. It is expected that subsequent to the disposal of the equipment at its salvage value, there will still be some Class 8 assets on hand and that the Class 8 undepreciated capital cost balance (UCC) will remain positive. Third, the company will be allowed an investment tax credit of 5 percent on the equipment's capital cost of $24,000. All of the credit is expected to be used at the end of the year of acquisition of the equipment.

First, we observe that under the ownership alternative, the company will be able to claim an investment tax credit of $1,200 (i.e., 5 percent of $24,000) at the end of the first year. The present value of this inflow discounted at the after-tax interest rate of 9 percent will equal $1,100 (approximately) (i.e., $1,200 \cdot PVIF_{.09,1 \text{ yr.}}$). However, for capital cost allowance purposes, the equipment's capital cost of $24,000 must be reduced by the amount of the investment tax credit. Therefore, the amount to be added to the existing Class 8 UCC balance (i.e., the balance prior to the acquisition of the equipment) will equal $22,800 (i.e., $24,000 − $1,200). This resulting increase in the UCC balance (ΔUCC_0) will generate incremental CCA deductions (ΔCCA's) and therefore tax savings beginning at the end of the first year. The ΔCCA deductions and the associated tax savings for the first 10 years are presented in Table 20.10.

Table 20.10[a] ΔCCA Deductions and Associated Tax Savings

Year	ΔUCC (1)	ΔCCA (to be claimed at year-end) (2) = 20% of (1)	$t \cdot \Delta CCA$ (tax savings) (3) = 40% of (2)	ΔUCC remaining after the deduction of ΔCCA at year-end (4) = (1) − (2)
1	$22,800	$4,560	$1,824	$18,240
2	18,240	3,648	1,459	14,592
3	14,592	2,918	1,167	11,674
4	11,674	2,335	934	9,339
5	9,339	1,868	747	7,471
6	5,591[b]	1,118	447	4,473
7	4,473	895	358	,578
8	3,578	716	286	2,862
9	2,862	572	229	2,290
10	2,290	458	183	1,832
↓	↓	↓	↓	↓
Limiting values ∞	0	0	0	0

[a]The values in this table have been rounded off to the nearest dollar.
[b]This value is the difference between the UCC of $7,471 at the end of year 5 and the proceeds of $1,880 from the equipment's salvage value.

As indicated in this table, the ΔUCC balance left at the end of the fifth year will equal $7,471. This balance, after the sale of the equipment at its residual value at the beginning of the sixth year, will be reduced to $5,591 (i.e., $7,471 − $1,880).* The firm will be entitled to ΔCCA deductions in future years on this remaining balance, even though the equipment will no longer be in the firm's Class 8 asset pool. Furthermore, as shown under column 2 of Table 20.10, these future deductions, under the declining balance method, will theoretically continue for an infinite number of years.

The calculation of the present value of the infinite series of the tax savings (column 3) associated with the perpetual ΔCCA deductions is an exceedingly cumbersome task. However, this calculation can be simplified by using the following formula (developed in the Appendix to Chapter 15):

$$\frac{\Delta UCC_0 \cdot d \cdot t}{k + d} - \frac{S \cdot d \cdot t}{k + d} \cdot \frac{1}{(1 + k)^n}$$

where

ΔUCC_0 = incremental UCC balance resulting from the acquisition of the asset

d = prescribed CCA rate for the asset class in which the asset is included

t = tax rate

S = residual or salvage value

k = discount rate

In our example, ΔUCC_0 = $22,800; d = .20; t = .40; S = $1,880; and k = .09. Therefore,

$$\text{PV of the tax savings from } \Delta \text{CCA deductions} = \frac{\$22,800 \cdot .20 \cdot .40}{.09 + .20} - \frac{1,880 \cdot .20 \cdot .40}{.09 + .20} \cdot \frac{1}{(1 + .09)^5}$$
$$= \$6,289.66 - \$337.10$$
$$= \$5,953 \text{ (approximately)}$$

The net cost under the borrowing-to-purchase alternative is, therefore, equal to
Amount of loan − PV of proceeds from salvage value
− PV of investment tax credit
− PV of the tax savings from ΔCCA deductions

Substituting the appropriate values in the preceding expression, we find that the net cost under the borrowing-to-purchase alternative equals

---

*As pointed out in Chapter 2, upon sale of an asset from an asset class, the lower of the proceeds of sale or the original cost of the asset sold must be deducted from the presale UCC balance of the class. In the example under discussion, the proceeds of sale, $1,880, are less than the equipment's original cost of $24,000. Hence, the presale UCC balance of $7,471 is reduced by $1,880.

$15,225 (i.e., $24,000 − $1,880 · $PVIF_{.09,5 \text{ yr.}}$ − $1,100 − $5,953).

A comparison of this amount with the net cost of the leasing alternative ($16,455) given in Table 20.8 shows that in contrast to the previous result, the purchase alternative will now be financially more attractive.* This reversal occurred because the assumptions regarding the equipment's residual value, the investment tax credit, and the method of calculating capital cost allowances were relatively more favourable to the purchase alternative in the present example.

It should be noted that the computation of the CCA-based tax shield under the purchase alternative may in some situations be more cumbersome than it was in the previous example. For example, if subsequent to the disposal of the equipment considered in the previous analysis, either no assets were left in the firm's Class 8 asset pool or the residual value had exceeded the aggregate book value (UCC) of the assets in the pool, the computation of the tax shield would be more complicated. In these situations, the recapture of CCA and capital gains or terminal losses may have to be recognized. For a detailed discussion of these tax complications, refer to the capital cost allowance section in Chapter 2.

There is still another possible factor that is sometimes relevant in the evaluation of the purchase alternative but has not been considered in the above analysis. This factor is the provision for accelerated capital cost allowances as a tax incentive for investment in manufacturing and processing machinery and certain types of pollution control equipment. As noted in Chapter 2, under this incentive provision the book value of the above types of assets can be written off in two years at a maximum rate of 50 percent in the first year. Clearly, where this provision applies, it increases the present value of the CCA-based tax savings and thereby reduces the net cost of the ownership alternative. However, as noted earlier, to the extent that the leasing market is competitive, the CCA-based tax benefits available to the owner-lessor would be shared with the lessee in the form of reduced lease payments.

SOME LIMITATIONS OF THE PRECEDING ANALYSIS

It is important to remember the limitations of the above lease-purchase decision analysis. The analysis cannot be used to decide whether or not a particular asset should be acquired. Since it assumes that the investment decision has already been made, it is concerned simply with the choice between two specific methods of *financing* the acquisition of the asset.[5] In other words, the analysis is based on the assumption that the

---

*If the purchase alternative involved the use of the equipment beyond the fifth year, then it would not be strictly comparable with the leasing alternative involving a five-year lease term. However, if it is assumed that under the leasing alternative, the firm could purchase the equipment at its residual value at the end of the lease term, then the two alternatives could be made comparable by including an additional cash outflow $[S - (S \cdot d \cdot t)/(k + d)]$, at the end of year 5, in the cash-flow stream of the leasing alternative. Also note that if the term loan to purchase the asset were available only with a certain percentage of the asset's purchase price as a down payment, then the analysis would have to be modified. For the analysis of lease purchase decisions under these conditions, see the article by L. D. Schall cited in the suggested readings at the end of this chapter.

firm's capital budgeting decisions can be separated from its financing decisions. Clearly, a more theoretically rigorous but also more complicated approach would involve a *simultaneous* consideration of the firm's investment and financing policies along with the lease and purchase alternatives.[6]

Another limitation of the analysis is that it views the general lease-or-buy decision as a choice between leasing the asset or purchasing it using *all* debt financing. In reality, the problem may not be so simple, since the purchase may be made from a combination of debt and equity funds. For example, the analysis presented before does not deal adequately with the situation where the asset is purchased with, say, 20 percent of the purchase price covered by cash and the remaining 80 percent by a bank loan.[7] However, since most well-run businesses generally do not have excess cash on hand, the simple analysis given here would be accurate enough for most cases. Furthermore, it has also been argued that a comparison of lease financing with debt financing is appropriate in a situation where a firm has a specified target capital structure and the convergence toward this structure requires undertaking of a fixed-charge obligation—either debt or a long-term noncancelable lease—to finance the acquisition of a fixed asset.

Finally, it should be noted that the method for the analysis of the lease-purchase decision presented here is but one of the several methods currently in use.[8] However, a 1977 survey showed that the present-value-comparison method discussed here is commonly used by the major U.S. corporations.[9]

Advantages and Disadvantages of Leasing

Leasing has a number of nonquantifiable advantages and disadvantages that should be considered in making a decision between leasing and owning. Although not all of these advantages and disadvantages hold in every case, it is not unusual for a number of them to be relevant to a given lease-purchase decision.

ADVANTAGES OF LEASING

The basic advantages commonly cited for leasing are the ability it gives the lessee to, in effect, depreciate land, its effects on financial ratios, its effect on the firm's liquidity, the ability it gives the firm to obtain 100-percent financing, the limited claims of lessors in the event of bankruptcy or reorganization, the opportunity for transferring the risk of obsolescence to the lessor, the lack of many restrictive covenants in the lease contract relative to the typical debt contract, and the possibility of piecemeal financings through leasing. Each of these often cited advantages is described and critically evaluated below.

Effective Depreciation of Land   It is sometimes stated that leasing of land has a cost advantage over owning land because the lease will allow the lessee to "depreciate" land for tax purposes. The basis of this argument is that by deducting the lease payments on the land as an expense for tax purposes, the lessee is in effect depreciating the cost of land because this cost has been included in the lease payments. This argument, however, overlooks the possibility that the value of the land may appreciate substantially over the lease period and that any appreciation in the value of the land accrues to the lessor and not the lessee.

Effects on Financial Ratios   Earlier in the chapter we described the effect leasing could have on certain financial ratios involving balance sheet data. Leasing, since it results in the receipt of service from an asset possibly without increasing the assets or liabilities on the firm's balance sheet, may be camouflaged on the balance sheet. With the CICA rulings concerning capitalization of financial leases discussed earlier in the chapter, this advantage no longer applies to financial leases. Even in the case of operating leases, the CICA requires disclosure of leases in a footnote to the firm's statements. Today, most analysts are aware of the significance of leasing for the firm's financial position and will not view the firm's financial statements strictly as presented; instead, they will make certain adjustments to these statements that will more accurately reflect the effect of any existing operating leases on the firm's financial position.

Increased Liquidity   The use of sale-leaseback arrangements may permit the firm to increase its liquidity by converting an *existing* asset into cash, which can be used as working capital. A firm short of working capital or in a liquidity squeeze can sell an owned asset to a lessor and lease the asset back for a specified number of years. Of course, this action binds the firm to making fixed payments over a period of years. The benefits of the increase in current liquidity are therefore tempered somewhat by the added fixed financial payments incurred through the lease. The various tax factors involved in the sale and leaseback arrangement must also be considered in assessing the net effect of the arrangement on the firm's liquidity.

100-Percent Financing   Another advantage attributed to leasing is that it provides 100-percent financing. Most loan agreements for the purchase of fixed assets require the borrower to pay a portion of the purchase price as a down payment. As a result, the borrower receives only 90–95 percent of the purchase price of the asset. In the case of a lease, the lessee is not required to make any type of down payment; he or she must make only a series of periodic payments. In essence, a lease permits a firm to receive the use of an asset for a smaller initial out-of-pocket cost than borrowing. However, since large initial lease payments are often required in advance, it is possible to view the initial advance payment as a type of down payment.*

Limited Claims in the Event of Bankruptcy or Reorganization   When a lessee-firm becomes bankrupt or is reorganized, the lessor can repossess the asset, but his or her claim to missed payments is typically limited to some specified amount usually equal to one year's obligations. On the other hand, the lender's claim includes the entire unpaid principal and interest charges.† However, whether or not the firm is better off leasing or owning in the event of distress depends on a number of unknown factors such as the market value of the asset at the time relative to the

---

*Since lease payments are normally made in advance, there is no guarantee that leasing a given asset provides more financing than borrowing; in many instances it may provide less financing than borrowing.

†In the case of a mortgage loan, the lender also can gain possession of the asset and sell it to satisfy the unpaid debt. Any proceeds in excess of the debt obligations accrue to the firm and any shortfall usually becomes an obligation of the firm.

remaining lease or debt obligations and whether or not the lessor is able to find other lessees for the asset.

Avoidance of the Risk of Obsolescence   Operating leases provide the lessee firm with an opportunity to shift the risk of obsolescence to the lessor. However, since lessors are likely to be well aware of such a risk, we can expect them to seek compensation for bearing it, usually directly in the form of higher lease payments. In other words, the lessee in effect buys insurance against the risk of obsolescence. Whether or not the transfer of this risk is worth the extra cost will depend upon the particular circumstances of the lessee and lessor. For example, suppose that the lessor can spread the risk of obsolescence over many lease contracts. To the extent the economic advantage of such diversification is passed on to the lessee in the form of lower lease payments, the economic cost of obsolescence will be lower to the user-firm under leasing than under purchase.

Avoidance of Restrictive Covenants Accompanying Debt   Although the firm's suppliers of funds will regard a lease commitment as similar to a debt contract, protective provisions of the lease contract, such as restrictions on dividend payments or additional debt, may be less stringent than those under some forms of debt.* Thus, lease financing may constrain the firm's future borrowing capacity to a lesser degree than would the borrow-to-purchase of the asset. On the other hand, the lessor, in return for relatively less restrictive provisions in the lease contract, may demand a higher rate of return as a compensation for the higher risk incurred. In this case, the lessee-firm must decide whether relatively less constrained future borrowing capacity is worth the added rental payment.

Piecemeal Financing   In the case of low-cost assets that are infrequently acquired, the firm may find leasing—especially operating leases—useful. Leasing may allow the firm to finance small asset acquisitions at a cost lower than the cost of issuing numerous small bond issues. Also through piecemeal financings of low-cost assets, the firm retains its ability to raise funds in economically preferred quantities at the right times, thereby helping to lower its overall cost of capital. However, there are other alternatives that may be cheaper than piecemeal lease financings. For example, a firm could temporarily finance its needs with short-term loans and then fund them with long-term bonds issued at economically preferred times.

DISADVANTAGES OF LEASING

The commonly cited disadvantages of leasing include high interest costs, the lack of claims to salvage values, the difficulty of making property improvements, and obsolescence considerations. Though not relevant in every case, they may bear importantly on

---

*An in-depth discussion of the various *restrictive covenants*, which are certain financial and operating constraints contractually placed upon the firm included in long-term loan agreements, is presented in Chapter 21. It is possible that even under a lease certain contractual constraints may be placed upon the firm as part of the lease agreement.

the lease-purchase decision in certain instances. Each of the often cited disadvantages is described and critically evaluated below.

High Interest Costs   As we pointed out earlier, a lease does not have an explicit interest cost; rather, the lessor builds a return for itself into the lease payment. In some leases the implicit return to the lessor may be quite high, so that the firm might be better off borrowing to purchase the asset. The lessee should estimate this return in the manner illustrated earlier in order to determine whether it is reasonable. The reasonableness of the lessor's required return should be judged in the light of factors such as the general credit-worthiness of the lessee and the lessor's obligations to provide unique or specialized services under the lease contract.

Lack of Salvage Value   At the end of the term of the lease agreement, the residual value of assets, if any, is realized by the lessor. Therefore, if an asset is expected to appreciate substantially in value over the term of the available lease option, it may be less expensive to own rather than lease the asset. However, it should be recognized that the anticipated residual value is usually a very uncertain estimate. As such, when a firm decides to own rather than lease a particular asset primarily on the basis of its estimated residual value, it is in effect taking a gamble. In some cases, the gamble may pay off, and in retrospect the firm may find that the decision to own rather than lease the asset was actually a superior decision. In others, the reverse may hold. Also, if the leasing market is competitive, potential residual values would tend to be recognized in lease payment negotiations. This again suggests that the potential residual value associated with an asset does not necessarily mean that the cost of owning the asset will materially differ from that of leasing it.

Difficulty of Property Improvements   Under a lease, the lessee is generally prohibited from making improvements on the leased property without the approval of the lessor. If the property were owned, this difficulty would not arise. Related to this disadvantage is the fact that it is often hard to obtain financing for improvements on leased property since it is difficult for the lender to obtain a security interest in the improvements. On the other hand, the lessor may agree in the initial lease contract to finance or make certain leasehold improvements specified by the lessee.

Obsolescence Considerations   If a lessee leases (under financial lease) an asset that subsequently becomes obsolete, it still has to make lease payments over the remaining life of the lease. This is true even if it is unable to use the leased assets. In many instances, a lessee will continue to use obsolete assets since it must pay for them. This type of situation can weaken a firm's competitive position by raising (or failing to lower) production costs and therefore forcing the sale price of its products to be increased in order to earn a profit.

Summary

This chapter has discussed a number of important aspects of leasing. A lease is a contractual arrangement with a specified term, series of lease payments, payment dates, penalties, and other important features. The basic types of leases are operating and financial leases. The noncancelability of the relatively longer term of the financial lease makes it quite similar to the debt contract. The form of debt which most closely approximates lease financing is the collateralized term loan. A financial lease can be initiated in two ways—as a direct lease or as a sale-leaseback arrangement. Under a direct lease, the lessor purchases specified assets from an outsider and leases them to the firm. Under a sale-leaseback arrangement, the lessor purchases the assets from the lessee and then leases them back to the same firm.

Most financial leases require the lessee to maintain, insure, and pay taxes on leased assets; operating leases, on the other hand, normally include maintenance clauses whereby the lessor absorbs these costs. Leases may be renewable, although most financial leases are not. The Department of National Revenue provides guidelines specifying which lease payments are tax-deductible.

Since lease payments are tax-deductible, the cost of leasing is reduced by the the tax shield provided. Most lease payments are made in advance, although the tax deduction cannot be taken until the service provided by the lease has been received. The amount of the annual lease payment is determined by the lessor, who seeks to assure itself of a certain return over the term of the lease.

The lessee firm is required by certain opinions and rulings of the Canadian Institute of Chartered Accountants (CICA) to disclose the existence of leases on its financial statements. In the case of financial (or capital) leases, the CICA now requires and outlines detailed procedures for capitalization of the lease commitment as an asset and corresponding liability. In the instance a lease obligation is not capitalized, traditional financial ratios can be misleading. Therefore, the capitalization of financial leases provides for a balance sheet that more accurately reflects the true financial condition of the firm.

By leasing rather than owning assets, the firm can incur certain significant opportunity costs such as the loss of the assets' residual values, any investment tax credits associated with the assets, and the loss of tax shields from the CCA deductions on the assets. A lease-purchase decision can be evaluated by comparing the present values of after-tax cash outflows associated with the lease and purchase alternatives. The most desirable alternative is one that has the minimum present value of after-tax cash outflows associated with it. In the present-value method of lease analysis presented in this chapter, the lease-or-purchase decision is viewed as a choice between leasing the asset or purchasing it using *all* debt financing. The choice of the discount rate to be used in the present-value analysis of the lease-purchase decision is highly controversial. However, since most components of cash flows under the leasing and borrowing-to-purchase alternatives are contractually determined and are therefore relatively certain, most analysts recommend that the firm's after-tax interest rate on debt is a reasonable rate to use in discounting after-tax cash flows of either alternative.

Commonly cited advantages of leasing include the ability to depreciate land, potential favourable ratio effects, increased liquidity, the ability to obtain 100-percent financing, limited claims of lessors in bankruptcy or reorganization, the avoidance of obsolesence risk, lack of many restrictive covenants, and the flexibility provided. Disadvantages include high interest costs, lack of salvage value, difficulty of property improvements, and obsolesence considerations.

Questions

20.1   What is leasing? What roles are played by the lessor and lessee? How are lease payments treated for tax purposes?

20.2   Why is leasing often viewed as a source of financing?

20.3   A firm has decided to acquire a new machine and is currently examining whether to lease or to borrow-purchase the machine. A comparison of these financing alternatives has indicated that leasing would have a financial cost advantage over the borrowing-to-purchase alternative. The firm also has sufficient cash available to purchase the machine. In view of this fact, the company's financial analyst has argued that to avoid the burden of fixed charges resulting from the lease commitment, the company should purchase the machine with cash. Do you agree with the analyst's reasoning?

20.4   What is an operating lease? What are its key characteristics?

20.5   Does the operating lease provide a mechanism for hedging against obsolescence risk without any cost to the lessee?

20.6   What are the circumstances under which an operating lease can be an attractive arrangement?

20.7   What is a financial lease? How is it different from an operating lease?

20.8   What is the difference between a *direct lease* and a *sale-leaseback arrangement?* Which of these is a quick source of cash for the firm? Why?

20.9   What are the major similarities and the major differences between lease and debt financing?

20.10   A leveraged lease is sometimes referred to as a "third-party lease." Why? Why is such a lease called a leveraged lease?

20.11   What sort of companies may act as lessors of assets? Under what conditions may a renewal be offered?

20.12   Define the term *lease capitalization.* Why is it argued that a firm's outstanding financial leases should be capitalized and reported on the firm's balance sheet?

20.13   How are lease payments timed? What effect might advance payments have on the tax benefits of a lease arrangement and the after-tax cash outflows associated with the lease?

20.14   "The riskier the firm that seeks financing, the greater the incentive for the supplier of capital to make the arrangement a lease rather than a loan." What is the reasoning behind this statement?

20.15   "By leasing rather than owning assets, the firm can incur certain significant opportunity costs." Which opportunity costs are referred to in this statement?

20.16   What are the key advantages and disadvantages of leasing as a source of financing? Which of these advantages and disadvantages are most important in a subjective lease-buy evaluation?

Problems

20.1   The Lima Company's lease on a warehouse requires annual lease payments of $40,000 to be made at the beginning of each year for the next 12 years. Determine the after-tax cash outflows each year, assuming the firm is in the 40-percent tax bracket.

20.2 Given the following lease payments and terms, determine the yearly after-tax cash outflows in each case assuming that lease payments are made at the start of each year and the firm is in the 40-percent tax bracket.

Firm	Annual lease payment	Term of lease
A	$100,000	4 years
B	$ 80,000	14 years
C	$150,000	8 years
D	$ 60,000	25 years
E	$ 20,000	10 years

20.3 Klondike Aviation Company Ltd. has just leased a facility costing $270,120 under a 10-year financial lease from Confederated Financial Corporation. The lease contract calls for lease payments that would fully amortize the leased facility's cost and would yield a 15-percent return on that amount over the lease period. The lease payments are to be made at the start of each year.
a. Determine the annual lease payments that Klondike must make under the lease contract.
b. Determine the annual after-tax cash outflows that would result from the lease undertaken by Klondike.

20.4 The Stampede Company Ltd. is considering either leasing or purchasing a new machine costing $60,000. If the machine is purchased, it will be depreciated straight-line (no salvage value) over a 20-year life. A $60,000, 10-percent loan will be used to finance the purchase. The company uses the same method for calculating its tax depreciation (CCA) and the depreciation expense for reporting purposes. The leasing arrangement would entail a 20-year lease requiring annual beginning-of-year payments of $6,300. The most recent financial statements of the company are given below.

Financial Statements
Stampede Company
Year Ending December 31

Income statement	
Sales	$200,000
Less: Cost of goods sold	140,000
Gross profits	$ 60,000
Less: Operating expenses excluding interest, depreciation, and lease expense	$ 10,000
Depreciation expense (CCA)	10,000
Lease expense	0
Interest expense	15,000
Profits before taxes	$ 25,000
Less: Taxes (.40)	10,000
Profits after taxes	$ 15,000

Continued on next page

Balance sheet	
Current assets	$ 30,000
Fixed assets (net)	120,000
Total assets	$150,000
Current liabilities	$ 20,000
Long-term debt	50,000
Total liabilities	$ 70,000
Shareholders' equity	$ 80,000
Total liabilities and shareholders' equity	$150,000

(handwritten annotations: "Borrowing Leasing B.S stays same."; "$150,000 – 210 000"; "50,000 – 110 000")

a. Recast Stampede's *income statement* on the assumption that, as a result of acquiring the new machine, sales increased to $280,000, the cost of goods sold to $196,000, and operating expenses excluding interest, depreciation, and lease expense to $40,000.
   (1) Show the income statement if borrowing is used to purchase the asset.
   (2) Show the income statement if the asset is leased.
b. Recast Stampede's *balance sheet* assuming that all items other than those affected by the new machine will remain unchanged.
   (1) Show the balance sheet if the borrowing alternative is selected.
   (2) Show the balance sheet if the leasing alternative is selected and the capitalized value of the lease is not reported on the balance sheet.
c. Based on the income statements and balance sheets generated for the borrowing and leasing alternatives, calculate the following ratios in each case.
   (1) The debt-equity ratio. *(handwritten: 1.375 & .625)*
   (2) The times interest earned ratio. *(handwritten: 1.48   1.85)*
   (3) The total asset turnover. *(handwritten: 1.30   1.9)*
   (4) The return on investment. *(handwritten: 2.85   50%)*
d. Discuss the effects of each of the alternatives (borrowing or leasing) on the firm's financial picture as indicated by the ratios calculated in **c.**

20.5 Given the following lease payments, years remaining until the lease terminates, and capitalization rates, calculate the capitalized value of each lease, assuming that lease payments are made annually at the beginning of each year.

Lease	Lease payment	Remaining life	Capitalization rate
A	$ 40,000	12 years	10%
B	$120,000	8 years	12%
C	$ 9,000	18 years	14%
D	$ 16,000	3 years	9%
E	$ 47,000	20 years	11%

20.6 The Walker Company Ltd. wishes to purchase an asset costing $117,000. The full amount needed to finance the asset can be borrowed at 11-percent interest. The terms of the loan require equal end-of-year payments for the next six years. Determine the total annual loan payment, the amount of interest, and the amount of principal paid for each year.

20.7 The Rocky Mountain Restaurant wishes to evaluate two plans, borrowing-to-purchase and leasing, for financing a new oven.

Purchase: The oven costs $20,000 and is expected to have a five-year life with zero residual value at the end of that time. The asset will constitute a single-asset CCA class in the company's tax records, and the CCA deductions for it will be taken on a straight-line basis over its useful life. The total purchase price will be financed by a five-year, 15-percent loan requiring equal annual end-of-year payments. The firm is subject to a 40-percent tax rate.

Leasing: The restaurant could lease the asset under a five-year lease requiring annual beginning-of-year payments of $5,000.

a. For the purchase plan, calculate the following:

(1) The annual end-of-year payment.

(2) The annual interest expense deductible for tax purposes for each of the five years.

(3) The after-tax cash outflows resulting from the purchase for each of the five years.

(4) Using the after-tax interest rate of 9 percent on the loan as the discount rate, the present value of the after-tax cash outflows.

b. For the leasing plan, calculate the following:

(1) The after-tax cash outflows each year.

(2) The present value of the after-tax cash outflows using the after-tax interest rate of 9 percent on the loan as the discount rate.

c. Compare the present value of each of the cash-flow streams (from each plan) and determine which would be preferable. Explain your answer.

20.8 The Tony Corporation is attempting to determine whether to lease or purchase a new plating mill. The firm's tax rate is 40 percent. The terms of the lease and the purchase are given next.

Purchase: The mill, costing $60,000, can be financed entirely with a 20-percent loan requiring annual end-of-year payments of $28,490 for three years. The CCA deductions for the asset (to be recorded as a single-asset pool) will be taken on a straight-line basis over its three-year life. The mill's residual value at the end of three years is expected to be zero.

Lease: Annual advance lease payments of $26,000 are required over the three-year life of the lease.

a. Calculate the after-tax cash outflows associated with each alternative.

b. Calculate the present value of each cash-flow stream using the after-tax cost of borrowing (12 percent) as the discount rate.

c. Which alternative would you recommend and why?

•20.9 The Moncton Warehouse Company Ltd. is in need of cash and is considering a sale and leaseback arrangement involving one of its warehouse buildings. The company has discussed such an arrangement with two potential lessors, R and S. Each potential lessor requires a five-year lease commitment with beginning-of-year lease payments. The cash amounts offered for the warehouse under consideration and the lease payments required by each potential lessor are as shown in the following table.

Lessor	Cash amount offered for the warehouse	Required beginning-of-year lease payments
R	$220,000	$80,000
S	200,000	75,000

The warehouse, originally aquired for $500,000, is part of the company's Class 3 asset pool for which the maximum CCA rate of 5 percent is allowed on the declining balance. The company has a policy of taking the maximum CCA allowed for any given year. The sale of the warehouse will not eliminate the company's Class 3 pool and the UCC balance for the class is expected to remain positive after the sale. The company is subject to a 40-percent corporate tax rate.

Which of the lessors should Moncton Warehouse do business with? Why? Assume that the appropriate discount rate for all the cash flows involved in the problem is 10 percent.

•20.10 Nanaimo Sea Products Ltd. has decided to expand its salmon processing plant in British Columbia. The equipment necessary for this expansion costs $100,000 and can be either purchased or leased. The purchase option requires the firm to take a $100,000, 15-percent bank loan to be amortized through level end-of-year payments over a five-year period. The leasing option involves a five-year noncancelable lease requiring advance annual lease payments. The lease payments would be set at a level that would fully amortize the equipment's cost of $100,000 and would provide the lessor with a 12-percent return on that amount. The lease would be set up as a net lease in that the maintenance, insurance, and other such costs on the equipment would be borne by Nanaimo. If purchased, the equipment will constitute a single-asset CCA class on the company's books, and the CCA deductions on it will be taken on a straight-line basis over its five-year life to a zero salvage value at the end of that period. The corporate tax rate is at 40 percent.

a. Which of the two options should Nanaimo use to finance the acquisition of the equipment? Assume that the firm's after-tax cost of borrowing (9 percent) is the appropriate discount rate to use in your analysis.

b. How would your evaluation of the purchase alternative be affected if the equipment's *minimum* disposable value at the end of its life (i.e., at the *beginning* of the sixth year) were equal to $1,000?

c. How would the purchase alternative compare with the leasing alternative if, in addition to the salvage value information given in part **b**, it is assumed that the equipment will be included in an asset pool for which CCA deductions will be claimed at the prescribed maximum rate of 20 percent on the declining balance; that after the disposal of the equipment, the book value (UCC) of the pool will remain positive; and that there will still be some assets left in the pool?

20.11 Bedeck Suppliers Ltd., a newly incorporated company, has decided to locate its head office in Montreal. As such, the company has found a suitable site in downtown Montreal for the purpose of constructing its head office building. Discussions with the owner of the land have indicated that Bedeck can either (1) buy the land for $100,000 and construct the building at an estimated cost of $300,000; or (2) have the land owner construct the building at the same estimated cost of $300,000, and then lease both the land and the building for 20 years. The lease would be a noncancelable commitment involving *end-of-year* lease payments of $55,000. These payments would fully amortize the total cost of $400,000 for the land and the building and would provide the lessor with an approximate yield of 12 percent on this amount. The maintenance, insurance, and other such costs associated with the building will be borne by Bedeck. Furthermore, Bedeck will have no option to purchase either the land or the building at the end of the lease period. The residual value of the building after the lease period is estimated to be zero.

If Bedeck were to accept the first option, then (1) in order to finance the acquisition of the land and the construction of the building, it will have to take a $400,000, 20-year, 15-percent bank loan to be repaid in equal end-of-year installments; (2) the building will become part of a single-asset pool on the company's books and will be subject to CCA deductions on a straight-line basis over its estimated useful life of 20 years with an expected residual value of zero at the end of that period; and (3) the land will be sold at its estimated market value of $300,000 at the end of 20 years. The corporate tax rate on ordinary income is at 40 percent with realized capital gains subject to an effective tax rate of 20 percent.

Which options should Bedeck accept? In your analysis, assume that the after-tax interest rate of 9 percent on the loan is the appropriate discount rate for computing the present value of *all* cash flows involved in the problem.

Notes

1. For a detailed discussion of leveraged leasing, see E. Richard Peckham, "An Analysis of the Risks of Leveraged Leasing," *Journal of Commercial Bank Lending* 57 (March 1975), pp. 2–29; and Robert C. Wier, "Economic Implications of Multiple Rates of Return in the Leveraged Lease Context," *Journal of Finance* 28 (December 1973), pp. 1275–1286.
2. For an analysis of the effect of this lag on the desirability of leasing relative to debt financing under the U.S. tax laws, see Richard S. Bower, Frank C. Herringer, and J. Peter Williamson, "Lease Evaluation," *Accounting Review* 41 (April 1966), pp. 257–265.
3. See, for example, Richard S. Bower, "Issues in Lease Financing," *Financial Management* 2 (Winter 1973), pp. 25–34.
4. More sophisticated approaches are available to deal with the uncertain residual value involved in the lease-purchase decision. See, for example, Harold E. Wyman, "Financial Lease Evaluation Under Conditions of Uncertainty," *Accounting Review* 48 (July 1973), pp. 489–493.
5. For an analysis of a lease viewed as an investment rather than a financing decision, see Robert W. Johnson and Wilber G. Lewellen, "Analysis of the Lease-or-Buy Decision," *Journal of Finance* 27 (September 1972), pp. 815–824. Also, see William L. Ferrara, "Should Investment and Financing Decisions Be Separated?" *Accounting Review* 41 (January 1966), pp. 106–147.
6. Such an approach is presented in Stewart C. Myers, David A. Dill, and Alberto J. Bautista, "Valuation of Financial Lease Contracts," *Journal of Finance* (June 1976), pp. 761–786.
7. For an analysis of the general lease-buy decision not using 100-percent debt financing, refer to L. D. Schall, "The Lease or Buy and Asset Acquisition Decisions," *Journal of Finance* 29 (September 1974), pp. 1203–1214.
8. For a comparison of the various methods in use, see Richard S. Bower, "Issues in Lease Financing," *Financial Management* 2 (Winter 1973), pp. 25–34.
9. See Paul F. Anderson and John D. Martin, "Lease vs. Purchase Decisions: A Survey of Current Practice," *Financial Management* (Spring 1977), pp. 41–47.

Suggested Readings

Anderson, Paul F. and John D. Martin, "Lease versus Purchase Decisions: A Survey of Current Practice," *Financial Management* 6 (Spring 1977), pp. 41–47.

Bierman, H., Jr., "Accounting for Capitalized Leases: Tax Considerations," *Accounting Review* 48 (April 1973), pp. 421–424.

Blum, James D., "Accounting and Reporting for Leases by Lessees: The Interest Rate Problems," *Management Accounting* 59 (April 1978), pp. 25–28.

Bower, Richard S., "Issues in Lease Financing," *Financial Management* 2 (Winter 1973), pp. 25–34.

———, Frank C. Herringer, and J. Peter Williamson, "Lease Evaluation," *Accounting Review* 41 (April 1966), pp. 257–265.

Cooper, Kerry and Robert H. Strawser, "Evaluation of Capital Budgeting Projects Involving Asset Leases," *Financial Management* 4 (Spring 1975), pp. 44–49.

Doenges, R. Conrad, "The Cost of Leasing," *Engineering Economist* 17 (Fall 1971), pp. 31–44.

Ferrara, William L., "Should Investment and Financing Decisions Be Separated?" *Accounting Review* 41 (January 1966).

———, "The Case for Symmetry in Lease Reporting," *Management Accounting* 59 (April 1978), pp. 17–24.

Ferrara, William L. and Joseph F. Wodjak, "Valuation of Long-term Leases," *Financial Analysts Journal* 25 (November-December 1969), pp. 27–32.

Financial Accounting Standards Board, *Financial Accounting Standards: Original Pronouncements as of July 1, 1978* (Stamford, Conn.: Financial Accounting Standards Board, 1978), Standard No. 13–"Accounting for Leases."

Franks, Julian and Stewart D. Hodges, "Valuation of Financial Lease Contracts: A Note," *Journal of Finance* 33 (May 1978), pp. 657–669.

Gordon, Myron J., "A General Solution to the Buy or Lease Decision: A Pedagogical Note," *Journal of Finance* 29 (March 1974), pp. 245–250.

Gritta, Richard D., "The Impact of the Capitalization on Leases on Financial Analysis," *Financial Analysts Journal* 30 (March-April 1974), pp. 1–6.

Honing, Lawrence E. and Stephen C. Coley, "An After-Tax Equivalent Payment Approach to Conventional Lease Analysis," *Financial Management* 4 (Winter 1975), pp. 18–27.

Jackson, James F., Jr., *An Evaluation of Lease Financing* (Austin: Bureau of Business Research, University of Texas, 1967).

Jenkins, David O., "Purchase or Cancelable Lease," *Financial Executive* 38 (April 1970), pp. 26–31.

Johnson, Robert W. and Wilbur G. Lewellen, "Analysis of the Lease-or-Buy Decision," *Journal of Finance* 27 (September 1972), pp. 815–823.

Levy, L. E., "Off Balance Sheet Financing," *Management Accounting* (May 1969), pp. 12–14.

Lewellen, Wilbur G., Michael S. Long, and John J. McConnell, "Asset Leasing in Competitive Capital Markets," *Journal of Finance* 31 (June 1976), pp. 787–798.

Long, Michael S., "Leasing and the Cost of Capital," *Journal of Financial and Quantitative Analysis* 12 (November 1977), pp. 579–586.

Miller, Merton and Charles W. Upton, "Leasing, Buying, and the Cost of Capital Services," *Journal of Finance* 31 (June 1976), pp. 761–786.

Mitchell, G. B., "After-Tax Cost of Leasing," *Accounting Review* 45 (April 1970), pp. 308–314.

Myers, Stewart C., David A. Dill, and Alberto J. Bautista, "Valuation of Financial Lease Contracts," *Journal of Finance* 31 (June 1976), pp. 799–819.

Nantell, Timothy J., "Equivalence of Lease versus Buy Analyses," *Financial Management* 2 (Autumn 1973), pp. 61–65.

Ofer, Aharon R., "The Evaluation of the Lease versus Purchase Alternatives," *Financial Management* 5 (Summer 1976), pp. 67–72.

Peckham, Richard E., "An Analysis of the Risks of Leveraged Leasing," *Journal of Commercial Bank Lending* 57 (March 1975), pp. 2–29.

Roenfeldt, Rodney L. and Jerome S. Osteryoung, "Analysis of Financial Leases," *Financial Management* 2 (Spring 1973), pp. 74–87.

Sartoris, William L. and Ronda S. Paul, "Lease Evaluation—Another Capital Budgeting Decision," *Financial Management* 2 (Summer 1973), pp. 46–52.

Schall, Lawrence D., "The Lease-or-Buy and Asset Acquisition Decisions," *Journal of Finance* (September 1974), pp. 1203–1214.

Stickler, Alan D. and Dunlop J. Bruce, *Financial Statement Presentation Requirements and Practices in Canada* (Butterworths, 1979).

Vancil, Richard F., "Lease or Borrow: New Method of Analysis," *Harvard Business Review* 39 (September-October 1967), pp. 68–83.

Weir, Robert C., "Economic Implications of Multiple Rates of Return in the Lease Context," *Journal of Finance* 28 (December 1973), pp. 1275–1286.

Wyman, Harold E., "Financial Lease Evaluation Under Conditions of Uncertainty," *Accounting Review* 48 (July 1973), pp. 489–493.

Chapter 21

LONG-TERM DEBT FINANCING

This chapter is devoted to the long-term debt financing (debt capital) of the business firm. The importance of long-term debt to the firm's capital structure was emphasized in earlier discussions of financial leverage, the cost of capital, and capital structure. The presence of debt in the firm's capital structure provides financial leverage, which tends to magnify the effects of increased or decreased operating income on the owners' returns. Since debt is normally the cheapest after-tax form of long-term financing, its presence may lower the firm's cost of capital, thereby permitting the firm to select a larger dollar value of acceptable investment alternatives.*

Long-term debt financing can be obtained directly through *term loans*. It can also be obtained through *bonds* and *debentures*. By selling bonds and debentures, the firm can sell small portions of the total required debt financing to various purchasers.

This chapter is divided into seven major sections. The first section discusses the general characteristics of long-term debt financing. The second section describes the various types of term loans available to the business borrower. The third section discusses project financing. The fourth section discusses the characteristics of corporate bonds. The fifth section discusses common types of bonds. The sixth section deals with international borrowings. The final section of this chapter discusses bond-refunding options, with special emphasis placed on the early retirement of outstanding bonds.

---

*This is commonly the case due to the tax deductibility of interest, which causes the explicit cost of debt (discussed in Chapter 17) to be quite low. Of course, as was pointed out in Chapter 18, the introduction of large quantities of debt into the firm's capital structure can result in high levels of financial risk, which may cause the firm's weighted average cost of capital to rise.

Characteristics of Long-Term Debt Financing

Although in Canada long-term debt is often defined as debt having a maturity of 10 or more years, we will define long-term debt as debt having a maturity of greater than one year.* The long-term debts of business firms typically have maturities of between 5 and 30 years. When a long-term debt is within a year of its maturity, many accountants will move the debt balance to the current liabilities account to reflect the fact that the long-term debt has actually become a short-term obligation at that point in time. Similar treatment is given to portions of long-term debts that are payable in the coming year. These entries are normally captioned the "Current Portion of Long-Term Debt."

STANDARD LOAN PROVISIONS

A number of standard provisions are included in long-term agreements to assure the lender that the firm will continue to exist and operate in a respectable and businesslike manner. Generally, the lender will not place a burden on the financially sound business firm. Five of these provisions are discussed below.

The Maintenance of Satisfactory Accounting Records   The borrower is required to maintain satisfactory accounting records in accordance with generally accepted accounting principles. This guarantees the lender that the financial data of the borrower is accurately presented and permits the easy interpretation of operating results.

The Rendering of Financial Statements   The borrower is required to supply, at certain dates, audited financial statements that provide the lender with the information for enforcing certain restrictive covenants and for monitoring the firm's progress. Often the lender requires the firm's bank account statements to evaluate the borrower's spending behaviour.

The Payment of Taxes and Other Liabilities   The borrower is required to pay taxes and other liabilities when due. The lender must ensure that the borrower does not default on any of its other payment obligations, since defaults could lead to bankruptcy.

Repair and Maintenance Requirements   The lender requires the borrower to maintain all its facilities in good working order so that the borrower does not let its assets deteriorate to the point where their market value is negligible.

Sale of Accounts Receivable   Borrowers may be prohibited from selling accounts receivable to generate cash, since selling accounts receivable may be viewed as a

---

*Some texts classify debts with maturities of 1–10 years as *intermediate-term debt*. This text uses a strict short-term–long-term classification. Debts with maturities of less than one year are considered short term, and debts with maturities greater than one year are considered long term. This type of classification is more in line with the firm's balance sheet classification of current liabilities and long-term debts.

sacrifice of the firm's long-run liquidity in order to satisfy short-term obligations. From a long-term lender's viewpoint, this behaviour is generally not desirable.

RESTRICTIVE LOAN PROVISIONS

Long-term lending agreements, whether resulting from a negotiated term loan or a bond issue, normally include certain "restrictive covenants." These contractual clauses place certain financial and operating *constraints* on the borrower for the life of the loan agreement. Since the lender is committing its funds for a long period, it seeks to protect itself against adverse financial developments affecting the borrower. Generally, these covenants include working capital restrictions, fixed-asset restrictions, constraints with respect to subsequent borrowing, prohibition on leases, combination restrictions, salary restrictions, management restrictions, constraints on security investment, constraints on the use of loan proceeds, and dividend restrictions.

Working Capital Restrictions   One of the most common restrictions requires the borrower to maintain a minimum level of net working capital at all times. If the net working capital of the firm falls below the predetermined negotiated level, this is construed as an indicator of a deteriorating financial position and entitles the lender to *call* the loan prior to the firm's downfall.* Thus, this provision gives the lender the opportunity to reevaluate the borrower's financial position and to decide whether or not to continue with the established lending arrangement.

In addition to a net working capital requirement, many loan agreements contain provisions specifying minimum levels of current assets or minimum current ratios, or both. These provisions are also aimed at forcing the firm to maintain its liquidity, since a failure to maintain short-run solvency makes the firm's long-run success rather questionable. However, the working capital requirements should not be so restrictive that they impede the firm's ability to achieve reasonable profits.

Fixed-Asset Restrictions   Long-term lenders often place constraints on the firm with respect to the liquidation, acquisition, and encumbrance of fixed assets.

The Liquidation of Fixed Assets   Lenders often prohibit the liquidation of fixed assets. A firm that does not have sufficient liquidity to make required payments can sell fixed assets in order to get cash. However, this is a dangerous strategy that may damage the firm's ability to repay a term loan. Some firms sell fixed assets because they are no longer useful; if this is the case, the lender may find the liquidation of assets acceptable. By including a restrictive covenant, the lender at least retains the right to pass judgment in such a situation.

*When a loan is "called," the lender demands immediate repayment. Violation of any standard or restrictive loan covenants generally gives the lender the right to call a loan. In other words, violation of the covenants means the borrower has failed to abide by the terms of the loan contract. The lender's recourse is to require the immediate return of its money along with any accrued interest. Sometimes the lender will merely request some type of concession such as representation on the borrower's board of directors as an alternative to calling the loan. Of course, the acceptance of such a concession is controlled by the lender—not the borrower.

The Acquisition of Fixed Assets   Lenders sometimes prohibit the borrower from making capital expenditures to acquire new fixed assets. They may specify a maximum dollar capital expenditure per year. The purpose of this restriction is to require the firm to maintain liquidity by keeping its dollars in current as opposed to fixed assets, and to ensure that the firm does not change its business risk by internally diversifying into new lines of business. A lender normally permits a level of capital expenditures sufficient to allow for adequate maintenance and repair of assets. It may waive the capital expenditure restriction if a large capital expenditure is shown to be justifiable.

The Encumbrance of Fixed Assets   Quite often lenders will prohibit the use of fixed assets as collateral for a loan. By forcing the borrower to leave fixed assets unencumbered, the lender protects itself in case of liquidation. This ensures that the proceeds from the liquidation of the unencumbered assets would be available to satisfy the term lender's claims.

Constraints on Subsequent Borrowing   Many lending agreements prohibit the borrower from incurring any additional long-term debt. Short-term borrowing, which is a necessity for a seasonal business, is not usually limited in the lending agreement. The restriction on long-term borrowing may require only that additional borrowing be unsecured or *subordinated* to the original loan. Subordination of subsequent debts means that the subordinated creditors agree to wait until all the claims of the existing or *senior debt* are satisfied prior to receiving any distribution of assets in the event of liquidation.*

Prohibition on Leases   Borrowers may be prohibited from entering into financial leases. Often a certain dollar limit is placed on the amount of lease liability acceptable to the lender. If the firm were permitted to make unlimited lease agreements, the effectiveness of restrictive provisions with respect to debt and capital expenditures would be minimal. The similarity between a lease and a long-term debt obligation was discussed in Chapter 20. The lender's objective is to ensure that financial lease commitments, which also are a form of long-term financing, are kept under control.

Combination Restrictions   Occasionally, the lender requires the borrower to agree not to combine in any way with another firm, unless the lender approves. Such an action could completely change the firm's financial and operating structure, and the changed structure could make the firm more risky than it was when the loan was initially negotiated.

Salary Restrictions   To prevent the firm's liquidation through large salary payments, the lender may prohibit salary increases over a certain annual percentage for

---

*Debts are quite often subordinated in such a way that the senior debt's recovery in liquidation is greater than that of the general creditors. An example of how the subordination feature works in liquidation is given later in this chapter.

specified employees. Restrictions on salary increases are intended to prevent the firm from paying out dollars that could be used to increase its liquidity and decrease its financial risk by increasing its operating income (earnings before interest and taxes). Normally included in this provision is a statement prohibiting employee loans or advances since the effect of either is similar to that of a large salary payment.

Management Restrictions   The lender may require the borrower to maintain certain "key employees" without whom the future success of the firm is uncertain. The lender may also retain the privilege of calling the loan or taking part in the selection of a new executive if a key executive were to resign. In order to protect itself in the event of the death of a key executive, the lender may also require the firm to maintain a "key man" life insurance policy on specified executives. The policies may be payable to the company or directly to the lender to retire the loan. These management-related provisions are needed only when the presence of certain individuals is critical to the future success of the firm.

Constraints on Security Investment   Occasionally the lender includes a covenant limiting the borrower's security investment alternatives. For example, the firm may be limited to investments in marketable securities. This is designed to increase the probability that the borrower will survive a liquidity crisis.

Constraints on the Use of Loan Proceeds   Occasionally a covenant specifically requiring the borrower to spend the borrowed funds on certain items is included in the loan agreement. This restriction assures the lender that the funds lent will not be diverted outside the company or to some less productive use than that for which the money was initially borrowed.

Dividend Restrictions   A relatively common provision is to limit the firm's cash dividend payout to a maximum of 50–70 percent of its net earnings. Occasionally the dividend restriction is stated as a maximum dollar amount per year. Many lenders also place restrictions on the *repurchase* of shares, which in essence is another method for distributing corporate earnings.

The preceding list of restrictive covenants merely contains the more common loan restrictions. In the process of negotiating the terms of long-term borrowing, the borrower and lender must ultimately both agree to the restrictive covenants. Whether the resulting restrictive covenants favour the borrower or the lender depends upon the relative bargaining power of the two parties.

The violation of any standard or restrictive provisions by the borrower gives the lender the right to demand the immediate repayment of accrued interest and the principal of the loan. The lender will not normally demand immediate repayment, but it will evaluate the situation to determine whether the violation is serious enough to jeopardize the loan. On the basis of this evaluation the lender may call the loan, or waive the violation and continue the loan, or waive the violation but alter the terms of the initial agreement.

Term Loans

A *term loan* is a loan with a maturity of *more than one year*. Term loans are made by various financial institutions—such as foreign and Canadian-owned banks, life insurance companies, and specialized term lenders—to business firms.* These loans generally have maturities of 2–15 years; bank loans generally have terms of 5 years or less, and insurance company loans generally have terms of 10–15 years. These loans are most often made to finance *fixed* working capital needs, to purchase machinery and equipment, or to liquidate other loans—either to change their maturities or to lower the interest cost. Since term loans are similar to privately placed bonds in that they are directly negotiated between the borrower and the lender, they have many of the advantages and disadvantages of privately placed bonds. This section discusses both the specific characteristics of term loan agreements and the interest cost of term loans to business.

TERM LOAN AGREEMENTS

The actual term loan agreement is a formal contract containing anywhere from a few to a few hundred pages. These agreements are normally prepared by the lender's attorneys. The following items are normally specified in the loan agreement: the amount and maturity of the loan, the type of interest rate charged, the interest cost of the loan, the timing and nature of payments, standard provisions, restrictive provisions, the collateral (if any), the purpose of the loan, the action to be taken in the event of default, and share purchase options. Of these basic factors, only the type of interest rate charged, the interest cost of the loan, payment dates, collateral requirements, and share purchase options remain to be discussed.

TYPE OF INTEREST RATE CHARGED

Basically, there are two types of interest rates charged on term loans—the variable rate and the fixed rate.

Variable Rate   The variable rate is the standard type of interest rate used on the term loans provided by the Canadian chartered banks. In this type of loan, the interest rate charged by the banks generally floats at a predetermined fixed percentage (*spread*) above the prime rate for the term or *duration* of the loan. The interest-rate premium above the prime rate, for a $200,000 five-year loan, is generally about three percentage points above the prime rate. Generally, a higher or lower premium over prime, or spread, is charged on loans with a longer or shorter term-to-maturity. As is shown in the following example, the premium over prime may be subject to renegotiation during the term of the loan.[1]

---

*The characteristics and differences in the term-lending policies of these institutions were discussed in Chapter 19.

EXAMPLE   In December 1976, Hydro-Quebec signed a $1.25-billion U.S. loan with a consortium of Canadian and foreign banks, headed by the Bank of Montreal. The loan, which had an 8½-year term-to-maturity, was to consist of two portions—a $750-million term loan, and a $500-million standby credit. Both portions of the loan carried an interest rate of 0.75 percentage points above the London Interbank Offered Rate (LIBOR), which is the key U.S.-dollar lending rate between British banks. In addition, the loan agreement had a provision that allowed Hydro to reopen (renegotiate) the terms of the loan after two years. After approximately two months of negotiation, the terms of the loan were successfully renegotiated in January 1980. The new terms reduced the interest-rate spread for both portions of the loan to 0.5 percentage points over LIBOR. Based on the renegotiated spread, Hydro would pay about $1.88 million [i.e., (0.75 − 0.50) · $750 million] less a year on the term portion of the loan. If Hydro used the standby credit, it would pay an additional $1.25 million less on the standby credit. Even with the new terms, interest on the $750-million term credit was costing Hydro about $9.4 million a month in January 1980, since LIBOR was at a near-record 14.5 percent.

Fixed Rate   The fixed rate is the typical type of interest rate used on term loans provided by Canadian subsidiaries of U.S. banks, insurance companies, and specialized term lenders, such as Roy Nat. In this type of loan, the interest rate charged by the lender is fixed for the term of the loan. To effectively compete with the foreign-owned banks operating in Canada, the Canadian chartered banks have become more active in fixed-rate term lending.

THE INTEREST COST OF TERM LOANS

The major factors affecting the cost of a term loan for a given borrower are the term-to-maturity of the loan, which determines the basic cost of money; the riskiness of the borrower; and the size of the loan. Each of these aspects will now be discussed.

The Basic Cost of Money   The *basic cost* of money is the starting point for determining the specific interest rate that a lender will charge a specific prospective borrower for a specific term loan. The basic cost of money is defined as the yield on virtually default-free debt issues, such as Government of Canada bonds. Thus, for a specific term loan, the yield on a government bond, with the same term-to-maturity as the loan, is used as the basic cost of money.

The relationship between the yield-to-maturity of debt and debt's term-to-maturity, when all other aspects of the debt are the same, is referred to as the *term structure of interest rates*.[2] The graphic illlustration of the term structure for a group of bonds that have the same risk of default at a particular point in time is called the *yield curve*. The yield curve is upward sloping, flat, or downward sloping depending upon whether short-term rates are lower than, equal to, or higher than long-term rates. Some of the possible shapes of yield curves are depicted in Figure 21.1.

There are two important factors that determine the shape of the yield curve for a specific group of bonds. The first factor is the *risk differential* between longer and

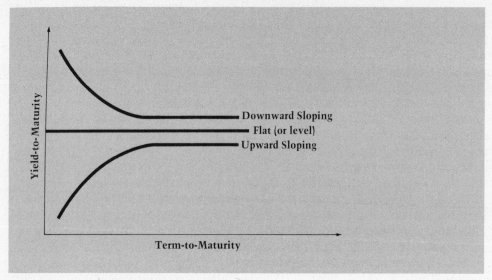

Figure 21.1   Some possible types of yield curves.

shorter-term bonds. At least two reasons account for investors' belief that the risk of a specific bond increases as its term-to-maturity increases. First, since investors find it more difficult to accurately forecast the financial position of the borrower as the term of the bond increases, investors perceive the risk of default increasing as the bond's term-to-maturity increases. Second, even for bonds that are vitually default-free, investors are exposed to a greater *interest-rate risk* by holding bonds with longer maturities, since the changes in the value of the bond to interest-rate movements increases as the term-to-maturity of the bond increases.* Since investors expect to be compensated for these additional risks, a *liquidity premium* must be offered to induce investors to invest in longer-term bonds. Thus, in the absence of a significant fall in future interest rates, the interest rates on longer-term bonds will be higher than the interest rates on shorter-term bonds, due to the liquidity premium being paid on longer-term bonds.

The second factor that determines the slope of the yield curve is the expectation of investors regarding the *future movement of interest rates.* Generally, when investors have expected interest rates to *rise,* the yield curve has been *upward sloping.* During such periods of time, lenders have generally used a higher basic cost of funds on longer-term as opposed to shorter-term loans. However, when both long-term and short-term interest rates have been relatively high, and investors have expected interest rates to *fall significantly,* the yield curve has been *humped and downward sloping.* During such periods of time, lenders have generally used a higher basic cost of funds on shorter-term as opposed to longer-term loans. Thus, whether a term loan's basic interest cost increases, stays constant, or decreases, as its term-to-maturity increases, depends upon the term structure of interest rates.

---

*However, borrowers, unlike lenders, prefer to borrow long-term, since this reduces the risk of being unable to meet principal payments.

The lender's expectations for future short-term interest rates may differ from that of the market. If the lender believes that long-term rates do not accurately reflect future interest rate movements, and the lender expects future short-term interest rates to increase, it may be wise for the lender to lend on a short-term and not on a long-term basis. Similarly, if the borrower believes that long-term rates do not accurately reflect future interest rate movements, and the borrower expects future short-term interest rates to increase, it may be wise for the borrower to borrow on a long-term and not on a short-term basis. Of course, the effectiveness of the lender's (or borrower's) decision will be greatly affected by the accuracy of his or her interest rate forecast.

To the basic cost of funds, the lender will add premiums related to such factors as the estimated (default) riskiness of the borrower and the size of the loan. Therefore, the actual rate of interest charged on a term loan is the basic cost of money adjusted for the borrower's riskiness and the size of the loan.

The Riskiness of the Borrower   The lender's main concern is with the ability of the borrower to repay the loan requested. If the lender's assessment of the borrower's riskiness (using, for example, the ratios discussed in Chapter 3) indicates that the requested loan will likely make the borrower unable to service all its debt, the loan will not be made. The overall assessment of the borrower's default risk, along with information on past payment patterns, is used by the lender in determining the risk premium to be added to the basic cost of a loan, if the loan is to be provided. It should be clear that a careful credit analysis of a borrower by the lender (or potential bondholder) is necessary to assess the riskiness of the prospective borrower.

Some lenders determine a prospective borrower's "risk class"* and find the rates charged on similar maturity loans to firms believed to be in the same risk class. Instead of having to determine a risk premium, the lender can use the yield curve to get the risk premium prevailing in the marketplace for similar loans. A key to the successful use of this approach is to be able to accurately measure and classify the riskiness of a given firm.

The Size of the Loan   The size of the term loan affects the interest cost of borrowing in an inverse manner. Loan administration costs are likely to decrease with increasing loan size, but the risk to the lender increases, since the more term debt incurred by the borrower, the greater the risk of default. The size of the loan sought by each borrower must be evaluated to determine the net administrative cost-risk trade-off. The size of the loan with respect to the lender's total funds also affects the interest cost. If a lender lends 50 percent of its money to one borrower, it will charge a rate reflecting the nondiversifiable riskiness of the loan to it. This risk will be high because of the lender's failure to diversify its loans.

*A *risk class* reflects the firm's overall risk profile. One must envision a continuum of risk, break it into discrete classes, and place the firm in an appropriate class. Looking at other firms perceived to be in the same risk class will help the lender to make certain decisions with respect to the appropriate rate of interest. For publicly traded firms, betas (see Chapter 16) are often used to classify firms into homogeneous risk classes.

OTHER FACTORS

The three remaining factors—payment dates, collateral requirements, and share-purchase options—will now be discussed.

Payment Dates   Term loan agreements generally require quarterly, semiannual, or annual payments. Generally, these equal payments fully amortize the principal and interest over the life of the loan. Occasionally a term loan agreement will require periodic payments over the life of the loan followed by a large lump-sum payment at maturity. This lump sum, or *balloon payment*, in some instances represents the entire loan principal since the periodic payments represent only interest. If the lending agreement specifies a large balloon payment, the borrower often is required to make periodic payments into a *sinking fund*, which is a type of deposit or investment that at maturity is equal to the required balloon payment. The use of sinking funds is much more common in the case of bond financing. Term loan agreements normally include prepayment penalties of 2–10 percent of the outstanding loan balance. This is because term lenders generally prefer to have their loans held to maturity.

Collateral Requirements   Term lending arrangements may be unsecured or secured in a fashion similar to short-term loans. Whether collateral is required depends on the lender's evaluation of the borrower's financial condition. Common types of collateral include machinery and equipment, plant, pledges of accounts receivable, and pledges of securities. The lender can obtain a security interest in any of these assets by publicly filing certain documents that become part of the term loan agreement. When fixed assets are used as collateral, the lender files a mortgage on them; in many instances the loan is actually made to finance the purchase of these fixed assets. If current assets such as accounts receivable and marketable securities are used as collateral, the lender requires continuous pledges of acceptable accounts and securities.

Share-Purchase Options   A recent trend in term lending is for the lender to require the borrower to provide share-purchase options (sometimes referred to as *equity sweeteners* or *equity kickers*) in addition to the required interest payments. Share-purchase options are *warrants* that allow the holder to purchase a stated amount of common shares in the firm at a specified price over a certain period of time. These options can be made available only by corporate borrowers. They are used to entice institutional lenders to make term loans. Warrants are discussed in greater detail in Chapter 23.

Project Financing[3]

Project financing is the financing of a particular economic unit (project) in which a lender (lessor) relies on the cash flows and earnings generated by the economic unit (project) for loan (lease) servicing, and on the assets of the economic unit (project) as collateral for the loan (lease). Such projects are significant in Canada, and include various energy and energy-related projects such as the development of major oil and gas fields (like the tar sands in Alberta), pipelines, refineries, and port facilities. Generally, these projects require investment financing that far exceeds a single firm's capacity. As a result, consortia of companies are often formed to share the construction, commercial, operating, and financial risks of undertaking such projects.

Generally, part of the funding for such projects consists of equity participation by the sponsors of the project, and the remainder of the funding consists of off-balance-sheet term loans or leases, on a nonrecourse or recourse basis. If the term loan or lease is on a nonrecourse basis, the lender or lessor is mainly interested in the percentage of equity invested in the project and the economic viability of the project. The economic viability of the project is of utmost importance since repayment of the funds borrowed for the project must be generated solely from the project's net cash flows. If the loan or lease is on a recourse basis, then each sponsor may either guarantee his or her share of the project's obligations or be jointly and severally responsible for the total project's obligations.* In this case, the lender or lessor is interested in the economic feasibility of the project and in the credit-worthiness and financial standing of the project's sponsors.

The maturity and repayment schedule of a project's loan or lease are generally set to match the expected net cash flows generated by the project over time. Thus, the maturity of such term loans and leases is often eight years or more.

When the project is situated in a foreign country, the project's sponsors not only are subjected to additional commercial risks, but also face various political and foreign exchange risks. As discussed in Chapter 19, many of these commercial and political risks can be reduced by obtaining insurance from the Export Development Corporation.

Characteristics of Corporate Bonds

A *bond* is a certificate indicating that a corporation has *borrowed* a certain amount of money on a long-term basis and promises to repay it at a specific future date.† The issuing corporation agrees to pay bondholders a stated amount of interest at specified time intervals (usually semiannually). Most bonds are issued with maturities of 10–30 years and in denominations of $1,000. However, maturities of less than 10 years and denominations of anywhere from $100 to $10,000 are not uncommon. Bonds with face values of less than $500 are referred to as *baby bonds*. The stated interest rate on a bond represents the percentage of the bond's face value that will be paid out annually. Purchasers of bonds (i.e., bondholders) are creditors who expect to receive specified periodic interest and repayment of the principal amount (i.e., the face value of the bond) at maturity.

*For a discussion of risk-sharing rules, see Chapter 2.
†Perpetual bonds are rarely used in Canada. Notable exceptions are the approximately $560 million 4-percent perpetual consolidated debentures issued by Canadian Pacific Ltd., which are still outstanding. An interesting feature of this issue is that the bondholders obtain the right to vote if there is a default on interest payments.

LEGAL ASPECTS OF CORPORATE BONDS

Since a corporate bond issue is often sold to numerous unrelated persons or entities, certain legal arrangements are required to protect the purchasers of the bond. Bondholders are legally protected primarily through the indenture and the trustee.

Bond Indenture   A *bond indenture,* or trust deed, is a quite complex and legal document stating the conditions under which a bond has been issued. It specifies both the rights of the bondholders and the duties of the issuing corporation. The actions that may be taken by bondholders if the issuer violates any of the clauses in the indenture are also clearly specified. In addition to specifying the interest and principal payments and dates, it contains various standard and restrictive provisions, sinking-fund requirements, and provisions regarding a security interest (if the bond is secured).

Standard and Restrictive Provisions   The standard and restrictive provisions of a bond issue are virtually the same as those discussed earlier in this chapter for term loan agreements.

Sinking-Fund Requirements   One other restrictive provision that is normally included in a bond indenture is a *sinking-fund* (or *purchase-fund*) requirement. The objective of this requirement is to provide for the systematic retirement or amortization of a bond issue over its life. There are two general types of sinking funds—the general sinking fund and the specific sinking fund. With the *general sinking fund,* the firm invests the sinking-fund payments in securities, such as Government of Canada bonds, which have the same term-to-maturity as the bond issue. With the more common *specific sinking fund,* the firm uses the payments to retire portions of the issue prior to the maturity of the issue. Usually, the stipulated sinking-fund payment is a mandatory *fixed* annual dollar amount. Sometimes, the stipulated annual payment can be a variable amount; for example, a certain percentage of annual sales or earnings. Even the fixed-payment plans sometimes provide for a "balloon payment" in order to retire outstanding bonds at maturity.

Under a specific sinking-fund requirement, the issuer can either purchase the bonds in the marketplace or "call" them at the specified call price. It will call bonds only when sufficient bonds cannot be purchased directly in the marketplace or when the market price of the bond is above the call price. When the market price is above the call price, random selection procedures are normally used to determine which bonds to call.

Security Interest   The bond indenture is similar to a loan agreement in that any collateral pledged against the bond is specifically identified in the document. Generally the title to the collateral is attached to the indenture and the disposition of the collateral in various circumstances is specifically described. The protection of bond collateral is quite crucial in order to increase the safety and thereby enhance the marketability of a bond issue.

Trustee   A *trustee* is a third party to a bond indenture. The trustee is chosen by the issuer and is usually a department of a trust company. As a representative of the bondholders, the trustee must ensure that the issuer lives up to the provisions in the bond indenture. If there is a violation of the provisions of the bond indenture, the trustee, as an agent of the bondholders, can take action to rectify the situation. If such actions are not successful, the trustee is generally required to report the violations to the bondholders. After obtaining their consent, the trustee can take action against the firm to force the firm to comply with the provisions of the bond indenture. The trustee also normally participates in the actual creation of the indenture, making sure that all necessary legal protections have been provided in the agreement. Bond indentures not only specify the provisions of the issue, but they also indicate the duties, rights, responsibilities, and conditions for removal of a trustee. In other words, the bondholders retain the right to hire trustees and fire them when they fail to fulfill their responsibilities. After the financial collapse of Atlantic Acceptance Corporation Ltd. and the Prudential Finance Company, Ontario amended its Business Corporations Act in 1970 to include sections dealing with the duties and responsibilities of trustees of public debt issues. Similar provisions now exist in the Canadian and British Columbia Business Corporations Acts.

THE GENERAL FEATURES OF A BOND

Three general features quite often found in a bond issue are a conversion feature, a call feature, and warrants. These features provide both the issuer (borrower) and the purchaser (lender) with certain opportunities for replacing, retiring, and/or supplementing the bond with some type of equity issue.

The Conversion Feature   The conversion feature of certain so-called *convertible bonds* allows the creditor (bondholder) to convert the bonds into a certain number of preferred or common shares. The creditor will convert his or her bonds only if the market value of shares becomes greater than the conversion price. The conversion feature is generally considered attractive by both the issuer and the purchaser of corporate bonds. A more extensive discussion of convertible bonds will be presented in Chapter 23.

The Call Feature   The call feature is included in almost all corporate bond issues. It gives the issuer the opportunity to repurchase bonds at a stated call price prior to maturity. The amount by which the call price exceeds the bond face value is commonly referred to as the *call premium*. The call premium is typically equal to one year's interest for the first year the bonds become callable. Thus, for the first year a $1,000 12-percent bond becomes callable, the call price would be $1,120 [i.e., $1,000 + 12% · $1,000]. For subsequent years, the call premium typically decreases at a constant rate. Bonds or debentures can be redeemed before maturity without paying the call premium if the debt holders approve such an action. This is illustrated in the following example.

EXAMPLE On February 13, 1980, a proposal by Reed Ltd. to retire $115 million worth of debentures before maturity without paying the required call premium was approved by 93.3 percent of the debenture holders (the trust deed specified a required two-thirds vote). The debentures had initially been issued in four series in 1975. The trustee was the Montreal Trust Company. Under the trust deed, call premiums were to be paid to debenture holders if the debentures were retired before maturity or if Reed sold its assets "as an entirety or substantially as an entirety." In December 1979, Reed sold its Ontario pulp and paper mill—an operation that represented about 40 percent of the value of Reed's total assets. This sale raised legal doubts as to whether Reed was in default of its trust deed. Thus, with the approval of debenture holders, Reed avoided the $10-million call-premium cost of the alleged violation of the trust deed.

The call feature is generally advantageous to the issuer. For example, when interest rates fall, an issuer can call an outstanding bond and issue a new bond at a lower interest rate. When interest rates rise, the call privilege will not be exercised, except possibly to meet sinking-fund requirements. Generally, the issuer must pay a higher interest rate on a callable bond than on a noncallable bond of equal risk. This interest premium depends directly on the expectations of both the issuer and the purchaser with respect to future interest rates. The call feature is helpful in forcing the conversion of convertible bonds when the conversion price of a share is below the market price.*

Warrants Warrants are occasionally attached to bonds as "sweeteners" or "kickers" to make the bonds more attractive to prospective buyers. A *warrant* is a certificate giving its holder the right to purchase a certain number of common shares at a specified price. An in-depth discussion of share purchase warrants is included in Chapter 23.

RETRACTABLE AND EXTENDIBLE FEATURES

Retractable and extendible features provide a bondholder with an option that entitles the bondholder to alter the maturity date of the bond.

Retractable Feature The retractable feature is like an option that gives the bondholder the right to retract or reduce the maturity date of the bond. After giving the issuer the proper advance notice, a retractable feature allows the bondholder to sell the bonds to the issuer at a specified time before the maturity date at the bond's par value. The retractable feature will be exercised by bondholders only if the interest rate on similar bonds is *higher* than the retractable bond's coupon rate.

---

*A discussion of how the call feature can be used to force conversion of a convertible security has been included in Chapter 23. Once the reader has obtained a feel for the various aspects of the conversion feature, the use of the call to force conversion will be better understood.

EXAMPLE   On April 5, 1978, Trizec Corporation Ltd. issued $25 million of a $10\frac{1}{2}$-percent issue of senior debentures, which were to retire on June 1, 1998. The debentures have a retractable feature that permits a debenture holder to redeem the debentures on June 1, 1988. To exercise this option, the debenture holder must notify Trizec of such an intention between September 1, 1987, and December 1, 1987.

Extendible Feature   The extendible feature is like an option that gives the bond-holder the right to extend the maturity date of the bond at the same coupon rate. Thus, an extendible feature allows the bondholder to extend the shorter-term debt into longer-term debt, at a fixed-coupon rate, on or before a specified future date. The extendible feature will be exercised by bondholders on the date on which it must be exercised only if the interest rate on similar bonds is *lower* than the exten-dible bond's coupon rate. Since both the retractable and extendible features (options) have potential value to bondholders, the yield on such bonds should be less than the yield on similar bonds that do not have these features.

EXAMPLE   Consolidated-Bathurst Inc. has an outstanding issue of 11-percent debentures, which are to retire on March 3, 1985. The debentures have an extendible feature that permits a debenture holder to extend the maturity date of the debentures to March 3, 1995. The debentures will continue to carry the same 11-percent coupon rate.

YIELD ON A BOND

The *yield* or *effective rate of return* on a bond is the discount rate that equates the present value of the bond's expected cash inflows with the bond's purchase price.* Thus, if a bond is sold prior to maturity, the bond's yield-to-maturity will probably differ from its holding-period yield, because the bond's current market value when sold prior to maturity will probably differ from its face value. As discussed in Chapter 13, the bond's market value will be less than its face value when the market interest rate on similar bonds is higher than the bond's coupon rate, and vice versa. An example should help to emphasize the possible difference between a bond's yield-to-maturity and a shorter holding-period yield.

*It should be emphasized that the calculated yield is a *nominal*, and not a *real*, return. Generally, during periods of *anticipated* inflation, bondholders do not suffer, since the market interest rate includes a premium to compensate for the market's expected inflation rate. However, during periods of *unantici-pated* inflation, bondholders suffer, since they incur a loss in *real* value. For example, if actual inflation is greater than anticipated inflation, then the bondholders will experience a more than anticipated erosion in the purchasing power of the cash inflows (interest plus principal repayment) generated by the bond investment.

EXAMPLE   Sue Ellen bought a $1,000, 12-percent, 11-year bond at par. If Sue Ellen held the bond until maturity, then the bond's yield-to-maturity would be equal to the bond's coupon rate of 12 percent. However, suppose that Sue Ellen sells the bond after one year, when the current interest rate for similar 10-year bonds is 10 percent. As discussed in Chapter 13, since the bond's market value must be such that it provides a 10-percent annual return, the bond's market value will be the *sum of* the present value of an annuity of $60 received semiannually for 10 years (discounted semiannually at 5 percent) *plus* the present value of a lump sum payment of $1,000 at the bond's maturity date (also discounted semiannually at 5 percent). Thus, the bond's market value will be approximately $1,125 [i.e., $60 · 12.462 + $1,000 · 0.377]. Sue Ellen's yield over the 1-year holding period, as discussed in Chapter 13, is the discount rate that *equates* the present value of the two $60 semiannual interest payments and the $1,125 selling price of the bond *with* the $1,000 original purchase price of the bond. Thus, Sue Ellen's holding-period yield is based on the solution for *i* (the semiannual discount rate) in the following:

$$1,000 = \$60 \, (PVIF_{i,1\,yr.}) + \$60 \, (PVIF_{i,2\,yrs.}) + \$1,125 \, (PVIF_{i,2\,yrs.}).$$

By trial and error, *i* is found to be approximately 12 percent. Thus, the annual yield for the 1-year holding period (2 · *i*) is approximately 24 percent. (If compounding is reflected in the annualization, the annual rate is 25.44 percent.)

MARKETING A BOND

Primary or new issues of corporate bonds can be made in two ways—through private placements or public offerings.

Private Placements   The private or direct placement of bonds involves the sale of a bond issue directly to one purchaser or a group of purchasers, normally large financial institutions such as life insurance companies and pension funds. Directly placed bond issues do not differ significantly from a long-term loan; there is virtually no secondary market for them. Since the bonds are placed directly, registration of the issue is not required. As discussed in Chapter 19, interest rates on directly placed bonds are slightly above those for similar public issues, due to their very limited marketability.

Public Offerings   Bonds sold to the public are generally sold by investment dealers.* The rate charged by the investment dealer is largely dependent on the size of the issue and the reputation of the issuer. Bonds issued through public offerings much be registered with the provincial securities commissions. The price at which bonds are publicly offered often differs from the bonds' stated or *face value*. If similar-risk debt instruments currently yield a higher interest rate than the bond's stated or *coupon rate*, the bond will have to be sold at a *discount* (i.e., below its face value); if the prevailing rate on similar-risk instruments is below the bond's coupon rate, the bond will be sold at a *premium* (i.e., above its face value).

---

*A more detailed discussion of the underwriting function was presented in Chapter 19. Also included in Chapter 19 was a description of the capital markets in which both corporate shares and bonds may be traded.

Table 21.1   Moody's, Standard & Poor's, and Canadian Bond Rating Service's Bond Ratings

Moody's	Interpretation	Standard & Poor's	Interpretation	CBRS	Interpretation
Aaa	Prime quality	AAA	Bank investment quality	A++	Highest quality
Aa	High grade	AA		A+	Very good quality
A	Upper-medium grade	A		A	Good quality
Baa	Medium grade	BBB		B++	Medium grade
		BB		B+	Lower-medium grade
Ba	Lower-medium grade or speculative	B	Speculative	B	Poor quality
B	Speculative	CCC		C	Speculative
Caa	From very speculative	CC		D	Default
Ca	to near or in default	C			
C		DDD	In default (rating	S	Rating suspended
		DD	indicates the relative		
		D	salvage value)		

Source: Moody's Investors Service, Inc; Standard & Poor's NYSE Reports; and CBRS Ltd.

BOND RATINGS

Three major financial services—the U.S.-based Moody's, and Standard & Poor's; and the Canadian-based Canadian Bond Rating Service (CBRS)—assess the default risk of publicly traded bonds, by using such factors as company size, leverage, interest coverage, earnings instability and level of subordination.* Based on their assessment of default risk, each firm provides a rating for each bond reviewed. The ratings used by the firms, along with a brief interpretation of each group of ratings, is summarized in Table 21.1.

There is normally an inverse relationship between the quality or rating of a bond and its interest rate or yield-to-maturity. As shown in Figure 21.2, higher-quality (higher-rated) bonds have lower yields than lower-quality (lower-rated) bonds. When considering bond financing, the financial manager must therefore concern him- or herself with the expected bond ratings, since these ratings can significantly impact upon the bonds' saleability and cost to maturity.

Types of Bonds

Bonds can be classified according to whether or not they are secured by pledges of specific assets. The following two sections discuss the various types of unsecured and secured bond issues. A summary of the key characteristics and priority of lenders' claims against the major types of bonds is included in Table 21.2, presented at the end of this section.

*In 1979, CBRS provided ratings on the bonds and debentures of approximately 190 Canadian-based companies (approximately 240 issues). It also provided ratings on the short-term promissory notes (such as commercial paper) and preferred shares of a number of Canadian-based companies. Also, the Canadian-based Dominion Rating Service provides rating services for short-term corporate paper and some long-term debt.

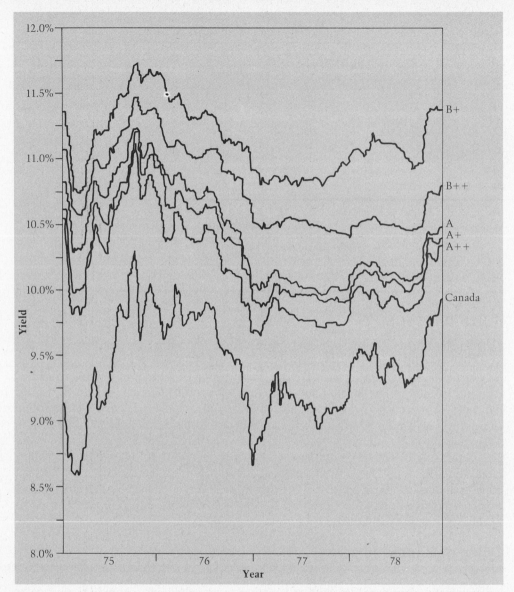

Figure 21.2   Corporate long-term bond yields. These long-term corporate bond yields are selected from a number of bonds that have been rated by the Canadian Bond Rating Service and are actively traded. These bonds are grouped by rating category and the average yield is computed and recorded weekly. SOURCE: Canadian Bond Rating Service, *An Introduction to Bond and Commercial Paper Rating* (Montreal, 1979), p. 4.

UNSECURED BONDS

Unsecured bonds are issued without the pledge of specific collateral. There are three basic types of unsecured bonds—debentures, subordinated debentures, and income bonds.

Debentures   Generally, *debenture holders*, as general creditors, have a claim on any of the firm's assets remaining once the claims of all secured creditors have been satisfied. The indenture under which a debenture is issued may contain restrictions on the issuance of future debentures and secured debt. Only quite credit-worthy firms are able to issue debentures.

Subordinated Debentures   *Subordinated debentures* are debentures that are subordinated to other types of debt.* Although the subordinated-debt holders rank below all other long-term creditors with respect to both liquidation and the payment of interest, their claims must be satisfied prior to those of common or preferred shareholders. The higher risk associated with subordinated debentures generally makes them a more expensive method of financing for the issuer. However, even when the dividend tax credit is considered, subordinated debentures offer a tax advantage over preferred shares. Convertible bonds are almost always subordinated. Also, commercial lending officers generally insist upon subordination of other debt incurred by the firm. Thus, subordination increases the percentage of assets available for the commercial lender's loans, and other forms of senior debt, in the event of liquidation. An example will clarify this point.

EXAMPLE   The Bell Company has $3 million worth of senior debt, $3 million worth of subordinated debentures, and $4 million worth of other ordinary unsecured creditor's claims outstanding. The total claims against the firm are therefore $10 million. The firm has just gone bankrupt and has been liquidated for only $6 million. All creditors do *not* receive their 60-percent (i.e., $6 million available ÷ $10 million in claims) share of the $6 million. Instead, the senior debt holder has a claim on both its and the subordinated-debenture holder's portion. Together, these amount to 60 percent (i.e., since each of them has a $3-million claim out of total claims of $10 million) of the $6 million, or $3.6 million. Since it needs $3 million to satisfy its claim, the senior debt holder receives this amount. The subordinated-debenture holder receives $600,000 (i.e., $3.6 million − $3.0 million), and the other ordinary unsecured creditors receive $2.4 million (i.e., 40% · $6 million). Rather than receiving its proportionate share of $1.8 million (i.e., 30 percent of $6 million), the senior debt holder receives full satisfaction of its claim.† Without the subordinated debentures, the senior debt holder would have received only a little more than half this amount (i.e., $1.8 million instead of $3.0 million).

---

*If secured, the security is a floating charge against all assets that are not specifically pledged.
†A more detailed example of the place of senior and subordinated debt holders in the liquidation process is included in Chapter 26. The example illustrates the rights of both debt and equity holders in the liquidation process.

Income Bonds   An *income bond* requires the payment of interest only when there are sufficient earnings from which to make the payment. Although they are not common in Canada, income bonds are used during the rehabilitation of a failed or failing firm. Since the interest payment on an income bond is not a *fixed* charge, such payments must be treated as if they were a dividend by both the bondholder and the firm for Canadian income tax purposes. Due to the weak claim of the income bondholders on the firm's assets, the stated rate of interest on income bonds is generally quite high.

SECURED BONDS

The basic types of secured bonds are mortgage bonds, collateral trust bonds, and equipment trust certificates. Secured bonds, like secured short-term loans, have specific assets pledged against them as collateral.* If the issuer defaults on any provisions of the secured bond indenture, the trustee can liquidate the collateral to satisfy the bondholder's claim. If the bondholder's full claim is not satisfied through liquidation of collateral, it becomes an ordinary unsecured creditor.

Mortgage Bonds   A *mortgage bond* is a bond secured with a lien on *real* property (land and buildings). When a *specific lien* is used, the security for the mortgage bond is a specifically designated real property. When a *blanket lien* is used, the security for the mortgage bond is all the real property currently owned by the firm. Thus, a blanket lien offers the bondholder more protection than a specific lien.

A *first-mortgage bond* gives the holder the first claim on secured assets. A *second-mortgage bond* gives the holder a secondary claim on assets already secured by the first mortgage. The first-mortgage bond is obviously the most secure since the holder has the first claim on the pledged assets. Although first and second mortgages are most common, subsequent mortgages can be filed. Mortgage bonds are purchased by trust companies, life insurance companies, and pension funds. A number of features may be included in a mortgage bond indenture.

Open-End Mortgages   An *open-end mortgage* permits the issuance of additional bonds under the same mortgage contract. This arrangement provides the issuer with some flexibility in its financing, but provides little protection for creditors.

Limited Open-End Mortgages   A *limited open-end mortgage* allows the firm to issue additional bonds for up to a specified maximum, which is typically stated as a percentage of the original cost of the pledged property. This arrangement provides more protection to existing bondholders than the open-end mortgage.

Closed-End Mortgages   A *closed-end mortgage* does not permit additional borrowing on a given mortgage. The only way additional funds can be raised is through a more "subordinated" mortgage. Creditors are well protected under this arrangement.

---

*In practice, there is often very little difference between the collateral backing of bonds and debentures. For example, the 9.75-percent debentures due in 1994 of Lake Ontario Cement Ltd. are secured by a first mortgage on the firm's manufacturing facility in Picton; by a floating charge on substantially all other property, plant, and equipment of the company; and by a pledge of the shares of the firm's U.S. subsidiaries.

After-Acquired Clauses   Many mortgages, especially open-end mortgages, contain an *after-acquired clause.* This clause provides that all real property subsequently acquired be added to the property already pledged as security under the first mortgage. The clause in effect protects the claim of current mortgage holders by giving them a lien on any additional property acquired by the firm.

Table 21.2   Summary of Characteristics and Priority of Claim of Bonds

Bond type	Characteristic	Priority of lender's claim
I. Unsecured		
Debentures	Only credit-worthy firms can issue them.	Claims are same as those of any ordinary unsecured creditor. May have other unsecured bonds subordinated to them.
Subordinated debentures	Claims are not satisfied until those of the creditors holding certain (senior) debts have been fully satisfied. Convertible bonds are normally subordinated debentures.	Claim is that of ordinary unsecured creditor but not as good as senior debt claim.
Income bonds	Payment of interest required only when earnings are available from which to make such payment. Often issued in rehabilitation of a failed or failing firm.	Claim is that of an ordinary unsecured creditor. Not in default when interest payments are missed since they are contingent only on earnings being available.
II. Secured		
Mortgage bonds	Secured by a specific or blanket lien on real property. Can be open-end (other bonds can be issued against collateral), limited open-end (a specified amount of additional bonds can be issued against collateral), or closed-end. May contain an after-acquired clause (property subsequently acquired becomes part of mortgage collateral).	Claim on proceeds from sale of mortgaged assets; if not fully satisfied, they become an ordinary unsecured creditor. The first-mortgage claim must be fully satisfied prior to distribution of proceeds to second-mortgage holders, and so on. A number of mortgages can be issued against the same collateral.
Collateral trust bonds	Secured by shares and/or bonds that are owned by the issuer. Collateral value is generally 25–35% greater than bond value.	Claim on proceeds from share and/or bond collateral; if not fully satisfied, they become ordinary unsecured creditors.
Equipment trust certificates	Used to finance "rolling stock"—airplanes, trucks, boats, railroad cars. A mechanism whereby a trustee buys equipment with funds raised through the sale of trust certificates and then leases the asset to the firm. After the final scheduled lease payment, the lessee receives title to the asset. It is a type of leasing.	Claim is on proceeds from sale of asset; if proceeds do not satisfy outstanding debt, trust certificate holders become ordinary unsecured creditors.

Collateral Trust Bonds   If the security held by a trustee consists of shares and/or bonds of other companies, the secured bonds issued against this collateral are called *collateral trust bonds*. Since the assets of *holding companies* generally consist of shares and bonds of their subsidiaries, holding companies are the primary issuers of collateral trust bonds.* Many of these bonds provide for the substitution of fixed assets as collateral as long as a predefined collateral premium over the amount borrowed is maintained. The value of the collateral generally must be 25–35 percent greater than the value of the bonds it supports.

Equipment Trust Certificates   Equipment trust certificates are commonly used to finance equipment, when obsolescence is not an important consideration. These certificates are used by transportation companies, such as railroads, airlines, and truck lines, to finance their "rolling stock"—planes, trucks, or boats. To obtain the equipment, a down payment of 20–25 percent is made by the purchaser (borrower) to the trustee, which is normally a trust company. To raise the additional funds required to purchase the equipment from the manufacturer, the trustee sells certificates, primarily to financial institutions. The purchaser makes periodic lease payments to the trustee, which then pays dividends to the trust certificate holders. The trust certificates mature serially and are retired by the trustee, using the balance of the lease payments. The final lease payment is used to retire any remaining certificates. After the final payment, the trustee passes title of the equipment to the borrower. The annual lease payment to the trustee is set to cover the cost of dividends, retiring certificates, and the expenses of the trust in each period of the trust agreement's life. Institutional investors find trust certificates as attractive an investment as senior secured debt for the following reasons: First, the equipment pledged is essential to the borrower's (lessee's) business; second, the pledged equipment can be easily transferred to another lessee, even in the event of the present lessee's insolvency, since the pledged equipment is owned by the trustee; and third, the risk and consequences of default decrease over time, since the ratio between the value of the pledged collateral and the value of the certificates outstanding increases over time. Although discussed in this chapter, it should be clear that equipment trust certificates are essentially a form of leasing.

International Borrowings[4]

For many firms and most levels of government in Canada, the bond market is international. Therefore, when considering possible bond markets, these borrowers have to consider the differences in interest rates and yield curves between different bond markets.

When issuing bonds in non-Canadian capital markets, the borrower must determine

---

*A *holding company* is a corporation having a controlling interest in one or more other corporations. In order to maintain this controlling interest, ownership of between 10 and 25 percent of the outstanding shares of a firm is normally required. A discussion of holding companies is included in Chapter 25.

the currency or currencies in which the debt is to be denominated. The debt can either be denominated in the firm's domestic currency (referred to as a *domestic-pay bond*) or in a foreign currency (referred to as a *foreign-pay bond*). For a Canadian issuer, a domestic-pay bond is a bond that is denominated in Canadian dollars; and a foreign-pay bond is a bond that is denominated in a non-Canadian currency (that is, a bond on which principal and interest payments must be made in non-Canadian currency). Foreign investors generally require a higher interest rate on domestic-pay bonds than on foreign-pay bonds, since on the former the investor bears the exchange-rate risk for the borrower.

The borrower must also decide whether it wants to sell debt on the larger and more active Eurobond market or on the foreign bond market. The *Eurobond market* is based in Europe and consists of foreign-pay bonds denominated in a currency or currencies other than the domestic currency of the investor or borrower. For example, a Canadian firm could sell Eurobonds denominated in U.S. dollars to French, German, and Italian investors. The *foreign bond market* consists of foreign-pay bonds denominated in the currency of the investor. For example, a Canadian firm could sell foreign-pay bonds denominated in Swiss francs to Swiss investors.

A firm issuing foreign-pay bonds must weigh the anticipated advantages and disadvantages of such a decision. The two major advantages are greater access to funds; and anticipated interest rate savings, after adjusting for anticipated shifts in exchange rates, due to a lower interest rate in the foreign market. The major disadvantage is that adverse movements in exchange rates may substantially increase the actual amount of Canadian dollars needed to service the interest payments and to repay the bond principal (face value). Remember, on a foreign-pay bond, the *borrowing company bears the exchange rate risk.* As noted in the following example, a firm with foreign (export) sales can reduce exchange rate risks by borrowing in the foreign currencies in which its sales are transacted.

EXAMPLE   In January 1980, Bombardier Inc., a Quebec-based manufacturer of snowmobiles, announced that it had finalized a bond issue on the Swiss financial market for 21 million Swiss francs (about 15.4 million Canadian dollars at the then current exchange rates). The bonds were due on July 31, 1992, and carried a 5.75-percent interest rate. (At that point in time, Government of Canada bonds, with approximately the same term-to-maturity, were offering a yield-to-maturity of approximately 12.9 percent!) According to the management of Bombardier, "Borrowing in Swiss currency gives Bombardier the advantage of a low interest rate." Furthermore, the anticipated rise in the value of the franc would be "partly offset by the fact that Bombardier, through its operations in Austria, trades in Austrian shillings, a currency that closely follows the rate of exchange of the Swiss franc."

Bond Refunding Options

A firm wishing to refund a bond prior to maturity has two basic options. Both require some foresight on the part of the issuer. Each of these options is discussed next.

SERIAL ISSUES

The borrower can issue *serial bonds*, a certain proportion of which come due each year. When serial bonds are issued, a schedule showing the yields, interest rates, and prices associated with each maturity is given. An example would be a $30 million, 20-year bond issue for which $1.5 million of the bonds mature each year. The interest rate associated with the shorter maturities would, of course, be lower than the rates associated with the longer maturities. Although serial bonds cannot necessarily be retired at the option of the issuer, they do permit the issuer to refund the debt over its life. Not only does this type of bond have appeal to the firm, it also can attract purchasers, since such an issue offers a variety of yields and maturities from which the investor can select.

REFUNDING BONDS BY EXERCISING A CALL PRIVILEGE

If interest rates drop after the issuance of a bond, the issuer may wish to refund the bond and issue new bonds at the lower interest rate. If a call feature has been included in the bond issue, the issuer can easily retire it. The desirability of such an action is not necessarily obvious, but can be determined by a type of cost-benefit analysis using present-value techniques. Before proceeding to an example, a few tax-related points should be clarified.

Bond Discounts and Premiums   If the new bonds are sold, or the old bonds were sold, at either a *discount* (i.e., for less than their face value) or a *premium* (i.e., for more than their face value), then the tax effects of such discounts or premiums must be included in the refunding evaluation. If the issue price and the coupon rate of a bond issue meet certain provisions stipulated in the income tax act,* then the firm can deduct all of the bond discount during the year in which the bond principal is *repaid*; otherwise, the firm is only allowed a partial deduction during the year in which the bond principal is repaid.†

Call Premiums   The amount by which the call price exceeds the face value of the bond is the *call premium*. It is paid by the issuer to the bondholder in order to buy back outstanding bonds prior to maturity. The call premium is not a tax-deductible expense in Canada, since it is considered a capital expense.

Flotation or Issuing Costs   In Canada, commissions, bonuses, or discounts paid to an underwriter are not a tax-deductible expense. Issue costs that are tax-deductible include the legal, accounting, and printing costs that are incurred *directly* by the issuer in preparing the issue.‡ These issue costs are allowable as a deduction for tax purposes during the year that they are incurred by the issuer.

---

*These provisions are designed to discourage firms from issuing bonds with "deep" discounts from their face value (that is, bonds with extremely low coupon rates). If the firm was permitted to deduct the full amount of the discount for tax purposes during the year of issue, "deep" discounting would in effect allow the issuing firm to take much of the total tax deductions associated with interest payments at the date of issue, instead of over the life of the bond.

†There are situations (such as serial bonds) when principal payments are made over a period of years. In such situations, the bond discount must be prorated for tax purposes.

‡For more specific information, refer to the Federal Income Tax Act.

EXAMPLE   The Flaherty Company Ltd. is contemplating calling $30 million of 30-year, $1,000 bonds that were issued 5 years ago at a coupon rate of 9 percent. The bonds have a call price of $1,090 and initially were sold at a discount of $30 per $1,000 bond. (Assume that the total discount is tax-deductible.) The initial flotation cost was $360,000 ($100,000 of which was tax-deductible). The Flaherty Company intends to sell $30,000,000 of 7-percent, 25-year bonds in order to have sufficient proceeds for retiring the old bond issue.* The firm intends to sell the new bonds at their face value of $1,000. The flotation costs on the new issue are estimated to be $440,000 ($140,000 of which is tax deductible). The firm is currently in the 40-percent tax bracket and estimates its after-tax cost of debt to be 5 percent.† The firm expects to need a 4-month overlap period, during which both the new and old bonds will be outstanding. The overlap period occurs because the new bonds are usually sold 1 or more months before the old bonds are redeemed, to avoid the consequences of a sudden adverse movement in interest rates. During the overlap period, interest must be paid on both the old and new bonds. Neither bond issue has a sinking-fund requirement.‡

The first step is to calculate the incremental initial outlay, or initial investment, involved in implementing the proposed plan. Table 21.3 presents the calculations required, which indicate that the Flaherty Company must pay out $3,264,000 now in order to implement the refunding plan. The second step in the analysis is to determine the annual cash savings that will result from the new bond. The annual cash savings are the same for the first 24 years. They differ in year 25 because the discount on the old bond is tax deductible during that year. Table 21.4 shows how the annual savings are calculated by subtracting the annual cash outflows of the new bond from the annual cash outflows of the old bond. The new bond results in cash savings of $360,000 per year for the first 24 years, and a cash saving of $0 in year 25.

The final step in the analysis is to compare the initial outlay of $3,264,000 required to retire the old bond and issue the new bond to the annual cash savings resulting from the issuance of the new bond. Because of the difference in the timing of these cash flows, the present value of the 24-year annuity of $360,000, and the present value of the cash saving of $0 in year 25 must be found using the after-tax cost of debt. (The *after-tax cost of debt* is used since the alternatives are equally risky contractual—not guaranteed—obligations that have very low risk.§ The same logic was used in Chapter 20 in the lease-purchase decision.) The present value of the $360,000 24-year annuity, discounted at 5 percent, is $4,967,640 (i.e., 13.799 · $360,000); the present value

---

*To simplify the analysis, the maturity of the new bonds has been set equal to the number of years to maturity remaining on the old bonds. The interested reader is referred to more advanced texts for a discussion of the situation in which new and old bonds have unequal maturities remaining.

†Ignoring any flotation costs, the firm's after-tax cost of debt would be 4.2 percent {i.e., [7% debt cost · (1 − .40 tax rate)]}. In order to reflect the flotation costs associated with selling new debt, the use of an after-tax debt cost of 5 percent was believed to be the applicable discount rate. A more detailed discussion of techniques for calculating a firm's after-tax cost of debt can be found in Chapter 17.

‡If a sinking-fund requirement existed, then the sinking-fund payments would have to be included in the analysis.

§Although a great deal of controversy surrounds the appropriate discount rate, the after-tax cost of debt is used to evaluate the bond refunding proposal because the decision itself involves the choice between two contractual alternatives having very low risk. If we were deciding whether a new bond should be sold—not making a refunding decision—the appropriate risk-adjusted rate, or cost of capital, would be used. In the bond refunding decision, we are only attempting to evaluate a possible replacement for an existing financing instrument. This is a very low-risk decision.

Table 21.3   Calculating the Incremental Initial Outlay for the Flaherty Company

Initial cash outflows	
Cost of calling old bonds ($1,090 · 30,000)	$32,700,000
Cost of issuing new bonds	440,000
Interest on old bonds during overlap period	
$(.09 \cdot \frac{4}{12} \cdot \$30,000,000)$	900,000
Total cash outflows	$34,040,000

Initial cash inflows	
Proceeds from new bond	$30,000,000
Tax shields[a]	
Cost of issuing new bonds (.40 · $140,000)	56,000
Discount on old bond ($900,000 · .40)	360,000
Overlapping interest	
$(.09 \cdot \frac{4}{12} \cdot \$30,000,000 \cdot .40)$	360,000
Total cash inflows	$30,776,000
Incremental initial outlay	$3,264,000

[a]These are treated as a cash inflow, although they actually represent a negative cash outflow.

Table 21.4   Calculating the Annual Cash Flows for the Flaherty Company

	Annual cash outflow	
Old bond	Years 1–24	Year 25
Annual interest (.09 · $30,000,000)	$2,700,000	$2,700,000
Less: Tax savings[a]		
Interest (.09 · $30,000,000 · .40)	($1,080,000)	($1,080,000)
Bond discount (year 25 only) ($900,000 · .40)	–	($360,000)
Annual cash outflows with old bond	$1,620,000	$1,260,000
New bond		
Annual interest (.07 · $30,000,000)	$2,100,000	$2,100,000
Less: Tax savings[a]		
Interest (.07 · $30,000,000 · .40)	($840,000)	($840,000)
Annual cash outflows with new bond	$1,260,000	$1,260,000
Annual cash flow savings from new bond	$360,000	0

[a]Tax savings are treated as cash inflows because of the tax shield they provide.

of the cash saving of $0 in year 25, discounted at 5 percent, is $0 (i.e., 0.295 · $0). The present value of the cash savings is thus $4,967,640 (i.e., $4,967,640 + $0). A comparison of the present value of the cash savings of $4,967,640 to the initial outlay of $3,264,000 shows that there is a net saving of $1,703,640 (i.e., $4,967,640 − $3,264,000). Since a net cash savings does result, the proposed refunding plan is recommended.*

Since the bond refunding is advantageous to the firm, it must be disadvantageous to the old bondholders. If the current yield on the new bonds is 7 percent, and the old bond issue has a 9-percent coupon rate, then the market value of the old bonds would have increased so that they also yield 7 percent. Unfortunately for the old bondholders, the firm, by using the call premium, forces the old bondholders to sell the old bonds at a value (the call price) that is less than the bond's current market value. In addition, if the proceeds of such a forced sale are to be reinvested in bonds of equivalent risk, then the coupon rate on the new bonds will be lower than that which was offered on the old bonds. This example illustrates the disadvantages of the call feature to bondholders. It also illustrates why a callable bond, with the same default risk and term-to-maturity as a noncallable bond, should be priced so that it provides a higher yield than the noncallable bond.

The analytical approach illustrated for bond refunding decisions can be applied to all refunding problems. Certain modifications may be required, but the basic process of finding the incremental initial outlay and annual cash flow savings and comparing the present value of the savings to the initial outlay in order to make the decision is always the same.

Summary

This chapter has discussed the various characteristics and types of long-term debt financing available to the business firm. Certain standard and restrictive loan provisions are common to all long-term borrowing arrangements. The standard provisions are generally concerned with the maintenance of satisfactory accounting records, the rendering of financial statements, the payment of obligations, the repair and maintenance of assets, and the sale of accounts receivable. Restrictive provisions are generally concerned with working capital minimums, the disposition of fixed assets in the event of liquidation, subsequent borrowing, financial lease commitments, business combinations, executive salaries, management, security investments, the disposition of loan proceeds, and dividend payments. The intention of all loan provisions is to protect the lender by permitting it to break the loan agreement and demand immediate repayment when the firm's financial position appears to be weakening as indicated by a violation of one or more loan provisions.

*Although the refunding operation would be profitable at this point in time, it may be *more* profitable to delay its implementation. For example, if interest rates are expected to decline further, a delay in the refunding operation may be desirable. In deciding whether or not to delay the implementation of the refunding operation, a financial decision maker must use a forecast of the distribution of future rates of interest at various future points in time.

The cost of long-term loans is normally higher than the cost of short-term borrowing. The difference depends on future interest rate expectations, the loan's maturity, the loan's size, and the riskiness of the borrower. Generally the key factor differentiating the rates on loans that have the same term-to-maturity is the financial position (standing) and risk of the borrower.

Long-term loans generally require quarterly, semiannual, or annual installment payments. Some loans provide for balloon payments at maturity; others require that sinking-fund payments be made to retire the loan. Term loans may be unsecured or secured; secured term loans are normally collateralized with fixed assets. Some term lenders require share purchase options, which give them an opportunity to take an equity interest in the borrowing company. These loans can be obtained directly from a number of financial institutions. Generally, Canadian chartered bank loans have a term of 5 years or less and carry a variable interest rate; while insurance company loans have terms of 10–15 years and carry a fixed interest rate.

Project financing is important for the financing of large energy and energy-related projects, since the required financing of these projects generally far exceeds the financial capacity of any single firm. The debt portion of a project financing is generally an off-balance sheet financing. If provided on a nonrecourse basis, then the lender must rely *solely* on the cash flows and earnings generated by the project for loan servicing, and on the assets of the project in case of loan default.

Bonds, which are certificates carrying a promise to pay interest and principal at specified future dates, are issued by businesses. The agreement under which the bond is issued is called an indenture, and the enforcement of the indenture is placed in the hands of a trustee. Bonds are typically in $1,000 denominations and may have long maturities. Many bonds have a conversion feature, a call feature, or share purchase warrants attached. Bonds, with either a retractable or extendible feature, allow the bondholder to alter the maturity date of the bond held. The yield-to-maturity of a bond is fixed at the time a bond is purchased. The holding-period yield, for a holding-period that is shorter than the bond's term-to-maturity, will depend upon the bond's market value (and thus interest rates) at the point at which the bond is sold by the bondholder. Bonds are sold through either private placements or public offerings; investment dealers are quite active in public offerings. Bond ratings, which are issued by independent companies such as Moody's, Standard & Poor's, and the Canadian Bond Rating Service, are important indicators of the risk of a proposed or existing bond. The higher the risk the lower the rating, and therefore the higher the interest cost, and vice versa.

Bonds may be unsecured or secured. Unsecured bonds are referred to as debentures. Some debentures are subordinated to other types of debt. Income bonds are another type of unsecured bond that pays interest only when earnings are available. The types of secured bonds include mortgage bonds, collateral trust bonds, and equipment trust certificates. The mortgage bond is the most common type of secured bond.

When issuing bonds, many firms must first compare the interest rates and yield curves in domestic and international bond markets. If a firm decides to issue bonds in a nondomestic capital market, it must then decide on the currency or currencies in which the bonds are to be denominated. If the bonds are denominated in a currency other than the issuer's domestic currency, then the issuer bears the exchange-rate risk for the lender.

Bond refunding is an important consideration for a firm. When serial bonds are issued, the refunding is on a planned basis since the bonds' maturities are originally set so as to provide for their orderly retirement. The inclusion of a call feature in a bond allows the issuer to refund a bond prior to maturity. Refunding is done when there is a drop in interest rates great enough to provide savings that are greater than the costs of calling the old bonds and issuing new bonds. Analytical techniques using present values should be used in making bond refunding decisions. The basic approach involves comparing the present value of the annual savings (discounted at the after-tax cost of debt) with the initial outlay required to initiate the refunding. The key variables considered include issue costs, discounts and/or premiums, interest, interest overlaps, and the call premium. A variety of tax adjustments are also required. If the present value of the savings exceeds the initial outlay, the refunding is made; otherwise it is rejected.

Questions

21.1 Why is long-term debt an important component of a firm's capital structure? What are the two key methods of raising long-term debt?

21.2 How do long-term debts differ from current liabilities? When will a long-term debt be reclassified as a current liability?

21.3 What motive does the lender have for including certain restrictive provisions in a loan agreement? How do these covenants differ from the so-called standard loan provisions?

21.4 What sort of working capital requirements are specified in loan agreements? What protection are they intended to provide for the long-term lender?

21.5 What sort of restrictions on fixed assets are included in loan agreements? How do these restrictions affect the liquidation, acquisition, or encumbrance of fixed assets?

21.6 What sort of negotiation process is required in settling on a set of restrictive covenants? What generally are the consequences of violation of a standard or restrictive loan covenant?

21.7 What is the general relationship between the cost of short-term and long-term borrowing? Why are long-term rates generally higher than short-term rates? How may interest rate expectations affect financing decisions?

21.8 How do the financial riskiness of the borrower and the size of a loan affect the cost of long-term financing? How is the actual cost of funds determined?

21.9 What types of interest and principal payment dates are generally associated with a term loan agreement? What are balloon payments? How do they differ from lump-sum payments?

21.10 What types of collateral are commonly used as security for term loans?

21.11 What is project financing? How does a lender evaluate whether or not it will provide the nonrecourse term loan portion of a project financing?

21.12 What sort of maturities, denominations, interest payments, and types of purchasers are associated with a typical corporate bond?

21.13 What is a bond indenture? What role does a trustee play with respect to a bond indenture?

21.14 What does it mean if a bond has a conversion feature? A call feature? Warrants?

21.15 What does it mean if a bond has a retractable feature? An extendible feature?

21.16   How may a primary bond issue be sold? Which method is more expensive? How are bonds rated, and why?

21.17   What are the basic types of unsecured bonds? What can happen to the subordinated-debt holder in the instance of bankruptcy?

21.18   How may a mortgage bond be secured? What are the various types of mortgage bonds? What is an after-acquired clause?

21.19   What are domestic-pay bonds and foreign-pay bonds? What are the Eurobond market and the foreign-bond market?

21.20   What two options may be available to a firm wishing to retire an outstanding bond issue prior to maturity? Must these options be provided for in advance of issuance? Why might the issuer wish to retire a bond prior to maturity?

21.21   What are (a) bond discounts and premiums and (b) call premiums?

Problems

21.1   Thompson and Thompson have $25 million of debentures currently outstanding; $15 million are straight debentures and the remaining $10 million are subordinated. The firm has recently become bankrupt; the assets have been liquidated for $15 million and there are $15 million of ordinary unsecured creditor claims.
a.   Determine how much of the $15 million will be distributed to each creditor.
b.   Calculate the percentage of each debt recovered by each creditor.
c.   Explain why debenture holders may permit the issuance of only subordinate debt when the firm raises new capital.

21.2   The Shoestring Company Ltd. currently has $10 million of unsecured debt outstanding. The unsecured debt has the following components:

Debt		Amount	Subordinated
Ordinary unsecured creditors' claims	.5	$1,000,000	No
Debenture A	1	2,000,000	No
Debenture B	1.5	3,000,000	No
Debenture C		2,000,000	Yes, to debenture A
Debenture D	1	2,000,000	Yes, to debentures A and B
Total		$10,000,000	

The firm has just become bankrupt and has no secured debt outstanding. The liquidation of the firm has produced $5 million.
a.   Determine the amount each debt holder would have gotten if all the creditors had been ordinary unsecured creditors.
b.   Given the actual nature of the firm's indebtedness, how much money, if any, will each creditor receive?
c.   Determine the percentage of claims recovered by each creditor, given the actual nature of the firm's indebtedness.
d.   Discuss the advantage to debenture holders of subordinating subsequent indebtedness.

21.3   For each of the bond issues in the next table, calculate the dollar amount of interest that must be paid during the interest overlap period.

Bond	Principal	Coupon rate	Interest overlap period
A	$ 2,000,000	9%	2 months
B	$60,000,000	8%	4 months
C	$40,000,000	10%	3 months
D	$10,000,000	8.5%	4 months
E	$25,000,000	9.5%	1 month

Also calculate the tax shield resulting from the overlapped interest if the firm is in the 40-percent tax bracket.

21.4 For each of the following callable bond issues, calculate the after-tax cost of calling the issue. Each bond has a $1,000 face value; the various issue sizes and call prices are summarized in the table. The firm is in the 40-percent tax bracket.

Bond	Size of issue	Call price
A	8,000 bonds	$1,080
B	10,000 bonds	$1,060
C	6,000 bonds	$1,010
D	3,000 bonds	$1,050
E	9,000 bonds	$1,040
F	13,000 bonds	$1,090

21.5 Chatham Marine Ltd. is contemplating calling an outstanding $30 million bond issue and replacing it with a new $30 million bond issue. The firm wishes to do this in order to take advantage of the decline in interest rates that has occurred since the initial bond issuance. The old and new bonds are described below. The firm is in the 40-percent tax bracket.
Old bonds: The outstanding bonds have a $1,000 face value and a 10-percent coupon rate. They were initially issued five years ago with a 25-year maturity. They were initially sold for their face value of $1,000, and the firm incurred $250,000 in tax-deductible issuance costs. They are callable at $1,060.
New bonds: The new bonds would have a $1,000 face value and an 8-percent coupon. They would have a 20-year maturity and could be sold at their face value. The tax-deductible issuance cost of the new bonds would be $400,000. The firm does not expect to have any overlapping interest.
a. Calculate the after-tax cash inflow from the issuance cost of the new bonds.
b. Calculate the after-tax cash outflow from the call premium required to retire the old bonds.
c. Determine the incremental initial outlay required to issue the new bonds.
d. Calculate the annual after-tax cash savings, if any, expected from the bond refunding and reissue.
e. If the firm has a 5-percent after-tax cost of debt, would you recommend the proposed refunding? Why or why not?

21.6 Lawrence Furniture Ltd. is considering calling an outstanding bond issue of $10 million and replacing it with a new $10 million issue. The firm wishes to do this to take advantage of the decline in interest rates that has occurred since the original issue. The two bond issues are discussed below; the firm is in the 40-percent tax bracket.

Old bonds: The outstanding bonds have a $1,000 face value and a 12-percent coupon rate. They were issued five years ago with a 20-year maturity. They were initially sold at a $20 discount from face value. Total tax-deductible issuance costs were $120,000. The bonds are callable at $1,080.

New bonds: The new bonds would have a 15-year maturity, a face value of $1,000 and a 9-percent coupon rate. It is expected that these bonds can be sold at face value for a tax-deductible flotation cost of $200,000. The firm expects the two issues to overlap for two months.

a. Calculate the incremental initial outlay required to issue the new bonds.
b. Calculate the annual after-tax cash savings, if any, expected from the bond refunding.
c. If the firm uses a discount rate of 6 percent to evaluate its least risky decisions, would you recommend refunding? Explain your answer.

21.7 The Korrect Copy Ltd. is considering the calling of an outstanding bond issue of $14 million and replacing it with a new $14 million issue. The details of both bond issues are outlined below. The firm has a 40-percent marginal tax rate.

Old bond: Korrect's old issue has a coupon rate of 10-percent, was issued six years ago, and had a 30-year maturity. The bonds sold at their $1,000 face value, tax-deductible flotation costs were $120,000, and their call price is $1,080.

New bond: The new issue is expected to sell at face value ($1,000), have a 24-year maturity, and have a tax-deductible flotation cost of $360,000. The firm will have a 3-month period of overlapping interest while it retires the old bond.

a. What is the initial outlay required to issue the new bonds?
b. What are the annual after-tax cash savings, if any, from refunding if:
   (1) The new bonds have an 8.5-percent coupon?
   (2) The new bonds have a 9.0-percent coupon?
c. Construct a table showing the net benefits of refunding under the two circumstances given in **b**, when
   (1) The firm has an after-tax cost of debt of 5 percent.
   (2) The firm has an after-tax cost of debt of 7 percent.
d. Discuss the set(s) of circumstances when the refunding is favourable and when it is not.
e. If the four circumstances were equally probable (i.e., each had .25 probability), would you recommend the refunding? Why or why not?

Notes

1. The particular variable rate used may be subject to change by the borrower over time. For example, Quintette Coal Ltd., an affiliate of Denison Mines Ltd., has a U.S. $5.3-million loan that matures in 1984. The loan bears interest at a variable rate, which can be changed by Quintette from time to time. The choices available to Quintette include the London Interbank Eurodollar market rate, the U.S. base rate, or the Canadian prime rate plus margins (spreads) of up to 0.75 percent.
2. There are a number of excellent basic surveys on the different hypotheses (such as the expectations hypothesis, the market segmentation hypothesis, and the eclectic hypothesis) on the term structure of interest rates. For example, see J. Van Horne, *Functions and Analysis of Capital Market Rates* (Englewood Cliffs, N.J.: Prentice-Hall, 1970), chap. 4.
3. For a more extensive discussion of project financing, the reader is referred to Larry Wynant, "Essential Elements of Project Financing," *Harvard Business Review* (May–June 1980), pp. 165–173.
4. For a more extensive discussion of this topic, refer to K. Stroetmann, *The Theory of Long-Term International Capital Flows and Canadian Corporate Debt Issues in the United States* (Unpublished Ph.D. Dissertation, University of British Columbia, May 1974); and P. Lusztig and B. Schwab, "Units of Account and the International Bond Market," *Columbia Journal of World Business,* (Spring 1975), pp. 74–79.

Suggested Readings

Ananthanarayanan, A. L. and Eduardo S. Schwartz, "Retractable and Extendible Bonds: The Canadian Experience," *Journal of Finance* 35 (March 1980), pp. 31–47.

Ang, James S., "The Two Faces of Bond Refunding," *Journal of Finance* 30 (June 1975), pp. 869–874.

Bierman, Harold, "The Bond Refunding Decision," *Financial Management* 1 (Summer 1972), pp. 22–29.

Black, Fischer and John C. Cox, "Valuing Corporate Securities: Some Effects of Bond Indenture Provisions," *Journal of Finance* 31 (May 1976), pp. 351–367.

Boot, John C. G. and George M. Frankfurter, "The Dynamics of Corporate Debt Management, Decision Rules and Some Empirical Evidence," *Journal of Financial and Quantitative Analysis* 7 (September 1972), pp. 1957–1966.

Bowlin, Oswald D., "The Refunding Decision: Another Special Case in Capital Budgeting," *Journal of Finance* 21 (March 1966), pp. 55–68.

Brown, Bowman, "Why Corporations Should Consider Income Bonds," *Financial Executive* 35 (October 1967), pp. 74–78.

Cox, John C., Jonathan E. Ingersoll, Jr., and Stephen A. Ross, "An Analysis of Variable Rate Loan Contracts," *Journal of Finance* 35 (May 1980), pp. 389–403.

Dobell, R. and T. Sargent, "The Term Structure of Interest Rates in Canada," *Canadian Journal of Economics* (February 1969), pp. 65–77.

Dyl, Edward A. and Michael D. Joehnk, "Sinking Funds and the Cost of Corporate Debt," *The Journal of Finance* (September 1979), pp. 887–893.

Emery, Douglas R., "Overlapping Interest in Bond Refunding: A Reconsideration," *Financial Management* 7 (Summer 1978), pp. 19–20.

Fullerton, D. *The Bond Market in Canada* (Toronto: Carswell, 1962).

Handorf, William C., "Flexible Debt Financing," *Financial Management* 3 (Summer 1974), pp. 17–23.

Johnson, Rodney and Richard Klein, "Corporate Motives in Repurchases of Discounted Bonds," *Financial Management* 3 (Autumn 1974), pp. 44–49.

Karna, Adi S., "The Cost of Private versus Public Debt Issues," *Financial Management* 1 (Summer 1972), pp. 65–67.

Kraus, Allan, "The Bond Refunding Decision in an Efficient Market," *Journal of Financial and Quantitative Analysis* (December 1973), pp. 793–806.

Laber, Gene, "Repurchase of Bonds Through Tender Offers: Implications for Shareholder Wealth," *Financial Management* 7 (Summer 1978), pp. 7–13.

Litzenberger, Robert H. and David P. Rutenberg, "Size and Timing of Corporate Bond Flotations," *Journal of Financial and Quantitative Analysis* 8 (January 1972), pp. 1343–1359.

Lusztig, P. and B. Schwab, "Units of Account and the International Bond Market," *Columbia Journal of World Business* (Spring 1975), pp. 74–79.

Mayor, Thomas H. and Kenneth G. McCoin. "The Rate of Discount in Bond Refunding," *Financial Management* 3 (Autumn 1974), pp. 54–58.

Morris, James R., "On Corporate Debt Maturity Strategies," *Journal of Finance* 31 (March 1976), pp. 29–37.

Ofer, Aharon, R. and Robert A. Taggart, Jr., "Bond Refunding: A Clarifying Analysis," *Journal of Finance* 32 (March 1977), pp. 21–30.

Peters, R., *Economics of the Canadian Corporate Bond Market* (Montreal: McGill–Queens University Press, 1971).

Pinches, George E., "The Role of Subordination and Industrial Bond Ratings," *Journal of Finance* 30 (March 1975), pp. 201–206.

Reilly, Frank K. and Michael D. Joehnk, "The Association Between Market-Determined Risk Measures for Bonds and Bond Ratings," *Journal of Finance* 31 (December 1976), pp. 1387–1402.

Riener, Kenneth D., "Financial Structure Effects of Bond Refunding," *Financial Management* 9 (Summer 1980), pp. 18–23.

Sibley, A. M., "Some Evidence on the Cash Flow Effects of Bond Refunding," *Financial Management* 3 (Autumn 1974), pp. 50–53.

Stroetmann, Karl, *The Theory of Long-Term International Capital Flows and Canadian Corporate Debt Issues in the United States* (Unpublished Ph.D. Dissertation, University of British Columbia, 1974).

Van Horne, James C., "A Linear-Programming Approach to Evaluating Restrictions Under a Bond Indenture or Loan Agreement," *Journal of Financial and Quantitative Analysis* 1 (June 1966), pp. 68–83.

Van Horne, James C., *Functions and Analysis of Capital Market Rates* (Englewood Cliffs, N.J.: Prentice-Hall, 1970), Ch. 4.

Weingartner, H. Martin, "Optimal Timing of Bond Refunding," *Management Science* (March 1967), pp. 511–524.

White, William L., "Debt Management and the Form of Business Financing," *Journal of Finance* 29 (May 1974), pp. 565–577.

Wynant, Larry, "Essential Elements of Project Financing," *Harvard Business Review* (May-June 1980), pp. 165–173.

Zinbarg, Edward D., "The Private Placement Loan Agreement," *Financial Analysts Journal* 31 (July-August 1975), pp. 33–35.

Chapter 22

COMMON AND PREFERRED SHARES

This chapter is devoted to the two *traditional* classifications of externally generated sources of equity capital—common and preferred shares.* The major internally generated source of equity capital, retained earnings, will be discussed in Chapter 24.

Chapters 17 and 18 discussed the firm's cost of capital and capital structure. The cost of capital discussion indicated that common shares are generally a more expensive after-tax source of financing for a firm than preferred shares, because investors generally perceive a common share investment as being more risky than a preferred share investment. The discussion of capital structure emphasized the need for an equity base, which is large enough to allow the firm to raise the sufficient low-cost debt to build an optimal capital structure.

This chapter is divided into four major sections. The first section discusses the characteristics, sale, values, advantages, and disadvantages of common shares. The second section presents the basic rights, special features, advantages, and disadvantages of preferred or preference shares. The third section examines the mechanics and use of share rights. The final section discusses why firms issue more than one type of financial security.

Common Shares

The true owners of a business firm are the common shareholders. They invest their money in the firm because of their expectations for future returns. A common shareholder is sometimes referred to as a *residual owner*, since in essence he or she receives

---

*Although the terms *share* and *stock* are used interchangeably, *share* is the preferred Canadian term.

what is left after all other claims on the firm's income and assets have been satisfied. It is the common shareholder's wealth that the firm's management should strive to maximize. Since the common shareholder has a very risky residual claim, he or she expects to be adequately compensated in terms of dividends and capital gains.

This section of the chapter discusses the characteristics of common shares, the sale of common shares, the basic values of common shares, and some of the chief advantages and disadvantages of common share financing.

CHARACTERISTICS OF COMMON SHARES

An understanding of the basic characteristics of common shares is essential to understand the nature of common share financing. Thus, in this section we shall discuss authorized, issued, and outstanding shares; par value; claims on income and assets; maturity; voting rights; right to examine company books and records; preemptive right; share repurchases; and classified common shares.

Authorized, Issued, and Outstanding Shares The maximum number of common shares that a firm is *authorized* to issue is specified in the firm's articles of incorporation. Since the approval of current shareholders is needed to increase a firm's authorized share position, firms generally attempt to authorize more shares than they currently plan to issue. This must be tempered by the fact that registration fees are based on the number of shares authorized.

After authorized shares have been sold by the firm, they become *issued. Outstanding* shares are the number of shares actually held by shareholders. The number of shares issued and outstanding for a firm will differ only when the firm has repurchased some of its shares. In that case, the number of shares outstanding will be less than the number issued. Repurchased shares are referred to as *treasury shares.* The amount of treasury shares is therefore found by subtracting the number of outstanding shares from the number of shares issued.

Par Value Common shares have historically been authorized with or without a par value. When common shares have had a par value, the value has generally been an arbitrary low value (such as $1 per share). If par value shares, with the exception of mining shares, are sold or issued for less than their par value, then the shares are *not* fully paid and are assessable. This means that the owners of the shares during a bankruptcy can be legally assessed an amount equal to the difference between the par value and the price initially paid for the shares. Under the current Federal Business Corporations Act, par value is no longer allowed. In addition, many firms have amended their articles to change their par value shares into shares without par value.* The accounting entries resulting from the sale of common shares that have a par value can be illustrated by a simple example.

---

*For example, at the annual general meeting of Denison Mines Ltd. held on February 9, 1979, a resolution to amend the articles of the company to change each of the company's shares with a par value of $1 into four shares without par value was approved by the shareholders.

EXAMPLE   The Clark Company Ltd. has issued 1,000 common shares of $2 par value, receiving proceeds of $50 per share. This results in the following entries on the firm's books.

Capital stock	
Authorized—2,000 shares with $2 par value	
Issued and fully paid—1,000 shares	$ 2,000
Contributed surplus	48,000
Shareholders' equity	$50,000

Firms are usually prohibited legally from distributing any of their contributed surplus as dividends.*

Claims on Income   Common shareholders have *no legal claim* to share in the earnings of a corporation until all the claims of all creditors, the government, and preferred shareholders have been satisfied; and the firm's board of directors have declared a cash dividend. If the firm's board of directors decides not to declare a cash dividend, then the only recourse available to common shareholders is to attempt to change the composition of the board of directors. If the firm's board of directors decides to declare a cash dividend, certain owners may have preference to dividends over other owners. Most corporations pay dividends quarterly as a result of the quarterly dividend meeting of the board of directors. Dividends may be paid in cash, shares, or merchandise. Cash dividends are most common, and merchandise dividends are least common. A firm's ability to make cash dividend payments may be constrained due to its cash position or certain loan covenants. Share splits, which have some similarity to share dividends, are sometimes used to supposedly enhance the trading activity of a share. The common shareholder is not promised a dividend, but he or she grows to expect certain dividend payments from the historical dividend pattern of the firm.

Because of the great importance of the dividend decision to the growth and valuation of the firm, Chapter 24 is devoted solely to a discussion of dividends and retained earnings.

Claims on Assets   Common shareholders not only have no guarantee of receiving dividends, but they are also not guaranteed anything in the event of forced liquidation. When the firm becomes bankrupt, the firm's assets are liquidated and the proceeds are distributed first to secured creditors, then to preferred creditors, then to ordinary unsecured creditors, then to deferred creditors, then to preferred shareholders, and finally to common shareholders.† Since the liquidation value of the firm's assets is generally below their book value, the common shareholders rarely receive the book value of their equity in the event of bankruptcy.

---

*The various legal and internal considerations regarding the payment of cash dividends are discussed in detail in Chapter 24. A firm can pay out more dollars in cash dividends than it earns in a given period if sufficient cash and retained earnings are available.

†The various procedures followed in bankruptcy proceedings are described in Chapter 26.

Maturity   Unlike most debt, common equity is a permanent form of financing.* It does not mature, and therefore the firm is not required to repay the initial amount invested in the common equity. Holders of common equity are able to liquidate their holding fairly easily if the equity is traded publicly. Even equity in closely held private corporations can be sold, although the process of finding a suitable buyer may be more difficult than in the case of large publicly held firms. Since equity has an infinite life, unless the firm is liquidated, the price that can be realized on a sale of common shares will fluctuate with the level of the firm's current and expected future prospects and risk.† Thus, the overall returns to common shareholders are generally quite risky.

Voting Rights   Generally, each common share entitles the holder to one vote in the election of directors or in other special elections.‡ Votes are generally assignable and must be cast at the annual shareholders' meeting. *Nonvoting common shares* can be issued when the firm's present owners wish to raise capital through the sale of common shares, but do not want to give up any voting power. When this is done, the common shares will be classified. A discussion of classified shares will be undertaken later in this section of the chapter. Three aspects of voting require special attention—proxies, majority voting, and cumulative voting.

Proxies   Since most small shareholders often cannot attend the annual meeting to vote their shares, they may sign a proxy statement giving their votes to another party. The solicitation of proxies from shareholders is closely controlled by the applicable provincial securities and companies acts. More specifically, management is required to provide shareholders with an information circular that contains specific information for soliciting proxies. The information circular must also be filed with the applicable securities commission. There are two reasons for these regulatory requirements. First, if proxy solicitation was completely controlled by management, there is a possibility that proxies would be solicited on the basis of misinformation and that incompetent management would self-perpetuate by using the resources of the firm to solicit proxies. Second, if it is too easy for minority shareholders to replace management, then there is the possibility that such groups will gain control of the corporation in order to temporarily reap personal benefits. The existing management generally receives the shareholders' proxies, since it is able to solicit them at company expense. Occasionally, when the ownership of the firm is widely disseminated, outsiders may attempt to gain control by waging a *proxy battle*. This requires soliciting a sufficient number of votes to unseat the existing management. To win a corporate election, votes from a majority of the shares voted— not outstanding—is required. Proxy battles generally occur when the existing manage-

---

*Perpetual debt is a notable exception.

†The market price of a firm's publicly traded shares *may* be affected not only by *fundamental* factors such as the firm's current and expected future prospects, but also by a number of *technical* and *behavioural* factors. These technical and behavioural factors include the time of the year and investor confidence.

‡It should be noted that if a company is a constrained share company, then the total number of shares that can be registered and voted by any one shareholder is limited. Canada Trustco Mortgage Company is an example of such a company.

ment is performing poorly; however, the odds of a nonmanagement group winning a proxy battle are generally slim.

Majority Voting   In the majority voting system, each shareholder votes for each position on the board of directors separately, and each shareholder is permitted to vote all of his or her shares for *each* director he or she favours. The directors receiving the majority of the votes are elected. It is impossible for minority interests to select a director under this system. An example will clarify this point.

EXAMPLE   The Baker Company Ltd. is in the process of electing three directors. There are 1,000 shares outstanding of which management controls 60 percent. The management-backed candidates are A, B, and C; the minority candidates are D, E, and F. By voting its 600 shares (60 percent of 1,000) for *each* of its candidates, management can elect A, B, and C. The minority shareholders, with only 400 votes for each of their candidates, cannot elect any directors. Management's candidates will receive 600 votes each, and the other candidates will receive 400 votes each.

Cumulative Voting   The Federal and Ontario Acts permit the use of a cumulative voting system to elect corporate directors, provided such provisions are included in the firm's articles or bylaws. Other acts, such as those in British Columbia and Alberta, do not prohibit such a voting system. The cumulative voting system gives a number of votes equal to the number of directors to be elected to each common share. The votes can be given to *any* director(s) the shareholder desires. The advantage of this system is that it provides the minority shareholders with an opportunity to elect at least some directors.

EXAMPLE   The Able Company Ltd., like the Baker Company Ltd., is in the process of electing three directors. In this case, however, each common share entitles the holder to three votes, which may be voted in any manner desired. Again, there are 1,000 shares outstanding, and management controls 600. It therefore has a total of 1,800 votes (3 · 600), while the minority shareholders have 1,200 votes (3 · 400). In this situation, the minority shareholders can select at least one director, if they give all their votes to one of their candidates.

A commonly cited formula for determining the number of shares necessary to elect a certain number of directors, *NE*, is given by Equation 22.1:

$$NE = \frac{O \cdot D}{T + 1} + 1 \tag{22.1}$$

where
      NE = the number of shares needed to elect a certain number of directors
        O = the total number of common shares outstanding
       D = the number of directors desired
       T = the total number of directors to be elected

Substituting the values in the example above for O and T and letting $D = 1, 2$, and 3 yields values of NE equal to 251, 501, and 751. Since the minority shareholders control only 400 shares, they can elect only one director. However, even with cumulative voting, certain election procedures, such as staggered terms for directors, can be used to prevent minority representation on a firm's board of directors. Also, the majority shareholders may control a large enough number of shares and/or the total number of directors to be elected may be small enough to prevent minority representation.

Right to Examine Company Books and Records   Although shareholders are legally entitled to examine specific books and records of the firm (such as the shareholder register), most firms discourage the exercise of such a right by shareholders. In fact, many corporate managements feel that the information disseminated by the corporation, such as the annual report, totally fulfills the shareholders' information requirements.

Preemptive Right   A *preemptive right* gives a firm's existing common shareholders the right to purchase a specified maximum number of shares of a new issue. The maximum number of shares that can be purchased by each existing shareholder is the same percentage of the new issue as the shareholder's present shareholding is of the firm's total number of shares outstanding. Thus, when new share issues are made by a firm, the preemptive right permits existing shareholders to maintain their proportionate voting control; it also protects against the dilution of their proportionate residual claims to the firm's earnings and assets.

Unlike the practice in the United States, there is no preemptive right in Canada, unless such a right has been specified in the issuer's articles of incorporation. The Federal, Ontario, and Alberta Acts permit the inclusion of a preemptive right in a corporation's articles of incorporation; the B.C. Act permits the inclusion of a preemptive right in a firm's articles for public companies, and requires it for private companies; and the current Canadian Bank Act requires the inclusion of the preemptive right in the articles of the chartered banks.

Share Repurchases   As stated earlier, shares that have been repurchased by a firm are called *treasury shares*. Firms occasionally repurchase shares in order to change their capital structure or to increase the returns to the owners. Since the effect of repurchasing common shares is similar to that of the payment of cash dividends to shareholders, share repurchases are given in-depth coverage in Chapter 24.

Classified Common Shares   Common shares are generally perfect substitutes; that is, one share has the same rights as any other share. When shares are grouped into classes (or *classified*), shares of different classes are no longer perfect substitutes, since they are different in terms of such factors as voting rights and/or the type of dividend they will receive.[*] In Canada, the class with preference is more properly

---

[*]Prior to December 31, 1978, firms were permitted to pay *tax-deferred dividends* from their tax-paid undistributed surplus. Since the right to pay this type of dividend expired, many firms have simplified their share structure. For example, Canada Trustco had two classes of common shares outstanding— Class A and Class B. The shares were freely convertible one into the other and were identical in all

referred to as *preferred* or *preference shares*. Preferred shares will be discussed in greater detail in the next major section of this chapter. The complexity involved with classified common shares is illustrated in the following example.

EXAMPLE   Reed Shaw Osler Ltd. is a firm that provides insurance brokerage and risk management services internationally. The firm has a share capital structure that consists of three classes of common shares—Classes A, B, and C. Each share in each class is entitled to one vote. Each Class B share may be converted at any point in time into one Class A share. Each Class C share may be converted into two Class B shares, if a new Class A share is issued by the company, or if the company should dispose of all or a substantial part of its assets (or undertakings), or if a takeover bid is made to the holders of the Class A shares. Class A and Class B shares are entitled to the same per-share dividend; Class C shares are entitled to twice the per-share dividend paid on a Class A or B share. However, dividends paid on the special preferred shares of A. R. Stenhouse & Partners Ltd. (a subsidiary of Reed Shaw Osler Ltd.) reduce the dividends paid on the Class B and C shares.

SALE OF NEW COMMON SHARES

New common share issues can be placed privately by the firm or through some type of share option or share purchase plan. Since these placement methods were discussed in Chapter 19, further discussion is not included here. New issues of common shares can also be placed publicly through an investment dealer or rights offering. An investment dealer is commonly used in situations in which rights offerings are not required or are unsuccessful. Although the sale of common shares through an investment dealer is generally more expensive than a private placement, the investment dealer does provide a convenient mechanism for selling new common shares. Since a detailed discussion of the functions, organization, and operation of the investment dealer in selling corporate securities was presented in Chapter 19, further discussion is not included here. Rights offerings will be discussed in a subsequent section of this chapter.

BASIC VALUES OF COMMON SHARES

The value of a common share may be measured in a number of ways. It has a book value, a liquidation value, a market value, and a theoretical or intrinsic value. The book value and the liquidation value do not reflect the value of the firm as a going concern. The book value measures the firm's common share value as the per-share amount of common share equity recorded on the firm's balance sheet. The liquidation value is calculated by taking the *market* value of the firm's assets, subtracting its liabilities and the claims of preferred shareholders from this figure, and dividing the result by the number of common shares outstanding.

---

rights except that the Class B shares received tax-deferred dividends. After seeking and receiving approval of a supplementary letters patent, Canada Trustco reclassified all its outstanding Class A and Class B common shares into one class of common shares on March 28, 1979.

Intrinsic value is the value that is justified based on the firm's current operations and *future* prospects. This value depends upon investors' anticipated returns and perceived risk from investing in such a firm. One accepted method of determining the intrinsic value of a common share is to use a common share valuation model, such as calculating the present value of all future per-share dividends expected over the firm's assumed infinite life. Refer to Chapter 17 for an in-depth discussion of this approach. Another accepted method of calculating the intrinsic value is to use the capital asset pricing model. Refer to Chapters 16 and 17 for an in-depth discussion of this concept.

ADVANTAGES AND DISADVANTAGES OF COMMON SHARES

Some of the basic advantages and disadvantages of common share financing are discussed below.

Advantages   The basic advantage of common shares stems from the fact that they are a source of financing that places a minimum of constraints on the firm. Since dividends do not have to be paid on common shares and their nonpayment does not jeopardize the receipt of payment by other security holders, common share financing is quite attractive. The fact that common shares have no maturity, thereby eliminating any future repayment obligation, also enhances the desirability of common share financing.

Another advantage of common shares over other forms of long-term financing is their ability to increase the firm's borrowing power. The more common shares the firm sells, the larger the firm's equity base and therefore the more easily and cheaply long-term financing can be obtained.

Disadvantages   The disadvantages of common share financing include the potential *dilution* of voting power and earnings. Only when rights are offered and exercised by their recipients can this be avoided. Of course, the dilution of voting power and earnings resulting from new issues of common shares may go unnoticed by the small shareholder.

Another disadvantage of common share financing is its high cost. Chapter 17 indicated that the after-tax cost of common equity is generally greater than the after-tax cost of debt or preferred shares. If one were to disregard the tax-deductible feature of interest, the cost of common equity financing would still be generally higher than the cost of debt financing. The firm must compensate suppliers of common equity more than suppliers of debt (or preferred shares), because the suppliers of common equity take a higher risk due to their secondary (residual) claim on the firm's income and assets. Although common equity is generally more costly, all business firms are initially capitalized with some common equity, and continual increases in common equity are generally necessary for a firm to grow and mature.

Preferred Shares

The term *preferred share* is not used in either the Federal or Ontario Business Corporations Acts. As discussed earlier, if a firm has two or more classes of shares, then the classes that have greater preferences or rights over the class with the least preferences or rights are properly referred to as preference shares. Thus, the legally oriented and traditional definitions of preferred shares differ somewhat. Traditionally, preferred shares refer to those *classes* of shares that are *nonvoting* under normal circumstances and have *certain privileges* or rights that make the claims of their holders senior to the claims of common shareholders but junior to the claims of bondholders.

Firms generally do not issue large quantities of preferred shares. The ratio of the dollar value of all classes of preferred shares to the dollar value of a firm's total capital position is normally quite small. Preferred shareholders are promised a fixed periodic return, which is stated either as a percentage or in dollars. In other words, 5-percent preferred shares or $5 preferred shares can be issued. The way the dividend is stated depends on whether or not the preferred share has a par value. Unlike common shares, preferred shares often have a par value. Such a value is relevant since the value determines the amount that preferred shareholders are entitled to in the event of liquidation. Generally, the annual dividend is stated as a percentage on par-value preferred shares and in dollars on *no-par* preferred shares. A 5-percent preferred share with a $100 par value is expected to pay $5 (5 percent of $100) in dividends per year.

BASIC RIGHTS OF PREFERRED SHAREHOLDERS

The basic rights of all classes of preferred shareholders with respect to voting, the distribution of earnings, and the distribution of assets are somewhat more favourable than the rights of common shareholders. Since preferred shares are a form of ownership and generally have no maturity date, their claims on income and assets are junior to those of the firm's creditors.

Voting Rights Preferred shareholders have many of the characteristics of both creditors and owners. Because preferred shareholders are promised a fixed periodic return similar to the interest paid creditors, but do not generally expect to have their invested capital repaid by the firm at a maturity date, they are often considered a *quasi-debt* supplier. The fixed return characteristic of debt coupled with the permanent nature of the preferred share investment suggest a *hybrid* type of security. Since the preferred share investment is generally permanent, it does not represent ownership; but because the preferred shareholders' claim on the firm's income is fixed and takes precedence over the claim of common shareholders, they do not expose themselves to the same degree of risks as common shareholders. Preferred shareholders are therefore not normally given the right to vote.

The Distribution of Earnings If the stated preferred share dividend is *passed* (i.e., not declared) by the board of directors, the payment of dividends to common shareholders is prohibited. It is this preference in dividend distributions that makes common shareholders the true risk takers regarding expected returns. Generally, preferred shares are *not* issued unless the directors are reasonably certain that funds will be available to pay preferred share dividends. This ensures that there is at least a possibility that some earnings will be distributed as dividends to common shareholders.

The Distribution of Assets   Although the preferred shareholders must wait until the claims of all creditors have been satisfied, their claims are normally given preference over those of the common shareholders. The amount of the claim of a class of preferred shareholders in liquidation proceedings is normally equal to the par or stated book (or liquidation) value of that class of preferred shares. If a firm desires to issue a class of preferred shares that has a higher priority than that on an existing class of preferred shares, then the firm must first obtain the approval of all the preferred shareholders of all junior classes and then must create a new class of preferred shares.

TREATMENT IN FINANCIAL ANALYSIS

Since preferred shares are a hybrid type of security, they can be considered as being equity or debt in a financial analysis. If the financial analysis is being undertaken by a lender, preferred shares are generally considered to be equity, because the claims of debtholders are senior to the claims of preferred shareholders. If the financial analysis is being undertaken by a common shareholder, preferred shares are generally considered to be debt, because like debt they are a leverage-inducing source of funds.

SPECIAL FEATURES OF PREFERRED SHARES

A number of features are generally included as part of a preferred share issue. These features, along with a statement of the share's par value, the amount of dividend payments, the dividend payment dates, and certain restrictive covenants, are specified in an agreement similar to a long-term loan agreement or bond indenture. Some of these features are discussed below.

Preferred Share Covenants   The restrictive covenants commonly found in a preferred share issue are aimed at assuring the continued existence of the firm and, most important, the regular payment of the stated preferred share dividends. Some of the more common covenants are discussed next.

Passing Preferred Dividends   Since the directors of the corporation make preferred dividend payment decisions, there may be a provision stating that if preferred share dividends are passed for a certain number of quarters (assuming quarterly payments are required), the preferred shareholders are entitled to elect a certain number of directors until the payment of preferred dividends resumes.

The Sale of Senior Securities   A preferred share issue may prohibit the issuance of any additional securities senior to the preferred shares or any additional preferred shares. The issuance of additional common shares is not viewed negatively by preferred shareholders, since the added funds are raised without impairing the preferred shareholders' claims on earnings and assets. If a clause does not prohibit new issues of debt and preferred shares, there may be a constraint on the amount of new funds that can be raised with senior securities.

Acquisitions, Amalgamations, and Sale of Assets   Often, preferred share issues prohibit the firm from combining with any other firm, or from selling all or a portion of the firm's assets. These actions may change the firm's asset and capital structures in a fashion believed to be detrimental to the interest of preferred shareholders.*

Working Capital Requirements   Working capital requirements similar to those for long-term debt are not uncommon in preferred share issues. The firm may be required to maintain a minimum amount of net working capital or a minimum current ratio. The motive for this requirement is to cause the firm to maintain sufficient liquidity to perpetuate itself over the long run.

Dividends and Share Repurchases   Preferred share issues may prohibit or limit the amount of common share cash dividends or common share repurchases the firm can make in any year. The reason for this prohibition is to ensure that the firm maintains adequate cash to provide a continuing stream of preferred share dividends.

The violation of restrictive covenants usually permits the preferred shareholders to force the retirement of their shares at their stated value plus a possible premium. When the firm defaults, the initiative is placed in the hands of the preferred shareholder.

Cumulation   Most preferred shares are *cumulative* with respect to any dividends passed.† That is, all dividends in arrears must be paid prior to the payment of dividends to common shareholders. (The arrearages, however, earn no return.) If preferred shares are *noncumulative*, passed dividends do not accumulate and only the most recent dividend must be paid prior to distributing earnings to common shareholders. A simple example may help clarify the distinction between cumulative and noncumulative preferred shares.

EXAMPLE   The Morgan Company Ltd. currently has outstanding an issue of $6.00 preferred shares on which quarterly dividends of $1.50 are to be paid. Due to the cash shortage, the last two quarterly dividends were passed. The directors of the company have been receiving a large number of complaints from common shareholders, who have of course not received any dividends in the past two quarters either. If the preferred shares are cumulative, the company will have to pay the preferred shareholders $4.50 per share ($3.00 of dividends in arrears plus the current $1.50 dividend) prior to paying out any earnings to the common shareholders. If the preferred shares are noncumulative, the firm will have to pay only the current $1.50 dividend to the preferred shareholders prior to paying out funds to the common shareholders. This example should make it quite clear why most preferred share issues are cumulative and why the dividends on cumulative preferred shares are normally paid when they are due.

---

*In other words, if a firm were to combine with or acquire a firm that had very high levels of debt, the post-combination firm would have more debt claims that are senior to the preferred shareholders' claims; therefore, the preferred shareholders would be in a more risky position with respect to the distribution of income and assets than they were prior to the combination.

†Most preferred shares are cumulative since it is difficult to market noncumulative shares. The common shareholders will obviously prefer noncumulative preferred to be issued since it does not place them in quite as poor a position, but they must recognize that it is often in the best interest of the firm to raise needed funds by selling cumulative preferred shares.

Participation   Most issues of preferred shares are *nonparticipating*, which means that the preferred shareholders receive only the required dividend payments. Occasionally, *participating* preferred shares are issued. This type of preferred share provides for dividend payments based on certain formulas that allow the preferred shareholders to participate with common shareholders in the receipt of dividends beyond a specified amount.

Series Provisions   Generally, the terms and features of a class of preferred shares cannot be changed by a firm unless the firm receives the approval of the shareholders of that class. Unfortunately, capital market conditions change over time. As a result, terms and features that were once attractive to investors may no longer be attractive to new investors. By using a series provision, a firm can avoid the cost and time delay of obtaining shareholder approval for changes in the terms and features of an existing class of preferred shares.

The series provision operates as follows. For a given class of preferred shares, there is an authorized amount of share capital, and all shares within the class have the same overall creditor position. As the firm decides to issue more authorized shares from the class, each issue becomes a series with its own designation, terms, and features. The series provision is best illustrated by an example.

EXAMPLE   Canada Trustco has a class of cumulative redeemable preference shares, with a $20.00 par value, which are issuable in series. As of December 31, 1979, the company had the following series outstanding:

	Shares	Amount
Authorized	4,862,591	$97,252,000
Issued and fully paid		
Series A—$8\frac{3}{4}$%	312,059	6,241,000
Series B—$7\frac{1}{4}$%, convertible	1,478,955	29,579,000
Series C—$7\frac{3}{4}$%, convertible	53,014	1,061,000
Series D—floating %, retractable	1,250,000	25,000,000
Series E—floating %, retractable	750,000	15,000,000
	3,844,028	$76,881,000

The dividend rates on Series A, B, and C are as given above. The dividend rate on Series D and E is adjusted quarterly and, expressed on a per-annum basis, is equal to the sum of (1) one-half of the average bank prime rate, and (2) 1.25 percent. Each series has separate terms and conditions respecting redemption, conversion, retraction, and purchase for cancellation. These features for Series B are given as follows: (1) redemption—June 1, 1979, at $20.87 reducing annually by $0.145 to $20.00 at June 1, 1985, and thereafter; (2) conversion—convertible into common shares at the option of the holder at a conversion price of $26.51 per common share at any time on or prior to May 31, 1985, or at any time prior to 10 days before the date specified for redemption of such shares, whichever is earlier; (3) retraction—not available; and (4) purchase for cancellation—a purchase fund should be established in 1981 and subsequent years. The amount thereof will not exceed $900,000.00 in 1981 and $1,800,000.00 in subsequent years, which funds shall be applied by the company to purchase shares for cancellation in the open market if available, at a price not exceeding the par value thereof plus the costs of purchase.

The Redemption Feature   Preferred shares are often *redeemable* or callable, which means that the issuer can retire outstanding shares within a certain specified period of time at a specified price(s). The redemption or call option generally cannot be exercised until a period of years has elapsed since the issuance of the preferred shares. It also cannot be exercised until all current dividends and all dividend arrearages have been paid by the firm. The redemption price is normally set above the initial issuance price and declines according to a predetermined schedule as time passes (as in the Canada Trustco example above).

The Conversion Feature   Preferred shares quite often contain a conversion feature (as in the Canada Trustco example above) that permits their conversion into a specified number of common shares. Sometimes the conversion ratio or time period for conversion changes according to a prespecified formula. The redemption feature is a useful tool for forcing the conversion of convertible preferred shares. A more in-depth discussion of conversion is presented in Chapter 23.

Retirement, Refinancing, and Recapitalization   There are a number of ways of providing for the retirement of preferred shares either for the purpose of refinancing or in order to recapitalize (i.e., change the capital structure of) the firm.

Planned Retirement   Many issues of preferred shares have a sinking or purchase fund feature, which provides for the gradual redemption of shares at a specified rate over a given period of time. This type of planned retirement makes the preferred shares quite similar to long-term debt—except that if the firm is unable to make a sinking-fund payment for preferred shares, bankruptcy will not result.

Refinancing   By including a redemption or call feature in a preferred share issue, the issuer may be able to replace an outstanding issue with a less expensive form of financing. The shares could be retired by purchasing them outright in the marketplace, but due to the difficulty and expense of this approach, the use of the redemption feature is almost a necessity.

Whether refinancing is justified depends on the present value of the cost of maintaining the preferred shares as opposed to the cost of a new issue of debt, preferred, or common shares. This decision is quite similar to the bond refunding decision discussed in Chapter 21, except for two considerations. First, preferred dividend payments are not tax deductible, and savings on future dividend payments generally accrue in perpetuity.

Recapitalization   A firm may want to retire preferred shares to change its capital structure. This can be accomplished by purchasing the preferred shares in the market, redeeming the preferred shares, or forcing their conversion.

TERM PREFERRED SHARES

As discussed previously, preferred shares generally have no maturity date and have a stated fixed dividend rate. *Term preferred shares* either have a *fixed* maturity date or have a number of provisions designed to *alter* the maturity date or the stated fixed dividend rate. Term preferred shares, which are issued with a fixed maturity date, are similar to bonds of equal term-to-maturity. Term preferred shares that have a retraction feature are very similar to a retractable bond. A retraction feature gives the holder of the preferred shares an (put) option to sell the preferred shares to the issuer at par value at some specified future date.* Term preferred shares, which are issued with a floating dividend rate, are similar to variable rate term loans (discussed in Chapter 21). They can also be thought of as being similar to preferred shares, which are redeemed and reissued at a new dividend rate on a regular specified schedule. For an example, refer to the previous Canada Trustco example.

The introduction and extensive use of term preferred issues has been a reaction to market conditions of high and uncertain interest and inflation rates. By using the above provisions to reduce the maturities of preferred shares, firms have shifted some of the effects of interest-rate movements and unanticipated inflation from investors to themselves. Thus, with the reduction in investors' exposure to interest-rate and inflation risks, firms can offer lower yields on term preferreds as compared to standard preferred shares.

ADVANTAGES AND DISADVANTAGES OF PREFERRED SHARES

It is difficult to generalize about the advantages and disadvantages of preferred shares due to the various features that may or may not be incorporated in a preferred share issue. The attractiveness of preferred shares is also affected by current interest rates and a firm's existing capital structure. Nevertheless, some key advantages and disadvantages can be discerned.

Advantages   The basic advantages of preferred shares are their ability to increase leverage, the flexibility of the obligation, and their use in business combinations.

Increased Leverage   Since preferred shares obligate the firm to pay only fixed dividends to its holders, its presence helps to increase the firm's financial leverage. The effects of preferred shares on a firm's financial leverage were discussed in Chapter 4. It is the fixed payment obligation of preferred shares that allows the firm's common shareholders to receive increased returns when earnings on total capital are greater than the cost of preferred shares. An example will help to illustrate this point.

EXAMPLE   The Robin Company Ltd. has the following capital structure.

Type of capital	Amount	Percentage of total capital
Long-term debt @ 8%	$ 30,000	30%
Preferred shares @ 10%	30,000	30
Common share equity	40,000	40
Total capital	$100,000	100%

---

*For example, Series D and E of the cumulative redeemable preference shares of Canada Trustco are retractable at the option of the holder at $20 (their par value) on April 1, 1987, and on April 1, 1988, respectively.

In the most recent period, the firm earned $10,000 *before interest and after taxes,* or 10 percent on its total capital. Since the firm is in the 40-percent tax bracket, the after-tax cost of debt is only 4.8 percent [i.e., 8 percent · (1 − .40)].* The firm must therefore pay its long-term creditors $1,440 (.048 · $30,000) and its preferred shareholders $3,000 (.10 · $30,000), leaving $5,560 ($10,000 − $1,440 − $3,000) available for the common shareholders. The return on the common share equity is therefore 13.9 percent ($5,560 ÷ $40,000). The presence of the preferred shares increases the firm's leverage and magnifies the return to the common shareholders since the return on the total capital is greater than the cost of fixed financing.

If the Robin Company had earned the same amount but had $30,000 worth of bonds, no preferred shares, and $70,000 worth of common shares, the earnings available for the common shareholders would have amounted to $8,560 ($10,000 − $1,440). The return on the common share equity would thus have been only 12.2 percent ($8,560 ÷ $70,000). The decreased return to the common shareholders is due to the decreased leverage resulting from the replacement of the $30,000 worth of preferred shares with an additional $30,000 worth of common shares. It should be clear from this example how preferred shares can be used to increase the firm's leverage, thereby magnifying the effects of increased earnings on the common shareholders' returns.

Flexibility   Although a preferred share does provide added leverage in much the same way as a bond, it differs from a bond in that the issuer can pass a dividend payment without suffering the consequences that result when an interest payment is missed.

Use in Business Combinations   Preferred shares have been used successfully to either combine or acquire firms. Often preferred shares are exchanged for the common shares of an acquired firm; the preferred dividend is set at a level equivalent to the historical dividend of the acquired firm. This lets the acquiring firm state at the time of the acquisition that only a fixed dividend will be paid. All other earnings can be reinvested to perpetuate the growth of the combined enterprise. This approach also permits the owners of the acquired firm to be assured of a continuing stream of dividends equivalent to what may have been provided prior to its acquisition. Quite often, preferred shares used for business combinations are convertible. The use of preferred shares in business combinations is discussed in greater depth in Chapter 25.

Disadvantages   The two major disadvantages of preferred shares are the seniority of the holders' claims and the cost of the shares.

Seniority of the Holders' Claims   Since holders of preferred shares are given preference over the common shareholders with respect to the distribution of both earnings and assets, the presence of preferred shares in a sense jeopardizes the common shareholders' returns. Adding preferred shares to the firm's capital structure creates additional claims

---

*Recall from Chapter 17, which was concerned with the cost of capital, that since interest is tax-deductible the after-tax cost of debt to the firm is generally calculated by multiplying the stated cost by 1 minus the tax rate. In this example, since the $10,000 represents earnings measured *before interest and after taxes,* to get earnings *after* interest and taxes, the interest cost times 1 minus the tax rate [interest · (1 − tax rate)] must be subtracted from the earnings before interest and after taxes.

prior to those of the common shareholders. If the firm's after-tax earnings are quite variable, its ability to pay at least token dividends to its common shareholders may be seriously impaired with the addition of preferred shares to the firm's capital structure.

Cost   Historically, the before-tax cost of preferred shares has been higher than the before-tax cost of comparable-grade bonds. This is due to the risk premium desired by investors to compensate for greater risks inherent in preferred shares. One of these risks is introduced by the longer (infinite) term-to-maturity associated with preferred shares. Another of these risks is due to the fact that payment of dividends to preferred shareholders is not guaranteed, whereas interest on bonds is.

Recently, the before-tax cost to the issuer of high-grade preferred shares has been lower than that of high-grade bonds. This is due to the different tax treatment of dividends and interest for investors. While interest is taxed at the investor's marginal tax rate, preferred dividends are tax free for intercorporate dividend payments, and the dividend tax credit makes the effective tax rate on dividends very low for investors in the low marginal tax brackets.* Thus, although the before-tax yield to these investors is lower on preferred shares than on bonds, the after-tax yield is higher on preferred shares than on bonds. Therefore, as expected, the after-tax yield is higher on preferreds due to their higher risk.

The after-tax cost to the issuer of preferred shares is still significantly greater than that of long-term debt. This is due to the fact that interest on long-term debt is tax-deductible, while preferred dividends must be paid from earnings after taxes.

In summary, the desirability of using preferred shares to raise funds depends not only on the firm's current financial structure and the state of the financial markets, but on the trade-offs among the cost, risk, and control of the alternate forms of long-term financing. The firm must weigh the long-run costs and benefits of preferred share financing against the advantages and disadvantages of both long-term debt and common share financing. Consideration must also be given to whether the shares will be cumulative or noncumulative, participating or nonparticipating, callable or noncallable, and convertible or nonconvertible.

Financing with Rights

Rights, which provide certain common share purchase privileges to existing shareholders, are an important tool of common share financing. Without them, a firm's present shareholders run the risk of losing their proportionate interest and control of the corporation. If a preemptive right (discussed previously) is contained in a firm's articles, then the firm must first offer any new common shares to existing shareholders. If the articles contain no preemptive right, then the firm may still decide to attempt to sell the new shares first to existing shareholders. In either case, the share issue will be called a *rights offering*. A *right* is a piece of paper providing its holder with an option to buy a certain portion of a new share. Generally, each existing shareholder receives one right for each share held, and more than one right is required to purchase a new common share. An example may help clarify the use of rights.

*Taxation is discussed in greater detail in Chapter 2.

EXAMPLE   The Maverick Company Ltd. currently has 100,000 common shares outstanding and is contemplating issuing an additional 10,000 shares through a rights offering. Each existing shareholder will receive 1 right per share, and each right will entitle the shareholder to purchase $\frac{1}{10}$ of a new common share (10,000 ÷ 100,000). Therefore 10 rights will be required to purchase 1 common share. The holder of 1,000 shares of existing common equity will receive 1,000 rights, each permitting the purchase of $\frac{1}{10}$ of a share of new common equity. Thus, he or she can purchase 100 new common shares. If the shareholder exercises his or her rights, he or she will end up with a total of 1,100 common shares, or 1 percent of the total number of (110,000) shares outstanding. This is the same proportion the shareholder had prior to the rights offering (i.e., 1,000 ÷ 100,000).

THE MECHANICS OF RIGHTS OFFERINGS

When a company makes a rights offering, the board of directors must set a *holder-of-record date*, which is the last date on which the recipient of a right must be the legal owner indicated in the company's share ledger. Due to the lag in bookkeeping procedures, shares are usually sold *ex rights* (i.e., without rights) two business days prior to the holder-of-record date. Prior to this point, the shares are sold *cum rights* or *rights on*, which means that purchasers of the shares will receive the rights.

The issuing firm sends rights to holders of record, who are free to exercise them, sell them, or let them expire. Rights are transferable, and many are traded actively. They are exercisable for a specified period of time, generally not more than a few months, at a share price, which is called the *subscription price*, set somewhat below the prevailing market price of a share. Since fractions of shares are not always issued, it is sometimes necessary to either purchase additional rights or sell any extra rights. The value of a right depends largely on the number of rights needed to purchase a share and the amount by which the right-subscription price is below the current market price of a share. If the rights have a very low value and an individual owns only a small number of shares, the rights may be permitted to expire.

MANAGEMENT DECISIONS

A firm's management must make two basic decisions when preparing for a rights offering. The first is the price at which the right holders can purchase a new common share. The subscription price must be set *below* the current market price, because this discount gives value to the rights. The size of the discount depends on management's evaluation of the sensitivity of the market to a price change, the degree of dilution in ownership and earnings expected, and the size of the rights offering. In general, the price discount is larger for more volatile shares, since the subscription price must be set so that the rights will be exercised even if there is a drop in the price of the firm's common shares.

Discounts as large as 40 or more percent have been observed, but the typical discount is between 10 and 20 percent. Management generally considers a rights offering as being successful if approximately 90 percent of the rights have been exercised.

Once management has determined the subscription price, it must determine the number of rights required to purchase a share. Since the amount of funds to be raised is known in advance, the subscription price can be divided into the amount of funds to be raised to get the total number of shares that must be sold. Dividing the total number of shares outstanding by the total number of shares to be sold will give management the number of rights required to purchase a share.

EXAMPLE   The Boone Company Ltd. intends to raise $1 million through a rights offering. The firm currently has 160,000 shares outstanding, which have been most recently trading for $53–$58 per share. The company has consulted an investment dealer, which has recommended setting the subscription price for the rights at $50 per share. It believes that at this price the offering will be fully subscribed. The firm must therefore sell an additional 20,000 shares ($1,000,000 ÷ $50 per share). This means that 8 rights (i.e., 160,000 ÷ 20,000) will be needed to purchase a new share at $50. Therefore each right will entitle its holder to purchase $\frac{1}{8}$ of a common share.

THE VALUE OF A RIGHT

Theoretically the value of a right should be the same if the share is selling *with rights on (cum rights)* or *ex rights*. However, the market value of a right may differ from its theoretical value (as discussed next).

With Rights On   Once a rights offering has been declared, shares will trade for only a few days with rights on. Equation 22.2 is used to find the value of a right when the share is trading with rights on, R_o.

$$R_o = \frac{M_o - S}{N + 1} \tag{22.2}$$

where

R_o = the theoretical value of a right when the share is selling rights on

M_o = the market value of the share with rights on

S = the subscription price of the share

N = the number of rights needed to purchase a share

EXAMPLE   The Boone Company's shares are currently selling with rights on at a price of $54.50 per share, the subscription price is $50.00 per share, and eight rights are required to purchase a new share. According to Equation 22.2, the value of a right is $0.50 [($54.50 − $50.00) ÷ (8 + 1)]. A right should therefore be worth $0.50 in the marketplace.

Ex Rights   When a common share is traded ex rights, meaning that the value of the right is no longer included in the share's market price, the share price is expected to drop by the value of a right. Equation 22.3 is used to find the market value of the share trading ex rights, M_e. The same notation is used as in Equation 22.2.

$$M_e = M_o - R_o \tag{22.3}$$

The value of a right when the common shares are trading ex rights, R_e, is given by Equation 22.4.

$$R_e = \frac{M_e - S}{N} \tag{22.4}$$

The use of these equations can be illustrated by returning to the Boone Company example.

EXAMPLE   According to Equation 22.3, the market price of a Boone Company share selling ex rights is $54.00 ($54.50 − $0.50). Substituting this value into Equation 22.4 gives us the value of a right when the common shares are selling ex rights, which is $0.50 [($54.00 − $50.00) ÷ 8]. The theoretical values of the right when the share is selling with rights on or ex rights are therefore the same.

Share-Split Effect   Some financial writers incorrectly maintain that a rights issue is detrimental to existing shareholders because there is a fall in the market price of the shares in the ex rights trading period. As shown above, the market value of the share trading ex rights will fall by the theoretical value of a right, whose value depends upon the difference between the share's rights-on market price and its subscription price. If the two prices are *not* equal, then the right will have a nonzero value, and the market price of the share will fall by the value of the right in the ex rights trading period. However, the combined market value of the right and the common share in the ex rights holding period will not decrease. Thus, as in the case of share splits, rights by themselves do *not* decrease the total market value of an existing shareholder's common equity holding.*

THE MARKET BEHAVIOUR OF RIGHTS

As indicated earlier, rights are negotiable instruments that are publicly traded. The market price of a right will generally differ from its theoretical value, since the holder of a right has a call option on a specified percentage of a firm's common shares. The extent of the difference will depend upon how the firm's share price is expected to behave during the period when the right is exercisable. By buying rights instead of the share itself, investors can achieve much higher returns on their investment when the share's price advances.

UNDER- AND OVERSUBSCRIBED OFFERINGS

Most rights offerings are made through investment dealers, who form a *soliciting dealer group* to facilitate the subscription of shares. For providing this service, the group receives a management fee. Generally, the investment dealer also agrees to a *standby arrangement*, which is a formal guarantee that any shares not subscribed to or sold publicly will be purchased by the investment dealer. This guarantee assures the firm

*Share splits are discussed in Chapter 24.

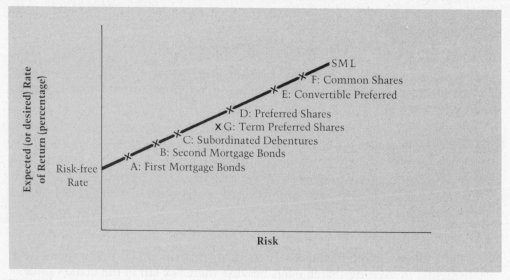

Figure 22.1   Expected rate of return and risk on the various classes of securities of Maple Leaf Co. Ltd.

that the entire issue will be sold; it will not be *undersubscribed.* The investment dealer, of course, requires an additional fee for making this guarantee. Rights offerings may also be made directly by the issuing company.

Most rights offerings include an *oversubscription privilege.* Under this provision, shares not sold, because rights were not exercised, are offered to interested shareholders on a pro rata basis at the stated subscription price. This privilege is a method of restricting ownership to the same group, although ownership proportions may change slightly. Shares that cannot be sold through the oversubscription privilege may be offered to the public. If an investment dealer is used, the disposition of unsubscribed shares may be totally at the dealer's discretion.

Rationale for Various Classes of Securities

In an *efficient* capital market, the various classes of a firm's securities would be priced so that their expected return reflects their level of risk. As was discussed in Chapter 16, the relationship between the expected returns and risks of the various classes of securities of all firms is linear, and is referred to as the security market line (SML). Figure 22.1 provides a graphic representation of the relationship for the various classes of securities of Maple Leaf Co. Ltd. for a one-year holding period.

Since different investors have different risk-return trade-off preferences, most firms offer various classes of securities, which differ in their risk-return characteristics, in order to appeal to as many investors as possible. In addition, by increasing the number of different classes of securities available to investors, a firm may also increase the diversification opportunities that are available to investors.

Figure 22.1 can also be used to illustrate why the management of a firm may issue shares of a class of securities that it believes is presently incorrectly priced by the market.* For example, suppose that management and their investment dealers believe that, since the market has overreacted in its evaluation of the dividend tax credit, the yield on term preferred shares is at present too low—see, for example, point G in Figure 22.1. In such a case, investors appear to be willing to accept an expected return less than that required in an efficient market. Thus, if the financing decision is based solely on relative cost, management should issue term preferred shares.

Summary

Both common and preferred shares are instruments for raising long-term equity funds. Both these securities represent forms of ownership and therefore the payment of dividends is not mandatory. Also, these securities generally have no maturity. Preferred shares are considered a security senior to common shares since the holders of preferred shares are given preference over common shareholders with respect to the distribution of both income and assets. Before dividends are paid or assets are distributed to the common shareholders, the claims of the preferred shareholders must be satisfied. In liquidation proceedings, the claims of preferred shareholders are paid immediately after the creditors' claims have been satisfied.

Common shareholders are the true owners of the firm because they subordinate their claims to those of all other parties. Various voting systems are available for providing minority representation on the firm's board of directors. Purchasers of common shares normally expect to receive some type of dividend; sometimes common shares are repurchased to meet any of a variety of objectives. Holders of common shares often receive a preemptive right that gives them an opportunity to purchase any new common share issues on a pro rata basis in order to maintain their proportion of votes and earnings. When shares are grouped into classes, the classes with preference are more properly referred to as preferred or preference shares. Common shares may be placed directly with the purchaser by the issuer or sold publicly by an investment dealer or by the use of a rights offering. Private placement can also be achieved through the use of share options and/or share purchase plans. The worth of a common share may be judged by its book value, liquidation value, market value, or intrinsic value. The basic advantages of common shares stem from the fact that they are a source of financing that places a minimum of constraints on the firm regarding periodic payments and retirement. Common shares also allow the firm to enhance its borrowing power. Disadvantages often cited for common shares include the potential dilution of voting power and earnings, and the relatively high cost of this form of financing.

Preferred shares are similar to debt in that they have a fixed (but not mandatory) annual payment. Since the preferred shareholder's claims are given preference over the claims of common shareholders, they are exposed to less risk than the common share-

---

*Note that whether or not capital markets are efficient is a very controversial subject when academics and practitioners meet!

holders. Generally, they have no voting privileges. Preferred shares may have certain restrictive covenants similar to those of bond issues. They may also have such features as cumulative dividends, participation in earnings, a series provision, a redemption feature, a conversion feature, and certain retirement options. Term preferred shares either have a fixed maturity date or have a number of provisions designed to alter the maturity date or the stated fixed dividend rate. The basic advantages cited for the use of preferred share financing include its ability to increase leverage, the flexibility of the obligation, and its use in business combinations. Disadvantages include its preference over the common shareholders, who are the firm's true owners, and its relatively high cost.

Rights are used to pass a purchase (call) option to the owners. A certain number of rights are required to purchase shares at a reduced price, which causes the rights to have a value. Rights may be sold, exercised, purchased, or allowed to expire.

In an efficient capital market, the various classes of a firm's securities are priced so that their expected returns reflect their risk levels. This relationship is given by the linear security market line (SML). By offering various classes of securities with different risk-return characteristics, the firm appeals to a greater group of investors.

Questions

22.1   How do debt and equity capital differ? What are the key differences between them with respect to ownership, claims on income and assets, and maturity?

22.2   Why is the common shareholder considered the true owner of a business firm? What risks do common shareholders take that other suppliers of long-term capital do not?

22.3   What is the difference between the number of common shares *authorized* and the number of shares actually *outstanding*? Why are firms likely to authorize more shares than they initially intend to issue?

22.4   What are proxies? How are they used? What are proxy battles, and why are they initiated? Why is it difficult for minority shareholders to win such a battle?

22.5   How do majority and cumulative voting systems differ? Which of these voting systems would be preferred by the small shareholder? Why?

22.6   What are the key advantages and disadvantages of using common share financing as a source of new capital funds?

22.7   What are preferred shares? What claims do preferred shareholders have on the firm's income and assets? How are the dividends on preferred shares stated?

22.8   What are cumulative and noncumulative preferred shares? Which is most common? Why?

22.9   What are participating and nonparticipating preferred shares? How is the degree of participation specified? In what circumstance would you expect participating preferred to be issued?

22.10 What is a redemption feature in a preferred share issue? When and at what price does the redemption usually take place? What benefit does the redemption feature offer the issuer of preferred shares?

22.11 What are the advantages of raising funds through issues of preferred shares? Are there any disadvantages to preferred shares as a source of financing?

22.12 What are share rights? How are they related to preemptive rights? Why might the issuance of share rights on a preemptive basis be an attractive and fast method of raising new equity capital?

22.13 What is the *holder-of-record date* for share rights? What do the terms *ex rights* and *cum rights* or *rights on* mean? Are share rights marketable?

22.14 What is a right subscription price? How is it determined? Given the subscription price, what must the firm know to determine the number of rights to offer?

22.15 How are a firm's various classes of securities priced in an efficient market? Why does a firm have a number of different classes of securities?

Problems

22.1 What accounting entries on the firm's balance sheet would result from the following cases?
a. A firm sells 10,000 shares of $1-par common at $13 per share.
b. A firm sells 20,000 shares of $2-par common and receives $100,000.
c. A firm sells 200,000 shares of no-par common for $8,000,000.
d. A firm sells 14,000 shares of common for the par value of $5 per share.

22.2 Max-an'-Maud's, a fast-food franchise, is electing five new directors to the board. The company has 1,000 shares of common outstanding. The management, which controls 54 percent of the common shares outstanding, backs candidates A–E, while the minority shareholders are backing candidates F–J.
a. If the firm uses a majority voting system, how many directors will each group elect?
b. If the firm uses a cumulative voting system, how many directors will each group elect?
c. Discuss the differences between these two approaches and the resulting election outcomes.

22.3 Determine the number of directors that can be elected by the minority shareholders using (1) majority voting and (2) cumulative voting in each of the following cases.

Case	Number of shares outstanding	Percentage of shares held by minority	Number of directors to be elected
A	140,000	20%	3
B	100,000	40%	7
C	175,000	30%	4
D	880,000	40%	5
E	1,000,000	18%	9

22.4 Sinderson, Schaefer, and Schloff has an outstanding issue of preferred shares with an $80 par value and an 11-percent annual dividend.
a. What is the annual dollar dividend? If it is paid quarterly, how much will be paid each quarter?
b. If the preferred shares are *noncumulative* and the board of directors has passed the preferred dividend for the last three years, how much must the preferred shareholders be paid prior to paying dividends to common shareholders?
c. If the preferred shares are *cumulative* and the board of directors has passed the preferred

dividend for the last three years, how much must be paid to the preferred shareholders prior to paying dividends to common shareholders?

22.5 In each of the following cases, how many dollars of preferred dividends per share must be paid to preferred shareholders prior to paying common dividends?

Case	Cumulative-noncumulative provision	Par value	Dividend per share	Periods for which dividends passed
A	Cumulative	$ 80	$ 5	2
B	Noncumulative	$110	8%	3
C	Noncumulative	$100	$11	1
D	Cumulative	$ 60	8.5%	4
E	Cumulative	$ 90	9%	0

22.6 The Korrect Kan Company Ltd. has outstanding an issue of 3,000 shares of participating preferred shares, having a $100 par value and an 8-percent annual dividend. The preferred shareholders participate fully with common shareholders in dividends of more than $9.00 per share for common shares. The firm has 5,000 shares of common outstanding.

a. If the firm pays the preferred shareholders their dividends and then declares an additional $100,000 of dividends, how much will be the total dividend per share for preferred and common shares, respectively?

b. If the firm pays the preferred shareholders their dividends and then declares an additional $40,000 in dividends, what is the total dividend per share for each type of shareholder?

c. If the firm's preferred shares are cumulative and the past two years' dividends have been passed, what dividends will be received by each type of shareholder if the firm declares a *total* dividend of $30,000?

d. Rework **c** assuming the total dividend payment is $20,000.

e. Rework **a** and **b** assuming the preferred shares are nonparticipating.

22.7 The Great Plains Corporation Ltd. had *earnings before interest and after taxes* of $300,000 last year. The firm has a marginal tax rate of 40 percent, and currently has the following capital structure:

Type of capital	Amount	Percent of capital
Long-term debt @ 10%	$600,000	25%
Preferred shares @ 11%	600,000	25
Common shares	1,200,000	50
Total capital	$2,400,000	100%

a. Calculate the firm's *before-interest and after-tax* return on its total capital.

b. Calculate the firm's after-tax return on common equity.

c. If the firm had raised the $600,000 of preferred share capital through the sale of $600,000 of additional common shares, what would its after-tax return on common equity have been?

d. If the firm had shifted the preferred share financing to debt (at the same 10-percent cost), what effect would this have had on the after-tax return on common equity?

e. Use the answers in **b** through **d** to evaluate the effects of preferred shares on the firm's financial leverage.

22.8 Zesto-Presto Ltd. currently has the following capital structure:

Type of capital	Amount	Percent of capital
Long-term debt @ 10%	$100,000	20%
Preferred shares @ 8%	50,000	10
Common shares	350,000	70
Total capital	$500,000	100%

The firm had earnings *before interest and after taxes* of $80,000 in the past year and has a 40-percent tax rate.

a. What was the firm's after-tax return on common equity?

b. What effect on the after-tax return on common equity would result from a $50,000 shift from long-term debt to preferred shares?

c. What effect on the after-tax return on common equity would result from a $50,000 shift from common equity to preferred equity?

d. What information concerning preferred share leverage is illustrated by **b** and **c**?

22.9 Indicate (1) how many shares one right is worth and (2) the number of shares a given shareholder, X, can purchase in each of the following situations:

Case	Number of shares outstanding	Number of new shares to be issued	Number of shares held by shareholder X
A	900,000	30,000	600
B	1,400,000	35,000	200
C	800,000	40,000	2,000
D	60,000	12,000	1,200
E	180,000	36,000	1,000

22.10 Manitoba Gas Ltd. wishes to raise $1,000,000 in common equity financing using a rights offering. The company has 500,000 outstanding common shares, which have recently traded for $25 to $28 per share. The firm believes if the subscription price is set at $25, the shares will be fully subscribed.

a. Determine the number of new shares the firm must sell in order to raise the desired amount of capital.

b. How many shares will each right entitle a holder of one share to purchase?

c. Reword **a** and **b** assuming the subscription price is $10.

d. What is the theoretical value of a right if the current market price of a share is $27 and the subscription price is $25? Answer for both the *rights-on* and *ex-rights* situations.

e. Rework **d** assuming the subscription price is $10.

f. Which subscription price ($10 or $25) will be more likely to assure complete subscription? Why?

22.11 Determine the theoretical value of a right when the common shares are selling (1) rights on and (2) ex rights in the following cases:

Case	Market value of a share, rights on	Subscription price of one share	Number of rights needed to purchase one share
A	$20.00	$17.50	4
B	$56.00	$50.00	3
C	$41.00	$30.00	6
D	$50.00	$40.00	5
E	$92.00	$82.00	8

22.12   The Flint Paper Corporation Ltd. is interested in raising $600,000 of new equity capital through a rights offering. The firm currently has 300,000 common shares outstanding. It expects to set the subscription price at $25 and it expects that a share will sell for $29 with rights on.

a.   Calculate the number of new shares the firm must sell in order to raise the desired amount of funds.

b.   How many rights will be needed to purchase one share at the subscription price?

c.   Cogburn Jones holds 48,000 common shares of Flint Paper. If he exercises his rights, how many additional shares can he purchase?

d.   Determine the theoretical value of a right when the shares are selling (1) rights on and (2) ex rights.

e.   Approximately how much could Jones get for his rights immediately after the shares go ex rights?

f.   If the holder-of-record date for the Flint Paper Company was Monday, March 15, on what days would the shares sell (1) rights on and (2) ex rights?

Suggested Readings

Bacon, Peter W., "The Subscription Price in Rights Offerings," *Financial Management* 1 (September 1972), pp. 59–64.

Bear, Robert M. and Anthony J. Curley, "Unseasoned Equity Financing," *Journal of Financial and Quantitative Analysis* 10 (June 1975), pp. 311–325.

Bildersee, John S., "Some Aspects of the Performance of Non-Convertible Preferred Stocks," *Journal of Finance* 28 (December 1973), pp. 1187–1202.

Brown, Michael J., "Post-Offering Experience of Companies Going Public," *Journal of Business* (January 1970), pp. 10–18.

Donaldson, Gordon, "In Defense of Preferred Stock," *Harvard Business Review* 40 (July-August 1962), pp. 123–136.

Duvall, Richard M. and Douglas V. Austin, "Predicting the Results of Proxy Contests," *Journal of Finance* 20 (September 1965), pp. 467–471.

Elsaid, Hussein H., "The Function of Preferred Stock in the Corporate Financial Plan," *Financial Analysts Journal* (July-August 1969), pp. 112–117.

Fewings, David R., "The Impact of Corporate Growth on the Risk of Common Stocks," *Journal of Finance* 30 (May 1975), pp. 525–531.

Fowler, David J., C. Harvey Rorke, and Vijay M. Jog, "Heteroscedasticity, R^2 and Thin Trading on the Toronto Stock Exchange," *Journal of Finance* (December 1979), pp. 1201–1210.

Furst, Richard W., "Does Listing Increase the Market Price of Common Stocks?" *Journal of Business* 43 (April 1970), pp. 174–180.

Keane, Simon M., "The Significance of Issue Price in Rights Issues," *Journal of Business Finance* 4 (September 1972), pp. 40–45.

Livingston, Miles, "Industry Movement of Common Stocks," *Journal of Finance* 32 (June 1977), pp. 861–874.

Lynch, J. E., "Accounting for Equity Securities," *Financial Management* 2 (Spring 1973), pp. 41–47.

McDonald, J. G. and A. K. Fisher, "New-Issue Stock Price Behavior," *Journal of Finance* 27 (March 1972), pp. 97–102.

McQuillan, P., *Going Public in Canada* (Toronto: Canadian Institute of Chartered Accountants, 1971).

Nelson, J. Russell, "Price Effects in Rights Offerings," *Journal of Finance* 20 (December 1965), pp. 647–660.

Pinches, George E., "Financing with Convertible Preferred Stock, 1960–1967," *Journal of Finance* 25 (March 1970), pp. 53–63.

Reilly, Frank K., "A Three Tier Stock Market in Corporate Financing," *Financial Management* 4 (Autumn 1975), pp. 7–16.

Shaw, David, "The Allocation Efficiency of Canada's Market for New Equity Issues," *Canadian Journal of Economics* (November 1969), pp. 546–556.

Sprecher, C. Ronald, "A Note on Financing Mergers with Convertible Preferred Stock," *Journal of Finance* 26 (June 1971), pp. 683–686.

Stevenson, Richard A., "Retirement of Non-Callable Preferred Stock," *Journal of Finance* 25 (December 1970), pp. 1143–1152.

Thompson, Howard E., "A Note on the Value of Rights in Estimating the Investor Capitalization Rate," *Journal of Finance* 28 (March 1973), pp. 157–160.

White, R. W. and P. A. Lusztig, "The Price Effects of Rights Offerings," *Journal of Financial and Quantitative Analysis* 15 (March 1980), pp. 25–40.

Ying, Louis, Wilbur Lewellen, Gary Schlarbaum, and Ronald Lease, "Stock Exchange Listings and Securities Returns," *Journal of Financial and Quantitative Analysis* (September 1977), pp. 415–432.

Chapter 23

CONVERTIBLE SECURITIES AND WARRANTS

The last two chapters discussed a number of financial instruments used in raising long-term funds externally. They discussed term loans, bonds, preferred shares, and common shares, emphasizing primarily the general characteristics of each of these financing sources. In this chapter, we shall focus on two optional features of security issues—conversion options and share purchase warrants.

Both conversion features and warrants allow the firm to shift its future capital structure automatically. The conversion feature, which may be attached to either a bond or preferred share, permits the firm's capital structure to be changed without increasing the total financing. Share purchase warrants may be attached to a long-term debt, a bond, a preferred share, or a common share. They permit the firm to raise added funds at some point in the future by selling common shares.

The use of warrants shifts the firm's capital structure toward a less highly levered position since new equity capital is obtained. Both conversion features and warrants are commonly used today as sweeteners to issues of shares or bonds. Thus, by utilizing these features, a firm can finance at a lower interest or dividend rate in exchange for giving new investors potentially valuable options. Thus, a firm must evaluate the cost-benefit trade-off of offering such options. Both convertible securities and warrants may be listed and traded on organized security exchanges and over the counter.

The major goal of this chapter is to present the key characteristics and considerations the financial manager must be aware of when contemplating the use of convertible securities or warrants as part of a financing package. The chapter has four major sections. The first section discusses the basics of option theory. The second discusses the characteristics of convertible securities, the motives for their issuance, and other managerial considerations. The third section discusses the various values that can be assigned to convertible securities. The final section is devoted to the general characteristics and values of share purchase warrants.

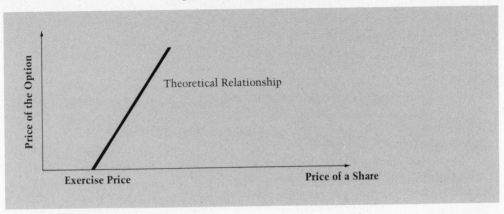

Figure 23.1   Theoretical value of an option.

• Options

Convertible securities, warrants, and rights (which were discussed in Chapter 22) are all types of options. An *option* can be defined as a contract that gives its holder the right to buy or sell an underlying asset on or before a specified expiry date. Since the basics of option markets were discussed in Chapter 19, this section will concentrate on the valuation of options. For ease of exposition, we shall concentrate on call options, where the underlying asset is a common share.

THE RELATIONSHIP BETWEEN THE VALUES OF THE OPTION AND THE UNDERLYING ASSET

The theoretical relationship between the value or price of a call option and the value or price of a common share is given by the 45-degree line in Figure 23.1. Whenever the exercise price of the option is greater than or equal to the underlying share's market price, the option has a theoretical value of zero. Whenever the exercise price of the option is less than the underlying share's market price, the option's theoretical value is simply derived by subtracting the exercise price of the option from the share's market price.

The market value of a "live" (unexpired) option will be equal to or greater than its theoretical value. That is, an option's market value may be positive, even if the underlying share's present market price is less than the option's exercise price, provided that there is some possibility that the price of the share will exceed the exercise price of the option before expiration of the option.

As depicted in Figure 23.2, the market price of an option also depends upon the time remaining to expiration. In general, the longer the time remaining to expiration, the greater the value of the option relative to its theoretical value, since there is more time

•While we feel that all students of finance should be exposed to the basics of option pricing, this section is not essential in the comprehension of subsequent sections of this chapter.

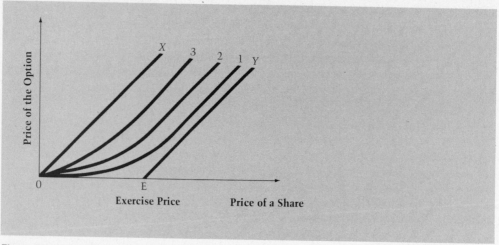

Figure 23.2   Relationship between the prices of the option and the underlying asset for various option expiration dates.

for the option to have value. The minimum or *floor value* of an option is given by line OEY in Figure 23.2. It is the option's theoretical value. As noted above, the theoretical value is the value of an option with only a moment before expiration. The maximum value of an option is given by line OX in Figure 23.2. It is the market value of the underlying asset. This value characterizes a perpetual option that will not be exercised prior to maturity. Thus, the market value of the option approaches the market value of the underlying asset, since the present value of the exercise price approaches zero as the time horizon becomes more distant.

The pricing relationship for most options is concave and lies between these two boundaries. When the time remaining to expiration is short (for example, line 1 in Figure 23.2), the relationship plots near the lower (minimum-value) boundary; when the time remaining to expiration is long (for example, line 3 in Figure 23.2), the relationship plots near the upper (maximum-value) boundary. The relationship is concave because of the leverage associated with purchase of an option. Since the purchase of an option requires a lower investment than purchase of the underlying asset, the percentage change in the option's market value will be greater than that for the underlying asset. Furthermore, the largest relative percentage change will occur when the price of the underlying asset is near the option's exercise price. Since the possibilities for large percentage gains decrease as the base price increases, higher option prices will reduce leverage opportunities. This, in turn, will reduce the spread between an option's market and floor values.*

An option's market value is also affected by three other factors—the variability in the price of the underlying asset, changes in the payments by the firm to holders of the underlying asset, and changes in interest rates. Thus, a greater variability in the price of the underlying asset will increase the market value of an option; while an increased cash payout on the underlying asset (e.g., dividend per share) will decrease an option's market

*This is similar to what happens to operating leverage. See Chapter 4 for more details.

value. Changes in relative proportions of the capital gain and dividend components of total return on the underlying asset will affect the value of the option, since the option's value depends upon the capital gain component of a security's total return. An increase in interest rates should increase an option's market price, since the present value of the future exercise price (that is, the cost of exercising the option) decreases as the interest rate increases.

EQUILIBRIUM VALUE OF AN OPTION

If an option or the underlying asset are "incorrectly" priced in the market, investors have an opportunity to earn a *riskless excess profit* by arbitrage. By taking a long position in the underlying asset and a short position in options, an investor can form a riskless hedge. The hedge is riskless because movements in the value of the long position will be completely offset by movements in the short position. As in all arbitrage arguments, investors who take such positions will influence relative prices so as to eliminate all excess returns.

Thus, in equilibrium, Black and Scholes have shown that the expected return on a fully hedged position of common shares and options should equal the risk-free rate in an efficient capital market.[*][1] The Black-Scholes model is an extremely important advance in the literature because of its theoretical importance for evaluating various contingent claim assets.[†] Since all such securities are combinations of basic option contracts, a theory of option pricing may lead to a general theory of contingent claims pricing. This, in turn, could lead to a unified theory that would explain the pricing of a firm's liabilities, the term structure of interest rates, and the theory of speculative markets.

Based on this very general discussion of option pricing, we now examine two specific types of options frequently used by business firms as financing sweeteners—the con-

---

[*]Black and Scholes have shown that the equilibrium value of a call option, w, is given by

$$w = x\,N(d_1) - ce^{-rt}N(d_2)$$

where

x = the current price of a common share
c = the exercise price of the option
r = the short-term interest rate
t = the time remaining to the expiration of the option
$N(d)$ = the value of the cumulative normal density function
$$d_1 = \frac{ln\,(x/c) + (r + 1/2\sigma^2)t}{\sigma\sqrt{t}}$$
$$d_2 = \frac{ln\,(x/c) + (r - 1/2\sigma^2)t}{\sigma\sqrt{t}}$$
ln = the natural logarithm
σ^2 = the variance rate of return on the common share

They also have shown that the equilibrium value of a put option, u, is given by

$$u = ce^{-rt}\,N(-d_2) - x\,N(-d_1)$$

[†]A contingent claim asset is an asset whose value (payoff) at any particular point in time is contingent (dependent) upon the particular value (outcome) that occurs for its underlying asset. For example, the theoretical value of a call option at any particular point in time is contingent upon the value of its underlying common share.

vertible security and the warrant. However, note that, because of its complexity, we will not show how the Black-Scholes model is used to value either convertible securities or warrants.*

Characteristics of Convertible Securities

A *conversion feature* is an option included as part of either a bond or preferred share issue. It permits the holder of the bond or share to convert his or her security into a different type of security.

TYPES OF CONVERTIBLE SECURITIES

Either corporate bonds or preferred shares may be convertible. These securities are most commonly convertible into common shares, although in the case of bonds conversion into preferred shares occurs in rare instances.† The most common type of convertible security is the bond. Both convertible bonds and convertible preferred shares normally have a *call feature*, which permits the issuer to force conversion if it so desires.

Convertible Bonds   A convertible bond is almost always a debenture or an unsecured bond with a call feature. It is most commonly convertible into a predefined number of common shares. Because the conversion feature provides the purchaser of a convertible bond with the possibility of becoming a shareholder on quite favourable terms, convertible bonds are generally a less expensive form of financing than nonconvertible or *straight bonds.*

Convertible Preferred Shares   Occasionally a preferred share will contain a conversion feature. Convertible preferred shares, because of the value of the conversion option, can normally be sold with a lower stated dividend than a similar-risk nonconvertible or *straight preferred share.* Convertible preferred shares are usually convertible over an unlimited time horizon; convertible bonds normally are convertible only for a specified period of years.

GENERAL FEATURES OF CONVERTIBLES

The general features of convertible securities include the conversion ratio, the conversion period, the conversion value, and the conversion premium. Each of these items is discussed below.

The Conversion Ratio   The conversion ratio can be given or calculated. For example, sometimes the conversion ratio is stated by indicating that the security is con-

---

*For such applications, refer to the references at the end of the chapter. See, for example, M. J. Brennan and E. S. Schwartz, "Convertible Bonds: Valuation and Optimal Strategies for Call and Conversion," *Journal of Finance* 32 (December 1977), pp. 1699–1715.
†The discussion throughout this chapter deals only with the near-universal case of convertible securities convertible into common shares.

vertible into *x* common shares. Thus, in order to find the *conversion price*, the face value (not the market value) of the convertible security must be divided by the conversion ratio.

EXAMPLE   Cudworth Potash Ltd. has outstanding two convertible security issues—a bond with a $1,000 face value convertible into 25 common shares and a preferred share with a par value of $114 convertible into 3 common shares. The conversion ratios for the bond and the preferred share are 25 and 3, respectively. The conversion price for the bond is $40 ($1,000 ÷ 25), and the conversion price for the preferred share is $38 ($114 ÷ 3).

Sometimes, only the conversion price is given. In this case, the conversion ratio can be obtained by dividing the face value of the convertible by the conversion price. Often the conversion price is not constant, changing in response to the length of time the issue has been outstanding or the proportion of the issue that has been converted. A convertible security could have a conversion price of $30 for the first 10 years and $35 thereafter. Or, the conversion price could be $30 for the first 30 percent of the securities converted and $35 for all subsequent conversions. These types of acceleration features are often included in a bond indenture or preferred share covenants in order to give the issuer the power to force conversion.

EXAMPLE   The Wakaw Grain Company has outstanding a convertible 20-year bond with a face value of $1,000. The bond is convertible at $50 per share into common shares for the next 5 years and at $55 for the remainder of the bond's life. The conversion ratio for the first 5 years is 20 ($1,000 ÷ $50), and for the remainder of the bond's life it is 18.18 ($1,000 ÷ $55).

When a conversion ratio indicates the issuance of *fractional shares*, the issuer may issue the fractional shares, permit the converter to purchase the balance of a fractional share in order to get a full share, or pay the converter the fractional share price upon conversion. The treatment of fractional shares on conversion is specified in the initial bond indenture or preferred share covenants.

The conversion price must be a price that the firm's common shares may reach at some time prior to the maturity of the convertible. If prospective purchasers do not expect conversion ever to be feasible, they will purchase a straight bond or a different convertible issue.

The Conversion Period   Convertible securities are often convertible only within or after a certain period of time such as two to five years after issuance. Convertible preferred shares are generally convertible for an unlimited time. Time limitations on conversion are imposed by the issuer to suit the firm's forecast long-run financial needs.

The Conversion Value   The *conversion value* of a convertible security is the value of the security measured in terms of the market value of the security into which it may be converted. It is found simply by multiplying the conversion ratio by the current market price of the resultant security.

EXAMPLE The Krohn Electronics Company Ltd. has outstanding a $1,000.00 bond that is convertible into common shares at $62.50 a share. The conversion ratio is therefore 16 ($1,000.00 ÷ $62.50). Since the current market price of the common is $65.00 per share, the conversion value is $1,040.00 (16 · $65.00). Since the conversion value is above the bond value of $1,000.00, conversion is a viable option for the owner of the convertible security. Of course, the security holder may anticipate a still greater conversion value and therefore maintain his or her present position if the issuer does not force conversion by using its call privilege.

The Conversion Premium The *conversion premium* is the percentage difference between the conversion price and the issuance price of a security. The conversion premium is normally set initially in the 10- to 20-percent range and depends largely on the nature of the company. If the company's shares are not expected to appreciate greatly over the coming years, a low premium will be used.

EXAMPLE The Oliver Book Company Ltd., a high-growth book publisher, has just issued a $1,000 convertible bond. The bond is convertible into 20 common shares at a price of $50 per share. Since the firm's common shares are currently selling at $42 per share, the conversion premium is $8 per share ($50 − $42), or $160 ($8 per share · 20 shares). For the Oliver Book Company, the conversion premium is approximately 19 percent (i.e., $8 ÷ $42), which would not be unusual for a high-growth company like Oliver.

MOTIVES FOR CONVERTIBLE FINANCING

The motives or advantages associated with convertible security financing are generally consistent with the long-run view of the firm's financial structure discussed in Chapters 17 and 18. A basic theme is the importance of timing security issues to best capitalize on varying financial costs (i.e., to exploit perceived market imperfections in the pricing of various financial instruments). This section discusses the use of convertibles as a form of deferred common share financing, as a sweetener for debt or preferred share financing, and for raising temporarily cheap financing.

Deferred Common Share Financing When a convertible security is issued, both the issuer and the purchaser expect the security to be converted into common shares at some point in the future. If the purchaser did not have this expectation, he or she would not accept the lower return normally associated with convertible issues. However, since the convertible security is sold with a conversion premium, conversion is initially not feasible.

The issuer of a convertible could sell common shares instead, but they could be marketed only at the current market price or below. By selling the convertible, the issuer in effect makes a deferred sale of common shares. Thus, by issuing convertible securities instead of common shares, the firm is able to decrease the dilution of both earnings and control. This benefit is illustrated in the following example.

EXAMPLE   The Green Manufacturing Company Ltd. needs $1,000,000 of new long-term financing. The firm is considering the sale of either common shares or a convertible bond. The current market price of the common is $20 per share. In order to sell the new issue, the shares would have to be underpriced by $1 and sold for $19 per share. This means that approximately 52,632 shares ($1,000,000 ÷ $19 per share) would have to be sold. The alternative would be to issue 30-year 9-percent, $1,000 face-value convertible bonds. The conversion price would be set at $25 per share and the bond could be sold at par (i.e., for $1,000). Thus 1,000 bonds ($1,000,000 ÷ $1,000 per bond) would have to be sold. The firm currently has outstanding 200,000 common shares. The most recent earnings available for common shares were $400,000 or $2 per share (i.e., $400,000 ÷ 200,000 shares).

If earnings available for common shares remain at the $400,000 level, the earnings per share associated with each financing alternative are as follows:

Financing alternative	Number of shares outstanding	Earnings per share
Common shares	252,632	$1.58
Convertible bond		
Before conversion	200,000	$1.73[a]
After total conversion	240,000	$1.67

[a]The additional interest expense on the convertible bond has been included as follows. If we assume a 40-percent tax rate, the $400,000.00 is reduced by the after-tax cost of debt of $54,000.00 [i.e., .09 · $1,000,000.00 · (1 − .40)], thereby resulting in earnings available for common shares of $346,000.00 (i.e., $400,000.00 − $54,000.00). Dividing the 346,000 of available earnings by the 200,000 shares outstanding, yields the earnings per-share value of $1.73.

In the foregoing example, the use of the convertible bond has not only resulted in a smaller dilution of earnings per share ($1.67 per share vs. $1.58 per share) but also in a smaller number of shares outstanding (240,000 vs. 252,632). This better preserves the voting control of the owners. In actuality, the firm's earnings would be expected to increase for either form of new financing. However, the per-share earnings increase would be larger with the convertible bond due to the smaller number of new shares issued.

A Sweetener for Financing   A second common motive for the use of convertible securities is the fact that the conversion feature often makes the bond or preferred share issue more attractive to the purchaser. Since the purchaser of the convertible security is given an option to share in the firm's future success, *convertibles can normally be sold with lower interest rates than nonconvertibles.* Therefore, from the firm's viewpoint, including a conversion feature as part of a bond or preferred share issue reduces the effective interest cost or preferred dividend at the cost of giving new investors potentially valuable options. The purchaser of the issue sacrifices a portion of his or her fixed return in order to have the benefit of exercising a potentially valuable call option on the firm's equity in the future.

Raising Temporarily "Cheap" Funds   The general pattern for a growing firm is to sell convertible securities to finance its expansion, thereby minimizing its present financial costs. Once expansion has been achieved and a higher level of revenues is being generated, the fixed payment obligations can be shifted to common equity, assuming that conversion is feasible.* With a larger equity base, the firm can obtain new low-cost debt funds for further expansion. In addition, a conversion feature may be the key factor that makes the sale of debt or preferred shares feasible during a period of tight money and high inflation.

OTHER CONSIDERATIONS

Two other considerations require discussion—forcing conversion and overhanging issues.

Forcing Conversion   A firm issues a convertible security with the expectations that the price of its common shares will rise by enough to make conversion attractive, and that at that point in time the purchaser will convert the security into common shares. However, in practice, there are at least two reasons why a convertible security holder may not convert the security when the firm's share price rises above the conversion price. The first is that the holder already has the market price benefit obtainable from conversion and still receives fixed periodic interest or dividend payments. The second reason for nonconversion is the belief by the holder of the convertible security that the market price of the common shares will not stay above the conversion price.†

As indicated earlier, virtually all convertible securities have a call feature that enables the issuer to force their conversion. The call price of the security generally exceeds the security's face value by an amount equal to one year's stated interest on the security. Due to this call premium, the call privilege is generally not exercised until the conversion value of the security is 10–15 percent above the call price. This type of premium above the call price helps to assure the issuer that when the call is made the holders of the convertible will convert it instead of accepting the call price. When the convertible holders believe the share price to be quite volatile, the conversion value must be considerably above the call price for the call to be effective in forcing conversion.

---

*The option to convert is actually placed in the hands of the purchaser of the security—not the issuing firm. The *call* feature can be used by the issuer to force conversion, although, as we shall see later, sometimes the economics of the situation result in an "overhanging issue." If the share price appreciates sufficiently above the conversion price, conversion should be automatic.

†Of course the holder of the convertible could convert the security and then sell the shares, but he or she would have to pay both brokerage fees and taxes on the sale. By converting and holding the shares or not converting at all, he or she delays or avoids these expenses.

EXAMPLE   The Felix Catfood Company Ltd. currently has outstanding a 9-percent $1,000.00 convertible bond. The bond is convertible into 50 common shares at $20.00 per share and callable at $1,090.00. Since the bond is convertible into 50 common shares, calling it would be equivalent to paying each common shareholder $21.80 per share ($1,090.00 ÷ 50 shares). If the firm issues the call when the common is selling for $23.00 per share, a convertible security holder is likely to take the $1,090.00 instead of converting the security, even though he or she realizes only $21.80 per share instead of $23.00. This is because the security holder recognizes that the share price is likely to drop as soon as the conversion occurs. Also, if the security holder wishes to sell the shares after conversion, he or she will have to pay taxes and brokerage fees on the transaction.

If the Felix Catfood Company waited until the market price exceeded the call price by 10–15 percent—if, say, the call was made when the market price of a share reached $24.50—most of the convertible holders would probably convert the security. The conversion price of $24.50 per share would be approximately 12.4 percent above the call price per share of $21.80—high enough to cover any movements in the share price or brokerage fees associated with conversion. At least 30 days advance notice is normally given prior to a call.

Increasing common share dividends is sometimes helpful in forcing conversion.

Overhanging Issues   In some cases the market price may not exceed the conversion price; in other cases the market price may rise to within a few percentage points of the call price per share. In either of these cases, conversion is not a viable alternative for the holders of the security. A convertible security that cannot be forced into conversion is called an *overhanging issue.*

An overhanging convertible issue can complicate a firm's capital structure management. For example, a firm might have expected conversion at a certain point in time to reduce its leverage position, so that it could issue more debt. However, if the convertible issue is overhanging at that particular point in time, then the firm will either have to call the issue and pay a call premium or issue new preferred or common shares.

Although convertible securities are an attractive type of deferred equity financing, the issuer must have confidence in its ability to use the funds to stimulate increases in the value of its common shares to make conversion feasible. The issuer must recognize the possibility that the convertible securities may not be converted and new equity financing may not be automatically forthcoming.

Determining the Value of Convertibles

The key characteristic of convertible securities that greatly enhances their marketability is their ability to minimize the possibility of a loss while providing a possibility of capital gains. Closely related to this characteristic is the fixed pattern of interest or dividend income from convertible securities. Based on these considerations, this section discusses the three values of a convertible security—the bond or preferred share value, the share or conversion value, and the market value.

BOND OR PREFERRED SHARE VALUE

The *bond or preferred share value* of a convertible security is the price of a *straight* bond or preferred share issued by a firm having the same risk. The bond or preferred share value is typically the floor, or minimum, price at which a convertible bond or preferred share will be traded.

Calculating the Straight Bond Value   The straight (bond) value of a convertible bond is equal to the present value of its interest and principal payments, when discounted at the straight bond interest rate.

EXAMPLE   The Rich Company Ltd. has just sold a $1,000.00, 20-year convertible bond with an 8-percent coupon rate. The bond interest will be paid at the end of each year and the principal will be repaid at maturity.* A straight bond could have been sold with a 10-percent coupon. The straight bond value of the convertible is calculated as follows:

Year(s)	Payment (1)	Present value factor @ 10% (2)	Present value (1) · (2) (3)
1–20	$ 80[a]	8.514[b]	$681.12
20	1,000	.149[c]	$149.00
		Straight bond value	$830.12

[a] $1,000 @ 8% interest per year.
[b] Present-value interest factor for an annuity, PVIFA, for 20 years discounted at 10 percent, from Table A-4.
[c] Present-value interest factor, PVIF, for $1 to be received at the end of year 20 discounted at 10 percent, from Table A-3.

The value, $830.12, is the minimum price at which the convertible bond is expected to sell.

Calculating the Straight Preferred Share Value   The minimum price at which a convertible preferred share can be expected to sell can be found in a similar manner. It is assumed to equal the present value of preferred dividends over an infinite life discounted at the yield on a straight preferred share. Thus, the straight value of a convertible share is given by d/r, where d is the annual preferred dividend and r is the appropriate discount rate.†

---

*As indicated earlier, since bond interest is typically paid semiannually, one must use semiannual discounting to find the present value of the stream of interest payments. Although the techniques for finding a bond value for a bond paying semiannual interest were described in Chapter 13, the technique will not be applied here in order not to complicate the concepts being presented.
†Calculation of the present value of an infinite-lived annuity, or *perpetuity*, was discussed in some detail in Chapter 13.

EXAMPLE   The Rich Company Ltd. has just issued a 9-percent convertible preferred share with a $100.00 par value. If the firm had issued a nonconvertible preferred share, the annual dividend yield would probably have been 11 percent. Dividends are paid at the end of each year. Dividing the annual dividend of $9.00 (9 percent of $100.00) by 11 percent yields a value for a preferred share of $81.81 (i.e., $9.00 ÷ 0.11). In otherwords, the straight or floor value of a preferred share is $81.81.

SHARE OR CONVERSION VALUE

The *share or conversion value* of a convertible security is measured in terms of the market price of the underlying common share. When the market price of the common share exceeds the conversion price, the share or conversion value is expected to exceed the straight bond or preferred share value of the convertible, as illustrated in the following example.

EXAMPLE   The Rich Company Ltd. convertible bond described earlier is convertible at $50.00 per share. This means that it can be converted into 20 shares, since it has a $1,000.00 face value. The conversion value of the bond for various share values is as follows:

Market price of a share	Conversion value
$40	$ 800
$50	$1,000
$60	$1,200
$70	$1,400
$80	$1,600

Since the straight value of this bond is $830.12, it will never sell for less than this amount, regardless of how low its conversion value is. If the market price per share were $40.00, the bond would still sell for $830.12—not $800.00—since its value as a bond would dominate. (Of course, its straight bond value will change as interest rates change.)

MARKET VALUE

The market value of a convertible is likely to be greater than either its straight value or its conversion value. The amount by which the market value exceeds the straight or conversion value is often designated the *market premium*. The market premium is larger the closer the straight value is to the conversion value. Even when the conversion value is below the straight value, a premium based on expected share price movements exists.

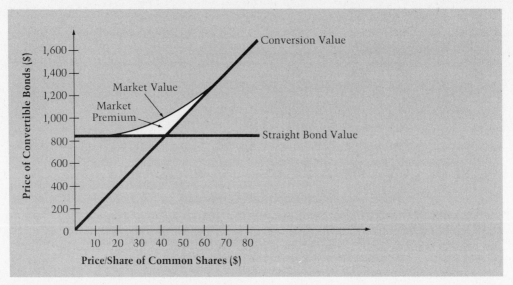

Figure 23.3   The values and market premium for the Rich Company's convertible bond.

The general relationship between the straight value, the conversion value, the market value, and the market premium of the Rich Company's convertible bond, described in the preceding examples, is shown in Figure 23.3.*

As Figure 23.3 shows, the straight bond value acts as a floor for the security's value, and when the market price of the share exceeds a certain value the conversion value of the bond exceeds the straight bond value. Also, due to the expectations of investors about movements in the price of the firm's common shares, the market value of the convertible often exceeds both the straight and the conversion value of the security, resulting in a market premium on the security.

SPECIAL CONSIDERATIONS

Unfortunately, the behaviour of convertible security values—specifically the straight value of a convertible—is not precisely as described. The straight value of a bond or preferred share is not necessarily fixed over a long period of time. It can be affected by a number of firm and capital market factors. If the firm runs into operating or financial difficulties, it is quite possible that its credit-worthiness will deteriorate and the risk associated with its securities will increase. Due to this increase in risk, the rate at which the payments associated with its bonds or preferred shares are discounted will rise, thereby lowering their straight value. It is also possible for the firm's credit rating to rise, so that the straight value of its convertible securities rises also.

---

*We have discussed the method of finding the market value, conversion value, straight value, and market premium associated with a convertible bond. The values of a convertible preferred share would be found in a similar fashion. Bond examples are used throughout the chapter because convertible bonds are more common than convertible preferred shares.

The second factor affecting straight values is interest rate movements in the capital markets. If money becomes tighter, interest rates will rise, causing the present value of the cash flows associated with a bond or a preferred share to decline, and vice versa.

Share Purchase Warrants

Share purchase warrants are quite similar to share rights, which were described in detail in Chapter 22. A *warrant* gives the holder a transferable option to purchase a certain number of common shares at a specified price, within a specified period of time.* Warrants also bear some similarity to convertibles, since they provide for the possible injection of additional equity capital into the firm at some future date.

CHARACTERISTICS OF WARRANTS

This part of the chapter is devoted to the use of warrants as sweeteners, exercise prices, warrant trading, a comparison of warrants and convertibles, and a comparison of warrants and rights.

Warrants As Sweeteners   Warrants are generally attached to debt or preferred share issues as sweeteners, in order to add to the marketability of the issue while lowering the required interest or preferred dividend rate. As sweeteners, warrants are quite similar to conversion features. When money is tight, the attachment of warrants may be the key factor enabling the firm to raise needed funds. Also, when a firm is believed to be financially risky, warrants may be the key factor enabling it to obtain debt or preferred share financing. Often, when a new firm is being capitalized, suppliers of debt or preferred shares will require warrants to permit them to share in whatever success the firm achieves. Since the initial capital is generally considered risk capital, its suppliers expect an opportunity to share in the rewards that (hopefully) will result from the use of the funds they supply. Warrants are quite often used to pay for the services acquired in business combinations and to compensate investment dealers for underwriting services.

Exercise Prices   The price at which holders of warrants can purchase the specified number of shares is normally referred to as the *exercise price* or the *striking price.* This price is normally set 10–20 percent above the market price of the firm's shares at the time of issuance. Until the market price of the shares exceeds the exercise price, holders of warrants would not be advised to exercise warrants, since they could purchase the shares more cheaply in the marketplace. Occasionally the exercise price of a warrant is not fixed, but changes at certain predefined points in time. An exercise price will rise in order to give holders of warrants an incentive to exercise them. The exercise price of a warrant is automatically adjusted for share splits and share dividends.

---

*Although perpetual warrants are rare in Canada, Canadian Gas and Energy Ltd. has an issue of perpetual warrants outstanding.

Warrant Trading   Since warrants are usually *detachable*, they are often listed and actively traded on the stock exchanges and in the over-the-counter market.

A Comparison of Warrants and Convertibles   The key difference between the result of exercising a warrant and converting convertibles is that the warrants provide an influx of new capital, while the convertible does not. The potential effects on the firm's capital structure of the exercise of warrants is best explained in light of the use of convertibles. One effect of the exercise of share purchase warrants is a dilution of earnings and control, since a number of new common shares are automatically issued. Of course, the conversion of a convertible security generally results in a greater dilution of earnings and control due to the considerably larger number of common shares issued.

The exercise of a warrant shifts the firm's capital structure to a less highly levered position, since new equity capital is created without any change in the firm's debt capital. If a convertible issue were converted, the reduction in leverage would be even more pronounced, since the new common equity would be created through a corresponding reduction in either debt or preferred shares. The exercise of warrants reduces the firm's leverage, but not to the degree that the conversion of a convertible security issue does.

A Comparison of Warrants and Rights   Both warrants and rights are types of options that result in new equity capital, although the warrant provides for deferred equity financing. The right provides for the maintenance of pro rata ownership by existing owners, while the warrant has no such feature. Rather, the warrant is generally used to make other forms of financing more attractive. The life of a right is typically less than a few months, whereas a warrant is generally exercisable for a period of years. Also, rights are issued with a subscription price below the prevailing market price of the common shares, while warrants are generally issued at an exercise price 10–20 percent above the prevailing market price.

THE VALUE OF WARRANTS

Like a convertible security, a warrant has both a theoretical and a market value. The difference between these values, or the *warrant premium*, depends largely on investor expectations and the ability of the investors to get more leverage from the warrants than the underlying common shares.

The Theoretical Value of a Warrant   The theoretical or floor value of a warrant is given by Equation 23.1.

$$TV = (P - E)N \qquad (23.1)$$

where

TV = the theoretical or floor value of a warrant
P = the market price of a common share
E = the exercise price of the warrant
N = the number of common shares obtainable with one warrant

EXAMPLE   The Classic Car Company Ltd. has outstanding warrants that are exercisable at $40 per share and entitle the holders to purchase three common shares. The warrants were initially attached to a bond issue to sweeten it. The common shares of the firm are currently selling for $47 per share. Substituting $P = \$47$, $E = \$40$, and $N = 3$ into Equation 23.1 yields a theoretical warrant value of $21 [i.e., ($47 − $40) · 3]. If investors are perfectly rational and their present expectations do not change, Classic's warrants should not sell for less than $21 in the marketplace.

The Market Value of a Warrant   The market value of a share purchase warrant is generally above its theoretical value. Only when the theoretical value of the warrant is very high are the market and theoretical values of a warrant quite close. The general relationship between the theoretical and market value of the Classic Car Company's warrants is presented graphically in Figure 23.4. The market value of the warrants generally exceeds the theoretical value by the greatest amount when the share's market price is close to the warrant exercise price per share.

Warrant Premium   The *warrant premium* is also shown in Figure 23.4. This premium results from a combination of investor expectations about the future price of a common share and the ability of the investor to obtain leveraged returns by trading in warrants rather than shares. An example will clarify the effect of expectations of share price movements and the greater leverage associated with warrants on warrant market values.

EXAMPLE   John J. Investor has $2,430 to invest in the Classic Car Company. Classic's common is currently selling for $45 per share, and its warrants are selling for $18 per warrant. Each warrant entitles the holder to purchase three shares of Classic's common at $40 per share. Since Classic's common is selling for $45 per share, the theoretical warrant value, according to Equation 23.1, is $15 [i.e., ($45 − $40) · 3].

The warrant premium is believed to result from investor expectations and leverage opportunities. John J. Investor could spend his $2,430 in either of two ways. Ignoring brokerage costs, he could purchase either 54 common shares at $45 per share or 135 warrants at $18 per warrant. If Mr. Investor purchases the shares, and the price rises to $48, and he then sells the shares, he will gain $162 ($3 per share · 54 shares). If, instead of purchasing the shares, he purchases the 135 warrants and the share price increases by $3 per share, Mr. Investor will make approximately $1,215. Since the price of a common share rises by $3, the price of each warrant can be expected to rise by $9, since each warrant can be used to purchase three common shares. A gain of $9 per warrant on 135 warrants means a total gain of $1,215 on the warrants.

The greater leverage associated with warrants works both ways. If the market price fell by $3, the loss on the shares would be $162, while the loss on the warrants would be close to $1,215. The leverage effect is not perfectly symmetrical, since the warrant premium varies depending on the price of the common shares, as depicted in Figure 23.4. Other factors affecting the warrant premium are the variability of common share

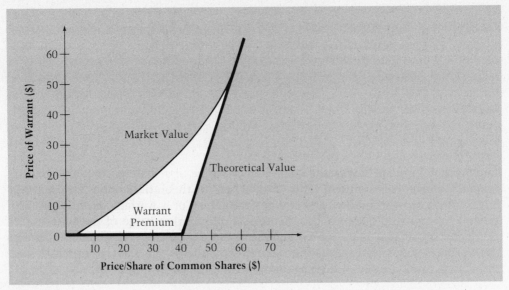

Figure 23.4   The values and warrant premium of the Classic Car Company's share purchase warrants.

prices, the nearness to the warrant's maturity or expiration date, the risk-free rate of interest, and the dividend policies of the firm.*

Summary

This chapter has discussed the basics of option theory and has presented an in-depth discussion of two optional features of long-term debt or preferred shares—convertibles and warrants. Both features are attractive due to their usefulness as sweeteners and as forms of deferred equity financing. Corporate bonds may be convertible into common or preferred shares although the conversion of bonds into preferred shares is relatively uncommon. Most convertibles have a call feature. A convertible's conversion ratio indicates the number of shares it can be converted into. A conversion privilege may have a limited life, or the conversion ratio may decrease at predefined points in time. Conversion is not an attractive alternative when a security is initially issued.

The major motives for the use of convertibles are to obtain deferred common share financing, to sweeten security issues, and/or to raise temporarily cheap funds. When the value of a share rises to a level at which conversion becomes attractive, the firm may use the call feature to force conversion. Usually conversion is not forced until the conversion value of the security is 10–15 percent above the call price. Sometimes the predefined decreases in the conversion ratio or changes in dividends on common shares can assist conversion. Occasionally, conversion does not become attractive and the firm cannot force it.

*The interested reader can determine the effect of a change in each of these factors on the warrant premium (and value) by referring to the basic concepts discussed in an earlier section on options.

The value of a convertible can be measured in a number of ways. Generally the minimum value at which a convertible will trade is the value of a straight (i.e., nonconvertible) security of the same company. The conversion value of a convertible is its value measured in terms of the securities into which it may be converted. The market value of a convertible is generally above these values, especially when the straight security value and conversion value are quite close. The amount by which the market value exceeds the straight or conversion value is called the market premium. The straight value of the convertible may fluctuate in response to changes in the firm's financial risk and capital market activity.

Share purchase warrants are generally attached to debt or preferred share issues to enhance their attractiveness and lower their cost. Sometimes warrants are used in business combinations or to compensate underwriters. A warrant provides the holder with the privilege of purchasing a certain number of common shares at a specified price, called the exercise or striking price. Warrants generally have limited lives. They are generally detachable, and many are traded on organized security exchanges and in the over-the-counter market. Warrants are quite similar to convertibles, but they have a less pronounced effect on the firm's leverage and bring in new funds. They are also similar to share rights, except that their exercise generally results in a dilution of ownership control and earnings. The life of a warrant is also generally longer than that of a right. The exercise price of a warrant is initially set above the underlying share's current price, while the subscription price of a right is set below the prevailing market price of the share.

The market value of a warrant is usually greater than its theoretical value due to market price expectations and the ability of investors to obtain considerably more leverage from trading warrants than from trading the underlying common share. The warrant premium, or amount by which the market value of a warrant exceeds its theoretical value, generally declines as the warrant approaches maturity or in response to certain internal firm factors.

Questions

23.1   What is an option? What happens if an option or its underlying asset are incorrectly priced in the market?

23.2   What are the key similarities and differences between *convertible securities* and *share purchase warrants*? What effect do these instruments have on the firm's capital structure?

23.3   What is a conversion ratio? How may it be stated? Is a conversion ratio always fixed over the conversion period?

23.4   What is the conversion value of a convertible security? How can the conversion value be calculated if one knows the conversion ratio and the current market value of the firm's common shares?

23.5   Why is convertible security financing often viewed as a form of deferred common share financing? Do issuers of convertibles expect them to be converted?

23.6   Why is a conversion feature often considered a type of sweetener to be used in raising debt or preferred share capital? What sort of compensation does the issuer receive in exchange for this sweetener?

23.7   When the share price of a convertible security rises above the conversion price, why may the security not be converted?

23.8   What is a call feature? Why do virtually all convertible securities have a call feature? At what level is the call price generally set, and how far above the call price must the conversion value be before the call is exercised?

23.9   What is an overhanging issue? Why is it often considered problematic?

23.10   What is meant by the bond or preferred share value of a convertible security? How is this *straight value* calculated, and why is it often viewed as a floor for the convertible's value?

23.11   What is meant by the share or conversion value of a convertible security? In what circumstances will a convertible sell for its share or conversion value?

23.12   Can you graphically depict the general relationship between the straight value, conversion value, market value, and market premium associated with a convertible security?

23.13   Why may the straight value of a convertible not be constant over a long period of time?

23.14   What are *share purchase warrants?* How do they differ from share rights? How are warrants issued, and how are they similar to convertibles?

23.15   What is the exercise or striking price of a warrant? What relationship does this price have to the share price at the time of issue?

23.16   What are the similarities and key differences between the effects of convertibles and warrants on the firm's ownership, its earnings per share, its capital structure, and its ability to raise new capital?

23.17   What is the general relationship between the theoretical and market value of a warrant? In what circumstances are these values quite close?

23.18   What factors other than the price of the associated common shares affect the warrant premium?

•23.19   Based on the basic concepts of option pricing—and assuming that all other factors remain constant—how will a warrant's premium change as the warrant approaches its expiration date? if the risk-free rate of interest increases? if the firm increases its cash payment on the underlying asset?

Problems

23.1   Calculate the conversion price for each of the following convertible issues.
a.   A $1,000 face-value bond convertible into 20 shares of common.
b.   Preferred share with a $104 par value and convertible into 13 shares of common.
c.   A $1,000 face-value bond convertible into 50 common shares.
d.   A $90 par-value preferred share convertible into 6 common shares.

23.2   What is the conversion ratio for each of the following securities?
a.   A $115 par-value preferred convertible into common at $20 per share.
b.   A $1,000 face-value bond convertible into common shares at $25 per share.
c.   An $80 par-value preferred share convertible into common shares at $5 per share.
d.   A $600 bond convertible into common shares at $30 per share.

23.3   What is the conversion value for each of the following convertible securities?
a.   A $1,000 bond convertible into 25 common shares. A common share is currently selling at $50 per share.

b. A $1,000 bond convertible into 12.5 preferred shares. A common share is currently selling for $42 per share.

c. A $1,000 bond convertible into 100 common shares. A common share is currently selling for $10.50 per share.

d. A $60 preferred convertible into 2 common shares. A common share is currently selling for $30 per share.

23.4   Market Manufacturing Company Ltd. has two convertible issues outstanding. One is an $85 par-value convertible preferred, convertible into common shares at $40 per share for the next year, after which it is convertible at $42.50 per share for the next three years. After four years, the conversion feature expires. The other convertible issue is a bond with a $1,000 face value. It is convertible into 20 common shares in the first year, and 18 common shares thereafter.

a. Calculate the conversion ratio for the preferred issue in the first year and in the following three years.

b. Calculate the conversion price for the convertible bond in the first year and thereafter.

c. Explain the rationale for increases in the conversion price (decreases in the conversion ratio) with the passage of time.

d. If the current market price of a common share is $35, which issue would you expect to be converted first? Explain your answer.

23.5   The Regina Medical Supply Corporation Ltd. has just issued a convertible bond with a face value of $1,000. The bond may be converted into 12.5 common shares. A share is currently selling at $73 per share.

a. What is the per-share conversion premium associated with this issue?

b. Calculate the total conversion premium for the bond.

c. State the conversion premium as a percentage of the current share price.

d. If the market price increased to $80, $85, and $100 per share of common, what would be the conversion value of the bond in each case?

23.6   Give the conversion value, conversion premium, and the conversion premium in percentage terms (of the current share price) for the following convertibles.

Convertible	Face value	Conversion ratio	Current market price of a share
A	$1,000	25	$42.25
B	$ 800	16	$50.00
C	$1,000	20	$44.00
D	$ 100	5	$19.50

23.7   The Kenora Grain Company Ltd. is considering two alternatives for raising a needed $1,000,000. Option A involves a sale of common shares at $37 per share, a $3 underprice relative to the current market price of $40. The alternative, option B, would be to sell $1,000 face-value convertible bonds. These carry a 10-percent interest coupon and can be sold at face value. The conversion ratio would be 22. The firm currently has 150,000 common shares outstanding. The earnings available for common shareholders are expected to be $600,000 per year for each of the next several years.

a. Determine the number of common shares outstanding and the earnings per share under the common share financing alternative.

b. Determine the number of common shares outstanding and the earnings per share associated with the bond prior to its conversion under the convertible bond financing alternative. (Ignore bond interest.)

c. Determine the number of shares outstanding and the earnings per share associated with the bond alternative once all bonds have been converted.

d. Discuss which of the two alternatives is preferable in terms of maximizing earnings per share.

23.8   Yellowhead Ice must decide whether to obtain a needed $2,000,000 of financing by selling common shares at its currently depressed price or selling convertible bonds. The firm's common shares are currently selling for $32 per share; new shares can be sold for $30 per share, an underpricing of $2 per share. The firm currently has 100,000 common shares outstanding. Convertible bonds can be sold for their $1,000 par value and would be convertible at $34. The firm expects its earnings available for common shareholders to be $200,000 each year over the next several years.

a. Calculate the earnings per share resulting from
   (1) The sale of common shares.
   (2) The sale of the convertible bonds prior to conversion. (Ignore bond interest.)
   (3) The sale of convertible bonds after all bonds have been converted.

b. Which of the two financing alternatives would you recommend the company adopt? Why?

23.9   Calculate the straight value for each of the following:

Case	Face or par value	Coupon or dividend	Coupon or dividend on equal-risk straight instruments	Years to maturity (bonds)
Bond A	$1,000	10%	11%	20
Preferred R	$ 80	8%	9%	—
Bond B	$ 800	8%	10%	14
Preferred S	$ 60	6%	7%	—
Bond C	$1,000	11%	13%	30
Preferred T	$ 50	7%	9%	—
Bond D	$1,000	10%	13%	25

23.10   The Western Clock Company Ltd. has an outstanding issue of convertible bonds with a $1,000 face value. These bonds are convertible into 40 common shares. They have an 8-percent coupon and a 20-year maturity. The interest rate on a straight bond of similar risk would be 10 percent.

a. Calculate the conversion value of the bond when the market price of a common share is $20, $25, $28, $35, and $50 per share.

b. Calculate the straight value of the bond.

c. For each of the share prices given in **a,** at what price would you expect the bond to sell? Why?

d. What is the least you would expect the bond to sell for regardless of the common share price behaviour?

23.11 Mrs. Tom Fish Company has an outstanding issue of convertible preferred with a $50 par value. These preferred shares are convertible into four shares of common. They have a 9-percent dividend while the coupon on straight preferred of similar risk is 10 percent.

a. Calculate the conversion value of a preferred share when the market price of a common share is $15.00, $12.50, $11.00, $13.00, and $20.00 per share.

b. Calculate the straight value of this preferred share.

c. For each of the common share prices given in **a**, at what price would you expect the preferred share to sell? Why?

d. Graph the conversion value and straight value of the preferred share for each common share price given. Plot the common share prices on the x-axis and the preferred prices on the y-axis. Use this graph to indicate minimum market price associated with each common share price.

23.12 Elmer's Electronics Ltd. has warrants that allow the purchase of three shares of its outstanding common shares at $50 per share. The share price and the warrant value associated with that share price are summarized as follows:

Common share price	Market value of warrant
$42	$ 2
46	8
48	9
54	18
58	28
62	38
66	48

a. For each of the values given, calculate the theoretical warrant value.

b. Graph on a set of common share price–warrant price axes the theoretical and market values of the warrant.

c. If the warrant value is $12 when the market price of common is $50, does this contradict or support the graph you have constructed? Explain why or why not.

d. Specify the area of warrant premium. Why does this premium exist?

e. If the expiration date of the warrants is quite close, would you expect your graph to look different? Explain.

23.13 Gayle Graham is evaluating the Ever-On Battery Company's shares and warrants in order to choose the best investment. The firm's shares are currently selling for $50 per share; its warrants to purchase three shares for $45 are selling for $20. Ignoring transactions costs, Ms. Graham has $8,000 to invest. She is quite optimistic with respect to Ever-On because she has certain "inside information" about the firm's prospects with respect to a large government contract.

a. How many shares and how many warrants can Ms. Graham purchase?

b. Suppose Ms. Graham purchased the common shares, held them one year, then sold them for $60 per share. Ignoring broker's fees and taxes, what return would she realize? What would be her rate of return on this investment?

c. Suppose Ms. Graham purchased warrants, held them for one year, and the market price of the shares increased to $60. Ignoring brokerage fees and taxes, what return would she realize if the market value of the warrants increased to $45 and she sold out?

d. What benefit, if any, would the warrants provide? Are there any differences in the risk of these two alternative investments? Explain.

23.14   Mark Christian can invest $5,000 in either the common shares or the warrants of Kettering Engineering. A common share is currently selling for $30 per share; its warrants, which provide for the purchase of two shares of common at $28 per share, are currently selling for $7. A share is expected to rise to a market price of $32 within the next year, so the expected value of a warrant over the next year is $8. The expiration date of the warrant is one year from the present.

a.   If Mr. Christian purchases the warrant, and converts to common shares in one year, what rate of return would he earn if the market price of common shares is actually $32 then? (Ignore brokerage fees and taxes.)

b.   If he purchases the shares, holds them for one year, and then sells them for $32, what is his rate of return? (Ignore brokerage fees and taxes.)

c.   Repeat **a** and **b** assuming the market price of the shares in one year to be (1) $30 and (2) $28.

d.   Discuss the two alternatives and trade-offs associated with them.

Notes

1.   See Fischer Black and Myron Scholes, "The Pricing of Options and Corporate Liabilities," *Journal of Political Economy* 81 (May-June 1973), pp. 637–654. Also, see Robert C. Merton, "A Rational Theory of Option Pricing," *Bell Journal of Economics and Management Science* 4 (Spring 1973), pp. 141–183. In equilibrium, Stoll has shown that there is a parity between the premiums on puts and calls (referred to as the put-call parity). For greater details, refer to Hans R. Stoll, "The Relationship Between Put and Call Option Prices," *Journal of Finance* (December 1969), pp. 801–824.

Suggested Readings

Alexander, Gordon J. and Roger D. Stover, "Pricing in the New Issue Convertible Debt Market," *Financial Management* 6 (Fall 1977), pp. 35–39.

Bacon, Peter W. and Edward L. Winn, Jr., "The Impact of Forced Conversion on Stock Prices," *Journal of Finance* 24 (December 1969), pp. 871–874.

Baumol, William J., Burton G. Malkiel, and Richard E. Quandt, "The Valuation of Convertible Securities," *Quarterly Journal of Economics* 80 (February 1966), pp. 48–59.

Black, Fischer and Myron Scholes, "The Pricing of Options and Corporate Liabilities," *Journal of Political Economy* (May-June 1973), pp. 637–659.

Brennan, Michael J., "The Pricing of Contingent Claims in Discrete Time Models," *Journal of Finance* 24 (March 1979), pp. 53–68.

Brennan, M. J. and E. S. Schwartz, "Savings Bonds, Retractable Bonds and Callable Bonds," *Journal of Financial Economics* (August 1977).

———, "Convertible Bonds: Valuation and Optimal Strategies for Call and Conversion," *Journal of Finance* 32 (December 1977), pp. 1699–1715.

Brigham, Eugene F., "An Analysis of Convertible Debentures: Theory and Some Empirical Evidence," *Journal of Finance* 21 (March 1966), pp. 35–54.

Chen, Andrew H. Y., "A Model of Warrant Pricing in a Dynamic Market," *Journal of Finance* 25 (December 1970), pp. 1041–1059.

Frank, Werner G. and Charles O. Kroncke, "Classifying Conversions of Convertible Debentures over Four Years," *Financial Management* 3 (Summer 1974), pp. 33–42.

Frank, Werner G. and Jerry J. Weygandt, "Convertible Debt and Earnings per Share: Pragmatism vs. Good Theory," *Accounting Review* 45 (April 1970), pp. 280–289.

Frankle, A. W. and C. A. Hawkins, "Beta Coefficients for Convertible Bonds," *Journal of Finance* 30 (March 1975), pp. 207–210.

Hayes, Samuel L., III and Henry B. Reiling, "Sophisticated Financing Tool: The Warrant," *Harvard Business Review* 47 (January-February 1969), pp. 137–150.

Horrigan, James O., "Some Hypotheses on the Valuation of Stock Warrants," *Journal of Business Finance and Accounting* 1 (Summer 1974), pp. 239–247.

Ingersoll, Jonathan, "An Examination of Corporate Call Prices on Convertible Securities," *Journal of Finance* 32 (May 1977), pp. 463–478.

Jennings, Edward H., "An Estimate of Convertible Bond Premiums," *Journal of Financial and Quantitative Analysis* 9 (January 1974), pp. 33–56.

Leabo, Dick A. and Richard L. Rogalski, "Warrant Price Movements and the Efficient Market Model," *Journal of Finance* 30 (March 1975), pp. 163–178.

Lewellen, Wilbur G. and George A. Racette, "Convertible Debt Financing," *Journal of Financial and Quantitative Analysis* 7 (December 1973), pp. 777–792.

Mehta, Dileep R., "The Impact of Outstanding Convertible Bonds on Dividend Policy," *Journal of Finance* 31 (May 1976).

Mumey, G., "Premiums on Convertible Bonds: Comment," *Journal of Finance* 25 (September 1970), pp. 928–930.

Pinches, George E., "Financing with Convertible Preferred Stocks, 1960–1967," *Journal of Finance* 25 (March 1970), pp. 53–64.

Rush, David F. and Ronald W. Melicher, "An Empirical Examination of Factors Which Influence Warrant Prices," *Journal of Finance* 29 (December 1974), pp. 1449–1466.

Samuelson, P. A. and R. C. Merton, "A Complete Model of Warrant Pricing That Maximizes Utility," *Industrial Management Review* 10 (Winter 1969), pp. 17–46.

Schwartz, Eduardo S., "The Valuation of Warrants: Implementing a New Approach," *Journal of Financial Economics* 4 (January 1977), pp. 79–94.

Shelton, John P., "The Relation of the Price of a Warrant to the Price of Its Associated Stock," *Financial Analysts Journal* 23 (May-June and July-August 1967), pp. 143–151 and 88–89.

Soldofsky, Robert M., "Yield-Rate Performance of Convertible Securities," *Financial Analysts Journal* 27 (March-April 1971), pp. 61–65.

Stevenson, Richard A. and Joe Lavely, "Why a Bond Warrant Issue?" *Financial Executive* 38 (June 1970), pp. 16–21.

Stone, Bernell K., "Warrant Financing," *Journal of Financial and Quantitative Analysis* 11 (March 1976), pp. 143–154.

Van Horne, James C., "Warrant Valuation in Relation to Volatility and Opportunity Costs," *Industrial Management Review* 10 (Spring 1969), pp. 19–32.

Walter, James E. and Augustin V. Que, "The Valuation of Convertible Bonds," *Journal of Finance* 28 (June 1973), pp. 713–732.

Chapter 24

DIVIDENDS AND RETAINED EARNINGS

Retained earnings are the primary internally generated source of long-term funds for the business firm. Like financial leases, long-term loans, bonds, preferred shares, and common shares, retained earnings provide capital to the firm. And like capital from other sources, such funds are not "free." Since the alternative to the retention of earnings is the payment of cash dividends, there is a reciprocal relationship between retained earnings and cash dividends.

Once a firm has satisfied its obligations to its creditors, the government, and its preferred shareholders (if any), any remaining earnings can be retained, paid out as cash dividends, or split between retained earnings and cash dividends. Retained earnings can be invested in assets that will help the firm to expand or to maintain its present rate of growth. If earnings were not retained, additional funds would have to be raised through one of the other sources of financing. A difficult and quite critical decision affecting the firm's overall objective of owners' wealth maximization revolves around the firm's retained earnings-dividend decision.

This chapter is devoted to both retained earnings and dividends. The primary emphasis is on the dividend decision. The chapter has five major sections. The first and second sections deal with certain procedural and theoretical considerations regarding retained earnings and cash dividends. The third section presents the key factors affecting the firm's cash dividend policy. Certain of these factors act as constraints on the corporate dividend decision. The fourth section discusses the types of dividend policies commonly in use. The final section of the chapter discusses two noncash methods of paying dividends—declaring share dividends (and the related topic of share splits) or making share repurchases.*

*To be consistent with U.S. terminology, these terms are commonly called *stock dividends*, *stock splits*, and *stock repurchases*, respectively, in Canada.

Procedural Considerations

This section discusses retained earnings as a source of financing and cash dividend payment procedures.

RETAINED EARNINGS AS A SOURCE OF FINANCING

As discussed in earlier chapters, a firm should accept and fund all investment projects that offer a return greater than the firm's cost of funds. In this context, dividend policy can be viewed as a financing decision, since a firm's source of funds (retained earnings plus external financings) must equal the firm's use of funds (dividends plus investments in assets). Thus, a firm will have to raise funds externally whenever it wants to pay dividends that exceed the portion of earnings that remain unspent after all new investment projects have been financed. A simple example will clarify this point.

EXAMPLE   The Miller Flour Company's balance sheet is presented in Table 24.1. The company decided to distribute the entire $40,000 of earnings available for common shareholders as cash dividends. Had Miller instead retained all $40,000 of its earnings available for common, the bottom portion of its income statement would have changed as follows:

Table 24.1   The Miller Flour Company's Balance Sheet When All Earnings Are Paid Out as Dividends

Balance sheet			
Assets		Liabilities and shareholders' equity	
Cash	$ 20,000	Total current liabilities	$ 200,000
Other current assets	340,000	Long-term debt	300,000
Total current assets	$ 360,000	Preferred shares at 8%	100,000
Fixed assets (net)	640,000	Common shares	300,000
		Retained earnings	100,000
Total assets	$1,000,000	Total liabilities and shareholders' equity	$1,000,000

	Total earnings	
	Paid out	Retained
Earnings available for common	$40,000	$40,000
Less: Common share dividends	40,000	0
To retained earnings	$ 0	$40,000

Table 24.2 presents the firm's balance sheet when it retains the $40,000 in earnings. A comparison of the balance sheet in Table 24.2 with that in Table 24.1 shows that Miller has available an added $40,000 of financing as a result of retaining (instead of paying out in common share dividends) the $40,000 of earnings available to be paid out to the common shareholders.*

---

*Firms can pay out in cash dividends more than the current period's earnings. The two items that may act as constraints are the amount of cash available and the total amount of retained earnings. The maximum amount of cash dividends a firm can pay in a given period is discussed later in the chapter.

Table 24.2   The Miller Flour Company's Balance Sheet When All Earnings Are Retained

Assets		Liabilities and shareholders' equity	
Cash	$ 60,000	Total current liabilities	$ 200,000
Other current assets	340,000	Long-term debt	300,000
Total current assets	$ 400,000	Preferred shares at 8%	100,000
Fixed assets (net)	640,000	Common shares	300,000
		Retained earnings	140,000
Total assets	$1,040,000	Total liabilities and shareholders' equity	$1,040,000

Had the firm paid out these earnings as dividends, it would have to borrow or sell common or preferred shares to attain the asset and financial structure shown in the balance sheet in Table 24.2. Retained earnings are actually funds obtained from the common shareholders, and are often viewed as a fully subscribed new issue of common shares. The implications of this fact for the firm's cost of capital were discussed in Chapter 17.

CASH DIVIDEND PAYMENT PROCEDURES

The payment of cash dividends to corporate shareholders only occurs when such payment is declared by the board of directors. The directors normally hold a quarterly or semiannual dividend meeting at which they evaluate the past period's financial performance to determine whether and when dividends should be paid.

Although most firms have a set policy regarding the amount of the periodic dividend, the firm's directors determine the amount at their periodic dividend meeting.

Relevant Dates   If the firm's directors declare a dividend, they typically issue a statement indicating their dividend decision, the dividend-record date, and the payment date. This statement is generally quoted in the *Globe and Mail Report on Business*, the *Financial Post*, and other financial news media.

The Dividend-Record Date   This is the date on which the company closes its *share transfer book* and compiles a list of its shareholders.* Because of the time needed to make bookkeeping entries when a share is traded, the share will sell *ex dividend* for two business days prior to the dividend-record date. The TSE and other stock exchanges allow two business days for recording changes of ownership. When a share is selling prior to the ex dividend date, it is said to be selling with *dividends on* or *cum dividends.*

The Payment Date   The payment date is generally set at a date that is two or three weeks after the dividend-record date. This allows for lags in cheque preparation and

---

*The *share transfer book* is the official book in which the records of the current owners of the firm's outstanding shares are kept. *Transfer agents*, which are generally the trust companies, maintain the share transfer book for most firms.

mailing. An example will clarify the various dates and accounting entries associated with the payment of cash dividends.

EXAMPLE   At the quarterly dividend meeting of the Wiseley Gun Company Ltd. on June 10, the directors declared an $0.80 per-share cash dividend for holders of record on Monday, July 1. The firm has 100,000 common shares outstanding. The payment date for the dividend is August 1. Before the dividend was declared, the key accounts of the firm were as follows:

Cash $200,000   Dividends payable $ 0
                            Retained earnings   1,000,000

When the dividend was announced by the directors, $80,000 (i.e., $0.80 per share · 100,000 shares) of the retained earnings was transferred to the dividends payable account. The key accounts thus became

Cash $200,000   Dividends payable $ 80,000
                            Retained earnings   920,000

The shares sold ex dividend for two business days prior to the date of record, which was June 7. Purchasers of Wiseley's shares on June 26 or earlier received the rights to the dividends, and those purchasing the shares on or after June 27 did not.* Prior to the August 1 payment date, the firm mailed dividend cheques to the holders of record as of July 1. This produced the following balances in the key accounts of the firm:

Cash $120,000   Dividends payable $ 0
                            Retained earnings   920,000

Thus the net effect of declaration and payment of the dividend was to reduce the firm's total assets (and shareholders' equity) by $80,000.

PAYMENT TO NONRESIDENTS

Many countries in a weak financial position closely regulate the payment of dividends to nonresidents, since such payments could unfavourably affect the country's balance of payments. The return implications of the existence or potential introduction of such regulations in a country are important factors when a Canadian investor or firm considers an investment in such a country.

Theoretical Viewpoints on the Relevance of Alternate Dividend Policies

A recurring topic in the theoretical literature of finance is whether or not a firm's dividend policy has an impact on the valuation of its shares. The two opposing schools

---

*A simple way to determine the first day on which the shares sell ex dividend is to subtract 2 from the dividend-record date; if a weekend intervenes, subtract 2 additional days. One business day prior to the first ex dividend day is the last day the shares will sell with dividends on.

of thought are attributable to Gordon and to Miller and Modigliani (MM). The Gordon position is that dividends are relevant and that the amount of dividends paid does affect the market value of the firm. The Miller and Modigliani position is the opposite: dividends are irrelevant and the amount of dividends paid does *not* affect the value of a firm.

Before proceeding to a discussion of the two opposing viewpoints, note that both groups agree that a firm should attempt to fund all investment projects that are acceptable when discounted at the firm's cost of capital. They also agree that if dividends are paid by reducing the funds allocated to acceptable investment projects, then paying increased dividends will reduce the value of the firm. However, given a fixed optimal investment policy for a firm and perfect capital markets,* the two opposing groups differ in their assessment of the impact of a firm's dividend policy on the market valuation of the firm.

THE RELEVANCE OF DIVIDENDS

The dividend relevance school's leading proponent, Myron Gordon, argues that the dividend decision affects the temporal (time) pattern of cash (i.e., dividend plus capital value change) payments to investors. Since future payments are uncertain and investors are believed to be risk averse, Gordon argues that the market value of a firm will depend upon the dividend policy it follows. More specifically, Gordon maintains that since investors prefer less risky current dividends to more risky future dividends,† the discount rate investors use to discount dividends increases with time. As a result, a firm's value will decrease, if any reduction in current dividends is invested by the firm to only yield the firm's cost of capital (assumed to be constant over time), and thus allow the firm to pay increased future dividends.

As noted by Brennan, Gordon's position essentially results from the inconsistency of using a constant discount rate to assess the desirability of new investments, and of using a discount rate that increases with time to assess the present value of alternate dividend streams over time.[1] However, there is no compelling theoretical reason to assume that the two discount rates should differ over time. Thus, if a firm "correctly" evaluates the desirability of investment projects by using a discount rate that fully reflects the preferences of investors as given in the capital markets, dividend policy again becomes strictly a financing decision and MM's position is again relevant.

THE IRRELEVANCE OF DIVIDENDS

The major arguments for the irrelevance of dividends were first propounded in 1961 by Miller and Modigliani (MM), who made three key assumptions. First, they assumed that capital markets were perfect in that there was equal and free access to information about any firm's future profits and investment opportunities, there was no transaction costs

---

*Some of the necessary conditions for perfect capital markets are: (1) there is equal and free access to information about any firm's future profits and investment opportunities; (2) there is no transaction costs (e.g., issuing and brokerage costs); and (3) there is no difference in the marginal tax rates for dividends or capital gains.

†This is often referred to as the "bird-in-the-hand" argument.

(e.g., issuing and brokerage costs), and there was no differences in the marginal tax rates for dividends or capital gains. Second, MM assumed that each investor was a rational wealth maximizer who viewed all other market participants and the total market as also being rational wealth maximizers. MM referred to this state as being "symmetric market rationality." Third, MM assumed that the investment policy of the firm was determined strictly by investment criteria and thus was independent of the level of a firm's dividend payments. This latter assumption allowed MM to view the dividend policy decision simply as a financing issue.

Given these three key assumptions, MM demonstrated analytically that the value of a firm was determined by the earning power and risk of the firm's portfolio of investment projects, and *not* by the amount of dividends it paid. Furthermore, MM argued that the appropriate rate for capitalizing (discounting) a firm's earnings (i.e., EBIT) was determined by the risk of the firm's earnings, and the risk of the firm's earnings did not depend upon the division of a firm's earnings into dividends and retained earnings (capital gains). MM also demonstrated analytically that in a world without taxes, or in a world with only corporate taxes, it made no difference whether or not shareholders received their cash flows as dividends or capital gains. Only when MM introduced personal taxes into their analysis did they suggest that dividends might affect the value of the firm.

While MM did rule out the possibility that a firm's dividend decision could affect a firm's investment decisions, they did not rule out the possibility that a firm's investment decisions could affect a firm's dividend decision.[2] For example, MM's arguments would suggest that a firm that lacks acceptable investment opportunities should distribute any unused internally generated funds to its shareholders, so they could then invest the proceeds in alternate acceptable investment opportunities. Thus, the *residual theory* of dividends is consistent with MM's dividend irrelevance theory.*

EFFECT OF MARKET IMPERFECTIONS

Although the dividend relevance issue has not yet been fully resolved, the nature of the debate was substantially altered by MM's paper. Since MM's paper, proponents of the position "that dividends may nonetheless still matter in practice" have concentrated on various market imperfections as the primary underlying cause. In this section, we will evaluate the possible effect of three of the commonly cited market imperfections— signaling aspect of dividends due to incomplete and unequal information, the existence of transaction costs, and the existence of differential personal taxes on dividends and capital gains.

Incomplete and Unequal Information   MM initially assumed that all investors had perfect knowledge about all firms' future profits and investment opportunities. In practice, investors have incomplete (and often unequal) information about a firm

---

*In the case of small firms, the treatment of dividends as a residual remaining after all acceptable investments have been initiated is quite common. This occurs since small firms do not normally have comparatively ready access to capital markets. The use of retained earnings therefore acts as a key source of financing for the firm's growth, which is generally an important goal of a small firm.

and its future prospects. Thus, when a firm raises or lowers its dividend payments, there may be a corresponding information-induced movement in the firm's share price.

According to MM, any effect a change in dividends has on share prices is attributable not to the dividend itself, but rather to the information a change in dividends conveys about expected future earnings. Since corporate management is both averse to reducing per-share dividends and likely to be more informed about a firm's future prospects and investment opportunities, MM argued that increases in cash dividends raise expectations about the level of future earnings, which in turn may cause investors to bid up share prices. Although the empirical evidence appears to support this signaling hypothesis, there is no conceptual conflict with MM's irrelevance position, since such information can be communicated to investors in other ways.[3]

Transaction Costs   MM argued that the negative effect of the dilution of earnings and ownership resulting from the sale of common shares on the firm's value is just offset by the positive effect of the dividends paid.* Thus, if there are no flotation or brokerage costs,† the cost of raising common equity through the retention of earnings or the sale of new shares is, in effect, the same for all firms.

However, once issuing (flotation) costs are introduced, each dollar paid in dividends can result in the firm raising more than a dollar of external financing. Since retained earnings are now a cheaper source of funds (see Chapter 17), it is no longer in the best interest of the firm's shareholders for a firm to simultaneously pay dividends and raise new funds externally. Thus, consideration of issuing expenses suggests that investors will prefer less dividends to more dividends.

On the other hand, when brokerage costs are introduced, investors should no longer be indifferent between receiving a cash dividend or obtaining an equivalent amount of cash by selling part of their equity holding. Since transaction costs make it less costly to obtain income by collecting dividends than by selling off securities, there will be a transaction-cost incentive to prefer dividends over capital gains. Thus, consideration of brokerage costs suggests that investors who require cash will have a dividend preference.

According to MM, since firms tend to attract an investor "clientele" drawn by the particular payout being followed, the effect of the transaction-cost incentive may be negligible, since one clientele is as good as another in terms of the valuation implied for the firm. The empirical evidence does lean toward the existence of a clientele effect.[4]

---

*Since retained earnings are not used to raise common share equity, then new common shares must be sold. The sale of new common shares may decrease the proportionate ownership and earnings claim of existing shareholders. MM argue that since this dilution is the cost associated with paying higher cash dividends (i.e., retaining less earnings) the impact of the increased dividend payment just compensates existing shareholders for any dilution they might experience. The share price is therefore unaffected by the dividend decision.

†It should be recalled from Chapter 17 that flotation costs are borne by the issuer of a security. This cost consists of two components: (1) underpricing costs, which reflect the fact that in a competitive market the price must be reduced to sell additional shares; and (2) underwriting costs, which include administrative and sales fees. This assumption also implies that prospective and existing shareholders do not have to pay any brokerage fees on purchase and sale transactions.

Personal Taxes It has been argued that in a world of personal taxes, there are at least two reasons why investors will prefer the receipt of capital gains as opposed to the receipt of dividends. First, an investor can postpone (or defer) the relevant tax payment on capital gains until the gains are actually realized by the sale of shares. Second, for investors who have used up their tax-free investment income allowances and are in high tax brackets, the tax paid on capital gains will generally be lower than that on dividends received. If this argument is valid, then firms should view dividends as a residual—a payment that should be made from the funds remaining after all profitable investments have been financed.

As discussed in Chapter 2, the current Canadian tax legislation has many complexities, such as the initial tax-free allowance on dividend and interest payments from Canadian sources, the dividend tax credit, and the reduced taxation of capital gains. When these complexities are considered, it is difficult to determine whether personal taxes result in a general and systematic tax-induced investor preference for dividends or for capital gains in the capital market. That is, in practice, an investor's preference for capital gain or dividend payments will depend upon the investor's marginal rate of taxation.* Thus, using MM's clientele argument, the tax-induced effect of personal taxes may be negligible, since one clientele is as good as another in terms of the valuation implied for the firm. In a more recent paper, Miller and Scholes demonstrate that even under the existing U.S. tax legislation, rational investors never have to pay more than the capital gains tax rate on dividend payments.[5] In addition, the available empirical evidence does not support the notion that an important dividend-tax clientele is in fact present.[6]

Conclusion The major justification for the relevance and practical importance of dividend policy must be due to one or more of the market imperfections discussed above. Unfortunately, we are still unable to unambiguously determine whether or not, and how, these imperfections can cause share prices to be a function of dividend policy. Nevertheless, in the remainder of this chapter we will make the realistic assumption that since flotation costs are associated with new issues of equity, firms prefer to finance with retained earnings. In the absence of flotation costs, a number of the factors discussed in the remainder of the chapter would not be important in developing or implementing a firm's dividend policy.

Factors Affecting Dividend Policy

Before discussing the common types of dividend policies, we should consider the factors involved in formulating dividend policy. These factors include certain legal, contractual, and internal constraints, the firm's growth prospects, owner considerations, and market considerations.

---

*As discussed in Chapter 2, the dividend tax credit is designed in such a manner that the *effective* marginal tax rate on dividend income increases *more than proportionally* with increases in an investor's *nominal* marginal tax rate. In fact, the effective marginal tax rate for investors with a low marginal tax rate can be negative. On the other hand, this is *not* the case with capital gains taxation, even when the general $1,000 deduction for dividends, interest, and capital gains is considered.

LEGAL, CONTRACTUAL, AND INTERNAL CONSTRAINTS

The firm's dividend policy is often constrained by certain legal, contractual, and internal factors. The legal factors result from the provincial and federal corporation acts, the contractual constraints typically result from certain loan covenants, and the internal constraints are the result of the firm's liquid asset position.

Legal Constraints   There are four basic legal constraints confronting the corporation regarding cash dividend payments. They concern capital impairment, net profits, insolvency, and retention of the preferred small business tax status.

Capital Impairment   Most corporation acts prohibit corporations from paying out as cash dividends any portion of the firm's capital. Capital impairment restrictions are generally established to provide a sufficient equity base to protect creditors' claims on the firm's assets.

Net Profits   The net profits requirement is similar to the capital impairment requirement in that it limits the amount of dividends to the sum of the firm's present and past earnings. In other words, the firm cannot pay more in cash dividends than the sum of its most recent and past retained earnings. This requirement has the same effect as the capital impairment rule where capital is defined as all paid-in capital. The reader should recognize, however, that *the firm is not prohibited from paying more in dividends than its current earnings.* *

EXAMPLE   The Miller Flour Company, illustrated earlier in this chapter, had $40,000 in earnings available for common share dividends. An analysis of the balance sheet in Table 24.1 indicates that the firm has past retained earnings of $100,000. Thus, it could legally pay dividends of up to $140,000 during the current period.

Insolvency   If a firm has overdue liabilities or is legally insolvent or bankrupt (i.e., if the fair value of its assets is less than its liabilities), most corporation acts prohibit the payment of cash dividends. This restriction is intended to protect the firm's creditors by prohibiting the liquidation of a near-bankrupt firm through the payment of cash dividends to owners. The payment of cash dividends by an insolvent firm could seriously impair its creditors' claims in bankruptcy.

Preferred Small Business Tax Status   As discussed in Chapter 2, the Canadian Income Tax Act provides for a reduced rate of taxation for the taxable income of smaller Canadian-controlled corporations, provided that the corporation's accumulated taxable income does not exceed a specified limit. Since small businesses are allowed to deduct four dollars from their accumulated taxable income for each three dollars of taxable

---

*A firm having an operating loss in the current period could still pay cash dividends as long as sufficient retained earnings were available and, of course, as long as it had the cash with which to make the payments.

dividends paid to shareholders, there is a tax-induced incentive for small businesses to pay dividends in order to retain their preferred tax status. The effects of this legal requirement were illustrated in Chapter 2.

Contractual Constraints   Often the firm's ability to pay cash dividends is constrained by certain restrictive covenants in a lease contract, a term loan agreement, a bond indenture, or a preferred share agreement. Generally these constraints either prohibit the payment of cash dividends until a certain level of earnings has been achieved or limit the amount of dividends paid to a certain amount or percentage of earnings. Since cash is required to pay dividends, constraints on dividend payments help to protect lessors, creditors, and preferred shareholders from losses due to insolvency on the part of the firm. Contractual constraints on dividend payments are quite common, and their violation is generally grounds for a request for immediate repayment by the affected supplier of funds.

Internal Constraints   The firm's ability to pay cash dividends is generally constrained by the amount of excess cash available. Lenders are not especially interested in lending money for dividend payments, since they produce no tangible or operating benefits that will help the firm repay the loan. It is important to keep in mind that although a firm may have high earnings, its ability to pay dividends may be constrained by a low level of liquid assets (cash and marketable securities).

EXAMPLE   The Miller Flour Company could legally pay $140,000 in dividends (since it has $100,000 in past retained earnings plus $40,000 in current earnings available for common). The firm has total liquid assets of $50,000 ($20,000 in cash plus marketable securities worth $30,000), but $35,000 of this is needed for operations. Therefore, the maximum dividend the firm can pay, without borrowing, is $15,000. It is important to recognize internal liquidity constraints when making the cash dividend decision.

GROWTH PROSPECTS

The growth prospects of the firm must be evaluated in establishing a dividend policy. Generally firms with greater growth possibilities are in constant and greater need for funds.

THE AVAILABILITY OF FUNDS

A firm must evaluate its financial position from both a profitability and a risk standpoint to develop insight into its ability to raise funds quickly at a minimum cost. Generally the large, mature firm has greater access to new capital than the firm in a state of rapid growth. For this reason, the funds available to the rapidly growing, especially small, firm may not be sufficient to support the numerous acceptable projects. Thus, a growth firm may have to depend heavily on internal financing through retained earnings in order to take advantage of the profitable projects available to it.

INFLATION

During periods characterized by large increases in the price level, a firm may find that the replacement cost of existing assets far exceeds the funds generated by capital cost allowance writeoffs. During such time periods, the reported operating income of the firm will in effect be overstated by an amount equal to the unrecovered real depreciation of the existing asset base. If management is subject to money illusion, it may increase the amount of dividends paid out of the inflated reported earnings, instead of retaining and reinvesting a larger portion of the earnings to maintain the firm's existing level of assets (and thus earning power).

OWNER CONSIDERATIONS

As noted, in establishing a dividend policy, the primary concern should be how to maximize the firm's owners' wealth over the long run. Although it is impossible to establish a policy that will satisfy each existing and potential owner, the firm must establish a policy that maximizes the market value of its common equity. Three factors that must be considered are the tax status of the owners, their other investment opportunities, and the dilution of ownership.

The Tax Status of the Firm's Owners   The tax status of a firm's owners can have a significant effect on the firm's dividend policy. If a firm has a large percentage of wealthy shareholders who are in a high tax bracket, the firm may decide to pay out a lower percentage of its earnings to provide its owners with income in the form of capital gains as opposed to dividends. Since the capital gains tax rate is considerably less than the ordinary tax rate, these wealthy owners should find their tax liability reduced. On the other hand, a firm may have mostly lower-income shareholders who need dividend income, are in a low tax bracket, and can utilize the full benefits of the dividend tax credit and the tax-free dividend and interest allowance. These owners may prefer a high payout of earnings.

It is quite difficult for the financial manager of a large, diversely held firm to know or cater to the tax status of the owners. If the directors, or some controlling group of shareholders, believe a low dividend payout is preferable, any owners disagreeing with this strategy can divest themselves of their holdings and purchase the shares of a firm paying out a high percentage of earnings. Thus, to some extent, a firm's dividend policy will determine its shareholder composition (referred to earlier as the clientele effect), and vice versa. Although as we indicated in a previous section, the tax status of owners may not be the primary factor in the dividend decision, it should be given some attention.

It should also be noted that some firms have attempted to cater to a group of shareholders with more heterogeneous dividend preferences (i.e., more than one clientele) by paying out a higher percentage of earnings while simultaneously providing investors with a dividend reinvestment plan. The features of such a plan are demonstrated by the following example.

EXAMPLE On February 22, 1980, the Canadian Development Corporation (CDC) announced a new common share dividend reinvestment plan for holders of the firm's Class B shares. The new plan was designed as a convenient means for shareholders to increase their equity holding in CDC by using their preferred share dividends to purchase new common shares from CDC at 5 percent below the average market price of CDC common shares for the five days preceding the first business day of the month of the reinvestment. Participants in the plan or CDC common share-holders could also purchase additional common shares from CDC at the average market price by making optional cash contributions to the plan of up to $3,000 per quarter. Participating share-holders were not charged brokerage fees. All administration fees connected with the plan were paid by CDC.

Owner Investment Opportunities A firm should not retain funds for investment in average-risk projects yielding returns that are less than the firm's cost of capital. Whatever the portion of earnings that remains unspent after all new acceptable investment projects have been financed should be paid out in dividends.

The Dilution of Ownership Since the most comparable alternative to the use of retained earnings as a source of equity financing is the sale of new common shares, consideration should be given to the dilution of ownership interests that may result from a high-payment dividend policy.

It is more important that the shareholders recognize the firm's motives for retaining or paying out a large percentage of earnings. Although the ultimate dividend policy depends on numerous factors, the avoidance of shareholder discontent is important. If the shareholders become dissatisfied with the existing dividend policy, they may sell their shares, increasing the possibility that control of the firm will be seized by some outside group. The "takeover" of a firm by outsiders is more likely when owners are dissatisfied with its dividend policy. It is generally in the financial manager's own self-interest to keep in touch with the shareholders' general attitudes toward dividends.

MARKET CONSIDERATIONS

Since the wealth of the firm's owners is reflected in the market price of the firm's shares, an awareness of the market's probable response to certain types of dividend policies is helpful in formulating a suitable dividend policy. The probable market response to fixed-dollar or increasing dividends and continuous dividend payments is discussed in this section.

Fixed-Dollar or Increasing Dividends Shareholders are believed to value a fixed or increasing level of dividends as opposed to a fixed payout ratio. If the *payout ratio*, which is found by dividing the dividends per share by the earnings per share, is held constant, the shareholders may receive no dividends in the lean periods and high dividends when earnings are high. Since paying a fixed or increasing dividend eliminates uncertainty about the magnitude of dividends, the earnings of the firm are likely to be discounted at a lower rate and the value of the firm's shares is likely to remain at a reasonably high level. In short, stable or gradually increasing dividends are considered preferable to the variable dividends that may result from a fixed payout ratio.

Continuous Dividend Payments The marketplace generally not only values a fixed or increasing dividend level, but also values a policy of continuous dividend payment. To reduce owners' uncertainty about returns, not only must the amount of the dividend payment be predictable but so must its frequency of receipt. The continuous payment of cash dividends, regardless of their magnitude, should reduce shareholder uncertainty.

As discussed earlier, the stability and continuous nature of dividends are important factors because of the information content of dividend payments. By paying fixed or increasing dividends on a continuous basis, the firm gives its owners a feeling of confidence in its continued success. On the other hand, if the firm passes a dividend payment in a given period due to a loss or very low earnings, shareholders are quite likely to react unfavourably. The nonpayment of the dividend creates uncertainty about the firm's future success, and this uncertainty may result in lower share values. Even if current earnings are low, a firm should continue its dividend payment to avoid conveying unfavourable information to owners and prospective investors. Owners and investors generally construe a dividend payment during a period of losses as an indication that the loss is temporary.

Types of Dividend Policies

Although there are an infinite number of possible dividend policies available to the business firm, three of the more commonly used dividend policies are briefly described in this section: a constant-payout-ratio dividend policy, a regular dividend policy, and a low regular-and-extra dividend policy. A particular firm's cash dividend policy may incorporate elements of each of these policies.

A CONSTANT-PAYOUT-RATIO DIVIDEND POLICY*

This type of dividend policy has been adopted by few firms. The firm simply establishes a certain percentage of earnings to be paid out each period. The problem with this type of policy is that if the firm's earnings drop or a loss occurs in a given period, the dividends will be low or even nonexistent. Since dividends have an information content, the firm's shares will most likely be adversely affected by this type of action. An example will clarify the problems stemming from a constant-payout-ratio dividend policy.

*The *payout ratio*, by definition, is the firm's cash dividend per share divided by its earnings per share. It indicates the percentage of each dollar earned that is distributed to the owners in the form of cash.

EXAMPLE   The Nader Motor Company Ltd. has a policy of paying out 40 percent of earnings in cash dividends. In periods when a loss occurs, the firm's policy is to pay no cash dividends. Nader's earnings per share, dividends per share, and average price per share for the past six years are as follows:

Year	Earnings/share	Dividends/share	Av. price/share
19X3	$4.50	$1.80	$50.00
19X4	2.00	.80	46.00
19X5	−1.50	.00	38.00
19X6	1.75	.70	48.00
19X7	3.00	1.20	52.00
19X8	− .50	.00	42.00

Dividends increased in 19X5–19X6 and 19X6–19X7 and decreased in 19X3–19X4, 19X4–19X5, and 19X7–19X8. It can be seen that in years of decreased dividends, the firm's share price dropped; when dividends increased, the price of a share increased.

A REGULAR DIVIDEND POLICY

This type of dividend policy has been adopted by most firms. It consists of the payment of a fixed-dollar dividend in each period, and is what is implied when we refer to "a stable dividend policy." Most firms when using this policy will increase the regular dividend once a *proven* increase in earnings has occurred. Under this policy, dividends are almost *never* decreased. An example will clarify how a regular dividend policy works.

EXAMPLE   The Gusher Oil Company's dividend policy is to pay annual dividends of $1.00 per share until per-share earnings have exceeded $4.00 for three consecutive years, at which time the annual dividend will be raised to $1.50 per share and a new dividend plateau established. The firm does not anticipate decreasing its dividend unless its liquidity is in jeopardy. Gusher's earnings per share, dividends per share, and average price per share for the past 12 years are as follows:

Year	Earnings/share	Dividends/share	Av. price/share
19X7	$3.00	$1.00	$35.00
19X8	2.80	1.00	33.50
19X9	.50	1.00	33.00
19Y0	.75	1.00	33.00
19Y1	3.00	1.00	36.00
19Y2	6.00	1.00	38.00
19Y3	2.00	1.00	38.50
19Y4	5.00	1.00	42.00
19Y5	4.20	1.00	43.00
19Y6	4.60	1.50	45.00
19Y7	3.90	1.50	46.50
19Y8	4.50	1.50	47.50

It can be seen that, regardless of the level of earnings, Gusher paid dividends of $1.00 per share through 19Y5. In 19Y6 the dividend was raised to $1.50 per share, since earnings of $4.00 per share had been achieved for three years. In 19Y6, the firm would also have had to establish a new earnings plateau for further dividend increases. It can be seen that Gusher Oil Company's average price per share exhibited a stable, increasing behaviour in spite of the somewhat volatile pattern of earnings per share.

Often, a regular dividend policy, such as that of the Gusher Oil Company, is built around a *target dividend-payout ratio*. The firm attempts to pay out a certain percentage of earnings; but, rather than let the dividends fluctuate, it pays a stated dollar dividend and adjusts it toward the target payout as proven increases in earnings occur. For instance, the Gusher Oil Company appears to have a target payout ratio of around 35 percent. The payout was about 33 percent ($1.00 ÷ $3.00) when the dividend policy was set in 19X7 and the dividend was raised to $1.50 (about a 38-percent payout ratio) when per-share earnings exceeded $4.00. The use of a target payout ratio with a regular dividend policy is not unusual.

A LOW REGULAR-AND-EXTRA-DIVIDEND POLICY

Some firms establish a policy of a low regular dividend accompanied by an additional dividend when earnings warrant it. If earnings are higher than normal in a given period, the firm may pay this additional dividend, which will be designated an *extra dividend*. Thus the firm avoids giving existing and prospective shareholders false hopes of increased dividends in coming periods. The use of the low regular-extra designation is especially common among companies that experience cyclical shifts in earnings.

Firms using this type of dividend policy must raise the level of the regular dividend once proven increases in earnings have been achieved. The extra dividend should not be allowed to become a regular event, or it becomes meaningless. The use of a target payout ratio in establishing the regular dividend level is advisable.

Noncash Dividends

Attention thus far in this chapter has been devoted to the payment of cash dividends. A number of alternatives or supplements to the payment of cash dividends are available to the firm. One uncommon approach, which will not be discussed in the text, is the payment of dividends in merchandise produced by the firm. However, two noncash methods of paying dividends—share dividends and share repurchases—as well as a closely related topic—share splits—are discussed in this section. Share dividends are easily recognizable as a dividend payment.

SHARE DIVIDENDS

Often, firms pay share dividends as either a replacement for or a supplement to the payment of cash dividends. Although share dividends do not have a real value, the firm's shareholders may believe that they represent something they did not have before, and therefore have value. By definition, a *share dividend* is a payment of shares to the firm's existing owners. The accounting and tax aspects, the shareholder's viewpoint, and the company's viewpoint of share dividends are discussed in this section.

Accounting Aspects   In an accounting sense, the payment of a share dividend is a "shifting of funds" between capital accounts rather than a use of funds. When a firm declares a share dividend, the general procedures with respect to its announcement and distribution are the same as those described earlier for a cash dividend. The difference is that the owner receives additional shares, which in actuality represent something he or she already owns. It does not change the shareholders proportional ownership or increase the assets of the firm. An example of the accounting entries associated with the payment of share dividends is given in the following example.

EXAMPLE   The J and L Company's current shareholders' equity on its balance sheet is as follows:

Preferred shares	$ 300,000
Common shares [100,000 shares without nominal or par value (n.p.v.)]	1,000,000
Retained earnings	700,000
Shareholders' equity	$2,000,000

If J and L declares a 10-percent share dividend and the market price of its shares is $15 per share, $150,000 (i.e., 10% · $15 per share · 100,000 shares) of retained earnings will be capitalized. The resulting account balances are as follows:

Preferred shares	$ 300,000
Common shares (110,000 shares n.p.v.)	1,150,000
Retained earnings	550,000
Shareholders' equity	$2,000,000

Since 10,000 (10 percent of 100,000) new shares have been issued and the prevailing market price is $15 per share, $150,000 ($15 per share · 10,000 shares) has been shifted from retained earnings to the common share account. Note that the firm's shareholders' equity has not changed; funds have only been redistributed between the shareholders' equity accounts.

It is important to recognize that since the payment of share dividends reduces the firm's retained earnings, it also reduces the aggregate amount of cash dividends that can be legally paid out. Because the availability of cash is typically more binding on the firm's ability to pay cash dividends, the reduction of retained earnings as the result of share dividend payments generally does not unfavourably impact on the firm.

Tax Aspects   Since the share dividends of private companies are considered a cash dividend distribution, they are taxed as regular income to a firm's shareholders. On the other hand, the share dividends of public companies have been taxed since March 31, 1977, as capital gains. The share dividends of public companies are given a zero net cost base for capital gains purposes when they are initially received by the firm's shareholders, and the total proceeds obtained when the shares are later sold by the shareholder are thus taxed as a capital gain.

The Shareholders' Viewpoint   The shareholder receiving a share dividend receives nothing of value. After the share dividend is paid, the per-share value of the shareholder's shares will decrease in proportion to the share dividend in such a way that the market value of his or her total holdings in the firm will remain unchanged. The shareholder's proportion of ownership in the firm will also remain the same. An example will clarify these points.

EXAMPLE   Mr. X owned 10,000 shares of the J and L Company. The company's most recent earnings were $220,000.00, and earnings are not expected to change in the near future. Before the share dividend, Mr. X owned 10 percent (10,000 shares ÷ 100,000 shares) of the firm's shares, which were selling for $15.00 per share. Earnings per share were $2.20 ($220,000.00 ÷ 100,000 shares). Since Mr. X owns 10,000 shares, his earnings were $22,000.00 ($2.20 per share · 10,000 shares). After receiving the 10-percent share dividend, Mr. X has 11,000 shares, which again is 10 percent (11,000 shares ÷ 110,000 shares) of the ownership. The market price of the shares can be expected to drop to $13.64 per share [$15.00 · (1.00 ÷ 1.10)], which means that the market value of Mr. X's holdings will be $150,000.00 (11,000 shares · $13.64 per share). This is the same as the initial value of his holdings (10,000 shares · $15.00 share). The future earnings per share will drop to $2.00 ($220,000.00 ÷ 110,000 shares), since the same $220,000.00 in earnings must now be divided between 110,000 shares. Since Mr. X still owns 10 percent of the shares, his portion of the total earnings is still $22,000.00 ($2.00 per share · 11,000 shares).

Sometimes when a firm issues a share dividend, it will maintain the cash dividend per share, thereby increasing the dividends paid out since more shares are outstanding. This type of action actually represents an increase in dividends and may result in an increased market value for the firm's shares. The effect of this increased dividend is dependent upon its informational content.

The Company's Viewpoint   Share dividends are more costly to issue than cash dividends, but the advantages of using them generally outweigh these costs. Firms find the share dividend a means of giving owners something without having to use cash. For example, when a firm is growing rapidly and needs internal financing to perpetuate this growth, a share dividend is used. As long as the investors recognize that the firm is reinvesting its earnings in a manner that should tend to maximize their future earnings, the market price of the firm's shares should not be adversely affected. If the share dividend is paid so that cash can be retained to satisfy past due bills, the market reaction may be less favourable.

SHARE SPLITS

Although not a type of dividend, *share splits* have a similar effect upon a firm's share price as do share dividends. Therefore share splits are briefly described here. Share splits are commonly used to lower the market price of a firm's shares in order to enhance their trading activity.

Accounting Aspects   A share split has no effect on the firm's financial structure. It most commonly increases the number of shares outstanding and reduces the share's par or stated value. In other words, in a 2-for-1 split, two new shares are exchanged for each old share; in a 3-for-2 split, three new shares are exchanged for each two old shares, and so on. It also reduces other financial measures such as earnings per share, book value per share, and market value per share.

EXAMPLE   The LEC Company Ltd. had 200,000 common shares and no preferred shares outstanding. Since the shares are selling at a high market price, the firm has declared a 2-for-1 share split. The before-and-after shareholders' equity is as follows:

Before

Common shares (200,000 shares outstanding without nominal or par value)	$4,400,000
Retained earnings	2,000,000
Shareholders' equity	$6,400,000

After

Common shares (400,000 shares outstanding without nominal or par value)	$4,400,000
Retained earnings	2,000,000
Shareholders' equity	$6,400,000

It should be clear that although a share dividend impacts on the firm's retained earnings, a share split has no effect on retained earnings and therefore does not have any impact on the aggregate amount of cash dividend payments a firm may legally make.

Shares can be split in any way desired. Sometimes *reverse share splits* are made. For example, in a 1-for-2 split, one new share is exchanged for two old shares; in a 2-for-3 split, two new shares are exchanged for three old shares, and so on. Reverse share splits are initiated when a share is selling at too low a price to appear respectable.*

*If a share is selling at a low price—possibly less than a few dollars—many investors are hesitant to purchase it because they believe it is "cheap." These somewhat unsophisticated investors correlate cheapness and quality, and they feel that a low-priced share is a low-quality investment. A reverse share split raises the share price and increases per-share earnings.

Price Effects   As is the case for share dividends, a share split should not have any impact on the total market value of a firm's equity, unless there is either an economic benefit or new information associated with the share split. No new economic benefits should be associated with the share split. That is, since the amount of total earnings and the appropriate market rate of capitalization should not change because of the share split, the total market value of the firm's equity should not change.

No new information that affects the total market value of the firm's equity should be associated with a share split. However, as has been empirically shown by Fama, Fisher, Jensen, and Roll, since dividend changes are often associated with share splits, the information content of such dividend changes (and not the share split itself) may affect the total market value of a firm's equity.[7]

SHARE REPURCHASES

Common shares are repurchased for a number of reasons, such as to obtain shares to be used in acquisitions, to have shares available for share option plans, to remove publicly held shares so the firm can go private,* or merely to retire outstanding shares. Repurchase of shares is permitted under a number of provincial corporations acts. For example, the British Columbia and Ontario acts permit a firm to repurchase its own shares, to hold repurchased shares on a nonvoting basis, and to later reissue such shares. The federal corporations act also permits the repurchase of shares by federally incorporated firms. However, under the federal act, any repurchased shares must be retired. This section is concerned with the repurchase of shares for retirement, since this type of repurchase may be used as a substitute for the payment of cash dividends. It covers the accounting entries resulting from repurchases, motives for the retirement of shares, and the repurchase process.

Accounting Entries   The accounting entries resulting when common shares are repurchased are a reduction in cash and the establishment of an asset account called "treasury shares," typically shown as a deduction from shareholders' equity.

Motives for the Retirement of Shares   When common shares are purchased for retirement, the underlying motive is to distribute excess cash to the firm's owners. The general rationale for this action is that as long as earnings remain constant the repurchase of shares reduces the number of outstanding shares, raising the earnings per share and therefore the market price per share. The retirement of common shares can be viewed as a type of reverse dilution, since the earnings per share and the market price of shares are increased by reducing the number of shares outstanding. A simple example will clarify this point.

---

*The "squeeze-out" of minority shareholders while firms go private by repurchasing shares has been a contentious regulatory issue in Canada during 1978 and 1979.

EXAMPLE   The Terrell Company Ltd. has released the following financial data:

Earnings available for common	$1,000,000
Number of shares outstanding	400,000
Earnings per share ($1,000,000 ÷ 400,000)	$2.50
Market price per share	$50
Price-earnings ratio ($50 ÷ $2.50)	20

The firm is contemplating paying cash dividends of $2 per share, which will raise the price of a share to $52 (since the market price is currently $50) while a share is selling with dividends on. The total amount of dividends to be paid by the firm will be $800,000 (400,000 shares · $2 per share). However, instead of paying $800,000 in cash dividends, the firm could repurchase shares at $52 per share. With $800,000, it could repurchase approximately 15,385 shares ($800,000 ÷ $52 per share). As a result of this repurchase, 384,615 shares (400,000 shares − 15,385 shares) of common shares would remain outstanding. Earnings per share would rise to $2.60 ($1,000,000 ÷ 384,615), and if a share still sold at 20 times earnings, its market price would rise to $52 per share. It should be noted that the market price per share would be the same, $52, regardless of whether the cash dividend was paid or shares were repurchased.*

The impact of the share repurchase illustrated is attributable to two key assumptions—(1) the shares could be repurchased at $52 each, and (2) the price-earnings ratio remains at 20 in either case (i.e., cash dividend or share repurchase). If the firm were to buy the shares for less than $52, the remaining shareholders would gain; while at more than $52, the remaining shareholders would lose. If the price-earnings ratio rose as a result of repurchase, the remaining shareholders would gain, and if it were to drop they would lose. In other words, the assumptions made with respect to both the purchase price and the price-earnings ratio significantly impact the analysis of a proposed share repurchase in lieu of paying cash dividends.

There are two advantages of share repurchases to shareholders. First, share repurchases result in a tax advantage for shareholders with high marginal tax rates. This tax advantage stems from the fact that while cash dividends are taxed at an investor's effective tax rate (i.e., the rate that reflects the dividend tax credit), the increase in the market value of the shares due to the share repurchase is taxed at the capital gains tax rate. Second, shareholders who do not need current income can defer the tax payment on the increased market value of their equity holding by not selling their shares.

There are two disadvantages of share repurchases to shareholders. First, share repurchases result in a tax disadvantage for shareholders with low effective tax rates or no taxable income. Second, if the firm repurchases shares at a price greater than their intrinsic value, the remaining shareholders lose.

Although the use of share repurchases to retire shares is most commonly viewed as a

---

*When a share is selling with dividends on, its price would be $52; once the dividend is paid, the share's price would drop by the $2-per-share dividend to $50. Of course, the shareholders would have gained the $2-per-share dividend, while in the case of the share repurchase, the remaining shareholders would have experienced a $2-per-share increase in the market price (i.e., from $50 per share to $52 per share).

dividend decision, some people view it as an investment or a financing decision. A share repurchase may be viewed as an investment decision in those cases where the firm has excess cash but no acceptable investment opportunities and the firm's shares are believed to be undervalued. The retirement of shares through repurchases may be considered a financing decision in the sense that it enables the firm to shift its debt-equity ratio to a more highly levered position. When debt or preferred shares are used to raise funds for a repurchase of shares, it is more likely to be viewed as a financing decision. However, our basic concern in this chapter is with the use of share repurchases as a form of cash dividend.

The Repurchase Process   When a company intends to repurchase a block of outstanding shares, it should make shareholders aware of its intentions. Specifically, it should advise them of the purpose of the repurchase (i.e., acquisitions, share options, retirement, and so forth) and the disposition (if any) planned for the repurchased shares (i.e., traded for shares of another firm, distribution to executives, held in the treasury, and so forth). Three basic methods of repurchase are commonly used. One is to purchase shares on the *open market*. This may place upward pressure on the price of shares if the number of shares being repurchased is reasonably large compared to the total number of shares outstanding. It is quite important in this case that the firm clearly state its intentions and make certain that the purchase price is fair and equitable in view of the interests and opportunities of the remaining shareholders in the firm.

The second method of repurchasing shares is through *tender offers*.* A tender offer is a formal offer by the firm to purchase a given number of shares at a specified price. The price at which a tender offer is made is set above the current market price in order to attract sellers. If the number of shares desired cannot be repurchased through the tender offer, open-market purchases can be used to obtain the additional shares. Tender offers are preferred when large numbers of shares are repurchased since the company's intentions are clearly stated and each shareholder has an opportunity to sell his or her shares at the tendered price.

The third method sometimes used to repurchase shares involves arranging to purchase on a *negotiated basis* a large block of shares from one or more large shareholders.

Summary

This chapter has discussed two closely related topics—dividends and retained earnings. The cash dividend decision is normally a quarterly decision made by the corporate board of directors. Any earnings remaining after cash dividends have been paid become retained earnings, which represent reinvested funds to the firm. Retained earnings are a source of long-term financing to the business firm. Since they are a source of capital,

---

*Tender offers are discussed in greater detail in Chapter 25. The motive for these offers may be to acquire control of another firm rather than to tender the firm's own shares.

they are an alternative to financial leases, long-term debt, bonds, preferred shares, or the sale of new common shares. Retained earnings may be viewed as a fully subscribed new issue of common shares since they represent new ownership capital.

Theoretical arguments have been made suggesting the irrelevance of dividends with respect to the market value of a firm. The major proponents of this belief are Miller and Modigliani. Another school of thought suggests that dividends are an important factor in maximizing the wealth of the firm's owners, since paying dividends reduces the owners' uncertainty concerning the future success of the firm, causing them to discount its earnings at a lower rate. The effect of this lower discount rate is to raise the market value of the firm's shares.

The firm must consider certain factors in setting its dividend policy. Federal and provincial corporation acts prohibit it from paying out capital. These acts limit dividends to an amount equal to current and past retained earnings only. Most acts prohibit insolvent firms from paying cash dividends. Lease contracts, loan covenants, bond indentures, and preferred share agreements quite often limit dividends to a certain amount. The amount of cash and marketable securities a firm has often acts as an internal dividend constraint. Other factors that require consideration by the firm are its growth prospects, availability of funds, inflation, the owners' tax status, the owners' other investment opportunities, dilution, and certain market considerations. Common dividend policies include a constant payout ratio, regular dividends, or low regular and extra dividends. A firm's dividend policy is often a combination of these policies. Firms commonly establish a target payout ratio, which they attempt to maintain by making discrete increases in dividends with proven increases in earnings. Most firms try to establish dividend policies that will not require them to decrease their dividends.

Occasionally, firms cannot pay cash dividends or can only pay low cash dividends. In order to provide owners with some indication that the firm is doing well, they may pay share dividends. Share dividends result from capitalizing retained earnings; they do not actually have a value to the recipient. Although not a type of dividend, share splits, which are used to supposedly enhance trading activity in a firm's shares, are sometimes initiated. They tend to have effects similar to a share dividend since they most often (except in the case of a reverse share split) increase the number of shares outstanding while not providing any inflow of new capital. In an accounting sense, the share split does not affect retained earnings; it merely results in a notational entry.

Another method of paying noncash dividends is to repurchase shares. Firms having excess cash can repurchase and retire shares to increase their earnings and market price per share. These increases occur if the firm can repurchase shares at a price equal to or below the share price with dividends on, and if the firm's post-repurchase price-earnings ratio remains unchanged or improves over the pre-repurchase price-earnings ratio. The actual repurchase decision would, of course, depend upon the reasonableness of such assumptions. Making share repurchases in lieu of cash dividend payments may provide tax benefits to the firm's owners by providing them with capital gains income, instead of ordinary income, which would be taxed at a higher rate. Some firms repurchase shares for acquisitions, for share options, for the purposes of going private, or for retirement. Share repurchases can be made either directly in the marketplace, through tender offers, or on a negotiated basis from holders of large blocks of shares.

Questions

24.1 How are retained earnings a source of funds to the business firm? If earnings were not retained, what might the financial consequences for the firm be?

24.2 Why must the firm view its dividend decision as a financing decision?

24.3 How does the dividend-record date relate to the payment of cash dividends? What do the terms *ex dividend* and *dividends on,* or *cum dividends,* mean? Who sets the dividend payment date?

24.4 What assumptions are used by Miller and Modigliani in support of the irrelevance of dividends?

24.5 What do MM say about the effect of dividends on share prices? Do they believe dividends affect share prices?

24.6 What effect do flotation (issue) costs have on the relevance of dividends?

24.7 What are some contractual and internal constraints on the firm's ability to pass dividends? Why do contractual constraints exist?

24.8 Why must the firm's dividend policy be based somehow on its growth prospects?

24.9 Why is the primary consideration with respect to dividend policy its effect on the firm's owners? How may the tax status of the owners affect a firm's dividend policy?

24.10 What effect do outside investment opportunities and the possible dilution of ownership have on the firm's determination of an acceptable dividend policy?

24.11 Why is there a tax-induced incentive for small businesses to pay dividends?

24.12 What are (1) a constant-payout-ratio policy; (2) a regular dividend policy; and (3) a low regular-and-extra-dividend policy? What are the ramifications of these policies?

24.13 What is a share dividend? Do share dividends have any value in and of themselves? Why are they issued?

24.14 What is a share split? Compare a share split with a share dividend. What is a reverse share split?

24.15 Explain how share dividends and share splits affect the firm's balance sheet and the firm's ability to pay dividends.

24.16 If it is more costly to issue shares than to pay cash dividends, why do firms issue share dividends? Are there any similarities between share dividends and share splits? What are they?

24.17 What motives prompt firms to repurchase their shares? What effect on balance sheet accounts does the repurchase of shares have?

24.18 What is the logic behind repurchasing of common shares in order to redistribute excess cash to the firm's owners? How might this raise the per-share earnings and market price of outstanding shares?

24.19 How may shares be repurchased by a firm? Why is it important that the firm's shareholders be made aware of the purpose of a repurchase and the planned disposition of repurchased shares?

Problems

24.1 Yukon Widget Ltd., at its quarterly dividend meeting, declared a cash dividend of $1.10 per share and a dividend-record date of Monday, July 10. The firm has 300,000 common shares outstanding and has set a payment date of July 31. Prior to the dividend declaration, the firm's key accounts were as follows:

Cash	$500,000	Dividends payable	$ 0
		Retained earnings	$2,500,000

a. Show the entries after the meeting adjourned.
b. When is the ex dividend date?
c. After the July 31 payment date, what would the key accounts be?
d. What effect, if any, will the dividend have on the firm's total assets?

24.2   The Gander Company's shareholders' equity account is as follows:

Preferred shares	$ 500,000
Common shares (400,000 shares n.p.v.)	2,600,000
Retained earnings	1,900,000
Total shareholders' equity	$5,000,000

The earnings available for common shareholders from this period's operations are $100,000, which have been included as part of the $1,900,000 retained earnings.
a. What is the maximum dividend per share the firm can pay?
b. If the firm has $160,000 in cash, what is the largest per-share dividend it can pay without borrowing?
c. Indicate what accounts, if any, will be affected if the firm pays the dividends indicated in a and b above. What changes would result from the dividends indicated in a and b?
d. Indicate the effects of an $80,000 cash dividend on the firm's shareholders' equity.

24.3   A firm has $800,000 in its common share account, retained earnings of $40,000 (including the current year's earnings), and 25,000 common shares outstanding. It earned $29,000 after taxes and preferred share dividends in the most recent year.
a. What is the most the firm can pay in cash dividends to each common shareholder?
b. What effect would a cash dividend of $0.80 have on the firm's balance sheet entries?
c. If the firm cannot raise any new funds from external sources, what do you consider the key constraint with respect to the magnitude of the firm's dividend payments? Why?

24.4   A firm has had the indicated earnings per share over the past 10 years (19X9–19Y8):

Year	Earnings per share
19Y8	$4.00
19Y7	3.80
19Y6	3.20
19Y5	2.80
19Y4	3.20
19Y3	2.40
19Y2	1.20
19Y1	1.80
19Y0	− .50
19X9	.25

a. If the firm's dividend policy was based on a constant payout ratio of 40 percent for all years with positive earnings and a zero payout otherwise, determine the annual dividend for each year.
b. If the firm had a dividend payout of $1.00 per share, increasing by $0.10 per share whenever the dividend payout fell below 50 percent for two consecutive years, what annual dividend did the firm pay each year?

c. If the firm's policy was to pay $0.50 per share each period except when earnings per share exceed $3.00, when an extra dividend equal to 80 percent of earnings beyond $3.00 would be paid, what annual dividend did the firm pay each year?

d. Discuss the pros and cons of each dividend policy described in **a** through **c**.

24.5 Given the following earnings per share over the 19X1–19X8 period, determine the annual dividend per share under each of the policies set forth in **a** through **d**.

Year	Earnings per share
19X8	$1.40
19X7	1.56
19X6	1.20
19X5	− .85
19X4	1.05
19X3	.60
19X2	1.00
19X1	.44

a. Pay out 50 percent of earnings in all years with positive earnings.

b. Pay $0.50 per share except when earnings exceed $1.00 per share, when there would be an extra dividend of 60 percent of earnings above $1.00 per share.

c. Pay $0.50 per share and increase to $0.60 per share whenever earnings per share rise above $0.90 per share for two consecutive years.

d. Combine policies in **b** and **c**. When the dividend is raised (in **c**), raise the excess dividend base (in **b**) from $1.00 to $1.10 per share.

e. Compare and contrast each of the dividend policies described in **a** through **d**.

24.6 FMA has a shareholders' equity account, given in the following table. The firm's common shares have a current market price of $30 per share.

Preferred shares	$100,000
Common shares (10,000 shares n.p.v.)	300,000
Retained earnings	100,000
Shareholders' equity	$500,000

a. Show the effects on FMA of a 5-percent share dividend.

b. Show the effects of (1) a 10-percent, and (2) a 20-percent share dividend.

c. In light of your answers to **a** and **b**, discuss the effects of share dividends on the firm's shareholders' equity.

24.7 Hadley-Walsh Steel Ltd. has a shareholders' equity account as given in the following table. The firm's common shares currently sell for $4.00 per share.

Preferred shares	$ 100,000
Common shares (400,000 shares n.p.v.)	600,000
Retained earnings	320,000
Shareholders' equity	$1,020,000

a. Show the effects on the firm of a $0.01, $0.05, $0.10, and $0.20-per-share *cash* dividend.

b. Show the effects on the firm of a 1-percent, 5-percent, 10-percent, and 20-percent share dividend.

c. Compare the effects in **a** and **b**. What are the significant differences in the two methods of paying dividends?

24.8 Alfred Clark currently holds 400 shares of Mountain Grown Coffee. The firm has 40,000 shares outstanding. The firm most recently had earnings available for common shareholders of $80,000 and its shares have been selling for $22 per share. The firm intends to retain its earnings and pay a 10-percent share dividend. The retention of earnings is deemed necessary to finance a planned expansion. The firm expects the rate of return on the expansion to equal the rate of return the firm now earns on shareholders' equity.

a. How much does the firm currently earn per share?

b. What proportion of the firm does Alfred Clark currently own?

c. What proportion of the firm will Mr. Clark own after the share dividend? Explain your answer.

d. At what market price would you expect a share to sell after the share dividend?

e. Discuss what effect, if any, the payment of share dividends will have on Mr. Clark's share of the ownership and earnings of Mountain Grown Coffee.

24.9 The Mission Company Ltd. has outstanding 50,000 common shares currently selling at $40 per share. The firm most recently had earnings available for common shareholders of $120,000, but it has decided to retain these funds and is considering either a 5-percent or a 10-percent share dividend in lieu of a cash dividend.

a. Determine the firm's current earnings per share.

b. If Jack Frost currently owns 500 shares of the firm, determine his proportion of ownership currently and under each of the proposed dividend plans. Explain your findings.

c. Calculate and explain the market price per share under each of the share dividend plans.

d. For each of the proposed share dividends, calculate the earnings per share after payment of the share dividend.

e. How much would the value of Mr. Frost's holdings be under each of the proposals? Explain.

f. As Mr. Frost, would you have any preference with respect to the proposed share dividends? Why or why not?

24.10 The Foothills Oil Company's current shareholders' equity account is as follows:

Preferred shares (5% cumulative, $100 par)	$ 400,000
Common shares (600,000 shares n.p.v.)	2,000,000
Retained earnings	800,000
Shareholders' equity	$3,200,000

a. Indicate the change, if any, expected if the firm declares a 2-for-1 share split.

b. Indicate the change, if any, expected if the firm declares a 1-for-$1\frac{1}{2}$ reverse share split.

c. Indicate the change, if any, expected if the firm declares a 3-for-1 share split.

d. Indicate the change, if any, expected if the firm declares a 6-for-1 share split.

e. Indicate the change, if any, expected if the firm declares a 1-for-4 reverse share split.

24.11 The Big Company Ltd. is considering a 3-for-2 share split. They currently have the shareholders' equity position shown below. The current share price is $120 per share. The most recent period's earnings available for common is included in retained earnings.

Preferred shares	$ 1,000,000
Common shares (100,000 shares n.p.v.)	2,000,000
Retained earnings	10,000,000
Shareholders' equity	$13,000,000

a. What effects on Big Company would result from the share split?
b. What change in share price would you expect to result from the share split?
c. What is the maximum cash dividend per share the firm could pay before and after the share split?
d. Contrast your answers to a through c with the circumstances surrounding a 50-percent share dividend.
e. Explain the differences between share splits and share dividends.

24.12   The following financial data on the Victor Share Company Ltd. are available:

Earnings available for common shareholders	$800,000
Number of shares of common outstanding	400,000
Earnings per share ($800,000 ÷ 400,000)	$2
Market price per share	$20
Price-earnings ratio ($20 ÷ $2)	10

The firm is currently contemplating paying cash dividends of $1 per share, which will raise the share price to $21 per share while dividends are on.
a. Approximately how many shares can the firm repurchase at the $21 per-share price using the funds that would have gone to pay the cash dividend?
b. Calculate earnings per share after the repurchase. Explain your calculations.
c. If a share still sells at 10 times earnings, how much will the market price be after the repurchase?
d. Compare and contrast the pre- and post-repurchase earnings per share. Discuss the tax implications of this action.
e. Compare and contrast the pre- and post-repurchase market price. Discuss your findings.

24.13   The Off Shore Steel Company Ltd. has earnings available for common shareholders of $2 million and 500,000 common shares outstanding at $60 per share. The firm is currently contemplating the payment of $2 per share in cash dividends.
a. Calculate the firm's current earnings per share and price-earnings multiple.
b. If the firm's shares are expected to sell at $62 per share with dividends on and the firm can repurchase shares at this price, how many shares can be purchased in lieu of making the proposed cash dividend payment?
c. How much will the earnings per share be after the proposed repurchase? Why?
d. If a share will sell at the old price-earnings multiple, how much will the market price be after repurchase?
e. Compare and contrast the earnings per share and market price per share before and after the proposed share repurchase.
f. Describe and discuss the differences, if any, in balance sheet entries resulting from the payment of cash dividends and the proposed share repurchase. Be specific.
g. What recommendations might you offer Off Shore with respect to the proposed share repurchase?

Notes

1. This discussion is based on Michael Brennan,"A Note on Dividend Irrelevance and the Gordon Valuation Model," *Journal of Finance* 26 (December 1971), pp. 1115–1121.
2. For Canadian data, Morgan and Saint-Pierre's empirical findings are consistent with the separability of the investment and dividend decisions of a firm. See I. G. Morgan and J. Saint-Pierre, "Dividend and Investment Decisions of Canadian Firms," *Canadian Journal of Economics* (February 1978), pp. 20–37.
3. S. A. Ross, "The Determination of Financial Structure: The Incentive-Signalling Approach," *The Bell Journal of Economics* (Spring 1977), pp. 23–40; and "Some Notes on Financial Incentive—Signalling Models, Activity Choice and Risk Preferences," *Journal of Finance* (June 1978), pp. 777–792.
4. R. R. Pettit, "Taxes, Transaction Costs and Clientele Effect of Dividends," *Journal of Financial Economics* (December 1977), pp. 419–436.
5. Merton Miller and Myron Scholes, "Dividends and Taxes," *Journal of Financial Economics* 6 (December 1978), pp. 333–364.
6. See, for example, Marshal Blume, Jean Crockett, and Irwin Friend, "Stock Ownership in the United States: Characteristics and Trends," *Survey of Current Business* 54 (November 1974), pp. 16–40; Richard Pettit, "Taxes, Transactions Costs, and the Clientele Effect of Dividends," *Journal of Financial Economics* (December 1977), pp. 419–436; and Wilbur G. Lewellen, Kenneth L. Stanley, Ronald C. Lease, and Gary G. Schlarbaum, "Some Direct Evidence on the Dividend Clientele Phenomenon," *Journal of Finance* 33 (December 1978), pp. 1385–1399.
7. Fama, Fisher, Jensen, and Roll found that the risk-adjusted rates of return for those common shares that had a dividend increase after a share split were on average marginally better than the market rate of return; while the risk-adjusted rates of return for those common shares that had a dividend decrease after a share split were on average below the market rate of return. They interpreted their findings as follows: Since corporate managements are averse to dividend reductions, any unanticipated change in dividends will convey new information to shareholders about management's expectations for the future prospects of their firm. In addition, shareholders expect an increased dividend to be associated with a share split, because firms that engage in share splits generally have promising future prospects. Thus, there is no significant impact on the rate of return after a split if dividends actually increased, since the increased dividends confirmed shareholders' pre-split expectations about post-split dividends. However, there is a significant drop in the rate of return after the split if dividends decreased, since the decreased dividend is a new and totally unexpected information event for the firm's shareholders. The interested reader is referred to Eugene Fama, Lawrence Fisher, Michael Jensen, and Richard Roll, "The Adjustment of Stock Prices to New Information," *International Economic Review* 10, No. 1 (February 1969), pp. 1–21.

Suggested Readings

Arditti, Fred D., Haim Levy, and Marshall Sarnat, "Taxes, Uncertainty, and Optimal Dividend Policy," *Financial Management* 5 (Spring 1976), pp. 46–53.

Black, Fischer and Myron Scholes, "The Effects of Dividend Yield and Dividend Policy on Common Stock Prices and Returns," *Journal of Financial Economics* 1 (May 1974), pp. 1–22.

Brennan, Michael, "Taxes, Market Valuation, and Corporate Financial Policy," *National Tax Journal* 23 (December 1970), pp. 417–427.

———, "A Note on Dividend Irrelevance and the Gordon Valuation Model," *Journal of Finance* 26 (December 1971), pp. 1115–1121.

Brigham, Eugene F. and Myron J. Gordon, "Leverage, Dividend Policy, and the Cost of Capital," *Journal of Finance* 23 (March 1968), pp. 85–104.

Elton, Edwin J. and Martin J. Gruber, "Marginal Stockholder Tax Rates and the Clientele Effect," *Review of Economics and Statistics* 52 (February 1970), pp. 68–74.

———, "The Effect of Share Repurchases on the Value of the Firm," *Journal of Finance* 23 (March 1968), pp. 135–150.

Fama, Eugene F. and Harvey Babiak, "Dividend Policy: An Empirical Analysis," *Journal of the American Statistical Association* 63 (December 1968), pp. 1132–1161.

Finnerty, Joseph E., "Corporate Stock Issue and Repurchase," *Financial Management* 4 (Autumn 1975), pp. 62–71.

Friend, Irwin and Marshall Puckett, "Dividends and Stock Prices," *American Economic Review* 54 (September 1964), pp. 656–682.

Gordon, Myron J., "Dividends, Earnings and Stock Prices," *Review of Economics and Statistics* 41 (May 1959), pp. 99–105.

——, *The Investment, Financing, and Valuation of the Corporation* (Homewood, Ill.: Irwin, 1962).

Higgins, Robert C., "The Corporate Dividend-Savings Decision," *Journal of Financial and Quantitative Analysis* 7 (March 1972), pp. 1527–1541.

Keane, Simon M., "Dividends and the Resolution of Uncertainty," *Journal of Finance and Accounting* 1 (Autumn 1974), pp. 389–393.

Khoury, N. and Keith Smith, "Dividend Policy and the Capital Gains Tax in Canada," *Journal of Business Administration* (Spring 1977).

Krainer, Robert E., "A Pedagogic Note on Dividend Policy," *Journal of Financial and Quantitative Analysis* 6 (September 1971), pp. 1147–1154.

Laub, P. Michael and Ross Watts, "On the Informational Content of Dividends," *Journal of Business* 49 (January 1976).

Lewellen, Wilbur G., Kenneth L. Stanley, Ronald C. Lease, and Gary Schlarbaum, "Some Direct Evidence on the Dividend Clientele Phenomenon," *The Journal of Finance* 33 (December 1978), pp. 1385–1399.

Lintner, John, "Distribution of Income of Corporations Among Dividends, Retained Earnings, and Taxes," *American Economic Review* 46 (May 1956), pp. 97–113.

——, "Dividends, Earnings, Leverage, Stock Prices, and the Supply of Capital to Corporations," *Review of Economics and Statistics*, 44 (August 1962), pp. 243–269.

——, "Optimal Dividends and Corporate Growth Under Uncertainty," *Quarterly Journal of Economics* 78 (February 1964), pp. 49–95.

Millar, James A. and Bruce D. Fielitz, "Stock Split and Stock Dividend Decisions," *Financial Management* 2 (Winter 1973), pp. 35–45.

Miller, Merton H., "Debt and Taxes," *Journal of Finance* 32 (May 1977), pp. 261–275.

Miller, Merton H. and Franco Modigliani, "Dividend Policy, Growth and the Valuation of Shares," *Journal of Business* 34 (October 1961), pp. 411–433.

Miller, Merton H. and Myron Scholes, "Dividends and Taxes," *Journal of Financial Economics* 6 (December 1978), pp. 333–364.

Morgan, I. G. and J. Saint-Pierre, "Dividend and Investment Decisions of Canadian Firms," *Canadian Journal of Economics* (February 1978), pp. 20–37.

Norgaard, Richard and Corine Norgaard, "A Critical Examination of Share Repurchase," *Financial Management* 3 (Spring 1974), pp. 44–50.

Pettit, R. Richardson, "The Impact of Dividend and Earnings Announcements: A Reconciliation," *Journal of Business* 49 (January 1976), pp. 86–96.

Smith, Keith V., "Increasing Stream Hypothesis of Corporate Dividend Policy," *California Management Review* 14 (Fall 1971), pp. 56–64.

Stewart, Samuel S., Jr., "Should a Corporation Repurchase Its Own Stock?" *Journal of Finance* 31 (June 1976), pp. 911–921.

Van Horne, James C. and John J. McDonald, "Dividend Policy and New Equity Financing," *Journal of Finance* 26 (May 1971), pp. 507–519.

Walter, James E., *Dividend Policy and Enterprise Valuation* (Belmont, Calif.: Wadsworth, 1967).

Watts, Ross, "The Information Content of Dividends," *Journal of Business* 46 (April 1973), pp. 191–211.

West, Richard R., and Alan B. Brouilette, "Reverse Stock Splits," *Financial Executive* 38 (January 1970), pp. 12–17.

Whittington, G., "The Profitability of Retained Earnings," *Review of Economics and Statistics* 54 (May 1972), pp. 152–160.

Wrightsman, Dwayne and James O. Horrigan, "Retention, Risk of Success, and the Price of Stock," *Journal of Finance* 30 (December 1975), pp. 1357–1359.

Part Eight

Expansion
and Failure

BALANCE SHEET

Assets	Liabilities and Shareholders' Equity
Current Assets	Current Liabilities
Fixed Assets	Long-Term Debt
	Shareholders' Equity

This part of the text is concerned with two areas of interest to the financial manager, who must make decisions with respect to the firm's future. The topics of acquisitions, amalgamations, and holding companies are discussed in order to provide a basic understanding of the principles of these types of external expansion. Often, firms seeking either to obtain additional capacity, to diversify, or to use excess liquidity will find external growth a viable alternative. Another area in which the financial manager unfortunately may become involved is business failure and rehabilitation. An understanding of the key concepts related to failure and rehabilitation may be of benefit not only when the firm itself is failing, but also when a customer or creditor of the firm is failing. Chapter 25 discusses the common types of business combinations, motives for combining, and procedures used. Chapter 26, the final chapter of the text, describes the key concepts and legal procedures related to business failures, rehabilitations, and liquidations. Both chapters are primarily concerned with the firm's equity position.

ACQUISITIONS, AMALGAMATIONS, AND HOLDING COMPANIES

Business firms often find external expansion through a business combination to be a viable alternative to internal growth. Typically, these firms are interested in rapidly expanding their productive capacity and earnings and in taking advantage of certain liquidity benefits. The methods of forming business combinations are the acquisition of assets, acquisition of shares, and statutory amalgamation. These methods may differ not only with respect to the procedures involved, but also with respect to their objectives.

In this chapter, the primary emphasis will be on viewing business combinations from the standpoint of the acquiring company. The chapter has four major sections. The first section presents certain fundamental information about the forms of business combinations, motives for forming business combinations, and relevant variables to be considered in contemplating such combinations. The second section discusses certain aspects of business combinations, including the negotiations involved in completing a combination. The third section discusses holding companies by placing primary emphasis on their major advantages and disadvantages. The final section discusses the role played by the Foreign Investment Review Agency (FIRA) in monitoring business combination activity in Canada.

The Fundamentals of Business Combinations

A *corporate combination* occurs when two or more limited companies come under common ownership or control, or both. The ultimate form of the combination may vary. It may result in two or more corporations emerging as one corporation, or it may result in a parent-subsidiary relationship. We will now discuss the various forms of business combinations.

FORMS OF BUSINESS COMBINATIONS

A company (referred to as the *acquiring* or *buying company*) can combine with at least one other company (referred to as the *target, selling,* or *acquired company*) by using one of the following three methods: (1) the acquirer can acquire the assets of the target, (2) the acquirer can acquire the outstanding shares of the target, or (3) the acquirer can amalgamate with the target.* The method chosen for a specific combination generally depends upon the legal and tax implications of each alternative.

Acquisition of a Target's Assets†   An acquiring company can purchase all or a portion of a target's total assets. Under the Federal and Provincial Business Corporations Acts, the shareholders of the target company must ratify the terms of the purchase offer. Any dissenting shareholders have an *appraisal right*, which means that the acquiring firm can be required to purchase their shares at an appraised price.‡

The payment to the target for the assets purchased can be either cash or shares of the acquiring company. If the payment for the purchased assets is cash, the management of the target company must then decide whether it should pay a liquidating dividend to its shareholders and wind up, whether it should use the cash to enter a new line of business, or whether it should become a holding company by purchasing shares in a number of corporations. If the payment for the purchased assets is shares of the acquiring company, the management of the target company must then decide whether it should become a holding company or whether the shares of the acquiring company should be first disbursed to the target's shareholders and then the target should be wound up. Often, the tax-free rollover provisions of the Federal Income Tax Act favour the latter alternative.§

Thus, a single corporate entity does not necessarily have to result from an asset purchase. However, since the method of payment for the purchased assets is generally shares of the acquiring company, a single corporate entity usually results when all the assets of a target company are purchased.

Acquisition of a Target's Shares   An acquiring company can purchase all or a portion of a target's outstanding shares. As in the case of a purchase of assets, the

---

*In the accounting literature, the acquiring company is often referred to as the *combinor*, and the acquired company is often referred to as the *combinee*.

†Two or more companies can also be "combined" by a lease of all or part of the assets and undertakings of one or more companies to another company. In such a case, the lessee company pays rent, which is distributed to the shareholders of each lessor company in the form of dividends. For a more detailed discussion of leasing, refer to Chapter 20.

‡The approval of the seller's bondholders is also required in those cases where such approval is stipulated in the bond indenture provisions.

§A *rollover* is the allowable transfer of capital (e.g., the acquiring firm's shares) and depreciable property under specified conditions from one taxpayer to another at a value that is less than the fair market value of the underlying property (e.g., the target's assets) in such a manner as to defer taking the gain into income until a predefined transaction or event takes place (e.g., the acquiring firm's shares are sold by the target's shareholders). Rollovers are covered under Sections 85, 85.1, and 97 of the Federal Income Tax Act; Subsection 20(1.2) of the *Income Tax Application Rules,* 1971; Part III of Chapter 63 of S.C. 1970–71–72; and Parts XLV and XLVI of the *Income Tax Regulations* (SOR/72–338).

shareholders of the target company must ratify the terms of the purchase offer, and any dissenting shareholders have an appraisal right.

The payment to the target's shareholders for their purchased shares can be either cash or shares of the acquiring company. Unless the share purchase is accompanied by a statutory amalgamation, all the corporate entities involved in a share purchase continue to exist. The relationship, however, becomes a parent-subsidiary relationship.

Amalgamation of the Acquiring and Acquired Companies   An acquiring company can amalgamate or combine with a target company according to the statutory provisions of the appropriate Business Corporations Acts. This also includes holding and subsidiary corporations. The shareholders of all amalgamating companies must ratify the terms of the amalgamation, as negotiated by the managements of the involved companies. Dissenting shareholders have an appraisal right.

After a statutory amalgamation, a single corporate entity will emerge. It may be either one of the combining corporations or it may be an entirely new corporation.

COMMON CLASSIFICATIONS OF BUSINESS COMBINATIONS

In practice, business combinations are often classified using the American legal definitions, which are based on the form of the entity that emerges from the combination. Under this scheme, business combinations are classified as consolidations and mergers.

Consolidations   A *consolidation* involves the combination of two or more limited companies to form a completely new corporate entity. The new corporation normally absorbs the assets and liabilities of the companies from which it is formed. The old corporations merely cease to exist. Consolidations normally occur when the firms to be combined are of similar size.

Mergers   A *merger* occurs whenever one of the limited companies in the combination of two or more limited companies assumes the assets and liabilities of the other companies, and the other companies cease to exist. Mergers are generally confined to combinations of firms that are unequal in size. Generally, the identity of the largest firm is maintained.

Because of the great similarity between consolidations, mergers, and amalgamations, and the fact that the distinctions between them are often not followed in common business usage, the remainder of this chapter will generally not differentiate between these forms of combination. *The term "combination" will be used to refer to amalgamations, consolidations, and mergers.*

MOTIVES FOR BUSINESS COMBINATIONS

Firms combine to fulfill certain objectives in addition to the maximization of their owners' wealth. The more common motives for combination—which include growth, risk reduction, synergistic effects, financial considerations, increased managerial skills, tax considerations, and increased ownership liquidity—are discussed in this section.

Growth   Companies desiring rapid growth either in *size* or in the *range of their products* may find that some form of business combination will better fulfill this objective. Instead of going through the time-consuming process of internal growth, the firm may achieve the same growth objective in a shorter period of time by acquiring or combining with an existing firm. Also, the risks associated with design, construction, and sale of new products are reduced if the acquiring firm can acquire a proven concern. Moreover, when a firm expands or extends its product line by acquiring another firm, it may also remove a potential competitor.

Business combinations may be used to achieve either horizontal, vertical, circular, or conglomerate growth. Each of these types of growth is briefly described next.

Horizontal Growth   Horizontal growth occurs when firms in the same line of business are combined. For example, the combination of two machine tool manufacturers is a form of horizontal growth. Certain economies may result from this type of growth, due to the elimination of certain staff and support functions to avoid duplication. For example, two vice presidents of finance or two purchasing agents may no longer be required. Economies are also expected to result through the purchase of merchandise in larger quantities and the elimination of duplicate sales channels. Horizontal growth is commonly referred to as *horizontal integration*.

Vertical Growth   Vertical growth occurs when a firm grows backward by acquiring suppliers of its raw materials or forward by acquiring purchasers of its finished products. In other words, vertical growth involves expansion either backward toward the firm's suppliers or forward toward the ultimate consumer. The economic benefits of vertical growth, which is commonly referred to as *vertical integration*, stem from the firm's greater control over the acquisition of raw materials or the distribution of finished goods. A firm that is *totally integrated* controls the entire production process from the extraction of raw materials to the sale of finished goods. An example of vertical growth would be the combination of a machine tool manufacturer with a supplier of castings.

Circular Growth   Circular growth occurs when firms with different products, which can be distributed through the same channel, combine. Economies are expected to result from the elimination of duplicate sales channels. An example of circular growth would be the combination of a department store chain and a travel agency, since the travel service can then be sold in the department stores and also be offered to the credit account customers of the department store.

Conglomerate Growth   Conglomerate growth involves the combination of firms in unrelated businesses.* An example would be the combination of a manufacturer of sporting goods with the manufacturer of aircraft components. Since a conglomerate consists of firms in unrelated businesses, no real operating economies (or synergies) are

---

*In the financial industry, a further distinction is made between a *financial conglomerate* and a *financial congeneric*. The former refers to diversification by a financial institution such as a bank into nonrelated fields such as real estate; and the latter refers to diversification by a financial institution such as a bank into several related areas of finance such as factoring, leasing, credit life insurance, and national credit card distribution.

expected from this type of growth. Risk reduction is supposedly the major benefit obtained by conglomerate growth.

Risk Reduction   Risk reduction is often used as an argument for external growth, and especially for conglomerate growth. Supporters of this position maintain that such growth will increase the market value of the firm. Since external growth should reduce the variability of the earnings of a combination of firms, and since investors are presumed to be risk averse, it is argued that investors will place a greater value on the more stable combined expected earnings stream.* Others have argued that corporate diversification by itself either will not affect current share-holders' wealth or it will decrease it. The latter group maintains that since investors can diversify their holdings by themselves, there is no reason to expect that they will be willing to pay a premium for corporate diversification.[1] The latter group maintains that since a conglomerate combination has no operating economies (i.e., synergistic effects), the total market value of the combined firm will not change as a result of the combination. Therefore, the increased market value of the combination's debt caused by the reduction of the debt's default risk (referred to as the *coinsurance* effect) must be offset by a corresponding decrease in the market value of the combination's equity. However, it can be argued that this decrease in the market value of equity will be offset by the debt-associated benefits of external diversification. More specifically, risk reduction should reduce the default risk of the combination's debts; which in turn should decrease the required rate of interest on the combination's debts; which in turn should increase the firm's maximum permissible debt capacity. Due to the tax shield associated with corporate debt, the value benefits of a greater amount of debt in the combination's capital structure will accrue to current shareholders.

Synergistic Effects   The synergistic effects of business combinations are the economies of scale due to the combination, which make the profits of the combination greater than the sum of the profits of the components operated independently.

Synergistic effects are said to be present when a whole is greater than the sum of its parts, or 1 plus 1 equals 3. The economies of scale that generally result from the combination of business firms lowers their combined overhead, thereby increasing their earnings to a level greater than the sum of their earnings as independent firms. Practitioners maintain that the economies of scale associated with business combinations are most significant in the research and development and marketing functions of a firm.[2]

Synergistic effects are most obvious when firms grow horizontally, especially when small plants are integrated.† Redundant staff functions in areas such as purchasing and sales can be eliminated during this type of combination. Synergistic effects also result when firms are combined vertically, since certain administrative functions can be elim-

---

*The theory of conglomerate diversification is drawn directly from the portfolio theory used for asset or security selection. A brief discussion of the key concepts underlying the portfolio-type approach to the diversification of risk was presented in Chapter 16.

†This is derived from a classical argument in economics; that is, as the firm grows in size (scale), its costs grow less than proportionally.

inated. For example, only one of the two presidents making $60,000 per year may be required after the combination of two firms.

Synergistic effects may also result when there are imperfect product markets for assets such as a loyal labour force, unpatentable knowledge, management and marketing expertise, and imperfections in the market for licensing trademarks. In such markets, firms may combine to more fully exploit a "specific" asset in order to earn "synergistic" profits.

Financial Considerations   Often firms combine to enhance their fund-raising ability. Quite often, especially in the case of conglomerates, a firm may combine with a firm having high liquid assets and low levels of liabilities. The acquisition of this type of "cash-rich" company can increase the firm's borrowing power and decrease its financial riskiness. In some cases, it may even be possible for the acquiring company to borrow to finance the purchase of the cash-rich company, and to make repayment out of the funds or debt-carrying capacity of the acquired company. Other firms, like Genstar Ltd., maintain that one of the advantages of a diversified combination is its ability to transfer financial resources among companies (referred to as *internalization*) more efficiently than the financial sector. In the case of Genstar, cash flows were transferred primarily into its land development and housing subsidiaries from its CCA-generating cement subsidiaries.

Increased Managerial Skills   Occasionally a firm will become involved in a business combination to obtain certain key management personnel that it could not hire independently. In addition, firms with underutilized management and staff expertise sometimes acquire relatively small and promising companies that cannot hire their own competent management and specialized staff services.

Tax Considerations   The tax laws can encourage external diversification. For example, a profitable company may combine with an unprofitable (or failing) company to utilize the acquired company's unused operating (noncapital) losses, unused investment tax credits, unused depletion allowances, and unused tax deferrals on credit sales against its own operating income. If the acquired operating (noncapital) losses cannot be first applied against current income, they must then be applied against the previous year's income, and then against the earliest available income of the five subsequent years.*

These tax benefits are useful only in amalgamations, and only if allowed by the taxation authorities. The probability of such approval is low if there are no other motives for the business combination other than tax considerations.

EXAMPLE   The Perkins Company Ltd. has a $450,000 operating income loss carryforward-carryback from last year (its first year of operations). To use this loss carryforward and to diversify its operations, the Brock Company has acquired Perkins Company through an amalga-

---

*Since a detailed discussion of the tax implications of operating losses was presented in Chapter 2, the reader should review that material if greater clarification is required.

mation. Brock had no operating income (before taxes) in its most recent fiscal year, and it expects to have an annual operating income of $300,000 for this year and the next five years. Assuming that these expected income values are realized, that the Perkins' portion of the combined firm just breaks even, and Brock is in the 40-percent tax bracket, then the total taxes paid by the two firms without and with the combination are calculated as follows.

Total combined taxes without the combination

	Year		
	0	1	2
Operating income	$300,000	$300,000	$300,000
Taxes (.40)	$120,000	$120,000	$120,000

Total combined taxes with the combination

	Year		
	0	1	2
Operating income	$300,000	$300,000	$300,000
Less: Operating income loss carryforward	300,000	150,000	0
Taxable income	$ 0	$150,000	$300,000
Taxes (.40)	$ 0	$ 60,000	$120,000

With the amalgamation, the total tax payments are less. The combination is able to deduct the operating income loss carryforward against operating income for the current year; then for the immediately preceding year (there was no income for that year); and then for each of the next five years. Using this procedure, the total operating income loss was exhausted at the end of year 1. The tax advantages resulting from a combination with a company with an operating income loss carryforward-carryback should be clear from this example.

Increased Ownership Liquidity and Diversification   Principal shareholders of small family-run businesses or closely held, nonpublicly traded businesses sometimes attempt to increase the diversification and liquidity of their personal shareholdings by combining their firm with a publicly traded firm. This combination motive is generally important when the principal shareholders of such firms plan to retire or when the principal shareholders desire to reorganize their estates (bequests) so that it will be easier for their heirs to pay estate taxes after their death.

For publicly traded firms, the combination of a small and a larger firm, or two small firms into a larger corporation, may provide the owners of the small firm(s) with greater liquidity. Instead of holding shares in a small firm having a very "thin" market, the owners will receive shares that are traded in a broader ("fat") market and can be liquidated more readily. Not only does the ability to convert shares into cash quickly have appeal, but owning shares for which market price quotations are readily available provides owners with an asset that has a higher collateral value.

Analyzing Prospective Combinations

This portion of the chapter is devoted to the various analytical decision-making techniques commonly used in evaluating and negotiating business combinations. Since a business combination should be undertaken only if it satisfies the major objective of the firm (i.e., shareholders' wealth maximization), the investment evaluation criteria derived in Chapters 14 and 15 should be used in analyzing prospective combinations. Also, to forecast the effects of a proposed combination on the firm's future financial performance, the financial manager must quantitatively evaluate the effect of the combination on certain key financial variables, such as earnings per share and market price per share. An important ratio in analyzing prospective combinations is the *price-earnings (P/E) ratio*.

The key topics in this section are cash purchases of companies, share exchange acquisitions, and negotiation of combinations.

CASH PURCHASES OF COMPANIES

When a firm is acquiring another firm for cash (for ease of exposition, debt is assumed to be the same as cash here), the use of simple capital budgeting procedures is required. Regardless of whether the firm is being acquired for its assets or as a going concern, the basic approach is quite similar.

Acquisitions of Assets   In some instances a firm is acquired not for its income-earning potential, but as a grouping of assets (generally fixed assets) needed by the acquiring firm. The cash price paid for this type of acquisition depends largely on which assets are being acquired, and is subject to bargaining between the buyer and seller. If the entire firm is acquired, the liquidation value of the firm is a reasonable price; if only certain key assets are purchased, no more than the market value of these assets should be paid. If the entire firm is purchased as an ongoing concern, consideration must also be given to the value of any business losses.

To determine whether the purchase of assets is financially justifiable, the firm must estimate both the costs and the benefits of the assets. This, in effect, is the classic capital budgeting problem. A cash outlay is made to acquire assets, and as a result of their acquisition, certain future cash benefits are expected. These cash benefits are primarily generated by the increased earnings (or reduced costs) derived from the combination.

EXAMPLE   The VW Company is interested in acquiring certain fixed assets of the Bug Manufacturing Company. Bug, which has had some operating losses over the past five years, is interested in selling out; but it wishes to sell out entirely, not just to get rid of certain fixed assets. A condensed balance sheet for the Bug Company is given in the following table.

VW Company needs only machines B and C and the land and buildings. However, it has made some inquiries and has arranged to sell the accounts receivable, inventory, and machine A for $23,000. Since there is also $2,000 in cash, VW will get $25,000 for the excess assets. Bug wants $20,000 for the entire company, which means that VW will have to pay the firm's creditors

Assets		Liabilities and shareholders' equity	
Cash	$ 2,000	Total liabilities	$ 80,000
Marketable securities	0	Shareholders' equity	120,000
Accounts receivable	8,000	Total liabilities and shareholders' equity	$200,000
Inventory	10,000		
Machine A	10,000		
Machine B	30,000		
Machine C	25,000		
Land and buildings	115,000		
Total assets	$200,000		

$80,000 and its owners $20,000. The actual outlay required by VW after liquidating the unneeded assets will be $75,000 [($80,000 + $20,000) − $25,000]. In other words, to obtain the use of the desired assets (i.e., machines B and C and the land and buildings) and the tax benefits of Bug's business losses, VW must pay $75,000. The *after-tax cash inflows* expected to result from the new equipment and business losses are $14,000 per year for the next five years and $12,000 per year for the following five years. The desirability of this acquisition can be determined by calculating the net present value of this outlay using the VW Company's 9-percent cost of capital, as shown in Table 25.1.

Since the net present value of $9,784 is greater than zero, VW should find acquisition of the Bug Company an acceptable investment. Of course, if VW has alternate and cheaper ways of obtaining similar assets, the acquisition should not be made. The importance of capital budgeting techniques in evaluating cash acquisitions of assets should be clear from this example. As long as the firm makes acquisitions having positive net present values, the market value of the firm should be enhanced.

Table 25.1   An Analysis of the Bug Company Acquisition by the VW Company

Years	Net cash flow (1)	P.V. factor @ 9% (2)	Present value (1) · (2) (3)
0	($75,000)	1.000[a]	$(75,000)
1–5	14,000	3.890[b]	54,460
6	12,000	0.596[a]	7,152
7	12,000	0.547[a]	6,564
8	12,000	0.502[a]	6,024
9	12,000	0.460[a]	5,520
10	12,000	0.422[a]	5,064
		Net present value	$ 9,784

[a]The present-value interest factors, PVIF, for $1 discounted at 9 percent for the corresponding years obtained from Table A-3.
[b]The present-value interest factor for an annuity, PVIFA, with a five-year life discounted at 9 percent obtained from Table A-4.

Acquisitions of Going Concerns   Cash acquisitions of going concerns are best analyzed using capital budgeting techniques. It is appropriate to evaluate the prospective acquisition *strictly as an investment decision if* the acquiring company intends
to maintain its existing capital structure over the long run. To undertake such an
analysis, the acquiring company must estimate the future net after-tax cash operating income (including any synergistic effects) that the acquired firm will add to
the acquiring firm. (That is, the cash-flow estimates should be after tax but before
financing charges.) Any required or anticipated new investments should be netted
against this operating cash-flow estimate.

If the acquisition is not expected to change the business risk of the acquiring company
as perceived by the suppliers of capital, then the appropriate rate of discount is the
acquiring company's after-tax cost of capital. If the acquisition is expected to change the
business risk of the acquiring company, then the effect of the acquisition on the acquiring company's cost of capital must be estimated using the techniques discussed in
Chapter 18. An example will clarify the application of capital budgeting techniques
when the cash acquisition of a going concern is being considered.

EXAMPLE   The Stockade Company is contemplating the acquisition of the Wall Company, which
can be purchased for $60,000 in cash. Stockade currently has a high degree of business risk,
which is reflected in its 13-percent cost of capital. Because of the low business risk of the Wall
Company, Stockade estimates its overall cost of capital will drop to 10 percent after the acquisition. Since the effect of the less risky company resulting from the acquisition of Wall Company
cannot be reflected in the *expected* cash benefits, the post-acquisition cost of capital (i.e., 10
percent) must be used to evaluate the cash flows expected from the acquisition. The incremental
cash inflows expected from the proposed acquisition are $5,000 for years 1–10; $13,000 for
years 11–18; $4,000 for years 19–30, and nothing thereafter. The net present value of the
acquisition is calculated in Table 25.2.

Table 25.2   An Analysis of the Wall Company Acquisition by the Stockade
Company

Years	Net cash flow (1)	P.V. factor @ 10%[a] (2)	Present value (1) · (2) (3)
0	($60,000)	1.000	($60,000)
1–10	5,000	6.145	30,725
11–18	13,000	(8.201–6.145)[b]	26,728
19–30	4,000	(9.427–8.201)[b]	4,904
		Net Present Value	$ 2,357

[a]Present-value interest factors for annuities, obtained from Table A-4.
[b]These factors are found using a shortcut technique that can be applied to annuities for periods of years beginning at some
point in the future. By finding the appropriate factor for the present value of an annuity given for the last year of the annuity
and subtracting the present value of an annuity factor for the year immediately preceding the beginning of the annuity, the
appropriate interest factor for the present value of an annuity beginning sometime in the future can be obtained. The
interested reader can check this shortcut by using the long approach and comparing the results.

Since the net present value of the acquisition is greater than zero ($2,357), the acquisition is acceptable. It is interesting to note that had the effect of the changed business risk not been considered, the acquisition would have been found unacceptable since the net present value at a 13-percent cost of capital is − $11,864.

SHARE EXCHANGE ACQUISITIONS

Quite often an acquiring firm will exchange its common shares for common shares of the target firm. The *ratio of exchange* of shares is determined in the combination negotiations. This ratio affects the various financial yardsticks used by existing and prospective shareholders in valuing the combined firm's shares. This section discusses the ratio of exchange and its effect on key financial variables.

The Ratio of Exchange When a firm intends to acquire another firm by an exchange of shares, it must first determine whether it has sufficient authorized and unissued and/or treasury shares to complete the transaction. Then, the acquiring and acquired firms must agree on the terms of the exchange. Because of the added complexities encountered in valuing nonpublicly traded firms, we will assume in this section that the shares of both firms are traded publicly. Generally, the final terms of the exchange are unlikely to be equal to the ratio of the per-share market prices of the acquired and acquiring firms. First, the acquiring firm is often quite willing to offer a higher than market price to obtain the expected synergistic or financial benefits of the combination. Second, a positive incentive must generally be offered to current shareholders of the target firm to induce them to exchange their shares for shares of the acquiring firm. Any difference between the actual price paid per share and the market price per share of the acquired company is referred to as the *combination premium*. Due to tax reasons, the combination premium is generally greater for cash as opposed to share acquisitions. Thus, *the actual ratio of exchange is merely the ratio of the amount paid per share of the acquired firm to the market price per share of the acquiring firm.* An example will clarify the calculation of the ratio of exchange.

EXAMPLE The Huge Company, whose shares are currently selling for $80 per share, is interested in acquiring the Tiny Company to integrate its operations vertically. Tiny's shares are currently selling for $50 per share, but in the combination negotiations, Huge has found it necessary to offer $56 per share. Since Huge does not wish to purchase the firm for cash, Tiny has agreed to accept Huge's shares in exchange for its shares. Since Huge's shares currently sell for $80 per share, and it must pay Tiny's shareholders $56 per share, the ratio of exchange is .7 (i.e., $56 ÷ $80). This means that the Huge Company must give .7 shares for each share of Tiny to Tiny's shareholders.

The Effect of the Ratio of Exchange on Key Financial Variables Owners of both the acquiring and acquired firm are concerned with the effect of the acquisition on certain financial variables. The *key* focus is on the resulting earnings and market price per share, but attention is sometimes given to dividends per share, book value per share, the business riskiness, and the capital structure of the combined company. Each of these financial variables will be briefly discussed and illustrated in this section.

The Effect on Earnings Per Share   The earnings per share of the firm are likely to change as a result of a combination. Generally, the resulting earnings per share differ from the precombination earnings per share for both the acquiring and the acquired firm. They depend largely on the ratio of exchange and the precombination earnings of each firm. It is best to view the initial and long-run effects of the ratio of exchange on earnings per share (eps) separately.

The Initial Effect   When the ratio of exchange is equal to 1 and both the acquiring and the acquired firm have the same precombination earnings per share (and thus the same price-earnings ratio), the combined firm's earnings per share will initially remain constant. In actuality, the earnings per share of the combined firm are generally above the precombination earnings per share of one firm and below the precombination earnings per share of the other firm, after making the necessary adjustments for the ratio of exchange. These differences can be illustrated by a simple example.

EXAMPLE   The Huge Company is contemplating acquiring the Tiny Company. The current financial data related to the earnings and market price for each of these companies are given in Table 25.3. Although Tiny's shares currently have a market price of $50.00 per share, Huge has offered it $56.00 per share. As we saw in the preceding example, this results in a ratio of exchange of .7.
　　To complete the combination and retire the 20,000 outstanding shares of Tiny Company, Huge will have to issue and/or use treasury shares totaling 14,000 shares (.70 · 20,000 shares). Once the combination is completed, Huge will have 139,000 shares of common (125,000 + 14,000) outstanding. If the earnings of each of the firms remain constant, the combined company will be expected to have earnings available for the common shareholders of $600,000.00 ($500,000.00 + $100,000.00). The earnings per share of the combined company should therefore equal approximately $4.32 per share ($600,000.00 ÷ 139,000 shares). At first, it would appear that the Tiny Company's shareholders have sustained a decrease in per-share earnings (from $5.00 to $4.32); but, since each original share of the Tiny Company is equivalent to .7 shares of the

Table 25.3   Huge Company and Tiny Company Financial Data

Item	Huge Company	Tiny Company
Earnings available for common	$500,000	$100,000
Number of shares of common outstanding	125,000	20,000
Earnings per share	$4	$5
Market price per share	$80	$50
Price-earnings ratio	20	10

Table 25.4   A Summary of the Effects on Earnings Per Share of a
Combination Between the Huge Company and the Tiny
Company at $56 Per Share

| | Earnings per share | |
Shareholders of	Before combination	After combination
Huge Company	$4.00	$4.32
Tiny Company	5.00	3.02[a]

[a]Based on .70 of the Huge Company's earnings per share.

combined company, the equivalent earnings per share are $3.02 ($4.32 · .70). In other words, as a result of the combination, the Huge Company's original shareholders initially experience an increase in earnings per share from $4.00 to $4.32 at the expense of the Tiny Company's shareholders, whose earnings per share drop from $5 to $3.02. These results are summarized in Table 25.4.

The easiest way to explain the increased eps for the original Huge Company shareholders and the decreased eps for the original Tiny Company shareholders is to compare the price-earnings ratio of the original company to that based on the price paid for the acquired company. The possible outcomes are presented in Table 25.5. The usefulness of the relationships in Table 25.5 can be illustrated by comparing the P/E ratios associated with the Huge-Tiny combination. The Huge Company's P/E ratio is 20, while the P/E ratio based on the share price paid the Tiny Company was 11.2 ($56.00 ÷ $5.00). Since the P/E based on the share price paid for the Tiny Company was less than the P/E of the Huge Company (11.2 vs. 20), the effect was to increase the eps for original holders of shares in the Huge Company (from $4.00 to $4.32) and to decrease the effective eps to original holders of shares in the Tiny Company (from $5.00 to $3.02).

Had Huge paid the Tiny Company $110.00 per share, which would result in a ratio of exchange of 1.375 ($110.00 ÷ $80.00), the effects on eps would be as shown in Table 25.6. The original shareholders of Huge Company would experience a drop in eps (from $4.00 to $3.93), while the original shareholders of Tiny Company would experience an increase in eps (from $5.00 to $5.40). This is because the P/E ratio based on the share price paid for Tiny's shares was 22 ($110.00 ÷ 5), while the P/E of a share of Huge Company was 20. As indicated in Table 25.5,

Table 25.5   The Effect of P/E Ratios on Earnings Per Share

| | Effect on eps | |
Relationship between P/E paid and P/E of acquiring company	Acquiring company	Acquired company
P/E paid > P/E of acquiring company	Decrease	Increase
P/E paid = P/E of acquiring company	Constant	Constant
P/E paid < P/E of acquiring company	Increase	Decrease

Table 25.6   A Summary of the Effects on Earnings Per Share of a
Combination Between the Huge Company and the Tiny Company
at $110 Per Share

	Earnings per share	
Shareholders of	Before combination	After combination
Huge Company	$4.00	$3.93[a]
Tiny Company	5.00	5.40[b]

[a] $\dfrac{\$500,000.00 + \$100,000.00}{(1.375 \cdot 20,000) + \$125,000} = \$3.93$

[b] $\$3.93 \cdot 1.375 = \$5.40$

---

whenever the P/E ratio based on the share price paid is greater than the P/E of the acquiring company, the earnings per share of the original owners of the acquiring company will initially decrease, while the effective eps of the original holders of the acquired company initially increases.

The previous example demonstrates how an acquiring firm could achieve a continuing growth in earnings per share by continually combining with firms having a lower price-earnings ratio than itself. This has been called *phantasmic growth* because such growth is the product of a series of financial transactions. In the absence of synergistic effects, such growth in eps is contrived because it has not resulted from a change in the earning power or potential of the combining firms.

The Long-Run Effect   The long-run effect of a combination on the earnings per share of the combined company depends largely on whether the earnings of the combined firm grow. It is generally expected that the earnings of either or both of the component firms will grow. When synergies are realized, the sum of the earnings of two firms will exceed the total of each firm when viewed separately.

An acquiring company, which initially experiences a decrease in eps, will experience higher future eps than it would have had without the combination if the earnings of the acquired company grow at a faster rate than those of the acquiring company. An example will clarify this point.

EXAMPLE   In 19X0, the Huge Company acquired the Tiny Company by exchanging 1.375 common shares for each common share of the Tiny Company. Other key financial data and the effects of this exchange ratio were discussed in the preceding example. The total earnings of the Huge Company are expected to grow at an annual rate of 3 percent without the combination, while the Tiny Company's earnings are expected to grow at a 7 percent annual rate without the combination. No synergistic effects are expected from the combination, and the same growth rates are

Table 25.7   The Effects of Earnings Growth on eps for the Huge Company Without and With the Combination with the Tiny Company

Year	Without the combination		With the combination	
	Total earnings	Earnings per share[b]	Total earnings[c]	Earnings per share[d]
19X0	$500,000	$4.00	$600,000	$3.93
19X1	515,000	4.12	622,000	4.08
19X2	530,450	4.24	644,940	4.23
19X3	546,364	4.37	668,868	4.39
19X4	562,755	4.50	693,835	4.55
19X5	579,638	4.64	719,893	4.72

[a]Based on a 3-percent compound growth rate.
[b]Based on 125,000 shares outstanding.
[c]Based on a 3-percent growth in the Huge Company's earnings and a 7-percent growth in the Tiny Company's earnings.
[d]Based on 152,500 shares outstanding [i.e., (1.375 · 20,000 shares) + 125,000 shares].

expected to apply to the component earnings streams with the combination. Table 25.7 shows the future effects on the eps for the Huge Company without and with the proposed combination with the Tiny Company, based on these growth rates.

Table 25.7 indicates that the earnings per share without the combination will be greater than the eps with the combination for the years 19X0 through 19X2; after 19X2, the eps will increase above what they would have been without the combination as a result of the faster earnings growth rate of the Tiny Company (7 percent vs. 3 percent). Although a few years are required for this difference in the growth rate of earnings to pay off, it can be seen that in the future the Huge Company will receive a payoff from combining with the Tiny Company at a 1.375 ratio of exchange. The relationships in Table 25.7 are graphed in Figure 25.1. The long-run eps effects of the combination are clearly depicted by this graph.

The type of analysis in the preceding example should provide the financial manager with useful information for making the combination decision. The presence of synergistic effects or differential growth rates of earnings may suggest that, even though the initial effect of the combination will be to lower eps, the long-run effect may be an increase in eps.

The Market Price Per Share   The market price per share does not necessarily remain constant after an acquisition; rather, adjustments take place in the marketplace in response to changes in expected earnings, the dilution of ownership, changes in operating and financial risk, and certain other financial and managerial changes. Using the ratio of exchange discussed in the preceding section, a *ratio of exchange in market price* can be calculated. This ratio, the *MPX*, is defined by Equation 25.1:

$$MPX = \frac{MP_{acquiring} \cdot RX}{MP_{acquired}} \tag{25.1}$$

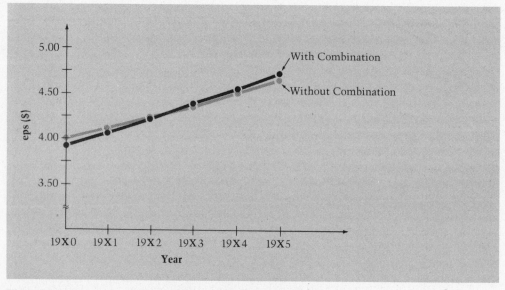

Figure 25.1   Future eps without and with the Huge-Tiny combination.

where

$$MPX = \text{market price ratio of exchange}$$
$$MP_i = \text{the market price for firm } i$$
$$i = \text{the acquiring or acquired firm}$$
$$RX = \text{the ratio of exchange}$$

A simple example can be used to illustrate the calculation of this ratio.

EXAMPLE   In the Huge-Tiny Company example used earlier, the market price of a share of the Huge Company was $80.00 and that of the Tiny Company was $50.00. The ratio of exchange was 1.375. Substituting these values into Equation 25.1 yields a market price ratio of exchange of 2.2 [($80.00 · 1.375) ÷ $50.00]. This means that $2.20 of the market price of the Huge Company is given for every $1.00 of the market price of the Tiny Company.

The ratio of exchange of market prices is normally greater than 1, which indicates that in order to acquire a firm a premium over its market price must be paid. The original owners of the acquiring firm may still gain because of synergistic effects. They may also gain if the market values the combined earnings at the higher of the two firms' price-earnings ratios, because investors mistakenly perceive the phantasmic growth in eps as being real growth in eps. Thus, if a firm with a higher P/E ratio acquires a firm with a lower P/E ratio and the combined company maintains the higher P/E ratio, a rise in the market price of the acquiring company's shares will result. This can be illustrated by a simple example.

EXAMPLE   The Huge Company and Tiny Company financial data in Table 25.3 can be used to explain the market price effects of a combination. If we assume that the ratio of exchange between the shares of the two companies was 0.7, then substituting into Equation 25.1 give us a ratio of exchange of market prices of 1.12 [($80 · .70) ÷ $50]. If the earnings of the combined companies remain at the precombination levels, and if a share of the combined companies sells at the Huge Company's precombination multiple of 20 times earnings, the values in Table 25.8 can be expected. Not only will the original company have higher earnings per share, but the market price of its shares will also be higher.

Table 25.8   Post-combination Market Price of the Huge Company Using a .7 Ratio of Exchange and a P/E Ratio of 20

Item	Combined company
Earnings available for common	$600,000
Number of shares of common outstanding	139,000
Earnings per share	$4.32
Price-earnings ratio	20
Expected market price per share (20 · $4.32)	$86.40

It should be noted that, in the absence of synergistic effects, the kind of price behaviour exhibited in the preceding example is quite unlikely, especially in capital markets that are efficient.[3] Such behaviour is possible when the shares of the acquired company have been selling at too low of a P/E due to market thinness.*

Dividends Per Share   The dividend per share does not normally enter into the combination decision, since the payment of dividends is a discretionary decision based on numerous firm and market factors. The primary concern of the acquiring firm is earnings per share, since earnings are a prerequisite to the payment of dividends. The dividend decision can be made once an acquisition has been consummated.

The Book Value Per Share   The book value per share, like the dividend per share, is irrelevant when a firm is acquiring a going concern. If the firm being acquired is being obtained only for its assets, then the book value per share may be helpful in determining the purchase price per share. When this type of acquisition is made, there is a great deal of concern about the liquidity in the form of working capital provided by the acquired firm. In this case, both the book value per share and the *working capital per share* are relevant. The post-combination book value depends to some extent on the accounting

*A *thin market* exists when a firm's shares are not actively traded due to the small number of owners or the small size of the enterprise. The shares of such firms are usually traded over the counter, and as a result of their relative inactivity, the price at which they are traded may not reflect their true or intrinsic value.

procedures used in constructing the combined firm's statements. A brief introduction to the accounting techniques used is presented in the next section of this chapter.

The Business Risk The business risk resulting from the combination must be considered in analyzing a potential combination. Generally, business risk, which reflects the stability of sales, is considered in making the initial combination inquiry. Since the nature of the business being acquired is studied by the acquiring firm, the business risk is implicitly considered.

The Capital Structure The fact that the precombination capital structure of the target firm differs from the acquiring firm is not very important in valuing the target firm, since after the combination the acquiring firm can easily modify the capital structure of the acquired firm. As noted earlier in the chapter, the target firm should be evaluated strictly as an investment decision if the acquiring company intends to maintain its existing (supposedly optimal) capital structure over the long run. Thus, the optimal and not the precombination capital structure of the target firm is important in valuing the target firm.

ACCOUNTING TREATMENT*

In Canada, the appropriate accounting treatment of a combination depends upon a single criterion—whether or not it is possible to identify one of the combining firms as the acquirer.† Since one of the combining firms can generally be identified as the acquirer, the *purchase method* of accounting is usually used. In those rare instances when one of the combining firms cannot be identified as the acquirer, the *pooling-of-interest method* is used.

Since in a purchase a new basis of accountability arises, fair values must be applied to the net assets or shares of the acquired firm. Four of the major characteristics of purchase accounting are as follows. First, *goodwill* (i.e., the excess of the purchase cost over the total book value of all identifiable assets purchased less the total value of all liabilities assumed by the purchaser) is reflected in the combined firm's financial statements. Second, the shareholders' equity section of the combined firm reflects the actual purchase price (including direct combination expenses), and is not a simple carryforward of the shareholders' equity section of the acquired firm. Third, a consolidated financial statement is only appropriate at the date of combination. Thus, the combination does not affect the earnings reported for prior reporting periods. And finally, the combination will probably affect future earnings adversely since goodwill will be amortized against income on a straight-line basis over the estimated life of the goodwill.‡

---

*For a comprehensive treatment of this topic, the reader is referred to any basic intermediate accounting textbook.

†A firm is considered to be the acquirer if (1) it distributes cash or other assets, or incurs liabilities, to obtain the assets or shares of another firm; and/or (2) its shareholders hold more than 50 percent of the voting shares of the combined firm.

‡If an acquiring firm's management attempts to maximize eps, then the acquiring firm's management may reject a potential combination that is advantageous to its shareholders but requires a purchase method of accounting. However, it should be noted that while the goodwill expense under the purchase method of accounting may have a substantial effect on the eps of the combination, it will have no effect on the cash flows of the combination because it is an after-tax expense.

Since in a pooling-of-interest no new accountability arises, the combining firms continue to be valued according to their precombination book values.* Four of the major characteristics of pooling-of-interest accounting are as follows. First, goodwill is *not* reflected in the pooled firm's financial statements. Second, the total assets and liabilities of the pooled firm are the carryforward of the established book values of the combining firms; that is, all accounting values are a simple summation of the corresponding values for the precombination combining firms. In general, the shareholders' equity of the pooled firm will be equal to the total shareholders' equity of the combining firms; and the retained earnings of the pooled firm will be equal to or less than the total retained earnings of the combining firms. Third, all financial statements of the combining firms are consolidated at the date of the combination for all reporting periods. Since continuity of ownership is assumed under pooling, the combining firms are considered to have always been combined, and thus earnings of prior reporting periods must be restated to accurately reflect the earnings of the pooled firm. Fourth, there is no direct impact on the future earnings of the pooled company. Thus, if given a choice, management would likely prefer to account for most business combinations under the pooling method.

EXAMPLE   On April 9, 1980, Hiram Walker-Gooderham and Worts Ltd. and Consumers' Gas Co. were effectively amalgamated to form Hiram Walker-Consumers Home Ltd. Since the acquiring company could not be identified, the pooling-of-interest method of accounting was used in amalgamating the two firms.

THE COMBINATION NEGOTIATION PROCESS

Many potentially attractive combinations fail during the negotiation process for every combination actually consummated. When the management of an acquiring firm has found a suitable combination candidate, it can negotiate either with the firm's management or directly with its shareholders. Typically, negotiation with the management is preferred, although if such negotiations fall through the acquiring firm may make a direct appeal to the other firm's shareholders through tender offers.

Management Negotiations   The acquiring firm must make an offer based on a certain exchange ratio to initiate the combination negotiation process. The target must then review the offer and, in light of alternate offers, agree or disagree with the terms offered. Normally, certain nonfinancial questions must be answered in the negotiations. These usually relate to the disposition and compensation of the existing management, product line policies, financing policies, and the autonomy of the acquired firm.

However, the most important of the terms is the price per share offered. If the acquired firm is offered a good premium over its market price, along with certain other guarantees, the combination may be consummated. In Canada, bidding seldom occurs during the negotiation process, because it is generally considered unethical for the seller to

---

*This assumes that all the combining firms had applied GAAP (i.e., generally accepted accounting principles) on a reasonably uniform basis.

"shop around" during the negotiation period.[4] In a few well-publicized instances, there have been negotiations in which the target has played one offer against another to obtain the best possible terms. In general, if the combination is to be consummated in a friendly manner, both parties must agree to the various financial and nonfinancial terms prior to combining.

When there are differences in the expectations between the sellers and the buyers as to the value of synergistic effects, certain *contingent payments* are built into the combination contract. These are generally effective because they tend to be valued more highly by the optimistic acquired company than by the more pessimistic acquiring company. In a cash transaction, *share purchase warrants* may be given to the management of a closely held company that is to be operated by its management as a subsidiary.[*] The warrants may be exercisable once the market price of the acquiring firm reaches a certain level; more commonly, however, they are tied somehow to the earnings of the subsidiary. The terms of this type of warrant generally state that if the subsidiary's accumulated earnings exceed a specified amount within a certain period of time, the management will be paid a certain percentage of earnings or will receive or be able to purchase at a prespecified price a certain number of the common shares of the acquiring firm. The level of performance necessary to receive the contingency payment may be geared to average annual earnings or some other financial value. The contingency payments in a share exchange transaction are quite similar.

The use of contingency payments as a *sweetener* to encourage the existing management of the acquired company to operate the firm, after it has been acquired, in a manner that will benefit the combined company is an attractive feature from both the acquiring and the acquired firm's viewpoint.

Tender Offers When management negotiations for an acquisition break down, tender offers may be used in an attempt to negotiate a combination directly with the target firm's shareholders. As we saw in Chapter 24, a tender offer is made at a premium above the market price and is offered by the acquiring company (referred to as the *bidder*) to the shareholders of the target firm. Shareholders accept the offer by returning their completed agreement to sell to the bidder's agent (typically a trust company). The offer may be conditional on the bidder obtaining a certain percentage of the outstanding shares of the target.

Legally, a tender offer is called a *takeover bid* if after the offer the acquiring company will own more than 20 percent of the outstanding listed shares of the acquired company. Regulations dealing with the form and procedures involved with takeover bids are included in most Provincial Securities Acts. For example, in Ontario, the bidder must file a takeover bid circular with the Ontario Securities Commission (OSC).

Sometimes a tender offer is made to add pressure to existing combination negotiations; in other cases, the tender offer may be made without warning to catch the management off guard. If the management is not desirous of a combination or believes that the premium in a projected tender offer is too low, it is likely to take certain defensive actions to ward off the tender offer. Common strategies include declaring an attractive

---

[*]Share purchase warrants were described in detail in Chapter 23. Review this material if greater clarification is desired.

dividend, informing shareholders of alleged damaging effects of being taken over, using the media, or attempting to sue the acquiring firm on even the slightest point of law. In the event of a non-Canadian tender offer, the target's management may utilize the review process of the Foreign Investment Review Act, by arguing that the proposed takeover offers no significant benefits to Canada. These actions may deter or delay a tender offer. Deterring the tender offer by filing suit gives the management that is fearful of a takeover time to find and negotiate a combination with a firm they would prefer to be acquired by. On the other hand, any vigorous defense by the management of the target firm will virtually assure their replacement if their defensive actions fail. It is the management's responsibility to make sure that any action it takes is consistent with the firm's overall objective of the long-run wealth maximization of the firm's owners.

Holding Companies

A *holding company* is a company that has voting control of one or more other companies (subsidiaries or divisions). Generally, there is virtually no formal organization above the level of the individual firm since each of the "controlled" firms is essentially autonomous. In order to have this voting control, the holding company may need to own only a small percentage of the outstanding shares. The number of shares required depends on the dispersion of ownership of the company. In the case of companies with a relatively small number of shareholders, as much as 30–40 percent of the shares may be required; in the case of firms having a widely dispersed ownership, 10–20 percent of the shares may be sufficient to gain voting control. A holding company desirous of obtaining voting control of a firm may use either direct market purchases or tender offers to obtain the needed shares.

ADVANTAGES OF HOLDING COMPANIES

The key advantages of the holding company arrangement are the leverage effect, protection from risk, legal benefits, tax benefits, and the fact that control can be obtained without negotiations.

The Leverage Effect   A holding company arrangement permits a firm to control a large amount of assets with a relatively small dollar investment. In other words, the owners of a holding company can *control* significantly larger amounts of assets than they could acquire through an amalgamation. A simple example may help illustrate the leverage effect.

EXAMPLE   The Moses Company currently holds voting control of two subsidiaries—company X and company Y. The balance sheets for the Moses Company and its two subsidiaries are presented in Table 25.9. It owns approximately 17 percent ($10 ÷ $60) of company X and 20 percent ($14 ÷ $70) of company Y. It is assumed that these holdings are sufficient for voting control.

Table 25.9   Balance Sheets for the Moses Company and Its Subsidiaries

Moses Company

Assets		Liabilities and shareholders' equity	
Common share holdings		Long-term debt	$ 6
Company X	$10	Preferred shares	6
Company Y	14	Common share equity	12
Total	$24	Total	$24

Company X

Current assets	$ 30	Current liabilities	$ 15
Fixed assets	70	Long-term debt	25
Total	$100	Common share equity	60
		Total	$100

Company Y

Current assets	$ 20	Current liabilities	$ 10
Fixed assets	140	Long-term debt	60
Total	$160	Preferred shares	20
		Common share equity	70
		Total	$160

The owners of the Moses Company's $12 worth of equity have control over $260 worth of assets (company X's $100 worth and company Y's $160 worth). This means that the owners' equity represents only about 4.6 percent ($12 ÷ $260) of the total assets controlled. From the discussions of ratio analysis, financial leverage, and capital structure in Chapters 3, 4, and 18, respectively, the reader should recognize that this is quite a high degree of leverage. If an individual shareholder or even another holding company owns $3 of Moses Company's shares, which is sufficient for its control, it will in actuality control the whole $260 of assets. The investment in this case would represent only 1.15 percent ($3 ÷ $260) of the assets controlled.

The high leverage obtained through a holding company arrangement greatly magnifies earnings and losses for the holding company. Quite often a *pyramiding* of holding companies occurs when one holding company controls other holding companies. This arrangement causes an even greater magnification of earnings and losses. It is important to recall that the greater the leverage, the greater the risk involved.

Risk Protection   Another advantage commonly cited for the holding company arrangement is that the failure of one of the companies held does not result in the failure of the entire holding company. The failure of a subsidiary should cost the holding company, at a maximum, no more than its investment in that subsidiary. Often, lenders to subsidiaries of holding companies will require the holding company to guarantee the subsidiaries' loans in order to protect themselves in the event that the subsidiary goes bankrupt.

Legal Benefits   A legal benefit of the holding company results from the fact that since each subsidiary is a separate corporation, any lawsuits or legal actions filed against the subsidiary will not threaten the remaining companies. Furthermore, for multinational firms, the parent can establish a separate legal entity in each of the national jurisdictions in which it operates.

Tax Benefits   A holding company can be used to reduce the overall tax payments of a group of companies belonging to the same overall corporate structure, especially in an international setting. For example, if a subsidiary situated in a country with low tax rates purchases goods and services at a below-market transfer price from a subsidiary situated in a country with high tax rates, then the profits of the buying subsidiary will be inflated at the expense of the profits of the selling subsidiary. This, in turn, should increase the combined after-tax profits of the two subsidiaries because of the difference in their applicable tax rates. Note that the relevant tax authorities will typically monitor such dealings between associated companies closely to ensure that tax revenues are not lost. In cases where transfer prices are deemed to be significantly below fair market values, the tax authorities may restate corporate profits upward and thus levy an additional tax liability on the selling subsidiary.

Lack of Negotiations   Another major advantage of the holding company arrangement is the relative ease with which control of a subsidiary can be acquired. The holding company can gain control of a company simply by purchasing enough of its shares discretely over a period of time in the marketplace. Shareholder or management approval is not generally required for a holding company to acquire control of a firm, whereas it usually is required for other business combinations.

DISADVANTAGES OF HOLDING COMPANIES

The key disadvantages commonly cited with respect to the holding company arrangement include multiple taxation, the magnification of losses, and high administrative expenses.

Multiple Taxation   When a taxable Canadian corporation receives a cash dividend from another taxable Canadian corporation, or from a controlled corporation resident in Canada, the dividend-receiving corporation does not have to pay taxes on the funds received. Thus, in these situations, there is no double taxation on intercorporate dividend payments. In all other cases (such as foreign dividend payments), some portion of the dividend payment will be lost to double taxation at the corporate level.

Magnification of Losses   As the discussion of the leverage resulting from the holding company arrangement indicated, both earnings and losses are magnified. The magnification of losses when general economic conditions are unfavourable may result in the collapse of the holding company. The degree of risk is to some extent a function of the degree of pyramiding and the general stability of the subsidiaries' earnings. However, since managers and shareholders are generally risk averse, this increased risk must be recognized as a very real disadvantage of holding companies. Furthermore, in the utility field, excessive pyramiding through holding companies makes rate regulation extremely difficult.

High Administrative Expenses   A holding company is generally a more expensive form of business organization to administer than a single company created by a business combination. The increased cost is generally attributable to the cost of maintaining each company as a separate entity and therefore not achieving all the economies available through a combination. Also, coordination between the holding company and its subsidiaries normally requires additional staff to maintain channels of communication.

Foreign Investment Review Agency (FIRA)

The Foreign Investment Review Agency (FIRA) is a federal crown corporation that has the power to significantly influence the nature and extent of business combination activity in Canada. In the 1974 Foreign Investment Review Act, FIRA was given the mandate to review prospective acquisitions of voting control (prospective takeovers) of Canadian businesses by non-Canadian investors and firms. Acquisition of control has been defined as the acquisition of more than 5 percent of the voting shares of a publicly traded corporation or more than 20 percent of the voting shares of a private corporation. FIRA's decisions are based on both the "no detriment" principle and the "significant benefit" principle. FIRA's checklist of the latter benefits includes items such as higher Canadian employment, additional Canadian exports, more Canadian resource processing or use of Canadian parts and services, and Canadian participation as shareholders or managers. Generally, FIRA will not approve a change of control unless the prospective non-Canadian acquirer makes a commitment to provide some of the above benefits.

Summary

This chapter has discussed the common methods of forming business combinations, which are the acquisition of assets, the acquisition of shares, and statutory amalgamations. A corporate combination occurs when two or more limited companies come under common ownership or control. The ultimate form of such a combination can be two or more corporations emerging as one corporation or it can be a parent-subsidiary relationship.

The motives for business combinations include growth, risk reduction, synergistic effects, financial considerations, increased managerial skills, tax considerations, and increased ownership liquidity and diversification. A firm can have horizontal, vertical, circular, or conglomerate growth. Horizontal growth involves acquiring firms in the same line of business, while vertical growth involves acquiring another firm in the same channel of production or distribution. Circular growth involves acquiring firms with different products that can be distributed through the same channel. Conglomerates are the result of acquiring unrelated firms to diversify risk. Risk reduction is often proposed as the rationale for conglomerate growth. Synergistic effects are economies of scale resulting from the lower overhead of combined firms. Managerial skill can be acquired, tax benefits through business loss carryforwards may be acquired, the marketability of shares may be increased, and the firm's fund-raising ability may be enhanced through the acquisitions of another firm. Some firms maintain that one of the advantages of a diversified combination is the increased ability of the combination to transfer financial resources among its various components more efficiently than the financial sector. These motives for combining are not mutually exclusive; generally a mixture of them provides justification for any particular business combination.

Business combinations can be transacted either by paying cash or through the exchange of shares. In either case, the firm being acquired may be acquired for its assets or as a going concern. If cash is paid, traditional capital budgeting procedures using net present value can be applied to determine the economic feasibility of the purchase. If the combination will significantly change the business risk of the acquiring firm, the cost of capital should be adjusted to take this into account. If an exchange of shares is used to acquire a firm, a ratio of exchange of shares must be established. The ratio of exchange can be stated as the ratio of the price paid for the acquired firm's shares to the acquiring firm's market price. The price paid must normally be greater than the acquired firm's market price to make the combination attractive.

In establishing the ratio of exchange, the effects on the key financial variables—the earnings per share and the market price per share of the combined firm—must be forecast for both the immediate future and the long run. Attention is sometimes given to the dividends per share, book value per share, business risk, and the capital structure of the combined firm. A key relationship affecting the combined firm's earnings per share and market price per share is the relationship between the price-earnings ratio paid for the acquired firm and the price-earnings ratio of the acquiring firm. Analytical schemes for evaluating these relationships are available.

The appropriate accounting treatment of a combination depends upon whether or not one of the combining firms can be identified as the acquirer. If one can be identified as the acquirer, the purchase method of accounting is used; if one cannot be identified as the acquirer, the pooling-of-interest method of accounting is used.

A combination can be negotiated either with the firm's management or directly with the firm's shareholders. Not only do negotiations with management require a favourable cash price or exchange ratio, but certain nonfinancial factors must be agreed upon. Often the management is given certain sweeteners as part of the payment price or to stimulate positive future performance. If a combination cannot be negotiated, tender offers can be used to purchase shares directly from the owners. Sometimes combination negotiations become quite competitive and cut-throat.

A holding company can be created by gaining control of other companies by purchasing as little as 10–20 percent of their voting shares. The chief advantages of holding companies are leverage effects, risk protection, legal benefits, possible tax benefits, and the fact that negotiations are not required to gain control of a prospective subsidiary.

The disadvantages commonly cited include multiple taxation if the prospective subsidiary is non-Canadian, the magnification of losses, and high administrative expenses.

The Foreign Investment Review Agency (FIRA) reviews prospective acquisitions of voting control of Canadian businesses by non-Canadian investors and firms. Generally, FIRA will only approve such acquisitions if such acquisitions will result in a "significant" benefit to Canada.

Questions

25.1   What is meant by a corporate combination? What are the three methods by which corporations can combine?

25.2   What are two common classifications of business combinations? How do they differ?

25.3   What is the difference between horizontal, vertical, and conglomerate growth? In which case could "total integration" result? Why?

25.4   How may business combinations increase the firm's fund-raising capability or its managerial skill? What broader justification must a business combination have?

25.5   Why and in what situations may the acquisition of a firm with a business loss carryforward-carryback be quite acceptable?

25.6   Why may business combinations be made to increase the liquidity and individual portfolio diversification of a firm's ownership? What types of firms are likely to combine for this motive?

25.7   What should be the financial manager's overriding concern in evaluating possible business combinations? What should the financial manager's viewpoint be with respect to (1) the dividend per share, (2) the book value per share, and (3) business risk?

25.8   What is the justification for the acquisition of companies not as going concerns, but rather for all or part of their assets? What other benefit may result from such acquisitions?

25.9   How should one evaluate the acquisition of a going concern? What difficulties are often encountered?

25.10   What is a ratio of exchange? Is it based on the current market prices of the shares of the acquiring and acquired firm? Why or why not?

25.11   When a share exchange type of acquisition is being evaluated, what are normally the key variables considered? Why?

25.12   What are the important considerations in evaluating the long-run impact of a combination on the combined firm's earnings per share? Why may a long-run view change a combination decision?

25.13   What is a tender offer? How might it be used to arrange a combination? Are tender offers the primary tool used to arrange combinations?

25.14   To discourage shareholders from accepting tender offers, what actions might the firm's management take?

25.15   What is a holding company? What are the companies held by a holding company called? How does the holding company arrangement differ from an amalgamation?

25.16   To obtain voting control in other companies, how many voting shares must a company control? On what does this depend?

25.17   What are the key advantages cited for the holding company arrangement? What leverage effect is involved?

25.18   What disadvantages are commonly cited for the holding company arrangement? What is pyramiding?

Problems

25.1 The Whitower Watch Company is contemplating the acquisition of the Sport-Watch Company, a firm that has shown large operating losses over the past few years. As a result of the acquisition, Whitower believes the total pretax operating income of the amalgamation will not change from its present level for five years. The total operating loss of Sport-Watch is $500,000, while Whitower projects annual operating income to be $280,000 per year for this year and for each of the next five years. This is unchanged from last year. The firm is in the 40-percent tax bracket.

a. If Whitower does not make the acquisition, what is the company's tax liability for last year, this year, and each of the next five years?

b. If the acquisition were made, how much would the company owe or save in taxes for last year, this year, and each of the next five years?

c. If Sport-Watch can be acquired for $225,000 in cash, should Whitower make the acquisition based on tax considerations?

25.2 Peterson's Pants has experienced operating losses in the past two years of $400,000 per year. Two firms are interested in acquiring Peterson's for its operating losses. The first potential acquirer, Stud Duds, expects its operating income to remain unchanged at $200,000 for the current and the next five years. Stud Duds has a cost of capital of 15 percent. The second potential acquirer, Glitter Threads, has realized and expected operating income as indicated:

Year	Glitter Threads operating income
−1	$ 80,000
0	120,000
1	200,000
2	300,000
3	400,000
4	400,000
5	500,000

Glitter Threads has a cost of capital of 15 percent. Both firms are subject to 40-percent tax rates on ordinary business income.

a. What is the annual tax advantage of the acquisition for Stud Duds?

b. What is the annual tax advantage of the acquisition for Glitter Threads?

c. If the decision is based solely on tax savings, what is the maximum cash price each interested firm would be willing to pay for Peterson's Pants?

d. Use your answers in a through c to explain why a potential acquisition can have different values to different potential acquiring firms.

25.3 The Gray Printing Company is considering the acquisition of the Multi-Color Press at a cash price of $60,000. The Multi-Color Press has liabilities of $90,000. Multi-Color has a large press that Gray needs; the remaining assets would be sold to net $65,000. As a result of acquiring the press, Gray would experience an increase in net cash flow of $20,000 per year over the next 10 years. The firm has a 14-percent cost of capital.

a. What is the effective or net cost of the large press?

b. If this is the only way Gray can obtain the large press, should the firm go ahead with the acquisition? Explain your answer.

c. If the firm could purchase a press that would provide slightly better quality, and $26,000 annual net cash flow for 10 years, for a price of $120,000, which alternative would you recommend? Explain your answer.

25.4 The Toma Fish Company is contemplating the acquisition of the Seaside Packing Company for a cash price of $180,000. Toma currently has a quite high business risk and therefore has a cost of capital of 14 percent. As a result of acquiring Seaside Packing, which is financed entirely with equity, Toma expects its business risk to drop and its cost of capital therefore to drop to 11 percent. The acquisition of Seaside Packing is expected to increase Toma's cash flows by $20,000 per year for the first 3 years and by $30,000 per year for the following 12 years.

a. Determine whether the proposed cash acquisition is desirable. Explain your answer.
b. If the firm's business risk would actually have remained unchanged as a result of the proposed acquisition, would this alter your recommendation? Support your answer with numerical data.

25.5 Elkheart Oil is being considered for acquisition by Onagonda Oil. Onagonda believes that the combination would increase its cash flows by $25,000 for each of the next five years and $50,000 for the following five years. Onagonda can expect its cost of capital to increase from 12 to 15 percent if the acquisition is made. The cash price of Elkheart is $125,000.

a. Would you recommend the acquisition?
b. If the cost of capital does not change with the acquisition, would your decision in **a** be different? Explain.

25.6 Flannagan's Dairy Ltd. is attempting to acquire Milk Bar Ltd. Certain financial data on these corporations are summarized as follows:

Item	Flannagan's Dairy Ltd.	Milk Bar Ltd.
Earnings available for common	$20,000	$8,000
Number of shares of common outstanding	20,000	4,000
Market price per share	$12	$24

Flannagan's has sufficient authorized but unissued shares to carry out the proposed acquisition. Assume that no synergies are expected from the combination.

a. If the ratio of exchange is 1.8, what will be the earnings per share based on the original shares of each firm?
b. If the ratio of exchange is 2.0, what will be the earnings per share based on the original shares of each firm?
c. If the ratio of exchange is 2.2, what will be the earnings per share based on the original shares of each firm?
d. Discuss the principle illustrated by your answers to **a** through **c**.

25.7 United Manufacturing Company is interested in acquiring the Boren Machine Company by exchanging four-tenths of a share for each share of Boren. Certain financial data on these companies are as follows:

Item	United Manufacturing	Boren Machine
Earnings available for common	$200,000	$50,000
Number of shares of common outstanding	50,000	20,000
Earnings per share	$4.00	$2.50
Market price per share	$50.00	$15.00
Price-earnings ratio	12.5	6

United has sufficient authorized but unissued shares to carry out the proposed acquisition.

a. How many new common shares will United have to issue in order to make the proposed acquisition?

b. If the earnings for each component of the combination remain unchanged, what will the post-combination earnings per share be?

c. How much, effectively, has been earned on behalf of each of the original common shares of Boren?

d. How much, effectively, has been earned on behalf of each of the original common shares of United?

25.8 Calculate the ratio of exchange of (1) shares, and (2) the market price in each of the following cases.

Case	Current market price per share Acquiring	Acquired	Price per share offered
A	$50	$25	$ 30
B	$80	$80	$100
C	$40	$60	$ 70
D	$50	$10	$ 12.50
E	$25	$20	$ 25

What does each ratio signify? Explain.

25.9 Gordo Enterprises, at the end of 19X0, had 80,000 common shares outstanding and most recently had net operating income of $160,000. The Potut Company, at the end of 19X0, had 10,000 common shares outstanding and earned $20,000 for common shareholders last year. Gordo's earnings are expected to grow at an annual rate of 5 percent, while Potut's growth rate in earnings should be 10 percent per year.

a. Calculate earnings per share for Gordo Enterprises for the next five years assuming there is no combination.

b. Calculate the next five years' earnings per share for Gordo assuming it acquires Potut at a ratio of exchange of 1.3.

c. Calculate the next five years' earnings per share for Gordo assuming it acquires Potut at a ratio of exchange of 1.1.

d. Graph the earnings-per-share figures from **a, b,** and **c.** Explain the differences.

e. Which plan—**b** or **c**—is preferable from the viewpoint of each of the firms? Why?

25.10 B. S. Books wishes to evaluate a proposed combination with Plain Cover Publications. B. S. had 19X0 earnings of $200,000, has 100,000 common shares outstanding, and expects earnings to grow at an annual rate of 7 percent. Plain Cover had 19X0 earnings of $800,000, has 200,000 common shares outstanding, and its earnings are expected to grow at 3 percent per year.

a. Calculate the expected earnings per share for B. S. Books for the next five years without the combination.

b. What would the B. S. Books shareholders earn over the next five years on each of their B. S. Books shares converted into Plain Cover shares at a ratio of (1) .6, and (2) .8 shares of Plain Cover for one share of B. S. Books?

c. Graph the pre- and post-combination earnings-per-share figures developed in **a** and **b.**

d. If you were a financial manager, what would you recommend from **b**—(1) or (2)? Explain your answer.

25.11 The Merwin Company Ltd. is considering the acquisition of the Lyle Company Ltd. by exchanging 1.25 common shares for each common share of Lyle Company. The Merwin

Company expects to sell at the same price-earnings multiple after the combination as before the combination.

Item	Merwin Company	Lyle Company
Number of common shares outstanding	90,000	15,000
Earnings available for common	$225,000	$50,000
Market price per share	$45	$50

a. Calculate the ratio of exchange of market prices.
b. Calculate the earnings per share and price-earnings ratio for each company.
c. Calculate the price-earnings ratio used to purchase the Lyle Company.
d. Calculate the post-combination earnings per share for the Merwin Company.
e. Calculate the expected market price per share of the combined firm. Discuss this result in light of your findings in **a**.

25.12 The Magna Company holds shares in company A and company B. For the companies, a simplified balance sheet is presented below. Magna has voting control over both company A and company B.

Magna Company

Assets		Liabilities and shareholders' equity	
Common share holdings		Long-term debt	$ 40,000
Company A	$ 40,000	Preferred shares	25,000
Company B	60,000	Common share equity	35,000
Total	$100,000	Total	$100,000

Company A

Assets		Liabilities and shareholders' equity	
Current assets	$100,000	Current liabilities	$100,000
Fixed assets	400,000	Long-term debt	200,000
Total	$500,000	Common share equity	200,000
		Total	$500,000

Company B

Assets		Liabilities and shareholders' equity	
Current assets	$180,000	Current liabilities	$100,000
Fixed assets	720,000	Long-term debt	500,000
Total	$900,000	Common share equity	300,000
		Total	$900,000

a. What percentage of the total assets controlled by the Magna Company does its common share equity represent?
b. If another company owns 15 percent of the common shares of the Magna Company and by virtue of this fact has voting control, what percentage of the total assets controlled does the outside company's equity represent?
c. How does a holding company effectively provide a great deal of control for a small dollar investment?

d. Given the following additional facts, answer questions **a** and **b**.

(1) Company A's fixed assets consist of $20,000 of common shares in company C. This provides voting control.

(2) Company C, which has total assets of $400,000, has voting control of company D, which has $50,000 of total assets.

(3) Company B's fixed assets consist of $60,000 of common shares in both company E and company F. In both cases, this gives it voting control. Companies E and F have total assets of $300,000 and $400,000, respectively.

Notes

1. The irrelevance of corporate diversification for valuation is presented in a more rigorous fashion by S. Myers, "Procedures for Capital Budgeting Under Uncertainty," *Industrial Management Review* (Spring 1968), pp. 1–19; and H. Levy and M. Sarnat, "Diversification, Analysis and the Uneasy Case for Conglomerate Mergers," *Journal of Finance* (September 1970), pp. 795–802.

2. For example, see The Provincial Bank of Canada, *Economic Review* 2 (July-August 1972).

3. This is supported by empirical findings. For example, Laiken studied the economic and financial performance of a sample of 369 Canadian-based firms that were listed on the Toronto Stock Exchange during the period of 1960–1970. The companies varied greatly in their external growth activity. Laiken found that greater levels of external growth activity were not associated with either larger increases in profit margins or increased price-earnings ratios. See S. N. Laiken, "Financial Performance of Merging Firms in a Virtually Unconstrained Legal Environment," *The Antitrust Bulletin* (Winter 1973).

4. Donald J. Lecraw and Donald N. Thompson, *Conglomerate Mergers in Canada: A Background Report* (Ottawa: Royal Commission on Corporate Concentration Report No. 32, May 1978), p. 6.

Suggested Readings

Austin, Douglas V., "The Financial Management of Tender Offer Takeovers," *Financial Management* 3 (Spring 1974), pp. 37–43.

Baesel, J. B. and D. Grant, *The Performance of Acquisition Oriented Canadian Companies: 1960–1975* (Ottawa: Unpublished report submitted to the Royal Commission on Corporate Concentration, 1976).

Birnie, David A. G., "Incorporation, Acquisition, Disposition and Reorganization," *Canadian Income Tax Revised* (Toronto: Butterworth and Co. (Canada) Ltd., 1974).

Cheney, Richard E., "Remedies for Tender-Offer Anxiety," *Financial Executive* 43 (August 1975), pp. 16–19.

Ellert, James C., "Mergers, Antitrust Law Enforcement and Stockholder Returns," *The Journal of Finance* 31 (May 1976), pp. 715–732.

Globerman, Steven, *Mergers and Acquisitions in Canada: A Background Report* (Ottawa: Royal Commission on Corporate Concentration, Report No. 34, April 1977).

Goudzwaard, Maurice B., "Conglomerate Mergers, Convertibles, and Cash Dividends," *Quarterly Review of Business and Economics* (Spring 1969), pp. 53–62.

Halpern, Paul J., "Empirical Estimates of the Amount and Distribution of Gains to Companies in Mergers," *Journal of Business* 48 (October 1973), pp. 554–575.

Haugen, Robert A. and Terence E. Langetieg, "An Empirical Test for Synergism in Merger," *Journal of Finance* 39 (June 1975), pp. 1003–1014.

Heath, John, Jr., "Valuation Factors and Techniques in Mergers and Acquisitions," *Financial Executive* 49 (April 1972), pp. 34–44.

Hogarty, Thomas F., "The Profitability of Corporate Mergers," *Journal of Business* 43 (July 1970), pp. 317–327.

Laiken, S. N., "Financial Performance of Merging Firms in a Virtually Unconstrained Legal Environment," *The Antitrust Bulletin* (Winter 1973).

Larson, Kermit D. and Nicholas D. Gonedes, "Business Combinations: An Exchange Ratio Determination Model," *Accounting Review* 44 (October 1969), pp. 720–728.

Lecraw, Donald J. and Donald N. Thompson, *Conglomerate Mergers in Canada: A Background Report* (Ottawa: Royal Commission on Corporate Concentration, Report No. 32, May 1978).

Lewellen, Wilbur G., "A Pure Financial Rationale for the Conglomerate Merger," *Journal of Finance* 26 (May 1971), pp. 521–537.

MacDougal, Gary E. and Fred V. Malek, "Master Plan for Merger Negotiations," *Harvard Business Review* 48 (January-February 1970), pp. 71–82.

Mandelker, Gershon, "Risk and Return: The Case of Merging Firms," *Journal of Financial Economics* 1 (December 1974), pp. 303–336.

Mason, R. Hal. and Maurice B. Goudzwaard, "Performance of Conglomerate Firms: A Portfolio Approach," *Journal of Finance* 31 (March 1976), pp. 39–48.

Melicher, Ronald W. and David F. Rush, "Evidence on the Acquisition-Related Performance of Conglomerate Firms," *Journal of Finance* 29 (March 1974), pp. 141–149.

Morin, D. and W. Chippindale, Eds., *Acquisitions and Mergers in Canada* (Toronto: Methuen, 1970).

Nielsen, James F. and Ronald W. Melicher, "A Financial Analysis of Acquisition and Merger Premiums," *Journal of Financial and Quantitative Analysis* 8 (March 1973), pp. 139–148.

Reilly, Frank K., "What Determines the Ratio of Exchange in Corporate Mergers?" *Financial Analysts Journal* 18 (November-December 1972), pp. 47–50.

Schwartz, G. B. and E. J. Kelly, "Bank Financing of Corporate Acquisitions: The Cash Tender Offer," *Journal of Commercial Bank Lending* 53 (August 1971), pp. 19–29.

Scott, James H., Jr., "On the Theory of Conglomerate Mergers," *Journal of Finance* 32 (September 1977), pp. 1235–1250.

Shick, Richard A., "The Analysis of Mergers and Acquisitions," *Journal of Finance* (May 1972), pp. 495–502.

Shick, Richard A. and Frank C. Jen, "Merger Benefits to Shareholders of Acquiring Firms," *Financial Management* 3 (Winter 1974), pp. 45–53.

Stapleton, R. C., "The Acquisition Decision as a Capital Budgeting Problem," *Journal of Business Finance and Accounting* 2 (Summer 1975), pp. 187–202.

Stevens, Donald L., "Financial Characteristics of Merged Firms: A Multivariate Analysis," *Journal of Financial and Quantitative Analysis* 8 (March 1973), pp. 149–158.

Woods, Donald H. and Thomas A. Caverly, "Development of a Linear Programming Model for the Analysis of Merger/Acquisition Situations," *Journal of Financial and Quantitative Analysis* 4 (January 1970), pp. 627–642.

Chapter 26

FAILURE, REHABILITATION, AND LIQUIDATION

The preceding 25 chapters of this text have presented various concepts, tools, and techniques for efficiently managing the finances of the business firm. Unfortunately, not all business firms, even if they use these techniques, are able to sustain themselves indefinitely; many firms fail each year as a result of one or a group of causes. In some instances, the failure of the firm may be due to temporary phenomena that can be overcome with the cooperation of outsiders. In other instances, certain legal procedures can be employed to rehabilitate the failed firm and eliminate its recognized weaknesses. If the weaknesses that caused the firm to fail cannot be eliminated, there are legal procedures for the orderly liquidation of the firm.

Although financial managers do not like to think of the financial rehabilitation or liquidation of the firm, it is important that they be aware of the consequences of failure and the remedies available to the failed firm. This knowledge is important not only when the firm itself fails, but also when the firm is a creditor of a failed firm. The procedures for collecting (if possible) at least a portion of the outstanding account when a customer of the firm that owes it money for the purchase of merchandise fails should be understood. A knowledge of the possible consequences of a business failure is important not only from the viewpoint of a failed or failing firm, but also from the viewpoint of the failing firm's suppliers of credit.

This chapter presents the fundamental concepts related to business failure. Attention is given to the remedies available to the failed firm and the satisfaction of creditor claims associated with a business failure. The chapter has five major sections. The first section presents a brief discussion of the nature and possible causes of business failure. The second section discusses the voluntary (and essentially "out-of-court") actions that can be taken to settle the claims of creditors. The third and fourth sections discuss legal remedies for the failed firm—commercial arrangements and bankruptcy liquidations. **815**

The fifth section presents some of the proposed changes to the present federal Bankruptcy Act.

The Nature and Causes of Business Failure

To provide the reader with a feel for the frequency and magnitude of business failure, some statistics on business failure have been given in Table 26.1. From the table, it is apparent that the frequency of business failures increased rapidly from 1977 onward and that the average debt of the failed firms was unusually high for 1976. This 1976 finding can be attributed to the slow growth experienced by the economy in 1975 (real growth in GNP of 1.1 percent), which resulted in a marked increase in the failure of larger firms (i.e., firms with liabilities greater than $100,000) in 1976.

Although the majority of firms that fail do so within the first year or two of their life, other firms grow, mature, and eventually fail. The failure of a business firm can be viewed in a number of ways and may be the result of one or more causes. This section presents both the types and major causes of business failure.

TYPES OF BUSINESS FAILURES

Business firms may fail either economically or financially.

Economic Failure   There are many definitions of economic failure. The most common definition states that a firm has failed when its revenues do not cover its costs. That is, a firm that consistently reports operating losses has failed to earn at a level that permits it to cover all its costs. From the point of view of prospective and existing shareholders, this type of performance is not desirable, and it will probably result in the deterioration of the value of the firm in the marketplace.

A second definition of economic failure is that a firm has failed if the firm's average return on investment has historically been less than its cost of capital. Although the consequences in the marketplace of economic failure can be great, outsiders generally cannot pressure the firm to liquidate. When returns are low, corrective action must be initiated and carried out by the owners and directors. Low returns, unless remedied, are likely to result eventually in financial failure.

Financial Failure   Financial failure is a more serious type of failure than economic failure. Financial failure includes the entire range of possibilities between technical insolvency and bankruptcy, both of which are discussed next.

Technical Insolvency   Technical insolvency occurs when a firm is unable to pay its liabilities as they come due. Although the firm cannot pay its bills as they come due, the firm's assets have not deteriorated and its liabilities have not increased to a point where they exceed the fair value of its assets. If some of the firm's assets can be converted into cash within a reasonable period, the firm may be able to escape complete failure. Nevertheless, a technically insolvent firm is illiquid and cannot continue to conduct business without certain changes.

Table 26.1 Business Failure Statistics 1970–1979

	Dun & Bradstreet[a]			Statistics Canada[b]				
						Number of failures according to size of liabilities		
Year	Number of failures	Average failure rate	Average liability per failure[a]	Number of failures	Average liability per failure	<$25,000	$25,000–$100,000	>$100,000
1970	2287	82	$115,826	3281	$ 78,527	1506	1284	491
1971	2627	90	$124,603	3270	$ 98,487	1444	1354	472
1972	2848	98	$ 87,748	3046	$100,851	1300	1314	432
1973	2718	91	$117,797	2945	$100,747	1132	1317	496
1974	2512	78	$150,290	2853	$114,111	1033	1261	559
1975	2863	84	$164,777	2091	$155,570	676	896	519
1976	2976	82	$394,291	2631	$460,656	732	1176	723
1977	4131	109	$232,824	3745	$177,185	862	1822	1061
1978	5119			4882	$128,711	1164	2432	1286
1979	5786			n.a.[b]	n.a.[b]	n.a.[c]	n.a.[c]	n.a.[c]

SOURCE: Dun & Bradstreet Ltd., *The Canadian Business Failure Record* (Toronto), various issues; and Statistics Canada, *Commercial Failures* (Ottawa: catalogue no. 61-002, quarterly), various issues. This compilation is limited to those bankruptcies filed under Federal legislation (the Bankruptcy and Winding-Up Acts) and does not include failures, sales, or seizures carried out under other legislation.
[a]Failure rate per 10,000 concerns.
[b]Not available because publication of this information was discontinued by Statistics Canada at the end of 1978. Similar information is now given in: Bureau of Corporate Affairs, *Bulletin: Canada Corporations Bankruptcy and Insolvency* (Ottawa: Consumer and Corporate Affairs, monthly). The two sources are not compatible, however, because the corresponding data from the latter source for 1978 was 5511 business failures with an average liability per failure of $109,840.
[c]No longer available.

Bankruptcy   Bankruptcy occurs when a firm's total liabilities exceed the fair value of its total assets. A bankrupt firm has a "real" net worth which is negative.

Although a less than competitive return on the firm's investment is not consistent with the firm's goal of owners' wealth maximization, such returns are not considered legal evidence of business failure. The law defines business failure as being financial failure (i.e., as being either technical insolvency or bankruptcy), since the law is designed to protect creditors. Thus, since our concern in this chapter is with what is legally considered to be business failure, we will use the term "failure" hereafter to refer only to financial failure (i.e., technical insolvency and bankruptcy).

MAJOR CAUSES OF BUSINESS FAILURE

The major causes of business failure are a lack of managerial skill, economic activity, and corporate maturity.

Lack of Managerial Skill   The primary cause of business failure is mismanagement, which indeed accounts for more than 70 percent of all business failures.* Specific managerial faults include overexpansion, poor financial advice, a poor sales force, and high production costs. Since a firm is generally organized and administered in a hierarchical form, the top manager, president, and board of directors all must share the responsibility for the failure of a firm as a result of mismanagement.

Economic Activity   Economic activity—especially economic downturns—can contribute to the failure of a business firm. If the economy goes into a recession, the firm's sales may decrease abruptly, leaving it with high fixed costs and insufficient revenues to cover these fixed operating and financial outlays. If the recession is prolonged, the likelihood of survival decreases. The impact of slow economic growth (e.g., 1975) on business failures (e.g., in 1976) can be seen in Table 26.1 and has been discussed earlier.

Not all firms and industries are equally affected by macroeconomic activity.† Thus, when the national economy may be doing well, the industry in which a firm operates may be in a slump and firms in the industry may fail. Increased competition is often a key cause of business failures during a recession. The failure of a firm during an economic boom, on the other hand, is more often attributable to mismanagement.

Corporate Maturity   Firms, like individuals, generally go through the stages of birth, growth, maturity, and eventually decline. Since our country can be considered industrially young (little more than 100 years old), the opportunity to observe the

---

*This is based on a compilation by Dun & Bradstreet of the underlying causes of business failure in Canada.

†The success of some firms runs countercyclical to economic activity, and other firms are unaffected by economic activity. For example, the sale of sewing machines is likely to increase during a recession, since people are more willing to make their own clothes and less willing to pay for the labour of others. The sale of boats and other luxury items may decline during a recession, while sales of staple items such as electricity are likely to be unaffected. In terms of "beta"—the measure of nondiversifiable risk developed in Chapter 16—a negative beta would indicate a firm whose stock market behaviour is countercyclical to economic activity (as measured by the return on a market index).

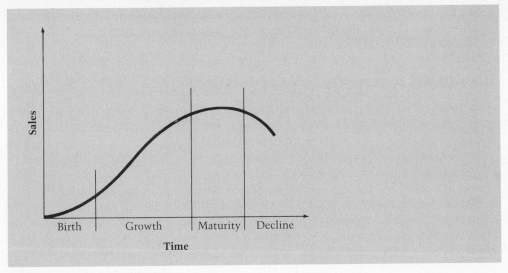

Figure 26.1   The life cycle of a firm.

failure of business firms due to old age has not been that profound. The life cycle of the firm, which is quite similar to a product's life cycle, is shown in Figure 26.1.

If a firm's life is to progress as depicted in the figure, it must first be fortunate enough to survive the birth phase, because the evidence indicates that the risk of failure is very high during a firm's first two years. The firm must then have competent and aggressive management during its growth phase. The management must be able to sustain growth through business combinations, research and development, technological innovation, new market development (e.g., export market), and exploration. At some point, due to a lack of management planning or foresight and/or misfortune, the firm will enter its maturity phase; and subsequently it may even enter into its decline phase. Obviously, some firms (such as IBM) have been successful in prolonging the growth phase of their life cycle; while other firms, such as single-product nondiversifying firms, have passed through all four phases before failing financially.

Voluntary Settlements

When a firm becomes either technically insolvent or bankrupt, it may arrange with its creditors an "out-of-court" settlement or discharge that leaves it in a position to continue operations. If the firm is technically insolvent, the voluntary settlement will probably permit the firm to continue operations, but if the firm is bankrupt the settlement may result in the liquidation of the firm. Regardless of whether the firm survives or is liquidated, a voluntary settlement enables it to bypass many of the costs involved in formal legal proceedings.* This is especially important for smaller firms. A possible

---

*This is not strictly true if the firm is liquidated through a formal or statutory assignment. This will be discussed later in this section.

disadvantage of a voluntary settlement is that since the debtor-firm generally retains control of the business, the value of the assets left with and operated by the debtor-firm can deteriorate further.

INITIATING A VOLUNTARY SETTLEMENT

A voluntary settlement is normally initiated by the debtor-firm, since such a settlement may enable it to continue to exist or to be liquidated in a manner that maximizes the owners' recovery of their investments. The debtor first files a proposal for an extension or a composition. Subsequently, the debtor, possibly with the aid of a key creditor, arranges a meeting with all its creditors.

The first item of business at the meeting is to select a committee of creditors to investigate and analyze the debtor's situation and recommend a plan of action. The committee generally consists of some of the largest creditors and one or two of the smaller creditors. Generally, a two-thirds majority vote of each class of creditors is needed before the proposal is both accepted and binding on all the members of the class.

A VOLUNTARY SETTLEMENT TO SUSTAIN THE FIRM

If the creditor committee recommends and the creditors agree to sustaining the firm's existence, a number of common plans may be used. The conditions necessary for sustaining the debtor-firm include (1) the debtor-firm shows the ability to recover; (2) the debtor-firm is a good moral risk; (3) it is reasonable to believe that the debtor-firm's recovery is feasible given expected business conditions; and (4) by sustaining the debtor-firm, the creditors can continue to receive business from it. Common strategies for sustaining the firm include extension, composition, creditor control, and a combination of these approaches.

Extension An *extension* is an arrangement whereby the creditors extend the required payment date of past-due obligations. Creditors often prefer an extension because they can receive payment in full. Extensions are arranged when the creditors feel that it is quite likely that the firm can overcome its problems and resume successful operations. Normally, when creditors give an extension, they require cash payments for purchases until the past debts have been satisfied. Occasionally a creditor may agree to subordinate its claims to those of new creditors. This is done to permit the firm to get back on its feet so that repayment is more likely to be forthcoming. Because of the uncertainties involved, the creditor committee will often insist on certain controls over the debtor-firm. It may take legal control (e.g., an assignment) of the debtor-firm's assets or common shares, take a security interest in certain assets (such as notes and mortgages), or reserve for itself the right to approve all disbursements.

When the creditor committee makes its recommendations to the creditors, it must present a plan providing for the immediate repayment of dissenting creditors. If a large enough number of creditors dissent to the committee's recommendations and no acceptable solution can be reached, liquidation may be the only alternative.

Composition   A *composition* is a pro rata cash settlement of creditor claims. Instead of receiving full payment of their claims, as in the case of an extension, creditors receive only a partial payment of their claims. A uniform percentage (e.g., 15 percent) of each dollar owed is paid as full settlement of each creditor's claim. The willingness of creditors to accept a composition arrangement depends greatly on their general evaluation of the effects of liquidation. The creditors must weigh their estimate of the amount they would recover in the event of liquidation against the composition and the prospect of future profits from the firm's continued existence. A composition arrangement can be quite similar to a commercial arrangement in the event of bankruptcy except that many of the legal and administrative procedures and expenses are bypassed, and the debtor-firm avoids the stigma of officially being declared bankrupt. As in the case of an extension, there may be dissenting creditors, in which case the primary alternatives are to pay them the full amount they are owed, let them recover a higher percentage of their claims, or liquidate the firm.

Creditor Control   Occasionally, the creditor committee's investigation results in the general finding that the current management cannot operate the debtor-firm if the firm is to have a reasonable chance of survival. In this case, the committee may take control of the firm and operate it until all claims have been settled, or it may recommend that a new management be installed. The real danger of attempting to sustain a failing corporation through creditor control is the opportunity it provides for mismanagement suits by shareholders.* For this reason creditors hesitate to take over the management of a failed corporation.

A Combination of Approaches   A plan involving some combination of extension, composition, and creditor control can result. An example would be a settlement whereby the debtor-firm agrees to pay 75 cents on the dollar in three equal annual installments of 25 cents on the dollar, while the creditors agree to sell additional merchandise to the firm on 30-day terms if the existing management is replaced by a new management acceptable to them. The important point for creditors to consider is that if a greater return is expected from liquidation, attempts to sustain the firm are an unacceptable course of action financially.

A VOLUNTARY SETTLEMENT RESULTING IN LIQUIDATION

When the estimated liquidation value of the firm is greater than its market value as a going concern, the only acceptable course of action is generally the liquidation of the firm.

---

*The existing ownership can sue creditors who are running the company and are unable to sustain the firm. In other words, if the creditor committee is in control when the firm fails, it can be held responsible instead of the firm's original management that placed the firm in technical insolvency or bankruptcy. Even if the creditor committee is assured of winning a mismanagement suit, the time and cost of the litigation are a serious drawback to such a course of action.

Objective   The objective of the liquidation process is two-fold. First, it is to recover as much per dollar owed as is possible. Second, it is to maximize the shareholders' recovered residual claim; that is, the amount remaining for shareholders after the claims of all other claimants have been satisfied.

Procedure   Liquidation can be effected through assignment or through the legal procedures provided by the bankruptcy laws.* *Assignment*, which is dealt with in this section of the chapter, is a liquidation procedure that need not go through the courts and can be used to fully satisfy the claims of all claimants "out-of-court." On the other hand, *bankruptcy*, which is dealt with in a subsequent section of the chapter, is a procedure conducted under the auspices of the courts for formally liquidating a business firm and in effect completely discharging the claims of the firm's creditors.

Thus, if the debtor is willing to accept liquidation, legal action need not be required. Generally, an orderly assignment is likely to be quicker, more efficient, and less costly in terms of accounting and legal expenses. Thus, it should produce noticeably higher settlements. However, all the creditors must agree to a liquidation by assignment for it to be feasible. Thus, firms with a small number of creditors, and no publicly held outstanding securities, are more likely to be liquidated in this way.

The assignment procedure begins with a meeting of the creditors at which all the creditors voluntarily agree to an assignment. An *assignment* is an agreement between the debtor and the creditors that legally assigns the power to liquidate the debtor-firm's assets to a third party (referred to as an *assignee* or *trustee*). Generally, an assignment trustee has more flexibility in the disposition of assets and has greater familiarity with resale markets than does a bankruptcy trustee. The two types of assignments are discussed next.

Informal or Common-Law Assignment   In an informal or common-law assignment, the creditors agree on an assignee or trustee. The assignee is entrusted with the title to the assets and the responsibility to liquidate them efficiently. Once the assignee has liquidated the firm's assets, he or she must distribute the recovered funds to the creditors and owners (if any funds remain for the owners).

The assignee may liquidate the assets through bulk or piecemeal auction or private sale. A bulk auction sale is generally preceded by sufficient advertising so that enough bids are received to ensure an orderly resale market. A piecemeal auction sale, conducted by a licensed auctioneer, is generally used to liquidate large and well-differentiated items such as machine tools.

Since the common-law assignment does not automatically discharge the debtor-firm from its obligations, the final action in an assignment is for the debtor-firm to obtain a signed release from the creditors attesting to the complete settlement of their claims. Generally, after the execution of the assignment and a careful review of all transactions,

---

* There is a major difference between the two liquidation procedures in terms of discharge for the owners of an unincorporated business. With a liquidation through bankruptcy, the owners of an unincorporated business are automatically discharged from the balance of their obligations; with a liquidation through assignment, the owners of an unincorporated business are not automatically discharged from the balance of their obligations.

the creditors' committee will recommend that such a release be granted. Although obtaining a release is generally not a necessary step for an incorporated business being wound up, there is always the possibility that if the release is not obtained the courts may hold the debtor-firm's management personally liable for any unsettled claims. On the other hand, it is obvious that for an unincorporated business, obtaining such a release is extremely important.

Statutory Assignment   Since a statutory assignment is conducted according to the statutes regulating assignment, it is similar but more formal than a common-law assignment. In a statutory assignment, the assignment instrument is recorded to provide official notice to all third parties, and the assignment proceedings are carried out under court order. Thus, the court selects the assignee and supervises the assignee's activities. As in the case of a common-law assignment, the debtor-firm is not automatically discharged from all its obligations unless it obtains a release from all its creditors.*

Commercial Arrangements†

When a firm has failed, it may not be willing or able to obtain a voluntary "out-of-court" settlement with its creditors. In such a situation, the failed firm can attempt to obtain a commercial arrangement (sometimes called a reorganization)‡ or a liquidation under the federal bankruptcy and insolvency laws.

The federal bankruptcy and insolvency laws have long been concerned with the allocational efficiency of resources.§ Thus, these laws have been designed to differentiate between a firm that has failed because of temporary adverse general economic conditions and a firm that has failed because it could not meet the rigours of competition. In the former case, the present laws facilitate proposals for commercial arrangements, because forcing such firms into costly bankruptcy procedures would not be allocationally efficient. In the latter case, the present laws attempt to minimize the cost and formality of the liquidation of such firms so that the recoverable resources can be transferred to more allocationally efficient uses. Before proceeding, it should be noted that commercial arrangements are discussed in this section of the chapter and liquidations under the bankruptcy laws are discussed in the next section of the chapter.

*Thus, in both types of assignments, the debtor-firm obtains a discharge of unsettled obligations by private negotiations with creditors (i.e., "out-of-court").

†An arrangement may be considered to be necessary for a firm even if the firm is not technically insolvent or bankrupt. Thus, under the federal Companies Act, the term *arrangement* is used to refer to any reorganization (or restructuring) of the share capital of a company. Examples include the division of shares into shares of different classes, the conversion of shares into shares of another class, the consolidation of shares of different classes, the modification of any provisions attached to shares of any class, and an amalgamation or reconstruction.

‡This is probably caused by U.S. terminology, since both arrangements and reorganizations are possible under the U.S. Chandler Act. Thus, in the United States, a debtor-firm can either file for an arrangement under Chapter XI of the Chandler Act or it can file for a reorganization under Chapter X of the Chandler Act. Since arrangements as defined in the United States relate only to unsecured debts and must be acceptable to *all* creditors, they are not commonly used in the United States.

§Allocational efficiency was defined and discussed in Chapter 19.

CHARACTERISTICS OF COMMERCIAL ARRANGEMENTS

Commercial arrangements are similar in purpose and form to extensions and compositions of a firm's outstanding obligations. Thus, a *commercial arrangement* may be necessary to *modify* or *eliminate* the *property rights* of the various classes of creditors and owners. Examples include the reduction of principal owed to secured and unsecured creditors, the lengthening of short-term debt maturities into longer-term maturities, and the elimination of fixed-payment securities by substituting shares for debt. A commercial arrangement may also be necessary to identify and rectify the underlying causes of a firm's failure and to increase the probability of a firm's survival by ensuring that the firm can raise funds for working capital and fixed-asset replacement and modernization.

MECHANICS OF COMMERCIAL ARRANGEMENTS

Most arrangement proposals of unregulated business corporations are made under Part III of the present Bankruptcy Act.* Under the Act, the debtor-firm is the only entity that can make the proposal. The debtor-firm can file a proposal before or after bankruptcy. Once a proposal is filed, it halts all legal actions to enforce claims against the debtor-firm by all creditors, with the exception of secured creditors and creditors whose debts are not dischargeable (such as suppliers of necessaries).† The stages in the formulation of a commercial arrangement are discussed next.

Preparation of the Proposal   The formalization of a commercial arrangement begins with the preparation of the proposal. The proposal must include a schedule for the payment of the claims of all the creditors according to the order of priority prescribed in the Bankruptcy Act. It must also provide for the payment of the fees and disbursements of the trustee. In addition, unless the proposal states otherwise, it is implied that the debtor-firm will continue to manage its business. Thus, unlike bankruptcy, the debtor-firm's property is not automatically vested in the trustee. Since the financial aspects of an arrangement proposal are quite important, they will be discussed in a separate section.

Lodging the Proposal with a Trustee   The debtor-firm can generally lodge the proposal with a trustee of its choice. In all other cases, it must lodge the proposal with the trustee appointed by the court to administer the estate. The trustee is required by the Bankruptcy Act to make an investigation and appraisal of the affairs and property of the debtor-firm. This is necessary so that the trustee can make a reasonably accurate estimate of the financial situation of the debtor-firm and the causes

---

*Unregulated business corporations can also make proposals under the Winding-Up Act or the Companies Creditors' Arrangement Act. The latter act only applies to companies that have a bond issue or other indebtedness evidenced under a trust deed in favour of a trustee. Banks and other financial intermediaries can only make proposals under the Winding-Up Act or the Companies Creditors' Arrangement Act.

†An application for the appointment of an interim receiver by the court requires the approval of at least 5 percent in number and 25 percent in value of the unsecured creditors.

of its financial distress. The trustee then files the proposal with the *Official Receiver* (the officer of the court for each bankruptcy district) and calls a meeting of the creditors.

Creditor Approval of the Proposal   In order for the proposal to be binding on all unsecured creditors, the proposal must be accepted by a simple majority in number and three-fourths in value of creditors voting on the proposal. In calculating the benefits of an arrangement, the creditors must first assess the likelihood and expected rewards of successful rehabilitation against the costs involved in restructuring their claims (i.e., the costs of rehabilitation). Then they must compare this estimated *net* going-concern value of the rehabilitated firm to the firm's net liquidation value. The option that promises the highest risk-adjusted return should be the option favoured by the creditors. If the creditors reject the proposal, the debtor-firm is deemed to be bankrupt.

Court Approval of the Proposal*   After receiving the required approval of the creditors, the trustee must then seek the required court approval of the proposal. The court's approval or disapproval of the proposal is based on the following standards.

Fair and Equitable   A proposal is considered fair and equitable if it maintains the priorities of the respective contractual (property) rights of the creditors, preferred shareholders, and common shareholders. For example, holders of first mortgage bonds must be given priority over common shareholders. It would also be unfair to eliminate the original common shareholders as owners if the valuation of the firm indicates that some equity still exists. Canadian courts implicitly assume that a proposal must be fair and equitable if it has been agreed to by all interested parties.

Feasible   The court must find the proposal not only fair and equitable, but feasible— meaning it must be *workable*. The rehabilitated firm must have sufficient working capital, sufficient funds to cover fixed charges, sufficient credit prospects, and a sufficient ability to service debt to retire or refund debts as given in the proposal. This requirement is intended to ensure that the rehabilitated firm can operate efficiently, compete with other companies in the same industry, and avoid future commercial arrangement or bankruptcy liquidation.

If the proposal is accepted by the court, it is binding on all creditors of the firm. (This must be confirmed by supplementary letters patent.) If the proposal is rejected by the court, or if it is later annulled by the court, the debtor-firm is deemed to be bankrupt.

---

*While the stages in a corporate arrangement in the United States are similar, those for a corporate reorganization in the United States differ as follows. First, the debtor-firm or three or more creditors file for a reorganization under Chapter X of the Chandler Act. The court then appoints a trustee to prepare the reorganization plan. The reorganization plan is then presented to the court to determine if the reorganization plan is fair, equitable, and feasible. Once approved, and if the indebtedness exceeds $3 million, the Securities and Exchange Commission (SEC) then reviews the plan and makes an advisory report that is attached to the plan before it is reviewed by the creditors and shareholders. Based on this input, the creditors and shareholders either accept or reject the reorganization plan.

FINANCIAL ASPECTS OF AN ARRANGEMENT PROPOSAL

Although there are many financial approaches to rehabilitating a firm, two common approaches are the recapitalization (or reorganization) of the firm and a composition-type arrangement with creditors. In preparing the financial aspects of an arrangement proposal based on a recapitalization of the firm, three steps are generally followed: (1) the determination of the total valuation of the debtor-firm; (2) the determination of the appropriate capital structure for the rehabilitated firm; and (3) the determination of all exchanges of old for new securities. Each of these steps is discussed below.

The Valuation of the Firm   Although the valuation of the rehabilitated firm is probably the most difficult step, it is very important because it determines whether a commercial arrangement is appropriate. Both the liquidation value and the going-concern value are generally estimated. Thus, if the firm's value as a going concern is less than its liquidation value, liquidation may be appropriate; and if the opposite is found to be true, a commercial arrangement may be appropriate. The technique used to determine the liquidation value of the firm is similar to that described in the discussion of valuation in Chapters 17 and 18. The technique generally used to estimate the going-concern value of the rehabilitated firm is the capitalization of earnings. This involves forecasting the firm's sales and then estimating the earnings likely to be generated from those sales. Information gathered from a survey and discussion with various experts are often used in both forecasts. Then, by applying an appropriate *capitalization rate* (i.e., price-earnings multiple), the present value of forecast earnings can be transformed into the value of the firm as a going concern. An example will clarify this approach.

EXAMPLE   The Weak Company Ltd. is preparing an arrangement proposal under Part III of the Bankruptcy Act. The firm has calculated its liquidation value (after expenses) to be $5,000,000. The firm has investigated its past operations and expected industry trends in order to estimate its future sales. On the basis of its estimate of future sales, the firm expects the rehabilitated firm to generate after-tax earnings of $600,000 annually. In view of the firm's changed capital structure and prevailing capital market conditions, a capitalization rate of 10 percent was used to evaluate the estimated earnings. Assuming the $600,000 annual earnings would continue indefinitely, and using the procedure for capitalizing an infinite-lived stream of earnings (Equation 13.26), a value was found for the Weak Company as a going concern—$6,000,000 [$600,000 · (1 ÷ .10)]. Since the firm's value as a going concern is estimated to be greater than its liquidation value ($6,000,000 vs. $5,000,000), the firm is confident in recommending a rehabilitation by commercial arrangement to its creditors.

Recapitalization   The next step is to determine what is the appropriate capital structure for the rehabilitated firm. Since most firms' financial difficulties result from high fixed charges, the capital structure is generally altered to reduce the fixed charges so that there will be an adequate coverage margin of fixed charges. Generally, debts are exchanged for equity or the maturities of debts are extended. Sometimes income bonds are exchanged for debentures and mortgage bonds.* In recapitalizing the firm, a great deal of emphasis is generally placed on obtaining a mix of debt and equity that allows the firm to service its debts and provide a reasonable level of earnings for its owners. It is important to recognize that the valuation of owners' returns after the recapitalization is one of the bases for the rehabilitation decision. An example will clarify the recapitalization process.

EXAMPLE   The Weak Company's current (i.e., before recapitalization) capital structure, according to its books, is as follows:

Debentures	$2,000,000
Mortgage bonds	4,000,000
Preferred shares	1,000,000
Common shares	3,000,000
Total capital	$10,000,000

The high leverage of this plan is obvious from the debt-equity ratio of 1.50 ($6,000,000 ÷ $4,000,000). Since the firm as a going concern was found to be worth only $6,000,000, a less highly levered capital structure with total capital of $6,000,000 was proposed.

Debentures	$1,000,000
Mortgage bonds	1,000,000
Income bonds	2,000,000
Preferred shares	500,000
Common shares	1,500,000
Total capital	$6,000,000

Since interest on an income bond does not have to be paid unless earnings are available to pay it, it can be treated like equity in evaluating the firm's leverage. The new debt-equity ratio is 0.50 ($2,000,000 ÷ $4,000,000), which indicates a considerably safer capital structure for the recapitalized Weak Company.

The Exchange of Obligations   Once an appropriate capital structure has been established in accordance with the firm's value as a going concern, the last step is to determine a plan for exchanging outstanding obligations for new securities. The guiding principle is the *absolute priority rule;* that is, all senior claims on assets must be satisfied in full prior to settling any junior claim(s). In order to comply with this principle, senior suppliers of capital must receive a claim on new capital equal to their previous claims. The common shareholders are the last to receive any new securities. It is not unusual for them to receive nothing. Security holders do not

---

*Although income bonds are generally considered not very desirable investments because of the high degree of uncertainty associated with the interest payment, they are very commonly used in corporate rehabilitations. Since income bonds are a form of debt, their holders have preference over equity holders with respect to the receipt of interest and the recovery of principal in liquidation.

necessarily have to receive the same type of security they held before. Quite often they receive a combination of securities. An example will clarify this process.

EXAMPLE   The exchange of securities involved in the recapitalization of the Weak Company were as follows:

1   The $2,000,000 in debentures were exchanged for $1,000,000 in new debentures and $1,000,000 in mortgage bonds.
2   The $4,000,000 in mortgage bonds were exchanged for $2,000,000 in income bonds, $500,000 of preferred shares, and $1,500,000 of common shares.
3   The preferred shareholders received nothing.
4   The common shareholders received nothing.

Since the valuation of the firm allowed a total capitalization of only $6,000,000, only the claims of the original debenture and mortgage bondholders were satisfied through the exchange process. The original preferred and common shareholders were virtually eliminated, and the original mortgage bondholders became the firm's new owners.

The Weak Company example should make clear the priorities in a rehabilitation by commercial arrangement and the close relationship between the value of the firm as a going concern, the recapitalization process, and the ultimate exchange process. In many cases, the original common shareholders will retain some ownership in the firm, although there is no guarantee of this.

As noted earlier, a firm can be rehabilitated by a commercial arrangement that uses a composition-type of settlement with creditors. Such a proposal may be an offer to make a cash payment of so many cents on the dollar in full satisfaction of unsecured claims, to make such a cash payment in installments over time, or to make such a payment in shares or bonds. In all cases, secured claims have to be settled in accordance with the terms of the security (or whatever accommodation can be negotiated); and preferred claims have to be paid in full before any payments can be made to unsecured creditors. Such an arrangement is best illustrated by the following example.

EXAMPLE   In April 1979, Ray Sportswear Inc. of St. Ludger, Quebec, made its first proposal for a commercial arrangement. Ray Sportswear was a manufacturer of blue jeans under the Ray and Danielle Laurent labels. A consolidated statement of the company at that time showed that the firms' liabilities of $2,600,000 exceeded its assets by $509,000. According to the firm's management, the firm's insolvency had been caused by a number of bankruptcies of the firm's customers. The proceedings were prompted by Ray Sportswear's largest secured creditor, the National Bank of Canada, which had become concerned about its outstanding loan balance of $692,155. Ray Sportswear had a total of 181 unsecured creditors with proven claims of $486,108. On May 29, 1980, 10 of the company's unsecured creditors voted 90 percent in favour of accepting $0.50 on the dollar. The proposal also provided for the full repayment of the seven secured creditors who had proven claims of $1,300,000. The trustee from Thorne Riddell & Co. noted that he would be asking the Quebec Superior Court to ratify the proposal within two weeks of the creditor meeting.

Liquidation by Bankruptcy[1]

When a firm has failed, it may not be willing or able to obtain a voluntary "out-of-court" settlement with its creditors. It may also not be able to successfully negotiate a commercial arrangement. In such a situation, the failed firm has only one remaining course of action. That course of action is to be declared legally bankrupt and to be liquidated according to the applicable bankruptcy and insolvency laws. A number of important aspects of such liquidations are discussed in this section.

BANKRUPTCY LEGISLATION

Since bankruptcy and insolvency are exclusively under federal jurisdiction in Canada, an insolvent company can generally only be liquidated under the federal Bankruptcy Act.* The present act was enacted in 1949 and was amended in 1966. The act applies to all insolvent debtors (firms and individuals), with the exception of building societies having share capital, incorporated banks, savings banks, insurance companies, trust companies, loan companies, and railways. The act has three objectives. The first is to protect the property-right claims of creditors against fraud by the debtor during liquidation. The second is to enable the assets of the bankrupt to be distributed fairly among the creditors, according to the priority of their property rights, and with a minimum of expense. The third is to relieve or discharge the bankrupt from the obligations it had incurred by being engaged in business, so that the bankrupt can make a fresh start in commercial life.

INITIATOR OF BANKRUPTCY PROCEEDINGS

Any debtor-firm that is not specifically precluded from filing under the Bankruptcy Act can *voluntarily* file for bankruptcy on its own behalf. Creditors can initiate an *involuntary* bankruptcy. More specifically, whenever the debtor-firm has committed an act of bankruptcy (discussed below) within the preceding six months, one or more creditors having provable aggregate claims of at least $1,000 can petition the court for a receiving order against the debtor-firm.

ACTS OF BANKRUPTCY†

Each of the 10 acts of bankruptcy is formulated on the premise that the debtor is either unable or unwilling to pay its debts. The 10 acts can be summarized as follows.

1 *Fraudulent conveyance.* Permitting any part of the debtor-firm's property to be transferred to a third party without adequate consideration to hinder, delay, or defraud creditors.

*The Winding-Up Act applies almost exclusively to the liquidation of solvent federally incorporated companies. However, it could be used in the winding-up of any federally or provincially incorporated insolvent corporation. Similarly, the provincial corporations acts are important in the liquidation of solvent provincially incorporated companies.
†These apply to both individuals and corporations.

2 *Concealment or removal.* Permitting any part of the debtor-firm's property to be concealed or removed to hinder, delay, or defraud creditors.

3 *Preference (or preferential transfer).* Transferring a portion of the insolvent firm's property to one or more creditors to favour those creditors over other creditors.

4 *General assignment.* Assigning assets for the benefit of specific creditors.

5 *Sudden departure.* Being unavailable to defeat or delay creditors.

6 *Outstanding execution order.* Failure by the debtor, within the time limits specified in the act, to redeem property that was seized under an execution or other process issued against the debtor.

7 *Default on a proposal.* Default by the debtor on a proposal for a commercial arrangement under the act.

8 *Notice to creditors.* Notice by the debtor to creditors that the debtor has suspended or will suspend payment(s) on its debts.

9 *Admission at a creditor's meeting.* The debtor presents a written admission of insolvency at a meeting of creditors, or the debtor presents a financial statement that shows insolvency.

10 *Technical insolvency.* The debtor is unable or fails to meet liabilities as they come due.

MECHANICS OF LIQUIDATION BY BANKRUPTCY

The stages in a liquidation by bankruptcy are discussed next.

Up to the Appointment of the Trustee The mechanics of an involuntary and voluntary bankruptcy differ up to the appointment of the bankruptcy trustee. In an involuntary bankruptcy, creditors petition the court for a receiving order against the debtor-firm. When the petition is filed in court, or at any point in time prior to the issuance of a receiving order, the petitioning creditor(s) can ask the court to appoint a licensed trustee as an interim receiver (called a *sequestrator* in Quebec).

Appointment of an Interim Receiver Before the court will appoint an interim receiver, the petitioning creditor(s) must convince the court that the debtor-firm's assets are in jeopardy. Upon appointment, the interim receiver takes possession of all the debtor-firm's property, and takes control of all the debtor-firm's receipts and disbursements. The interim receiver does not, however, interfere in the conduct of the debtor-firm's affairs. The total cost of the interim receivership is generally a first charge on the assets of the bankrupt's estate.

Issuance of a Receiving Order The bankruptcy petition is heard by the court having jurisdiction in bankruptcy. If the court is satisfied that the debtor-firm is bankrupt, the court declares the debtor-firm bankrupt by issuing a *receiving order* against the debtor-firm. The court also appoints a licensed trustee to the bankrupt's estate. The bankruptcy trustee is generally the trustee who acted as the interim receiver. Once the receiving order is issued, it halts all legal actions to enforce claims against the bankrupt.

On the other hand, in a voluntary bankruptcy, the debtor-firm files with the official receiver. There is generally no petition or receiving order. The official receiver appoints a trustee to take possession and ownership of the bankrupt's estate.* From this point on, the mechanics for an involuntary and a voluntary bankruptcy are identical.

The Trustee   The trustee is licensed by the Superintendent of Bankruptcy and is an officer of the court. Upon appointment to a bankrupt's estate, the trustee takes immediate possession of all the property, books, and records of the bankrupt, makes an inventory of the bankrupt's assets and liabilities, and informs himself or herself of the identity of all the bankrupt's creditors. The trustee has wide powers. With the permission of the inspectors of the estate, the trustee can sell any of the bankrupt's property, can continue the bankrupt's business, can make compromises, can initiate or defend legal actions, or can approve or disapprove any creditor's claim in whole or in part.† The creditors, by a special resolution at a creditors' meeting, can replace the trustee.

The First Meeting of Creditors   Within 5 days of his or her appointment, the trustee must notify all the creditors of the calling of the first meeting of the creditors.‡ The meeting must be held not later than 15 days from the date of the mailing of the notice to creditors. The purpose of the first meeting, which is usually held at the office of the official receiver, is to discuss the affairs of the bankrupt; to confirm the appointment of the trustee (or by special resolution to elect a replacement); to direct the trustee in the administration and distribution of the bankrupt's estate; and to appoint one to five inspectors to represent the creditors in the bankruptcy proceedings.§ At this meeting and any subsequent meeting, a simple majority in number and three-fourths in value of the creditors voting is sufficient to approve a special resolution; and a simple majority in both number and value of creditors voting is sufficient to approve any other resolution.‖

Up to the Distribution of the Estate   After the first meeting of the creditors, the trustee, with the guidance and approval of the inspectors, liquidates the estate of the bankrupt (except for the verified claims of secured creditors). The trustee also completes all the returns required by law, and determines the validity and value of all the claims filed by creditors against the bankrupt. In due course, the trustee prepares a report on the bankrupt, a statement of receipts and disbursements, and a (liquidating) *dividend list* (i.e., the list used in distributing the estate to creditors).

---

*Since the bankrupt's estate is considered to be a new legal entity (i.e., distinct from the bankrupt itself), interest on debt ceases to accrue and rental leases can be terminated.

†The trustee can disallow certain transactions (such as gifts, settlements, and fraudulent preferences) that occurred within certain time periods before the bankruptcy.

‡Proof of claim and proxy forms, which must be completed and filed by the creditors, are sent along with this notice. It is important that creditors return the completed proof of claim form to legally establish their claims and to be able to vote at the meeting of creditors.

§Like the directors of a corporation, the inspectors are supposed to maintain policy control over the administrative decisions of the trustee.

‖Because creditors have little interest in estates with few assets, they often do not attend the first meeting. Thus, obtaining the required quorum (i.e., three creditors in person or by proxy) is often difficult.

The statement of receipts and disbursements and the dividend list also require the approval of the Superintendent of Bankruptcy and of the court.

Distribution of the Estate   The trustee distributes the assets of a bankrupt's estate (except for the verified claims of secured creditors) on an absolute priority basis. Thus, until all the assets have been distributed, the trustee settles verified claims in the following order: each of the classes of creditors, then preferred shareholders, and then common shareholders. Under the present Bankruptcy Act, creditors are divided into four general classes—secured, preferred, ordinary unsecured and restricted (or deferred) creditors. Each of these classes is now discussed.[2]

Secured Creditors   Secured creditors are creditors holding bonds, chattel mortgages, and assignments of book debts. Although a secured creditor is considered to be outside of the statutory distribution scheme, a secured creditor has several options. The secured creditor can take possession of his or her security and make no further claim against the estate (i.e., remain outside of the statutory distribution scheme); the secured creditor can realize his or her security by selling it and filing an unsecured claim against the bankrupt's estate for any deficiency or reimbursing the bankrupt's estate for any surplus; or the secured creditor can surrender the security to the bankrupt's estate and file an ordinary unsecured claim against the bankrupt's estate for the total debt. On the other hand, the trustee can redeem the security by fully settling the secured portion of the secured creditor's claim. This is necessary because the secured creditor has an absolute priority to the extent of his or her security interest. A secured creditor's security interest can be a specific charge on identifiable assets, or it can be a floating charge on present and future-acquired revolving assets, such as inventories and accounts receivable (as was discussed in Chapter 12). Since the floating charge becomes a fixed charge at the moment of bankruptcy or upon the appointment of a receiver, few, if any, assets may be left to be liquidated by a bankruptcy trustee.

Preferred Creditors   Preferred creditors are creditors who have legally been given special priority to ensure that the estate is administered or to ensure a greater equity among a bankrupt's claimants. Preferred creditor categories, ranked in descending order of their legal priority in the distribution of the bankrupt's estate, are funeral expenses (for individual bankrupts); expenses and fees of the trustee; legal costs of administering the estate; the levy payable to the Superintendent of Bankruptcy; arrears of wages, salaries, and commissions (e.g., the wages for the three months prior to bankruptcy to the extent of $500 in each case); arrears of municipal taxes (for the two years prior to bankruptcy); three month rent arrears; cost of making first seizure; U.I.C. and workman's compensation withholdings; claims for injuries to employees not covered by workman's compensation; and arrears of federal and provincial debts. If sufficient proceeds are not available to pay any specific category in full, then the available proceeds are distributed rateably to the verified claimants of that specific category. *Note that the order of priority is strict; that is, no payment is made to a lower priority category of creditors until full payment has been made to all higher priority categories of creditors.*

Ordinary Unsecured Creditors   After the preferred claims are paid in full, the ordinary unsecured creditors are paid in full, or rateably if there are insufficient funds for a full payment. Ordinary unsecured creditors include trade creditors, debenture holders, and unsatisfied secured creditors. While subordinated debt holders are in this creditor class, they must relinquish their share of the distribution to senior debt holders, until the claims of the senior debt holders have been fully satisfied.

Restricted (or Deferred Creditors)   If funds remain to be distributed after the unsecured creditors have been paid in full, then they are paid rateably to restricted creditors. Restricted creditors either have no claim against the estate until all the other creditors have been paid in full, or are deprived of their preferential claim because of their relationship with the bankrupt. For example, the claim for unpaid wages of an officer of the bankrupt would fall into this creditor class. In practice, the class of restricted creditors generally does not receive any payment during the distribution of the estate.

An Illustration   The application of the above priorities by a bankruptcy trustee in the distribution of a bankrupt's estate can be illustrated by a simple example.

EXAMPLE   The Failed Company Ltd. has the balance sheet presented in Table 26.2. The trustee, as was her obligation, has liquidated the firm's total unencumbered assets, obtaining the highest amounts she could get. She managed to obtain $2,300,000 for the firm's current assets. She also determined that the fair value of the firm's fixed assets was $2,000,000. It should therefore be clear that the firm is legally bankrupt, since the firm's $5,600,000 of liabilities exceeds the $4,300,000 (i.e., $2,300,000 + $2,000,000) fair value of its total assets.

Table 26.2   The Balance Sheet of the Failed Company Ltd.

Assets		Liabilities and shareholders' equity	
Cash	$ 10,000	Accounts payable	$ 200,000
Accounts receivable	1,090,000	Notes payable—finance co.	1,000,000
Marketable securities	5,000	Accrued wages[a]	400,000
Inventory	3,100,000	Accrued rent[b]	100,000
Prepaid expense	5,000	Taxes payable	300,000
Total current assets	$4,210,000	Total current liabilites	$2,000,000
Land	$2,000,000	First mortgage[c]	$1,800,000
Net plant	1,810,000	Second mortgage[c]	1,000,000
Net equipment	80,000	Subordinated debentures[d]	800,000
Total fixed assets	$3,890,000	Total long-term debt	$3,600,000
		Preferred shares (5,000 sh.)	$ 400,000
		Common shares (10,000 sh.)	2,000,000
		Retained earnings	100,000
		Shareholders' equity	$2,500,000
Total	$8,100,000	Total	$8,100,000

[a]Represents wages of $400 per employee earned within three months of filing bankruptcy for 1,000 of the firm's employees.
[b]Rent owed for the use of machinery received within three months preceding the filing of bankruptcy.
[c]Mortgages on the firm's total fixed assets.
[d]Subordinated to the notes payable to the bank.

The holders of the first and second mortgages, as secured creditors, realized on their security (i.e., the fixed assets) by selling it for its fair market value of $2,000,000. As a result, the first mortgage holders were fully paid; the second mortgage holders were partially paid from the remaining $200,000 (i.e., $2,000,000 − $1,800,000) of the proceeds from the liquidation of the fixed assets. The second mortgage holders also filed an ordinary unsecured claim against the estate of the Failed Company for the $800,000 deficiency of their claim (i.e., $1,000,000 claim less $200,000 partial realization).

Table 26.3   The Distribution of the Estate of the Failed Company Ltd.

Proceeds from liquidation	$2,300,000
− Expense of administering bankruptcy	$ 800,000
− Wages owed workers	400,000
− Taxes owed governments	300,000
− Rent owed lessor	100,000
Funds remaining for ordinary unsecured creditors	$ 700,000

The next step in the liquidation process for the trustee is to distribute the proceeds to the various creditors. The only liability not shown on the balance sheet is an $800,000 expense for administering the bankrupt estate. The distribution of the $2,300,000 among the firm's creditors is shown in Table 26.3. It can be seen from the table that once all prior claims on the proceeds from liquidation have been satisfied, the ordinary unsecured creditors get to divide the remaining funds on a pro rata basis. The distribution of the $700,000 between the ordinary unsecured creditors is given in Table 26.4. Since the claims of the ordinary unsecured creditors have not been fully satisfied, the preferred and common shareholders receive nothing.

Table 26.4   The Distribution of Funds Among the Ordinary Unsecured Creditors of the Failed Company Ltd.

Ordinary unsecured creditors' claims	Amount	Settlement @ 25 percent[a]	After subordination adjustment[b]
Unpaid balance of second mortgage	$ 800,000[c]	$200,000	$200,000
Accounts payable	200,000	50,000	50,000
Notes payable—finance co.	1,000,000	250,000	450,000
Subordinated debentures	800,000	200,000	0
Total	$2,800,000	$700,000	$700,000

[a]The 25-percent rate is calculated by dividing the $700,000 available for this creditor class by the $2,800,000 owed all the ordinary unsecured creditors. Each creditor of the class is entitled to a pro rata share.
[b]The subordination adjustment concerns the notes payable to which certain debentures are subordinated. The debenture holders must pay what they can from their proceeds *up to* an amount sufficient to satisfy fully the claims of the holder of the notes payable (the finance company).
[c]This figure represents the difference between the $1-million second mortgage and the $200,000 payment on the second mortgage from the proceeds from the sale of the collateral remaining after satisfying the first mortgage.

It is interesting to note that of the ordinary unsecured creditors the finance company holding the notes payable fares the best, thanks to the debentures that are subordinated to these notes.* As a result of the subordination, the finance company receives 45 percent of its claims ($450,000 ÷ $1,000,000), while the other unsecured creditors receive only 25 percent of their claims. Of course, the subordinated debenture holders receive nothing as a result of the subordination of their obligation to the finance company. The consequences in liquidation of subordinated debt for both the subordinated debt holders and the holders of debts to which other debts have been subordinated should be clear from this example. It is understandable that the firm must normally pay a higher interest rate in order to raise funds through sale of subordinated debts. They are simply more risky.

Discharge   A bankrupt corporation can only apply for a discharge from bankruptcy when it has fully paid the claims of all creditors. However, the effect of a bankruptcy proposal, accepted by the required majority of creditors and the court, is similar to a discharge. In such a case, the directors and officers are relieved from their legal responsibilities unless it has been demonstrated that they were legally responsible for the bankruptcy (for example, through fraud).

Proposed New Bankruptcy Act[3]

The purpose of the proposed new Bankruptcy Act is to consolidate four statutes—the Bankruptcy Act, the Winding-Up Act, the Companies' Creditors Arrangement Act, and the Farmers' Creditors Arrangement Act—into one act. In addition, the proposed new act attempts to introduce an administrative structure that will permit a greater administrative efficiency in the arrangement and liquidation procedures.

A primary objective of the proposed new act is to provide a new, integrated, and flexible procedure for facilitating and encouraging arrangements. The proposed new act attempts to eliminate many of the formidable obstacles presently encountered by proponents of arrangement proposals. For example, the proposed new act introduces a notice of intention, which will automatically stop *all* legal proceedings against the debtor by *all* creditors (including secured creditors) for a period of 10 days (or longer if agreed to by the court). Thus, the proposed new act recognizes that a debtor must have sufficient time, free from pressure or harassment, to prepare a carefully considered and workable proposal for an arrangement. Further, the proposed new act would allow outside parties (such as creditors, the bankruptcy trustee, the liquidator, a trustee appointed under a trust deed, or a receiver) to make a proposed arrangement for the debtor.

---

*If the notes payable had been bank financing, it would have been secured. As was discussed in Chapter 12, most of the short-term business loans provided by the Canadian chartered banks involve the pledge of short-term assets (in particular, accounts receivable and inventories). Secured bank financing has been assumed in Problem 26.10.

The proposed new act contains numerous other amendments, such as the following:

1 The proposed new act stipulates an order of priority for estate distribution that reduces considerably the categories of preferred creditors, that clarifies the position of ordinary unsecured creditors, and that makes explicit the rights of deferred creditors. Thus, governmental creditors (at all levels of government) will almost always be treated as ordinary unsecured creditors.

2 The proposed new act increases the priority of the claims of wage earners; wages up to $2,000 per employee (and $500 in benefits) will come behind the costs of administration and before all other preferred claims.

3 The proposed new act introduces several new provisions concerning the status and personal liability of directors and officers of corporations. For example, the act makes the directors and former directors of the bankrupt company jointly and severally liable for unpaid employee wages of up to $2,500 per employee. It also makes a director or officer of the bankrupt firm personally liable for specific unsettled claims against the bankrupt firm's estate. This liability will have occurred when a director or officer in his or her own interest continued to conduct a business that was not in the interest of the corporation, continued to conduct business by resorting to sales below cost or similar improper means, conducted business with a view of delaying or defrauding creditors, or committed specified bankruptcy offences.

4 To deal with a frequent and particularly intractable problem when a lessee becomes bankrupt, the proposed new act has a number of provisions to specify the respective rights, duties, and powers of a lessor, lessee, and the trustee.

Summary

This chapter has been devoted to the important but unpleasant topic of business failure. The financial manager should be aware of the causes and possible remedies for failure. This information is important not only in preventing or dealing with the firm's own failure but also applies when the firm is a creditor of a failed business. The firm's owners and management may consider low or negative earnings a form of business failure, but these do not necessarily result in the rearrangement or liquidation of the firm. Technical insolvency or bankruptcy are more commonly considered indicators of business failure. The technically insolvent firm cannot pay its bills; the bankrupt firm's liabilities exceed the fair market value of its assets. Both technical insolvency and bankruptcy are considered legal forms of bankruptcy. The major causes of business failure are a lack of managerial skill, economic activity, and corporate maturity.

The financially failed firm has three basic alternatives. One alternative is to arrange a voluntary settlement with its creditors. Voluntary settlements are initiated by the debtor and can take one of a number of forms. To sustain the firm, an extension, a composition, creditor control of the firm, or a combination of these strategies can be arranged. An extension is an arrangement in which creditors eventually receive full payment. Composition involves paying off debts on a pro rata basis. Creditor control involves the management of the firm by the creditors until their claims have been satisfied. Often a combined strategy using extension, composition, and creditor control is implemented. The creditors must agree to any of these plans. If they do not, they may recommend voluntary liquidation through assignment, which bypasses many of the legal requirements of bankruptcy. If the firm is liquidated through assignment, the firm legally assigns the power to liquidate its asets to an assignee or trustee. There are two types of assignment—an informal or common-law assignment and a statutory assignment.

A failed firm that cannot or does not want to arrange a voluntary "out-of-court" settlement can attempt to obtain a commercial arrangement. Commercial arrangements are used to modify or eliminate the property rights of the various classes of a debtor's creditors and owners. These include extensions, compositions, and restructuring of the debtor-firm's outstanding obligations. Most arrangement proposals of unregulated business corporations are made under Part III of the present Bankruptcy Act. The mechanics of an arrangement are as follows: The debtor-firm prepares a proposal that must include a schedule for the payment of the claims of all the creditors according to the order of priority prescribed in the Bankruptcy Act. The debtor-firm generally lodges the proposal with a trustee of its choice. The trustee investigates and appraises the affairs and property of the debtor-firm. The trustee files the proposal with the official receiver and calls a meeting of the creditors. If approved by the creditors, the trustee must then seek the required court approval of the proposal. If the proposal is deemed fair, equitable, and feasible by the court, it is binding on all the creditors of the firm. If the proposal is rejected by the court, the debtor-firm is deemed to be bankrupt.

An insolvent debtor-firm that is unable or unwilling to obtain a voluntary out-of-court settlement or a commercial arrangement with its creditors is liquidated. An insolvent firm can voluntarily or involuntarily become bankrupt by petitioning for bankruptcy or committing an act of bankruptcy under the federal Bankruptcy Act. There are 10 acts of bankruptcy. The responsibility for liquidation is placed in the hands of a court-appointed trustee, whose responsibilities include the liquidation of assets, the distribution of the proceeds, and an accounting of all his or her actions. The proceeds must be distributed in accordance with the priority of claims established by the Bankruptcy Act. The order of priority is strict. Thus, no payment is made to a lower priority class or class category of creditors until full payment has been made to all higher priority classes or class categories of creditors. A bankrupt corporation can only be discharged from bankruptcy if it has fully paid the claims of all creditors.

Questions

26.1 How can a business firm that meets all its debt obligations technically be considered to have failed? Are firms that just break even each period considered failures? Why or why not?

26.2 What is the difference between *technical insolvency* and *bankruptcy?* How do the courts view these two situations?

26.3 Are poor returns recognized as a form of business failure by the courts? What is the primary purpose of the laws relating to business failure?

26.4   What are the primary causes of business failure? What types of actions commonly cause business failure?

26.5   What is a voluntary settlement? What probable actions will result from a voluntary settlement of the technically insolvent or bankrupt firm? What is the advantage of a voluntary as opposed to a legal settlement?

26.6   Who initiates a voluntary settlement? What are the procedures for the first meeting?

26.7   What is meant by an extension? What type of settlement, if any, do creditors receive under this arrangement? What is normally done when creditors disagree with a proposed extension?

26.8   What is meant by composition? What type of settlement, if any, do creditors receive under this arrangement? What happens if creditors dissent to a proposed composition?

26.9   How may an extension and composition be combined to form a settlement plan that permits the continued existence of the firm?

26.10   What is the objective of a voluntary liquidation? What is the initial step in a voluntary liquidation by assignment? What are the two types of assignments that can be used for a voluntary liquidation?

26.11   What options are available to a firm that has failed but is not willing or able to obtain a voluntary out-of-court settlement with its creditors? How do the federal bankruptcy and insolvency laws differentiate between firms that have failed because of temporary adverse general economic conditions and firms that have failed because they could not meet the rigours of competition?

26.12   What are the purposes of commercial arrangements? What must be included in a commercial arrangement proposal? How do the creditors determine if a commercial arrangement proposal is acceptable?

26.13   What three steps are generally followed in preparing the financial aspects of an arrangement proposal based on a recapitalization of the firm? What role does the *absolute priority rule* have in such an arrangement proposal? What other type of arrangement proposal is used?

26.14   How are *voluntary* and *involuntary* bankruptcy different? What conditions must be satisfied in order to file an involuntary bankruptcy?

26.15   How do the steps involved in a voluntary and an involuntary bankruptcy differ up to the appointment of the bankruptcy trustee?

26.16   What role is played in the liquidation by bankruptcy process by the bankruptcy trustee? by the inspectors?

26.17   In what order would the following claims be settled in bankruptcy proceedings.
   a.   Claims of preferred shareholders.
   b.   Any deficiency of secured creditors remaining after they have realized on their security interest.
   c.   Expenses of administering the bankrupt's estate.
   d.   Claims of common shareholders.
   e.   Claims of ordinary unsecured creditors.
   f.   Municipal taxes legally due.
   g.   Rent incurred within three months of the bankruptcy.
   h.   Wages of $500 per employee incurred within three months of the bankruptcy.

Problems

26.1 Classify each of the following voluntary settlements as an extension, a composition, or a combination of the two.
a. Paying all creditors $0.30 on the dollar in exchange for complete discharge of the debt.
b. Paying all creditors in full in three periodic installments.
c. Paying a group of creditors with claims of $10,000 in full over two years, and immediately paying the remaining creditors $0.75 on the dollar.

26.2 For a firm with outstanding debt of $125,000, classify each of the following voluntary settlements as an extension, a composition, or a combination of the two.
a. Paying a group of creditors in full in four periodic payments, and paying the remaining creditors in full immediately.
b. Paying a group of creditors $0.90 on the dollar immediately, and paying the remaining creditors $0.80 on the dollar in two periodic payments.
c. Paying all creditors $0.15 on the dollar immediately.
d. Paying all creditors in full in six months.

26.3 The Peachtree Business Forms Company Ltd. recently ran into certain financial difficulties that have resulted in the initiation of voluntary settlement procedures. The firm currently has $150,000 in outstanding debts and approximately $75,000 in liquidable short-term assets. Indicate, in each plan below, whether the plan is an extension, a composition, or a combination of the two. Also, indicate the cash payments and timing of those payments required of the firm under each plan.
a. Each creditor will be paid $0.50 on the dollar immediately, and the debts will be considered fully satisfied.
b. Each creditor will be paid $0.80 on the dollar in two quarterly installments of $0.50 and $0.30. The first installment is to be paid in 90 days.
c. Each creditor will be paid the full amount of its claims in three installments of $0.50, $0.25, and $0.25 per dollar. The installments will be made in 60-day intervals beginning in 60 days.
d. A group of creditors having claims of $50,000 will be immediately paid in full; the remainder will be paid $0.85 on the dollar, payable in 90 days.

26.4 The following table summarizes the earnings after taxes, capitalization rate, and liquidation value of the six firms indicated. Earnings are expected to remain constant over an infinite time horizon.

Firm	Earnings after taxes	Capitalization rate	Liquidation value
A	$ 25,000	9%	$ 250,000
B	$140,000	12%	$1,200,000
C	$200,000	12%	$1,500,000
D	$ 40,000	10%	$ 500,000
E	$ 60,000	14%	$ 400,000
F	$150,000	8%	$1,875,000

a. Calculate the value of the firm as a going concern in each case.
b. Should each firm be sustained or liquidated?

26.5   Wrightsman Supply Ltd. is in financial difficulty. The firm has a liquidation value of $1,000,000 and has estimated after-tax earnings of $150,000 per year indefinitely. The firm has a capitalization rate of 12 percent. Wrightsman's management has recommended the following proposed capital structure based on its valuation of the firm's worth.

	Amount	
Type of capital	Current	Proposed
Debentures	$ 500,000	$ 250,000
Mortgage bonds	1,250,000	250,000
Income bonds	0	500,000
Preferred shares	250,000	0
Common shares	500,000	750,000
Total	$2,500,000	$1,750,000

a. Calculate the value of Wrightsman as a going concern. Would you recommend liquidation of the firm or sustaining the firm by restructuring its capital structure? Why?
b. Calculate and discuss the degree of leverage in the current and proposed capital structures. (Consider income bonds as being equity.)
c. Discuss the exchanges that would result from the proposed recapitalization. Indicate what amount, if any, and what type of capital each of the original suppliers of funds would receive under the absolute priority rule.

26.6   The Cannon Paper Company Ltd. has an estimated liquidation value of $1,000,000. The firm's earnings are expected to remain at approximately $125,000 indefinitely, and its cost of capital is estimated to be 8 percent. The firm's current and proposed capital structures are given:

	Amount	
Type of capital	Current	Proposed
Debentures	$ 500,000	$ 100,000
Mortgage bonds	450,000	200,000
Income bonds	0	400,000
Preferred shares	25,000	0
Common shares	925,000	300,000
Total	$1,900,000	$1,000,000

a. Calculate the value of the firm as a going concern. Would you recommend liquidation or rehabilitation by capital restructuring? Why?
b. Calculate and discuss the financial leverage in the current and proposed capital structures.
c. Discuss the exchanges that would result from the proposed recapitalization. Be sure to indicate what amount, if any, and type of capital each of the original fund suppliers would receive.
d. Discuss the requirements of a capital restructuring plan and the role of priorities in the exchange process.

26.7   The current capital structure and five proposed capital structures for the Ralston Company Ltd. are presented.

	Amount		
Type of capital	Current	A	B
Debentures	$2,000,000	$ 500,000	$ 0
Mortgage bonds	3,000,000	2,000,000	0
Income bonds	0	1,000,000	3,000,000
Preferred shares	1,000,000	0	0
Common shares	2,000,000	1,500,000	2,000,000
Total	$8,000,000	$5,000,000	$5,000,000

	Amount		
Type of capital	C	D	E
Debentures	$1,000,000	$1,500,000	$1,000,000
Mortgage bonds	0	0	1,000,000
Income bonds	2,000,000	0	1,000,000
Preferred shares	500,000	0	1,000,000
Common shares	1,500,000	3,500,000	1,000,000
Total	$5,000,000	$5,000,000	$5,000,000

a. Calculate the degree of financial leverage in the current and each of the proposed plans. (Treat income bonds as a form of equity capital.) Compare the plans' financial leverage.

b. Indicate, for each of the proposed plans, the exchanges that would result from the recapitalization. Indicate what amount, if any, and type of capital each of the original fund suppliers would receive.

c. Viewing the proposals from the current owners' viewpoint, indicate which arrangement plan you believe to be the most equitable. Explain your answers.

26.8   The Langston Company Ltd. recently failed and was left with the following balance sheet.

a. The bankruptcy trustee liquidated the firm's unencumbered assets, obtaining net proceeds of $2,200,000. The fair value (realizable value) of the firm's fixed assets was $2,500,000. In the process of liquidating the unencumbered assets, the bankruptcy trustee incurred expenses totaling $400,000.

   (1) Prepare a table indicating the amount, if any, to be distributed to each claimant except the ordinary unsecured creditors. Indicate the amount to be paid, if any, to the group of ordinary unsecured creditors.

   (2) After the secured creditors have realized on their security, how much, if any, is still owed the second mortgage holders?

   (3) Prepare a table showing how the remaining funds, if any, would be distributed to the firm's ordinary unsecured creditors.

   (4) Discuss what effect, if any, the presence of subordinated debentures has on the payment to the holder of the notes payable.

b. Rework a(1) through a(4) assuming that the secured creditors realized $2,000,000 on the fixed assets instead of $2,500,000.

c. Compare, contrast, and discuss your findings in **a** and **b**.

Assets		Liabilities and shareholders' equity	
Cash	$ 80,000	Accounts payable	$ 400,000
Accounts receivable	1,090,000	Notes payable—finance co.	800,000
Marketable securities	10,000	Accrued wages[a]	600,000
Inventory	2,300,000	Accrued rent[b]	50,000
Prepaid expenses	20,000	Taxes payable	250,000
Total current assets	$3,500,000	Total current liabilities	$2,100,000
Land	$1,000,000	First mortgage[c]	$2,000,000
Net plant	2,000,000	Second mortgage[c]	800,000
Net equipment	1,500,000	Subordinated debentures[d]	500,000
Total fixed assets	$4,500,000	Total long-term debt	$3,300,000
		Preferred shares (10,000 sh.)	$ 300,000
		Common shares (5,000 sh.)	1,800,000
		Retained earnings	500,000
		Shareholders' equity	$2,600,000
Total	$8,000,000	Total	$8,000,000

[a]Represents wages of $300 per employee earned within three months of filing bankruptcy for 2,000 of the firm's employees.
[b]Rent owed for the use of machinery received within three months preceding the filing of bankruptcy.
[c]The first and second mortgages are on the firm's total fixed assets.
[d]Subordinated to the notes payable to the finance company.

26.9 A firm has $450,000 in funds to distribute to its ordinary unsecured creditors. Three possible sets of ordinary unsecured creditor claims are presented as follows:

Ordinary unsecured creditors' claims	Case I	Case II	Case III
Unpaid balance of second mortgage	$300,000	$200,000	$ 500,000
Accounts payable	200,000	100,000	300,000
Notes payable	300,000	100,000	500,000
Subordinated debentures[a]	100,000	200,000	500,000
Total	$900,000	$600,000	$1,800,000

[a]Subordinated to notes payable.

a. Calculate the settlement, if any, to be received by each creditor in each case *ignoring* the subordination.
b. Determine the settlement, if any, to be received by each creditor in each case after adjusting for subordination.
c. Discuss the effect of subordination on the settlement to be received by the senior issue, or notes payable, in each case.

26.10 The Mindy Corporation Ltd. recently failed and was liquidated by a court-appointed trustee who charged $300,000 for her services. The pre-liquidation balance sheet is given:

Assets		Liabilities and shareholders' equity	
Cash	$ 40,000	Accounts payable	$ 200,000
Accounts receivable	620,000	Notes payable—bank[a]	300,000
Marketable securities	30,000	Accrued wages[b]	50,000
Inventory	1,200,000	Accrued rent[c]	30,000
Prepaid expenses	10,000	Taxes payable	20,000
Total current assets	$1,900,000	Total current liabilities	$ 600,000
Land	$ 300,000	First mortgage[d]	$ 700,000
Net plant	400,000	Second mortgage[d]	400,000
New equipment	400,000	Subordinated debentures[e]	300,000
Total fixed assets	$1,100,000	Total long-term debt	$1,400,000
		Preferred shares (15,000 sh.)	$ 200,000
		Common shares (10,000 sh.)	700,000
		Retained earnings	100,000
		Shareholders' equity	$1,000,000
Total	$3,000,000	Total	$3,000,000

[a]As is usual for bank financing (see the footnote on page 835), the bank's financing was secured. In this case, Mindy had pledged all its accounts receivable and inventory as security for the bank note.
[b]Represent wages of $500 per employee earned within three months of filing bankruptcy for 100 of the firm's employees.
[c]Rent owed for use of machinery received two months prior to filing bankruptcy.
[d]The first and second mortgages are on the firm's total fixed assets.
[e]These debentures have been subordinated to the other debentures.

a. The bankruptcy trustee liquidated the firm's unencumbered assets (i.e., the current assets other than accounts receivable and inventory) obtaining net proceeds of $70,000. She also liquidated the firm's encumbered current assets (i.e., the accounts receivable and inventory) for the bank obtaining net proceeds of $1,230,000. The trustee for the first and second mortgage bondholders seized and liquidated the firm's fixed assets obtaining net proceeds of $1,200,000.

   (1) Prepare a table indicating the amount to be distributed to each claimant. Indicate if the claimant is an ordinary unsecured creditor.

   (2) How much, if any, is owed to first-mortgage holders and second-mortgage holders as ordinary unsecured creditors?

   (3) Do the firm's owners receive any distribution of funds? If so, in what amounts?

   (4) What effect, if any, does the presence of the subordinated debentures have on the payments to the holders of the debentures?

b. The bankruptcy trustee liquidated the firm's unencumbered assets (i.e., the current assets other than accounts receivable and inventory) obtaining net proceeds of $70,000. She also liquidated the firm's encumbered current assets (i.e., the accounts receivable and inventory) for the bank obtaining net proceeds of $1,130,000. The trustee for the first and second mortgage bondholders seized and liquidated the firm's encumbered fixed assets obtaining net proceeds of $600,000. Given these changes, answer questions a(1) through a(4).

c. Compare, contrast, and discuss your findings in **a** and **b**.

Notes

1. The following has been extremely helpful in the preparation of this section: Consumer and Corporate Affairs, *Background Papers for the Bankruptcy and Insolvency Bill* (Ottawa: Government of Canada, 1979).
2. In general, it has been found that the administrative costs of a bankruptcy are high, that the time needed to complete such an administration is long, and that unsecured creditors receive little or nothing from the distribution of a bankrupt's estate. For example, for a sample of 48 bankrupts situated in Nova Scotia, Dipchand and George found that administrative costs averaged 40.6 percent of liquidation proceeds; that it took on average 21 months to complete the administration of an estate; that unsecured creditors received an average of 36.2 percent of the liquidation proceeds; and that for approximately one-third of the cases, the unsecured creditors received no liquidation proceeds. See Cecil R. Dipchand and Roy E. George, "The Cost of Bankruptcy," *CA Magazine* 110, No. 7 (July 1977), pp. 28–30. These findings are quite similar to the Canadian statistics for 1975. In 1975, $33.7 million was realized on 5,999 closed estates. Administrative fees were 44.1 percent of the realizations. Included in administrative fees are trustee fees, which were 23.4 percent of realizations. See Superintendent of Bankruptcy, *Annual Report* (Ottawa: Consumer and Corporate Affairs, March 31, 1976), p. 17.
3. The following has drawn extensively on Consumer and Corporate Affairs, *Background Papers for the Bankruptcy and Insolvency Bill* (Ottawa: Government of Canada, 1979). Also note that the proposed Bankruptcy Act has taken the form of Bill C-60, Bill S-11, Bill S-14, and Bill C-12.

Suggested Readings

Altman, Edward I., *Corporate Bankruptcy in America* (Lexington, Mass.: Heath, 1971).

———, "Corporate Bankruptcy, Potential Stockholder Returns and Share Valuation," *Journal of Finance* 24 (December 1969), pp. 887–900.

———, "Financial Ratios, Discriminant Analysis and the Prediction of Corporate Bankruptcy," *Journal of Finance* 23 (September 1968), pp. 589–609.

Beaver, William H., "Financial Ratios As Predictors of Failure," *Empirical Research in Accounting: Selected Studies, Journal of Accounting Research* supplement (1966), pp. 71–111.

———, "Market Prices, Financial Ratios, and the Prediction of Failure," *Journal of Accounting Research* 6 (Autumn 1968), pp. 179–192.

Consumer and Corporate Affairs, *Background Papers for the Bankruptcy and Insolvency Bill* (Ottawa: Government of Canada, 1979).

Deakin, E. B., "A Discriminant Analysis of Predictors of Business Failure," *Journal of Accounting Research* 10 (Spring 1972), pp. 167–169.

Dipchand, Cecil R. and Roy E. George, "The Cost of Bankruptcy," *CA Magazine* 110 (July 1977), pp. 28–30.

Donaldson, Gordon, "Strategy for Financial Emergencies," *Harvard Business Review* (November-December 1969), pp. 67–79.

Dun & Bradstreet Canada Limited, *The Canadian Business Failure Record* (Toronto, annual and weekly).

Edmister, Robert O., "An Empirical Test of Financial Ratio Analysis for Small Business Failure Prediction," *Journal of Financial and Quantitative Analysis* 7 (March 1972), pp. 1477–1493.

Eisenbeis, Robert A. "Pitfalls in the Application of Discriminant Analysis in Business, Finance and Economics," *Journal of Finance* 32 (June 1977), pp. 875–900.

Gordon, Myron J., "Towards a Theory of Financial Distress," *Journal of Finance* 26 (May 1971), pp. 347–356.

Higgins, Robert C. and Lawrence D. Schall, "Corporate Bankruptcy and Conglomerate Merger," *Journal of Finance* 30 (March 1975), pp. 93–113.

Johnson, Craig G., "Ratio Analysis and the Prediction of Firm Failure," *Journal of Finance* 25 (December 1970), pp. 1166–1168.

Joy, Maurice O. and John O. Tollefson. "On the Financial Applications of Discriminant Analysis," *Journal of Financial and Quantitative Analysis* 10 (December 1975), pp. 723–739.

Moyer, R. Charles, "Forecasting Financial Failure: A Re-examination," *Financial Management* 6 (Spring 1977), pp. 11–17.

Murray, Roger F., "The Penn Central Debacle: Lessons for Financial Analysis," *Journal of Finance* 26 (May 1971), pp. 327–332.

Scott, James H., Jr., "Bankruptcy, Secured Debt, and Optimal Capital Structure," *Journal of Finance* 32 (March 1977), pp. 1–20.

Stanley, David T. and Marjorie Girth, *Bankruptcy: Problem, Process, Reform* (Washington, D.C.: Brookings Institution, 1971).

Tamari, M. "Financial Ratios As a Means of Forecasting Bankruptcy," *Management International Review* 4 (1966), pp. 15–21.

Walter, James E., "Determination of Technical Insolvency," *Journal of Business* 30 (January 1957), pp. 30–43.

Weston, J. Fred, "The Industrial Economics Background of the Penn Central Bankruptcy," *Journal of Finance* 26 (May 1971), pp. 311–326.

FINANCIAL TABLES

TABLE A–1 Compound-value interest factors for one dollar, CVIF

Year	1%	2%	3%	4%	5%	6%	7%	8%	9%	10%
1	1.010	1.020	1.030	1.040	1.050	1.060	1.070	1.080	1.090	1.100
2	1.020	1.040	1.061	1.082	1.102	1.124	1.145	1.166	1.188	1.210
3	1.030	1.061	1.093	1.125	1.158	1.191	1.225	1.260	1.295	1.331
4	1.041	1.082	1.126	1.170	1.216	1.262	1.311	1.360	1.412	1.464
5	1.051	1.104	1.159	1.217	1.276	1.338	1.403	1.469	1.539	1.611
6	1.062	1.126	1.194	1.265	1.340	1.419	1.501	1.587	1.677	1.772
7	1.072	1.149	1.230	1.316	1.407	1.504	1.606	1.714	1.828	1.949
8	1.083	1.172	1.267	1.369	1.477	1.594	1.718	1.851	1.993	2.144
9	1.094	1.195	1.305	1.423	1.551	1.689	1.838	1.999	2.172	2.358
10	1.105	1.219	1.344	1.480	1.629	1.791	1.967	2.159	2.367	2.594
11	1.116	1.243	1.384	1.539	1.710	1.898	2.105	2.332	2.580	2.853
12	1.127	1.268	1.426	1.601	1.796	2.012	2.252	2.518	2.813	3.138
13	1.138	1.294	1.469	1.665	1.886	2.133	2.410	2.720	3.066	3.452
14	1.149	1.319	1.513	1.732	1.980	2.261	2.579	2.937	3.342	3.797
15	1.161	1.346	1.558	1.801	2.079	2.397	2.759	3.172	3.642	4.177
16	1.173	1.373	1.605	1.873	2.183	2.540	2.952	3.426	3.970	4.595
17	1.184	1.400	1.653	1.948	2.292	2.693	3.159	3.700	4.328	5.054
18	1.196	1.428	1.702	2.026	2.407	2.854	3.380	3.996	4.717	5.560
19	1.208	1.457	1.753	2.107	2.527	3.026	3.616	4.316	5.142	6.116
20	1.220	1.486	1.806	2.191	2.653	3.207	3.870	4.661	5.604	6.727
21	1.232	1.516	1.860	2.279	2.786	3.399	4.140	5.034	6.109	7.400
22	1.245	1.546	1.916	2.370	2.925	3.603	4.430	5.436	6.658	8.140
23	1.257	1.577	1.974	2.465	3.071	3.820	4.740	5.871	7.258	8.954
24	1.270	1.608	2.033	2.563	3.225	4.049	5.072	6.341	7.911	9.850
25	1.282	1.641	2.094	2.666	3.386	4.292	5.427	6.848	8.623	10.834
30	1.348	1.811	2.427	3.243	4.322	5.743	7.612	10.062	13.267	17.449
35	1.417	2.000	2.814	3.946	5.516	7.686	10.676	14.785	20.413	28.102
40	1.489	2.208	3.262	4.801	7.040	10.285	14.974	21.724	31.408	45.258
45	1.565	2.438	3.781	5.841	8.985	13.764	21.002	31.920	48.325	72.888
50	1.645	2.691	4.384	7.106	11.467	18.419	29.456	46.900	74.354	117.386

TABLE A–1 Compound-value interest factors for one dollar, CVIF (continued)

Year	11%	12%	13%	14%	15%	16%	17%	18%	19%	20%
1	1.110	1.120	1.130	1.140	1.150	1.160	1.170	1.180	1.190	1.200
2	1.232	1.254	1.277	1.300	1.322	1.346	1.369	1.392	1.416	1.440
3	1.368	1.405	1.443	1.482	1.521	1.561	1.602	1.643	1.685	1.728
4	1.518	1.574	1.630	1.689	1.749	1.811	1.874	1.939	2.005	2.074
5	1.685	1.762	1.842	1.925	2.011	2.100	2.192	2.288	2.386	2.488
6	1.870	1.974	2.082	2.195	2.313	2.436	2.565	2.700	2.840	2.986
7	2.076	2.211	2.353	2.502	2.660	2.826	3.001	3.185	3.379	3.583
8	2.305	2.476	2.658	2.853	3.059	3.278	3.511	3.759	4.021	4.300
9	2.558	2.773	3.004	3.252	3.518	3.803	4.108	4.435	4.785	5.160
10	2.839	3.106	3.395	3.707	4.046	4.411	4.807	5.234	5.695	6.192
11	3.152	3.479	3.836	4.226	4.652	5.117	5.624	6.176	6.777	7.430
12	3.498	3.896	4.334	4.818	5.350	5.936	6.580	7.288	8.064	8.916
13	3.883	4.363	4.898	5.492	6.153	6.886	7.699	8.599	9.596	10.699
14	4.310	4.887	5.535	6.261	7.076	7.987	9.007	10.147	11.420	12.839
15	4.785	5.474	6.254	7.138	8.137	9.265	10.539	11.974	13.589	15.407
16	5.311	6.130	7.067	8.137	9.358	10.748	12.330	14.129	16.171	18.488
17	5.895	6.866	7.986	9.276	10.761	12.468	14.426	16.672	19.244	22.186
18	6.543	7.690	9.024	10.575	12.375	14.462	16.879	19.673	22.900	26.623
19	7.263	8.613	10.197	12.055	14.232	16.776	19.748	23.214	27.251	31.948
20	8.062	9.646	11.523	13.743	16.366	19.461	23.105	27.393	32.429	38.337
21	8.949	10.804	13.021	15.667	18.821	22.574	27.033	32.323	38.591	46.005
22	9.933	12.100	14.713	17.861	21.644	26.186	31.629	38.141	45.923	55.205
23	11.026	13.552	16.626	20.361	24.891	30.376	37.005	45.007	54.648	66.247
24	12.239	15.178	18.788	23.212	28.625	35.236	43.296	53.108	65.031	79.496
25	13.585	17.000	21.230	26.461	32.918	40.874	50.656	62.667	77.387	95.395
30	22.892	29.960	39.115	50.949	66.210	85.849	111.061	143.367	184.672	237.373
35	38.574	52.799	72.066	98.097	133.172	180.311	243.495	327.988	440.691	590.657
40	64.999	93.049	132.776	188.876	267.856	378.715	533.846	750.353	1051.642	1469.740
45	109.527	163.985	244.629	363.662	538.752	795.429	1170.425	1716.619	2509.583	3657.176
50	184.559	288.996	450.711	700.197	1083.619	1670.669	2566.080	3927.189	5988.730	9100.191

TABLE A–1 Compound-value interest factors for one dollar, CVIF (continued)

Year	21%	22%	23%	24%	25%	26%	27%	28%	29%	30%
1	1.210	1.220	1.230	1.240	1.250	1.260	1.270	1.280	1.290	1.300
2	1.464	1.488	1.513	1.538	1.562	1.588	1.613	1.638	1.664	1.690
3	1.772	1.816	1.861	1.907	1.953	2.000	2.048	2.097	2.147	2.197
4	2.144	2.215	2.289	2.364	2.441	2.520	2.601	2.684	2.769	2.856
5	2.594	2.703	2.815	2.932	3.052	3.176	3.304	3.436	3.572	3.713
6	3.138	3.297	3.463	3.635	3.815	4.001	4.196	4.398	4.608	4.827
7	3.797	4.023	4.259	4.508	4.768	5.042	5.329	5.629	5.945	6.275
8	4.595	4.908	5.239	5.589	5.960	6.353	6.767	7.206	7.669	8.157
9	5.560	5.987	6.444	6.931	7.451	8.004	8.595	9.223	9.893	10.604
10	6.727	7.305	7.926	8.594	9.313	10.086	10.915	11.806	12.761	13.786
11	8.140	8.912	9.749	10.657	11.642	12.708	13.862	15.112	16.462	17.921
12	9.850	10.872	11.991	13.215	14.552	16.012	17.605	19.343	21.236	23.298
13	11.918	13.264	14.749	16.386	18.190	20.175	22.359	24.759	27.395	30.287
14	14.421	16.182	18.141	20.319	22.737	25.420	28.395	31.691	35.339	39.373
15	17.449	19.742	22.314	25.195	28.422	32.030	36.062	40.565	45.587	51.185
16	21.113	24.085	27.446	31.242	35.527	40.357	45.799	51.923	58.808	66.541
17	25.547	29.384	33.758	38.740	44.409	50.850	58.165	66.461	75.862	86.503
18	30.912	35.848	41.523	48.038	55.511	64.071	73.869	85.070	97.862	112.454
19	37.404	43.735	51.073	59.567	69.389	80.730	93.813	108.890	126.242	146.190
20	45.258	53.357	62.820	73.863	86.736	101.720	119.143	139.379	162.852	190.047
21	54.762	65.095	77.268	91.591	108.420	128.167	151.312	178.405	210.079	247.061
22	66.262	79.416	95.040	113.572	135.525	161.490	192.165	228.358	271.002	321.178
23	80.178	96.887	116.899	140.829	169.407	203.477	244.050	292.298	349.592	417.531
24	97.015	118.203	143.786	174.628	211.758	256.381	309.943	374.141	450.974	542.791
25	117.388	144.207	176.857	216.539	264.698	323.040	393.628	478.901	581.756	705.627
30	304.471	389.748	497.904	634.810	807.793	1025.904	1300.477	1645.488	2078.208	2619.936
35	789.716	1053.370	1401.749	1861.020	2465.189	3258.053	4296.547	5653.840	7423.988	9727.598
40	2048.309	2846.941	3946.340	5455.797	7523.156	10346.879	14195.051	19426.418	26520.723	36117.754
45	5312.758	7694.418	11110.121	15994.316	22958.844	32859.457	46897.973	66748.500	94739.937	134102.187
50	13779.844	20795.680	31278.301	46889.207	70064.812	104354.562	154942.687	229345.875	338440.000	497910.125

TABLE A–1 Compound-value interest factors for one dollar, CVIF (continued)

Year	31%	32%	33%	34%	35%	36%	37%	38%	39%	40%
1	1.310	1.320	1.330	1.340	1.350	1.360	1.370	1.380	1.390	1.400
2	1.716	1.742	1.769	1.796	1.822	1.850	1.877	1.904	1.932	1.960
3	2.248	2.300	2.353	2.406	2.460	2.515	2.571	2.628	2.686	2.744
4	2.945	3.036	3.129	3.224	3.321	3.421	3.523	3.627	3.733	3.842
5	3.858	4.007	4.162	4.320	4.484	4.653	4.826	5.005	5.189	5.378
6	5.054	5.290	5.535	5.789	6.053	6.328	6.612	6.907	7.213	7.530
7	6.621	6.983	7.361	7.758	8.172	8.605	9.058	9.531	10.025	10.541
8	8.673	9.217	9.791	10.395	11.032	11.703	12.410	13.153	13.935	14.758
9	11.362	12.166	13.022	13.930	14.894	15.917	17.001	18.151	19.370	20.661
10	14.884	16.060	17.319	18.666	20.106	21.646	23.292	25.049	26.924	28.925
11	19.498	21.199	23.034	25.012	27.144	29.439	31.910	34.567	37.425	40.495
12	25.542	27.982	30.635	33.516	36.644	40.037	43.716	47.703	52.020	56.694
13	33.460	36.937	40.745	44.912	49.469	54.451	59.892	65.830	72.308	79.371
14	43.832	48.756	54.190	60.181	66.784	74.053	82.051	90.845	100.509	111.119
15	57.420	64.358	72.073	80.643	90.158	100.712	112.410	125.366	139.707	155.567
16	75.220	84.953	95.857	108.061	121.713	136.968	154.002	173.005	194.192	217.793
17	98.539	112.138	127.490	144.802	164.312	186.277	210.983	238.747	269.927	304.911
18	129.086	148.022	169.561	194.035	221.822	253.337	289.046	329.471	375.198	426.875
19	169.102	195.389	225.517	260.006	299.459	344.537	395.993	454.669	521.525	597.625
20	221.523	257.913	299.937	348.408	404.270	468.571	542.511	627.443	724.919	836.674
21	290.196	340.446	398.916	466.867	545.764	637.256	743.240	865.871	1007.637	1171.343
22	380.156	449.388	530.558	625.601	736.781	866.668	1018.238	1194.900	1400.615	1639.878
23	498.004	593.192	705.642	838.305	994.653	1178.668	1394.986	1648.961	1946.854	2295.829
24	652.385	783.013	938.504	1123.328	1342.781	1602.988	1911.129	2275.564	2706.125	3214.158
25	854.623	1033.577	1248.210	1505.258	1812.754	2180.063	2618.245	3140.275	3761.511	4499.816
30	3297.081	4142.008	5194.516	6503.285	8128.426	10142.914	12636.086	15716.703	19517.969	24201.043
35	12719.918	16598.906	21617.363	28096.695	36448.051	47190.727	60983.836	78660.188	101276.125	130158.687
40	49072.621	66519.313	89962.188	121388.437	163433.875	219558.625	294317.937	393684.687	525508.312	700022.688

TABLE A-2 Compound-value interest factors for a one-dollar annuity, CVIFA

Year	1%	2%	3%	4%	5%	6%	7%	8%	9%	10%
1	1.000	1.000	1.000	1.000	1.000	1.000	1.000	1.000	1.000	1.000
2	2.010	2.020	2.030	2.040	2.050	2.060	2.070	2.080	2.090	2.100
3	3.030	3.060	3.091	3.122	3.152	3.184	3.215	3.246	3.278	3.310
4	4.060	4.122	4.184	4.246	4.310	4.375	4.440	4.506	4.573	4.641
5	5.101	5.204	5.309	5.416	5.526	5.637	5.751	5.867	5.985	6.105
6	6.152	6.308	6.468	6.633	6.802	6.975	7.153	7.336	7.523	7.716
7	7.214	7.434	7.662	7.898	8.142	8.394	8.654	8.923	9.200	9.487
8	8.286	8.583	8.892	9.214	9.549	9.897	10.260	10.637	11.028	11.436
9	9.368	9.755	10.159	10.583	11.027	11.491	11.978	12.488	13.021	13.579
10	10.462	10.950	11.464	12.006	12.578	13.181	13.816	14.487	15.193	15.937
11	11.567	12.169	12.808	13.486	14.207	14.972	15.784	16.645	17.560	18.531
12	12.682	13.412	14.192	15.026	15.917	16.870	17.888	18.977	20.141	21.384
13	13.809	14.680	15.618	16.627	17.713	18.882	20.141	21.495	22.953	24.523
14	14.947	15.974	17.086	18.292	19.598	21.015	22.550	24.215	26.019	27.975
15	16.097	17.293	18.599	20.023	21.578	23.276	25.129	27.152	29.361	31.772
16	17.258	18.639	20.157	21.824	23.657	25.672	27.888	30.324	33.003	35.949
17	18.430	20.012	21.761	23.697	25.840	28.213	30.840	33.750	36.973	40.544
18	19.614	21.412	23.414	25.645	28.132	30.905	33.999	37.450	41.301	45.599
19	20.811	22.840	25.117	27.671	30.539	33.760	37.379	41.446	46.018	51.158
20	22.019	24.297	26.870	29.778	33.066	36.785	40.995	45.762	51.159	57.274
21	23.239	25.783	28.676	31.969	35.719	39.992	44.865	50.422	56.764	64.002
22	24.471	27.299	30.536	34.248	38.505	43.392	49.005	55.456	62.872	71.402
23	25.716	28.845	32.452	36.618	41.430	46.995	53.435	60.893	69.531	79.542
24	26.973	30.421	34.426	39.082	44.501	50.815	58.176	66.764	76.789	88.496
25	28.243	32.030	36.459	41.645	47.726	54.864	63.248	73.105	84.699	98.346
30	34.784	40.567	47.575	56.084	66.438	79.057	94.459	113.282	136.305	164.491
35	41.659	49.994	60.461	73.651	90.318	111.432	138.234	172.314	215.705	271.018
40	48.885	60.401	75.400	95.024	120.797	154.758	199.630	259.052	337.872	442.580
45	56.479	71.891	92.718	121.027	159.695	212.737	285.741	386.497	525.840	718.881
50	64.461	84.577	112.794	152.664	209.341	290.325	406.516	573.756	815.051	1163.865

TABLE A-2 Compound-value interest factors for a one-dollar annuity, CVIFA (continued)

Year	11%	12%	13%	14%	15%	16%	17%	18%	19%	20%
1	1.000	1.000	1.000	1.000	1.000	1.000	1.000	1.000	1.000	1.000
2	2.110	2.120	2.130	2.140	2.150	2.160	2.170	2.180	2.190	2.200
3	3.342	3.374	3.407	3.440	3.472	3.506	3.539	3.572	3.606	3.640
4	4.710	4.779	4.850	4.921	4.993	5.066	5.141	5.215	5.291	5.368
5	6.228	6.353	6.480	6.610	6.742	6.877	7.014	7.154	7.297	7.442
6	7.913	8.115	8.323	8.535	8.754	8.977	9.207	9.442	9.683	9.930
7	9.783	10.089	10.405	10.730	11.067	11.414	11.772	12.141	12.523	12.916
8	11.859	12.300	12.757	13.233	13.727	14.240	14.773	15.327	15.902	16.499
9	14.164	14.776	15.416	16.085	16.786	17.518	18.285	19.086	19.923	20.799
10	16.722	17.549	18.420	19.337	20.304	21.321	22.393	23.521	24.709	25.959
11	19.561	20.655	21.814	23.044	24.349	25.733	27.200	28.755	30.403	32.150
12	22.713	24.133	25.650	27.271	29.001	30.850	32.824	34.931	37.180	39.580
13	26.211	28.029	29.984	32.088	34.352	36.786	39.404	42.218	45.244	48.496
14	30.095	32.392	34.882	37.581	40.504	43.672	47.102	50.818	54.841	59.196
15	34.405	37.280	40.417	43.842	47.580	51.659	56.109	60.965	66.260	72.035
16	39.190	42.753	46.671	50.980	55.717	60.925	66.648	72.938	79.850	87.442
17	44.500	48.883	53.738	59.117	65.075	71.673	78.978	87.067	96.021	105.930
18	50.396	55.749	61.724	68.393	75.836	84.140	93.404	103.739	115.265	128.116
19	56.939	63.439	70.748	78.968	88.211	98.603	110.283	123.412	138.165	154.739
20	64.202	72.052	80.946	91.024	102.443	115.379	130.031	146.626	165.417	186.687
21	72.264	81.698	92.468	104.767	118.809	134.840	153.136	174.019	197.846	225.024
22	81.213	92.502	105.489	120.434	137.630	157.414	180.169	206.342	236.436	271.028
23	91.147	104.602	120.203	138.295	159.274	183.600	211.798	244.483	282.359	326.234
24	102.173	118.154	136.829	158.656	184.166	213.976	248.803	289.490	337.007	392.480
25	114.412	133.333	155.616	181.867	212.790	249.212	292.099	342.598	402.038	471.976
30	199.018	241.330	293.192	356.778	434.738	530.306	647.423	790.932	966.698	1181.865
35	341.583	431.658	546.663	693.552	881.152	1120.699	1426.448	1816.607	2314.173	2948.294
40	581.812	767.080	1013.667	1341.979	1779.048	2360.724	3134.412	4163.094	5529.711	7343.715
45	986.613	1358.208	1874.086	2590.464	3585.031	4965.191	6879.008	9531.258	13203.105	18280.914
50	1668.723	2399.975	3459.344	4994.301	7217.488	10435.449	15088.805	21812.273	31514.492	45496.094

TABLE A–2 Compound-value interest factors for a one-dollar annuity, CVIFA (continued)

Year	21%	22%	23%	24%	25%	26%	27%	28%	29%	30%
1	1.000	1.000	1.000	1.000	1.000	1.000	1.000	1.000	1.000	1.000
2	2.210	2.220	2.230	2.240	2.250	2.260	2.270	2.280	2.290	2.300
3	3.674	3.708	3.743	3.778	3.813	3.848	3.883	3.918	3.954	3.990
4	5.446	5.524	5.604	5.684	5.766	5.848	5.931	6.016	6.101	6.187
5	7.589	7.740	7.893	8.048	8.207	8.368	8.533	8.700	8.870	9.043
6	10.183	10.442	10.708	10.980	11.259	11.544	11.837	12.136	12.442	12.756
7	13.321	13.740	14.171	14.615	15.073	15.546	16.032	16.534	17.051	17.583
8	17.119	17.762	18.430	19.123	19.842	20.588	21.361	22.163	22.995	23.858
9	21.714	22.670	23.669	24.712	25.802	26.940	28.129	29.369	30.664	32.015
10	27.274	28.657	30.113	31.643	33.253	34.945	36.723	38.592	40.556	42.619
11	34.001	35.962	38.039	40.238	42.566	45.030	47.639	50.398	53.318	56.405
12	42.141	44.873	47.787	50.895	54.208	57.738	61.501	65.510	69.780	74.326
13	51.991	55.745	59.778	64.109	68.760	73.750	79.106	84.853	91.016	97.624
14	63.909	69.009	74.528	80.496	86.949	93.925	101.465	109.611	118.411	127.912
15	78.330	85.191	92.669	100.815	109.687	119.346	129.860	141.302	153.750	167.285
16	95.779	104.933	114.983	126.010	138.109	151.375	165.922	181.867	199.337	218.470
17	116.892	129.019	142.428	157.252	173.636	191.733	211.721	233.790	258.145	285.011
18	142.439	158.403	176.187	195.993	218.045	242.583	269.885	300.250	334.006	371.514
19	173.351	194.251	217.710	244.031	273.556	306.654	343.754	385.321	431.868	483.968
20	210.755	237.986	268.783	303.598	342.945	387.384	437.568	494.210	558.110	630.157
21	256.013	291.343	331.603	377.461	429.681	489.104	556.710	633.589	720.962	820.204
22	310.775	356.438	408.871	469.052	538.101	617.270	708.022	811.993	931.040	1067.265
23	377.038	435.854	503.911	582.624	673.626	778.760	900.187	1040.351	1202.042	1388.443
24	457.215	532.741	620.810	723.453	843.032	982.237	1144.237	1332.649	1551.634	1805.975
25	554.230	650.944	764.596	898.082	1054.791	1238.617	1454.180	1706.790	2002.608	2348.765
30	1445.111	1767.044	2160.459	2640.881	3227.172	3941.953	4812.891	5873.172	7162.785	8729.805
35	3755.814	4783.520	6090.227	7750.094	9856.746	12527.160	15909.480	20188.742	25596.512	32422.090
40	9749.141	12936.141	17153.691	22728.367	30088.621	39791.957	52570.707	69376.562	91447.375	120389.375
45	25294.223	34970.230	48300.660	66638.937	91831.312	126378.937	173692.875	238384.312	326686.375	447005.062

TABLE A–2 Compound-value interest factors for a one-dollar annuity, CVIFA (continued)

Year	31%	32%	33%	34%	35%	36%	37%	38%	39%	40%
1	1.000	1.000	1.000	1.000	1.000	1.000	1.000	1.000	1.000	1.000
2	2.310	2.320	2.330	2.340	2.350	2.360	2.370	2.380	2.390	2.400
3	4.026	4.062	4.099	4.136	4.172	4.210	4.247	4.284	4.322	4.360
4	6.274	6.362	6.452	6.542	6.633	6.725	6.818	6.912	7.008	7.104
5	9.219	9.398	9.581	9.766	9.954	10.146	10.341	10.539	10.741	10.946
6	13.077	13.406	13.742	14.086	14.438	14.799	15.167	15.544	15.930	16.324
7	18.131	18.696	19.277	19.876	20.492	21.126	21.779	22.451	23.142	23.853
8	24.752	25.678	26.638	27.633	28.664	29.732	30.837	31.982	33.167	34.395
9	33.425	34.895	36.429	38.028	39.696	41.435	43.247	45.135	47.103	49.152
10	44.786	47.062	49.451	51.958	54.590	57.351	60.248	63.287	66.473	69.813
11	59.670	63.121	66.769	70.624	74.696	78.998	83.540	88.335	93.397	98.739
12	79.167	84.320	89.803	95.636	101.840	108.437	115.450	122.903	130.822	139.234
13	104.709	112.302	120.438	129.152	138.484	148.474	159.166	170.606	182.842	195.928
14	138.169	149.239	161.183	174.063	187.953	202.925	219.058	236.435	255.151	275.299
15	182.001	197.996	215.373	234.245	254.737	276.978	301.109	327.281	355.659	386.418
16	239.421	262.354	287.446	314.888	344.895	377.690	413.520	452.647	495.366	541.985
17	314.642	347.307	383.303	422.949	466.608	514.658	567.521	625.652	689.558	759.778
18	413.180	459.445	510.792	567.751	630.920	700.935	778.504	864.399	959.485	1064.689
19	542.266	607.467	680.354	761.786	852.741	954.271	1067.551	1193.870	1334.683	1491.563
20	711.368	802.856	905.870	1021.792	1152.200	1298.809	1463.544	1648.539	1856.208	2089.188
21	932.891	1060.769	1205.807	1370.201	1556.470	1767.380	2006.055	2275.982	2581.128	2925.862
22	1223.087	1401.215	1604.724	1837.068	2102.234	2404.636	2749.294	3141.852	3588.765	4097.203
23	1603.243	1850.603	2135.282	2462.669	2839.014	3271.304	3767.532	4336.750	4989.379	5737.078
24	2101.247	2443.795	2840.924	3300.974	3833.667	4449.969	5162.516	5985.711	6936.230	8032.906
25	2753.631	3226.808	3779.428	4424.301	5176.445	6052.957	7073.645	8261.273	9642.352	11247.062
30	10632.543	12940.672	15737.945	19124.434	23221.258	28172.016	34148.906	41357.227	50043.625	60500.207

TABLE A–3 Present-value interest factors for one dollar, PVIF

Year	1%	2%	3%	4%	5%	6%	7%	8%	9%	10%
1	.990	.980	.971	.962	.952	.943	.935	.926	.917	.909
2	.980	.961	.943	.925	.907	.890	.873	.857	.842	.826
3	.971	.942	.915	.889	.864	.840	.816	.794	.772	.751
4	.961	.924	.888	.855	.823	.792	.763	.735	.708	.683
5	.951	.906	.863	.822	.784	.747	.713	.681	.650	.621
6	.942	.888	.837	.790	.746	.705	.666	.630	.596	.564
7	.933	.871	.813	.760	.711	.665	.623	.583	.547	.513
8	.923	.853	.789	.731	.677	.627	.582	.540	.502	.467
9	.914	.837	.766	.703	.645	.592	.544	.500	.460	.424
10	.905	.820	.744	.676	.614	.558	.508	.463	.422	.386
11	.896	.804	.722	.650	.585	.527	.475	.429	.388	.350
12	.887	.789	.701	.625	.557	.497	.444	.397	.356	.319
13	.879	.773	.681	.601	.530	.469	.415	.368	.326	.290
14	.870	.758	.661	.577	.505	.442	.388	.340	.299	.263
15	.861	.743	.642	.555	.481	.417	.362	.315	.275	.239
16	.853	.728	.623	.534	.458	.394	.339	.292	.252	.218
17	.844	.714	.605	.513	.436	.371	.317	.270	.231	.198
18	.836	.700	.587	.494	.416	.350	.296	.250	.212	.180
19	.828	.686	.570	.475	.396	.331	.277	.232	.194	.164
20	.820	.673	.554	.456	.377	.312	.258	.215	.178	.149
21	.811	.660	.538	.439	.359	.294	.242	.199	.164	.135
22	.803	.647	.522	.422	.342	.278	.226	.184	.150	.123
23	.795	.634	.507	.406	.326	.262	.211	.170	.138	.112
24	.788	.622	.492	.390	.310	.247	.197	.158	.126	.102
25	.780	.610	.478	.375	.295	.233	.184	.146	.116	.092
30	.742	.552	.412	.308	.231	.174	.131	.099	.075	.057
35	.706	.500	.355	.253	.181	.130	.094	.068	.049	.036
40	.672	.453	.307	.208	.142	.097	.067	.046	.032	.022
45	.639	.410	.264	.171	.111	.073	.048	.031	.021	.014
50	.608	.372	.228	.141	.087	.054	.034	.021	.013	.009

TABLE A–3 Present-value interest factors for one dollar, PVIF (continued)

Year	11%	12%	13%	14%	15%	16%	17%	18%	19%	20%
1	.901	.893	.885	.877	.870	.862	.855	.847	.840	.833
2	.812	.797	.783	.769	.756	.743	.731	.718	.706	.694
3	.731	.712	.693	.675	.658	.641	.624	.609	.593	.579
4	.659	.636	.613	.592	.572	.552	.534	.516	.499	.482
5	.593	.567	.543	.519	.497	.476	.456	.437	.419	.402
6	.535	.507	.480	.456	.432	.410	.390	.370	.352	.335
7	.482	.452	.425	.400	.376	.354	.333	.314	.296	.279
8	.434	.404	.376	.351	.327	.305	.285	.266	.249	.233
9	.391	.361	.333	.308	.284	.263	.243	.225	.209	.194
10	.352	.322	.295	.270	.247	.227	.208	.191	.176	.162
11	.317	.287	.261	.237	.215	.195	.178	.162	.148	.135
12	.286	.257	.231	.208	.187	.168	.152	.137	.124	.112
13	.258	.229	.204	.182	.163	.145	.130	.116	.104	.093
14	.232	.205	.181	.160	.141	.125	.111	.099	.088	.078
15	.209	.183	.160	.140	.123	.108	.095	.084	.074	.065
16	.188	.163	.141	.123	.107	.093	.081	.071	.062	.054
17	.170	.146	.125	.108	.093	.080	.069	.060	.052	.045
18	.153	.130	.111	.095	.081	.069	.059	.051	.044	.038
19	.138	.116	.098	.083	.070	.060	.051	.043	.037	.031
20	.124	.104	.087	.073	.061	.051	.043	.037	.031	.026
21	.112	.093	.077	.064	.053	.044	.037	.031	.026	.022
22	.101	.083	.068	.056	.046	.038	.032	.026	.022	.018
23	.091	.074	.060	.049	.040	.033	.027	.022	.018	.015
24	.082	.066	.053	.043	.035	.028	.023	.019	.015	.013
25	.074	.059	.047	.038	.030	.024	.020	.016	.013	.010
30	.044	.033	.026	.020	.015	.012	.009	.007	.005	.004
35	.026	.019	.014	.010	.008	.006	.004	.003	.002	.002
40	.015	.011	.008	.005	.004	.003	.002	.001	.001	.001
45	.009	.006	.004	.003	.002	.001	.001	.001	.000	.000
50	.005	.003	.002	.001	.001	.001	.000	.000	.000	.000

TABLE A–3 Present-value interest factors for one dollar, PVIF (continued)

Year	21%	22%	23%	24%	25%	26%	27%	28%	29%	30%
1	.826	.820	.813	.806	.800	.794	.787	.781	.775	.769
2	.683	.672	.661	.650	.640	.630	.620	.610	.601	.592
3	.564	.551	.537	.524	.512	.500	.488	.477	.466	.455
4	.467	.451	.437	.423	.410	.397	.384	.373	.361	.350
5	.386	.370	.355	.341	.328	.315	.303	.291	.280	.269
6	.319	.303	.289	.275	.262	.250	.238	.227	.217	.207
7	.263	.249	.235	.222	.210	.198	.188	.178	.168	.159
8	.218	.204	.191	.179	.168	.157	.148	.139	.130	.123
9	.180	.167	.155	.144	.134	.125	.116	.108	.101	.094
10	.149	.137	.126	.116	.107	.099	.092	.085	.078	.073
11	.123	.112	.103	.094	.086	.079	.072	.066	.061	.056
12	.102	.092	.083	.076	.069	.062	.057	.052	.047	.043
13	.084	.075	.068	.061	.055	.050	.045	.040	.037	.033
14	.069	.062	.055	.049	.044	.039	.035	.032	.028	.025
15	.057	.051	.045	.040	.035	.031	.028	.025	.022	.020
16	.047	.042	.036	.032	.028	.025	.022	.019	.017	.015
17	.039	.034	.030	.026	.023	.020	.017	.015	.013	.012
18	.032	.028	.024	.021	.018	.016	.014	.012	.010	.009
19	.027	.023	.020	.017	.014	.012	.011	.009	.008	.007
20	.022	.019	.016	.014	.012	.010	.008	.007	.006	.005
21	.018	.015	.013	.011	.009	.008	.007	.006	.005	.004
22	.015	.013	.011	.009	.007	.006	.005	.004	.004	.004
23	.012	.010	.009	.007	.006	.005	.004	.003	.003	.003
24	.010	.008	.007	.006	.005	.004	.003	.003	.002	.002
25	.009	.007	.006	.005	.004	.003	.003	.002	.002	.001
30	.003	.003	.002	.002	.001	.001	.001	.001	.000	.000
35	.001	.001	.001	.001	.000	.000	.000	.000	.000	.000
40	.000	.000	.000	.000	.000	.000	.000	.000	.000	.000
45	.000	.000	.000	.000	.000	.000	.000	.000	.000	.000
50	.000	.000	.000	.000	.000	.000	.000	.000	.000	.000

TABLE A–3 Present-value interest factors for one dollar, PVIF (continued)

Year	31%	32%	33%	34%	35%	36%	37%	38%	39%	40%
1	.763	.758	.752	.746	.741	.735	.730	.725	.719	.714
2	.583	.574	.565	.557	.549	.541	.533	.525	.518	.510
3	.445	.435	.425	.416	.406	.398	.389	.381	.372	.364
4	.340	.329	.320	.310	.301	.292	.284	.276	.268	.260
5	.259	.250	.240	.231	.223	.215	.207	.200	.193	.186
6	.198	.189	.181	.173	.165	.158	.151	.145	.139	.133
7	.151	.143	.136	.129	.122	.116	.110	.105	.100	.095
8	.115	.108	.102	.096	.091	.085	.081	.076	.072	.068
9	.088	.082	.077	.072	.067	.063	.059	.055	.052	.048
10	.067	.062	.058	.054	.050	.046	.043	.040	.037	.035
11	.051	.047	.043	.040	.037	.034	.031	.029	.027	.025
12	.039	.036	.033	.030	.027	.025	.023	.021	.019	.018
13	.030	.027	.025	.022	.020	.018	.017	.015	.014	.013
14	.023	.021	.018	.017	.015	.014	.012	.011	.010	.009
15	.017	.016	.014	.012	.011	.010	.009	.008	.007	.006
16	.013	.012	.010	.009	.008	.007	.006	.006	.005	.005
17	.010	.009	.008	.007	.006	.005	.005	.004	.004	.003
18	.008	.007	.006	.005	.005	.004	.003	.003	.003	.002
19	.006	.005	.004	.004	.003	.003	.003	.002	.002	.002
20	.005	.004	.003	.003	.002	.002	.002	.002	.001	.001
21	.003	.003	.003	.002	.002	.002	.001	.001	.001	.001
22	.003	.002	.002	.002	.001	.001	.001	.001	.001	.001
23	.002	.002	.001	.001	.001	.001	.001	.001	.001	.000
24	.002	.001	.001	.001	.001	.001	.001	.000	.000	.000
25	.001	.001	.001	.001	.001	.000	.000	.000	.000	.000
30	.000	.000	.000	.000	.000	.000	.000	.000	.000	.000
35	.000	.000	.000	.000	.000	.000	.000	.000	.000	.000
40	.000	.000	.000	.000	.000	.000	.000	.000	.000	.000
45	.000	.000	.000	.000	.000	.000	.000	.000	.000	.000
50	.000	.000	.000	.000	.000	.000	.000	.000	.000	.000

TABLE A–4 Present-value interest factors for a one-dollar annuity, PVIFA

Year	1%	2%	3%	4%	5%	6%	7%	8%	9%	10%
1	.990	.980	.971	.962	.952	.943	.935	.926	.917	.909
2	1.970	1.942	1.913	1.886	1.859	1.833	1.808	1.783	1.759	1.736
3	2.941	2.884	2.829	2.775	2.723	2.673	2.624	2.577	2.531	2.487
4	3.902	3.808	3.717	3.630	3.546	3.465	3.387	3.312	3.240	3.170
5	4.853	4.713	4.580	4.452	4.329	4.212	4.100	3.993	3.890	3.791
6	5.795	5.601	5.417	5.242	5.076	4.917	4.767	4.623	4.486	4.355
7	6.728	6.472	6.230	6.002	5.786	5.582	5.389	5.206	5.033	4.868
8	7.652	7.326	7.020	6.733	6.463	6.210	5.971	5.747	5.535	5.335
9	8.566	8.162	7.786	7.435	7.108	6.802	6.515	6.247	5.995	5.759
10	9.471	8.983	8.530	8.111	7.722	7.360	7.024	6.710	6.418	6.145
11	10.368	9.787	9.253	8.760	8.306	7.887	7.499	7.139	6.805	6.495
12	11.255	10.575	9.954	9.385	8.863	8.384	7.943	7.536	7.161	6.814
13	12.134	11.348	10.635	9.986	9.394	8.853	8.358	7.904	7.487	7.103
14	13.004	12.106	11.296	10.563	9.899	9.295	8.746	8.244	7.786	7.367
15	13.865	12.849	11.938	11.118	10.380	9.712	9.108	8.560	8.061	7.606
16	14.718	13.578	12.561	11.652	10.838	10.106	9.447	8.851	8.313	7.824
17	15.562	14.292	13.166	12.166	11.274	10.477	9.763	9.122	8.544	8.022
18	16.398	14.992	13.754	12.659	11.690	10.828	10.059	9.372	8.756	8.201
19	17.226	15.679	14.324	13.134	12.085	11.158	10.336	9.604	8.950	8.365
20	18.046	16.352	14.878	13.590	12.462	11.470	10.594	9.818	9.129	8.514
21	18.857	17.011	15.415	14.029	12.821	11.764	10.836	10.017	9.292	8.649
22	19.661	17.658	15.937	14.451	13.163	12.042	11.061	10.201	9.442	8.772
23	20.456	18.292	16.444	14.857	13.489	12.303	11.272	10.371	9.580	8.883
24	21.244	18.914	16.936	15.247	13.799	12.550	11.469	10.529	9.707	8.985
25	22.023	19.524	17.413	15.622	14.094	12.783	11.654	10.675	9.823	9.077
30	25.808	22.397	19.601	17.292	15.373	13.765	12.409	11.258	10.274	9.427
35	29.409	24.999	21.487	18.665	16.374	14.498	12.948	11.655	10.567	9.644
40	32.835	27.356	23.115	19.793	17.159	15.046	13.332	11.925	10.757	9.779
45	36.095	29.490	24.519	20.720	17.774	15.456	13.606	12.108	10.881	9.863
50	39.197	31.424	25.730	21.482	18.256	15.762	13.801	12.234	10.962	9.915

TABLE A-4 Present-value interest factors for a one-dollar annuity, PVIFA (continued)

Year	11%	12%	13%	14%	15%	16%	17%	18%	19%	20%
1	.901	.893	.885	.877	.870	.862	.855	.847	.840	.833
2	1.713	1.690	1.668	1.647	1.626	1.605	1.585	1.566	1.547	1.528
3	2.444	2.402	2.361	2.322	2.283	2.246	2.210	2.174	2.140	2.106
4	3.102	3.037	2.974	2.914	2.855	2.798	2.743	2.690	2.639	2.589
5	3.696	3.605	3.517	3.433	3.352	3.274	3.199	3.127	3.058	2.991
6	4.231	4.111	3.998	3.889	3.784	3.685	3.589	3.498	3.410	3.326
7	4.712	4.564	4.423	4.288	4.160	4.039	3.922	3.812	3.706	3.605
8	5.146	4.968	4.799	4.639	4.487	4.344	4.207	4.078	3.954	3.837
9	5.537	5.328	5.132	4.946	4.772	4.607	4.451	4.303	4.163	4.031
10	5.889	5.650	5.426	5.216	5.019	4.833	4.659	4.494	4.339	4.192
11	6.207	5.938	5.687	5.453	5.234	5.029	4.836	4.656	4.487	4.327
12	6.492	6.194	5.918	5.660	5.421	5.197	4.988	4.793	4.611	4.439
13	6.750	6.424	6.122	5.842	5.583	5.342	5.118	4.910	4.715	4.533
14	6.982	6.628	6.303	6.002	5.724	5.468	5.229	5.008	4.802	4.611
15	7.191	6.811	6.462	6.142	5.847	5.575	5.324	5.092	4.876	4.675
16	7.379	6.974	6.604	6.265	5.954	5.669	5.405	5.162	4.938	4.730
17	7.549	7.120	6.729	6.373	6.047	5.749	5.475	5.222	4.990	4.775
18	7.702	7.250	6.840	6.467	6.128	5.818	5.534	5.273	5.033	4.812
19	7.839	7.366	6.938	6.550	6.198	5.877	5.585	5.316	5.070	4.843
20	7.963	7.469	7.025	6.623	6.259	5.929	5.628	5.353	5.101	4.870
21	8.075	7.562	7.102	6.687	6.312	5.973	5.665	5.384	5.127	4.891
22	8.176	7.645	7.170	6.743	6.359	6.011	5.696	5.410	5.149	4.909
23	8.266	7.718	7.230	6.792	6.399	6.044	5.723	5.432	5.167	4.925
24	8.348	7.784	7.283	6.835	6.434	6.073	5.747	5.451	5.182	4.937
25	8.422	7.843	7.330	6.873	6.464	6.097	5.766	5.467	5.195	4.948
30	8.694	8.055	7.496	7.003	6.566	6.177	5.829	5.517	5.235	4.979
35	8.855	8.176	7.586	7.070	6.617	6.215	5.858	5.539	5.251	4.992
40	8.951	8.244	7.634	7.105	6.642	6.233	5.871	5.548	5.258	4.997
45	9.008	8.283	7.661	7.123	6.654	6.242	5.877	5.552	5.261	4.999
50	9.042	8.305	7.675	7.133	6.661	6.246	5.880	5.554	5.262	4.999

TABLE A–4 Present-value interest factors for a one-dollar annuity, PVIFA (continued)

Year	21%	22%	23%	24%	25%	26%	27%	28%	29%	30%
1	.826	.820	.813	.806	.800	.794	.787	.781	.775	.769
2	1.509	1.492	1.474	1.457	1.440	1.424	1.407	1.392	1.376	1.361
3	2.074	2.042	2.011	1.981	1.952	1.923	1.896	1.868	1.842	1.816
4	2.540	2.494	2.448	2.404	2.362	2.320	2.280	2.241	2.203	2.166
5	2.926	2.864	2.803	2.745	2.689	2.635	2.583	2.532	2.483	2.436
6	3.245	3.167	3.092	3.020	2.951	2.885	2.821	2.759	2.700	2.643
7	3.508	3.416	3.327	3.242	3.161	3.083	3.009	2.937	2.868	2.802
8	3.726	3.619	3.518	3.421	3.329	3.241	3.156	3.076	2.999	2.925
9	3.905	3.786	3.673	3.566	3.463	3.366	3.273	3.184	3.100	3.019
10	4.054	3.923	3.799	3.682	3.570	3.465	3.364	3.269	3.178	3.092
11	4.177	4.035	3.902	3.776	3.656	3.544	3.437	3.335	3.239	3.147
12	4.278	4.127	3.985	3.851	3.725	3.606	3.493	3.387	3.286	3.190
13	4.362	4.203	4.053	3.912	3.780	3.656	3.538	3.427	3.322	3.223
14	4.432	4.265	4.108	3.962	3.824	3.695	3.573	3.459	3.351	3.249
15	4.489	4.315	4.153	4.001	3.859	3.726	3.601	3.483	3.373	3.268
16	4.536	4.357	4.189	4.033	3.887	3.751	3.623	3.503	3.390	3.283
17	4.576	4.391	4.219	4.059	3.910	3.771	3.640	3.518	3.403	3.295
18	4.608	4.419	4.243	4.080	3.928	3.786	3.654	3.529	3.413	3.304
19	4.635	4.442	4.263	4.097	3.942	3.799	3.664	3.539	3.421	3.311
20	4.657	4.460	4.279	4.110	3.954	3.808	3.673	3.546	3.427	3.316
21	4.675	4.476	4.292	4.121	3.963	3.816	3.679	3.551	3.432	3.320
22	4.690	4.488	4.302	4.130	3.970	3.822	3.684	3.556	3.436	3.323
23	4.703	4.499	4.311	4.137	3.976	3.827	3.689	3.559	3.438	3.325
24	4.713	4.507	4.318	4.143	3.981	3.831	3.692	3.562	3.441	3.327
25	4.721	4.514	4.323	4.147	3.985	3.834	3.694	3.564	3.442	3.329
30	4.746	4.534	4.339	4.160	3.995	3.842	3.701	3.569	3.447	3.332
35	4.756	4.541	4.345	4.164	3.998	3.845	3.703	3.571	3.448	3.333
40	4.760	4.544	4.347	4.166	3.999	3.846	3.703	3.571	3.448	3.333
45	4.761	4.545	4.347	4.166	4.000	3.846	3.704	3.571	3.448	3.333
50	4.762	4.545	4.348	4.167	4.000	3.846	3.704	3.571	3.448	3.333

TABLE A-4 Present-value interest factors for a one-dollar annuity, PVIFA (continued)

Year	31%	32%	33%	34%	35%	36%	37%	38%	39%	40%
1	.763	.758	.752	.746	.741	.735	.730	.725	.719	.714
2	1.346	1.331	1.317	1.303	1.289	1.276	1.263	1.250	1.237	1.224
3	1.791	1.766	1.742	1.719	1.696	1.673	1.652	1.630	1.609	1.589
4	2.130	2.096	2.062	2.029	1.997	1.966	1.935	1.906	1.877	1.849
5	2.390	2.345	2.302	2.260	2.220	2.181	2.143	2.106	2.070	2.035
6	2.588	2.534	2.483	2.433	2.385	2.339	2.294	2.251	2.209	2.168
7	2.739	2.677	2.619	2.562	2.508	2.455	2.404	2.355	2.308	2.263
8	2.854	2.786	2.721	2.658	2.598	2.540	2.485	2.432	2.380	2.331
9	2.942	2.868	2.798	2.730	2.665	2.603	2.544	2.487	2.432	2.379
10	3.009	2.930	2.855	2.784	2.715	2.649	2.587	2.527	2.469	2.414
11	3.060	2.978	2.899	2.824	2.752	2.683	2.618	2.555	2.496	2.438
12	3.100	3.013	2.931	2.853	2.779	2.708	2.641	2.576	2.515	2.456
13	3.129	3.040	2.956	2.876	2.799	2.727	2.658	2.592	2.529	2.469
14	3.152	3.061	2.974	2.892	2.814	2.740	2.670	2.603	2.539	2.477
15	3.170	3.076	2.988	2.905	2.825	2.750	2.679	2.611	2.546	2.484
16	3.183	3.088	2.999	2.914	2.834	2.757	2.685	2.616	2.551	2.489
17	3.193	3.097	3.007	2.921	2.840	2.763	2.690	2.621	2.555	2.492
18	3.201	3.104	3.012	2.926	2.844	2.767	2.693	2.624	2.557	2.494
19	3.207	3.109	3.017	2.930	2.848	2.770	2.696	2.626	2.559	2.496
20	3.211	3.113	3.020	2.933	2.850	2.772	2.698	2.627	2.561	2.497
21	3.215	3.116	3.023	2.935	2.852	2.773	2.699	2.629	2.562	2.498
22	3.217	3.118	3.025	2.936	2.853	2.775	2.700	2.629	2.562	2.498
23	3.219	3.120	3.026	2.938	2.854	2.775	2.701	2.630	2.563	2.499
24	3.221	3.121	3.027	2.939	2.855	2.776	2.701	2.630	2.563	2.499
25	3.222	3.122	3.028	2.939	2.856	2.776	2.702	2.631	2.563	2.499
30	3.225	3.124	3.030	2.941	2.857	2.777	2.702	2.631	2.564	2.500
35	3.226	3.125	3.030	2.941	2.857	2.778	2.703	2.632	2.564	2.500
40	3.226	3.125	3.030	2.941	2.857	2.778	2.703	2.632	2.564	2.500
45	3.226	3.125	3.030	2.941	2.857	2.778	2.703	2.632	2.564	2.500
50	3.226	3.125	3.030	2.941	2.857	2.778	2.703	2.632	2.564	2.500

Appendix B

ANSWERS TO SELECTED END-OF-CHAPTER PROBLEMS

The following list of answers to selected problems (and portions of problems) is included to provide "check figures" for use in preparing detailed solutions to end-of-chapter problems requiring calculations. For problems that are relatively straightforward, the key answer is given, while for more complex problems answers to a number of parts of the problem are included. Detailed calculations are not shown—only the final and, in some cases, intermediate answers, which should help to confirm whether or not the correct solution is being developed. For problems containing a variety of cases for which similar calculations are required, the answers for only one or two cases have been included. The only verbal answers included are simple "Yes or No" or "Choice-of-Best Alternative" responses; answers to problems requiring detailed explanations or discussion are not given.

The problems (and parts of problems) for which answers have been included were selected randomly; therefore there is no discernible pattern to the choice of problem answers given. It is important to recognize that the answers given are based on what are believed to be the most obvious and reasonable assumptions related to the given problem; in a number of cases, other reasonable assumptions could result in equally correct answers.

2.1 b. (1) $4,000 terminal loss
(2) $6,000 recaptured depreciation
2.2 b. $75,000 capital gain; will increase 1979 tax liability by $17,250
c. Will increase 1980 tax liability by $2,484
2.4 Maximum tax savings in 1978 = $12,712
2.5 a. $24,930.81
b. $15,600

2.7 $40,500

2.8 Mr. Roberts will get a tax credit of $170, and Mr. Dummer will pay federal tax of $870 on his dividend income.

3.1 a. Current ratio: 19X0 = 1.88; 19X1 = 1.74; 19X2 = 1.79; 19X3 = 1.55

3.2 a. Inventory turnover = 3.69

3.3 a. Average age of accounts receivable = 45 days

3.4 a. Debt to total capital = .60
       Total debt coverage = 1.29

3.5 a. 19X7 = 22.18% Raimer; 16.97% Industry

3.6 Current ratio = 1.67
       Average age of accounts receivable = 29.7 days
       Inventory turnover = 7.89
       Debt-equity ratio = .38
       Total asset turnover = .83
       Net profit margin = 6.6%
       Return on common equity = 8.97%
       Earnings per share = $15.25
       Total debt coverage = 3.54

4.1 a. 20,000 books; **c.** 16,000 books

4.2 a. R = 4,000 units; **b.** S = $56,000; T = $125,000

4.3 a. $20,000

4.4 a. $254,000; **c.** Units 10%; EBIT 50%

4.5 d. 60,000/0

4.6 a. $0.375

4.7 a. $10,000; **c.** $20,000

4.8 a. DFL = 1.5

4.9 a. Common share plan DFL = 1.25

4.10c. 5,000 units

4.11a. Operating = 175,000 units; Total = 233,333 units
    d. DTL = 2.4

4.12a. DTL of A = 2.14
    b. DTL of B = 2.14

5.1 Five are sources. Seven are uses.

5.2 a. $2,000 = use

5.3 a. Total sources = $3,600
    b. Total sources = $3,000

5.4 a. Total sources = $90,800
    b. Total sources = $72,900

5.5 Expected cash receipts for July = $82,500

5.6

	May	June	July
Net cash flow	$3,000	− $21,000	− $13,000
Loans (investments)	X	X	$26,000

5.7 a. Nov. = $33,000; Dec. = $14,000; Jan. = −$7,000; Feb. = $37,000
Mar. = $65,000; Apr. = $154,000
5.8 a. First month = $5,000
   b. First month—pessimistic = −$14,000
First month—optimistic = $24,000

6.1 a. Pro forma income A/T = $67,500
   b. Total assets = $697,500
6.2 a. Total assets = $9,080,000
6.3 a. Labor per unit = P_1, 2 hrs.; P_2, 1.2 hrs.
   b. Overhead allocation for P_1 = $6.12 per unit
   c. Total cost/unit for P_2 = $19.68
6.4 a. Production of product X = 4,600 units
   c. Cost per unit of product X = $22.89
6.5 Pro forma income after taxes = $64,605
6.6 Accounts receivable = $21,375
Inventory = $39,038
Total assets = $285,062

7.1 a. Profits on total assets = $2,700.
Financing costs = $1,920
Net profits = $780
Current ratio = 3.0
ROI = 3.9%
7.2 a. (1) Net profit = $1,950
Current ratio = 2.0
ROI = 1.6%
7.3 Annual loan cost = $640
7.4 a. (1) Aggressive plan financing cost = $440,000
(2) Conservative plan financing cost = $1,120,000
7.5 a. Conservative plan financing cost = $288,000
   b. Aggressive plan financing cost = $54,000
7.7 a. Conservative plan financing cost = $20,000

8.1 a. Cash cycle = 120 days
8.2 c. $97,000
8.3 Current cash cycle = 120 days
   b. Cash cycle = 105 days
8.5 Annual savings = $70,000
8.6 a. $3,000,000
8.7 b. −$6,300
8.8 Yes
8.10 Savings = $4,800
8.11a. No
   c. Yes

8.12a. 5.00%
  b. 7.50%
  d. 4.04%
  e. 6.00%, select *e*

9.1 b. $102,000
  c. $120,000
9.2 a. $125,000
9.3 a. Fixed costs, without = $180,000,000
9.4 a. $5,000
9.5 Yes
9.6 No
9.7 b. $28,000
  c. No
  d. Yes
9.8 a. $11,900
  b. Changes in bad debts = $3,150.00; cost of incremental investment in A/R = $7,283.33
9.9 Don't ease collection

10.1 Approx. four A items
  Approx. five B items
  Approx. seven C items
10.2 b. $33,333
10.3 a. $43,750
10.4 a. $2,857
10.5 Recommend no change.
10.6 Addition to profits = $20,000
10.7 a. For 1,000 units: Annual order cost = $2,000; carrying cost = $125; and total cost = $2,125
  For 5,000 units: Annual order cost = $400; carrying cost = $625; and total cost = $1,025
10.8 a. (1) EOQ = 5,000 units; average level of inventory = 2,500 units; number of orders = 20; total cost of inventory = $1,000
10.9 Level = 150 tons
10.10a. 200 units
  c. 33.33 units
10.11 Consolidate the divisional cash accounts to generate savings of $800.

11.1 a. Dec 25; **c.** Jan 15; **e.** Nov. 25
11.2 b. 18.18%; **d.** 31.81%; **f.** 55.67%
11.4 Annual savings = $18,000
11.6 a. 6%
  b. 10%

12.1 a. 13.75%
   b. 13.75%
   d. The revolving credit account is the best.
12.2   14.29%
12.4 a. A: $20,000, G: $27,000, H: $19,000
   b. $72,000
   c. $54,000
12.6 a. $1,173.30
   b. Funds available $88,000.000
12.7 b. $3,318
12.8 a. Effective interest rate = 12%
12.9 a. Intercity: $625
     Second Canadian: $660.67
     North Mall: $950
   c. Effective interest rate of (1/10 net 40) = 12.12%. Borrowing, even an average amount of $60,000, costs the firm $7,272. This is not superior to borrowing from Intercity Bank.

13.1   A = $530.60; C = $23,670; E = $62,345
13.2 b. $338
13.3 a. Annual = $7,345, 8%
     Semiannual = $7,400, 8.16%
     Quarterly = $7,430, 8.2%
   d. 8.33% for part **a,** 12.8% for part **b,** and 8.33% for part **c**
13.4 a. $12,650
13.6 $17.63
13.7 b. Take $2,000 in three years.
13.8 b. $4,467
13.9 $370
13.11 $442.44
13.12   C = $698.84
13.13   He should take projects A and C.
13.14a. B = 4.75%
   b. C = 2.5%
13.16 $36,730
13.17a. A, present-value interest factor = 12.5
   b. C, present value of perpetuity = $50,000
13.18b. He should take loan B.

14.2 b. The initial cash outlay will be reduced by $4,000.
14.3 a. CCA = $12,000 per year
   c. Annual cash inflow = $17,400
14.4 b. Incremental CCA = $1,000 per year; tax savings = $400 per year
   c. Annual cash inflow $30,400
14.5 b. Incremental CCA = $6,000 for years 19X1 and 19X2
   c. Cash inflows $14,400, $14,400, $12,000, $12,000, and $12,000 for years 19X1 through 19X5

15.1 a. 6 years
15.2 c. The firm will take the first machine.
15.3 a. NPV = $840; accept
    c. NPV = − $805; reject
15.4 a. 9%
    b. NPV = − $320
15.6 c. IRR = 12%
15.7 a. IRR = 10%
    b. 18 years
    c. $12,243.48
15.8 NPV and PI rankings differ; take project X.
15.12a. B is preferred on the basis of NPV; A is preferred on the basis of IRR.
    f. Yes
15.13a. A is preferred on the basis of NPV; IRR = 20% for both A and B. Hence, both are equally desirable on the basis of IRR.
    b. Because such a choice will imply that the firm will obtain an incremental net cash flow of $4,000 in year 2 but will sacrifice an incremental net cash flow of $4,800 in year 3; that is, the firm will lose an opportunity of earning 20% (greater than the cost of capital of 15%) on $4,000.
15.14 Initial investment = $18,400
15.16b. Incremental UCC = $16,000
    e. NPV = $4,376 (approx.)
    f. NPV = − $5,342.60
    g. NPV = − $4,841.60
15.16 NPV = $3,740 > 0; therefore, develop the program.
15.17 Select outlets 4, 5, and 2.
15.18 NPV of $7,405

16.1 a. Project A, range = $1,600
    b. Project B, range of NPV = $1,702.80
    d. Recommend project B.
16.2 b. Camera R, expected cash inflow = $750
16.3 b. Line B, expected cash inflow = $835
16.4 b. Project X, expected NPV = $33,450
16.5 b. Project A, expected cash inflow = $300
    c. Project B, std. dev. of cash inflows = $89.44
16.6 a. Project I, coefficient of variation = 1.5
16.7 a. (3) Project 473, std. dev. = $106.10
    (4) Project 297, coef. of var. = .367
    c. Project 473
16.8 a. A and B, B and D—projects positively correlated
    A and D—projects negatively correlated
    A and D, B and C, C and D—projects not correlated
    b. Project A, std. dev = $1,000
    Project C, std. dev. = $0
    c. Project AB, std. dev. = $1,899.80

16.9 a. Project B, rate of return = 10.25%

Project D, rate of return = 5.0%

16.10b. Recommended game is Signs Away.

16.12b. −$4,681

16.13a. Yes

16.14b. (1) Project A, std. dev. = 2,828; coef. of var. = 1.414

(2) Project A, risk-adjusted discount rate = 13.5%

17.1 a. Bond A, k_b = 8.47%; after-tax cost of debt k_i = 5.09%

17.2 a. k_p = 8.21%

b. k_p = 6.67%

17.4 a. g = 3% (approx.)

c. k_c = 6.85%

d. k_r = 6.48%

17.5 k_e = 15%

17.7 a. k_e = 16.48%

b. k_c = 16.66%

c. Use k_c = 16.66% based on the marginal cost principle

e. Use k_r = 16.48%

17.8 a. g = 10%

b. P_o will decline to $13.43 (approx.).

17.9 a. Both Alpha and Beta corporations will have k_e = 14%.

17.10a. k_e = 22%

b. 12%

c. Accept

d. No

e. k_e = 26%

17.13a. k_i = 6.40%; k_p = 10.1%; k_c = 15.58%; and k_r = 15.40%

b. 11.36%

c. Reject, NPV = −$2,394,366

d. Market value will decline by −$2,394,366.

e. No effect

17.14a. $1 million

b. $600,000

c. 12%

d. 9.6%

e. Mr. Quixote should use a discount rate of 11.2%.

18.1 Plan 1: eps = $2.00; Plan 2: eps = $3.40; Plan 3: eps = $5.27

18.2 a. Plan 1: eps = $1.20; Plan 2: eps = $2.04; Plan 3: eps = 3.16

b. No, the eps ranking is unchanged.

18.4 a. Plan 1: expected eps = $1.20; Var. eps = .22

Plan 2: expected eps = $1.44; Var. eps = .90

c. Adoption of Plan 2 will have an adverse effect.

18.5 a. S = $2,837, 837.80 for C

b. V = $3,484,848 for C

c. B = $647,011 for C

18.6 a. $S = \$708,000; V = \$1,068,000$
    b. $k_o = 8.99\%$
    c. Debt-equity ratio $= .508$
    d. $V = \$906,000; k_o = 10\%$. Reject the plan because it will reduce the firm's market value or alternatively increase the firm's k_o.

18.7 b. $k_o = 8.46\%$
    d. $k_o = 8.19\%$. Recommend the action because it will reduce k_o from 8.46% to 8.19% and therefore will increase the firm's value.

18.8 e. Capital structure B is recommended because k_o is the lowest for B and correspondingly V is maximized.

18.9 b. $k_e = .10, .102, .106, .112,$ and $.133$ for Plans 1 through 5, respectively

18.10a. (1) $V_L = V_U = \$40,000$
      (3) $V_L = \$48,000$
    b. $k_o = .12, .116, .113, .11,$ and $.106$ for Plans 1 through 5, respectively.

18.11b. No, the $1,200 total transaction cost is greater than the $1,000 arbitrage profit.

19.2   A $= \$1,278.75;$ C $= \$50,760$
19.3 a. B $= \$570;$ D $= \$4,176.57$
    b. A $= \$50;$ C $= \$29.80$
19.4 b. $411.53
    d. 22.18%
19.5 a. A $= \$6,045;$ C $= \$5,156.25$
    b. B $= \$253.13$
    c. C $= \$771.87$
    d. B $= -28.67\%$
    e. A $= \$1,814.68$
    f. B $= -13.07\%$
19.6 a. (1) 400 shares
19.7 a. A $= -\$500;$ C $= -\$2,512.50$
    b. B $= \$6,720$
19.8 b. $-\$1,200$
19.9   Three long positions
    One short position
19.10 $3.60 per share
19.11b. $94,750,000
    c. Selling group receives $750,000.

20.1 $40,000 for year 0, $24,000 for years 1–11, and $-\$16,000$ for year 12
20.3 a. $46,798
20.5   Lease A capitalized value $= \$299,800$
20.7 c. Leasing is preferred.
20.8 b. Purchase $PV = \$40,805;$ leasing $PV = \$44,959$
    c. Purchase alternative is preferred.
20.9   Accept the deal offered by lessor R, because it will cost $8,972 versus $23,217 cost of deal offered by lessor S.
20.10a. Borrow-to-purchase
    b. The net cost of borrow-to-purchase alternative will be reduced by $412.

20.11   Accept the borrow-to-purchase option with net cost = $298,946 as against the $301,257 net cost of the leasing option.

21.1 a. Debentures get $9,375,000, ordinary unsecured creditors get $5,625,000, and subordinated debt holders get nothing.

     b. Debentures get 62.5%, ordinary unsecured creditors get 37.5%, and subordinated debt holders get 0.0%.

21.2 a. Debenture B would get $1,500,000.

     b. Ordinary unsecured creditors get $500,000.
     Debenture B gets $2,500,000.

     c. Ordinary unsecured creditors get 50%.
     Debenture B gets 83.3%.

21.3   A, Interest = $30,000; C, Interest = $1,000,000
     B, Tax shield = $640,000; D, Tax shield = $113,333.33

21.5 a. $160,000

     b. $1,800,000

     c. $2,040,000

     d. $360,000

     e. NPV = $2,446.30 > 0; therefore, refunding is recommended.

21.6 a. $960,000

     b. $180,000 for years 1–14; $100,000 for year 15

     c. NPV = $754,800 > 0; therefore, refunding is recommended.

21.7 a. $1,546,000

     d. Refunding is favourable when the coupon rate is 8.5% and the after-tax cost of debt is 5%.

     e. Expected PV of savings will equal − $219,430 < 0; therefore, the bond refunding is not desirable.

22.2 a. Majority: A, B, C, D, E; Minority: none

     c. Cumulative voting gives the minority shareholders a better chance of electing directors.

22.3   A: Majority voting 0, cumulative voting 0
     B: Majority voting 0, cumulative voting 3

22.4 a. $8.80

     b. $8.80

     c. $35.20

22.5   A: $15.00
     D: $25.50

22.6 a. Preferred shares: $14.875 per share
     Common shares: $15.875 per share

     c. Preferred dividends = $10.00 per share
     Common dividends = $0.00 per share

     e. (a) Preferred dividends = $8.00 per share
         Common dividends = $20.00 per share

22.7 a. 8.5%

     b. 6.5%

  c. 8%

  d. 9%

22.8 a. 20.57%

  b. 20.28%

  d. Preferred shares can magnify earnings and generate an optimal leverage.

22.9   A: Number of shares per right = 0.033; number of shares X can buy = 20.

   D: Number of shares per right = .20; number of shares X can buy = 240.

22.10a. 40,000 shares

  b. 0.08 share

  f. $10 would be more likely to assure complete subscription, because the market price is less likely to decline below $10 per share.

22.11   Case A: (1) R_o = $0.50; (2) M_e = $19.50, R_e = $0.50

22.12a. 24,000 shares

  b. 12.5 rights

  e. approx. $0.30 per right or more

23.1 a. $50 per share

  b. $8 per share

23.2 b. 40 shares

  c. 16 shares

23.4 a. After first year = 2 shares

  b. First year = $50 per share

23.5 b. $87.50

  d. At $85 per share = $1,062.50

23.6   A, Conversion value = $1,056.25

   B, Conversion premium percentage = 0.0%

23.7 a. Earnings per share = $3.39

  b. Number of shares of common outstanding = 150,000

  c. Earnings per share = $3.49

23.8 a. (3) $1.26 per share

  b. Convertible bonds

23.9   Preferred R = $71.11

   Bond B = $681.90

23.10a. At $25 = $1,000

   At $35 = $1,400

  b. $830.12

23.11a. At $11 = $44

   At $13 = $52

  c. At $15 = $60

23.12a. At $46 = − $12; at $58 = $24

23.13a. Number of warrants = 400

  b. Return on investment = 20%

23.14b. 6.67%

  c. (1) For warrants, rate of return = − 42.85%

24.1 b. Wednesday, July 5

  d. Decrease in total assets

24.2 a. $4.75 per share
  d. A decrease in retained earnings and hence shareholders' equity by $80,000
24.3 b. A $20,000 decrease in cash and retained earnings
  c. Cash, because a firm cannot pay more in dividends than it has in cash, unless it borrows or liquidates some assets.
24.4 a. 19X0 = $0.00; 19X4 = $1.28
  b. 19X3 = $1.00; 19X7 = $1.40
  c. 19X2 = $ .50; 19X8 = $1.30
24.5 a. 19X3 = $ .30; 19X7 = $ .78
  b. 19X5 = $ .50; 19X8 = $ .74
  c. 19X1 = $ .50; 19X6 = $ .50
  d. 19X4 = $ .53; 19X8 = $ .78
24.6 a. Retained earnings = $85,000
  c. Shareholders' equity has not changed.
24.7 a. $0.05 per-share cash dividend; retained earning = $300,000.
  c. Share dividends do not affect shareholders' equity. Cash dividends reduce retained earnings and hence shareholders' equity.
24.8 a. $2 per share
  d. $20 per share
24.9 a. $2.40 per share
  b. Ownership proportion under 5% share dividend plan = 1%
24.10b. Common shares = $1,800,000 (400,000 shares at $4.50 par)
  d. Common shares = $1,800,000 (3,600,000 shares at $0.50 par)
24.11a. The shares outstanding will increase to 150,000.
  b. The share price would decrease by one-third to $80 per share.
  c. Before share split: $100 per share
    After share split: $66.67 per share
24.12a. 19,047 shares
  c. $21.00 per share
24.13a. Price-earnings multiple = 15
  c. $4.13 per share

25.1 a. Yr. 1 = $112,000; yr. 3 = $112,000
  b. Yr. 2 = $ 24,000; yr. 4 = $112,000
25.2 a. Yr. 2 = $160,000; yr. 4 = $240,000
  b. Yr. 1 = $0.00;   yr. 3 = − $60,000
  c. $620,000
25.3 a. $85,000
  c. Acquire Multi-Color.
25.5 a. Desirable
25.6 a. $1.029 per share Flannagans; $1.853 per share Moon Bar
25.7 a. 8,000 shares
  c. $1.72 per share
25.8   A, Ratio of exchange of shares = .6
    C, Ratio of exchange of shares = 1.75
    B, Ratio of exchange of market price = 1.25
    D, Ratio of exchange of market price = 1.25

25.9 a. Yr. 1 = $2.10 per share; yr. 3 = $2.315 per share
   b. Yr. 2 = $2.157 per share; yr. 4 = $2.406 per share
   c. Yr. 3 = $2.328 per share; yr. 4 = $2.459 per share
25.10a. Yr. 2 = $2.29 per share; yr. 4 = $2.62 per share
   b. (1) Yr. 1, ratio of .6 = $2.395 per share
        Yr. 3, ratio of .6 = $2.58 per share
     (2) Yr. 2, ratio of .8 = $3.079 per share
        Yr. 4, ratio of .8 = $3.32 per share
25.11a. 1.125
   b. Merwin Company, eps = $2.50
     Lyle Company, P/E Ratio = 15
   d. $2.529 per share
   e. $45.52 per share
25.12a. 2.5%
   d. For **a,** equity as a percent of total assets = 1.37%.
     For **b,** equity as a percent of total assets = .206%.

26.3 a. Cash payment = $75,000 at present.
   c. Cash payment = $75,000 in 60 days; $37,500 in 120 days; $37,500 in 180 days
26.4 a. B = $116,667; D = $400,000
   b. A, sustain; C, sustain
26.6 a. Rehabilitation by restructuring of capital structure
   c. Mortgage bondholders get $200,000 in income bonds and $250,000 in common shares.
26.7 b. A, Debenture holders get $500,000 in debentures and $1,500,000 in mortgage bonds.
    C, Mortgage bondholders get $1,000,000 in bonds, $500,000 in preferred shares, and $1,500,000 in common shares.
   c. Since in all cases common and preferred shareholders get nothing, they would probably not consider any of the five plans to be equitable.
26.8 a. (1) Employees get $600,000.
    (2) $300,000
    (3) Subordinated debenture holders get $0.00.
   b. For **a,** (1) Government (taxes) gets $250,000.
    For **a,** (2) First mortgage holders fully paid; therefore no proceeds remained to be paid to the second mortgage holders, who then filed an ordinary unsecured claim for the total amount of debt.
    For **a,** (3) Second mortgage holder gets $276,800.
26.9 a. Case I, accounts payable get $100,000.
    Case II, notes payable get $75,000.
    Case III, subordinated debentures get $125,000.
   b. Case I, notes payable get $200,000.
    Case II, subordinated debentures get $125,000.
    Case III, Accounts payable get $75,000.
26.10b. For **a,** (2) First mortgage holder is owed $100,000.
    For **a,** (3) No

Glossary

ABC Inventory Control System A system of dividing a firm's inventory into three groups—A, B, and C—according to the contribution of the items to the firm's overall investment in inventory. A items are those requiring the largest investment, B items are those requiring the second largest investment, and C items are those requiring the smallest investment. Inventory control techniques can be applied in light of this breakdown.

Absolute Priority Rule The guiding principle in the recapitalization of a firm. Under the rule, all senior claims on assets must be satisfied in full prior to settling any junior claim(s).

Accept-Reject Approach Evaluating capital expenditure proposals to determine whether the projects meet the minimum acceptance criteria established by the firm.

Accrual Basis The basis on which an accountant typically views the revenues and expenses of a business firm. Generally, revenues are recognized at the point of sale and expenses when they are incurred, although, in actuality, since sales and purchases are often made on credit, cash flows may not occur at these points.

Accruals A current liability commonly found on balance sheets. Accruals represent obligations of the firm for certain services received for which payment is not yet due. The most common accruals are accrued wages, accrued rent, and accrued taxes. Accruals are an inexpensive form of financing for the business firm.

Acid-Test Ratio A measure of liquidity used when a firm is believed to have illiquid inventories. It is calculated by dividing the firm's current assets minus its inventory by its current liabilities. The higher this ratio is, the more liquid the firm is considered.

Active Business Income Income from ordinary business transactions as opposed to income derived from property.

Aggressive Approach Financing a firm's short-term outlays (seasonal needs) with short-term funds and its long-term outlays (permanent needs) with long-term funds. A high-profit–high-risk approach to financing.

Aging of Accounts   The evaluation of a firm's accounts receivable or accounts payable to determine the percentages that are current and the percentages that are past due.

Amalgamation   The combination of two or more companies, according to the statutory provisions of the appropriate Business Corporations Acts. After a statutory amalgamation, a single corporate entity will emerge that will be either one of the combining corporations or an entirely new corporation.

Amortization   The process of allocating an expense or a loan payment to certain periods of time. An amortized loan schedule is one that requires equal loan payments in each period over the life of the loan, using a specified rate of interest.

Annual Cleanup   A provision normally included in a line-of-credit agreement. It requires the borrower to "clean up" its loans (have a zero loan balance) for a specified time during one or more periods a year. This requirement ensures that funds obtained by borrowing against a line of credit will be kept only for the short term.

Annuity   A pattern of cash flows that are equal in each year; often referred to as an equal annual pattern of cash flows.

Arbitrage   The simultaneous purchase and sale of the same good, or its perfect substitute, for a profit. The arbitrage argument is extremely important in analytically solving many of the problems in finance, such as the derivation of the Black-Scholes option pricing model.

Asset Structure   The mix and types of assets on a firm's balance sheet. The mix of assets depends on the current-fixed-asset breakdown; the type of assets depends on which current and fixed assets are best for a given firm. The management of the firm's asset structure is an important function of the financial manager.

Assignment   An agreement between the debtor and the creditors that legally assigns the power to liquidate the debtor-firm's assets to a third party. This party is called an *assignee* or *trustee.*

Average Age of Accounts Payable   A ratio indicating the average amount of time taken by a firm to pay its accounts payable. The credit-worthiness of a firm can be evaluated by comparing the average age of its payables to the credit terms extended to it.

Average Age of Accounts Receivable   The average amount of time required to collect an account receivable. A useful measure for evaluating the firm's credit and collection policies in light of the credit terms extended by it.

Average Investment in Accounts Receivable   The actual amount of dollars a firm has tied up in its receivables. This is a function of the marginal cost per unit of product, the annual credit sales, and the average amount of accounts receivable on the firm's books.

Average Investment in Inventory   The average amount of money a firm has tied up in its inventory. This is a function of the cost of goods sold and inventory turnover.

Average Rate of Return   A measure for evaluating proposed capital expenditures. It is calculated by dividing the average profits after taxes expected from a project by the average investment required by the project.

Average-Risk Investment or Project   The project having the same business risk as the typical or average investments historically undertaken by the firm.

Average Tax Rates   The quotient found by dividing the amount of taxes owed by the related amount of taxable income. For individuals, including sole proprietors and partnerships, the average tax rate will increase with increasing levels of taxable income due to the progressive nature of the federal income tax structure.

Bad Debt Expense   The percentage of credit sales for which payment was not received or is not expected to be received. Bad debt expenses are often estimated as a percentage of sales, and a reserve is established to cover them.

Balloon Payment   A large final payment on a loan. Often the balloon payment consists of the entire principal; in other cases, it is only a disproportionately large final payment.

Banker's Acceptance   A short-term instrument arising through international trade transactions. A safe security because a number of parties become liable for its payment at maturity. Yields on banker's acceptances are similar to yields on negotiable certificates of deposit.

Bankruptcy   The situation when a firm's total liabilities exceed the fair value of its total assets. Filing for bankruptcy under the Bankruptcy Act can be voluntary or involuntary, depending upon the circumstances.

Benefit-Cost Ratio (B-C Ratio)   Sometimes called a *profitability index*. B-C ratios are used to evaluate capital expenditure proposals. They are calculated by dividing the present value of net cash flows from a project by the initial investment in it. If the B-C ratio is greater or equal to 1, a project is acceptable; otherwise, it should be rejected.

Beta Coefficient, *b*   A measure of *nondiversifiable risk*. It is an index of the degree of responsiveness or comovement of the asset return with the market return. The beta for the market portfolio is equal to 1; all other betas are viewed relative to this value. They may be positive or negative; positive betas are much more common. The higher the beta, the more responsive the asset's return, and therefore the greater the nondiversifiable risk and vice versa.

Bond   A certificate indicating that a corporation has borrowed a certain amount of money on a long-term basis and promises to repay it at a specific future date.

Bond Discount or Premium   If a bond is sold at a *discount*, it is sold for less than its face value; if it is sold at a *premium*, it is sold for more than its face value.

Bond Indenture   A legal document that specifically states the conditions under which a bond has been issued, the rights of the bondholders, and the duties of the issuing corporation. An indenture normally contains a number of standard and restrictive provisions, including a sinking-fund requirement and a statement of the security if the bond is secured.

Bond Rating   The riskiness of publicly traded bonds is assessed by financial services such as *Moody's, Standard & Poor's,* and the *Canadian Bond Rating Service.* Their ratings are based on the overall quality of the bonds, which depends upon the *safety of principal* and interest.

Bond Refunding   The process of retiring outstanding bonds—typically in order to issue new securities at a lower interest rate than those retired. Bonds may be refunded through a preplanned arrangement involving the sale of *serial bonds* or by the exercise of a *call privilege*. Quantitative procedures are available for making bond refunding-reissue decisions.

Bond Value   The current worth of a bond, which can be estimated by calculating the present value of all the cash inflows associated with it. The present value is found by discounting the cash inflows at a specified rate or at the prevailing rate of interest for a similar term-to-maturity and risk instrument.

Book Value   The accounting value of an asset, a liability, or an equity. The *book value per share of common* is equal to the per-share equity plus any retained earnings.

Breakeven Analysis   A technique for evaluating the relationship between a firm's fixed costs, variable costs, profits, and sales. The *breakeven point* is the volume of sales at which the firm's revenues just equal its total operating costs. It can be measured in terms of either units or dollars.

Business Risk   The risk inherent in the general operations of a business firm. It is sometimes referred to as *economic risk* or *operating risk*, and is reflected in the variability of the firm's operating earnings (earnings before interest and taxes).

Call Feature   Included in most bond issues, it gives the issuer the opportunity to repurchase the bonds at a specified price prior to their maturity. Preferred shares are often callable or *redeemable*. The call or redemption price is normally set above the initial issuance price and declines according to a predetermined schedule as time passes.

Capital Asset Pricing Model (CAPM)   A basic theory dealing with the market-determined relationship between risk and return, which was developed primarily to explain the behaviour of financial asset prices under conditions of equilibrium in capital markets. Three important relationships derived in the CAPM are the capital market line (CML), the security market line (SML), and the characteristic line (CL).

Capital Budgeting   The total process of generating, evaluating, selecting, and following up on capital expenditure alternatives.

Capital Cost   The cost of a depreciable asset permitted for capital cost allowance purposes under the Income Tax Act.

Capital Cost Allowance (CCA)   The portion of the capital cost of an asset permitted as an annual tax-deductible expense.

Capital Expenditure   An outlay made by a firm for a fixed or an intangible asset from which benefits are expected to be received over a period greater than a year.

Capital Gain   The excess of proceeds of sale of an asset over the asset's original cost (or adjusted cost base if the asset was purchased after 1972).

Capital Loss   A loss resulting from the sale of a nondepreciable asset for less than its original cost (or adjusted cost base if the asset was purchased after 1972). For tax purposes, such losses are first netted against the capital gains realized in the year. If there is a net capital gain, then one-half of it is included as a *taxable capital gain* in the year's taxable income and taxed at regular tax rates. If a net loss occurs, then one-half of the net loss, referred to as an *allowable capital loss*, can be applied against other income of the year or carried back and/or forward under the prescribed rules.

Capital Market   A structure created by a number of institutions and arrangements whereby the suppliers and demanders of long-term funds make transactions. Participants in this market include individuals, business, and the government. The backbone of the capital market is the organized *security exchanges*.

Capital Market Line (CML)   It is the market-determined relationship between return and risk. Since the risk-free asset and the market portfolio are not correlated, the CML is a linear combination of the risk-free asset and the market portfolio of risky assets.

Capital Rationing   A situation in which there is a ceiling on the amount of funds available for capital expenditures during a given period.

Capital Structure   The mix of the various types of debt and equity capital maintained by a firm. The more debt capital a firm has in its capital structure, the more highly *levered* the firm is considered to be. There are conflicting views on whether or not an *optimal capital structure* that maximizes the firm's value exists.

Capitalize   The process of converting a future stream of cash flows into its present value. This is done merely by discounting the cash flows at the appropriate cost or *capitalization rate.*

Cash Breakeven Analysis   An approach for finding a firm's breakeven point recognizing that it is cash—not accounting profits—that is most important in meeting the firm's obligations. It is calculated using fixed *cash* costs, which are found by subtracting any noncash charges from the firm's fixed costs prior to calculating the breakeven point.

Cash Budget   A statement of various cash receipts and disbursements expected by a firm during the coming year, generally on a month-by-month basis. It is a short-term financial planning tool. By determining the *net cash flows* for each period and adjusting for any beginning cash, the firm can determine when financing will be required and when surpluses will occur. If a surplus is expected, the firm can arrange certain short-term investments. The cash budget is sometimes called a *cash forecast.*

Cash Cycle   The period of time from the point a firm makes an outlay to purchase raw materials to the point cash is collected from the sale of the associated finished good. The cash cycle represents the amount of time the firm's cash is tied up.

Cash Discount   A feature often included in a firm's credit terms. It allows a firm's customers to pay less than the sale price of merchandise if payment is made within a certain number of days after the beginning of the credit period.

Cash Discount Period   The number of days between the beginning of the credit period and the last day on which a customer can take a cash discount.

Cash Flows   The actual payment or receipt of dollars by the firm. Cash flows do not necessarily occur at the point at which an obligation is incurred or an item is sold. The financial manager operates using a cash-flow point of view, since cash is the lifeblood of the firm.

Cash Turnover   The number of times each year a firm's cash is turned over. It can be calculated by dividing the firm's cash cycle in days into the number of days in the year. The higher a firm's cash turnover, the more efficiently cash is being used, and vice versa.

Certainty Equivalent   That single certain cash payoff that a decision maker requires to make him or her indifferent between choosing the certain cash payoff and an uncertain cash payoff; that is, a distribution of possible cash payoffs.

Certainty Equivalent Approach   One of the most theoretically preferred approaches for the risk-adjusted evaluation of projects. In evaluating projects using this approach, the decision maker first adjusts for risk by converting the expected cash flows to their corresponding certainty equivalents; then the certainty-equivalent cash-flow values are discounted at the risk-free rate to get their net present values.

Clientele Effect   The effect on a firm's value of attracting shareholders whose preferences regarding the pattern and stability of dividends correspond to the firm's preferences.

Coefficient of Variation   A relative measure of the variability of the outcomes associated with an event. It is calculated by dividing the standard deviation of outcomes by the mean.

Collection Policies   The procedures a firm follows when attempting to collect accounts receivable as promptly as possible once they are due. Collection letters, telephone calls, personal visits, the use of collection agencies, and legal action are all possible collection techniques. A firm's bad-debt expense reflects the effectiveness of its collection policy.

Comaker Loan   A loan secured by another, more credit-worthy party (the *cosigner,* or *comaker*). Cosigners generally have some interest in the borrowers for whom they cosign.

Commercial Arrangement   A modification or elimination of the property rights of the various classes of a firm's creditors and owners under the federal bankruptcy and insolvency laws. It is generally attempted when a firm has failed and is neither willing nor able to obtain a voluntary "out-of-court" settlement with its creditors.

Commercial Finance Company   A financial institution without a bank charter that makes business loans secured with accounts receivable, inventory, or chattel mortgages. Commercial finance companies generally accept much higher risks than chartered banks.

Commercial Paper   A short-term, unsecured, interest-bearing promissory note issued by a corporation or a finance company, which has a very high credit standing. These instruments have maturities of anywhere from 24 hours to one year or longer.

Commitment Fee   A fee charged on the total authorized credit under a revolving credit or line-of-credit arrangement. This fee is typically one-half to three-quarters of one percent of the total (i.e., used and unused) line of credit.

Common Shares   Shares held by the "true owners" of the business firm, who are the last to receive any distribution of earnings or assets. The common shareholder is the "residual owner" of the firm's assets since he or she, in essence, takes what is left. Most common shareholders have voting rights.

Compensating Balance   A requirement sometimes found in a line of credit or other short-term borrowing arrangement with a chartered bank. The borrower is required to maintain a chequing account balance of between 10 and 20 percent of the outstanding loan. A compensating balance requirement raises the effective cost of borrowing.

Composition   A pro rata settlement of creditor claims, instead of receiving full payment of their claims, creditors receive only a partial payment.

Compound Interest   Interest that is paid both on the initial principal deposited in an account and on interest earned on the initial principal in previous periods. The interest earned in one period becomes, in effect, part of the principal in a following period.

Compound Value of an Annuity   The future amount accumulated at a certain point, assuming that an equal annual deposit into a medium earning at a specified rate is made.

Concentration Banking   The use of geographically dispersed collection centers to speed the collection of receivables and reduce the firm's need for cash.

Conglomerate   A firm that grows by acquiring virtually unrelated firms. The key benefit claimed for this type of firm is the diversification of risk across various industries.

Conservative Approach   In financing, the use of long-term funds to cover all expected financing requirements and the use of short-term funds to cover only unexpected financial needs. A low-profit–low-risk approach.

Contribution Margin   The percent of each sales dollar that remains after satisfying all variable costs. This percentage represents the proportion of each sales dollar available for meeting fixed costs and profits.

Conversion Feature   An option included as part of either a bond or a preferred share issue that permits the holder of the bond or share to convert the held security into a different type of security.

Conversion Premium   The percentage by which the issuance price of a security exceeds the conversion price. Usually the conversion premium is in the 10- to 20-percent range.

Conversion Price   Equal to the face value of the convertible security divided by the conversion ratio.

Conversion Ratio   The ratio by which a convertible security can be converted into common shares. It represents the number of common shares the convertible can be exchanged for.

Conversion Value   The value of a security in terms of the market value of the securities into which it can be converted. In most cases, it equals the conversion ratio times the current market price of common shares.

Convertible Security   A bond or preferred share that may be converted into another class of security, typically common shares, at the option of the holder at a specified price over a specified period of time.

Corporate Combination   When two or more limited companies come under common ownership or control or both. The ultimate form of the combination can result in two or more corporations emerging as one corporation, or it can result in a parent-subsidiary relationship.

Corporation   A form of business organization in which all the owners, or shareholders, have *limited liability* and have their earnings taxed at a special corporate tax rate. Payments to the owners in the form of dividends are taxed as personal income. In terms of business receipts and net profits, the corporation is the dominant form of business organization.

Correlation   A statistical relationship between series of numbers representing anything from cash flows to test data. If series move together, they are *positively correlated;* if they move in opposite directions, they are *negatively correlated.*

Correlation Coefficient   A statistical measure of correlation. It ranges from $+1$ for perfectly positively correlated series to -1 for perfectly negatively correlated series.

Cost of Capital   The rate of return the firm must earn on its existing investment in order for its market value (and hence the market value of the shareholders' equity) to remain unchanged. It can also be the minimum rate of return a firm must earn on new investment to satisfy all of the firm's suppliers of capital.

Coupon Rate   The stated rate of interest on a bond. The annual interest payment is the product of the coupon rate and the face value of the bond.

Coverage Ratios   Ratios, such as the times interest earned, total debt coverage, and overall coverage ratio, that measure the ability of a firm to meet its fixed financial obligations. The higher these ratios, the better.

Credit Analysis   The process of determining whether a credit applicant meets the firm's credit standards and what amount of credit it should receive.

Credit Period   The amount of time given a credit purchaser to remit the full payment for credit purchases. Accounts not paid by the end of the credit period are considered past due.

Credit Policy   Guidelines for determining whether to extend credit to a customer and how much credit to extend. Credit standards, credit information, and credit analyses are the important components of credit policy.

Credit Standards   The minimum criteria for the extension of credit to a customer. Credit ratings, credit references, and the like are used in setting credit standards.

Credit Terms   The repayment terms extended by a firm to its credit customers. They include the cash discount and cash discount period, if any, the net period, and the beginning of the credit period.

Cumulative Preferred Shares   Most preferred shares are cumulative, which means that all dividends in arrears must be paid prior to distributing any dividends to common shareholders. *Noncumulative* preferred shares do not entitle the holder to the eventual receipt of "passed" dividends, but require the issuer to pay only the current dividend prior to paying common shareholders.

Cumulative Voting   A voting system in which each common share entitles the holder to as many votes as there are directors to be elected. This system gives minority shareholders an opportunity to elect some directors.

Current Ratio   A measure of liquidity calculated by dividing a firm's current assets by its current liabilities. The higher this ratio is, the more liquid the firm is considered.

Debenture   An unsecured bond whose holders have a claim on a firm's assets after the claims of all secured creditors have been satisfied. Unsecured bonds subordinated to these bonds become *subordinated debentures.*

Debt Capital   Any type of *long-term* debt. Debt capital can be obtained by negotiated borrowing or through the sale of bonds.

Debt-Equity Ratio   A measure of a firm's financial leverage, calculated by dividing the firm's long-term debt by its equity. The higher this ratio, the more highly levered the firm.

Decision Trees   An analytical technique for making sequential decisions among alternatives in an objective and consistent manner. Decision trees are diagrams that permit various alternatives and payoffs, as well as their probabilities of occurrence, to be mapped out in a clear and easy-to-analyze fashion.

Degree of Financial Leverage (DFL)   A measure of a firm's *financial leverage;* the higher the DFL, the greater the financial leverage and therefore the greater the *financial risk.*

Degree of Operating Leverage (DOL)   A measure of a firm's *operating leverage;* the higher the DOL, the greater the operating leverage and therefore the greater the *operating risk.*

Degree of Total Leverage (DTL)   A measure of a firm's *total leverage;* the higher the DTL, the greater the total leverage and therefore the greater the *total risk.*

Demand Deposit   A chequing account in a chartered bank.

Depreciation   A charge against current income for a portion of the historical cost incurred with the acquisition of fixed assets.

Dilution   A decrease in the proportional share of various owners in a firm. Dilution may result from new share issues. The dilution of ownership usually results in the dilution of earnings, although the long-run effect may be to increase per-share earnings.

Direct Placement   The sale of a bond or other security directly to one or a group of purchasers, normally large financial institutions such as life insurance companies and pension funds.

Discount Rate   The rate at which a series of future cash flows are discounted in order to determine their present value. The *opportunity rate* or *cost of capital* used in capital budgeting.

Discounted Cash-Flow (DCF) Methods   Methods for evaluating and ranking capital expenditure proposals based on the concept of the time value of money. The three major DCF methods are (1) the internal rate of return method, (2) the net present value method, and (3) the benefit-cost ratio or profitability index method.

Diversifiable Risk   The portion of an asset's risk that can be eliminated through diversification. It results from the occurrence of uncontrollable or random events such as labour strikes, lawsuits, regulatory actions, loss of key accounts, and so forth. The events generating this type of risk vary from firm to firm. It is assumed that any investor can create a portfolio in which this risk, sometimes called *unsystematic risk*, is completely eliminated through diversification.

Dividend   Payment made by a firm to its owners. Dividends may be paid either in *cash* or in *shares*. The firm's directors periodically meet to decide whether to pay dividends and to determine the amount and form of the dividend payment. An effect similar to a share dividend is often achieved through a *share split*. A variety of types of *dividend policies* are commonly used by firms.

Dividend Gross-up   An amount equal to 50 percent of an individual's dividend income. This amount is added to actual dividends received to obtain an individual's taxable amount of dividend income.

Dividend Tax Credit   A federal tax credit calculated as 75 percent of the dividend gross-up and applied against the federal tax payable by an individual. It reduces the effective tax rate on an individual's dividend income.

Dividend Yield   The annual dividend on a share divided by its prevailing per-share market price. The first term of the *Gordon Model* represents its dividend yield.

DuPont Formula   A formula relating a firm's net profit margin and total asset turnover to its *return on investment (ROI)*. The return on investment is equal to the product of the net profit margin and total asset turnover.

EAC   Earnings available for common shareholders.

Earning Assets   A term commonly used to describe fixed assets, since they generally provide the basis for a firm's earning power. Without plant and equipment, a manufacturing firm could not produce a product.

EBIT   Earnings before interest and taxes.

EBIT-eps Analysis   A technique used to evaluate various capital structures in order to select the one that best maximizes a firm's *earnings per share* (eps). The financing plans are often shown graphically on a set of EBIT (x-axis) – eps (y-axis) axes.

Economic Order Quantity (EOQ) Model   A technique for determining the optimum quantity of items to order or produce based on the trade-off between inventory ordering and carrying costs. The optimum quantity is that which *minimizes* the total cost of inventory or the sum of the ordering and carrying cost.

Economically Dependent Projects   A project is economically dependent on another if its operating cash flows and/or the likelihood of its acceptance are affected by the acceptance or nonacceptance of the other project. A project is *economically independent* if it is *not* economically dependent on any other existing or prospective project of the firm.

Effective Annual Interest Rate   Annual interest rate actually earned on a deposit when the interest is compounded monthly, weekly, or daily. The effective annual interest rate when the interest is compounded m times a year equals $(1 + i/m)^m - 1$, where i is the nominal annual interest rate. In the case of *continuous compounding* (i.e., compounding every microsecond), the effective annual interest rate equals $e^i - 1$.

Efficient Market   There are three common measures of market efficiency. *Operational efficiency* measures the relative cost incurred in the provision of intermediation services between the suppliers and demanders of funds. *Allocational efficiency* measures the ability of a market to maintain equivalent rates of return (or financing costs) on investments of equal risk. A market is *informationally efficient* when security prices always "fully reflect" all available public information.

Efficient Portfolio   A portfolio that provides a maximum expected return for a given level of risk or a minimum risk for a given level of expected return.

eps   Earnings per share; found by dividing the earnings available for common shareholders (EAC) by the number of common shares outstanding.

Equity Capital   Long-term funds provided by a firm's owners that do not mature at a future date, but have an infinite life. The basic sources of equity capital are preferred shares, common shares, and retained earnings.

Ex Dividend or Ex Right   Indicates that a share is selling without a recently declared dividend or right. The ex-dividend date is generally two business days prior to the *dividend-record date.* If a share is not selling ex dividend or ex rights, then it is selling *cum dividend* or *cum rights.*

Exercise Price   The price at which holders of *warrants* can purchase the number of shares on which they have an option. This price, which is set above the market price when issued, is sometimes called the *option price.*

Expected Value   A measure of central tendency. It can be found by calculating the average value of the expected outcomes. If probabilities are attached to expected outcomes, the expected value can be calculated as the weighted average return, in which the weights used are the probabilities of the various outcomes.

Extension   An arrangment whereby creditors extend the required payment date of past-due obligations. Extensions are arranged when the creditors feel that it is quite likely that the firm can overcome its problems and resume successful operations.

Factoring   The administration of the credit process by a factor or commercial finance company for a client firm. Canadian factoring can include credit payment guarantees by the factor of the approved accounts receivable generated by a client firm; it can include a provision that allows the client firm to draw advances (borrow) against uncollected (and not due) accounts.

Finance   A body of principles, theories, and empirical findings dealing with the generation and allocation of scarce resources (primarily money) by various decision-making units such as individuals, businesses, and governments. Finance deals with how these parties allocate scarce resources through a market-pricing system based on the valuation of risky assets (i.e., contingent claims).

Financial Analysis and Planning   A function of the financial manager. The use and transformation of financial data into a form that can be used to monitor and evaluate a firm's financial position, to plan future financing, and to evaluate the need for increased capacity.

Financial Breakeven Point   The level of EBIT necessary for a firm to be just able to meet its fixed financial obligations. In other words, the level of EBIT at which the eps just equals zero. The higher the financial breakeven point, the more financially risky the firm is considered.

Financial Intermediary   An institution that accumulates and then distributes savings to those needing funds. The process by which savings are accumulated by financial institutions and then lent or invested is generally referred to as *intermediation*.

Financial Leverage   The ability of fixed financial charges, such as interest and preferred share dividends, to magnify the effect of changes in EBIT on the firm's earnings per share (eps). The more fixed financial charges a firm must meet, the higher its financial leverage is.

Financial Markets   The markets for short-term and long-term loans and investments. The two key financial markets are the *money market* and the *capital market*.

Financial Risk   The risk of being unable to cover financial costs. The greater a firm's *financial leverage* is, the higher its financial risk is.

Financial Structure   The mix and type of financing on the firm's balance sheet. The mix is determined by the amount of short-term as opposed to long-term financing; the type of financing is determined by the specific instruments used. The management of a firm's financial structure is an important function of the financial manager.

Float   The amount of money tied up in cheques that have been written but not yet collected. Float exists because of the banking system's cheque-clearing procedures. Many firms are known to "play the float," which involves writing cheques against nonexistent deposits and depositing the money to "cover" the cheques sometime prior to their presentation for payment.

Flotation Costs   Sometimes called *issuance costs*. The costs of preparing, consulting, underwriting, and selling a new security issue. These costs are amortized over a security's life.

Foreign-Pay Bond   Debt that is denominated in a foreign currency. When debt is denominated in the firm's domestic currency, it is referred to as a *domestic-pay bond*.

Gordon Valuation Model   A commonly used equity valuation model. It is based on the premise that the value of a share to investors is the present value of all future dividends to be paid by the issuing firm to the holder of the share. The cost of equity capital can be calculated using the model.

Gross Profit Margin   The percentage of each sales dollar remaining after a firm has paid for its goods. It is calculated by dividing gross profits by net sales.

Growth Rate   The compound annual rate (stated as a percentage) at which a stream of cash flows or earnings or dividends grows over a period of years.

Holders of Record   Owners of a firm's shares on the holder-of-record date indicated on the firm's share ledger. Holders of record receive share rights or dividends when they are announced.

Holding Company   A company that has voting control of one or more other companies (subsidiaries or divisions). Generally, there is virtually no formal organization above the level of the individual firm since each of the "controlled" firms is essentially autonomous.

Homogeneous Risk Classes   A homogeneous risk class, according to MM, occurs when the expected EBIT of firms in the same risk class are perfectly correlated and therefore differ by, at most, a "scale factor."

Horizontal Growth   Growth caused by the combination of firms in the same line of business.

Income Bonds   A bond on which the payment of interest is required only when earnings are available from which to make the payment. Commonly used during the rehabilitation of a failing or failed business firm.

Industry Capitalization Approach   A valuation technique whereby the expected per-share earnings of the firm are capitalized at the *earnings-price ratio*, which is commonly referred to as the industry capitalization rate.

Initial Investment   The cash outflow that should be considered in evaluating a prospective capital expenditure. It is found by netting all inflows and outflows occurring at time zero for a proposed project.

Integer Programming   A mathematical programming technique for optimizing an objective function given certain constraints, one of which is that all solutions be integer values. This technique is often used in *capital rationing* in order to select the best group of projects.

Interest   Payments made on money borrowed or received on money lent. The amount of interest depends on the amount of principal borrowed or lent.

Intermediation   The process by which savings are accumulated in financial institutions and then lent out or invested. The reverse of this process, *disintermediation*, often occurs during inflationary periods since the high interest rates available from other financial media cause the movement of funds out of financial institutions and into these media.

Internal Rate of Return (IRR)   A sophisticated way of evaluating capital expenditure proposals. The discount rate that causes the net present value of a project to just equal zero. If a project's IRR is greater than the cost of capital, the project is acceptable; otherwise, it should be rejected. The IRR is often referred to as the *yield* on a project.

Intrinsic Value   The value that is justified based on the firm's current operations and future prospects. It depends upon investors' anticipated returns and perceived risk from investing in such a firm.

Inventory Turnover   A ratio calculated by dividing the cost of goods sold by the average inventory. The number of times per year an item of inventory is sold. In general, a high inventory turnover is preferred.

Investment Opportunities Schedule (IOS)   A schedule or graph that lists the best (i.e., highest) internal rate of return (IRR) to the worst (ie., lowest IRR) investment opportunities available to the firm at a given point in time.

Investment Tax Credit   A tax credit allowed to both individuals and corporations for certain capital assets acquired during a prescribed time period. It is applied on a regional basis; for most areas it is calculated as 5 percent of the capital costs of the eligible assets.

Lead Time   The amount of time that elapses between the placement of an order and the actual receipt of an order. To allow for the uncertainty that surrounds an expected lead time, most firms maintain a *safety stock* of inventory.

Lease Capitalization   The disclosure of a capital or financial lease directly on the balance sheet. The gross amount of an asset under a capital lease and related amortization are shown on the asset side of the balance sheet. The present value of the *minimum* future lease payments (i.e., lease payments excluding insurance, maintenance charges, and provincial sales taxes), discounted at an appropriate discount rate, is shown on the liability side of the balance sheet.

Leasing Obtaining the use of specific fixed assets without actually taking title to them. The *lessee* receives the services of the assets *leased* to it by the *lessor*, which owns the assets. A periodic tax-deductible lease payment is required. An *operating lease* is generally a short-term cancelable arrangement, while a *financial* or *capital lease* is a long-term noncancelable agreement.

Leverage A term commonly used in finance to describe the ability of fixed costs to magnify returns to a firm's owners resulting from changes in the firm's revenues.

Leveraged Lease A type of lease involving three parties: the lessor, the lessee, and the lender, who provides a portion of the purchase price of the leased asset.

Lien A legal term meaning "a claim on the property of another," such as a security interest obtained as collateral for the payment of a legal debt. A *floating lien* is a general claim on a group of assets that can not easily or economically be identified by serial numbers.

Limited Liability A type of liability that protects owners of a business firm from losing more than their initial investment in the business. Owners of sole proprietorships and partnerships generally do not have limited liability, while shareholders in corporations do. If the liability of owners is not limited, then it is unlimited.

Line of Credit The maximum amount of money or merchandise a lender or supplier, respectively, will extend to a firm without performing a further credit analysis. The firm can borrow or purchase on credit against the line as long as the amount owed is current and does not exceed the amount of the line.

Liquidation Value The value of a firm if all its assets are valued at their liquidation price and the resulting proceeds are reduced by the firm's debts and obligations to preferred shareholders. Also, the price at which a usable asset can currently be sold.

Liquidity The ability to pay bills as they come due. The liquidity of a firm is directly related to the level of cash, marketable securities, and other current assets it holds.

Liquidity Crisis A situation in which a firm is unable to meet due bills; a period of "technical insolvency."

Lock-Box System An arrangement whereby a firm has its customers mail their payments to geographically dispersed post office boxes, which are opened by its bank. The receipts are deposited in the firm's account, and any other enclosures are forwarded to the firm. This system speeds the collection process by reducing the time needed to mail, deposit, and clear cheques.

Long Term In finance, a period greater than one year. Fixed assets, noncurrent liabilities, and equity are the long-term assets, liabilities, and equities of the firm, respectively. Assets and liabilities with maturities of one to ten years are sometimes referred to as intermediate-term items.

Majority Voting A voting system in which each shareholder may cast one vote for each director for each share held. This system is to the advantage of the majority shareholders.

Marginal Analysis One of the basic principles that has been adopted from economics and has been used extensively in finance. It is the principle that an investment (or action) should be undertaken only when its marginal benefits exceed its marginal costs.

Marginal Tax Rate   Tax rate on an incremental dollar of taxable income.

Margin Purchases   Purchases of securities made by borrowing a portion of the purchase price. The *margin requirement* indicates the minimum percentage of the purchase price the purchaser must put up; the remainder may be borrowed from the broker at a stated cost.

Market Makers   In the over-the-counter market, individuals or firms that *make markets* in certain securities by offering to buy or sell them at a stated price. The *bid* and *ask* prices represent, respectively, the highest price offered to purchase a given security and the lowest price at which the security is offered for sale.

Market Premium   The amount by which the market price of a convertible security exceeds its *straight value*. The market premium is larger the closer the straight value is to the conversion value.

Market Return   The expected rate of return on the market portfolio of assets that can be viewed as the average rate of return on all assets. The TSE 300 Composite Index or some other share index is commonly used as a proxy for the market.

Marketable Securities   Short-term debt securities that can be readily converted into cash without sustaining a loss of principal. They include treasury bills, negotiable certificates of deposit, banker's acceptances, and repurchase agreements.

"Me-First" Rule   A contractual arrangement or agreement giving the firm's claimants (e.g. bondholders) veto power over any change in the investment and/or financing policy of the firm, whenever such a change adversely affects the market value of the claimant's claim on the firm's cash flows, assets, or both. An example is a *restrictive covenant* in a bond trust indenture.

Minimum Operating Cash   A firm's minimum operating cash can be estimated by dividing the firm's annual cash outlays by its cash turnover. The resulting value represents the minimum amount of cash or liquidity the firm is estimated to need during the year, assuming that there is a small degree of seasonality in the business.

Modified DuPont Formula   A formula relating the firm's *return on investment (ROI)* to the *return on equity (ROE)*. The return on equity is calculated by dividing the return on investment, which can be found using the DuPont formula, by 1 minus the *debt ratio*, which is equal to the total liabilities divided by the total assets.

Monetary Assets   Assets, such as cash and accounts receivable, whose value is defined in terms of a fixed monetary unit, such as a Canadian dollar or a Japanese yen.

Monetary Balance   The difference between monetary assets and monetary liabilities for a specific monetary unit. A negative balance, which occurs when monetary assets exceed monetary liabilities for a specific currency, indicates that the firm is a net monetary creditor in that currency; a positive balance indicates that the firm is a net monetary debtor in that currency.

Monetary Liabilities   Obligations, such as accounts payable, which are payable in a fixed monetary unit, regardless of whether or not the value (i.e., purchasing power) of that unit changes.

Money Market   An intangible market created by the suppliers and demanders of short-term funds. Not an organized security exchange, but a communications network through which marketable security transactions are made.

Monte Carlo Simulation   A statistically based approach for generating a probability distribution of outcomes (such as net cash flow) or measures of profitability (such as NPV).

Mortgage Bonds   A bond secured with a lien on real property or buildings. Under a *blanket mortgage,* all assets are held as collateral. A *first-mortgage bond* gives the holder the first claim on secured assets; a *second-mortgage bond* gives the holder a secondary claim on the assets already secured by the first mortgage.

Mutually Exclusive Projects   A group of capital budgeting projects that competes with one another in such a way that the acceptance of one eliminates all the others in the group from further consideration.

Negotiable Certificates of Deposit (CD's)   Negotiable instruments representing the deposit of a certain number of dollars in a chartered bank. Negotiable CD's have a good secondary market and a relatively high yield. The face value and maturity of a negotiable CD is usually tailored to the investors' needs.

Net Present Value (NPV)   The most common of the sophisticated tools for evaluating capital expenditure proposals. It is calculated by subtracting the initial investment required by a project from the present value of the forecasted cash inflows. If a project's NPV is greater than zero, the project is acceptable; otherwise, it should be rejected.

Net Present-Value Profile   A graph or schedule that depicts the net present value of a project (*y*-axis) for various discount rates (*x*-axis). This graph clearly depicts the project's *internal rate of return* as the *x*-axis intercept.

Net Working Capital   A measure of a firm's liquidity that is useful in time-series comparisons. It is calculated by taking the difference between the firm's *current assets* and *current liabilities.* It is sometimes defined as the portion of a firm's current assets financed with long-term funds.

Nominal Annual Interest Rate   Stated annual interest rate on a deposit or a loan.

Noncash Charges   Items that are deducted for tax purposes on a firm's income statement, but which require no actual cash outlay. Depreciation, amortization, and depletion charges are the most common noncash charges.

Nondiversifiable Risk   A risk that is not diversifiable and is attributed to forces that affect all firms and therefore are not unique to the given firm. Factors such as war, inflation, international incidents, and political events account for an asset's nondiversifiable risk. This risk, which is often called *systematic* or *relevant risk,* cannot be eliminated through diversification. It is measured by *beta, b.*

Note   A paper representing a single-payment or installment loan received by the firm. A note generally represents a single-payment short-term loan.

Operating Leverage   The power of fixed operating costs to magnify the effects of changes in a firm's sales revenue on its earnings before interest and taxes (EBIT). The greater a firm's fixed operating costs, the higher its operating leverage.

Operating (Noncapital) Loss   Occurs when a firm has a negative before-tax profit that can be carried back one year and forward up to five years to reduce taxable income.

Operating Risk   The risk of being unable to cover operating costs measured by the variability of a firm's EBIT. Increased *operating leverage* increases a firm's operating risk. It is also commonly referred to as *economic* or *business risk.*

Opportunity Cost   The return a firm can earn on the best alternative similar-risk investment opportunity available at a given time. In some cases, the cost of borrowing or the savings that would result from repayment of an existing debt.

Option   A contract between two investors that gives its owner the right to *buy* (a *call* *option*) or *sell* (a *put option*) the common shares of a particular company before the expiry date of the option at the option's exercise (*striking*) price.

Organized Security Exchanges   Centrally located organizations on whose premises securities are traded. The key Canadian exchange is the Toronto Stock Exchange (TSE).

Overhanging Issues   Convertible securities that are not converted because the market price of the associated securities does not reach a level sufficient to stimulate conversion.

Over-the-Counter Exchange   Not a specific institution; a way of trading securities resulting from an intangible relationship among the purchasers and sellers of securities. Active traders in this market are linked by a telecommunications network.

Par Value   The stated or face value of shares or bonds. Generally no par-value shares are issued.

Participating Preferred Shares   Preferred shares whose holders receive more than the stated dividends by participating with common shareholders in dividend distributions beyond a certain level. Most preferred shares are *nonparticipating*.

Partnership   A business organization owned by two or more individuals. Partnerships are the least common form of business organization. The partners' income is taxed as personal income; the partners generally have *unlimited liability*, although certain partners in a *limited partnership* may have limited liability.

Payback Period   The number of years required for a firm to recover the initial investment required by a project from the cash inflows it generates. Short payback periods are preferred.

Payoff Matrix   A table indicating the payoff associated with each of a number of possible *states of nature*, or outcomes.

Payout Ratio   A firm's cash dividend per share, divided by its earnings per share. This ratio indicates the percentage of each dollar that is distributed to the owners in the form of cash.

Percentage Income Statement   An income statement in which each item is shown as a percentage of net sales. The firm's *gross profit margin, operating profit margin,* and *net profit margin* are readily available from this statement. It is useful for both time-series and cross-sectional comparisons.

Perpetuity   An annuity with an infinite life; in other words, an annuity that never stops providing the holder with *x* dollars at the end of each year.

Pledge of Accounts Receivable   Another term for the *assignment of accounts receivable.* The securing of a short-term loan with certain of the firm's accounts receivable, generally on a "trust" basis.

Portfolio   A combination of investments that may consist of securities, fixed assets, or a mixture of both.

Portfolio Risk Effects in Capital Budgeting   Refers to two opposing viewpoints on whether portfolio risk effects should be considered when evaluating a capital expenditure. The *risk-interdependence* viewpoint maintains that portfolio risk effects should be considered; while the *risk-independence* viewpoint maintains that portfolio risk effects can be ignored.

Preemptive Right   Gives a firm's existing common shareholders the right to purchase a specified maximum number of shares of a new issue. When new share issues are made by a firm, the preemptive right permits existing shareholders to maintain their proportionate voting control; it also protects against the dilution of their proportionate residual claims to the firm's earnings and assets.

Preferred or Preference Shares   A type of equity whose holders are given certain privileges, chiefly the right to receive a fixed periodic dividend. The claims of preferred shareholders are senior to those of the common shareholders in liquidation. Preferred shares are sometimes considered a form of *quasidebt*, since they have a fixed periodic dividend associated with them. Preferred shareholders normally do not receive voting rights.

Price-Earnings (P/E) Ratio   The ratio of the market price of a share to the annual per-share earnings.

Prime Interest Rate   The rate of interest charged by the Canadian chartered banks on business loans to the best business borrowers. The prime rate fluctuates with changing supply and demand relationships for short-term funds and is very dependent upon the rediscount rate set by the Bank of Canada.

Principal   The amount of money on which interest is earned by a depositor or an investor or the amount of money on which interest is paid by a borrower.

Probability   The percentage chance of a certain outcome occurring. If an outcome is expected to occur seven out of ten times, the probability associated with that outcome is .7, or 70 percent.

Profitability-Risk Trade-off   A trade-off common to many financial decisions. The most common area of concern is in the management of working capital. The lower a firm's liquidity is, the greater the risk of *technical insolvency* and the higher the expected profits. This relationship between the profitability and risk works both ways.

Pro Forma Statements   *Projected* financial statements. Pro forma income statements and balance sheets are typically prepared for the coming year. The cash budget and pro forma income statement act as inputs to the pro forma balance sheet. The sales forecast is the key input to all these statements.

Project Financing   The term-loan financing of a particular economic unit (project) in which a lender relies on the cash flows and earnings generated by the economic unit (project) for loan servicing, and on the assets of the economic unit (project) as collateral for the loan. The financing can also involve leasing.

Prospectus   A document issued to describe a new issue of securities. Before beginning issue, it is reviewed by the Securities Commissions in the provinces where the issue is to be sold. The Commissions' staff analyzes the preliminary prospectus to determine if there are any factual omissions or misrepresentations.

Proxy   A statement in which the holder of shares transfers his or her voting rights to another party. Sometimes *proxy battles* erupt when outside groups attempt to gain control of a firm's management.

Range   The most basic statistical measure of risk or variability, calculated by subtracting the lowest (i.e., worst or pessimistic) outcome from the highest (i.e., best or optimistic) outcome. The larger the range of a project, the more variability, or risk, it is said to have.

Ranking Approach   Evaluating the relative attractiveness of capital projects on the basis of some predetermined criterion.

Ratio Analysis   The use of various financial ratios for measuring various aspects of a firm's performance. Commonly grouped into liquidity and activity ratios, debt ratios, and profitability ratios. The key inputs to ratio analysis are the firm's income statement and balance sheet.

Ratio Comparisons   The most common types of ratio comparisons are *time-series* and *cross-sectional* comparisons. Time-series comparisons evaluate the same firm's performance over time; cross-sectional comparisons compare the performance of similar firms at the same point in time. Sometimes industry averages are used in cross-sectional comparisons.

Ratio of Exchange   A relevant measure when an acquiring firm plans to exchange its common shares for common shares of the target firm; the ratio of the amount paid per share of the acquired firm to the market price per share of the acquiring firm.

Recapitalization   The process of changing a firm's capital structure by altering the mix of debt and equity capital without increasing the total amount of capital. This often occurs as part of a commercial arrangement under the bankruptcy laws.

Recaptured Depreciation   The numerical value of a negative year-end UCC balance of a class of depreciable assets deemed as income for the year and taxed at the regular tax rate.

Refunding   The process of selling a new security in order to retire an existing security with the proceeds. This is often done to lower financial costs or to change a firm's capital structure.

Relevant Cash Inflows   The incremental after-tax net operating cash inflows (i.e., the combined incremental after-tax cash operating incomes and the tax savings for each period) and the salvage value expected to result from the investment.

Reorder Point   The level or inventory at which the firm places an order. It may be stated as a specific number of items or as a certain level of items in a bin.

Repurchase Agreements   An agreement whereby a bank or security dealer sells specific marketable securities to a firm agreeing to repurchase the securities at a specified price at a specific time.

Residual Theory of Dividends   A theory suggesting that a firm pay cash dividends if and only when acceptable investment opportunities for these funds are currently unavailable. In other words, cash dividends are viewed as residual funds that cannot be used in some acceptable investment opportunity.

Restrictive Loan Provisions   Provisions that place constraints on the operations of term borrowers, such as restrictions on working capital, fixed assets, future borrowing, combinations, salaries, security investments, the use of loan proceeds, and the payment of dividends. Sometimes called "restrictive covenants."

Retained Earnings   The portion of after-tax earnings not paid out as dividends. The balance sheet entry for retained earnings represents the earnings retained through the balance sheet date.

Retractable and Extendible Features   Retractable and extendible features provide a bondholder with an option that entitles the bondholder to alter the maturity date of the bond. The *retractable feature* gives the bondholder the right to retract or reduce the maturity date of the bond. The *extendible feature* gives the bondholder the right to extend the maturity date of the bond at the same coupon rate.

Return on Common Equity   A ratio calculated by dividing the earnings available to common shareholders by the common shareholders' equity. This ratio measures the rate of return earned on the owners' book investment.

Return on Equity (ROE) A ratio measuring the return earned on the owners' (both preferred and common shareholders') investment; calculated by dividing net profit after taxes by shareholders' equity. It represents the end result of the *Modified DuPont Formula*.

Return on Investment (ROI) Sometimes called the *return on total assets*. It can be calculated by dividing the firm's net profits after taxes by its total assets or by multiplying its net profit margin by the total asset turnover. The relationship between the net profit margin, total asset turnover, and return on investment is often referred to as the *DuPont Formula*.

Revolving Credit Agreement A guaranteed line-of-credit arrangement in which the bank guarantees that, regardless of economic conditions, it will make available the amount of the line at any time during the term of the agreement. Often these agreements are written for two-year terms; they are more expensive than a simple line of credit.

Rights Offering An offering of a new issue of common shares to the firm's current shareholders on a pro rata basis. A *right* is a piece of paper providing its holder with an option to buy a certain portion of a new share.

Risk Used interchangeably with the term *uncertainty* to refer to the variability of returns associated with a project or forecast values of the firm. In a statistical sense, risk exists when a decision maker can estimate the probabilities associated with various outcomes.

Risk-Adjusted Discount Rate A discount rate used in capital budgeting decisions that has been adjusted for the firm or the project's risk. The risk-adjusted rate is determined by adding an appropriate *risk premium* to the *risk-free rate of return*.

Risk-Free Rate The rate of return commonly required on a risk-free security. It is usually measured by the yield on a government security such as a treasury bill. The beta for a risk-free security is equal to zero.

Risk Positioning The process of classifying projects as being of high, low, or average risk.

Risk Premium The amount by which the required return on an asset or security j, $\overline{k}_j$, exceeds the risk-free rate, R_F. In terms of the capital asset pricing model (CAPM), it can be expressed as $b_j \cdot (\overline{k}_m - R_F)$, where b_j is the asset's beta coefficient and $\overline{k}_m$ is the required return on the market portfolio.

Safety of Principal The risk that the market value of a security will drop below the amount paid to purchase it. Concern over the safety of principal is especially important when making *marketable securities* investments. It can be viewed as the likelihood of loss in principal.

Safety Stock An amount of inventory maintained in excess of that needed to meet expected usage in view of the expected *lead times* to receive orders. It provides a cushion for fulfilling demand in the event that the actual usage exceeds expected usage or a delay in receipt of orders occurs.

Sale-Leaseback Arrangement An arrangement whereby a firm sells its existing assets to a leasing company, which then leases them back to the firm. This is often done to generate cash. This arrangement differs from a *direct lease* of assets originally owned by the lessor.

Sales Forecast   Sales forecasts are an important input to the firm's financial planning process. *Internal sales forecasts* are obtained from the sales force; *external sales forecasts* are based on regression analysis and the consideration of certain macroeconomic factors.

Salvage Value   The expected value of a depreciable asset at the end of the asset's usable life. For depreciation purposes, salvage values must be estimated.

Secondary Market   A market for outstanding securities (i.e., those that are not new issues).

Security   Used interchangeably with the term *collateral* to refer to the specific items used by a borrower to back up a loan.

Security Market Line (SML)   A simple linear relationship between expected return and risk for individual assets and inefficient portfolios. It is a straight line that reflects for each beta (*x*-axis) the associated required return (*y*-axis). As traditionally graphed, the SML presents the required or expected returns associated with all positive betas.

Semivariable Costs   Costs that are fixed over a certain range of volume and change to a different level beyond that volume.

Sensitivity Analysis   The analysis of the effect of changes in certain variables on an outcome in order to get a feel for the variability of outcomes, or risk, associated with a cash budget, a project, or other risky situations.

Serial Bonds   Bonds issued in such a fashion that a certain proportion of them come due each year. Serial bonds allow the issuer to gradually refund debt.

Share Dividend   A payment of shares to a firm's existing owners. It actually represents the distribution of something the owners already have. The effect of this action is merely to capitalize a portion of the firm's retained earnings.

Share Options   Options generally extended to members of a firm's management that permit them to purchase a certain number of shares at a stated price over a specified period. They are intended to motivate the management to perform well.

Share Purchase Plans   Fringe benefits occasionally offered to employees that allow them to purchase their firm's shares at a discount or on a matching basis with the firm absorbing part of the cost. These plans do provide the firm with an "internal source" of new equity capital.

Share Repurchases   The act of buying back the firm's own common shares. The repurchased shares are called *treasury shares*, and represent the difference between the number of shares *issued* and the number of shares *outstanding*. Share repurchases are sometimes used in lieu of paying cash dividends. The repurchase can be made by purchase in the open market, through *tender offers*, or on a negotiated basis from a group of large shareholders.

Share Split   A method of either increasing or decreasing (by a reverse split) the number of shares outstanding, while lowering or raising the market price per share. Shares are split to stimulate trading activity.

Short Sale   A share transaction made in anticipation of a drop in a security's price. The short seller sells shares belonging to another person or firm, promising to buy them back at a future date in order to replace them. The idea is to sell high and buy low, so that the initial proceeds exceed the outlay required to repurchase the securities. Brokers facilitate short-sale transactions.

Short Term   A period of time less than a year. Current assets are short-term assets, and current liabilities are short-term liabilities.

Simple Cash-Flow Pattern   A pattern of cash flows in which an initial outlay is followed by a series of inflows. Other *nonsimple* patterns do exist.

Sinking Fund   A deposit or investment account into which borrowers are required to make periodic payments to provide funds for the retirement of their debt. A sinking fund is normally established in such a way that the deposits accumulate to the maturity value of the debt.

Small Business Deduction   A federal tax credit available to relatively small Canadian-controlled private corporations. It serves to reduce the basic federal corporate tax rate of 46 percent to 25 percent on the first $150,000 of active business income of eligible corporations.

Sole Proprietorship   A business owned by one person, who operates it for his or her own profit. This is the most common form of business organization. The earnings of the sole proprietor are taxed as ordinary income, and the proprietor's liability is unlimited.

Source and Use of Funds Statement   A statement of the various sources and uses of funds for a firm over a certain period. The inputs to this statement are balance sheets for the beginning and end of the period and an income statement covering the period. It can be prepared using either cash or net working capital as the pivotal value. This statement is sometimes referred to as *source and application of funds statement.*

Sources of Funds   Sources of funds include a decrease in an asset, an increase in a liability, net profits after tax, depreciation and other noncash charges, and the sale of securities.

Split Financing   The joint financing of a firm's short-term financing needs by a chartered bank and a commercial finance company.

Spread   The difference between the price paid for a security by an investment dealer and the sale price. Also, the difference in interest rates between various debt instruments.

Standard Deviation   A statistical measure of the variability of outcomes associated with a specified event; the square root of the average squared deviations from the mean. It is used as a measure of risk.

Standby Arrangement   An arrangement whereby an underwriter agrees to purchase shares not subscribed to as a result of a rights offering. An issue of shares that is not fully subscribed is said to be *undersubscribed.*

Standby Fee   A fee charged on the unused portion of the credit under a revolving credit or line-of-credit arrangement.

Statistical Dependence   Refers to the statistical relationship between the operating cash flows of projects and generally occurs when the project's cash flows are similarly affected by common external factors, such as the business cycle.

Straight Value   The value of a *convertible security* when viewed solely on the basis of the interest or dividends it provides. This value is found by discounting the stream of interest or dividends at the rate that would be earned on a similar-risk security not having the conversion feature.

Stretching Accounts Payable   A strategy of paying bills as late as possible as long as the firm's credit rating is not damaged, taking into consideration any cash discounts offered. By stretching its accounts payable, a firm "leans on the trade" and thereby reduces the amount of operating cash it requires.

Subordinated Debt   Debt whose holders have a claim on the firm's assets only after the claims of holders of *senior debt* (the debt to which the subordinated debt is subordinated) have been satisfied. The subordinated debt holder is in a much riskier position than the senior debt holders.

Subscription Price   The price at which the holder of share rights can purchase a common share. To make the rights attractive, the subscription price is generally set below the prevailing market price of a share at the time of the rights offering.

Synergistic Effects   The results of certain economies of scale that cause the total value of an organization to be greater than the value of the components summed. Synergistic effects often act as an impetus for business combination.

Tax Credit   A tax deduction permitted directly against tax otherwise payable.

Technical Insolvency   A firm is technically insolvent if it is unable to pay its bills as they come due. Technical insolvency normally precedes *bankruptcy*. A firm can overcome technical insolvency through borrowing in many cases.

Tender Offer   A formal offer by a firm to purchase a given number of its own shares or the shares of another company at a specified price. The price at which a tender offer is made is usually set above the prevailing market price to attract sellers. Tender offers are used to repurchase the firm's own shares or in takeover attempts in which management negotiations have failed.

Terminal Loss   The positive UCC balance of a class of depreciable assets remaining after the sale of the last asset from the class.

Term Lenders   Term loans are made by various financial institutions to business firms. These institutions include foreign and Canadian-owned banks, life insurance companies, and specialized term lenders.

Term Loan   A loan having an initial maturity greater than one year; a *long-term loan*.

Term Loan Interest Rates   There are two types of interest rates charged on term loans. On a *variable-rate loan*, the interest rate charged floats at a predetermined fixed percentage (spread) above the prime rate for the loan (or duration) of the loan. On a *fixed-rate loan*, the interest rate charged by the lender is fixed for the term of the loan.

Term Preferred Shares   Preferred shares that either have a fixed maturity date or have a number of provisions designed to alter the maturity date or the stated fixed dividend rate.

Term Structure of Interest Rates   The relationship between the yield-to-maturity of debt and debt's term-to-maturity, when all other aspects of the debt are the same.

Thin Market   A situation in which a firm's shares are not actively traded, due either to the small number of shareholders or to the small float of the firm. Many of the shares with a thin market are traded over the counter.

Total Asset Turnover   A ratio indicating the efficiency with which a firm uses its assets. It is calculated by dividing annual sales by total assets. The higher this ratio is, the more efficient the firm's use of assets is assumed to be.

Total Leverage   The power of fixed costs—both operating and financial—to magnify the effects of changes in a firm's sales revenue on its earnings per share (eps). The greater the firm's fixed costs, the higher its total leverage. It reflects the combined effect of *operating leverage* and *financial leverage* on the firm's risk.

Total Risk   The risk that a firm will be unable to meet its operating and financial costs. The higher a firm's operating and financial *leverage*, the greater its total risk.

Trade Credit   Credit obtained through open-account purchases, represented by an *account payable* by the recipient and an *account receivable* by the grantor.

Trade-Off Approach   A financial strategy in which the firm finances a portion of its forecast seasonal funds need with long-term funds. This strategy represents a trade-off between the high-profit–high-risk *aggressive approach* and the low-profit–low-risk *conservative approach*. The exact trade-off used depends largely on the decision maker's attitude toward risk.

Treasury Bill   A short-term obligation of the federal and provincial governments. Treasury bills are issued weekly. They have virtually no risk and therefore provide a low yield.

Treasury Shares   Shares that have been issued and then repurchased by a firm. Occasionally, shares are repurchased as a way of paying dividends.

Trust Receipt   A loan made against specific collateral that remains in the hands of the borrower, but which can usually be identified by serial numbers. Trust receipt loans involving inventory are referred to as *floor-planning* arrangements.

Trustee (Bond)   The third party to a bond indenture; typically a department of a trust company, whose responsibility it is to make sure the user lives up to the numerous conditions in the bond indenture. The trustee is paid a fee and acts to protect the interests of the bondholders.

UCC Balance   Undepreciated capital cost balance of a class of depreciable assets. The UCC balance of a class is increased by the capital costs of new assets included in the class and is reduced by the proceeds of asset disposals from the class. The maximum amount of CCA permitted for a class is calculated by applying the prescribed CCA rate for the class to its year-end UCC balance.

Uncertainty   Commonly used interchangeably with the term *risk* to refer to the variability of outcomes associated with a specific project or event. In a statistical sense, uncertainty exists when a decision maker has no historical data from which to develop a probability distribution.

Underwriting   The investment dealer's function of guaranteeing the issuer of a security that it will receive at least a specified minimum amount for the issue. The underwriter of an issue accepts the risk that it will not sell. Often an investment dealer will aid in the *private placement* of an issue or agree only to a *best-efforts* offering whereby the risk of selling the issue is avoided.

Uneven Stream of Cash Inflows   A stream of cash inflows that does not reflect any particular pattern. Any pattern of cash inflows other than an *annuity* is considered an uneven stream.

Unlisted Securities   Securities not listed on an organized security exchange, but traded in an over-the-counter market.

Uses of Funds   Uses of funds by a firm include increases in assets, decreases in liabilities, net losses, payments of cash dividends, and the repurchase or retirement of shares.

Utility Function   A curve indicating the risk-return preferences of a decision maker.

Valuation   The process of measuring the value of an asset or liability. A term typically used to describe the overall process of estimating the worth of a business firm or a financial asset using its *book value, liquidation value, market value,* the *industry capitalization* rate, the *Gordon model,* or the CAPM.

Variable Costs   Costs that vary directly with a firm's sales, and are a function of volume, not time.

Venture Capitalist   Any individual or institution that provides "high-risk" debt or equity capital unavailable from traditional sources, for the growth (or seed funding) of small businesses at any stage before they go public.

Vertical Growth   When a firm grows backward by acquiring suppliers of its raw materials or forward by acquiring purchasers of its finished products.

Voluntary Settlement   An "out-of-court" settlement or discharge with a firm's creditors that leaves a technically insolvent or bankrupt firm in a position to continue operations or to be liquidated. A voluntary settlement enables the firm to bypass many of the costs involved in formal legal proceedings.

Warehouse Receipt Loan   A loan secured with inventory that is controlled by the lender and can be removed for sale only with the lender's approval. Both *terminal* and *field* warehousing arrangements are used. A *warehouse receipt* is issued by the *warehouseman* to the lender; it describes the various items of collateral under his control.

Warrant   A certificate giving its holder the right to purchase a certain number of common shares at a specified per-share price. A warrant is usually detachable, meaning that the recipient can sell it without selling the security to which it was attached. Quite often, warrants are used to "sweeten" a debt or preferred share issue, or are used in business combinations. Warrants are traded on the security exchanges and may or may not have limited lives.

Warrant Premium   The difference between the market value and the theoretical value of a *share purchase warrant*. The amount of the warrant premium typically depends upon investors' expectations as well as their ability to get more leverage from the warrants than the underlying shares. This premium is typically largest when the market price of the shares and the warrant *exercise price* are close together.

Wealth Maximization   The strategy of maximizing the value of the owners' or shareholders' interest (investment) in a firm, which is generally measured by the market value of the firm's shares. This strategy is not necessarily consistent with a strategy of profit maximization.

Weighted Average Cost of Capital (WACC)   A measure of the cost of capital calculated by weighting the marginal cost of each type of capital (i.e., debt, preferred shares, common equity, etc.) by the proportion of that type of capital in the firm's capital structure.

Working Capital Management   An area of finance concerned with the management of a firm's current accounts, which include its *current assets* and *current liabilities*. The management of working capital is quite important, since if the firm cannot maintain a satisfactory working capital position it may become technically insolvent and may be forced into bankruptcy.

Yield   The actual return received by an investor in a security. It depends on the price paid for the security and the annual interest or dividend payment expected. It is sometimes viewed as the internal rate of return on an investment. The phrase *yield-to-maturity* is used to refer to the yield of a bond held to maturity.

Yield Curve   The graphic illustration of the term structure for a group of bonds that have the same risk of default at a particular point in time. The yield curve can be upward sloping, flat, or downward sloping.

INDEX

Index

Index

Index

Index

Index

Index

Index

Index

PRESENT-VALUE INTEREST FACTORS FOR A ONE-DOLLAR ANNUITY, PVIFA

Year	1%	2%	3%	4%	5%	6%	7%	8%	9%	10%
1	.990	.980	.971	.962	.952	.943	.935	.926	.917	.909
2	1.970	1.942	1.913	1.886	1.859	1.833	1.808	1.783	1.759	1.736
3	2.941	2.884	2.829	2.775	2.723	2.673	2.624	2.577	2.531	2.487
4	3.902	3.808	3.717	3.630	3.546	3.465	3.387	3.312	3.240	3.170
5	4.853	4.713	4.580	4.452	4.329	4.212	4.100	3.993	3.890	3.791
6	5.795	5.601	5.417	5.242	5.076	4.917	4.767	4.623	4.486	4.355
7	6.728	6.472	6.230	6.002	5.786	5.582	5.389	5.206	5.033	4.868
8	7.652	7.326	7.020	6.733	6.463	6.210	5.971	5.747	5.535	5.335
9	8.566	8.162	7.786	7.435	7.108	6.802	6.515	6.247	5.995	5.759
10	9.471	8.983	8.530	8.111	7.722	7.360	7.024	6.710	6.418	6.145
11	10.368	9.787	9.253	8.760	8.306	7.887	7.499	7.139	6.805	6.495
12	11.255	10.575	9.954	9.385	8.863	8.384	7.943	7.536	7.161	6.814
13	12.134	11.348	10.635	9.986	9.394	8.853	8.358	7.904	7.487	7.103
14	13.004	12.106	11.296	10.563	9.899	9.295	8.746	8.244	7.786	7.367
15	13.865	12.849	11.938	11.118	10.380	9.712	9.108	8.560	8.061	7.606
16	14.718	13.578	12.561	11.652	10.838	10.106	9.447	8.851	8.313	7.824
17	15.562	14.292	13.166	12.166	11.274	10.477	9.763	9.122	8.544	8.022
18	16.398	14.992	13.754	12.659	11.690	10.828	10.059	9.372	8.756	8.201
19	17.226	15.679	14.324	13.134	12.085	11.158	10.336	9.604	8.950	8.365
20	18.046	16.352	14.878	13.590	12.462	11.470	10.594	9.818	9.129	8.514
21	18.857	17.011	15.415	14.029	12.821	11.764	10.836	10.017	9.292	8.649
22	19.661	17.658	15.937	14.451	13.163	12.042	11.061	10.201	9.442	8.772
23	20.456	18.292	16.444	14.857	13.489	12.303	11.272	10.371	9.580	8.883
24	21.244	18.914	16.936	15.247	13.799	12.550	11.469	10.529	9.707	8.985
25	22.023	19.524	17.413	15.622	14.094	12.783	11.654	10.675	9.823	9.077
30	25.808	22.397	19.601	17.292	15.373	13.765	12.409	11.258	10.274	9.427
35	29.409	24.999	21.487	18.665	16.374	14.498	12.948	11.655	10.567	9.644
40	32.835	27.356	23.115	19.793	17.159	15.046	13.332	11.925	10.757	9.779
45	36.095	29.490	24.519	20.720	17.774	15.456	13.606	12.108	10.881	9.863
50	39.197	31.424	25.730	21.482	18.256	15.762	13.801	12.234	10.962	9.915